Maurizio Galia
Presents:

Progressive Rock
Around the World in Fifty Years

Picked and reviewed by
**Claudio Aloi, Giuseppe Di Spirito, Maurizio Galia
Roberto Vanali, Franco Vassia, Donato Zoppo.**

A very special thanks goes to
Peter Gabriel and **Aldo Tagliapietra**
for their precious contribution to the foreword

PROG 50: Progressive Rock around the World in Fifty Years
an Original Concept by Claudio Aloi & Maurizio Galia

This book is dedicated to the loving memory of David Watts, friend and precious counselor

Authors:
Claudio Aloi, Maurizio Galia.

Foreword & Introductions
Peter Gabriel, Aldo Tagliapietra, Maurizio Galia, Franco Vassia

Hystorical and Archive research:
Claudio Aloi, Giuseppe Di Spirito, Maurizio Galia,
Roberto Vanali, Franco Vassia, Donato Zoppo.

English Version: Christine Colomo

Music Counselor: Luca Andriolo

Layout and Graphic Design:
Maurizio Galia.

Illustrations:
Cover: *"Watcher of the skies expanded"* Acrylic on canvas/Digital art by Maurizio Galia.
Inner chapters: *"Vinyl Dreams"*, *"Major Arcane"*, 5 acrylic & gouache by Maurizio Galia

Photos:
Aldo Tagliapietra: Armando Gallo, Gianni Facca.
Maurizio Galia: Francesco Alecce
Donato Zoppo: Francesca Grispello.
Genesis live page 471: Armando Gallo.
Genesis live page 480: Bruno Zampaglione.
Peter Gabriel page 3: Armando Gallo, Virgin Music and other press photographers.
Peter Gabriel live page 480: Francesco Leone.
Pink Floyd live page 470: Pink Floyd archives.
Maurizio Galia and Carlo Massarini: Valerio Giulianelli.
Maurizio Galia and Donato Zoppo': Franco Vassia.
Maurizio Galia and Athos Enrile: Franco Vassia.
Maurizio Galia and Peter Gabriel: Laura Grenci.
Libero Robba and Giancarlo Bertelle page 465: Sergio Cippo.
Osanna page 2: Marco Antonio Baldassari.

Other pictures from this book are from the authors' personal archives or official press reviews.

Printed in July 2025 by: **Press Up**, Zona Industriale Zettevene, 01036 VITERBO
ISBN 978-88-89571-16-3

PROGRESSIVE ROCK:
Musical minds out of any boxes.

I was introduced to Maurizio through his charming puppets and illustrations, which used to make me smile.

He has made a life following his imagination and letting it run wild. That makes him a perfect candidate to produce a book on Progressive Rock, or what he calls the free music of Prog Rock, or in this case – the Prog Rock 50.

Prog, at its best, doesn't follow the normal rules and conventions of composition, it's playful and inventive, free to explore whatever interests. I remember one of Genesis' first reviews referred to us as a *Folk, Blues Mystical group*, a genre that seems to have disappeared these days.

Borders were there to be broken and many of us grouped together in this much derided Prog rock, had a lot of pleasure letting our musical minds wander far and wide and straight out of any boxes we were thrown in.

Despite all the repeated warnings of the critics, there are an increasing number of young people exploring this rich and quirky vein of music. This book will be a very useful introductory guide to them and a welcome collection of memories for the prog fans of my generation.

Maurizio's prog collection is full of fruit, brought to life by his passion and good-humoured enthusiasm for the music that he loves so much. He has carefully assembled all the artists that he feels belong here, from different periods, different countries and different musical backgrounds; a veritable army of progsters; all mounted and ready - ready to challenge any non-believers, in whatever shape or form they are found.

Peter Gabriel

PROGRESSIVE ROCK:
In its 50ies but too young to die.

Progressive is undoubtedly the music of freedom of composition for it knows no boundaries or constraints. It is the adult-age of Rock: born in England in the late '60s, it rose from the ashes of Psychedelia when some Rock musicians found they urged to stray from the metrical structures adopted till then. No more songs using a two verse/chorus/verse/chorus pattern, but real suites with more elaborate rhythmic, harmonic and melodic developments, also inspired by Classical music and Jazz.

This was also a need in the audience of the time and that's why Prog hit the top of the charts and stayed there for an entire decade. What was once "non-commercial" became commercial and record labels started signing up progressive groups one after the other.

Following the footsteps of what was happening in England, Italy proved to be the most receptive country for the genre. New groups, new ideas and new music started to show up and Italian Prog became famous all over the world. From Beat to Psychedelia and on to Prog, this was the wonderful musical journey that my generation experienced.

At the end of the '70s it reached its highest peak, when suddenly, from America, Disco music appeared and, together with the generational change, wiped out everything that had been built before. It took 15 years to re-evaluate the '70s and now that things have been restored, an old adagio of those years comes to mind: <<Now he's too old to Rock'n'Roll but he's too young to die>>. So I open my guitar-case and play it over with in my heart endless gratefulness.

Aldo Tagliapietra

INTRODUCTION

When I met **Claudio Aloi** for the first time, I immediately sensed he was a passionate music connoisseur and collector, just like me. After many inspiring discussions, over beer or coffee, on possible projects we could cooperate on, we both agreed that something was still missing in the publishing world: a book that extensively narrated the history of Progressive Rock from its beginnings to our present day, the story of over 50 years of music.

So we went and bought most of the existing literature on the subject, realizing that all the traceable material stopped at the end of the '70s, completely ignoring what's happened later and that perhaps was still going on.

I here recall fondly the moment when Claudio totally surprised me by saying: <<*Maurizio! Let's write this book together!*>> A proposal which, at first, left me dumbfounded as my gut replied: <<*But I'm not a professional writer!*>> Then my sense of belonging to the family of Progressive Rock got me all excited when I pictured the challenge.

I therefore decided to organize a team of true professionals, as motivated and passionate as we both were, but with the better knowledge I lacked. I immediately turned to my good friend **Franco Vassia**, very influential and well known in the Italian music culture, as well as the creator and director of one of the best Italian magazines on Progressive Rock: *Nobody's Land*. Above all, Franco also had first hand experience of the early '70s Prog golden era in the genre.

Then I contacted **Donato Zoppo** and **Peppe Di Spirito**, two young Prog experts who wrote and published their studies and researches on the best web sites and magazines, with special regards to Donato's complete essays on some of the world's most famous artists.

That done, who else could I now involve to access certain records mostly unavailable? **Mauro Moroni**, also a dear friend with whom I worked for many years, was my best choice, being one of the most important collectors and figures of the Italian music industry of Progressive Rock and Psychedelic music. He introduced me to **Roberto Vanali**, another high profile collector and expert, and we all set to work in gathering a selected choice of titles and names from around the world, in order to give this book the completeness it deserved.

After months of tough negotiations and lively discussions on a topic which had hundreds of names to choose from, we applied the wisest decision possible: to agree on the fact that we disagreed. Every one of us finished writing his part with a shake of the head and muttering about some of the choices, but we all had the certainty we were nevertheless doing the right thing: filling up this gap in History.

The fact that some of the authors, like me, were directly involved as musicians, or indirectly, like Mauro being a music producer, or Franco through his books, should not lead to the impression we may attempt to seek promotion or personal advantage from this project. On the other hand, the fact that this work was done by people from a Prog background is the best guarantee that you will be reading a quality book. So please enjoy it as we enjoyed writing it for you!

Maurizio Galia

INTRODUCTION TO PROG:
HEROES, TALES & STORIES FROM ONCE UPON A TIME

To understand how important the significance of Progressive Rock was for those lucky enough to cross the threshold between the '60s and the '70s, we would need to spread through an incredibly broad range of studies, to a point historians would probably frown on our creation of certain comparisons, that may even appear disrespectful. Because of the vastness and versatility of its musical, literary and pictorial value, it may eventually be considered as one of the major artistic and creative periods of the entire History of Music, similar to (with the utmost humility and the proper proportions) the extraordinary process called Renaissance that, from the late Middle-Ages and the beginning of Modern Age, revolutionized the whole of civilization.

In our case it is Music that charts the course, becoming a bright beacon for the new generations to come. Detaching itself from the prevailing trends and deliberately losing along the way the leisure and disenchantment of those times, Pop was trying to take on the features of a new Art, trying to land at the court of a parallel world in which there existed only one single, iron-clad rule: listening. A meticulous, careful, scrupulous and almost religious listening. A new spark was lit, like a reverberation, an unexpected light that could blind the eyes, but which was also seen as a stream in which to mirror and bask.

The history of Prog Rock (or Art-Rock, to define the brave artists of that period) begins in the late '60s, flying on the Winds of Change that arose from the coasts of England, gradually blowing so hard, they managed to eradicated atavistic and overt beliefs. With a strong desire to return Europe to its primary role of Golden Cradle of Culture, ever flowing under the surface and never far from its roots, a wind that not only cleansed and cleared up the sky, but which picked up the sand and rocks jamming the gears of commercial music. After many years of delirium, the coughing engine of the market was forced, reluctantly, to a desperate retreat and to a painful and deep analysis.

The Beatles, who for some time already had been listening to the noise of scrap metal, were collecting all the junk and debris of this illness and, along with *Sgt. Pepper and his Lonely Hearts Club Band*, they had sharpened their weapons to dictate yet another Table of Commandments, but not before having lifted the bar upwards, fixing the cardinal points for a new musical perspective.

Rock was shedding skin and nothing would stop it. It was like a fever that, once healed, left the body with a feeling of well-being and a strong desire of starting over. A ramification of veins mixed with a blend of good heat conductors, capable of filtering and then of regenerating all the different currents of the period: from Classical music to Jazz, poetry to literature, graphics to painting, filmmaking to comics. A spread of the arts which competed in blending into one another and, all alike, ready to give birth to an endless rosary of savory records with lyrics intended for libraries and covers fit for art galleries, or perhaps a shrink's waiting room.

The pioneers of this new course (many harbored from the wreck left by the downfall of Beat) wore names bound to glory such as **Procol Harum**, whom with "A Whiter Shade of Pale" (a free rearrangement of "Aria on the G String Suite No. 3 BWV 1068", by **Johann Sebastian Bach**) hit the top of the charts all over the world, and **The Moody Blues**, authors of *Days of Future Passed* (based on the "New World" from Symphony No.9 by **Antonin Dvorak**), which is widely referred to as <<*the founding album of the New Progressive course*>>.

Other artists will soon revive the genre's glory days: decisive precursors like **Raymond Vincent**'s **Wallace Collection** (eccentric violinist in high credit with **Sonja Kristina** and **Darryl Way**'s band **Curved Air**); **Keith Emerson** led the group **The Nice** (before a hilarious reading along with **E.L.& P.** of *Pictures at an Exhibition* by **Modest Mussorgsky**) with the beautiful *The Thoughts of Emerlist Davjack* and *Ars Longa Vita Brevis*; the magical flute of **Jan Anderson** used for "Bouré" by **Jethro Tull**, yet another work borrowed from **Bach**'s ever steady genius.

Thus songs disappeared (or rather, were relegated to festivals and sideshows) giving way to full albums just like real suites in the classical genre, becoming complex and structured with various movements more or less epic, but all with the same common denominator: while musicians waded through proper instrumental scores from Classical themes (alternating them with back-beat breaks and integrating them with majestic and solemn fugues), lyricists extracted subjects and mythological symbols, religious and folkloric texts, to build meaningful and sublime poetry. Instead of rhyming couplets, all the simulacra of the new culture that protruded beyond this hemisphere appeared and, as in a game of domino, in addition to **Van Der Graaf Generator**'s lost pioneers, pieces of reminiscences from **Gabriel**'s Tiresias and Narcissus can be found on the way up to *Tarkus*, the monster, and down to the tables of the submerged oceanic tales by **Yes**; the bearded child from "The Musical Box", the dirty and coarse beggar of *Aqualung*, *Octopus*, the sea monster from **Gentle Giant**, the knights of the Round Table by **Rick Wakeman**; "21st Century Schizoid Man" by **King Crimson**, **Hammill**'s "Refugees"... and so many more. An enchanted world of characters, stories and passions that seem to come from the remotest and ancestral corners of the mind.

A beautiful season, flourished with a series of albums not to be missed. If *In the Court of The Crimson King* by **King Crimson** (*In the Wake of Poseidon*, *Lizard* and *Island* should also be mentioned), can be seen as the cornerstone of an entire progressive frame, there are many who recognize **Genesis** as the brightest star of this movement. Guided by a histrionic **Peter Gabriel**, **Genesis** (more than anyone else) was able to create the right conditions for a series of masterpieces: Trespass, *Nursery Cryme*, *Foxtrot* and *Selling England by the Pound* (*The Lamb Lies Down on Broadway*, despite being an excellent record, belongs to a period that perhaps should be more correct to define as post-prog) have all the features of a **Rossini** crescendo, able to turn and rehabilitate the preconceptions of the ruling critique (what disturbs the most, with the exception of the Italian magazine Ciao 2001 and the English Melody Maker, was the total dislike of the press). The stylistic virtuosity of **Genesis**, the mannerisms, the taste of theatricality and transvestism supported by an incredible series of brilliant performances, shoots them right to the top of their fame.

If the first two places of the progressive pedestal are occupied by **Genesis** and **King Crimson**, the third is a highly subjective choice: competing groups are **Van der Graaf Generator** (*The Least We Can Do Is Wave To Each other*, *H to He, Who Am the Only One*, *Pawn Hearts* and *Godbluff*), **Yes** (*The Yes Album*, *Fragile*, *Close to the Edge*, *Yessongs*, *Tales from the Topographic Oceans*), **Emerson, Lake & Palmer** (*Emerson, Lake & Palmer*, *Tarkus*, *Pictures at an Exhibition*, *Trilogy*, *Brain Salad Surgery*), **Jethro Tull** (*This Was*, *Stand Up*, *Benefit*, *Aqualung*, *Thick as a Brick*, *a Passion Play*), **Pink Floyd** (*Ummagumma*, *Atom Heart Mother*, *The Dark Side of the Moon*, *Wish You Were Here*, *Animals*, *The Wall* and *The Final Cut*), **Gentle Giant** (*Gentle Giant*, *Acquiring the Taste*, *Three Friends*, *Octopus*, *The Glass House*) and in alternative, **Camel**, **Caravan**, **Audience** and **Curved Air**.

But if England had once again begun by moving the first pieces, we have to recognize that Italy was among the first to respond to the calling and, unlike in the past (where groups were limited exclusively to cover major worldwide hits) was able to produce albums of great vigor. After recovering famous castaways from the raft of a shipwrecked Beat (**New Trolls**, **Le Orme**), Italy soon became a melting pot of intents.

Capable of generating extraordinary groups that not only had the merit of revitalizing the dying scenario, it also showed further genius in names such as **Premiata Forneria Marconi (PFM)**, **Banco del Mutuo Soccorso (BMS)**, **Balletto di Bronzo**, **Osanna**, **Rovescio della Medaglia**, **Raccomandata con Ricevuta di Ritorno**, **Arti & Mestieri**. Recordings, published with the rhythms and cycles of an assembly line, were greeted by fans as manna from the sky. You could tell that things were changing when in the stores appeared (with long queues) *Storia di un minuto* by **PFM** and **BMS**'s self-titled albums.

While **PFM**'s record (which gathered some of the best musicians of the time), calibrating Mediterranean sounds on the wake of the Anglo-Saxon **King Crimson**, **Yes** and **Soft Machine**, gave birth to a mixture so prepared to circulate and affect even foreign markets; **BMS**'s album instead, tried to regain expressive codes of popular culture, using the strong lyrical impact of the melodramatic opera, they managed to mix Ariosto's tales with avant-garde social issues.

In Genoa, **New Trolls** (also exiles of Beat) responded with *Concerto Grosso* (written by future Grammy award **Luis Enriquez Bacalov**), a didactic album, majestic and poignant, that recovers glories from the Baroque period, contrasting them with rock music; in Venice, **Le Orme** released *Collage*, a remarkably and impressive album that took them directly to **EL&P**'s royal court; in Naples, **Osanna** issued *Palepoli*, a delightful and provocative reinterpretation of their hometown. Groups, titles and dates which, while losing sight of their space and time, are still destined to be the monoliths of an extraordinary Golden Age.

But, like all movements, fashions and revolutions, Prog set a steady pace creating a crisis, subject to certain exceptions, that decreed its untimely end. Even if the years to come still lit the sky with a few new bright stars, rain clouds began to gather on the horizon at the end of the '70s.

The crisis arrived on the clock and while recordings took the shape of inanimate and sometimes cheesy objects, concerts which use to take place in front of massive walls of public, now overlooked desolate and empty spaces. As Saturn devoured his children, even Prog (for fatigue, fatality or perhaps just pure narcissism) gobbled his own. Stunned by success and fame, **EL&P** entertained expensive tours with all the stems for bankruptcy; **Rick Wakeman** snuck away from **Yes**, populating lakes with flaming dragons while his music continued to admire itself in the mirror.

The end of Prog (that however continued to sprout new bands inheriting the legacy albeit with questionable results, often discontinuous as **Marillion**, **IQ**, **Pendragon**, **Spock's Beard**, **Flower Kings**) was also helped by the record industry which, feeling it lost the goose of the golden eggs, at first turned to Disco music and then resolved through Punk, whose concept was of convincing young people that they could become rock stars, even if untalented and unable to read a single note.

Nowadays I feel creativity is almost gone, watered down and suffocated by the vulgarity and hedonism of the media. This book is meant to be a tribute and a thank you to the heroes of that era:

their music, despite everything, is now safe, placed on the shelves of our hearts. There it will stay and, just like a shell, whenever we may be in need, it will readily bring to our ears the sound of the sea.

Franco Vassia

SMALL GLOSSARY OF WORDS AND ABBREVIATIONS

AOR:
Adult Oriented Rock, often wrongly confused with *Art Oriented Rock*, though it has practically the same meaning. It refers to an easy listening Pop-Rock, mostly American-styled, pompous but with elements close to the Prog genre.

CANTERBURY SOUND or SCHOOL:
It's not the name of an institute or a school itself, but a universally accepted term to indicate the musical genre born inside Prog from Canterbury artists such as **Wilde Flowers**, **Soft Machine**, **Matching Mole**, **Caravan** among others, who created a peculiar sound and style, rich in references to avant-garde Jazz.

KRAUT ROCK:
Inspired by the Teutonic typical dish *Sauerkraut*, it indicates the majority of Rock music produced by German artists, even those tied to Prog. A clear recognition of German music in a global context: the original use of electronics and psychedelic sounds, different from Californian and English, often related to the German cabaret of the Weimar Republic. Within the term *Kraut* we find listed bands like **Tangerine Dream**, **Popol Vuh** and the early **Kraftwerk**, also described as *Cosmic Couriers* because of their dreamy electronic and metaphysical music inspired by the early experimental **Pink Floyd**.

RIO:
Abbreviation of *Rock In Opposition*, it indicates a specific movement within the Prog genre, very related to the Canterbury school, but definitely more avant-garde and highly politicized towards the Left. Quick examples are **Henry Cow**, **Etron Fou Leloublan** and in Italy, **Stormy Six**.

ZEUHL:
This word derives from the most imaginative literary invention of the Progressive era: the Kobaïan language, invented by **Christian Vander** from **Magma**. Meaning *Celestial, Universal*, the term has come to refer to the concept of a Universal Progressive Sound, typical of all those artists inspired by **Magma**'s dark, mysterious, yet charming and creative music.

SUMMARY

THE TEAM: pag 10

Chapter One:
KINGS: pag 11

Europe:
Austria: pag.12
Belgium: pag.13
Czechoslovakia: pag.15
Danemark: pag.18
Estonia: pag.20
Finland: pag.21
France: pag.24
Germany: pag.36
Great Britain: pag.57
Greece: pag.93
Holland: pag.96
Hungary: pag.100
Italy: pag.103
Norway: pag.121
Poland: pag.122
Portugal: pag.125
Romania: pag.127
Spain: pag.128
Sweden: pag.138
Turkey: pag.145
Yugoslavia: pag.147
Indochina e North Asia:
Japan: pag.148
North America:
Canada: pag.154
United States of America: pag.159
Oceania:
Australia: pag.168
New Zealand: pag.172
Sud America:
Argentina: pag.174
Brazil: pag.177

Chapter Two:
KNIGHTS: pag.179

Europe:
Belgium: pag.180
Czechoslovakia: pag.182
Danemark: pag.183
Finland: pag.185
France: pag.187
Germany: pag.194
Great Britain: pag.204
Greece: pag.218
Holland: pag.219
Hungary: pag.222
Israel: pag.223
Italy: pag.224
Norway: pag.237
Poland: pag.238
Portugal: pag.239
Russia: pag.240
Spain: pag.241
Sweden: pag.247
Switzerland: pag.251
Turkey: pag.252
Yugoslavia: pag.253
Indochina & North Asia:
Indonesia: pag.254
Japan: pag.255
Philippines: pag.257
North America:
Canada: pag.258
United States of America: pag.260

Oceania:
Australia: pag.267
South America:
Argentina: pag.268
Brazil: pag.271
Chile: pag.273
Mexico: pag.274
Perù: pag.276
Venezuela: pag.277
International Cooperations: pag.278

Chapter Three:
TROOPERS: pag.279

Europa:
Austria: pag.280
Belgium: pag.281
Bulgaria: pag.284
Czechoslovakia: pag.285
Estonia: pag.287
Finland: pag.288
France: pag.291
Germany: pag.307
Great Britain: pag.320
Greece: pag.339
Holland: pag.340
Hungary: pag.344
Iceland & Greenland: pag.346
Israel: pag.348
Italy: pag.349
Norway: pag.382
Poland: pag.386
Portugal: pag.389
Romania: pag.390
Russia: pag.391
Spain: pag.394
Sweden: pag.401
Switzerland: pag.407
Turkey: pag.410
Yugoslavia: pag.412
Indochina & Asia:
Japan: pag.415
Korea: pag.419
North America:
Canada: pag.420
United States of America: pag.428
Oceania:
Australia: pag.441
New Zealand: pag.443
South Africa:
South Africa: pag.444
South America:
Argentina: pag.445
Brazil: pag.450
Chile: pag.453
Mexico: pag.454
Perù: pag.457
Venezuela: pag.458
South West Asia:
Ex-Sovietic Republics: pag.459
It's almost Prog!: pag.462

APPENDIX: pag.469

PROG ON STAGE a conversation with Libero Robba.: pag.470

BIBLIOGRAPHY AND WEBSITES: pag.472

ARTISTS INDEX: pag.473

THE TEAM

C.A. - CLAUDIO ALOI (Caselle Torinese, 1960): agronomist, researcher, music lover, collector. Breast-fed with milk & Beat, he gradually discovers and studies Soul music, then flirts with Rock-Blues just before giving in to his attraction towards the newborn cries of the '70s sophisticated Pop. Always interested in the phenomenon of Pop music in all its forms, he analyses the aspects that have most influenced the Music industry from the '50s, to better appreciate the magical world of music through the knowledge of its historical and cultural implications. Since 1996 he co-authors *Discomania* with his friend Giorgio Prigione, the only Italian guide to collector records at the time. In 2000 he publishes the book *Viaggio Magico E Misterioso* dedicated to **The Beatles** discography. He also organizes exhibitions and cultural events related to the music industry and has taken part in radio broadcasts (*Raistereo 1, Raistereonotte, Notturno Italiano*) as a musical expert.

G.D.S. - GIUSEPPE DI SPIRITO (Napoli, 1973): a 360 degrees music lover, especially fond of Progressive Rock, which he seeks in all its manifestations, spreading his opinions on websites such as *Arlequins* and *Rotters' Club* (of which he is a founding member). He participates in the brief adventure of the fanzine *Trespass*, collaborates with the Finnish magazine *Colossus* and with the Italian magazine *Metal Shock*. Member of the *Gnosis Project*, he occasionally writes for the weekly magazine Unico. His actual geographical proximity to Donato Zoppo has created a bond made of exchanges and continuous interactions ongoing to this very day.

M.G. - MAURIZIO GALIA (Moncalieri, 1963): painter, illustrator and graphic designer, he graduates from the Fine Arts Academy in Turin. Author of many illustrated books for schools and children, he is best known for a comic strip made in 1987 on the mystery of Mozart's death, titled *Requiem*. In 2003 and 2006 he helps organize, together with ATIF, two personal exhibitions of Paul Whitehead in Turin, publishing his first and only existing catalog. Seriously committed to divulging Prog since 1979, he is also a musician and a composer, founder of the group **Aquael**. In the same year he releases three solo albums using the pseudonym **Maury e i Pronomi**, before finally reforming the aforementioned group in 2008. In 2012 he is the artistic consultant of Viterbo's Italian Prog Rock festival called Le Radici del Rock.

R.V. - ROBERTO VANALI (Varazze, 1961): surveyor, musician, writer, he navigates Prog since 1972, researching with passion recordings coming from all over the world, with a preference for the Canterbury Sound and for more complex compositions. He writes reviews for the famous Progressive web-zine *Arlequins* since 2004, with articles and specials. As far as music is concerned, he was born a drummer in the '70s, but is now devoted only to singing and to Prog compositions. After taking part in various bands, he militates with **Armalite** since 1992, a group selected for the *Trilogy Edition (Inferno, Purgatorio, Paradiso)* published by Musea for the Finnish *Colossus Project* and for *The Progressive Battles* compilation. Recently, he has written a esoteric novel soon to be published.

F.V. - FRANCO VASSIA (Candia Canavese, 1949): an advertising graphic-artist and deep analyst of Rock music; since the '70s he collaborates with *Ciao 2001* and *Super Sound*. Among the founders of Radio Vogue, one of the first free radios, he elaborates a series of workshops and forums for schools and literary clubs on music, to privilege not only the artistic side, but also the social and political aspects. In the '90s he gives birth to the magazine *Nobody's Land: Frammenti Dell'utopia Progressiva*, which is still a reference point for lovers of the sector. In 2001 he publishes *I Campi Della Memoria*, first volume of a trilogy that gathers the interviews and opinions of some of the greatest musicians of the era. Author of the lyrics in the album *I Supplicanti* by **Camera Astralis**, he wrote the preface of the book *...E mi viene da pensare* by **Banco del Mutuo Soccorso**. He also wrote *Resistere a Mafiopoli* together with Giovanni Impastato.

D.Z. - DONATO ZOPPO (Salerno, 1975): journalist and borderline Prog-Rock & Jazz music lover, he writes for the magazines *Jam, Wonderous Stories* and *L'Idea*. Among the founders of the popular web-zine *MovimentiProg*, he is the music responsible for the free-magazine Metromorfosi in Rome. Author of *Premiata Forneria Marconi 1971-2006: 35 Anni Di Rock Immaginifico* (Editori Riuniti 2006) and *La Musica dei Lingalad* (Bastogi 2008), he participates in Racconti a 33 giri (2003) and *100 Dischi Ideali Per Capire Il Rock*, edited by Ezio Guaitamacchi (Editori Riuniti 2007). Also radio conductor of two lucky broadcasts of Radio Città BN: *Rock City Nights* and *A Day In The Life*. Author of Zen stories such as *Stop Over Bombay* (second award for the Premio Freequency - MEI 2005), he coordinates the project TranSonanze, collaborating with Vocidentro Films and **Malaavia Carovana Eterea**. He's also director of the press office Synpress 44. In 2011, he publishes for Arcana Editrice *Prog: Una Suite Lunga Mezzo Secolo*, an essay which can be considered complementary to the book you are now reading, and other recent essays related to artists of the music world.

C.C. - CHRISTINE COLOMO (Planet Earth, 1973): born on American soil in an African Colony before moving to Singapore till the age of 10, she is an English-Italian native speaker, fluent also in French. The rest of her life was based in Turin, Italy, with souvenirs of British, Malay and Chinese customs, ethnocentrically filtered through her new cultural background. Graduated in Languages for duty and in Anthropology for pleasure, she writes tales and short stories, often lyrical, where the boundaries of reality and the limits of her perception of the facts are blended together through the walls of emotion. Today she lives casually, capturing memories in the blurry images of the mind. Music? It depends on the mood of the day. She was probably the only chance to help transpose these 6 rambling Progsters into some kind of an English version.

KINGS
Chapter One

Genesis - *Watcher of the Skies*

Europe: AUSTRIA

KLOCKWERK ORANGE

Herman Delago – *guitars, keyboards, trumpet, vocals,* **Markus Weiler** – *keyboards,* **Guntram Burt** – *bass, guitars, vocals,* **Wolfgang Boeck** – *drums, percussions.*

In 1970, teenager **Herman Delago** was already holding concerts in the Tirol region. In love with European Rock, he forms **Satisfaction of Night** in Innsbruck with some other high-school kids. They played simple songs, many of which were covers, especially from the **The Beatles** and **The Rolling Stones**, but also "The Nile Song" by **Pink Floyd** and **Black Sabbath**'s "Paranoid". When English Prog however reached him, the desire to experiment those sounds and symphonic themes caught on, so in 1974 he forms **Klockwerk Orange**, a name that had nothing to do with Kubrick's film, but was inspired by the colour of **Boeck**'s drum-set. In those days **Delago**'s small rehearsal room became the meeting point for various hippy groups. The magical and relaxed atmosphere naturally led to long music sessions, with influences going from **Bruckner** to **Mozart**, from **King Crimson** to **Emerson Lake & Palmer**, and added elements of Tirol folk-tavern music. They sign up with CBS for their only album published in 1975 titled *Abra-Kadabra*: two long tracks on one side and one long suite on the other, characterized by the dynamic and ever-changing symphonic Prog, with excursions into German and Austrian music and an eye on classical and traditional authors. A mixture on the verge of sobriety, or better, of fake relaxation and hidden simplicity, that brought this album to very high levels, but unfortunately without the slightest success. Textures and movements have nothing simple to them and the almost circus-style trumpet combined with the many organ layers involved, give a certain oddness to the enti-

re work. Short pieces of experimental electronics, even if derived from previous German studies and not only, blend well with parts almost sounding like from a movie score, where one would often expect to see Pinocchio or Buster Keaton jump out of the scene, only to abruptly steer towards a more openly symphonic **Emerson**-ian and epic sound, led by the organ and supported by **Pink Floyd** styled choirs, as in "The Key" or in the title-track's ending. After another sudden break, there comes a Bolero or a Hispanic chivalry theme, then another choir, a slight guitar pattern and again that unfailing tense and dramatic trumpet-playing. We can only imagine the satisfaction of a high-school student whom, at the end of the course, instead of bringing an album chosen randomly according to taste, had one of his very own making. Perhaps part of the great value of this work is due to the fact that they were, as a matter of fact, just kids. **Delago** will later pursue his artistic activities, no longer in a band, but by studying Ambient, New Age and Tirol music, with the extensive use of what would become his favorite instrument, the didgeridoo. **R.V.**

DISCOGRAPHY:
ABRAKADABRA *(1975, CBS).*

Europe: BELGIUM

PRESENT

Roger Trigaux, Reginald Trigaux - *guitar, keyboards*, Daniel Denis, Dave Kerman, Dave Davister - *drums*, Alain Rochette, Pierre Chevalier - *keyboards*, Christian Genet, Ferdinand Philippot, Bruno Bernas, Jean-Pierre Mendes, Kevin Macksoud - *bass*, Maria-Anne Polaris - *vocals*, Yuval Mesner, Matthieu Safatly - *cello*, Dominic Ntoumos, Fred Becker - *horns*.

<<**Present**'s music touches the listener better when it's performed live. Live we are extremely powerful and the music acts directly on the public's emotions. **Present**'s music is made of emotions. It is pure emotion!>>
In this statement by **Roger Trigaux** we find the key to understanding his creature: the importance of emotions, impact, physicality and the power of Rock.
Trigaux first discovers the guitar in 1967, fascinated by **Jimi Hendrix**'s music, and in 1974 he founds **Univers Zero** together with Daniel Denis. They are the true mind of the ensemble until 1979, when they start a new project called **Present**, also involving **Christian Genet**. While still bearing some ties to the band of origin, the debut album's ironic title *Triskaidekaphobie (Fear of number 13)* was a their answer to *1313* by **UZ**, although more nervous and electronic. Despite their frenzy rhythm and themes, Present do not forget the main role of rock-riffs, almost a core to their long compositions.

The second LP released in 1985, more fluid and dynamic, combines the complexity of intellectual writing with the sound stains of **Miles Davis**' *Bitches Brew* and the thickness of the Belgian Avant-rock, through the dazed vocals recalling **Polaris** and the *Fripp*-ish styled guitar playing of their leader. If **Univers Zero** are considered the fathers of Belgian rock, **Present** are the children in search of identity: the first, absorb and use Classical music with some repetitive Rock rhythms and sounds, the latter bring to an extreme its obsessive and heavy matrix echoing **King Crimson** and **Magma**.
After a long pause, in 1989 the label Cuneiform reissues both albums stimulating a rediscovery of **Present**. In the early '90s **Roger** organizes a guitar-duo with his son **Reginald**, a talented guitarist (label Gazul publishes *C.O.D. Performance* only in 1999, a minimalist and noise print album with evocative guitar raids, almost an evolution of **Fripp** and **Göttshing**'s experiments).

Meanwhile **Trigaux** reunites them with a new line-up for a concert, but the actual return of the band (with **Denis Rochelle** and **Guy Segers**) takes place in 1998 with the vehement album *Certitudes*. Although still in a harmonious relationship with **UZ**, **Trigaux**'s writing is the other side of **Daniel Denis**: a dark, shady minimal-rock, influenced both by the barbarisms of intellectual music and by a certain gloomy and morbid post-romanticism. Trigaux manages to involve drummer **Dave Kerman** (**5uu's**, **U Totem**, **Thinking Plague**) and producer Udi Koomran in the birth of *#6*, with two excellent suites, inspired and credible. This new incarnation overwhelms the audience with its experiments with horns and in the visceral and titanic work *High Infidelity*. These adventurous tours are immortalized in a very good live album of 2005.
After 6 albums, many memorable performances and the textbook Avant-rock style, Present is now a very influential name: without it, bands such as **NeBeLNeST**, **Far Corner** and **Guapo** would never have been born. **D.Z.**

DISCOGRAPHY:

TRISKAIDEKAPHOBIE *(Atem, 1981)* **LE POISON QUI RENDE FOU** *(Cuneiform, 1985)* **LIVE!** *(live, Cuneiform 1996)* **CERTITUDES** *(Cuneiform, 1998)* **C.O.D. PERFORMANCE** *(Gazul, 1999)* **N. 6** *(Carbon 7, 1999)* **HI-INFIDELITY** *(Carbon 7, 2001)* **A GREAT INHUMANE ADVENTURE** *(live, Cuneiform 2005)* **BARBARO(Ma non Troppo)** *(Ad Hoc, 2009)*.

Europe: BELGIUM

UNIVERS ZERO

Daniel Denis - *drums*, **Michel Berckmans, Dirk Descheemaeker, Ariane De Bievre, Bart Maris, Serge Bertocchi** - *winds*. **Marcel Dufrane, Patrick Hanappier, Jean-Luc Aime, Thierry Zaboitzeff, André Mergen, Marc Verbist, Igor Semenoff, Aurelia Boven** - *strings*, **Christian Genet, Guy Segers, Reginald Trigaux, Eric Platain** - *bass*, **Emmanuel Nicaise, Andy Kirk, Jean-Luc Plouvier** - *keyboards*, **Roger Trigaux, Michael Delory, Christophe Pons** - *guitars*, **Jean Debefve** - *hurdy-gurdy*, **Ilona Chafe** - *vocals*, **Bart Quartier** - *percussion*, **Louision Renault** - *accordion*.

Gloomy, dark, apocalyptic and above all revolutionary: **Univers Zero**. Definitions abound, the most effective is found on its website: <<*If Stravinsky had a rock band, it would sound like this.*>> In quantitative terms, Belgium has given little to progressive rock, but the weight and quality of a group like **Univers Zero** are absolutely essential for the development of all modern Rock world wide. Describing their style as Chamber Rock means simplifying a brave project of synthesis between Rock, Jazz and classic Avantgarde. Embryo of the **UZ** phenomenon is the **Arkham** avant-rock trio, led by drummer **Daniel Denis** who, in 1972, joins **Magma** with keyboardist **Jean-luc Manderlier**, subsequently founding **Necronomicon** which will finally become **Univers Zero** in 1974. The tight Rock rhythms are engaged by oboe, bassoon and viola, developing a collective writing and a good interplay between both electric and acoustic instruments: the result is a first self-titled album, later reissued as 1313, a debut in deep contrast with the controversial Punk music of 1977. The following year **UZ** begin their famous tour Rock In Opposition and in '79 *Heresie* is released becoming soon known as their funeral album. It's the kind of album you either love or hate, no in between: horrific and desperate atmospheres mark the three long tracks with abnormal chamber music that have no equal, not even in their kinship with **Magma**. It is a historic moment where **King Crimson** and **Henry Cow**'s dream will finally come true: a Euro-rock, freed from all connections with the American matrix, able to incorporate the legacy of **Bartok, Stravinsky** and **Webern** with some folk and the Old Continent's intellectual music. **Roger Trigaux** moves on to found **Present** and with the arrival of keyboardist **Andy Kirk**, the composition becomes broader: like in the album *Ceux Du Dehors*, which looks for a more vivid and dynamic language, always in line with the group's style, linked to the progressive development of themes and sounds. After a short break, **UZ** returns with *Uzed*, a smart and mature sequel of the previous work, using grim fanfares and rock ribbings. *Heatwave* is instead the beginning of a fruitful partnership with label Cuneiform and a massive use of synths.

In 1986 **UZ** breaks up for financial reasons. yet its status of cult band grows all around the world and groups are inspired by their music, from the Italian **Gatto Marte** to the American **Thinking Plague** and, for certain aspects, **Rachel**. In the meantime **Daniel Denis** begins a long-term collaboration with the French **Art Zoyd**, releases two solo LPs. In the second half of the '90s he works on the rebirth of **UZ**. *The Hard Quest* is their comeback and, along with *Rhythmix* and *Implosion*, constitutes the second phase of this band. Shorter tracks with rhythm and sound both oriented towards electronic music, and the help of director **Philippe Seynaeve** or the creation of multimediatic performances of great beauty. It is incorrect to speak of contamination with regards to **UZ**: inspired by the process of synthesis already operated by **Frank Zappa**, in which Rock - in terms of electricity and rhythmic force - has a decisive role, along with Electric Jazz, in a more refined and elegant stylistic dimension. The 2006 live album, their last release, fully confirms this conclusion. **D.Z.**

DISCOGRAPHY:
UNIVERS ZERO (1313) (*Univers Zero, 1977*) **HERESIE** (*Atem, 1979*) **CEUX DU DEHORS** (*Atem, 1981*) **TRIOMPHE DES MOUCHES** (*EP Atem,, 1981*) **CRAWLING WIND** (*EP, Caos International, 1983*) **UZED** (*Cryonic, 1984*) **HEATWAVE** (*Cuneiform, 1986*) **THE HARD QUEST** (*Cuneiform, 1999*) **RHYTHMIX** (*Cuneiform, 2002*) **IMPLOSION** (*Cuneiform 2004*) **LIVE** (*live, Cuneiform, 2006*).

Europe: **CZECHOSLOVAKIA**

COLLEGIUM MUSICUM

Marián Varga - *piano, organ, synthesizer,* **Fedor Frešo** - *bass guitar,* **Dušan Hájek** - *drums,* **Karel Witz** - *electric guitar,* **Pavol Hammel** - *vocal,* **František Griglák** - *guitars.*

No doubt in eastern European countries the lesson of groups such as The **Nice**, **EL&P** and **Ekseption** was learned like nowhere else. **Collegium Musicum** too points its musical horizons towards a form of Symphonic Rock with slight Goth infiltrations, strongly inspired by **Deep Purple**'s *Concert For Group And Orchestra*. The originality this band is clearly expressed in a first self-titled album published in 1971: the Baroque inflection of their sound is supported by a Hammond organ played with unmatched technique and surrounded by guitars with a bass that always rises to the occasion. Both this first album and the next, *Konvergencie*, contain long compositions in which the group is able to express all its energy, played with enviable skill: it is not a coincidence that **Marián Varga** is repeatedly mentioned among the best keyboardists in the world, superior to superstars like **Rick Wakeman**. The classical background of the group produces endless sequences of small gems, inspired by pieces from **Bach** and **Vivaldi** with a mix of very pleasant melodies, never predictable nor tedious. Undeniable praise goes to the arrangements that, especially in this last album, give a touch of orchestral class, beyond the limits of majestic, to the whole work.

Their third release of 1973 is a live album that meant to show the most creative side of this band, thanks to a series of improvisations not included in the studio performances. The truth is that it fails to properly stir the audience's emotions for it strangely and inexplicably lacks in energy and pathos. In the meantime **Varga** begins several artistic collaborations with **Pavol Hammel** and **Radim Hladík**, among others, producing some important recordings.

Zelena Posta is a collection of songs inspired by Classical music, with a very personal interpretation based on the virtuosity of the musicians, who engage in a sort of competition to prove their worth. Only flaw: the texts are in Slovak. *Na Druhom Programe Sna* is more affected by **Hammel**'s presence and is overall a good Prog album, strongly inspired by themes dear to **Emerson, Lake & Palmer**.

In 1978 *Continuous* is published as their last and most controversial album, to love or to hate, with no shades of grey; at the same time it represents the coming of age of **Varga** and his desire to move on and experiment with new sounds and artistic horizons, forecasting a good solo career, unfortunately far from Prog.

C.A.

DISCOGRAPHY:
COLLEGIUM MUSICUM *(Supraphon, 1970)* **KONVERGENCIE** *(Opus, 1971)* **ZELENE POSTA** *(Opus, 1972)* **NA DRUHOM PROGRAME SNA** *(Opus, 1976)* **CONTINUO** *(Opus, 1978)* **ON A ONA** *(Opus, 1979)* **SPEAK, MEMORY** *(Live CD-DVD, Pavian, 2010).*

Europe: CZECHOSLOVAKIA

FERMATA

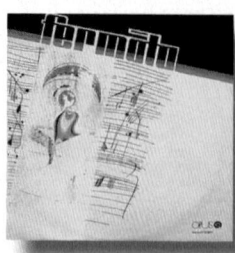

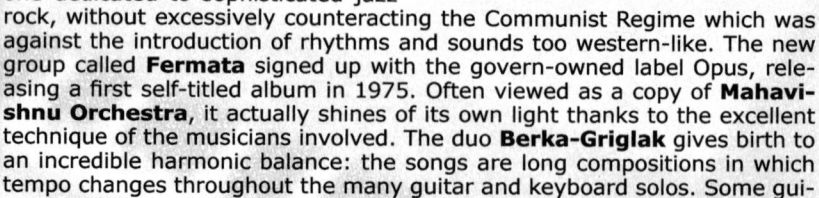

Thomas Berka - *keyboards,* **Frantisek Griglak** - *guitars,* **Ladislav Lucenic** - *bass,* **Karol Oláh** - *drums,* **Anton Jaro** - *bass,* **Milan Tedla** - *violin.*

In 1973 **Collegium Musicum**'s guitarist **Frantisek Griglak** leaves the band and together with keyboardist **Thomas Berka** forms another one dedicated to sophisticated jazz rock, without excessively counteracting the Communist Regime which was against the introduction of rhythms and sounds too western-like. The new group called **Fermata** signed up with the govern-owned label Opus, releasing a first self-titled album in 1975. Often viewed as a copy of **Mahavishnu Orchestra**, it actually shines of its own light thanks to the excellent technique of the musicians involved. The duo **Berka-Griglak** gives birth to an incredible harmonic balance: the songs are long compositions in which tempo changes throughout the many guitar and keyboard solos. Some guitar passages inevitably pay their tribute to **John McLaughlin**, but it's the keyboards and synthesizer mix which provides a winning recipe.

Two years later *Pieseň Z Hôľ-Song from Ridges* incredibly confirms the musicians' artistic talents and is one of the best jazz rock albums of the '70s. Despite some changes in line-up, the band's sound remains vital and pleasant and the contribution of

violinist **Milan Tedla** adds atmosphere and melody to a more symphonic album than the previous, yet still remarkably oriented towards a fusion genre interpreted with skill.

In 1977 *Huascaran* is released: a concept album that narrates the tragedy of the 1970 earthquake that shook Peru. Recorded without bassist **Jaro**, replaced by **Lucenic**, this album is considered **Fermata**'s masterpiece: jazz rock dips into miraculous ethnic reflections without offending its classy and elegant spirit, an experiment that precedes what **Weather Report** will undergo several years later. Regretfully their potential will remain unspoken for,

partially due to the ostracism of a country stifled by a repressive regime.

Biela Planeta in 1980 steers them definately towards Fusion, while maintaining the high levels of technical quality. The same happens with their next album *Generation*, while *Ad libitum* of 1984 is more a return to Rock record, slightly more catchy too. The rest of their production is far from Prog.

C.A.

DISCOGRAPHY:
FERMATA *(Opus, 1975)* **PIESEN Z HOL** *(Opus, 1976)* **HUASCARAN** *(Opus, 1977)* **BIELA PLANETA** *(Opus, 1980)* **GENERATION** *(Opus, 1981)* **AD LIBITUM** *(Opus, 1984)* **SIMILE** *(UMSK, 1991)* **AD REAL TIME** *(ENA, 1994)* **X** *(BMG-Ariola, 1999).*

Europe: **CZECHOSLOVAKIA**

MODRY EFEKT

Radim Hladik - *guitar*, **Vlado Cech** - *drums*, **Milos Svoboda** - *guitar*, **Jiri Kozel** - *bass*, **Fedor Freso** - *bass*, **Lesek Semelka** - *keyboards*.

Rightly regarded as the most representative among Czechoslovakia's Prog bands, they form in the late '60s as **Blue Effect**. in the wake of those bands that reinterpreted classic Rock-Blues and Rhythm & Blues from overseas and was therefore severely opposed by the country's censorship, which compelled them to change their name, too blatantly western.
They begin their adventure influenced by the early '70s works of **Yes**, **King Crimson** and **Jethro Tull**. *Modrý Efekt & Jazzový orchestr Čs. rozhlasu: Nová Syntéza*, their first album, has this new style and is a real surprise: Rock sounds placed in a big-band context. An extremely brave experiment which marries diverse musical genres, quite the opposite from each other, a bit like what **Deep Purple** did with their famous *Concerto For Group And Orchestra*. This experiment was a resounding success and gave them the opportunity to continue with very particular musical styles, supported by excellent quality artists.
The sequel manages to improve their initial intentions thanks to the inclusion of **Lesek Semelka**'s brilliant voice. Technically flawless, well arranged and balanced, the album swings between sweet melodies, gentle Jazz and more Rock-ish sounds. Full of dreamlike atmospheres, similar to some of the most inspired **Pink Floyd** moments, and short bursts of Space-Rock create a setting in between Symphonic Prog and experimental Jazz Rock.
The band's magic flows on with *Modry Efekt & Radim Hladik*, almost an entirely instrumental work with references to a song already included in *Nova synteza 2*, rearranged in a more dynamic key; as for the rest, beautiful the flute insertions which duet with the keyboards, accompanied by particularly inspired guitars.

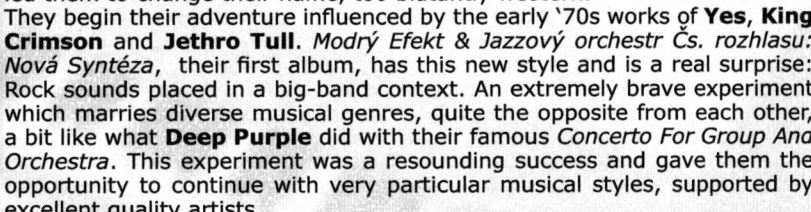

After this record the line-up changes, aggregating among others, **Fedor Freso** from **Collegium Musicum**, thus forming a sort of Czech super-group now called **M Efekt**, which publishes in 1977 the wonderful *Svitanie*. This album is the culmination of all the personal experiences gathered so far by the quartet, still strongly inspired by **Yes** for the majesty of their sound, though the Jazz-Rock origins still affects the composition. An almost complete absence of vocals does not diminish the artistic potential, but indeed, thanks to the exquisite arrangements and clever positioning of the solos, creates a wonderfully harmonious balance.
The following album *Svet Hledaku* is still good despite **Freso**'s absence, credited more to the artistic ambitions of **Hladik** than to the group itself. References to fusion disappear in the footsteps of **Yes**. *33* was released in 1981 as an attempt to recover some of the sounds forgotten along the way, but the chemistry is no longer there: the flavour is not what it used to be a few years earlier and although the album is a good exercise of musical technique, it does not convey the same vibrations. **C.A.**

DISCOGRAPHY:
MEDITACE *(Supraphon, 1969)* **KINGDOM OF LIFE** *(English version of "MEDITACE", Supraphon-Artia, 1970)* **CONJUNCTIO** *(Supraphon, 1970)* **NOVÁ SYNTÉZA** *(Panton, 1971)* **NOVÁ SYNTÉZA 2** *(Panton, 1974)* **MODRY EFEKT & RADIM HLADIK** *(Supraphon, 1974)* **THE BLUE EFFECT A BENEFIT OF RADIM HLADIK** *(English version of "MODRY EFEKT" & "RADIM HLADIK"(Supraphon-Artia 1975)* **SVITANIE** *(Supraphon, 1977)* **SVET HLEDAKU** *(Panton, 1978)* **33** *(Supraphon, 1981)*.

Europe: DANEMARK

ALRUNE ROD

First lineup 1969 – 1971:
Giese – *guitar, vocals,* **Kurt Ziegler 'Pastor'** - *keyboards,* **Claus From** – *drums,* **Leif Roden** – *vocals, bass.*
Second lineup 1972 – 1975:
Leif Roden – *vocals, bass,* **Karsten Høst** – *drums,* **Mikael Miller** – *guitar,* **Ole Poulsen** – *guitar.*

Founded in 1968, they were in love with the '60s Psychedelia and Beat music, able to incorporate in their style a strong and rough sound, containing also neat and light shades held together through a very innovative drive. In the beginning the group's balance was based on strenuous organ excursions and searing guitar strumming, that suddenly subside to make way for almost intimate moments, with **Roden**'s voice extending from the thinnest whisper to the relentless drama and most strangled scream.

A debut single released by Sonet came out that same year as a perfect prelude to the Danish movement in embryo at the time, and of which they were among the protagonists. At the beginning of 1969 their first LP, *Alrune Rod*, is released bringing out a natural tendency towards dilated atmospheres and prolonged tracks. Certain references to **Pink Floyd**, **Vanilla Fudge** and **The Grateful Dead** are clear enough, but it is important to emphasize how the solutions and vocals of this record are incredibly similar

and sometimes precursors of **Van Der Graaf Generator**'s intuitions of that same period, as in the song 'Bjergsangen' and its 11 minute wonders.

Coherent but obtaining a different result is the definitely more Space-Rock oriented second album *Hej Du* (1970) and its monumental **Floyd**-ian suite 'Perlesøen', almost 22 minutes of psychedelia chases between hazy **Hendrix** themes, **Gilmour** wavering sounds and a rich, present and often protagonist organ. In the suite, the group also makes wise use of electronics, noises, various dissonances and elements of Kraut-Rock Avant-garde.

In 1972 another psychedelic record full of rich implications and new ideas is released, but this work proves to be more Rock orien-

ted (well underlined by the title *Alrune Rock*), while maintaining mixed features of styles and forms: from the progressive "Om At", to the rousing and rhythmic Rock of "Rock Soster", ending with an ethereal, folkish and hippie "Kender du det". This work is clearly the last of the band's first phase, as they appears a year later in a different line-up led by **Roden** and completely redefined, with two guitars, the total loss of keyboards and a new label. Needless to say that *Spredt For Vinden* (1973) presents a sharp change in sound: the well intertwined guitars push a gap between the arrangements and Prog, moving towards a softer Psychedelic Pop with elements from Beat, Folk, Hippie and Americana. Even worse fate for the album *4 Vejs* made of simple and conventional Pop songs. In 2002 their last reunion with a slightly different line-up and a series of forgettable concerts.

R.V.

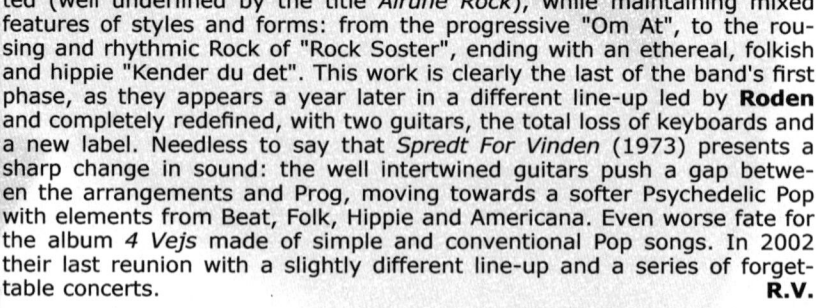

DISCOGRAPHY:

TÆL ALDRIG IMORGEN MED (single) *(1968, Sonet)* **ALRUNE ROD** *(1969, Sonet)* **HEJ DU** *(1970, Sonet)* **ALRUNE ROCK** *(1972, Sonet)* **SPREDT FOR VINDEN** *(1973, Mandragora)* **4-VEJS** *(1974, Mandragora)* **TATUBA TAPES** *(1975, Mandragora)* **ALRUNEN LIVE IN AALBORG** *(2002, Ohm Records)* **RAGNAROCK LIVE '74** *(2004, Karma Music).*

Europe: DANEMARK

BURNIN RED IVANHOE

Kim Menzer - *winds, piano, percussion*, **Ole Fick** - *guitars, vocals*, **Karsten Vogel** - *keyboards, saxophones*, **Jess Staer** - *bass, acoustic guitar*, **Bo Thrige Andersen** - *drums, percussion*.

It was on one spring evening in 1967, at the end of an afternoon full of discussions, that **Burnin' Red Ivanhoe** took its musical form. Not yet sealed into their final line-up, the band was well aware of its potential and began to compose songs that combined Blues, Jazz and Rock in a very personal and innovative mix, which later will take the shape of a Progressive Jazz-Blues. When in 1969 they finally make their way to a recording studio for the first time, the songs are already plenty, so for the debut album *144 M* they have to opt for a double vinyl. A choice that initially did not favor sales, but paid back once the rumors spread along with positive reviews. The songs appear in a rather heterogeneous way, with clear hard Psychedelic references and Acid late-Beat implications. Among the 20 tracks of the original record (brought to 26 in the CD version) "Purple Hearts", "Brondbyerne Ivanhoe", the proggier "Marsfesten", the Jazz-Rock of "Antique Peppermint" or the distortion of themes dear to **The Rolling Stones** such as 'Ivanhoe in the Woods'. The immediate start on a second release led to what is considered their best effort: the 1970 self-titled album. Compared to the previous it has a broader stretch in the time lapse of execution; but for what seemed

to be functional in "Across The Windowsill", "Gong-Gong", "The Elephant Song" or the experimental "Secret Oyster Service", the same cannot be said for "Rotating Irons", a long and quite bland slow-Blues.

W.W.W., their third work published in 1971, proved to be far more Prog, conceptually more elaborate, with references to **Traffic**, **Colosseum** and some of the finest **Jethro Tull**. Emblematic the iridescent "2nd Floor" and "Croydon"; important experimental **Pink Floyd** moments in the track "WWW"; a great dynamic Prog in both "Avez-Vous Kaskelainen" and "Kaske-Vous Karsemose".

6 Elefantskovcikadeviser is a very different story: of that same year but with guest singer **Povl Dissing**, it has clear Folk trends, except for the mini-suite "2 Tingel Tangelmanden", a fantasy Prog track. After 1972, the band takes a break, developing similar side projects such as *Secret Oyster* and *Day Of The Phoenix*. Finally 1974 gives birth to *Right On*, which still reaches a good level though, with some Funky Rock tendencies. The band then breaks up again until 1980 when they reunite under a different label. The following album *Shorts* is a simple Pop Rock album with no pretensions of any kind. Same thing happens with the second reunion at the end of the '90s with the release of *Lack Of Light*, followed by several years of live performances, from nostalgic old songs to the attempt of an easy listening Pop. **R.V.**

DISCOGRAPHY:

M 144 *(1969, Sonet)* **BURNIN' RED IVANHOE** *(1970, Sonet)* **W.W.W** *(1971, Sonet)* **6 ELEFANTSKOVCIKADEVISER** [Povl Dissing With Burnin' Red Ivanhoe] *(1971, Sonet)* **MILEY SMILE - STAGE RECALL** *(1972, Sonet)* **RIGHT ON** *(1974, Sonet)* **SHORTS** *(1980, Pick Up Pulp)* **BURNIN' LIVE 1971-72** *(1991, DMA)* **LACK OF LIGHT** *(1998, Bri)*

Europe: ESTONIA

MESS
(Sven Grünberg)

Sven Grünberg - *keyboards, vocals*, **Elmu Värk** - *guitars*, **Ivar Sipra** - *drums, percussions*, **Matti Timmermann** - *bass*, **Andrus Vaht** - *drums (on the track "Tiik")*, **Härmo Härm** - *electronic instruments*, **Leho Lätte** - *horns*, **Valdek Põld** - *horns*, **Rold Uusväli** - *organ*, **Tõnu Kaljuste* - *vocals*.

Brainchild of keyboardist and composer **Sven Grünberg**, they were the first Soviet group ever to play a Symphonic Rock of clear Progressive dye. Perhaps due to the proximity to Scandinavia, perhaps due to the great musical intelligence and intuitiveness of their leader, their approach was easily identifiable with a trend that moved in parallel across the rest of Europe, unlike in the remaining Soviet Union areas where we find a certain delay in the development of the Prog genre.
Their beginning in 1973/1974 was probably not an easy one, considering that the Regime imposed itself also on how to play music, but the result was still very high and certainly not inferior to the works of more famous bands abroad. **Sven**, passionate with synthesizers and other electronic devices of the time, found his perfect alter ego in **Härmo Harm**, an expert in electronics, who personally assembled western-styled synths especially for him. Unfortunately all the material produced since 1974 was published only in 1980 with the release of a record containing songs that fade out before the real ending of the track. The German label Bella Musica will finally issue almost all rest of the available material in 1995. Also here the quality is penalized by the too early faded endings and the partitions and subdivisions of some of the songs. The recordings are still not fully satisfactory, but allow to present a band of extraordinary ability and its very creative composer.

An album that really gathers their most representative material is Strangiato Records 2004 *Kusi Eneselt* where **Grünberg** is given the opportunity to clean and re-master his original tapes, publishing it in two versions, standard and deluxe, also containing a second CD with high quality bonus tracks and live performances (the title track goes from 10 to 16 minutes compared to the previous 1995 version, allowing to appreciate the entire song: a rare progressive combination between the Symphonic

and Space genres). Not being a self-centred person, **Grünberg** leaves ample room to each of the musicians involved, creating complex and intricate guitar and horn passages of incomparable beauty. Tracks like "Tilk" or "Rohelised Leed" are an ethereal sonic bliss, thanks to atmospheres that partially recall **Genesis**, **Yes** and **Pink Floyd** and the Canterbury school. **Sven Grünberg** also produced some soloist material that unfortunately did not achieve the same remarkable levels.

R.V.

DISCOGRAPHY:
SVEN GRÜNBERG'S PROGE-ROCK GROUP (MESS) *(1995, Bella Musica)* **KÜSI ENESELT** *(2004, Strangiato Records)*, **SVEN GRÜNBERG: HINGUS** *(Melodya, 1981)*.

Europe: FINLAND

HAIKARA

Vesa Lehtinen - *vocals, percussion,* **Vesa Lattunen** - *vocals, guitars, piano, bass, keyboards,* **Harry Pystynen** - *sax, flute,* **Timo Vuorinen** - *bass,* **Markus Heikkerö** - *drums, percussion,* **Auli Lattunen** - *vocals,* **Matti Heinanen** - *vocals,* **Jan Schaper** - *sax, flute,* **Tommi Mäkinen** - *bass,* **Jukka Teerisaari** - *drums,* **Saara Hedlund** - *vocals,* **Hannu Kivilä** - *cello.*

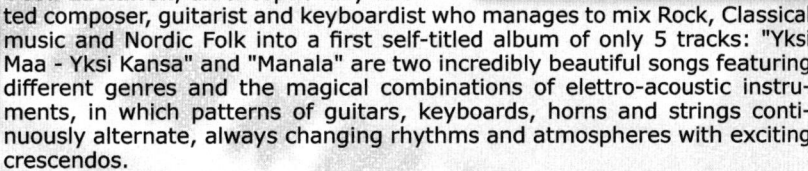

Formed in 1971 around the figure of **Vesa Lattunen**, an exceptionally talented composer, guitarist and keyboardist who manages to mix Rock, Classical music and Nordic Folk into a first self-titled album of only 5 tracks: "Yksi Maa - Yksi Kansa" and "Manala" are two incredibly beautiful songs featuring different genres and the magical combinations of elettro-acoustic instruments, in which patterns of guitars, keyboards, horns and strings continuously alternate, always changing rhythms and atmospheres with exciting crescendos.

The second album *Geafar*, out two years later, maintains the same level of the previous, confirming all the good things with the addition of sweet vocals performed by the leader's sister. The dynamic Rock of "Change" introduces to a whole series of well crafted compositions, in which guitar and sax take turns with sublime moments of melancholy and sweetness, the band's trademark.

In *Iso Lintu* dated 1975 sees them taking a step backwards with more commercial songs, although there are a few good moments as in part of "Kuutamo", suite for orchestra and rock-band, that unfortunately never had an official publication. After issuing some singles of little interest, they break-up because of their different views, only to return in 1998 with a new line-up and a high quality album called *IV Domino*. The tracks owe their beauty to the fact they reflect the old style of the band. This new found youth is confirmed both in the remake of "Yksi Maa - Yksi Kansa" for a tribute to Finnish Prog and, above all, by the 2001 release *Tuhkamaa* iin which, even given the reduction of the compositions' length, we still find the strong personality and quality of the first two works.

The subsequent participation in projects of the fanzine Colossus in *(Kalevala* and *The Spaghetti Epic)* shows a band at its fullest, especially in the wonderful, majestic and classical suite "The West", also full of eccentricities and which can be considered one of the highest peaks achieved by **Haikara**. Unfortunately, while working on new projects, **Lattunen** suddenly dies putting an end to one of the most beautiful musical adventures in the history of Prog. **G.D.S.**

DISCOGRAPHY:
HAIKARA *(RCA, 1972)* **GEAFAR** *(RCA, 1974)* **ISO LINTU** *(private press, 1976)* **IV DOMINO** *(Metamorphos, 1998);* **TUHKAMAA** *(Mellow, 2001).* **Participations:** **TUONEN TYTAR** *(Mellow, 2001)* **KALEVALA** *(Musea, 2003)* **THE SPAGHETTI EPIC** *(Musea, 2004).*

Europe: FINLAND

TASAVALLAN PRESIDENTTI

Jukka Tolonen - *guitar*, **Måns Groundstroem** - *bass*, **Vesa Aaltonen** - *drums*, **Frank Robson** - *keyboards*, **Juhani Aaltonen** - *sax, flute*, **Eero Raittinen** - *vocals*, **Pekka Pöyry** - *sax, flute*, **Heikki Virtanen** - *bass*.

Parallel to the birth of **Wigwam**, the disbandment of **Blues Section** also leads to the creation of **Tasavallan Presidentti**. This new band already shows its amazing personality in their 1969 self-titled debut, which combines different styles of music and moods, Prog Rock with Jazz and English Blues influences, resuming and expanding certain ideas already carried out by **Traffic**. The musical apparatus is first category, with a big spot light on **Jukka Tolonen**'s top-notch guitar qualities.

The sequel *Tasavallan Presidentti II* a year later, not only confirms the instrumental prowess of the band, but allows the stylistic creativity to shine, placing them among the most important Finnish Prog artists. The important collaboration with Folk-rock singer and songwriter **Pekka Streng** leads to the album *Magneettimiehen Kuolema* in 1970, but it is with the next, *Lambertland* (1972) that they will leave a mark: a fantastic record that outlines a decisive trend towards a very original Jazz-rock, where the patterns between **Pekka Pöyry**'s sax and flute, and **Tolonen**'s electric guitar shine in a very particular manner. As a matter of fact, the well arranged instrumental passages are the main attraction of this work, with rhythmic cavalcades that decisively fit the Rock style of the time. A praise however, goes to the beautiful vocal melodies and warm voice of **Eero Raittinen**, which interprets them to perfection.

These features are also to be also found in 1973's *Milky Way Moses*, which reproduces the energy of some of the best **Colosseum** material. After this LP, and a tour through Scandinavia and Great Britain, the band disappears for nearly three decades. 2001 sees their reunion with a come-back album, *Still Struggling For Freedom*, a live recording that documents their well known skills on stage and eagerness to continue in the footsteps of their glorious past. *Six Complete* follows in 2006, a good record, even if it does not add anything new to their style. **Jukka Tolonen**'s solo career which begins in 1971 with the label Love Records publishing four highly recommended albums: *Tolonen!* (1971), *Summer Games* (1973), *The Hook* (1974) and *Hysterica* (1975), all containing a Progressive Blues-rock inspired by **Hendrix** with heavy Jazz insertions. **G.D.S.**

DISCOGRAPHY:
TASAVALLAN PRESIDENTTI *(1969, Love Records)* **TASAVALLAN PRESIDENTTI II** *(1970, Columbia)* **LAMBERTLAND** *(1972, Love Records)* **MILKY WAY MOSES** *(1973, Love Records)* **STILL STRUGGLING FOR FREEDOM** *(2001, Akbazar)* **SIX COMPLETE** *(2006, Presence Records)* **POP-LIISA-1** *(2016, Swart Records)*.

Europe: FINLAND

WIGWAM

Jukka Gustavson - *keyboards, vocals,* **Jim Pembroke** - *vocals, piano, guitar,* **Ronnie Österberg** - *drums,* **Mats Huldén** - *bass,* **Nikke Nikamo** - *guitar,* **Pekka Pohjola** - *bass,* **Pekka Rechardt** - *chitarra,* **Måns Groundstroem** - *bass,* **Hessu Hietanen** - *keyboards.*

The origin of Finnish prog is usually traced back to 1968, when the legendary blues-rock band **Blues Section** disbands and from its ashes rise two icons such as **Wigwam** and **Tasavallan Presidentti**. **Jim Pembroke**, **Vladimir Nikke Nikamo**, **Mats Huldén**, **Ronnie Österberg** and **Jukka Gustavson**, the first core of **Wigwam**, publish *Hard'n'Horny* in 1969, an album which goes from Blues to Symphonic Pop, combining Folk connotations vaguely recalling **Traffic**. The group sees its turning point with the entry of **Pekka Pohjola**, present in *Tombstone Valentine* (1970) and, more importantly, in what represents one of the symbols of Finnish prog, *Fairyport*, published in 1971, a magnificent and balanced compendium of Canterbury sounds, Jazz-rock and romantic atmospheres (**Frank Zappa**'s *Hot Rats* is also a clear source of inspiration).

They replicate in 1973 with another excellent work of extraordinary quality with the same style, entitled *Being*, but the golden moment is short and a revolution in the line-up imminent: the defections of **Pohjola** and **Gustavson** and the entry of **Pekka Rechardt** and **Måns Groundstroem**, direct the band's sound towards a less Progressive Rock, yet still quite effective. After *Live Music From the Twilight Zone* they publish *Nuclear Nightclub* and *Lucky Golden Stripes* and *Starpose*, their greatest successes, and they are also launched on the British market by Virgin. Beautiful albums such as *Nuclear Nightclub* (a classic of Finnish Rock) are characterized by a classy Rock style with only a few digression into Prog and Folk, prelude to the work *Dark Album*, slightly plainer and with no real drive to it.

Österberg's suicide in 1980 marks the end to the first part of their story. In the 90ies **Pembroke**, **Rechardt** and **Groundstroem** reunite the band with a variety of interesting Pop-rock works, an eye on the past and the other on Psychedelia. Among these, the double live *Wigwam Plays Wigwam*, where they are in enviable shape, celebrating themselves in a partial remake of their repertoire.

Pohjola, **Gustavson** and **Pembroke** all have brilliant solo careers too: while **Pohjola** will be treated in another section of this book, on **Gustavson** we wish to point out the amazing *Jaloa Ylpeyttä Yletän* (1978, Love Records), containing a very wide range of instruments for an orchestral sound and with original styles between Jazz and Symphonic Rock.   **G.D.S.**

DISCOGRAPHY:
HARD 'N' HORNY (1969, Love Records) **TOMBSTONE VALENTINE** (1970, Love Records) **FAIRYPORT** (1971, Love Records) **BEING** (1973, Love Records) **LIVE FROM THE TWILIGHT ZONE** (1975, Love Records) **NUCLEAR NIGHTCLUB** (1975, Love Records) **LUCKY GOLDEN STRIPES AND STARPOSE** (1976, Love Records) **DARK ALBUM** (1978, Love Records) **LIGHT AGES** (1993, Polarvox) **WIGWAM PLAYS WIGWAM - LIVE** (2001, EMI) **TITANS WHEEL** (2002, EMI) **SOME SEVERAL MOONS** (2005, Major Leidén Productions).

Europe: FRANCE

ANGE

Christian Decamps - *vocals, keyboards*, **Francis Decamps** - *keyboards, vocals*, **Jean-Michel Brezovar** - *guitar, flute, vocals*, **Daniel Haas** - *bass*, **Gérard Jelsch** - *drums*, **Claude Demet** - *guitar, flute*, **Gerald Renard** - *bass*, **Serge Cuenot** - *guitar*, **Jean Claude Potin** - *drums*, **Laurent Sigrist** - *bass*, **Didier Visieux** - *bass*, **Robert Defer** - *guitar*, **Francis Meyer** - *drums*, **Jean-Pierre Guichard** - *drums*, **Tristan Decamps** - *keyboards, vocals*, **Hassan Hajdi** - *guitar*, **Thierry Sidhoum** - *bass*, **Hervé Rouyer** - *drums*, **Caroline Crozat** - *vocals*, **Benoît Cazzulini** - *drums*.

Formed in 1969, they start off with a live tour, performing the opera *La Fantastique Epopée du General Machin* (documented later in their 1978 album *En Concert*), in which the band proposes a very theatrical Rock, the beginning of an extraordinarily brilliant career. After publishing a first single, things start to get more serious and their Symphonic Rock debut *Caricatures* is published in 1972 containing slightly dark atmospheres exhibited with a certain emphasis and highlighted by the charismatic singer **Christian Decamps**.

After this, a series of very high level albums mark indelibly the history of French Symphonic Prog (*Le Cimetiére des Arlequins*, *Au Delà Du Délire*, *Emile Jacotey*, *Par les Fils de Mandrin*) and the live performance *Tome VI*. with its noisy and spooky organ will become the trademark of **Ange**. The theatricality with which all is presented and the precise placement of guitar and flute, do the rest.

For a while the history of the group coincides with that of many colleagues of the time: the strong Punk and Disco music trend had majors labels searching for more and more marketable products, thus they begin to move towards a more direct and accessible Pop-rock, which had just the right touch of aggressiveness. They also record an album with cover songs of French singers, but the golden era seems to be over. *Fou!* in 1984 opens to new opportunities as also *Seve Qui Peut* and *Les Larmes du Dalai Lama* where the symphonic sounds return with new vigor, yet in 1995 they go on a farewell tour. Luckily they issue a few other albums and **Christian Decamps** reforms the band together with his son **Tristan** and other young talents. *The Voiture à Eau*, the spectacular *Culinaire Lingus*, *?*, are all excellent examples of their modern Symphonic Rock. They begin this new incarnation with a foot in the past, emanating contemporary sounds through a dash of electronic music and an overwhelming energy that has few equals. **Ange** are among the few giants that were able to update their sound without denying what was done before. The cohesion between the leader's experience and his companions' verve is high and they prove it on stage (very interesting too are *Le Tour de la Question* and celebratory *Zenith An II*). **G.D.S.**

RECOMMENDED RECORDINGS:

CARICATURES *(1972, Philips)* **LE CIMETIÉRE DES ARLEQUINS** *(1973, Philips)* **AU DELAÀ DU DÈLIRE** *(1974, Philips)* **EMILE JACOTEY** *(1975, Philips)* **PAR LES FILS DE MANDRIN** *(1976, Philips)* **BY THE SONS OF MANDRIN** *(1976, Philips)* **TOME VI** *(1977, Philips)* **EN CONCERT** *(1978, RCA)* **GUET-APENS** *(1978, Philips)* **VU D'UN CHIEN** *(1980, Philips)* **MOTEUR!** *(1982, Philips)* **A PROPOS DE...** *(1983, Philips)* **LA GARE DE TROYES** *(1983, Phonogram)* **FOU!** *(1984, Trema)* **EGNA** *(1984, Trema)* **TOUT FEU TOUT FLAMME** *(1987, Marianne)* **SEVE QUI PEUT** *(1989, Celluloid)* **LES LARMES DU DALAÏ LAMA** *(1992, Phonogram)* **UN P'TIT TOUR ET PUIS S'EN VONT** *(1995, ADN; reissued on CD as* **Rideau!** *And* **A... Dieu**) **LA VOITURE À EAU** *(1999, Un Pied dans la Marge)* **RÊVES-PARTIES** *(2000, Un Pied dans la Marge)* **CULINAIRE LINGUS** *(2001, Un Pied dans la Marge)* **TOME 87** *(2002, Musea)* **EN CONCERT – PAR LES FILS DE MANDRIN MILLÉSIMÉ 77** *(2003, Musea)* **?** *(2005, Un Pied dans la Marge)* **LE TOUR DE LA QUESTION** *(2007, Un Pied dans la Marge)* **ZENITH AN II** *(2007, Musea)* **SOUFFLEURS DE VERS** *(2008, Un Pied dans la Marge)*.

Europe: FRANCE

ART ZOYD

Patricia Dallio - *piano, electric piano* - **Gérard Hourbette** - *viola, violin, keyboards, percussions* - **Didier Pietton** - *saxophones, percussions* - **Jean-Pierre Soarez** - *trumpet, horns, percussions* - **Theirry Zaboitzeff** - *bass, cello, guitars, tapes, keyboards.*

Cemented to the foundations of the best European Avant-garde, they represent one of the highest levels of expression, smartness and innovation in France. Initially strongly influenced by **Frank Zappa** and **Captain Beefheart**. their first single Sangria was officially launched in 1969. Nothing really relevant happened, so they focused more on live performances, often improvised, with long passages full of Blues and Free Jazz, but traditionally played with a clear Rock attitude. In 1971 the harmony of the group started to collapse and some musicians left, replaced by **Gérard Hourbette** and **Thierry Zaboïtzeff**, two artists with a very innovative impulse, unfortunately refrained till 1975, when the founding members finally also quit the band, leaving them free to explore every possible avant-garde path. A first self-produced album is then released with an absolutely atypical line-up (violin, cello, trumpet, bass and piano) and a first real tour begins as opening act for **Magma**. Their music was one of the most unusual you could hear at the time, embracing Classical, Contemporary, Chamber music, Electronic, Jazz, Zeuhl and Minimalist experimentation. This new way of conceiving music, open and wholesome with no preconceived notion or caged-in scheme, saw them become a bridge between old and new for their being so traversal and indefinable.

In 1978 their joining **Chris Cutler**'s movement Rock In Opposition came natural and they took part in many music events. Between 1979 and 1982 three albums of great value were released: absolute relevance is given to *Phase IV* which fully demonstrates the great innovative and compositional skills of both leaders. The band, even without guitar and drums, was appreciated by the inveterate Avant-garde fans, also capturing the Rock intellectuals attention. Songs of incredible energy and an ever-changing formula that owe very much to the development of electronic devices that always provided new cues of interest.

1983 sets a new era of collaboration between music and image, through the ballet choreography of *Le Mariage du Ciel et de l' Enfer* which brought them to play in the temple of classical music, La Scala in Milan, and later also to feature in many cult film soundtracks such as *Nosferatu* (1988), *Faust* (1995), *Haxan* (1997) and *Metropolis* (2002).

In 1997 **Zaboitzeff** leaves and the band will somehow become a different kind of creature, with dozens of musicians composing different kinds of music, having almost exclusively electronic and synthetic sounds, yet always maintaining a good level in quality. **R.V.**

DISCOGRAPHY:
SYMPHONIE POUR LE JOUR OÙ BRÛLERONT LES CITÉS *(1976, Art Zoyd self product / Atem)* **MUSIQUE POUR L'ODYSSÉE** *(1979, Atem / Cryonic)* **GÉNÉRATION SANS FUTUR** *(1980, Atem / Cryonic)* **PHASE IV** *(1982, RE)* **LES ESPACES INQUIETS** *(1983, Mantra / COM)* **LE MARIANE DU CIEL ET DE L'ENFER** *(1985, Cryonic / MAD)* **BERLIN** *(1987, Cryonic / COM)* **NOSFERATU** *(1988, Atonal / ACD)* **ART ZOYD / J.A. DEANE / J. GREINKE** *(1990, EAR Rational)* **MARATHONNERRE I** *(1993, Atonal / ACD)* **MARATHONNERRE II** *(1993, Atonal / ACD)* **FAUST** *(1995, Atonal / ACD)* **HÄXAN** *(1997, Atonal / ACD)* **u.B.I.Q.U.e.** *(2001, Impossibile Records)* **METROPOLIS** *(2002, Impossibile Records)* **MUSIQUES NOUVELLES ENSEMBLE** Expériences De Vol # 1, 2, 3 *(2002, Sub Rosa)* **MUSIQUES NOUVELLES ENSEMBLE - Expériences De Vol # 4, 5, 6** *(2005, Impossibile Records)* **LE CHAMP DES LARMES** *(2006, Impossibile Records)* **LA CHUTE DE LA MAISON HUSHER** *(2008, Impossibile Records).*

Europe: FRANCE

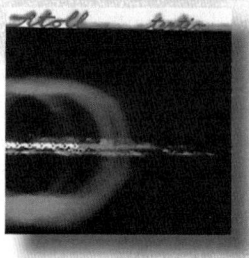

ATOLL

André Balzer, Raul Leininger - *vocals,* Alain Gozzo, Gilles Bonnabaud, Mathieu Bonaddio, Michael Altmayer, Niko Wege - *drums,* Jean-Luc Thillot, John Wetton, Jean-Pierre Klares, Roman Belliot - *bass,* Luc Serra - *guitars, keyboards,* Michael Taillet, Bruno Gehin, Nathalie Geschier, Olivier Sosin - *keyboards,* Christian Beya, Jean-Jacques Flety - *guitar,* Richard Aubert, Jean Dehé - *violin,* Stella Vander, Lisa Deluxe, André Teitschaid - *backing vocals.* Pascal Meyer - *percussion.* Michaël Kadi, Julienne Petit - *horns.*

With the advent of British Prog, Europe discovers the opportunity to base a new Rock language upon melodies, rhythmic patterns, harmonics and national Folk tunes. Italy, Germany, Sweden and Spain all go through a blooming of the Arts, with festivals and new experiences in the music production. Despite the traditional chansonniers and the skepticism towards this new found British Rock, it is yet France whom assimilates best, emphasizing the peculiarities, seemingly ill suited for Rock structures, and a theatrical expressiveness that will become the French's business card.
Apart from the **Magma** experience, so unique to go beyond any typical French dimension, **Ange**, **Pulsar**, **Mona Lisa** and **Halloween** create a style that still gains the international interest. But France has also known the exceptional story of **Atoll**: Musiciens-Magiciens is a stunning example, for it is so rare to see a non-English debut of such creativity, a gem of dreamy Flash-rock that derives from **Yes** the taste for quick successions in themes and imagery, from **Gentle Giant** the rhythmic skills and perfect vocal openings and from **Genesis** the acoustic suspense. **PFM** would be the closest reference for their wide tonal range and the constant changing nature of sound or the jazzy and acoustic nuances; yet the sparkling spaghetti-rock transcends Italian borders while **Atoll** rremain tightly tied to the French territory, even if their singer is a notch better. Proof in how *L'Araignée Mal* is ranked higher by legions of progsters on their charts of masterpieces, in particular thanks to the title-track's dynamism, a suite that highlights their style. Here the sextet is less disperse, drier and less gentle, playing a more rousing **Mahavishnu Orchestra** styled jazz-rock, whose eccentric and unconventional touch also influences **Balzer**'s emphatic singing. The exit of **Luc Serra**, replaced by guitarist **Chris Beya** and violinist **Richard Aubert**, does not affect the group's eclecticism, which beautifully blends synths and guitars or mellotron and electric piano with great skill in the arrangements and in the writing, enhancing both collective and solo spaces. **Atoll** becomes an authority of French Rock and does not miss a chance to show its qualities even during live performances.
In 1977 times had changed and in Art-rock the **Camel** model becomes a safer choice: *Tertio* pushes towards an immediate but not ordinary Symphonic Rock with a Fusion aftertaste; *Rock Puzzle* is a typical end of the decade Rock album, developing the group's peculiar mood in the formal popular song (the future CD version features **John Wetton** who discovers **Atoll** and takes part for a while in the project, as far as to record songs like "Here Comes The Feeling" between '80 and '81 (which he will bring with him to the group **Asia**). After years of silence **Beya** reunites the band and releases the mediocre *L'Ocean*, followed 15 years later by the pleasant concept album *Illian*: two similar recordings, unfortunately far from the magical '70s

D.Z.

DISCOGRAPHY:
MUSICIENS-MAGICIENS *(Eurodisc, 1973)* **L'ARAIGNEE MAL** *(Eurodisc, 1975)* **TERTIO** *(Eurodisc, 1977)* **ROCK PUZZLE** *(Eurodisc, 1979)* **L'OCEAN** *(King Records, 1989)* **TOKYO C'EST FINI** *(live, King Records, 1990)* **CHRIS BEYA ATOLL: ILLIAN - J'ENTENDS GRONDER LA TERRE** *(Musea Records, 2004).*

Europe: FRANCE

CATHARSIS

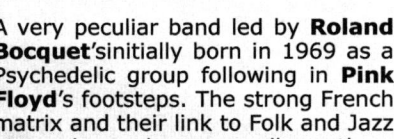

Roland Bocquet - *keyboards*, **Patrik Moulia** - *guitars, percussion*, **Charlie Eddi** - *drums, percussion*, **Yves de Roubaix** - *bass, guitars*, **Allain Geoffroy** - *piano, charango*, **Charlotte** - *vocals, violin, percussion*.

A very peculiar band led by **Roland Bocquet**'s initially born in 1969 as a Psychedelic group following in **Pink Floyd**'s footsteps. The strong French matrix and their link to Folk and Jazz atmospheres however, allows them to rise over the veil of simple inspiration or tout-court derivation. In 1971 they release a first album titled *Masq* with heterogeneous results, ranging from Psychedelia to Beat, from the short hippie outbursts of talented **Charlotte**'s dragging lunar vocals, to some odd Arabian moments, all mixed into an experimental Prog, enriched by clean and intriguing percussions. A typical core example of their live performances is "4 Art 6". *Les Chevrons* is published the following year with a line-up of only four elements, essentially confirming the original sound, but with more symphonic traits. In the following years they begin to experiment with the inclusion of texts by French poets within the musical textures. This produces the two projects *Rimbaud, C'est Toi* (1972) and *Pop Poems* (1973) often omitted in some of their discographies. The result however is not very different from other works of the time. Another essential release in 1973 is *Volume III 32 Mars*, which in 23 minutes, probably the shortest French record ever, sees their sound become more experimental. *Illuminations* brings their typical style closer to a certain Avant-garde bands such as **Faust** and **Amon Düül II** or **Opus Avantra**. **Bocquet**'s Farfisa organ is the truly unique feature of their

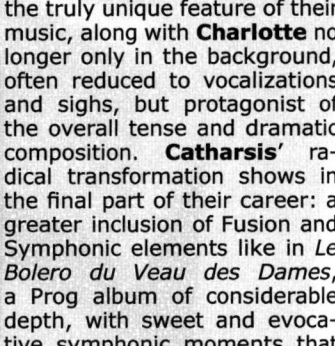

music, along with **Charlotte** no longer only in the background, often reduced to vocalizations and sighs, but protagonist of the overall tense and dramatic composition. **Catharsis**' radical transformation shows in the final part of their career: a greater inclusion of Fusion and Symphonic elements like in *Le Bolero du Veau des Dames*, a Prog album of considerable depth, with sweet and evocative symphonic moments that sometimes also refer to certain Italian bands like **Le Orme**, or to the greater British **Camel** of *The Snow Goose*. The last episode *Et s'aimer... et mourir...* was a sort of reunion of the historical formation, yet maintaining the latest sonorities rather than evoking those of the early times. Unfortunately there is a loss of strength in the composition and a drop of tension in favour of easy-listening arrangements, more to the service of a catchy Funky Fusion than in that of Prog, saved only in the last track "Et Mourir", sweet epitaph for a band that, perhaps wrongly, is remembered for the shortness of their records rather than for their contents. **R.V.**

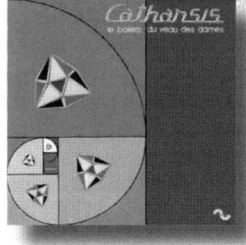

DISCOGRAPHY:
VOLUME I – MASQ *(1971, Saravah Records)* **VOLUME II – LES CHEVRONS** *(1972, Saravah Records)* **RIMBAUD, C'EST TOI** *(1972, Pathè Marconi)* **POP POEMS** *(1973, Pathè Pes)* **VOLUME III – 32 MARS** *(1973, Festival Records)* **VOLUME IV – ILLUMINATIONS** *(1975, Festival Records)* **VOLUME V – LE BOLERO DU VEAU DES DAMES** *(1976, Festival Sonopresse)* **VOLUME VI – ET S'AIMER ... ET MOURIR** *(1976, Festival Records)*.

Europe: FRANCE

ETRON FOU LELOUBLAN

Jo Thirion - organ, piano, trumpet, vocals, **Bernard Mathieu** - saxophones, **Guigou Chenevier** - drums, saxophones, vocals, **Ferdinand Richard** - bass, guitars, vocals, **Fred Frith** - violin, guitar.

Artistic creation of actor and musician **Chris Chanet**, this band begins in 1973 as the trio **Etron Fou** (Crazy Excrement). For many years their initial activity is exclusively on stage, with ironic, prankster and cabaret performances full of strange sounds coming from all European cultures and affected by the follies of **Frank Zappa** and the warm deranged atmospheres of **Captain Beefheart**. Only in 1976, during a tour as opening act for **Magma**, is the appendix **Leloublan** added to the name, as they manage, thanks to **Vander**'s help, to obtain a contract. A few months later their first album *Batelages* is released with a certain immaturity, but offering a remarkable variety of styles and themes. The album is a precursor of trends that will begin a few years later and that will go on for decades. Here we find gathered Punk, Math-rock, Jazz-rock, Cabaret, cacophonies and free forms of all kinds, Circus fanfares, Yodel, electronic noises with spoken and industrial vocals sung in French, German, English and Italian.

Chanet leaves soon after the debut, replaced by **Francis Grand** in order to complete the trio for the recording of *Les fous Perdegagnent 3 (Au pays des...)* in early 1978, with the introduction of additional new sounds from Space-Rock or like in the opening track's ethnic elements. That Spring they are invited to play in **Henry Cow**'s festival of Avant-garde rock in London, where they subscribe to Rock In Opposition, the manifesto of all major festivals in Europe and worldwide, opening a window through all the most important avant-garde realities of the time, like **Henry Cow** themselves, but also **Stormy Six**, **Samla Mammas Manna**, **Univers Zero** and **Art Zoyd**. Saxophonist

Bernard Mathieu joins just in time for the beginning of a U.S. tour, summarized in 1979 live album *En Public aux Etats-Unis d'Amérique*. An often unbalanced work, which shows how difficult it was to pack up such surreal and extremely complex performances. Once back in France the group decides to expand, allowing the entry of multi-instrumentalist **Jo Thirion**.
In 1980, they join **Henry Cow**'s guitarist **Fred Frith** in his album *Speechless* released in 1981. **Frith** will produce Fou's following album *Les Poumons Gonflés,* in which he also appears as a guest star, for a more mature and compact sound with no sign of weakness. **Mathieu** exits leaving sax to

Bruno Meillier for the remarkable recording of *Les Sillons De La Terre* that completes a path of unsettling melodies, truncated and articulated musical phrases, a better use of dissonances, sudden changes of pace and atmospheres and, altogether, about as far away from conventional song-writing as possible. In the end the band returns to being a trio and, yet again with **Frith**'s help, they record *Face Aux Eléments Dechaínés*, a masterpiece worthy of being their last.   **R.V.**

DISCOGRAPHY:
BETELAGES *(1977, Gratte-Ciel)* **LES 3 FOUS PERDEGAGNENT (Au pays des...)** *(1978, Tapioca)* **EN PUBLIC AUX ÉTATS-UNIS D'AMÉRIQUE** *(1979, Celluloid-CEL)* **LES POUMONS GONFLÉS** *(1982, Turbo-TMSA)* **LES SILLONS DE LA TERRE** *(1984, Turbo-TMSA)* **FACE AUX ELÉMENTS DECHAÍNÉS** *(1985, Recommended Records)*.

Europe: FRANCE

HELDON

Richard Pinhas - *guitars, synthesizers*, **Patrick Gauthier** - *keyboards, synthesizers*, **Klaus Blasquiz** - *vocals*, **George Grunblatt** - *mellotron, keyboards - guitars*, **François Auger**: *drums, synthesizers, percussions*, **Didier Batard** - *bass*.

Despite a degree in philosophy and a prestigious job at the Sorbonne University of Paris, **Richard Pinhas**, founder and leader of **Heldon**, decides to drop everything and become a full-time musician. Already leader of a band called **Schizo**, with 2 singles out in 1972, and before that, of another called **Blues Convention** with singer **Klaus Blasquiz** (future member of **Magma**), he is a great science fiction fan, taking his band's new name from a novel by **Norman Spinrad**, later also one of the group's lyric collaborator.

Electronique Guerilla comes out in 1974 as his own record, with some guests on two tracks, including **Patrick Gauthier** from **Magma**. The music is strongly influenced by the insights of **Robert Fripp** and **Brian Eno** and by the German movements of the early '70s, with scratchy riffs on a powerful and aggressive guitar and specific cyclic keyboard backgrounds. The result is very innovative and extremely convincing, as in anything that revolved around Avant-garde and the research of new sounds or musical forms.

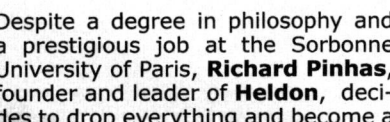

George Grunblatt, already playing synths in a piece from the previous album, takes part in all the tracks of *Allez Teia* (1975) with an ample use of Mellotron. A softer and lighter work, with Folk and Psychedelic traits, closer to **King Crimson** rather than to the German electronic sound, while maintaining several contact points especially with the early **Tangerine Dream**. The dedication in the first track's title "In the wake of King Fripp" is eloquent and a clear indication of **Pinhas**' modus operandi. 1975 is an extremely prolific year and, before its end, the ambitious double album *It's Always Rock And Roll* is released: a very heterogeneous record that unites pure electronic Avant-garde and songs that confirm the already proposed style, perhaps still with one eye on the Cosmic German genre. The compositions are longer and the guitar more and more distorted and recognizable, introducing a sort of industrial Hard-noise of which the group was an absolute precursor.

Another turning point is the 1976 experimental *Agneta Nilsson*, where the long and massive songs appear sometimes majestic and symphonic and sometimes metronomic and convulsive, maintaining the **King Crimson** touch, but also diverting towards more experimental Space Kraut elements. Still of 1976 *Un Reve Sans Consequence Speciale*, also featuring this hard-industrial noise with strong throbbing rhythms, but also inserting strange mixtures of hard-jazz with percussive ethnic breakouts. With 1978's *Interface* and the homonym suite, **Heldon** reaches a peak of absolute excellence, with Avant-garde sounds lying on a bed of very creative electronic backgrounds. The group's masterpiece is however remains *Stand By*, a work of amazing perfection that blends **Ravel**, **Tangerine Dream**, **King Crimson** and the most solid Zeuhl features, touching even higher levels in the long and splendid "Bolero". **Pinhas** will entertain his own prolific solo career until 2001, when for a sort of reunion comes to mind and he decides to re-evoke the name **Heldon** for the album *Only Chaos Is Real* using material recorded since 1998, an epic fail. **R.V.**

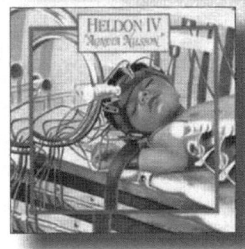

DISCOGRAPHY:
ELECTRONIQUE GUÉRILLA *(1974, Disjuncta)* **ALLEZ TEIA** *(1975, Disjuncta)* **SOUTIEN À LA RAF** *(1975, Disjuncta- Single)* **IT'S ALWAYS ROCK AND ROLL** *(1975, Disjuncta)* **AGNETA NILSSON** *(1976, Disjuncta/Urus Rec.)* **PERSPECTIVE 1 BIS COMPLÉMENT / PERSPECTIVE 4 BIS** *(1976, Disjuncta/Urus Rec. - Single)* **UN RÊVE SANS CONSÉQUENCE SPÉCIALE** *(1976, Cobra COB)* **THE PARIS CONCERT** *(1976 EP - CD Promotional copy - King Records)* **INTERFACE** *(1978, Cobra COB)* **STAND BY** *(1979, Egg Rec.)* **ONLY CHAOS IS REAL** *(2001, CD Musea)*.

Europe: FRANCE

LARD FREE

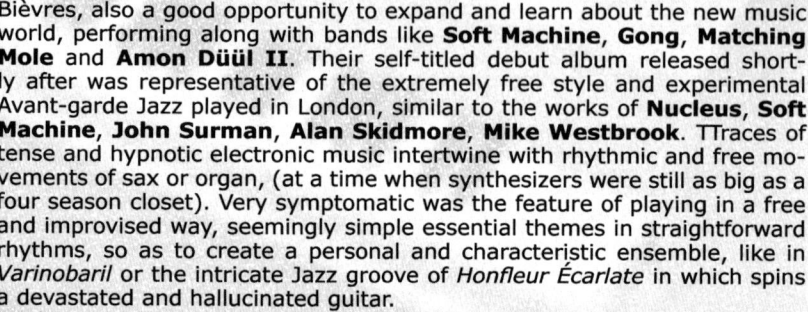

Gilbert Artman - *piano, drums, saxophones, vibes,* **Richard Pinhas** - *guitars, synth, bass,* **Alain Audat** - *saxophones, synth,* **Antoine Duvernot** - *saxophones, flute.*

The structural base of the band was laid in 1970 by **Gilbert Artman**, who at the time was a drummer in a big Jazz band. The great exploratory atmosphere he lived in encouraged him to pursue a different career. Most of his material was composed in two years, partly also performed live around 1998 and finished posthumously in the live collection titled *Unnamed*.

Great visibility was given by their participation in 1972 to the French festival of Alternative music in Bièvres, also a good opportunity to expand and learn about the new music world, performing along with bands like **Soft Machine**, **Gong**, **Matching Mole** and **Amon Düül II**. Their self-titled debut album released shortly after was representative of the extremely free style and experimental Avant-garde Jazz played in London, similar to the works of **Nucleus**, **Soft Machine**, **John Surman**, **Alan Skidmore**, **Mike Westbrook**. Traces of tense and hypnotic electronic music intertwine with rhythmic and free movements of sax or organ, (at a time when synthesizers were still as big as a four season closet). Very symptomatic was the feature of playing in a free and improvised way, seemingly simple essential themes in straightforward rhythms, so as to create a personal and characteristic ensemble, like in *Varinobaril* or the intricate Jazz groove of *Honfleur Écarlate* in which spins a devastated and hallucinated guitar.

In the sequel *I'm Around About Midnight* (1975), the Free-Jazz element gives way to more cyclic and insightful sounds inspired by **Fripp**, with unchanging rhythms sustaining them. Here also appears the great **Richard Pinhas** from **Heldon**, whose guitar gives a strong characteristic touch to the overall sound. In this sense also *Does East Bakestan Belong To Itself* follows the same path, with its percussions, flute and guitar arrangements magically exposed on the shelf of **King Crimson** experimentations.

In 1977 the third album is recorded with a completely different line-up, except for **Artman**, and presents a strong deviation mainly towards German electronic sounds, but also with similarities to the first works **Clearlight** and **Heldon**. *Spiral Malax* contains two long tracks with Kraut elements and highly experimental moments of Space Prog, yet never losing sight of the Jazz component and of the **Fripp & Eno** duo concepts. As aforementioned, all 1971/1972 live material was gathered in a collection full of Free Prog Jazz, both in intent and content.

R.V.

DISCOGRAPHY:
GILBERT ARTMAN'S LARD FREE *(Vamp, 1973)* **I'M AROUND ABOUT MIDNIGHT** *(Vamp, 1975)* **III (Spirale Malax)** *(Cobra, 1977))* **UNNAMED** *(Live, Spalax Records, 1997).*

Europe: FRANCE

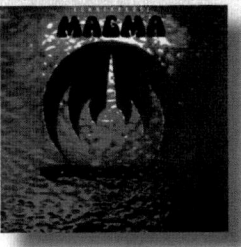

MAGMA

Note: the number of musicians who played, if only for a brief period, in Magma is huge; the ones mentioned can be considered the most significant.

Christian Vander - drums, vocals, **Klaus Blasquiz** - vocals, **François Cahen** - piano, **Francis Moze** - bass, **Teddy Lasry** - clarinet, sax, flute, **Claude Engel** - guitar, flauto, **Richard Raux** - sax, flute, **Alain Charlery** - trumpet, percussion, **Laurent Thibault** - bass, **Yochk'o Seffer** - sax, **Louis Toesca** - trumpet, **Jannick Top** - bass, **Jean-Luc Manderlier** - keyboards, **René Garber** - clarinet, vocals, **Claude Olmos** - guitar, **Stella Vander** - vocals, **Gérard Bikialo** - keyboards, **Michel Grailler** - keyboards, **Brian Godding** - guitars, **Bernard Paganotti** - bass, **Gabrid Federow** - guitars, **Didier Lockwood** - violin, **Benoit Widemann** - keyboards, **Jean-Luc Chevalier** - bass, **Patrick Gauthier** - keyboards, **Isabelle Feuillebois** - vocals, **Antoine Paganotti** - vocals, **Jean-Christophe Gamet** - vocals, **Julie Vander** - vocals, **Claude Lamamy** - vocals, **James Mac Gaw** - guitar, **Emmanuel Borghi** - keyboards, **Philippe Bussonet** - bass, **Himiko Paganotti** - vocals, **Frédéric d'Oelsnitz** - keyboards.

Unique, phenomenal, innovative, **Magma** is one of the most symbolic bands of prog, responsible for the creation of zeuhl, whose obsessive and edgy characteristics make it a genre apparently for few. **Christian Vander**, the brain of the group, is also a great drummer. He grows up listening to **Coltrane** and firmly decides to create something as shocking too, surrounding himself with brave musicians (the line-up will undergo profound changes over time) and debuting in 1970 as **Magma**, with a self-titled double album containing a peculiar form of Avant-garde Jazz-rock, slightly recalling **Soft Machine**, but definitely more reckless. The themes developed also in the following album concerning sci-fi adventures between Earth and the (fake) planet **Kobaia,** all sung in an invented language, phonetically reminiscent of the Teutonic countries. *1001° Centigrades* pushes even farther this thematic, which comes to its completeness in *Mekanik Destruktïw Kommandöh*, a unique masterpiece combining the Jazz teachings of **Coltrane** with cutting edge avant-garde, contemporary music and the choral and majestic sound of **Orff**. Absolutely fundamental is the rhythmic section's role, which pulses in a fierce as skillful manner. In 1974 other wonders appear, such as *Wurdah Itah* and *Kohntarkosz*, which lightens slightly up the sound: obsessiveness and anxiety remain, but the atmosphere becomes more mysterious and rarefied. . With **Didier Lockwood** and his fierce violin, they publish Live, a testimony of their concerts and one of the best live recordings of all times. In *Udu Wudu* their sound goes back to being granitic: the suite composed by **Jannick Top**, "De Futura", stands out with his terrific and powerful bass playing. *Attahk* is further proof of their great class, but after two other live albums, they record *Merci* in 1984, which instead turns out to be rather weak, demonstrating how hard the '80s were, even for **Magma**. A renewal comes with their transformation into the band **Offering**, a new project that gives birth to some very valuable modern Jazz tracks and a mostly acoustic album. Only in the '90s will **Magma** return under this glorious name, with new young and talented musicians and an intense stage performance activity, issuing a first monumental triple live album called *Theusz Hamtaahk* and then again with *K.A.*, yet another masterpiece in their most classic Zeuhl style.

G.D.S.

RECOMMENDED RECORDINGS:
MAGMA *(1970, Philips, aka Kobaia)* **1001° CENTIGRADES** *(1971, Philips)* **MEKANIK DESTRUKTIW KOMMANDOH** *(1973, Vertigo/A&M)* **WURDAH ITAH** *(1974, Barclay, aka Tristan et Yseult, Vander's soloist project)* **KOHNTARKOSZ** *(1974, Vertigo/A&M)* **LIVE** *(1975, RCA Utopia)* **UDU WUDU** *(1976, RCA/Tomato)* **INÉDITS** *(1977/Tapioca)* **ATTAHK** *(1975, Eurodisc/Tomato)* **RETROSPEKTIW VOL. 3** *(1981, RCA)* **RETROSPEKTIW VOLL. 1 & 2** *(1981, RCA)* **MERCI** *(1984, Jaro)* **FLOE ESSI / EKTAH** *(1998, Seventh Records, mini cd)* **THEUSZ HAMTAAHK** *(2000, Seventh Records)* **K.A** *(2004, Seventh Records)*.

Europe: FRANCE

MONA LISA

Dominique Le Guennec - *vocals, flute,* **Jean-Paul Pierson** - *piano, keyboards,* **Jean-Luc Martin** - *bass, vocals,* **Francis Poulet** - *drums, percussion,* **Christian Gallas** - *guitars,* **Gilles Solves** - *guitars,* **Pascal Jardon** - *guitars.*

When it comes to classic French symphonic prog, the first name that comes to mind is **Ange**; immediately after we definitely find **Mona Lisa**. This band from Orléans, revolves around the exuberance of **Dominque Le Guennec**, singer and flute player who, with his stage presence (for which he continues to be compared to **Peter Gabriel**) aand his personality, has always shown an out of the ordinary charisma. The first album entitled *L'Escapade* was released in 1974 and contains a series of compositions that alternate French theatricality, similar to the **Ange** experiences, and a romantic touch vaguely recalling **Genesis**.

After a good beginning, they start their real escalation with the album *Grimaces*, that shows a much greater drive than the previous. The theatrical Rock band on this occasion is perhaps at its highest, thanks to a series of well-guessed musical themes, the emphatic instrumental parts and to the in-a-state-of-grace **Le Guennec** at his most expressive peak. Songs like the seemingly light-hearted and very addictive "La Mauvais Réputation"

(adaptation of a **Brassens**' composition), "Brume", "Accroche-toi", "Suis-moi", resounding and dramatic echo of *The Lamb Lies Down On Broadway* by **Genesis**, and "Au Pays de Grimaces", beautifully recited by the leader in the midst of sudden tempo changes with wonderfully intertwining guitars and keyboards, belong to the hexagon's history of Symphonic Rock.

Another two albums, *Le Petit Violon de Mr. Gregoire* and *Avant qu'il Ne Soit Trop Tard*, follow on the same wave-length and are highly appreciated by fans. After **Le Guennec** leaves, the band publishes a very uninspired album then vanishes from the scenes. The name reappears in 1998 when **Le Guennec** himself reintroduces it with a completely renewed line-up, involving musicians from **Versailles**, a modern and very valuable French Prog group. *De l'Ombre à la Lumière* is a beautiful studio album that updates the sound of the old incarnation, making it a little more energetic. *Progfest 2000* is a live recording of their performance at the homonym U.S. festival, with a DVD that allows to understand how important the visual part on stage is, with **Le Guennec** constantly changing costumes and showing off all his front-man and mime/actor skills.

G.D.S.

DISCOGRAPHY:
L'ESCAPADE *(1974, Arcane)* **GRIMACES** *(1975, Arcane)* **LE PETIT VIOLON DE MR. GREGOIRE** *(1977, Crypto)* **AVANT QU'IL NE SOIT TROP TARD** *(1978, Crypto)* **VERS DEMAIN** *(1979, Crypto)* **DE L'OMBRE À LA LUMIÈRE** *(1998, Musea)* **PROGFEST 2000** *(2000, Musea)*.

Europe: FRANCE

PULSAR

Gilbert Gandil - *guitar, vocals*, **Victor Bosch** - *drums, percussion* **Roland Richard** - *flute, saxophones, strings*, **Jacques Roman** - *keyboards, bass*.

This band literally rises from the ashes of **Free Sound**, a group that played mainly **Pink Floyd** and early **Soft Machine** covers since 1972. They consolidate the line-up around in 1974 and finally issue a first album titled *Pollen*. **Pulsar**'s intent of exploring the Psychedelic Space genre of **Pink Floyd** is clear, yet treating it with a Symphonic touch, very evocative and dreamlike, with Classical and Romantic references. Aided by a never intrusive drummer, **Roland Richard**'s beautiful, lyrical and ethereal flute parts blend into the soft harmonic textures of guitarist and singer **Gilbert Gandil**, whose theatricality sometimes reminds us of **Peter Hammill** and **Christian Décamps**; but also with large majestic explosions of symphonic crescendos, a distorted guitar and **Jacques Roman**'s broad patterns of Mellotron.

In 1976 *The Strands Of The Future* is released, a more mature album with greater openness towards the Symphonic themes, containing a magical Space suite played with Classical tones and more personality, showing throughout the entire album an expressiveness and a versatile musical touch, always dramatic and sometimes rarefied or rich of restless aggressiveness.

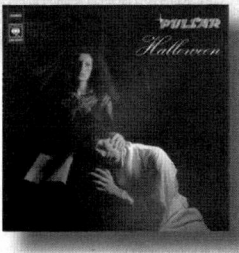

While **Pulsar** maintain the **Pink Floyd** traits, sounds from **Klaus Schulze** can be detected, as well as some interesting excursions on the shores of their fellowmen **Clearlight**, or even **King Crimson** styled arpeggios. This quality leap, widely acknowledged by the critics, earned them, as well as sales of all due respect, a new contract with prestigious CBS, publishing in 1977 the successful *Halloween*: 40 minutes divided simply into Part I and II, with 9 movements composed as one long suite in a twirl of high-class sound and effect. Mellotron, synths, strings, caressing voices and obscure and electrical parts, with crescendos that make it a marvelous Prog album, with some brief references to the early **Genesis**.

After a few years pause and a reshuffle in the line-up, the band returns with the fascinating and particular work *Bienvenue au Conseil d'Administration* (1981), initially born for the theater, with spoken parts and electronic experiences taken from the New Prog and New Wave trends of the time, with sounds close to contemporary **Vangelis** or **Steve Hillage**, faster rhythms yet maintaining extremely dramatic atmospheres, where **Richard** makes a fairly massive use of his saxophone.

Another long break leads to *Görlitz* in 1989, a record that wants to bridge their early sounds to a future that still isn't sure of its significance. The result has some good parts but is poor in ideas and full of repetitive forms. Surprisingly *Memory Ashes*, born from their reunion in 2007, brings them back to their very strong **Pink Floyd** ideas of Space Music, combining persuasive and intriguing Post-Rock themes.   **R.V.**

DISCOGRAPHY:
POLLEN *(1975, Kingdom Rec.)* **THE STRANDS OF THE FUTURE** *(1976, Kingdom Rec.)* **HALLOWEEN** *(1976, CBS)* **BIENVENUE AU CONSEIL D'ADMINISTRATION** *(1981, Theatre Rec.)* **GÖRLITZ** *(1989, Musea)* **MEMORY ASHES** *(2007, Cypress Music).*

Europe: FRANCE

WAPASSOU

Freddy Brua - *piano, keyboards*
Jacques Lichti - *violin*
Karen Nickerl - *guitar, vocals*

In 1973 the classically trained pianist **Freddy Brua** set up in Strasbourg one of the most original and unusual bands of all the Progressive world, starting from a very strange line-up with no rhythmic section and a singular musical style, quite indefinable. **Wapassou** immediately began by composing songs when the group was forced to evaluate, for the recording of a self-titled album in 1974, the inclusion of some guests. The choice of using percussions for certain pieces in order to adapt to a Rock structure, was not always a good one, as in the first track "Femmes-fleurs" where several inaccuracies can be heard. Anyway the record managed with great honor to merge Chamber Music and Prog together. A bleak scene dominated by the Crumar organ, complemented by faint vocals, delicate arpeggios and gloomy violin patterns. Hard to find similar contemporary examples at the time. With some light references to **Robert Wyatt**, or passages vaguely linked to German groups such as **Popol Vuh** or to their fellowmen **Chene Noir** or even to the British **Curved Air**, all tracks give the impression of an extremely personal and seminal group, in the attempt of combining the Classical music of **Bach** to the progressive genre.

required a lengthy study with the imperative of leaving out rhythmic instruments in order to allow a stronger homogeneity in sound. It consists in one long track and is considered refined and unmistakable for the greater cohesion between musical movements which enables the perfect union between symphony, avant-garde and soundscapes. Singer **Eurydice** takes part momentarily in the project well integrating her skills as a high soprano, especially when the violins melt with her vocal tones. The following year *Salammbô* is recorded as an hypothetical soundtrack to the novel by Gustave Flaubert. The sound is ever more rarefied and full of atmosphere, with liquid guitars, rare romantic vocals and a persistent background organ, sometimes interrupted by the fuzz guitar. The musical progression between fullness and void is emotional and intense. In the coming years electronics play a main role: sounds are mostly synthetic, bringing them closer to other experimenters such as **Schulze** or **Vangelis**, but their romantic and classic central-European style, however, keeps them apart. *Ludwig - A Roi Pour L' Eternité* is published in a moment

of decadence: perhaps the avant-garde ambitions were exhausted and the work was nothing more than a pale electronic watercolour on the threshold of New Wave. Even truer for *Genuine*, which will lead to the dissolution of the group. A latter reunion will bring to the release of *Le Lac D'Argent* in 1986, without adding more to what has already been said.   **R.V.**

DISCOGRAPHY:
WAPASSOU *(1974, Prodisc)* **MESSE EN RÉ MINEUR** *(1976, Crypto)* **SALAMMBÔ** *(1977, Crypto)* **LUDWIG - UN ROI POUR L'ETERNITÉ** *(1979, Crypto)* **GÉNUINE** *(1980, Sterne)* **ORCHESTRA 2001 - LE LAC D'ARGENT** *(1986, OM France)*.

Europe: FRANCE

ZAO

François Cahen - *piano, keyboards*, **Yochk'o Seffer** - *sax, clarinet*, **Jean-My Truong** - *drums*, **Joël Dugrenot** - *bass*, **Jean-Yves Rigaud** - *violin*, **Mauricia Platon** - *vocals*, **Gerard Prevost** - *bass*, **Pierre Guignon** - *percussion*, **Didier Lockwood** - *violin*, **Manu Katché** - *drums*, **Hamed Belhocine** - *trombone*, **François Debricon** - *sax*, **Michel Seguin** - *percussion*, **Patrick Tilleman** - *violin*, **Dominique Bertram** - *basso*, **François Causse** - *drums*, **Cynthia Saint - Ville** - *vocals*, **Akihisa Tsuboy** - *violin*.

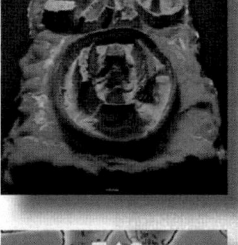

Formed by **Yochk'o Seffer** and **François Cahen** in 1972 after ending their adventure in the early **Magma**. Over the years a good number of valuable musicians will cooperate with them, allowing the creation of a series of great quality albums. The first, *Z = 7L* (released in 1973) is an imaginative crossroad between **Magma** and a jazz-rock contamination of central European flavours (in fact **Seffer** has Hungarian roots) with extravagant female vocals and continuous instrumental acrobatics. It

is, among the rest, the one closest to Zeuhl, since already with *Osiris* (lacking the voice of **Mauricia Platon** present in the debut) this component is lessened in favour of a more dynamic Jazz, at the same time more elegant and solid. After this experience, the ambitious *Shekinah* is published containing a number of excellent compositions, where the expressions of Free-Jazz approach contemporary Classical music and Avant-garde thanks to the use of a string quartet. With *Kawana*, however, they return to Jazz-rock and this will be their last great album.

Seffer leaves the band and from **Magma** arrives violinist **Didier Lockwood**. In 1977 this new line-up performs on stage (the result can be appreciated in the posthumous *Live!*)

showing considerable improvisational skills and new incursions into eastern European folk-rock. They record *Typhareth*, good but at a lower level than the previous. In 1993 the historic core **Seffer**, **Cahen** and **Truong** will reunite with the help of **Patrick Tilleman** and **Dominique Bertram**, publishing *Akhenaton*, a Progressive Jazz-rock oriented album, with flakes of Fusion that still denote a certain mannerism. Then again, silence until 2004 when they hold a series of concerts in Japan, and the two founders are this time sided by **Prevost**, **Causse**, singer **Saint-Ville** and by the acrobatic violinist **Akihisa Tsuboy** appreciated

for his work with **KBB**, one of the most prominent Japanese bands of the recent years. From these performances derives the live album *In Tokyo* published three years after, showing all the exuberance and class of this new incarnation. **G.D.S.**

DISCOGRAPHY:

Z=7L *(1973, Vertigo)* **OSIRIS** *(1975, Disjuncta)* **SHEKINA** *(1975, RCA)* **KAWANA** *(1977, RCA)* **TYPHARETH** *(1977, RCA)* **AKHENATON** *(1994, Musea)* **LIVE!** *(2003, Musea)* **IN TOKYO** *(2007, Musea)*.

Europe: GERMANY

AGITATION FREE

Lutz "Lüül" Ulbrich, Jörg "Joski" Schwenke, Stefan Diez, Gustav Lütjens, Mickie Duwe - *guitars*, **Michael "Fame" Günther** - *bass*, **Christopher Franke, Burghard Rausch, Dietmar Burmeister, Harald Grosskopf** - *drums*, **Micheal "Höni" Hoenig, Bernhard Arndt, Manfred Opitz, Christian Kneitzel** - *keyboards*, **Johannes "Alto" Pappert** - *sax*.

Berlin 1967: the merge of bands **Fame** and **Sentries**, creates this explosive German ensemble, among the first to specialize in concerts using lightings and projections on stage, crafted by their mentor (artistic and political) **Folke Hanfield**, inspired by the shows from the famous British underground scene of **Pink Floyd**. The Zodiac Club audience in Berlin loves their wild improvisations, but the encounter with Swiss composer **Thomas Kessler** stimulates them to expand their knowledge and work more seriously with electronics.

After the exit of **Axel Genrich** (who joins **Guru Guru**) and **Chris Franke** (who joins **Tangerine Dream**), the line-up becomes a quintet that debuts with a peculiar tour in Egypt, Lebanon, Jordan and Greece (sponsored by the Goethe Institute): an opportunity to confront with different cultures leaving its mark in the album *Malesch*, out at the end of 1972. Starting from a **Pink Floyd** base, Cosmic Rock quenches its thirst with Electronics and World Music through haunting melodies and exotic atmospheres that recall the desert, the pyramids, the bazaars and the sea. The title (meaning never mind in Arabic) indicates the propensity to mild and soothing sound environments and is a sensational news for the growing German music, that has so far expressed its neutrality towards Acid-rock bands such as **Amon Düül II**, **Ash Ra Tempel** or the majestic electronics of **Tangerine Dream**.

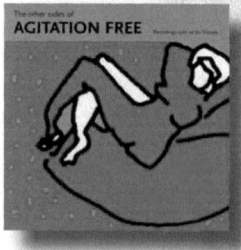

The band performs live a lot, earning trust and credibility abroad (along with a remarkable French tour) and in the summer of 1973 they start recording 2nd, which turns out to be a step ahead from the previous: **Agitation Free** lets go totally in fluid and ecstatic instrumental expansions, driven by guitars drenched in Jazz-rock and entwined in electronic drapes. It is a dreamy Space-rock, perfect for expressing the physical and mental condition of an ideal post-trip, bringing Berliners closer to **The Grateful Dead**.

The frenetic concerts and significant changes of line-up (**Lutz** remains in Paris with his partner **Nico**; **Hoenig** works with **Klaus Schulze**) weaken the band, which see the ghost of routine appearing and therefore decide to close the experience holding a last concert in Berlin on November 14th 1974, a teutonic Last Waltz with the participation of old and new friends (some tracks are also in *Fragments*, 1995).

All members start projects of their own: **Lutz** works with **Gottsching** and **Ashra Tempel** and then embarks on solo adventures; **Hoenig** joins **Tangerine Dream**; **Rausch** founds **Bel Ami**. In 1976 a brilliant live album is recorded: *Last*, with three long tracks on both sides. The first side exhibits the typical acid loss in which **Agitation Free** excels (with a statuary "Laila Part II"), while the second is more rarefied and experimental. It is the first step to the posthumous revaluation of the 90ies that issues many live recordings with unreleased tracks, until the band finally reunites in 1998 with the placid *River Of Return*. **Hoenig** is now a popular soundtrack composer and works in electronics; **Ulbrich** continues with **Ashra**, joins the astonishing band **17 Hippies** and the Wax Museum in Tokyo even dedicates him a statue.

D.Z.

DISCOGRAPHY:

MALESCH *(Vertigo 1972)* **2ND** *(Vertigo 1973)* **LAST** *(Barclay 1976)* **FRAGMENTS** *(Musique Intemporelle 1995)* **AT THE CLIFFS OF RIVER RHINE** *(live, Garden Of Delights 1998)* **THE OTHER SIDES OF AGITATION FREE** *(live, Garden Of Delights 1999)* **RIVER OF RETURN** *(Prudence 1999)*.

Europe: GERMANY

AMON DÜÜL I & II

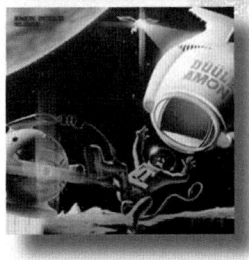

Ella Bauer, Angelika Filanda, Renate Knaup, Joy Alaska - *vocals*, **Rainer Bauer** - *vocals, guitars*, **Ulrich Leopold, Dave Anderson, Lothar Meid, Robby Heibl, Klaus Ebert** - *bass*, **Dadam, Klaus Esser, John Weinzierl, Nando Tischer** - *guitars*, **Chris Karrer** - *guitars,, violin, horns*, **Hansi, Olaf Kubler** - *winds*. **Helge Filanda, Peter Leopold, Dieter Serfas, Danny Fichelscher** - *drums*, **Ushci Obermeier, Noam, Shrat** - *percussion*, **Wolfgang Krischke, Falk-Ulrich Rogner, Jimmy Jackson, Stefan Zauner** - *keyboards*, **Al Gromer** - *sitar*.

One of the most famous hippy communities was born in Munich under the name of **Amon Düül** (the Egyptian god and a character in a Turkish novel). It gathered a dozen bohemians who lived together producing multimedia shows. Among these were many talented musicians, above all the heterodox Jazz musician **Chris Karrer**. During the Essen Songtagen Festival (October '68) the community splits in two: **Amon Düül I** - the politicized faction - signs up with Metronome holding an epic 48-hour party from which they derive 4 albums (one of the most incredible psychedelic madness in Europe), published between '71 and '73. The other faction, **Amon Düül II**, debuted in 1969 with the triumphant *Phallus Dei*, recorded in just three days. A completely new sound, with possible contaminations from **Mothers Of Invention** and from a certain American acid-rock. It was the dawn of Kraut Rock. In the early 70's comes their second masterpiece *Yeti*, strongly supported by **Andrew Lauder** of **Liberty**: it is one of the highest rock peaks of the time and consecrates the band abroad. Long jams, acid-folk, pre-punk riffs, ragamuffin, jazz and the reunion with **Amon Düül I** in "Sandoz In The Rain" with **Renate Knaup** singing (vocally between **Yoko Ono** and **Grace Slick**) makes it an authentic cult. Their success and the various defections (**Shrat** founds **Sameti**, **Dave Anderson** joins **Hawkwind**, **Knaup** and **Rogner** exit) do not affect the giant space rock double album *Tanz Der Lemminge*, born under the guidance of **Karrer** and **Weinzierl**. A forth very inspired *Carnival In Babylon*, with the track "All The Years Round" adored by **John Peel**, still reaches the previous' high levels, bringing them to their first UK tour. In the summer of '72 *Wolf City* comes to light, confirming **AD II**'s vision of prog with its dark and dreamlike sounds, but it also marks the beginning of a downward spiral: proof is the uncertain *Vive La Trance*, the first step towards the normalization of their sound, now more regular. *Hijack* signs **AD II**'s first line-up as a rock-band, more common in all respects: hypnotic rock oriented with a ting of funk, always keeping its kraut mood, yet less dreamier and enlightened than before. Their last big hit is the third double album, *Made In Germany*, an ambitious and ironic Rock-opera, dedicated to the glorious Teutonic past (*Hansi Kraut* is kidnapped on planet *Krautopia* and meets famous people from German history). A more ordinary *Pyragony 10th* marks a further change while *Only Human* attempts to give an appearance of eccentricity to their sound, that is already unfortunately 6 feet under. The *Vortex* reunion doesn't help much, and even less will the attempt of **Weinzierl** and **Anderson** to resurrect **Amon Düül II** by recording a handful of English sounding albums. Some revivals of the old group reminisce in the mid-'90s until **Peter Leopold**, a central figure in the history of the group, dies in 2006.
D.Z.

DISCOGRAPHY:
AMON DÜÜL I: PSYCHEDELIC UNDERGROUND *(Metronome, 1969)* **COLLAPSING** *(Metronome, 1970)* **PARADIESWÄRTS DÜÜL** *(Ohr, 1971)* **DISASTER** *(Basf, 1973)* **EXPERIMENTE** *(Timewind, 1982)*. **AMON DÜÜL II: PHALLUS DEI** *(Liberty, 1969)* **YETI** *(Liberty, 1970)* **TANZ DER LEMMINGE** *(Liberty, 1971)* **CARNIVAL IN BABYLON** *(United Artists, 1972)* **WOLF CITY** *(United Artists, 1972)* **VIVE LA TRANCE** *(United Artists, 1973)* **LIVE IN LONDON** *(live, United Artists, 1974)* **HIJACK** *(Nova, 1974)* **MADE IN GERMANY** *(Nova, 1975)* **PYRAGONY 10TH** *(Nova, 1976)* **ALMOST ALIVE** *(Nova, 1977)* **ONLY HUMAN** *(Strand, 1978)* **VORTEX** *(Telefunken, 1981)* **BBC RADIO 1 LIVE IN CONCERT PLUS** *(live Windsong, 1992)* **NADA MOONSHINE #** *(Mystic, 1996)* **FLAWLESS** *(Mystic, 1998)* **LIVE IN TOKYO** *(live, Mystic, 1999)*.

Europe: GERMANY

ASH RA TEMPEL

Manuel Göttsching, Lutz Ulbrich - *guitars, keyboards,* **Klaus Schulze, Wolfgang Müller, Harald Grosskopf** - *drums,* **Hartmut Enke** - *bass,* **Rosi Müller** - *vocals,* **Michael Hoenig, Steve Baltes** - *keyboards.*

Manuel Gottsching is one of the world's most influential musicians in the electronic field; he starts off with blues becoming some kind of kraut rock **Richard Sinclair**. Master mind of the band, together with **Hartmut Enke** and **Klaus Schulze** (who recently left **Tangerine Dream**) he gives birth to the stratospheric albums *Ash Ra Tempel* and *Schwingungen*. In the early '70s the three Berliners propose themselves as a transfigured power-trio, a sort of paroxysmal expansion of **Cream** and **Blue Cheer**, aalso thanks to the electronic equipment brought in directly from London, that encourages them to paint an aggressive and, at the same time, rarefied sound. A long track on each side, a constant alternation between feedback, walls of sound, dramatically open Blues riffs, Electronic ramblings, violence and ecstasy, Free-rock and visions.

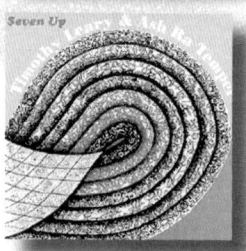

Boss of the label Ohr, **Rolf-Ulrich Kaiser** falls in love with them and they fall in love with the <<*most dangerous man in the world*>> according to Nixon, the LSD prophet **Timothy Leary**, refugee in Switzerland: the three engage his cause, which leads to the inevitable *Seven Up* in which **Leary** appears as a guest star. It is a revolutionary album, first release of **Kaiser**'s new project: the label Die Kosmischen Kuriere will sign up the controversial but legendary epic **Cosmic Jokers**, of which **Gottsching** is one of the most

determinant names. Another two long improvisations in *Join Inn* and a greater versatility in *Starring Rosi* (with his girlfriend **Rosi Müller** and **Harald Grosskopf** from **Wallenstein**) close this first phase.
After a cosmic hangover, **Gottsching** has another of his insights, simple but memorable: referring to the beloved **Riley**, **Reich** and **Glass**, he overdubs never ending guitar riffs, creating a very pleasant album, more appealing than **Fripp** and **Eno**'s experiment. *Inventions For Electric Guitar* is a cyclic solo guitar album and marks the difference from his previous, launching a new more sophisticated stylistic approach. With **Lüül** from **Agitation Free**,

Manuel works on a series of catchy and remarkably consistent albums, adding to his riff walls, certain hypnotic and pounding rhythms (influenced by Funk and by **Kraftwerk**), perfect base for his fluid guitar-playing.
From *New Age Of Earth* onward, even the name changes, since the label Virgin prefers **Ashra**: a soft lounge Space-rock genre, in a climate of reflux, which however, anticipates many musical trends to come. The most striking example of **Manuel**'s insights is *E2 - E4*: an album of worship inspired by the most strict dictates of minimalism, built on a sequence that is repeated throughout the album and that some Italian DJ re-elaborated successfully.
Since then **Gottsching** continues with reprints, mature works such as *Walkin' The Desert*, the rare monumental project *Private Tapes*, some live albums, collaborations and shows in Japan. In *Concert For Murnau*, he creates a fascinating audio commentary for the expressionist masterpiece *The Castle of Vogelod* (1921). **Zeitkratzer**'s tribute will place him in a prestigious position among contemporary European composers. **D.Z.**

DISCOGRAPHY:
ASH RA TEMPEL *(Ohr, 1970)* **SCHWINGUNGEN** *(Ohr, 1971)* **SEVEN UP** *(Die Kosmischen Kuriere, 1972)* **JOIN INN** *(Ohr, 1973)* **STARRING ROSI** *(Kosmische Musik, 1973)* **INVENTIONS FOR ELECTRIC GUITAR** *(Kosmische Musik, 1975)* **NEW AGE OF EARTH** *(Isadora, 1976)* **BLACKOUTS** *(Virgin, 1978)* **CORRELATIONS** *(Virgin, 1979)* **BELLE ALLIANCE** *(Virgin, 1980)* **E2-E4** *(In Team 1984)* **WALKIN' THE DESERT** *(Navigator, 1989)* **DREAM & DESIRE** *(1977)* (Musique Intemporelle, 1991) **TROPICAL HEAT** *(1985/87) (Navigator, 1991)* **LE BERCEAU DE CRISTAL** *(1975) (Spalax, 1993)* **EARLY WATER** *(1996) (Spalax, 1993)* **THE PRIVATE TAPES** *(Manikin, 1996)* **SAUCE HOLLANDAISE** *(live, Manikin 1998)* **@SHRA** *(Think Progressive, 1998)* **FRIENDSHIP** *(Manikin, 2000)* **GIN ROSÈ** *(Manikin, 2000)* **@SHRA VOL. 2** *(1997) (live, MG.Art, 2002)* **MANUEL GÖTTSCHING: DIE MULDE** *(MG.Art, 2005)* **E2-E4 LIVE** *(live, MG.Art, 2005)* **CONCERT FOR MURNAU** *(MG.Art, 2005).*

Europe: GERMANY

CAN

Irmin Schmidt - *keyboards*, **Holger Czukay** - *bass, tapes, electronic devices*, **Michael Karoli** - *guitars, violin, vocals*, **Jaki Liebezeit** - *drums, horns*, **Malcolm Mooney, Kenji "Damo" Suzuki** - *vocals*. **Rosko Gee** - *bass, vocals*, **Reebop Kwaku Baah** - *percussion*.

Anarchists and indefinable, **Can** is Germany's most original experience from the '60s & '70s, coming from an intellectual environment and looking at New Rock with great interest. Composer and pianist from Berlin **Irmin Schmidt** studies **Messiaen** and **Cage**, takes part in NY's Avant-garde movement and attends **Stockhausen** and **Berio**'s courses in Darmstadt where he meets **Holger Czukay**, a Polish bassist and music teacher dazzled by The Beatles he discovered thanks to his young student **Michael Karoli**, a curious explorer of guitar sounds. **Schmidt** enrolls American bassist **David Johnson** and professional drummer **Jaki Liebezeit**, just back in Germany after years of Jazz-playing in Spain: **Inner Space** is hence founded with the aim of overcoming boundaries between musical genres, using the new Electronic expressiveness in a highly experimental and Psychedelic context.

The band finds its headquarters in Cologne, in the castle of Schloss Nörvenich, where they set up a studio with **Manni Löhe**: after producing soundtracks for films of dubious quality and meeting the weird Afro-American singer **Malcolm Mooney**, they become **The Can** (from 1970, only **Can**) publishing the album *Monster Movie*. The rhythmic engine brings to extremes the hypnotic style of **Velvet Underground**, where the singer penetrates walls of distortion and dissonances; **Czukay** juggles with **Teo Macero**-styled tape-loops and cut-ups and by composing subtraction, he achieves few obsessive, relentless cords.

Mooney's psychological issues force him to return to New York, but his time with **Can** left an extraordinary amount of ideas, as the brilliant posthumous album Delay 1968. **Mooney** is replaced by **Kenji "Damo" Suzuki**, a mysterious Japanese vagabond with an appealing voice, so perfect for his monotonous ritual sound. In *Tago Mago* their music is sublimated: monotonous but not boring, minimal but not empty, shiny and bizarre, brainy and furious at the same time, described as new chamber music for its distance from the rumble of rock. Raw and visionary sounds, between magic, noise, writing and clandestine recordings are contained in this double album that consecrates the originality of German music and influences generations of punk, new wave and industrial bands, including **Sonic Youth** and **Radiohead**. The delightful *Ege Bamyasi* exploits the success of the hit single "Spoon" (which leads **Can** to their English tour) and contains less random pieces such as "Future Days", more relaxed and quiet, on the threshold of ambient. After **Damo Suzuki**'s exit, they begin to mimic **Amon Düül II** playing a more regular kind of music, but still sensual and intriguing: *Soon Over Babaluma* is a mix of funk, reggae and world music, even if their more structured style does not allow comparisons with the wild charm of the first albums. *Landed* is issued after signing up with a different label and is more conventional; *Flow Motion* is closer to **Embryo**'s exotic atmosphere; *Saw Delight* features "Gee and Baah" from **Traffic**.

Can's new direction disappoints **Czukay**, who exits only to return for a last self titled album, after which they will all go their own way. In '89 they gather for *Rite Time*, a decent album, but **Karoli**'s death in 2001 puts an end to any further revival of this unforgettable band. **D.Z.**

DISCOGRAPHY:
THE CAN: MONSTER MOVIE *(Music Factory, 1969)* **SOUNDTRACKS** *(Liberty, 1970)* **TAGO MAGO** *(United Artists, 1971)* **EGE BAMYASI** *(United Artists, 1972)* **FUTURE DAYS** *(United Artists, 1973)* **SOON OVER BABALUMA** *(United Artists, 1974)* **LIMITED EDITION** *(United Artists, 1974)* **LANDED** *(Harvest, 1975)* **UNLIMITED EDITION** *(Harvest, 1976)* **FLOW MOTION** *(Harvest, 1976)* **SAW DELIGHT** *(Harvest, 1977)* **OUT OF REACH** *(Harvest, 1978)* **CAN** *(Harvest, 1978)* **DELAY 1968** *(Spoon, 1982)* **RITE TIME** *(Mercury, 1989)*.

Europe: GERMANY

ELECTRA

Bernd Aust - *saxophones*, **Wolfgang Riedel** - *bass*, **Ekkehard Berger** - *guitar*, **Peter Ludewig** - *drums, vocals*, **Karl-Heinz Ringel** - *keyboards*, **Stephan Trepte** - *vocals*, **Peter Sandkaulen** - *guitar*, **Rainer Uebel** - *keyboards*, **Manuel Von Senden** - *vocals*.

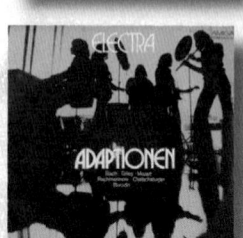

Formed in 1969 as **Electra Combo**, they start playing in dance halls for a few years without neglecting their Classical studies, that will leave an indelible imprint in the musical orientation. Finally in 1974 they manage to record a self-titled debut album, though pretty disappointing, lacking vigor, uninspired and suspended halfway between the desire for a viable artistic expression and the need to provide a commercial product. With *Adaptionen* they become more daring: tracks taken from Classical music are adapted to Prog, with a large deployment of highly inspired organ and guitar moments.

Unfortunately label Amiga requires them to publish *3*, a mixture of past discarded pieces and new compositions: a pastiche of themes that leave an awkward sense of fraud. However *Die Sixtinische Madonna* manages to restore the balance and gives the group back their title of Masters of Kraut Rock. This is a Rock-Opera, based on the contrast between communist ideology and the religious icon, that lives off the absolute intertwining between the sound produced by keyboards and guitars, backed up by the masterful voice of **Manuel von Senden**. More creative than **Yes**, more passionate than **Ekseption**, less sophisticated than **EL&P** and much more symphonic than **Jethro Tull**, **Electra** poses as founder of a certain model of Kraut, less experimental and a little more romantic, farther from Hard-Rock and more devoted to choral music transplanted from certain Goth-inspired religious themes, rich in mystery and openly symphonic. The long suite that

bares the title of the album is one of the masterpieces of the band and can be declared as a manifesto of a more mature Kraut movement.

The '80s lead to profound line-up transformations that will inevitably affect their artistic orientation: *Ein Tag wie eine Brücke* pays a high price to the winds of innovation which, under the name of New Wave are lashing out on the music world. This time it is the Progressive genre to be contaminated, dirtied inside by artistic germs hardly compatible with the sounds from which it was built and tempered. It will take a few years for the band to collect the pieces and find the energy to release another incredible album, harshly opposed by critics, but of great musical depth: *Augen der Sehnsucht*, which brings them back to their highest levels of inspiration and interpretation. The concert tours to promote the album become more intense and their performances are more and more complex and engaging. This is their farewell to the Prog scene, since the following *Tausend und ein Gefühl* and all that will come after, can be classified as Pop Rock, elegant and delightfully packaged, but terribly far from the path taken in 1974.

C.A.

RECOMMENDED RECORDINGS:
ELECTRA COMBO *(Amiga, 1974)* **ADAPTIONEN** *(Amiga, 1974)* **3** *(Amiga, 1979)* **DIE SIXTINISCHE MADONNA** *(Amiga, 1980)* **EIN TAG WIE EINE BRUCKE** *(Amiga, 1981)* **AUGEN DER SEHNSUCHT** *(Amiga, 1985).*

Europe: GERMANY

ELOY

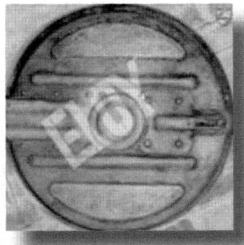

Frank Bornemann - *guitar, vocals, percussions,* **Klaus-Peter Matziol** - *bass, bass-pedal, vocals,* **Jürgen Rosenthal** - *drums, percussions,* **Detlev Schmidtchen** - *keyboards, vocals, percussions.*

In 1969 guitarist **Frank Bornemann** founds **Eloy** inspired by the futuristic race featured in Herbert G. Wells' *The Time Machine*. The original musical approach is marked by a turbulent beat and an ever present guitar, but the widespread trend for innovation soon leads to a new way of mixing sounds, that will be published in their self-titled 1971 album, nothing more than a decent and fairly conventional Hard-Rock, not yet revealing the band's clear inclination towards Prog. During the following two years, before issuing a sequel, **Bornemann** evaluates new proposals coming especially from England and begins drawing inspiration from compositional groups such as **Pink Floyd** and **Van Der Graaf Generator**. He is also interested in the use of classic melodic rock music. *Inside* (1973) and *Floating* (1974) are two very different albums: songs become longer, **Manfred Wieczorke**'s keyboards begin to take shape and the Progressive tendencies start to stand out, but the continuous changes in line-up do not help musical stability.

In 1975, *Power and the Passion* represents another quantum leap and after its release, **Wieczorke** leaves the group to join **Jane**. The new structure brings to a better line-up and to better records under every aspect. The composition turns out to be punctual and instrumentally impeccable. *Dawn, Ocean* and *Silent Cries and Mighty Echoes* (also called the *Cosmic Trilogy*) sell out largely, also in time, confirming the remarkable quality achieved.

As with many historical groups the turn of the decade seems to be difficult. The following works, while still offering good ideas, don't have the strength and inventiveness of the previous. Other line-up changes, especially the loss of their powerful and precise drumme **Rosenthal**, shift the balance. Tracks shrink in order to accompany easier and less aggressive melodies. *Colors* (1980) is a typical transition album, waiting for the band to regroup their ideas and re-establish themselves.

With the return of drummer **Fritz Randow**, who joins till 1975, two inspired and very bright science-fiction concept albums are published, opening to the new synth sounds. Unfortunately after *Planets* and *Time To Run* begins a phase of heavy downfall. Undeniably sparse puffs of quality here and there are to be found among the rare albums released several years apart, until the last episode in 1998, a sort of thematic repetition of their masterpiece: *Ocean 2* tries to revive the past with no luck at all.
R.V.

DISCOGRAPHY:
ELOY *(1971, Philips)* **INSIDE** *(1973, EMI Electrola)* **FLOATING** *(1974, EMI Electrola)* **POWER AND THE PASSION** *(1975, EMI Electrola)* **DAWN** *(1976, EMI Electrola)* **OCEAN** *(1977, EMI Electrola)* **ELOY LIVE** *(1978, EMI Electrola)* **SILENT CRIES AND MIGHTY ECHOES** *(1979, EMI Electrola)* **COLOURS** *(1980, EMI Electrola)* **PLANETS** *(1981, EMI Harvest)* **TIME TO RUN** *(1982, EMI Harvest)* **PERFORMANCE** *(1983, EMI Harvest)* **METROMANIA** *(1984, EMI Harvest)* **CODENAME WILDGEESE** *(1985, SW Milan)* **RA** *(1988, ACI Records)* **DESTINATION** *(1992, ACI Records)* **THE TIDES RETURN FOREVER** *(1994, SPV)* **OCEAN 2** *(1998, BMG)*.

Europe: GERMANY

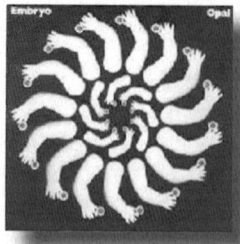

EMBRYO

Christian Burchard - *drums, percussion, vibes, keyboards, vocals*. **Edgar Hofmann** - *winds, violin*. **Hansi Fischer, Charlie Mariano** - *horns*. **Jimmy Jackson, Hermann Breuer, Mal Waldron, Dieter Miekautsch, Michael Wehmeyer** - *keyboards*, **Ralph Fischer, Jörg Evers, David King, Uwe Müllrich, Gerard Hartwig Luciano** - *bass*. **John Kelly, Al Jones, Julius Schittenhelm, Sigi Schwab, Roman Bunka** - *guitars*, **Maria Archer** - *vocals*, **Trilok Gurtu** - *percussion*.

The band forms thanks to the will of a curious percussionist called **Christian Burchard**, a lover and student of Jazz whom, together with Classical violinist **Edgar Hofmann**, plays in the quartet of pianist **Mal Waldron**. The boys make their way through an increasingly artistic Munich and in October 1970 debut with *Opal*, a perfect merge of Jazz, Psychedelia, World Music and Blues, with that languid and hypnotic mood that will be the trademark of all Teutonic productions.
The band receives immediate credit also during their on-stage performances, publishing *Embryo's Rache*, enriched by **Jackson**'s Mellotron and the rather unusual rhythms for a Rock act due to the more improvisational approach. It is a hit, so the new quartet publishes next *Father, Son & Holy Ghosts*, a more intimate work with essential ethnic tints, to the point that the Goethe Institute even decides to sponsor an African tour, just like for

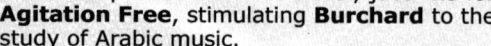

Agitation Free, stimulating **Burchard** to the study of Arabic music.
In '73 the label Brain releases *Steig Aus* and *Rocksession*: recorded with **Waldron** between '71 and '72, but at the time rejected by the other label United Artists for their excessive experimentation. The albums prove them to be at ease between the fusion of free rock, jazz and African-American influences. The association with **Charlie Mariano** gives way to

a series of African, Middle East and funky soaked sounds, while the growing influence of **Roman Bunka** brings the band to India for a collaboration with percussionist **Trilok Gurtu**.
At the end of the decade they resist through the various storms, managing to cross into the '80s deepening their studies with significant international travels (especially in southeast Asia) and fine works, now wide open to the entire ethnic musical world. *Embryo's Reise* and *Turn Peace* (celebrating the twentieth anniversary of the group) are proof of how they do not melt nor yield to the revival of the '90s either, but continue in their eclectic path undisturbed. **Burchard** is always present in large-scale projects, collaborating with **Waldron** or other young artists such as the Italian **Mandara Alhambra**. After nearly 40 years of career their name still evokes experimentation, artistic freedom, peaceful and fruitful collaboration. The Great Spirit of Kraut dwells here.

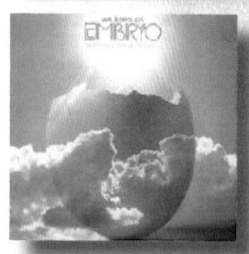

D.Z.

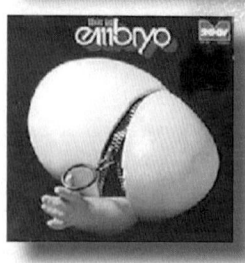

DISCOGRAPHY:
OPAL *(Ohr, 1970)* **EMBRYO'S RACHE** *(United Artists, 1971)* **FATHER, SON & HOLY GHOSTS** *(United Artists, 1972)* **STEIG AUS** *(Brain, 1973)* **ROCKSESSION** *(Brain, 1973)* **WE KEEP ON** *(Brain, 1974)* **SURFIN'** *(Buk, 1975)* **BAD HEADS AND BAD CATS** *(April, 1977)* **LIVE** *(April, 1977)* **APO CALYPSO** *(April, 1978)* **EMBRYO'S REISE** *(Schneeball ,1979)* **LIFE!** *(Schneeball, 1980)* **LA BLAMA SPAROZZI** *(Schneeball, 1982)* **ZACK GLÜCK** *(Materiali Sonori, 1984)* Embryo & **YORUBA DUN DUN ORCHESTER** *(Schneeball, 1985)* **AFRICA** *(Materiali Sonori, 1987)* **JAZZBÜHNE BERLIN** *(Amiga, 1989)* **TURN PEACE** *(Schneeball, 1990)* **IBN BATTUTA** *(Indigo Schneeball, 1994)* **NI HAU** *(Indigo Schneeball, 1996)* **LIVE IN BERLIN** *(live, United Records, 1998)* **ISTANBUL - CASABLANCA TOUR 98** *(live, Indigo Schneeball, 1999)* **INVISIBLE DOCUMENTS - LIVE 74** *(live, Diskonforme, 1999)* **ONE NIGHT AT THE JUAN MIRÒ FOUNDATION** *(live, Diskonforme 2000)* **LIVE 2000 VOL. 1** *(Indigo Schneeball, 2000)* **LIVE 2001 VOL. 2** *(Indigo Schneeball, 2001)* **BREMEN 1971** *(live, Garden Of Delights, 2003)* **HALLO MIK - LIVE RECORDINGS 2002-2003** *(live, Schneeball, 2003)* **LIVE IN WENDLAND** *(live, Schneeball, 2007)* **FREEDOM IN MUSIC** *(Schneeball, 2008)*.

Europe: GERMANY

FAUST

Rudolf Sossna - *guitar, keyboards,*
Hans-Joachim Irmler - *keyboards.*
Jean-Hervé Peron - *bass,* **Gunter Wüsthoff** - *horns, keyboards,* **Werner Diermeier, Arnulf Meifert** - *drums.*

More of an experiment than of a group, their live debut in Hamburg does not receive a very good response from the audience. A project like this could only be born in the '70s and in the cradle of a unique experimental lab: a Germany driven by an irresistible impulse for freedom. It is a favorable period for the country's Rock music: **Can, Tangerine Dream** and **Amon Düül II** are appreciated in England and the phenomenon of kraut rock is gaining ground. Radical journalist Uwe Nettelbeck gathers a group of musicians in a studio in Wümme, with the involvement of technical sound engineer Kurt Graupner. Here they can use all the technology available and are allowed to pioneering trials in the manipulation of sounds. Even the cover of their self-titled album, with the x-ray of a fist (**Faust** in German means fist) is avant-garde, especially attracting British attentions. Inspired by the early **Soft Machine, Pink Floyd, the Velvet Underground** and the experimental *Lumpy Gravy* by **Frank Zappa**, the band combines the most hypnotic Garage-rock with a liberal and ironic use of cut-ups. *Faust* is a revolutionary work and such a success in England, that the label Polydor will publish *Faust So Far* at first for the UK market: the album improves the ideas of the previous one, drawing the band closer to **Can** by increasing the anarchic component and the Psychedelic Rock, also shocking for the all-black cover and illustrations of each song. Thanks to Graupner and the enlightened leadership of Uwe **Faust** lives the studio as an authentic creative dimension, anticipating **Kraftwerk** and **Brian Eno**. It will be in Wümme that keyboardist **Anthony Moore** will record *Pieces From The Cloudland Ballroom* (with *Diermeier* on the drums), before founding **Slapp Happy**, produced by the same Nettelbeck.

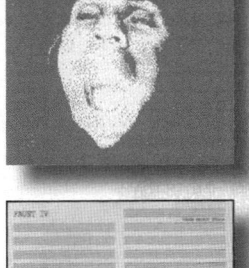

In love with NY's culture, in 1972 they meet violinist **Tony Conrad** (**Theater Of Eternal Music**, better known as the **Dream Syndicate**) and the three of them take part in one of his works, focusing on a mystic **Cale-Riley** type of Minimalism. The album is released by the label Caroline in the economic series, and Virgin will pursue the same policy for *Faust Tapes* (a compilation recorded between 1971 and 1973), helping them reach a higher place in the charts. **Faust** becomes a cult in England and the performances destabilize the audience with provocative and experimental live-acts, using pinball machines connected to synths. Virgin recordings affect only part of *Faust IV*, a more acid, corrosive and **Syd Barrett**-styled album, which shines for its visionary foresight. After some changes in the line-up and the refusal of Virgin to publish new material, the adventure ends. In the '80s **Chris Cutler**'s label Recommended is interested in the group, in its own way a forerunner of the RIO movement, and publishes archival material: their cult starts over, considered among the most influential European groups of the '70s and more and more mythologized. A reunion in the '90s sees important collaborations with **Jim O' Rourke** - deus ex machina of post-rock - who features in *Rien*. Bands like **Einsturdenze Neubauten** and **Ulan Bator** declare their love for **Faust** and **Julian Cope**, who plays a crucial role in the rediscovery of international kraut, considering their avant-rock a milestone of this era. **D.Z.**

DISCOGRAPHY:

FAUST *(Polydor, 1971)* **FAUST SO FAR** *(Polydor, 1973)* **TONY CONRAD WITH FAUST: Outside The Dream Syndicate** *(Caroline, 1973)* **FAUST TAPES** *(Virgin, 1973)* **FAUST IV** *(Virgin, 1973)* **MÜNICH AND ELSEWHERE** *(Recommended, 1986)* **LAST LP** *(Recommended, 1988)* **RIEN** *(Table Of The Elements, 1995)* **FAUST CONCERTS, VOL. 1: LIVE IN HAMBURG 1990** *(live, Table Of The Elements, 1996)* **FAUST CONCERTS, VOL. 2: LIVE IN LONDON 1992** *(live, Table Of The Elements, 1996)* **UNTITLED** *(1996)* **YOU KNOW FAUST** *(Recommended, 1997)* **EDINBURGH 1997** *(live, Klangbad, 1997)* **FAUST WAKES NOSFERATU** *(Klangbad, 1998)* **RAVVIVANDO** *(Klangbad, 1999)* **THE LAND OF RAUKKO & RAUNI LIVE** *(Ektro, 2001)* **BBC SESSIONS** *(live, Recommended, 2001)* **FREISPIEL** *(Klangbad, 2002)* **PATCHWORK 1971-2002** *(Staubgold, 2002)* **LIVE IN KRAKOW 2006** *(live, LTC 2007)* **DISCONNECTED** *(Art-errorist, 2007)*.

Europe: GERMANY

GROBSCHNITT

Stefan Danielak (Wildschwein) *guitars, vocals*, **Joachim Ehrig (Eroc)** - *drums, percussion, tape effects, vocals*, **Wolfgang Jäger (Popo)** - *bass*, **Volker Kahrs (Mist)** - *keyboards*, **Gerd-Otto Kühn (Lupo)** - *guitars*.

Born in 1970 from the ashes of a German band called **Crew** (since 1966), they began playing as **Grobschnitt** with an intense on-stage activity. From the beginning the group shows great technical skills and an extremely versatile musical approach, originating from the Blues and opening its horizons to very interesting symphonic forms, together with strong theatrical and cabaret acts especially during live performances. Towards the end of the 1971 tour, label Brain Records gives them the opportunity to record a first self-titled studio album published in 1972. It immediately pointed out their personal extravagance which combined moments of classic Symphonic Prog with Latin American rhythms and a **Santana** inspired guitar, a **Hendrix** Hard-Blues. The Kraut-Space openings are of exquisite workmanship with small interferences and brief marches or any other kind of noise made by drummer **Eroc** (**Joachim Ehrig**) on synths.

1973 was dedicated to live concerts and saw the addition of keyboardist **Mist** (**Volker Kahrs**) which, with his extremely positive entry, gave a consistent qualitative contribution to the composition. The second album's titled was taken from the fat chief of the Roadies, whose nickname was *Ballermann* (in the group everyone had a nickname), suggesting the idea of an introspective journey between real and lysergic, becoming their eponymous double album. It contained the long "Solar Music", a Space-jam of great effect that would further on become the key moment of every concert, with a lot of moaning and Cosmic shifts balanced by a perfect execution technique. This suite is perhaps what brought them closer to the Kraut movement, instead of on the side where they had always been.

Already the following year *Jumbo* sees them at a turning point: sung in English and German, it appears more incline to less complex and experimental sounds. Unquestionably a good work, it however has the defect of playing less as **Grobschnitt** and more as the leading British groups of the time (**Yes, Camel, Pink Floyd, Genesis**). The same fate for the next recording *Rockpommel Land*, but with a decidedly more substantial song-writing, containing the famous title-track, a suite full of events in succession, worthy of the great band they had always been. After 1978's long tour, they release the remarkable *Solar Music - Live*, a perfect epitome of what the band was on stage, despite missing the visual aspect, an essential element of each of their representations. The next phase of their career is downhill, and so, even if some good ideas could still be felt in *Merry Go Round* and *Illegal*, the following *Volle Molle*, *Razzia* and so forth, result poor and weak, with the exception of few live performances. The official end of the group takes place in Hagen with a 1989 farewell concert. **R.V.**

DISCOGRAPHY:

GROBSCHNITT *(1972, BRAIN)* **BALLERMANN** *(1974, BRAIN)* **JUMBO** *(1975, BRAIN)* **ROCKPOMMEL'S LAND** *(1977, BRAIN)* **SOLAR MUSIC - LIVE** *(1978, BRAIN)* **MERRY GO-ROUND** *(1979, BRAIN)* **VOLLE MOLLE** *(1980, BRAIN)* **ILLEGAL** *(1981, BRAIN)* **RAZZIA** *(1982, BRAIN)* **KINDER UND NARREN** *(1984, BRAIN)* **SONNENTANZ - LIVE** *(1985, BRAIN)* **FANTASTEN** *(1987, Teldec)* **LAST PARTY LIVE 1989** *(1990, BRAIN)* **THE GROBSCHNITT STORY 4 ILLEGAL LIVE 1981** *(2003, WOL)*.

Europe: GERMANY

GURU GURU

Mani Neumeier - *drums, percussions, vocals, tape effects, keyboards,*
Uli Trepte - *bass, tape effects,*
Ax Genrich - *guitars,*
Konrad Plank - *Sound Engineering.*

Among the founders of the German movement later identified as Krautrock, the band **Guru Guru** is also the oldest representative, starting off in 1968 and still in business. During their career, the only common element of each line-up is their creator, the amazing drummer **Mani Neumeier**. From the beginning (known as **Guru Guru Groove Band**) their music is distinguished by a strong traversal and fusion component, which combines experimental and avant-garde, jazz tints, sometimes tending to free forms, large doses of psychedelia, open tendencies to space rock and strong traces of rock blues. The style is inspired by **Frank Zappa** and **Jimi Hendrix**, but also by great Jazz improvisers like **Coltrane** and **Monk** are always present in their compositions.

During the recording of a first album, **Neumeier** fires guitarist **Edy Nageli** in favour of **Ax Grenich** coming from **Agitation Free**. His undoubted qualities turn out to be decisive for the band and the album *UFO* in 1970 was put out on a market where these sounds had just began to be of a certain interest. Very strong the bluesy and acid matrix of the forever-lasting tracks, but with a space jam flavour: the leading guitar, mixed with dazed vocals as out of nowhere, creates the strange ethereal atmosphere of **Gong**'s contemporary works. The state of pure psychedelic avant-garde of the title track that, with its compositional weirdness, will heavily mark the band's production. The initial phase proves to be a raging river with very high content albums flowing one after another: *Hinten* (1971), *Känguru* (1972), their best work ever also thanks to **Konrad Plank (Conny Plank)**, and *Guru Guru* (1973).

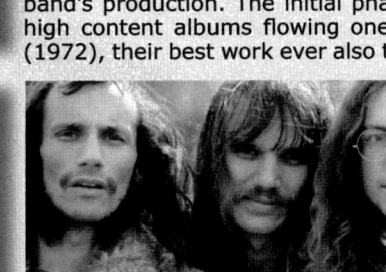

Musicians leaves and join continuously, especially after the anomalous abandonment of phenomenal bassist **Trepte**. When **Plank** quits, the first real change in their music starts to show, while **Neumeier** fueled a dense series of interesting collaborations outside the group. *Don't Call Us We Call You* (1973) and the live *Dance Of The Flames* (1974) are both transitional albums with great insight and significant moments, alternating others more trivial and prone to pop.

The concept of combining styles led to all sorts of inventions, determining oddities (techno, yodel, funky and tango) on a conceptually higher level. The decadent 80ies' releases are simply copies, with space rock trends, often very similar to **Hawkwind**. Over the next decade the band goes through a kind of re-birth of expression, also determined by successful external collaborations, in particular with phenomenal guitarist **Luigi Archetti** and his contribution of deconstructed jazz. Fewer releases thereafter, but of good quality, up to the recent and very decent *Psy*. **R.V.**

DISCOGRAPHY:
UFO *(1970, Ohr)* **HINTEN** *(1971, Ohr)* **KÄNGURU** *(1972, Brain)* **GURU GURU** *(1973, Brain)* **DON'T CALL US WE CALL YOU** *(1973, Atlantic)* **DANCE OF THE FLAMES** *(1974, Atlantic)* **MANI UND SEINE FREUNDE** *(1975, Atlantic)* **TANGO FANGO** *(1976, Brain)* **GLOBETROTTER** *(1977, Brain)* **GURU GURU LIVE** *(1978, Brain)* **HEY DU!** *(1979, Brain)* **MANI IN GERMANI** *(1981, GBD)* **GURU MANI NEUMEIERS NEUE ABENTEUER** *(1983, Biber)* **JUNGLE** *(1987, Casino)* **GURU GURU 88** *(1988, Casino)* **LIVE 72** *(1988, United Dairies, RRRecords)* **SHAKE WELL** *(1993, ZYX-Music)* **WAH WAH** *(1995, Think Progressive)* **MASK** *(1996, Think Progressive)* **MOSHI MOSHI** *(1997, Think Progressive)* **30 JAHRE LIVE** *(1998, Revisited Records)* **2000 GURUS** *(2000, Funfundvierzig)* **ESSEN 1970** *(2003, Amber Soundroom)* **IN THE GURU LOUNGE** *(2005, Revisited Records)* **WIESBADEN 1972** *(2007, Garden Of Delights)* **PSY** *(2008, Trance-Music)*.

Europe: GERMANY

HOELDERLIN

Christian Grumbkow - *guitars,*
Joachim Grumbkow - *keyboards, cello, flute, vocals,*
Hans Bäär - *bass, rhythm guitar,*
Michael Bruchmann - *drums, percussions,*
Christoph Noppeney - *viola, acoustic guitar, flute, piano, vocals.*

The group starts its musical career in 1970 when various musicians coming from different experiences, from Rock to Jazz to Folk, begin to play together with brothers **Christian** and **Joachim Grumbkow**. As the band settles and increases in number, songs take shape and, after a few concerts, comes their first release in 1972: with up to nine instrumentalists, *Hölderlins Traum* proves to be an excellent debut and for many, their best work. The music is very rich, sophisticated and sometimes resounding, with great female vocals, it is the result of each member's different experience, which can be resumed as Symphonic Prog with a very personal and engaging Folk and acoustic element. This earned them numerous and extremely positive reviews, an obvious incentive to continue.

A tour of 80 dates in Germany alone brings them to TV appearances and festivals of all kinds, including concerts in prisons, inevitably keeping them away from the studio. Only in 1975 are they able to start working on a second and more intense compositional phase, releasing three excellent albums. *Hoelderlin* (1975) keeps intact the acoustic Folk element but leaving behind the Psychedelic ingredient that, surely because of a greater contemporary involvement, was still present in their beginnings. Instead the symphonic component expands to the benefit of sounds that somehow remind us of the early **Genesis**, but also of other groups of the same period, like **Camel** or **Curved Air**. However undeniable is how **Hoelderlin** was able to maintain the band's great personality and standard of excellence, made of fascinating and appealing sounds. *Clowns & Clouds* (1976) and *Rare Birds* (1976) are both remarkable works which confirm the beautiful composition and executive value of these musicians. *Hoelderlin Live-Traumstadt* (1978) gathers some of their most recent performances, even with a smaller formation and therefore slightly more in line with the demands of the time. A massive line-up shuffle, with the entry of, among others, **Eduard Schicke** from the trio **Schicke**, **Führs** and **Fröhling**, brought a heavy change in sounds. *New Faces* (1979) expresses this well already in the title, with only a vague relation to Prog, instead mainly composed by tracks of peaceful Pop Rock, without any pretense. Worse fate for the following *Fata Morgana* (1981) with its simple and at times even pleasant Melodic Prog.

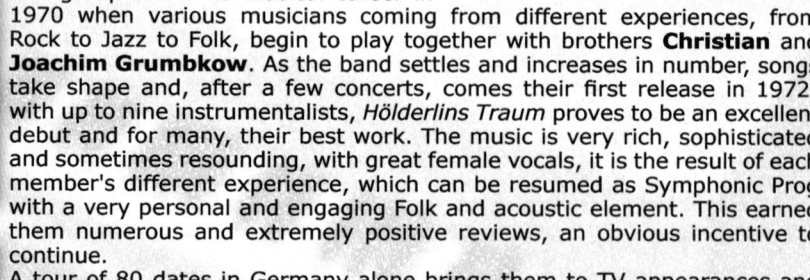

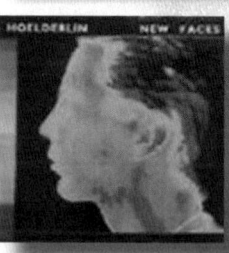

Pushed by **Bruchmann**, they reunite in studio, publishing a somewhat lovable album, with a beautiful female voice and soft, subtle textures, although still far from the wonderful sounds of the past. **R.V.**

DISCOGRAPHY:
HÖLDERLINS TRAUM *(1972, Pilz)* **HOELDERLIN** *(1975, Spiegelei)* **CLOWNS AND CLOUDS** *(1976, Spiegelei)* **RARE BIRDS** *(1972, EMI)* **HOELDERLIN LIVE - TRAUMSTADT** *(1978, Spiegelei)* **NEW FACES** *(1979, Intercord)* **FATA MORGANA** *(1981, Intercord)* **EIGTH** *(2007, Odeon/EMI)*.

Europe: GERMANY

KRAAN

Hellmut Hattler - *bass*
Peter Wolbrandt - *guitar, vocals*
Johannes Pappert - *saxophones*
Jan Fride - *drums, percussions*
Ingo Bischof - *keyboards.*

Formed in 1970 playing an undefined musical genre with typical Rock elements combined to forms of Free-Jazz. This mix generates strange results and even stranger attitudes in those who listen: seen as a Jazz band by Rock fans and as Rock band by the Jazz audience, both are right. The first two 1972 albums *Kraan* and *Wintrup* summarize the characteristics of their beginnings, presenting a solid and technically prepared group which knows how to smoothly switch from defined to improvised parts. There are no particularly experimental sections and neither blatantly easy-going melodies. In the songs, oriental and ethnic sounds coexist with rich atmospheres, wrapped in very tight rhythms and dynamics.

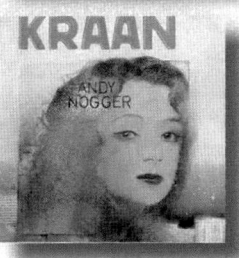

With the rapid rise in popularity they move to Berlin, soon ready for their masterpiece *Andy Nogger*, released in 1974, and a massive double live album out the following year. Here Prog Rock Jazz is present in all its glory. In the live versions, songs expand making room for each musician with great technical improvised parts and high-impact sounds. The first phase ends more or less like this.

They moves again, creating a community in Wintrup where they combine song-writing with political themes, as in vogue at the time. Keyboardist **Ingo Bischof** joins permanently and the compositions grow closer to Symphonic Fusion, with intrusions of Funk moments and with rhythmic grooves, anticipating a few years the trends that will be normal towards the end of this decade. The open character of their structure allows, during the years, a certain rotation of musicians, such as exceptional drummer **Udo Dahmen**, while maintaining the original consistency. The tendency is to include more funky arrangements, especially in the '80s, sometimes recorded separately as in *2- Schall Platten* of 1983. The band later that year takes a pause which will last nearly five years, during which they were thought to be over. Then in 1988, they too reunite until 1991 with four other works.

Regardless of the ups and downs, Kraan proves to still be great on stage, and publishes *Kraan Live '88*. Then something breaks again, bringing them to another halt. This allows the musicians to work in other activities until a second reunion in 1998. Their latest album *Psychedelic Man* released in 2007, presents echoes of Psychedelia, Rock, Funk, Jazz and Electronics, always skilfully mixed by addressing themes with their usual coherence. **R.V.**

DISCOGRAPHY:

KRAAN *(1972, Spiegelei)* **WINTRUP** *(1972, Spiegelei)* **ANDY NOGGER** *(1974, Passport)* **KRAAN LIVE** *(1975, Spiegelei)* **LET IT OUT** *(1975, Passport)* **WIEDERHÖREN** *(1977, EMI Harvest)* **FLYDAY** *(1979, EMI Harvest)* **TOURNEE - LIVE** *(1980, EMI Harvest)* **NACHTAHRT** *(1982, Boots/ Gee Bee Dee)* **2 SCHALL-PLATTEN** *(1983, Boots/Gee Bee Dee)* **X** *(1983, Teldec)* **KRAAN LIVE 1988** *(1988, Interecord)* **DANCING IN THE SHADE** *(1989, Interecord)* **SOUL OF STONE** *(1991, Interecord)* **THE FAMOUS YEARS COMPILED** *(1998, IRS INT)* **KRAAN LIVE 2001** *(2001, Bassball Recordings)* **BERLINER RING** *(2001, Bassball Recordings)* **TROUGH** *(2003, Bassball Recordings)* **PSYCHEDELIC MAN** *(2007, EMI)* **DIAMONDS** *(2010, Bassball).*

Europe: GERMANY

KRAFTWERK

Ralf Hütter & Florian Schneider - *sinthesizers, electronic devices, programming, vocals,* **Andreas Hohmann, Klaus Dinger, Wolfgang Flür, Karl Bartos, Fritz Hilpert, Henning Schmitz** - *drums, electronic percussion,* **Plato Kostic, Klaus Roeder** - *guitar.* **Emil Schult** - *flute.*

More than thirty years after the album in which they presented their philosophical and sonic project, Kraftwerk still collects credit from bands like **Autechre, Rammstein, Coldplay, Daft Punk** and **Orbital**, along with movements like New Wave, Techno-Pop, Ambient and Industrial. In addition, the genesis of this group explains the closeness of the popular phenomenon and of intellectual music in Germany: proof are the inclinations of **Ralf Hütter** and **Florian Schneider**, both **Karlheinz Stockhausen**'s students at Düsseldorf Remschied Kunstakademie, both working at an experimental project with electronic sounds that don't deny their German origin.

Under the name **Organisation** these two musicians publish an album between **Can**'s repetitiveness and **Popol Vuh**'s acoustic sounds, yet soaked with ethno-psychedelic references (with flutes and percussions), which will affect the works thereafter. Changed to **Kraftwerk** (meaning Power Station), they set up the Kling Klang Studio and publish two self-titled albums similar to the previous *Tone Float*, but with a certain tendency towards minimal repetition with electronic percussions and researched sound. **Conny Plank**'s production ensures a quality not to be found in other contemporary albums: the covers are inspired by Pop Art, with **Klaus Dinger** on drums (later founder of **Neu!**) and **Michael Rother**, who with **Florian** will later appear on TV.

If *Ralf & Florian* sees the two alone with primitive synthesizers and drum machines, *Autobahn* radicalizes sound and philosophy: the relationship between man and the machine, technology, art and music, popular and culture, authority and freedom, all expressed in a fundamental album inspired by the monotony of the long German highways. Some speak of kling klang music, in the future it will be called Synth-Pop: their sound is Spartan, stern and martial, but its secret lies in the technological concept which allows to electronically generate rhythmic patterns and modify entries. It is an international success, henceforth the austere (but ironic) **Kraftwerk** becomes a phenomenon that intrigues and shocks, and they soon begin to publish for the international market.

With percussionists **Bartos** and **Flür** their most famous line-up takes place releasing a remarkable trilogy: *Radio-Activity*, inspired by radio waves and nuclear power; the famous *Trans-Europe Express* (1977 is the year of punk); the perfect *The Man-Machine*, which goes down in history for the final expression of **the Kraftwerk** philosophy and for the use of dummies instead of real musicians. **Ralf** and **Florian**'s music is concrete and up to date, accessible and sometimes dance-able: the boom of New Wave and Elettro-Rock is due to them, as is the evolution of Electronics since their studies in Milan's University of Phonology at RAI.

The '80s and '90s are more enigmatic with less releases and all in the field of music technology: *Computer World* and *Tour De France* are state of the art regarding the new frontiers of sound. The colossal *Minimum-Maximum* is their first live album. Absolutely Kraut.   **D.Z.**

DISCOGRAPHY:
THE ORGANISATION: TONE FLOAT *(RCA 1970)* **KRAFTWERK** *(Philips 1970)* **KRAFTWERK 2** *(Philips 1972)* **RALF & FLORIAN** *(Philips 1973)* **AUTOBAHN** *(Philips 1974)* **RADIO-ACTIVITY** *(Capitol 1975)* **TRANS-EUROPE EXPRESS** *(Capitol 1977)* **THE MAN-MACHINE** *(Capitol 1978)* **COMPUTER WORLD** *(EMI 1981)* **ELECTRIC CAFÉ** *(EMI 1986)* **THE MIX** *(EMI 1991)* **TOUR DE FRANCE SOUNDTRACKS** *(EMI 2003)* **MINIMUM-MAXIMUM** *(live, EMI 2005)* **3D (DER KATALOG)** *(Kling Klang, 2017).*

Europe: **GERMANY**

NEKTAR

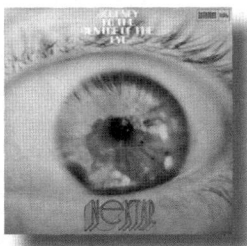

Roye Albrighton, Dave Nelson - *guitar, vocals.*
Derek "Mo" Moore, Carmine Rojas, Randy Dembo, Peter Pichl - *bass.* **Ron Howden, Dave Prater, Ray Hardwick** - *drums.* **Allan "Taff" Freeman, Larry Fast, Tom Hughes, Klaus Henatsch** - *keyboards.* **Mick Brockett** - *visual effects, light engineering.*

<<*Not the #1 German band in England, but the #1 British band in Germany!*>> This was written on posters advertising **Nektar** concerts in 1973. During the early '70s it was less common for British groups to concentrate activities in Germany, while bands like **Can**, **Amon Düül II** and **Faust** acquired success in Britain through concerts and with their own records at the top of the charts. Moreover **Nektar** managed to seal a bond so tight with its Teutonic land to be considered the Germans tout court! If **Beatles**, **Deep Purple** and **Pink Floyd** consolidate their following in Germany, **Nektar**, despite no special connection if not a certain psychedelic feeling, put down roots through kraut rock.

The adventure begins in the mid-'60s, a time when many British musicians played in Hamburg at the famous Star Club: it is here that **Prophecy** (**Taff Freeman**, **Rob Howden** and **Mo Moore**) meet the great Rainbows' guitarist **Roye Albrighton**. A valuable partnership strengthened by the collaboration with creative light-designer **Mick Brockett**, who gives the group beautiful visual stimuli. **Moore** organizes a detailed action plan and **Nektar** concerts manage to conquer the interest of an American manager, that unfortunately will later on let them down. Once back in Germany they sign a contract with Peter Hauke and the prestigious Bacillus (owned by Bellaphon), which will support their long discography thereon.

Journey To The Center Of The Eye is a terrific debut: a space opera meant to be represented on stage with **Brockett**'s dazzling light-shows. Even better is *A Tab In The Ocean*: the long instrumental moments are inspired by **Pink Floyd** and anticipate that certain indolent trait by **Camel**; "King Of Twilight" will even be covered by **Iron Maiden** in '84. The grandeur and strength of the sounds make **Nektar** one of a kind.

The quartet is excellent at live performances, as proven in their tours (the boys also open for **Frank Zappa**) and issue the live studio double album *Sounds Like This* (recorded with **Dieter Dierks** and even praised by **Elton John**). The formula is finally refined in a memorable concept album *Remember The Future*: a huge suite characterized by an art-rock linked to **Yes** and a cosmic rock with large spaces and epic sounds with strong evocative power. Brilliant for the balance between all components, it also sells a lot in the U.S. and determines their international success, also among critics.

The downward phase then begins: Bellaphon presses for more concise and radio broadcast-able songs to which they reply with *Down To Earth*, about the circus world (even the band dresses up accordingly) written with **Bob Calvert**, with a more rock and melodic approach, less resounding. *Recycled* can easily compete with the giants of pomp-rock; in the weak *Magic Is A Child* **Albrighton** is absent and the genius of synths **Larry Fast** (head of the **Synergy** project and then right-hand man of **Peter Gabriel**) does what he can. The revival of prog and the illness from which **Roye** recovers, stimulate a reunion in 2002, publishing three decent albums, and featuring in some important prog international festivals. **D.Z.**

DISCOGRAPHY:

JOURNEY TO THE CENTER OF THE EYE *(Bellaphon/Bacillus 1971)* **A TAB IN THE OCEAN** *(Bellaphon/Bacillus 1972)* **...SOUNDS LIKE THIS** *(Bellaphon/Bacillus 1973)* **REMEMBER THE FUTURE** *(Bellaphon/Bacillus 1973)* **SUNDAY NIGHT AT LONDON ROUNDHOUSE** *(live, Bellaphon/Bacillus 1974)* **DOWN TO EARTH** *(Bellaphon/Bacillus 1974)* **RECYCLED** *(Bellaphon/Bacillus 1975)* **MAGIC IS A CHILD** *(Bellaphon/Bacillus 1976)* **LIVE IN NEW YORK** *(live, Bellaphon/Bacillus 1978)* **MORE LIVE IN NEW YORK** *(live, Bellaphon/Bacillus 1978)* **MAN IN THE MOON** *(Ariola 1980)* **THE PRODIGAL SON** *(Bellaphon 2001)* **UNIDENTIFIED FLYING ABSTRACT** *(live, Bellaphon 2002)* **GREATEST HITS LIVE** *(live, Classic Rock 2003)* **EVOLUTION** *(Dream Nebula 2004)* **DOOR TO THE FUTURE** *(Eclectic discs 2005)* **BOOK OF DAYS** *(Bellaphon 2008)*.

Europe: GERMANY

NOVALIS

Hartwig Biereichel - *drums, percussions*, **Detlef Job** - *guitars, vocals*, **Fred Mühlböck** - *lead vocals, acoustic guitar, flute*, **Lutz Rahn** - *keyboards*, **Heino Schünzel** - *bass, vocals*.

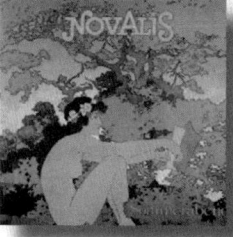

Among one of the best examples of romantic German Prog, and certainly that with the highest number of imitators, this band forms in 1971 thanks to a lucky add, as it often happened, which leads to a first line-up and immediately after, to their contract with label Brain. Nearly two years later, the first fascinating album *Banished Bridge* is published, with its incredible keyboards and an extensive use of Mellotron and guitars that often tend to search for more Hard-Rock solutions. Sounds are inspired by British bands such as **Camel** and **Pink Floyd**, even if they are absolutely not imitations or clones, as the Teutonic component is clear. The album opens with the homonym suite, a high level work, as is the rest of the record, like the beautiful "Laughing" with its very appealing jazzy intrusions.

The group begins a huge live activity which often sees them alongside of other Prog bands such a **Jane** and **Emergency**. The great lyrical and melo-

dic expressiveness of the band does not go unnoticed by **Achim Reichel** (producer and former musician from **AR and The Machines**) that joins in just in time. *Novalis* is issued in 1975, combining the romance of the first with a more accurate compositional attention.

There is a great instrumental understanding and balance between the guitar and keyboards parts, with a sweet atmosphere filling in every space. Considered by many their best, the third album *Sommerabend* is a mature work of extremely rich and varied arrangements, both in terms of melody and for its non obvious refinement of solutions. Especially this suite rises to a high level of prog, with a softer frame, never conceptually complex and increasingly targeted towards the spontaneity of forms; a great success with substantial sales, certainly among the largest for a rock band.

Their name also lands in Japan and their sales here reach peaks that only the **Scorpions** (among German bands) achieve. *Novalis Konzerte* is such an excellent live album that a worthy sequel to this record was not an easy thing, yet 1977 *Brandug*, although not on the very same level, did not come out so bad, shifting towards more immediate and sometimes verging-on Pop Rock sounds, especially in vocals. Same fate for the next, resulting at a much lower level of compositional choices, commercially made, yet rewarding them on the German charts. The following period sees them aligned to contemporary trends, in addition to changes in line-up, with a further drift towards a rather trivial Pop with elements of very linear Neo-Prog, from popular ballads to almost New Age electronics. **R.V.**

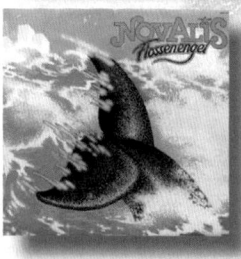

DISCOGRAPHY:
BANISHED BRIDGE *(1973, BRAIN)* **NOVALIS** *(1975, BRAIN)* **SOMMERABEND** *(1976, BRAIN)* **NOVALIS KONZERTE** *(1977, BRAIN)* **BRANDUNG** *(1977, BRAIN)* **VIELEICHT BIST DU EIN CLOWN?** *(1978, BRAIN)* **FLOSSENENGEL** *(1979, Teldec)* **AUGENBLICKE** *(1980, Teldec)* **NEUMOND** *(1982, Phonogram)* **STERNTAUCHER** *(1983, Phonogram)* **VISIONEN** *(1983, Ahorn)* **BUMERANG** *(1984, Teldec)* **NACH UNS DIE FLUT** *(1985, Phonogram)* **NOVALIS LEBT! - LIVE 1981/1984** *(1993, Castle Communications)*.

Europe: GERMANY

OUT OF FOCUS

Remigius Drechsler - *guitar,* **Hennes Hering** - *keyboards,* **Moran Neumüller** - *vocals, saxophones, flute,* **Stephan Wiesheu** - *bass,* **Klaus Spöri** - *drums,* **Ingo Schmid-Neuhaus** - *sax,* **Peter Dechant** - *guitar,* **Hermann Breuer** - *keyboards,* **Michael Thatcher** - *keyboards,* **Grand Roman Langhans** - *percussion,* **Wolfgang Göhringer** - *guitar, vocals,* **Evelyn Drechsler** - *bass.*

Ranked among the most influential bands of the Progressive Kraut-rock movement, with only three albums which all stand out for their originality and technical expertise, **Out of Focus** are artistically inspired by the British prog culture, with particular reference to groups oriented towards more complex musical horizons, such as **Colosseum** and **Pentangle**. Already their debut album leaves an important mark: *Wake Up* and its Psychedelic sounds mix and blend to sweet Folk tunes, brilliantly played by a flute and an organ supported by simple but extremely catchy rhythms.

Out of Focus is the second chapter of this extraordinary experience, experimental and technically close to perfection, it plays out wisely by setting the sound on intimate combinations of organ and guitar, over which the flute tops moments of extraordinary beauty. Deliberately interpreted as if it were a sound check before a concert, every song lives on the musicians' improvisational strength and their incredible team spirit. The Psychedelic past from which they come from is still present, but their musical trend towards a well-structured form of Jazz Rock is clear and nicely underlined by the saxophone intrusions.

The vocals are penalized by inadequate texts and **Neumuller**'s performances lie in the background behind the many instrumental moments. *Four Letter Monday Afternoon* cannot be considered only as a Jazz-rock album for the Jazz inclinations of the band were already obvious in the previous self-titled album: the most typical elements of German Krautrock are interpreted through the excellent use of organ and flute and the greatly effecting guitars in the first LP. Their Jazz ambitions are confined to the third and fourth side, emerging with a proud session of horns (saxophone, trombone) which steal the scene from the vocals. Critics are deeply divided on *Four Letter Monday Afternoon*, but it is actually an artistic operation of great courage, issued on a double LP in order to create the suitable space to better express the sonic dimension made of large orbits and complex passages, extraordinarily immediate. Notes are spiced up by skilfully created rhythms and intertwining instrumental patterns, musical duels, dreams and not nightmares. Then the disbandment creating a space in time devoted to collections, compilations and nostalgic operations. **C.A.**

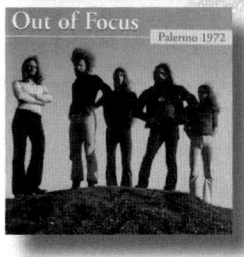

DISCOGRAPHY:
WAKE UP *(Kuckuck, 1970)* **OUT OF FOCUS** *(Kuckuck, 1971)* **FOUR LETTER MONDAY AFTERNOON** *(Kuckuck, 1972).*

Europe: GERMANY

POPOL VUH

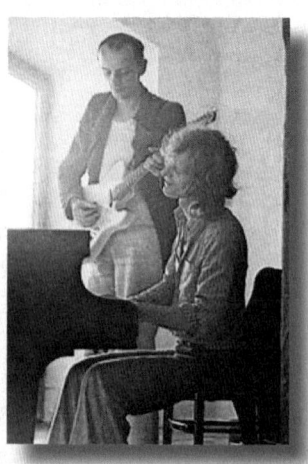

Florian Fricke, Frank Fiedler, Guido Hyeronimus - *keyboards, piano, synthesizers.* **Holger Trülzsch, Klaus Wiese, Shana Kumar** - *percussion.* **Conny Veit, Daniel Fichelscher, Bernd Wippich** - *guitars.* **Robert Eliscu, Olaf Kübler, Matthias V. Tippelskirch, Susan Goetting, Chris Karrer** - *horns.* **Djong Yun, Renate Knaupp** - *vocals.* **Fritz Sonnleitner** - *violin.* **Al Gromer** - *sitar.* **Anne-Marie O'Farell** - *Harp.*

Less cerebral than **Froese**, less freak than **Gottsching**, less eclectic than **Karrer**, **Florian Fricke** did not invent any new sound or style, as he followed with devotion the genre of sacred music, creating modern and non dogmatic liturgies, hard to label under the genre of popular music. Together with **Holger Trülzsch** and **Frank Fielder**, he founds **Popol Vuh** (taken from the name of a sacred text of the Quiche Indios from Guatemala) which will become his alter-ego. Label Liberty invites him to experience the power of a modular Moog, but he does not want to mimic **Walter Carlos**: *Affenstunde* is the first step in a mystical mosaic, an album for synths and percussions, akin to the experiments of the early **Tangerine Dream**.

After signing up with label Pilz, they become more accurate: *In Den Gärten Pharaos* is an album of rare power with reduced electronic ambitions. Partly recorded in a church it contains two majestic songs enriched by a pipe-organ. The group becomes a chamber ensemble and religious inspiration (both Christian and Veda) goes hand in hand with the disappearance of electronics, whilst minimalist shades and electric hints begin to rise: *Hosianna Mantra* is an intimate and serene chapel mass, among the most beautiful works of the second part of 1900. **Julian Cope** writes: <<I've never heard anything like it>>.

While feeding on religious texts, oriental and classical music, **Fricke** does not ignore electronic sounds: the extraordinary *Seligpreisung* - inspired by Matthew's Gospel - is enhanced by the entry of **Daniel Fichelscher** which improves the piano and guitar patterns and adds a never intrusive drumming. The partnership between the two will last for many years and the next two albums will continue to explore the sacred texts, with a harsh but never difficult language, sometimes joyful, truly inspired, distant from the cosmic musicians directed by **Kaiser**. **Popol Vuh** slowly turn towards world-music, almost a complementary adventure to that of **Embryo**, placing them undoubtedly as the forerunners of the new age and as one of the German groups that will exercise their influence in the future. *Letzte Tage, Letzte Nächte* is another high-flying composition that opens itself to Indian music, as is the end of the decade's trend. In parallel **Florian** weaves a fruitful collaboration with director **Werner Herzog**, who will commission numerous soundtracks for films such as *Aguirre* and *Nosferatu*.

In the 80ies and 90ies **Fricke** also produces less material and with his son, publishes electronic works of dubious taste. The only part worth saving is the re-elaboration of some **Mozart** pieces for piano. In 1999 **Fricke** composes the superb installation *Messa di Orfeo* as his farewell since he dies in 2001.

D.Z.

DISCOGRAPHY:
AFFENSTUNDE (Liberty 1971) **IN DEN GÄRTEN PHARAOS** (Pilz 1971) **HOSIANNA MANTRA** (Pilz 1972) **SELIGPREISUNG** (Kosmische Musik 1973) **EINJÄGER & SIEBENJÄGER** (Kosmische Musik 1975) **DAS HOLELIED SALOMOS** (United Artists 1975) **AGUIRRE** (Barclay 1975) **LETZTE TAGE, LETZTE NÄCHTE** (United Artists 1976) **YOGA** (PDU 1976) **HERZ AU GLAS - COEUR DE VERRE** (Egg 1977) **NOSFERATU - ON THE WAY TO A LITTLE WAY** (Egg 1978) **BRÜDER DES SCHATTENS, SÖHNE DES LICHTS** (Brain 1978) **DIE NACHT DER SEELE (Tantric Songs)** (Brain 1979) **Sei Still, Weisse ICH BIN** (IC 1981) **AGAPE - AGAPE LOVE - LOVE** (Uniton 1982)**SPIRIT OF PEACE** (Cicada 1985) **COBRA VERDE** (Milan 1987) **FLORIAN FRICKE SPIELT MOZART** (Bell 1991) **CITY RAGA** (Milan 1995)**SHEPHERD'S SYMPHONY** (Mystic 1997) **MESSA DI ORFEO** (Spalax 1999).

Europe: GERMANY

KLAUS SCHULZE

Klaus Schulze - *keyboards and programming, drums, percussion,* **Ernst Walter Siemon, Arthur Brown, Michael Garvens, Ian Wilkinson, Elfi Schulze, Roloef Oostwoud** - *vocals,* **Rainer Bloss, Andreas Grosser, George Stettner, Jörg Schaaf** - *keyboards,* **Harald Grosskopf, Fred Severloh, Mike Shrieve, Ulli Schober** - *drums,* **Wolfgang Tiepold** - *cello,* **Manuel Göttsching** - *guitars.*

Phenomenal. There can be no other word to describe the discography of **Klaus Schulze**. Together with **Edgar Froese, Holger Czukay, Florian Fricke** and **Hutter & Schneider**, he is the major exponent of the most well-known *kraut movement*. Loved by enthusiasts and acclaimed by critics, as a musician he takes his distance from the popular genre, from which he actually comes from, to express himself in a language that is typical of contemporary and electronic music. He begins his career in Berlin as the drummer of **Psy Free** and after graduating in Engineering, he studies composition with names such as **Ligeti, Winkel, Kessler** and **Blacher**. **Edgar Froese** summons him to play in **Tangerine Dream** as the drummer for the epic *Electronic Meditation*, but soon after he leaves the trio for **Ash Ra Tempel**'s first LP. After leaving **Gottsching** and **Enke**, , he publishes the revolutionary *Irrlicht* in 1972, not a commercial success yet a great piece of work, at the height of **Stockhausen, Xenakis, Maderna** and **Riley**: the electronically processed organ, the brave use of the orchestra, a thorough arrangement of the sound, the expansion of small and repeated moments, the concept of a fading tempo in favour of open and dreamlike spaces, all give the birth to *Kosmische Muzik*.

Klaus is a decisive presence in the history of the **Cosmic Jokers** and with Kaiser they publish *Cyborg*: another colossal work which will influence, among others, **Vangelis, Jarre** and **Kitaro**. Even before **Mike Oldfield** and **Brian Eno**, he is the prototype of a creative studio solo-musician and his records testify the evolution of music technology. He begins a long collaboration with the explosive Progressive division of label Metronome, called Brain, with which he publishes *Blackdance* (introducing synths and a more pronounced rhythmic pattern) and finally issues *Picture Music* which was in standby for over a year.

TimeWind - dedicated to **Wagner** - ideally closes the first historic and visionary stage; from *Moondawn* on **Klaus** explores the more concrete sequencer/drums couple, welcoming also collaborators such as **Harald Grosskopf, Wolfgang Tiepold** and **Rainer Bloss** (companion in the great 1983 European tour). Sometimes he also lends his art as a producer and opens his own label Innovative Communication, later re-named as In Team. Unlike others which lose their glow, **Schulze**'s discography is always brilliant: albums as *X, En=Trance* and *Audentity* are compellingly inspired. Under the pseudonym of **Richard Wahnfried**, he also launches a small parallel discography. His activity proceeds unabated in the '90s too, with several titles like the disturbing *Kontinuum* which confirms his inimitable style, and *Farscape* - with the charming vocalist **Lisa Gerrard** - which brings him back to the attention of the media.   **D.Z.**

DISCOGRAPHY:
IRRLICHT *(Ohr 1972)* **CYBORG** *(Kosmische Musik 1973)* **BLACKDANCE** *(Brain 1974)* **PICTURE MUSIC** *(Brain 1975)* **TIMEWIND** *(Brain 1975)* **MOONDAWN** *(Brain 1976)* **BODY LOVE** *(Brain 1977)* **MIRAGE** *(Brain 1977)* **BODY LOVE II** *(Brain 1978)* **X** *(Brain 1978)* **DUNE** *(Brain 1979)* **...LIVE...** *(live, Brain 1980)* **DIG IT** *(Brain 1980)* **TRANCEFER** *(Innovative Communication 1981)* **AUDENTITY** *(IC 1981)* **DZIEKUJE POLAND LIVE 1983** *(live, IC 1983)* **ANGST** *(In Team 1984)* **INTER*FACE** *(Brain 1985)* **DREAMS** *(Brain 1986)* **EN=TRANCE** *(Brain 1988)* **MIDITERRANEAN PADS** *(Brain 1990)* **THE DRESDEN PERFORMANCE** *(live, Virgin 1990)* **BEYOND RECALL** *(Virgin 1991)* **ROYAL FESTIVAL HALL VOL. 1** *(live, Virgin 1992)* **ROYAL FESTIVAL HALL VOL. 2** *(live, Virgin 1992)* **THE DOME EVENT** *(live, Virgin 1993)* **LE MOULIN DE DAUDET** *(Virgin 1994)* **GOES CLASSIC** *(ZYX 1994)* **TOTENTAG** *(ZYX 1994)* **DAS WAGNER DISASTER - LIVE** *(ZYX 1994)* **IN BLUE** *(ZYX 1995)* **ARE YOU SEQUENCED?** *(WEA 1996)* **DOSBURG ONLINE** *(WEA 1997)* **LIVE@KLANGART 1** *(live, Ranhorse 2001)* **LIVE@KLANGART 2** *(live, Rainhorse 2001)* **MOONLAKE** *(SPV 2005)* **KONTINUUM** *(SPV 2007)* **FARSCAPE** *(SPV 2008).*

Europe: GERMANY

STERN COMBO MEISSEN

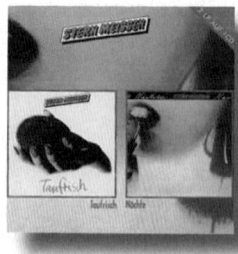

Bernd Fiedler - *bass*, **Reinhard Fißler** - *vocals*, **Norbert Jägervoce** - *percussion, keyboards*, **Lothar Kramer** - *keyboards*, **Thomas Kurzhals** - *keyboards*, **Martin Schreier** - *drums*.

After a few years spent fiddling with cover songs of Anglo-Saxon and American pop groups, **Stern Meissen** start a musical career destined to push them towards the top of German kraut-rock. With their self-titled album recorded in 1977, they immediately direct their sound towards dreamlike atmospheres, intergalactic travels and sound effects stolen from **Pink Floyd**: oscillating with extraordinary ease between **UFO** and **Hawkwind**'s galactic rock and the symphonic and luxurious sound of **Yes**, in a continuous dialogue between synth and keyboards. Accused of trying to copy **Pink Floyd**'s *Wish You Were Here*, they nevertheless show an amazing energy in the live album where they have the brilliant idea of keeping two excellent keyboardists in the band, creating around them great sound balance.

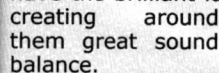

They will record in studio the following year *Weisses Gold*, in which both keyboards, supported by a stern drumming, are given a lot of space, confirming the band's original potential. The German vocals provide the musicality with a certain austerity and harshness, which will be one of their main features.

Der Weite Weg sees some classical contaminations ("La Primavera" by **Vivaldi** is interpreted in an extraordinarily delicate and melancholy way), vocals being less harsh and in general based on softer tones; sound effects are sparse and focus more on calm and sweet atmospheres, extremely pleasant and of great effect. Followed by *Reise Zum Mittelpunkt des Menschen* which has far more sophisticated musical textures, the continuous insistence of the double keyboards is brought to an exasperation of research, whilst vocals lose their importance almost disappearing in the instrumental complexity. A true manifesto of krautrock, essential and inimitable, to love or to hate with no other alternative.

Stundenschlag (1980) is a rather contradictory episode which lacks the initial energy: the refined sound is taken from Pop Rock, with dull passages of Lounge music and a good technicality, yet uninspired. *Taufrisch* (1985) has the same unsurprising style. Despite the latter, the band is still among the most innovative of eastern Germany, capable of imposing both an aggressive and melodic sound, without too heavily imitating some of the big names of European Prog. Recommended the anthology *40 Jahre* in which they reinterpret the most important moments of their exciting experience.

C.A.

DISCOGRAPHY:
STERN COMBO MEISSEN (Amiga, 1977) **WEISSES GOLD** (Amiga, 1978) **DER WEITE WEG** (Amiga, 1979) **REISE ZUM MITTELPUNKT DES MENSCHEN** (Amiga, 1980) **STUNDENSCHLAG** (Amiga, 1980) **TAUFRISCH** (Amiga, 1985) **40 JAHRE** (Bush Funk, 2004).

Europe: GERMANY

TANGERINE DREAM

Edgar Froese - *keyboards, bass, guitars, synthesizers,* **Peter Baumann** - *keyboards, synthesizers, flute,* **Christoph Franke** - *keyboards, synthesizers.*

In September 1967 **Edgar Froese** founds **Tangerine Dream** in West Berlin, the band that most inspired the *Cosmic Courier* movement (one of the most extreme colonies of prog). Their name seems to derive from **The Beatles**' *Sgt Pepper's Lucy in the Sky with Diamonds* (tangerine trees and marmalade skies) and becomes a true musical logo which condenses the cathartic atmospheres of **Pink Floyd** with avant-garde technology (since 1972 their sound will be almost exclusively based on the use of synthesizers). To be noted the album of 1967 *Tangerine Dream* by the English band **Kaleidoscope** has never been confirmed as a declared source.

The debut album *Electronic Meditation* (1969), except certain rather confusing passages, is a surprising electronic work which elaborates the psychedelic lessons coming from England. Two years later *Alpha Centauri*, their most worthy album, opens the Cosmic Music season (a visionary and dreamlike legion at the borders of contemporary classical music). In 1972 *Zeit* is published as a four-movement suite on a double album that testifies the growth of a truly homogeneous group with the Progressive touch. The following year they sign up with Ohr (a prestigious German label) and publish *Atem*, another beautiful album with which they hit the top of the charts. That same year *Green Desert* is recorded but will see the light only 12 years later.

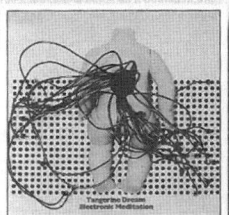

A contract with legendary Virgin Records (the label behind **Oldfield**'s *Tubular Bells* myth) helps **Tangerine Dream** realize what for many is seen as their masterpiece: *Phaedra*, an extraordinary album, capable of sinking under your skin from the very beginning. It is 1974 and the band begins a prestigious tour intended for the main European cathedrals (their debut in Reims, France, was attended by **Nico**, the **Velvet Underground** muse). **Edgar Froese** publishes *Aqua*, his first solo album which retrieves the moods and the stimuli left by the band.

The subsequent years are particularly prolific: the studio albums, *Rubicon* (1975) and *Stratosfear* (1976) add up to two beautiful live recordings, *Ricochet* (1975) and *Encore* (1977, double album). Curious and particularly characteristic was their presentation on stage, playing their backs turned to the audience. Unfortunately their magic moment comes to an end and despite a worrying creative void, the next works, with a few small exceptions (*Poland*, 1984), will come pouring out, flooding an already saturated market which was going the opposite way. During the 90s the band becomes exclusive property of **Froese** who adds his son **Jerome** to the lineup. The following albums will be repetitive maintaining the same sounds, updated only for technology. **Edgar Froese** dies in 2014 closing all future acts.

F.V.

RECOMMENDED RECORDINGS:
ELECTRONIC MEDITATION *(Ohr, 1970)* **ALPHA CENTAURI** *(Ohr, 1971)* **ZEIT** *(Ohr, 1972)* **ATEM** *(Polydor, 1973)* **PHAEDRA** *(Virgin, 1974)* **RUBICON** *(Virgin, 1975)* **RICOCHET** *(Virgin, 1975)* **STRATOSFEAR** *(Virgin, 1976)* **ENCORE** *(Virgin, 1977)* **SORCERER** *(MCA, 1977)* **CYCLONE** *(Virgin, 1978)* **FORCE MAJEURE** *(Virgin, 1979)* **TANGRAM** *(Virgin, 1980)* **THIEF** *(Virgin, 1980)* **EXIT** *(Virgin, 1981)* **WHITE EAGLE** *(Virgin, 1982)* **LOGOS** *(Virgin, 1982)* **HYPERBOREA** *(Virgin, 1983)* **WAVELENGHT** *(Varese-Sarabande, 1983)* **RISKY BUSINESS** *(Virgin, 1983)* **FIRESTARTER** *(MCA, 1984)* **FLASHPOINT** *(EMI, 1984)* **POLAND** *(Jive-Electro, 1984)* **LE PARC** *(Jive-Electro, 1985)* **DREAM SEQUENCE** *(Virgin, 1985)* **HEARTBREAKERS** *(Virgin, 1985)* **LEGEND** *(Virgin, 1986)* **UNDERWATER SUNLIGHT** *(Jive-Electro, 1986)* **TYGER** *(Jive-Electro, 1987)*.

Europe: GERMANY

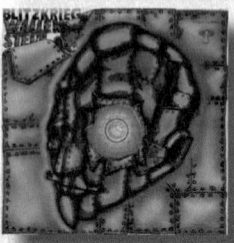

WALLENSTEIN

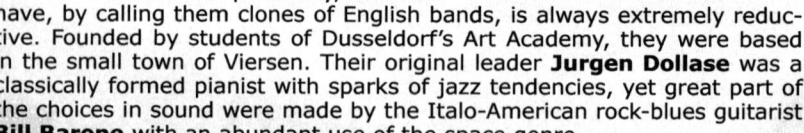

Bill Barone - *guitar*, **Jürgen Dollase** - *keyboard, percussions, vocals*, **Harald Großkopf** - *drums, percussions*, **Dieter Meier** - *bass*, **Joachim Reiser** - *violin*.

To cut short a band like **Wallenstein** with terms such as symphonic or cosmic-couriers or even more superficially, as some have, by calling them clones of English bands, is always extremely reductive. Founded by students of Dusseldorf's Art Academy, they were based in the small town of Viersen. Their original leader **Jurgen Dollase** was a classically formed pianist with sparks of jazz tendencies, yet great part of the choices in sound were made by the Italo-American rock-blues guitarist **Bill Barone** with an abundant use of the space genre.

At the beginning they chose the name **Blietzkrieg**, soon abandoned and kept only as the title of their first 1972 album. The four long tracks here contained, as the amazing "Lunatic" stands out, are the perfect summary of the experiences of these musicians always caught between electronics and the often aggressive fugues of **Barone**'s Gibson and the ethereal watercoloured keyboards and vocals of **Dollase**, all patched together by a precise and never out of line rhythmic section. The album brought them excellent reviews and the public seems to appreciate the formula that is maintained also for their second album, which unfortunately has a non-homogeneous feel to it. In fact *Mother Universe* appears as a less concentrated album, with more concessions to the song dimension and with a strong stylistic difference among the suites going from, for example, the syncopated parts of "Shackspearesque" to the hard blues atmospheres of "Braintrain", or from the ballad styles of "Relics of Past" to the rude elements in "Dedicated to Mistery Land".

On a totally different level is the following year's album, the amazing *Cosmic Century*. This quality leap is due to violinist **Joachim Reiser** joining in: songs become evermore complete, airy, highly structured and lively developed. Space interludes stride along with great symphonic overtures containing more jazzy portions, sometimes recalling some of the interesting works of **Mahavishnu Orchestra**, such as the brilliant "Silver Arms", the dynamic "Rory Blanchford" and the soft piano textures of "Gran Piano". Unfortunately this outstanding album is also the end of their so-called golden period.

The next release *Stories, Songs and Symphonies* is still a good album, alternating excellent moments to not too interesting stuff. It shows an almost total renounce of progressive music in favour of reducing themes to a more classic rock. More space is given to violin and piano, sacrificing Mellotron and synths. The beautiful progressions of "Your Lunar Friends" and the interesting development of "Sympathy for Bela Bartock" are still quotable, but the rest is a Rock genre closer to Songwriters such as **Bowie** or **Hammill**.

Their career officially ends in 1981 with a pale Pop taste, often for the charts, changes in line-ups and absolutely nothing to be added on the Prog side. **R.V.**

DISCOGRAPHY:
BLITZKRIEG *(1971, PILZ)* **MOTHER UNIVERSE** *(1972, PILZ)* **COSMIC CENTURY** *(1973, Kosmische Musik)* **STORIES, SONGS & SYMPHONIES** *(1975, Kosmische Musik)* **NO MORE LOVE** *(1977, RCA)* **CHARLINE** *(1978, RCA)* **BLUE EYED BOYS** *(1979, RCA)* **FRAULEINS** *(1980, EMI Harvest)* **SSSSSSTOP!** *(1981, RCA)*.

Europe: GREAT BRITAIN

KEVIN AYERS

Unstable, cheerful, playful, romantic, unpredictable, childish and ingenious, these are the traits of **Kevin Ayers**, one of the most influential and peculiar musicians of the British scene. A childhood (until the age of 12) wandering around the world with his father, a BBC producer, may have been the cause of a certain verve of character, marked by total instability, always chasing after success and running away from it when it finally came his way. In college he met other young music fans and in particular a group of them which had formed a band with the exotic name of **Wilde Flowers**. They took him in not for his capacities, rather modest at the time, but for his extraordinary and very long blonde hair. The Canterbury Sound adventure was to begin. Soon the **Wilde Flowers** divided into **Caravan** and **Soft Machine**. Ayers stayed with the latter playing bass, guitar and singing some of the songs, where he stood out for his strong baritone voice. With the group **Soft Machine** he records a first 45 rpm and a whole album, alternating vocals with **Robert Wyatt**, and guitar with Australian **Daevid Allen**. Ayers had already abandoned his companions when beginning to record a second album. He sold his instrument to **Jimi Hendrix**'s bass player **Noel Redding**, and retired to Spain with **Allen**, where he prepared the songs for his first solo album, returning to England alone while **Allen** was forced to stay in France (for Visa issues) where he creates **Gong**. So towards the end of 1969, thanks to the efforts of his friend **Syd Barrett** from **Pink Floyd**, he signs up with the newborn label Harvest and releases his first album *Joy of a Toy*, combining songwriting to the Canterbury Sound flavour of psychedelia, experimental, jazz, blues and rock, obtaining memorable ballads with symphonic parts, folk or avant-garde fragments. Essential the contribution of composer and conductor **David Bedford** for the latter, **Luigi Nono**'s pupil and a great contemporaneous experimenter. Not even a year later, a second album called *Shooting at the Moon* was released. For the occasion **Ayers** decided to have a backing band he called **Whole World**, and among others he recruited a very young **Mike Oldfield**, his friend **Robert Wyatt** and a flutist re-known for turning upside down melodic forms, **Lol Coxhill**. It was another amazing masterpiece, with great attention to the compositional and decompositional parts and with songs that will be forever fixed points of **Ayers**' musical career. The collaboration with **Bedford** continued in *Whatevershebringswesing* and *Bananamour*, good the first, rather modest the second. A good qualitative recovery is felt in *The Confessions Of Dr Dream And Other Stories* and its fairly good homonym suite.

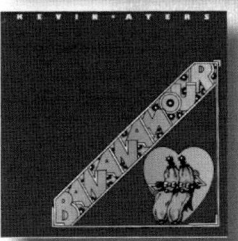

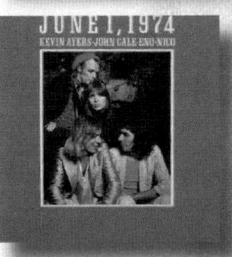

That same year the concert with **Brian Eno**, **Nico** and **John Cale** was published as *June, 1 1974*. Little or no relevance to the rest of his compositional career, made up of few and rare albums in which stand out sporadically some good pieces but nothing more. Worth of notice is instead a broadcast by BBC released in 2005, a double box rich of interesting things and not just a simple exercise of memorabilia. **Kevin** dies in 2013. **R.V.**

DISCOGRAPHY:
JOY OF A TOY *(1969, Harvest)* **SHOOTING AT THE MOON** *(1970, Harvest)* **WHATEVERSHEBRINGSWESING** *(1971, Harvest)* **BANANAMOUR** *(1973, Harvest)* **THE CONFESSIONS OF DR. DREAM AND OTHER STORIES** *(1974, Island)* **JUNE 1, 1974** *(with Nico, John Cale and Brian Eno - 1974, Island 1974)* **LADY JUNE'S LINGUISTIC LEPROSY** *(with Lady June and Brian Eno - 1974, Caroline/Virgin)* **SWEET DECEIVER** *(1975 Island)* **YES WE HAVE NO MAÑANAS (So Get Your Mañanas Today)** *(1976, Harvest)* **RAINBOW TAKEAWAY** *(1978, Harvest)* **THAT'S WHAT YOU GET BABE** *(1980, Harvest)* **DIAMOND JACK AND THE QUEEN OF PAIN** *(1983, Charly)* **DEIÀ... VU** *(1984, Blau)* **AS CLOSE AS YOU THINK** *(1986 Illuminated)* **FALLING UP** *(1988 Virgin)* **STILL LIFE WITH GUITAR** *(1992 FNAC)* **THE UNFAIRGROUND** *(2007, LO-MAX)*.

Europe: GREAT BRITAIN

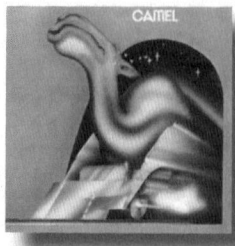

CAMEL

Andy Latimer - *guitars, flute, vocals,* **Peter Bardens, Brian Eno, Dave Sinclair, Jan Scheelas, Kit Watkins, Duncan MacKay, Guy Le Blanc, Ton Scherpenzel** - *keyboards,* **Andy Ward, Paul Burgess, Dave Stewart, Denis Clement** - *drums.* **Doug Ferguson, Richard Sinclair** - *bass, vocals,* **Mel Collins** - *horns,* **Colin Bass** -*bass, keyboards.*

Prog is already on the verge of decadence when **Camel** publishes its first albums, therefore less interest is shown by the press; but this somehow allows the band to work better on their very own sound, releasing a couple of masterpieces in the Punk era and in the early '80s and thus earning the love of a passionate crowd that sustains them to this very day.
The Rock-Blues trio **The Brew** meet keyboardist **Peter Bardens**, former musician in **Them** and in **Shotgun Express**, founding **Camel**, a quartet breathing Canterbury sound, not eccentric as in **Gong** or jazzy as **the Soft Machine**, but closer to **Caravan** with an eye on the **Pink Floyd** evolution.
Their second LP *Mirage* receives better attention, recharging them with the energy to break through with a new idea: putting into music **Paul Gallico**'s tale *The Snow Goose: A Story Of Dunkirk* (1941). The album is one of the last symphonic rock works, interpreted in the light of the chameleon personality that prefers elegant solo excursus rather than putting weight on the whole. It is a success and following the times, **Camel**'s language smooths up in *Moonmadness*: nice and fresh, it is the last product of the original line-up, that pursues balance among instrumental digressions and melody, avoiding hyperbolic gimmicks.

Punk explodes, Disco music makes booties shake, yet for **Camel** it is the moment for yet another jewel: the arrival of **Richard Sinclair** and **Mel Collins** unveils a latent vein of Jazz-rock in *Rain Dances*, an ethereal LP with a great solo singer, embellished by an influential guest such as **Brian Eno** (head of the Berlin period of **David Bowie**), played by a band in pretty good shape.

The decade ends with a memorable live-album, the **Caravan**-oriented *Breathless* (last work by **Bardens**, replaced not by chance by former **Caravan Dave Sinclair** and **Jan Schelhaas**) and *I can See Your House From Here*, more conventional but containing the magnificent "Ice", a last great **Camel** fresco. The original band doesn't exist anymore but the attachment to a romantic sound, dreamy and open to instrumental escapes, even if refreshed by opportune Pop hooks, is at the base of the 80ies: intriguing concept albums (the excellent *Nude* above all) few of which fortunate, oriented towards a concrete pop-rock between **Alan Parsons Project** and the new **Pink Floyd**, are the legacy of Andy Latimer, who takes a break in 1984.

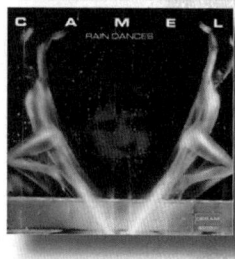

Tempted by the revival of Prog during the '90s, **Camel** returns to the scenes with albums (self-produced) which update old sonorities through the always convincing guitar of their protagonist **Latimer**. *Dust And Dreams* (inspired by John Steinbeck's Fury) recalls the 1975 formula and *Harbour Of Tears* stands out for its intimacy; nostalgia surfaces in the pleasant *Rajaz*, while **Peter Bardens** with his super-band **Mirage** proposes live covers of classic **Camel** songs. The keyboardist dies in 2002 and **Andy Latimer** dedicates *A Nod And A Wink* to him. Weakened by his health too, he now remains the only depository of this kind and melancholic sound. **D.Z.**

DISCOGRAPHY:
CAMEL (MCA 1973) **MIRAGE** (Deram 1974) **MUSIC INSPIRED BY THE SNOW GOOSE** (Decca 1975) **MOONMADNESS** (Decca 1976) **RAIN DANCES** (Deram 1977) **A LIVE RECORD** (Decca 1978) **BREATHLESS** (Deram 1978) **I CAN SEE YOUR HOUSE FROM HERE** (Deram 1979) **NUDE** (Gama 1981) **THE SINGLE FACTOR** (Decca 1982) **STATIONARY TRAVELLER** (Decca 1984) **PRESSURE POINTS: Live In Concert** (Decca 1984) **DUST AND DREAMS** (Camel 1991) **HARBOUR OF TEARS** (Camel 1996) **COMING OF AGE** (live, Camel 1998) **RAJAZ** (Camel 1999) **A NOD AND A WINK** (Camel 2002) **THE SNOW GOOSE** (New re-recorded version, Camel 2013).

Europe: **GREAT BRITAIN**

CARAVAN

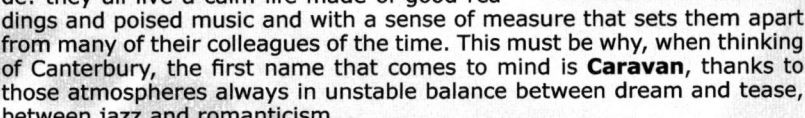

Richard Sinclair, John G. Perry, Mike Wedgwood, Dek Messecar, Jim Leverton - *bass, vocals,* David Sinclair, Steve Miller, Jan Schelhaas - *keyboards,* Pye Hastings, Phil Miller, Doug Boyle - *guitar, vocals,* Richard Coughlan - *drums,* Jimmy Hastings, Lol Coxhill, Mel Collins - *horns.* Geoffrey Richardson - *viola.*

Nostalgic melodies, relaxed rhythms, sprays of Jazz, hints of Rock and a detached ironic attitude: they all live a calm life made of good readings and poised music and with a sense of measure that sets them apart from many of their colleagues of the time. This must be why, when thinking of Canterbury, the first name that comes to mind is **Caravan**, thanks to those atmospheres always in unstable balance between dream and tease, between jazz and romanticism.
After the **Wilde Flowers** experience, **Hastings**, **Coughlan** and cousins **Richard** and **David Sinclair** decide not to follow **Soft Machine**'s new path but to pursue instead the road towards a lighter lunatic Pop, just above the lines with a Psychedelic jazzy taste to brighten it up a touch. Their 1968 debut is an obvious embryo project signed up with the American label Verve (same as extremists like **Zappa** and **Velvet Underground**); with a little bit of work they manage to ignite with a fantastic second LP that intertwines three incredible suites with the typical **Caravan** style. *If I Could do it All Over Again* reveals their true talent, followed shortly after by a second masterpiece: *In The Land Of Grey And Pink*, their Canterbury sound manifesto, but also one of the most effervescent works of the '70s, born at just the right time with a peculiar sound ranging from the organ fuzz to an elegant falsetto, of sober and gentle classicism, never austere. The suite "Nine Feet Underground" is a continuous crescendo of brilliant melodic ideas and solo interludes gracefully assembled.
With **Dave Sinclair**'s exit and the entry of **Steve Miller** (from **Delivery**), the band sheds skin: characterized by the insistent sound of an electric piano, *Waterloo Lily* is a pleasant rock-jazz album, deprived however of a certain **Caravan** taste, resulting slightly more sour and rock-oriented. With **Richard** (who founds **Hatfield And The North**) the band loses its magic formula and rolls recklessly towards pop. At the end of 1973 – historically late for this kind of things - **Caravan** collaborates with an orchestra: although directed by **Simon Jeffes** (which was about to create **the Penguin Café Orchestra**), it is not the appropriate partner for a band so subtle and phlegmatic. *Cunning Stunts* is a turning point: a varied and versatile album, probably the last interesting work of the band which inexorably declines towards catchy scheme-songs, deprived of inventiveness and imagination.
In 1982 the historical quartet re-groups and lives a moment of grace (*Back To Front*) only to dismantle once again. **Pye Hastings** will brings them back nearly ten years later, wandering among nostalgic revivals (with unplugged re-makings), recovering archived material and publishing some new albums. The last of this **Caravan** lineup is *The Unauthorized Breakfast Item*, an album of mature and square melodic rock, without great pretension, yet still making a good impression along side with the new trend of Brit pop (**Coldplay, Travis, Elbow, Doves**). **D.Z.**

DISCOGRAPHY:

CARAVAN (Verve 1968) **IF I COULD DO IT ALL OVER AGAIN, I'D DO IT ALL OVER YOU** (Decca 1970) **IN THE LAND OF GREY AND PINK** (Deram 1971) **WATERLOO LILY** (Deram 1972) **FOR GIRLS WHO GO PLUMP IN THE NIGHT** (Deram 1973) **CARAVAN & THE NEW SYMPHONIA** (live, Deram 1974) **CUNNING STUNTS** (BTM 1975), **BLIND DOG AT ST. DUNSTANS** (BTM 1976) **BETTER BY FAR** (Arista 1977) **THE ALBUM** (Kingdom 1980), **BACK TO FRONT** (1982) **BATTLE OF HASTINGS** (HTD 1995) **ALL OVER YOU** (HTD 1996) **THE UNAUTHORIZED BREAKFAST ITEM** (Eclectic 2003).

Europe: GREAT BRITAIN

COLOSSEUM

Jon Hiseman - *drums,* **Tony Reeves, Louis Cennamo, Mark Clarke** - *bass,* **James Litherland, Dave "Clem" Clempson** - *guitars,* **Dick Heckstall-Smith, Barbara Thompson** - *horns,* **Dave Greenslade** - *keyboards,* **Chris Farlowe** - *vocals*

The origins of Progressive Rock should not only be searched on the Psychedelic scene: in the second half of the '60s in England we find a memorable blossoming of White Blues that, on the one hand is a basic formula for groups like **The Rolling Stones** and **the Animals**, while on the other it becomes the land of angry blues-men that do not recognize themselves in the lovable tunes of the "Fab Four" **Beatles**. **John Mayall** and **Alexis Korner** are undisputed pioneers and masters, and their bands **Bluesbreakers** and **Blues Incorporated** are authentic gym parlours: here an entire generation of talents has the opportunity to develop new instrument research that engages on classic Blues with references to rock, jazz and acid music, expanding the usual forms through improvisation. The ripest fruit coming from this school is **Cream**, but Brit Blues knows another two highly trained cubs, **Dick Heckstall-Smith** and **Jon Hiseman**: with the **Graham Bond Organisation** in 1966 they publish *Solid Bond* and in 1968 *Bare Wires* with the **Bluesbreakers** whose disbandment will stimulate them to continue together. They pick up bassist **Reeves** along the way and work on an ambitious goal: the development of a new language starting from a rock-blues extraction, which will use the nonchalance of jazz without ignoring the symphonic pop of **Nice** and **Procol Harum**.

Majestic already in their name, **Colosseum** debut with *Those Who Are About To Die Salute You*: the album immediately reveals a phenomenal technical background, particularly **Hiseman** (which will become one of the most influential drummers of the time) and organist **Dave Greenslade** who cites **Bach** and vividly communicates through horns, immediately creating a trademark. Vertigo (the Philips brand for the new prog generations, as Deram was for Decca and Harvest for EMI) invests all on **Colosseum**: *Valentyne Suite* is not only the first catalog number for the new label, but also a historic album which contributes to the very definition of progressive, including its cover (**Marcus Keef**). Masterpiece of the quintet, it contains one of the earliest and most complete suites, with an already perfect balance between Rock, Jazz, Blues, Classical patterns and **Coltrane**-like recollections, collective expressions and solos. It is curious that the best line-up coincides with a not so good album (*Daughter Of Time*), but the new combo shows great harmony in *Colosseum Live*: **Chris Farlowe**'s mighty voice (from **Thunderbirds**), **Mark Clarke**'s solid bass playing and **Clem Clempson**'s torrential guitar (from **Bakerloo**) are the secret of a band ever so overwhelming, that they sound as if they were playing for the last time.

1971 sees them separate and flee in different directions: **Hiseman** and **Clarke** found the **Tempest**; **Greenslade** form the **Greenslade** with **Reeves**; **Farlowe** joins the **Atomic Rooster**; **Clempson** joins the **Humble Pie**. In 1975 the drummer recovers the old name releasing three highly technical albums of rock-jazz but quite anonymous, very similar to **Brian Auger**'s fate. 1971's line-up returns in 1994 with great concerts and a couple of new albums; **Heckstall-Smith** departs in 2004 and is replaced by **Barbara Thompson**, wife of leader **Hiseman**. **D.Z.**

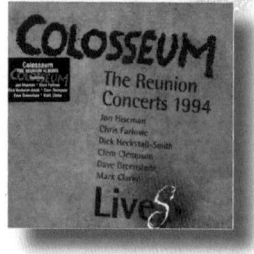

DISCOGRAPHY:
THOSE WHO ARE ABOUT TO DIE SALUTE YOU *(Fontana 1969)* **VALENTYNE SUITE** *(Vertigo 1969)* **THE GRASS IS GREENER** *(Dunhill 1970, only USA)* **DAUGHTER OF TIME** *(Vertigo 1970)* **COLOSSEUM LIVE** *(Vertigo 1971)* **COLOSSEUM II: Strange New Flesh** *(Bronze 1976)* **COLOSSEUM II: Electric Savage** *(MCA 1977)* **COLOSSEUM II: War Dance** *(MCA 1977)* **COLOSSEUM LIVES: The Reunion Concert** *(Intuition 1994)* **BREAD AND CIRCUSES** *(Temple Music 1997)* **TOMORROW'S BLUES** *(Temple Music 2003)*.

Europe: **GREAT BRITAIN**

CURVED AIR

Sonja Kristina - vocals, **Darryl Way** - violin, keyboards, **Francis Monkman** - guitar, keyboards, **Florian Pilkington-Miksa** - drums, **Robert Martin** - bass, **Ian Eyre** - bass, **Mike Wedgewood** - bass, **Eddie Jobson** - violin, **Kirby Gregory** - guitar, **Jim Russell** - drums, **Stewart Copeland** - drums, **Tony Reeves** - bass, **Mick Jacques** - guitar.

Curved Air is one of the most original Symphonic Rock bands active in the '70s, even if it did not achieve the same success as some of the bigger names of the time. Leaders are the two charismatic figures of **Sonja Kristina**, charming and talented vocalist and **Darryl Way**, exceptional violinist whom indelibly marked the band's sound with his instrument. Great guitarist **Francis Monkman** and the rhythmic duo formed by **Florian Pilkington-Miksa** and **Robert Martin** complete the first line-up. *Air Conditioning* (1970); *Second Album* (1971) and *Phantasmagoria* (1972) represent the most important assets of this group, which create an alchemical blend of Symphonic Prog extraction, Pop-Rock and Folk, topped by the right touch of experimentation. These albums contain just about all their features and the songs that made them famous. "Vivaldi" led by a Baroque theme and a crazy electric violin, the special melodies of "It Happened Today" and "Propositions", the straightforward and engaging energy of "Back Street Luv" and "Marie Antoinette", the sweet and melancholic ballad "Melissa", the spirit of research in "Screw", "Jumbo" and "Piece of Mind", is a beautiful demonstration of **Curved Air**'s greatness.

Unfortunately, in the midst of this magical moment, the group falls apart. Of particular note is the defection of **Darryl Way**, leaves to form **Wolf**. Another great violinist, **Eddie Jobson**, takes his place managing to keep up with the pace. Although they do not reach the quality peaks of their early years, they publish *Air Cut* in 1973; built on pre-existing foundations it presents a hardening in sound, very close to hard-rock. New variations in line-up come with the exit of **Wedgwood** and **Jobson**, and the return of prodigal son **Way** yields the live album *Live*. **Kristina** and **Way** are soon joined by **Stewart Copeland**, **Tony Reeves** and **Mick Jacques** and another good album, *Midnight Wire*, is released, although far from the prog of their beginnings.

Airborne, issued in 1976, displays a certain fatigue of composition. On December 23rd that same year a farewell concert is held thinking it would be their last. From 1978 **Stewart Copeland** co-founds **the Police** together with contrabass/bass player **Gordon Sumner (Sting)** and guitarist **Andy Summers**, a genius coming from important projects like **Soft Machine** and **Gong**. A reunion of **Curved Air** in 1990 will bring to the recording of *Alive*, after which some previously unreleased recordings will come to life such as *Lovechild* from 1973 and *Live at the BBC*. Another two reunions give birth to *Reborn* in 2008 and *Northstar* in 2014 in the wake of a new Prog revival in the last decade, and we hope to see another one yet to come.   **G.D.S.**

DISCOGRAPHY:

AIR CONDITIONING *(1970, Warner Bros)* **SECOND ALBUM** *(1971, Warner Bros)* **PHANTASMAGORIA** *(1972, Warner Bros)* **AIR CUT** *(1973, Warner Bros)* **LIVE** *(1975, Dream)* **MIDNIGHT WIRE** *(1975, BTM)* **AIRBORNE** *(1976, BTM)* **ALIVE** *(1990, Private Pressing)* **LOVECHILD** *(1990, Castle)* **LIVE AT THE BBC** *(1995, Strange Fruit)* **REBORN** *(2008, Avalon)* **RETROSPECTIVE** *(2010, Repertoire)* **LIVE ATMOSPHERE** *(2012, Cherry red)* **AIRWAVES (Live at the BBC)** *(2012, Cleopatra)* **NORTHSTAR** *(2014, Cherry red)*.

Europe: **GREAT BRITAIN**

EMERSON LAKE & PALMER

Keith Emerson - *keyboards, piano,*
Greg Lake - *bass, vocals, guitars,*
Carl Palmer - *drums, percussion.*

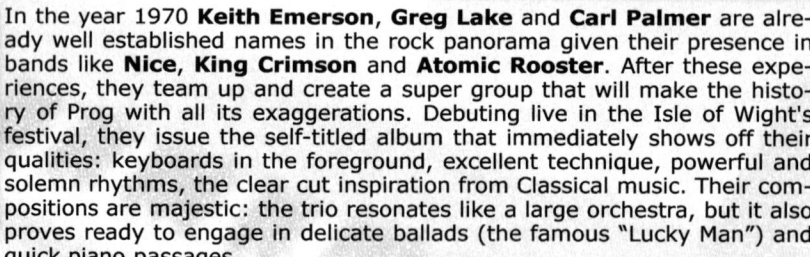

In the year 1970 **Keith Emerson**, **Greg Lake** and **Carl Palmer** are already well established names in the rock panorama given their presence in bands like **Nice**, **King Crimson** and **Atomic Rooster**. After these experiences, they team up and create a super group that will make the history of Prog with all its exaggerations. Debuting live in the Isle of Wight's festival, they issue the self-titled album that immediately shows off their qualities: keyboards in the foreground, excellent technique, powerful and solemn rhythms, the clear cut inspiration from Classical music. Their compositions are majestic: the trio resonates like a large orchestra, but it also proves ready to engage in delicate ballads (the famous "Lucky Man") and quick piano passages.

In 1971 they release *Tarkus*, in which features the eponymous suite, one of the manifestos of the band, with over 20 minutes of acrobatics and symphonic flavored virtuosity. The other side of the album, despite some good intuition, is not fully convincing. **ELP** are exuberant also in concert, with lavished and spectacular shows; it is live that they record their next album *Pictures at an Exhibition*, an adaptation of the famous Rock-Opera by **Mussorgsky**, , key to their performances since their beginnings.

After this flashy episode of their career, comes their most beautiful and balanced album, *Trilogy*. Here romance reaches its highest peak and the harmony between musicians is at its top, with no moments of fatigue. At this point they found their own music label Manticore (through which they will launch Italian bands lik **PFM** and **Banco del Mutuo Soccorso** in England). They release the album *Brain Salad Surgery*, based on the long and monumental track "Karn Evil 9", a complex, unbridled, technological and memorable piece. To celebrate this first part of their career a triple live album is also issued. The next chapter opens with *Works vol.1*, a double LP with three sides occupied by solo experiments (**Emerson** engages in a concert for piano and orchestra, **Lake** in some ballads and **Palmer** in Classical music for percussions and drums) and one last side made of two beautiful compositions by the group in their consolidated style. After this they lose momentum and after another two disappointing works, they are swallowed up by their delusions of grandeur: **Keith Emerson** will have his small moment of fame in Italy in the early '80s thanks to two theme songs for the TV program *Odeon* and for his soundtrack of the film *Inferno* by Dario Argento; **Palmer** will instead join **Asia**, where he finds a place for **Lake** in a brief tour. In 1992 the album *Black Moon* is a decent comeback, although far from the splendor of the '70s. The next *In the Hot Seat* is a CD with no true meaning, which marks the sad ending of the trio's studio recordings. Many the re-editions of famous concerts, as for the latest and perhaps unnecessary live-album *High Voltage*. **Keith Emerson**'s suicide in 2016 and **Greg Lake**'s death after a terrible illness close definitely any further plans.

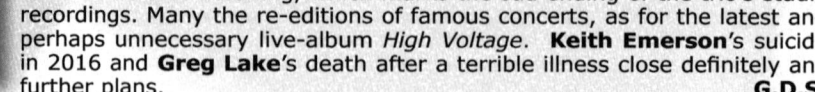

G.D.S.

DISCOGRAPHY:

EMERSON, LAKE & PALMER *(1970, Island)* **TARKUS** *(1971, Island)* **PICTURES AT AN EXHIBITION** *(1971, Island)* **TRILOGY** *(1972, Island)* **BRAIN SALAD SURGERY** *(1973, Manticore)* **WELCOME BACK MY FRIENDS TO THE SHOW THAT NEVER ENDS** *(1974, Manticore)* **WORKS VOL. 1** *(1977, Atlantic)* **WORKS VOL. 2** *(1977, Atlantic)* **LOVE BEACH** *(1977, Atlantic)* **IN CONCERT** *(1979, Atlantic)* **BLACK MOON** *(1992, Victory)* **LIVE AT THE ROYAL ALBERT HALL** *(1993, Victory)* **WORKS LIVE** *(1993, Victory)* **IN THE HOT SEAT** *(1994, Victory)* **LIVE AT THE ISLE OF WIGHT FESTIVAL** *(1997, Sanctuary)* **KING BISCUIT FLOWER HOUR** *(1997, BMG)* **LIVE IN POLAND** *(1997, Manticore)* **THEN & NOW** *(1998, Eagle Records)* **HIGH VOLTAGE** *(2010, Sanctuary)*.

Europe: **GREAT BRITAIN**

FAMILY

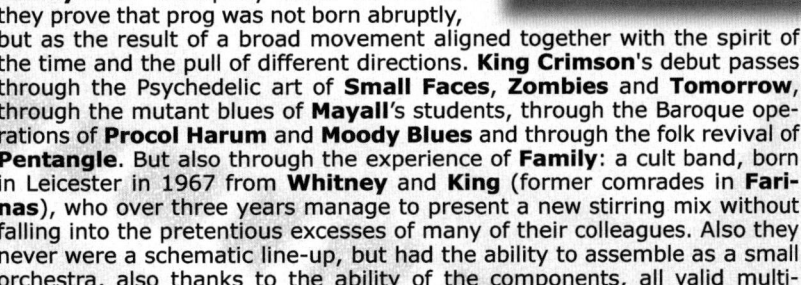

Roger Chapman - *vocals, harmonica, sax,* **John "Charlie" Whitney** - *guitars,* **Jim King** - *horns,* **Ric Grech** - *bass, violin, cello,* **Rob Townsend** - *drums,* **John "Poli" Palmer** - *vibes, flute, violin,* **John Weider, John Wetton, Jim Cregan** - *bass, vocals,* **Tony Ashton** - *keyboards.*

Family is an exemplary band: first of all they prove that prog was not born abruptly, but as the result of a broad movement aligned together with the spirit of the time and the pull of different directions. **King Crimson**'s debut passes through the Psychedelic art of **Small Faces**, **Zombies** and **Tomorrow**, through the mutant blues of **Mayall**'s students, through the Baroque operations of **Procol Harum** and **Moody Blues** and through the folk revival of **Pentangle**. But also through the experience of **Family**: a cult band, born in Leicester in 1967 from **Whitney** and **King** (former comrades in **Farinas**), who over three years manage to present a new stirring mix without falling into the pretentious excesses of many of their colleagues. Also they never were a schematic line-up, but had the ability to assemble as a small orchestra, also thanks to the ability of the components, all valid multi-instrumentalists.

Summer of 1968: **Soft Machine**, **Caravan** and **Jethro Tull** are about to release their debut-album; **Yes**, **King Crimson** and **Genesis** are getting ready to begin, and **Family** churn out their first masterpiece. The 12 songs in *Music In A Doll's House* absorb the mood of the period, which goes from acid-rock to R&B, passing through mystical **Beatles**-ish echoes, pop paintings from **the Kinks** and folk-rock from **The Band**. **Roger Chapman**'s voice stands out: gritty, expressive, with that unmistakable vibrato so influential for **Peter Gabriel**. The closest reference is **Traffic** to which they are intertwined: **Ric Grech** is their bassist whom soon will pass on to **Winwood**; **Dave Mason** is their producer, thanks to whom **Family** keeps in balance their many influences. Eight months later the same line-up, acclaimed by critics and audiences, repeats itself with the sequel *Family Entertainment*: a perfected formula containing an anthology piece like "The Weaver's Answer". The band is yet another anomaly and since they aspire for grandeur in the States, they start avoiding long suites and alternating acoustic, electric, dirty rock and refinement. **Family** embark in their first controversial American tour with **The Nice** and **Ten Years After** and soon lose **Grech** who joins **Blind Faith** instead. They perform as opening group to **The Rolling Stones** in a huge Hyde Park concert and later on in the Isle of Wight. *A Song For Me* opens the new decade with a more electric and aggressive sound, experimental and messy, but prized in the charts. At the end of 1970 they record *Anyway*, a one side live - one side studio album, at the Fairfield Halls, followed by the successful *Fearless*: this fifth LP presents a young **John Wetton**, who, in order to join **Family**, refuses **Robert Fripp**'s first invitation to join **King Crimson**. It is an excellent album, widely regarded as their best for the compactness, the significant contribution of **Wetton** and the once in a lifetime performance of an overwhelming **Chappo**. After such high levels, the next releases, *Bandstand* and *It's Only A Movie*, can only be more conventional and predictable. On October 13, 1973 a farewell concert is held and they will never reunite, leaving the individual musicians to pursue their careers with numerous side projects.

D.Z.

DISCOGRAPHY:
MUSIC IN A DOLL'S HOUSE *(Reprise 1968)* **FAMILY ENTERTAINMENT** *(Reprise 1969)* **A SONG FOR ME** *(Reprise 1970)* **ANYWAY** *(Reprise 1970)* **FEARLESS** *(Reprise 1971)* **BANDSTAND** *(Reprise 1972)* **IT'S ONLY A MOVIE** *(Raft 1973)* **FAMILY LIVE** *(live, Mystic 2003).*

Europe: GREAT BRITAIN

ROBERT FRIPP

One of the most fervent and imaginative minds of Prog, innovator and experimenter as few are found, **Robert Fripp** was born May 16, 1946 in Wimborne Minster, southern England. By his own admission, in the beginning he did not have a musical ear, nor sense of rhythm; he was also left-handed but wanted to play with his right and his shyness prevented him to appear in public. Yet he still took lessons together with another young student, **Greg Lake**, and for the examination piece he chose **Paganini** adapted for the guitar, leaving everyone agasp.

His recording career began in 1968 with brothers **Peter** and **Mike Giles**. *The Cheerful Insanity of Giles, Giles & Fripp* turned out to be a quite immature album, but the songs signed by **Fripp** showed a glimpse of remarkable ideas and technique. The following year he began the extraordinary adventure of **King Crimson**, full of events, beginning one of the most important progressive discographies ever. This did not prevent him from having a close and fruitful series of collaborations, productions and side projects.

The **Van Der Graaf Generator**, without a guitarist on a permanent basis, call him for the solos in *H to He* (1970) and *Pawn Hearts* (1971). In that same period he involves 50 musicians from the best of London's Jazz and the Canterbury's Sound panorama, in the huge **Centipede** project from which 80 minutes of Avant-garde music are recorded in the album titled *September Energy* he also produces.

In 1972 he starts a collaboration with **Brian Eno**, already exited from **Roxy Music**, which will lead to two pillars of avant-garde and experimental music such as *No Pussyfooting* (1973) and *Evening Star* (1975). Here the new engraving sound carpet techniques were created with the aid of sequence recording tapes (reel to reel), known as **Frippertronics**.

Then came a period of total detachment from the music world, which also interrupted **King Crimson**'s production. After three years of research he appears alongside **David Bowie** and subsequently 1979 brought to his first real solo album, *Exposure*, hovering between experimentalism and song, born from the collaboration with **Peter Hammill**, **Daryl Hall**, **Peter Gabriel**, **Michael Walden** and **Phil Collins**.

The '80s bear more of his projects and collaborations: **The League of Gentlemen**, **Andy Summers** of **The Police**, **Talking Heads** and **Toyah Willcox** who will become his wife. Very important and prolific is his work with **David Sylvian**, but more importantly the resurrection of the **King Crimson** project with three new records, before another temporary disbandment.

Always in parallel he continues his soloist works with guitar ensembles such as **The League of Crafty Guitarists**, still playing with **David Sylvian** and, in the '90s his new technique called **Soundscapes** will basically replace **Frippertronics**, with the aid of electronics instead of using reel to reel.

New partnerships form with his old friend **Brian Eno** leading to the discovery of themes from the '70s with *Equatorial Stars*. **Fripp**'s collaborations continue along with **King Crimson** albums, his productions and his solo activities.

R.V.

RECOMMENDED RECORDINGS:

THE CHEERFUL INSANITY OF GILES, GILES & FRIPP (Giles, Giles & Fripp - 1968, Deram) **NO PUSSYFOOTING** (Fripp & Eno - 1973, EG) **EVENING STAR** (Fripp & Eno - 1975, EG) **EXPOSURE** (1979, EG) **GOD SAVE THE QUEEN/UNDER HEAVY MANNERS** (1980, Polydor) **THE LEAGUE OF GENTLEMEN** (Robert Fripp & The League of Gentlemen - 1981, EG) **I ADVANCE MASKED** (Andy Summers/Robert Fripp 1982, A&M) **GOD SAVE THE KING** (1985, EG) **THE LEAGUE OF CRAFTY GUITARISTS LIVE** (Robert Fripp & The League of Crafty Guitarists - 1986, EG) **THE FIRST DAY** (David Sylvian & Robert Fripp - 1993, Virgin) **DARSHAN** (David Sylvian & Robert Fripp - 1993, Virgin) **1999 SOUNDSCAPES: LIVE IN ARGENTINA** (1994, DGM) **THE EQUATORIAL STARS** (Fripp & Eno - 2005, Opal) Jakszyk, Fripp, Collins - (A King Crimson ProjeKct) - **A SCARCITY OF MIRACLES** (2011, DGM).

Europe: **GREAT BRITAIN**

PETER GABRIEL

In the aftermath of a gigantic tour called *The Lamb Lies Down on Broadway*, **Peter Gabriel** leaves **Genesis** in 1975 and takes a break for family reasons. His comeback to the world of entertainment is an album produced by **Bob Ezrin** in 1977, simply titled *Peter Gabriel*. This first attempt to take distance from the mother group contains good songs with very American-style Rock sounds and a couple of hits like "Here comes the flood" and "Solsbury Hill".

After a triumphant tour, in which none of his theatrical tricks inaugurated with **Genesis** appear, **Peter** has his second album produced by **Robert Fripp**, again with only his name on the cover, but this time, thanks to **Fripp** himself, with slight innovations that will place it among the tantalizing promises of the Rock scene in the late '70s.

Peter openly declares his intention of growing apart from the fairy-tale sound that he helped create: not yet 30, he wants to renew himself. He plans meticulously this change and, in interviews given at the time, he foresees needing at least three to four albums to establish his very own style.

As a matter of fact he becomes recognizable already in the 1980 album *Peter Gabriel III* containing a new hit titled "Games without frontiers" along with songs filled by new arrangements that will improve moreover in 1982 with *Peter Gabriel IV*.

In 1979 **Peter** is struck by the listening of a soundtrack from an African film and decides to contaminate with tribal rhythms both albums *PG III* and *PG IV*. Nothing new when speaking of mingling Afro to Rock, yet it is the way he does it: he dives as deep as to create **Womad** in 1982 (a festival of World Music culture) and seven years later he founds his very own label named **Real World**.

The renewal of music through the internationalization of musical language itself is why this is still Prog, even though he is not always successful in doing so. His most famous album *So* of 1986 is a sensational return to traditional patterns and easy-listening songs such as "Sledgehammer", although he does this with unmatched class. *Passion*, soundtrack to Martin Scorsese's *The Last Temptation of Christ*, is truly a masterpiece of blended musical influences from different ethnic groups.

The next album *Us* is a good mix between *Passion* and more commercial songs, sewn together with touching and precious lyrics taken from his personal sphere. A multimedia tour follows, crowned by the release of *Secret World Live*, then he dwells in silence for the ten years to come.

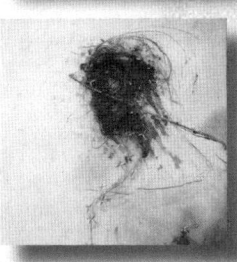

He also records an interactive game for computers called *Eve*, which contains alternative and genius versions of his songs: he believes it complete nonsense to stay anchored to one same arrangement and in fact publishes countless re-editions of his material. Even if his latest comeback *Ovo* in 2000 and *Up* in 2002 will be somewhat disappointing to many, his reinterpretation of songs by others in *Scratch My Back* and the revival of some of his classics with one voice and an orchestra in *New Blood*, is still to most synonymous of great class.   **M.G.**

DISCOGRAPHY:
PETER GABRIEL *(Charisma, 1977)* **PETER GABRIEL II** *(Charisma, 1978)* **PETER GABRIEL III** *(Charisma, 1980)* **PETER GABRIEL IV** *(Charisma, 1982)* **PLAYS LIVE** *(Charisma, 1983)* **BIRDY** *(Charisma, 1985)* **SO** *(Charisma/Virgin 1986)* **PASSION** *(Real World, 1989)* **SHAKING THE TREE** *(Virgin, 1990)* **US** *(Real World, 1992)* **SECRET WORLD LIVE** *(Real World, 1994)* **OVO** *(Real World, 2000)* **OVO: The Millennium Show** *(Real World, 2000)* **LONG WALK HOME** *(Real World, 2002)* **UP** *(Real World, 2002)* **HIT** *(Real World/Virgin, 2003)* **SCRATCH MY BACK** *(Real World/Virgin 2010)* **NEW BLOOD** *(Real World/Virgin 2011)* **LIVE BLOOD** *(Real World/Virgin 2012)* **SCRATCH MY BACK/AND I'LL SCRATCH YOURS** *(Real World/Virgin 2013)* **RATED PG** *(Real World/Virgin 2020)*.

Europe: GREAT BRITAIN

GENESIS

Peter Gabriel - *flute, percussion, vocals, (1968/1975)*, **Chris Stewart, John Silver** - *drums (1968-1969)*, **John Mayhew** - *drums (1970)*, **Phil Collins** - *drums, backing vocals (1971/1992), vocals (1975/1992)* **Mike Rutherford** - *bass, guitars*, **Tony Banks** - *keyboards*, **Anthony Phillips** - *lead guitar (1968/1970)*, **Steve Hackett** - *lead guitar (1970/1977)*, **Ray Wilson** - *vocals, (1997/1999)*.

Genesis represents the archetype of a Progressive Rock band. No one thereafter is immune to tributes and constant referrals to this mythical group of musicians who in 1969, barely in their twenties, release *From Genesis to Revelation*, a not fully ripe album containing numerous biblical references and musically already showing off their incredible talent.
Their true birth as a band is felt to be achieved with *Trespass*, where their great ability in the construction of songs like "The Knife" and "Stagnation", reaches peaks of unsuspected talent for so young musicians. *Nursery Cryme*, the next album, born after the shocking departure of **Anthony Phillips**, is instead an absolute masterpiece. All the songs are characterized by the particular suite structure, filled with imperious breaks, sudden changes in rhythm and incredible fugues, also thanks to the arrival of two fundamental elements: **Phil Collins** and **Steve Hackett**. Songs rich in cultural and traditional references like "The Musical Box" are portrayed by the charismatic gestures and facial expressions of the extraordinary **Peter Gabriel**, who thus gives birth to the so-called theatrical rock.

In 1972 *Foxtrot*, another masterpiece, is released containing "Supper's Ready", a beautiful suite which incarnates the highest level ever reached by the band for music, lyrics and theatricality. **Genesis** concerts are more like a whirlpool of visions and sensations, so disturbing to stick indelibly in the mind of the spectator, and *Genesis Live* becomes the manifesto of all concerts in those years, yet unfortunately insufficient alone to describe what was going on on stage. It is not until more recently that films are released to show it to the public of today.

In October 1973 *Selling England by the Pound* nearly reaches perfection. It is a seductive and enchanting album containing "Dancing With the Moonlit Knight", "Firth of Fifth" and "The Cinema Show" which are like jewels to pass on to posterity. The following year *The Lamb Lies Down on Broadway*, a double concept album, is released and mistakenly regarded by many as **Gabriel**'s first solo album since he wrote all the lyrics himself. It is an excellent album with sounds unheard of in previous works, but seemed to marginalize contributions from other members as if they were barely supporting actors. Inevitable will be the separation to come. The albums *A Trick of the Tail* and *Wind and Wuthering*, still jewels of poetry and inventiveness, see **Gabriel** already replaced by **Phil Collins** as the lead singer.
The departure of **Steve Hackett** in 1977 closes the progressive time lapse for the band. A new phase in Pop will soon begin leading **Genesis** to their worldwide success in this genre. 1980's album *Duke* is still worthy of notice as it is full of references to their glorious past, after which we find them escalating the Pop charts with top hits of easy-listening music of another kind. A last breath could be *Calling all Stations* where we find singer **Ray Wilson** instead of **Collins**.   M.G.

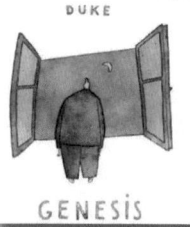

DISCOGRAPHY:
FROM GENESIS TO REVELATION *(Decca, 1969)* **TRESPASS** *(Charisma, 1970)* **NURSERY CRYME** *(Charisma, 1971)* **FOXTROT** *(Charisma, 1972)* **GENESIS LIVE** *(Charisma, 1973)* **SELLING ENGLAND BY THE POUND** *(Charisma, 1973)* **THE LAMB LIES DOWN ON BROADWAY** *(Charisma, 1974)* **A TRICK OF THE TAIL** *(Charisma, 1976)* **WIND & WUTHERING** *(Charisma, 1977)* **SECONDS OUT** *(Charisma, 1977)* **AND THEN THERE WERE THREE** *(Charisma, 1978)* **DUKE** *(Charisma, 1980)* **ABACAB** *(Charisma, 1981)* **THREE SIDES LIVE** *(Charisma, 1982)* **GENESIS** *(Charisma, 1983)* **INVISIBLE TOUCH** *(Charisma, Virgin, 1986)* **WE CAN'T DANCE** *(Virgin, 1991)* **THE WAY WE WALK, VOLUME ONE: THE SHORTS** *(Virgin, 1992)* **THE WAY WE WALK, VOLUME TWO: THE LONGS** *(Virgin, 1993)* **CALLING ALL STATIONS** *(Virgin, 1997)* **LIVE OVER EUROPE** *(Virgin, 2007)*.

Europe: GREAT BRITAIN

GENTLE GIANT

Ray Shulman - *bass, guitar, violin,* **Derek Shulman** - *vocals, bass, guitar,* **Phil Shulman** - *horns, vocals,* **Gary Green** - *guitar,* **Kerry Minnear** - *keyboards, cello, vibes, flute, vocals,* **Martin Smith, Malcolm Mortimore, John Weathers** - *drums.*

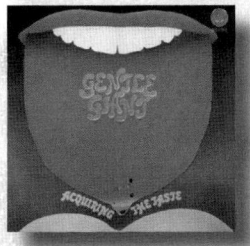

Among the great groups of symphonic rock, **Gentle Giant** is one that chose the most difficult path. Despite the Baroque glints and the fairy-tale atmospheres, they concentrate on developing very complex compositions which help their extraordinary technical abilities to shine as the very talented and skilled musicians they are, also able to exploit a very ample and variegated range of instruments. Another characteristic is the very particular harmonies they create with vocals, often recalling certain solfeggio exercises.
They debut in 1970 with a fresh and mature self-titled Rock-based album, like in the track "Giant", but containing so many other influences like Classical, Medieval and Folk. Their rightful intuitions increase in the following album *Acquiring the Taste*, a superb painting of inimitable and very personal style: the sound becomes lighter and softer, creating a halo of magic like a fascinating enchantment, only interrupted a couple of times by a certain amount of energy. The unpredictable instrumental dynamics of which the band is capable of, become even more evident in *Three Friends*, a concept-album of huge level, prelude to *Octopus* and *In a Glass House*, other two incredible albums that need no compromises: here dwells the true essence of **Gentle Giant**: the refined sound, the tenacious Rock, the Classical themes, the acrobatic rhythms, the singing originality, the spirit of adventure

and the experimentation. Tracks like "The Advent of Panurge", "Knots", "The Boys in the Band", "The Runaway", "Way of Life" are icons of their repertoire, baffling when performed live.
In a Glass House, a true masterpiece, is misunderstood and seams to be a commercial failure. The musicians luckily do not give up and they continue fearlessly along the chosen path, convinced of their means and of their art, giving birth to other albums such as *The Power and the Glory*, *Free Hand*, *Inter'view* and the live album *Playing the Fool*. They start a downward phase with *The Missing Piece*, which nevertheless contains some very good pieces. Fewer good tracks in *Giant for a Day*. Their fate as giants is slightly upheld by *Civilian* though the band appears tired and in fact soon breaks up.
Many rumors of an eventual reunion but this is a dream not come true yet. The partial reunion of three of the components (**Minnear, Mortimor** and **Green**, calling themselves the **Three Friends**) may not seem enough (excluding the **Shulman** Brothers) but fans are quenched by the numerous posthumous publications released. **G.D.S.**

RECOMMENDED RECORDINGS:
GENTLE GIANT *(1970, Vertigo)* **ACQUIRING THE TASTE** *(1971, Vertigo)* **THREE FRIENDS** *(1972, Vertigo)* **OCTOPUS** *(1973, Vertigo)* **IN A GLASS HOUSE** *(1973, WWA)* **THE POWER AND THE GLORY** *(1974, WWA)* **FREE HAND** *(1975, Chrysalis)* **INTER'VIEW** *(1976, Chrysalis)* **PLAYING THE FOOL – LIVE** *(1976, Chrysalis)* **THE MISSING PIECE** *(1977, Chrysalis)* **GIANT FOR A DAY** *(1978, Capitol Records)* **CIVILIAN** *(1980, Chrysalis)* **THE LAST STEPS** *(1996, Red Steel Music)* **UNDER CONSTRUCTION** *(1997, Alucard)* **KING BISCUIT FLOWER HOUR** *(1998, King Biscuit Flower Hour)* **OUT OF THE FIRE – THE BBC CONCERTS** *(1998, hux Records)* **TOTALLY OUT OF THE WOODS – THE BBC SESSIONS** *(2000, Hux Records)* **INTER'VIEW IN CONCERT** *(2000, Glass House)* **LIVE IN ROME 1974** *(2000, Glass House)* **ENDLESS LIFE** *(2002, Glass House)* **ARTISTICALLY CRYME** *(2002, Glass House)* **THE MISSING FACE** *(2002, Glass House)* **LIVE AT THE BICENTENNIAL 1776-1976** *(2014, Alucard)* .

Europe: GREAT BRITAIN

GONG

Daevid Allen - *guitar, vocals*, **Gilli Smyth, Miquette Giraudy, Sandy Colley** - *vocals*, **Didier Malherbe, Theo Travis** - *horns*, **Christian Tristch, Hansford Rowe** - *bass, guitar*, **Pip Pyle, Laurie Allan, Pierre Moerlen, Orlando Allen** - *drums*, **Tim Blake, Francis Moze, Patrice Lemoine** - *keyboards*, **Mike Howlett** - *bass,* **Steve Hillage** - *guitars*, **Rachid Hourai, Mirelle Bauer, Benoit Moerlen, Mino Cinelu** - *percussion*, **Jorge Pinchevsky, Darryl Way** - *violin*.

Instructions for use: <<*Turn On, Tune In, Drop Out*>> advises **Timothy Leary**. Gather your vinyls and surround yourself with strange doodles of flying teapots and dwarfs with pointy heads, going from a temporary termination of the mind to entering the world of contradictions, just as they represent the last fortress of the hippy utopia, though being a historical Prog band. **Daevid Allen** was stranded in France due to passport issues: this is how the Australian musician meets **Gilli Smyth** in 1968, when a sudden vision gongs him in the direction of a new path, recording the crazy solo album *Banana Moon* with some friends (**Pyle, Wyatt**), then a soundtrack for an eccentric motorcycle film and finally the album *Camembert Electrique*. Landing on planet **Gong** means following blindly the Great Chief towards illumination: music is part of this happy colored multinational commune in which everything (**Didier Malherbe** becomes **Bloomdido Bad De Grasse**) is all mixed up in a cauldron of Space-Rock and **Zappa**-ries, Fusion and Acid resistances, anarchy and marijuana. Then comes the *Radio Gnome Trilogy: Flying Teapot, Angel's Egg* and *You*, an authentic mythology about a cosmic Gnome Radio, the hero 'Zero' and a crowd of allegorical characters. The three gnomophonic albums live off the most unconditional creative liberty, with novelties like the **Gilli Smyth**'s song ("Spatial whisper") and **Daevid**'s famous glissando guitar; a chameleon sequence of Jazz, Rock, contextualism, Cabaret, esoterism and Psychedelia, without form but making sense through an impeccable instrumental imprint, given the level of the musicians. **Gong** is an **Allen**-ian creature, proven in the excellent (and a greatly sold) *Shamal*; after 1976 **Pierre Moerlen** leads the group and a completely different sound is born as the more serious and composed **Pierre Moerlen's Gong** proposes a pulsating Jazz-Rock, with ample use of melodic percussions and many guest collaborations (**Holdsworth, Winwood, Lockwood, Oldfield**). After the solo albums and the **Gongmaison** parenthesis, Allen himself recalls 'Zero The Hero' in 1990 with a come-back: *Shapeshifter* and *Zero To Infinity* (fourth and fifth episode of *Radio Gnome*) with updated sounds and close to Trance or to the new Electronics style of **The Orb**. While **Gong**'s legacy survives as an apparently insane and on the verge of musical imagination band, **Allen**'s career is active with numerous collaborations (the Japanese **Acid Mothers Temple, University Of Errors** and **Brainville 3** with **Fred Frith** and **Chris Cutler**), various projects and the usual live performances. In 2010 they are back with a new album and the return of **Steve Hillage** and **Miquette Giraudy**. Another good album in 2014, *I see You*, is somewhat a last farewell to **Allen** who dies the following year, leaving in heritage the band's name to some new musicians who release the first Gong album without its founder, *Rejoice! I'm dead*!

D.Z.

RECOMMENDED RECORDINGS: *(Pierre Moerlen's GONG albums not included):*
MAGICK BROTHER/MYSTIC SISTER *(BYG 1969)* **CONTINENTAL CIRCUS** *(Philips 1971)* **CAMEMBERT ELECTRIQUE** *(BYG 1971)* **Radio Gnome Invisible Part I - FLYING TEAPOT** *(Virgin 1973)* **Radio Gnome Invisible Part II - ANGEL'S EGG** *(Virgin 1973)* **Radio Gnome Invisible Part III - YOU** *(Virgin 1974)*, **SHAMAL** *(Virgin 1976)*, **GAZEUSE!** *(Virgin 1977)* **EXPRESSO II** *(Virgin 1978)* **LIVE AU BATACLAN** *(Mantra 1989)*, **SHAPESHIFTER** *(Celluloid 1992)*, **25TH BIRTHDAY PARTY** *(Voiceprint 1995)*, **ZERO TO INFINITY** *(Snapper 2000)*, **LIVE 2 INFINITEA** *(Snapper 2000)* **ACID MOTHERHOOD** *(Voiceprint 2004)* **2032** *(G-Wave 2009)* **I SEE YOU** *(Mad Fish 2014)* **REJOICE! I'M DEAD!** *(Mad Fish 2016)* **THE UNIVERSE ALSO COLLAPSED** *(K-scope 2019)*.

Europe: GREAT BRITAIN

STEVE HACKETT

Already in 1975 while he was still playing in **Genesis**, guitarist **Steve Hackett** publishes his first solo album *Voyage of the Acolyte*, a very beautiful work which clearly proves the importance of his presence in the economy of the **Genesis**' sound: wonderful compositions, skilled and intense executions, baroque glimpses, majestic crescendos and some eccentricity, show how his talent and class are infinite.
In 1977 **Hackett** chooses to leave the band that brought him to fame and to fully devote to his career, not disdaining here and there other collaborations. *Please Don't Touch*, *Spectral Mornings* and *Defector* represent a dense trio, containing some fantastic songs and solos gone down in the history of the six strings. They also help understand how eclectic he is in his sound experimentations and research of the many different genres: the baseline remains Symphonic Prog, yet his desire to explore will always give originality to his works although they may swing high and low. Albums like *Cured* and *Highly Strung* (also the **GTR** project with **Steve Howe**), almost push towards a top ten Rock style, close to the American one of AOR. On the other hand acoustic guitar recordings are published like little precious gems of their own kind (*Bay of Kings* and *Momentum*). From the 90ies onward **Hackett** comes out even stronger with this will to juggle different genres with acceptable results. Electronic works prove his heterogeneity (like the sombre *Darktown* or the multicolored *To Watch the Storms*), good classical music publishings in which he is accompanied by an orchestra (*A Midsummer Night's Dream* and *Metamorpheus*) or by his brother **John** (*Sketches of Satie*). We even find him dealing with Blues in *Blues with a Feeling*.
He also releases commemorative albums such as *Genesis Revisited* with part of the old band's repertoire, and the live recording *The Tokyo Tapes* in which, with other superstars such as **John Wetton**, **Ian McDonald**, **Chester Thompson** and **Julian Colbeck**, he plays both his own compositions as well as tracks from **Genesis**, **King Crimson** and **Asia**. This should not be mistaken as opportunism. After a justified rejection of **Genesis** in his first soloist years, **Hackett** reaches the rightful decision of acknowledging what he also contributed to creating. Particularly interesting are also the numerous live albums, both electronic and acoustic performances, also commemorating his career, like the stupendous 4 CD box *Live Archive* which gathers exhibitions from the '70, '80 and '90.
In 2009 another surprise comes after his divorce with Kim Poor and his exit from Camino Records: a new and very imaginative electric album with **Chris Squire** and **Anthony Phillips** as special guests! And as if this were not enough, yet an other album is released plus the second chapter of *Genesis Revisited*.

G.D.S.

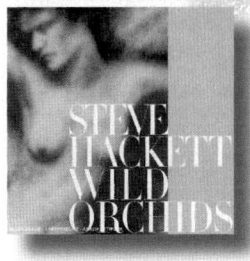

DISCOGRAPHY:
VOYAGE OF THE ACOLYTE *(1975, Charisma)* **PLEASE DON'T TOUCH** *(1978, Charisma)* **SPECTRAL MORNINGS** *(1979, Charisma)* **DEFECTOR** *(1980, Charisma)* **CURED** *(1981, Charisma)* **HIGHLY STRUNG** *(1983, Charisma)* **BAY OF KINGS** *(1983, Lamborghini)* **TILL WE HAVE FACES** *(1984, Lamborghini)* **MOMENTUM** *(1988, Start Records)* **TIME LAPSE – LIVE** *(1992, Kudos)* **GUITAR NOIR** *(1993, Kudos)* **BLUES WITH A FEELING** *(1994, Kudos)* **THERE ARE MANY SIDES TO THE NIGHT** *(1995, Kudos)* **A MIDSUMMER NIGHT'S DREAM** *(1997, EMI Classic)* **GENESIS REVISITED** *(1997, Reef Recordings)* **THE TOKYO TAPES** *(1998, Camino Records)* **DARKTOWN** *(1999, Camino Records)* **SLETCHES OF SATIE** *(con John Hackett, 2000, Camino Records)* **FEEDBACK 86** *(2000, Camino Records)* **LIVE ARCHIVE** *(2001, Inside Out)* **LIVE ARCHIVE 70** *(2001, Camino Records)* **SOMEWHERE IN SOUTH AMERICA... LIVE IN BUENOS AIRES** *(2002, Camino Records)* **TO WATCH THE STORMS** *(2003, Camino Records)* **LIVE ARCHIVE NEARFEST** *(2003, Camino Records)* **HUNGARIAN HORIZONS** *(2003, Camino Records)* **LIVE ARCHIVE 03** *(2004, Camino Records)* **LIVE ARCHIVE 04** *(2004, Camino Records)* **METAMORPHEUS** *(2005, Camino Records)* **LIVE ARCHIVE 05** *(2005, Camino Records)* **LIVE ARCHIVE 83** *(2006, Camino Records)* **WILD ORCHIDS** *(2006, Camino Records)* **TRIBUTE** *(2008, Camino Records)* **OUT OF THE TUNNEL'S MOUTH** *(2009, Wolfwork)* **BEYOND THE SHROUDED HORIZON** *(2011, Inside Out)* **GENESIS REVISITED II** *(2012, Inside Out)* **WOLFLIGHT** *(2015, Inside Out)* **THE NIGHT SIREN** *(2017, Inside Out)*.

Europe: GREAT BRITAIN

PETER HAMMILL

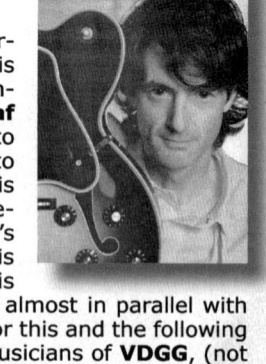

Certainly one of the most coherent and inspired artists of the Prog movement, perhaps the greatest, his boundless and rich production, never ending in comparison to that of his original band - **Van Der Graaf Generator** - creates a serious difficulty in trying to describe him in just this one page. Better to stick to the highlights, which are many but more defined. His soloist debut *The Aerosol Grey Machine*, though precedent to that of the **VDGG**, went under the band's name due to contractual quibbles. Therefore what is considered his first album in 1970, *Fool's mate*, is published only after the first breakup of the band, almost in parallel with *Pawn Hearts* that has a place on the wall of fame. For this and the following albums **Peter** will collaborate with almost all the musicians of **VDGG**, (not really definable as ex-companions since they not only collaborate but also play together in the many reunions up to this very day) and in fact, a part from him singing and his more introspective writings, he will always be tightly tied to this band. **Peter**'s voice is one of a kind: **Robert Fripp** says: <<Hammill does with his voice what Hendrix did with his guitar.>> A very extreme comparison, but quite the truth. When in 1975 *Nadir's Big Chance* is released, **Hammill** becomes the interest of the rising punk generations: **Johnny Rotten** is a declared fan and despite him showing off a <<I Hate Pink Floyd>> T-shirt, he wouldn't miss the **VDGG** in concert at Marquee. **Hammill**'s extraordinarily expressionistic warblings are innovative and inimitable, and the lyrics that spring out from these existential depths are present in all of his production. In the '80 he moves closer to the idea of a parallel production and to the work of **Peter Gabriel**, and *Sitting Targets*, *Enter K* and *Patience* make their way along side the best New Wave genre of the time. Dark bands like **Joy Division** (later **New Order**), **The Cure**, **Siouxie and the Banshees** openly paid their respects to **Hammill**. Just listen to **K-group** (with many ex **VDGG**!) and have a blast.

At the beginning of the '90 **Hammill** increases his production also thanks to the advent of digital support. He founds his own label, Fie!, releasing albums that are considered for the few, far from radio broadcasts or charts, but the creativeness and quality of his production is always there. *Fireships* and *Roaring Forties* contain episodes that don't make us regret the **VDGG** and a suite like "Headlong stretch" is the best proof. More recent albums like *This* and others (so many!) made before the actual reunion of the **VDGG**, such as *Veracious* were often recorded with the piano alone and **Stuart Gordon** on the violin, apparently too simple, but made warm and involving by his unmistakable voice.

M.G.

RECOMMENDED RECORDINGS (Collaborations not included):
FOOL'S MATE *(1970, Charisma)* **CHAMELEON IN THE SHADOW OF THE NIGHT** *(1972, Charisma)* **THE SILENT CORNER AND THE EMPTY STAGE** *(1974, Charisma)* **IN CAMERA** *(1974, Charisma)* **NADIR'S BIG CHANCE** *(1975, Charisma)* **OVER** *(1976, Charisma)* **THE FUTURE NOW** *(1978, Charisma)* **pH7** *(1979, Charisma)* **A BLACK BOX** *(1980, Mercury)* **SITTING TARGETS** *(1981, Virgin)* **ENTER K** *(1982, Mercury)* **PATIENCE** *(1983, Mercury)* **THE MARGIN (live with K-group)** *(1984, Virgin)* **THE LOVE SONGS** *(1984, Virgin)* **SKIN** *(1986, Virgin)* **AND CLOSE AS THIS** *(1986, Virgin)* **IN A FOREIGN TOWN** *(1988, Line)* **OUT OF WATER** *(1989, Enigma)* **ROOM TEMPERATURE LIVE** *(1990, Enigma)* **THE FALL OF THE HOUSE OF USHER** *(1990, reissued in 1999, Fie!)* **FIRESHIPS** *(1991, Fie!)* **THE NOISE** *(1992, Fie!)* **LOOPS AND REELS** *(1993, Fie!)* **THERE GOES THE DAYLIGHT***(1993, Fie!)* **ROARING FORTIES** *(1994, Fie!)* **X MY HEART** *(1996, Fie!)* **SONIX** *(1996, Fie!)* **EVERYONE YOU HOLD** *(1997, Fie!)* **THIS** *(1998, Fie!)* **TYPICAL** *(1999, Fie!)* **NONE OF THE ABOVE** *(2000, Fie!)* **WHAT, NOW?** *(2001, Fie!)* **SONIX** *(2001, Fie!)* **THE THIN MAN SINGS BALLADS (Compilation)** *(2002, Fie!)* **CLUTCH** *(2002, Fie!)* **INCOHERENCE** *(2004, Fie!)* **VERACIOUS (Live With Stuart Gordon)** *(2006, Fie!)* **SINGULARITY** *(2006, Fie!)*.

Europe: **GREAT BRITAIN**

HATFIELD AND THE NORTH

Phil Miller - *guitars,* **Dave Stewart, Sophia Domancich** - *keyboards,* **Richard Sinclair** - *bass, vocals,* **Pip Pyle** - *drums,* **Robert Wyatt** - *vocals,* **Geoff Leigh, Jimmy Hastings, Mont Campbell, Lindsay Cooper, Tim Hodgkinson** - *horns,* **Amanda Parsons, Barbara Gaskin, Ann Rosenthal (The Northettes)** - *vocals,* **Jeremy Baines** - *pixiphone.*

Hatfield And The North is part of the great Canterbury dream, probably the highest and most typical moment of the anomalous and fleeting wave: a project that is not the simple sum of its single members but a unique synergy, a meeting point of different artistic paths. **Phil Miller** and **Pip Pyle** played in **Delivery** from 1966, the first joining **Matching Mole**, the second **Gong**. **Richard Sinclair** and **Steve Miller**, brother of **Phil**, leave **Caravan** and the four play under the name of **Steve Miller**'s **Delivery** until the exit of the keyboardist, so with the arrival of the renegade **David Sinclair**, the band changes name (speaking of deviations: leaving London there is big sign highlighting communications toward the North, and one in Hatfield). **David** - not really at ease with improvisation and composed rhythms - is replaced by pianist **Dave Stewart**, young but very talented, not quite the jazz lover but a prepared musician coming from bands like **Uriel**, **Egg** and **Khan**. It is the February of 1974 when Virgin publishes their striking debut album: **Richard** brings his oblique melodies and eccentric singing, **Pyle** is perfectly swimming in irregular tempos and mutating rhythms, **Stewart**'s Fender Rhodes replies steadily to **Ratledge** and **Sinclair**'s fuzz-organ. It is an unusual album composed of small passages forming an imaginary suite: the baseline is similar to jazz-rock but **HATN** go beyond using richer shades, compact writing and improvisation, this aura of perennial nonsense and the magic of melodies such as "Calyx" written by **Phil Miller** for an exceptional **Wyatt**. With a sense of humor: since **Phil Spector** had the **Ronettes**, the **Hatfields** have three vocalists called the **Northettes**. *The Rotters' Club* follows its predecessor with a soft and lunatic rock, performed with elegant interplay, openings to jazz and to intellectual music, dreamy and bizarre at the same time, clearly expressed in the structure of **Stewart**'s suite "Mumps". **HATN** manage to sublime the characteristics of their groups of origin and the personality - strong and defined - of each single musician: the fluid and coherent guitar playing in **Miller**, the legacy of the best **Caravan**, the intellectual and demanding vision in **Stewart**, horn and clarinets of guests from **Henry Cow** and **Jimmy Hastings**. Besides the band is his strong answer to the dying art-rock: if **Yes**, **Jethro Tull** and **ELP** conquer, **HATN** is a continuous gathering of little and eccentric ideas assembled with inimitable compositional talent on the intriguing lyrics by **Pip**. A pity they do not gather the same amount of fans: for a couple of years they perform in universities and theaters, but despite the appreciations of the critics, they break up giving birth to other projects such as the **National Health**. In 1990 we have an episodic reunion for a television broadcast (with **Pyle**'s partner **Sophia Domancich**,); 15 years later a come back with **Alex Maguire** on keyboards and **Mark Fletcher** who will take **Pyle**'s place after his death. Two albums with studio recordings and collaborations in important international festivals bring the **Hatfields** back to fame and the novel by Jonathan Coe (*The Rotters' Club*, Viking 2001) contributes to preserving their memory.   **D.Z.**

DISCOGRAPHY:
HATFIELD AND THE NORTH (*Virgin 1974*) **THE ROTTER'S CLUB** (*Virgin 1975*) **AFTERS** (*Virgin 1980*) **LIVE 1990** (*live, Demon 1993*) **HATWISE CHOICE: ARCHIVE RECORDINGS 1973-1975, VOLUME 1** (*Burning Shed 2005*) **HATTITUDE: ARCHIVE RECORDINGS 1973-1975, VOLUME 2** (*Burning Shed 2006*).

Europe: GREAT BRITAIN

HAWKWIND

Dave Brock – *rhythm guitar*, **Nik Turner** – *flute and sax*, **Lemmy Kilmister** - *bass*, **Dik Mik Davies, Del Dettmar** - *keyboards*, **Simon King** - *drums*, **Robert Calvert** - *vocals*, **Michael Moorcock** - *lyrics*

Since their first appearance in 1969 only one thing do the 42 different line-ups have all in common: founding member **Dave Brock**, heart and soul of **Hawkwind** and composer of most of their music and lyrics. Impossible to quote every single instrumentalist or singer that has taken part in the group, however, among others, **Lemmy Kilmister** as founder of **Motorhead**, Tim Blake from **Gong**, Dave Anderson from **Amon Düül II** and the immense **Ginger Baker** drummer from **Cream**.

At the beginning they simply called themselves **Group X**, then **Hawkwind Zoo**, then again another abbreviation. Fundamental for the musical growth of the band is the first period, between 1969 and 1970, in which a long tour saw them placed side by side with the **Pink Faires**. The members of these two groups mixed and they often improvised together. This material was what brought to 1970's *Hawkwind*, a strongly soaked in Psychedelia and Electronics album with enough clear references to the first **Pink Floyd**, but without forgetting a pinch of **John Cale** and **Terry Riley**. The musical expression of the group had the intent of producing a lysergic effect without the assumption of drugs. It would guide the sounds and rhythms in order to create small riffs, made hypnotic by their being repeated, bringing you into a sort of altered state of conscience.

In the following years many albums followed and they would participate frequently in underground musical festivals with eccentric and memorable exhibitions, rich of long improvisations that will be also used as material for future releases. In the first years of the '70 they in fact create their best poetic, visionary, imaginary, freak and alternative works, as hard and dark as they get. *In Search of Space, Doremi Fasol Latido* and *Space Ritual Alive* which is perhaps the best of the entire production. Other fundamental year was 1976 with their passing from United Artists to Charisma and the release of *Astounding Sounds, Amazing Music*. Their fame leads them to become the protagonists of a novel of science fiction.

The band suffered, as almost everyone under the events of the end of this decade, with breakups, changes in name and exits. Then the comeback in the '80 with the usual changes in line-up, label and sometimes good albums like *Levitation* and *Sonic Attack*, sometimes less meaningful ones like *Out & Intake* or *Church of Hawkwind*. The 90ies flow without notice. Today **Hawkwind** is reduced to a trio that rotates around the charisma of the usual **Brock** that among his soloist projects and many live albums or sometimes questionable operations of recovery, continues the adventure.

R.V.

RECOMMENDED RECORDINGS:
HAWKWIND *(LP, Liberty/United Artists, 1970)* **IN SEARCH OF SPACE** *(LP, United Artists, 1971)* **DOREMI FASOL LATIDO** *(LP, United Artists, 1972)* **THE SPACE RITUAL ALIVE** *(2LP, United Artists, 1973)* **HALL OF THE MOUNTAIN GRILL** *(LP, United Artists, 1974)* **WARRIOR ON THE EDGE OF TIME** *(LP, United Artists;, 1975)* **ASTOUNDING SOUNDS AMAZING MUSIC** *(LP, Charisma, 1976)* **QUARK STRANGENESS & CHARM** *(LP, Charisma, 1977)* **HAWKLORDS: 25 YEARS ON** *(LP, Charisma, 1978)* **PXR5** *(LP, Charisma, 1979)* **LIVE 79** *(LP, Bronze, 1980)* **LEVITATION** *(LP, Bronze, 1980)* **SONICK ATTACK** *(LP, RCA Active, 1981)* **CHURCH OF HAWKWIND** *(LP, RCA Active, 1982)* **CHOOSE YOUR MASQUES** *(LP, RCA Active, 1982)* **ZONES** *(LP, Flicknife, 1983)* **OUT & INTAKE** *(LP, Flicknife, 1987)* **THE XENON CODEX** *(LP, GWR, 1988)* **SPACE BANDITS** *(LP, GWR, 1990)* **PALACE SPRINGS** *(LP, GWR, 1991)* **ELECTRIC TEEPEE** *(CD, Castle Communications, 1992)* **ALIEN** *(CD, Emerge, 1995)* **DISTANT HORIZONS** *(CD, Emerge, 1997)* **TAKE ME TO YOUR FUTURE** *(CD Hawkwind Dual Disc 2006)*

Europe: **GREAT BRITAIN**

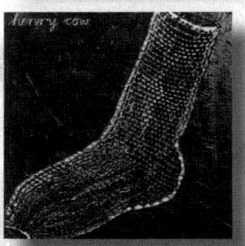

HENRY COW

Fred Frith - *guitar, viola, violin, piano, vocals,* **Tim Hodgkinson** - *organ, piano, horns, vocals,* **Geoff Leigh, Lindsay Cooper, Mongezi Feza, Muchsin Campbell, Nick Evans, Anne-Marie Roefels** - *horns,* **John Greaves** - *bass, piano, vocals,* **Chris Cutler** - *drums, vocals,* **Robert Wyatt** - *vocals.* **SLAPP HAPPY: Dagmar Krause** - *vocals,* **Peter Blegvad** - *guitar, vocals,* **Anthony Moore** - *piano.*

<<There's a lot of fantastic stuff going on. Devastation if you look ahead. There is a guitarist, Fred Frith. He plays with Henry Cow. He manages some extraordinary things with the fuzz-box. Think Yardbirds sleeping with Giorgy Ligeti among the smoking ruins of a divided Berlin>>. Malcolm's description (one of the young protagonists of Jonathan Coe's novel "The Rotter's club", p. 50) gives us a fair idea of what **Henry Cow** represented in 1974: Rock and Jazz heritages, hookups with intellectual music, an explicit Progressive engagement. Politicized, experimental, brave.
Their debut album is published only in 1973, but they were already playing since 1968: **Fred Frith** and **Tim Hodgkinson** studied in Cambridge but their mind was bent towards musical exploration and to the counter-culture, therefore they put together a combo that immediately abandons blues to research sounds more within the **Soft Machine** and **Frank Zappa Mothers**' style. Despite the changes in line-up, they perform live (Glastonbury, Edinburgh) and collaborate in drama or dance projects, arousing the interest of Virgin which had just released the famous *Tubular Bells* album. With **Ray Smith**'s unmistakable sock on the front cover, Leg End is immediately perceived as something different. Classical wind instruments, a free and deconstructed Jazz language, episodic Electronic hints, sounds of European derivation: some collocate them in the Canterbury area but there are only light ties to the early **Soft Machine**. After a tour with **Faust**, the new album needs to be released so the band resorts to improvisation and studio experimentation, making Unrest rich and unpredictable yet provocative and difficult. By now they are far away from the concept of Rock band: their 'total music' is born from a modern and traversal Chamber ensemble, that meets another anomaly **Slapps Happy**. Together with this Anglo-German trio they record *Desperate Straights* and *In Praise Of Learning*, bringing the sound from a serious instrumental dimension to a more surreal and dadaistic formula (embracing **Schoenberg** and **Captain Beefheart, Kurt Weill** and Robert Wyatt), with the eccentric voice of **Dagmar Krause** as lead singer and an even more engaged connotation to their style <<Art is not a mirror - it is a hammer>> is written on the second album. The fusion of the two bands brings tension: the **Slapps** break up and **Krause** remains in **Henry Cow** going with them on a long European tour; their radicalism makes **Frith** and his musicians distance themselves even more from England and from Virgin and in the summer of '75 they are invited to Italy thanks to political contacts in the PCI party the related festivals across the country. They return to London in '77 taking part in the **The Orckestra** project only to break up immediately due to financial and artistic issues. *Western Culture* is in fact their last album. Just before its publication they appear on the stage in the New London Theatre on March 12th 1978, with **Univers Zero, Stormy Six, Etron Fou Leloublan** and **Samla Mammas Manna** giving birth to the manifesto Rock In Opposition (RIO) and later to the coordination of independent, progressive and experimental groups, critical toward the policies of the record industry and in general to a stylistic and conceptual idea that still unites bands all over the world. **Henry Cow** break up definitely in 1979 but their legacy will survive in the flow of publications by its single members, in the Recommended Records catalog, and wherever there is musical liberty and artistic integrity. **D.Z.**

DISCOGRAPHY:
LEG END *(Virgin 1973)* **UNREST** *(Virgin 1974)* **SLAPP HAPPY/HENRY COW: Desperate Straight** *(Virgin 1975)* **SLAPP HAPPY/HENRY COW: In Praise Of Learning** *(Virgin 1975)* **HENRY COW CONCERTS** *(Compendium 1976)* **WESTERN CULTURE** *(Broadcast 1979).*

Europe: GREAT BRITAIN

IQ

Peter Nicholls - *vocals*, **Mike Holmes** - *guitar*, **Mark Westworth, Neil Durant** - *keyboards, vocals*, **John Jowitt** - *bass, vocals*, **Andy Edwards** - *drums (2005)*, **Martin Orford** - *keyboards (1982/2007)*, **Paul Menel** - *(1987/1989)*, **Tim Esau** - *bass (1982/1983)*, **Paul Cook** - *drums (1982/2005)*.

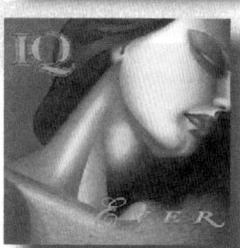

Born from the ashes of **Lens** a group led by guitarist **Mike Holmes**, IQ start their band activity in 1982 with the very particular voice of **Peter Nicholls** (very resembling physically and vocally **Peter Gabriel**), keyboardist **Martin Orford**, **Tim Esau** on the bass and **Paul Cook** for drums. Criticized by the predominant musical press (oriented to defend Punk and New Wave) maybe even more than **Marillion** for their **Genesis** inspired style (from which **Nicholls** also takes his theatrical art of disguise), IQ record *Seven Stories Into Eight*, an album that leads them to perform in the mythical Marquee.

In 1983, full New Prog era, *Tales from the Lush Attic* is released with its persuasive atmospheres and impetuous rhythms. Two years later they publish *The Wake*, a masterpiece that will consecrate them to fame. The first crisis begins when **Nicholls** leaves to found **Niadem's Ghost** (an experience that will reveal itself rather disappointing), forcing the band to replace him with **Paul Menel**. Two more albums, *Living Proof* (live) and *Nine In a Pond is Here* (a recovery of old recordings), then finally comes a new contract with Squawk (owned by Polygram), which releases *Nomzamo* and *Are You Sitting Comfortably?*, two confused albums but rewarded by a good commercial success. Despite sales, the band is dismissed by Squawk. **Paul**

Menem and **Tim Esau** both disappointed and embittered leave the group to continue the commercial research recently undertaken.

Once back into the Progressive flow, IQ ask for **Peter Nicholls'** return, who does together with a new bass player, the dynamic **John Jowitt**. This reassessment period coincides with the publication of minor compositions in *J'ai Pollette of Arnou*. In 1993 their precious jewel *Ever* for the first time manages to bring out a strong cohesive personality and above all it is far from the original sound inspiration. It contains a handful of extraordinary passages destined to

become some of their very best. This renewed success forces Giant-spv to publish *Forever Live*, a wonderful double album and video recording of the concert. Four years later another double album *Subterranea* becomes their absolute masterpiece with compositions that have the right mixture of prog perfectly embroided into the taste of the time with its keyboard fugues. At the end of the century *The Lost Attic* gathers a collection of scattered rare pieces of the band. In 2000 *The Seventh House*, *Dark Matter* and *Frequency* still see them brightly shining high in the progressive sky.

F.V.

DISCOGRAPHY:
TALES FROM THE LUSH ATTIC *(Private pressing, 1983)* **THE WAKE** *(Sahara Records, 1985)* **LIVING PROOF** *(Samurai Records, 1986, live)* **NINE IN A POND IS HERE** *(MSI (Private pressing),1987)* **NOMZAMO** *(Squawk, 1987)* **ARE YOU SITTING COMFORTABLY?** *(Squawk, 1989)* **J'AI POLLETTE D'ARNU** *(Giant-spv, 1990)* **EVER** *(Giant-spv, 1993)* **FOREVER LIVE** *(Giant-spv, 1993, live)* **SUBTERRANEA** *(Giant-spv, 1997)* **SEVEN STORIES INTO NINETY EIGHT** *(Giant-spv, 1998, reissue of the tape SEVEN STORIES INTO EIGHT originally from 1982)* **THE LOST ATTIC** *(1999, anthology of previously unreleased tracks)* **SUBTERRANEA: THE CONCERT** *(Giant-spv, 2000)* **THE SEVENTH HOUSE** *(Giant-spv, 2000)* **DARK MATTER** *(Giant-spv, 2004)* **FREQUENCY** *(Giant-spv, 2009)* **THE ROAD OF BONES** *(Giant-spv, 2014)*

Europe: **GREAT BRITAIN**

JETHRO TULL

Ian Anderson - *vocals, flute, sax, guitar, mandolin, keyboards,* **Mick Abrahams, Tony Iommi, Martin Barre** - *guitar,* **Glen Cornick, Jeffrey Hammond-Hammond, John Glascock, Tony Williams, Dave Pegg, David Goodier** - *bass,* **Clive Bunker, Barriemore Barlowe, Mark Craney, Gerry Conway, Paul Burgess, Doane Perry, James Duncan** - *drums,* **John Evan, David Palmer, Peter-John Vettese, Martin Allcock, Don Airey, Andrew Giddings, John O' Hara** - *keyboards,* **Eddie Jobson** - *violin.*

Jethro Tull has the fundamental role of embodying the evolution from a simple Blues band and revolutionizing the history of rock for its use of the transverse flute. Their debut album *This Was* immediately proves its originality through the right combination of Rock and Jazz, with a harsh flute inspired by **Roland Kirk**'s "Serenade To To Cuckoo". **Mick Abrahams** then goes off to create the **Blodwyn Pig** leaving his place to the imaginative **Martin Barre**. They publish *Stand Up* which surprises for the rough mixture of Rock-Blues with archaic folk atmospheres and suggestive orchestral arrangements; the fancy jazzing of **Bach**'s famous *Bourée* (Suite for lute in Mi minor BWV 996) consecrates **Ian Anderson**. The band draws closer to the dominant progressive genre: **John Evan** plays out live his adventurous fantasies in *Benefit* and the triumphal *Aqualung* (considered a concept album despite **Anderson** saying quite the contrary) is yet another confirmation of success: brave and destabilizing, it is about religion, social criticism and surreal characters, containing great pieces which go from acoustic sketches to orchestral suites, Jazz and Hard Rock blends. In 1972 their Prog masterpiece is published: for the first time ever a one track suite extends over both sides of the concept album *Thick As A Brick* once again confirming the intents and true compositional maturity of the band. Keyboards are added to the original flute-guitars couplet, elaborating complex rhythmic scores with their very personal classical inspiration - recovering Baroque dances, marches and popular ballads - and unleashing an amazing sequence of ideas with the right amount of irony. **Jethro Tull** find their maximum expression in this epic project between Troubadour and Free-rock, whilst the allegorical *A Passion Play* or the lazy *War Child* are controversial works that exceed in the conceptual structure. Only in 1975's maybe too long *Minstrel In The Gallery* does the balance of *Aqualung* return (anticipating the Folk trilogy of 1977-79, at its highest in *Songs From The Wood*, a crystalline and airy album), unbelievably achieved given the surrounding fury of Punk. The first half the '80 is harmful to the band, that does not manage to compare itself to the rising **Genesis** and **Yes**, drowning in a pathetic Electronic Rock. Only in 1987, with the pleasant *Crest Of a Knave* do the rejuvenated **Tull** return to a more dignified and rock sound recalling **Dire Straits** or AOR. Despite the instability of the line-ups, they make it through the 90ies steadily (*Catfish Rising*) and somewhat influenced by Ethno/World Music (*Roots To Branches*). **Anderson** and **Barre** issue some soloist projects while the name **Jethro Tull** still remains inimitable through all the classic rock catalogs out thereafter. After many lineup changes, the collaboration between **Anderson** and **Barre** ends. The name of the band is banned from use in court, although the old leader still releases under the name **Ian Anderson's Jethro Tull** where an unmistakable sound fills repetitive and tired ideas.

D.Z.

DISCOGRAPHY:
THIS WAS *(Island1968)* **STAND UP** *(Island 1969)* **BENEFIT** *(Island 1970)* **AQUALUNG** *(Chrysalis 1971)* **THICK AS A BRICK** *(Island 1972)* **LIVING IN THE PAST** *(Island 1972)* **A PASSION PLAY** *(Island 1973)* **WARCHILD** *(Chrysalis 1974)* **MINSTREL IN THE GALLERY** *(Island 1975)* **TOO OLD TO ROCK 'N' ROLL, TOO YOUNG TO DIE** *(Chrysalis 1976)* **SONGS FROM THE WOOD** *(Chrysalis 1977)* **HEAVY HORSES** *(Island 1978)* **BURSTING OUT** *(live, Island 1978)* **STORMWATCH** *(Island 1979)* **A** *(Island 1980)* **BROADSWORD AND THE BEAST** *(Chrysalis 1982)* **UNDER WRAPS** *(Chrysalis 1984)* **CREST OF A KNAVE** *(Chrysalis 1987)* **ROCK ISLAND** *(Chrysalis 1989)* **CATFISH RISING** *(Chrysalis 1991)* **A LITTLE LIGHT MUSIC** *(live, Chrysalis 1992)* **ROOTS TO BRANCHES** *(Chrysalis 1995)* **J-TULL DOT COM** *(Fuel 2000, 1999)* **LIVING WITH THE PAST** *(live, Fuel 2000 2002)* **THE JETHRO TULL CHRISTMAS ALBUM** *(Fuel 2000, 2003)* **NOTHING IS EASY: LIVE AT THE ISLE OF WIGHT** *(Eagle, 2004)* **AQUALUNG LIVE** *(Eagle, 2005)* **LIVE AT MONTREUX 2003** *(Fuel 2000, 2007).*

Europe: GREAT BRITAIN

KING CRIMSON

Robert Fripp - *guitars, mellotron*, **Mike Giles, Ian Wallace, Andy McCulloch, Bill Bruford, Bill Rieflin, Jeremy Stacey, Pat Mastelotto, Gavin Harrison** - *drums*, **Peter Giles, Tony Levin, Trey Gunn** - *bass, stick*, **Greg Lake, Boz Burrell, John Wetton, Gordon Haskell** - *vocals, bass*, **Ian Mc Donald, Mel Collins** - *sax, flute, mellotron*, **David Cross**: *violin*, **Jamie Muir** - *percussion*, **Adrian Belew, Jakko Jakszyk** - *guitars, vocals*, **Pete Sinfield, Richard Palmer-James** - *lyrics*.

Creature of one genius **Robert Fripp**, only constant denominator in the articulated story of this band, which he simply defines <<*a way of doing things*>>. *In The Court Of The Crimson King*, October 12th 1969: an epic, fabulous, majestic, grotesque, romantic and visionary album, in one word, stunning. Although important influences can be traced (**The Beatles, The Moody Blues**, improvisation and jazz...), this is the turning point that still holds an ascendant over whoever ventures in any kind of Art-rock composition, defining a new style that, with its dark and tenebrous shades, gives a clean cut to the hopes of the smiley hippy generation. It finally marks the moment when European Rock conquers over the American sovereignty. An esoteric and Progressive portrait defined also by the apocalyptic cover: this is the first use ever of the mellotron combined to **Peter Sinfeld**'s alchemic lyrics and a structure that recalls the scheme of a symphonic concert. Their success was passed on mouth to mouth after their apparition as opening band in the famous **Rolling Stones** concert in Hyde Park on July 5th 1969, then the triumph and a year later a photocopy of the latter, *In The Wake Of Poseidon*, but still valuable and inspired. 1970 *Lizard* is a more complex progressive-jazz classical blend, with **Tippett**'s collaboration and **Fripp**'s orchestral direction inspired by the best **Gil Evans** and **Miles Davis**. A first phase ends with the airy *Islands*, which mixes with maturity European intellectual traditions to the Electronic language. In the '73 **Fripp** creates a second incarnation of the band with three mysterious Metal albums that redefine Art Rock and launch a signal into the future: with violinist **David Cross**, insane drummer **Jamie Muir** and two gigantic **Bill Bruford** and the late **John Wetton**, (who dies in 2017) and elaborates a stripped to the bone style in which he inserts the pictorial **Hendrix**-ian guitar playing on **Bartòk**'s quartet for arcs and **Stravinskji**'s barbarisms. Alongside another handful of parallel projects with **Eno, Gabriel, Bowie**, and also his Sufi and Frippetronics research, then **Fripp** moulds his third **Crimson**-ian Golem: it is the dawn of the 1980s when new wave triumphs and **King Crimson** go back to geometric and tight rhythms publishing *Discipline*, a web of sounds embellished by the ironic refinement of the guitar insertions. Ten years go by and the fourth epiphany materializes as a double trio recording the claustrophobic *Thrak*, a new **King Crimson** for a new millennium. They issue good level albums, a neverending flow of live performances, mini albums and experimental operations like **ProjeKcts**. Contextually **McDonald, Collins** and the **Giles** brothers reform the very first **King Crimson** (without **Fripp** and **Lake**) under the name of **21st Century Schizoid Band**, devoting to a pure and simple revival of 'another way of doing things' compared to **Fripp**'s projects. All of this convinces old **Bob Fripp** to renovate his 'court' once more with a new lineup engaging **Collins, Jakszyk, Levin** and three drummers (!): they begin a triumphal tour in 2014 playing a repertoire that covers all the different ages of this extraordinary band with great satisfaction of their audience.

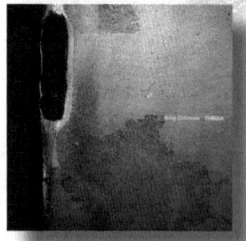

D.Z.

RECOMMENDED RECORDINGS:
IN THE COURT OF THE CRIMSON KING *(Island, 1969)* **IN THE WAKE OF POSEIDON** *(Island, 1970)* **LIZARD** *(Island, 1970)* **ISLANDS** *(Island, 1971)* **EARTHBOUND** *(live, Island, 1972)* **LARKS' TONGUES IN ASPIC** *(Island, 1973)* **STARLESS AND BIBLE BLACK** *(Island, 1974)* **RED** *(Island, 1974)* **USA** *(live, Island, 1975)* **DISCIPLINE** *(1981)* **BEAT** *(EG 1982)* **THREE OF A PERFECT PAIR** *(EG, 1984)* **THE GREAT DECEIVER** *(live, Virgin 1992)* **VROOOM** *(DGM, 1994)* **THRAK** *(DGM, 1995)* **THE CONSTRUKCTION OF LIGHT** *(DGM, 2000)* **HEAVY CONSTRUKCTION** *(live, DGM, 2000)* **HAPPY WITH WHAT YOU HAVE TO BE HAPPY WITH** *(DGM, 2002)* **THE POWER TO BELIEVE** *(DGM,2003)*. **LIVE AT THE ORPHEUM** *(DGM,2014)* **LIVE IN TORONTO** *(DGM,2015)* **RADICAL ACTION** *(Live CD-DVD - DGM,2016)* **LIVE IN CHICAGO** *(DGM,2017)* **MELTDOWN** *(DGM,2018)*.

Europe: GREAT BRITAIN

MARILLION

Derek William Dick (Fish) - *vocals e lyrics (1982/1988)*, **Steve Rothery** - *guitars*, **Mark Kelly** - *keyboards, vocals, programming*, **Pete Trewavas** - *bass, guitar, vocals*, **Mick Pointer** - *drums (1982/1983)*, **Steve Hogarth** - *vocals (1989/2014), guitar, percussion*, **Ian Mosley** - *drums, percussion (since 1984)*.

If after a decade from its birth, prog rock manages to come out of its sepulcre, this is above all thanks to a band called **Marillion**, (from Tolkien's Silmarillion), connecting them directly to the fables and the fantasy they borrowed. The band lead by **Fish** shows the courage and ability to reweave the threads shredded by the archangel **Gabriel** and is capable of starting over from the exact point in which the genre had been cut off. 1983 *Script for a Jester's Tear* is a first sublime album which can be considered a perfect bridge, with its beautiful songs, blooming as flowers freshly picked from the **Genesis** garden. The sweet and dilated atmospheres spread like honey over a bread of lyrics baked by **Fish**, an incredible stage performer and probably **Gabriel**'s true heir. "He Knows You Know", "The Web", "Garden Party", "Chelsea Monday" and "Forgotten Sons", with their seductive pace and almost liturgical outcome, make it an album to be hung high up in the sky of the whole progressive firmament.

In 1984 *Fugazi* is released and again is well above the average with tracks like "Emerald lies", "Punch and Judy" and, above all, the dynamic and cathartic "Assassing". Imperious and perfect rhythms with perturbing atmospheres add up to **Fish**'s prodigal voice making **Marillion**'s sound truly one of a kind. And nothing changes with *Misplaced Childhood* the following year, taking them to the top of the charts in half of Europe, thanks to two very particular songs like "Lavender" and sales' record-breaker "Kayleigh". Fascinating down to the album covers, all perfectly illustrated by painter **Mark Wilkinson**. In 1987 *Clutching at Straws*, about alcoholism, is still a good album even if smaller in comparison to its precedents. Then due to personal and artistic divergences, **Fish** abandons the group devoting to a prolific solo career.

The double live album, *The Thiewing Magpie*, is released in 1988 with a collection of the band's best moments. **Steve Hogarth**'s voice, however seductive, results diametrically opposite to that of **Fish**: whereas in medicine it is called a rejection crisis, here instead it brings the band to completely forget the past, undertaking a highway leading straight to an easy-listening Rock. Albums are good and still above average (*Season's End, Holidays In Eden*...). One last worth mentioning album is 1994's *Brave*, while the following projects do not seem to make it to the hall of fame and are either financed through early subscriptions online or with the downloading of songs from the Internet, sometimes even inviting fans to post their live videos on You Tube.
F.V.

DISCOGRAPHY (Collections and compilations not included):
SCRIPT FOR A JESTER'S TEAR *(EMI, 1983)* **FUGAZI** *(EMI, 1984)* **REAL TO REEL** *(EMI, 1984, live)* **MISPLACED CHILDHOOD** *(EMI, 1985)* **CLUTCHING AT STRAWS** *(EMI, 1987)* **THE THIEVING MAGPIE** *(EMI, 1988, double live)* **SEASONS END** *(EMI, 1989)* **HOLIDAYS IN EDEN** *(EMI, 1991)* **BRAVE** *(EMI, 1984)* **AFRAID OF SUNLIGHT** *(EMI, 1995)* **MADE AGAIN** *(Raw Power, 1996, live)* **THE STRANGE ENGINE** *(Castle Music, 1997)* **RADIATION** *(Raw Power, 1998)* **MARILLION.COM** *(Castle Music, 1999)* **ANORAKNOPHOBIA** *(EMI, 2001)* **ANORAK IN THE UK** *(EMI, 2002, doppio, live)* **BRAVE LIVE** *(Racket, 2002, live)* **MARBLES** *(Intact, 2004)* **POPULAR MUSIC** *(Racket, 2005, double live)* **MARBLES LIVE** *(Racket, 2005, live)* **MARBLES BY THE SEA** *(Racket, 2005, live)* **HAPPINESS IS THE ROAD** *(Intact, 2008)* **LESS IS MORE** *(Racket Records, 2009)* **SOUND CAN'T BE MADE** *(Racket Records, 2012)* **F.E.A.R.** *(EarMusic, 2017)*.

Europe: **GREAT BRITAIN**

THE MOODY BLUES

Ray Thomas - *Harmonica, flute, vocals,* **Graeme Edge** - *drums,* **John Lodge** - *bass,* **Mike Pinder, Patrick Moraz** - *keyboards,* **Justin Hayward** - *guitar.*

What is the name of the album capable of dividing the sea into Beat and Progressive Rock? Or better said, who gave birth (and when) to Prog between **The Beatles**'s *Sgt. Pepper Lonely Hearts Club Band* in 1967 and **King Crimson** with *In the Court of the Crimson King* two years later?
If we want to remain objective, we would certainly opt for the first without however forgetting the most precious and conclusive contribution of **The Moody Blues** (until then known for only one song, "Go Now") with the epic *Days of Future Passed* published that same year. Judged at first pompous, redundant and emphatic, the album (freely inspired by **Antonín Dvorák**'s Symphony n.9) was instead a challenging glove thrown, like a dam against the flow, in the face of music, where on one bank the cheap crop would grow while on the other side a new nourishment was preparing the life to begin, like a mill ready to bring fresh water and Classical influences to the crowd of groups to be.

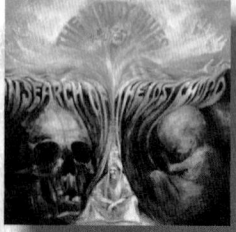

Days of Future Passed is endowed with beauty and extraordinary sweetness, flawless to this very day. Guided by **Mike Pinde**r's liquid and prolific Mellotron and graced by **Ray Thomas**' transverse flute, **The Moody Blues** exploit the orchestral sound in the best of possible ways and, under the direction of a professional like **Peter Knight**, they draw arabesques of unusual beauty until then unexplored. The beginning of "Nights in White Satin" with its painful recalling and continuous absences, seem to refer to Samuel Beckett's *Waiting for Godot*. But instead, unlike Godot, it arrives

when you less expect it, without knocking and it storms in with the full power of its seductive fragrance and with a dramatic stormy explosion. It goes as far as to nearly hurt.
From 1968 to 1972, they publish a rosary of incisions of great depth and amazing beauty such as *In Search of the Lost Chord, On the Threshold of a Dream, To Our Children's Children's Children, To Question of Balance, Every Good Boy Deserves Favour* and *Seventh Sojourn*. The very talented line-up counts among its

crew, besides **Pinder** and **Thomas**, musicians such as **Justin Hayward** and **John Lodge** (co-authors of the wonderful 1975 "Blue Jays") and of drummer **Graeme Edge**. Their compositional skills manage to maintain unaltered their symphonic and orchestral structure even when traveling in the more foreign territories of Rock, easily passing from a killer ballad ("Question") to the electric roots in "I'm Just a Singer (In a Rock'n'Roll Band)". Defined since their beginnings as a small traveling orchestra, they make it through the '70s and '80s with joys and pains, as well as some worrying defections (inauspicious that of **Michael Pinder**, replaced by ex-**Yes** keyboardist **Patrick Moraz**). The following albums, even if pleasant, result however abundantly unprovided of that elegant aura that made them famous.

F.V.

DISCOGRAPHY:

THE MAGNIFICENT MOODIES *(Decca, 1965)* **DAYS OF FUTURE PASSED** *(Deram, 1967)* **IN SEARCH OF THE LOST CHORD** *(Deram, 1968)* **ON THE THRESHOLD OF A DREAM** *(Deram, 1969)* **TO OUR CHILDREN'S CHILDREN'S CHILDREN** *(Deram, 1969)* **A QUESTION OF BALANCE** *(Deram, 1970)* **EVERY GOOD BOY DESERVES FAVOUR** *(Deram, 1971)* **SEVENTH SOJOURN** *(Deram, 1972)* **CAUGHT LIVE+5** *(Deram, 1977)* **OCTAVE** *(Deram, 1978)* **LONG DISTANCE VOYAGER** *(Deram, 1981)* **THE PRESENT** *(Deram, 1983)* **THE OTHER SIDE OF LIFE** *(Deram, 1986)* **SUR LA MER** *(Deram, 1988)* **KEYS OF KINGDOM** *(Deram, 1991)* **A NIGHT AT RED ROCK WITH THE COLORADO SYMPHONY ORCHESTRA** *(Deram, 1993)* **STRANGE TIMES** *(Deram, 1999)* **DECEMBER** *(Deram, 2003)*.

Europe: **GREAT BRITAIN**

NATIONAL HEALTH

Dave Stewart, Alan Gowen - *keyboards,* **Phil Miller** - *guitars,* **Neil Murray, John Greaves, Rick Biddulph** - *bass,* **Pip Pyle** - *drums,* **Jimmy Hastings, Paul Nieman, Phil Minton, Keith Thompson, Elton Dean, Annie Whitehead, Ted Emmett** - *horns,* **John Mitchell, Selwyn Baptiste** - *percussion,* **Georgie Born** - *cello,* **Amanda Parsons, Peter Blegvad, Richard Sinclair, Barbara Gaskin** - *vocals.*

Themes, compositional trends, stylistic attitudes, influences and resulting achievements have made artists of Prog the greatest anomalies in the history of Rock. Without mentioning the whole Canterbury situation. A 'thinking' musician like **Dave Stewart** is the living proof: preparation, study, research, coherence are his characteristics and more in general those of a whole generation of colleagues. **Stewart** was born in 1950 and at the age of only 18 he begins to plays the organ with **Steve Hillage, Clive Brooks** and **Mont Campbell** in a new born band called **Uriel** oscillating between acid-blues and strong influences coming from **Nice**. After **Hillage**'s exit it becomes the trio **Egg**, one of the first English avant-garde rock bands, publishing two albums and then breaking up. **Stewart** joins **Khan** where **Hillage** is already playing and in 1973 replaces **David Sinclair** in the early **Hatfield And The North** going from playing the organ to the electric piano, which will soon become his trademark. In the **HATN** he is the main composer and at the end of the project - after a tour with **Gong** - he is stimulated to continue on that eccentric and experimental path, in clear antithesis with the trends of the period. **Dave** addresses Gilgamesh's keyboardist **Alan Gowen**, whom which he had played with a couple of years before in **HATN**, with the idea of forming a sort of rock orchestra with a double keyboard and double partitions. They recruit an wide group of musicians (among which **Bill Bruford, Phil Miller, Mont Campbell**) and call themselves the **National Health**. The band performs live but times change and the attentions of the music industry had diverted towards Punk. Labels turned their backs to the very Rock bands they had contributed to bring to success and as a reaction, many initiatives are born such as Rock In Opposition. **NH** also pay for certain changes in line-up (**Pyle** replaces **Bruford**; **Neil Murray** arrives from Gilgamesh only to be replaced by **Greaves** from **Henry Cow**) finding themselves with a thinner group for the recording of their debut self-titled album, then published a year later by Affinity (owned by label Charly). **National Health** is a good project and releases at the end of that same year *Of Queues And Cures*. Both homogeneous albums have a circle-like pattern recalling the opening theme in the end, and are fruit of an ambitious formation with very clear ideas, that looked towards the Classical world absorbing its dynamics, organicity and completeness. This is the last act of the Great Canterbury Saga and the **NH** propose themselves as a more articulated version of the **HATN**, with catchy and ironic loose moments, even if the composition is of a more meditated jazz-rock, with complex rhythmic elaborations. If the tracks are mainly fruit of **Stewart** refined pen, we find **Miller** not simply reduced to **Gowen**'s mere substitute, but playing his guitar in a non conventional sophisticated way. It is a happy combination of Art-rock and Jazz, that doesn't bend on any side and convinces both for the collective and solo partitions. **NH** succeed in performing live with regularity (**Gowen** returns in '79) but after the Scandinavian concerts at the beginning of the 80ies the band breaks up. **Stewart** plays in **Bruford**'s solo albums and forms the **Rapid Eye Movement** with whom he hits the charts in October of 1981 also thanks to their cover of "It's My Party" with **Barbara Gaskin**. As a touching tribute to Alan Gowen, who dies by leukemia that year, **Stewart** and **Miller** rearrange the old material written by keyboardist before his departure under the old band's name, gathering in the album *D.S. Al Coda* many guests like **Richard Sinclair, Elton Dean, Annie Whitehead** and it results to be a good technological evolution of the **NH** sound. **D.Z.**

DISCOGRAPHY:
NATIONAL HEALTH *(Affinity 1978)* **OF QUEUES AND CURES** *(Charly 1978)* **D.S. AL CODA** *(Europa 1982)* **MISSING PIECES** *(East Side Digital 1996)* **PLAYTIME** *(Digital 2001).*

Europe: GREAT BRITAIN

THE NICE

Brian Davidson – *drums, percussions,*
Keith Emerson – *keyboards,*
Lee Jackson – *guitars, bass, vocals,*
David O'List - *guitar, horns, vocals.*

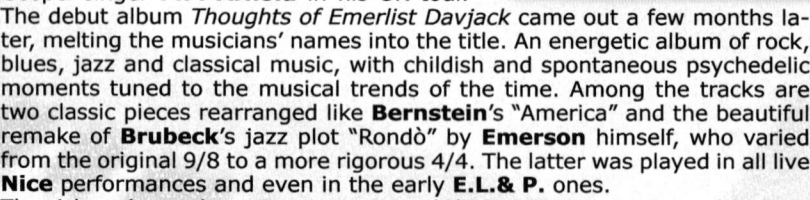

The band starts off in 1967 with an experience as supporter group for the Soul & Gospel singer **P.P. Arnold** in his UK tour.

The debut album *Thoughts of Emerlist Davjack* came out a few months later, melting the musicians' names into the title. An energetic album of rock, blues, jazz and classical music, with childish and spontaneous psychedelic moments tuned to the musical trends of the time. Among the tracks are two classic pieces rearranged like **Bernstein**'s "America" and the beautiful remake of **Brubeck**'s jazz plot "Rondò" by **Emerson** himself, who varied from the original 9/8 to a more rigorous 4/4. The latter was played in all live **Nice** performances and even in the early **E.L.& P.** ones.
The rich and complex arrangements and this mixing genres in such an unlabeling way, upset the most orthodox critics, but those were the years of the innovations that led shortly to the greatest rock and prog works ever.

During a concert at the Royal Albert Hall in London, after the execution of particularly roughly played "America", **Emerson** burned the stars and strips flag in front of the American consul, leading him to be banned from this country till 1992.
When beginning to record their second album *Ars Longa Vita Brevis* in 1968, perhaps not at the technical height of the others or perhaps overpowered by **Emerson**'s charisma, guitarist **O'List** leaves the band (even **Steve Howe**, then with **Yes**, auditioned as a replacement). But the idea was of carrying on without him as a keyboard-lead trio. **Emerson** became

officially the leader as well as one of the most famous keyboardists in the history of rock. This second album results more organic and coherent. While **Emerson**'s technical abilities shine through the arrangements of some Classical themes, here he completely distorts, emphasizes or reduces **Sibelius** and **Bach** to a minimum, mixing Dada to experimental parts and Psychedelic with traces of Beat, showing how this could be the new musical trend.

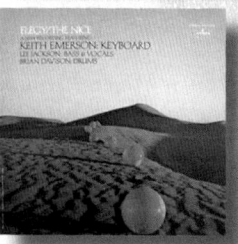

A third album *Nice* was recorded half live and half in the studio, containing also a longer and revised version of **Bob Dylan**'s "She Belongs to Me". Other material was published posthumous the group's disbandment, and **Emerson** already playing in the famous trio with **Lake** and **Palmer**, while **Davidson** and **Jackson** formed with **Patrick Moraz** (later with **Yes** and **The Moody Blues**) the band **Refugee**. To be mentioned *Elegy*, a gathering of unpublished tracks rearranged in different versions, *Five Bridges*, a live album with orchestra and *Vivacitas*, another good live performance recorded in 2002 in Glasgow with the band reunited just for the occasion.   **R.V.**

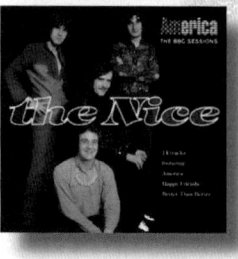

DISCOGRAPHY:
THE THOUGHTS OF EMERLIST DAVJACK *(Immediate, 1967)* **ARS LONGA VITA BREVIS** *(Immediate, 1968)* **NICE / EVERYTHING AS NICE AS MOTHER MAKES IT** *(Immediate, 1969)* **FIVE BRIDGES** *(Charisma, 1970)* **ELEGY** *(Charisma, 1971)* **VIVACITAS** *(Sanctuary, 2004)*.

Europe: GREAT BRITAIN

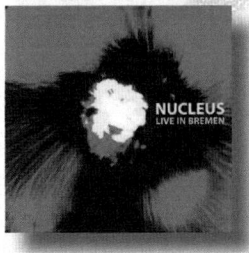

NUCLEUS

Ian Carr - *trumpet, flugelhorn, electric piano,* **Karl Jenkins** - *oboe, sax, electric piano, piano,* **Brian Smith, Kenny Wheeler, Tony Roberts, Tony Coe, Bob Bertles, Phil Todd, Harry Beckett** - *horns,* **Chris Spedding, Allan Holdsworth, Jocelyn Pitchen, Ken Shaw, Mark Wood** - *guitar,* **Jeff Clyne, Ron Matthewson, Roy Babbington, Roger Sutton, Billy Christian, Dill Katz, Mo Foster, Steve Berry, Tony Levin** - *bass, contrabass,* **John Marshall, Clive Thacker, Bryan Spring, Roger Sellers** - *drums,* **Chris Karan, Trevor Tomkins, Aureo De Souza, Richard Burgess, Chris Fletcher** - *percussion,* **Keith Winter, Paddy Kingsland, Geoff Castles, Neil Ardley** - *synthesizers,* **Dave McRae, Gordon Beck** - *electric piano,* **John Taylor** - *organ,* **Norma Winstone, Kieran White, Joy Yates** - *vocals.*

The geographic proximity and a certain affinity with **Soft Machine** places them as part of the Canterbury sound. As a matter of fact their contribution to the '70s (although not in a famous way, probably due to the difficulty of labeling them) is essential as they are the most loyal and rigorous interpreters of the Electric Jazz played with a **Davis**-styled matrix. It is not by chance that the master mind of this project, **Ian Carr** (born in 1933), is also **Miles Davis**'s biographer. And just like **Miles**' line-ups at the end of the '60, **Nucleus** acted like a gym for the training of formidable talents such as **Chris Spedding**, **Allan Holdsworth**, **Kenny Wheeler** and many others. A first album immediately materializes after the epic release of *Bitches Brew*, but in some way **Nucleus** anticipate the times: just before the **Davis** diaspora gives birth to **Return To Forever**, **Mahavishnu Orchestra** and **Headhunters**, and before the debut of **Weather Report**, **Carr** manages an elaborate repertoire worthy of notice: in the early '60 he is studying in Newcastle and plays his trumpet with the **Emcees Five**; later he goes to London and first creates the **Rendell-Carr Quintet** and finally, in 1969, **Nucleus**. *Elastic Rock* - a self explanatory title! - clearly follows the new direction music was taking and is carried out proudly by Vertigo. After winning the Montreux Jazz Festival, their performance in Newport and the addition of other musicians make **Nucleus** an open group. **Carr** introduces new ideas in the two following albums, also very appreciated across borders (**Area** often recognize being inspired by them). If **Davis**' shamanic music evokes the heart of Africa and is soaked in Funk, **Carr** manages a **European** interpretation, more poised and cultured, less overwhelming but never deprived of energy and vitality, with an impeccable organization of the horn section. The dynamic jazz-rock of the band is not eccentric as **Matching Mole** or **Hatfield And The North**, but closer to a post-**Wyatt Soft Machine** which **Jenkins** and **Marshall** decide to join. The loss of the two core members starts a crisis to which **Carr** reacts composing the formidable *Belladonna* and the suite *Labyrinth*, both audacious experiments of progressive-fusion. In the mid '70s they open up to funk and soul but seem to show a loss of inspiration. In '77 **Carr** also joins **Jon Hiseman**, **Barbara Thompson** and **Charlie Mariano** playing in the **United Jazz & Rock Ensemble**, continuing his activity of writing about jazz (already in '73 he published the prestigious *Music Outside*). He pursues leading **Nucleus** up to the early '80ies, with top class songwriting, never too low or loud or excessive. Lately some live performances have been published helping younger people get to know this precious and fundamental band. **D.Z.**

DISCOGRAPHY:
ELASTIC ROCK *(Vertigo 1970)* **WE'LL TALK ABOUT IT LATER** *(Vertigo 1970)* **IAN CARR WITH NUCLEUS: SOLAR PLEXUS** *(Vertigo 1971)* **IAN CARR: BELLADONNA** *(Vertigo 1972)* **LABYRINTH** *(Vertigo 1973)* **ROOTS** *(Vertigo 1973)* **UNDER THE SUN** *(Vertigo 1974)* **SNAKESHIPS ETCETERA** *(Vertigo 1975)* **ALLEYCAT** *(Vertigo 1975)* **IN FLAGRANTI DELICTO** *(Capitol 1977)* **OUT OF THE LONG DARK** *(Capitol 1979)* **AWAKENING** *(Mood 1980)* **IAN CARR'S NUCLEUS: LIVE AT THE THEATERHAUS** *(Mood 1985)* **IAN CARR FEAT. NUCLEUS: OLD HEARTLAND** *(EMI 1988)* **LIVE IN BREMEN** *(Cuneiform 2003)* **THE PRETTY REDHEAD** *(Hux 2003)* **HEMISPHERES** *(Hux 2006)* **UK TOUR '76** *(MLP 2006)*

Europe: GREAT BRITAIN

MIKE OLDFIELD

English multi-instrumentalist endowed with an almost infinite talent, his production is as long as a phone book, owing a big part (if not all) of his popularity to the extraordinary debut album *Tubular Bells*, launched by Virgin (the mythical label founded by future multi-millionaire **Richard Branson**), which literally traced the tracks that divide classic rock and all the other musical contaminations to come. Published right in the middle of Prog's reign (May 1973), it can be considered as one of the fundamental moments of the entire music industry. The album discloses like a shell and after gathering all the sounds and moods of the universe, it shatters, analyzes, counts, divides and recomposes them. **Oldfield** plays about ten instruments in it also thanks to a wise study of layers, making *Tubular Bells* a sonorous collage of unusual beauty, dreamy and therapeutic, a true corollary of emotions. The score was used as the introduction for a film by **William Friedkin**, *The Exorcist* helping it stay at the top of the charts for 247 weeks. This inspires another symphonic project, *The Orchestral Tubular Bells* produced by **David Bedford**, a talented classical musician **Oldfield** played with in **Whole World** created by ex-Soft Machine guitarist **Kevin Ayers**.
The following year the eclectic and very seductive *Hergest Ridge* does not however seem to possess the same charm of its predecessor. On a different level entirely results *Ommadawn*, again another long suite that, despite a lukewarm reception from the critics, proves itself able of showing and elaborating **Oldfield**'s elasticity and extraordinary abilities in using ethnic music: the neverending, perturbing and obsessive tribal singing, which

closes the first part of the album, seems to be the soundtrack of a dream that can't wait to fly over the African sands. In 1978 the celestial and ethereal *Incantations* is released with the use of incredible voices such as **Maddy Prior** from **Steeleye Span** and his sister **Sally Oldfield**, and female choirs that poker-dot the composition. Unfortunately this album also closes the circle opened with *Tubular Bells*. From *Platinum* onward **Oldfield** starts to grow farther apart from conceptual music, bending more on a commercial and catchy trend like **QE2** and **Crises**.
A slight sign of redemption seemed to be *The Killing Fields* (a beautiful score to the tragedy of the Cambodian people in the film by Roland Joffé), but the following years are almost entirely devoted to re-proposing live versions of *Tubular Bells* and some other rare gems (*Islands*, *The Songs of Distant Earth*, *Music of the Spheres*) that nevertheless carry the embarrassing aftertaste of a heated soup nearly gone sour. **F.V.**

DISCOGRAPHY (Compilations not included):

TUBULAR BELLS (Virgin, 1973) **HERGEST RIDGE** (Virgin, 1974) **THE ORCHESTRAL TUBULAR BELLS** (Virgin, 1975) **OMMADAWN** (Virgin, 1975) **INCANTATIONS** (Virgin, 1978) **EXPOSED** (Virgin, 1979) **PLATINUM** (Virgin, 1979) **IMPRESSIONS** (Virgin, 1979) **AIRBORN** (Virgin, 1980) **QE2** (Virgin, 1980) **MUSIC WONDERLAND** (Virgin, 1980) **EPISODES** (Virgin, 1981) **FIVE MILES OUT** (Virgin, 1982) **CRISES** (Virgin, 1983); **DISCOVERY** (Virgin, 1984) **THE KILLING FIELDS** (Virgin, 1984) **ISLANDS** (Virgin, 1987) **EARTH MOVING** (Virgin, 1989) **AMAROK** (Virgin, 1990) **HEAVEN'S OPEN** (Virgin, 1991) **TUBULAR BELLS II** (Warner, 1992) **ELEMENTS** (Warner, 1993) **THE SONGS OF DISTANT EARTH** (1994) **VOYAGER** (Warner, 1996) **TUBULAR BELLS III** (Warner, 1998) **GUITARS** (Warner, 1999) **THE MILLENNIUM BELL** (Warner, 1999) **TRES LUNAS** (WEA, 2002) **TUBULAR BELLS 2003** (Warner, 2003) **LIGHT & SHADE** (Mercury, 2005) **MUSIC OF THE SPHERES** (Universal classic, 2008) **MAN ON THE ROCKS** (Universal classic, 2014) **RETURN TO OMMADAWN** (Universal classic, 2017).

Europe: GREAT BRITAIN

ANTHONY PHILLIPS

A certain stage-phobia and an aversion to the music business, pushes guitarist **Anthony Phillips** to leave **Genesis** after recording *Trespass* in 1970. This doesn't prevent his soloist career, far from the spotlights yet prolific and full of gracious and touching albums. *The Geese & the Ghost* (1977) is probably still the most praised with its Pastoral spirit inspired by the bucolic sounds coming from his **Genesis** past. Fairy-tale atmospheres, delicate ballads and the medieval sounds of "Henry: Portraits from Tudor Times" (with ample use of classical instruments and, among the others, the participation of **Phil Collins** and **Mike Rutherford**) show his talent as a musician of great class.

Wise After the Event is a bit more electric but still good even if it slightly results less inspired than the predecessor. The following step is represented by the first of a series of volumes entitled *Private Parts and Pieces*, in which Ant often inserts compositions from the past, creating juicy guitar or piano solos. From 1979 with the elegant Pop-Rock *Sides*, he begins to explore different genres going from the experimentation and electronics of *1984*, to the classical or new age of *Private Parts and Pieces*, to the unsuccessful attempt of *Invisible Men*.

1988 sees the sublime *Tarka* (in collaboration with **Harry Williamson**) make its way with its seductive acoustic guitars playing up to developing in orchestral movements, often driven by the horns or the string section. It is an exceptional album that, perhaps more than any other, proves his extraordinary skills in composition along with his depth as a musician. He cannot be defined any longer just as **Genesis**' ex-guitarist and as a matter of fact in some collaborations with **Guillermo Cazenave** and **Mike Rutherford**, he is also an exquisite keyboardist.

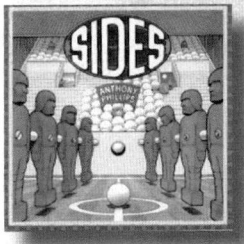

Other two albums worthy of mention are what we many consider to be his masterpiece, *Slow Dance*, a suite built over melodies that give the shivers, with hints of Classical music and the correct pinch of Electronics, and "Gypsy Suite" where acoustic guitars are the absolute protagonists. Another series of albums under the title *Missing Links* (the last issued in 2009) contain recordings of TV broadcasts and unpublished tracks, as well as other material (in particular the one published on *The Archive Collection vol.1* containing "F Sharp", an embryonic version of "The Musical Box" confirming once more how much **Phillips** contributed to the first **Genesis**. Recently he will appear as a special guest in **Steve** (his successor in **Genesis**!) and **John Hackett**'s new album.   G.D.S.

DISCOGRAPHY:

THE GEESE & THE GHOST *(1977, Hit & Run)* **WISE AFTER THE EVENT** *(1978, Arista)* **PRIVATE PARTS AND PIECES** *(1978, Arista)* **SIDES** *(1979, Passport Records)* **PRIVATE PARTS AND PIECES II – BACK TO THE PAVILION** *(1980, Passport Records)* **1984** *(1981, RCA)* **PRIVATE PARTS AND PIECES III – ANTIQUES** *(1982, Passport Records)* **INVISIBLE MEN** *(1983, Passport Records)* **PRIVATE PARS AND PIECES IV – A CATCH AT THE TABLES** *(1984, Passport Records)* **PRIVATE PARTS AND PIECES V – TWELVE** *(1984, Passport Records)* **PRIVATE PARTS AND PIECES VI – IVORY MOON** *(1986, Passport Records)* **PRIVATE PARTS AND PIECES VII – SLOW WAVES SOFT STARS** *(1987, Audion Records)* **TARKA** *(with Harry Williamson, 1988, Prt Records)* **FINGER PAINTING (Missing Links vol. 1)** *(1989, Occasional Records)* **SLOW DANCE** *(1990, Virgin)* **PRIVATE PARTS AND PIECES VIII – NEW ENGLAND** *(1992, Virgin)* **MISSING LINKS VOL. 2 – THE SKY ROAD** *(1994, Brainworks)* **SAIL THE WORLD** *(1994, Resurgence Records)* **GYPSY SUITE** *(with Harry Williamson, 1995, Voiceprint)* **THE LIVING ROOM CONCERT** *(1995, Voiceprint)* **THE MEADOWS OF ENGLEWOOD** *(with Guillermo Cazenave, 1996, Astral Records)* **PRIVATE PARTS AND PIECES IX – DRAGONFLY DREAMS** *(1996, Blueprint)* **MISSING LINKS VOL. 3 – TIME & TIDE** *(with Joji Hirota, 1997, Blueprint)* **LIVE RADIO SESSIONS** *(with Guillermo Cazenave (1998, Discmedi Blau)* **THE ARCHIVE COLLECTION VOL. 1** *(1998, Blueprint)* **PRIVATE PARTS AND PIECES X – SOIRÉE** *(1999, Blueprint)* **RADIO CLYDE** *(2003, Blueprint)* **THE ARCHIVE COLLECTION VOL. 2** *(2004, Blueprint)* **FIELD DAY** *(2005, Blueprint)* **WILDLIFE** *(with Joji Hirota, 2008, Voiceprint)* **PATHWAYS AND PROMENADES - MISSING LINKS VOL. 4** *(2009, Voiceprint)* **PRIVATE PARTS & PIECES XI: CITY OF DREAMS** *(2012, Voiceprint)* **STRINGS OF LIGHT** *(2019, Esoteric Antenna).*

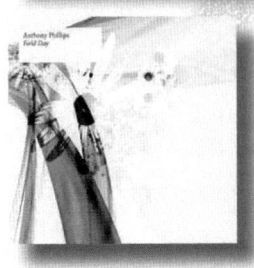

Europe: GREAT BRITAIN

PINK FLOYD

Syd Barrett - *guitar, vocals* (1967-1968)
David Gilmour - *guitar, vocals,*
Nick Mason - *drums,*
Roger Waters - *bass, vocals*
Richard Wright - *keyboards, vocals.*

Pink Floyd's long artistic career has lived three separate moments: the first and shortest one was characterized by *The Piper at the Gates of Dawn*, almost entirely written by **Syd Barrett** and universally recognized as the pillar of English Psychedelia. The forced exit of **Barrett** due to his state of health exacerbated by the use of drugs, inaugurated a second artistic moment, the longest and most meaningful, and perhaps the true birth of a Progressive **Pink Floyd**: with *A Saucerful of Secrets* they begin a real collective project that characterizes the band up to the album *Animals* nine years later. In fact *More* (score for a film by **Barbet Schroeder**) and *Ummagumma*, still maintaining the clear Psychedelic elements, are premonition of a more elaborate and rich debate contained in the two masterpieces *Atom Heart Mother* (with the aid of a real orchestra and a symphonic choir) and the more personal *Meddle* that contains the beautiful suite "Echoes". The band is the preferred icon of the Flower Power movement and of all LSD based parties (even if the musicians take their distance). They are summoned to compose scores like *Obscured by Clouds* (for **Schroeder**, 1972) and *Zabriskie Point* (for **Michelangelo Antonioni**, 1970) because of this. But they have something else in mind. In 1973 their absolute masterpiece *The Dark Side of the Moon* is released as a jewel of sonorous perfection, a fascinating collection of songs that will capture the public of not just that generation. Success however is always an issue. The last truly balanced album is *Wish You Were Here* (1975), a tribute to **Barrett**. Then gradually **Roger Waters** will start to prevail and the aforementioned *Animals* of 1977 is the first fruit of this hegemony.
Pink Floyd are also one of the only bands to have a unique and inimitable stage apparatus. The apotheosis is the live performance of *The Wall* in 1979, recorded in a double album of planetary success, where a wall of white bricks would gradually cover the band from sight during a concert, with films and huge dancing dolls created by **Gerald Scarfe**. The songs are written almost entirely by **Waters** except for 3 tracks which he wrote together with **David Gilmour**. Keyboardist **Richard Wright** cannot deal with the despotic situation anymore and abandons the band at the end of the tour. The album becomes a film directed by **Alan Parker** in 1982, just before another album written again by **Waters**, *The Final Cut*, where he still speaks of war. At this point the band's disapproval is at its peak and **Waters** decides to leave. **Wright** returns and with **David Gilmour** and **Nick Mason** they continue the project, not without starting their very own war in court, which **Waters** will lose.
Another two albums and relative titanic tours will take place: *A Momentary Lapse of Reason* and *The Division Bell* which bring the band back twenty years. Some other good works and recorded live collections of their very best are published and finally in July 2005 the reconciliation with **Waters** for the concert *Live 8* on stage in London. **Wright** dies in September 2008, two years after the departed but unforgotten **Barrett**.
Surprisingly, twenty years after their last studio album, a new record is released, *The Endless River*, an instrumental work containing tracks assembled from the 1993 sessions, the last with **Wright** still playing in the band.
M.G.

DISCOGRAPHY (Compilations not included):
THE PIPER AT THE GATES OF DAWN *(Columbia, 1967)* **A SAUCERFUL OF SECRETS** *(Columbia, 1968)* **MORE** *(Columbia, 1969)* **UMMAGUMMA** *(Harvest, 1969)* **ATOM HEART MOTHER** *(Harvest, 1970)* **MEDDLE** *(Harvest, 1971)* **OBSCURED BY CLOUDS** *(Harvest, 1972)* **THE DARK SIDE OF THE MOON** *(Harvest, 1973)* **WISH YOU WERE HERE** *(Harvest, 1975)* **ANIMALS** *(Harvest, 1977)* **THE WALL** *(Harvest, 1979)* **THE FINAL CUT** *(Harvest, 1983)* **A MOMENTARY LAPSE OF REASON** *(EMI, 1987)* **DELICATE SOUND OF THUNDER (Live)** *(EMI, 1988)* **THE DIVISION BELL** *(EMI, 1994)* **PULSE (Live)** *(EMI, 1995)* **IS THERE ANYBODY OUT THERE? (the Wall Live 1980-81)** *(EMI, 2000)*. **THE ENDLESS RIVER** *(Parlophone, 2014)*.

Europe: GREAT BRITAIN

PROCOL HARUM

Gary Brooker - *piano, vocals,* **Barry B.J. Wilson** - *drums,* **David Knights, Alan Cartwright** - *bass,* **Matthew Fisher, Chris Copping** - *keyboards,* **Robin Trower** - *guitar,* **Keith Reid** - *lyrics.*

Fundamental group without which, with every probability, the Progressive Rock generator would never have been activated. **Procol Harum** managed to capitalize and to mix symphonic music with the most seductive side of rock, creating legions of followers. "Seven Stones", from **Genesis**' album *Nursery Cryme*, could be seen as just an example of how their influence inspired and can be viewed as the point of astral conjunction between **Gary Brooker**'s golden phase and that to come with **Peter Gabriel**.
The world famous "A Whiter Shade of Pale" is a composition cleverly structured upon a harmonic turn drawn from the "Secondo Movimento dell'Aria sulla Quarta Corda" (Suite for Orchestra n. 3 BWV 1068 by **Johann Sebastian Bach**). **Keith Reid**'s visionary and highly poetic lyrics are accompanied by both piano and Hammond organ playing arrangements by **Brooker**. The song was recorded in a studio thanks to the contribution of **Matthew Fisher** and other capable session-men. Practically forced by this success, **Brooker** is compelled to create the first line-up of the band composed by the already quoted **Fisher** and **Reid**, **Ray Royer**, **David Knights** and drummers **Bobby Harrison** and **Bill Eyden**. After only a few months they release another hit single "Homburg", with great atmosphere and permeated by atypical and decadent lyrics. The band which adapted itself around the historical trio (**Brooker-Reid-Fisher**), assumes a greater dynamism with the entry of guitarist **Robin Trower** and drummer **B.J. Wilson**. The choice to eliminate from their first real album "A Whiter Shade of Pale" (instead included in the American edition) creates a rather hybrid and embarrassing situation, since at the time LPs were mainly composed by songs, usually of success, gathered randomly.

The following year the album *Shine on Brightly* is published, and though it does not achieve the magnificence of their debut, it maintains all the same characteristics intact and, for some verses, it results to be even more innovative especially in the splendid suite "In Held Twas in I", a classical incursion structured in 5 movements. The title track "Shine on Brightly", is also another great song based on Classical and Rock music and in order to contain the numerous versions (which at least in Italy were more than their sales), **Procol Harum** make their own Italian version called "Il tuo diamante".

In 1969 the melancholy album *A Salty Dog* is recorded, containing the homonym song which becomes one of their favourites, played in all concerts. The following works are decidedly of less importance and take them away from the charts they had gotten so used to be on top of, with their planetary first success. The crisis becomes irreversible with the abandonment of **Fisher** and **Knights**. After the disappointing *Home*, **Robin Trower** momentarily takes the lead producing *Broken Barricades*, a tough album, very distant from the original style of the band confusing the fans.

To have another great album it is necessary to wait for the year 1972 when *Live with the Edmonton Symphony Orchestra* comes to life, a project that, thanks to the use of a band plus a symphonic orchestra, re-lights their popularity. Chronologically their last, great album is *Grand Hotel*, 1973, streaked by such decadent melancholy to almost result tragical.

F.V.

DISCOGRAPHY (Compilations not included):
PROCOL HARUM *(Regal Zonophone/Deram Records, 1967)* **SHINE ON BRIGHTLY** *(Regal Zonophone/A&M, 1968)* **A SALTY DOG** *(Regal Zonophone/A&M, 1969)* **HOME** *(Regal Zonophone/A&M, 1970)* **BROKEN BARRICADES** *(Island Records/Chrysalis, 1971)* **PROCOL HARUM LIVE WITH THE EDMONTON SYMPHONY ORCHESTRA** *(Island Records/Chrysalis, 1972)* **GRAND HOTEL** *(Chrysalis, 1973)* **EXOTIC BIRDS AND FRUIT** *(Chrysalis, 1974)* **PROCOL'S NINTH** *(Chrysalis, 1975)* **ROCK ROOTS** *(Cube Records, 1976)* **SOMETHING MAGIC** *(Chrysalis, 1977)* **THE PRODIGAL STRANGER** *(RCA, 1991)* **THE LONG GOODBYE** *(RCA, 1995)* **THE WELL'S ON FIRE** *(Eagle, 2003)*.

Europe: **GREAT BRITAIN**

RENAISSANCE

***Renaissance 1:* Jim McCarty** - *drums, percussion, vocals,* **Keith Relf** - *vocals, guitar,* **Jane Relf** - *vocals,* **John Hawken** - *piano, keyboards,* **Louis Cennamo** - *bass.*

***Renaissance 2:* Michael Dunford** - *guitars, vocals,* **John Tout** - *keyboards, vocals,* **Jon Camp** - *bass, cello, vocals,* **Terry Sullivan** - *drums, percussion, vocals,* **Annie Haslam** - *vocals,* **Stephanie Adlington** - *vocals,* **Phil Mulford** - *bass,* **Dave Dowle** - *drums,* **Stuart Bradbury** - *guitar,* **Andy Spillar** - *keyboards,* **Mickey Simmonds** - *keyboards,* **Rave Tesar** - *keyboards,* **David Keyes** - *bass.*

Born from the cinders of the **Yardbirds, the Renaissance** start out with **JimMcCarty, Keith Relf**, his sister **Jane, John Hawken** and **Louis Cennamo** recording refined albums (*Renaissance* and *Illusion*) characterized by an elegant romantic Pop contaminated by Classical, Jazz and Folk music. After an unbelievable series of circumstances that push them to make many changes, by 1972 the line-up is completely different, based on the quintet **Michael Dunford, John Tout, Jon Camp, Terry Sullivan** and the divine **Annie Haslam**, one of the most gifted singers in the history of rock, both for vocal extension and her incredible sweetness of tone.

Between '72 and '75 enchanting albums are recorded such as *Prologue, Ashes are Burning* (perhaps the best of this period), *Turn of the Cards* and *Scheherazade and other Stories*, all containing a very elevated classical component to their prog. Thus the music becomes very resonant, artfully guided by the keyboards (often accompanied by an orchestra) and by **Haslam**'s acute notes, without ever losing the feeling brought by delicate melodies and passages close to folk. The live performance *Live at Carnegie Hall* precedes their best album, *Novella*, a persuasive Symphonic Rock with the presence of a never intrusive orchestra and a series of spectacular majestic compositions, with marvelous dynamics.

A Song for All Seasons is their last great album. The style remains the usual one but the songs are shorter and a tendency toward an easy-listening Pop is sensed throughout. The decrease in quality becomes clearer in the following works, that contain shallow sounds that don't properly convince the public. The band has no signed contract and disappears in 1987 after recording a few acoustic concerts that will be published only years after as *Unplugged Live at the Academy of Music*. 1994 sees a come back under the name **Annie Haslam's Renaissance** with *Blessing in Disguise* and *The Other Woman* and **Dunford's Renaissance** used by **Dunford** together with singer **Stephanie Adlington**. Both albums are characterized by an elegant Pop that doesn't really make a hit. A couple of cds containing rearrangements of old classics or unpublished material are issued and in 2000. **Haslam** and **Dunford** get back together recording first the interesting *Tuscany* and then the beautiful live performance *In The Land of the Rising Sun*. **Dunford** dies in 2013 leaving all the future of **Renaissance** to **Haslam** alone who seems to want to continue. **G.D.S.**

DISCOGRAPHY:

RENAISSANCE *(1969, Island)* **ILLUSION** *(1971, Island)* **PROLOGUE** *(1972, Sovereign/EMI)* **ASHES ARE BURNING** *(1973, Sovereign/EMI)* **TURN OF THE CARDS** *(1974, Btm)* **SCHEHERAZADE AND OTHER STORIES** *(1975, Btm)* **LIVE AT CARNEGIE HALL** *(1976, Btm)* **NOVELLA** *(1977, Sire/Warner Bros)* **A SONG FOR ALL SEASONS** *(1978, Sire/Warner Bros)* **AZURE D'OR** *(1979, Sire/Warner Bros)* **CAMERA CAMERA** *(1981, Irs)* **TIME LINE** *(1993, Irs/A&M)* **THE OTHER WOMAN** *(1995, Htd)* **OCEAN GYPSY** *(1997, Htd)* **SONGS FROM RENAISSANCE DAYS** *(1997, Htd)* **LIVE AT THE ROYAL ALBERT HALL PART ONE** *(1997, King Biscuit Flower Hour)* **LIVE AT THE ROYAL ALBERT HALL PART TWO** *(1997, King Biscuit Flower Hour)* **BBC SESSIONS** *(1999, Wounded Bird)* **TUSCANY** *(2000, Toshiba/EMI)* **UNPLUGGED LIVE AT THE ACADEMY OF MUSIC** *(2000, Mooncrest)* **CAN YOU HEAR ME** *(2001, Disky)* **MOTHER RUSSIA** *(2002, Disky)* **IN THE LAND OF THE RISING SUN** *(2002, Giant Electric Pea)* **BRITISH TOUR '76** *(2006, Major League Productions).*

Europe: **GREAT BRITAIN**

SOFT MACHINE

Mike Ratledge - *keyboards*, **Robert Wyatt** - *drums, vocals*, **Kevin Ayers** - *guitar, bass, vocals*, **Daevid Allen**- *guitar, bass*, **Hugh Hopper** - *bass, vocals*, **Elton Dean, Theo Travis** - *horns* **John Marshall** - *drums*, **Karl Jenkins** - *horns*, **Roy Babbington** - *guitar, bass*, **Allan Holdsworth** - *guitar*, **John Etheridge** - *guitar*.

In conjunction with the Beat Generation, Swingin' London's artistic temptations, Jazz and the counterculture, a new Rock genre and the '900's European Avant-garde, **Soft Machine** are among the most influential names of the late '60. A sound lab considered the fulcrum of what will be defined as the Canterbury scene. The placid English panorama is revived when **Daevid Allen**, an odd Australian beatnik, fond of poetry, LSD and of tape-loops, arrives: with **Robert Wyatt** and **Hugh Hopper** he founds the **Daevid Allen Trio** then, in 1964 **The Wilde Flowers** that breakup to give birth in the August of 1966 to the **Soft Machine**, a name derived from **William Burroughs**' novel of 1961. The quartet formed by **Allen, Wyatt, Mike Ratledge** and **Kevin Ayers** creates a traversal music, in unstable balance between Free Jazz, poetry reading, Dadaism and Acid-Pop, fully fitting a heterodox style, distant from the capricious Psychedelia of their many colleagues.

After a formidable apprenticeship on the stages of London's underground and an American tour with **Jimi Hendrix**, they release their first two albums between 1968 and 1969, probably the best European answer to **Zappa & The Mothers**. The first LP is unexpectedly successful in the USA and few months later the second beats it. **Hopper** replaces **Ayers** marking the entry of great jazz influences and of a certain aleatoric music, in an unpredictable and eccentric album, that reveals the difference from **Wyatt**'s spontaneous and grotesque tendency and the rigorous musical research of **Ratledge**, still both being complementary to one another.

Keith Tippett's example of a horn section (**Elton Dean, Dobson, Evans, Charig**), helps them define their own sound through **Ratledge**'s incisive Lowrey organ, **Hopper**'s hypnotic fuzz bass, **Wyatt**'s hard drumming and nonsense singing, achieving this unique balance in the ambitious 1970 album *Third*. It becomes the maximum expression of the band, one of the highest moments of the '70: a superb double album - with one suite on each side - in which the Electric Jazz of **Miles Davis** cohabits with **Terry Riley**'s minimal music, the experimentation on magnetic tape with what remained of the dreamy psychedelic season.

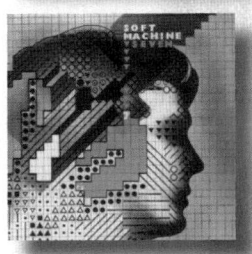

The serious instrumental direction tends to prevail, so **Wyatt** leaves after the publication of *Fourth* (in which he only plays the drums): from 1971 on they then become a prolific jazz-rock machine, austere but smartly conceived like the album *Six*, with **Karls Jenkins** (**Nucleus**) taking over the lead after the exit of **Ratledge**. The group inexorably grows farther apart from their psychedelic origins and the original line-up (by 1976 no founding member was left in it), pursuing Fusion with guitar ace **Allan Holdsworth** (*Bundles*) and then coming to a halt in 1978, though **Hopper** and **Dean** try to resuscitate the old glamour with a band called **Soft Heap**. The old name reappears in 1981 with the lame *Land Of Cockayne*, and will live different incarnations in the following years (**SoftWhere, Soft Works, Soft Machine Legacy**). A brand new album in 2018: *Hidden Details*.

D.Z.

DISCOGRAPHY:

SOFT MACHINE *(Probe, 1968)* **VOLUME TWO** *(Probe, 1969)* **THIRD** *(CBS, 1970)* **FOURTH** *(CBS, 1971)* **FIFTH** *(CBS, 1972)* **SIX** *(CBS,1972)* **SEVEN** *(CBS, 1973)* **BUNDLES** *(Harvest, 1975)* **SOFTS** *(Harvest, 1976) 1976)*, **ALIVE AND WELL RECORDED IN PARIS** *(Harvest 1978)* **LAND OF COCKAYNE** *(EMI 1981)* **JET PROPELLED PHOTOGRAPHS** *(Decal 1989 , recordings from 1967)*, **LIVE AT THE PARADISO 1969** *(Voiceprint 1996)* **HIDDEN DETAILS** *(Dyad/Tonefloat, 2018).*

Europe: GREAT BRITAIN

TRAFFIC

Steve Winwood - *organ, guitar, bass, vocals, percussion,* **Jim Capaldi, Jim Gordon, Roger Hawkins, Walfredo Reyes Jr.** - *drums, vocals,* **Dave Mason, Michael McEvoy** - *guitar, keyboards, bass, vocals,* **Chris Wood** - *horns, organ, percussion,* **Randall Bramblett** - *horns,* **Ric Grech, David Hood, Rosko Gee** - *bass,* **Reebop Kwaku Baah** - *percussion.*

Traffic's story is of the utmost importance given the talent of the musicians who took part in the project and due to the period of great artistic and musical changes which created the relation between R&B, Psychedelia and Prog. Like **the Kinks**, **Colosseum** and **Trinity**, they were just as pioneeristic. **Steve Winwood** is the enfant prodige of English Pop, symbol of the **Spencer Davis Group** with which he records the two classics "Gimme Some Lovin'" and "I'm A Man" between 1963 and 1967. Swingin' London's overwhelming movida changes his perspectives and Chris Blackwell's label Island decides to invest on him. Together with **Chris Wood**, **Jim Capaldi** and **Dave Mason** (already met by playing in **Hellionses**), he retires to a calm Berkshire cottage indulging in night jams and composing their first pieces, just like the **Hawks** (later known as **The Band**) were doing in a pink house near Woodstock.

After the hit singles "Paper Sun" and "Hole In My Shoe", **Traffic** finally release *Mr. Fantasy*, the key moment in which psychedelic folk and vaudeville, blues and Asian melt in a pot of relaxed atmospheres mixed with the mastery of **Jimmy Miller** and without exaggerating the electronics. After a collaboration with **Hendrix** for the majestic *Electric Ladyland*, the new self-titled album *Traffic* is published: more concrete than the first it highlights the soul in **Winwood**'s voice and the eclectic blend of acoustic instruments, jazzy hints, horns and percussions resulting as truly soothing and never too show off.

The following American tour increases the inside dissensions and **Mason** leaves the band. In 1969 they breakup as do **Cream**: **Clapton** and **Baker** meet **Winwood**, take **Grech** away from **Family** and create a super group called **Blind Faith**: a great promise for the Acid-blues genre that however last the lapse of an album and a tour. In the meantime the former band members are playing as **Wooden Frog** when Island publishes *Last Exit*, a collection of unpublished works and live-tracks.

Winwood starts to think of recording *Mad Shadows* as solo album, improving what was done with **Traffic** and **Blind Faith**; **Capaldi** and **Wood**'s rejoining the band convinces him to use the old name **Traffic** instead. In the summer of 1970 the trio releases the marvelous *John Barleycorn Must Die*, a mixture of Folk Jazz, Soft Rock inclinations and Blues echoes that create a balance between structure and jam, the secret of an epic album that overcomes similar ones done by **Family** and **Jethro Tull** for its elegance. Rock evolves thanks to all these new bands and so do Traffic through their instrumental density and their recovery of English folk, just like this famous title-track. Success strengthens the wholeness of the group, **Mason** returns, the line-up grows and after a live performance they publish three homogeneous albums that receive great appreciation in America: nevertheless '71-'74 **Traffic** lose their unpredictability in long Rock-Jazz songs that tire and wear out. The definitive breakup arrives in 1974. **Wood** dies in 1983, **Winwood** and **Capaldi** start bright solo careers. In 1994 they surrender to idea of a reunion, trying to re-live the greatness of the past. The drummer's death in 2005 puts an end to any further nostalgic project. **D.Z.**

DISCOGRAPHY:
MR. FANTASY *(Island 1967)* **TRAFFIC** *(Island 1968)* **LAST EXIT** *(Island 1969)* **JOHN BARLEYCORN MUST DIE** *(Island 1970)* **WELCOME TO THE CANTEEN** *(live, Island 1971)* **THE LOW SPARK OF HIGH HEELED BOYS** *(Island 1971)* **SHOOT OUT AT THE FANTASY FACTORY** *(Island 1973)* **ON THE ROAD** *(live, Island 1973)* **WHEN THE EAGLE FLIES** *(Island 1973)* **FAR FROM HOME** *(Virgin 1994).*

Europe: GREAT BRITAIN

TWELFTH NIGHT

Geoff Mann - *vocals*, **Andy Sears** - *vocals (1985/1987)*, **Brian Devoil** - *drums, percussions*, **Clive Mitten** - *bass, keyboards*, **Andy Revell** - *guitars*.

Twelfth Night's presence in the Prog circle is often controversial for they have a very strong New Wave component to their rhythms, compositions, guitar and Korg Polysix sounds, that create personal amalgamates in unstable balance between Prog intentions and New Wave results. They begin in 1978, when **Andy Revell**, **Brian Devoil** and **Clive Mitten** found the band and begin to record long compositions based on the guitarist's melodic style. Part of this initial material is gathered in two audio tapes of the early '80s to which **Rick Battersby**'s keyboards are added and later also with the voice of **Electra McLeod**, an American singer.
Live at the Target is released as an entirely instrumental album, extremely beautiful to the point of revealing their compositional qualities which only still missed a true vocalist. Since the beginning they had this artist with them creating the concert backdrops and writing critiques for the local papers, without realizing he would soon be the man to turn their fate around: **Geoff Mann**, endowed with a very involving and supple vocal expressiveness, warm or scratchy according to the lyrics.
At the end of 1981, a first tape *Smiling At Grief* is recorded, still rather anchored to the English New Wave that was at its highest at the time; however among the songs some great passages prelude to their best album issued later in 1982, *Fact and Fiction*, followed by extremely positive critiques. This album shortly became a milestone for the music of this period in a traversal way, given the deep and intelligent lyrics and the unique singing, capable of giving a different meaning to every sentence according to the words used.

Success seemed to be just behind the door when suddenly **Geoff Mann** decides to leave the group for a solo career. Vocalist **Andy Sears** replaces him but inevitably the group is not the same anymore. Already the next album's compositions lose strength. A mini-album entitled *Art and Illusion*, significantly lower in quality, as is even more evident in the modest *XII* published in 1986 which leads to the final breakup. In 1993 **Mann** dies of cancer, yet they still manage to work together publishing rearrangements or other unpublished songs or live recordings.   **R.V.**

RECOMMENDED RECORDINGS:
THE FIRST TAPE ALBUM *(Stereo 7 tape, fan club release, recordings of 1980)* **TWELFTH NIGHT (aka. Early Material, The Electra Tape)** *(Stereo 7 tape, Twelfth Night Records, 1980)* **LIVE AT THE TARGET** *(LP, Twelfth Night Records, 1981)* **SMILING AT GRIEF** *(Stereo 7 tape, Twelfth Night Records, 1982)* **FACT AND FICTION** *(LP Twelfth Night Records, 1982)* **LIVE AND LET LIVE** *(LP Music For Nations, 1984)* **TWELFTH NIGHT (aka. XII - The Virgin Album)** *(LP Virgin, 1986)* **COLLECTORS ITEM** *(Food For Thought Records, 1991)* **ENTROPY** *(Private Pressing, 2006)* **MMX (Live May 2010)** *(Private Pressing, 2010)*.

Europe: GREAT BRITAIN

VAN DER GRAAF GENERATOR

Peter Hammill - *vocals, guitar, piano,* **David Jackson** - *flute, sax,* **Guy Evans** - *drums,* **Hugh Banton** - *organ, bass,* **Keith Ellis, Nic Potter** - *bass,* **Graham Smith** - *violin,* **Charles Dickie** - *cello.*

Science fiction, literature, chemistry, philosophy and spirituality: with **Van Der Graaf Generator** rock finally becomes an adult and drinks from other sources of knowledge, not only musical. The tantrums of English Psychedelia, fascinated by childhood and by the playful vision of Victorian England, are by now overcome: man has to face his own insecurity and solitude, a place between ghosts and fears. Before the sunset of an era made of illusions and collective awareness, **VDGG** sing the dismay of man through an Art-rock both aggressive and graceless as poetic and dreamy. **Peter Hammill** can be seen as more than just a poet, for he sings of a personal philosophical system, almost as if he were the Leopardi of Rock accompanied by one of the most original bands of the time.

VDGG formed in 1967 in Manchester university. They face numerous changes in line-up and in 1969 release a raw debut which initially was supposed to be **Hammill**'s solo album. After signing up with **Tony Stratton-Smith** from Charisma Records, they literally explode. Probably the entire Progressive production doesn't come even close to the three highly inspired and powerful albums released between 1970 and 1971: *The Least We Can Do...*, *H To He* and *Pawn Hearts*.

In a decade where every band develops their own personality, **VDGG** go beyond: in the ambitiously unique *Pawn Hearts* they define an intellectual project lead by **Hammill**'s complex vision of the world. They create a dynamic and acute sound, that alternates moments of grandeur to dives in sepulchral obscurity, sudden flashes and agonizing melodies branded by **Hammill**'s emphatic voice, the absence of guitars, the abrasive interlacing of horns and organ with **Evans**' tight rhythms all wisely guided by **John Anthony**. We do not find the **Genesis** fables, nor **Yes**' interstellar escapes or **Jethro Tull**'s bucolic wanderings, but instead here goes the musical score to nightmares and painful discoveries. After 1971's masterpiece, **Hammill** begins his solo career that for quality and quantity will become a unique case in the history of Rock (also for the constant collaboration with his ex-colleagues). In 1975 he returns with **Generator** publishing four less complex studio recordings, calmer and meditative, and a rough live album in '78, after which they retire. A pity since they are the only ones showing real claws in the full midst of the Punk period (see the interesting *The Quiet Zone*, with **Graham Smith** from **String Driven Thing**), so much as to have the unexpected **Johnny Rotten** from **Sex Pistols** among their fans. Confirming **VDGG**'s uniqueness, the 2005 reunion starts with the release of the double album *Present* which has no nostalgic intentions. It bares the research of a new kind of music and despite a good live tour that brings them for the first time in front of thousands of fans that had never seen them sees in action, different opinions lead **David Jackson** to leave the band. They exorcise his exit by becoming for the first time a trio and publishing the intriguing *Trisector*. Since 2011 other 4 albums are released: *A Grounding In Numbers*, *ALT*, *Merlin Atmos* (Live) and the last *Do Not Disturb*.

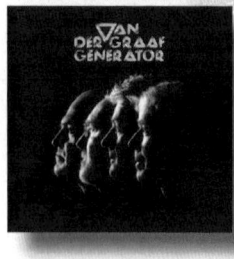

D.Z.

DISCOGRAPHY:
THE AEROSOL GREY MACHINE (Mercury 1969) **THE LEAST WE CAN DO IS WAVE TO EACH OTHER** (Charisma 1970) **H TO HE, WHO AM THE ONLY ONE** (Charisma 1970) **PAWN HEARTS** (Charisma 1971) **GODBLUFF** (Charisma 1975) **STILL LIFE** (Charisma 1976) **WORLD RECORD** (Charisma 1976) **THE QUIET ZONE/THE PLEASURE DOME** (Charisma 1977) **VITAL** (live, Charisma 1978) **PRESENT** (EMI 2005) **REAL TIME** (live, Fie! 2006) **TRISECTOR** (Virgin/EMI 2008) **LIVE AT THE PARADISO** (Voiceprint 2009) **A GROUNDING IN NUMBERS** (Esoteric Records 2011) **ALT** (Esoteric Records 2011) **MERLIN ATMOS** (Esoteric Records 2015) **DO NOT DISTURB** (Esoteric Records 2016).

Europe: **GREAT BRITAIN**

ROBERT WYATT

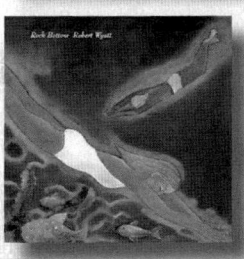

Pink Floyd's drummer and archivist **Nick Mason** said **Wyatt** was the Rock'n'Roll answer to Lenin. In this edition **Robert Wyatt**, whose last name is actually **Ellidge**, is mentioned many times as in the pages related to the **Daevid Allen Trio, Wilde Flowers, Soft Machine** and **Matching Mole**, and for his undeniable influence on many other artists of the so-called Canterbury school (**Hatfield and the North, Caravan, Kevin Ayers, Gong**). An artist of vigorous and surreal talent who truly lived two very separate lives due to an accident on the night of 1st June 1973 in which, after a party, he falls out of a window drunk, losing the use of his legs and therefore having to abandon forever the drums.

This tragedy didn't really influence the quality of his career, though he did of course need to adapt to his new reality. **Wyatt** came out stronger than ever, both as singer and an author, proving the consistence of the artist within. In 1970 with *The End Of An Ear* (as the end of a way of listening to music) **Wyatt** starts to improve his Avant-garde concept, already anticipated in "Moon in June" from the album *Soft Machine III*, creating in 1974 the masterpiece of his second life, *Rock Bottom*, produced by the already quoted **Nick Mason** (**Pink Floyd** will devolve a whole concert income to help **Robert**). This album contains marvelous songs such as "Sea song", while "Alifib" and "Alife" contain the love anagrams dedicated to his partner in life, **Alfreda Benge**.

Wyatt's songs are deeply tied to his taste for Jazz and in his albums we find some of the best jazz players around at the time (**Fred Frith, Gary Windo, Hugh Hopper, David Sinclair, Mark Charig** and **Mike Oldfield**). This preferred genre doesn't however prevent him to compose his version of **Neil Diamond**'s "I'm a believer", that hits the charts in 1975

(famous the cover by **Monkees**). His extremely melodious and unique voice even conquers **Elvis Costello** who will write "Shipbuildings" especially for him in 1983 (a sad song on British navy shipyards during the Falklands war). He also makes a personal cover of "Biko" by **Peter Gabriel**, but nobody will ever reproach his choices since he is a world of his own. His declared political commitment to the Left wing and his always being on the side of the weak, confine him to a small, but artistically rich universe.

His production becomes rarefied towards the end of the '70s and, although not exclusively of a Prog nature, they are still full of inventiveness and charm. Worth listening to are certainly the albums *Old Rottenhat*, *Dondestan* and the more recent *Shleep* recorded with the fundamental help of **Phil Manzanera**. 1998 sees most of the Italian artists reunited in a tribute album of his songs, *The Different You*, which he presents during the Turin Music Fair, containing remarkable tracks sung by **Max Gazzè, Cristina Donà, Battiato** and one by **Robert** himself. After another two good albums before he definitely retires from the scenes.   **M.G.**

DISCOGRAPHY (partecipations and singles not included):

THE END OF AN EAR *(1970, CBS)* **ROCK BOTTOM** *(1974, Virgin)* **THE PEEL SESSIONS** *(1974, Strange Fruit)* **RUTH IS STRANGER THAN RICHARD** *(1975, Virgin)* **THE ANIMALS FILM** *(1982, Rough Trade EP)* **NOTHING CAN STOP US** *(1982, Rough Trade)* **WORK IN PROGRESS** *(1984, Rough Trade EP)* **OLD ROTTENHAT** *(1985, Rough Trade)* **DONDESTAN** *(1991, Rough Trade)* **A SHORT BREAK** *(1992, Voiceprint)* **SHLEEP** *(1997, Hannibal)* **DONDESTAN (Revisited)** *(1998, Hannibal)* **SOLAR FLARES BURN FOR YOU** *(BBC archive recordings, 2003, Cuneiform)* **CUCKOOLAND** *(2003, Hannibal/Rikodisc)* **THEATRE ROYAL DRURY LANE (Robert Wyatt & Friends in Concert - 8/9/1974)** *(2005, Hannibal/Rikodisc)* **COMICOPERA** *(2007, Domino Records)*.

Europe: GREAT BRITAIN

YES

Jon Anderson, Trevor Horn. Benoit David, Jon Davison - *vocals,* Chris Squire - *bass, vocals,* Peter Banks, Steve Howe, Trevor Rabin, Billy Sherwood - *guitar, bass, vocals,* Tony Kaye, Rick Wakeman, Patrick Moraz, Geoff Downes, Igor Khoroshev, Oliver Wakeman - *keyboards,* Bill Bruford, Alan White - *drums.*

Born in 1968 they reach the highest peak of the entire Prog movement with a fifth album, an elegant sound that maintains a Classical and dynamic structure, mixing melodies, graveness and aggressive arrangements. True anomaly for influences and themes, life-styles and success, **Yes** is also the most responsible for a slight decadence of the genre, by now hyperbolic and further away from the Rock matrix. After a couple of albums between Post-Beat, Baroque mannerism and cheesy covers, *The Yes Album* embodies their unique style (marked by the arrival of ex-Tomorrow guitarist **Steve Howe**). **Rick Wakeman** joins them in 1971 for *Fragile*: a perfect line-up and even if the song type is old-fashioned, the melodic foundations are solid and the amazing technical ability serves a windmill of ideas. The formula repeats in *Close To The Edge*, subliming the perfect synergy of these prodigious instrumentalists who collectively are superb. The addition of **Roger Dean**'s visual painting to their sound makes them a real cult, and the triple live album *Yessongs* only confirms their talent. Immediately after *Close To The Edge*, Anderson's leadership starts to stagger, so the redundant *Tales From Topographic Oceans* seems more of a pantomime. Relayer has a more slender structure and sees the entry of **Patrick Moraz**. They then take a year to pursue solo projects until Wakeman returns. *Going For The One* convinces for its balance and elegance while Tormato and *Drama* (the latter with **Trevor Horn** singing and **Geoff Downes** on keyboards) close the decade with a pompous Rock and the simplest but less fascinating lyrics. In 1983 South African **Trevor Rabin**, together with **Tony Kaye**, brings to the new, winning formula of Elettro/Pop-Rock: 90125 goes down in history for its freshness and careful sounds, thanks also to a incredible production operated by ex-singer Trevor Horn that guarantees the survival of the group in such a difficult time. The recovery of Art-rock in the '90s stimulates **Yes**, that after the commemorative *Union* and the dignified *Talk*, returns to the old ways: 1972's line-up is now updated and they publish a series of albums that inject in the Classical concept a more modern and bold spirit. Their last true legacy is the solemn *Magnification* in 2001 recorded with an orchestra. Ten years later *Fly From Here*, born from a new questionable line-up decided by young **Benoit David** replacing **Anderson**, sees **Downes** back on keyboards and Horn as their producer. Then **Jon Davison** replaces **Benoit** while **Billy Sherwood** replaces **Squire** who died in 2015. **D.Z.**

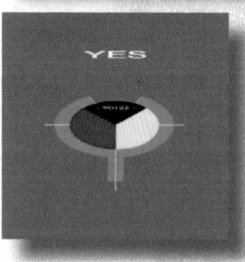

DISCOGRAPHY:
YES *(Atlantic 1969)* **TIME AND A WORD** *(Atlantic 1970)* **THE YES ALBUM** *(Atlantic 1971)* **FRAGILE** *(Atlantic 1972)* **CLOSE TO THE EDGE** *(Atlantic 1972)* **YESSONGS** *(live, Atlantic 1973)* **TALES FROM TOPOGRAPHIC OCEANS** *(Atlantic 1973)* **RELAYER** *(Atlantic 1974)* **GOING FOR THE ONE** *(Atlantic 1977)* **TORMATO** *(Atlantic 1978)* **DRAMA** *(Atlantic 1980)* **YESSHOWS** *(Atlantic 1980)* **90125** *(Atco 1983)* **90125 LIVE: THE SOLOS** *(Atco 1985),* **BIG GENERATOR** *(Atco 1987),* **ANDERSON BRUFORD WAKEMAN HOWE** *(Arista 1989),* **UNION** *(Arista 1991)* **TALK** *(Victory 1994),* **KEYS TO ASCENSION** *(Essential 1996)* **KEYS TO ASCENSION 2** *(Essential 1997)* **OPEN YOUR EYES** *(Eagle 1997),* **THE LADDER** *(Eagle 1999)* **HOUSE OF YES - live from House of Blues** *(Eagle 2000)* **MAGNIFICATION** *(Eagle 2001)* **LIVE AT MONTREUX 2003** *(Eagle 2007)* **FLY FROM HERE** *(Frontiers Records 2011)* **IN THE PRESENT (live)***(Frontiers Records 2014)* **HEAVEN AND EARTH** *(Frontiers Records 2014)* **LIKE IT IS (Volume 1 - Live)** *(Frontiers Records 2014)* **LIKE IT IS (Volume 2 - Live)** *(Frontiers Records 2015).*

Europe: GREECE

APHRODITE'S CHILD

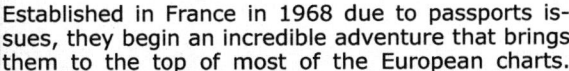
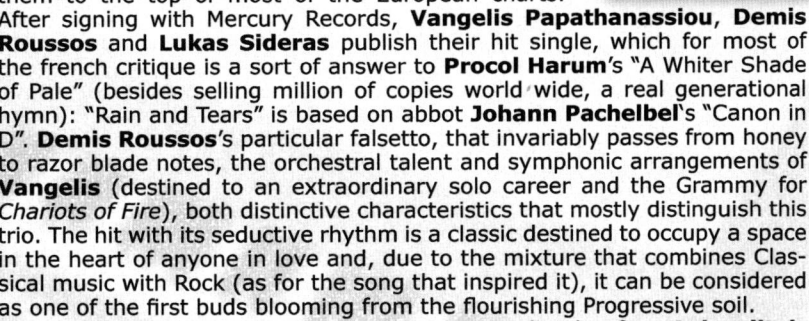

Vangelis Papathanassiou - *keyboards,*
Demis Roussos - *vocals, bass,*
Lukas Sideras - *drums.*

Established in France in 1968 due to passports issues, they begin an incredible adventure that brings them to the top of most of the European charts. After signing with Mercury Records, **Vangelis Papathanassiou**, **Demis Roussos** and **Lukas Sideras** publish their hit single, which for most of the french critique is a sort of answer to **Procol Harum**'s "A Whiter Shade of Pale" (besides selling million of copies world wide, a real generational hymn): "Rain and Tears" is based on abbot **Johann Pachelbel**'s "Canon in D". **Demis Roussos**'s particular falsetto, that invariably passes from honey to razor blade notes, the orchestral talent and symphonic arrangements of **Vangelis** (destined to an extraordinary solo career and the Grammy for *Chariots of Fire*), both distinctive characteristics that mostly distinguish this trio. The hit with its seductive rhythm is a classic destined to occupy a space in the heart of anyone in love and, due to the mixture that combines Classical music with Rock (as for the song that inspired it), it can be considered as one of the first buds blooming from the flourishing Progressive soil.
With "End of the World", which followed immediately after, **Aphrodite's Child** goes beyond the borders and the structures until then established by commercial music: the track slowly moves towards a cathartic pulse and mutates to the point of leaving you torn under the strength of the most incandescent magma. While **Vangelis**' Hammond traces extraordinary arabesques touching almost inaccessible skies, **Demis**' voice is draped in the clothes of the Angel of Death.
In that same period (1969) they record a first album, *Aphrodite's Child*, which contains some good ideas still in embryo, but which still respect the trend of the time by gathering few great successes followed by a collection of b-sides. The phenomenon continues with other great singles ("It's Five O'clock", "Spring", "Summer", "Winter and Fall" and "I Want to Live") not as famous as the first but still with the power to place the band at the top of the market.
After recording "Lontano dagli occhi" by **Sergio Endrigo** and "Quando l'amore diventa poesia" for the Sanremo Song Festival to which however, they won't take part, **Vangelis** wants to pursue Avant-garde new paths, while **Demis** is for maintaining their staus quo. This divergence of opinions brings to the inevitable breakup. So after *It's Five O'Clock* (1970) and *The Best of Aphrodite's Child* the following year, **Vangelis** records *666* (number of the Beast), a double album which, despite being titled under the band's name, is his actual first real solo album. Too far apart from the usual patterns and diametrically opposite to the themes of **Aphrodite's Child** (a masterpiece of progressive rock)(a masterpiece of Prog) it will be cast aside on the shelves of the record label and published only after their breakup. **F.V.**

DISCOGRAPHY (Less important anthologies not included):
END OF THE WORLD *(Mercury, 1968)* **APHRODITE'S CHILD** *(Mercury, 1970 - Brazilian release)* **IT'S FIVE O'CLOCK** *(Mercury, 1970)* **BEST OF APHRODITE'S CHILD** *(Mercury, 1971)* **666** *(Vertigo, 1972).*

Europe: GREECE

AXIS

Christos Stassinopoulos - *drums*, **Demis Visvikis** - *vocals, organ*, **Demetris Katakuzinos** - *acoustic guitars, bass, vocals*, **Alexandros Fantis** - *bass*, **George Chatziathanassiou** - *drums, percussion, vocals*, **Alecos Caracandas** - *guitars, vocals*, **Christian Stassinopoulos** - *percussion*.

One of the few groups of Greek origins able get some recognition out of the borders of its country, they are an answer to the more famous **Aphrodite's Child** with which it contended popularity within the Hellenic music business. They got together in France in 1970 under the wing of **Eddie Barclay**, heir manager, producer and inspiration, engraving a handful singles that sold well enough. Their first album is from 1971 and is a discreet success on a European level, also thanks to the English version of the famous "Song of Osanna" by **Delirium**, simply titled "Osanna"; in that same summer they participate to Festivalbar in Italy and thereafter have the opportunity of performing in some concerts where they surprise the public for the freshness of their sound, full of energy and rhythms, true heirs of the **Stassinopoulos** and **Chatziathanassiou** brothers. In Italy and in good part of Europe they are remembered above all for *Ela Ela*, a good chart success derived from the Greek Folk heritage and rearranged in a Prog version.

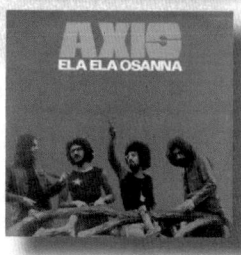

The band's style gradually sharpens growing closer to the Canterbury sound, though in a more energetic key, deeply Prog thanks also to **Visvikis'** great job on the organ. Fundamental characteristic of their sound is really the obsessive presence of percussions that not only accompanies, but often guides the sound with enthusiastic rhythm. Critics have often associated them with **Uriah Heep** but the secret of their originality is that of recalling many big names without resembling to none of them at all.

Their second album *Axis* brings the band into the Olympus of European Prog: an amazing mix of traditional Greek elements, ground into the extraordinary scenery of Canterbury sounds. With their third album they confirm their intention to pursue the Canterbury path through some complex guitar riddles recalling the first **King Crimson** while the general atmosphere is of Hard Rock inspiration, with the organ always in great evidence. The album is not easily available, printed originally only for the French market where it received scarce interest from the public. It has been recently re-issued as a CD.

Due to the commercial failure of their last project and partly to the fact that **Eddie Barclay**'s interests were changing, the band breaks-up and the members manage to effectively recycle themselves into other groups.   **C.A.**

DISCOGRAPHY:
OSANNA *(Riviera, 1971)* **AXIS** *(Riviera, 1972)* **ELA ELA/OSANNA** *(Riviera, 1972)* **AXIS** *(Riviera, 1973)*.

Europe: GREECE

PLJ BAND
TERMITES

Laurentis Machairitsas - *vocals, 12 strings guitar, keyboards*, **Antonis Mijelos** - *guitars*, **Jimmy Vasalakos** - *bass, backing vocals*, **Pavlos Kikrilis** - *rhythm guitar, nylon guitar*, **Tolis Skamajouras** - *drums, percussion*.

This Greek band published in 1982 one of the most original and looked for albums of the history of Prog, *Armageddon*, which owes its rarity to the fact that it was seized and convicted to be destroyed by the Authorities because they reputed its content blasphemous. Only 300 copies were saved. Needless to say how very valuable to collectors (more than 300 dollars each) they are. The band also auto-produced *Gaspar* has a really unique sound for being a Greek band; *Armageddon* is pure Prog tied to strong sparks of Psychedelic Folk with hints of German Space Rock. It also has a beautiful cover painted by an artist that reproduces perfectly the style of Salvador Dalì, crowning in an appropriate way the content (the Catalan artist often desecrated in his works anything that tasted bigot, as his experimental films together with Louis Buñuel in the '30s).

After the fiasco of this first album and the troubles it went through, the band decided to change style. They also changed their name into **Termites** and they started over with a more traditional Rock, publishing five good albums sung in Greek: *Termites* (1983), *A Martoli Maria* (1984), *Tsimentenia trena* (1986), *Tsimentenio concerto* (1987), *Perimenontas Ti Vroxi* (1988).

In 1988 they breakup mainly because of the abandonment of their singer **Laurentis Machairitsas** who wanted a solo career. Their

last concert was recorded in an album of great success. Since then **Machairitsas** issued eleven solo albums and worked a lot as an author for other Greek musicians. Also his band partners tried solo careers and, except for **Antonis Mijelos**, none were successful. In 1998, ten years after their last concert, a commemorative reunion sees them together for one evening, in the Basket stadium Irinis Kai Filias, playing in front of 20.000 fans. This concert was recorded and published two years later on CD and DVD as *Termites - I synaulia*. **M.G.**

DISCOGRAPHY:
GASPAR *(EP, 1979, Self- produced)* **ARMAGEDDON** *(1982, Second Battle /2006, CD Universal)* **TERMITES** *(1983, Vertigo)* **A MARTOLI MARIA** *(1984, Vertigo)* **TSIMENTENIA TRENA** *(1986, Virgin)* **TSIMENTENIO CONCERTO** *(1987, Virgin)* **PERIMENONTAS TI VROXI** *(1988, Virgin)* **TERMITES - I SYNAULIA** *(2000, Minos)*.

Europe: HOLLAND

FOCUS

Thijs Van Leer - *flute, keyboards, vocals,* **Jan Akkerman** - *guitar, vocals,* **Bert Ruiter** - *bass,* **Pierre Van Linden** - *drums.*

One of the best Dutch groups of the Progressive scene and probably the most well-known abroad, **Jan Akkerman** and **Thijs Van Leer**'s band influenced deeply a certain type of Prog ramification of the early '70s, setting the baseline of the ephemeral yet important Dutch Pop: of Classical extraction and education, they start to crystallize from 1969 when they begin to taste the intoxicating novelty of combining Classical to Pop music, or better rearranging classics like **Bach** in a Pop key.

When *In and out of Focus* is published they immediately get noticed as the band who opened an important new path and the fans start to gather. Even if this debut album has a lot defects, it is intense, rich of exciting, simple but beautiful songs like "House Of The King", and makes a smart use of the flute. Yet the whole album must be appreciated for the delicate and harmonic balance obtained by melting the novelties of British Pop at the end of the '60s with the innovative Psychedelic sound and classical Music. The atmosphere springing from the record are vaguely Baroque, refined and sweet, with rare and more vigorous parts.

The next, a more mature album, *Focus II* (or *Moving Waves*) was recorded in 1972 and represents an unbelievable breakthrough for the group that consolidates its sound expressing it with unsuspected energy. The track "Hocus Pocus", perhaps too exploited by the radios (memorable for the yodel) sees **Akkerman** give his very best on the electric guitar while **Van Leer** builds walls of sounds on the keyboards, playing with great intensity and once again his flute enchants and surprises; "Eruption" is a song that amazes for the intensity of the composition, pure energy produced by keyboards and guitars never so inspired.

Focus III is a double album, incredibly involving and never boring where the organ traces skilled paths which are followed by the hard and sharp electric guitar with solos inspired by the great **Frank Zappa**. The atmosphere sometimes becomes more relaxed, going from Jazz to sweet melodies with the flute appearing and disappearing like gems of poetry. Then the sudden exit of **Van der Linden** followed soon by **Akkerman** and finally by **Van Leer**. New members will keep the band playing up to the mid '80s with nothing worth of real notice for the purposes of our book.

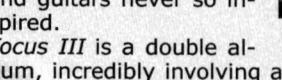

C.A.

RECOMMENDED RECORDINGS:

IN AND OUT OF FOCUS *(Polydor, 1970; Holland: FOCUS PLAY FOCUS, Imperial 1970)* **MOVING WAVES** *(Polydor, 1972; Holland: FOCUS II, Imperial 1971)* **FOCUS III** *(Polydor, 1972)* **FOCUS AT THE RAINBOW** *(Polydor, 1973)* **HAMBURGER CONCERTO** *(Polydor, 1974)* **MOTHER FOCUS** *(Polydor, 1975)* **FOCUS CON PROBY** *(EMI, 1977)*.

Europe: **HOLLAND**

GROUP 1850

Peter Sjardin - *flute, organ, vocals,* **Beer Klaasse** - *drums,* **Daniël van Bergen** - *guitar, piano,* **Ruud van Buuren** - *bass.*

Since their debut **Group 1850** was considered the most Avant-garde band of the musical Dutch panorama, technically superior even to the more famous **Outsiders**. When their first album *Agemo's Trip to Mother Earth* was published in 1968, it immediately seemed clear which path they were undertaking: British Psychedelia but soaked with references from the US's Acid West-Coast experience. Published with a 3-D cover and special glasses, their first LP is an authentic pearl in the panorama of Psych-Rock: particularly Acid guitars, organ, the rhythmic section in good evidence and above all, excellent arrangements, make it a pillar of the genre. The question to why they remained so fairly unknown even in Holland is a mystery, also since they were signed up with a great label such as

Philips. The album came out in England too, yet no trace of its appearance here is left. In 1969 *Paradise Now* is released, less Acid than the previous and slightly more conform to the record market by request of their new label Discofoon: over 50.000 copies were sold (a small win for an Lp in those years). Musically very complex in comparison to the style that the band had when playing live, it is the result of a good studio recording with effects similar to *A Saucerful Of Secrets* by **Pink Floyd**, with a very predominant organ and bass. Unfortunately also the new label's attempt of exporting their sound in Great Britain and the United States resulted a failure bringing them soon to a breakup. During the '70s they sometimes reunite ("Fire" 1971) and will release a live album in 1974 mostly of their old Psychedelic tracks. It is an example of how a potentially great band sometimes doesn't find the right opportunity to emerge.   **C.A.**

DISCOGRAPHY:
AGEMO'S TRIP TO MOTHER EARTH *(Philips, 1968)* **PARADISE NOW** *(Discofoon, 1969)* **POLYANDRI** *(Rubber, 1975)* **LIVE** *(Orange, 1975)* **LIVE ON TOUR** *(Rubber, 1976)* **THE GREAT SINGLE TRACKS** *(Twilight Zone, 1993)* **1967-1968** *(Mercury, 1993)* **MOTHER NO-HEAD - THEIR 45S** *(Pseudonym, 2012)* **PARADISE NOW / AGEMO'S TRIP TO MOTHER EARTH** *(Pseudonym, 2013).*

Europe: HOLLAND

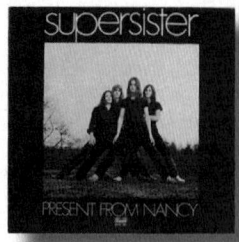

SUPERSISTER

Robert Jan Stips - *keyboards, vocals,* **Sacha van Geest** - *flute, vocals, sax,* **Ron van Eeck** - *bass,* **Herman van Boeyen** - *drums,* **Charlie Mariano** - *sax.*

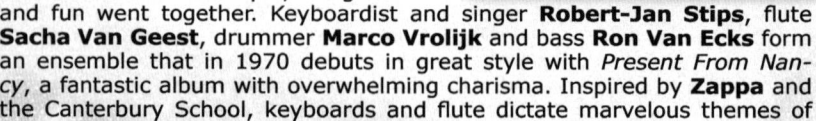

Supersisters is an exceptional group who managed to create a personal sound in which technique, imagination and fun went together. Keyboardist and singer **Robert-Jan Stips**, flute **Sacha Van Geest**, drummer **Marco Vrolijk** and bass **Ron Van Ecks** form an ensemble that in 1970 debuts in great style with *Present From Nancy*, a fantastic album with overwhelming charisma. Inspired by **Zappa** and the Canterbury School, keyboards and flute dictate marvelous themes of great impact as they follow the continuous rhythmic changes imposed by the drums. Same sound for the studio albums *To the Highest Bidder*, *Pudding en Gisteren* (with the title-track's fabulous 20 minutes) and *Superstarshine*. The musicians show great ability in creating complex music, at the same time being involving and direct.

Some discussions bring to a change in line-up: **Van Boeyen** and **Mariano** join and Iskander is published with producer **George Gomelski** (known for his collaborations with **Soft Machine**, **Magma** and **Gong**). Different from the previous it contains a particular form of Jazz-Rock and this version of the **Supersisters** is fully convincing too. After other musician turnovers, *Spiral Staircase* is published: practically a solo album by **Van Geest** though he goes under the first name adopted by the band: **Sweet OK Supersister**. The album is a sort of playful experimentation flooded with irony and eccentricity. The magic continues in the following album even if confusion in the band brings them however to a final break-up and the various musicians will hook up in different projects.

In 2000 an album of old recordings, *Memories New Macaws*, brings them to play together in the original line-up for the American Progfest and in other various concerts in their country. From these performances a double live *Supersisterious* seems to give the band a renewed energy when tragedy breaks the spell: a terminal illness takes **Van Geest**, truncating all expectations of one of the most radiant wonders of European Prog. **G.D.S.**

DISCOGRAPHY:
PRESENT FROM NANCY *(1970, Polydor)* **TO THE HIGHEST BIDDER** *(1971, Polydor)* **PUDDING EN GISTEREN** *(1972, Polydor)* **SUPERSTARSHINE** *(1972, Polydor)* **ISKANDER** *(1973, Polydor)* **SPIRAL STAIRCASE** *(1974, Polydor)* **MEMORIES ARE NEW** *(2000, Soss)* **SUPERSISTERIOUS** *(2001, Biem/Stemra).*

Europe: HOLLAND

TRACE

Rick Van Der Linden - *keyboards,* **Jaap Van Eik** - *bass, vocals, guitar,* **Pierre Van Der Linden** - *drums,* **Ian Mosley** - *drums.*

After the experience in **Ekseption**, keyboardist **Rick** forms a trio with drummer **Pierre** (from **Brainbox** and **Focus**) and with bass-player **Jaap** (previously in **Cuby & the Blizzards, The Motion, Solution, Living Blues**). They call themselves Trace and become one of the best imitators of **Emerson, Lake & Palmer**: their sound is pompous, technical and tied to Classical music. Since their 1974 debut-album the band proves to have clear ideas of making the keyboards the absolute protagonists (synthesizers, Hammond and church organs, mellotron, piano). Wild Symphonic Prog with vivid and ever-changing rhythms create splendid compositions like "Gaillarde" (which blends a concert of **Bach** and a traditional Polish dance) and "Ounces and Progression". To promote the LP they play live also as support group for **Curved Air**.

For some time the musicians move to England and it is in this period that drummer **Ian Mosley** joins after answering an add on a newspaper, replacing **Pierre Van Der Linden**. With this line-up *Birds* is published in 1975 maintaining the same sound as a clear photocopy

of their debut, where the best parts are the rearrangements of **Bach** (as in "Opus 1065" making their music even more Baroque with **Darryl Way** on the violin) and "King-Bird", a 22 minute Symphonic Rock delight. Nevertheless, they do not receive large scale attention and **Ian** and **Jaap** exit. **Ian Mosley** will appear in the early '80s playing for **Steve Hackett** and in **Marillion** from their second album Fugazi onward, a career he still pursues. **Rick Van Der Linden** instead publishes in 1976 *The White Ladies* as **Rick Van Der Linden And Trace** (19 short songs that form one long suite), milder than the previous, romantic like **Camel** and with refined orchestrations. The album is very beautiful

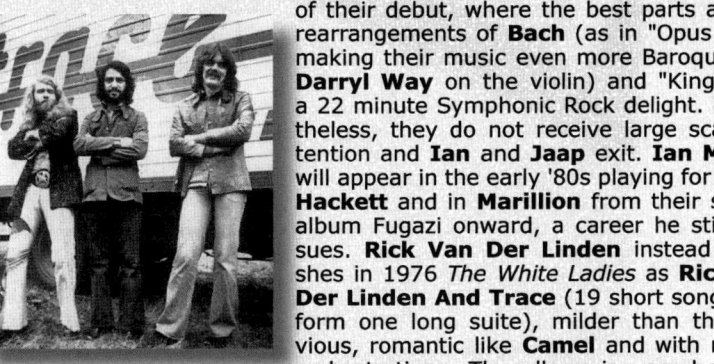

but it doesn't satisfy the fans so at this point the leader decides to put an end to **Trace** and reforms **Ekseption** while simultaneously pursuing his solo career.

G.D.S.

DISCOGRAPHY:
TRACE *(1974, Philips)* **BIRDS** *(1975, Philips)* **THE WHITE LADIES** *(1976, RCA).*

Europe: **HUNGARY**

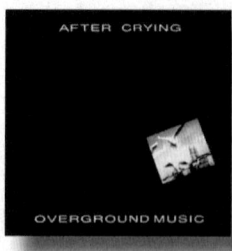

AFTER CRYING

Zoltán Bátky-Valentin - *vocals,* **Gàbor Egervári** - *flute,* **Tamás Görgényi** - *lyrics,* **Zoltán Lengyel** - *keyboards, piano,* **Zsolt Madai** - *drums, percussion,* **Ferenc Torma** - *guitar, synthesizer,* **Pèter Pejtsik** - *bass, cello,* **Balázs Winkler** - *trumpet, keyboards.*

Born in 1986, they represent an interesting anomaly in Prog's panorama: a Contemporary Classical music ensemble or a Symphonic Rock band? These talented musicians play acoustic Classical instruments such as cellos, trumpets, pianos, flutes; of course there are many other contemporary groups with similar features, but their approach does not come from a Rock based structure. **After Crying**'s 30 years of dedicated career is of rare and not just Hungarian experience: their initial aim was of creating quality Classical music that could be understood by a wider audience than the usual fans of this type of genre. Therefore the compositions cannot be synthesized as moments between classical and modern, acoustic and electric, and so forth, as for most of their colleagues: they should be considered as an authentic twenty-first century Chamber orchestra.

The debut album *Overground Music*, is perhaps their most representative given the absence of traditional Rock instruments (electric guitars and drums) and it is a great example of how the voice is often used in dissonance with the rest of the melodies creating an interesting mix. "Shining" sounds like a song from a **Steve Hackett** album and is pure delight to any true Prog fan, since often eastern European artists are suspiciously viewed as plain copy-cats of

English Symphonic Rock, adding little creativeness or originality. Not only do they stay away from the standards set by Anglo-Saxon trends of Blues and Rock'n'roll, but they openly refuse them driving inspiration from the Russian Classical tradition of 19th century instead. Some of their works transpire an unexpected darkness while others seem to betray influences from **Emerson, Lake & Palmer**, especially during the Hammond partitions.

In 1996 they issue a project that marks a change of attitude from the band's previous classical purism: *De Profundis*. Here they blend into Folk with clearly Pop styled vocals and a very present drum session. The whole album seems to echo references from the Dutch band of the '80s called the **Flairck**.

The next four recordings are good but less relevant. They continued to play live in world wide tours for a while, but then took a 10 years pause with no real break-up. In fact after **Gábor Egervári**'s recovery from a non specified illness, they publish another two albums and have resumed their musical career.

M.G.

DISCOGRAPHY:
OVERGROUND MUSIC *(Periferic, 1990)* **MEGAL·ZOTTAK ÈS MEGSZOMORÌTOTTAK** *(Quint, 1992)* **FOLD ES EG** *(Periferic, 1994)* **DE PROFUNDIS** *(Periferic, 1996)* **AFTER CRYING 6** *(Periferic, 1997)* **SHOW** *(Periferic, 2003)* **STRUGGLE FOR LIFE** *(Periferic, Live, 2000)* **BOOTLEG SYMPHONY** *(Periferic, Live, 2001)* **CREATURA** *(Periferic, Live, 2011).*

Europe: **HUNGARY**

OMEGA

János Kóbor - *vocals, guitars*, **Laszlo Benko** - *trumpet, flute, keyboards*, **András Kovacsics** - *guitar*, **István Varsányi** - *bass*, **Péter Láng** - *sax*, **László Harmath** - *bass, sax*, **Mária Wittek** - *vocals*, **József Laux** - *drums*, **Tamás Mihály** - *bass*, **Gabòr Presser** - *keyboards*, **György Molnár** - *guitar*, **Ferenc Debreceni** - *drums*.

Always from and within the Hungarian musical panorama, with rare raids outside their country, this band's career shifts from clear Beat experiences to the Anglo-Saxon trends, using Psychedelia and pale Folk tendencies. Their first albums are appreciated by collectors and fans, but **Omega** are in reality an opaque attempt to imitate the Psychedelic Beat of **Kinks**, **Hollies**, **Pretty Things**, without particular success, also given the difficult musicality of the Hungarian language.

The change happens in 1970 with *Ejszakai Orszagùt* (One night on the road) where they manage to create complex dark atmospheres, alternated to melodic ballads with distorted guitars and heavy percussions. The splendid cover is the work of Hungarian painter E.Szasz. The album's success and the enthusiasm of the fans during their concerts, bring the group to a next recording called *Elö*, a live album full of energy and technically perfect.

In 1973 *Omega 5* is published, a great project with ample space for keyboards and guitars, also issued in an English version. The following *200 Years after the Last War*, is similar to the previous but published directly in

the English version. The next studio album, *Omega 6*, is a excellent job, more clearly inspired by **Yes** and **Rick Wakeman**, iin which electric sounds prevail with more Symphonic Rock arrangements on the verge of Hard Rock.

In 1975 the band's masterpiece *The Hall Of Floaters In The Sky*, is recorded in England with the participation of well known special guests. It is a concept-album sung almost entirely in English even if maintaining a certain accent. This is probably **Omega**'s most elevated artistic moment, with all the ingredients typical of British Prog Rock from the best **Gentle Gian**t inspiration. After a couple of years they publish the Space Rock album, *Time Robbers*, inspired by **David Bowie**. The following *Idörablö* diverts to an easy-listening Pop Rock which will in fact be a sales hit on the Hungarian market. The next, *Csillagok Útján* of 1978, returns to more Progressive themes (the English version is titled *Skyrover*) and is actually the last Prog chapter of their career, thereafter converted to the Pop Rock genre. Since *Gammapolis* (1979) is a collection of tracks discarded from the original *Skyrover* recording, it can still be worth of note to our cause. Today **Omega** keeps publishing less interesting works and can be seen performing here and there in concert.   **C.A.**

RECOMMENDED RECORDINGS:
TROMBITAS FREDI ES A RETTENETES EMBEREK *(Qualiton, 1968)* **10000 LEPES** *(Qualiton, 1968)* **EJSZAKAI ORSZAGUT** *(Qualiton, 1970)* **ELÖ** *(Pepita, 1972)* **OMEGA** *(Bacillus, 1973)* **OMEGA 5** *(Pepita, 1975)* **200 YEARS AFTER THE LAST WAR** *(Bacillus, 1974)* **OMEGA VI: NEM TUDOM A NEVED** *(Pepita, 1975)* **THE HALL OF FLOATERS IN THE SKY** *(Bacillus, 1976)* **TIME ROBBER** *(Bacillus, 1976)* **IDÖRABLÖ** *(Pepita, 1977)* **GAMMAPOLIS** *(Pepita, 1977)* **CSILLAGOK ÚTJÁN** *(Pepita, 1977)* **RHAPSODY** *(Edel, 2010)* **GYÖNGYHAJÚ LÁNY** *(Hungaroton, 2015)*.

Europe: HUNGARY

SOLARIS

István Cziglán - *guitar, keyboards*, **Róbert Erdész** - *keyboards*, **Attila Kollár** - *flute, keyboards*, **Tamás Pócs** - *bass*, **László Gömör** - *drums*, **Csaba Bogdan** - *guitar*, **Gábor Kisszabó** - *bass*.

In 1980 some Hungarian university students gather and form **Solaris**, choosing the name from Lem's science fiction novel. They start off playing live as much as possible and as a prize for winning a certain contest, they finally manage to record a hit single. Three years later their line-up consolidates with musicians **Cziglán**, **Erdész**, **Kollár**, **Gömör** and **Pócs** and this quintet gives life to one of the most thrilling Prog-albums of the '80s:

Marsbeli Kronikak (Martian Chronicles, title inspired by Bradbury's famous book). It is an entirely instrumental Symphonic Prog album, with hints of Electric and Space-rock music, especially in some keyboard synthetic sounds, a feature that confirms them as a cult-band. The contrasts and combinations of keyboards, guitars and the massive dose of flute partitions are absolutely brilliant and very appreciated by the public.

As in most eastern European Regimes which didn't promote this kind of subversive artistic forms, and being the label partly owned by the government, the band still manages to publish *1990*, another excellent work, before the label lets them go. The musicians take different roads until 1995 when surprisingly they reunite thanks to Greg Walker's invitation to participate in Progfest where **Solaris** play wonderfully and are

included in the double cd recording *Live in Los Angeles* out one year later (which also contains an interesting unpublished studio track). Their enthusiasm returns but the moment is spoiled by the news of **Cziglan**'s cancer that eventually kills him at the end of 1998.
The band issues a new album the following year, *Nostradamus. The Book of Prophecies*, a discreet job that confirms their style even if it is very different from all the previous. The next 15 years will be mainly characterized by live performances with no real new works except for the re-edition of older publishings and archive recordings, until the end of 2014 when they finally publish *Martian Chronicles II*. Of their solo experiences the most interesting perhaps concerns **Attila Kollar** and his **Musical Witchcraft** band in which the flute obviously plays a leading role. **G.D.S.**

DISCOGRAPHY:
MARSBELI KRONIKAK - MARTIAN CHRONICLES *(1984, Start)* **1990** *(1990, Start/Pepita)* **LIVE IN LOS ANGELES** *(1996, Solaris Music Production)* **NOSTRADAMUS – THE BOOK OF PROPHECIES** *(1999, Periferic)* **BACK TO THE ROOTS... – SOLARIS ARCHIV 1** *(2000, Periferic)* **NOAB – SOLARIS ARCHIV 2** *(2005, Periferic)* **MARSBELI KRONIKAK II - MARTIAN CHRONICLES II** *(2014, Solaris Music)*.

Europe: ITALY

AREA

Demetrio Stratos - *vocals, organ, percussion,* **Giulio Capiozzo, Walter Calloni** - *drums,* **Patrick Djivas, Ares Tavolazzi, Hugh Bullen, Paolo Dalla Porta** - *bass, contrabass,* **Patrizio Fariselli** - *keyboards, horns, percussion,* **Paolo Tofani** - *guitars, synthesizers,* **Victor Busnello, Steve Lacy, Larry Nocella, Guido Guidoboni, Luciano Biasutti** - *horns,* **Paul Lytton, Anton Arze, Josè Arze** - *percussion,* **Umberto Benedetti Michelangeli** - *strings quartet.*

Area are quite a unique experience, close to that of **Art Ensemble Of Chicago** or to **Henry Cow**, but only to speak of them as a music band is limiting, since they were something else too: the long soundtrack of the 1968 wave that crossed Italy at the time. <<*From clash, creativity is born*>>: their goal was to create a total and traversal music genre. **International POPular Group** was not an advertising gimmick but the perfect synthesis of experiences and different extractions of 1972 Milan city: the Greek **Demetrio Stratos** was the voice of **I Ribelli** of the song "Pugni chiusi", **Capiozzo** played Jazz studying Ethnic percussions, **Fariselli** played in his father's Ball orchestra, **Djivas** was of French origin and of gypsy spirit, **Busnello** was a jazz player transplanted in Belgium, **Tofani** a hippy in love with technology who had just returned from London; and as for **Gianni Sassi**, genius art director, founder of the independent pioneer label Cramps, he would manage lyrics, image and communication.

Arbeit Macht Frei is the beginning of a series of revolutionary and far-sighted albums. Compositions roam from Rock-Jazz to Arabic and Balkan melodies, Concrete music, Surrealism and non dogmatic militancy, going off like a bomb in the hands of such a team. The debut album is a lightening bolt: a cardboard P38 springs from the vinyl, an Arabic voice introduces the listener to a cauldron of overwhelming sounds, with themes such as Palestine and alienation. The following LP is even more extreme since it deepens - with the famous "Lobotomia" - the research on noise; *Crac!* instead is a return to more accessible sonorities, although when playing live the provocation of this band is always intransigent. Taking **Davis**'s sonorous environments and inheriting a certain rhythmic vigor from **Nucleus**, **Area** give Jazz-Rock a myriad of influences (from World Music to Ambient), also researching complex rhythmic patterns. Technically inimitable, they collaborate with giants like **Steve Lacy** and **John Cage**, gaining also international credibility thanks to **Stratos**' vocal studies of technique that will become an inestimable inheritance. The voice as an instrument is among the characteristic elements of the group, that brings to its extreme consequences the concept of improvisation (*Event '76*). They become part of the cultural and musical change, participating in Alternative festivals (ex. Lambro Park in Milan), though they have little in common with the Italian Pop movement, as proven in the concept of *Maledetti* which is fruit of an open group foreseeing a dangerous futuristic society. In 1978 they lose **Tofani**, leave Cramps and publish 1978, an album with shorter songs tied to a more vivid Fusion genre. The death of **Demetrio Stratos** (June 13th 1979) and the memorable tribute concert in the Arena of Milan become a symbol: the '70s are over and worries crack open into the future. They continue as **Area II** with a canonical Electric Jazz and some also begin solo careers. In 1997 they issue their last album as **Area**: **Capiozzo** dies in 2000, **Fariselli** continues his work with Jazz, soundtracks and in keeping the memory of **Area** alive. In 2010 an unexpected reunion of the three surviving members **Fariselli-Tavolazzi-Tofani** is held with new concerts and a new Live album containing unpublished songs entitled *Live 2012*. **D.Z.**

DISCOGRAPHY:
ARBEIT MACHT FREI *(Cramps 1973)* **CAUTION RADIATION AREA** *(Cramps 1974)* **CRAC!** *(Cramps 1975)* **ARE(A)ZIONE** *(live, Cramps 1975)* **MALEDETTI (Maudits)** *(Cramps 1976)* **1978 GLI DEI SE NE VANNO, GLI ARRABBIATI RESTANO** *(Ascolto 1978)* **EVENT '76** *(live, Cramps 1979)* **TIC & TAC** *(Ascolto 1980)* **AREA II: AREA II** *(Gala 1986)* **AREA II: CITY SOUND** *(Gala 1987)* **CHERNOBYL 7991** *(Sony 1997)* **CONCERTO TEATRO UOMO** *(live, Cramps 1997)* **PARIGI-LISBONA** *(live, Cramps 1997)* **LIVE 1977** *(live, Akarma 2002)* **LIVE 2012** *(live, BTF 2012).*

Europe: ITALY

ARTI & MESTIERI

Beppe Crovella, Antonino Salerno, Marco Cimino, Piero Mortara - *keyboards*, **Gigi Venegoni, Willy Fugazza, Slep, Marco Roagna** - *guitars*, **Furio Chirico** - *drums*, **Giovanni Vigliar, Corrado Trabuio, Lautaro Acosta** - *violin*, **Arturo Vitale, Claudio Montafia, Guido Scategni, Flavio Boltro, Alfredo Ponissi** - *horns*, **Marco Gallesi, Gigino Fregapane, Umberto Mari, Roberto Cassetta, Roberto Puggioni** - *bass*. **Gianfranco Gaza, Rudy Passuello, Ivano Nicolò** - *vocals*.

At the beginning of the '70s, **Furio Chirico** was a young drummer but already well known for playing in some beat bands such as **Martò and the Judas, New Beat, I Ragazzi del Sole** and **The Trip**. In 1971 in a Turin jazz club, **Furio** sees a concert by **Sogno di Archimede**: the young band rearranges songs from **King Crimson** but also proposes original ones between Canterbury, ethnic music and jazz rock (some will be published in 2001 in the album *Articollezione*). Since he was already meditating on new operations between prog and jazz, he keeps in contact with this band and exits **The Trip** (that shortly after breaks up). **Beppe Crovella** (keyboards from **Mystics**) joins him and finally the **Arts** take form, later known as **Arti & Mestieri**, when a very interested Franco Mamone invites them to perform at the Festival of Re Nudo on June 15th 1974 in Milan's Lambro Park. **Gigi Venegoni** is a **Fripp** and **Zappa** fan while **Crovella** is influenced by **Vanilla Fudge** and by other classic bands, same as for **Vigliar** who comes from a conservatory extraction, and last but not least **Furio** who pays great attention to Jazz, Rhythm & Blues and to American percussionists in general. Record label Cramps promotes the innovative mixture of the sextet and publishes Tilt: it is a first excellent album, that recovers a lot of ideas from

Sogno di Archimede with the funnel-illustrated cover, one of the most famous of the prog world, that will become the very symbol of **A&M**. Ideal point break of fusion between the steep rock-jazz of **Mahavishnu Orchestra** and the Orchestral Rock of **Yes**, this band doesn't aim for a pure technical impact, but towards a global and colorful dimension, a structure that leaves free spaces with limited solos, melodic and catchy themes (like in the hymn "Gravity 9.81") and acute Mediterranean humor. **A&M** conquers the favors of both critics and public, so they are granted the opportunity to play as opening group to **Gentle Giant** and **PFM**. Less radical than **Area** and more sophisticated than the **Perigeo**, their second album *Giro Di Valzer Per Domani* is published: the entrance of the ex-**Procession** singer **Gianfranco Gaza** and a new found research of synthesis in the compositions, make

this second LP a more fluid and complete work without altering their style. **A&M**'s personality is compact and adamant: on a tight rhythmic structure, the combination between keyboards, horns, violins and guitars makes them a sort of rock-jazz orchestra. After some years of pause the renewed lineup gives birth to *Quinto Stato*, a work with funk and pop-jazz references, with lyrics that reflect the political contradictions of the time. After another long break, in which excellent projects (**Venegoni & Co., Esagono**) are pursued, in the mid '80s **A&M**, lead only by **Chirico**, return with two LPs of conventional Jazz Fusion. During the '90s **Beppe Crovella**'s label Electromantic produces some New-Prog bands and will guide the return of **A&M** with *Murales*, an album of elegant and contaminated fusion. They punctually begin to publish new live-albums and Electromantic opens its archives releasing *Extractions*, a new studio album which recovers some old ideas, and the album *33* which is another glorious tribute to their past. In 2015 **Venegoni** and **Chirico** consolidate **A&M** by publishing a new masterpiece, *Universi Paralleli*, proving their creativity is more alive than ever. **D.Z.**

RECOMMENDED RECORDINGS:
TILT - IMMAGINI PER UN ORECCHIO *(Cramps, 1974)* **GIRO DI VALZER PER DOMANI** *(Cramps, 1975)* **QUINTO STATO** *(Cramps, 1979)* **ACQUARIO** *(Studio, 1983)* **CHILDREN'S BLUES** *(Augusta, 1985)* **LIVE** *(live, Vinyl Magic 1990)*, **MURALES** *(Electromantic, 2000)* **ARTICOLLEZIONE** *(Electromantic, 2002)* **LIVE 1974/2000** *(live, Electromantic, 2002)* **PROGDAY SPECIAL** *(live, Electromantic, 2003)* **ESTRAZIONI** *(Electromantic, 2005)* **FIRST LIVE IN JAPAN** *(live, Electromantic, 2006)* **33** *(Electromantic, 2008)* **UNIVERSI PARALLELI** *(Sfera/Cramps/Sony, 2015)*.

Europe: ITALY

IL BALLETTO DI BRONZO

Gianni Leone - *keyboards, vocals,* **Marco Cecioni, Lino Ajello** - *guitars,* **Gianchi Stinga** - *drums,* **Michele Cupaiolo, Vito Manzari** - *bass.*

At the origin of the geography of Italian Prog we find **Battitori Selvaggi**, one of the first bands of Naples' beat, founded in 1963 by **Raffaele Cascone**: spooling between London and Naples, he immediately becomes a key character in the change of Neapolitan music and in '72 he will become the DJ of a TV broadcast called Per voi giovani. After the exit of **Cascone** the band becomes **Big Ben** and then **Balletto di Bronzo**, inspired by the painting *Bronze Ballet* by Edward Wardsworth. They issue some songs until the debut album arrives: *Sirio 2222* is like a bomb, not even **New Trolls** and **Le Orme** dared as much. Though still bond to beat melodies and lyrics, this hard-rock has an innovative strength without equal in Italy: loud and psychedelic, akin to **Led Zeppelin** and **Cream**. In parallel another band was making its way: **Lino Vairetti**'s *Città Frontale* (once **Volti Di Pietra**). Playing among their lines was young organist **Gianni Leone**, who studied piano from the age of eight and was looking for a place to explore his non conventional ideas. He joins **BDB** upsetting the balance of the group and the encounter with **Vito Manzari** (former in **Quelle Strane Cose Che**) will mark the end of a first line-up, and the start of **Gianni** as their new leader. In love with **Emerson**, **Zappa**, **Schoenberg** and **Brian Auger**, he discovers a book about the submerged island of Ys and elaborates a concept that recalls those mysterious atmospheres. Published by Polydor, *YS* is another revolutionary album where any trace of heavy or post-beat disappears. The band's new language becomes difficult, complex, unpredictable, closer to **King Crimson**'s *Lizard* or to certain sophisticated solutions by **Egg**. It is the story of the last man on the Earth, who faces three encounters before disappearing, just like for the legendary Breton islet: the five movements compose one long suite to which also participates a choir directed by Detto Mariano. The Symphonic Rock of **BDB** has little in common with **ELP** or **Genesis**: it reminds us of the structures and dynamics of **Yes**, but the Gothic choirs, the visionary lyrics, the horrific atmospheres, sometimes morbid or grotesque, make it a great deal more personal. Just like **Renaissance** between their second and the third lp, also **BDB** are playing now in an entirely new line-up, more acrobatic than before, and they see an histrionic **Leone** as their deus ex machina surrounded by modern and ancient keyboards. Yet success brings them to the end of their story: the band experiments with every type of excess in their new country house in Rimini, but they actually do not conclude anything concrete and will close their fairy-tale despite the fact **Eddie Offord**, producer of **Yes** in England, is showing them some interest. Fed up with art-rock, **Leone** then moves to New York where he follows the new wave becoming **LeoNero**. He and publishes *Vero* ('77), then goes off to Hollywood and releases *Monitor* ('81): the first is a mix of electronic rock, **Bowie** and memoirs of **BDB**, the second is more in line with the electro-pop genre. In the '90 fans all around (particularly Japanese and South Americans) show an increasing attention to *YS*: this induces **Gianni** to look through his repertoire despite the difficulty of creating a stable line-up. In 1999 Mellow Records issues *Trys*, a good live album that reveals modern arrangements and new ideas, while the legend of **BDB** still reaps the appreciation of old and new fans who never skip a concert of the charismatic **Gianni Leone**. Following this renewed interest, **Cecioni** and **Ajello** resurrected the original sound of the band and publish a brand new album entitled *Cuma 2016 D.C.* with **Leone** participating as special guest. **D.Z.**

DISCOGRAPHY:
SIRIO 2222 *(RCA, 1970)* **YS** *(Polydor, 1972)* **IL RE DEL CASTELLO** *(Raro! 1990)* **TRYS** *(live, Mellow Records, 1999)* **"CUMA 2016 D.C"** Balletto di Bronzo di Ajello e Cecioni *(BTF, 2016)*

Europe: ITALY

BANCO DEL MUTUO SOCCORSO

Francesco Di Giacomo, Tony D'Alessio - *vocals*, **Marcello Todaro, Filippo Marcheggiani, Nicola Di Già, Rodolfo Maltese** - *guitars, trumpet*, **Pierluigi Calderoni, Fabio Moresco** - *drums*, **Renato D'Angelo, Marco Capozi** - *bass*, **Gianni Nocenzi, Vittorio Nocenzi**, - *keyboards*.

Fundamental group in the national economy of Prog Rock, **Banco del Mutuo Soccorso** is the band that managed to capitalize more than any other in an independent key and to re-read the Progressive code of the new musical wave coming from the UK. *Banco del Mutuo Soccorso* iis their first album (better known as *Money-Bank* for the Avant-garde cover). A very structural, incisive, refined, complex and passionate project both for the essence and quality and the lucidity shown in the brave attempt to preserve a historical page of the Italian patrimony such as the Melodrama. Built on a Symphonic framework, **Francesco Di Giacomo**'s vocal chords give it heart and lyricism and brothers **Vittorio** and **Gianni Nocenzi** on keyboards (organ and piano) make it soon become incandescent lava. Songs like "R.I.P.", "Metamorfosi" and "Il giardino del Mago" are not only worthy for their musical structure but also for the excellent lyrics that, like blades, lacerate the meats and become food for the brain: the aversion for wars, the regret, the nightmares and the ancestral memories that permeate the album, draw apocalyptic sceneries as many as the holes in the soul. *Darwin!*, their second album, is a sweet and yearning arrangement of the great scientist's theory on evolution: "L'evoluzione", "La conquista della posizione eretta", "750.000 anni fa... l'amore?" and "Cento mani e cento occhi" are simply sublime and they manage to insinuate more than one question. In 1973 *Io Sono Nato Libero* was released, another great album that, although not reaching the previous heights, contains excellent concepts and at least two songs destined to outlive them like "Non mi rompete" and "Canto nomade per un prigioniero politico".

Some time later, as for others before them, they try the English path and they record *Banco* for **Greg Lake**'s label Manticore (bass and voice of **E.L.&P.**) which translates some of their most famous songs. *Come in un'ultima cena*, of 1976 still has good intuitions and great energy and the European tour with **Gentle Giant** makes them famous. In the same period they publish *Garofano Rosso* (soundtrack of the homonym film by Luigi Faccini), an instrumental project that will give them the courage to record the extraordinary *...di terra*, without singing parts, proof of their state of grace.

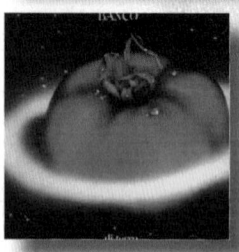

At the end of the decade *Canto Di Primavera* and the live performance *Capolinea* will unfortunately mark the end of an era. The cultural and musical crisis of the 80s forces them to an abrupt commercial swerve. *Urgentissimo, Buone Notizie* and *...E Via* bring them further apart from the charts and from the heart of the fans. The rebirth comes thanks to the re-editing of the first two albums published as *Da Qui Messere Si Domina La Valle*, extraordinary example of how music, just like the Arab Phoenix, knows how to be rise from its own ashes and become immortal. Sadly in 2014 **Di Giacomo** dies in a car crash. **Nocenzi** pays tribute to him at once releasing the album: *Un Idea Che Non Puoi Fermare* where several artists are singing **BMS** songs. One year later, also **Rodolfo Maltese**, dies after a long illness opening the future of this band to new musicians. **F.V.**

DISCOGRAPHY (compilations not included):
BANCO DEL MUTUO SOCCORSO *(Ricordi, 1972)* **DARWIN!** *(Ricordi, 1972)* **IO SONO NATO LIBERO** *(Ricordi, 1973)* **BANCO** *(Manticore, 1974)* **GAROFANO ROSSO** *(Manticore, 1976)* **COME IN UN'ULTIMA CENA** *(Manticore, 1976)* **AS IN A LAST SUPPER** *(Manticore, 1976)* **...DI TERRA** *(Ricordi, 1978)* **CANTO DI PRIMAVERA** *(Ricordi, 1979)* **CAPOLINEA** *(Ricordi, 1979)* **URGENTISSIMO** *(CBS, 1980)* **BUONE NOTIZIE** *(CBS, 1981)* **BANCO** *(CBS, 1983)* **...E VIA** *(CBS, 1985)* **DONNA PLAUTILLA** *(Raro!, 1989)* **DA QUI MESSERE SI DOMINA LA VALLE** *(Virgin, 1991)* **IL 13** *(EMI, 1994)* **NUDO** *(EMI, 1997)* **NO PALCO** *(Sony, 2003)* **...SEGUENDO LE TRACCE** *(Maracash, 2005)* **UN'IDEA CHE NON PUOI FERMARE.** *(SELF, 2014)* **TRANSIBERIANA** *(Inside-Out, 2019)*

Europe: ITALY

FRANCO BATTIATO

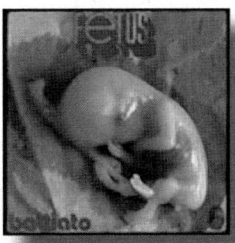

One of the greatest musicians and Italian artists ever, who passed away in the past 2021. He was musically formed at the end of the '60s and already collaborating with artists among like **Giorgio Gaber**.
After having recording some commercial singles, he decides for a total makeover and publishes *Fetus* in 1972, with the experimental label Bla Bla. Since this debut he immediately shows his propensity towards Electronic and contemporary Intellectual music which will grow and consolidate in the next works. It is this constant research and his charming creation of musical plots, with the aid of the VCS3 synthesizer, that puts him among the first pioneers of Italian Prog. He is also an innovator regarding lyrics, full of sophisticated and Experimental references like singing backwards sentences, only apparently senseless.
In the early '70s his ties to the underground Italian culture are tight: memorable his collaboration to **Collettivo Frankenstein** with **Gianni Sassi** and **Sergio Albergoni,** and the foundation of *Osage Tribe* that he quic-

kly abandons. His participation to this entourage creates long lasting friendships with other artists such as **Juri Camisasca**.
His prog masterpiece *Sulle corde di Aries* (1973) is rich in instrumental parts, anticipating by years what later will become World Music and the interest in Middle-Eastern cultures, in particular his personal interest in Sufis and in the doctrines of **Gurdjieff**, (Russian-Armenian philanthropist founder of a school of thought devoted to the attainment of a harmonic development of mankind). Immediately after the first three albums, **Battiato** will enter the realms of contemporary Avantgarde musical research, winning the **Karl Heinz Stockhausen** prize with *L'egitto Prima Delle Sabbie* (1978), last chapter of his sound analysis that will consecrate him as artist in the cultural elìte. **Battiato** will always remain a true Prog artist and innovator, even though with a puzzling change of route, in 1979 he publishes apparently Commercial music (helped by violinist **Giusto Pio**) that will bring him to the top of the charts and to the notoriety he still maintains. This new status will not prevent his continuous desire to also experiment, like the hit songs he wrote together with philosopher **Manlio Sgalambro**, or the lyrical operas like *Genesi* and *Gilgamesh* that prove his compositional depth. From the end of the '90s to today we also assist the recovery of his Electronic sonorities and Psychedelic Prog, typical of his first works, such as *Gommalacca*, *Dieci stratagemmi*, *Apriti Sesamo* and the last *Joe Patti's Experimental Group*, which only confirms his great coherence and unique and inimitable style.. **M.G.**

DISCOGRAPHY (Compilations and live albums not included):

FETUS *(Bla Bla, 1972)* **POLLUTION** *(Bla Bla, 1972)* **SULLE CORDE DI ARIES** *(Bla Bla, 1973)* **CLIC** *(Bla Bla, 1974)* **MADEMOISELLE LE GLADIATOR** *(Bla Bla, 1975)* **BATTIATO** *(Ricordi, 1977)* **JUKE BOX** *(Ricordi, 1978)* **L'EGITTO PRIMA DELLE SABBIE** *(Ricordi, 1978)* **L'ERA DEL CINGHIALE BIANCO** *(Emi, 1979)* **PATRIOTS** *(Emi, 1980)* **LA VOCE DEL PADRONE** *(Emi, 1981)* **L'ARCA DI NOE'** *(Emi, 1982)* **ORIZZONTI PERDUTI** *(Emi, 1983)* **MONDI LONTANISSIMI** *(Emi, 1985)* **GENESI** *(Fonit Cetra, 1987)* **FISIOGNOMICA** *(Emi, 1988)* **COME UN CAMMELLO IN UNA GRONDAIA** *(Emi, 1991)* **GILGAMESH** *(Emi, 1992)* **CAFFE' DE LA PAIX** *(Emi, 1993)* **MESSA ARCAICA** *(Emi, 1994)* **L'OMBRELLO E LA MACCHINA DA CUCIRE** *(Emi, 1995)* **L'IMBOSCATA** *(Emi, 1996)* **GOMMALACCA** *(Emi, 1998)* **FLEURS** *(Columbia/Sony, 1999)* **CAMPI MAGNETICI** *(Sony Classical, 2000)* **FERRO BATTUTO** *(Columbia/Sony, 2001)* **FLEURS 3** *(Columbia/Sony, 2002)* **DIECI STRATAGEMMI** *(Columbia/Sony, 2005)* **IL VUOTO** *(Columbia/Sony, 2007)* **FLEURS 2** *(Universal, 2008)* **INNERES AUGE** *(Universal, 2009)* **TELESIO** *(Sony Classical, 2011)* **APRITI SESAMO** *(Universal, 2012)* **JOE PATTI'S EXPERIMENTAL GROUP** *(Universal, 2014)*

Europe: ITALY

LUCIO BATTISTI

The majority of his fans never probably really understood the hugeness of his Art. They will forever remember the songs written with **Mogol** (**Giulio Rapetti**, poet and author) which changed the history of Italian Commercial music. The albums listed here as a matter of fact, belong to works that mainly are among those less liked by his the greater audience, yet they represent the true nature of this great singer, songwriter and musician.

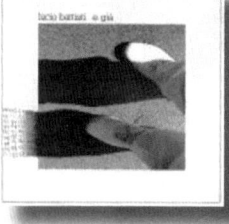

Since the beginning **Lucio Battisti** had the luck of working with the best musicians and Italian instrumentalists available. In his first true album *Amore e non Amore* conceived as a project and not as a collection of successes, he can immediately count on the help of the entire **Premiata Forneria Marconi** and the result is evident: free and fresh music as a good underground album would require. Three years later his most misunderstood masterpiece *Anima Latina*, is published. Loved and hated by critics and public, it contains original and genius Prog intuitions for that time. After eight years of success he will break his artistic association with **Mogol** to publish *E già* entirely recorded and produced with **Greg Walsh** and using only synthesizers and drum machines. A fascinating experiment that no other Italian artist will ever dare emulate.

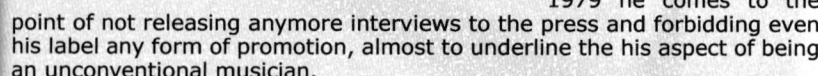

Many will always criticize **Lucio Battisti**'s behavior, bashful and shy: he will stop performing live from 1972, choosing to construct his music with perfectionism and maniacal care inside some of the best recording studios known at the time. His conceptual idea was clear and precise: the will to communicate only through his art, so from 1979 he comes to the point of not releasing anymore interviews to the press and forbidding even his label any form of promotion, almost to underline the his aspect of being an unconventional musician.

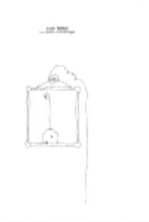

True revolution is *Don Giovanni*, masterpiece of musical sensitivity and first episode of an artistic association that will bring to desperation his tireless fans and at the same time is the joy of any true passionate of this unpredictable artist. With lyrics by the Avant-garde poet **Pasquale Panella**, he will publish another four albums using almost exclusive Electronic arrangements with a language that, for the Italian song-making, was totally unheard of and innovative. Besides the already quoted *Don Giovanni* are *La Sposa Occidentale* and *Hegel*, his very last albums. Death parts us from this irreplaceable genius in 1998, at only 55 years of age. All of his works, including those more experimental, live on and still are looked up to by the best.

M.G.

DISCOGRAPHY:

LUCIO BATTISTI *(Ricordi, 1969)* **EMOZIONI** *(Ricordi, 1970)* **AMORE E NON AMORE** *(Ricordi, 1971)* **VOLUME 4** *(Ricordi, 1971)* **UMANAMENTE UOMO : IL SOGNO** *(Numero Uno, 1972)* **IL MIO CANTO LIBERO** *(Numero Uno, 1972)* **IL NOSTRO CARO ANGELO** *(Numero Uno, 1973)* **ANIMA LATINA** *(Numero Uno, 1974)* **LA BATTERIA, IL CONTRABBASSO, ECCETERA...** *(Numero Uno, 1976)* **IO, TU, NOI TUTTI** *(Numero Uno, 1977)* **UNA DONNA PER AMICO** *(Numero Uno, 1978)* **UNA GIORNATA UGGIOSA** *(Numero Uno, 1980)* **E GIA'** *(Numero Uno, 1982)* **DON GIOVANNI** *(Numero Uno, 1986)* **L'APPARENZA** *(Numero Uno, 1988)* **LA SPOSA OCCIDENTALE** *(Sony, 1990)* **COSA SUCCEDERA' ALLA RAGAZZA** *(Sony, 1992)* **HEGEL** *(Numero Uno, 1994)*.

Europe: ITALY

DEUS EX MACHINA

Claudio Trotta - *drums,*
Alessandro Porreca - *bass,*
Maurino Collina - *guitar,*
Alessandro Bonetti - *violin,*
Luigi Ricciardiello - *keyboards,*
Alberto Piras - *vocals,*
Fabrizio Puglisi - *keyboards.*

Prog music is clearly in crisis at the end of the '80s also in Italy. Many bands start to form and they publish works that tend more towards Symphonic Rock or New-Prog, drawing inspiration both from the great British teachers and from their own fellow countrymen. In this panorama **Deus Ex Machina** are somewhat like a white whale with the greatest courage. Discovered by Kaliphonia Records' owner **Raoul Caprio**, master in recognizing progressive talents, this band based its sound

on a sort of personal Jazz-Rock with very aggressive traits, like **Area**, and particularly elevated technical ability, that allows the musicians to move in complex compositions with more than one execution difficulty. Their singer **Alberto Piras** is universally appreciated for his excellent vocals and is one of the best heirs of the unforgotten **Demetrio Stratos**. They debuts with *Gladium Caeli* in 1990 proving immediately their uncommon talent. Curiously all lyrics are in Latin, yet the album is greeted warmly by the Prog community as a beautiful gust of freshness.

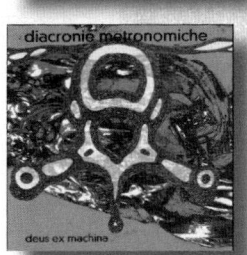

The name **Deus Ex Machina** starts to spread around the underground circuits (and not only) and to an already notable debut follows a even greater work, the self-titled 1992 album, in which they manage to improve the peculiarities of the previous. With *De Repubblica*, dated 1994, the qualitative levels have become impressive: the band touches its artistic peak with a CD full of good ideas and of fanciful compositions, in which their instrumental ability never ceases to amaze. It soon will become one of the most accredited works of contemporary Prog.

After the beautiful live recording *Diacronie Metronomiche*, confirmation of their state of grace, they release in 1998 *Equilibrismo da Insofferenza* in which the Jazz component is given more space thanks to the abundant use of brass instruments. *Cinque* of 2002 is the first issued record by Cuneiform after their breakup with Kaliphonia: closer to RIO, it helps consolidates their name, by now immediately recognizable. Their last work *Imparis*, is a superb album of Jazz-rock closer to **Mahavishnu Orchestra**. Recorded in two days in the Parisian club 'Le Triton' (2006) it came out two years later with a radiant live DVD concert. Ten years before a brand new album in 2016, *Devoto*, where they go back to their roots rediscovering an aggressive Hard Jazz-Rock with their incredible Fusion performances.

G.D.S.

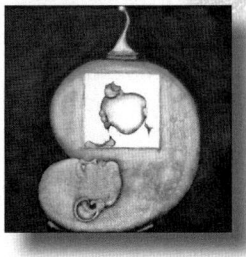

DISCOGRAPHY:

GLADIUM CAELI *(1990, Kaliphonia)* **DEUS EX MACHINA** *(1992, Kaliphonia)* **DE REPUBLICA** *(1995, Kaliphonia)* **DIACRONIE METRONOMICHE** *(1996, Kaliphonia)* **NON EST ARS QUAE AD EFFECTUM CASUS VENIT** *(1997, Kaliphonia, live, solo in LP)* **EQUILIBRISMO DA INSOFFERENZA** *(1998, Kaliphonia)* **CINQUE** *(2002, Cuneiform Records)* **IMPARIS** *(2008, Cuneiform Records)* **DEVOTO** *(2016, Private Pressing).*

Europe: ITALY

FINISTERRE

Fabio Zuffanti - *bass, vocals,* **Boris Valle, Agostino Macor** - *keyboards,* **Stefano Marelli** - *guitars, vocals,* **Marco Cavani, Marcello Mazzocchi, Andrea Orlando** - *drums,* **Sergio Grazia, Marco Moro, Francesca Biagini** - *flute, vocals,* **Edmondo Romano** - *horns,* **Sergio Caputo** - *violin.*

The utopia of new prog and its revival after years of being forgotten, the return to a musical research, the conquest of a new artistic dignity: speaking of **Finisterre** means entering a dream come true, but that unfortunately did not last long. Among the many Italian and international New Prog bands, better than others, this band managed to bring the authentic spirit of Art-rock to the contemporary culture, with freshness, vigor, nostalgia and without denying themselves anything at all. Here we find the debut of excellent bassist and composer **Fabio Zuffanti**, at the very beginning of his restless career and numerous future parallel projects.

Finisterre begin in 1993 with the trio **Zuffanti, Marelli, Valley**. The newborn Mellow Records invests on the group and records *Finisterre* in the January of 1995: a pleasant first album, even if quite impersonal due to the long compositions that recall **PFM**, **Yes** and **Jethro Tull**, rrearranged lightheartedly with the only defect of the absence of an important lead singer.

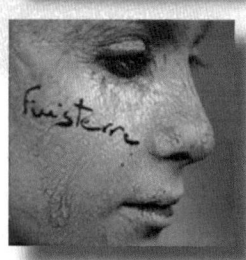

Their masterpiece In Limine is one of the most beautiful pages of the history of Italian Rock: a delicate and overwhelming album, with an eye on both Classical and Contemporary music, Jazz and Ethnic from a Rock perspective: immediate references from **King Crimson**'s *Lizard* for the balance of the arrangements and the wider dimension of the ensemble. They gain notoriety abroad too, charming when performing live, they participate in all the main Prog festivals recording excellent live albums and are present in many tributes (**Genesis, Van Der Graaf, Camel**, other minor Italian prog bands) of this so effervescent and magic period. *Ai Margini Della Terra Fertile* confirms them as heirs of **PFM**, not only for evident stylistic affinities but also for the ability to hold the stage with involvement and passion. Nevertheless, a more uncertain period is about to begin: the sense of borders, with which they already had to deal with before, becomes ever more stressing, the need to cross the tight Prog label and their encounter with producer **Roberto Colombo**'s Iridea is decisive. *In Ogni Luogo* is a change in sound which leaves back the sumptuous Prog of the early years and leads them to a new and more concrete form of Art-rock, dry and nervous and using mainly guitars. Influenced by names such as **Giardini di Mirò** and **Bluvertigo**, it is an album that doesn't conquer the fans but will be re-evaluated in the long run because of the good quality and level of its production.

The time for a healthy pause comes and some musicians develop parallel projects, but **Zuffanti** has all the intentions of recording a third LP: the label Immaginifica owned by **Franz di Cioccio** from **PFM** takes interest in the band and supports them for *La Meccanica Naturale* released in 2004, which proposes a new path in the Prog genre, not necessarily heading towards Indie or Alternative Rock, oscillating between **Battiato** and **Genesis, Yes** and **CSI**. Intellectual Rock? Certainly. **Fabio Zuffanti** then moves on to new projects with **Höstsonaten**, and **La Zona** (Post-Rock), **Maschera di Cera** (Symphonic Vintage Rock), **Aries** (Prog-Folk), **Quadraphonic** (Electronics) and the more recent **Rohmer**: a creative and prolific talent of which Italy should be proud.

D.Z.

DISCOGRAPHY:

FINISTERRE *(Mellow Records, 1995)* **IN LIMINE** *(Mellow Records, 1996)* **LIVE... AI MARGINI DELLA TERRA FERTILE** *(live, Mellow Records, 1996)* **IN OGNI LUOGO** *(Iridea, 1998)* **LIVE AT PROGDAY 1997** *(live, Proglodite, 2000)* **STORYBOOK** *(live, Moonjune, 2001)* **HARMONY OF THE SPHERES** *(Mellow Records, 2002)* **LA MECCANICA NATURALE** *(Immaginifica, 2004)* **MEMOIRS** *(Mellow Records, 2014).*

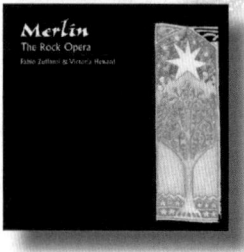

Europe: ITALY

GOBLIN

Claudio Simonetti, Maurizio Guarini - *keyboards*, **Fabio Pignatelli** - *bass*, **Walter Martino, Agostino Marangolo** - *drums*, **Massimo Morante, Carlo Pennisi** - *guitar*, **Antonio Marangolo** - *horns*.

In Giovanni Aloisio's book *Un mondo a parte* (2005) he considers **Goblin** to be a phenomenon, an anomaly: one of the most prolific European bands, that in the era of festivals, preferred studio recording to a concert, and produced independent and double albums with OST for films, idolized abroad but looked down upon in Italy.

At the end of the '60s **Claudio Simonetti** and **Walter Martino** create the band **Ritratto di Dorian Gray**, a quintet performing covers from **Yes**, **Deep Purple** and **King Crimson**. This band participates in '71 to the Festival of Caracalla and the following year is invited to open **Van Der Graaf Generator**'s concert at the Piper Club. Re-named **Seconda Generazione** and later on **Oliver**, they go to London as **Cherry Five** acquiring singer **Clive Haynes**, and contact **Eddie Offord** for their audition in Manticore that doesn't go well. So they sign up with the label Cinevox owned by **Enrico Simonetti** (**Claudio**'s father) who dislikes **Clive**'s voice replacing him with **Tony Tartarini** from *Uovo di Colombo*. Here they become **Goblin**, but all previous material will be published in 1976 still as *Cherry Five*.

Film director **Dario Argento** is now working at his forth thriller with a soundtrack written by the great jazz player **Giorgio Gaslini**. His desire to use a rock band convinces him to assign the execution to **Goblin**, that add some of their own songs and ultimate the OST of *Profondo Rosso*. It is a triumph: the film is one of the most innovative thrillers world wide. The relation between images and music feels complete and the album stays for a very long time at the top of the charts. It is a moment of great glory for progressive rock. Two years earlier William Friedkin used *Tubular Bells* for his film The Exorcist: **Goblin** derive inspiration from **Oldfield**'s initial arpeggio creating a more hypnotic and visionary key, with sharp Rock guitars.

Marangolo (ex **Flea** and **Etna**) and **Guarini** revive the band and participate to **Riccardo Cocciante**'s tour. Then in 1976 they release an excellent album unrelated to the film making business, *Roller*, considered to be their true debut with influences from **Yes** and **ELP**, but with a more dynamic sound, vivid and funky with incisive Jazz-rock hookups and a personality by now recognizable also in the expressiveness of its single members. In 1977 **Simonetti**'s morbid and dark musical atmospheres accompany the memorable initial sequence of *Suspiria* taking them back into the film biz. In the '78 the concept *Il Fantastico Viaggio Del 'Bagarozzo' Mark* inspired midway by **Wakeman** and **Kraftwerk**, introduces greatly sung tracks but still a commercial failure. Same for *Volo*, a pop album that **Pignatelli** produces with **Antonello Venditti**'s band with which he has many past collaborations. **Simonetti** recovers Classical atmospheres founding 2 new groups, **Horror Project** and **Daemonia**; **Pignatelli** and the others return as **Goblin** in 2005 reintegrating **Simonetti** only in 2011 with a new tour and a new live album. At the moment the name is bouncing from one court to another because of the disputes between musicians who are using different names like **Goblin Rebirth**, **Enrico Simonetti's Goblin** and **Goblin 4**.

D.Z.

DISCOGRAPHY:

PROFONDO ROSSO *(Cinevox, 1975)* **ROLLER** *(Cinevox, 1976)* **SUSPIRIA** *(Cinevox, 1977)* **IL FANTASTICO VIAGGIO DEL "BAGAROZZO" MARK** *(Cinevox, 1978)* **ZOMBI** *(Cinevox, 1978)* **SOLAMENTE NERO** *(Cinevox, 1978)* **LA VIA DELLA DROGA** *(Cinevox, 1978)* **BUIO OMEGA** *(Cinevox, 1979)* **SQUADRA ANTIGANGSTERS** *(Cinevox, 1979)* **AMO NON AMO** *(Cinevox, 1979)* **PATRICK** *(Cinevox, 1979)* **CONTAMINATION** *(Cinevox, 1980)* **VOLO** *(Cinevox, 1982)* **SIMONETTI-MORANTE-PIGNATELLI: TENEBRE** *(Cinevox, 1982)* **NOTTURNO** *(Cinevox, 1983)* **PHENOMENA** *(Cinevox, 1984)* **LA CHIESA** *(Cinevox, 1989)* **NON HO SONNO** *(Cinevox, 2000)* **BACK TO THE GOBLIN 2005** *(Goblin, 2005)* **HORROR BOX** *(Cinevox, 2000)* **GOBLIN REBIRTH** *(Goblin, 2005)*.

Europe: ITALY

MUSEO ROSENBACH

Giancarlo Golzi - *drums, percussion, vocals,* **Alberto Moreno** - *bass, piano,* **Enzo Merogno** - *guitar, vocals,* **Pit Corradi** - *keyboards,* **Stefano "Lupo" Galifi** - *lead vocals,* **Andrea Biancheri** - *vocals,* **Marco Balbo** - *guitar,* **Marioluca Bariona** - *keyboards.*

When in 1970 the mythical group **Il Sistema** breaks up, some of its musicians join **Quinta Strada** soon changing name to **Museo Rosenbach**. So begins one of the most charming stories of Italian Prog, since the band was already set into the spirit of research that in those years pushed the genre to widen its borders. After some concerts they audition for Ricordi Records which signs them up. They publish the extraordinary *Zarathustra* of 1973, a pillar of Italian Prog with its spectacular and original Symphonic matrix, far from any attempt of imitating the British models.
The album is perfect, focused on keyboards

without technicalities, but which rather aim to create refined atmospheres, at times powerful and always packed with pathos with a Classical aftertaste. Unfortunately the Nietzsche themes on which the album is based and the bust of Mussolini on the cover create some issues. This misunder-

standing and the consequent unfair accusation of fascism is inevitable. Plus the musicians disagree on the path to follow and soon break-up taking very different roads. **Giancarlo Golzi** for one, joins **J.E.T.** that in 1974 sees the entry of **Antonella Ruggiero** as lead singer and the band is renamed **Matia Bazar**.
Twenty years go by and in 1992 some archive material is published in *Live 72*, containing a concert they held

just before issuing *Zarathustra*, with the songs in different versions from the album and brass playing by **Leonardo Lagorio**, future **Celeste** member. Rare & Unreleased is a collection of recordings held during the Ricordi audition, when finally they reunite with a partially new line-up, publishing *Exit* in 2000 and a more conventional Pop-rock style. In 2003 they participate in the project by label Colossus, a triple cd entitled *Kalevala*, along with **Museo Rosenbach**. In 2012 and 2013 another live version of *Zarathustra* is published and the new studio album *Barbarica* ends this tale. **Giancarlo Golzi** dies suddenly in august 2015 after a strong heart attack and now the band's destiny lies in the hands of his colleagues guided by **Galifi**.
G.D.S.

DISCOGRAPHY:
ZARATHUSTRA *(1973, Ricordi)* **LIVE 72** *(1992, Mellow Records)* **RARE & UNRELEASED** *(1992, Mellow Records)* **EXIT** *(2000, Carisch)* **ZARATHUSTRA LIVE IN STUDIO** *(2012, Immaginifica)* **BARBARICA** *(2013, Immaginifica)* **Participations:** **KALEVALA** *(2003, Musea).*

Europe: ITALY

NEW TROLLS

Vittorio De Scalzi, Giorgio Usai, Maurizio Salvi - *keyboards, flute, vocals,* **Giorgio D'Adamo, Frank Laugelli** - *bass,* **Gianni Belleno, Alfio Vitanza** - *drums, vocals,* **Nico Di Palo, Ricky Belloni** - *guitars, bass, vocals.*

After cruising the charts with their Psychedelic raids, this band will be the first to bring Italian music away from Beat and into a more intellectual song-writing dimension. This happens with the album *Senza Orario Senza Bandiera* (lyrics by **Fabrizio De André** and **Riccardo Mannerini**) which also results being the first concept-album in the history of all Italian music, landing **New Trolls** directly into the Prog genre without knocking on the front door.

Their next, *Concerto Grosso per i New Trolls*, is composed by **Luis Enriquez Bacalov** (grammy award for the OST of Giuseppe Tornatore's film *Il Postino*) and contains Shakespeare inspired lyrics with the merit of remodeling the Baroque experience (originally based on two different instruments dueling in a continuous game of procrastination) into a real Classical orchestra.

The album is a combustion of emotions and elements that will soon become a pillar of Prog Rock thanks to its amazing success. *Searching for a Land* is a rather different situation: even if it doesn't obtain the same success, it however proves them to be in continuous evolution and gives us one of their most beautiful songs, "In St. Peter's Day". After this a series of parallel projects begin, among which the band **N.T. Atomic System** (**Vittorio De Scalzi** and **Giorgio D'Adamo**) and *Nico, Gianni, Frank and Maurizio* (**Ibis**).

With the entry of **Ricky Belloni**, in 1976, the band goes back to its original nucleus and issues *Concerto Grosso n. 2*, a superlative album, though slightly inferior to the precedent masterpiece. In "Le Roi Soleil" they try to mimic **Queen**'s "Bohemian Rhapsody" with a good result. The albums that follow are more easy-listening, leading them in a different direction and causing new and incurable frictions.

The impossibility of using the original name creates further problems, but also three new entities: **La Storia Dei New Trolls** (lead by **De Scalzi** and **Di Palo**) which go on tour with the *Concerto Grosso* albums and a real orchestra; **Il Mito dei New Trolls** (with **Usai, Belleno** and **Belloni**); and more recently the **UT New Trolls** (**Belleno** and **Maurizio Salvi**, oriented towards a more technical Prog Rock). In 2006, **De Scalzi** and **Di Palo** start a new and strange *Concerto Grosso* called *The Seven Seasons*. This inspires their fellow musicians and sees the rejoining of **Belleno, D'Adamo** and **Bacalov** to a new *Concerto Grosso N°3* released in 2013. **D'Adamo** dies and the others carry on their separate projects leaving fans to hope for a tribute concert someday.   **F.V.**

DISCOGRAPHY (Compilations not included):
SENZA ORARIO SENZA BANDIERA *(Fonit Cetra, 1968)* **NEW TROLLS** *(Fonit Cetra, 1970)* **CONCERTO GROSSO** *(Fonit Cetra, 1971)* **SEARCHING FOR A LAND** *(Fonit Cetra, 1972, doppio)* **UT** *(Fonit Cetra, 1972)* **N.T. Atomic System: N.T. ATOMIC SYSTEM** *(Magma, 1973)* **N.T. Atomic System: TEMPI DISPARI** *(Magma, 1974)* **Ibis: CANTI D'INNOCENZA, CANTI DI SPERANZA** *(Fonit Cetra, 1973)* **Ibis: SUN SUPREME** *(Polydor, 1974)* **Ibis: IBIS** *(Polydor, 1975)* **CONCERTO GROSSO N. 2** *(Magma, 1976)* **LIVE** *(Magma, 1976)* **REVIVAL** *(Magma, 1977)* **ALDEBARAN** *(WBT, 1978)* **NEW TROLLS** *(WBT, 1979)* **FS** *(Fonit Cetra, 1981)* **AMERICA OK** *(Fonit Cetra, 1983)* **TOUR** *(Fonit Cetra, 1985)* **AMICI** *(Ricordi, 1988)* **QUELLI COME NOI** *(WEA, 1992)* **THE SEVEN SEASONS** *(Aerostella/Edel, 2007)*. **UT (Uno Tempore): Live in Milan** *(Aerostella/Immaginifica, 2012)* **CONCERTO GROSSO N°3** *(Aerostella/Immaginifica, 2013)* **La leggenda NEW TROLLS: CONCERTO GROSSO N°1-2-3** *(Live - Aerostella/Immaginifica, 2014)* **UT New Trolls: DO UT DES** *(Aerostella/Immaginifica, 2013)* **UT New Trolls: È** *(Maracash, 2015)*

Europe: ITALY

LE ORME

Aldo Tagliapietra - *vocals, bass, guitar, sitar,* **Tony Pagliuca, Francesco Sartori, Michele Bon, Andrea Bassato** - *keyboards,* **Michi Dei Rossi** - *drums,* **Claudio Galieti** - *bass,* **Nino Smeraldi, Tolo Marton, Germano Serafin** - *guitars,* **Jimmy Spitaleri** - *vocals.*

Born as a beat band, a genre always leaving traces in their melodies, these pioneers from Venice gather in 1966 to record some singles the following year and a full album in 1968, *Ad Gloriam*: a Psychedelic pearl influenced by **The Beatles**, **Small Faces** and **The Kinks**, but with a melodic attitude already peculiar to their style. **Le Orme** pay great attention to the new Symphonic Pop coming from abroad like **ELP** and **Quatermass**, their idols, and they decide to carry out a similar project in Italy with the 1971 phenomenal album *Collage*, the first Italian project truly speaking a Pop language at the same level of their English competitors. The keyboards dominate the scene quoting **Alessandro Scarlatti** and echoing **Keith Emerson** and **Dave Greenslade**, with solid rhythms and **Aldo**'s ethereal voice, which will be their famous trademark.

Uomo Di Pezza is instead a concept album on enigmatic female figures: they are a trio greatly inspired by **Bach**, blending ballads and surreal atmospheres which hit the top of the charts also thanks to the controversial song "Gioco di Bimba".
After a tour with **Peter Hammill** as supporting act (he had just left **Van Der Graaf Generator**), their most important studio recording *Felona and Sorona* is published: a conflict among two planets symbolizing good and evil, with a sumptuous rock that permeates the music, and **Wagner**-ian hints, well structured and free from the residual bonds of traditional song writing. **Peter Hammill** translates their lyrics for the English version produced by label Charisma, and the band goes on a successful UK tour.

In 1974 *In Concerto* is published, the first live-album of Italian prog. They deepen their research and issue a more complex album, *Contrappunti*, where **Pagliuca** and **Tagliapietra** reach their compositional peak, accompanied by producer **Giampiero Reverberi** on piano. Then the downfall begins while they try adding a guitarist, but nothing really seems to surprise anymore. 1975 to 1977 sees a foreign recorded trilogy: *Smogmagica* (published in Los Angeles with for cover a painting by **Paul Whitehead**), *Verità nascoste* (in London), *Storia o leggenda* (in Paris). The band then closes the decade with *Florian*, a genial acoustic album issued at the peak of Disco music, using ancient instruments, Classical music, Minimalism, ballads and exoticism. Appreciated by the critique but not by the public, that also neglects their following album. *Venerdi* is the LP which changes this lack of interest and wins them a participation in the Sanremo Festival, but electronic pop is not their path. 1996 sees another mystical trilogy, *Il Fiume*, *Elementi* and *L'Infinito* (the last two have covers by **Paul Whitehead**). Concerts multiply and prog-fans worldwide are bewitched. Yet in 2009 **Aldo Tagliapietra** leaves the band and **Michi De Rossi** recruits **Jimmy Spitaleri** as lead singer, publishing a new album, *La Via Della Seta*, and more recently a rather needless new version of *Felona and Sorona*. **Dei Rossi** is of today the only original band member actively playing under the band's name.
D.Z.

DISCOGRAPHY:
AD GLORIAM *(Car Juke Box, 1968)* **L'AURORA** *(Car Juke Box, 1970)* **COLLAGE** *(Philips, 1971)* **UOMO DI PEZZA** *(Philips, 1972)* **FELONA E SORONA** *(Philips, 1973)* **FELONA & SORONA** *(Charisma, 1973)* **IN CONCERTO** *(live, Philips, 1974)* **CONTRAPPUNTI** *(Philips, 1974)* **SMOGMAGICA** *(Philips, 1975)* **VERITÀ NASCOSTE** *(Philips, 1976)* **STORIA O LEGGENDA** *(Philips, 1977)* **FLORIAN** *(Philips, 1979)* **PICCOLA RAPSODIA DELL'APE** *(Philips, 1980)* **VENERDÌ** *(DDD 1982)* **ORME** *(Polygram 1990)* **IL FIUME** *(Tring, 1996)* **AMICO DI IERI** *(Tring, 1997)* **ELEMENTI** *(Crisler, 2001)* **L'INFINITO** *(Crisler, 2004)* **LIVE IN PENNSYLVANIA** *(live, Self 2008)* **LA VIA DELLA SETA** *(Love Music/Self 2011)* **FELONA E SORONA 2016** *(BTF/Self 2016).*

Europe: ITALY

OSANNA

Lino Vairetti - *vocals, guitars, keyboards,* **Danilo Rustici, Gigi Borgogno, Fabrizio Fedele, Pako Capobianco** - *guitars,* **Elio D'Anna, Vito Ranucci, David Jackson** - *horns,* **Lello Brandi, Enzo Petrone, Nello D'Anna, Enzo Cascella** - *bass,* **Fabrizio D'Angelo Lancellotti, Luca Urciuolo, Oderigi Lusi, Sasà Priore** - *keyboards,* **Massimo Guarino, Gennaro Barba** - *drums,* **Irvin Luca Vairetti** - *keyboards, vocals.*

In the Naples the great rock prophets of 1970 are called **Osanna**. This band lived the '60s postwar period, when bands grew like mushrooms: at first called **Battitori Selvaggi** then as **Volti Di Pietra** (**Lino Vairetti**) and later as **Città Frontale**, they were initially influenced by Blues Rock. They change name for the last time when **Gianni Leone** exits and they meet **Elio D'Anna**. In 1971 the band acts as a support for **Arthur Brown**'s concert and participates in the most important Italian festivals, noticed at once by **Renzo Arbore** and **Fabrizio Zampa**. Signed up with Fonit Cetra, they publish a memorable LP entitled *L'Uomo*: n album with a foldable cover that becomes a poster of them dressed up in long robes and painted faces. Their sound lies between Hard-Rock, Jazz, Folk and political engagements with the volcanic expressiveness of **Vairetti**'s warm voice well blends with **Rustici**'s **Hendrix**-ian guitar and **D'Anna**'s charisma, echoing **Led Zeppelin** and **Jethro Tull**. On stage **Osanna** seem to perform theatrical music shows and support **Genesis**' Italian tour in August 1972 due to their visual choices that impress even **Peter Gabriel** (who had not yet worn the famous fox head). Fonit and **Luis Bacalov** involve them in a Rock-Orchestra challenge for the OST of the noir movie *Milano Calibro 9* by Fernando di Leo. But **Osanna** cultivates a more ambitious dream, *Palepoli*, an extraordinary Rock Opera based on a concept about Naples and its past, which strengthens the relation with the new environment of Neapolitan art. They also involve photographer Umberto Telesco, film director Tony Neiwiller and a group of actors among which Tonino Taiuti. If *L'Uomo* created a fracture with the Neapolitan melody, **Osanna** now recover more traditional roots: the two suites are fruit of a creative, passionate band influenced by **King Crimson** and **Van Der Graaf**, without sacrificing their own ideas flowing in a visceral and dynamic sound pot. The multimedia show tours Italy. **Osanna** also organize the historical festival **Be-In** of 1973, but the fatigue and some misunderstandings force them to a break. In 1974 *Landscape Of Life* proves to be a more cerebral Art-rock album, conceived for the foreign market, after which the band breaks up definitely. **Danilo Rustici** and **D'Anna** move to London and found **Uno**, then later with **Corrado Rustici** and others they also form the band **Nova**; **Vairetti** and **Guarino** instead set out to create **Città Frontale**. In 1978 **Osanna** reunite with the Fusion album *Suddance*, anticipating **Pino Daniele** and the Naples Power genre of the '80s. Despite the good critical response, the band is forced to break up once more. At the end of the '90s **Vairetti** returns with a young and trained Rock band, reforming **Osanna** in a completely new line-up. He rearranges old songs collected in the album *Taka Boom* and from the end of 2008 publishes *Prog Family* with **David Jackson** (escaped from **VDGG**) and other guests. In 2012 *Rosso Rock* is recorded partly live, with unpublished songs; the last releases are *Palepolitana* (double album where one of the two contains a live version of their famous *Palepoli*, while the other contains brand new songs) and *Papè Satan Aleppe* performed live. In 2021 the celebration of their 50 years comes out with a brand new album and a documentary film. **D.Z.**

DISCOGRAPHY:

L'UOMO *(Fonit Cetra 1971)* **PRELUDIO TEMA VARIAZIONI CANZONA** *(Fonit Cetra, 1972)* **PALEPOLI** *(Fonit Cetra, 1973)* **LANDSCAPE OF LIFE** *(Fonit Cetra, 1974)* **SUDDANCE** *(CBS, 1978)* **TAKA BOOM** *(Afrakà, 2001)* **LIVE - UOMINI E MITI** *(live, Suoni dal sud, 2004)* **PROG FAMILY** *(Afrakà/BTF, 2008)* **ROSSO ROCK** *(Afrakà/BTF, 2012)* **PALEPOLITANA** *(Afrakà/Maracash, 2015)* **PAPÈ SATAN ALEPPE** *(Afrakà/Maracash, 2016)* **50 IL DIEDRO DEL MEDITERRANEO** *(Afrakà/Maracash, 2021)*.

Europe: ITALY

PERIGEO

Giovanni Tommaso - bass, contrabass, synthesizers, vocals, **Franco D'Andrea** - piano, electric piano, synthesizers, **Claudio Fasoli** - horns, **Tony Sidney** - guitars, **Bruno Biriaco** - drums, **Tony Esposito** - percussion.

When **Perigeo**, at the apex of their career, opened for **Weather Report**, poor **Joe Zawinul** wasn't very happy that the public appreciated them so much. Thanks to a consolidated formula, this is one of the most talented bands of the European '70s with an unusual history, not only for the different musical language, but also for age and extraction.
Giovanni Tommaso is one of the most authoritative Italian jazz players of 1971: among the founders of **Quintetto di Lucca** at the end of the '50s, he played in the US wit **Sonny Rollins** and was of the closest partner of **Chet Baker** during his Italian stay. Like **Miles Davis** he felt that Jazz at the end of the '60s was at a dead end and in need of something new: the revolution of Electric Jazz is a decisive signal.
While in an orchestra in Rome, he looks for the right companions for his venture with a new modal language and electronic tools. Here he meets **Bruno Biriaco**, a young drummer from Rome and already quoted for his illustrious collaborations (**Schiano**, **Basso**, etc.); **Franco D'Andrea**, a pianist from Trento already working with **Gato Barbieri** and founder of the **Modern Art Trio**; the Venetian sax **Claudio Fasoli**,also in search of new horizons. All names of some worth in the Italian Jazz panorama, all except **Tony Sidney**, Italo-American Hard-Rock guitarist ever present in Florence's Space Elettro-jams, who played in the band **Le Madri Superiori**.
Despite RCA's doubts and the indifference of certain purists, **Perigeo** publishes *Azimut* in 1972, an already suggestive debut album though still somewhat undefined. Three others follow between '73 and '75, born after many experimented and appreciated concerts with a wide use of electric guitars and synthesizers, spacing from Funk to centre European or Latin melancholy atmospheres to acoustic music. The band fully inserts itself in the Jazz-Rock wave, with echoes from **Colosseum** in the brass/guitar duets and the use of a Fender Rhodes recalling the **Return To Forever**. The quintet's sound distinguishes itself for a smart narrative and development of the themes (at times sung) and for the fascinating melodies and rhythmic power enriched by **Tony Esposito** in *La Valle Dei Templi*. **Perigeo** decide not to choose between expressive tools, widely using electric guitars and synthesizers, spacing from funk to centre European or Latin melancholy atmospheres to acoustics music. It is also an influential band: jazz-rock Italian bands like **Agorà** and **Baricentro** who owe a lot to the sonorities of their album *Genealogia*.
In 1975 they began opening concerts for **Weather Report** and touring around the world. Then a fifth album made in Toronto, which also went out in the USA as *Fata Morgana*, a less convincing work to the point that **Tommaso** decides to put an end to the adventure. In 1980 RCA proposes him an ambitious project, a musical and a tour inspired to *Alice In Wonderland*, with guests like **Lucio Dalla**, **Rino Gaetano** and **Anna Oxa**; the following year as **New Perigeo**, but without his old colleagues, he publishes an album with songs by **Vanera**, AKA **Pasquale Panella**. The five musicians actively pursue their own careers and in 2006 - 30 years after the breakup - **Tommaso** will found **Apogeo**.

D.Z.

DISCOGRAPHY:

AZIMUT (RCA, 1972) **ABBIAMO TUTTI UN BLUES DA PIANGERE** (RCA, 1973) **GENEALOGIA** (RCA, 1974) **LA VALLE DEI TEMPLI** (RCA, 1975) **NON È POI COSÌ LONTANO** (RCA, 1976) **PERIGEO SPECIAL: ALICE** (RCA, 1980) **NEW PERIGEO: EFFETTO AMORE** (RCA, 1981) **NEW PERIGEO: Q CONCERT** (RCA, 1981) **LIVE 1976** (Contempo, 1990) **LIVE AT MONTREUX** (RCA, 1993).

Europe: ITALY

PREMIATA FORNERIA MARCONI

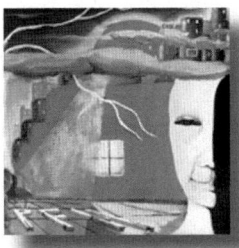

Franz Di Cioccio- *drums, percussion, vocals,* **Roberto Gualdi, Walter Calloni,** - *drums, percussion,* **Franco Mussida, Marco Sfogli** *- guitars, vocals,* **Flavio Premoli, Alessandro Scaglione, Alberto Bravin** - *keyboards, vocals,* **Giorgio Piazza, Patrick Djivas** - *bass,* **Mauro Pagani** - *flute, violin,* **Bernardo Lanzetti** – *vocals,* **Greg Bloch, Edoardo De Angelis** - *violin, keyboards,* **Lucio Fabbri** - *violin, guitars, keyboards.*

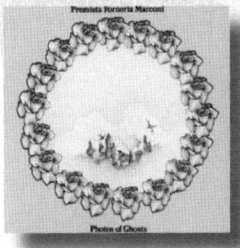

Premiata Forneria Marconi represents the highest quality and notoriety peak ever reached by a band of Italian Prog. They actually belong to that small list of names that invented it in Italy. During a long career playing for singers such as **Mina, Celentano, De Andrè, Battisti**, the future band components leaded by **Franz di Cioccio** exercise on songs by **King Crimson, Jethro Tull** and **Uriah Heep**. Then in 1971 as **PFM** they open the concert in Bologna for **Deep Purple** with immediate success.
At the beginning of 1972 they publish *Storia Di Un Minuto*, a masterpiece that not only contains the incredibly famous track "Impressioni di Settembre", but also a rock-suite loaded with colours and energy, a balanced choral construction. More sophisticated and outlined, *Per Un Amico* gives further courage to the band always searching for international visibility. **Greg Lake** and Manticore fall in love with **PFM** and assign them to **Pete Sinfield**, ex- **King Crimson**, that will help with the lyrics and production of *Photos Of Ghosts*, their first international album containing the best of the first two. They hit charts abroad and begin a European tour with guests like **Sinfield** and **Mel Collins**.

After the formidable *L'Isola di Niente*, a passionate Mediterranean album, finally the moment of a USA tour arrives. It is the first time for an Italian band to play in front of oceanic audiences, participating in festivals with **Santana, Allman Brothers, ZZ Top** and **Bad Company**. They release *Live In USA* (entitled *Cook* in the American market). They meet singer **Bernardo Lanzetti** from **Acqua Fragile** and record *Chocolate Kings*, with songs felt as unkind towards the stars & the stripes culture so they become unwanted in the US. In Japan instead sales are gold, and after the exit of **Mauro Pagani** they start working on a new rock-jazz album in California, *Jet Lag*, with **Greg Bloch** on the violin. They return to the Italian language with *Passpartù* and then embark in an extraordinary live project with **Fabrizio De André** which will establish in unequivocal way a new kind of music-writing in Italy. With the passing of time they choose a more Pop Rock sound, clearly expressed in *Suonare Suonare* (1980) and *Come Ti Va In Riva Alla Città* (1981), and at the end of the '90s with *Ulisse* (1997), *Dracula* (2005) and *Stati Di Immaginazione* (2006). In 2012 a tour as will consecrate them. In *PFM in Classic* they play with a Symphonic orchestra the reinterpretation of their classics with inserts of unpublished songs and a mastery only they possess. Other new albums are released in the recent times.

D.Z.

DISCOGRAPHY:
STORIA DI UN MINUTO *(Numero Uno, 1972)* **PER UN AMICO** *(Numero Uno, 1973)* **PHOTOS OF GHOSTS** *(Manticore, 1973)* **L'ISOLA DI NIENTE** *(Numero Uno, 1974)* **THE WORLD BECAME THE WORLD** *(Manticore, 1974)* **LIVE IN USA** *(live, Numero Uno, 1974)* **CHOCOLATE KINGS** *(Numero Uno, 1976)* **JET LAG** *(Numero Uno, 1977)* **PASSPARTÙ** *(Zoo 1978)* **FABRIZIO DE ANDRE', ARRANGIAMENTI PFM: IN CONCERTO VOL. 1** *(Ricordi, 1979)* **IN CONCERTO VOL. 2** *(Ricordi, 1980)* **SUONARE SUONARE** *(Numero Uno, 1980)* **COME TI VA IN RIVA ALLA CITTÀ** *(Numero Uno 1981)* **PerForMance** *(live, Numero Uno, 1982)* **PFM? PFM!** *(Numero Uno, 1984)* **MISS BAKER** *(Ricordi 1987)* **10 ANNI LIVE 1971-1981** *(live, RTI 1996)* **ULISSE** *(RTI, 1997)* **www.pfmpfm.it (il Best)** *(live, RTI, 1998)* **SERENDIPITY** *(Sony, 2000)* **LIVE IN JAPAN 2002** *(live, Sony 2002)* **PFM + PAGANI: PIAZZA DEL CAMPO** *(live, Sony 2003)* **DRACULA - OPERA ROCK** *(Sony, 2005)* **STATI DI IMMAGINAZIONE** *(Sony, 2006)* **PFM CANTA DE ANDRE'** *(Aerostella, 2008)* **A.D. 2010 LABUONA NOVELLA** *(Aerostella, 2010)* **LIVE IN ROMA PFM con Ian Anderson** *(Immaginifica 2012)* **CELEBRATION 1972 -2012 Special Box Set** *(Sony Music, 2012)* **PFM IN CLASSIC** *(Immaginifica, 2012)* **EMOTIONAL TATTOOS** *(Inside Out, 2017)* **I DREAMED OF ELECTRIC SHEEP - Ho Sognato Pecore Elettriche** *(Inside Out, 2021).*

Europe: ITALY

SENSATION'S FIX

Franco Falsini - *guitar, keyboards, vocals,*
Richard Ursillo, Gary Falwell - *bass,*
Keith Edwards - *drums,*
Stephen Head - *keyboards, drums.*

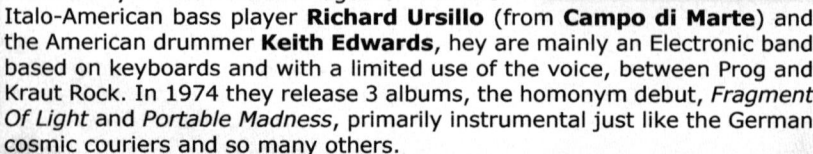

Founded by **Franco Falsini** together with the Italo-American bass player **Richard Ursillo** (from **Campo di Marte**) and the American drummer **Keith Edwards**, hey are mainly an Electronic band based on keyboards and with a limited use of the voice, between Prog and Kraut Rock. In 1974 they release 3 albums, the homonym debut, *Fragment Of Light* and *Portable Madness*, primarily instrumental just like the German cosmic couriers and so many others.
As a matter of fact even if they participate in the music festivals of the '70s, they are fairly unknown in Italy, their music being distant from the common tastes of the young public of the time and far from the common Prog standards. If we also add that they completely self-produce themselves, with results that penalize the quality of their sound, the difficulty of taking over a larger audience is understandable.

With the entry of **Stephen Head** on keyboards, a fourth album is recorded *Finest Finger*, containing good vocal parts. Also *Boxes Paradise* will pursue a greater immediateness. They move to California, where *Vision's Fugitives* is recorded for the US market, but with no success despite the new American sound. A last album *Flying Tapes* is out in 1978 with songs from the previous ones.

In 1979 they change name into **Sheriff**, with **Falsini**, **Ursillo** and **Edwards** in the line-up. The LP *Sheriff Observatory* is released using nicknames (**Falsini** is **Frank Filfoyt**), again for the US market and characterized by a very Rock sound. **Ursillo** goes back to Italy leaving the band to the three remaining musicians. **Gary Falwell** will play the bass for all 1979, with only one live appearance, until they definitely breakup when **Falsini** decides to move to New

York and work as sound engineer. **Keith Edwards** remains in the US until he discovers to be seriously ill and commits suicide. **Falsini** publishes a solo album in 1975, *Cold Nose*, soundtrack to the same titled film. He vanishes for many years and some rumors see him as Techno-music producer in London at the beginning of the '90s. **Richard Ursillo** kept playing in various bands in Florence and returned to collaborate in a reunion of **Campo di Marte** in 2003. A recent concert sees **Falsini** and **Ursillo** introducing a new album of reissues and remastered recordings, proving a reinvigorated passion in proposing their timeless electronic music. **M.G.**

DISCOGRAPHY:
SENSATION'S FIX (Polydor, 1974) **FRAGMENTS OF LIGHT** (Polydor, 1974) **PORTABLE MADNESS** (Polydor, 1974) **FINEST FINGER** (Polydor, 1976) **BOXES PARADISE** (Polydor, 1977) **VISION'S FUGITIVES** (All Ears, 1977 released only in USA) **FLYING TAPES** (Polydor, 1978) **Sheriff: SHERIFF OBSERVATORY** (OR 1996, 1979, released only in USA) **ANTIDOTE** (Habla, 1989) **MUSIC IS PAINTING IN THE AIR** (2012, RVNG).

Europe: ITALY

LE STELLE DI MARIO SCHIFANO

Nello Marini – *keyboards, vocals,*
Urbano Orlandi – *guitar, vocals,*
Giandomenico Crescentini – *bass, vocals,*
Sergio Cerra – *drums.*
Francesca Camerana – *recitative vocals.*

History tells us that the group originated from the encounter of the ex bass player from **New Dada**, **Giandomenico Crescentini**, with guitarist **Urbano Orlandi** from Rome. Through common friends, the band met **Mario Schifano**, artist and painter already of great fame. In 1967 **Schifano** takes them under his wing a bit like what **Andy Warhol** did with **Velvet Underground**. The desire to experiment mixing Psychedelic with Traditional singing, Beat with noise improvisation, dissonances derived by contemporary Classical music or Jazz and Blues, becomes imperative after seeing a **Pink Floyd** concert at the Piper in Rome. But theirs was neither emulation nor inspiration: only the confirmation that the path they were on was right and that what they were doing had a parallel activity going on in England.

Initially as backing band of **Schifano**'s artistic representations, events during which they played live as part of the exhibit, exalting the Acidity and Psychedelia of the paintings. Between events the band moved to Turin for a series of concerts and records the album *Dedicato a* in the Fono Folk Stereostudio. Their music flows with moments of deep Psychedelia and very complex parts, that find their apex in the memorable suite of the first side. Very curious the participation of countess **Francesca Camerana**, a well known high society character of Turin's club life. With more than 17 minutes of strange acrobatics, often more mental than musical, the song "Le ultime parole di Brandimarte, dall'Orlando Furioso, ospite Peter Hartman e fine - da ascoltare con TV accesa senza volume", (Brandimarte's last words, from the Orlando Furioso, featuring Peter Hartman - to be heard with the TV on mute)

is the insane title preluding to a universe of Avantgarde which bloomed first, for a strange series of events, in Italy than in the rest of the world. The second side of the album introduces shorter songs but always of great intelligence. Fundamental the splendid "Susan Song" or the rich lyricism of "Molto alto - a colori" (very loud - colours) - songs that will be, for their musical themes, inspiration for Italian Pop and for bands like **Le Orme** or **New Trolls**. In the months following the release, **Schifano**'s interest waned and after one more album the band broke up for good. This vinyl immediately became an unbelievable rarity until it was reprinted in 1992 on CD. **R.V.**

DISCOGRAPHY:
DEDICATO A ... *(BDS - M&F, 1967, CD Mellow Records, 1992)* **E IL MONDO VA / SU UNA STRADA** *(1968, CBS).*

Europe: ITALY

THE TRIP

First lineup 1967 – 1972
Billy Gray - *guitars, vocals,*
Joe Vescovi - *keyboards, vocals,*
Arvid "Wegg" Andersen - *bass, vocals,*
Pino Sinnone - *drums.*
Second lineup 1972 – 1973:
Joe Vescovi - *keyboards, vocals,*
Arvid "Wegg" Andersen - *bass, vocals,*
Furio Chirico - *drums.*

Group of English origin formed by drummer **Jan Broad, Arvid Andersen, Billy Gray** and guitarist **Ritchie Blackmore** hey arrive in Italy following **Ricky Maiocchi**, already singer in the **Camaleonti** at the end of 1966, giving birth to a brief project named **Maiocchi & The Trip** based in Turin. Psychedelia and a Rock derived from Hard Blues were the matrix of their sound. Unsatisfied with some of the band's choices, **Blackmore** will soon go home and found **Deep Purple**.

The band feels they need an organist as the Hammond was seen as an essential element by most. They contact **Joe Vescovi** who perfectly integrates with their style. After a while **Broad** exits abruptly giving way to **Pino Sinnone**'s entry on the drums, and with this line-up they sign a contract for RCA in Rome, after a concert at the Piper, publishing a Bolero Rock album entitled *The Trip*. The release was very appreciated both by critics and public, with its sonorous rich plots though still quite Psychedelic-Beat, full of Hard Rock and experimentation with many Classical Symphonic hints.

A film production involves them in a series of episodes similar to the **Monkees**, but after the first shooting, for economic reasons, everything shut down. **The Trip** locks up once more in **Vescovi**'s house where they prepared a second album *Caronte* released in 1971, inspired from his idea of the ferryman transporting the newly dead **Jimi Hendrix** and **Janis Joplin** to the other side. Musically growing, more Prog than the previous and with greater space for keyboards, it also maintained the Symphonic Hard-prog style. When they complicate the musical plots and

begin to write longer and more complex songs, their success collapses, and after a theft of their musical instruments and various other discussions, **Sinnone** abandons the band. Also **Gray** leaves trying a soloist career that fails. Superb drummer **Furio Chirico** finally joins the trio and they publish *Atlantide*, very professional and mature, fully Progressive with leading keyboards giving great space to rhythms with an incredible drum solo. The success of the band, especially in their live performances, did not increase sales which brought several doubts, though it did not change their choices; rather it enriched them in the last 1973 episode, *Time of Change*, a complex and structured album which will be appreciated only years later in the light of what will go on in Europe in that period.

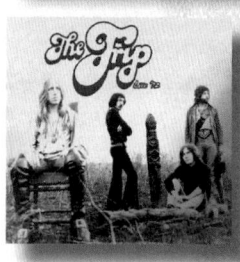

Chirico leaves the band to form **Arti & Mestieri** and they will continue with drummer from **Osage Tribe** till the break up. In 2010 **The Trip** triumphantly appear in concert with the trio and the aid of two assistant musicians, at the Prog Exhibition in Rome. A tour in Japan follows and when **Andersen** dies they will still play live in some minor festivals. In 2013 **Joe Vescovi** also dies leaving to **Pino Sinnone** (the only survivor!) license to use the legendary name. The story continues with a renewed band lead by an over 70 years old drummer still alive and kicking! **R.V.**

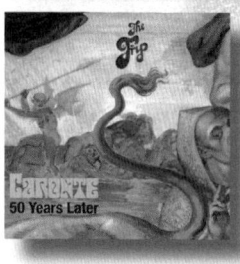

DISCOGRAPHY:
THE TRIP *(1970, RCA)* **CARONTE** *(1971, RCA)* **ATLANTIDE** *(1972, RCA)* **TIME OF CHANGE** *(1973, Trident)* **PROG EXHIBITION (Box CD-DVD Live)** *(2011, Aereostella/Immaginifica/Edel)* **LIVE '72** *(2016, Black Widow)* **CARONTE 50 Years Later** *(2021, Maracash)* **NOW THE TIME HAS COME** *(2023, Maracash).*

Europe: NORWAY

JUNIPHER GREENE

Helge Grøslie - vocals, keyboards, **Bent Åserud** - guitars, flute, harp, vocals, **Øyvind Vilbo** - bass, vocals, **Geir Bøhren** - drums, vocals, **Freddy Dahl** - vocals, guitars, vibes.

Perhaps the first, perhaps the best, perhaps the most famous, certainly fundamental for the birth and development of Prog in Norway (and in the whole of Scandinavia). They begin their activity already in 1966 playing a Blues, Beat, Jazz mixed to the rising Psychedelia and even though very young and essentially influenced by what was going on in England, the boys were able to show they had the right numbers.

The first line-up saw **Bøhren**, **Vilbo**, **Åserud** and **Sønstevold** facing essentially live activities, creating a great understanding among them and the possibility to work on their own compositions. Brief songs inspired by all kinds of new musical tides took form with time, often uniting and originating longer and articulated compositions. *Friendship* was released only in 1971 and due to the quantity of material available, as a double-album. The first had shorter songs closer to Psychedelic Blues, Canterbury Jazz (like "Try to understand"), Hard Acid and Psychedelic Rock with jazz elements. The second entirely devoted to their historical suite "Friendship" with over 26 minutes of progressive pirouetting flutes, organs, guitars and powerful voices. The album immediately achieved the status of masterpiece in Norwegian Rock and still today it is considered one of the best Prog albums ever made in the land of the fjords.

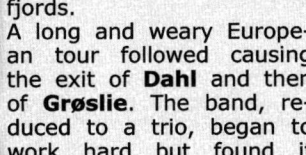

A long and weary European tour followed causing the exit of **Dahl** and then of **Grøslie**. The band, reduced to a trio, began to work hard but found it difficult to repeat the magic of their debut without all of the original elements. The result was *Communication* (1973) with very American sonorities and clear AOR tendencies, Hard Country and Pop Rock sung flat and simple. Among the songs is a 12 minute title-track and some short inspired moments here and there, but globally an absolutely disappointing album, nothing like the band of two years before. Even if there was never a real break-up, the activity of the band became almost exclusively private, publishing in 1982 *Forbudte Formiddagstoner* with a nearly complete change of musicians and a sound closer to New Wave and to **Simple Minds**. In 1981 *Rewind* also came out containing some unpublished tracks from the '60s and some rearranged songs, material altogether negligible.

R.V.

DISCOGRAPHY:
FRIENDSHIP *(1971, Sonet)* **A SPECTRE IS HAUNTING THE PENINSULA/TRY TO UNDERSTAND** *(single - 1971, Sonet)* **UGHA MUGHA SUNSHINE BOY/EASY FLYING** *(single - 1973, On Records)* **COMMUNICATION** *(1974, On Records)* **REWIND** *(1981, Hammer)* **FORBUDTE FORMIDDAGSTONER** *(1982, Musikkselskapet)* **SLARAFFENLIV/ALLA TOYA** *(single - 1983, Musikkselskapet).*

Europe: POLAND

CZESLAW NIEMEN

Czeslaw Juliusz Wydrzycki aka **Niemen** begins his career very young with traditional Polish and Belarusian instruments, besides the piano and the bassoon. Founder of bands like **Niebiesko-Czarnis**, he had a nonconformist and eccentric image given by his way of dressing up or by his polemic streaks that angered censorship in his country. Czeslaw's Beat period brings him also to Italy where he records some albums in Italian. Here he comes closer to Jazz while experimenting in different musical experiences like with the Hammond organ and the synthesizer. He releases *Enigmatic*,

which has a deep, classical inspiration with strong inserts of Jazz and Blues. The long suite dedicated to polish hero Jozef Bem contains a homage to the emerging English Prog, soaked with gloomy and sad sounds and underlined by guitars played in the best Blues tradition. It is 1969 and for music in Poland this is an authentic revolution.

The magic continues in 1971 with *Enigmatic II*, first act of a double-album that features all the musical instruments he had encountered until then: Hard Rock mixed to Classical passages of an organ, guitar solos stolen from **Santana**, articulated melodies played on a Hammond and aggressive tunes like **Iron Butterfly** would play, are the ingredients which make it a masterpiece. *Niemen I* and *Niemen II* are then released shortly one after the other, confirming the desire of the artist to always explore new artistic horizons. Jazz Rock with dark and Goth shades with great instrumental complexity. When he signs up with CBS, Niemen suddenly finds the western markets wide open and waiting. He collaborates for a long time with Blood Sweat & Tears giving the impression of wanting a permanent role.

Strange Is This World of 1972 is all in English and the music creates soft landscapes of Rock Blues with some hot tempered outlines. *Ode to Venus* in 1973 is less inspired being a collection of old unpublished songs, where the violin adds a melancholy vein to the already decadent and dark themes. In the same year CBS (interested in the Russian market) releases his *Russiche Lieder*, another collection of Folkish songs, more a stylistic exercise that interested very little the market after all. In 1974 *Mourner's Rhapsody* is recorded

with high-class musicians like **Steve Kahn** or **Jan Hammer**, somewhat a classy Pop album, far from the experiments of the first years, with wise and delicate use of choirs and catchier sounds for a wider audience. At the end of the CBS adventure, **Niemen** returns to experiment more Avant-garde situations, forming **Aerolits**.

They record *Niemen Aerolit* where Jazz Rock intimately winds around Electronic sounds imported by German Krautrock. Also the following album *Katharsis* echoes clearly of European Prog, particularly through the use of keyboards: no more songs but sounds that run after each other in an organized disorder. The growing repression of the '80s in Poland brought the artist deep disappointment and his abandonment of musical research. **Niemen** dies in 2004.

C.A.

RECOMMENDED RECORDINGS:
DZIWNY JEST TEN SWIAT *(1967, Polskie Nagrania Muza)* **SUKCES** *(1968, Polskie Nagrania Muza)* **CZY MNIE JESZCZE PAMIETASZ** *(1968 , Polskie Nagrania Muza)* **NIEMEN ENIGMATIC** *(1969, Polskie Nagrania Muza)* **NIEMEN ENIGMATIC 1** *(1970, Polskie Nagrania Muza)* **NIEMEN ENIGMATIC 2** *(1971, Polskie Nagrania Muza)* **STRANGE IS THIS WORLD** *(1972, CBS)* **NIEMEN VOL. 1** *(1972, Polskie Nagrania Muza)* **NIEMEN VOL. 2** *(1972, Polskie Nagrania Muza)* **ODE TO VENUS** *(1973, CBS)* **RUSSICHE LIEDER** *(1973, CBS)* **MOURNER'S RHAPSODY** *(1974, CBS)* **NIEMEN AEROLIT** *(1974, Polskie Nagrania Muza)* **KATHARSIS** *(1975, Polskie Nagrania Muza)* **IDEE FIXE** *(1977, Polskie Nagrania Muza).*

Europe: POLAND

SBB

Jozef Skrzek - *keyboards, bass, vocals*, **Apostolis Antymos** - *guitar, percussion, drums*, **Jerzy Piotrowski** - *drums*, **Slawomir Piwowar** - *guitar, bass, keyboards*, **Myroslaw Muzykant** - *drums, percussion*, **Paul Wertico** - *drums*, **Irek Slyk** - *drums*, **Gabor Nemeth** - *drums*.

After the collaboration with **Czeslaw Niemen**, **SBB** forms officially as the trio **Skrzek, Antymos** and **Piotrowski**, debuting in 1974 with an album recorded live that shows an incredible band: aggressive improvisations, a dirty sound and a Hard Blues vein which extends towards experimentation and innovation. The first studio recorded LP, *Nowy Horyzont* came from this desire of research in a personal Symphonic Rock sometimes recalling ELP, sometimes more Avantgarde.

During the years they consolidate their name with boiling hot concerts as the symbolic *Karlstad Live* which testifies their amazing improvisational abilities. *Pamiec* and *Ze Slowem Biegne Do Ciebe* are both important, combining Classical reminiscences, Jazz-rock and so much energy into their Prog. The unpredictable dynamics of the compositions that alternate light atmospheres, sudden sonorous outbursts and symphonic majesty, smartly converge in one direction different styles and the disruptive energy, characteristic of this exceptional band at ease with long suites performed to perfection. SBB prove they have nothing to envy with the most famous names of Prog. To confirm this, they release another album also known as **Wolanie** or *Brzek Szkla*, whilst the later *Jerzyk* goes the opposite way with a series of brief passages, directed toward Jazz-rock.

Another two suites on *Follow My Dream* introduce some direct and catchy moments, always maintaining an elevate quality. In quartet with **Slawomir Piwowar** they publish in 1980 the sublime symphonic *Memento z Banalnym Tryptykiem*, far from fashions and containing the amazing 21 minutes title-track, brought to conclusion only by an epic guitar.

Then the breakup: a long period of silence (with **Skrzek** always playing solo) until the come-back in the '90s, at first with concerts and live albums, then with new works in which class and experience emerge without adding originality. The formidable creative vein of the band is documented instead by numerous posthumous tracks, among which "Sikorki" where we find the famous Jazz player **Tomasz Stanko**, and in *The Lost Tapes* (18 CDs), with an impressive quantity of unpublished material that deserves the maximum close examination. **G.D.S.**

DISCOGRAPHY:
SBB *(1974, Muza)* **2 – NOWY HORYZONT** *(1975, Muza)* **PAMIEC** *(1975, Muza)* **ZE SLOWEM BEIGNE DO CIEBIE** *(1976, Muza)* **SBB** *(aka Wolanie o Brzek Szkla 1977, Supraphon)* **JERZYK** *(1977,)* **FOLLOW MY DREAM** *(1978, Spiegelei)* **AMIGA ALBUM** *(1978, Amiga)* **WELCOME** *(1979, Spiegelei)* **MEMENTO Z BANALNYM TRYPTYKIEM** *(1980, Muza)* **LIVE 1993** *(1994, Stuff Records)* **LIVE IN AMERICA '94** *(1994, Radio Katowice)* **ABSOLUTELY LIVE '98** *(1999, Yesterday)* **W FILHARMONII: AKT 1***(1999, Yesterday)* **W FILHARMONII: AKT 2** *(1999, Yesterday)* **GOODBYE – LIVE IN CONCERT** *(2000, Moskito)* **THE GOLDEN HARP** *(2001, autoproduzione)* **KARLSTAD LIVE '75** *(2001, Koch)* Budai **IFJUSAGI PARK – LIVE '77** *(2001, Metal Mind)* **NASTROJE** *(2002, Metal Mind)* **TRIO – LIVE TOURNÉE 2001** *(2002, Cd-Silesia.com)* **FREEDOM – LIVE SOPOT '78** *(2002, Cd-Silesia.com)* **22.10.1977 GOTTINGEN ALTE ZIEGELEI** *(2004, Metal Mind)* **SIKORKI** *(2004, Metal Mind)* **WICHER W POLU DMIE** *(2004, Metal Mind)* **ODLOT – LIVE 2004** *(2004, Slaska Witryna Muzyczna)* **NEW CENTURY** *(2005, Metal Mind)* **LIVE IN THEATRE 2005** *(2005, Metal Mind)* **THE LOST TAPES VOL. 1** *(2005, Metal Mind)* **LIVE IN SPODEK 2006** *(2006, Metal Mind)* **THE LOST TAPES VOL. 2** *(2006, Metal Mind)* **THE ROCK** *(2007, Metal Mind)* **LIVE IN MARBURG 1980 – THE FINAL CONCERT** *(2007, Metal Mind)* **FOUR DECADES** *(2007, Metal Mind)* **COMPLETE TAPES 1974** *(2007, Metal Mind)*.

Europe: POLAND

SKALDOWIE

Andrzej Zielinski - *vocals, keyboards,* **Jacek Zielinski** - *vocals, trumpet, violin,* **Jerzy Tarsiński** - *guitar,* **Konrad Ratyński** - *bass, vocals,* **Jan Budziaszek** - *drums.*

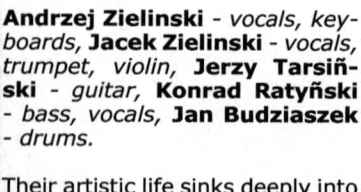

Their artistic life sinks deeply into the roots of Beat music of the mid '60s, when working with cover bands of British Beat was the rule. The first albums of this band are in fact good executions in **Mersey** Beat style that denote the good artistic personality of the two **Zielinski** brothers, founders of the group. They are basically a Top 40 band with rather catchy and commercial songs and a discreet number of fans. In the '70s the group broadens its horizons drawing closer to Pop with light Psychedelic veins. At the end of a tour in North America they discover the Hammond organ and listen to this music that was changing (a rare and unusual event for a band belonging to the eastern European block). History tells us that the north American experience inspired the realization of *Od Wschodu Do Zachodu Slonca*, a first timid approach to Prog. After releasing the albums *Ty* and *Wszystkim Zakochanym* and a tour in Germany, their conversion to Prog was complete. *Krywan, Krywan* in 1973 confirms this with its 18 minutes opening track and the frequent use of Classical passages (exceptional the reference to **Rossini**'s "William Tell overture").

The LP sparked the curiosity of the public and attracted the interest of the critics whom appreciated the integration of foreign musical influences with elements of Polish Pop Folk. *Szanujmy Wspomnienia* and *Stworzenia Swiata Czesc Druga* are the ideal sequels of the undertaken artistic vein, always with the use of the Hammond sustained by an energetic rhythmic base; the latter refers to motives drawn by the world of Classical music with its lengthy suites. Unfortunately the stylistic evolution of the band drives

them toward a more commercial Pop, gradually losing all the elements of Prog. With *Droga Ludzi* for the 1980 Olympic games in Moscow, they begin to decline until their final break-up. Then of course a reunion, actually a revival for that one time and nothing more. **C.A.**

RECOMMENDED RECORDINGS:
SKALDOWIE *(Pronit, 1967)* **WSZYSTKO MI MOWI ZE MNIE KTOS POCOCHAL** *(Pronit, 1968)* **CALA JESTES W SKOWRONKACH** *(Pronit, 1969)* **OD WSCHODU DO ZACHODU SLONCA** *(Muza, 1970)* **WSZYSTKIM ZAKOCHANYM** *(Muza, 1973)* **TY** *(Muza, 1971)* **KRYWAN KRYWAN** *(Muza, 1973)* **SZANUJMY WSPOMNIENIA** *(Muza, 1976)* **STWORZENIA ŚWIATA CZĘŚĆ DRUGA** *(Muza, 1976)* **DROGA LUDZI** *(Pronit, 1979)*.

Europe: **PORTUGAL**

JOSE' CID

José Cid is one of the greatest Portuguese musicians, founder of **Quarteto 1111**, he often collided with censorship for the lyric content. After the break-up he begins to deepen his knowledge of Prog and records alone *Vida (Sons Do Quotidiano)*, mini Rock Opera in which is described in only 12 minutes the mystery of life from birth to death (and the album ends with the noise of a car crash).

His career steps up with the publication in 1978 of *10.000 Anos Depois Entre Venus e Mars* considered by the critics one of the hundred best albums of Prog Rock in the world. Sung in Portuguese, it attracts the listener with its sweet melody of sublime interaction between keyboards, guitars and synths: narrating the tale of a man and a woman, last survivors on Earth, destined to return home to give new life to the human race. The mellotron wisely adds great atmosphere and, particularly in the passage "O Caos", he creates a fine vocal feeling before surrendering to the guitar solos. Genius the insertion

of arcs playing in the background. The title-track is addressed instead toward outer-space atmospheres, mostly created by a great melange of synthesizer and guitars, in the wake of the best **Moody Blues** style. Useless to underline how the album initiated a florid artistic stream in Portugal.

After this remarkable experience, **Cid** instead turns to a more classy Pop genre, effective but no more definable as Progressive, often on air in TV shows. He will even reunite **Quarteto 1111** in 1984 for a television program and in 1989 a special *Christmas with Josè Cid* is broadcast. This, however doesn't prevent him from colliding with the media and during the '90s he creates scandal appearing naked only covered by an LP to protest against the power of radios that penalize Portuguese music in favour of foreign artists. Nothing however can breach his popularity: in 2004 his concert at Coliseu dos Recreios is filmed and aired by RTP, with the appearance of musicians from **Quarteto 1111**. A triumph. In 2007 the whole band reappears and he is idolized as a true legend.   **C.A.**

RECOMMENDED RECORDINGS:

LISBOA PERTO E LONGE *(Columbia/EMI, 1971)* **CAMARADA** *(Columbia/EMI, 1972)* **VIDA (SONS DO QUOTIDIANO)** *(Decca, 1978)* **10.000 ANOS DEPOIS ENTRE VENUS E MARTE** *(Discos Orfeu, 1978)* **COISAS SUAS** *(Discos Orfeu, 1979)* **MY MUSIC** *(Discos Orfeu, 1980)* **XI CORAÇÃO** *(Polygram, 1986)* **JOSÉ CID** *(Universal, 1989)* **CAMÕES, AS DISCOBERTAS E NOS** *(Universal, 1991)* **ENTRE MARGENS** *(Universal, 1997)* **ODA A FEDERICO GARCIA LORCA** *(Universal, 1997)* **AO VIVO NO CAMPO PEQUENO** *(Farol, 2008)* **COISAS DO AMOR E DO MAR** *(Farol, 2009)* **QUEM TEM EIEDO DE BALADAS** *(Farol, 2011)*.

Europe: PORTUGAL

PETRUS CASTRUS

Pedro Castro - *Vocals, guitar, bass,*
José Castro – *vocals, keyboards,*
Urbano Oliveira – *drums, percussions.*

Formed in 1971 as the musical creature of the **Castro** brothers, especially of **Pedro Castro** who transposed his own name in Latin for the band. In the beginning they were more, with **Júlio Pereira** on guitars, **José Mario** on percussions and with a different drummer, **João Seixas**. The sound of the origins was essentially that of their single passions, not having found a common road yet. Mainly the themes were of Psychedelia, echoing **Pink Floyd**, **The Nice**, **Jimi Hendrix**, **Renaissance** and **Procol Harum**.
Initially a couple of singles, the very first one, *Marasmo* (1971), well represents the music of the period, ethereal, sweet and Psychedelic, recalling atmospheres of certain Italian Rock bands of the time. Dominated by piano and organ and by almost Jazz vocals, it resulted as a very classy starting point for their sound. The next single *Tudo Isto, Tudo Mais* was perhaps more of in a French song-writing key, with a dynamic and jazzy piano. Other extremely interesting tracks were composed thereafter but oddly never included in the two official albums, yet luckily gathered posthumous in a very rare LP. There are some **Santana** moments, some Brazilian intrusions, a lot of English atmospheres (**Traffic**, **Pink Floyd**) and Canterbury hints.
The first true LP was released only in 1973 as *Mestre*. Album in which we find songs of great spontaneity and lyrical beauty like "Mestre" or "Tiahuanaco", together with the saucier Foxtrot of "Macaco" or the Rock'n'Roll of "Velho Avarento". Immediately after **Pereira** leaves, the group breaks-up for the first time until in 1977 when the two brothers recruit drummer Oliveira,

recording jazzy *Candida* and the dramatic *No Concelho De Cà*, between Canterbury sounds and Brazilian music. The following year a last episode, *Ascenção e Queda*, album of great stylistic maturity, with perfect musical technique and of composition, alternating moments rich of nostalgic pathos and of the greatest stylistic Prog complexity. The concept is the rise and fall in the life of a man, and starts with the melancholy piano and the screeching of seagulls of "A Chegada", developed on unbelievably sad lyrics, ending with Fusion moments of strange and shiny intent, given that the album is instead dominated by reflexive themes and a notable pathos, also thanks to the splendid choral parts of **Helena Águas**, like in "Ascenção".

R.V.

DISCOGRAPHY:
MESTRE *(1973, Sassetti Records)* **ASCENÇÃO E QUEDA** *(1978, Decca Portugal).*

Europe: ROMANIA

PHOENIX

Nicolae Covaci – *guitar, vocals, flute,* **Iosif Kappl** – *bass, vocals, violin, flute,* **Mircea Baniciu** – *vocals, guitar,* **Ovidiu Lipan** – *drums, percussions,* **Gunter Reininger** – *keyboards.*

In 1962 fifteen-year-old **Nicolae Covaci** began to play with his friend as Sfintii (**The Saints**), a name that was absolutely not digested by the Regime, but that however lasted up to 1965, when the band was forced to change it in order to keep on playing. Essentially a cover band of Rock'n'Roll, Beat or local Folk songs, also from **The Beatles**, **The Rolling Stones** and **The Who** and toward the end of the '60s they finally began to write their own lyrics, recording an EP between 1968 and 1969. In the same period they also performed in some theatrical shows, however it is not until 1972 that they publish a first LP produced in Romania: *Cei Ce Ne-Au Dat Nume* represents their true debut, for many their best, clearly pointing out the direction they had taken, with ample Folk parts and a great use of acoustic tools, but also Symphonic environments, using more complex and dynamic electric or acoustic sounds, with Beat, Blues and Hard Rock inserts, but maintaining the typical local Folk which resulted in an extremely personal style. Unfortunately, given the times, the album had to pass under the heavy scissors of censorship and

sound, lyrics and style were somehow (in good and bad) imposed.
In 1973 they composed a Rock Opera called *Meşterul Manole*, absolutely not approved by the regime that boycotted and cut it leaving a very small part intact, mixed with old songs of the group. The following year a second official album *Mugur De Fluire*, inferior to the precedent on the Prog side, perhaps because of censorship, but

however an interesting piece dominated by the "Lasa, Lasa" theme and with 5 brief parts distributed among the songs as a connection, creating a sort of concept of very traditional aspects, between Folk, Hard Rock, Psychedelia, Blues and Beat, seen in a very rural and personal way.
1975 *Cantafabule* (in origin *Zoosophia*) is a very variegated and heterogeneous double album, where purely Folks songs ("Stima Casei") are mixed to Hard Blues moments, passing by traditional Rock or Rock'n'Roll with some hints of Space rock and Zeuhl ("Zoomahia"), perhaps unintentionally sounding like **Jethro Tull** and **Gentle Giant**. All guided by the immense bass rhythms of **Iosif Kappl** and those unmistakable choirs.

A troubled period began with various escapes from the country even hiding in amp casings to get out. Some of them founded parallel groups in Germany or, for those who stayed, in Romania. Things were reestablished only in the '90s, with the end of the Regime and the definitive come-back of the members that were abroad. At the beginning with the excuse of some concerts and then also to take back the activity, recording good quality albums, even though with some Pop hints. Theoretically the group still exists. **R.V.**

DISCOGRAPHY:
CEI CE NE-AU DAT NUME *(1972, Electrecord Romania)* **MUGUR DE FLUIER** *(1974, Electrecord Romania)* **CANTOFABULE** *(1975, Electrecord Romania)* **TRANSSYLVANIA-PHOENIX** *(1981, Bellaphone)* **SYMPHONIX – TIMIŞOARA** *(1992, Eurostar)* **IN UMBRA MARELUI URS** *(2000, Cat Music)* **BABA NOVAK** *(2005, Phoenix Records)* **VINO, TEPEŞ!** *(2014, Phoenix Records).*

Europe: SPAIN

ATILA

Eduardo Niebla – *guitars*, **Juan Puñet** – *drums*, **Benet Nogue** – *keyboards*, **Miguel A. Blasco** – *bass*.

The brief but important history of **Atila** substantially coincides with that of its founder **Eduardo Niebla**, gifted and extrovert Catalan guitarist who since his teens created a series of unlikely bands like **Los Helios**, **Guevara Group** or **Metafora**, often together with one of his 10 brothers. Only in 1973 (age 18) did he decide to take it seriously, choosing music as profession and, after finding the right partners, he founded **Atila**.

The anomalous debut was a live album with a half an hour long track entitled *Beginning Of The End*. It was 1975 and, although in the Progressive genre much had been already eviscerated, it soon dominated the Symphonic market of best Classical inspiration with its **Bach** fugues and interesting, though sometimes naif, rearrangements of Classical themes, with Hard Prog moments between **ELP** and certain italic Arias similar to **The Trip**'s style, but also important Space jam parts with Psychedelic hints not distant from **Pink Floyd**. What strikes is the scarce influence of Spanish music here and in all their future works, perhaps clearly wanting to maintain their distance from other local groups that always kept one foot inside the folk genre.

They often tour in France, where they are warmly welcomed, with memorable painted stage scenes. In 1976 a second record simply titled *Intencion* holds on tight to their Classical Symphonic imprint. They prove to have acquired a great maturity that finally manages to shines through, thanks to the good instrumental quality of the musicians. The second part of the album is entirely covered by a suite which is the rearrangement of their debut under the Spanish title "El Principio del Fin". The track, reduced to half its length and purged of various frills, is rethought in sounds and solos, maintaining however the entire intro for organ of **Bach**'s "Toccata and Fugue in D minor". A general sense of Space Rock guides the album as well as the typical **Hendrix** styled-guitar intrusions, main feature of **Niebla**'s style. Also the first part has an electric romanticism to it, unifying themes that often develop rapidly, with sudden changes and unexpected climaxes.

Reviure is published the year following and proves the band's constant evolving in style and maturity. The composition is ever so intense and enriched with personal touches, contaminated by Jazz rock, Latin music, atmospheres similar to **Camel** ("Somni"), **Santana** ("Atila") and sometimes closer to Spanish Symphonic Prog ("Al Mati"), resulting in one of their best works.

Niebla, after collaborating with artists linked to Canterbury (**Coxhill**, **Gong**, **Dobson**, **Malherbe**, etc.) still plays guitar with people like **George Michael** (dead in 2016) or **Belinda Carlisle**. R.V.

DISCOGRAPHY:
BEGINNING OF THE END *(1975, New Promotion)* **INTENCION** *(1976, BASF)* **REVIURE** *(1977, EMI)*.

Europe: SPAIN

BLOQUE

Juan Carlos Guitiérrez - *keyboards, vocals,* **Juanjo Respuela** - *guitars, vocals,* **Sixto F. Ruiz** - *guitars, bass,* **Tivo Martinez** - *drums,* **Luis M. Pastor** - *sound engineer, vocals.*

It was 1975 when **Juan José Respuela**, greatly fond of American Rock especially that of **Allman Brother Band**, formed a group with some friends to perform his own music. The year after **Juan Carlos Gutierrez** joined in bringing his personal touch to the sound, derived by the listening of English Classical Prog. From this mixture came their style made of a solid basic Rock with Progressive fugues.
Their debut essentially happened playing live in the various festivals of the northern Spanish coast, then making their way through a series of gigs all the way up to the capital, until they were noticed by Chapa Discos label manager that signed them up immediately.
Their first album *Bloque* is published only in 1978, decisively imposing itself for how they managed to condense their sonorous characteristics in a studio recording, with not very long tracks, but rich in researched lyricism and yearning melancholy. The American Rock component is dominant recalling classics and southern songs, especially in the second part of the album, with strong references to English Symphonic Prog, never leaving out traditional melodies about freedom, social aspects and human values.

In 1979 *Hombre, Tierra y Alma* proves their great compositional skills, always with songs unusually short for being Prog, where the themes would be concentrated into just a few minutes. Stronger the Prog attitude, with an imposing mellotron, yet keeping the typical elements of '60s & '70s Rock: the quick and precise notes of **Ruiz**'s bass, the solos of **Guitiérrez**'s keyboards and **Respuela**'s dynamic guitar which often would anticipate certain New Prog sounds of the years immediately to come.
Their 1980 album is perhaps considered as their best work: a romantic acoustic and electronic beginning, the strong heterogeneous sound jumps them straight into the following decade bringing to Spain sonorities from **The Who** (in "Alquimista Soy"), or more typical Prog structures ("La Danza del Agua", with its changing rhythms from a Symphonic 11/8 to the 6/8 of Flamenco), peaks of Latin romanticism like in **PFM** "El Hijo del alba"), Hard Prog tracks like the mini suite in 4 parts "El silencio de las esferas".
With extraordinary stylistic coherence, and despite the decadence period, the band publishes the following year *Musica Para la Libertad*, true son of the times both for composition and sounds. The rhythms are more Rock yet the instrumental parts are selected carefully generating a kind of greatly dynamic AOR-symphonic Blues. Despite the freshness of the album, they break-up with a live performance revival, to come back only after almost 20 years.   **R.V.**

DISCOGRAPHY:
BLOQUE *(1978, Chapa)* **HOMBRE, TIERRA Y ALMA** *(1979, Chapa)* **EL HIJO DEL ALBA** *(1980, Chapa)* **MUSICA PARA LA LIBERATAD** *(1981, Chapa)* **EN DIRECTO** *(1999 Live, Enfasis).*

Europe: SPAIN

COMPANYIA ELECTRICA DHARMA

Joan Fortuny - *saxophones*, **Josep Fortuny** - *drums*, **Lluis Fortuny** - *Trumpet*, **Jordi Soley, Maria Fortuny** - *keyboards*, **Carles Vidal** - *Bass*, **Pep Rius** - *guitar*.

This is the most legendary of all Catalan bands, founded by the **Fortuny** brothers **Esteve, Joan** and **Josep** in 1974, who manage to bring the traditional Folklore into Iberian music mixing it with Jazz Rock. One of the characteristic instruments of their music is in fact a sax soprano that imitates the tenor voices of songs from Catalogna. The **Fortuny** brothers begin as kids in the '60s, learning from **The Beatles** and **The Rolling Stones**. They start out with live gigs in small places and in church, pursuing a great number of events that give them a solid reputation as a concert band.

When **Carles Vidal** enters, **Joan** leaves him the bass and takes over the sax, with **Jordi Soley** on keyboards (years later to be substituted by **Maria Fortuny**). They close themselves inside a hippie commune in Girona calling the band **Companyia Elèctrica Dharma** after Kerouac's The Dharma Bums, a book rich of oriental and Indian culture, very trendy at the time.
They are quickly ready for their first album *Diumenge* which is an immediate success gaining them more than 100.000 spectators in about ten years of concerts.
The band still exists, ever active and their albums prove a longevity typical of that creativeness which withstands time, yet all publications connected to the revival phenomenon do not obtain the same effect of public. They leave us with a good repertoire destined to connoisseurs and passionates of the genre, who accept the new editions deprived of any surprise, yet faithful to a language that can still create proselytes.

M.G.

DISCOGRAPHY:
DIUMENGE *(Edigsa, 1975)* **L'OUCOMBALLA** *(Edigsa, 1976)* **TRAMUNTANA** *(Edigsa, 1977)* **L'ANGEL DE LA DANSA** *(Edigsa, 1978)* **ORDINÀRIES AVENTURES** *(Edigsa, 1979)* **L'ATLÀNTIDA** *(Belter, 1981)* **AL PALAU DE LA MÚSICA CATALANA AMB LA COBLA MEDITERRÀNIA** *(Belter, 1982)* **CATALLUNA** *(Polydor, 1983)* **FORÇA DHARMA!** *(PDI, 1985)* **NO VOLEM SER** *(PDI, 1986)* **HOMENATGE A ESTEVE FORTUNY** *(PDI, 1987)* **FIBRES DEL COR** *(PDI, 1989)* **TIFA HEAD** *(PDI, 1991)* **QUE NO ES PERDI AQUEST SO** *(PDI, 1993)* **20 ANYS DE C.E.DHARMA** *(Picap, 1994)* **FORÇA 20 ANYS DHARMA** *(PDI, 1994)* **EL VENTRE DE LA BÉSTIA** *(Picap, 1996)* **RACÓ DE MÓN** *(Picap, 1998)* **SONADA!** *(Mondicor, 2000)* **LLIBRE VERMELL** *(Discmedi, 2002)* **DHARMASSERIA** *(Discmedi, 2004)* **30 ANYS. LA DHARMA L'ARMA. EL JOC DE LA COBLA I EL ROCK.** *(Música Global, 2006)* **EL MISTERI D'EN MILES SERRA I LES MÚSIQUES MUTANTS** *(Picap, 2008)*

Europe: SPAIN

FUSIOON

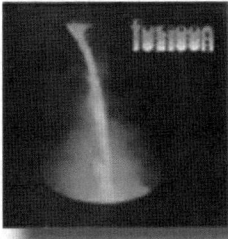

Manel Camp - *piano, eyboards, vocals,* **Jordi Camp** - *bass, vocals,* **Marti Brunet** - *guitar, vocals,* **Santi Arisa** - *drums, vocals, flute.*

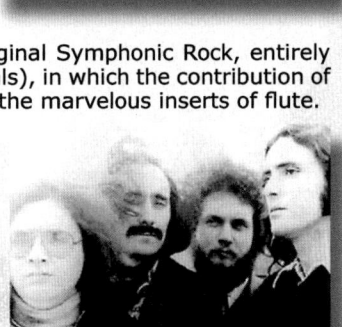

From Barcelona, they publish three magnificent albums in the first half of the '70s, becoming one of the most important bands of Iberian Prog. They immediately introduce themselves through a self-titled album in which they re-elaborate a series of Spanish Folk songs: an original Symphonic Rock, entirely instrumental (except for some sporadic vocals), in which the contribution of keyboards is particularly highlighted as are the marvelous inserts of flute.

In their second self-titled album, remembered for the crocodile drawing on the cover, the musicians subsequently improve their proposal with a more personal sound that unites in the best of ways Latin warmth and rock energy. The instrumental interlacements are more articulated and they detach the electrifying dialogues between guitar and keyboards, that sometimes go as far as Jazz-rock. In the tracks "Tritons" and "Concerto Grosso" a Classical streak is dominating (particularly in the first song where they rearrange a theme by **Tchaikovsky**).

The artistic growth of the band reaches its peak with *Minorisa*, a masterpiece which directly places them in the history of Prog. Here music becomes even more complex and the spirit of research is maximized. The first side of the LP is entirely occupied by the suite "Ebusus", almost 19 minutes in which

the band proposes an eccentric Symphonic Rock, articulated, with continuous changes of atmosphere, insertions of curious vocal parts and a pinch of Electronics and experimentation.

The creativeness of **Fusioon** reaches the top with the spectacular title-track, once more in contact with their roots, elaborating again, in a fanciful way, three traditional themes through an extraordinary mix of Prog Rock and Folklore. Closing the album is "Llaves del Subcosciente", in which emerges even more clearly the desire to experiment, with this curious passage in which the electronic keyboards, the mellotron and the guitar distortions seem to echo some of the exponents of the German cosmic messengers' scene like **Tangerine Dream**, **Popol Vuh** or **Klaus Schulze**.   G.D.S

DISCOGRAPHY:
FUSIOON *(1972, Belter)* **FUSIOON (Crocodile)** *(1974, Belter)* **MINORISA** *(1975, Ariola).*

Europe: SPAIN

GUALBERTO GARCIA PEREZ

Formidable artist, rich of ideas and musical inventiveness, **Gualberto** goes to the music school of Seville, playing in bands (**Bats**, **Smash**) of brief duration. An experience in America allows him to come in contact with a different artistic reality, from which he learns many innovative elements and in particular how to play the sitar. Back in Spain he takes all these learnings and puts them into *A La Vida Al Dolor*, an album of great effect in which the sitar and the tabla confer a touch of amazing novelty. It is divided in two contrasting parts: in the first one "A la vida" predominates a typically European taste, with Folk ballads soaked with sad streaks and melancholy; in the second "Al dolor" the traditional Andalusian taste emerges, a sort of Flamenco-rock contaminated by oriental sounds with a great finale of electric guitars, absolutely innovative for the genre.

A year later *Vericuetos* is issued, authentic masterpiece for its complexity: realized with the aid of first-quality musicians, this album is the sum of the artist's intellectual experiences, with typically Prog sounds build on synth bases and keyboards, penetrated by sitar, violin, acoustic and electric guitar in a formidable mixture endowed with great energy.

The last Prog act of **Gualberto** is *Sin Comentario*, n entirely instrumental album in which the artist becomes a one man band, playing all the instruments from the electric and classical guitars to the sarod or Persian guitar. The atmosphere that springs is a footstep ahead from his previous works, slightly Jazz imposed and under the influence of **Frank Zappa**, that he had the chance of knowing during his stay in the US, unquestionably well organized and undoubtedly extremely pleasant. It is worth spending two words for the album *Gualberto* containing recordings belonging to when he went from the experience in **The Smash** to his solo career: although these are very raw tracks, sometimes excessively commercial, in them we find the seeds of the artistic evolution that **Gualberto** will hereafter undertake.   **C.A.**

DISCOGRAPHY:
A LA VIDA AL DOLOR *(Movieplay, 1975)* **VERICUETOS** *(Movieplay, 1976)* **OTROS DIAS** *(Movieplay, 1979)* **GUALBERTO Y AGUJETAS** *(Movieplay, 1979)* **GUALBERTO Y RICARDO MIÑO** *(Aries del Sur, 1983)* **SIN COMENTARIO** *(Lost Vinyl, 1996)* **GUALBERTO** *(Wah-Wah, 2003)*.

Europe: SPAIN

ICEBERG

José "Kitflus" Mas - *keyboards*, **Joaquín "Max" Suñe** - *guitar*, **Jordi Colomer** - *drums, percussions*, **Primitivo Sancho** - *bass*.

An extremely compact band which succeeded in producing with regularity, and with the same line-up, 5 records of absolute and indisputable value. Their genre is a Jazz-prog Symphonic-rock with moments referable to as Fusion (mainly resembling **Chick Corea, Mahavishnu Orchestra** and **Santana**). After various experiences beginning at the end of the '60s with groups of different extraction, from Folk to Jazz, from Rock to Psychedelia, in 1974 keyboardist **Josep Mas Portet** aka **Kitflus** meets the right people and founds in Barcelona a band of great technique and great musical spirit. In opposition to the great energy of the sound, he decides to call it **Iceberg**.

The following year's debut is rather pretentious, with a concept of episodes on the life of the famous Pharaoh *Tutankhamon*. The album has the naif thematic of a first record, and alongside purely lyrical tracks like "Lying On The Sand" or "Close To God", we find unbelievably Prog ones such as "Amarna" or "Amenophis IV" with great rhythmic acrobatics and technical solos. Some small references to the great classics of English Prog (**Yes, Mahavishnu**) appear, but also from projects like *Jesus Christ Superstar*.

Their direction becomes clearer in the second release *Coses Nostres* of 1976, more prone to Jazz-rock. When the band loses their singer and saxophonist **Angelo Riba**, they will still produce an extremely variegated and rich conceptual Symphonic-prog through Joaquin Suñe's peculiar use of the guitar (between **Steve Howe** and **John McLaughlin** styles) together with the great keyboard playing of **Mas**. The album, dynamic in execution and result, contains the song "Nova", that will become one of the strongest pieces of all their live performances. Every track is an elegant representative of their style, by now defined, like in the beautiful "11/8", rich of really personal hints.

Style confirmed in the following album *Sentiments* of 1977 which, a part from the slightly Funky "Magic", introduced tracks of great depth like "Alegries del Mediterrani" or "A Sevilla". *Iceberg En Directe* published in 1978 is a powerful live album that knows how to highlight the extraordinary abilities of the band and their more cheerful and playful side, underlining the true pleasure of making music and giving us one of the best live editions of the time.

Their last gift, *Arc-En-Ciel*, arrives just before the break-up, opening with "El caminant nocturn", probably containing the best guitar solo of the band, in full Santana-style. The break-up sees **Mas** and **Suñe** joining the super band **Pegasus**, but this is different story. **R.V.**

DISCOGRAPHY:
TUTANKHAMON *(1975, Bocaccio Records)* **COSES NOSTRES** *(1976, Bocaccio Records)* **SENTIMENTS** *(1977, Bocaccio Records)* **ICEBERG EN DIRECTE** *(1978, Bocaccio Records)* **ARC-EN-CIEL** *(1979, Bocaccio Records)*.

Europe: SPAIN

ITOIZ

Juan Carlos Perez - *guitar and vocals,* **Jose Garate** – *bass,* **Jose Antonio Fernandez** – *keyboards,* **Joseba Erkiaga** – *flute,* **Estanis Osinalde** – *drums.*

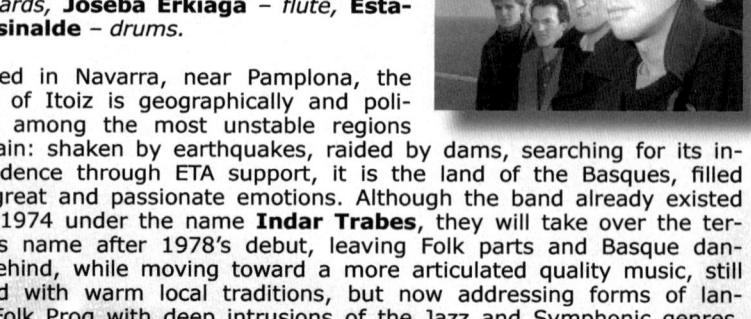

Situated in Navarra, near Pamplona, the valley of Itoiz is geographically and politically among the most unstable regions of Spain: shaken by earthquakes, raided by dams, searching for its independence through ETA support, it is the land of the Basques, filled with great and passionate emotions. Although the band already existed since 1974 under the name **Indar Trabes**, they will take over the territory's name after 1978's debut, leaving Folk parts and Basque dances behind, while moving toward a more articulated quality music, still soaked with warm local traditions, but now addressing forms of languid Folk Prog with deep intrusions of the Jazz and Symphonic genres. *Itoiz* reveals itself as an extremely winning mixture, becoming one of the most important records of what is to be the second wave of Spanish Prog. The choice of singing in Basque, a language distant from other typical Prog idioms and more in general from the international music scene, completes the idea of being presented in an alternative way on the market. Also very interesting are the possible references to the **Genesis** of *Trespass*, to the romantic side of **Yes** and to other Folk groups of the early '70s. Overall the sound results similar to the French, above all to colleagues like **Carpe Diem** and **Shylock**, obviously nicely sewed under the skin of the Basque tradition.

Perez's particular voice, together with important flute sections, creates an enchanting sound and the choice of not using synthesizers (at the time all too common) allowed their music to be timeless, keeping intact their charm up to this very day. After almost two years they finally release a masterpiece: *Ezekiel* came at a moment of strong decadence for Prog, but perhaps because the genre took off late in Spain, it actually was a great success. The clear and mature composition, the careful research of instruments and sounds always in the right place, the liaise of Symphonic parts with delicate acoustic moments and delicious Jazz intrusions to the plot, perfectly balancing the whole to a point of rare perfection. A refined concept, untiringly pleasant also thanks to the widening of the organic with sax and violin. The following *Alkolea* (1982) is not at the same level also perhaps given the line-up change which introduced a weaker compositional aspect, drier in rhythmic choices and more synthetic in sounds. Nevertheless there are some good songs like "Hire Bideak" and "Beheko Plaza", among others of doubtful choice such as "Ixilik Egon Hadi....Ixili" in which appears a glimpse of the **Bee Gees**' Disco sound. Then they rediscovered a Dance soul and everything else up to the 1988 break-up becomes a form of well manufactured Pop, commercial music, repetitive and distant from any form of Prog. **R.V.**

DISCOGRAPHY:

ITOIZ *(1978, XOXOA)* **EZEKIEL** *(1980, XOXOA)* **ALKOLEA** *(1982, Elkar)* **MUSIKAZ BLAI** *(1983, Elkar)* **ESPALOÍAN** *(1985, Elkar)* **AMBULANCE** *(1987, Elkar)* **EREMUKO DUNEN ATZETIK DABIL** *(1988 Live, Elkar).*

Europe: SPAIN

NEURONIUM

Michel Huygen - *keyboards,* **Carlos Guirao** - *keyboards, guitar,* **Albert Giménez** - *keyboards, guitar,* **Santi Picó** - *guitar, 1980.*

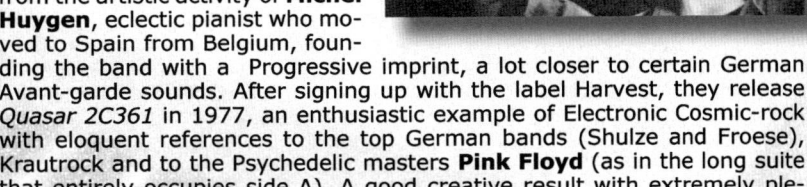

The **Neuronium** project was born from the artistic activity of **Michel Huygen**, eclectic pianist who moved to Spain from Belgium, founding the band with a Progressive imprint, a lot closer to certain German Avant-garde sounds. After signing up with the label Harvest, they release *Quasar 2C361* in 1977, an enthusiastic example of Electronic Cosmic-rock with eloquent references to the top German bands (Shulze and Froese), Krautrock and to the Psychedelic masters **Pink Floyd** (as in the long suite that entirely occupies side A). A good creative result with extremely pleasant sounds, onyric and Cosmic atmospheres which have a extraordinarily relaxing effect and decidedly introspective melodic tones.

Huygen's unstoppable artistic creativeness brings to a second masterpiece, *Vuelo quimico* in 1978, in which guest singer **Nico** from **The Velvet Underground** appears reciting verses of Edgar Allan Poe. The album is a real pearl, musically similar to the precedent with a greater use of guitars that blend perfectly with **Nico**'s unmistakable voice. After this they enjoy great popularity taking part in live tours and festivals while neglecting studio sessions. **Huygen** meets **Vangelis** in this period and they collaborate in some of his projects, thus changing deeply the **Neuronium** formula, which since 1980 also changed label and therefore artistic orientation.

What is published thereafter is but a pale memoir of the first two masterpieces; while *Digital Dreams* recalls paths dear to artists such as **Jean Michel Jarre**. *Chromium Echoes* of 1982 deserves special note and is played in all the band's concerts of the '80s. **Huygen** disbands and reunites **Neuronium** to his pleasure, while undertaking a solo career or involving dozens of world famous musicians in his projects, which are more New Age by now than Progressive. Still active to this very day and have evolved toward a classy and positive Electronic music, with great energy. They do not disappoint though nothing of their beginnings is there any longer.

C.A.

DISCOGRAPHY:
QUASAR 2C361 *(Harvest, 1977)* **VUELO QUIMICO** *(Harvest, 1978)* **DIGITAL DREAMS** *(Auvi, 1980)* **THE VISITOR** *(Auvi, 1981)* **CHROMIUM ECHOES** *(Auvi, 1982).*

Europe: SPAIN

ÑU

François André - *violin*, **Enrique Ballesteros** - *drums*, **Jorge Calvo** - *bass*, **José Carlos Molina** - *vocals, flute, mellotron*, **José María García Sini** - *guitar*.

An explosive mixture of sounds between **Greenslade** and **Jethro Tull** is the best definition of **Ñu**, a Spanish band from the mid '70s led by keyboardist and singer **Josè Molina**. Anglo-Saxon Progressive follower but also deeply attracted by the hardest sounds of Hard Rock, he acts exactly as **Ian Anderson** did with **Jethro Tull**: artistic guide to the limit of despotism.

Their debut album is dated 1978, *Cuentos De Ayer Y De Hoy*, already pointing out what their musical themes would become: Hard Rock interposed with melodic passages of violin, flute and mellotron. Some songs recalling **Deep Purple**'s *Fireball*, and in general high energy played with a good alternation of harder parts and more melodic moments. Unfortunately the Spanish lyrics sound too rough for the very British context in which they are sung.

The following *A Golpe De Latigo* is published after a change in line-up imposed by **Molina**, that brings to the exclusion of guitarist Sini. The sound is always on the Hard Rock borderline, but the keyboards increase in importance, paying an inevitable tribute to **ELP**; the flute is perfectly set among the guitar solos and the violin. Still in Spanish the lyrics, limiting thus the project and its potential abroad.

Accorralado Por Ti arrives with the inevitable change in line-up. "Romance ghost" is the best song it contains, where the mixture of keyboards and guitars and the elegant background of choirs brings us back to the glorious '70s. The rest is more of a Heavy Metal album: the abandonment of Prog does not cause however the end of this band. Once chosen their path they will continue to publish good music and to perform in concerts that are constantly sold out.   **C.A.**

DISCOGRAPHY:
CUENTOS DE AYER Y DE HOY *(Chapa, 1978)* **A GOLPE DE LATIGO** *(Chapa, 1980)* **FUEGO** *(Chapa, 1981)* **ACCORRALADO POR TI** *(Chapa, 1984)* **NO HAY NINGUN LOCO** *(Barrabas, 1986)* **EL MENSAJE DEL MAGO** *(Barrabas, 1987)* **VAMOS A LIO'!** *(Barrabas, 1988)* **DOS ANOS DE DESTIERRO** *(Avispa, 1990)* **IMPERIO DE PALETOS** *(Barrabas, 1992)* **LA DANZA DE LAS MIL TIERRA** *(SMD, 1994)* **VEINTE ANOS Y UN DIA** *(Kainos, 1995)* **LA TABERNA ENCANTADA** *(A la caza del N, 1997)* **LA NOCHE DEL JUGLAR** *(A la caza del Nu, 1999)* **CUATRO GATOS** *(A la caza del Nu, 2000)* **REQUIEM** *(PIES, 2002)* **TITERES** *(PIES, 2003)* **DAMA DE HONOR** *(Foque, 2004)* **VIEJOS HIMNOS PARA NUEVOS** *(Santo Grial, 2011)*.

Europe: SPAIN

TRIANA

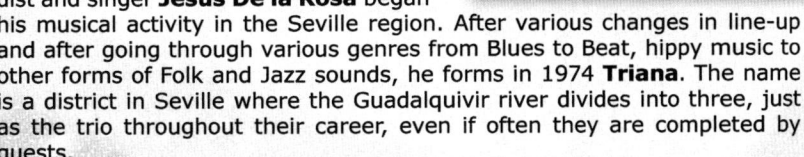

Jesùs De La Rosa – *keyboards, vocals*, **Juan Reina** – *vocals*, **Juan Jose Palacios** – *drums, percussions*, **Andrés Herrera Ruiz, Eduardo Rodriguez** - *guitars*.

Already in the mid '60s young keyboardist and singer **Jesus De la Rosa** began his musical activity in the Seville region. After various changes in line-up and after going through various genres from Blues to Beat, hippy music to other forms of Folk and Jazz sounds, he forms in 1974 **Triana**. The name is a district in Seville where the Guadalquivir river divides into three, just as the trio throughout their career, even if often they are completed by guests.

Born from the common passion for English Prog and Flamenco, it is this very mixture that will define their first phase with the birth in 1975 of *El Patio*: seven tracks of great charm made to plunge the public into this new way of playing Prog, thanks to the unique contamination. From "Abre la Puerta" to "Recuerdos de una Noche" we find a great demonstration of healthy cohabitation among electric and acoustic sounds, dominated by the warm voice of **De La Rosa**, naturally spun to sing with sweet melancholy the different states of the mind, dominated by themes of memory and passion.

The album did not sell well but was compensated by a great and crowded tour which brought them to the right amount of notoriety, and the exit of *Hijo Del Agobio* (1977). The traversal characteristic through Bulerías, Tango, Blues, Prog, Seguirillas and Symphonic Rock, remained intact and introduced the hit single "Rumor." The album was greatly welcome in America and the band was chosen as the best of the Latin area. Technically this work probably represents the apex of the trio. The lyrics are mostly on the passing from Franco's dictatorship to a democracy, very evocative and full of social feelings, perfect to obtain the interest of the whole nation.

Director Gonzalo Garciapelayo in 1979 produces their third work *Sombra Y Luz*, also good yet with a deviation toward commercial Pop music, through which they achieve great sales. Among the songs to remember are the title-track and "Hasta Volver", of absolute Prog value compared to the others. Future successes will distinguish them, despite the more commercial attitude, for their compositional standard: sometimes very intimate, sometimes made of radiant electric rides, making sure pure Prog songs sit alongside less elaborate Pop ones. **De La Rosa** dies in a car crash in 1983 just after a concert. This tragedy breaks up the band until drummer **Palacios**, in 1996 decides to exhume the name with a couple of nice but not too Prog albums. In 2002 also **Palacios** dies and **Triana** will be continued by **Juan Reina** as last singer of the band, with a sincere attempt in 2007 to pursue the path so tragically interrupted twice. **R.V.**

DISCOGRAPHY:
EL PATIO *(1975, Movieplay)* **HIJOS DEL AGOBIO** *(1977, Movieplay)* **SOMBRA Y LUZ** *(1979, Movieplay)* **UN ENCUENTRO** *(1980, Movieplay)* **TRIANA** *(1981, Movieplay)* **EN DIRECTO** *(1981, Movieplay)* **LLEGÓ EL DIA** *(1983, Movieplay)* **UN JARDIN ELECTRICO** *(1996, Omni)* **EN LIBERTAD** *(1999, PIES Compañia Discográfica)* **UN CAMINO POR ANDAR** *(2007, Fecha Edición)*.

Europe: SWEDEN

FLÄSKETT BRINNER

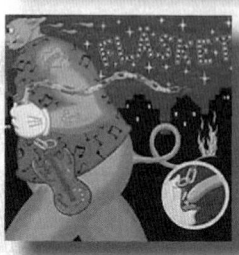

Bengt Dahlen - *guitar*, **Sten Bergman** - *keyboards, flute*, **Gunnar Bergsten** - *sax*, **per Bruun** - *bass*, **Erik Dahlbäck** - *drums*, **Mikael Ramel** - *guitar, vocals*.

With only two albums issued in 1971 and 1972, this band remains one of the most important, influential and involving bands of the entire Scandinavian scene because of their total expressive freedom and for the effervescent verve that stands out in their vinyls and even more in their incandescent live performances. Their music is a hard-prog based sound with continuous raids into the Swedish Folk genre, Jazz, Symphonic Rock, improvisation and very ironic and almost circus styled fragments. All, obviously, with the right amount of crazy and genius that continually pop out, clearly notifying the presence of **Zappa**'s chromosome (see *Hot Rats* or *The Grand Wazoo*).

Bo Hansson also collaborates on this project, both in studio and in concert. After the double LP *Fläsket* (half studio, half live) published in 1972, the band plans a next album but is interrupted. Yet the concerts continue and in fact, they find on stage their natural habitat and will keep playing for another decade.

Recently a four cd box was issued as the *Swedish Radio Recordings 1970-1975* containing loads of material of an impressive artistic quality: vivacious sounds with the chameleon ability to manage more styles, fabulous instrumental parts, at times even unbelievably improvised where guitar, organ and brass plunge in passionate tour-de-force, alternating brilliant solo parts that bring out the musicians' uniqueness. And, as if not enough, in two of the cds we find **Hansson** guest starring with his splendid executions (also present in the keyboardist's albums).

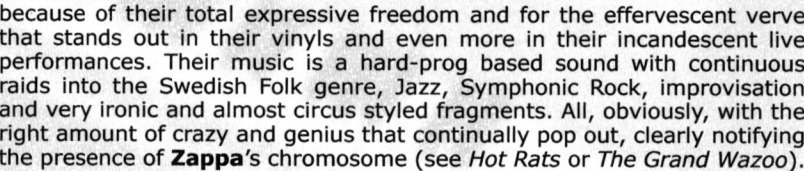

To be noted that guitarist **Mikael Ramel** issued some works in the '70 under his name with the collaboration, among others, of his companions from **Fläskets Brinner**. These are eccentric albums which take some of the most colourful sounds of the band and divert them toward paths closer to Psychedelia and to a more lunatic Folk genre.

G.D.S.

DISCOGRAPHY:
FLÄSKET BRINNER *(1971, Silence)* **FLÄSKET** *(1972, Ljudspår)* **THE SWEDISH RADIO RECORDINGS 1970-1975** *(2003, Mellotronen)*.

Europe: SWEDEN

BO HANSSON

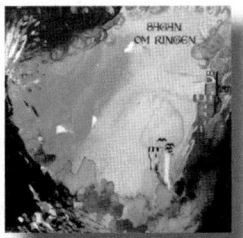

Teenager **Bo Hansson** joins his parents in Stockholm where he immediately begins to take an interest in Rock'n'roll as a self-taught guitarist, playing in a band called **Rock-Olga**. Going through all of Rock's evolutions, from Jazz to Blues, he will then join a band called **Slim' Notini's Blues Gang** in a project comparable to **John Mayall's Bluesbreakers**. Later **Hansson** will found the **Merrymen** with whom he opens **the Rolling Stones**' concert during their first Scandinavian tour.
After watching Jazz organist **Jack McDuff** play live, he is so impressed to decide to widen his musical horizons by purchasing a Hammond for himself. He leaves the **Merrymen** and through his former band member **Bill Öhrström**, who had become a producer for the Swedish Polydor branch, signs up along with drummer **Janne Karlsson**. his innovative style on the Hammond launches the duo **Hansson & Karlsson** publishing three albums between 1967 and 1969. Even **Jimi Hendrix** will notice them and after a jam together at Klub Filips, he will record a version of **Hansson**'s "Tax free".
Yet **Hansson**'s true debut occurs when, after reading Tolkien's The Lord of the Rings, he withdraws to a cottage on an island near Stockholm and then publishes *Sagan Om Ringen* with Silence Records, first independent Swedish label, in the autumn of 1970, selling a great deal of copies. This success actually makes it to GB where Tony Stratton Smith, head of Charisma, will publish the English version *Music Inspired by Lord of the Rings*, also hitting top sales in the U.K.

Encouraged by this he edits a following work with guitaris **Kenny Håkansson**, *Ur Trollkarlens Hatt*, issued by Silence Records toward the end of 1972 and by Charisma as *Magician's Hat* in 1973: it will not achieve the same success, despite the favors of the critics. This does not hurt his popularity in Sweden where he is pressured for a new tour, cancelled for he prefers recording a third studio album, *Mellanväsen*, always with Silence Records in October 1975, which will take the title *Attic Thoughts* under Charisma in the February of 1976. This is perhaps his best album but unfortunately achieves even less success than the others. The beautiful opening song "Rabbit Music" will inspire **Hansson** for the following album.

Once made partner in Silence Records, he will manage to receive better treatment with Charisma and, inspired by Richard Adams' Watership Down, he publishes the studio recording with producer Pontus Olssen in 1977: *El 'Ahrairah*(tale of the bunny hero titled *Music Inspired by Watership Down* for Charisma and Sire Records in America). Again sales are disappointing, forcing **Hansson** to retire from the scenes. He still collaborates with other musicians and his very last Swedish record is exclusively published in Sweden in 1985 as *Mitt I Livet* (Half life) for Silence Records. Then the curtain definitively closes with only some sporadic rumors on health and poverty issues, with some a rare live performance in a tiny club here and there, till he finally disappears in 2010.   **M.G.**

DISCOGRAPHY:
SAGAN OM RINGEN *(SRS, 1970)* **UR TROLLKARLENS HATT** *(SRS, 1972)* **LORD OF THE RINGS** *(Charisma, 1972)* **MAGICIAN'S HAT** *(Charisma, Sire, 1973)* **ATTIC THOUGHTS** *(Charisma, Sire, 1975)* **MELLANVÄSEN** *(SRS, 1975)* **EL-AHRAIRAH** *(YTF, 1977)* **MUSIC INSPIRED BY WATERSHIP DOWN** *(Charisma, Sire, 1977)* **THE BEST OF BO HANSSON** *(Charisma, 1983)* **MITT I LIVET** *(SRS, Bahama 1985)* **LORD OF THE RINGS (extended version)***(SRS, 1986)*.

Europe: SWEDEN

KAIPA

Hans Lundin - *keyboards, vocals,* **Roine Stolt** - *guitar, vocals,* **Tomas Eriksson** - *bass, vocals,* **Ingemar Bergman** - *drums, vocals,* **Mats Löfgren** - *vocals,* **Mats Lindberg** - *bass,* **Max Ahman** - *guitar,* **Mats Lindberg** - *bass (homonym of the previous),* **Pelle Andersson** - *drums.*

After the break-up of the band **San Michaels**, **Hans Lundin** and **Tomas Erikssons** form a new band by recruiting **Ingemar Bergman** and enfant prodige guitarist **Roine Stolt**. As **Kaipa**, these musicians move their first steps performing live and are immediately noticed by the famous label Decca which offers them a record contract. The self-titled debut album published in 1975, is an elegant Symphonic and dreamy fresco, sung in Swedish. **Lundin**'s talent here emerges since he signs great part of the compositions, and **Stolt** proves his true value. The band is good and coherent in creating a tale-ish sound that bestows a certain calm with its soft melodies, vague **Camel** romantic echoes and some hints of Classical music and Swedish Folk tunes.

Inget Nytt Under Solen issued in 1976 will consolidate the style of their debut with more articulated plots and will bring them closer to the British experiences of **Genesis**, **Yes** and **Camel**. Despite these influences, their strong personality emerges and the solemn suite "Skenet Bedrar" goes to prove it, representing at the same time one of the absolute hits of the band, in this album in a more Classical version.

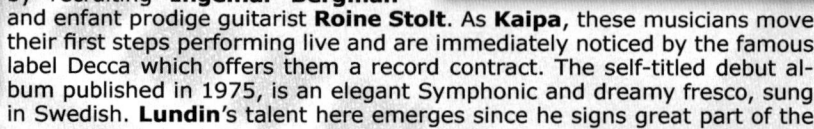

Meanwhile **Stolt**'s importance grows to the point that *Solo* dated 1978 sees the guitarist in the leading role. The sound is still romantic and the musicians manage well even in shorter tracks. **Stolt**'s departure in 1979 sees the band go through a crisis since **Lundin** directs the sound toward more commercial music that doesn't convince the public at all, not in *Händer* (1980) nor in *Nattdjustid* (1982).

The magical adventure seems to have come to a halt until 20 years later, when **Lundin** reforms **Kaipa** involving **Stolt** once again, who in the meantime had achieved a certain visibility with his **Flower Kings**. They so publish four cds (though the guitarist leaves before the last one is finished), particularly interesting *Notes from the Past*, but it almost looks as if tending to imitate the **Flower Kings** with a predictable yet well played Symphonic Rock. **G.D.S.**

DISCOGRAPHY:
KAIPA *(1975, Decca)* **INGET NYTT UNDER SOLEN** *(1976, Decca)* **SOLO** *(1978, Decca)* **HÄNDER** *(1980, Polar)* **NATTDJUSTID** *(1982, Pigglet)* **NOTES FROM THE PAST** *(2002, Inside Out)* **KEYHOLDER** *(2003, Inside Out)* **MINDREVOLUTIONS** *(2005, Inside Out)* **ANGLING FEELINGS** *(2007, Inside Out).*

Europe: **SWEDEN**

ISILDURS BANE

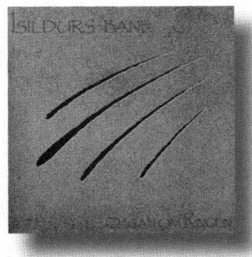

Klas Assarsson - *percussion,* **Mats Nilsson, Tommy Nilsson, Jay Schiffer, Dan Andersson, Bo N Roth, Jonas Christophs, Mats MP Persson** - *guitars,* **Jan Severinsson** - *horns, violin, percussion, keyboards,* **Ingvar "Lingon" Johansson, Stigge Ljunglof, Fredrik Janacek, Fredrik Emilsson** - *bass,* **Joachim Gustafsson** - *violin,* **Mats Johansson, Lars Hägglund, Christian Hierov** - *keyboards,* **Kjell Severinsson** - *drums, percussion,* **Bengt Johansson, Bjorn Lindh** - *horns,* **Mariette Hansson, Christof Jeppsson, Anna Lönnberg** - *vocals.*

Together with other few enlightened bands holding up high the Prog flag during the dawn of the '80s, like **Univers Zero, Kenso** and **Miriodor**, they embody the authentic Prog spirit and develop a project/concept through this most difficult decade. They settle into their last line-up by 1977 with the entrance of keyboardist **Johansson** playing alongside founders **Jan** and **Kjell Severinsson**. The name of the group is inspired by Tolkien, as is their debut album (a limited edition tape that officially sees the light in 1988) which connects them to the famous *Sagan Om Ringen* of fellow countryman **Bo Hansson**, reliving stories and characters of the Lord of the Rings: a modern, fantastic and lively Art-rock, with acoustic passages, Jazz-rock deviations in pure **Camel** style and a disruptive rhythmic compartment. It is an amazing debut for the time and for the inclination to be more of a small orchestra than of a rock band.

After a tour their first true LP is out in 1984 as *Sagan Om Den Irländska Älgen* mixing impressionistic Rock and Swedish Folk totally inspired by **Frank Zappa**'s style. If the contemporary paladins of new prog chose to relive the romantic rock of **Genesis** with updated sounds, IB preferred the **Yes** and **Gentle Giant** onto which they sewed various influences, from Classical to Jazz, avoiding excesses and prolixity. The fancy *Sea Reflections* is an instrumental album, a Fusion pause of exotic aftertaste with a notable horn section and links to **Weather Report** and **Uzeb**. The next recording, *Eight Moments Of Eternity* points them into finding a balance between art, literature and spirituality, molding the band into an intellectual Rock genre. Their next step is *Cheval*, a suite for rock band and orchestra, in search of the perfect synthesis among Rock, the Classical world, experimentation and communication. A sumptuous job played with the **Hallardsensemblen Orchestra**, that relives Ferdinand Cheval's great dream: the 30 years construction of the Palais Idéal. In fact they work very hard to build an ideal sound, a peaceful place where the most disparate expressive forms cohabit.

Their Art-rock becomes re-known and in their concerts they elaborate futuristic and multiform shows: *The Voyage*, inspired by Swiss artist Adolf Wölfli and composed with a Classical trio and a choir, is indeed a monumental and complex album, a further exploration of the possible interlacements between popular and contemporary music.

Not yet void of imagination and ideas, **IB** give way to the ambitious project *MIND (Music Investigating New Dimensions)*, a sonorous adventure in 5 volumes issued between 1997 and 2005, recorded both in studio and live with new techniques and collaborations: a vast mosaic which embraces a new Chamber Rock with Electronics, futurist Art-pop, improvisations and the **Zappa** legacy.   **D.Z.**

DISCOGRAPHY:

SAGAN OM RINGEN *(Isildurs Bane, 1981)* **SAGAN OM DEN IRLÄNDSKA ÄLGEN** *(Isildurs Bane, 1984)* **SEA REFLECTIONS** *(Isildurs Bane, 1985)* **EIGHT MOMENTS OF ETERNITy** *(Isildurs Bane, 1987)* **CHEVAL - VOLONTÉ DE ROCHER** *(1989)* **THE VOYAGE - A TRIP TO ELSEWHERE** *(Isildurs Bane, 1992)* **LOST EGGS** *(Isildurs Bane, 1994)* **MIND VOLUME I** *(Svenska Unikum, 1997)* **MIND VOL. 2 - LIVE** *(live, Record Heaven 2001)* **ISILDURS BANE & METAMORFOSI TRIO: MIND VOL.3** *(Ataraxia, 2003)* **MIND VOL. 4 - PASS** *(Ataraxia, 2003)* **MIND VOL. 5 - THE OBSERVATORY** *(DVD, Ataraxia, 2005).*

Europe: SWEDEN

MADE IN SWEDEN

Georg Wadenius - *guitars, keyboards, vocals,* **Bo Häggström** - *bass, guitar, mellotron,* **Tommy Borgudd** - *drums, percussions.*

Swedish prog has among its first creatures **Made In Sweden** founded by **Georg Wadenius**, only present member from beginning to end. He essentially preferred Blues and Jazz sounds borrowed from the American and English genres, but went beyond the scholastic idea of orthodox schemes that no longer were satisfactory, carrying out with the rest of the band a more traversal concept (something similar was going on in **Yes**'s first album with **Peter Banks** and on the other side of the ocean with **Frank Zappa**).

At the end of 1967, when the band had settled, they prepared the material for the recording of *Made In Sweden (With Love)* the year after. Here we find the Prog Jazz of "Saucery", the more traditional Blues of "Little Charlie", the turning inside out of the "Peter Gunn" theme, to the Jazz cover of "A Day In A Life" by **The Beatles**. It also contains some funny references like from the country western "Little Dame" or from the "Harry Lime Theme" (OST of the war film The Third Man), and still is probably one of the best debuts of the time.

After a short while they issue a second album *Snakes In a Hole* (1969), in which we find a consolidated heterogeneity of sounds between Prog Jazz and Blues with hints from **Zappa** like in "Discotheque People", hints from **Hendrix** like in "Give Me Whiskey" and the jazz rock of "Kristallen Den Grymma" and "Big Cloud".

A tour followed and led to the album *Live At The Golden Circle* (1970), with a good choice in songs though often longer than usual. This same year a third studio album was recorded, *Made In England,* known also as *Mad River*. Here again is the strange mixture of Jazz and Blues moments inside the same song, where the parts alternate in a very determined way, flowing sometimes even into an acoustic Folk of great level. We find unforgettable songs like "Mad River", but also some funny stuff like the Rock'n'roll of "Blind Will".

After a pause of more than five years the band returns heavily transformed with the respectable Funky Fusion of *Where Do We Begin?*. Among the new entries are **Pekka Pohjola** and **Vesa Aaltonen**, well known in the Swedish Prog scenario, although from Finland. Apparently a good project but lacking the success to continue the adventure. **R.V.**

DISCOGRAPHY:
MADE IN SWEDEN *(With Love)* *(1968, Sonet)* **SNAKES IN A HOLE** *(1969, Sonet)* **LIVE AT THE GOLDEN CIRCLE** *(1970, Sonet)* **MADE IN ENGLAND** *(1970, Sonet)* **WHERE DO WE BEGIN?** *(1976, Polydor).*

Europe: **SWEDEN**

SAMLA MAMMAS MANNA

Lars Hollmer - *keyboards, vocals*, **Coste Apetrea** - *guitar, vocals*, **Hasse Bruniusson** - *drums, percussions, vocals*, **Lasse Krants** - *bass, vocals*.

They began as trio at the end of the '60s thanks to composer and pianist **Lars Hollmer**. representing the very essence of an extraordinary ironic Avant-garde begun with **Frank Zappa** and spread out to the four corners of the earth. Their technical ability and innovative strength brings to a debut in 1971 with a self titled album, already incredibly mature and effective, containing so much Jazz and Folk but also circus music, experimentations, Dadaism and lots of joy incarnated in sounds of voices, spoken parts and background vocals. Many are the Canterbury references (as in "Vidgat Läge") in this mostly instrumental project, ingredients that later will be essential to the RIO movement. A special highlight goes to drummer **Bruniusson**'s rare inventiveness and dynamic ability.

In 1972 **Coste Apetrea** joins the band, a guitarist of great musical and compositional abilities, that brings to their sound new and strong Jazz-rock elements though maintaining the initial unprejudiced Avant-garde spirit. With the new line-up *Måltid* of 1973 well represents **Samla**'s resources and true possibilities with effervescent tracks, rich of nonconformism and witty eccentricity both in the use and in the dosing of the instruments, and for the elaboration of the musical structure.

In 1974 *Glossa Knapitatet* is published giving us other great quality executions grazing perfection, all tied together with stylistic mastery. The Avant-garde moments often interlace simple and catchy melodies, creating a particular sonorous syncretism. 1975 was a year dedicated to tours and live performances so the next album comes out in 1976: *Snorungarnas Symfoni*, a symphony written in origin by **G. To. Fitzpatrick**. Divided into 4 parts it had more of a Symphonic Rock tendency than their Classical Avant-garde style. However many define this as their best work, able to maintain their histrionic spirit and the complex, intimate weirdness. Inside discussions bring to a break-up until **Eino Haapala** joins in replacing **Apetrea** and the name of the band becomes **Zamla Mammaz Manna**. In 1978 *Schlagerns Mystick/For Aldre Nybegynnare* is issued dominated by improvisations and by the complexity of its plots, a real change in style. The album caught **Chris Cutler**'s attention and **Hollmer** becomes one of his R.I.O. adepts. In 1979 **Bruniusson** leaves his place to **Vilgot Hansson** for the summer tour and still plays in the following album *Familiesprickor* (1980).

Hollmer and **Haapala** record many other tracks together under the name **Von Zamla**: *Zamlaranamma* (1982) and *No Make Up* (1984) with **Michel Berckmans** from **Univers Zero**. A classic reunion with the historical line-up takes place for the millennium, to which two other interesting albums follow.

R.V.

DISCOGRAPHY:

As Samla Mammas Manna:
SAMLA MAMMAS MANNA *(1971, Silence)* **MÅLTID** *(1973, Silence)* **KLOSSA KNAPITATET** *(1974, Silence)* **SNORUNGARNAS SYMFONI** *(1976, Musiknätet Waxholm MNW)* **KAKA** *(1999, AMCD)* **DEAR MAMA** *(live 2002, Krax).*

As Zamla Mammaz Manna:
SCHLAGERNS MYSTIK / FÖR ÄLDRE NYBEGYNNARE *(1978, Silence)* **FAMILIESPRICKOR** *(1980, Silence).* *As Von Zamla:* **ZAMLARANAMMA** *(1982, Urspår)* **NO MAKE UP** *(1984, Urspår)* **VON ZAMLA 1983** *(1999, Cuneiform).*

Europe: SWEDEN

TRETTIOÅRIGA KRIGET

Stefan Fredin - *bass*, **Dag Lundqvist** - *drums, violin*. **Robert Zima** - *vocals*, **Christer Åkerberg** - *guitars*. **Mats Lindberg** - *keyboards, saxophones*. **Olle Thörnvall** - *lyrics*.

In the '70s every nation gives birth to creative bands that face the phenomenon of Art-rock with broad imagination and passion. For Scandinavia this is a decisive historical moment and Sweden responds with a movement known as Progg, rich of musical and political aspects that will mold all the militant Folk and Rock bands to come. Some of the best known names are **Samla Mammas Manna**, **Bo Hansson** and **Kaipa** but the Swedish progg scene sees among its rows another fundamental band, **Trettioåriga Kriget**, capable of playing English Rock with great personality, leaving their mark and acting as influencer for future groups such as **Änglagård**, **Landberk** and **Anekdoten**.

The name literally means "War of the 30 years" and was chosen by this sextet of young students from the outskirts of Stockholm. They began playing in 1970 with two drummers, an Austrian vocalist named **Robert Zima** and song-writer **Olle Thörnvall** that, influenced by **Sinfield** and **Reid**, will leave his harmonica to focus only on the lyrics. In 1972 talented guitarist **Åkerberg** joins in and **TK** becomes a quartet. They will continue rehearsing in the Grunden studios developing their really peculiar sound until they catch CBS's attention. In 1974 a self-titled debut album is published, followed by a tour and by Krigssang: a dynamic Prog, classic but never deprived of imagination, clearly cut for the guitar and with rich rhythmic drives, focusing on complex arrangements and the typical mellotron partitions. They sing in Swedish allowing the songs to keep their mysterious and emphatic mood. If the first LP has a more vehement impact, the tenebrous and melancholy atmospheres of the latter defines a style that will be still imitated 20 years later. They never fail to perform live and in 1976 they embark on a fortunate English tour but lose the contract with CBS. After a few years' break, they integrate with keyboardist **Lindberg** and publish Hei På Er!, an album with good commercial satisfaction and, even if it tends toward the American New Wave, it still withholds a certain artistic dignity, which cannot be said for the following Mot Alla Odds.

They synthesize their name to **Kriget** (as in Italy for **PFM** and **Banco**), index of a search for simplicity, and after an album named this way, they disband up to the mid '90s when label Mellotronen decides to reprint some of their initial works. Reuniting for some concerts between 2004 and 2007, they publish two new exceptional albums directly connected to their first works: Elden Av Ar a solid and powerful project, and The Borjan Och Slutet with its magnetic and mature atmospheres. Their participation in all the main international festivals allows the younger generations to get to know this historical band, formidable and still kicking.

D.Z.

DISCOGRAPHY:

TRETTIOÅRIGA KRIGET *(Epic, 1974)* **KRIGSSANG** *(CBS, 1975)* **HEI PÅ ER!** *(Mistlur, 1978)* **MOTT ALLA ODDS** *(Mistlur, 1979)* **KRIGET: KRIGET** *(Mistlur, 1981)* **WAR MEMORIES** *(Mellotronen, 1995)* **GLORIOUS WAR** *(Mellotronen, 2004)* **ELDEN AV AR** *(Mellotronen, 2004)* **I BORJAN OCH SLUTET** *(Mellotronen, 2007)* **WAR YEARS** *(live, Mellotronen, 2008)* **EFTER EFTER** *(Mellotronen, 2011)* **SEASIDE AIR** *(Mellotronen, 2016)*.

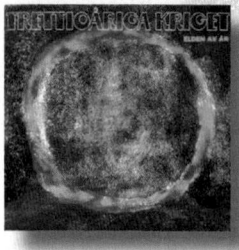

Europe: TURKEY

ERKIN KORAY

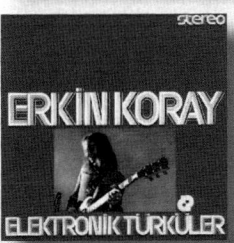

Born in 1941, for many he is actually the first artist to play Rock'n'roll in Turkey when in 1957 he begins his career with covers of songs by **Elvis Presley** and **Fats Domino**. For sure he was the first to be seen in the country with an electric guitar and a modern-day amp. His exceptional sense of timing sees his taste for Psychedelia transposed into Anatolic Rock as a great success. He soon publishes his own single "Anma Arkada" (1967) to which other songs follow, strengthening his reputation as a Rocker and putting him also in trouble with the authorities which were not accustomed to young people with long hair (since the government is a military institution with a large Muslim majority).

During the first years of the '70s he founds a trio called **Ter** with which he records only one hit single, "Hor Görme Garibi". Despite their success, the label, Istanbul Records, refuses to support since it considered their underground musical choices (rich of long guitar solos and Progressive arrangements) rather annoying, a clear sign of how the Turkish market was still unprepared to certain novelties. **Erkin** therefore inaugurates his solo career, encouraged by the interest of the fans, and in 1973 he finally issues a first self-titled album: practically a collection of songs as per the label's request.

By now the relation with Istanbul Records had reached its end and in 1974 he signs up with Doglan Records publishing his masterpiece *Elektronik Turkuler* (Electronic Ballads), a real album conceived just as such and no longer as a collection of singles. Rich in Prog Rock mixed to inspired local traditional Folk music, it was a huge success. From here on he begins a very satisfactory career touching the heart of a very large Turkish audience. His peers and colleagues often call him 'Erkin Baba' (Father Erkin) as a sign of affection, which goes to show how much they love

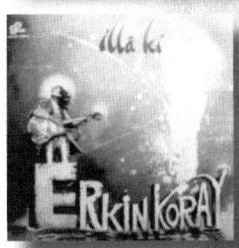

and respect him. Defined as the pioneer of modern Turkish music, being also the inventor of an instrument called the 'electric Baglama', or rather a kind of Turkish lute you can hear in many of his works, between 1990 and 2000, with the return of interest for the Psychedelic genre, his music has finds new vigor not only in Turkey, but all over the world. More recently and meant for the German market, in 2005 a documentary film on his life was made with many young artists paying him tribute. **M.G.**

DISCOGRAPHY:

ERKIN KORAY *(LP Istanbul, 1973)* **ELEKTRONIK TURKULER** *(LP Dogan, 1974)* **ERKIN KORAY 2** *(LP Dogan, 1976)* **ERKIN KORAY TUTKUSU** *(LP Kervan, 1977)* **BENDEN SANA** *(Kotas, 1982)* **ILLA KI** *(LP EMRE 1983)* **CEYLAN** *(LP EMRE, 1985)* **GADDAR** *(MC Uzelli, 1986)* **CUKULATAM BENIM** *(MC Armoni, 1987)* **HAY YAM YAM** *(MC Mega Müzik, 1989)* **TAMAM ARTIK** *(MC Mega Müzik, 1989)* **TEK BASINA KONSER** *(CD/MC Kalite, 1991)* **GUN OLA HARMAN OLA** *(CD Mega Müzik, 1996)* **DEVLERIN NEFESI** *(CD Ada Müzik, 1999)*.

Europe: TURKEY

BARIŠ MANÇO

Barıš Manço (or **Baris Mancho** as he is named in some European articles) was born in Istanbul in 1943 and is one of the greatest composers and singers of the Turkish Rock genre, with more than 200 songs translated in various languages. He was also a TV producer and a celebrity in all eastern Europe and the middle-east, wearing his hair long until his death in 1999 for a personal rebellion, due to the fact that as a pupil he was forced to cut it short to prevent lice. Seduced by Rock'n'roll and **Elvis Presley** as a boy, he creates many bands but always with the intent of blending Rock to traditional Turkish Folk and stuffing it with Progressive sounds. From 1963 he travels in Europe collaborating with various musicians and he begins to publish songs in English, in French and naturally in Turkish. After an accident that harms his face, he adds to his look a mustache that he will never take off again. Fed up of musicians from different nationalities, he founds an all Turkish band called **Kaygisizlar** with **Mazhar Alanson** and **Fuat Guner**, future members of the soon to be famous band called **MFÖ**.

In 1970 he records a first hit single "Daglar Daglar" which will sell over 700.000 copies and will remain one of his most popular songs. After this success he publishes a couple of tracks with the **Mogöllar** (The Mongols), another legend in the Turkish rock panorama. Shortly after his first true solo album *Dünden Bugüne* is released and then in 1972 he founds **Kurtalan Ekspres**, his personal band that will, from then on, always accompany him. In 1976 he decides to go international and records *Baris Mancho*, (playing with the phonetics of his name) with the aid of the **George Hayes Orchestra.** From 1977 to 1980 other successes will follow containing good music and in 1981 he will issue what is considered one of his most popular works, *Sözüm Meclisten Dıšarı*. Then again more good music such as in the albums *Degmesin Yaglı Boya* (1986), *Sahibinden Ihtiyaçtan* (1988) and *Darısı Bašınıza* (1989), which confirm his greatness.

In 1988 he becomes a TV producer for a music and culture broadcast on TRT 1, the Turkish national channel, traveling around more than 150 countries. Unfortunately this new activity, even if rich of satisfactions, will take up most of his time. His works become tired and without real enthusiasm, except maybe for his famous children's song "Ayi" (the bear). He makes time however for a last tour in Japan in 1995, from which the live album *Live In Japan* (1996) is recorded. He dies just before the publication of his studio album *Mançoloji* (Mançology or Manchology) in 1999.   **M.G.**

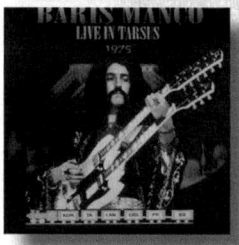

DISCOGRAPHY:
DÜNDEN BUGÜNE *(1971, Sayan)* **2023** *(1975, Yavuz Plak)* **SAKLA SAMANI GELIR ZAMANI** *(1976, Yavuz)* **BARIS MANCHO (uscito come NICK THE CHOPPER IN TURKEY)** *(1976, CBS, Yavuz LP)* **YENI BIR GÜN** *(1979, Yavuz)* **20 SANAT YILI DISCO MANÇO** *(1980, Türküola)* **SÖZÜM MECLISTEN DIŠARI** *(1981, Türküola)* **ESTAGFURULLAH... NE HADDIMIZE!** *(1983, Türküola)* **24 AYAR MANÇO** *(1985, Türküola)* **DEGMESIN YAGLI BOYA** *(1986, Emre Plakçılık)* **30 SANAT YILI FULAKSESUAR MANÇO - SAHIBINDEN IHTIYAÇTAN** *(1988, Emre Plakçılık)* **DARISI BAŠINIZA** *(1989, Yavuz)* **MEGA MANÇO** *(1992, Emre Plak)* **MÜSAADENIZLE ÇOCUKLAR** *(1995, Emre Plak)* **BARIŠ MANÇO LIVE IN JAPAN** *(1996, Emre Plak)* **MANÇOLOJI** *(1999, Emre Plak)* .

Europe: YUGOSLAVIA

KORNI GRUPA
KORNELYANS

Kornelije Kovac - *keyboards*, **Josip Bocek** - *guitars*, **Bojan Hreljac** - *bass*, **Vladimir Furduj** - *drums*, **Zlatko Pejakovic** - *lead vocals*.

Formed at the end of the '60s in a not exactly cultural-friendly Yugoslavia, this band manages nevertheless to pursue their own artistic goals far from the political context, interpreting a Prog genre of clear Italian inspiration. **Korni Grupa** were caught in between the market's demand for easy-listening songs and their personal tastes.

From 1970 to 1974 the line-up undergoes a series of changes, mainly due to the musicians' temptations of a soloist career. In 1972 their debut album is published, although in strong opposition with the Regime being somewhat of a Rock revolution, a hazardous step for the times. It is a milestone for the Slavic panorama, with songs disguised as Pop commercial tracks of a non excessive length, in order to avoid embarrassment and in non-association with the western enemies.

The fair share of keyboards and guitar partitions play a vaguely Jazzy Fusion genre with excellent technicality. Without excessive virtuosities, the next album follows above all the teachings of **Yes**'s Symphonic Rock style, with inevitable references to the Italian bands **Le Orme** and **PFM**. *Not An Ordinary Life* is published directly in English due to the attempt of trying to make more sales on the western markets: an unfortunate failure. After this record they bossily assume the role of best Balkan Rock band, but must provisionally change their name to **Kornelians**: history tells how after a difficult 1974 tour, leader **Kovac** abandons the group, de facto disbanding it. A few months later a double album, partially recorded live, increases the feeling of having lost a fundamental pillar of the Prog genre. In 1999 the band reunites for the exclusive creation of the music to a TV fiction called *1941*, as is their last album.

C.A.

DISCOGRAPHY:
KORNI GRUPA *(PGP, 1972)* **NOT AN ORDINARY LIFE** *(RICORDI PGP, 1974)* **MRTVO MORE** *(PGP, 1975)* **1941** *(PGP, 1979)*.

Indochina & North Asia: JAPAN

COSMOS FACTORY

Tsutomu Izumi - *keyboards, piano, vocals,* **Hisashi Mizutani** - *guitar, vocals,* **Toshikazu Taki** - *bass, vocals,* **Kazuo Okamoto** - *drums, percussion.*

They form in 1970 and soon move to Tokyo where they begin with the self-titled album of 1973 that immediately is a great hit. Known also as *An Old Castle of Transylvania*, it is a gem in which the band proves their great value: with keyboards dominating the scene, the fanciful moog solos and Hammond organ playing Classical echoes, the guitar breaks vaguely into **Fripp**-styled cut-edge melodies. The first five tracks alternate this majestic sound with stronger moments or more peaceful and melodic ones; then comes the spectacular and thrilling suite "An Old Castle of Transylvania" with its skillful keyboards and mellotron, creating dark atmospheres that subsequently intensify a dreamy Space-rock with hints recalling *Ys* from **Balletto di Bronzo**'s magic.
Though this remains the band's best work, some of their next projects are worthy of attention such as the eccentric Psychedelic Prog of *A Journey With the Cosmos Factory* published in 1975, with its strange melodies and symphonic moments similar to the debut-album. It contains ten tracks, not so long for the genre, all happily inspired by their chameleonic ability to extricate through different styles maintaining however a certain cohesion: schizoid guitars, **Pink Floyd** echoes, delicate ballads, majestic keyboards and visionary experimentation.

The following year they issue the excellent *Black Hole*, strongly influenced by **King Crimson**'s *Larks' Tongues in Aspic* and *Red* (even if references to **Pink Floyd** are always present): the harshness dissolves into carpets of mellotron full of good intuitions. After composing some soundtracks for TV purposes and Toshiba/Express's publishing in 1975 of the EPs *Fantastic Mirror*, *The Endless Universe of Our Mind* and *Days in the Past*, (which will become soon rare and valuable for collectors), in 1977 they undergo a last metamorphosis with *Metal Reflection*, a Hard-rock album of good quality, yet perhaps of minor interest. **G.D.S.**

DISCOGRAPHY:
AN OLD CASTLE OF TRANSYLVANIA *(1973, Columbia)* **A JOURNEY WITH THE COSMOS FACTORY** *(1975, Toshiba EMI/Express)* **BLACK HOLE** *(1976, Toshiba EMI/Express)* **METAL REFLECTION** *(1977, Toshiba EMI/Express).*

Indochina & North Asia: JAPAN

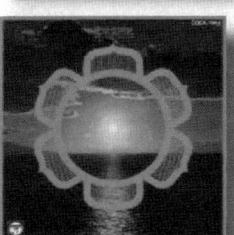

FAR EAST FAMILY BAND

Far Out:
Fumio Miyashita - *vocals, nihon-bue, acoustic guitar, harmonica, keyboards* , **Eiichi Sayu** – *guitars, keyboards, vocals* , **Kei Ishikawa** – *vocals, bass, electric sitar*, **Manami Arai** - *drums, nihon-daiko, vocals*.
Far East Family Band:
Fumio Miyashita - *guitar, keyboards, vocals* , **Masanori Takahashi (Kitaro)** - *keyboards, percussion*, **Akira Fukakusa** – *bass*, **Akira Ito** – *keyboards*, **Hirohito Fukushima** - *guitar, vocals*, **Shizuo Takasaki** - *drums*.

They originate from a previous band called **Far Out**, with a self-titled album published in 1973, essential to obtain a real knowledge of the Japanese Prog scene: composed by two long side tracks (in the recent CD version other 7 tracks were added), their music is a union of **Pink Floyd**'s Space-rock and traditional folk atmospheres; a large use of electric and electronics, Hammond and guitars (alternating Hendrix and Gilmour accordingly), choirs and vocals inspired by **Pink Floyd**'s *A Saucerful Of Secrets*.
After the break-up their leader **Fumio Miyashita** founds the **Far East Family Band** together with **Masanori Takahashi 'Kitaro'**, future master of Japanese New Age. Their initial activity was the rearranging of some old tracks of the previous group in order to be performed with the new line-up. In 1974 a truly new album is published entitled *The Cave Down To The Earth*, where the strong connection between **Pink Floyd**'s Space-rock style and traditional Folk music is very clear. Characteristic are the English titled songs, though lyrics are still in Japanese and sung with the typical dynamics of the local folklore (blending toward themes recalling *Meddle* or *The Dark Side Of The Moon*)

and making this debut album a very peculiar and unique one. The keyboards pave the way to a new naturist and floral age, pushing rich choral melodies or Psychedelic acid themes, driven by **Gilmour**-inspired guitar liquid notes, as in "Transmigration" with its great impact of high and low tones.
The following *Nipponjin* (1975) is a partial recovery of songs by the old group: the title-track, for example, is taken from the original song "Nihonjin", slightly shorter, achieving a new modern touch and maintaining the melodious vocal strings. This album may be slightly less appreciated than the predecessor because of certain repetitions and revivals in topics, but it is however an epic and overwhelming project, just like the emblematic last track "River Of Soul". Also the next, *Parallel World* (1976), will be produced by **Klaus Schulze**: perfect in expressing Cosmic themes, Electronic, hypnotic and strongly rhythmic, yet another a masterpiece. **Kitaro**, **Ito** and **Takasaki** leave their place in the band and **Yujin Harada** (from Samurai) joins in just in time to record a last episode, *Tenkujin* (1977). Here the sound returns to the origins and, even with some simplification of the rhythmic section, still results as an excellent last trail.   **R.V.**

DISCOGRAPHY:
FAR OUT (FAR OUT) *(1973, Mu Land)* **THE CAVE DOWN TO THE EARTH** *(1974, Mu Land)* **NIPPONJIN** *(1975, Vertigo)* **PARALLEL WORLD** *(1976, Columbia Coca)* **TENKUJIN** *(1977, All Ears)*.

Indochina & North Asia: JAPAN

FLOWER TRAVELLIN' BAND

Remi Aso, Yuya Uchida, Akira "Joe" Yamanaka - *vocals*, **Joji "George" Wada** - *drums*, **Hideki Ishima, Sosumu Oku, Katsuhiku Kobayashi** - *guitar*, **Ken Yashimoto, Jun Kowzuki, Jun Kobayashi** - *bass*. **Nobuhiko Shinohara** - *keyboards*.

Irresistible, the cover of their second album *Anywhere*, with the band riding naked on their motorbikes, is quite a treat and is used by **Julian Cope** for the front of his cult-book "Japrocksampler".
The **Flower Travellin' Band** are one of the most representative of the country and are not immune to the ritual of evolving from actual group to the restlessness of a Rock individuality, common in the '70s. Their leader **Yuya Uchida** was already active during the '50s and decides to follow the Pop evolution more closely moving to London and Paris, where he sees in action **The Beatles**, **Pink Floyd**, **Soft Machine** and many others. Once back he finds some talented musicians such as guitarist **Hideki Ishima** and vocalist **Remi Aso**, for a first line-up called simply **Flowers**. They start as the live-music performing-act of the multimedia art-work by **Toshi Ichiyanagi**, (ex husband of **Yoko Ono**) and the recordings of these improvisations will be published only many years later, in 1995, as *From Pussys To Death*.

Their official debut *Challenge* contains some cover songs of **Joplin**, **Cream** and **Hendrix**, resulting an eccentric acid-rock. Enlightened by vocalist **Joe Yamanaka**'s concert, **Uchida** decides to disband **Flowers** and re-found them as **Flower Travellin' Band** for the recording of **Kuni Kawachi**'s (keyboardist from **Happening Four + 1**, one of the first Japanese Symphonic groups) excellent solo album *Kirikryogen*, that will be published also some time later. Therefore lacking original material for a proper new album of their own, the newly christened **FTB**s decide to publish rearranged longer versions of songs by **Black Sabbath**, **Animals** and **King Crimson** for the above mentioned LP *Anywhere*, to at least shower the market and prove their actual talent.

In 1971 their masterpiece *Satori* is an imposing and epic suite in 5 movements that anticipates the Hard Prog of **Rush** yet closer to **Atomic Rooster** and **Black Widow**. Thanks to the label Atlantic, **FTB**s achieves notoriety abroad and plays in Toronto as opening act to **Lighthouse** and to **ELP**. The following year *Made In Japan* is recorded in Canada with the help of producer **Paul Hoffert**, keyboardist from **Lighthouse**: an eccentric Hard Rock album structured, yet in balance between **Tony Iommi**'s square riffs and the rituality of **Amon Duul II**.

Uchida decides to publish a live-album entitled *Make Up* packaged as a skin handbag, after which the musicians go rogue: **Joe** as a soloist; **Hideshi** projects the ambitious 'sitarla', a new instrument between a sitar and an electric guitar; in 2002 Yuya and Joe participate in the film 'Deadly Outlaw: Rekka' by Takashi Miike (who uses *Satori Pt. 2* for the OST). In 2008 they reunite and publish their ideal closure to *Anywhere*, called *We Are Here*. **D.Z.**

DISCOGRAPHY:
YUYA UCHIDA &THE FLOWERS: CHALLENGE (Synton, 1969) **FLOWER TRAVELLIN' BAND: ANYWHERE** (Atlantic, 1970) **KUNI KAWACHI & FLOWER TRAVELLIN' BAND: KIRIKYOGEN** (1970) **SATORI** (Atlantic, 1971) **MADE IN JAPAN** (Atlantic, 1972) **MAKE UP** (live, Atlantic, 1973) **FROM PUSSYS TO DEATH IN 10.000 YEARS OF FREAK-OUT** (Apex, 1995) **WE ARE HERE** (Pony Canyon, 2008).

Indochina & North Asia: JAPAN

KENSO

Yoshihisa Shimizu - *guitars, keyboards*, **Ichiro Karamatsu, Atsushi Makiuchi, Kazuyuki Morishita, Kenichi Oguki, Toshihiko Sahashi, Hiroyuki Namba, Kenichi Mitsuda** - *keyboards*, **Masayuki Tanaka, Kimiyoshi Matsumoto, Shunji Saegusa** - *bass*, **Shiro Yajima** - *flute*, **Haruhiko Yamamoto, Masayuki Muraishi, Keisuke Komori** - *drums*. **Masaki Inoue, Kumiko Tanabe, Yoshiaki Tsukahira, Junna Kaku, Tsunekatsu Takagi, Keiko Kawashima** - *vocals*.

Authentic precursors since their very first album, guitarist **Yoshihisa Shimizu** forms the band in 1974 but freezes the project due to his studies in medicine. This is mainly why their self-titled and auto-produced debut is published only in 1980, a year in which the world of the New Prog was already taking its first steps. Their Hard Rock beginnings develop in the next two albums toward an effervescent Jazz-rock, closer to the dynamism of **Yes**, **Brand X** and **UK**, the eccentricity of **Egg** and **National Health**, the melodic flavour of **Camel**. Just like **PFM** and Ange in their respective environments, **Kenso** manages to colour with exotic and oriental charm the melodies, that result in a predominance of instrumental parts similar to the American **Happy The Man**. After a three years pause and a live recording, *Sparta* is published confirming their orchestral taste through a profuse use of keyboards clearly inspired by **Joe Zawinul**'s style (from **Weather Report**). Then they publish *Yume No Uka*, for the first time without their drummer **Yamamoto**: an elegant and mature Fusion that recalls **Bruford** and **Holdsworth**, leading them away from their Symphonic past.

After this **Shimizu** is less prolific and eight years go by before being able to record their new album *Esoptron*, the first of a more harsh nature, still always impeccable.

It is a good historical moment for the band, recognized among the masters of Jazz Rock in Europe also thanks to the re-issues of their previous works. In Japan they are also looked upon as inspirations by excellent groups such as **Six North**, **KBB** and **Side Steps**. Yet they continue their career and publish a dynamic and more Ethnic album, *Fabulis Mirabilibus De Bombycosi Scriptis*, and the more futuristic, *Mono Utsuroi Yuku*. **Kenso** will thereafter keep performing live up to this very day (worthy of mention the 2005 concert held for NEARFest in Trenton) until a last album in 2014. Their indisputable role in the history of Progressive rock has endowed them with the reputation of authoritative, coherent and rigorous musicians, explorers of boundaries between Rock, Jazz and Experimentation.

D.Z.

DISCOGRAPHY:

KENSO *(Pam, 1980)* **KENSO II** *(Pam, 1982)* **KENSO III** *(King Records, 1985)* **KENSO IN CONCERT** *(Music For Five, Unknown Musician) (1986)* **SPARTA** *(1989)* **YUME NO UKA** *(Dream Hill) (1991)* **LIVE '92** *(1992)* **SORA NI HIKARU-EARLY LIVE VOLUME 1** *(live, 1994)* **INEI NO FUE-LIVE VOL. 2** *(live, 1995)* **ZAIYA LIVE** *(live, 1995) In The West (live, Musea 1998)* **ESOPTRON** *(1999)* **FABULIS MIRABILIBUS DE BOMBYCOSIS SCRIPTIS** *(Musea, 2000)* **KEN-SON-GU-SU** *(live, Pathograph 2000)* **CHILLING HEAT – LIVE IN TOKYO 2004** *(live 2005)* **LIVE IN USA - NEARFEST 2005** *(live, Musea 2006)* **UTSUROI YUKU MONO** *(2006)*.

Indochina & North Asia: JAPAN

SHINGETSU

Makoto Kitayama – vocals,
Akira Hanamoto – keyboards,
Haruhiko Tsuda – guitars,
Naoya Takahashi - drums,
Shizuo Suzuki - bass.

For a long time and unjustly so, this band was considered to be strongly oriented towards the **Genesis** sound of the **Gabriel** era, certainly the most famous Symphonic Prog band of Japan. Their career begins in the second half of the '70s, when musicians from cover bands like **Serenade**, **Hal** and **Belladonna** decide to compose their own songs. This transition period is well documented in *Kagaku No Yoru*, a collection of 1977/1979 recordings published only later in 1995, quite a while after the break-up. The official self-titled debut with original tracks is of 1979 and opens with the magical "Oni", an intense and touching hit of almost 10 minutes that, without exaggerating, is probably one of the best compositions of Symphonic Rock in the whole history of Prog. If only the entire album was on this same level we would be in front of a majestic opera: instead the rest are excellent songs, but far from the unbelievably incredible "Oni", that not only recalls the early **Genesis**, but also certain

atmospheres of Italian prog like **PFM**, from which they probably took their name (**Shingetsu** means Moon New, like "Luna Nuova" which is a song from **PFM**). Particularity however is their traditional ethnicity that prevents them from becoming a simple clone.
After this album and some concerts, they disband joining other symphonic groups like **Asturias** and **Aquapolis**. Under the **Shingetsu** name nothing else but some live recordings or unpublished outtakes are issued, for example the recovery by Musea of concerts held on 25-26 July 1979, gathered in a CD (2004), where the atmosphere and the dimension of those events, between musical and theatrical, is palpable. New Prog groups such as IQ derived great inspiration from this Japanese band, like from their long and splendid "Voyage For Killing Love Part 2". In 1998 singer **Makoto Kitayama** revives the band as **Shingetsu Project** for an album of oldies still with Musea, *Hikaru Sazanami*, and in 2005 Avalon produces a beautiful 5 CD box called *Zenshi* containing the old studio album and many other live outtakes, unpublished tracks and lost tapes. **R.V.**

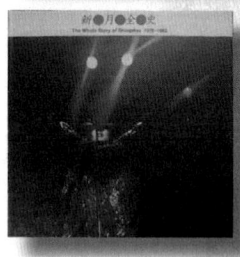

DISCOGRAPHY:
SHINGETSU *(1979, LP Zen Records)* **KAGAKU NO YORU (Serenade + Shingetsu)** *(1995, Belle Antique)* **AKAI ME NO KAGAMI LIVE '79** *(1979, Belle Antique)* **SHINGETSU LIVE 25-26 JULY 1979** *(2004, Musea)* **ZENSHI** *(2005, Avalon)*.

Indochina & North Asia: JAPAN

YONIN BAYASHI

Katsutoshi Morizono – *guitars, vocals,* **Hidemi Sakashita** – *keyboards,* **Shinichi Nakamura** – *bass, bass pedals, vocals,* **Daiji Iwao** – *drums, percussions*

At the beginning of the '70s they were playing a form of Psychedelic Rock with balanced moments of acid guitars and intriguing keyboards, clearly inspired by **Pink Floyd** and **Deep Purple**. The Four Musicians publish their first album *Aru Seishun/Nijûsai No Genten* in 1973, composed as the sound track of a film for a young director. It contains very short songs with acoustic and electric parts in continuous rotation and a strong dose of Psychedelic organ melodies full of effects. Lyrics are in Japanese thus creating a bridge towards more traditional aspects of the genre.

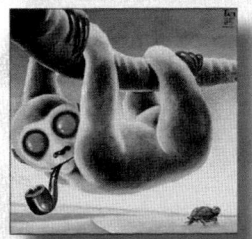

The following year a second record called *Isshoku Sokuhatsu*, much more mature and personal, famous also for the particular cover with a kind of monkey hanging from an elephant's trunk and smoking a pipe. The sound introduces an abundance of new Psychedelic sonorities sometimes to the advantage of a **Zappa** styled Jazz-rock, sometimes with greater references to the Mediterranean area such as **Perigeo**, other times of Canterbury tendency with a great electric piano and some intrusions of a Camel-Santana kind of Latin American music. Very defined the symphonic component, with string keyboards that do not only fill the voids, but often are clue to the dynamic and general result.

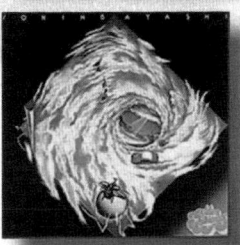

Subsequently this very album, with added live tracks and a light remixing of some parts, was printed for the foreign markets: the title is a translation from the original into the English: *Dangerous Situation*.

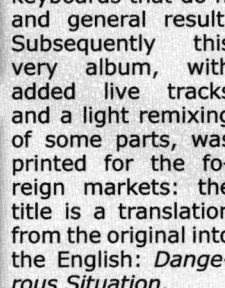
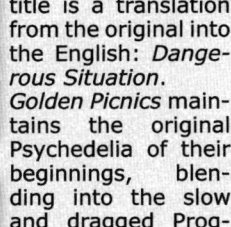

Golden Picnics maintains the original Psychedelia of their beginnings, blending into the slow and dragged Prog-Blues of "Flying", or into the deformed echo of **The Beatles** sonorities of "Carnival", or plunging into the depths of Kraut-rock like in the long and twisted "Bird's and Nessi's."

Then a huge change both in the genre and in the line-up (only keyboardist **Sakashita** remains) occurs: their music simplifies and becomes a more immediate and direct Rock, with shorter tracks. *Printed Jelly*, is strongly subject to these new choices in direction and so will be the rest of their future production. The 1979 break-up will lead to a couple of reunions and a debatable Funky-Disco-New Wave album called Dance, while the rest of their career twists towards Pop. **R.V.**

RECOMMENDED RECORDINGS:
ARU SEISHUN/NIJÛSAI NO GENTEN *(1973, Tam Ax)* **ISSHOKU SOKUHATSU** *(1974, Tam Ax)* **DANGEROUS SITUATION (LIVE)** *(1975, CBS)* **GOLDEN PICNICS** *(1976 CBS)* **PRINTED JELLY** *(1977, See Saw)* **BAO** *(1978, See Saw)* **'73 LIVE** *(1978, Tam Ax)* **NEO - N** *(1979, See Saw).*

North America: CANADA

HARMONIUM

Serge Fiori - *guitars, flute, zither harp, vocals,*
Michel Normandeau - *chitarra, voce,* **Louis Valois** - *bass, piano, vocals,* **Serge Locat** - *piano, keyboards,* **Pierre Daigneault** - *flute, sax, clarinet.*

Guitarist **Serge Fiori** together with **Michel Normandeau** and **Louis Valois** form the band and record their self-titled debut in 1974, containing a series of Folk, acoustic and Pastoral ballads guided by refined guitar arpeggios and sweet vocal melodies sung in French.
Their second project, *Si On Avait Besoin d'une Cinquième Saison* (1975) is simply sensational: **Serge Locat** and **Pierre Daigneault** join the original trio creating a bucolic and delicate sound with symphonic and suggestive Folk Prog elements, in which the acoustic guitars and vocals keep their leading roles, but give way to the more elaborate instrumental passages of piano, flute, keyboards and mellotron.

The first four songs are the ideal representation of each season, yet the cherry on the cake is the last 17 minutes suite, "Histoires Sans Paroles", inspired by a hypothetical fifth season in which their symphonic vein explodes in melodies of rare beauty and charm, elegantly balancing flute, Mellotron, keyboards and of course the guitars. In 1976 they widen the line-up and succeed in repeating the quality of this previous work with the double album *L'Heptade*, where the Classical genre greatly weighs on the compositions underlined by the orchestral tones. The sound results more majestic yet seems to maintain the band's characteristic lightness and elegance.

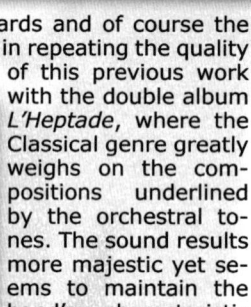

The public adores their live performances (their last concert before the break-up is toward the end of 1978) and two years after the disbandment a double LP called *En Tournée* is published. Worthy of mention is the collaboration between **Fiori** and **Richard Séguin** in the marvelous album published by CBS in 1978, "Deux Cents Nuits à l'Heure", to which many musicians from their last line-up participate. After this experience **Fiori** tries a solo career but shortly later will abandon the scenes for good, dedicating himself to production and studio engineering techniques.

G.D.S.

DISCOGRAPHY:
HARMONIUM *(1974, Polygram)* **SI ON AVAIT BESOIN D'UNE CINQUIÈME SAISON** *(1975, Polygram)* **L'HEPTADE** *(1976, CBS)* **EN TOURNÉE** *(1980, CBS).*

North America: CANADA

MANEIGE

Alain Bergeron - keyboards, flute, saxophones, **Jérome Langlois** - keyboards, guitars, **Vincent Langlois** - keyboards, percussion, **Denis Lapierre** - guitar, **Yves Léonard** - bass, **Gilles Schetagne** - drums, **Paul Picard** - percussion.

Casually noticed in Quebec by Harvest and given the opportunity to sign up with this label, famous for finding new talents in the Progressive world. Their Fusion style integrates brilliantly Jazz to Classical elements and Folk, rich of improvisations and solos that highlight each musician's excellent qualities.

A first album was published in 1975 and is an eloquent manifesto of their art: only four tracks and almost entirely instrumental, more adequate to a proper orchestra of Classical formulation than to a Pop-rock band. The music results to be a delicate mixture of harmonies that are never trivial and that confer extraordinary cohesion to the different styles placed side by side with wise mastery.

Yet their best is the second album, *Les Porches*, in which they develop the themes of the previous and manage to exasperate with great conviction their Rock Jazz Fusion with elements of the Classical genre. The title suite is composed of six parts, alternating acoustic to electric sounds with amazing results, embellished by the vocals (very rare for this band). Keyboards are clearly inspired by groups of European Prog, mainly **Genesis**, but what makes them unique is their ability to draw from Classical music and to succeed in blending it into a peculiar styled Jazz.

Unfortunately already in their third project the Progressive sonorities regress leaving more space to Jazz: songs are shorter and so are the solo parts, reminding us of certain **Frank Zappa** structures filtered through a vision close to the **Weather Report**'s *Black Market*. Inferior to expectations also their forth, *Libre Service-Self Service*, considered by the critics a true Fusion album, although some references to the Canterbury sound can be found, and the only Prog here seems to be the piano theme in "Noemi".

C.A.

DISCOGRAPHY:
MANEIGE *(Harvest, 1975)* **LES PORCHES** *(Harvest, 1975)* **NI VENT... NI NOUVELLE** *(Polydor, 1977)* **LIBRE SERVICE-SELF SERVICE** *(Polydor 1978).*

North America: CANADA

MIRIODOR

Pascal Globensky - *keyboards, guitars,* **Rémi Leclerc** - *drums,* **Sabin Hudon, Claude Saint-Jean, James Darling, Jean-Denis Levausser, Ivanhoe Jolicoeur, Marie-Chantal Leclair, Némo Vemba, Lisa Millet** - *horns,* **François Èmond** - *keyboards, horns, violin,* **Marc Petitclerc** - *keyboards,* **Denis Robitaille** - *bass, guitars,* **Bernard Falaise, Nicolas Masino** - *guitars, bass, keyboards,* **Stefka Iordanova** - *vocals,* **Stephanie Simard, Marie-Solail Bélanger** - *violin.*

Globensky speaks of his musical creature as <<*the greatest soundtrack to the weirdest film you have ever seen*>>. New Prog wasn't made of only mere copy-cats of **Genesis**, **Yes** and **Pink Floyd**, but also from audacious researchers such as the **Miriodor**, pursuing proudly the adventures of **Henry Cow**, **Slapp Happy**, **Faust**, and in general of the RIO movement. In 1980 **Pascal Globensky** and **François Èmond** form the band in Quebec City. Three years later the line-up becomes a sextet and self-produces *Rencontres*, a Classical Rock debut with amazing interlacements of horns and keyboards similar to the **Van Der Graaf Generator** and with an eccentric irony closer to **Soft Machine**. In a New Wave and Synth-Pop period of radios blasting triumphs from **Genesis** and **Yes** and placing on top of the charts **Marillion**, this still very fresh band proves to be a visionary revolution for the '80s.

After signing with Cuneiform, **Miriodor** confirm their style with a charming self-titled album in which they perform as a small Prog orchestra, evolving from **Egg** through **Univers Zero** to **The Enid**. The technological improvements help them to achieve a fuller sound and they begin a period of aimed international exposure with concerts and a participation in the Festival Internationalle De Musique Actuelle. *Third Warning* closes the first phase of this Canadian band and marks their opening towards an odd Rock-cabaret influenced by **Frank Zappa**, with fanfares and circus music.

Guitarist **Bernard Falaise** joins in on the next project completing them with an even more intriguing dimension: *Elastic Juggling* confirms **Miriodor**'s sound of blending Jazz impros and researched compositions, non conventional Theater and Art-rock. In this same period they take part to both Progscape and Montreal Jazz festivals and after creating a sound track for the documentary 'Almanach', **Hudon** leaves.

A fifth LP *Mekano* is issued using a new horn section that broadens their sound toward new influences of Jazz Fusion. It is a great success and the band performs and bewitches the Prog audience of NEARFest 2002 (concert recorded live on the second cd of *Parade*, 2005). Swedish **Lars Hollmer** (**Samlas Samma Manna**) lends a hand in this adventurous project, following **Globensky**'s objectives who was always careful to incorporate references from **Gentle Giant** and **Happy the Man** in contexts that also pleased fans of **Nyman** and **Garbarek**; same for *Avanti!* of 2009 and *Cobra Fakir* of 2013.

D.Z.

DISCOGRAPHY:
RENCONTRES *(Miriodor, 1984)* **TOT AU TARD** *(Miriodor, 1985)* **MIRIODOR** *(Cuneiform, 1988)* **THIRD WARNING** *(Cuneiform, 1991)* **ELASTIC JUGGLING** *(Cuneiform, 1995)* **MEKANO** *(Cuneiform, 2001)* **PARADE + LIVE AT NEARFEST** *(Cuneiform, 2005)* **AVANTI!** *(Cuneiform, 2009)* **COBRA FAKIR** *(Cuneiform, 2013)* .

North America: CANADA

MORSE CODE TRANSMISSION

Christian Simard - *keyboards, vocals,* **Jocelyn Julien** - *guitars,* **Daniel Lemay** - *guitars, flauto,* **Raymond Roy** - *drums,* **Michel Vallée** - *bass, vocals.*

Their beginnings are tied to the structures divulged in Quebec by the British and US Psychedelic wave made of sounds, colours and good vibrations with references to a more energetic Pop Rock on the wake of **Deep Purple**'s *The Book Of Taliesyn*, but without possessing the vocal qualities of these super-groups.

After shortening their name to **Morse Code**, the band matures into a new phase influenced by European Prog, going back to singing in French on typically British Prog melodies. Too easily labeled as a Symphonic Rock band, they are instead among the most sincere exponents of a Romantic Rock Prog with French lyrics, inspired by **Genesis**, but elegantly personalized.

Three finally interesting albums are published, well structured and happily inspired by the Anglo-Saxon trend, built on simple yet pleasantly elaborate sounds based on keyboards, bass, guitar, drums and flute: *La Marche Des Hommes* is still slightly inexperience according to the new rules of the Prog genre; with *Procreation* they find their right dimension made of fairy-tale and magical atmospheres between dream and reality evoked by unbelievable interlacements of keyboards and guitars; *Je suis le Temps* was severely critiqued yet it introduces a more credible and mature band whose Prog sound is filtered by the long solos and duets of piano and guitar.

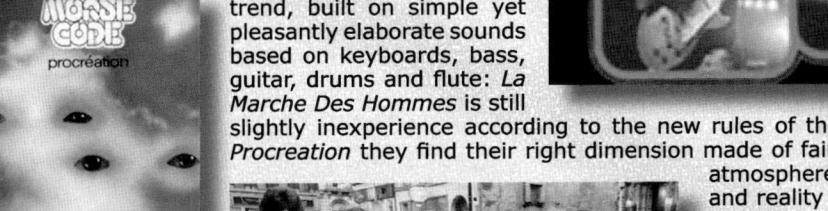

At the end of their career a collection of their very best is issued after the break-up as *Les Grands Success des Morse Code*, meant as the final curtain for a band that is still considered a cult in Quebec. **C.A.**

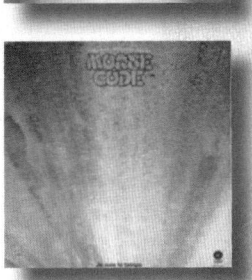

DISCOGRAPHY:
MORSE CODE TRANSMISSION *(RCA, 1971)* **II** *(RCA, 1972)* **LA MARCHE DES HOMMES** *(Capitol, 1975)* **PROCREATION** *(Capitol, 1976)* **JE SUIS LE TEMPS** *(Capitol, 1977)* **LES GRANDS SUCCESS DES MORSE CODE** *(Capitol, 1978)*.

North America: CANADA

RUSH

Geddy Lee - *bass, keyboards, vocals,* **Alex Lifeson** - *guitars,* **John Rutsey, Neil Peart** - *drums.*

Born in 1968 from the ashes of **Projection**, these unusual musicians begin their career in 1974 with a self-titled debut which mimics **Led Zeppelin** to the core, proving their musical immaturity. **Rutsey** is soon replaced by a more restless drummer and eclectic lyricist, **Neil Peart** and this renewed verve in the line-up brings them to publish three incredible futuristic studio recordings. Their sound and style is beautifully summarized in the last of these three, the concept album *2112*: a Hard Rock style that extends over the articulate constructions and sophisticated arrangements of their long suites. They maintain the Classical riff structure developing it with skillful maturity, also thanks to producer **Terry Brown**'s wise direction.

The following live-album confirms their unbelievable talent and closes a first phase and that inaugurates the tendency to schematize each different episode of their career. Success is immediate though the critics snob the phenomenon: the public loves them and so they begin a long international tour. From 1977 to 1981 another four creative albums with strong references to **Yes** and **Genesis**: **Peart**'s songwriting becomes more mature and consolidated, deepening the philosophical aspects of literary and intellectual texts. Synths here are used profusely, in tune with the Hard-rock themes of the times and the profound atmospheres of Prog. *Hemispheres* and *Moving Pictures* are among the best of this ever-changing period in which they fit perfectly with their enigmatic covers and an indisputable personality.

The '80s are **Rush**'s so-called 'keyboard era': synths are placed alongside the guitars and technology also becomes a dominant feature in the lyrics. Yet it is also a period of comprehensible low inspiration, prelude to the following decade: **Terry Brown** lets them go and the band, under the wing of many other producers, opens to influences such as from **Police** and **U2**, though never being truly conditioned by New Wave and Synth Pop. Their peculiarity is well expressed in the refined *Hold Your Fire*. The skills of each member have by now reached the highest of peaks, especially for **Peart** who receives many prizes and recognitions.

A fourth phase starts after signing up with Atlantic and publishing a couple of lame albums, followed by the harsh *Counterparts*: it is the golden moment for Prog Metal and bands like **Dream Theater** and **Fates Warning** greatly derive their inspiration from **Rush**. The monumental live recording *Different Stages* closes this glorious era, opening to another difficult one as **Neil Peart** loses both wife and daughter. The band fears a break-up but the drummer reacts with new found inspiration, also in a literary sense for he will publish three books. The next two LPs *Vapor Trails* and Snakes And Arrows reflect these emotions with their aggressive and concrete sound.

The fifth and last phase is still ongoing and begins with Feedback, a pleasant album with covers from Yardbirds, Cream etc.., while the last studio album *Clockwork Angels* of 2012 confirms them as a cult band for their genre.   **D.Z.**

DISCOGRAPHY:

RUSH *(Mercury, 1974)* **FLY BY NIGHT** *(Mercury, 1975)* **CARESS OF STEEL** *(Mercury, 1975)* **2112** *(Mercury, 1976)* **ALL THE WORLD'S A STAGE** *(live, Mercury, 1976)* **A FAREWELL TO KINGS** *(Mercury, 1977)* **HEMISPHERES** *(Mercury, 1978)* **PERMANENT WAVES** *(Mercury, 1980)* **MOVING PICTURES** *(Mercury, 1981)* **EXIT... STAGE LEFT** *(live, Mercury, 1981)* **SIGNALS** *(Mercury, 1982)* **GRACE UNDER PRESSURE** *(Mercury, 1984)* **POWER WINDOWS** *(Mercury, 1985)* **HOLD YOUR FIRE** *(Mercury, 1987)* **A SHOW OF HANDS** *(live, Mercury, 1989)* **PRESTO** *(Atlantic, 1989)* **ROLL THE BONES** *(Atlantic, 1991)* **COUNTERPARTS** *(Atlantic, 1993)* **TEST FOR ECHO** *(Atlantic, 1996)* **DIFFERENT STAGES - LIVE** *(Atlantic, 1998)* **VAPOR TRAILS** *(Atlantic, 2002)* **RUSH IN RIO** *(live, Atlantic, 2003)* **FEEDBACK** *(Atlantic, 2004)* **SNAKES AND ARROWS** *(Atlantic, 2007)* **SNAKES AND ARROWS LIVE** *(live, Atlantic, 2008)* **CLOCKWORK ANGELS** *(Anthem, 2012)*.

North America: UNITED STATES

DJAM KARET

Gayle Ellett, Mike Henderson - *guitars, keyboards, electronic percussion*, **Henry J. Osborne, Aaron Kenyon** - *bass, keyboards, percussion*, **Chuck Oken Jr.** - *drums*, **Andy Frankel, Marc Anderson** - *percussion*, **John Glass**, **Jeff Greinke, Walter Holland, Loren Nerell, Steve Roach, Kit Watkins, Carl Weingarten, Michael Ostrich** - *synthesizers*, **Judy Garp** - *violin*, **Dion Sorrell** - *cello*.

When **Frank Zappa** gave his music to **Clive Davis**, powerful owner of CBS, the reply was a dry <<No commercial potential!>> which with usual irony **Zappa** adopted as his slogan; when **Tangerine Dream** proposed their *Electronic Meditation* to **Rolf-Ulrich Kaiser** of label Ohr, it went slightly better: <<Ok, you may not have commercial potential but we will sign you up anyway>>; **Edgar Froese** made 'No Commercial Potential' his pride and a dozen years later **Djams Karet** used it for the debut of their long career. Born in a 1982 Post-Punk New-Psychedelia infested California, this eccentric band starts playing long Rock impros as **Happy Cancer**. The metamorphosis happens when in 1984 guitarist Gayle Ellett joins in and the quartet becomes **Djam Karet** ('elastic time' in Indonesian). They start off as live performers by recording tapes from their concerts in college campuses, such as the 1985 self-produced *No Commercial Potential*, to which follows *The Ritual Continues*.

Reflections From The Firepool is an unsettling Free-rock which well blends Hard-rock, Electronics, Minimalism, World Music, Fusion and Oriental themes inspired by **Ash Ra Tempel**, **King Crimson** and **Pink Floyd**; *Burning The Hard City* is a sharp and loud Heavy-prog; *Suspension And Displacement* is full of melancholy and persuasive Ambient; *Collaborator* is an Electronic Prog with prestigious guests (such as **Steve Roach** and **Kit Watkins**) that collaborate from afar by sending fragments which **Ellett** and his partners assemble in studio.

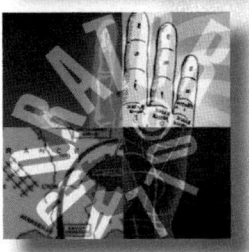

In 1997 the inevitable encounter with Cuneiform, the label most into recruiting talents of Avant-rock. They sign a contract and publish the compact and versatile *The Devouring*, an astounding work awarded Album of the Year, giving them further notoriety. Studio improvisation here is their main characteristic, with a predominant violin hanging above Mellotron pavements of lysergic arrangements penetrated by the hammering Jazz-rock soundscapes and Ethnic rhythms.

Two live recordings will follow: *Still No Commercial Potential* is a studio-live recorded without overdubs; *Live At Orion* is the proof of their exemplary dialogue with the audience. 10 years after these twin albums, the Techno-rock sequel *New Dark Age* and the Acid-rock, Folk and New Age album *Ascension* - first of a series of self-produced cds and limited editions. In 2003 *A Night For Baku* is published with its more dark Jam-rock, featuring an overwhelming rhythmic section. As a quintet they release *Recollection Harvest*, containing a disruptive Prog-fusion opposed to a World/Ambient genre that gives us two albums in one. **Djam Karet** is a very esoteric band that continues its coherent and confident career, creating songs with an authentically Progressive soul. **D.Z.**

DISCOGRAPHY:
NO COMMERCIAL POTENTIAL (HC, 1985) **THE RITUAL CONTINUES** (HC, 1987) **KAFKA'S BREAKFAST** (Auricle 1988) **REFLECTIONS FROM THE FIREPOOL** (HC, 1989) **BURNING THE HARD CITY** (HC, 1991) **SUSPENSION AND DISPLACEMENT** (HC, 1991) **COLLABORATOR** (HC, 1994) **THE DEVOURING** (Cuneiform, 1997) **STILL NO COMMERCIAL POTENTIAL** (HC, 1998) **LIVE AT ORION** (live, Cuneiform, 1999) **NEW DARK AGE** (Cuneiform, 2001), **ASCENSION** (HC, 1991) **#1** (HC, 2001) **AFGHAN** (live, Djam Karet 2001) **#2** (HC, 2001) **A NIGHT FOR BAKU** (Cuneiform 2003) **LIVE AT NEARFEST 2001** (Djam Karet, 2004) **RECOLLECTION HARVEST** (Cuneiform, 2005).

North America: UNITED STATES

ECHOLYN

Ray Weston - *vocals*, **Brett Kull** - *guitars, keyboards, vocals*, **Christopher Buzby** - *keyboards, vocals*, **Jesse Reyes, Thomas Hyatt** - *bass*, **Paul Ramsey, Jordan Perlson** - *drums*.

During the '70s the Knights of Prog built imposing careers, influenced armies of artists and bewitched million of fans thanks to the favorable spirit of the times and to the strong disco-graphic market. In the '90s New-Prog dwells between dream and utopia with its strong desire to preserve the artistic dignity of this glorious movement. **Echolyn** is one of the most beloved and representative groups from this decade and is also an emblematic expression of American Prog, at the same levels of **Kansas**, **Cathedral** and **Happy The Man**.
1In 1988 guitarist **Brett Kull** and drummer **Paul Ramsey** both leave the cover band **Narcissus** and plan a new musical project with keyboardist **Chris Buzby**. After including singer **Ray Weston** and bass player **Jesse Reyes** (later replaced by **Tom Hyatt**) they auto-produce a self-titled debut, that immediately sells out and is still cherished by collectors, followed by the splendid *Suffocating The Bloom* and the unplugged EP *And Every Blossom*. These first three works introduce the band's intentions, style and objectives: their peculiarity consisted in filtering the best English Art-rock from **Yes**, **Gentle Giant** and **Jethro Tull** into contemporaneity with Jazz-rock hints and catchy American melodies. The epic "A Suite For Everyman" contained in the second LP also proves that, in their hands, a long composition can result refined, intellectual and not excessive.

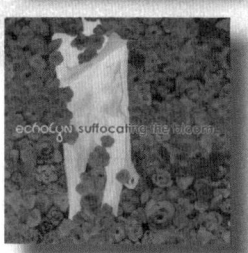

Sony signs them up for a contract to another 7 albums. The unexpected challenge pushes their enthusiasm and opens them to new artistic boundaries. They create their masterpiece *As The World*, which still is a milestone for New-prog: fresh, dynamic and amazing, touching for the passionate emotions and skillful execution. Their Art-rock is full of good ideas, well develop and polished. The vocal harmonization and rhythmic junctures shine through the melodic and sophisticated arrangements of Fusion matrix. They result confident and unleashed, their personality revealed: it is one of those rare cases in which New-prog finds itself on the same level with the classics of Prog. Unfortunately Sony withholds its support and stops promoting their concerts. Once again they find themselves auto-producing *When The Sweet Turns Sour* before breaking up.

The Rock-oriented musicians (**Paul**, **Ray** and **Brett**) form the band **Still** (which later will become **Always Almost**) while **Chris** devotes to Rock-jazz by joining **Finneuses Gauge**. In 2000 **Echolyn** reunite and record *Cowboy Poems Free*, a pleasant album, clearly inspired by **Steely Dan**, **Supertramp**, **Electric Light Orchestra** and not appreciated by the fans. Having by now accepted their auto-production karma, the five return to the style of their beginnings with the ambitious *Mei*: a long and passionate suite, symbol of a newly acquired artistic maturity and praised by the international Prog community. It is somewhat a new beginning, hosting frequent concerts and reissuing their first LPs, but also working on new projects like the Funky Jazz-rock of *The End Is Beautiful* and *Echolyn* that allows a first European tour. In 2015 *I Heard You Listening* keeps the dream alive...

D.Z.

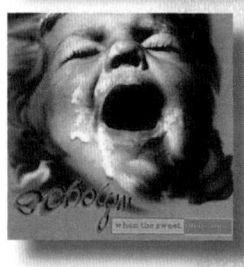

DISCOGRAPHY:
ECHOLYN (Bridge Records, 1991) **SUFFOCATING THE BLOOM** (Echolyn, 1992) **... AND EVERY BLOSSOM** (Bridge Records, 1993) **AS THE WORLD** (Sony, 1995) **WHEN THE SWEET TURNS SOUR** (Cyclops, 1996) **COWBOY POEMS FREE** (Velveteen, 2000) **MEI** (Velveteen, 2002) **PROG-FEST 94 (The Official Bootleg)** (live, Echolyn, 2002) **JERSEY TOMATO VOL. 2 (Live At The Metlar-Bodine Museum)** (live, Velveteen, 2004) **THE END IS BEAUTIFUL** (Echolyn, 2005) **ECHOLYN** (Echolyn, 2012) **I HEARD YOU LISTENING** (Echolyn, 2015)

North America: UNITED STATES

HAPPY THE MAN

Stanley Whithaker - *guitars, vocals,* **Frank Wyatt** - *piano, sax, flute,* **Kit Watkins** - *piano, keyboards, flute,* **Rick Kennell** - *bass,* **Ron Riddle** - *drums,* **Mike Beck** - *drums, percussion,* **Coco Roussel** - *drums,* **David Rosenthal** - *keyboards.*

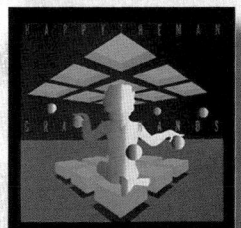

Prog 'made in USA' is thought to be more superficial and less of quality, yet in the mid '70s **Happy the Man** nearly achieved a collaboration with **Peter Gabriel** after signing with label Arista. Instead in 1977 they publish their self-titled debut which opens with the delicate and dreamy "Starborne", floating on the keyboards' melodic plots. From the second track "Stumpy Meets the Firecracker in Stencil Forest" the album pulls out that fizzy verve that will characterize their sound: uneven rhythms, majestic combinations of guitar, keyboards and brass instruments and the musical contamination from a personal Jazz-Rock ready to jump into the fresh oasis of Romanticism. "Knee Bitten Nymphs in Limbo", "Hidden Moods", "New York Dream's Suite" are other songs of great intensity that are ever present in their live performances.

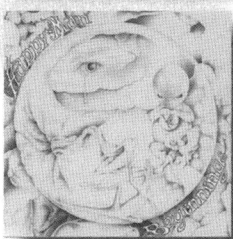

The incredible "Carousel" is the cherry on top, opening with an elegant piano and then developing into other instrumental textures. The Canterbury school experience lives both here and in the following *Crafty Hands* of 1978 which opens with the marvelous "Servi-

ce with a Smile" (only two minutes and a half, but of unbelievable intensity) confirming the band's peculiar style. Unfortunately the following year they break-up fundamentally for two reasons: the commercial failure and **Kit Watkins**'s joining **Camel**. In the '90s some unpublished recordings are issued, like the demo tracks from 1974-75 collected in *Beginnings* and a good concert recorded in the album *Live*. They reunite at the end of the century with the original line-up (only **Watkins** is replaced by **David Rosenthal**) and their concerts are widely attended by the fans. Their last work *The Muse Awakens* of 2004 is proof that they are back on track, picking up where they left over twenty years before. Then the musicians disband once more, some of which (**Whitaker**-**Wyatt**) start a new interesting band called **Oblivion Sun** with the cd *Pedal Giant Animals*.   **G.D.S.**

DISCOGRAPHY:
HAPPY THE MAN *(1977, Arista)* **CRAFTY HANDS** *(1978, Arista)* **BEGINNINGS** *(1990, Cuneiform Records)* **3RD "BETTER LATE..."** *(1990, Cuneiform Records)* **LIVE** *(1997, Cuneiform Records)* **DEATH'S CROWN** *(1999, Cuneiform Records)* **THE MUSE AWAKENS** *(2004, Inside Out).*

North America: UNITED STATES

KANSAS

Phil Ehart - drums, **Kerry Livgren** - guitar, **Dave Hope** - bass, **Robby Steinhardt** - violin, vocals, **Steve Walsh** - vocals, keyboards, **Richard Williams** - guitars, **John Elefante** - vocals, keyboards, **Steve Morse** - guitar, **Billy Greer** - bass, **David Ragsdale** - violin, guitar, **Greg Robert** - keyboards, vocals.

Kansas are famous for their ability to unite English Symphonic Rock to a more American Hard-Rock, especially in their '70s music with its resonant compositions, classy Pop, elegant ballads, energetic and deadly riffs. **Phil Ehart, Kerry Livgren, Dave Hope, Robby Steinhardt, Steve Walsh** and **Richard Williams** are the core of this band, promoted by producer Don Kirschner. Their second album *Song for America* is where they actually begin to shine, with songs of Symphonic taste that will go down in history like the phenomenal "Incomudro" and "Lamplight Symphony". After *Masque*, another good album, success really arrives with *Leftoverture*, in which their style merges with a closer approach to certain melodies typical of American rock, like the famous "Carry on Wayward Son", "Miracles Out of Nowhere", "Cheyenne Anthem", "The Wall").

Point of Know Return, the live performances of *Two For the Show* and *Monolith* only consolidate their reputation in the rock panorama. In the '80s a glimpse of stylistic change comes with *Audio-Visions* and from this moment on the band will be pushed toward the typical AOR genre, due also to the continuous changes in line-up (**Walsh** exits in '81, then follow **Steinhardt** and **Livgren**, while keyboardist and singer **John Elefante**, extraordinary guitarist **Steve Morse** from **Dixies Dregs** and bass player **Billy Greer** join in). The new course makes its way with a particularly inspired concept-album, *In the Spirit of Things* of 1988, the best of this decade, full of great songs, energetic and with an eye open to prog.

After some other line-up shifts, the '90s are directed on a New Prog path with *Freaks of Natures*, in which the violin returns to its fundamental role bringing out the Symphonic elements that seemed by now lost in time. They also record *Always Never the Same*, an interesting operation of rearranging some of their classics together with the London Symphony Orchestra. A final album *Somewhere to Elsewhere*, sees them once again in the original line-up, infusing abundant doses of energy and wondrousness.   **G.D.S**

DISCOGRAPHY:

KANSAS *(1974, Epic/Legacy)* **SONG FOR AMERICA** *(1975, Kirschner)* **MASQUE** *(1975, Kirschner)* **LEFTOVERTURE** *(1976, Kirschner)* **POINT OF KNOW RETURN** *(1977, Kirschner)* **TWO FOR THE SHOW** *(1978, Kirschner)* **MONOLITH** *(1979, Kirschner)* **AUDIO-VISIONS** *(1980, Epic/Legacy)* **VINYL CONFESSIONS** *(1982, Epic/Legacy)* **DRASTIC MEASURES** *(1983, Epic/Legacy)* **POWER** *(1986, MCA)* **IN THE SPIRIT OF THINGS** *(1988, MCA)* **LIVE AT THE WHISKEY** *(1992, Intersound)* **FREAKS OF NATURE** *(1995, Intersound)* **ALWAYS NEVER THE SAME** *(1998, River North Records)* **LIVE ON THE KING BISCUIT FLOWER HOUR** *(1998, King Biscuit Flower Hour)* **SOMEWHERE TO ELSEWHERE** *(2000, SPV)* **DEVICE, VOICE, DREAM** *(2002, SPV)* **DUST IN THE WIND** *(2002, EMI)*.

North America: UNITED STATES

THE MUFFINS

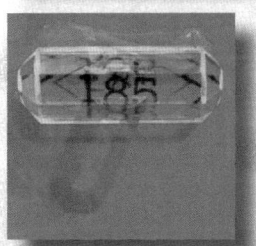

Stuart Abramowitz - *drums, vocals,*
Dave Newhouse - *keyboards, flute, sax, vocals,* **Tom Scott** - *clarinet, flute, sax, oboe, vibes, vocals,* **Billy Swann** - *bass, percussion, vocals,*
Mike Zenter - *guitar, violin, harmonica, vocals,* **Paul Sears** - *drums, percussion.*

In over thirty years of activity and nine albums, **The Muffins** have pleased quite a lot of fans with their avantgarde music. Born in 1973 the band consolidates its line-up only around 1976. During these early years the musicians are however very active, devoting mostly to concerts and recordings that will be published many years later. 1976 to 1978 instead is their moment of greater creativeness, that brings to the splendid debut *Manna/Mirage*: thanks to the diversity of instrumentation that allows them to jump from the electricity of rock to an acoustic brass and sax jam, the sound is very colored and pushes toward a form of clear Canterbury jazz-rock, seasoned with charming romanticism. The electric piano and sax pour us into that magic world where **Hatfield and the North** and **Soft Machine** left us a few years back.
Then the encounter with **Fred Frith** that leads them to participate in his soloist album *Gravity* and to record a studio album of their own called *<185>*, a difficult work to listen to, full of dissonances and experimentation closer to the extreme wing of the R.I.O. movement. **Frith** also produces and participates to this

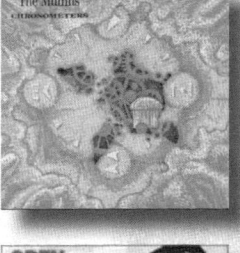

album of 1981, a time in which the record market had changed from the previous decade: the scarce sales discourages the band and they breakup.
In the '90s they reunite for the magnificent *Chronometers* and decide to issue the collection of unpublished works from their early years under the title *Open City*. They find a renewed desire for improvisation and for the exploration of a kind of whole music similar to certain ideas from **Zappa** and again from the Canterbury and R.I.O. concepts of their past.
They are fully back on track at the end of the '90s, with a series of concerts that fruit the avant-garde jazz of *Loveletters* in 2001 and the excellent studio album *Bandwidth* the following year, full of those sweet Jazz-Rock atmospheres created by a fully operating brass section. Two years later *Double Negative* is recorded with amazing symphonic inserts and ever present keyboards, slightly different from the usual style of **The Muffins**. After 2010 another two good albums are published confirming them as a band and opening horizons to novelty for the fans. **G.D.S.**

DISCOGRAPHY:
MANNA/MIRAGE *(1978, Private Pressing)* **<185>** *(1981, Private Pressing)* **CHRONOMETERS** *(1993, Cuneiform Records)* **OPEN CITY** *(1994, Cuneiform Records)* **LOVELETTER** *(2001, Contorted)* **BANDWIDTH** *(2002, Cuneiform Records)* **DOUBLE NEGATIVE** *(2004, Cuneiform Records)* **LOVELETTER #2** *(2005, Private Pressing).*

North America: UNITED STATES

PAVLOV'S DOG

David Surkamp - vocals, guitar
David Hamilton - keyboards
Doug Rayburn - mellotron, flute
Mike Safron - drums, percussions
Rick Stockton - guitars, bass
Siegfried Carver - violin, sitar, viola
Steve Scorfina - lead guitar.

From the warm and damp St. Louis of the 1970s, **Pavlov's Dog** represents one of the most explosive debuts in the American Rock panorama. Drummer **Mike Safron**, famous for his collaborations with **Bo Diddley** and **Chuck Berry**, wanted to form a band that would go beyond the current musical patterns of the south. He recruits **Doug Rayburn**, met playing for **Chuck Berry**, violinist **Siegfried Carter** and singer **David Surkamp** with his powerful voice, similar to **Geddy Lee** from **Rush**. Surkamp was the perfect person: he knew how to compose, write and loved English myths as did **Robert Wyatt**, one of his idols. Yet only after **Steve Scorfina**'s arrival in '74 (from **Guilty Speedwagon**) were they ready to finally record a first complete album, assuming a recognizable sound of their own: this debut will be published only a year later as *Pampered Menial* (after many trials and tracks that will instead be published in 2014 as *The Pekin Tapes*), thanks to a million dollar contract with ABC.

It was an extraordinary and unexpected success: a particularly compact, charming and balanced work that united the delicacy of Folk ballads to more aggressive Electric tendencies, not distant from AOR. The wise and non invasive use of mellotron, flute and violin in simple and never trivial arrangements are tied to melancholy and reflexive atmospheres which emanate from **Safron**'s blues touch, **Surkamp**'s idealistic folk, Carter's fancy Jazz playing and **Scorfina**'s scorching solos. The opening track "Julia"

makes you fall in love instantly but so do all the other songs, that plunge you into a unique world of melody and constructive wisdom, like in the fantasy of the typically prog closing track "Of Once And Future Kings".

The enormous success strongly solicited the band which lost its balance and was overcome by disputes on their future musical orientation, also strongly conditioned by signing up with CBS: their producer wanted songs which would make an immediate radio hit and called for some international collaborations such as **Bill Bruford** from **Yes** and **Andy Mckay** from **Roxy Music**. They recorded in an American studio but the mixing took place in London: *At The Sound Of The Bell*, finally published in 1976, was an album that ideally continued the style of the first one, but in reality contained only beautiful commercial songs. The result brought to a contract breech and to a sort of disgregation and line-up change: the musicians tried at first to publish a more personal album (under the title *Has Anyone Here Seen Siegfried?*) but the project was blocked, so the recording came out illegally in 1977 as *Third*, and then officially in 1994.

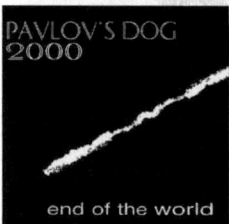

In 1990 a surprise reunion with some of the original members brings to the mediocre *Lost In America*. In 1995 **Safron**, decides to issue his **Pavlov's Dog 2000** *End Of The World*, under the band's name, but singing a very different genre. Much better instead *Echo & Boo* of 2010, which sees **Surkamp** back at the head of this controversial story. **R.V.**

DISCOGRAPHY:

PAMPERED MENIAL *(ABC-Dunhill, 1975)* **AT THE SOUND OF THE BELL** *(CBS, 1976)* **THIRD** *(TRC Records, 1977 - 1994)* **LOST IN AMERICA** *(Telectro, 1990)* **HAS ANYONE HERE SEEN SIEGFRIED?** *("Third" Reissue - Rockville, 1994)* **PAVLOV'S DOG 2000 End of the world** *(Kanned Goose, 1995 - Mini CD)* **ECHO & BOO** *(Rockville, 2010)* **THE PEKIN TAPES** *(Rockville, 2014)*.

North America: UNITED STATES

TODD RUNDGREN & UTOPIA

Todd Rundgren - *guitar, piano vocals*, **M.Frog** - *synthesizers*, **Roger Powell** - *keyboards*, **John Wilcox** - *drums*, **John Siegler** - *bass*, **Ralph Schuckett** - *keyboards*.

He plays guitar in several bands during the '60s (a 1969 psychedelic blues album with **Woody's Truck Stop**) forming **Nazz** in 1967 with a first couple of albums released the following years. Simultaneously he becomes a producer and sound engineer for Bearsville Records, later forming **Runt** in 1970 and publishing a pair of works that are actually all him. In the meantime his success as a technician allows him to produce his own power pop-oriented double album *Something/Anything?* in 1972, with him playing every instrument on it. The eclectic Post-Psychedelic *A Wizard, A True Star* and the more prog album *Todd* (with several lengthy, experimental synth oriented instrumentals) precede the decision of founding **Utopia** (a band with three keyboardists) and the Psychedelic Rock influences with Avant-garde Jazz Fusion from **Mahavishnu Orchestra** and **Frank Zappa**. Their first album *Todd Rundgren's Utopia* has only four tracks very close to **EL&P**, but exaggeratedly pharaonic, turning the band into an orchestra gone wild, with the famous song "The Ikon". *Initiation* proves **Rundgren**'s endless musical talent with an album of meticulous arrangement and production,

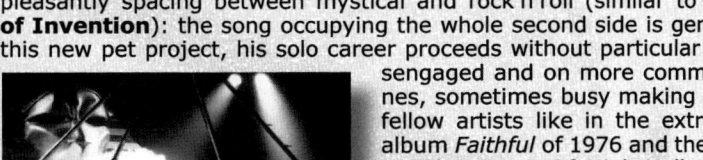

pleasantly spacing between mystical and rock'n'roll (similar to **Mothers of Invention**): the song occupying the whole second side is genius. With this new pet project, his solo career proceeds without particular aims, di-

sengaged and on more commercial tones, sometimes busy making fun of his fellow artists like in the extraordinary album *Faithful* of 1976 and the amazing 1978's *Hermit Of Mink Hollow* with its series of melodic ballads, playing all the instruments himself with that certain melancholy typical of American songwriters towards whom he directs his irony. Keyboardist **Roger Powell** joins in on the album *RA* in 1977: **Rundgren** ceases his experimental extremes and presents a beautiful and typically prog sound with good melodies and an energetic and spectacular sound. The quartet finally manages to be all equally involved, like in "Singring and the Glass Guitar", a splendid composition which hosts solos of each musician. During the late '70s **Rundgren** produces many artists including **Patti Smith**, **Tom Robinson** and **The Tubes**. He forms **TR-i** in 1991, releasing the computerised, Electronic sounding *No World Order* and other similar works throughout the decade. Good albums but low sales see him spend the rest of the '90s as a DJ, founding **PatroNet**, a device allowing users to download music directly from his site.

M.G.

RECOMMENDED RECORDINGS:
Todd Rundgren: **SOMETHING, ANYTHING** *(Bearsville, 1972)* **A WIZARD A TRUE STAR** *(Bearsville, 1973)* **TODD** *(Bearsville, 1974)* **FAITHFUL** *(Bearsville, 1976)* **HERMIT OF MINK HOLLOW** *(Bearsville, 1978)* **BACK TO THE BARS** *(Bearsville, 1979)*. Utopia: **TODD RUNDGREN'S UTOPIA** *(Bearsville, 1974)* **ANOTHER LIVE** *(Bearsville, 1975)* **RA** *(Bearsville, 1977)* **OOPS! WRONG PLANET** *(Bearsville, 1978)* **ADVENTURES IN UTOPIA** *(Bearsville, 1979)* **DEFACE THE MUSIC** *(Bearsville, 1980)*.

North America: UNITED STATES

WEATHER REPORT

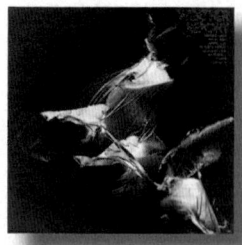

Joe Zawinul - *keyboards*, **Wayne Shorter** - *saxophone*, **Miroslav Vitous**, **Alphonso Johnson**, **Jaco Pastorius**, **Victor Bailey** - *bass*, **Airto Moreira**, **Mino Cinelu**, **Jose Rossy**, **Robert Thomas, Jr.**, **Manolo Badrena**, **Don Alias**, **Dom Um Romão**, **Alyrio Lima** - *tambourine, congas, vocals, timbales, percussion*, **Alphonse Mouzon**, **Eric Gravatt**, **Ishmael Wilburn**, **Skip Hadden**, **Leon "Ndugu" Chancler**, **Chester Thompson**, **Narada Michael Walden**, **Alex Acuñ**, **Peter Erskine**, **Omar Hakim** - *drums*.

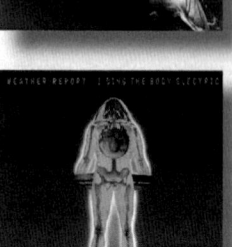

Joe and **Wayne** played together briefly in 1959 with **Maynard Ferguson**'s Band, keeping in touch and collaborating again with **Miles Davis**, until they finally decide to form their own band in 1970. The main feature of their music was a form of modern Jazz full of improvisations similar to those of *Bitches Brew*, with Experimental Electronic sounds filtered by the instruments, **Zawinul** on the electric piano and organ, **Vitous** on his double bass played with a fiddle stick. They release an album almost every year, the first in 1971 with **Alphonse Mouzon** on drums and winning the nomination of Jazz Album of the Year: an Experimental album, rich of electronic instruments and among the classics of Fusion Jazz. That same year a second album titled *Sing the Body Electric* is issued featuring the ARP 2600 synthesizer. *Mysterious Traveler* is one of their best works from the pre-**Jaco** era. While other Fusion acts relied heavily on the electric guitar, they instead managed to transcend anything done with Jazz-based music before. In 1976 *Black Market* is recorded, more melodic and concise or commercial pieces (with the participation of **Chester Thompson**, employed as second drummer by **Genesis** from 1977), sequeled by *Heavy Weather* after the entry of bass player **Jaco Pastorius**, who by then was already a driving force in the group: a big success and Grammy Award winner, particularly with the hit single "Birdland" (a song covered by **The Manhattan Transfer** and by **Buddy Rich**).

The band's decline starts when **Jaco** leaves in 1982, due to his commitment to lead the big band **Word of Mouth**, and **Erskine** is replaced by **Omar Hakim**. The group disbands after the completion of *This Is This* in 1986 to follow each their own solo projects (**The Zawinul Syndicate**). Their contribution to Prog inspired many artists like **Phil Collins** and **John Goodsall**'s Brand X. **Jaco Pastorius** dies tragically in 1987 followed by **Zawinul** in 2007 after a long struggle against cancer.   **M.G.**

RECOMMENDED RECORDINGS:
WEATHER REPORT *(Columbia, 1971)* **I SING THE BODY ELECTRIC** *(Columbia, 1972)* **LIVE IN TOKYO** *(CBS, 1972)* **SWEETNIGHTER** *(Columbia, 1973)* **MYSTERIOUS TRAVELLER** *(Columbia, 1974)* **TALE SPINNIN** *(Columbia, 1975)* **BLACK MARKET** *(Columbia, 1975)* **HEAVY WEATHER** *(Columbia, 1977)* **MR. GONE** *(Columbia, 1978)* **8:30** *(Columbia, 1979)* **NIGHT PASSAGE** *(Columbia, 1980)* **THIS IS THIS** *(Columbia, 1986)*.

North America: UNITED STATES

FRANK ZAPPA

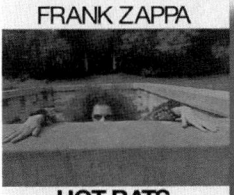

Frank Zappa, Elliot Ingber, Jim Fielder, Art Tripp, Lowell George - *guitar,* **Ray Collins, Captain Beefheart, Flo & Eddie** - *vocals,* **Jimmy Carl Black, Billy Mundi, Ron Selico, Paul Humphrey, Aynsley Dunbar, John Guerin** - *drums,* **Roy Estrada, Shaggie Otis, Max Bennett, Jim Pons** - *bass,* **Bunk Gardner, Euclid James "Motorhead" Sherwood, Buzz Gardner, Sal Marquez** - *horns,* **Don Preston, George Duke, Bob Harris** - *keyboards,* **Ian Underwood** - *keyboards, horns,* **Ruth Underwood** - *marimba, vibes,* **Jean-Luc Ponty, Don "Sugarcane" Harris** - *violin.*

Frank Zappa is a complex figure for any music genre. He cannot be enclosed or labeled for he never played Rock in a narrow sense, but should be considered a composer tout-court. For Prog's sake his first phase is the best since it will deeply inspire all the future young artists of Art-rock to come. Born in 1940, he grows experiencing Rhythm & Blues through the discovery of **Varése**, **Stravinskij** and **Webern** who conditioned his way of conceiving music.
After a decade of playing in low level bands, composing B-movie soundtracks and of avant-garde, in 1965 he founds **The Mothers of Invention**: inimitable and talented, they publish a debut in 1966 called *Freak Out*. Together with **Bob Dylan**'s *Blonde On Blonde* of that same year, this is the first double album of the history of rock: **Zappa** uses the long duration to express a synergy among all the genres, intellectually refined or popular, blending acid-rock with doo-wop, cabaret with electronic shuffles (as in "The Return Of The Son Of Monster Magnet" that covers the whole fourth side). This is the year in which **The Beatles** (*Revolver*) and **The Beach Boys** (*Pet Sounds*) begin their pop revolution, yet **The Mothers** were already one step ahead with *Absolutely Free*, a title-manifesto for an extraordinary futuristic album, full of perfect ideas, arrangements and quotes. The music is a whole by definition, as for all his production: free of embarrassment and taboo, it results as a corrosive and desecrating assembly sparing nobody. An example is *We're Only In It For The Money*'s sardonic attack on **The Beatles**' *Sgt. Pepper....* (between experimentation and rock-comedy) and on the entire Hip generation; *Ruben & The Jets* is a mocking homage to the greasy songs of the '50s. *Lumpy Gravy* acknowledges **Zappa** as a more serious composer of Concrete music and the majestic ultra-rock of *Uncle Meat* consolidates his reputation through his experiments of new recording techniques. The genius rock-jazz suite "King Kong" from this last album will be also proposed by violinist **Jean-Luc Ponty** in his own repertoire when **The Mothers** disband shortly after. Contemporaneously with **Miles Davis**' *Bitches Brew*, **Zappa** records *Hot Rats*, building a greater bridge between Rock and Jazz, always playing with the top notch musicians and important guests like **Ponty** and **Captain Beefheart**. He himself is a very talented guitarist and performs with a sort of Fusion orchestra, again ahead for the times. The early '70s see him exploring ways of blending the Jazz genre of the big bands and Avant-garde, as in his last album of this first phase, *Waka/Jawaka*. The rest of **Frank Zappa**'s extraordinary career can be found and referenced under many other contaminations, but to the story of prog, our tale ends here.   **D.Z.**

RECOMMENDED RECORDINGS:
THE MOTHERS OF INVENTION: FREAK OUT (Verve, 1966) **ABSOLUTELY FREE** (Verve, 1967) **WE'RE ONLY IN IT FOR THE MONEY** (Verve, 1968) **CRUISING WITH RUBEN & THE JETS** (Verve, 1969) **UNCLE MEAT** (Bizarre, 1969) **BURNT WEENY SANDWICH** (Bizarre, 1970) **WEASELS RIPPED MY FLESH** (Bizarre, 1970) **FILLMORE EAST, JUNE 1971** (live, Bizarre, 1971) **JUST ANOTHER BAND FROM L.A.** (Bizarre, 1972) **THE GRAND WAZOO** (Bizarre, 1972) **FRANK ZAPPA: LUMPY GRAVY** (Verve, 1967) **HOT RATS** (Bizarre, 1969) **CHUNGA'S REVENGE** (Bizarre, 1970) **200 MOTELS** (Bizarre, 1971) **WAKA/JAWAKA** (Bizarre, 1972).

Oceania: AUSTRALIA

ALEPH

Mary Carpenter - keyboards, **Ron Carpenter** - drums, **Dave Froggett** - guitar, **Mary Hansen** - keyboards, **David Highett** - bass, **Joe Walmsley** - vocals.

From Sydney, this sextet devoted to the celebration of a Symphonic Rock inspired by **Yes** and **Genesis**. They played live on hundreds of stages in Australia before landing their one and only studio album in 1977 called *Surface Tension*. The rather unusual line-up saw two extremely talented female keyboardists, whose sole presence steered them naturally toward this genre, sometimes with average but very effective results derived from American references like **Styx** or **Foreigner**.
Guitarist **Dave Froggett** and singer **Joe Walmsley** join the band mid-recordings, creating a perfect musical balance that reflects on side B, as in the suite "The Mountaineer", where piano, synthesizers and guitar pave the way to the warm and winding vocals. Alternating instruments and overwhelming solos that come and go in a rich and sumptuous atmosphere, smartly guided by the producer, the album closes with the melodic and relaxed themes of "Heaven's archaepelago", persuasive and highly involving.
Due to the many internal disagreements with the other members, **Walmsley** abandons the project before this last album even reaches the stores; the band, incapable of properly replacing him, abandons forever the scenes and Surface tension becomes incredibly hard to find for years. It is today made available on CD by a Korean label.

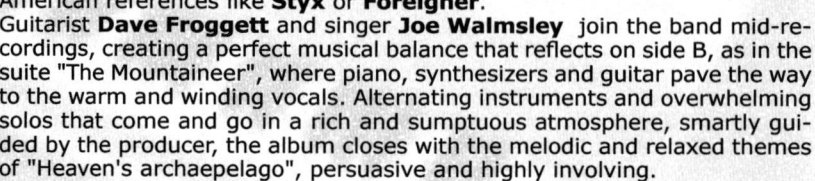

C.A.

DISCOGRAPHY:
SURFACE TENSION *(Transatlantic, 1977).*

ARAGON

Les Dougan – vocals, drums, **Tom Behrsing** – keyboards, **John Poloyannis** – guitars, mandolin.

Australia has never had a prolific army of Rockers among its troops (the **Bee Gees** were actually English residents) especially in the Prog genre. The inversion of this trend happened in the early '90s (though it lasted for a short moment, as all things beautiful), with the band **Aragon**:an ensemble that picked up musicians coming from every part of Europe, disciples and true followers of **Marillion**. They release their first album *Don't Bring the Rain* containing the song-manifesto "Cry Out" that underlines both the musical similarity and the great vocal-theatricality of **Les Dougan**'s performance, able to imitate **Fish** in an incredible way. Unfortunately already with the following last album *The Meeting*, they start to lose ground and start publishing tasteless songs aimed to a more easy listening market.

F.V.

DISCOGRAPHY:
DON'T BRING THE RAIN *(Ugum, 1990)* **THE MEETING** *(Si Records, 1992)* **ROCKING HORSE** *(Si Records, 1990)* **MOUSE** *(Si Records, 1990)* **THE ANGEL'S TEAR** *(Labra D'or, 1990).*

Oceania: AUSTRALIA

SEBASTIAN HARDIE

Mario Millo - *guitars, vocals,* **Peter Plavsic** - *bass,* **Alex Plavsic** - *drums, percussion,* **Toivo Pilt** - *keyboards.*

Considered the first and most important Prog Rock band from Australia, they publish their debut album only in 1975 but are actually active since 1967 when guitarist **Graham Ford** founds the **Sebastian Hardie Blues Band** playing a standard Soul-Rhythm & Blues. That same year the Italian **Mario Millo**, age 12 and already a phenomenal guitarist, was forming his first band; his ambition will soon make him join **Sebastians Hardie** along with keyboardist **Toivo Pilt** and brothers **Peter** and **Alex Plavsic** in 1973, the true birthday of Australian Rock. The quartet composes its own music but when in concert they also enjoy to indulge and perform **Oldfield**'s *Tubular Bells*. They sign up with Polydor and finally issue *Four Moments*, that will sell 35.000 copies in no time and award them a Grammy: a marvelous album, although inspired from the already existing Brit masters, it has its own expressiveness probably due to the fact it was recorded live in studio in just 6 days. The sound is romantic with dreamy melodies, soft tones and never excessive, an

emotional intensity that creates a sense of great space and a delicate pathos that is capable of moving and involving immediately. The album's structure is just like **Yes**' *Close To The Edge*, with a suite on the first side and two songs on the second, with constant references also to **Camel** and **Genesis**.
Millo is the main composer, developing themes through his instrument on the wake of **Latimer** and **Akkerman**, with the plasticity of **Santana**. **Pilt** is none the less with his refined atmospheres like in the organ arrangements of "Openings". The single "Rosanna"

(with its majestic sound similar to Queen) gives them further popularity to the point of becoming the opening acts for **Lou Reed**, **Osibisa** and **Santana** himself.
Windchase will follow on the same model of the previous album but in a less striking way. This unexpected failure will bring the band to a first break-up: brothers **Plavsics** will keep the name, while **Millo** and **Pilt** form **Windchase** and publish the beautiful *Symphinity*, that combines the classic atmospheres of **SH** with a Jazz-rock between **Santana** and **Al Di Meola**. At the end of the '70s, a critical moment for all Prog bands, Millo begins to compose soundtracks for movies and TV shows, yet he will also find the time to issue three solo digressions: *Epic III* (in line with his older projects), *Human Games* (radio hit) and *Oceans Of The Mind* (symphonic AOR Prog, evolved from the project *Men From Mars*). In 1994 **SH** reunite with the original line-up for Progfest '94 in LA and again in 2003 to play as supporter for the Australian **Yes** Tour.   D.Z.

DISCOGRAPHY:
FOUR MOMENTS *(Polygram 1975)* **WINDCHASE** *(Polygram 1976)* **WINDCHASE: Symphinity** *(Festival 1977)* **MARIO MILLO: Epic III** *(EMI 1979)* **MARIO MILLO: Human Games** *(1983)* **SEBASTIAN HARDIE - LIVE IN L.A.** *(live, Avalon 1997)* **MARIO MILLO: Oceans Of The Mind** *(Red Moon 2002).*

Oceania: AUSTRALIA

MASTER'S APPRENTICES

Glen Wheatley - *bass,* **Doug Ford** - *guitars,* **Colin Burgess** - *drums,* **Jim Keays** - *vocals, guitars.*

After understanding that the bass was not his instrument, **Jim Keays** decides to become a singer and joins a band called **Mustang**, whom up till then had only performed instrumental songs. In 1966 they issue the cover album *From Mustang to Masters*, containing mainly rearrangements of **Bo Diddley** or **Chuck Berry**, full of amusing hippy-styled Pop. Their initial sound is therefore a blend of Rhythm & Blues with some Beat and Psychedelia, similar to **The Shadows**. A common passion for their idol and master **John Lee Hooker** brings them to identify as his pupils and therefore to change the name into **Master's Apprentices**. Under this new christening they issue a first album in 1967 containing some of the songs of the previous and other unpublished works.

In the meantime they exhausted themselves in concert by traveling up and down the coast, so all new recordings were done in an irregular manner, with different line-ups and also in different studios found along the way. When in 1970 *Masterpiece* is finally published, it was welcomed with a certain chill due to its lack of homogeneity. The songs are elegant and well structured: probably with the right push they would have gained a better consensus given the mixture of Hard Rock, Pop, Psychedelia, Beat and R&B.

A more organic and complete album arrives the following year with *Choice Cuts*, containing always short tracks, but with a more Progressive tendency. Hints from **Led Zeppelin** and **Jethro Tull** are all over "Our Friend Owsley Stanley III", as are traces of **The Moody Blues** and **Procol Harum**, however played in a very personal key thanks to the particular vivid and dry voice of **Keays**. In 1971 they record *Nickelodeon* from one of their concerts, proving the band's great energy on stage, capable of dilating time with dynamic clarity and maintaining the intents of a great impact harsh Psychedelia.

Master's Apprentices' last work before the break-up is *A Toast To Panama Red*, with important hits like "Games We Play" and "Beneath The Sun", underlining their great yet underestimated talent (**Keays** will then record a couple of concept albums like the futuristic *The Boy From The Stars* in 1974). 15 years later one brief reunion to record *Do What You Wanna Do* of 1988 and the story ends. **R.V.**

DISCOGRAPHY:
THE MASTER'S APPRENTICES *(1967, Astor)* **MASTERPIECE** *(1970, Columbia)* **CHOICE CUTS** *(1971, Columbia)* **NICKELODEON** *(Live 1972, Columbia)* **A TOAST TO PANAMA RED** *(1972, Columbia)* **DO WHAT YOU WANNA DO** *(1988, Virgin).*

Oceania: **AUSTRALIA**

SPECTRUM

Mike Rudd - *vocals, guitars, harmonica*, **Bill Putt** - *guitars, bass*, **Mark Kennedy** – *drums years 1969-70* , **Ray Arnott** – *drums years 1970-73*, **Lee Neale** - *keyboards, years 1969-72*, **John Mills** - *keyboards, years 1972-73*.

Spectrum orbits around the figure of **Mike Rudd**, a fan of American Blues and of R&B. After leaving New Zealand he lands in Melbourne in 1966 playing at first with the **Chants R&B** and then with **The Party Machine**. In 1969 he decides to follow his personal calling toward Blues and forms Spectrum, performing live songs from **Pink Floyd**, **Soft Machine** and **Traffic**. After various attempts to structure the band in a more stable way, they finally sign up with the label Harvest and in 1971 publish *Spectrum Part One*. The album opens in extremely anomalous way for the Prog genre: a Country-Blues that had really nothing to do with the rest of the songs which were instead more Jazzy or Avant-garde. Well recognizable, **Rudd**'s powerful voice of a clear Hard Blues and southern American matrix. "Fiddling Fool" is probably the reason why this album had such a success, from its fluid dynamics to the Canterbury hints, with a keyboard playing mid **The Doors**, **Egg** and the most Psychedelic **Pink Floyd**. Also the instrumental parts in "Superbody" and "Make Your Stash" are worthy of note.

Kennedy decides to leave and is replaced by **Ray Arnott** for the second album of 1972, *Milesago*. This is probably Australia's first double-album and it represents the double soul of the band and highlights **Rudd**'s prominent talent as a composer. On one side a Hard-country-blues, often with standard short songs like "Play a Song That I Know" or "A Fate Worse Than Death"; on the other more dilated, complex tracks with more loaded Prog keyboards as in "Your Friend and Mines", "Fly Without Its Wings" or the title-track.

In parallel to the band's activity, **Rudd** spins-off a side project he names **Indelible Murtceps**, to underlined the more frivolous aspect of Spectrum, introducing brief Folk-country-blues songs in an album of 1973 entitled *Warts Up Your Nose*. A true two-sided coin he then decides to toss in the alternation of songs contained in *Testimonial*, where both groups play resulting not very credible, if not for the brief instrumental moments or in the beautiful "Essay In Paranoia."

Their career seems to end in 1974 with the double live-album *Terminal Buzz*, when in 2008 they publish the average *Breathing Space* with the following declaration: <<*We are a blues band, we can play for your birthday party or for your wedding!*>>. A pity that in 2013 they bury **Putt** and with him any future project. **R.V.**

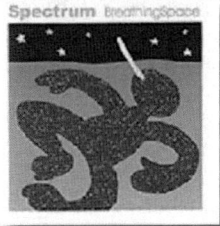

DISCOGRAPHY:
SPECTRUM PART ONE *(1970, Harvest)* **MILESAGO** *(1972, Harvest)* **WARTS UP YOUR NOSE (Indelible Murtceps)** *(1973, EMI)* **TESTIMONIAL** *(1973, EMI)* **TERMINAL BUZZ** *(1974, EMI)* **GHOSTS: POST-TERMINAL REFLECTIONS (compilation with unreleased tracks) (Spectrum Murtceps)** *(1991, Raven)* **BREATHING SPACE** *(2008, Aztec Music)*.

Oceania: NEW ZEALAND

DRAGON

Ivan Thompson - *keyboards*, **Ray Goodwin** - *guitars, vocals*, **Marc Hunter** - *vocals, percussion*, **Neil Storey** - *drums*, **Todd Hunter** - *bass, vocals*.

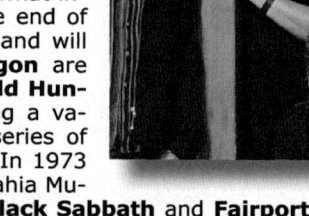

Their early years in New Zealand is what interests us the most, since after the end of 1975 the band moves to Australia and will start playing exclusively Pop. **Dragon** are formed around the character of **Todd Hunter** in 1972, when he starts picking a variable number of musicians for a series of concerts in the north of the island. In 1973 they perform in The Great Ngaruawahia Music Festival, alongside groups like **Black Sabbath** and **Fairport Convention**. Here Vertigo Records notices them and decides to sign a contract for a first album.

In the meantime **Todd**'s younger brother **Marc Hunter** joins in thus completing the line-up for *Universal Radio*, a mature work ready for an immediate success not only in their country. The sound is sweet and well harmonized, creating a soft Prog without excesses, with more peaceful atmospheres that sometimes become aggressive, but never crossing the line of delicacy. Certain tracks have a **Santana** taste to them, or the early **Camel** sound, with the eclectic attitude of **Barclay James Harvest** or **Supertramp**. Marc Hunter's delicate but firm voice shares similarities with **Steve Walsh** from **Kansas** and the beautiful Jazzy keyboards complete the never arrogant or exaggerated arpeggios of the **Gilmour** inspired guitars. The songs unravel full of references to the first **Pink Floyd** and to the last **Beatles**;

hints from Platina in "Avalanche", a richly Hammond-paved track, rhythmically moving on sweet Jazzy tempos.

To achieve notoriety quickly, their manager Graeme Nesbitt organizes a mighty national tour at the end of which they record their second studio album *Scented Gardens for the Blind*, out in the spring of 1975. It opens with the hit single "Vermillion Cellars", a rather meaningless song of cheap Pop Rock. Fortunately from the next track onward, "La Gash Lagoon", things change toward a beautiful Symphonic Prog, varied and full of keyboards, just like the following "Sunburst" with its long intro of organ recalling **Kansas**, while the good title-track decidedly comes closer to the music of **Yes**. At the end of the year they take the drastic decision to transfer to Sidney and change their guitarist replacing him with **Robert Taylor**, more oriented to a defined Pop genre. From then on they will undergo different and continuous line-up changes also due to deceases or break-ups, yet the band still plays on.

R.V.

RECOMMENDED RECORDINGS:
UNIVERSAL RADIO *(1974, Vertigo Records)* **SCENTED GARDENS FOR THE BLIND** *(1975, Vertigo Records)* **RUNNING FREE** *(1977, Portrait)* **SUNSHINE** *(1977, CBS)*.

Oceania: NEW ZEALAND

RAGNAROK

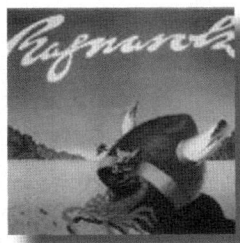

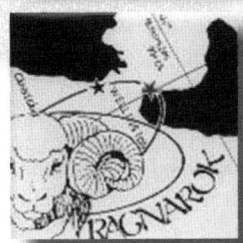

Andre Jayet - *drums, keyboards, synths, vocals*, **Ross Muir** - *bass, synths, vocals*, **Lea Maalfrid** - *vocals*, **Mark Jayet** - *drums, percussions, vocals*, **Ramon York** - *guitar synth, vocals*.

Among the bands who used the name **Ragnarok**, these are probably the less famous. From Auckland they were one of the few who proposed Prog in the region. The initial line-up was formed on the ashes of the former **Sweet Feet**, with a very gifted singer **Lea Maalfrid** and her precise and delicate voice. Under this name they publish in 1975 a first self-titled LP with on its cover a viking helmet and a big red scorpion, two completely foreign elements to the land of New Zealand, making it clear that their musical intents were very distant from where they were born, linked and inspired by the production of **Pink Floyd**, **Led Zeppelin**, **Yes** and **David Bowie**. And this is exactly what we find in their never too long songs, rising from an arpeggio or under a dry rhythm, in a vocal chord, a mellotron or synth moment, in their Rock'n'roll way of playing. The album is a success also abroad.

Perhaps not adequately acknowledged, **Lea Maalfrid** decides for a solo career, also in consideration of the fact that every member wanted to share the vocal partitions. First in Sydney then to LA, she opts for easy-listening Pop songs, also becoming a talent scout, a producer and a songwriter for **Sheena Easton** and **Bonnie Raitt**.

Reduced to a quartet they issue the single "Five New Years/The Fourteenth Knock" in 1976, prelude to the album *Nooks*: musically comparable to the previous, it is strengthened however by a more Progressive style, as in "Waterfall - Capt. Fagg" where the complex Prog theme transforms into an overwhelming Rock, worthy of **David Bowie**'s *Ziggy Stardust*. Notwithstanding the beautiful title track, the sweet "Paths Of Reminiscence" or the Psychedelic Symphonic drama of "The Volsung", it was a failure and brought them to break-up.

A following album also exists, *Live In New Zealand* of 1977, yet it was never approved by the band, who declared it non official and said they had no idea of how it became public: they blamed the imaginary buyer of a recorder they sold where the forgotten recording was probably found. This concert of November 1976 is by all means still a valid document that underlines the live atmospheres of their concerts, when they also use to play covers of **Led Zeppelin**'s "Whole Lotta Love", a medley of **Pink Floyd**'s "Us And Them" or "I Fall Apart" by **Rory Gallagher**.   R.V.

DISCOGRAPHY:
RAGNAROK *(1975, Revolution Record)* **NOOKS** *(1976, Polydor)* **LIVE IN NEW ZEALAND** *(Private press, 1977)*.

South America: ARGENTINA

ALMENDRA

Luis Alberto Spinetta - *guitar, vocals*, **Edelmiro Molinari** - *guitar, vocals*, **Emilio del Guercio** - *bass, vocals*, **Rodolfo García** - *drums*.

Undoubtedly fundamental for the Argentinian Rock genre, in 1967 **Almendra** rose from the ashes of two Folk Beat bands called **Los Sbirros** and **Los Larkings.** The following year, they issue a 45 RPM introducing two poetic songs, written with the clear intention of stepping beyond the threshold of Beat, immediately welcomed with enthusiasm and this strong initial interest translated into a continuous request for concerts and live events both nearby and even in the neighboring Peru. A second single strengthens their notoriety and the audience's desire of a complete LP. *Almendra* is finally published at the beginning of 1969 consolidating the harmonic class and compositional skills of usually brief songs but rich in pathos, endowed with a strong melodic structure, foreign to Argentina at the time. It contained sweet mixtures of Jazz, Beat and Latino atmospheres, like in "Que El Viento Borró Tus Manos." The presence of the rather long "Color Humano" was anomalous, with its hard guitar playing (inspired by **Hendrix**)

that served to counter the melodic balance. It is often seen as one of the best Rock albums in the history of Argentina, also thanks also to the harmonized vocals. After another long and successful tour across South America, the band gathers ideas they collect during this time in a double album simply called *Almendra II*, 1970. It essentially strengthens their Rock sound, also introducing Blues tracks of Southern-Country taste. The guitars harshen electrically while the rhythms thicken and the melodies immediately become more striking. Interesting is the long "Agnus Dei", with its many references to **The Moody Blues** and **Procol Harum**, however keeping in mind that they played with two guitars and absolutely no keyboards, therefore creating a completely different impact. After a long and weary tour that ends with the great concert at the famous Argentinian festival B.A. Rock., they break-up. The following year **Spinetta** founds **Pescado Rabioso** continuing a musically coherent career. By surprise and due to the strong insistence of their producer, the band reunites in 1979 with the excuse of an invitation to a big concert held in the stadium of Obras. The event is successful and recorded in two live albums issued separately that same year. They also record a new studio-album in 1980 called *El valle interior*, with slow pleasant songs that flow from Pop Prog to Fusion. **R.V.**

DISCOGRAPHY:
ALMENDRA I *(1969, BMG)* **ALMENDRA II** *(1970, BMG)* **ALMENDRA EN OBRAS I (LIVE)** *(1980, BMG)* **ALMENDRA EN OBRAS II (LIVE)** *(1980, BMG)* **EL VALLE INTERIOR** *(1980, BMG)*.

South America: ARGENTINA

ARCO IRIS

Ara Tokatlián - *horns*, **Guillermo Bordarampé** - *bass*, **Gustavo Santaolalla** - *guitar, vocals*, **Horacio Gianello** - *drums, percussion*.

RCA record label signs them up in 1969 with the idea of conquering the Argentinian market. Their self-titled debut is published the following year resulting to be a still immature album, that nevertheless proves how the band graduates in Pop and in the Psychedelic culture, expressing their sound also through the difficult Latin American Folk rhythms and blending them with a rudimental Jazz-rock (that still had to be born). The arrangements are hasty and approximate yet however it is a valid starting point for the band's great ambitions, despite the terrible art-work on the cover. The material discarded and some other songs, published as singles, will be gathered in *Suite #1* sung entirely in English. Beyond the obvious fact that this makes the cohesion among the songs difficult, the sound results Acid yet with delicate tones, pleasant and slightly Psychedelic. RCA decides to let them go yet they manage to produce their third work with Music Hall: *Tiempo De Resurrection*, never was a title so prophetic. **Arco Iris** finally find their true dimension here, melting Latin Folk with the genres coming from abroad: Jazz, Psychedelia and Space-prog. This success brings them to hold many concerts and to go on long promotional tours. The charismatic figure of **Gustavo Santaolalla** strongly emerges in this last work for his unmistakable guitar style, capable of interpreting and blending

with unique creativeness the different genres. **Santaolalla**'s personality leads them to the ambitious double album *Sudamerica or el Regreso a la Aurora*, perhaps the first in Spanish, rich of Folk references and Jazz contaminations. Considered as their masterpiece, it confirms their inimitable skills of stylistic Fusion by using atypical instruments like the chacarera, the malambo, the kena or the charango to obtain their amazing effects and experimentations. These first symptoms of change toward more sophisticated musical styles explode disruptively through the entire album *Inty Raymi*, devoted to the legendary adoration of the Inca Sun God and are even more evident in *Agitor Lucens V*, where the band unequivocally plunge into Symphonic Rock, maintaining a vague Jazzy style and the more typical tonalities of Andean music. Here the combination of sax and vocal parts is absolutely splendid as are the guitar and organ solos with hints of the best **ELP** inspiration. **Santaolalla** suddenly leaves the band to form **Soluna** without notice and at the highest of their success. **Ignacio Elizabetsky** replaces him but lacks the creative pulse of his predecessor and the album *Los Elementales* of 1977 will be the last for Prog interest for they will continue their career playing an average Jazz Rock that will flow into New Age. Worthy of mention the collaboration with **Herbie Hancock** in 1985 but Prog is nowhere to be found.   **C.A.**

RECOMMENDED RECORDINGS:
ARCO IRIS *(RCA, 1969)* **SUITE #1** *(RCA, 1970)* **TIEMPO DE RESURRECTION** *(Music Hall, 1972)* **SUDAMERICA O EL REGRESO A LA AURORA** *(Music Hall, 1972)* **INTY RAYMI** *(Music Hall, 1973)* **AGITOR LUCENS V** *(Music Hall, 1974)* **LOS ELEMENTALES** *(Cabal, 1977)*.

South America: ARGENTINA

PESCADO RABIOSO

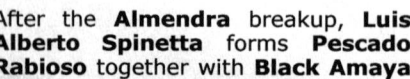
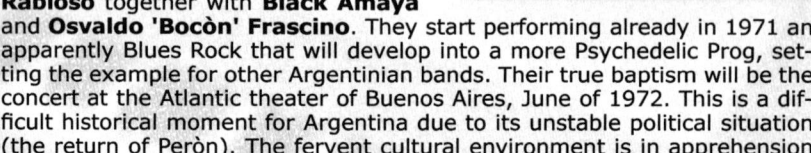

Luis Alberto Spinetta - *guitars, vocals*, **Black Amaya** - *drums*, **Carlos Cutaia** - *keyboards*, **David Lebón** - *bass, guitars, vocals*, **Osvaldo Frascino** - *bass, guitars, vocals in "Desatormentandonos"*.

After the **Almendra** breakup, **Luis Alberto Spinetta** forms **Pescado Rabioso** together with **Black Amaya** and **Osvaldo 'Bocòn' Frascino**. They start performing already in 1971 an apparently Blues Rock that will develop into a more Psychedelic Prog, setting the example for other Argentinian bands. Their true baptism will be the concert at the Atlantic theater of Buenos Aires, June of 1972. This is a difficult historical moment for Argentina due to its unstable political situation (the return of Peròn). The fervent cultural environment is in apprehension and at the end of the '70s the government will become a Military dictatorship, ending in the bloodshed war of 1982 (Falkland/Malvinas), lost against the UK. A first studio album *Desatormentándonos* is recorded featuring on keyboards **Carlos Cutaia** that will definitely join the line-up with **David Lebòn**, from **Color Humano** replacing **Frascino**. Immediately after they are hired to compose the soundtrack of "Hasta que se ponga el sol", a film by Anìbal Uset. In January 1973 a double-album full of guest stars such as **Emilio Del Guercio**, **Rodolfo García** and **Gustavo Spinetta**, is published entitled *Pescado 2*: its length and complicated articulation is more of a handicap for the time and does not go well. This accelerates the eventual break-up, but **Spinetta**'s contract with Microfòn obliges them to issue a last 45RPM in 1976 as **Pescado Rabioso**. Meanwhile, always bound to his contract and with the help of his former colleagues, he puts together a solo album, *Artaud*, using songs that were originally destined to the band, almost to underline that it was all the same creature. The album was promoted with various concerts (also in the Astral theater) and, even if it was not at the level of his previous works, it is still a good inspiration for many followers. Among the collection recordings that came after the disbandment, the two main ones are *Le Mejor de Pescado Rabioso* of 1976 and *Obras Cumbres* of 2001. **M.G.**

DISCOGRAPHY:
DESATORMENTÁNDONOS *(Microfòn, 1972)* **PESCADO 2** *(Microfòn, 1973)* **ARTAUD** *(Sony, BMG, 1974)* **LO MEJOR DE PESCADO RABIOSO** *(Sony Music, 1976)* **OBRAS CUMBRES - PESCADO RABIOSO** *(Sony Music, 2001)*.

South America: BRAZIL

OS MUTANTES

Rita Lee - *vocals*, **Rogerio Duprat** - *producer, arranger*, **Sergio Baptista** - *bass, guitars*, **Arnaldo Baptista** - *bass, keyboards*.

Imagine a Beat band, born in Brazil with the intention of emulating **The Beatles** and **The Beach Boys**, that wins a contract with Polydor and begins to record hit singles and one album that will be considered the manifesto of the dawning Brazilian Psychedelia... this is the genesis of **Os Mutantes**.
A typically '60s line-up (guitar, bass, drums, keyboards and singer) which gradually evolves into a more Progressive atmosphere with shy attempts of experimentation. The debut is similar to the structure of *Sgt.Pepper's Lonely Hearts Club Band* and they are invited to participate in musical events all over the country (including TV broadcasts). Polydor introduces them to producer and arranger **Rogerio Duprat**, in charge of the amazing second album containing great Psychedelia partitions seasoned with tastes of Brazilian Folk.

With the third, *A Divina Comedia Ou ando Meio Desligado*, their sound finally turns more Prog as a first footstep toward true artistic maturity. The album is not cohesive enough and perhaps lacks a suitable vocal part, but it reveals the talent of the other musicians. In 1971 *Jardim Electrico* sends a polemic message regarding the political and social situation, obviously not warmly welcomed by the authorities. To avoid further issues of censorship Polydor suggests a rather quick recording for a new album, *E Seus Cometas No País do Baurets*, where the sarcasm and the political satire are forgotten in favor of a crafty fusion in musical styles, from Rock-a-billy to Folk through Jazz and commercial Latin rhythms, without neglecting more Prog elements as in the long title-track suite.

Unfortunately strong inside tensions with **Rita Lee** leave her out of the following album, *OAEOZ*, that still results surprisingly valid with its flowing keyboards, guitars and wise use of percussions on the wake of **ELP**, disguising the unexceptional vocal qualities of **Dias** and **Baptista**. It was considered a masterpiece for Latin America's Prog, compared to *Nursery Cryme* by **Genesis** and to *Trilogy* by **ELP**, from which they differ for the simplicity of their sound, less majestic but surely as fresh and of great technique.

With *Tudo Foi Feito Pelo Sol* of 1974 they reach the top of their success achieving to perfectly combine the Rock Symphonic style dear to **Yes**, with the inevitable Folk and Ethnic influences, involving also unusual instruments for a Brazilian Prog band (sitar). Rich of dreamlike atmospheres, delicate and very complex melodies, it was misunderstood for a concept-album but the songs were in reality not tied together by a topic. Worthy of mention is the live recording *Ao Vivo* of 1976, again poorly appreciated by the audience and therefore the last for this band, who gave so much to the musical history of their country. **C.A.**

DISCOGRAPHY:
OS MUTANTES *(Polydor, 1968)* **MUTANTES** *(Polydor, 1969)* **A DIVINA COMEDIA OU ANDO MEIO DESLIGADO** *(Polydor, 1970)* **JARDIM ELETRICO** *(Polydor, 1971)* **E SEUS COMETAS NO PAIS DO BAURETS** *(Polydor, 1972)* **O A E O Z** *(Som Livre, 1973)* **TUDO FOI FEITO PELO SOL** *(Som Livre, 1974)* **AO VIVO** *(Som Livre, 1976)*.

South America: BRAZIL

O TERÇO

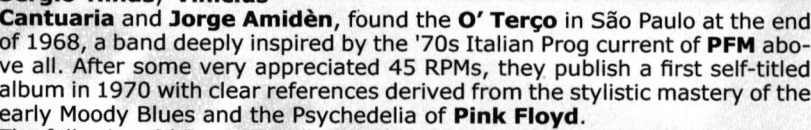

Sérgio Hinds - *guitars*, **Flávio Venturini** - *piano, synthesizers*, **Vinicius Cantuária** - *drums*, **César das Mercês** - *bass, flute*, **Jorge Amidèn** - *bass*, **Sérgio Magrão** - *bass*.

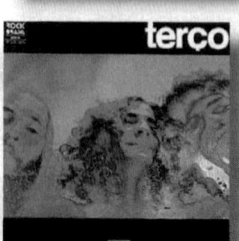

After playing in small Garage music bands, **Sergio Hinds**, **Vinicius Cantuaria** and **Jorge Amidèn**, found the **O' Terço** in São Paulo at the end of 1968, a band deeply inspired by the '70s Italian Prog current of **PFM** above all. After some very appreciated 45 RPMs, they publish a first self-titled album in 1970 with clear references derived from the stylistic mastery of the early Moody Blues and the Psychedelia of **Pink Floyd**.
The following *O' Terço II*, will reproduce the same themes with rather brief, well arranged songs of good Psychedelia; the sound hardens, slightly recalling examples of **Led Zeppelin** and **Black Sabbath**.

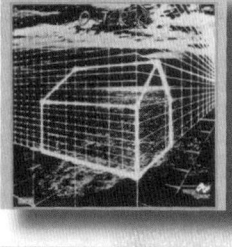

Cesar das Merces, who previously replaces **Jorge Amiden** on the bass, in this third album of 1975 begins his own musical evolution: *Criaturas Da Noite* is a fusion of acoustic guitars with truly inspired keyboards and a powerful bass, balanced by the vocals that create a perfect atmosphere. **Sergio Hinds** is the creative soul (a kind of Brazilian **Robert Fripp**) that guides and inspires, but **Flavio Venturini**'s con-

tribution on the keyboards proves to be priceless. The following year *Casa Encantada* matches the level of its predecessor, rich of delicate melodies of romantic Prog 'made in Italy', but elaborated with a typical Brazilian taste mixed of joy and melancholy.
The first signals of a slow but inexorable change toward more easy-listening Folk music is sensed already during the concerts that were held immediately after. *Mudanca de Tempo*, 1978, proposes once more the same rhythms and recipes yet with smaller conviction of the quintet, which starts to look upon a more commercial Pop Rock. *Som mais puro* is the confirmation of this trend, though a certain recovery of Prog is attempted, but the only original survivor is a tired **Sergio Hinds** that opts for a more calm and less experimental genre. From here onward their Prog adventure is to be considered over. All the rest of their material is forged as a romantic Pop with good references to American Rock of a radio broadcast liking.

C.A.

DISCOGRAPHY:
O TERÇO *(Phonodisc, 1970)* **O TERÇO II** *(Phonodisc, 1972)* **CRIATURAS DA NOITE** *(Copacabana, 1975)* **CASA ENCANTADA** *(Copacabana, 1976)* **MUDANCA DE TEMPO** *(Copacabana, 1978)* **SOM MAIS PURO** *(Elektra, 1982)*.

KNIGHTS
Chapter Two

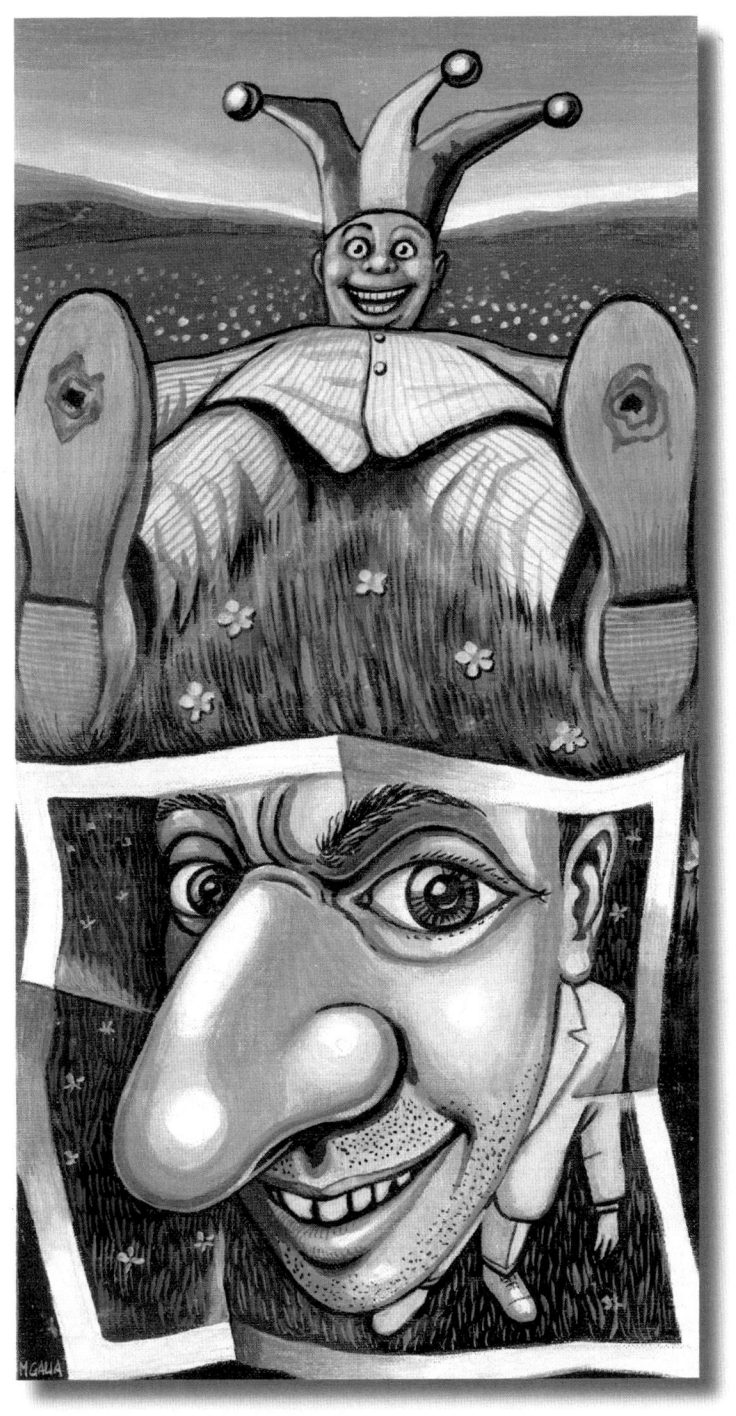

Pink Floyd - *Brain Damage*

Europe: BELGIUM

AKSAK MABOUL

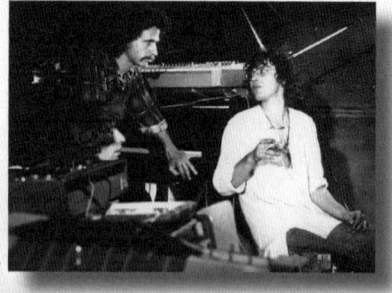

Marc Hollander – *keyboards, horns, percussion, drum machine*, **Vincent Kenis** – *guitar, keyboards, bass, percussioni*.

The strange name of this band, born from the mixture of Arabic and French forms meaning to express an unusual and limping path, is well coupled with the proposition of their music, close to an avant-garde pop and the RIO movement. **Aksak Maboul** is the materialization of **Hollander** and **Kenis**'s idea, recording a first excellent album in 1977, rich of Canterbury references like from **Wyatt** and **Henry Cow**. This album sees the participation of some members from **Univers Zero**. In 1979 they met **Chris Cutler**, who obviously wanted them to join the R.I.O. movement to which the band finally adheres. In that same year they begin to collaborate both with **Cutler** and **Frith**, bringing them to a second darker album, sad and less simple to listen to.

RECOMMENDED RECORDINGS: ONZE DANSES POUR COMBATTRE LA MIGRAINE *(1977, Kamikaze)* ***UN PEU DE L'ÂME DES BANDITS*** *(1980, Crammed).*

M.G. & C.C.

BANZAI

Peter Torfs – *keyboards, vocals*, **John MC O** – *guitars*, **Ludwig Kemat** – *percussion, saxophones*, **Evert Verhees** – *bass, vocals*, **Erry Foix** – *drums, percussion*.

Symphonic prog with some jazz elements is the proposal of a band born in the first part of the 70's and strongly influenced by the English wave, above all by **Yes**. Extremely interesting and fascinating, their music was recorded in one single album after which they break-up forever (together with the label that had them under contract). With beautiful keyboards and complex guitar mixtures, the sound is mainly homogeneous, with fast changing parts and solos that leave no boring moments, especially in the two mini suites. In the second edition of the album, other 6 songs are added and not good as the others, maybe derived from the early sessions but abandoned because of their clear inferiority.

DISCOGRAPHY: HORA NATA *(Delta, 1974).*

M.G. & C.C.

COS

Pascale Son – *vocals, oboe*, **Daniel Schell** – *guitar, flute*, **Charles Loos** – *keyboards*, **Alain Goutier** – *bass*, **Robert Dartsch** – *drums*, **Steve Leduc** – *percussion*, **Marc Hollander** – *keyboards*.

An important band for Belgium's prog proposing a very complex kind of music with Canterbury sounds and **Hatfield and the North**'s elements. Born from the ashes of **Classroom**, a group led by **Schell** at the end of 60's, they were contemporary colleagues of **Magma** and **Zao**. The first album published in 1974 is a fantastic debut with amazing instrumental parts containing jazz and zeuhl elements elegantly managed. Decidedly beautiful also the second album of 1976, with solo parts inspired from the best **Wyatt** moments and complex Canterbury styled jazz scores. The rest of their career will be made of redundant repetitions and stylistic simplifications.

RECOMMENDED RECORDINGS: POSTAEOLIAN TRAIN ROBBERY *(Plus / EMI, 1974)* ***VIVA BOMA*** *(EMI, 1976).*

M.G. & C.C.

Europe: BELGIUM

IRISH COFFE

William Souffreau - *vocals, guitar,* **Jean van der Schueren** - *guitar,* **Willy de Bisschop** - *bass,* **Paul Lambrechts** - *organ,* **Hugo Verhoye** - *drums.*

In addition to several singles, this band published a very nice and inspirational Hard Prog album, with pressing rhythms and wonderful melodies bouncing to and fro from Hammond organ to electric guitar. As a matter of fact, their sound is quite dirty, but of the kind that warms you up: they are clearly are putting their hearts souls into the music they play, recalling sometimes **Deep Purple** and **Uriah Heep** or certain works of the Italian **Biglietto Per L'inferno**. The singer's skills are remarkable, while other more quiet and relaxing parts are also very nice. The story of this band ends tragically when their keyboardist dies in a car accident.

DISCOGRAPHY: IRISH COFFEE *(1971, Trinagle).*   M.G. & C.C.

LAGGER BLUES MACHINE

Christian Duponcheel - *organ,* **Jean-Luc Duponcheel** - *drums,* **Jose Cuisset** - *guitars,* **Michel Maes** - *bass,* **Vincent Mottoulle** - *keyboards,* **Carmelo Pilotta** - *flute, sax.*

Active since the beginning of the '70s, this band should be proud of its high-quality album, greatly inspired by some of the best and famous groups of the time like **Soft Machine**, **Frank Zappa** and **Magma**, infused with a dark Symphonic Rock. Their originality, based on contaminations from very different styles, is blessed by the vintage sound of the keyboards that stand out, though always in balance with the sweetness of the acoustics, the fierceness of the electric guitars and the liveliness of the horn section. The theme compositions are articulated and have a very complex structure, especially the two long parts of "Symphonie". Their live album *Tanit*, is published well after the break-up, with a terrible audio quality, but it remains an interesting historical document.

DISCOGRAPHY: LAGGER BLUES MACHINE *(1972, CBS)* **TANIT** *(live 1970, 1992 Fricrivan).*   M.G. & C.C.

JENGHIZ KHAN

Tim Brean - *keyboards, vocals,* **Big Frisma** - *guitars, vocals,* **Christian Servranckx** - *drums, percussion, backing vocals,* **Pierre Rapsat** - *bass, lead vocals.*

Positioned on the verge of Prog and Hard Rock, this Belgian group had a very intense first phase made of live performances (on stage with **Black Sabbath**, **Yes**, and **Genesis**) and recorded only one album, published in 1971, Well Cut. The band's style is clearly closer to the music of **Ten Years Later** and **Iron Butterfly**, with some major Prog-Rock inflections. **Rapsat**'s bass playing is very customized and perfectly integrates **Frisma**'s guitar, while on the keyboards **Brean** recalls some sounds of the early **Vanilla Fudge**. The band breaks-up right after the album's publishing and **Rapsat** starts a promising solo career, while **Brean** joins the **Pebbles**, and **Frisma** plays for some time with **Wallace Collection**.

DISCOGRAPHY: WELL CUT *(Barclay, 1971).*   C.A. & C.C.

Europe: **CZECHOSLOVAKIA**

FLAMENGO

Vladimír Mišík - *vocals, congas*, **Jan Kubík** - *sax, flute, clarinet, vocals*, **Pavel Fort** - *guitars, vocals*, **Ivan Khunt** - *keyboards, vocals*, **Vladimir Kulhánek** - *bass, vocals* **Jaroslav Šedivý** - *drums*.

They all start with different experiences in various bands during the Beat movement in Czechoslovakia, finally pooling, in the '70s, into one talented band called **Flamengo**. After signing up with the label Supraphon, they publish a series of singles of remarkable Rock-Blues quality. Eventually they record *Kure v Hodinkách* (the rooster in the watch), a Rock album with Jazz influences and faint Psychedelic streaks that recall **Jethro Tull**. Unfortunately, the label's management had appointed the famous poet Josef Kainar to write the lyrics at a time when he became an uncomfortable figure for the Czech Communist Party. Politically this was a perfect opportunity to boycott the subversive genre and the album could not be distributed on the market. It was sold in a private form to a club of musicians (or this is the official version).

DISCOGRAPHY: KURE V HODINKACH *(Supraphon, 1972).*   **C.A. & C.C.**

JAZZ Q

Martin Kratochvil - *keyboards, piano*, **Lubos Andrst** - *guitars*, **Vladimir Padrunek** - *bass*, **Michal Vrbovec** - *drums*, **Frantisek Francl** - *guitars*, **Premysl Faukner** - *bass*, **Libor Laun** - *drums*, **Jiri Helesic** - *drums*, **Pavel Trnavsky** - *drums*, **Joan Duggan** - *vocals*.

Since the early '70s the talented **Martin Kratochvil** leads his band Jazz Q toward the kind of Electric Jazz created by **Miles Davis** at first, and then developed by **Weather Report**, **Mahavishnu Orchestra** and other similar groups. After a collaboration with the **Blue Effect**, they release *Pozorovatelna*, a fantastic first album in the wake of the most exciting traditional Prog Jazz-Rock. In each of the five complex tracks, the sound of the electric piano played by the group's leader is outstanding, ready to engage in masterly solos and creating peculiar atmospheres in duets with the guitar. The band progresses into a more formal mannerism, also exploring the Fusion genre, yet maintaining exceptional quality at all times.

DISCOGRAPHY: POZOROVATELNA *(1974, Pantom)* **SYMBIOSIS** *(1975, Supraphon)* **ELEGIE** *(1977, Supraphon)* **ZVESTI** *(1979, Supraphon)* **HODOKVAS** *(1980, Supraphon)* **HVEDZON** *(1984, Supraphon)* **LIVE 1974-75** *(1991, Bonton Records).* **CONIUNCTO** *(1971, Supraphon, with Blue Effect).*   **M.G. & C.C.**

PROGRESS ORGANISATION
(Barnodaj - Progres 2)

Zdenek Kluka - *drums, keyboards, guitars, vocals*, **Pavel Vane** - *chitarre, vocals*, **Jan Sochor** - *keyboards, vocals*, **Pavel Pelc** - *basso, vocals*.

Rather famous in Brno at the end of the '60s, they had to change name because **Progress Organization** was too British for the political point of view in 1968. Opting for a more Slavic yet meaningless name, **Barnodaj**, their first album however, was still published as **Progress Organisation**: a beautiful work of art at the border with psychedelia. Half of the album includes original tracks in Czech, while the other half contains British rock covers of **the Beatles**, **Cream** and other main bands. Seven years later a second album this time published as *Barnodj*, titled *Maugli* as a tribute to the famous novel by R. Kipling. Unfortunately here they lack the freshness of their debut, but maintain part of the psychedelic vigor as evidenced by the presence of unusual instruments, like the sitar. Then they change name once more to **Progres 2** and release a rock project called *Dialog Vesmirem* that, despite being ostracized by the government, had an enormous success in sales.

DISCOGRAPHY: BARNODAJ*(Supraphon, 1971)* **MAUGLI** *(Supraphon, 1978)* **DIALOG VESMIREM** *(Panton, 1980).*   **C.A. & C.C.**

Europa: **DANEMARK**

ACHE

Peter Mellin - *keyboards,* **Finn Olafsson** - *guitar, vocals,* **Torsten Olafsson** - *bass, vocals,* **Glenn Fischer** - *drums, percussion.*
Their story begins in the 60's, with the founding members divided in two beat bands called **The Harlows** and **McKenzie Set**; once disbanded, the musicians unite in 1968 and create **Ache**: essentially intended as a symphonic prog band, they eventually find themselves mixing hard-rock keyboards with dramatic tones, to parts of psychedelic blues with the clear predominance of guitars. Given the time they can be defined as precursors just like others such as **Nice** or **Vanilla Fudge**. Their first album in particular is composed of two long suites that highlight the great technique of both **Mellin** and **Olafsson**. Valid and coherent is also the second album *Green Man*. The band will publish another two albums, yet not as good as the previous.
RECOMMENDED RECORDINGS: **DE HOMINE URBANO** *(1970, Philips)* **GREEN MAN** *(1971, Philips).* M.G. & C.C.

CULPEPER'S ORCHARD

Cy Nicklin - *vocals, guitars, mandolin,* **Michael Friis** - *bass, organ, piano, sitar, vocals,* **Nils Henriksen** - *guitars, vocals, keyboards,* **Ken Gudman** - *drums.*
Singer and guitarist **Nicklin** is an English-transplanted-in-Denmark musician that played in a former folk beat trio called **Cy, Maia & Robert**. He later becomes the leader of **Culpeper's Orchard** and proposes a prog genre with some distinctive but extremely various hard elements, sometimes taken from the blues, sometimes from psychedelia or from beat, often also using references from some southern American or West Coast rock. Their first album is pretty good, with country vocals interlacing electric guitars and Hammond melodies. Also the second is a good one, maybe a little repetitive of the previous, but still with inspired references from **Led Zeppelin** or **Allman Brother**. Decidedly inferior the next album and the last bootlegs.

RECOMMENDED RECORDINGS: **CULPEPER'S ORCHARD** *(1971, Polydor)* **SECOND SIGHT** *(1972, Polydor).* M.G. & C.C.

IRON DUKE

Hans Resen - *basso, vocals, guitars, moog,* **Jens Olesen** - *keyboards.* **Tommy Hansen** - *guitars, moog, backing vocals,* **Claus Sarup** - *drums.*
If **Emerson Lake & Palmer** can be seen as masters, **Iron Duke** can be considered their most faithful pupils. In both their albums *First Salvo* and *Gammel Dansk* the comparison materializes in the obsessive presence of keyboards and the transposition of classical melodies into conventional pop-rock. The resulting music doesn't always meet the expectations of the most demanding palates, since the frequent quotes of classics such as **Haendel** and **Grieg** end up boring due to the exorbitant length of the tracks. The lack of technical skills and the exaggerated mix of rock and classical music actually handicaps the whole result. The second album, released three years later, appears to be slightly better and gives more space to the skills of the musicians. Both LPs are quite rare in their original version.
DISCOGRAPHY: **FIRST SALVO** *(Polydor, 1974)* **GAMMEL DANSK** *(Sonet, 1977).* C.A. & C.C.

Europe: DANEMARK

THE OLD MAN & THE SEA

Ole Wedel - *vocals*, **Benny Stanley** - *electric guitars*, **Tommy Hansen** - *organ, piano, vocals*, **Knud Lindhard** - *basso, vocals*, **John Lundvig** - *drums*.

Among the best prog records from northern Europe in the '70s, their one and only true album is full of warm Hammond organ and electric guitar melodies that recall some of the best of **Atomic Rooster**, yet avoiding their excessively dark sides. Capable of brilliant instrumental moments, this band enchants with a fascinating and cohesive work, tempting hints from **The Beatles**' and vocals passages that recall **CSNY**. Unfortunately they break-up without further activity after their marvelous debut, although a CD is released in 1999 containing demos and live recordings from their first years.

DISCOGRAPHY: THE OLD MAN & THE SEA *(1972, Sonet)* **1972-75** *(1999, Karma Music)*.　　　　　　　　　　　　　　　　　　　　　　　　**M.G. & C.C.**

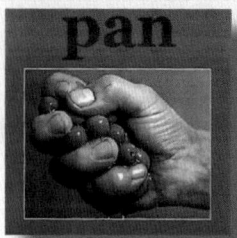

PAN

Robert Lelievre - *vocals, guitar*, **Thomas Puggard-Müller** - *guitar*, **Henning Verner** - *piano, organ, vibes*, **Arne Würgler** - *bass, cello*, **Micharl Puggard-Müller** - *drums*.

Like their fellow countrymen **The Old Man and the Sea**, this band also records only one gem in 1970, after which nothing will ever follow. Even **Pan**'s style shares some similarities, with a pretty lively and personal prog, led by the exchanges between organ and guitars. Yet they diverge from their colleagues by adding brilliant contaminations of classical, folk, blues and jazz to their marvelous melodies, also considering the period in which this album is released (therefore amplifying it's musical value). Their lead singer **Lelievre**, author of both music and lyrics, will eventually commit suicide in 1974 after a demising solo experience.

DISCOGRAPHY: PAN *(1970, Sonet)*.　　　　　　　　　　　　**M.G. & C.C.**

SECRET OYSTER

Karsten Vogel - *saxophones, keyboards*, **Claus Bøhling** - *guitar, sitar*, **Kenneth Knudsen** - *keyboards*, **Jess Stæhr** - *bass*, **Ole Streenberg** - *drums*.

This is a sort of Danish super-band formed on the ashes of **Burnin' Red Ivanohe**, **Coronorias Dans** and **Hurdy Gurdy**. They play a dynamic and never boring symphonic jazz rock, as in their debut of 1973, Furtive Pearls, where they unite themes from **Weather Report**, **Soft Machine** and **Frank Zappa**'s more jazzy period. Their evolution in time maintains rare quality and coherence, as do all four albums that result important for different aspects: the first has an innovative fierce character and is relevant to the Danish fusion genre, the second and specially the third, for the amazing scores, and the last for the quality of its ideas, similar to bands like **Brand X**.

RECOMMENDED RECORDINGS: SECRET OYSTER *(1973, CBS)* **SEA SON** *(1974, CBS)* **VIDUNDERLIGE KÆLLING** *(1975, CBS)* **STRAIGHT TO THE KRANKENHAUS** *(1976, CBS)*.　　　　　　　　　　　　**M.G. & C.C.**

Europe: FINLAND

FANTASIA

Roul Helantie - *piano, synthesizers, hammond organ,* **Hannu Lindblom** - *guitar, vocals,* **Harri Piha** - *bass,* **Karl-Erik Ronngard** - *drums.*

Prog rock in Finland produced a hoard of premier league talents who achieved success and attention; other equally talented bands in this country achieved an equally interesting quality yet remaining somewhat anonymous. Among the latter **Fantasia** stands out with their self-titled album released in 1975 of which very little is known. Analyzing the music, one must admit the fascinating work, saturated with fine romanticism (in **Camel** style) with beautiful organ parts and a guitar that pushes towards the jazz-rock genre in ways not dissimilar to **Wigwam**. This record in its original vinyl version costs a fortune because of its extreme rarity and, if not as a bootleg, it has never been officially published as a CD. The band produced this album thanks to the prize they won in a musical competition. The limited duration of the album (shortly over thirty minutes) is due to the producer's decision to avoid complex tracks (apparently due to technical limits) and extensions that are typical of a prog band. Their best known song is "Tulen Pisara".
DISCOGRAPHY: FANTASIA *(1975, Hi Hat).*

G.D.S.

FINNFOREST

Pekka Tegelman – *guitars, bass,* **Jussi Tegelman** – *drums,* **Jukka Rissanen** - *keyboards.*

This band derived great inspiration from **Mahavishnu Orchestra**, **Caravan**, **Camel** and (why not?) the Italian band **Arti e Mestieri**. Their sound is clearly of a symphonic jazz rock imprint, with complex and articulated structures and incredible guitar and keyboards plots. In their first album, as a trio, the band was compared also to **Wigwam** and **Focus** because of their excellent keyboardist **Rissanen**'s style, who after the exit of the album, leaves. The following year, with a more extended line up of 6 elements, they publish **Lahto Matkalle**, an album of great overtures and of fascinating atmospheres, with a more careful eye toward the composition and the clarity of sounds, sometimes, and wrongly, perceived as cold virtuosity.
RECOMMENDED RECORDINGS: FINNFOREST *(1975, Love Records)* **LÄHTÖ MÄTKALLE** *(1976, Love Records).*

M.G. & C.C.

GROOVECTOR

Kalle Aalto - *drums, percussion,* **Mikko Heininen** - *keyboards, programmaing, vocals,* **Teemu Niemelä** - *bass, vocals,* **Rauli Viitala** - *guitars,* **Teemu Huunonen** - *flute.*

Among one of the first exponents of Finnish prog-rock to revitalize the prog genre at the beginning of the new millennium, they debut with the extraordinarily beautiful *Ultramarine*, an instrumental romantic rock album, played with great class, slightly vintage (especially for the neverending sounds of the hammond organ and of the graceful transverse flute) and with clear references to **Camel** and **Bo Hansson**. Their second album, *Enigmatic Elements*, changes course, with shorter and more direct tracks, genre contaminations, very technological sounds and more modern pitches, with incredibly clean recordings. A third album *Darklubing at Tavastia* reaches incredible quality peaks and gives us a vision of the band during a live performance.
DISCOGRAPHY: ULTRAMARINE *(2000, Mellow Records)* **ENIGMATIC ELEMENTS** *(2003, Mellow Records)* **DARKLUBING AT TAVASTIA** *(2005, Mellow Records).*

M.G. & C.C.

Europe: FINLAND

NIMBUS

Hari Suilamo - *guitar*, **Pekka Rautio** - *keyboards*, **Pasi Saarelma** - *vocals*, **Juha Pekka Jokiranta** - *bass*, **Matti Jokiranta** - *drums*.

This band rises from the ashes of a previous named **Mafia**, and will record only one album of six tracks which are not so long, only one reaches seven minutes, yet achieving an exceptional quality: *Obus* is a very ingenious work where rock music tends to emerge although saturated with elements from classical and traditional northern folk. The keyboards are more symphonic while the guitar creates psychedelic sounds, with inserts of violin which paint a somewhat bucolic atmosphere, close to the best **Wigwam** due to the skilled instrumental parts and some jazzy arrangements. The deeply blues' mood enhances the chemistry flowing from these compositions making this one of the most beautiful Finnish prog records that truly deserves its place in history.

DISCOGRAPHY: OBUS (1974, Satsanga). M.G. & C.C.

NOVA

Antti Ortamo - *keyboards, vocals*, **Milla Vasenius** - *guitar*, **Jouko Helatie** - *guitar*, **Petri Peltola** - *bass*, **Jukka Marjala** - *drums*.

Atlantis is an album of 1976, based on a very classical symphonic prog, lacking none of the features which attract the many aficionados of this music genre: four ample tracks mainly guided by guitars and organ deeply influenced by British bands like **Yes**, **Camel** and **Pink Floyd**, as well as by local contaminations from their motherland with inserts which are not distant from jazz and blues (the comparison with Wigwam cannot be avoided). The tracks "Se Vuosi" and "Atlantis" are beautiful although this band sings in their native tongue. Even if this record is not very famous, especially abroad, probably also because of the language, the band defines a very precise historical period for Finland due to the new musical interests that were rising. Therefore in absence of demand for concerts in their genre, Nova disappears very quickly into oblivion.

DISCOGRAPHY: ATLANTIS (1976, Love Records). M.G. & C.C.

PEKKA POHJOLA

Former **Wigwam** member, **Pekka Pohjola** is a multi-instrumentalist who at a certain point of his career decides to go solo. He is also known and respected as a session-man for other famous artists with whom he collaborates. The first two solo albums immediately prove his genius with a very personal form of progressive jazz-rock: ample space is given to the horn section supported by a complex rhythmic structure, echos of Canterbury and classical music with hints of the great **Frank Zappa**. The third album, *Keesojen Lehto* is his most famous also for the presence of guest-star **Mike Oldfield**: a very peculiar work, lively and dreamy at the same time. One of the most recent recordings among the many in his discography is *Views* (2001), an enchanting mix of jazz and contemporary music.

RECOMMENDED RECORDINGS: PIHKASILMÄ KAARNAKORVA *(1972, Love)* **HARAKKA BIALOIPOKKU** *(1974, Love)* **KEESOJEN LEHTO** *(1977, Love;* **"Mathematicians Air Display"**, *1977, Virgin, U.K. Edition)* **VISITATION** *(1979, Dig It)* **SINFONIA NO. 1** *(1990 Flamingo Music)* **LIVE IN JAPAN** *(1995, Belle Antique)* **HEAVY JAZZ – LIVE IN HELSINKI AND TOKYO** *(1995, Pohjola Records)* **PEWIT** *(1997, Pohjola Records)* **VIEWS** *(2001, Pohjola Records)*. M.G. & C.C.

Europe: FRANCE

ALICE

Jean-Pierre Auffredo - *oboe, flute, saxophones, violin, guitar, piano, percussion, vocals,* **Bruno Besse** - *guitar, percussion,* **Sylvain Duplant** - *bass, guitar, percussion, vocals,* **Alain Suzan Orgue** - *piano, percussion, vocals, bass,* **Alain Weiss** - *drums, percussion, tubular bells, vocals.*

Born in 1969 from the first wave of French prog, this very unstable band did not last long. Both albums, recorded with two very different line-ups, show their awareness of being innovators in the dominant songwriting panorama: the excellent and fresh melodies where often underlined by dramatic moments and sometimes rhythmically anomalous odd-time signatures (probably among the first to use them). This first album of 1970 was recorded in London in order to give it a more English sound, managing thus to close the gap between their hippie, psychedelic and folk style and the **Jethro Tull** and **Traffic** targets despite the french lyrics. The second work is a concept album of true prog released two years later by Polydor and followed by its English version due to the success achieved.

RECOMMENDED RECORDINGS: ALICE *(Byg, 1970)* **ARRÊTEZ LE MONDE** *(Polydor, 1972).*

M.G. & C.C.

ARTCANE

Jack Mlynski - *guitars, vocals,* **Alain Coupel** - *keyboards, vocals,* **Stanislas Belloc** - *bass, vocals,* **Daniel Locci** - *drums.*

So strongly influenced by **King Crimson** that at times it feels like a sister album from *Larks' Tongues In Aspic*, their one and only album *Odyssee* was released in 1977: a series of finely structured tracks with guitar parts clearly inspired by **Robert Fripp**, that sometimes lose themselves in hard rock solos, leaving the rest of the band to itself, creating intriguing spacey atmospheres where the dialogue between keyboards and guitars becomes crystal clear. This symphonic rock album owes its publishing to the label Philips, who still believed in the genre despite the period of great musical change. The instrumental richness still manages to give way to some singing that recalls the tradition of French prog and its theatrical twist.

DISCOGRAPHY: ODYSSEE *(1977, Philips).*

M.G. & C.C.

ASIA MINOR

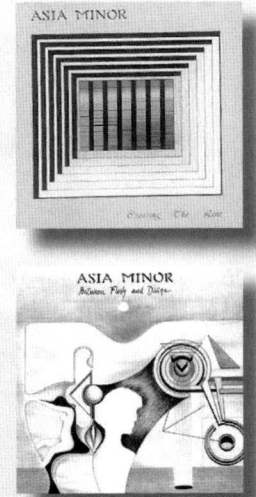

Eril Tekeli - *flute, guitars, bass,* **Setrak Bakirel** - *vocals, guitars, bass,* **Lionel Beltrami** - *drums, percussion,* **Robert Kempler** - *keyboards, bass,* **Nicolas Vicente** - *keyboards.*

Two Turkish students give birth to this band with their debut *Crossing The Line* in 1979. This romantic prog rock album is a wonderful fresco of the time, with the enchanting harping guitars, the emotional flute melodies and the epic sounds of the keyboards that give a vague oriental flavour to this first work. Of the nine tracks, two are instrumental, two are sung in Turkish and the remaining in English. The following year *Between Flesh And Divine* is released, maintaining the style and standards of the previous, though increasing perhaps certain references to British prog bands like **Camel** and **Yes**.

DISCOGRAPHY: CROSSING THE LINE *(1979, Wam)* **BETWEEN FLESH AND DIVINE** *(1980, Wam).*

M.G. & C.C.

Europe: **FRANCE**

CAN AM DES PUIG

Juan Arcocha - *vocals, flute, guitar,* **Leslie Mackenzie** - *tambourine, vocals, lyrics & concept,* **Daevid Allen** *production,* **Gillie Smyth** - *vocals,* **Stephanie Shepard, Pat Meadows** - *flute,* **Phil Shepherd, Lally Murray** - *percussion, vocals,* **Jerry C. Hart** - *guitar, drums, synthesizer, 12 string guitar,* **Tony Bullocks** - *vocals,* **Carmetta Mansilla** - *lead vocals,* **Jean-Paul Vivini** - *synthesizer,* **Rabbi Gaddy Zerbib**- *vocals.*

Meaning the 'House of Am on the Hill' in Catalan, nickname given to the Ibiza and Deia homes of founders **Juan** and **Leslie**: <<*While we were never a 'band' as such and never played gigs or any public performances, attributing the music to the house where the music was played and recorded is very appropriate*>>. It starts on a trip in India (1973) and the publishing of an etched book (Dawn) with lyrics derived from religious and philosophical songs or poems. Its success led to a second book in 1975, based upon three other parts (Morning, Afternoon, Evening) with 25 etchings finished in 1977. The initial idea was of accompanying the art-works with improvisations, so they go to the hippy town of Deia in search of **Robert Graves** who had already made his English version of the Welsh poem "Song of Amergin", also included in their booklets. Here they meet **Daevid Allen** (**Soft Machine, Gong**) who is happy to help produce their *Book of Am* as a double concept-album, recorded in 1978. Due to the funds, only the first record is released while the second will wait the limited edition re-issue of 2006. The music is a sublime work of mystic folk that clearly derives from the hippie psychedelia it was born in.
***DISCOGRAPHY:* BOOK OF AM** *(1978, Virgin).*   C.C.

DÜN

Laurent Bertaud - *drums,* **Jean Geeraerts** - *guitars,* **Bruno Sabathe** - *piano, keyboards,* **Alain Termol** - *percussion,* **Thierry Tranchant** - *bass,* **Pascal Vandenbulcke** - *flute.*

A sextet which had to auto-produce their own music due to the wrong timing in choice of genre: Eros was published in 1981, an album with only four long compositions of devastating musical complexity that encompasses zeuhl and jazz. Active during the reign of punk and disco-music, this band bravely focused on their very personal style by creating articulated and brilliant jazz-rock songs, very creative and free from any inhibition of invention whatsoever. All the instruments are played with great skill, masterly mixing and crossing with phenomenal accelerations and an unpredictable flow of rhythm and beats. They did not release anything else, which is a pity for a band that opened the concerts of **Magma** at the end of the '70s.
***DISCOGRAPHY:* EROS** *(1981, Private Pressing).*   M.G. & C.C.

EIDER STELLAIRE

Michel Le Bars - *drums,* **Patrick Singery** - *bass,* **Jean-Claude Delachat** - *guitars,* **Pierre Gerard-Hirne** - *keyboards,* **Veronique Perrault** - *vocals,* **Marie Anne Le Bars** - *flute,* **Pierre Minevielle** - *keyboards,* **Ann Stewart** - *vocals,* **Franck Coulard** - *electric piano,* **Isabelle Nuffer** - *piano.*

Founded by drum player **Michel Le Bars**, this French band is probably the one that best follows the blazing route left by **Magma**. Active during the '80s they release excellent records in the purest of zeuhl styles, with powerful rhythms, sharp guitars, obsessive themes and atmospheres. Of their three albums, the first featuring **Veronique Perrault** stands out, thanks to her immense class and voice and to the incredible talent she proves in singing 'vocalese', completing the extremely pleasant digressions of vibrant jazz-rock. The following albums do not reach the same heights yet still maintain very good levels in quality.

***DISCOGRAPHY:* EIDER STELLAIRE** *(1981, K)* **EIDER STELLAIRE II** *(1986, K2)* **EIDER STELLAIRE III** *(1987, Musea).*   M.G. & C.C.

Europe: FRANCE

ESKATON

Paule Kleynnaert - *vocals*, **André Bernardi** - *bass*, **Gérard Konig** - *drums*, **Gilles Rozenberg** - *keyboards*, **Marc Rozenberg** - *electric piano*, **Amara Tahir** - *vocals*, **Eric Guillame** - *electric piano*, **Alain Blésing** - *guitar*, **Patrick Lemercier** - *violin*.

A self-produced cassette-tape they recorded in 1979 (later published on CD in 1995 as a second edition), *4 Visions* is the first work for this band that reveals their quality in managing a peculiar interpretation of the zeuhl genre through a powerful musical structure, strong rhythms and an intriguing female voice. The similarities with **Magma** increase with *Ardeur*, released the following year, with the reiterated themes that radiate anxiety and restlessness. Another excellent album in full blown zeuhl style is *Fiction*, although it does not reach the same heights of its predecessors. The latest CD version also contains some added tracks that should have been part of a fourth record, that never saw the light.

DISCOGRAPHY: **4 VISIONS** (1979, Private Pressing) **ARDEUR** (1980, Musique Post Atomique-E) **FICTION** (1983, Musique Post Atomique -E).   **M.G. & C.C.**

MELODY

Gèrard Batrya - *bass*, **Diana Chase** - *vocals*, **Didier Dupard** - *keyboards*, **Patrick Frehner** - *vocals, percussion*, **Jean-Luc L'Hermitte** - *guitars, vocals*, **Phil Louvet** - *drums*, **Paul Amsellem** - *keyboards (second album)*, **Jean-Michel Le Meur** - *drums (second album)*.

A symphonic band active in the second half of the '70s which published the good but badly produced album *Come Fly With Me*. The second excellent *Yesterlife* was instead released by a major label and therefore recorded spending an appropriate budget. Their music stands in between **Genesis**, **Renaissance** and **Camel** for the refined arrangements and the sophisticated melodies. The crystal clear voice of the female singer reminds us of **Sally Oldfield** or, at times, even of **Rose Podwojny** from **Sandrose**.

DISCOGRAPHY: COME FLY WITH ME (1976, Pole) **YESTERLIFE** (1977 Vogue).   **M.G. & C.C.**

MINIMUM VITAL

Thierry Payssan - *keyboards, accordion*, **Eric Reberyol** - *bass*, **Christophe "Cocof" Godet** - *drums*, **Jean Luc Payssan** - *guitars, vocals*, **Anne Colas** - *flute*, **Antoine Fillon** - *drums*, **Pascale Jakubovsky** - *vocals*, **Antoine Guerber** - *vocals*, **Sonia Nedelec** - *vocals*, **Jean-Baptiste Ferracci** - *vocals*, **Charly Berna** - *drums*, **Didier Ottaviani** - *drums*.

Irresistible like no other, between the end of the '80s and the beginning of the '90s this is one of the bands who pushed the most toward a personal prog vision achieving excellent results. Their music is inspired, overwhelming and joyful, mixing rock, medieval themes, Hispanic-French folk, jazz and latino rhythms with an incredible passion. The lyrics are sung in an imaginary language and have a warm phonetic sound to them that enhanced the playfulness of the tracks. They released a series of excellent albums among which *Les Saisons Marines*, *Sarabandes*, and *Esprit d'Amour* are probably the best.

DISCOGRAPHY: ENVOL TRIANGLES (1985, Private Pressing) **LES SAISONS MARINES** (1988, Musea) **SARABANDES** (1990, Musea) **LA SOURCE** (1993, Musea) **ESPRIT D'AMOUR** (1996, Musea) **AU CERCLE DE PIERRE** (1998, Musea) **ATLAS** (2004, Musea).   **M.G. & C.C.**

Europe: FRANCE

MOVING GELATINE PLATES

Maurice Helminger - *organ, trumpet, sax, flute,* **Gérard Bertram** - *guitars, vocals,* **Didier Thibault** - *bass, vocals, 12 strings guitar,* **Gérard Pons** - *drums, percussion.*

Their fascinating career starts in the middle of '60s although their first record is published only in 1971. This is a great start with an adventurous jazz-rock inspired by the Canterbury school, where guitars and sax take lead alternating throughout the album. The following year they release *The World Of Genius Hans* and it can be considered as their masterpiece: the music is a visionary mix between **Santana** & **Frank Zappa**, yet full of personal ideas and originality. Unfortunately they disband and reunite only seven years later when **Thibault** attempts to renew the line-up and a revise the band's name: *Moving* of 1980 is therefore credited to **Come Moving**, a more concise album with a special guest from **Gong** for the horn section, **Didier Malherbe**. Again a very long pause sees them silent for 25 years until the release of a new CD with new musicians but the original name restored: *Removing* of 2006 is a refined album of high class jazz played with an actual orchestra and richer instrumentation.

DISCOGRAPHY: MOVING GELATINE PLATES *(1971, CBS)* THE WORLD OF GENIUS HANS *(1972, CBS)* REMOVING *(2006, Musea)*, COME MOVING: MOVING *(1980, Amo).* M.G. & C.C.

ONE SHOT

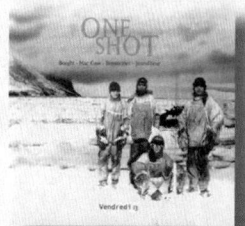

Daniel Jeand'heur - *drums,* **James MacGaw** - *guitar,* **Philippe Bussonet** - *bass,* **Emmanuel Borghi** - *keyboards.*

Created in 1999 by keyboard player **Emmanuel Borghi** and guitarist **James McGaw**, both ex-**Magma** musicians, they are completed by bassist **Philippe Bussonnet** and drummer **Daniel Jeand'heur** for the release of a first debut in 1999, originally only a demo tape. They describe their sound as a jazz-rock prog inspired by Zeuhl, strongly influenced by the **Mahavishnu Orchestra**. Their second record Vendredi 13 was recorded live in 2001 and contains long instrumental compositions closer to **Magma** and **King Crimson**. In 2006 the band release a third album called *Ewaz Vader*, with four long compositions with a harder edge, sometimes on the verge of the metal genre.

DISCOGRAPHY: ONE SHOT *(1999, autoproduzione)* VENDREDI 13 *(2001, Soleil Zeuhl)* EWAZ VADER *(2006, Le Triton)* DARK SHOT *(2008, Le Triton).* M.G. & C.C.

PENTACLE

Claude Menetrier - *keyboards, piano,* **Gérard Ruez** - *guitars, lead vocals,* **Richard Treiber** - *bass, acoustic guitar,* **Michel Roy** - *drums, vocals.*

La Clef Des Songes is their only album of 1975 made of a symphonic rock influenced by **Ange** and by the romantic sound of **Camel**. The tracks are played with enviable mastery and refined solutions, yet do not result as pompous as their contemporary colleagues, never self-indulging like the others, their delicate instrumental parts are impressed with a melancholic vein and the final result is very compelling. It's a pity that after this success they decide to disband without further notice. Of course the album is hard to find in the original version but recently it has been reissued on CD by the label Musea.

DISCOGRAPHY: LA CLEF DES SONGES *(1975, Arcane).* M.G. & C.C.

Europe: FRANCE

RIALZU

Christophe Mac Daniel - *organ, Fender electric piano, synth, vocals*, **François Mac Daniel** – *bass, vocals*, **Dominique Gallet** – *violin, vocals*, **Gilles Renne** – *guitars*, **Olivier Renne** – *drums, percussions*, **Jean-Philippe Gallet** – *vocals*, **Françoise Augé** - *vocals*.

Probably the only prog band from Corsica, they begin their career in the second half of the '70s inspired by the great French zeuhl bands: their sound tends to unite the Mediterranean soul with a powerful jazz-rock sung in Corsican using lyrics of local poets. The result is of great effect and spread over three compositions: two long and fascinating complex structures, with moments of zeuhl-fusion, recalling of course **Magma**'s style, or containing other more refined parts of clear **Pink Floyd** taste embedding native elements through the band's strong personality; the shorter track, "A Mubba", is more similar to the **PFM** of *Jet Lag* or to **Perigeo**. A recent release on CD with two added long live bonus guarantees the necessary accessibility.

RECOMMENDED RECORDINGS: RIALZU *(Ricoridu, 1978)*.   M.G. & C.C.

CATHERINE RIBEIRO

Catherine Ribeiro was born in Lyon and begun her career as an actress for film director Godard. She was convinced to become a singer by producer Patrice Moullet and begun this new version of herself with a first prog masterpiece in 1969, where she performs with the band **2Bis**. The album contains folk mixed with avant-garde and burning psychedelia; **Catherine**'s voice is very expressive, sometimes delicate and emotional and sometimes full of feeling and desperation. From her third album onward she sings with another band called **Alpes** and publishes probably her best works like the impressive *Paix* (1972) and *Libertes?* (1975) where influences of **Pink Floyd**, **Amon Düül**, **Gong**, **Magma** and **Neu** are merged together and guided by her vocals very similar to **Nico** and **Edith Piaf**. After 1980 the songs become shorter, still interesting and always intensely emotional, sophisticated and innovative, supported by fantastic musicians like **Davis Rose**, **Renè Werneer** and **Mireille Bauer**.

RECOMMENDED RECORDINGS: CATHERINE RIBEIRO + 2 BIS *(Festival, 1969)* NO.2 *(Festival, 1970)* PAIX *(Philips, 1972)* **(LIBERTES?)** *(Philips, 1975)* LE BLUES DE PIAF *(Philips, 1977)* PASSIONS *(Philips, 1979)* LA DEBOUSSOLE *(Philips, 1980)*.   M.G. & C.C.

SANDROSE

Rose Podwojny - *vocals*, **Jean-Pierre Alarcen** - *guitar*, **Christian Clairefond** - *bass*, **Henri Garella** - *organ, mellotron*, **Michel Julline** - *drums, percussion*.

Sandrose is a band born in 1972 from the ashes of a previous project called **Eden Rose**. They published only one powerful self-titled album where organ and mellotron dominate the entire record. However, the music contains delicate moments where the charismatic voice of **Rose Podwojny** goes from sensitive lyrics to sometimes dramatic words spoken out loud. An outstanding lead guitar performed by **Jan Pierre Alarcen** completes the arrangements of this fantastic band of symphonic rock inspired by the British masters, although managing their own personality. The wonderful long suite "Underground Session (Chorea)" merges perfectly classical music with rock, revealing a record with no weak moments that belongs among the best romantic rock albums of French prog.

DISCOGRAPHY: SANDROSE *(1972, Polydor)*.   M.G. & C.C.

Europe: FRANCE

SHYLOCK

Frédéric L'Épée - *guitars, bass,* **Didier Lustig** - *keyboards,* **André Fisichella** - *drums, percussion,* **Serge Summa** - *bass.*

A band active in the middle of the '70s playing a compelling symphonic rock based upon the intriguing and electrifying guitar of **Frédéric L'Epée** (influenced by **Genesis** and **King Crimson**) and the epic and atmospheric keyboards of Didier Lustig. They debut with the wonderful *Gialorgues* proving their talent at its best: high school melodies, rhythm changes and refined arrangements. The following and last album *Ile De Fiévre* is the natural stylistic development and quality confirmation of their standard. Rediscovered twenty years later as the source of inspiration for Swedish groups like **Änglagård** and **Anekdoten**.

DISCOGRAPHY: GIALORGUES *(1976, Gialorgues)* **ILE DE FIÈVRE** *(1977, CBS).* M.G. & C.C.

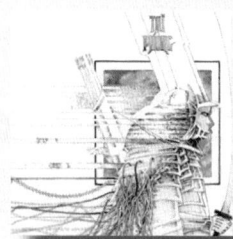

TAI PHONG

Khanh Mai – *vocals, guitar,* **Tai Shin** – *vocals, bass,* **Jean-Alain Gerdet** – *keyboards,* **Jean-Jaques Goldman** – *guitars, vocals,* **Stephan Caussarieu** – *drums, percussions.*

A mixed French and Vietnamese musical creature singing in English a power-prog of clear AOR legacy, with **Yes**, **Barclay James Harvest** and *Pavlov's Dog* inspirations. The compositions develop around the vocal's very high tonalities with sometimes rock-oriented keyboard playing or with more complex symphonic parts. In the second work *Windows* (1976), the symphonic parts finally prevail, creating a more compact and homogeneous album, rich of true lyrical moments. Singer Tai leaves and after consolidating a new line-up, their third album titled *Last Flight* is released three years later: the AOR themes are confirmed (**Styx**, **Supertramp**) through the best sumptuous sounds of the genre. The band disappear until 2000 when they publish the romantic, lyric and nostalgic new album *Sun*.

RECOMMENDED RECORDINGS: WINDOWS *(Warner, 1976).* M.G. & C.C.

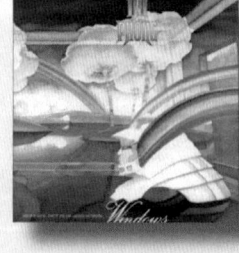

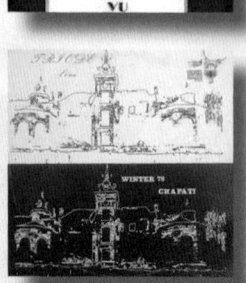

TRIODE

Michel Edelin - *flute,* **Pierre Chéreze** - *guitar,* **Pierre Yves Sorin** - *bass,* **Didier Hauck** - *drums.*

Flute player **Michel Edelin** is the leader of this band playing a prog full of contamination between various genres with impressive melodies and creative solutions, although they show an average personality of their own. Unforgettable the guitars of **Pierre Chéreze** as he is a well known rock blues performer in France, and his mastery is at its best in the cover song of **The Beatles** "Come together", contained in their only album of 9 mainly instrumental tracks: *On N'a Pas Fini D'avoid Tout Vu* of 1971 is deeply affected by psychedelic rock, Traffic and some Canterbury elements.

DISCOGRAPHY: ON N'A PAS FINI D'AVOIR TOUT VU *(1971, Futura).* M.G.

Europe: FRANCE

IGOR WAKHEVITCH

Friend of Dalì and **Wyatt**, this artist beholds the chaotic dynamism of a feather caught in the wind of pure experimentation: composer of unreal and powerful music, his voice screams with the darkest obstinacy of his art. A symphonic psychedelia covered by the obscure and deep velvet drapes of fear, ghostly dangling its chains in an atmosphere where everything can be expressed with its direct opposite. The enigmatic and obsessive creations lead anywhere just through the very thought that comes to the imagination and the electronic choreography evokes ballets of the soul and mind between the pillars of an ancient cloister. The doomed dimension generated by his compositions swirl out since the early '70s and still keep haunting the musical panorama.

***DISCOGRAPHY:* LOGOS** *(1970, Pathé)* **DR. FAUST** *(1971, Pathé)* **HATHOR** *(1973, Atlantic)* **LES FOUS D'OR** *(1975, Emi)* **NAGUAL** *(1977, Emi)* **LET'S START** *(1979, Emi)* – **DONC ...** *(6 CD boxset 1999, Fractal).* M.G. & C.C.

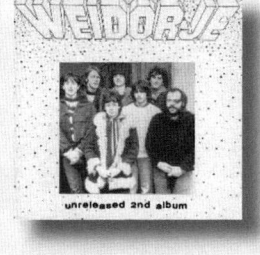

WEIDORJE

Bernard Paganotti - *bass, vocals,* **Patrick Gauthier** - *keyboards,* **Michel Ettori** - *guitar,* **Kirt Rust** - *drums,* **Alain Guillard** - *saxophones,* **Yvon Guillard** - *trumpet, vocals,* **Jean-Philippe Goude** - *keyboards.*

In 1976 former Magma musicians **Bernard Paganotti** and **Patrick Gautier** found a band by recruiting other talented French jazz-rock-zeuhl artists. The ensemble represents the best in talent and creativity and the resulting debut album *Weidorje* of 1978 is stunning and spectacular. It contains only three powerful tracks with obsessive vocals and the perfect union of electronic sounds and horn arrangements, also very close to the style of **Magma**. The track "Elohims Voyage" has a strong bass line and represents one of the highest moments of zeuhl music in the history of prog. Unfortunately they breakup immediately after, in pursuit of other personal projects of their own: **Gauthier** founds **Bebe Godzilla**, **Paganotti** founds **Paga** and **Goude** founds **Drones**.

***DISCOGRAPHY:* WEIDORJE** *(1978, Cobra).* M.G. & C.C.

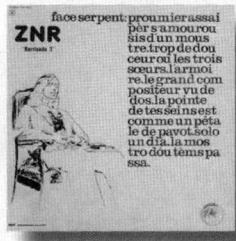

ZNR

Hector Zazou, Joseph Racaille - *various instruments.*

This is a duo who performed mainly in the French venues during the end of '70s, playing a more jazz-experimental avant-garde genre than actual prog. They published only two albums: the first, *Barricade 3* (1976) is difficult to label given the collection of fragments arranged with piano, synthesizers and other keyboards, where the guitars, drums and sax are sometimes inserted. The second *Traitè De Mecanique Populaire* is not far from the previous, but gains in communication and simplicity: classical melodies are mixed with strange hints of dance music for an album of extreme and personalized vision.

***DISCOGRAPHY:* BARRICADE 3** *(Isadora, 1976)* **TRAITE' DE MECANIQUE POPULAIRE** *(Scopa, 1979).* C.A. & C.C.

ANNEXUS QUAM

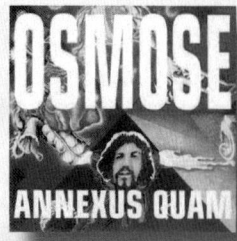

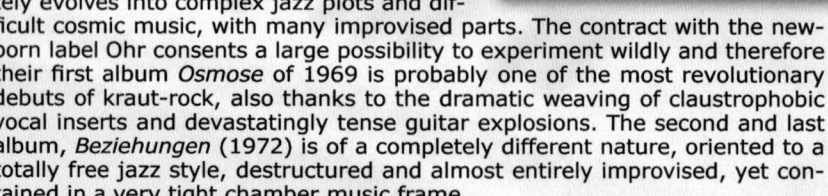

Peter Werner - *guitar, vocals, percussions*, **Uwe Bick** - *vocals, percussions*, **Harald Klemm** - *winds, percussions*, **Jürgen Jonuschies** - *bass, vocals, percussions*, **Werner Hostermann** - *clarinet, vocals, percussions*, **Hans Kämper** - *guitar, vocals, percussions, flute, trumpet*, **Ove Volquartz** - *sax*.

Founded in Dusseldorf in 1967, they start playing a strong psychedelia that immediately evolves into complex jazz plots and difficult cosmic music, with many improvised parts. The contract with the newborn label Ohr consents a large possibility to experiment wildly and therefore their first album *Osmose* of 1969 is probably one of the most revolutionary debuts of kraut-rock, also thanks to the dramatic weaving of claustrophobic vocal inserts and devastatingly tense guitar explosions. The second and last album, *Beziehungen* (1972) is of a completely different nature, oriented to a totally free jazz style, destructured and almost entirely improvised, yet contained in a very tight chamber music frame.

RECOMMENDED RECORDINGS: **OSMOSE** (Ohr, 1970).   M.G. & C.C.

ANYONE'S DAUGHTER

Matthias Ulmer – *keyboards, vocals*, **Harald Bareth** – *vocals, bass*, **Uwe Karpa** – *guitars*, **Kono Konopik** – *drums (until 1981)* **Peter Schmidt** – *drums (since 1981)*.

This is a clear example of bridge-band, linking the '70s to the '80s prog genre. Their first album of 1979 contains complex symphonic songs with fascinating structures sung in English; same for the following work, but resulting very open and elegant with its fusion hints. The third is a concept album rotating around the writings of **Herman Hesse**, with excellent instrumental acoustic parts and some portions narrated in German. Also in German the albums *In Blau* (1982) and *Neu Sterne* (1983). They seem to lose inspiration after a last release and in fact disband until 2000 when they come back with another line-up and with decidedly less interesting works. Excellent instead the live material recorded in 1980-1983 and recently published.

RECOMMENDED RECORDINGS: **ADONIS** (Music Is Intelligence, 1979) **ANYONE'S DAUGHTER** (Music Is Intelligence, 1980).   M.G. & C.C.

BRÖSELMASCHINE

Peter Bursch - *vocals, acoustic guitar, sitar, flute*, **Jenni Schucker** - *vocals, flute, percussions*, **Willi Kismer** - *vocals, guitar, harp*, **Mike Hellbach** - *percussions, mellotron*, **Lutz Ringer** - *bass, percussions*.

This band was born thanks to an intuition of guitarist **Peter Bursh**, who decided to gather in 1967 some good elements coming from the German folk genre. A first homonym album is finally released in 1971 containing thus very interesting forms of folk soaked with the hippie flower power and a use of ethnic instruments from India's traditional music (the sitar and the tabla). The surreal and imaginative lyrics are written especially for the female lead singer **Jenny Shucker** and the compositions couple with a male vocal counter melody. The second side of the album is very different, with two more experimentally acid longer tracks. The other records are not at the same level and are often released under the band name **Peter Bursch Und Die Bröselmaschine**.

RECOMMENDED RECORDINGS: **BRÖSELMASCHINE** (PILZ, 1971). M.G.

Europe: GERMANY

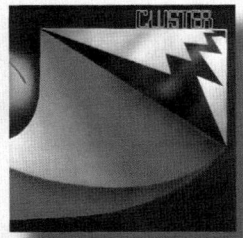

CLUSTER (KLUSTER)

Dieter Moebius, Hans Joachim Roedelius, Conrad Schnitzler - *various instruments, synthesizers, percussion.*

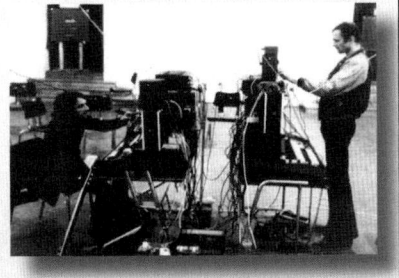

This band was founded by three students of Dusseldorf's Fine Arts Academy in 1969. In 1970 they publish as **Kluster** two albums which place them among the most interesting novelties from Germany: *Klopfzeichen* and *Osterei* reflect the themes of aesthetic improvisation learned

at the Academy. A third album will be published shortly after together with another band called **Eruption**, containing long improvisations recorded live. **Schnitzler** leaves in 1971 and the remaining duo **Moebius-Roedelius** renames the project as **Cluster**, playing ambient music, electronic experimentations and cold sounds. Sometimes their tracks are anguishing and not easy to listen, but their influence on kraut rock and on other German artists to come like **Schulze** and **Kraftwerk** is undeniable.

DISCOGRAPHY: **KLOPFZEICHEN** *(Schwann, 1970)* **OSTEREI** *(Schwann, 1970)* **CLUSTER** *(Philips, 1971)* **CLUSTER II** *(Brain, 1972)* **ZUCKERZEIT** *(Brain, 1974)* **SOWIESOSO** *(Sky, 1976).*

C.A. & C.C.

DZYAN

Reinhard Karwatky - *bass, keyboards,* **Peter Giger** – *drums, percussions,* **Eddy Marron** – *guitar, sitar, saxophones,* **Jochen Leuschner** – *vocals, percussions.*

Born in 1972 as a quintet, the line-up shifts from three to four musicians during their short career, keeping as the unique common element founder **Karwatky**. Though deriving somewhat inspiration from **Mahavishnu Orchestra** or from the Canterbury school, they distinguish their jazz-rock oriented parts for the strong coherence and personality of the more experimental sounds and rhythmic partitions that merge to a particularly

ethnic music, especially from India. It is yet with the second and third album that they truly achieve excellency for certain ideas and the good maturity of their style.

RECOMMENDED RECORDINGS: **TIME MACHINE** *(Bellaphone, 1973)* **ELECTRIC SILENCE** *(Bellaphone, 1975).*

M.G. & C.C.

EPIDAURUS

Christiane Wand, Ekhard Lander - *vocals,* **Günther Henne, Gerd Linke** - *keyboards,* **Heinz Kunert** - *bass,* **Manfred Struck, Voler Oehmig** - *drums,* **Uwe Asshoff** - *guitars.*

In 1977 **La Locanda delle Fate** closes the golden age of the Italian Prog '70s publishing their first album, that will become a cult. In that same year **Epidaurus** did something similar: their first album *Earthly Paradise* will become a German prog cult too: deeply influenced by **Genesis**, **Renaissance** and **Eloy**, they perform a delicate and romantic music. Just like **Locanda delle Fate** they had two talented keyboardists and just like **Renaissance** the lyrics are sung by a female vocalist. Immediately after this debut, the band breaks-up also due to the giant wave of punk and disco that captured the interest of the music labels also in Germany. **Henne**, **Kunert** and **Linke** found another band called **Choice** publishing one album before disappearing. Reunited 15 years later, **Epidaurus** comes back with a brand new album entitled *Endangered*, a disappointing record compared to the previous.

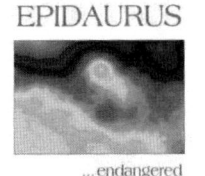

DISCOGRAPHY: EARTHLY PARADISE *(Gema, 1977)* **ENDANGERED** *(Garden Of Delights, 1994).*

M.G. & C.C.

Europe: GERMANY

EULENSPYGEL

Mulo Maulbetsch - *vocals*, **Detlev "Keucher" Nottrodt, Günther Marek** - *guitars*, **Matthias "Till" Thorow** - *guitars, violin*, **Cornelius Hauptmann** - *horns*, **Karlheinz Grosshans** - *keyboards*, **Ronnie Libal, Peter Weber** - *bass*, **Günther Klinger, Peter Garattoni** - *drums*.

Born from the ashes of **Royal Servants**, this is the classic German band politically sided, playing a powerful kraut-rock very close to the RIO movement. Looking like drunk hippies and with a Japanese vocalist (like **Can**), their debut, simply entitled *2*, is one of the first jazz-rock albums in Germany containing an eccentric music of clear **VdGG** hints with mellotron, guitars and horns brilliantly merging together. Their second album of 1972 is a more ambitious project: recorded at the Abbey Road studios in London, it is a strange sort of rock-opera, creatively politicized and eclectic. Disputes with their label and internal discussions among the musicians bring the band to a halt. After seven years they resume their career by publishing another two albums, confirming their intentions of pursuing their stubborn ideas in a very changed world: they struggle for several years until a definitive disbandment in 1984.
DISCOGRAPHY: *2 (Spiegelei 1971)* **AUSSCHUSS** *(Spiegelei 1972)* **EULENSPYGEL** *(Bellaphon 1979)* **LAUT UND DEUTLICHT** *(Neue Welt 1983).* **M.G.**

FRUMPY

Inga Rumpf – *vocals*, **Jean-Jacques Kravetz** – *keyboards*, **Karl-Heinz Schott** – *bass*, **Carsten Bohn** – *drums*, **Rainer Baumann** - *guitars*.

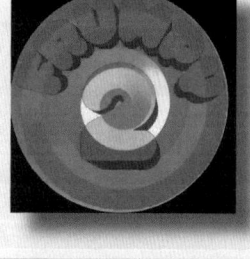

Born from the ashes of the German '60s folk-blues band **City Preachers** when French **Jean Jaques Kravetz** decides to join in with his very personal keyboard playing, also changing their name. Two are in fact the unmistakably recognizable elements of their sound: first, as mentioned, the keyboards ranging from blues, to classical and symphonic or developing around particular acid melodies which merged to certain effects and guitar solos that together with the strong rhythmic base created a very involving jazz-rock. Secondly **Inga Rumpf**, an almost a masculine lead voice, talented singer endowed with a powerful flexibility. Among the few of albums, their debut *All Will Be Changed* is very good, yet probably *Frumpy 2* reaches their highest with its four long and unforgettable tracks
RECOMMENDED RECORDINGS: **ALL WILL BE CHANGED** *(Philips 1970)* **FRUMPY 2** *(Philips, 1972).* **M.G. & C.C.**

GILA

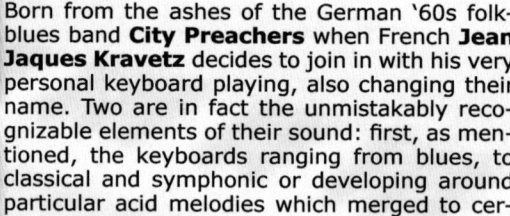

Conny Veidt – *guitar, percussions, vocals, sound effects*, **Daniel Alluno** – *drums, percussions*, **Fritz Scheyhing** – *keyboards, percussions, sound effects*, **Walter Wiederkehr** – *bass*.
Born in 1969 this band from Stuttgart was among the first to experiment kraut themes and the cosmic space genre oriented towards a more psychedelic sound. The band lived in a hippy community and they reflected this life style also in their musicality through very long jams and impros. The label BASF signed them up for a first LP in 1971, rich of various instruments yet obtaining a very balanced result. The ever present organ and the spacey guitars often run into or after more ethnic sounds, simulating the sitar for example. Some **Pink Floyd** echoes appear, but the great personality of this band remains predominant. A second album follows two years later featuring only **Veidt**, with **Fricke** and **Fichelscher** from **Popol Vuh** playing as if it where more their album than one of **Gila**.

RECOMMENDED RECORDINGS: **GILA - FREE ELECTRIC SOUND** *(BASF, 1971)* **BURY MY HEART AT WOUNDED KNEE** *(Warner, 1973).* **M.G. & C.C.**

Europe: **GERMANY**

GOMORRHA

Helmut Pohl – *drums, flute,* **Ali Claudi** – *guitar, vocals,* **Eberhard Krietsch** – *keyboards, bass, vocals,* **Ad Ochel** – *guitars, vocals, vibes,* **Peter Otten** – *lead vocals,* **Mike Eulner** - *bass (since 1972).*
This band is the hard psychedelic soul of kraut-rock, where the typical American west-coast style transpires from every track. The first homonym album was a partially home-made recording together with the help of the minor label Cornet. When BASF finally signs them up they decide to re-record their debut entitling it *Trauma* (1971), due to the poor quality of the previous release and adding some songs in English. This project had a double personality: psychedelic-pop in the shorter songs while experimental kraut space dominated the long title track, a very interesting piece born from the collaboration of **Conrad Plank**. The following year they change label and record a new good hard-rock album of psychedelic and experimental inclinations. Then they simply disappear.

RECOMMENDED RECORDINGS: **TRAUMA** *(BASF, 1971)* **I TURNED TO SEE WHOSE VOICE IT WAS** *(Brain, 1972).* M.G. & C.C.

M.L. BONGERS PROJECT

Marcel L. Bongers - *vocals,* **J. Georg Kobeck** - *keyboards,* **Joe Grande** - *guitar,* **Jacques Thysen** - *bass, guitar,* **Günter Heinz** - *drums, percussion.*
A shady band, among the minor artists of kraut-rock, who published an album *Pacific Prison* in 1978 (the years when punk and disco flogged Europe) conceived more as fantastic soundtrack to an imaginary movie than as a true music compilation: although the quality was seriously compromised by the average production, a halo of mystery surrounds this band and helped them gain a satisfying role in the kraut-rock music panorama. Full of the typical elements of German symphonic rock, the delicate flute perfectly interlaces with the keyboards playing compelling melodies that result in a smooth and well balanced sound that manages to capture the imagination. Recently issued on CD, the original LP is a collectors' item.
DISCOGRAPHY : PACIFIC PRISON *(Private Pressing, 1978).* C.A. & C.C.

MAMMUT

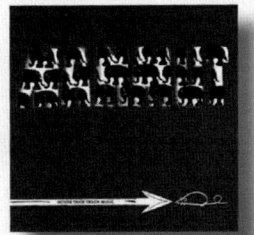

Klaus Schnur, Peter Schnur - *vocals, lead guitar,* **Rainer Hoffmann** - *piano, organ,* **Tilo Herrmann** - *bass, flute, backing vocals,* **Gunter Seier** - *drums, percussion.*
Born from the union of **The Rope Set** and **Those**, they began playing in the Stuttgart jazz-rock panorama, later mixing this experience with a harder type of rock, closer to **Deep Purple**'s style with results comparable to **Embryo** and **Amon Düül**. Their sound recalls **Canned Heat, Tomorrow's Gift** and **Frumpy** for a one shot album that is an excellent example of German prog, although damaged by the approximate production of the label Orschwall, who printed only a small quantity of copies, making it almost impossible to find. It was therefore reissued and distributed under another label, yet the band disappeared immediately after the last copy was sold.

DISCOGRAPHY: MAMMUT *(Orschwahl, 1971).* M.G. & C.C.

Europe: GERMANY

MINOTAURUS

Peter Scheu - *vocals*, **Lucky Hofstetter, Micky Helsberg** - *guitars*, **Dietmar Barzen** - *keyboards*, **Bernd Maciej** - *bass*, **Ulli Poetschulat** - *drums*.

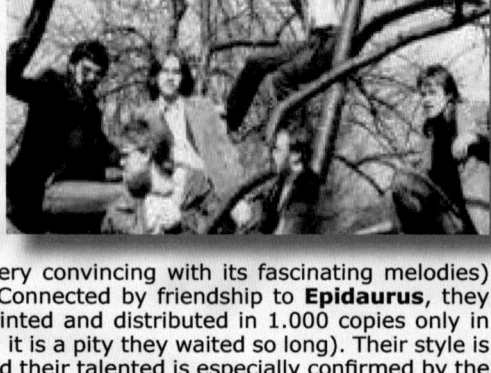

During a time when the music storm of change was turning the attention to more ancestral beats, between 1976 and 1977 a bunch of progsters took harbor in pursuing a resistance of the prog-rock genre. **Minotaurus** was one of these and as many others, they too release a prog album (average yet very convincing with its fascinating melodies) before disappearing into darkness the following year. Connected by friendship to **Epidaurus**, they shared the same studio and self produce *Fly Away*, printed and distributed in 1.000 copies only in 1978 (considering they were active since the early '70s, it is a pity they waited so long). Their style is deeply marked by **Genesis, Yes** and **King Crimson** and their talented is especially confirmed by the powerful live performances of tracks like "7117", where they play with Kubrick film images projected on their backs.

DISCOGRAPHY: FLY AWAY (Minotaurus 1978).   M.G. & C.C.

MYTHOS

Harald Weisse - *bass*, **Eberhard Hildebrand** - *drums*, **Stephan Kaske** - *flute, guitar, vocals, keyboards*.

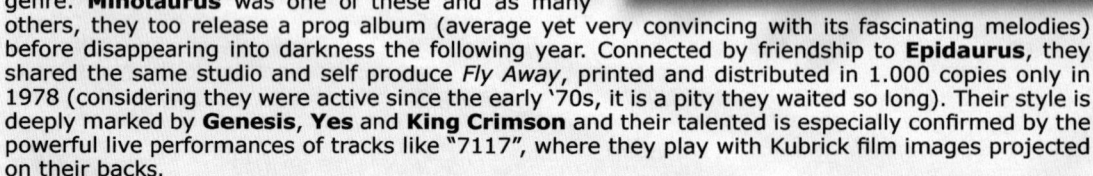

A band from Berlin founded at the end of the '60s playing classic kraut-rock mixed with space music and exotic atmospheres. In fact their first two albums *Mythos* and *Dreamlab* are very interesting and pleasant. An outstanding flute is well supported by the other instruments recalling some **Jethro Tull** moments. The stylistic evolution

of this band goes from electronic to hard rock: the large use of synthesizers contributes to create new dimensions to their music. The fourth album *Concrete city* of 1979, although appreciated in the underground scenes, is deeply influenced by the new contemporary sounds while their last recording, *Quasar* of the following year, opens the door to the dominating new wave.

DISCOGRAPHY: MYTHOS (Ohr, 1972) **DREAMLAB** (Kosmische Music, 1975) **STRANGE GUYS** (Venus, 1978) **CONCRETE CITY** (Venus, 1979) **QUASAR** (Sky, 1980).   C.A. & C.C.

MY SOLID GROUND

Bernhard Rendel - *guitar, vocals*, **Karl-Heinrich Dorfler** - *bass, vocals*, **Andreas Wurshing** - *drums*, **Ingo Werner** - *keyboards*.

Another one shot band who released their self titled album in 1971 becoming a respected reality of kraut-rock. Inspired by space music and psychedelic rock, they mingle with mastery other musical influences coming from the roots of rock'n'roll. The vocal parts are wonderful and evoke acid atmospheres sustained by a steady bass; the guitar solos play like gems inserted into the crowning piano and layers of keyboards, sometimes resounding like thunder over apocalyptic scenes. The track "Dirty Yellow Mist" is a valid example to understand how deep and complex their music is, while other moments are more rough and simple achieving a pleasant and never trivial result. Their album was censored for a while because of the pig's genitals on the front cover.

DISCOGRAPHY: MY SOLID GROUND (Bacillus, 1971).   C.A. & C.C.

Europe: GERMANY

THOMAS NATSCHINSKI

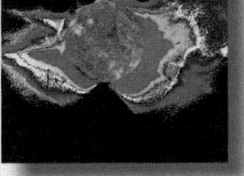

Almost unknown to Europe and in the rest of Germany, **Natschinski** is a strange character of the German prog panorama: son of musicians and talented pianist, he suffered the unlucky situation of East Germany's economic policy and the poor life of his many fellow citizens during '60s and '70s. However he was capable of assimilating the contemporary British beat genre into his band **Team 4** which he later renames **Thomas Natschinsky und seine gruppe**. Starting from a revision of beat adapted for a German palate, he slightly develops his project approaching prog-rock. In fact the third and last album *Wir Uber Uns* of 1972 is probably the best of his career, where good easy listening melodies highlight the excellent piano performances and give birth to pleasant psychedelic-pop songs. From 1981 to 1984 he played the keyboards in the famous East German rock band **Karat**. Today he is still active and appreciated as a songwriter and composer.

***DISCOGRAPHY:* DIE STRASSE** *(Amiga, 1968)* **GESCHICHTEN** *(Amiga, 1970)* **WIR UBER UNS** *(Amiga, 1972).*

C.A. & C.C.

PARZIVAL

Lothar Siems - *guitar, vocals,* **Thomas Olivier** - *drums,* **Walter Quintus** - *violin, bass, organ, piano,* **Walter von Seydlitz** - *cello.*

Parzival is one of the rare German band not involved in kraut-rock, but oriented toward a strange form of folk and very soft progressive rock, with sounds of ancient medieval music. They published only two albums at the beginning of the '70s entitled *Legend* and *Barock*. The first is probably their best and the most genuine: the sound is elegant and balanced with delicate symphonic touches that create these medieval atmospheres. Sometimes the sound becomes dark, like a journey into the past among the old castles of Bavaria. The choice to give a predominant acoustic sound to everything is without a doubt very brave, making *Legend* one of the best albums of this genre. The second record *Barock* is an attempt to mix the good results of the previous to a more commercial and rock oriented music, but fails to achieve the same appreciation. Maybe this interesting experiment should have been developed more but unfortunately the fascinating ensemble disbands shortly after this failure.

***DISCOGRAPHY:* LEGEND** *(Telefunken, 1971)* **BAROCK** *(Telefunken, 1973).*

C.A. & C.C.

SFF

Eduard Schicke - *drums, percussion,* **Gerhard Führs** - *piano, keyboards,* **Heinz Fröhling** - *bass, guitars, keyboards.*

After the disbanding of **Spektakel**, their former drummer **Schicke** and bass player **Fröhling** meet keyboardist **Führs** and decide to found the trio **SFF**, a wonderful band that finds its place in Germany's prog history with important works of fine symphonic rock. Their sound owes much to a large use of moog, mellotron and the overwhelming keyboards that builds particular song structures and original atmospheres. The debut of 1976 entitled *Symphonic Pictures* is probably the best of their albums and will most certainly inspire future bands like **Änglagård** twenty years later. The following two albums are also wonderful although not at the same level. Once disbanded, **Führs** and **Fröhling** found a duo publishing another two less interesting albums.

***DISCOGRAPHY:* SYMPHONIC PICTURES** *(1976, Brain)* **SUNBURST** *(1977, Brain)* **TICKET TO EVERYWHERE** *(1978, Brain).*

M.G. & C.C.

Europe: GERMANY

THIRSTY MOON

Jürgen Drogies - *guitar, percussion,* **Norbert Drogies** - *drums, percussion,* **Michael Kobs** - *electric piano,* **Harald Konietzko** - *bass, 12 string guitar, percussion, vocals,* **Erwin Noack** - *congas, percussion,* **Willi Pape** - *sax, clarinet, flute, percussion,* **Hans Werner Ranwig** - *organ, percussion, vocals.*

Before this band from Bremen descends into the wells of a more pop funky dance genre, they manage to record two excellent albums of a personal and elegant jazz-rock, with apparently simple plots which are actually very complex and well composed. They begin at the end of the '60s and after several years sign up with the label Brain for a good first homonym album in 1972 ("Big City" and "Love me"). Their sound is a jazzy inspired American rock, rich of woodwinds and rhythmic balances merged brilliantly with the experimental German kraut themes. Better, more complex and mature, the following *You'll Never Come Back*, with the amazing avant-garde title track and its excellent Fender piano.

RECOMMENDED RECORDINGS: **THIRSTY MOON** *(Brain, 1972),* **YOU'LL NEVER COME BACK** *(Brain, 1973).*   M.G. & C.C.

TOMORROW'S GIFT

Bernd Kiefer - *bass,* **Ellen Meyer** - *vocals,* **Gerd Paetzke** - *drums,* **Manfred Rürup** - *keyboards,* **Wolfgang Trescher** - *flute,* **Jochen Petersen** - *saxophones,* **Carlo Karges** - *guitar.*

They begin by playing blues an R&B in small clubs until the release of a first homonym record published as double album in 1971, a rarity for a debut band. Their music is deeply influenced by **Curved Air** although they still manage to remain faithful to their blues-rock past. Very appreciated for their original solutions, they were nevertheless strongly criticized by the press for the approximate English singing of their female vocalist **Ellen Meyer**. Few months after this first album they disband and reunite again the following year with a renewed line-up and some new ideas. The efforts bring to the recording in 1972 of a new album *Goodbye Future*, far from the previous style, now based upon the heavy use of keyboards and oriented toward a sophisticated jazz-rock. This second life ends briefly after and some of the former musicians start a new chapter called **Release Music Orchestra**.

DISCOGRAPHY: **TOMORROW'S GIFT** *(Plus, 1971)* **GOODBYE FUTURE** *(Spiegelei, 1972).*   C.A. & C.C.

TROYA

Elmar Wegmann - *guitar, flute, vocals,* **Klaus Pannewig** - *drums, vocals,* **Wilhelm Weischer** - *bass,* **Peter Savelsberg** - *keyboards.*

One of the less known bands of German prog, they release only one album in 1976 entitled *Point of Eruption*. This is a volcanic example of symphonic rock, in the wake of certain other German colleagues like **Jane**, **Mammut** and **Wallenstein**: rich of rhythmic changes, it contains large instrumental partitions where the sharp lead guitars and the compelling flutes are supported by an intense and strong keyboard layer. The romantic component is crowned by good vocal melodies and the final result is an album of brilliant ideas yet unfortunately affected by the poor production and approximate recording.

DISCOGRAPHY: **POINT OF ERUPTION** *(1976 Troya/Förderturm Records).*   M.G. & C.C.

Europe: GERMANY

TWENTY SIXTY SIX & THEN

Geff Harrison – *lead vocals*, **Gagey Mrozeck** – *guitars*, **Veit Marvos** – *keyboards*, **Dieter Bauer** – *bass*, **Steve Robinson** – *keyboards*, **Konstantin Bommarius** – *drums*, **Wolfgang Schönbrot** – *flute*, **Curt Cress** – *second drums*.

Born from the collaboration of very talented musicians at the end of 1971, their only album results as an intense and intriguing prog genre, full of waves rich in pathos and loaded by **Harrison**'s descriptive voice. Very fascinating the keyboard playing of **Marvos**, not just as simple accompaniment but being a true focal point in competition with the heavier guitar of **Mrozeck**. The themes are nostalgic and sad, sometimes explosive too as in the unforgettable song "Autum" or in the long title track "Reflections on the Future". The clarity of ideas and the expressiveness of the compositions prove their maturity, yet unfortunately the insufficient commercial success reduced them to a one-shot band that lived only in the span of one lonely album.

RECOMMENDED RECORDINGS: REFLECTIONS ON THE FUTURE *(United Artist, 1972)*.

M.G. & C.C.

ACHIM REICHEL'S MACHINES

Achim Reichel is a very inspired musician who at first begins creating the beat band Rattles and gaining great popularity in Germany. Following his artistic calling he merges into the kraut-rock spirit of the early '70s and leaves his contribution through the album *Die Grüne Reise* of

1971: the musicians that play here are personally picked by him and gathered under the name **The Machines**, who will become his backing band. His previous psychedelic ideas develop into a more mature and dreamy music, full of oriental philosophy and hypnotic experiences in perfect syntony with the contemporary hippie's movement. **Achim Reichel's Machines** influence some very famous bands like **Kraftwerk** and **Tangerine Dream** and it is a pity that after this beautiful album he closes his prog exploration in favour of more traditional folk music revisited according to his personal taste yet using and modern solutions.

RECOMMENDED RECORDINGS: DIE GRÜNE REISE *(Polydor, 1971)*. C.A.

WALPURGIS

Jürgen Dollase – *keyboards*, **Jerzy Sokolowski** - *guitar, vocals*, **Manfred Stadelmann** - *drums, vocals*, **Ryszard Kalemba** – *guitar*, **George Fruchtenicht** – *bass*, **Jan Sundermeyer** - *congas, flute*.

Among the most famous beacons of the kraut-rock movement (**Wallenstein**, **Cosmic Jokers**), **Jurgen Dollase** began his compositional and band experience with **Walpurgis**, an ensemble born in the early '70s from a blend of Polish and German artists who were playing more experimental concepts than the typical kraut, marrying the ideas of a **Pink Floyd** kind of prog and with evident references to the American psychedelia of **Grateful Dead**. An incisive and rough music that developed with a space attitude through slow and dreamy moments that plunged into the **Hendrix** acidity of guitars that lingered on expanding melodies in the best **Gilmour** style. The percussions marked the rhythmic section also using more ethnic instruments that supported the almost infinite organ chords.

RECOMMENDED RECORDINGS: QUEEN OF SABA *(Ohr, 1972)*.

M.G. & C.C.

Europe: GERMANY

WANIYETULA

Heinz Kuhne - *guitars*, **Hermann Beckert** - *bass*, **Thomas Goerdten** - *drums*, **Norbert Abels** - *keyboards*.

This particular German band has a weird and singular history: founded at the end of '60s they are forced to release their debut album *Nature's Clear Well* in 1978 (recorded in 1975) under the name **Galaxy** because their real name was rejected by the record label. The following years of their career the band pursues its dream of writing a rock opera inspired by **Edgar Allan Poe**'s novels, but due to numerous internal disagreements or to simple delays on their schedule, *A Dream Within A Dream* is released only in 1983. The sound proposed by **Waniyetula** is sometimes very researched, impressing with its refined, romantic atmospheres and for the majestic impact inspired by **Yes**. Sometimes the songs seem slightly tending toward New Wave, but like other existing concept albums, it must be considered in its whole.

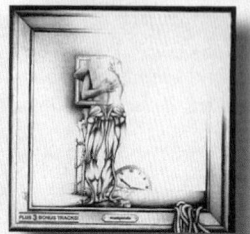

DISCOGRAPHY: NATURE'S CLEAR WELL (Import Records, 1978 as GALAXY) **A DREAM WITHIN A DREAM** (Klangkunst, 1983). **C.A. & C.C.**

WIND

Steve Leistner - *vocals, harmonica, flute, percussion*, **Thomas Leidenberger** - *guitars, vocals*, **Andreas Büeler** - *bass, vocals*, **Lucian Büeler** - *organ, piano, vocals, percussion*, **Lucky Schmidt** - *drums, percussion, vibes, clavinet, piano*.

This band is often described as part of the kraut-rock genre yet they are actually more inspired by the sound of American west coast bands like **The Grateful Dead**. Founded in the early '70s, their first album *Seasons*, published in 1971, is an absolutely marvelous manifesto of the rising psychedelic prog of those years, in this case also close to **Pink Floyd**'s *A Saucerful Of Secrets* with background vocals stolen from the early **King Crimson**. The next album of 1973 is entitled *Morning*. Very distant from the previous successes, it is more of a collection of boring short tracks, far from the fantasy and inventiveness of their beginnings. Of course they break-up and drummer **Lucky Schmidt** joins the band **Aera**.

DISCOGRAPHY: SEASONS (Plus, 1971) **MORNING** (CBS, 1973). **C.A. & C.C.**

VIRUS

Werner Monka - *guitar*, **Jorg-Dieter Krahe** - *organ*, **Bernd "Molle" Hohmann** - *vocals, flute*, **Reinhold Spiegelfeld** - *bass*, **Wolfgang Rieke** - *drums*.

From Bielefeld, a village in the North of Germany, they are among the psychedelic ramifications of kraut-rock, recording two albums in their short career. The first, *Revelation* of 1970, recalls the cosmic sounds of the early **Pink Floyd**, reinforced by compelling keyboards and powerful guitars. The dreamy track "Endless Game" is a small masterpiece of psychedelia with excellent vocal parts inspired by **Traffic**. The album also contains a rearranged cover version of **The Rolling Stones**' "Paint it Black" in a slightly more acid key. Their last recording is published the following year, after many line-up changes: the space atmospheres are by now forgotten and *Thoughts* becomes more concrete in its vigorous minimalist hard rock with songs deeply influenced by **Uriah Heep**.

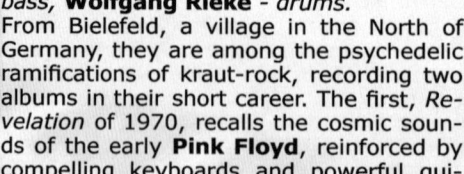

DISCOGRAPHY: REVELATION (BASF, 1970) **THOUGHTS** (Pilz, 1971). **C.A.**

Europe: GERMANY

XHOL

Tim Belbe, Hansi Fischer - *horns.* **Jammie Rhodes, Ronnie Swinson** - *vocals,* **Werner Funk** - *guitars,* **Klaus Briest** - *bass,* **Gerhard "Öcki" Von Brevern** - *keyboards,* **Gilbert "Skip" Van Wyck III** - *drums.*

Like for **Colosseum** and **Showmen**, this band is one of the best synthesis of the transition from rhythm & blues to a more composite jazz-rock. In the mid '60s their eccentric horn section, composed by **Tim Belbe** and **Hansi Fischer**, found the r&b duo **Soul Caravan** for the album *Get In High*. With the hippie movement they transform into **Xhol Caravan** and in 1969 release the epic *Electrip*: opened by the noise of a toilet-flush, this record brings for the first time to Germany certain vivid and eclectic sounds between **Zappa**, psychedelia, **Chicago** and rock-jazz. Crazy also during their live acts, they are the true pioneers of this new German rock. When **Fischer** joins **Embryo**, they become **Xhol** and publish *Hau-RUK* with its great electric jazz improvisations. Their last formidable album will collect some unpublished material dating from the '70s.

DISCOGRAPHY: Soul Caravan: GET IN HIGH (CBS 1967) **Xhol Caravan: ELECTRIP** (Hansa 1969) **Xhol: HAU-RUK** (Ohr 1970) **MOTHERFUCKERS G.M.B.H. & CO KG** (Ohr 1972).

M.G. & C.C.

YATHA SIDRA

Rolf Fichter - *keyboards, flute, electric piano, acoustic guitar, vocals,* **Klaus Fichter** - *drums, percussion,* **Matthias Nicolai** - *guitars, bass,* **Peter Elbracht** - *flute.*

Among the most important members of the German cosmic scene, they tend to mix the ethereal spirituality of **Popol Vuh** with the sensual temptations of oriental music. Their only album of 1974, *A Meditation Mass*, is a great example of contamination without boundaries in which elements of prog, psychedelia, classical music, jazz and folk lead the mind to wander lightly through day-dreams and emotions. Structured as one suite divided into four parts, it mystically fascinates from the opening to the finale with particularly intriguing blends of electronic sounds, keyboards, acoustic flute melodies, guitars and percussions.

DISCOGRAPHY: A MEDITATION MASS (1974, Brain).

M.G. & C.C.

ZARATHUSTRA

Ernst Zerzner - *vocals,* **Wolfgang Reimer** - *guitars, vocals, percussion,* **Michael Just** - *bass, vocals,* **Klaus Werner** - *organ,* **Wolfgang Behrmann** - *drums, percussion.*

Despite the name, this band from Hamburg has nothing to do with Nietzsche's philosophy, being one of the most powerful groups of the dark kraut-rock movement. Like many bands of this period, they are deeply influenced by the hard and essential sounds of **Uriah Heep**, **Atomic Rooster** and **Deep Purple** rich in keyboards and guitar solos: it is not a mistake, in these cases, to consider labeling them as heavy-prog. Their only recording, *Zarathustra*, is published in 1971 and is a clear example of this sub-genre. **Klaus Werner**'s keyboards stand out perfectly and blend beautifully with **Ernst Herzner**'s voice, while the rhythmic base provides a valuable support; The album is today a very rare item in its original version and has recently been released on CD.

DISCOGRAPHY: ZARATHUSTRA (Metronome, 1971).

C.A. & C.C.

Europe: GREAT BRITAIN

ARGENT

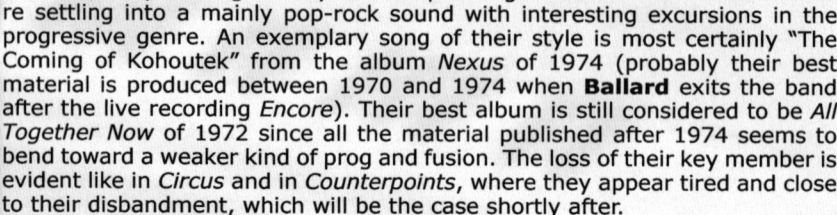

Rod Argent – *vocals, keyboards,* **Mac MacLeod** – *bass,* **Jim Rodford** – *bass,* **Chris White** – *bass,* **Robert Henrit** – *drums,* **Russ Ballard** – *vocals, guitar, keyboards,* **John Verity** – *guitar, vocals,* **John Grimaldi** - *guitars.*

Founded in 1968 by **Rod Argent**, former **The Zombies** member, they undergo many a line-up change before settling into a mainly pop-rock sound with interesting excursions in the progressive genre. An exemplary song of their style is most certainly "The Coming of Kohoutek" from the album *Nexus* of 1974 (probably their best material is produced between 1970 and 1974 when **Ballard** exits the band after the live recording *Encore*). Their best album is still considered to be *All Together Now* of 1972 since all the material published after 1974 seems to bend toward a weaker kind of prog and fusion. The loss of their key member is evident like in *Circus* and in *Counterpoints*, where they appear tired and close to their disbandment, which will be the case shortly after.

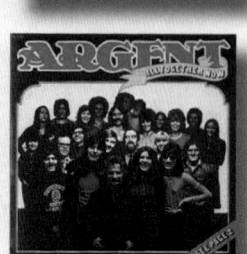

RECOMMENDED RECORDINGS: **ARGENT** *(Epic, 1970)* **RING OF HANDS** *(Epic, 1971)* **ALL TOGETHER NOW** *(Epic, 1972)* **IN DEEP** *(Epic, 1973)* **NEXUS** *(Epic, 1974)* **ENCORE: LIVE IN CONCERT** *(Epic, 1974).* **M.G**

ASIA

Geoff Downes – *keyboards,* **John Wetton** – *bass, vocals,* **Carl Palmer** – *drums,* **Steve Howe** – *guitars.*

The fact that at the end of 1980 the four original members all came from four major bands (**King Crimson, Yes, UK, ELP**) made this the superband of super bands. They take over a form of AOR pop-prog only partially close to the true progressive genre, and release a first album in 1981 containing simple songs, even though full of prog fiddle-fuddles. The second work consolidated these themes but after its release the band starts changing its line-up: only *Downes* will remain for the next recordings until in 2008 the original founders reunite for the album *Phoenix*. The market's renewed interest brings them to hold a new world wide tour and to the subsequent studio-albums *Omega* (2010) and *XXX* (2012). *Wetton* death in 2017 closes their career definitively.

RECOMMENDED RECORDINGS: **ASIA** *(Geffen, 1981)* **ARENA** *(Bullet Proof, 1996)* **AURA** *(Spitfire, 2001)* **PHOENIX** *(Frontiers/EMI, 2008).* **M.G. & C.C.**

ATOMIC ROOSTER

Vincent Crane - *keyboards, vocals,* **Carl Palmer, Paul Hammond, Ric Parnell, Preston Hayman** - *drums,* **John DuCann, Steve Bolton, Johnny Mandala** - *guitars,* **Nick Graham** - *bass,* **Peter French, Chris Farlowe** - *vocals.*

Even if considered as a minor group, they still played a role in the definition of prog-rock. When the band **Crazy World Of Arthur Brown** collapsed, former keyboardist **Vincent Crane** decides to create a solid power trio with young **Carl Palmer** and **Nick Graham**, for the recording of a debut where the Hammond was a clear protagonist. After this successful beginning, they are joined by guitarist **DuCann** from **Andromeda** for the following albums *Death Walks Behind You*, a jewel of sepulchral rough hard-prog, and *In Hearing Of*. The rest of their production is characterized by the incorporation of a lead singer, **Chris Farlowe**, and the compositions adapt in becoming less dramatic in favor of groove and melody. The unmistakable Hammond organ playing of **Vincent Crane** dies with him in 1989 ascending to immortality.

RECOMMENDED RECORDINGS: **ATOMIC ROOSTER** *(B&C, 1970)* **DEATH WALKS BEHIND YOU** *(Elektra, 1971)* **IN HEARING OF ATOMIC ROOSTER** *(Elektra, 1972),* **HEADLINE NEWS** *(Towerbell, 1983).* **M.G. & C.C.**

Europe: GREAT BRITAIN

AUDIENCE

Howard Werth - *guitars, vocals,* **Trevor Williams** - *bass, vocals,* **Keith Gemmell** - *saxophones, clarinet, flute,* **Tony Connor** – *drums, percussion,* **Patrick Neubergh** – *saxophones,* **Nick Judd** - *keyboards,* **John Fisher** – *drums (since 2005).*

Not exactly a true prog band, they incorporate many of the typical elements of the genre and are still loved as a cult by progsters around the world. The voice of their singer vaguely resembles **Peter Hammill**'s and the horn section is probably their main feature as in the albums *Friend's Friend's Friend* and *House On The Hill*. "Raid", "Jackdaw" and "Priestess" are three classics from this band, songs of great quality which give great space to the engaging instrumental parts. They end a first phase of their career in 1972 with the concept-album *Lunch*, an interesting project yet unsuccessful from a sale's point of view. They broke-up for more than three decades to reunite in 2005 for the joy of their fans.

RECOMMENDED RECORDINGS: **AUDIENCE** *(1969, Polydor)* **FRIEND'S FRIEND'S FRIEND** *(1970, Carisma)* **HOUSE ON THE HILL** *(1971, Charisma)* **LUNCH** *(1972, Charisma).*

M.G. & C.C.

BARCLAY JAMES HARVEST

John Lees – *vocals, guitars,* **Les Holroyd** – *vocals, bass, guitars, keyboards,* **Stuart Wolstenholme** – *vocals, keyboards,* **Mel Pritchard** – *drums.*

A particular prolific discography for these English gentlemen considered as one of the most important prog bands of the '70s. Not very cerebral or intellectually researched, they opt for a more cheesy and melodic sound full of orchestral arrangements adorned with pathos and great fugues, harps and very powerful vocals. Very famous in Germany, the success was such to regard it as their second country, their style manages to contaminate all of Eastern Europe. After a series of particular fascinating albums (*Barclay James Harvest*, *Once Again*, *Barclay James Harvest and Other Short Stories*, *Baby James Harvest*, *Time Honoured Ghosts*, *Octoberon*), their musical importance diminishes through the years into a weak shadow of their glorious past.

RECOMMENDED RECORDINGS: **BARCLAY JAMES HARVEST** *(Harvest, 1970)* **ONCE AGAIN** *(Harvest, 1971)* **BABY JAMES HARVEST** *(Harvest, 1972).*

M.G. & C.C.

BEGGARS OPERA

Martin Griffiths - *vocals,* **Alan Park** - *keyboards,* **Ricky Gardener** - *guitar, vocals,* **Marshall Erskine** - *bass, horns,* **Virginia Scott** - *keyboards,* **Raymond Wilson** - *drums,* **Colin Fairley** - *drums,* **Linnie Peterson** - *vocals,* **Gordon Seller** - *bass,* **Clem Cattini** - *drums.*

This Scottish band debuts with *Act One*, an album which contains a bit of all the exaggerations typical of Baroque Prog, with its continuous recalling of songs from classical operas, re-adapting them in a rock key (**Bach**, **Grieg**, **Mozart**, **Rossini** and more). It is a beautiful record with good intuitions, but inevitably labeled as kitsch. Their second work is even better than the first: *Waters Of Change* focuses on a symphonic rock where the keyboards are played swiftly and with great technique elaborating very dreamy atmospheres. All the following works still contain good ideas (especially *Pathfinder*) but progressively decreases in quality.

DISCOGRAPHY: **ACT ONE** *(1970, Vertigo)* **WATERS OF CHANGE** *(1971, Vertigo)* **PATHFINDER** *(1972, Vertigo)* **GET YOUR DOG OFF ME** *(1973, Vertigo)* **SAGITTARY** *(1974, Jupiter Records)* **BEGGAR'S CAN'T BE CHOOSERS** *(1979, Jupiter Records)* **LIFELINE** *(1980, Vertigo)* **THE FINAL CURTAIN** *(1996, Scratch).*

M.G. & C.C.

Europe: GREAT BRITAIN

BLACK WIDOW

Jim Gannon, John Culley - *guitars,* **Jess "Zoot" Taylor** - *keyboards,* **Kip Trevor, Rick E, Kay Garret** - *vocals,* **Clive Jones** - *horns,* **Bob Bond, Jeff Griffith** - *bass,* **Clive Box, Romeo Challenger** - *drums.*

In 2002 **Ozzy Osbourne** declared that with **Black Sabbath** <<*we couldn't conjure up a fart*>>. Well, **Black Widow** was the real thing! Their rock-theater brought on scene sacrifices and acts of black magic with a music meant to be the clear antithesis to a smiling flower-power utopia, like in the famous song "Come To The Sabbath". Born on the smokey ashes of **Pesky Gee**, this sinister band delivers three beautiful albums in the early '70s (plus one, recorded in 1972 but released only in 1997) before re-plunging into darkness. **Black Widow** is the definition of a cult-band, at the point of inspiring a famous Italian label to wear the same name: this record label from Genoa is responsible for publishing the posthumous recording of their fourth album and for the recovery of the very first version of *Sacrifice* (entitling it *Return To The Sabbath*), with **Kay Garret**'s voice singing all the songs before she decides to abandon the project.

DISCOGRAPHY: **SACRIFICE** *(CBS, 1970)* **BLACK WIDOW** *(CBS, 1970)* **III** *(CBS, 1971)* **IV** *(1972, LP Postumo: Black Widow, CD: Mystic Records, 1997)* **RETURN TO THE SABBATH (Sacrifice)** *(LP: Black Widow, CD: Mystic Records, 1997).*   M.G. & C.C.

BLOSSOM TOES

Brian Belshaw - *bass, vocals,* **Jim Cregan** - *guitars, vocals,* **Brian Godding** - *lead guitar, piano,* **Poli Palmer** - *drums,* **Barry Reeves** - *drums,* **Shawn Phillips** - *12 strings guitar.*

Blossom Toes are an invention of producer **Giorgio Gomelsky** (who molded them since their birth as **Ingoes**) who directed them toward the rising sun of British psychedelia in the second half of the '60s. Their first album *We Are Ever So Clean* (in Italy released as *The Psychedelic Sound Of Blossom Toes*) is certainly more sincere and fresh, showing how they overcame the clichés of the British beat phenomenon, managing to penetrate the universe of sounds that the new heir of Sgt. Pepper's Pop was producing. The following work, *If only for a moment*, is always driven by the winds of a very accentuated psychedelia, but with the tendency to stand on a minimal and dynamic hard rock. The 70's were dawning and also due to economic reasons, the label Marmalade does not renew their contract and the group splits. We will find the musicians later engaged as session men in various groups of the progressive British epic.

DISCOGRAPHY: **WE ARE EVER SO CLEAN** *(Marmalade, 1967)* **IF ONLY FOR A MOMENT** *(Marmalade, 1969).*   C.A. & C.C.

BRAND X

John Goodsall - *guitar,* **Percy Jones, John Giblin** - *bass,* **Robin Lumley, Peter Robinson, Frank Pusch** - *keyboards,* **Phil Collins, Kenwood Dennard, Chuck Burgi, Michael Clark, Steve Short, Frank Katz** - *drums,* **Morris Pert, Ronnie Ciago** - *percussion,* **Raf Ravenscroft, Danny Wilding** - *horns,* **Marc Wagnon** - *keyboards, vibes.*

This band is famous for having hosted **Phil Collins** as their drummer for a while, and the albums he appears in are often used by the **Genesis** die-hard fans to prove the talent of their idol. Yet **Brand X**'s role in London's music panorama was far more important: in *Unhortodox Behaviour, Moroccan Roll* and *Livestock* jazz-rock and prog have very thin boundaries, revealing how the liquidity of electric jazz and art-rock architectures can coexist. Their last work under this name is the tech-fusion album *X Communication*, then **Brand X** spins off into a band called **Tunnels**, where **Percy Jones** and **John Goodsall** continue their lead. In 2016 the old name reappears with a surprise line-up that sees **Chris Clark** on the keyboards and **Scott Weinberger** on the drums for an all new **Brand X** tour.

RECOMMENDED RECORDINGS: **UNHORTODOX BEHAVIOUR** *(Charisma, 1976)* **MOROCCAN ROLL** *(Charisma, 1977)* **LIVESTOCK** *(live, Charisma 1 977).*   M.G. & C.C.

Europe: GREAT BRITAIN

PETE BROWN's
BATTERED ORNAMENTS

Pete Brown's biographical profile is quite varied and hardly definable in one word: poet, writer, musician, songwriter and composer, session man, producer, this full blown artist provided English Prog with a powerful breeze of psychedelic energy. He began songwriting, singing and playing percussions in 1967 with **Cream** then founding the band **Battered Ornaments** for his most creative albums. The label Harvest signs him up for the production of *A Meal You Can Shake Hands With In The Dark* where the experience with **Baker**, **Bruce** and **Clapton** happily surfaces through the psychedelic background where exceptional jazz and blues tones paint dark shades upon light and delicate guitar walls. The success is repeated with *Mantel Piece*, also thanks to the collaboration of **Chris Spedding**, for an excellent album of a particularly boogie kind of rock. Unfortunately the relation with **Chris** goes south and he seems to be excluded from his own band. **Pete** moves on immediately creating **Piblokto**, into which some of the other musicians will converge, following their leader into more melodic projects.
DISCOGRAPHY: **A MEAL YOU CAN SHAKE HANDS WITH IN THE DARK** *(Harvest, 1969)* **MANTLE PIECE** *(Harvest, 1969).* **C.A. & C.C.**

CATAPILLA

Anna Meek - *vocals,* **Robert Calvert** - *sax,* **Graham Wilson** - *guitar,* **Thierry Reinhardt** - *sax, flute, clarinet,* **Hugh Eaglestone** - *sax,* **Dave Taylor** - *bass,* **Malcolm Frith** - *drums,* **Ralph Rolinson** - *keyboards,* **Carl Wassard** - *bass,* **Brian Hanson** - *drums.*

Undoubtedly one of the most interesting and original bands of the British underground, they are already a phenomenon in both the 1971 homonym debut and with their second album *Changes*, a gem of very rare beauty not only for the Prog genre but for the entire musical universe. Here a visionary rock sound is tinted with jazz highlights, psychedelia and sinister atmospheres. The long tracks develop through the rich instrumental compositions, featuring hallucinating guitars, an ecstatic Hammond organ and an incredibly intense saxophone. And then there is the voice of **Anna Meek**, moody, lazy, disturbing and terribly fascinating.

DISCOGRAPHY: **CATAPILLA** *(1971, Vertigo)* **CHANGES** *(1972, Vertigo).* **M.G.**

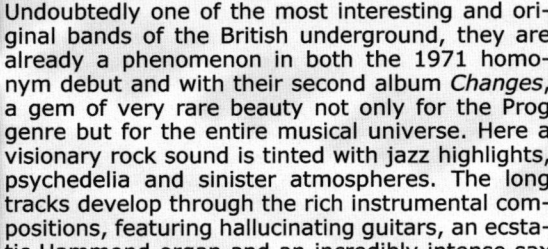

COMUS

Roger Wootton - *vocals, acoustic guitar,* **Bobbie Watson** - *vocals, percussion,* **Andy Hellaby** - *bass,* **Gordon Coxon** - *drums,* **Glen Goring** - *guitar, vocals,* **Colin Pearson** - *violin, viola,* **Rob Young** - *keyboards, flute, oboe.*

Comus will always be remembered for their extraordinary debut record *First Utterance* (1971): far from the fairy-tale atmospheres that were trending at the time, they grew directly from the lawn of a earthier underground genre. Their devious but evocative music is characterized by a restlessness that emerges from very acid and obscure folk sounds with a particularly dramatic use of the vocals. Charismatic and unique the songs are averagely short, containing absurd and hallucinating guitar-guided ballads; the two long tracks of progressive interest are "The Herald" and "Drip Drip", with their grim ritual dances, where the estranged violin and the incessant percussive rhythms play the leading roles. A very dark and funerary visionary album.

DISCOGRAPHY: **FIRST UTTERANCE** *(1971, Dawn)* **TO KEEP FROM CRYING** *(1974, Virgin).* **M.G. & C.C.**

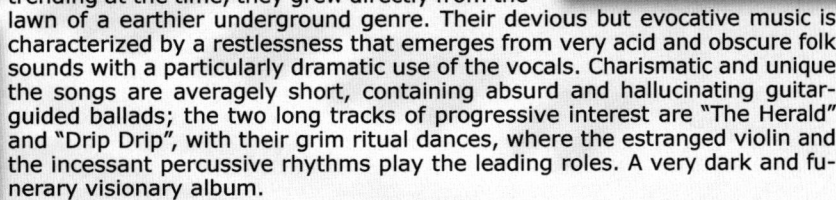

Europe: GREAT BRITAIN

CRESSIDA

Angus Cullen - vocals, **John Heyworth, John Culley** - guitar, **Peter Jennings** - keyboards, **Kevin McCarthy** - bass, **Iain Clark** - drums, **Harold McNair** - flute.

When defining proto-prog and cult-bands, the name **Cressida** immediately comes to mind: two incredible albums in perpetual balance between baroque, pastoral melodies, Canterbury flavors and acoustic structures which will affect the tidal wave of bands to come, from **Fruupp** to **Hostsonaten**. Beyond the sweet and delicate fascination of their music, **Cressida** are exemplary to understand the dynamics of the transition from post-beat to true prog: 'Troilus and Cressida' is a Shakespearian tragedy from which they derive their name and found in 1969 the band. The label Vertigo finds them very interesting and signs the group up for a first live studio album and then a second, more elaborate and with the presence of a real orchestra. They will break-up soon after this last recording, **Culley** joining **Black Widow** and **Clark** joining **Uriah Heep**.

DISCOGRAPHY: CRESSIDA (Vertigo, 1970) **ASYLUM** (Vertigo, 1971). **M.G.**

EAST OF EDEN

Dave Arbus – violin, flute, sax, horns, **Ron Caines** – sax, organ, vocals, **Dave Dufont** – drums, percussion, **Geoff Nicholson** –guitars, vocals, **Steve York** – bass, harmonica, piano.

This band grows around the charismatic figure of **Dave Arbus**, playing a vivid prog made of strong, sometimes hard sounds dominated by the sax and the violin which alternate with the very evocative melodies of a powerful guitar. Incredible for the variety and quality, their first two albums contain musical styles that go from rock-blues to jazz, circus to folk, psychedelia and classical themes inspired by **Bèla Bartòk**. Their personal and particular experimentations included tapes played in loop or backwards and fascinating flanging effects. Already the second very beautiful album sees a first line-up change until **Arbus** decides to abandon the project and move to Germany. In 1996 his come back in a jazz-rock key, together with **Caines** and the band for some good records.

RECOMMENDED RECORDINGS: MARCATOR PROJECTED (Deram, 1969) **SNAFU** (Deram, 1970). **M.G. & C.C.**

EGG

Dave Stewart - keyboards, **Clive Brooks** - drums, **Mont Campbell** - bass, vocals, horns, **Henry Lowther, Mike Davis, Bob Downes, Tony Roberts, Lindsay Cooper, Tim Hodkongson, The Wind Quartet** - horns, **Steve Hillage** - guitar, **Amanda Parsons, Barbara Gaskin, Ann Rosenthal** - vocals.

Directly involved in the Canterbury environment, this is one of the most pioneering experiences of adult rock, which anticipates by far the language of **Universe Zero** and **Art Zoyd**. **Steve Hillage** leaves **Uriel** and **Dave Stewart** transforms them into **Egg**, the authors of three embryo avant-garde rock records. The world of classical music and classical contemporary music (**John Cage, Terry Riley**) meets electric jazz through the embodiment of this powerful rock ensemble. The unusual and irregular rhythms of the perfect pair **Brooks** and **Campbell**, support the sophisticated walls of classical quotes (**Bach, Grieg**) coming from **Stewart**'s unique organ style, making **Egg** a band that goes beyond time and the space of the early '70s. It's no coincidence that **Stewart** will later join **Hatfield And The North**.

DISCOGRAPHY: EGG (Deram, 1970) **THE POLITE FORCE** (Deram, 1971), **THE CIVIL SURFACE** (Caroline, 1974). **M.G. & C.C.**

Europe: GREAT BRITAIN

THE ENID

Robert John Godfrey, William Gilmour, Tony Freer, Martin Wallis - _keyboards,_ **Stephen Stewart, Francis Lickerish, Nick May** - _guitars,_ **Glenn Tollet, Martin Russel, Terry Pack, Neil Feldman, Max Read** - _bass,_ **Chris North, Dave Storey, Damian Risdon, Wayne Cox, Steve Hughes** - _drums,_ **Troy Donockley** - _flute,_ **Geraldine Connor** - _vocals._
Majestic, romantic, orchestral, more than a band, this creature is carefully bred by composer **Robert John Godfrey** whom, after directing the **Barclay James Harvest Orchestra** and releasing the solo album _The Fall Of Hyperion_, founds _The Enid_ in 1974 with his trusted colleague **Stephen Stewart**. Already from the early stages they sail across very different moments of diverse inspiration, building a monumentally epic sound that lasts over 10 great albums of devoted classical prog, a coherent discography that confirms a very personal style of unmistakable symphonic traits. Never caring for trends and fashions, this band operates the highest and most complete synthesis between rock and classical music, creating around them the most deserving allure of true cult band.
RECOMMENDED RECORDINGS: ROBERT JOHN GODFREY: **THE FALL OF HYPERION** (Charisma, 1974) **THE ENID:** **IN THE REGION OF THE SUMMER STARS** (Deram, 1976) **AERIE FAERIE NONSENSE** (Honeybee, 1977).
M.G. & C.C.

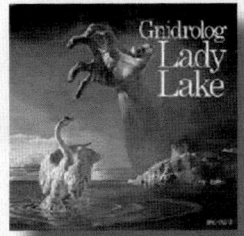

GNIDROLOG

Colin Goldring - _lead vocals, guitars, flute, sax, horn, harmonica,_ **Stewart Goldring** - _guitar, vocals,_ **Peter Cowling** - _bass, cello,_ **Nigel Pegrum** - _percussion, flute, oboe, piano,_ **John Earle** - _sax, flute, vocals._
Capable of mixing intricate textures of **Gentle Giant** inspiration, to vocal melodies in the best **Van der Graaf Generator** style and certain romantic moods of **Genesis**, this very valuable band leaves two remarkably rich albums, very well-known to the prog community. Already in their debut _In Spite Of Harry's Toe_ nail, the technical skills are coupled with a discreet amount of fantasy, but it is with _Lady Lake_ (also remembered for the fabulous cover) that the band goes beyond its limits and toward a very dynamic symphonic rock, refined through infinite instrumental combinations, where a howling sax is balanced by the gentleness of flute and oboe, stunning accelerations and delicate pastoral passages.

DISCOGRAPHY: **IN SPITE OF HARRY'S TOE-NAIL** (1972, RCA) **LADY LAKE** (1972, RCA) **LIVE 1972** (1999, Audio Archives) **GNOSIS** (2000, Snails).
M.G. & C.C.

GRYPHON

Richard Harvey – _keyboards, percussions, vocals, krumhorn_, **Brian Gulland** – _horns, percussions, krumhorn,_ **David Oberlé** – _drums, percussions,_ **Graeme Taylor** - _guitars,_ **Philip Nestor** – _bass._
This project of 1971 revolves around the figures of **Harvey** and **Gulland**, distinguishing itself for the very personal folk prog sound achieved by the insertion of Renaissance and Medieval themes and the use of traditional acoustic and electric instruments. Already in the first work _Gryphon_ (1973), they begin the  interesting musical contaminations, yet it is with the second album, _Midnight Mushrumps_ (1974), containing an over 18 minutes title-track suite where they express their real value and the originality of the ideas. _Red Queen To Gryphon Three_ (1974) is undoubtedly their masterpiece and fundamental to the genre, with its 4 long instrumental tracks, more symphonic and airy. Not at the same level is the rest of discography, even if some good hints can be still found in _Raindance_ of 1975.
RECOMMENDED RECORDINGS: **GRYPHON** (Transatlantic, 1973) **MIDNIGHT MUSHRUMPS** (Transatlantic, 1974) **RED QUEEN TO GRYPHON THREE** (Bell, 1974).
M.G. & C.C.

Europe: GREAT BRITAIN

ROY HARPER

Coming from the '60s English folk-beat generation, **Roy Harper** earned the label of uncomfortable artist for his independent temper and attitude. His character reflects all over his productions, which are a river full of stylistic themes poured onto a folk rock base. *Folkjokeopus* is the experimental transition towards new musical trends; *Flat Baroque and Berserk* and *Stormcock* reveal him as an extraordinary

musician who succeeds in combining a most intimate and folk acoustic side with the most electrical prog accents of his musicality; *Lifemask* further emphasizes the experimental aspect, leading directly to *Valentine*, a masterpiece of intimate music; *HQ* is an energetic rock album full of guests, featuring **John Paul Jones**, **Bill Bruford**, **Chris Spedding**, **David Gilmour** and **Steve Broughton**. **Harper** also collaborates with **Pink Floyd** singing "Have a Cigar" in the album *Wish You Were Here*. After taking his distance from the label Emi, he begins a new project involving his son **Nick**.
RECOMMENDED RECORDINGS: **FOLKJOKOEPUS** (Liberty, 1968) **FLAT BAROQUE AND BERSERK** (Harvest, 1970) **STORMCOCK** (Harvest, 1971) **LIFEMASK** (Harvest, 1973) **VALENTINE** (Harvest, 1974) **HQ** (Harvest, 1975) **BULLINAMINGVASE** (Harvest, 1977). C.A. & C.C.

HIGH TIDE

Tony Hill - *guitar*, **Simon House**, **Dave Tomlin** - *violin*, **Peter Pavli**, **Android Fullen** - *bass*, **Roger Hadden**, **Drachen Theacker** - *drums*, **Sushi Krishnamurti** - *vocals*.
If **Jethro Tull** consecrates a leading role to the flute, **High Tide** deserves the credit of inserting a main violin into the rock genre: bands like **It's A Beautiful Day** and **Family** were of course experimenting with it, **Curved Air** and **PFM** will find ways to highlight its use, but the way that **Simon House** plays his mysterious and gothic violin takes **High Tide** to an unimaginable role in the rock panorama. The 1969 dark and obscure heavy-prog album contains loud guitar and violin interlacements which bring on dilated and funerary atmospheres that explode in absolute freedom, like a mantra of folk and jazz reminiscence. The band then seems to fade away for decades while **Simon House** joins **David Bowie** and his band for the 1977 - 1978 tours. When **Tony Hill** returns to reunite them in 1987 through a different line-up, he is highly criticized by the media.

DISCOGRAPHY: **SEA SHANTIES** (Liberty, 1969) **HIGH TIDE** (Liberty, 1970) **INTERESTING TIMES** (1987) **PRECIOUS CARGO** (Cobra, 1989) **THE FLOOD** (SPM 1990) **A FIERCE NATURE** (SPM 1990) **ANCIENT GATES** (SPM 1990) **THE REASON OF SUCCESS** (SPM, 1992). M.G. & C.C.

JADE WARRIOR

Tony Duhig – *guitar, bass, keyboards, percussions*, **Jon Field** – *harp, flute, cello, guitar, percussions*.
When the psychedelic band July breaks-up, **Tony Duhig** and **Jon Field** moved on to formed **Jade Warrior** with the intention of pursuing their inspirations and passions. Their career begins in 1971 and goes on up to our very days with a psychedelic genre to

which they add jazz, blues, latino and experimental music, fusion or sometimes a more aggressive kind of rock and ethnic music derived from African and Japanese cultures (a peculiarity that will mark their entire career). Around these two musicians and their prolific discography revolve many important names such as **Steve Winwood**, **Theo Travis**, **David Cross** or **Fred Frith** and regular guests **Dave Duhig** (guitar) and **Allan Price** (drums). In 1991 **Tony Duhig** prematurely dies yet **Jon Field** still carries on his adventure with old and new friends.

RECOMMENDED RECORDINGS: **LAST AUTUMN'S DREAM** (1972, Vertigo) **WAVES** (1975, Island) **WAY OF THE SUN** (1978, Island). M.G. & C.C.

Europe: GREAT BRITAIN

KALEIDOSCOPE

Peter Daltrey - *vocals, keyboards*, **Eddie Pumer** - *guitars*, **Steve Clark** - *bass*, **Danny Bridgman** - *drums*.

After producing two masterpieces of the most authentic psychedelia, they will change name to **Fairfield Parlour** in order to avoid legal issues with the already existing American band Kaleidoscope. Guided by the ingenious **Peter Daltrey**, eclectic keyboardist and singer-songwriter, they debut with a few singles and the album *Tangerine Dream* in 1967, laying the foundations of a true British psychedelic realm. Rich of mysterious sounds, vivid colors and dreamy atmospheres, the 3-dimensional visions seem to masterfully overlap and deepen in the second album *Faintly Blowing*, where the visions become of a more avant-garde nature, with choirs playing a greater role. Their sound grows closer to the experience of the first **Soft Machine** and of **Pink Floyd**'s *The Piper At The Gates Of Dawn*. **Eddy Plumer**'s guitar greets **Daltrey**'s keyboards creating surrounding sounds that evoke unreal scenarios where flute, drums, and sound effects complete an abstract, ever-moving picture.

DISCOGRAPHY: TANGERINE DREAM *(Fontana, 1967)* **FAINTLY BLOWING** *(Fontana, 1969).*
C.A. & C.C.

KHAN

Steve Hillage - *guitars, vocals*, **Nick Greenwood** - *bass, vocals*, **Eric Peachey** - *drums*, **Dave Stewart** - *keyboards*.

The 'Submarine Captain' of **Gong**'s spacecraft, **Steve Hillage**, has also pre-**Gong** past worthy of attention: one of the most inventive guitarists of an era, he has a good solo discography and is a well-known producer too (**Simple Minds**). Due to his studies, **Steve** leaves definitively **Dave Stewart**'s **Arzachel/Egg** and in 1971 founds the trio **Khan** publishing the intriguing *Space Shanty*, a vigorous space-rock album with ample jazz and lysergic spirals, well balancing guitar and organ in the best Canterbury school style. Immediately after he decides to join **Daevid Allen** for his psychedelic space-prog project **Gong**, with whom he plays until 1974. In 1977 he recovers fragments of the hypothetical second **Khan** album and instead releases his first solo debut. In 2009 **Hillage** and his wife **Miquette Giraudy** re-join **Gong** until the death of its futuristic leader, **Daevid Allen**.

DISCOGRAPHY: SPACE SHANTY *(Deram, 1972).*
M.G. & C.C.

MATCHING MOLE

Robert Wyatt - *drums, vocals, keyboards*, **Phil Miller** - *guitar*, **David Sinclair, Dave McRae, Brian Eno** - *keyboards*, **Bill McCormick** - *bass*, **Alfreda Benge** - *vocals*.

Games with names: when **Robert Wyatt**, creator of **Soft Machine**, is thrown out of his own band, as an act of revenge he founds **Matching Mole** (soft machine in french is translated 'machine molle', which pronounced in English gives this peculiar name to his new band). They publish two albums of eccentric and fanciful British jazz-rock and are one of the Canterbury school's most delightful expressions. Of course echoes of the former band are ever present being his previous creature, yet **Wyatt** obtains even higher compositional and vocal results with indolent melodies, acute irony, tasty covers and the dreamy atmospheres. The homonym debut album contains the famous "O Caroline" and is proof of his more mature song-writing. The following *Little Red Record* is produced by **Robert Fripp** and features **Brian Eno** as a special guest. The band breaks-up at the end of 1972.

RECOMMENDED RECORDINGS: MATCHING MOLE *(CBS, 1972)* **MATCHING MOLE'S LITTLE RED RECORD** *(CBS, 1972).*
M.G. & C.C.

Europe: GREAT BRITAIN

OZRIC TENTACLES

Ed Wynne, Gavin Griffith, Steve Hillage - *guitars*, **Joie Hinton, Tom Brooks, Steve Everett, Seaweed, Harry Waters** - *synths*. **Roly Wynne, Zia Geelani, Brandi Wynne** - *bass*. **Tig, Merv Pepler, Rad, Stuart Fisher, Metro** - *drums*, **Paul Hankin Marcu C. Diess, Generator John, Jim O' Roon** - *percussion*, **John Egan** - *flute*.

If **Pink Floyd** and **Hawkwind** the founding fathers of space-rock, **Ozric Tentacles** are their bizarre but prolific children. They debut in 1984 in the lysergic 'Stonehenge Free Festival' and in a quarter century they publish over 20 albums and perform in thousands of concerts all over the world. The '70s cosmic-rock is the son of psychedelia and the **OT** teleport it into the 80's and stuff it with electronics, dub, funk and techno, making it a delicious sound especially appreciated by youngsters. During the early years, this band from Somerset starts by recording on cassette tapes until 1989, when they finally sign up with an indie label for a first album entitled *Pungent Effulgent*: unmistakable their cosmic jams and the irresistible mascot character they named Erp on the cover. Ironic and surreal, **Ed Wynne**'s band is the most credible heir to **Gong**.

RECOMMENDED RECORDINGS: **PUNGENT EFFULGENT** *(Demi Monde, 1989)* **ERPLAND** *(Dovetail, 1990)* **JURASSIC SHIFT** *(Dovetail, 1993).* **M.G. & C.C.**

PATTO

Michael "Mike Patto" McCarthy - *vocals*, **Peter "Ollie" Halsall** - *guitar, vibes, vocals*, - **Clive Griffiths** - *bass, vocals*, **John "The Admiral" Halsey** - *drums*.

Once there was **Timebox** that became **Patto** when psychedelic pop ended its spell. The innovative verve and the desire to compose, cast the band with a curse of great talent and even greater misfortune. Genial compositions played wonderfully with a guitarist of uncommon musical style and sung by the soul voice of their singer; the hard jazzy blues touches mixed to a certain psychedelia and the avant-garde of a complex rhythmic plot were the ingredients of a debut album that confirms the clarity of their ideas, but it is with the second *Hold your Fire* (1971) that comes the real masterpiece. They will carry on performing until the spring of 1973 until they break-up in search of other paths. Over the years Fate tolled its bell upon the musicians ending tragically any idea of reunion in this incredible tale: an overdose for **Ollie** (1992), cancer for **Patto** (1979), car accident with irreversible damages for the other two.

RECOMMENDED RECORDINGS: **PATTO** *(Vertigo, 1970)* **HOLD YOUR FIRE** *(Vertigo, 1971).* **M.G. & C.C.**

PENDRAGON

Nick Barrett – *vocals, guitars*, **Pete Gee** – *bass*, **Clive Nolan** – *keyboards*, **Fudge Smith** – *drums* (1986/2006), **Joe Crabtree** – *drums* (since 2006).

Together with **Marillion**, **IQ** and **Pallas**, this band began in 1978 as pioneers of the newly set progressive course, flowing down the river and inevitably into the '80s. Excellently lead by singer and guitarist **Nick Barrett**, their true soul explodes when the keyboards of **Clive Nolan** join in, giving the band its final shape. Despite its good musical quality in both arrangements and live performances, they are so irredeemably attached to the bow of a long gone past, emulating more than creating, that it is only in 1993 that their music achieves a well-deserved maturity: elegant and rich of passion, *The Window of Life* (and its beautiful cover) represents the tip of their efforts. The following works are also good (*The Masquerade Overture* and *Not Of This World*) though they will never be able to match it.

RECOMMENDED RECORDINGS: **THE WINDOW OF LIFE** *(Toff/Snapper, 1993)* **THE MASQUERADE OVERTURE** *(Toff/Snapper, 1996).* **M.G. & C.C.**

Europe: GREAT BRITAIN

PORCUPINE TREE

Steve Wilson - *vocals, guitars*, **Richard Barbieri** - *keyboards*, **Chris Maitland** - *drums, backing vocals*, **Colin Edwin** - *bass*, **Gavin Harrison** - *drums*.

A **Steve Wilson**'s project of the early 80's, **Porcupine Tree** is a truly innovative rock band for the new English prog genre. Born from the dreamiest and most overwhelming British psychedelia, **Wilson** strolls his guitar down the path of long compositions, where melodic songs alternate with symphonic suites, recreating the magical atmospheres of an authentic prog spell. Flowing bright among the many albums are *Signify* and *Lightbulb Sun*, with their references to the the '60s psychedelic rock, filtered through more contemporary eyes. The ingredients are always the same: fairy tales, delicate melodies, manipulated sounds that create dreamy effects, all cleverly arranged to obtain a great final result.

DISCOGRAPHY: **ON THE SUNDAYS OF LIFE...**(*Delerium, 1991*) **UP THE DOWNSTAIRS** (*Delerium, 1992*) **THE SKY MOVES SIDEWAYS** (*C&S, 1994*) **SIGNIFY** (*Delerium, 1995*) **COMA DIVINE** (*Delerium, 1997*) **STUPID DREAM** (*Snapper, 1999*) **LIGHTBULB SUN** (*Snapper, 2000*) **METANOIA** (*Delerium, 2001*) **IN ABSENTIA** (*Lava, 2002*) **DEADWING** (*Lava, 2005*) **FEAR OF A BLANK PLANET** (*Lava, 2007*) **THE INCIDENT** (*Roadrunner, 2009*).
C.A. & C.C.

QUATERMASS

John Gustafson - *bass, vocals*, **Peter Robinson** - *keyboards*, **Mick Underwood** - *drums*.

A typical example of how a one shot band can become a myth, Quatermass belongs to the original prog era of **Atomic Rooster**, **Dr. Z** and **Gravy Train**. A true power trio without guitars, they derive inspiration from **Keith Emerson** and **Crane** (avoiding exaggerated baroque styles) and push

hard on the aggressive and rough sounds as much as on a extensive use of ballads and orchestral arrangements. Heavy-prog at its peak in the famous "Black Sheep Of The Family" and instrumental quality to each musician that will make them among the most demanded session men. Their music, like the song "Post War Saturday Echo", will influence deeply tracks of the Italians **Le Orme** ("Collage"). In 1990 drummer **Mick Underwood** will experiment a sort of come-back naming the new band **Quatermass II** and publishing the album *The Long Road* practically on his own: a modest work, different from the previous, yet keeping somewhat intact the original myth. Rumors of any further true reunion die with the passing of **Gustafson** in December 2014.

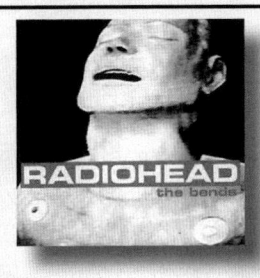

DISCOGRAPHY: **QUATERMASS** (*Harvest 1970*) **QUATERMASS II: The Long Road** (*Angel Air, 1990*).
M.G. & C.C.

RADIOHEAD

Thom Yorke - *vocals, guitars, keyboards*, **Johnny Greenwood** - *guitars, keyboards*, **Ed O' Brien** - *guitars*, **Colin Greenwood** - *bass*, **Phil Selway** - *drums*.

Prog: approach or style? Calling or Genre? This band couldn't be labeled further away from the idea of progressive sound, yet they the musical approach is comparable to the

best experimental **Pink Floyd** or **Can**. Originally bred by the post Brit-pop era, they find their way exploring the fields of various stylistic forms. This eternal research results in two revolutionary albums: the futurism and art-rock of *Ok Computer* wins the title of <Sgt. Pepper of the '90s>, while the heavily psychedelic *Kid A* is so electronically experimental to bewilder completely being so different and less straightforward. 2007 sees the release of *In Rainbows* that gives a further shake to the record market with its downloadable LP version (first world wide to do so).

DISCOGRAPHY: **PABLO HONEY** (*Parlophone, 1993*) **THE BENDS** (*Parlophone, 1995*) **OK COMPUTER** (*Parlophone, 1997*) **KID A** (*Parlophone, 1999*), **AMNESIAC** (*Parlophone, 2001*) **HAIL TO THE THIEF** (*Parlophone, 2003*) **IN RAINBOWS** (*Radiohead, 2007*).
M.G. & C.C.

Europe: GREAT BRITAIN

SECOND HAND

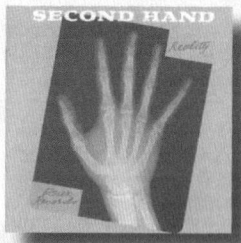

Ken Elliot - *keyboards, vocals,* **Kieran O'Connor** - *drums,* **Bobby Gibbons** - *lead guitar,* **Nick South** - *bass,* **Chris Williams** - *flute, cello, violin, saxophones,* **George Hart** - *bass, violin,* **Moggy Mead** - *guitar,* **Rob Elliot** - *vocals.*
Born in 1965 as **The Next Collection**, leader and keyboardist **Ken Elliot** signs them up with Polydor Records which immediately decides to change their name to **Second Hand**. Since their first album *Reality* is dated 1968, it can actually be defined as proto-prog for the psychedelic shades that blend naturally into an embryonic prog genre. After nearly three years of line-up and label changes, **Ken**'s brother **Rob** joins the band as lead singer for their second album of 1971 *Death May Be Your Santa Claus*. This record confirms the psychedelic and prog trend with dark sounds and excellent arrangements that slightly recall **Arthur Brown**. Unfortunately, some members leave and they become **Chillum** for a last homonym album, also of 1971, before the disbandment. Contained within is the famous track "Brain Strain", recorded live in studio during a first rehearsal of guitarist **McGill** with an impressive groove built on the **O'Connor** and **Hart** rhythmic section. The record was reissued on CD with previously unreleased added tracks (including a longer version of "Brain Strain").

DISCOGRAPHY: REALITY *(Polydor, 1968)* **DEATH MAY BE YOUR SANTA CLAUS** *(Mushroom, 1971).* **M.G. & C.C.**

SPOOKY TOOTH

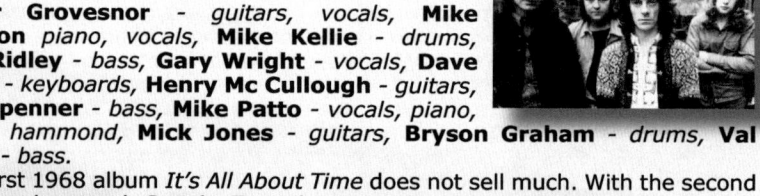

Luther Grovesnor - *guitars, vocals,* **Mike Harrison** *piano, vocals,* **Mike Kellie** - *drums,* **Greg Ridley** - *bass,* **Gary Wright** - *vocals,* **Dave Moore** - *keyboards,* **Henry Mc Cullough** - *guitars,* **Alan Spenner** - *bass,* **Mike Patto** - *vocals, piano, organo hammond,* **Mick Jones** - *guitars,* **Bryson Graham** - *drums,* **Val Burke** - *bass.*
Their first 1968 album *It's All About Time* does not sell much. With the second avant-garde record, *Spooky Two*, the story changes and becomes even more complicated when their label Island publishes *Ceremony* without permission: after a short pause that looked a lot like a true break-up, they return with *The Last Puff*, an album of good impact and progressive traits. With *You Broke My Heart So I Busted Your Jaw* the band finally obtains the deserved success, despite the constant line-up changes that create constant internal disputes. *The Mirror* is published in 1974 and marks the top of their career, which ends here. **Spooky Tooth** will live on in bands like **Humble Pie**, **Mott the Hoople** and **Foreigner**.

RECOMMENDED RECORDINGS: IT'S ALL ABOUT TIME *(Island, 1968)* **SPOOKY TWO** *(Island, 1969)* **THE LAST PUFF** *(Island, 1970)* **THE MIRROR** *(Island, 1974).* **C.A. & C.C.**

SPRING

Pat Moran - *vocals, mellotron,* **Ray Martinez** - *guitars, mellotron,* **Adrian "Bone" Maloney** - *bass,* **Kipps Brown** - *keyboards,* **Pick Withers** - *drums.*
A one shot-band author of an album that enchanted millions by describing in only 40 minutes all the dreams and aspirations of an entire movement. **Spring** is the evolution of a sound born with **The Moody Blues**, then enhanced by **Beggars Opera** and **Cressida** and developed by **Barclay James Harvest**: a symphonic rock without excesses and redundancies, composed and executed with gentleness, lyricism and pathos. Produced in 1971 by **Gus Dudgeon** with the magnificent cover photo by **Marcus Keef**, *Spring* is an album full of mellotron waterfalls, awesome melodies and a rock structure that opens to acoustic horizons. The band from Leicester unfortunately breaks-up after starting the sessions of a new, unfinished LP and the members will continue as sessionmen: **Pick Withers**, for example, will pursue a wonderful career ending up with the **Knopfler** brothers as the drummer of **Dire Straits** at the end of the '70s.

DISCOGRAPHY: SPRING *(Neon 1971).* **M.G. & C.C.**

Europe: **GREAT BRITAIN**

STRAWBS

Dave Cousins – vocals, guitars, **Dave Lambert** – vocals, guitars, bass, **Rick Wakeman** – keyboards, **Richard Hudson** – drums, **John Ford** – vocals, bass, **Blue Weaver** – keyboards.

The 1969 historical band led by guitarist **Dave Cousins**, initially begins its career with the extraordinary voice of folk singer **Sandy Denny** and the great keyboard playing of **Rick Wakeman** (whom some years later will join legendary **Yes**). Clearly deriving from folk roots, particularity they will maintain in all their works, they will publish their major successes in the first half of the '70s: albums of great charm and singular beauty which will become a beacon for future folk-rock and prog bands. Recently they reunited for a celebratory concert to which even **Wakeman** participated with his old band mates.

RECOMMENDED RECORDINGS: STRAWBS *(A&M,1969)* **DRAGONFLY** *(A&M, 1970)* **JUST A COLLECTION OF ANTIQUES AND CURIOUS** *(A&M, 1970)* **FROM THE WITCHWOOD** *(A&M, 1970)* **HERO AND HEROINE** *(A&M, 1974).*
M.G. & C.C.

THIRD EAR BAND

Glen Sweeney - percussion, **Richard Coff, Dave Tomlin, Ursula Smith, Simon House, Paul Buckmaster, Alan Samuel, Neil Black** - violin, viola, cello, **Paul Minns, Lynn Dobson** - horns, **Mel Davis** - cello, pipes, **John Peel** - jew's harp, **Denis Bridges, Mick Carter, Mike Merchant** - guitars.

Very similarly to **Popol Vuh** and **Aktuala**, this band from Canterbury experiments in acoustic ex-temporary compositional forms, far from the trends of esoteric atmospheres. It's a chamber music ensemble which explores ritual improvisations based on percussions, flute, oboe and violin, thus retrieving ancestral melodies, indie Rāga music and jazz, through the repetition of rhythmic cells and drones that lead to minimalism. They signs up with Harvest Records and publish two albums, unique to the international scene which at the end of the '60s had not yet invented world music as a genre. The band will participate in tv and cinema scores (for **Roman Polanski**'s *Macbeth* in 1972 for example) before breaking up for nearly two decades. **Glen Sweeney** will reunite the group in Italy in the late '80s with an updated but still intriguing formula.

RECOMMENDED RECORDINGS: **ALCHEMY** *(Harvest 1969)* **THIRD EAR BAND (ELEMENTS)** *(Harvest 1970)* **MUSIC FROM MACBETH** *(EMI 1972)* **ABELARD & HELOISE** *(Blueprint 1999).*
M.G. & C.C.

TOMORROW

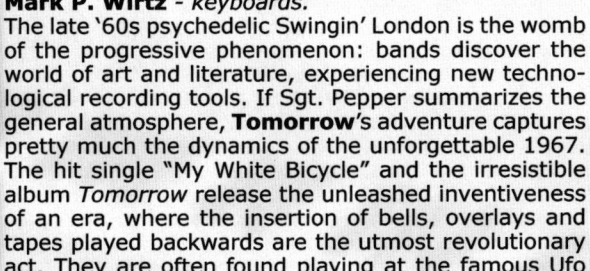

Keith West - vocals, **Steve Howe** - guitars, **John "Junior" Wood** - bass, **John "Twink" Alder** - drums, **Mark P. Wirtz** - keyboards.

The late '60s psychedelic Swingin' London is the womb of the progressive phenomenon: bands discover the world of art and literature, experiencing new technological recording tools. If Sgt. Pepper summarizes the general atmosphere, **Tomorrow**'s adventure captures pretty much the dynamics of the unforgettable 1967. The hit single "My White Bicycle" and the irresistible album *Tomorrow* release the unleashed inventiveness of an era, where the insertion of bells, overlays and tapes played backwards are the utmost revolutionary act. They are often found playing at the famous Ufo Club, conquering London's music scene before breaking-up in 1968: **West** founds the pioneering **Teenage Opera Project** and later pursues his solo career; **Twink** joins **Pretty Things** while **Steve Howe** will join permanently **Yes** after a short **Bodast** experience.

DISCOGRAPHY: **TOMORROW** *(Parlophone 1968).*
M.G. & C.C.

Europe: GREAT BRITAIN

TREES

Bias Boshell - *guitar, bass, vocals,* **Celia Humphris** - *keyboards, vocals,* **Unwin Brown** - *drums, vocals,* **Barry Clarke** - *guitars,* **David Costa** - *guitars.*

Fundamental British folk-prog and acoustic band (together with **Pentangle** and **Fairport Convention**) they choose the sweet voice of **Celia Humphris** to develop the musical plots of both albums released in 1970: the first perhaps a little too fresh but still heterogeneous, contains the song "Sally Free and Easy", a milestone for the progressive genre. They managed to balance the perfect electro-acoustic sounds with smart and pressing guitar riffs through an excellent song-writing where talent of each musician could emerge. Unfortunately the absolute indifference of the market did not help them find reasons not to disband. The progressive abandonment of its components ended in 1972 when the hope of a tour with **Byrds** vanished bringing to a final break-up. **Celia Humphris** pursued a career as an actress and a speaker; today the London Tube announcements are all given through her beautiful voice.

RECOMMENDED RECORDINGS: **THE GARDEN OF JANE DELAWNEY** (CBS, 1970) **ON THE SHORE** (CBS, 1970). C.A. & C.C.

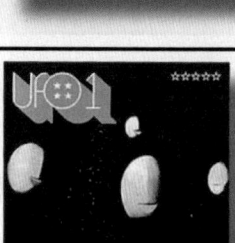

UFO

Phil Mogg - *vocals,* **Mick Bolton** - *guitars,* **Pete Way** - *bass,* **Andy Parker** - *drums.*

Launched by the label Beacon in 1970, this English band is characterized for their very own boogie and rock-blues style of strong psychedelic contaminations. It is however with their second album *Flying* that the space-rock experiences reach a higher peak like in the songs "Star Storm" and "Flying". Though their music was appreciated by the media, sales were not particularly good both in the UK and in the USA, while they exploded in Japan. In fact after their far-east tour a third album *UFO Live* was recorded taking tracks played during these concerts. **Mick Bolton**'s exit in 1972 sees the entry of German guitarist **Michael Schenker** and a change of style for the band, turning towards a rather commercial form of hard rock, but this is another story.

RECOMMENDED RECORDINGS: **UFO** (Beacon, 1970) **FLYING** (Beacon 1971) **UFO LIVE** (Beacon 1972). C.A. & C.C.

U.K.

Eddie Jobson - *keyboards, violin,* **John Wetton** - *bass, vocals,* **Allan Holdsworth** - *guitars,* **Bill Bruford** - *drums,* **Terry Bozzio** - *drums.*

It is rare for a partnership of technically great musicians to be so well-established: **Jobson**, **Wetton**, **Holdsworth** and **Bruford** debut with a homonym album featuring a powerful symphonic rock, open to contaminations of jazz-fusion with overwhelming guitar riffs and valuable instrumental parts. A new line-up without guitar and with **Terry Bozzio** on the drums sees the release in 1979 of another good record, *Danger Money*, where the keyboards cover the leading role. Inevitable the break-up. A series of live albums will follow proving the band's skills and qualities in the concert dimension. Recently there were rumors of a reunion, but **Wetton** and **Holdsworth**'s recent deaths closed any future possibility.

DISCOGRAPHY: **UK** (1978, Polydor) **DANGER MONEY** (1979, Polydor) **NIGHT AFTER NIGHT LIVE** (1979, Polydor) **CONCERT CLASSIC VOL. 4** (1999, Renaissance Records). M.G. & C.C.

Europe: GREAT BRITAIN

URIAH HEEP

Mick Box - *guitars,* **Ken Hensley** - *keyboards,* **David Byron** - *vocals,* **Paul Newton, Mark Clarke, Gary Thain, John Wetton** - *bass,* **Alex Napier, Nigel Ollson, Keith Baker, Ian Clarke, Lee Kerslake** - *drums.*

Hard-rock and prog relations are tight: **Deep Purple** anticipate this, **Rush** confirm it and **Uriah Heep** are an obvious example. The technical preparation of the band's musicians (**Ken Hensley**'s magnificent keyboard), the musical environment melting pot (**John Wetton** from Family and later with **King Crimson**; **Roger Dean** illustrated all the **Yes** covers; Vertigo publishes their first two LPs), the memorable suite "Salisbury" played with a real orchestra, place **Uriah Heep** in the prog-rock cradle. Initially the critics snob the band considering it an imitation of **Deep Purple** but the records from 1970 to 1976 (with the unforgettable **Dave Byron**) will soon become myths in the history of rock.

DISCOGRAPHY: **VERY EAVY... VERY UMBLE** *(Vertigo 1970)* **SALISBURY** *(Vertigo 1971)* **LOOK AT YOURSELF** *(Bronze 1971)* **DEMONS & WIZARDS** *(Bronze 1972)* **THE MAGICIAN'S BIRTHDAY** *(Bronze 1972)* **URIAH HEEP LIVE** *(live, Bronze 1973)* **SWEET FREEDOM** *(Bronze 1973)* **WONDERWORLD** *(Bronze 1974)* **RETURN TO FANTASY** *(Bronze 1975)* **HIGH AND MIGTHY** *(Bronze 1976).*

M.G. & C.C.

ROGER WATERS

Roger Waters, bass player, song writer and composer (all lyrics from *The Dark side of the Moon* to *The Final Cut* are actually his), co-founder and artistic leader of **Pink Floyd** until his controversial exit, he will pursue a solo career of great interest for the prog genre. His first album *Music from the Body* recorded with **Ron Geesin** in 1970 is declared of minor interest being a pseudo-documentary score so we should consider the material published after

1984: *The Pros and Cons of Hitch Hiking* is a brilliant concept album featuring **Eric Clapton** on the guitars; beautiful though a bit too '80s is the following *Radio Kaos* released in 1987; definitely a masterpiece the studio album *Amused to Death* of 1992 featuring **Jeff Beck** on guitars (the incredible music and lyrics are second only to his previous cult *The Wall* with **Pink Floyd**). After 25 years **Roger** returns with a brand new album: *Is this the life we really want?* Where his style is confirmed and we can find a sum of everything he wrote in the previous recordings.

RECOMMENDED RECORDINGS: **THE PROS AND CONS OF HITCH HIKING** *(Harvest, 1984)* **AMUSED TO DEATH** *(Sony, 1992)* **IS THIS THE LIFE WE REALLY WANT?** *(Sony, 2017)*

M.G. & C.C.

THE ZOMBIES

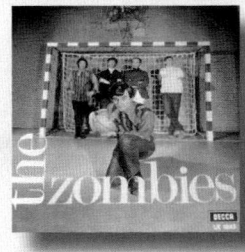

Rod Argent - *keyboards,* **Colin Blunstone** - *vocals,* **Chris White** - *bass,* **Paul Atkinson** - *guitars,* **Hugh Grundy** - *drums.*

Although belonging to the notorious Brit-beat, **Rod Argent**'s band was able to go beyond the genre targeting more mature sounds. In the first album *Begin Here* of 1965, there is so much energy to risk an explosion. After breaking the contract with Decca that required hit songs and a good boys' image on the cover of music maga-

zines, the five sign up with CBS and begin their navigation of the psychedelic phenomenon: the original album's title 'Odyssey and Oracle' was misspelled *Odessey And Oracle* by the graphic studio and printed on the covers, thus keeping the mistake. Recorded in the fall of 1966 but released only in 1968, it is a manifesto of British psychedelic pop that will open the doors to the future Prog standards. When the album is ready to sell, **The Zombies** no longer exist and each musician is already devoted to a new career or musical experience (**Rod** moves on to found his **Argent**).

DISCOGRAPHY: **BEGIN HERE** *(Decca, 1965)* **ODESSEY AND ORACLE** *(CBS, 1968).*

C.A. & C.C.

Europe: GREECE

AKRITAS

Stavros Logarides - *bass, vocals, acoustic guitar*, **Aris Tasoulis** - *organ, piano, keyboards*, **Giorgos Tsoupakis** - *drums, guest musicians:* **Dimis Papchristou** - *guitars*, **John Papadopoulos** - *organ.*

Coming from other musical experiences and from other bands, **Stavros Logarides** and **Aris Tasoulis**, find in **Akritas** the ideal place to create an adrenalin multiform album. The broad use of organ and keyboards remind us of the best **ELP** with highly symphonic moments and strong bonds to classical music. When playing altogether the band's rhythmic section applies continuous changes of tempo and atmospheres that recall **Frank Zappa** or **Aphrodite's Child** moods or even inspired by the dreamlike-ancestral shades of the German cosmic couriers.

DISCOGRAPHY: AKRITAS *(1973, Polydor).*

M.G. & C.C.

APOCALYPSIS

Vasilis Dertilis - *keyboards*, **Yiannis Palamidas** - *vocals*, **Stavros Sidiropoulos** - *drums*. **Harris Photopoulos** - *bass*, **Achiles Spyrou** - *guitars*, **Kimon Vassilopoulos** - *vocals (second album)*, **Lambras Tselentis** - *bass (second album)*, **Kostas Stratigopoulos** - *guitars (second album).*

Considered as the Greek **Genesis**, they publish a first homonym album in 1980, right in the middle of the World Wide prog crisis. Actually their sound is closer to the early works of the Belgian **Machiavel**, with good keyboard and guitar dialogues and an enthusiast theatrical singer. The next and last album, unfortunately, is far below the previous levels, largely dominated by a colorless pop that tries to recall the **Alan Parsons Project** and only at times manages to achieve contemporary sounds close to the style of **Twelfth Night**'s *Fact and Fiction*.

DISCOGRAPHY: APOCALYPSIS *(1980, Minos)* **NO** *(1982, Minos).* M.G. & C.C.

SOCRATES
(Socrates Drank The Conium)

Antonis Tourkoyorgis - *bass, guitar, vocals*, **Yannis Spathas** - *guitar*, **George Trantalidis** - *drums.*

Coming from a strong rock blues experience (**Hendrix**, **Free** and **Cream**) this band signs up with Polydor and immediately releases three excellent albums: *Socrates drank the Conium* (this was their original full name) and *Taste of Conium* both of 1972 are of unquestionable beauty, with the voice of Tourkogiorgis in great evidence and perfectly at ease with the English lyrics. In 1973 *On the wings* is recorded adding a second guitarist, **Gus Doukakis**, to the line-up who together with **Spathas** create a rougher sound, almost raw. Yet it is with Vertigo and the 1974 album that the band reaches its artistic peak, reducing its name to **Socrates**. *Phos* is produced with **Vangelis**' direct production and participation therefore conferring a much more progressive style to the sound. Also the critics unanimously consider it one of the highest moments for the Greek prog genre.

DISCOGRAPHY: SOCRATES DRANK THE CONIUM *(Polydor, 1972)* TASTE OF CONIUM *(Polydor, 1972)* ON THE WINGS *(Polydor, 1973)* PHOS *(Vertigo, 1974).*

C.A. & C.C.

Europe: **HOLLAND**

ALQUIN

Ferdinand Bakker – *guitars, vocals, piano, violin,* **Job Tarenskeen** – *vocals, saxophones,* **Hein Mars** – *vocals, bass,* **Ronald Ottenhoff** – *saxophones, flute,* **Dick Franssen** - *organ, piano,* **Paul Weststrate** - *drums.*
Born in the early '70s they release a first truly prog album entitled *Marks* in 1972, with an interesting mixture of jazz, rock, pop and classical elements. The arrangements derive a certain inspiration from the Canterbury sound and from **Curved Air**, adding a more personal touch through the south-American latino melodies enhanced by a vivid brass section playing in an rhythm & blues style. Excellent also the second work, *The Mountain Queen*, which hardens slightly leaving the prog genre to a more general sense of the term, with the ever present clarity of a Hammond organ and the beautiful alternation of rhythms. A third decidedly more rock-blues oriented album is released in 1973, still sufficiently prog but with funkier elements.

RECOMMENDED RECORDINGS: **MARKS** *(1972, Polydor)* **THE MOUNTAIN QUEEN** *(1973, Polydor).*

M.G. & C.C.

EARTH & FIRE

Jerney Kaagman - *vocals,* **Ton van de Kleij** - *drums,* **Chris Koerts** - *guitars,* **Gerard Koerts** – *guitars, keyboards,* **Hans Ziech** – *bass.*
Among the first to take over prog in Holland, the initial impact of their sound comes from the powerful, amazing and flexible voice of **Jerney Kaagman** that enhances the ethereal atmospheres of her colleagues. They debut with a great homonym album in 1970, even if the times were not yet ripe, and their second release *Song of Marching Children*, (with its amazing title-track suite) only goes to confirm the warm and melodious sounds of this never aggressive ensemble and their tremendous evocative force. Decidedly good also *Atlantis* of 1973 with the rich melodic start of the title-suite that covers side A.

RECOMMENDED RECORDINGS: **SONG OF THE MARCHING CHILDREN** *(1971, Polydor)* **ATLANTIS** *(1973, Polydor).*

M.G. & C.C.

EKSEPTION

Rick van der Linden - *keyboards,* **Huib van Kampen** - *guitar, saxophones,* **Cor Dekker** - *bass ,* **Rob Kruisman** - *flute, saxophones, guitar, vocals ,* **Rein van der Broek** - *trumpet,* **Peter de Leeuwe** - *drums,* **Michel van Dijk** - *vocals,* **Dick Remelink** - *saxophones.*
Important for their peculiar use of the classical music genre, **Linden** and **Broek** master the art of rearranging Bach and Gershwin by exploiting the most symphonic prog and jazz techniques. The compositions initially inspired by **The Nice** and **Keith Emerson** tend towards a large use of the electronic keyboards and woodwinds making immediately clear their strong intentions of going beyond just emulating themes already in the debut of 1969. Twelve albums for a not always great discography since their music often descends into a self indulging magniloquence that often results in tedious and sterile rides. The band is by now totally dismantled given the decease of most of the musicians.

RECOMMENDED RECORDINGS: **BEGGAR JULIE'S TIME TRIP** *(1969, Philips)* **OO.O4** *(1972, Philips).*

M.G. & C.C.

Europe: HOLLAND

KAYAK

Ton Scherpenzeel - *keyboards, vocals,* **Max Werner** - *vocals, mellotron,* **Johan Slager** - *guitars, vocals,* **Cees van Leeuwen** - *bass, vocals,* **Pirn Koopman** - *drums, vocals.*
Since their birth in 1973 they always tried to embrace a more melodic and easy-listening type of prog, with clear references to **Genesis** (and, in a second phase, to **Camel**, when keyboardist **Scherpenzeel** pursued a parallel career in and out as a session-man). Their essentially based keyboard sound is never complex and never contains strange rhythms, always characterized by sweet melodic phrases of romantic, evocative and nostalgic taste. Some works, especially in the '80s, are particularly critiqued given their commercial choices but they maintained themselves coherent and faithful to the initial idea. Surely interesting the album *Royal Bed Bouncer*, more dynamic and various.

RECOMMENDED RECORDINGS: **SEE SEE THE SUN** *(1973, EMI)* **ROYAL BED BOUNCER** *(1975, EMI).* M.G. & C.C.

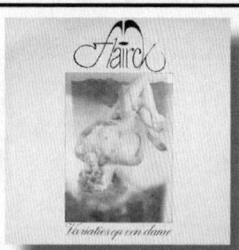

FINCH

Jan Van Nimwegen - *guitars,* **Cleem Determejer** - *keyboards,* **Peter Vink** - *bass,* **Beer Klaasse** - *drums.*
Klaasse and **Vink** are two Dutch blues musicians previously playing in **Q65**. They form **Finch** with the other colleagues, generating symphonic instrumental compositions made of complex and fascinating scores, with strong, rich and elegant hard prog elements. Three excellent albums in only three years, the first is the most affected by the English **Yes** and **ELP** while the second becomes more personal. Then a change in the line-up sees the exit of **Klaasse** and **Determejer** replaced respectively by **Hans Bosboom** (drums) and **Ad Wammes** (keyboards and flute); from this variation unexpectedly comes their best work, *Galleons of Passion* (1977), an album charged with symphonic parts, melodies of **Camel** inspiration.

RECOMMENDED RECORDINGS: **GLORY OF THE INNER FORCE** *(1975, Negram)* **BEYOND EXPRESSION** *(1976, Negram)* **GALLEONS OF PASSION** *(1977, Bubble).* M.G. & C.C.

FLAIRCK

Erik Visser - *guitars, sitar, mandolin,* **Peter Weekers** - *flute,* **Judy Schomper** - *viola, violin,* **Hans Visser** - *guitars,* **Fred Krems** - *percussion, vibes.*
Merging folk, classical and prog to a particular blend of various ethnic acoustic traditional instruments (hints of Celtic and Mediterranean music too), this band constantly underwent changes in its line-up making it close to impossible the definition of a specific formation. The only common denominator present in the entire discography is guitarist **Erik Visser**, elegant and talented musician of Indonesian origins. Under the progressive aspect, the best works are probably the first two of 1978 and 1980, plus a fantastic live album that immediately followed the latter. Their style is always elegant and evocative with ever evolving sounds that maintain a good quality level.

RECOMMENDED RECORDINGS: **VARIATIES OP EEN DAME** *(1978, Polydor)* **GEVECHT MET DE ENGEL** *(1980, Polydor)* **LIVE IN AMSTERDAM** *(1980, Polydor)* **CIRCUS** *(1981, Polydor).* M.G. & C.C.

Europe: HOLLAND

OUTSIDERS

Appie Rammers - *bass*, **Leendert Busch** - *drums*, **Ronald Splinter** - *guitars*, **Tom Krabbendam** - *guitars*, **Wally Tax** - *guitars, vocals*.

This great garage-beat band from Amsterdam published a series of discreet commercial hit singles in Holland and is appreciated for its rough style, devoted to an incurable form of proto-psychedelia. Their first album *The Outsiders* is a live recording released in 1967, where the angry voice of **Wally Tax** is undoubtedly comparable **Mick Jagger**'s.
The following year they publish *CQ*, an album of musical farsightedness pretenses, perhaps not yet fully in their reach: truly psychedelic, some songs recall **The Moody Blues** experience, but the interesting guitars are still unfortunately slightly too anchored to the garage band mentality. The break-up in 1969 ends too soon the career of one of the best Dutch performers of the '60s, pioneers of the Nederpop genre (a natural coming of age of the hippy-beat generation).
DISCOGRAPHY: THE OUTSIDERS (Relax, 1967) **CQ** (Polydor, 1968). **C.A.**

Q65

Frank Nuyens - *guitars*, **Jay Baar** - *drums*, **Joop Roelofs** - *guitars*, **Peter Vink** - *bass*, **Willem Bieler** - *vocals*, **Beer Klaasse** - *drums*.

If only this band had been able to keep the promises made with its first amazing album *Revolution*, they probably would have written one of the brightest pages in the history of European pop rock. Instead, after this 1966 release, they go into a deep experimentation, that often fails since the quintet wades in prog swamps with no true artistic skill and without the adequate production back-up. This is evident already in the following work *Revival* of 1969, and even more so for the production of the controversial *Afghanistan* in 1970, where they are clearly uncomfortable with their own attempt to harden the sounds, making it overall even less credible. Their music becomes ever more disappointing, like in We're gonna make it where the pale progressive traits drown under the strain of their incapacity. The band breaks-up in 1972.
RECOMMENDED RECORDINGS: REVOLUTION (Decca, 1966) **REVIVAL** (Decca, 1969) **AFGHANISTAN** (Negram, 1970). **C.A. & C.C.**

SOLUTION

Willem Ennes - *keyboards*, **Guus Willemse** - *bass, vocals*, **Tom Barlage** - *saxophones*, **Hans Waterman** - *drums*.

They begin their career in 1971 and play on for the entire decade, their sound resulting in a very interesting jazz-rock having much in common with the Canterbury school, especially in the atmospheres recalling the after-**Wyatt Soft Machine**. Not always well-balanced, the compositions even in their best albums sometimes lack of coherence, alternating complex jazz-rock to pure soul or rhythm & blues moments and, in the last period, also to funky. Very interesting nevertheless the first and second albums. These discontinuities increase with the production of **Gus Dudgeon** (also **Elton John**'s producer) and the release of *Fully Interlocking* in 1977. Then when former **Traffic** member **Jim Capaldi** becomes their next producer and songwriter, the prog seems to disappear completely ending here our narration.

RECOMMENDED RECORDINGS: SOLUTION (1971 Catfish) **DIVERGENCE** (1972 Harvest) **FULLY INTERLOCKING** (1977 Rocket). **M.G. & C.C.**

Europe: **HUNGARY**

EAST

Géza Pálvölgyi - *keyboards,* **János Varga** - *guitar,* **István Kárily** - *drums,* **Péter Mózcán** - *bass,* **József Tisza** - *vocals.*

This Hungarian pop rock band is greatly inspired by the progressive scene of the '70s, confirming a sound and style closer to the acid and psychedelic space genre between **Pink Floyd** and **Hawkwind**. In 1981 they publish the excellent *Jatekok*, which will be immediately also issued in an English version entitled *Games*. This great success leads to the following *Huseg* in which their prog is tainted by the new wave invading Europe at the time: the guitars harden and the keyboards become more obsessive. Curiously, the album's cover is identical to *Jatekok*, but in color instead of the original black and white artwork, probably meaning an achieved maturity of their musical language. The third LP, *Resek At Falon* is no longer a prog disciple since the new wave and taste for more elaborate and rich lyrics divert the band to other horizons.

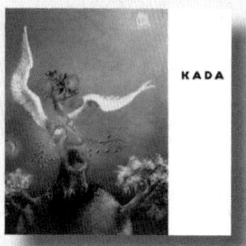

RECOMMENDED RECORDINGS: JATEKOK *(Start, 1981)* **GAMES** *(Start, 1981)* **HUSEG** *(Gong, 1982).*
C.A. & C.C.

KADA

Gergely Ballay - *drums,* **Attila Boros** - *bass,* **Gergely Katona** - *trumpet, horn, trombone,* **Gábor Kollmann** - *sax,* **Gyözö Mogyoró** - *percussion,* **Dániel Váczi** - *sax,* **László Válik** - *guitr, effects,* **Kornél Mogyoró** - *percussion.*

After an already brilliant debut, it is with the 2001 double album *Búcsúzás* that this band confirms its great value: an instrumental jazz-rock avant-garde band that gives great space to improvisation and live performances. Their jazz personality emerges through the use of electric guitars, not far from the style of **Robert Fripp**, where the trumpet represents the main element, straight from the school of **Miles Davis**; all the compositions are dosed with the right amount of electronics, dissonances and particular effects that recall the R.I.O. movement. Recorded live, the large number of instruments skillfully play through the many improvised parts, a feature that predictably characterizes also the next excellent live album of 2004, *Ohoáé*.

DISCOGRAPHY: KADA *(1999, Periferic)* **BÚCSÚZÁS** *(2001, Periferic)* **OHOÁÉ** *(2004, Periferic).*
M.G. & C.C.

ILLÉS ENSEMBLE

Levente Szàrényi - *guitar, vocals,* **Jànos Bròdy** - *rhythm guitars, flute, vocals,* **Szabolcs Szàrényi** - *bass, vocals,* **Lajos Illés** - *vocals, keyboards,* **Zoltàn Pàsztory** - *drums.*

One of the greatest ostracized Hungarian rock-beat bands already active since 1960, they are often compared to **The Beatles** in relation to their first musical period and well represent the psychedelia of the time. The name comes from founding member **Lajos Illés** and the first release dates 1967 though it actually is the soundtrack of *Ezek a Fiatalok* (= these youngsters), a film that sees the participation of other crucial Hungarian bands such as **Omega** and of female pop singer **Koncz Zsuzsa**. After incautiously criticizing their own government, they will be banned for a whole year from performing in any show or concert. Further political pressures will nevertheless force them to break-up in 1973, only to purposely reunite at the fall of the regime in 1990, for a great concert with **Omega** and **Metròs**. **Illés** dies in 2007 at the age of 64.

RECOMMENDED RECORDINGS: EZEK A FIATALOK *(1967 - film soundtrack)* **NEHËZ AZ ÜT** *(Qualiton, 1969)* **ILLÈSEK ÈS POFONOK** *(Qualiton, 1969)* **HUMAN RIGHTS** *(Qualiton, 1971).*
M.G. & C.C.

Europe: ISRAEL

CHURCHILLS
(Jericho Jones)

Robb Huxley - *guitar, vocals*, **Ami Triebich** - *drums*, **Haim Romano** - *guitars, congas, mandolin*, **Michael Gabrielle** - *bass, vocals*, **Danny Shoshan** - *vocals, congas*.

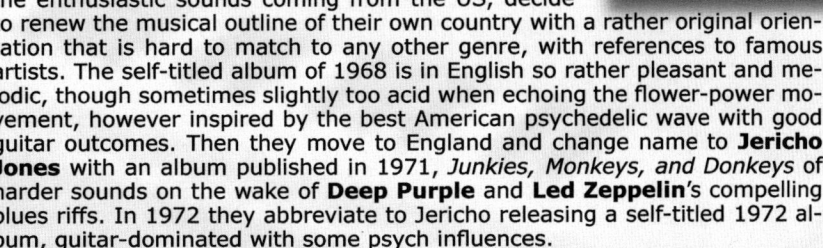

A group of young Israeli musicians who, amazed by the enthusiastic sounds coming from the US, decide to renew the musical outline of their own country with a rather original orientation that is hard to match to any other genre, with references to famous artists. The self-titled album of 1968 is in English so rather pleasant and melodic, though sometimes slightly too acid when echoing the flower-power movement, however inspired by the best American psychedelic wave with good guitar outcomes. Then they move to England and change name to **Jericho Jones** with an album published in 1971, *Junkies, Monkeys, and Donkeys* of harder sounds on the wake of **Deep Purple** and **Led Zeppelin**'s compelling blues riffs. In 1972 they abbreviate to Jericho releasing a self-titled 1972 album, guitar-dominated with some psych influences.

RECOMMENDED RECORDINGS: **Churchills: THE CHURCHILLS** (Ban, 1968) **Jericho Jones: JUNKIES, MONKEYS, AND DONKEYS** (Ban, 1971- Broadley 2010). **C.A. & C.C.**

SHLOMO GRONICH
(NoNames - Ktsat Acheret)

Shlomo Gronich - *keyboards, vocals*, **Shlomo Ydov** - *guitar, bass, percussion, vocals*, **Shem-Tov Levy** - *flute, piano, percussion, vocals*.

In 1971 he releases the first Israeli prog-rock album *Why Didn't You Tell Me?*, ranging from classical to jazz, underground, traditional and cabaret music. After a live project with **Mathi Caspi** (Behind The Sounds) the The Yom Kippur War puts a halt to all musical activities for some time: **Gronich** teams with **Shem Tov Levy** and **Shlomo Ydov** as **NoNames** (known in Hebrew as Ktsat Acheret) recording in 1974 an album reflecting the anguish of war, greatly inspired by **Yes** and **Rick Wakeman**, with a large use of keyboards and flute in the early **Genesis**'s style, though the atmosphere is very different, less evocative and psychedelic with a dose of jazz, classical, avant-garde and middle-eastern music. They split and he leaves for the US, returning in 1980 with the jazz-prog album, *Cotton Candy*. In 1983 he records with Levy *Family Album* before continuing his own prolific career.

RECOMMENDED RECORDINGS: **NoNames: KTSAT ACHERET** *(Hed-Arzì, 1974)* **Shlomo Gronich:COTTON CANDY** *(Hed-Arzì, 1983).* **C.A. & C.C.**

SHEM TOV LEVY
(Sheshet)

Shem Tov Levy (former **Ktzat Acheret**) records his first solo album in 1976 with influences of the usual suspects (**Gentle Giant**, **Yes** and **Mahavishnu Orchestra**) and his trademark sound of classical, jazz and Middle Eastern sonorities. After this he forms Sheshet with female singer **Yehudith 'Judith' Ravitz** and several veteran musicians of jazz and rock backgrounds. The band soon splits but a label notices them in concert and reunites them to record a self titled album in 1977: a soft jazz-rock (highly influenced **Chick Corea**'s *Return to Forever*) interpolating light melodies and delicate symphonic prog with Arabic and Balkan elements and their traditional folk. After this brilliant style contamination, they record an unreleased soundtrack for the film *The Stretcher Mark* before the final break-up. Levy pursues his own career with the 1983 album *Happy Family* released with **Shlomo Gronich**.

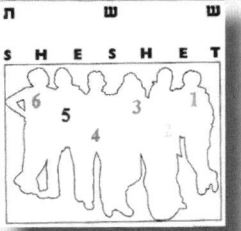

RECOMMENDED RECORDINGS: **SHESHET** *(1977, NMC).* **M.G. & C.C.**

Europe: ITALY

AKTUALA

Walter Maioli, Daniele Cavallanti, Otto Corrado - *horns*, **Antonio Cerantola, Attilio Zanchi** - *guitar*, **Laura Maioli, Lino Capra Vaccina, Trilok Gurtu** - *percussion*, **Marjon Klok** - *harp*, **Marino Vismara** - *cello*, **Maurizio Dones** - *viola*.

Born in the intellectual and political womb of the Italian industrial capital of the '70s, Milan, this is a band of true acoustic sounds and collective improvisation. Though both are seen as pioneers of the soon to become World Music genre, unlike the tribal ethnicity sought by his colleague **Glen Sweeney** (**Third Ear Band**), the composer and flute magician **Walter Maioli** plunges into jazz for his musical explorations: involving the poly-instrumentalist **Daniele Cavallanti** in this project, the three albums greatly echo **Coltrane**, **Don Cherry** and the **Art Ensemble Of Chicago** in their intersections of esoteric folk and north-African tunes that converge into an exotic and warm Mediterranean blues. The ensemble plays in squares and streets, signing up with the experimental label Bla Bla and collaborating with **Trilok Gurtu**. They move to Morocco and after their third album they break-up. **Maioli** continues his ethno-musical research and **Aktuala** is acknowledged as one of the first international examples of world-music.

DISCOGRAPHY: AKTUALA *(Bla Bla, 1973)* **LA TERRA** *(Bla Bla, 1974)* **TAPPETO VOLANTE** *(Bla Bla, 1976)*. M.G. & C.C.

ALPHATAURUS

Michele Bavaro - *vocals*, **Pietro Pellegrini** - *keyboards, vocals, vibes*, **Guido Wasserman** - *guitars*, **Alfonso Oliva** - *bass*, **Giorgio Santandrea** - *drums*.

One of the many brilliant meteors of the '70s' Italian progressive genre goes by the name of **Alphataurus**. Their homonym album is a successful merge of the anglophone symphonic prog to the Mediterranean experience. The musicians show great cohesion through songs in which the keyboards constantly push towards the classical side with their majestic rides and where the guitar contributes in a finishing touch of true rock or of delicate acoustic passages. They sing in their mother tongue yet manage to get away with it brilliantly. They start working on a second project but after recording all the instrumental parts (released posthumous in the interesting document *Dietro L'uragano*) they disband.

DISCOGRAPHY: ALPHATAURUS *(1973, Magma)* **DIETRO L'URAGANO** *(1993, Mellow Records)*. M.G. & C.C.

A PIEDI NUDI

Nicola Gardinale - *guitar*, **Mirko Schiesaro** - *vocals*, **Christian Chinaglia** - *keyboards*, **Simone Bighetti** - *bass*, **Carlo Bighetti** - *drums, flute, vocals*, **Enrico Barchetta** - *french horn*, **Mirko Andreassi** - *vocals*.

After a first album that results more like a trial than a real debut, the band records two CDs that will become a symbol of the Italian prog of the '90s: *Creazione* and *Eclissi*. Guitarist **Nicola Gardinale** leads them towards a particularly hard prog in the most violent **Fripp** style, but in which, above all, the claustrophobic atmospheres of **Balletto di Bronzo** are celebrated. **A Piedi Nudi** seem to tell fairy tales in shades of black, with a dark and aggressive symphonic sound. After the break-up, their former leader returns with the project **Nic-G and the Mogsy**, a band more oriented towards a modern hard-blues rock.

DISCOGRAPHY: A PIEDI NUDI *(1993, Mellow Records)* **CREAZIONE** *(1995, Mellow Records)* **ECLISSI** *(1997, Mellow Records)*. M.G. & C.C.

Europe: ITALY

APOTEOSI

Marcello Surace - *drums*, **Federico Ida** - *bass, flute*, **Franco Vinci** - *guitar, vocals*, **Silvana Ida** - *vocals*, **Massimo Ida** - *keyboards*.

This for long underestimated band proves their classical inspiration through the keyboards and piano streams of music, loaded with Mediterranean melodies in the vocal parts and with the more typical romanticism in the instrumental compositions (which sometimes recall **PFM**, or **Genesis** and **ELP**), without disregarding some space-rock temptations in the closings. Full of groove, their only album of 1975 is also characterized by a beautiful dynamic alternation of delicate flute passages, acoustic guitar and piano to others of great electricity and swift rhythms. Recently re-evaluated abroad through the reborn love of the progressive genre, it is listed in all foreign sites as one of the best products of the Italian pop wave of the '70s.

DISCOGRAPHY: **APOTEOSI** *(1975, Said Record).* M.G. & C.C.

ASGARD

Massimo Michieletto - *guitar*, **Marco Michieletto** - *drums*, **Chris Bianchi d'Espinosa** - *bass, guitar, vocals*, **Alberto Ambrosi** - *keyboards, flute, vocals*, **Francesco Grosso** - *vocals*, **Marco Ferrero** - *drums*, **Sergio Ghiotto** - *guitar*, **Peter Bachmayer** - *drums*, **Ivo Gallo** - *vocals*.

One of the most active in relaunching Italian prog in the early '90s, this band's sound is a monolithic, symphonic music with the right amount of energy that thickens their epic character, like in *Götterdämmerung* and *Arkana*, resulting in a mix of new-prog, baroque and hard-rock (in *Imago Mundi* closer to heavy-rock). *Esoteric Poem* is instead an awkward attempt to be more experimental: originally meant to be an EP, it was then released as a real album, but ending up to be pretty boring in this longer version. They renew the line-up for *Drachenblut*, maintaining a decent quality but still a bit far from the previous early heights.

DISCOGRAPHY: **GÖTTERDÄMMERUNG** *(1991, WMMS)* **ESOTERIC POEM** *(1992, WMMS)* **ARKANA** *(1992, WMMS)* **IMAGO MUNDI** *(1993, WMMS)* **DRACHENBLUT** *(2000, Dragon's Music).* M.G. & C.C.

IL BIGLIETTO PER L'INFERNO

Claudio Canali - *vocals, flute, french horn*, **Baffo Banfi, Giuseppe Cossa** - *keyboards*, **Marco Mainetti, Pier Panzeri** - *guitar*, **Fausto Branchini, Enrico Fragnoni** - *bass*, **Mauro Gnecchi** - *drums*, **Mariolina Sala** - *vocals*, **Raniero Fumagalli** - *uillean pipes*, **Renata Tomasella** - *horns*, **Carlo Redi** - *violin*.

A hard-prog Italian band with an explosive and engaging style that sounds very much like the dreamy rock of **Genesis** and **Yes** or of **Deep Purple** and **Uriah Heep**. The sextet publishes in 1974 an exceptional debut album, dark and aggressive but full of the melodic atmospheres created by the twin-keyboards and supported by both the scratchy sounding guitar and the theatrical voice of **Canali** (whom becomes a friar immediatelt after). They begin recording a second LP but unfortunately disband so this project will actually see the light only in 1992 thanks to an independent label. After forty years **Cossa** and **Gnecchi** reunite the band in 2009 with new elements, using folk arrangements and the convincing mix of traditional and theatrical of singer **Mariolina Sala**.

RECOMMENDED RECORDINGS: **IL BIGLIETTO PER L'INFERNO** *(Trident, 1974)*, **IL TEMPO DELLA SEMINA** *(Mellow Records, 1992)* **TRA L'ASSURDO E LA RAGIONE** *(BTF, 2009)* **VIVI LOTTA PENSA** *(BTF, 2015).* M.G. & C.C.

Europe: ITALY

CAMPO DI MARTE

Enrico Rosa - *guitar, vocals,* **Richard Ursillo** - *bass,* **Mauro Sarti** - *drums, flute,* **Carlo Felice Marcovecchio** - *drums,* **Alfredo Barducci** - *horns, keyboards.*

Florence's only art-rock band that the label United Artists tried to produce for their **Led Zeppelin** hard-sounding baroque fusion and atmospheres, mixed to a certain **Yes** dynamism and romance. The band disbands before even releasing the album, which manages to make it to the record market anyway, with all their musical philosophy surviving inside it. This homonym concept album contains seven tracks, as in seven episodes narrated by two drums, the electric and acoustic guitars, flutes and french horns, all in battle against War, an unusual topic for the genre. After this, guitarist **Enrico Rosa** will pursue his career in the jazz-fusion genre, while **Richard Ursillo** joins **Sensation's Fix** as their bass player. The reunion in 2003 for a series of concerts gives birth to an impeccable live-album.

DISCOGRAPHY: **CAMPO DI MARTE** *(United Artists 1973)* **CONCERTO ZERO** *(BTF 2004).*   M.G. & C.C.

CELESTE

Ciro Perrino - *drums, percussion, flute, keyboards, vocals,* **Leonardo Lagorio** - *keyboards, flute, sax,* **Mariano Schiavolini** - *guitar, violin,* **Giorgio Battaglia** - *bass.*

Born in 1974 as a spin-off of the band **Sistema**, they immediately record their album *Principe Di Un Giorno*, yet release it only two years later. A sophisticated, symphonic and pastoral album with continuous mellotron cascades, an extensive use of the flute and a very delicate guitar. This spectacular debut was followed by a second recording in 1977, *Second Plus*, yet again released only in 1991 due to the break-up: despite the poor audio quality, it is another amazing album and surprisingly different in style, a vivid Canterbury jazz-rock. Drummer **Ciro Perrino**, co-founder of label Mellow Records, was the one who recovered the old tapes for this second LP and then put together a third in 1994 entitled I suoni di una sfera, always recuperating unpublished tracks.

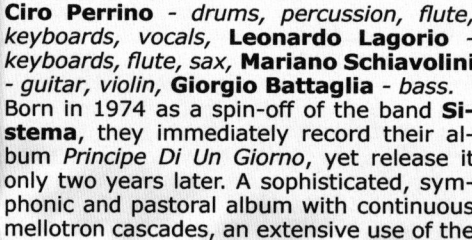

DISCOGRAPHY: **PRINCIPE DI UN GIORNO (aka Celeste)** *(1976, Grog)* **SECOND PLUS** *(1991, Mellow Records)* **I SUONI DI UNA SFERA** *(1994, Mellow Records).*   M.G. & C.C.

CERVELLO

Corrado Rustici - *guitars, flute, vibes,* **Gianluigi Di Franco** - *vocals, flute,* **Giulio D'Ambrosio** - *horns,* **Antonio Spagnolo** - *bass, guitar,* **Remigio Esposito** - *percussion.*

Naples '70s is a concentration of creativity and breaks from traditional melodic songwriting: Showmen are the pioneers, **Osanna** the standard-bearers and **Cervello** probably the best followers of this new Partenopean sound. The group explores the theatrical possibilities of rock, inspired by Greek tragedy and perform live wearing costume themes. *Melos* is a magical album embedded with flute and choirs which create surreal and unusual melodies between **King Crimson**'s *Lizard* and **Osanna** (Corrado is the brother of the famous **Danilo Rustici**). The band breaks-up in 1974: **Gianluigi Di Franco** (dead in 2005) collaborates with **Tony Esposito** ("Kalimba de Luna") and later will become a music therapist; **Corrado Rustici** joins **Nova** following them to the USA and later becoming a famous international producer.

DISCOGRAPHY: **MELOS** *(Ricordi 1973).*   M.G. & C.C.

CHERRY FIVE

Tony Tartarini - *vocals*, **Claudio Simonetti, Gianluca De Rossi** - *keyboards*, **Massimo Morante, Ludovico Piccinini** - *guitar*, **Fabio Pignatelli, Pino Sallusti** - *basso*, **Carlo Bordini** - *drums*.

From the ashes of this group will rise the more famous band **Goblin**. As a matter of fact, their only album as **Cherry Five** comes out posthumous in 1976 when they had already transitioned, yet it was recorded a couple of years before and put on hold probably to comply with some contractual clause. This highly technically skilled band is greatly inspired by the most classic British symphonic rock of **ELP** and **Genesis**. The songs are sung in English and the vocal partitions result very convincing. Despite the derivative nature of the long compositions, the interaction between **Simonetti**'s keyboards and **Morante**'s guitar-playing is successfully supported by the rapid rhythm changes. Most recently the founding members **Bordini** and **Tartarini** reunited with the help of new young musicians, resurrecting the band and publishing a new brand album in 2015.

DISCOGRAPHY: CHERRY FIVE (1976, Cinevox) **IL POZZO DEI GIGANTI** (2015, Black Widow).

M.G. & C.C.

DE DE LIND

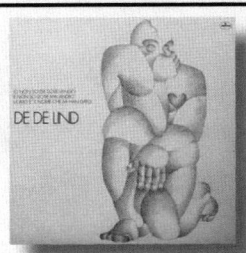

Matteo Vitolli - *guitars, percussion, piano, flute*, **Gilberto Trama** - *flute, sax, piano, organ, horn*, **Vito Paradiso** - *vocals, acoustic guitar*, **Eddy Lorigiola** - *bass*, **Ricky Rebajoli** - *drums, percussion*.

The name from a Miss Playboy of 1967, christens this underrated band that is actually a progressive legend since they manage to rise above the British emulations of their Italian colleagues with personality and an extraordinary originality. An exceptionally inspired album of evocative and charming hard-prog with passionate finishing touches: *Io non so da dove vengo e non so dove mai andrò, Uomo è il nome che mi hanno dato* (I don't know where I come from and I don't know where I will ever go, Man is the name they gave me). The electric and acoustic sounds of **Vito Paradiso**'s guitars and **Gilberto Trama**'s flute merge perfectly into a wonderful and fundamentally flawless composition. Rumors of a soon to be reunion are flying but not yet landed.

DISCOGRAPHY: IO NON SO DA DOVE VENGO E NON SO DOVE MAI ANDRÒ. UOMO È IL NOME CHE MI HAN DATO (1973, Mercury-Phonogram).

M.G. & C.C.

DELIRIUM

Ivano Fossati - *vocals, flute*, **Martin Grice** - *horns*, **Mimmo Di Martino, Rino Dimopoli, Roberto Solinas** - *guitar, vocals*, **Marcello Reale, Fabio Chignini** - *bass*, **Ettore Vigo** - *keyboards*, **Peppino Di Santo** - *drums*.

Together with **Le Orme**, **The Trip** and **Osanna**, this is one of the first bands of Italian prog, but instead playing the typical symphonic or hard rock, the band from Genova is inspired by a more folk traditional music in between Jethro Tull and Traffic. The soft and delicate debut album makes large use of both guitars and flute, fulling the atmosphere with dreamy ballads. Their most famous song is "Jesahel", a hit presented at the Festival of Sanremo which is still today a classic cult. Soon after this first release **Ivano Fossati** exits the band for a solo career that will transform him into the most important songwriters and singer still active this very day. The second album features jazz-rock elements that will be even more pronounced in the following one, rich of new ideas and intuitions. They break-up in the mid '70s and reunite some thirty years later with a new line-up and tour that leads to a passionate live recording and a recent studio album produced by the label Black Widow.

DISCOGRAPHY: DOLCE ACQUA (Fonit Cetra, 1971) **LO SCEMO E IL VILLAGGIO** (Fonit Cetra, 1973) **DELIRIUM III (Viaggio negli arcipelaghi del tempo)** (Fonit Cetra, 1974) **LIVE - VIBRAZIONI NOTTURNE** (Black Widow, 2007).

M.G. & C.C.

Europe: ITALY

DFA

Alberto De Grandis - *drums*, **Alberto Bonomi** - *keyboards*, **Luca Baldassarri** - *bass*, **Silvio Minella** - *guitars*.

Jazz-rock never really prospered in Italy, yet the few active ensembles in this field were exceptional: **Perigeo**, **Napoli Centrale**, **Picchio Dal Pozzo**, **Deus Ex Machina** and the **D.F.A**. The acronym stands for **Duty Free Area** since their sound is actually a sort of free trade area for the symphonic and psychedelic genre, a fusion prog beacon of more recent times. The band from Verona held high the international credibility of Italian prog by interpreting the Canterbury language in a contemporary and imaginative way. A demo-tape for their debut of 1997, a couple of good albums at the end of the decade, an excellent live album and a third more mature record represent the essential production of this quartet.

DISCOGRAPHY: **LAVORI IN CORSO** (Scolopendra, 1997) **DUTY FREE AREA** (Mellow Records 1999) **WORK IN PROGRESS LIVE** (Moonjune, 2001) **4TH** (Moonjune 2008). M.G. & C.C.

DEVIL DOLL

Mr. Doctor – *vocals*, **Francesco Carta** – *piano*, **Sasha Olenjuk** – *violin*, **Bor Zuljan** – *guitars*, **Jani Hace** – *bass*, **Davor Klaric** – *keyboards*, **Roman Ratej** – *drums*.

Absolute fans of the movies by **Tod Browning**, the Italian-Slovenian band derive not only their name from one of his films (Devil Doll) but also the nickname of singer **Mario Pancera** that hid his identity under the alias of 'Mr. Doctor'. Their story is a real enigma of darkness assisted by an amazing media circus that suck vital lymph directly out from the vein of charming esoteric stories such as the *Phantom of the Opera*, *The Portrait of Dorian Gray*, *The Hunchback of Notre Dame* and *Faust*. Among the most sublime albums of their discography: *Eliogabalus* of 1990 (inspired from the opera of **Antonin Artaud**) and *Sacrilegium* of 1992.

RECOMMENDED RECORDINGS: **ELIOGABALUS** (Hurdy Gurdy, 1990) **SACRILEGIUM** (Hurdy Gurdy, 1992). M.G. & C.C.

ETNA

Carlo Pennisi - *guitar, mandolin*, **Elio Volpini** - *bass, contrabass*, **Agostino Marangolo** - *drums, percussion*, **Antonio Marangolo** - *keyboards, clarinet*.

Already playing an average Italian pop prog as **Flea** since 1971 (*Flea on the Honey*), the core musicians decide to take a step further into the genre founding **Etna** and changing direction from the previous experiences by taking on a rich jazz-rock of an entirely instrumental nature. Their sound maintains the Mediterranean flavor, guided by the clever interlacing of guitars and keyboards with the electric piano and the ever-changing rhythmic section. The record is a success, warm and skillfully played, a kind of idealistic middle ground between **The Mahavishnu Orchestra** and **Baricentro**.

DISCOGRAPHY: **ETNA** (1975, Catoca). M.G. & C.C.

Europe: ITALY

EZRA WINSTON

Mauro di Donato - *synths, bass, vocals,* **Daniele Iacono** - *drums.* **Mauro Bianchi** - *synths,* **Paolo Lucini** - *flute,* **Fabio Palmieri** - *guitars.*

The '80s was a good moment in Italy for this group of brave pioneers: young bands such as **Malibran, Nuova Era, Aton's, Notturno Concertante** were working in the new underground progressive panorama. In 1988 **Ezra Winston** publishes their first real album of this new Italian prog, *Myth of the Crisavides*. This band from Rome, active since 1984,

immediately inspired many other musicians. Italian fans were given hope thanks to this renewed symphonic prog inspired by **Genesis, Gentle Giant, Yes** and other great English bands, with the return of sumptuous and complex arrangements and the recovery of fairy tales and surrealistic atmospheres. Their second album of 1990, Ancient afternoons sees the participation of a special guest: **Aldo Tagliapietra** from **Le Orme** and his wonderful voice. After this and another few concerts, the group apparently breaks up and each musician is involved in different other projects. Today there are rumors of an imminent return running through the grapevine.

DISCOGRAPHY: MYTH OF THE CHRYSAVIDES (Ezra Works 1988) **ANCIENT AFTERNOONS** (Angel 1990). **M.G. & C.C.**

GARYBALDI

Bambi Fossati - *guitar, vocals,* **Lio Marchi** - *keyboards,* **Angelo Traverso** - *bass,* **Maurizio Cassinelli** - *drums,* **Sandro Serra** - *bass.*

Born on the ashes of **The Gleemen** (who released only one good album of Italian Rock in 1970), Garybaldi is the project of guitarist **Bambi Fossati**, a great musician strongly influenced by **Jimi Hendrix**, who performed live also with **Santana, VDGG, Uriah Heep** and **Bee Gees**. In fact Jimi's sound is recognizable at once when listening to

the first track "Maya Desnuda" from the debut album *Nuda*. The whole record is ignited by an aggressive hard blues guitar, full of enthusiastic acid solos. The album cover is a fantastic work of art, a masterpiece by the famous illustrator Guido Crepax. Their second album *Astrolabio* of 1973 widens the prog elements with two long suites which fill the whole record of psychedelic and almost cosmic sounds, leaving great space to improvisation. The following incarnation of this group will be based upon the figure of their new leader **Fossati**, changing name accordingly to **Bambibanda e le Melodie** or **Bambi Fossati and Garybaldi**, until his death in 2014.

RECOMMENDED RECORDINGS: NUDA (1972, CGD) **ASTROLABIO** (1973, Fonit) **BAMBI FOSSATI & GARYBALDI** (1990, Artis) **BAMBI COMES ALIVE** (1993, Mellow Records). **M.G. & C.C.**

IL GIRO STRANO

Alessio Feltri - *keyboards,* **Mariano Maio** - *sax, flute,* **Mirko Ostinet** - *vocals,* **Mario Pignata** - *bass, guitars,* **Delio Sismondo** - *drums,* **Valentino Vecchio** - *guitar,* **Riccardo Gabutti** - *bass.*

One of the best posthumous discoveries of Italian prog in the '70s is **Giro Strano**, an unlucky band who performed live many times with great appreciation of the audience.

Sadly their only album, recorded between 1972 and 1973, was released twenty years later thanks to Mellow Records: *La Divina Commedia* (1992) is a good album of symphonic prog, with dark melodies and jazz rock inserts, fast and vibrant rhythms where the Sax is absolutely outstanding. This may be the reason of their wrongful comparison to VDGG, while the textures of organ and guitar are more directly compared to **Colosseum** and **Tonton Macoute**. Worthy of mention is lead vocalist **Mirko Ostinet** and his powerful and scratching voice, perfect for the lyrics (sometimes naif), although this is a common characteristic of many Italian bands of the '70s.

DISCOGRAPHY: LA DIVINA COMMEDIA (1992, Mellow Records). **M.G. & C.C.**

Europe: ITALY

JUMBO

Alvaro Fella - *vocals, guitar*, **Daniele Bianchini** - *guitar*, **Vito Balzano, Tullio Granatello** - *drums*, **Aldo Gargano, Paolo Guglielmetti** - *bass*, **Dario Guidotti** - *flute*, **Sergio Conte, Paolo Dolfini** - *keyboards*.

A band from Milan who plays powerful electric rock with provocative lyrics defending social themes. Their songs are not the average protest of some politicized Italian writer, but rather a harsher music inspired by **Led Zeppelin** and **Jethro Tull**. We can find this characteristic in their first self titled album of 1972, whilst in the second, *DNA*, we find longer songs with many instrumental jams. The third, *Vietato Ai Minori Di 18 Anni* (X-rated under 18) is definitely their masterpiece: **Alvaro Fella**'s scratching voice and their powerful music describe raw stories of alcoholism, alienation and homosexual victims. **Jumbo** disbands in 1976 with some sporadic reunions in 1983 and 1989. On the wake of a renewed interest for Italian Prog during the '90s, **Daniele Bianchini** reunites the band in 1992, without **Fella**, publishing an interesting album of new songs, even though not as good as the previous.

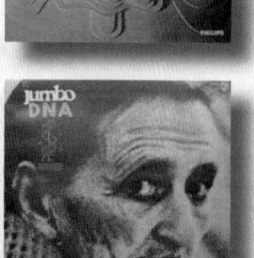

RECOMMENDED RECORDINGS: JUMBO (Philips, 1972) **DNA** (Philips, 1972) **VIETATO AI MINORI DI 18 ANNI** (Philips, 1973) **LIVE** (Mellow Records, 1992) **PASSING BY** (Jumbo, 2001). **M.G. & C.C.**

LOCANDA DELLE FATE

Leonardo Sasso - *vocals*, **Michele Conta, Oscar Mazzoglio** - *keyboards*, **Ezio Vevey** - *guitar, flute*, **Alberto Gaviglio** - *guitar*, **Luciano Boero** - *bass*, **Giorgio Gardino** - *drums*.

The death of **Demetrio Stratos** (**Area**, page 103) symbolically represents the end of the fabulous Italian Pop era of the '70s. **Locanda delle Fate**'s first album can instead be considered as the very last one for this phase: Forse le lucciole non si amano più (1977) was published by Polydor, but probably came out too late to be properly appreciated given the invasion of punk and disco music. Although tastes were inevitably changing in Italy, this record remains the gem that survived the dark ages between the end of the '70s and the mid '80s. It is still a favorite for any prog fan and recognized as a masterpiece in the history of progressive rock. The band was deeply influenced by **Genesis** and followed the same compositional structure of **Banco del Mutuo Soccorso**, using two keyboards, two guitars and a series of melancholic songs sung by **Leonardo Sasso**'s superlative voice (very similar to **Francesco Di Giacomo**). After more than twenty years from their break up, they reform in 1999 with a new album and restart their career as the cult band that they were.

RECOMMENDED RECORDINGS: **FORSE LE LUCCIOLE NON SI AMANO PIÙ** (Polydor 1977). **M.G. & C.C.**

MAXOPHONE

Sergio Lattuada - *keyboards, vocals*, **Marco Tomasini, Roberto Giuliani** - *guitars, piano, vocals*, **Leonardo Schiavone** - *horns*, **Maurizio Bianchini** - *horn, trumpet, vibes, percussion, vocals*, **Marco Croci** - *bass, vocals*, **Alberto Ravasini** - *bass, acoustic guitar, flute, lead vocals*, **Sandro Lorenzetti, Carlo Monti** - *drums*.

An extraordinary band who released a powerful prog rock album performed with strong personality and the typical rock line-up to which they added classical instruments like horns and strings. From the combination of these various elements rises a splendid album of great symphonic heights, with well structured songs, changes of tempo, classical pauses, rock sounds and a certain Jazz influence that nevertheless maintains a seductive Mediterranean atmosphere. The comparison with **Genesis** and **PFM** is purely indicative since **Maxophone** write their own songs and shine with their own light. Just like all the other bands facing the prog genre crisis at the end of '70s, they breakup after the release of an English version of their album in 1975 and, just like all their colleagues, they reunited twenty years later due to the renewed interest of the fans. In 2016 the latest Japanese Tour that led to their new studio album *La Fabbrica Delle Nuvole*.

DISCOGRAPHY: MAXOPHONE (1975, Produttori Associati) **LIVE IN TOKYO** (2014, Immaginifica- SELF) **LA FABBRICA DELLE NUVOLE** (2017, AMS). **M.G.**

Europe: ITALY

LA MASCHERA DI CERA

Fabio Zuffanti - bass, **Agostino Macor** - keyboards, **Alessandro Corvaglia** - vocals, **Andrea Monetti** - flute, sax, **Marco Cavani** - drums, **Maurizio Di Tollo** - drums.

At the beginning of the new millennium **Fabio Zuffanti** founds a band called **La Maschera di Cera** (the wax mask), releasing their debut in 2002, clearly inspired by the '70s' Italian musical genre. The audience immediately reacts fondly to the vintage atmospheres that recall **Museo Rosenbach** or **Metamorfosi**: a symphonic dark rock with **Agostino Macor** playing superbly his keyboards in duet with the flute of **Andrea Monetti**, both harmonized by **Alessandro Corvaglia**'s compelling voice (one of the best Italian singers so far, today in **Delirium**). The following albums are all at the same high quality level and adding more power to their style. Their participation in the Prog Exhibition of 2010 in Rome opens them to new horizons and, given the success, they issue a last album in 2013, *Le Porte Del Domani*, that can be seen as a curious sequel to *Felona and Sorona* by **Le Orme**.

DISCOGRAPHY: LA MASCHERA DI CERA *(2002, Mellow Records)* IL GRANDE LABIRINTO *(2003, Mellow Records)* IN CONCERTO *(2004, Mellow Records)* LUXADE *(2006, Immaginifica)* LE PORTE DEL DOMANI *(2013, AMS/BTF).* M.G. & C.C.

METAMORFOSI

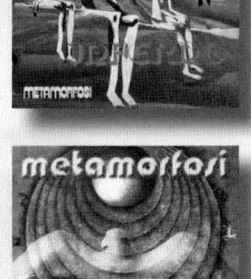

Davide Spitaleri - lead vocals, flute, **Enrico Olivieri** - piano, keyboards, flute, vocals, **Roberto Turbitosi** - bass, guitar, vocals, **Luciano Tamburro** - guitar, **Mario Natali** - drums, percussion, **Gianluca Herygers** - drums, percussion, **Leonardo Gallucci** - bass, acoustic guitar, **Fabio Moresco** - drums.

After an interesting but weak debut, **Metamorfosi** achieve greater quality with their second release *Inferno*, a mature album which ignites their career and puts them among the best bands of the Italian Prog scene in the '70s. This album is meant to be the first chapter of a trilogy that will last over 4 decades! Based on Dante's Divine Comedy, it is a superlative work of symphonic prog, coloured by dark atmospheres, precious evocative vocals (**Jimmy Spitaleri**) and led by the keyboards of **Enrico Olivieri**. It was targeted by the critics because of a certain naivety of lyrics, yet remains without a doubt one of the most important albums of Italian Prog. After a break of about thirty years, the sequel *Paradiso* is published, a convincing return, very close to the previous but less darker. The consequent success is enough to start working on other new projects, live performances and their third closing chapter *Purgatorio* in 2015.

RECOMMENDED RECORDINGS: ... E FU IL SESTO GIORNO *(1972, Vedette)* INFERNO *(1973, Vedette)* PARADISO *(2004, Progressivamente).* M.G. & C.C.

MOONGARDEN

Cristiano Roversi - bass, stick, keyboards, **Simone Baldini Tosi, Riccardo Tonco, Luca Palleschi** - vocals, **David Cremoni, Dimitri Sardini, Marco Tafelli** - guitar, **Luca Dell'Anna** - keyboards, **Mirko Tagliasacchi** - bass, **Adolfo Bonati, Max Sorrentini, Mau Di Tollo** - drums.

Among the crowded Prog scenario of the '90s, **Moongarden** represents a possible evolution from the standard new symphonic rock to a more complex modern art-rock. Since their debut they are deeply influenced by **Genesis**, **Camel** and **IQ** and their most significant work *The Gates of Omega* is more than just a sum of these styles: it is a milestone for European New Prog. After this important and well appreciated work, they undergo a simplification without losing their elaborate sound. In fact the following albums are more mature, inspired by great bands such as **Radiohead** and **Porcupine Tree** and great authors like **Peter Gabriel**, but with a more balanced use of technology and more accessible melodies. Their leader **Cristiano Roversi** is a talented composer and an eclectic performer: his collaborations with **Mangala Vallis** and the parallel project **Submarine Silence** are worthy of mention.

RECOMMENDED RECORDINGS: MOONSADNESS *(Mellow Records 1994)* THE GATES OF OMEGA *(Mellow Records 2001).* M.G. & C.C.

Europe: ITALY

OPUS AVANTRA

Donella Del Monaco - *vocals,* **Alfredo Tisocco** - *keyboards,* **Luciano Tavella, Vincenzo Caroli** - *flute,* **Pierdino Tisato, Tony Esposito, Paolo Siani, Saverio Tasca** - *percussion,* **Enrico Professione, Pieregidio Spiller, Riccardo Perraro, Manuela Rizzo** - *strings,* **Renato Zanella, Tony Lee** - *electric guitar.*

Opus Avantra is an ensemble of very talented musicians (like **Donella Del Monaco**, soprano and nephew of the famous tenor **Mario Del Monaco**) and the philosopher/lyricist **Giorgio Bisotto**. They manage to unite classical music and the finest modern Pop: in fact the name itself is a synthesis of the words 'avantgarde' and 'tradition'. Re-known journalist and producer **Renato Marengo** (who will add keyboardist **Alfredo Tisocco** and drummers **Tony Esposito** and **Paolo Siani** to the recording) helps release their marvelous debut, Introspezione, undisputed for creativity and perfection. After a second album full of symbolism, **Donella** decides to pursue an irregular solo career publishing two chill out projects, Strata and Lyrics. After this momentary break up, as many bands of the times, **Opus Avantra** reunite in 2004 with a new album Venetia Et Anima and a Japanese tour in 2008.
DISCOGRAPHY: OPUS AVANTRA - Donella Del Monaco (Introspezione) *(Trident 1974)* **LORD CROMWELL (Plays Suite For Seven Vices)** *(Suono 1975)* **VENETIA ET ANIMA** *(Opus Avantra 2004).*   M.G. & C.C.

IL PAESE DEI BALOCCHI

Armando Paone - *keyboards, vocals,* **Fabio Fabiani** - *guitars,* **Marcello Martorelli** - *bass,* **Sandro Laudadio** - *drums, vocals.*

1972 is a fruitful year for Italian Prog: **Il Paese dei Balocchi** (the land of fun games) is the interesting self-titled concept album, and sadly the only one, for this formidable band. A beautiful gem containing ten tracks performed as separate episodes of the same suite. Its symphonic rock is closer to classical music than to rock and their sound is represented by a majestic use of keyboards, even in the more delicate passages. Another main feature is the presence of a strong string section, just like a little Orchestra supporting the band with continuity, interactive to all their performances. All the dramatic parts are empathized without being too kitsch and the final result is fascinating, well balanced and close to perfection.

DISCOGRAPHY: IL PAESE DEI BALOCCHI *(1972, CGD).*   M.G. & C.C.

PICCHIO DAL POZZO

Aldo De Scalzi - *keyboards, vocals,* **Paolo Griguolo** - *guitars, vocals,* **Giorgio Karaghiosoff, Claudio Lugo, Roberto Romani** - *horns,* **Andrea Beccari** - *bass, vocals.* **Aldo Di Marco** - *drums.*

This band from Genova, guided by **Aldo De Scalzi** (brother of **Vittorio De Scalzi** from **New Trolls**), represents a unique experience for Italy. **Picchio Dal Pozzo** interprets at its best the Canterbury lessons, using surreal humor, impeccable performances, brilliant compositions and an open concept of band. Two compelling albums are released in the second half of the '70s, greatly inspired by **Zappa** and **Hatfield and the North**. The first is a journey through jazz, avant-garde and psychedelia, while the second perfects the rhythmic solutions. Disbanded in 1980, all the musicians will be divided in their own activities and **De Scalzi** himself will be employed as composer of movie soundtracks. After over twenty years the label Cuneiform releases Camere Zimmer Rooms in 2000 gathering unpublished old tapes and recordings. This renewed interest brings them back together and in 2004 they publish a new studio album containing vocal samples of the late **Demetrio Stratos**.

DISCOGRAPHY: PICCHIO DAL POZZO *(Grog 1976)* **ABBIAMO TUTTI I SUOI PROBLEMI** *(L'Orchestra 1980)* **CAMERE ZIMMER ROOMS** *(Cuneiform 2000)* **PIC_NIC@VALDAPOZZO** *(Auditorium 2004).*   M.G. & C.C.

Europe: ITALY

PIERROT LUNAIRE

Gaio Chiocchio - *guitars, keyboards, percussion, vocals,* **Arturo Stàlteri** - *piano, keyboards, vocals,* **Vincenzo Caporaletti** - *guitars, flute, bass,* **Jaqueline Darby** - *vocals,* **Massimo Buzzi** - *drums.*

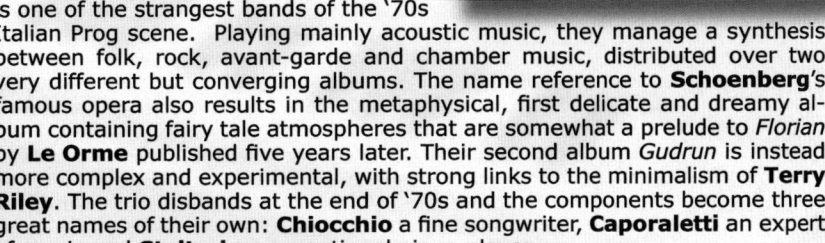

The trio from Rome, **Pierrot Lunaire**, is one of the strangest bands of the '70s Italian Prog scene. Playing mainly acoustic music, they manage a synthesis between folk, rock, avant-garde and chamber music, distributed over two very different but converging albums. The name reference to **Schoenberg**'s famous opera also results in the metaphysical, first delicate and dreamy album containing fairy tale atmospheres that are somewhat a prelude to *Florian* by **Le Orme** published five years later. Their second album *Gudrun* is instead more complex and experimental, with strong links to the minimalism of **Terry Riley**. The trio disbands at the end of '70s and the components become three great names of their own: **Chiocchio** a fine songwriter, **Caporaletti** an expert of music and **Stalteri** an exceptional piano player.

DISCOGRAPHY: **PIERROT LUNAIRE** *(IT, 1974)* **GUDRUN** *(IT, 1977).* **M.G.**

PROCESSION

Gianfranco Gaza, Samuele Alletto - *vocals,* **Roby Munciguerra, Marcello Capra** - *guitars,* **Angelo Girardi, Paolo D'Angelo, Enzo Martin** - *bass,* **Giancarlo Capello, Francesco Froggio Francica, Nico Spallino** - *drums,* **Maurizio Gianotti** - *horns,* **Mario Bruno, Stefano Carrara** - *keyboards.*

After playing as a cover band in various clubs, **Procession** sign a contract for two different but fascinating albums: *Frontiera* is focused bitterly on the concept of immigration, deeply influenced by **Led Zeppelin** and **Cream**, with the participation guitarists **Capra** and **Munciguerra** and the powerful voice of **Gianfranco Gaza** (often compared to **Robert Plant**). The second album, *Fiaba*, sees a line-up evolution with Munciguerra alone on the guitar (**Capra** leaves for Army duty) and **Maurizio Gianotti** joining in on flute and sax. It is more connected to the prog rock genre, with echoes of **Jethro Tull** and of the best British prog. They disband in 1975 pursuing separate careers (**Gaza** as singer of **Arti & Mestieri** for a while). **Capra** instead decides to create his own acoustic trio called **The Glad Tree**. In 2013 he will discover some old live recordings of a concert with the original **Procession** line-up (preceding their first album) and without **Munciguerra**: these tapes will be published as *9 Gennaio 1972*, not perfect in sound but still a fascinating document.

RECOMMENDED RECORDINGS: **FRONTIERA** *(Fonit Cetra, 1972)* **FIABA** *(Fonit Cetra, 1974),* **9 GENNAIO 1972** *(Electromantic, 2012).* **M.G.**

QUELLA VECCHIA LOCANDA

Massimo Roselli - *keyboards, vocals,* **Giorgio Giorgi** - *vocals, flute,* **Patrick Traina** - *drums, percussion,* **Romualdo Coletta** - *bass,* **Raimondo Maria Cocco** - *guitar, vocals,* **Donald Lax, Claudio Felice** - *violin.*

Quella Vecchia locanda (that old inn) deserves a notable place in the Italian Prog panorama. They released two wonderful albums with incredible and colorful art works on their covers, are both characterized by an elaborated and powerful symphonic rock, refined by the baroque elements though maintaining the Mediterranean melodic traits. The compositions are rich and interesting, creating a vibrant prog of Italian taste, greatly inspired by PFM and Antonio Vivaldi, although played with a style belonging to the best Gentle Giant, King Crimson and Traffic.

DISCOGRAPHY: **QUELLA VECCHIA LOCANDA** *(1972, Help!)* **IL TEMPO DELLA GIOIA** *(1974, RCA)* **LIVE** *(1993, Mellow Records).* **M.G.**

Europe: ITALY

SAINT JUST

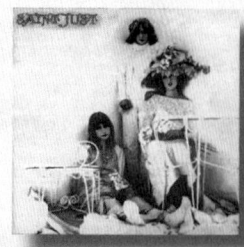

Jenny Sorrenti - *vocals* **Tony Verde** - *bass, guitar, vocals*, **Mario D'Amora** - *keyboards*, **Robert Fix** - *winds*, **Gianni Guarracino, Tito Rinesi, Andrea Faccenda** - *guitars*, **Fulvio Maras, Marcello Vento** - *drums*, **Tony Esposito** - *percussion*. Guided by lead singer **Jane** (**Jenny**) **Sorrenti**, their first homonym album is a superlative work that mixes perfectly all the reminiscences that, in that period, were in the air: from folk (especially French) to prog, from the electric bolts of rock to the baroque sonorities. More than a band, a real melting pot of intentions: mostly from the Naple's area, they lived in a hippy-style community of artists on the Bracciano lake (near Rome), a gathering point able to welcome fellow musicians creating some of the best experiences in their sound. The second and last album, *La Casa Del Lago* (the house on the lake), differs deeply from the previous enhancing the prog genre with a psychedelic spirits closer to the American west-coast bands. Then the 1974 break-up that leads Jenny toward a successful solo career. In 2010 her husband **Marcello Vento** (drummer in **Saint Just**) strongly supports her in hosting a come-back of the band and will release the album *Prog Explosion* in 2011 under the name **Saint Just Again**. **Marcello** dies in 2013 at the age of 63 due to an incurable illness, yet Jenny still progs on with her renewed band.
DISCOGRAPHY: SAINT JUST *(Harvest, 1973)* **LA CASA DEL LAGO** *(Harvest, 1974)* **PROG EXPLOSION** *(Raro Records, 2010)*.   M.G. & C.C.

SEMIRAMIS

Paolo Faenza - *drums, percussion, vibes*, - **Marcello Reddavide** - *bass*, **Giampiero Artegiani** - *guitars, keyboards*, **Michele Zarrillo** - *guitars, vocals*, **Maurizio Zarrillo** - *piano, keyboards*
Semiramis are one of the best Italian 'one shot' bands of the '70s. Founded by the **Zarrillo** brothers, excellent teenage musicians, they release their only record in 1973: *Dedicato a Frazz* is a fantastic album with a fascinating art-work cover. Performed with impressive mastery, the keyboards and guitars tend towards a jazzy classical rock. All seven tracks develop elaborate arrangements with continuous tempo-changes, balancing wisely the use of each instrument by proving a unique skill in mixing electric and acoustic moments. It's a pity they didn't last longer: **Michele Zarrillo** pursues his own career as a famous pop-melodic song-writer, singing in the best Italian Festivals like Sanremo or on TV shows to this very day; **Giampiero Artegiani** is a well-known songwriter and arranger. After more than forty years three of them reunite (**Artegiani, Zarrillo** and **Faenza**) for some live performances together with new young musicians to complete the lineup. Despite the unexpected death of **Maurizio Zarrillo** a new album and a live DVD/CD version of *Frazz* is scheduled to be released in 2017.
DISCOGRAPHY: DEDICATO A FRAZZ *(1973, Trident)*.   M.G. & C.C.

SHOWMEN (Showmen 2)

Mario Musella - *vocals, bass*, **James Senese** - *sax, flute, percussioni, vocals*, **Elio d'Anna** - *sax, flute*, **Giuseppe "Pepè" Botta** - *guitar*, **Luciano Maglioccola** - *keyboards*, **Franco Del Prete** - *drums, percussion*, **Gianmichele Mattiuzzo** - *keyboards, vocals*, **Mario Archittu** - *trombone, piano*, **Piero Alonso** - *guitar*.
A band born in Naples at the end of the '60s playing rhythm and blues: **Mario Musella** and **James Senese** start off by re-elaborating some famous classic Italian songs of the time like "Non si può leggere nel cuore" and "Un'ora sola ti vorrei" and gathering them in two self-titled albums of melodic taste and black music mood. In 1970 they breakup and **Musella** pursues his solo career until his death in 1979, while **Elio D'Anna** together with **Lino Vairetti** and **Danilo Rustici** found the **Osanna**. In 1971 Senese, Botta and Del Prete reunite as **Showmen 2** adding new musicians to the line-up like **Mattiuzzo, Archittu** and **Alonso**. This time they tend toward a more powerful jazz-rock prog sound in their album of 1972, but sadly it is barely noticed and they decide to quit once more. All but **James Senese**, fantastic saxophonist, that will create his own jazz-rock band called **Napoli Centrale** (see page 364).
DISCOGRAPHY: THE SHOWMEN *(1969, RCA)* **SHOWMEN** *(1970, RCA)* **SHOWMEN 2** *(1972, B.B.B.)*.   M.G. & C.C.

Europe: ITALY

IL SISTEMA

Luciano Cavanna - bass, vocals, **Leonardo Lagorio** - sax, flute, electric piano, **Enzo Merogno** - guitar, vocals, **Ciro Perrino** - drums, percussion, flute, vocals, **Floriano Roggero** - organ.

This band, formed at the end of the '60s and active until the beginning of the '70s, was re-discovered and revealed to the world only in 1992. Despite their relevance as mother-band for two other great Italian groups (**Museo Rosenbach** and **Celeste**), all their recordings went lost for over twenty years and were published later by drummer and producer **Ciro Perrino**, co-owner of Mellow Records. Their forgotten album *Il Viaggio Senza Andata* (the trip without departure) is a collection of mainly instrumental tracks, well performed by talented musicians. The heavy use of long improvisations and variations of classical themes (like "A night on Monte Calvo" of **Mussorgsky**), recall the contemporary **Concerto Grosso** by **New Trolls**, although without achieving the same quality: as a matter of fact their concepts and ideas were truly original but poorly developed, while their colleagues only the following year manage to elaborate them to perfection.

DISCOGRAPHY: **IL VIAGGIO SENZA ANDATA** *(1991, Mellow Records).*   M.G.& C.C.

ALAN SORRENTI

Two albums in 2 years (*Aria* and *Come Un Vecchio Incensiere All'alba Di Un Villaggio Deserto*), enough to celebrate an artist who, despite his natural talent, chose the commercial music genre with rather easy-listening and ephemeral songs. The first 1972 album's side A is covered by the title-track "Aria", structured as a suite, while the other 3 songs on the other side are more dreamy and psychedelic, like the high-flying and wonderful "Vorrei incontrarti". Overall a surreal and fabulous album in which his great singing qualities recall the best vocalizing elements of **Tim Buckley** and **Peter Hammill**, with the guttural contortions of a voice used as a proper musical instrument. Supported by a group of well-known collaborators (**Jean-Luc Ponty**, **Albert Prince** and **Tony Esposito**), Alan applies such hermetic and cerebral concepts to result almost impenetrable. His second album of 1973 closes this prog phase of his career losing him definitely to pop and disco.

RECOMMENDED RECORDINGS: **ARIA** *(Harvest, 1972)* **COME UN VECCHIO INCENSIERE ALL'ALBA DI UN VILLAGGIO DESERTO** *(Harvest, 1973)* **ALAN SORRENTI** *(Harvest, 1974)* .   M.G.& C.C.

SITHONIA

Orio Cenacchi - drums, percussion, **Oriano Dasasso** - keyboards, **Roberto Magni** - guitar, bass, **Paolo Nannetti** - keyboards, vocals, **Paolo Marcheselli** - vocals, **Andrea Guglielmi** - bass, **Gabriele Inglese** - flute, **Marco Giovanninni** - vocals, **Valerio Roda** - bass, **Sauro Musi** - guitar.

Among the first bands who relaunch prog rock in Italy between the '80s and '90s, their debut *Lungo il Sentiero di Pietra* contains elaborate songs that manage to detach from the classic British models, with good instrumental parts, melodic taste and compelling flute inserts. With the second album *Spettacolo Annullato* their proposal to rejuvenate the prog genre becomes more refined and they mature a recognizable strong personality, revealed in the suite "La recita del silenzio" and in all the other tracks. After the live recording *Folla Di Passaggio*, other two studio albums follow, clearly inspired by **BMS** and **PFM**: more modern and communicative for the time (less '70s and more into the '90s sound).

DISCOGRAPHY: **LUNGO IL SENTIERO DI PIETRA** *(1989, Camerun Records)* **SPETTACOLO ANNULLATO** *(1992, Mellow Records)* **FOLLA DI PASSAGGIO** *(1994, Mellow Records)* **CONFINE** *(1995, Mellow Records)* **HOTEL BRUN** *(1998, Mellow Records).*   M.G.& C.C.

Europe: ITALY

STANDARTE

Daniele Caputo - *drums, vocals.* **Michele Profeti** - *keyboards,* **Stefano Gabbani** - *bass,* **Daniele Nicolini** - *guitars.*

The '90s New Prog genre was mainly divided into two waves: the first characterized by bands searching, experimenting and exploring for solutions; the other by those who simply reproduced the '70s sound, more like pale copycats of the greater Anglophone masters of British Prog Rock. **Standarte** stands right in the midst of both for their sound is no real imitation of old ghosts but never too avant-garde either. Their debut in 1994 well absorbs the spirit of **Atomic Rooster**, **Rare Bird**, **Velvet Fogg** and **Gracious**, ignited by psychedelia and the dark atmospheres of a certain kind of prog. The following album, *Curses And Invocation*, is a pearl of symphonic rock performed by majestic vintage keyboard that makes it sound deranged and threatening. Sadly, the third magnetic album *Stimmung* is their last. After their solid contribution in create the image of their label Black Widow, and participating to some tribute albums, all will come to a halt (some will carry on by creating a post-beat oriented band called **London Underground**).

DISCOGRAPHY: STANDARTE *(Black Widow, 1994)* **CURSES AND INVOCATION** *(Black Widow, 1996)* **STIMMUNG** *(Black, Widow 1999).* **M.G.& C.C.**

IL ROVESCIO DELLA MEDAGLIA

Enzo Vita - *guitars,* **Stefano Urso** - *bass,* **Pino Ballarini** - *vocals, flute,* **Gino Campoli** - *drums,* **Franco Di Sabbatino** - *keyboards.*

A self-righteous and loud band that began its career playing in many rock Festivals of the '70s, **Il Rovescio Della Medaglia** (the other side of the medal) is one of the most popular bands of traditional Italian Prog. The first album *La Bibbia* of 1971 is a majestic hard rock, although broadened by good compositional arrangements, while the second release, *Io come io*, is more philosophical with a powerful and concrete music. For example, **Stefano Urso** is a revolutionary rock bassist who plays like a soloist. The real masterpiece of **RDM** is their third album *Contaminazione* of 1973 where the band, helped by **Luis Bacalov**, plays one of the best symphonic prog of all times, on the wake of **New Trolls** and **Osanna**. An outstanding record that was re-issued two years later, in 1975, in an English version. This same year they breakup and reunite only twenty years later thanks to **Enzo Vita**, following the new interest for the prog genre. Since 1995 the band is still performing to this very day, with another three good albums that unfortunately do not confirm the old energy of this cult band, probably due to the absence of their original singer.

DISCOGRAPHY: LA BIBBIA *(RCA, 1971)* **IO COME IO** *(RCA, 1972)* **CONTAMINAZIONE** *(RCA, 1973)* **CONTAMINATION** *(RCA, 1975)* **IL RITORNO** *(DB, 1995)* **VITAE** *(Vinyl Magic, 1999).* **M.G.& C.C.**

UNIVERSAL TOTEM ORCHESTRA

Dauno Giuseppe Buttiglione, Yanni Lorenzo Andretta - *bass,* **Ana Torres Fraile** - *vocals,* **Uto Giorgio Golin** - *drums,* **Marco Zanfei, Fabrizio Mattuzzi** - *keyboards,* **Daniele Valle** - *guitars,* **Antonio Fedeli** - *horns.*

Probably the best Italian disciples of **Magma** and of their idol **Christian Vander**, this band was deeply fascinated by the zeuhl revolution, as many others in Europe: of all the artists in the world that were devoted to his music, few were as credible and convincing as the **UTO**. Very talented musicians from Trento and former components of **Runaway Totem** (see page 369), they decide to abandon the modern symphonic rock dimension and form **Universal Totem Orchestra**, with a completely new sound which blended rock, jazz, classical, esoteric and gothic atmospheres. Their debut *Rituale Alieno* is a milestone of Italian New Prog: opera vocals, breathtaking rhythms and space-rock sounds creating a compelling record. A second album will be published almost ten years later, *The Magus*, a majestic and overwhelming project that confirms the value of this band.

RECOMMENDED RECORDINGS: RITUALE ALIENO *(Black Widow, 1999)* **THE MAGUS** *(Black Widow, 2008).* **M.G.& C.C.**

Europe: NORWAY

AUNT MARY

Bjørn Kristiansen – *vocals, guitar,* **Svein Gundersen** - *bass, vocals,* **Ketil Stensvik** - *drums,* **Jan Groth** - *vocals, keyboards,* **Bengt Jenssen** – *keyboards, vocals.*

Inspired by the music coming from England, at the beginning of 1970 this Norwegian band starts off with a hard prog album rich in beautiful keyboard melodies and excellent inserts of flute (**Ivar Fure**, present only in this first album). As part of this first prog wave they had little success until later on, maybe for the simplicity of some tracks that result roughly cut and somewhat incomplete. The beat-blues-folk formula is slightly amplified in the following work by adding more symphonic instrumental parts in an **ELP** style with more complex psychedelic elements. But it is their third album *Janus* of 1973 that finally conquers the market proving to be more complete, mature and personal. The art work on the cover is awkwardly very similar to **Pink Floyd**'s *The Division Bell* which was published twenty years later: a coincidence?

RECOMMENDED RECORDINGS: **JANUS** *(1973, Vertigo).*   M.G. & C.C.

HØST

First Line-up: **Geir Jahren** - *vocals,* **Bernt Bodahl** - *bass,* **Svein Rønning** - *guitars, keyboards, flute, vocals,* **Lasse Nilsen** - *guitars,* **Knut R. Lie** - *drums.* *Second Line-up:* **Geir Jahren** - *vocals,* **Bernt Bodahl** - *bass,* **Fezza Ellingsen** - *guitars, flute,* **Halvdan Nedrejord** - *keyboards,* **Willy Bendiksen** - *drums.*

Norway 1971 sees the rise this deeply bipolar band, essentially due to the two different line-ups that will create two very distinct albums: *Pa Sterke Vinger* (1974) contains a powerful hard prog with two interlacing guitars and many analogies with similar English and, for the expressiveness, Italian bands; *Hardt Mot Hard* (1976) is instead a more symphonic-prog work, almost totally composed by their new guitarist **Ellingsen**, a radical change with more complex structures and with particular and very interesting vocal phrases. They are still active in live performances though no true novelty has yet been released.

RECOMMENDED RECORDINGS: HARDT MOT HARDT *(1976, ON).* M.G.&C.C.

RUPHUS

Kjell Larsen - *guitar,* **Asle Nilsen** - *bass, flute,* **Gudny Aspaas** - *vocals,* **Håkon Graf** - *keyboards,* **Thor Bendiksen** - *drums,* **Hans Petter Danielsen** - *guitar,* **Rune Østdahl** - *vocals.*

Together for fun since 1970 they had no discographic intentions until Polydor decided to sign them up for a first album, *New Born Day*, in 1973. Their sound featured hard prog themes with a symphonic touch characterized by the guitars and the magniloquent keyboards; decidedly an excellent debut with obvious hints from **Yes**, **Focus** and **Uriah Heep**. Ranshart was released the following year and contained more structured compositions with beautiful partitions of flute and voices. Then famous Norwegian guitarist **Terje Rypdal** became their producer for the album *Let Your Light Shine* directing them towards a high-end jazz-rock. *Inner Voice*, even if with some stylistic repetitions, maintained the same good levels of quality, while the last two works were more simple and melodic.

RECOMMENDED RECORDINGS: **RANSHART** *(1974, Polydor)* **LET YOUR LIGHT SHINE** *(1976, Polydor).*   M.G. & C.C.

Europe: POLAND

BREAKOUT

Tadeusz Nalepa – *vocals, guitar,* **Mira Kubasińska** - *vocals,* **Krzysztof Dlutowski** - *organ,* **Janusz Zieliński** - *bass,* **Jòzef Hajdasz** – *drums,* **Wlodzimierz Nahorny** – *sax, flute,* **guest musicians...**

Born in Warsaw in 1968 and disbanded in 1979, the **Breakout** is one of the best rock groups of the European East. The passive resistance they manage through their music and art by bringing the western language into their country as an act against the Communist Regime, is praiseworthy. They are not exactly a prog rock band since they tend more toward a rock-blues with flute and sax inserts which open the sound to new horizons resulting sometimes closer to the **Jethro Tull** and other times to **Traffic**. Ten albums in ten years with many a line-up change, all orbiting around their leader and founder **Tadeusz Nalepa**, this band is still truly loved and respected today by their Polish fans. Although very popular in their country, all their albums are a rarity and very hard to find.

RECOMMENDED RECORDINGS: **NA DRUGIM BRZEGU TÒCZY** *(Pronit, 1969)* **70a** *(Pronit, 1970).* **M.G. & C.C.**

BUDKA SUFLERA

Romuald Lipko - *keyboards, bass guitar,* **Andrzej Ziolkowski** *guitars,* **Zbigniew Zielinski** - *batteria,* **Cugowski Krzysztof** - *vocals,* **Zeliszewski Tomasz** - *drums,* **Szczodrowski Andrzej** - *bass,* **Stefankiewicz Marek** - *hammond organ.*

Budka Suflera is a band from Lublin that began playing at the end of the '60s. They split around 1972, reuniting some years later but transforming their sound from a certain late beat music to a clear pop prog. The first album of this new course is released in 1975, *Cien Wielkiej Gûry* (the shadow of the great mountain), immediately greatly appreciated and becomes at once the manifesto of Polish Rock. Also the following *Przechodniem Bylem Miedzy Wami* (I was only leaving you) confirms their skills and popularity, after which the lineup deeply changes, pushing the band toward more commercial horizons and an obstinate top of the charts quest that nevertheless helped them to be known outside the borders of their country.

DISCOGRAPHY: **CIEN WIELKIEJ GÛRY** *(Muza, 1975)* **PRZECHODNIEM BYLEM MIEDZY WAMI** *(Muza, 1977)* **NA BRZEGU SWIATLA** *(Pronit, 1978)* **ONA PRZYSZLA PROSTO Z CHMUR** *(Muza, 1980).* **C.A. & C.C.**

LABORATORIUM

Janusz Grzywacz - *piano, keyboards,* **Marek Stryszowski** - *clarinet, sax, vocals,* **Mieczyslaw Gorka** - *drums, percussion,* **Maciej Gorski** - *bass,* **Waclaw Lozinski** - *flute, percussion,* **Pavel Scieranski** - *guitar,* **Krysztof Scieranski** - *bass.*

Relevant to the Polish Prog panorama, **Laboratorium** is a band who grew up with the music of **Niemen** and **Stanko**, distilling an intriguing blend of jazz and rock. They begin playing in little clubs, winning small contests and an appearance on the entire side of an LP for a music award. This could be considered their debut but their first real album is published only in 1976, *Modern Pentathlon*, where one whole side is a long suite of compelling guitars, keyboards and sax with non-sense vocalized lyrics or words treated with electronic effects. The other side contains shorter and more immediate funky styled songs. More good prog albums will follow, especially *Aquarium Live*, *Diver* and *Quasimodo* with their effervescing jazz-rock, but the latest ones are just average records with less originality.

DISCOGRAPHY: **LABORATORIUM** *(1974, Muza)* **MODERN PENTATHON** *(1976, Muza)* **AQUARIUM LIVE** *(1977, Polijazz)* **DIVER** *(1978, Helocon)* **QUASIMODO** *(1979, Muza)* **NOGERO** *(1980, View Records)* **LIVE – THE BLUE LIGHT PILOT** *(1982, Helicon)* **NO. 8** *(1984, Pronit)* **ANATOMY LESSON** *(1986, Face Music).* **M.G. & C.C.**

Europe: PORTUGAL

GONÇALO PEREIRA

Gonçalo Pereira is a very talented Portuguese guitarist who not only figures as a solist, but collaborates also in the two albums of the **Paulo Gonzo's Band**, *Quase tudo* and *Suspeito*. His style is an in-between **Steve Vai** and **Paul Gilbert**, with strong latin colours inspired by the ever present **Carlos Santana**. His three solo albums are a mix of heavy metal, prog and fusion, though never exaggerating in virtuosisms: from *GoncaloPereira@gspot* of 2004 the most representative tracks for his sound are "Retrosaria tricot", "Sessao geleia" and the beautiful "Pastel de nata". Other songs like "Contratempo" and "The Hypnotizer" are more delicate frescos of latin pop, where the guitar lies in the background in favour of the whole groove feeling. In the final suite "Trip to Kabul", his guitar

is back on the front line narrating crazy voyages of Oriental rhythms and Brazilian sambas through the progressive and indispensable latin melody.
DISCOGRAPHY: TRICOT NO PAYS DAS MARAVILHAS *(Ohr, 1998)* **UPGRADE** *(Ohr, 1999)* **GONÇALOPEREIRA@GSPOT** *(Ohr, 2004).*   M.G.

QUARTETO 1111

Miguel Artur da Silveira - *drums*, **Josè Cid** - *vocals, keyboards*, **António Moniz Pereira** - *guitars*, **Jorge Moniz Pereira** - *bass*.
The quartet derives playfully its names from **Michel Pereira**'s phone number and is the creature of a not yet famous **Josè Cid**. They released many EPs and singles before being able to record a true LP containing psychedelic acid pop and songs full of political and social themes, racism and human rights. Obviously they were censored at once by Salazar's government, forcing the band to continue with more neutral lyrics. A second album featuring the famous singer **Frei Camara** is published but despite all the precautions it was censored too. After this experience **Cid** leaves the band for a couple of years, until the return of democracy in Portugal. 1974's *Onde Quando Como Porquè Cantamos Pessoas Vivas* will be their last record containing compelling experimental music true to the best Brit prog rock teachings of the '70s.

DISCOGRAPHY: QUARTETO 1111 *(Columbia, 1970)* **BRUMA AZUL DO DESEJADO** *(EMI, 1973)* **ONDE, QUANDO, COMO, PORQUÊ, CANTAMOS PESSOAS VIVAS** *(Decca,1974).*   C.A. & C.C.

TANTRA

Armando Gama, Peter Luis, Guillherme Da Luz, Luis Ramos, Pedro Sales - *tastiere*, **Americo Luis, Dedos Tubarão, Pedro Codinho** - *basso*, **Manuel Cardoso, Bruno Silva** - *chitarre, voce*, **To-Zè Almeida, Bebè** - *batteria*.
Portugal's Prog panorama during the '70s is made of very few but good artists: **Petrus Castrus, Josè Cid, Sergio Godinho** and last but not least, the **Tantra**. This band, born at the end of this fabulous decade, published two wonderful albums inspired by **Camel** and **Yes**, yet following a genre closer to certain Mediterranean jazz-rock (**Arti & Mestieri**), expressive and colorful, sung in Portuguese. In 1980 Tantra caught the attention of **Peter Gabriel**, even though in the end he will opt for **Simple Minds** as opening act for his tour. A year later they release a last album, an average record, distant from the previous, published during a bad time also for prog rock. In 2002, after a twenty year pause, *Cardoso* reunites them for two new albums of loud symphonic rock, two respectable jobs but less fresh than their original sound: *Delirium* is nevertheless worthy of note.

DISCOGRAPHY: MISTEROS EN MARAVIHLAS *(Tantra, 1978)* **HOLOCAUSTO** *(Tantra, 1979)* **HUMANOID FLESH** *(Tantra, 1981)* **TERRA** *(Tantra, 2002)* **LIVE RITUAL** *(live, Tantra 2002)* **DELIRIUM** *(Tantra 2006).*   M.G.

Europe: RUSSIA

ARSENAL

Alexey Kozlov - *alto & soprano saxophones*, **Igor Saulsky** - *piano, organ*, **Vitaliy Rosenburgh** - *guitars*, **Victor Zaikin** - *bass*, **Anatoli Sizonov** - *trumpet*, **Vadim Akhmetgareyev** - *trombone*, **Stanislav Korosteliov** - *drums*.

From Moscow, these are one of the best progressive bands not only of Russia but of the whole Eastern Europe. Barely known abroad and to the western world, they start their career at the end of the '70s by publishing two wonderful albums: in 1977 the self-titled debut in the best prog rock tradition, playing music full of jazz, classical tunes and fusion, performed with good improvisations and always in search of fantastic and mysterious melodies. Without diminishing the recordings, this band was even better in concert, creating magical moments with their fantastic interpretations and long instrumental performances. Disbanded at the beginning of '80s they truly deserve to be re-discovered, although all three albums are very hard to find.

DISCOGRAPHY: ARSENAL *(Melodiya, 1977)* **SCORCHED BY TIME** *(Boheme, 1980)* **CREATED WITH THEIR OWN HANDS** *(Melodiya, 1982).* **C.A.**

HORIZONT (Gorizont)

Sergey Kornilov - *keyboards*, **Vladimir Lutoshkin** - *guitars, flute*, **Alexey Eremenko** - *bass, guitars*, **Andrey Krivilev** - *vocals, keyboards*, **Igor Pokrovsky** - *vocals*, **Valentin Sinitsin* - *drums*.

Excellent symphonic prog band from Gorky, this ensemble starts its career in the second half '70s following keyboardist **Kornilov**'s neoclassic contaminated compositions that ranged between **Yes** and **Genesis**' style and an avant-garde type of chamber music experimentation. The band recorded their debut album, *Summer in Town*, only in 1985 containing a suite and two longer tracks of fascinating, varied and complex atmospheres. A second album is released in 1989 with darker plots and richer concepts, generating a great avant-garde work where their inspiration became closer to bands like **Univers Zero**.

RECOMMENDED RECORDINGS: SUMMER IN TOWN *(1985, Boheme Music)* **THE PORTRAIT OF A BOY** *(1989, Boheme Music).* **M.G. & C.C.**

SEPSIS

Alexis Romanov - *guitars, guitar synth*, **Alexander Beriozkin** - *bass, vocals & screams*, **Ivan Fedenko** - *drums e percussion*.

The halo of mystery that surrounds this Russian one shot band of the early '90s deeply contributes in consecrating them as a cult band: *Liturgia Bezumia* (a liturgy of madness) was published in 1991 containing dark and obscure partitions with screams and noises distributed across the entire record. Their style does not seem to belong anywhere though some try to compare them to the energy of **Yes**. Probably they fit certain standards of the AOR or of an '80s Pop Rock, but truly recognizable for their own originality and powerful sound, made of highly abused guitar riffs and the compelling and definitely involving drum rhythms. Not a real masterpiece for the Prog genre but still an interesting album, not easy to find in its original version even if recently reissued on CD as *A Liturgy Of Madness* and repackaged with a different cover. The music is mainly instrumental, distinctly original and also at least slightly more complex and intricate than the music of **Rush**'s famous 2112.

DISCOGRAPHY: LITURGIA BEZUMIA *(Arton, 1991).* **C.A. & C.C.**

Europe: SPAIN

EDUARDO BORT

Eduardo Bort – *guitar*, **Alfonso Gimeno** – *keyboards*, **Vicente Alcañiz** – *drums*, **Marino Hernández** - *bass.* Ospiti: **Max Sunyer** – *guitar*, **Marcos Mantero** – *keyboard*, **Miguel Galán** – *guitar*.

Very talented Spanish guitarist, **Bort** develops his prog career around one homonym debut album in 1974. Essentially devoted to the psychedelic genre in which he would insert moments of space or symphonic music, sometimes hard, sometimes with fusion elements, similar to artists such as **Steve Hillage**, **Jimi Hendrix**, or **Santana**. Of course his compositions are rich of electric and acoustic guitars, but also contain a good use of the mellotron with many varied rhythmic changes and loud distortions or arpeggios like in the long track "Paseando Sobre la Hierba". Nine years after he releases a second album called *Silvia*, which is more simple and ballad oriented with some soft hints recalling **Pink Floyd**.

DISCOGRAPHY: EDUARDO BORT *(Movieplay, 1975)* **SILVIA** *(Bambulè, 1983).*

M.G. & C.C.

CAI

Diego Fopiani Macias - *drums, vocals*, **Jose A. Fernandez Mariscall** - *guitars*, **Francisco Delgado Gonzalez** - *guitars*, **Sebastian Dominguez Lozano** - *keyboards*, **Jose Velez Gomez** - *bass, vocals*.

Spanish quintet from Cadiz, from which the name **Cai** (in andalusian), they publish a first album *Mas Alla De Nuestras Mentes Diminutas* in 1978, raising great appreciation from the Spanish press and critique. This record divided into four parts ("Alameda", "Mas alla de nuestras mentes diminutas", "Solucion a un viejo problema", "Pasa un dia") contains the rhythms and sounds of the traditional andalusian guitars that sometimes is described as flamenco-rock. Also the second album *Noche Abierta* was a success: here the instrumental parts are expanded and skillfully developed adding to the structure the suggestive colours of andalusian culture. A third and last LP, *Cancion De La Primavera*, will bring them down to an average and more commercial music, losing the original overwhelming impact of the previous two.

DISCOGRAPHY: MAS ALLA DE NUESTRAS MENTES DIMINUTAS *(Trova, 1978)* **NOCHE ABIERTA** *(Epic, 1980)* **CANCION DE LA PRIMAVERA** *(Epic, 1981).*

C.A. & C.C.

LOS CANARIOS

Teddy Bautista - *keyboards, vocals*, **Mathias Sanuellian** - *keyboards, violin*, **Antonio Garcia De Diego** - *guitars, vibes, lyre, harpsychord, vocals*, **Christian Mellies** - *bass, theremin*, **Teddy Richard** - *drums, percussion*.

Their most famous work is *Ciclos*, an ambitious double concept-album based upon *The Four Seasons* by **Antonio Vivaldi**. The plot turns into the more unconventional narration of the life, from the birth to death, of a man symbolized by the changing seasons. **Vivaldi**'s music lies always in the background where a compelling symphonic rock aided by a real choir goes from fascinating to somewhat pretentious. Divided into four suites, one on each side, the music is full of all sorts of keyboards, simulating orchestras or electronic sounds. This targeted the criticism of many reviews, although the results are well-balanced and close to other examples like **Walter/Wendy Carlos**'s *A Clockwork Orange* and **New Trolls**' *Concerto Grosso*. Without a doubt a very recommended example of great Spanish prog-rock.

DISCOGRAPHY: CICLOS *(1974, Ariola).*

M.G. & C.C.

Europe: SPAIN

ENBOR

Inaki Gutierrez - *vocals, guitars,* **Manu Urretxaga** - *vocals, horns,* **Ramon Gardeazabal** - *vocals, acoustic guitar,* **Laguntzaileak Jimenez** - *saxophones,* **Aitor Amezaga** - *keyboards,* **Paco Diaz** - *drums.*

As for most of the bands coming from the Basque regions of Spain, this band begins playing their typical folk prog only in the late '70s. Their sound features a predominance of electric instruments with jazz moments of more rhythmic immediacy, often based upon a more simple form of rock music. Fundamental the figure of singer **Urretxaga** (also for his excellent flute and clarinet partitions), who sung in basque, confirming the strong sense of identity that historically characterizes his people. The lyrics are complex and strange yet merge beautifully with the melody. Only two records for this band, the first (1978) more song oriented and the second (1980) decidedly more prog like the wonderfully dynamic title-suite "Katebegiak".

RECOMMENDED RECORDINGS: **KATEBEGIAK** *(Elkar, 1980).*   M.G. & C.C.

GOMA

Antonio Rodríguez - *drums,* **José Lagares** - *bass,* **Pepe Sánchez** - *sax,* **Manuel Rodríguez** - *guitar,* **Alberto Toribio** - *keyboards.*

The 14th April of 1974, five musicians with very different backgrounds gather in Sevilla for their first rehearsal as a band and scheduling an album to be released on the 14th April of the following year. This is why their debut album goes under the title of *14 Abril*. A small masterpiece of their own progressive rock with the delicate textures of keyboards and saxophone that alternate jazz melodies and more aggressive tracks. An Andalusian tribute to music invading Europe during 1975. The apex culminates in the wonderful "Un nuevo Abril sin sal" where jazzy rhythms blend to certain **Deep Purple** sounds creating a powerful music mix, more oriented toward the British atmospheres than to true Andalusian or Spanish traditions.

DISCOGRAPHY: **14 ABRIL** *(Movieplay, 1975).*   C.A. & C.C.

GRANADA

Carlos Carcamo - *flute, violin, piano, mellotron, harpsychord, 12 strings guitar, percussione vocals,* **Michael Vortreflich** - *electric guitar,* **Antonio Garcia Oteyza** - *bass,* **Juan Bona** - *drums, vocals.*

From Madrid, this band of the early '70s releases a debut album in 1975, strongly influenced by the standards of contemporary European prog. Echoes of **Yes**, **Jethro Tull** and **Le Orme** emanate from the preponderating keyboards and the excellent flute arrangements. The following album *Espanya Año 75* is a further step along the same path: although still deeply inspired by the sounds of their idols, here they become more varied and original. The third and last album *Valle Del Pas* is rather ambitious and definitely ambiguous: an excessive production with heavily elaborated sounds where the violins and mandolins create a world orbiting **Frank Zappa** and further away from the initial stars that had led them to fame.

DISCOGRAPHY: **HABLO DE UNA TIERRA** *(Movieplay, 1975)* **ESPANYA AÑO 75** *(Movieplay, 1976)* **VALLE DEL PAS** *(Movieplay, 1978).* **C.A. & C.C.**

Europe: SPAIN

IMÁN CALIFATO INDEPENDIENTE

Marcos Mantero - *keyboards*, **Manuel Rodriguez** - *guitars, vocals*, **Urbano Moraes** - *bass*, **Kiko Guerrero** - *drums, percussion*.
Band from Madrid, they start playing together since 1976 and consolidate both the line-up and their final name when keyboardist **Mantero** joins in the following year. Their sound is a symphonic fusion proposal with some links to **Weather Report** and to the Canterbury school, creating a sort of blend that recalled very much the style of **Camel**. Talented and with a good technique, they are noticed by CBS who will produce their works: a first album in 1978 containing excellent instrumental parts with very fascinating and evocative atmospheres close to **Genesis**; a second good album of 1980, always on the same line, but mainly resulting as a repetition of thematics.
DISCOGRAPHY: CALIFATO INDEPENDIENTE *(CBS, 1978)* **CAMINO DEL ÁGUILA** *(CBS, 1980)*.
M.G. & C.C.

MAQUINA!

Jaime Paris - *guitar fuzz*, **Lluis Cabanach** - *guitar wah-wah*, **Jaime Vilaseca 'Tapi'** - *drums*, **Jordi Batiste** - *vocals, bass, flute*, **Enric Herrera** - *organ, piano*.
Before becoming officially **Maquina!**, they start off as musicians for the folk singer **Sisa**, accompanying him in neverending and exhausting tours. Finally quitting this uncomfortable role, they publish two 45 RPM for the label Diabolo and in 1970 their first album *Why?* reveals them as the formidable band they were and hits the Spanish charts among the first ten best albums. Their music is an alchemy of drums, organ, wah-wah guitars and powerful vocals, close to the best of **Brian Auger & Trinity**, jumping from R&B to jazz or prog and psychedelia. Brilliant live performers, their talent is best recorded in the album *En Directo* of 1972, which sadly also represents their farewell.

DISCOGRAPHY: WHY? *(Diabolo, 1970)* **EN DIRECTO** *(Diabolo,1972)*. **C.A.**

MEDINA AZAHARA

Manuel Martinez - *vocals*, **Miguel Galan** - *guitar*, **Pablo Rabadan** - *keyboards*, **Manuel Molina** - *bass*, **Jose A. Molina** - *drums*.
Historical band from Cordoba, born in the late '70s and still active with a line-up that preserves only its singer **Martinez**, they represent the harder side of Andalusian prog. The sound is of clear symphonic rock with inclinations towards the new prog trend, specially in some guitar or keyboards' passage. Predominant feature is **Martinez**'s powerful and precise voice of singing in Spanish, which has a main role over the instrumental parts. The excellent homonym first album of 1979 contains their song-manifesto "Paseando por la Mezquita", today one of Andalusia's 'patriotic' themes. Very good also the second album *La Esquina Del Viento* (1980) where hard rock prevails.
RECOMMENDED RECORDINGS: MEDINA AZAHARA *(Cbs, 1979)* **LA ESQUINA DEL VIENTO** *(Cbs, 1980)*.
M.G. & C.C.

Europe: SPAIN

MEZQUITA

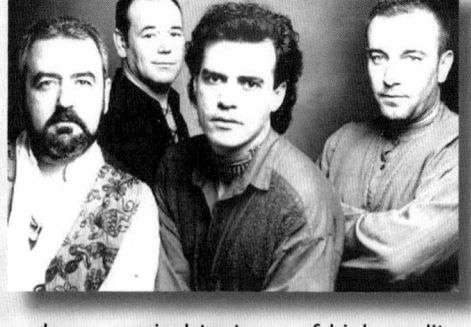

Jose Rafael Garcia - *guitars, vocals,* **Randy Lopez** - *bass, percussion, vocals,* **Roschka Lopez** - *keyboards, vocals,* **Rafael Zorrilla** - *drums, percussion, vocals.*
They start off in 1979 with the overwhelming *Recuerdos De Mi Tierra* and its powerful, spectacular title-track of an incredibly involving flamenco-prog. Their success is immediate and reveals very talented musicians with good

compositional skills and songwriting, dense musical textures of high quality levels performed with great enthusiasm and personality. Guitars and keyboards ignite sparking duels of incendiary effects. Their second album *Califas Del Rock* is more commercial but doesn't lose those typical flamenco moments and the Spanish vocals, essential for a band who performs with a true latino soul.
***DISCOGRAPHY:* RECUERDOS DE MI TIERRA** *(1979, Chapa)* **CALIFAS DEL ROCK** *(1981).* **M.G. & C.C.**

MODULOS

Pepe Robles - *vocals, guitars, flute, oboe, bongos,* **Tomás Bohórquez** - *Hammond organ, mellotron, accordion, moog,* **Emilio Bueno** - *bass,* **Juan Antonio García Reyzábal** - *drums, electric violin.*
They start in Madrid as a cover band coming from the ultimate Beat generation. In fact their first album of 1970, *Realidad*, contains songs of **The Beatles** and **Hollies** although re-interpreted with originality and more personal ideas, closer to the beat-psychedelic genre just like **Vanilla Fudge** did with their own material. The evolution toward prog rock is more evident in their second release, *Variaciones* of 1971, where they undertake the difficult realms of rock with classical contaminations and psychedelic-beat, always looking upon what **Vanilla Fudge** was doing. The following album *Plenitud* is where they climax with a more complex symphonic rock becoming the easy target of criticism for their new style was too close to **Yes**. The decline begins and two years later the fourth and last album *Modulos 4* (1974) sees them radically changed playing a more commercial music that will lead to them to a halt. When in 1980 the reactivate the band, their sound is no where near the progressive rock genre anymore.

***DISCOGRAPHY:* REALIDAD** *(Hispavox, 1970)* **VARIACIONES** *(Hispavox, 1971)* **PLENITUD** *(Hispavox, 1972)* **MODULOS 4** *(Hispavox, 1974).* **C.A. & C.C.**

MUSICA URBANA

Joan Albert Amargó - *piano, electric piano, keyboards, sax, clarinet, flute, trombone, violin,* **Lluis Cabanach** - *guitars,* **Carles Benavent** - *bass, contrabbas, acoustic guitar,* **Salvador Font** - *drums, percussion.*
They debut in 1976 with a fresh jazzy rock mixed to folk atmospheres and echoes of the Canterbury school. It is a successful instrumental record, greatly influenced by **Hatfield and the North**, performed with mastery and full of rhythmic changes. Main feature of their sound are the electroacoustic tunes that make it all the more powerful and resounding with the remarkable insert of horns that shadow the electric piano and guitar arrangements with wonderful fantasy. The second album *Iberia* of 1978 is also a good job although slightly weaker than the previous one.

***DISCOGRAPHY:* MUSICA URBANA** *(1976, Edigsa)* **IBERIA** *(1978, RCA).* **M.G.**

Europe: SPAIN

ORQUESTRA MIRASOL

Ricard Roda - *horns*, **Pedrito Díaz** - *percussion*, **Miquel Lizandra** - *drums* , **Xavier Batllés** - *bass* , **Víctor Ammann** - *keyboards*, **Toti Soler** - *guitars*.

Representatives of the Catalan progressive movement that reached its peak in the mid '70s, **Orquestra Mirasol** was greatly inspired by **Soft Machine**, **Herbie Hancock**, **Chick Corea** and **Miles Davis** and in fact takes on a particularly jazzy prog rock. Their album *Salsa Catalana* is a high quality product inspired by the most modern American jazz-rock currents mixed to Spanish folk and Catalan sonorities. After this successful debut another similar recording, *Doca A Oca I Tira Que Et Toca*, is published in 1975 but without the same results in sales or critique. Before the definitive split, the band changes line-up many times losing their original image and sound.

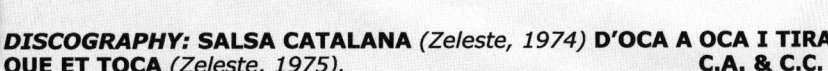

DISCOGRAPHY: **SALSA CATALANA** *(Zeleste, 1974)* **D'OCA A OCA I TIRA QUE ET TOCA** *(Zeleste, 1975).*

C.A. & C.C.

PAU RIBA

Defined as the "Catalan Kevin Ayers" by many reviews, this Catalan artist, political activist, eclectic musician and attentive follower of the worldwide folk generation, contributes to the history of Prog with albums of great artistic value, some also thanks to the collaboration of **Daevid Allen** from **Gong**. Riba was an inconvenient figure, a real outsider, very difficult to keep within conventional borders. He often took serious risks by wandering through culturally weird topics and subversive adventures like sexual liberation or the catalan independentist movements. His music linked to the Catalan folk tradition is ignited by psychedelic elements, futuristic sounds and naif geniality, such as *Eletroccid Acid Alquimistic Xoc And Licors*, two incredible albums were his unleashed creativity is without limits.

DISCOGRAPHY: **DIOPTRIA I** *(Concentric, 1970)* **DIOPTRIA II** *(Concentric, 1971)* **JO, LA DONYA I EL GRIPAU** *(Edigsa, 1971)* **ELECTROCCID ACCID ALQUIMISTIC XOC** *(Movieplay, 1975)* **LICORS** *(Movieplay, 1977)* **AMARGA CRISI** *(Edigsa, 1981).*

C.A. & C.C.

MIGUEL RIOS

Miguel Rios' immense discography also contains three episodes that perfectly fit into the Prog Rock description, specifically material from 1974 to 1978 contained in three compelling albums full of sonorities stolen from the British Prog tidal wave: *Memorias De Un Ser Humano* was a great success despite the strong censorship it underwent by the label Hispavox; *La Huerta Atomica* of 1976 is a brave uncensored concept album in a rock blues key, regarding delicate topics against nuclear weapons and the military power, very appreciated by both press and public; in *Al Andalus* of 1978 Rios' wonderful voice perfectly harmonizes with the instruments of **Los Guadalquivir** playing Arabian and folk melodies are mixed to jazz and space rock atmospheres.

RECOMMENDED RECORDINGS: **MEMORIAS DE UN SER HUMANO** *(Hispavox, 1974)* **LA HUERTA ATOMICA** *(Polydor, 1976)* **AL ANDALUS** *(Polydor, 1978).*

C.A. & C.C.

Europe: SPAIN

JAUME SISA

Albert Batiste - *bass*, **Emilio Baleriola** - *guitar*, **Raimon Casals** - *drums*, **Pere Riera** - *saxophones*, **Xavier Riba** - *violin*, **José María Pagán** - *piano*, **Dolores Palau** - *flute, vocals*, **Jaume Sisa** - *guitars, vocals*.

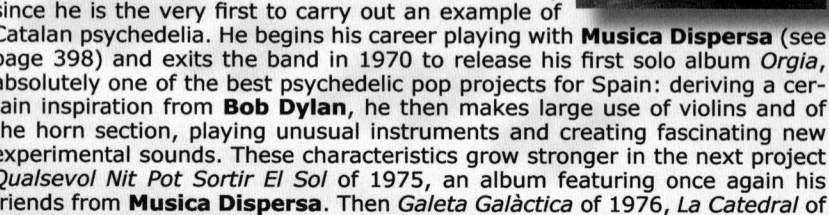

Misunderstood at the time, this musician and artist is an essential contribution to Spanish rock's history since he is the very first to carry out an example of Catalan psychedelia. He begins his career playing with **Musica Dispersa** (see page 398) and exits the band in 1970 to release his first solo album *Orgia*, absolutely one of the best psychedelic pop projects for Spain: deriving a certain inspiration from **Bob Dylan**, he then makes large use of violins and of the horn section, playing unusual instruments and creating fascinating new experimental sounds. These characteristics grow stronger in the next project *Qualsevol Nit Pot Sortir El Sol* of 1975, an album featuring once again his friends from **Musica Dispersa**. Then *Galeta Galàctica* of 1976, *La Catedral* of 1977 and *Antaviana* of 1978 complete the narrative of his evolution.

DISCOGRAPHY: **ORGIA** (Edigsa, 1971) **QUALSEVOL NIT POT SORTIR EL SOL** (Edigsa, 1975) **GALETA GALACTICA** (Edigsa, 1976) **LA CATEDRAL** (Edigsa, 1977) **ANTAVIANA** (Edigsa, 1978). C.A. & C.C.

SMASH

Gualberto Garcia Perez - *guitar, sitar*, **Julio Matito** - *vocals, bass, flute*, **Antonio Rodríguez** - *drums*, **Henrik Liebgott** - *guitar, violin*.

Greatly inspired by American West Coast groups like **Byrds**, **Buffalo Springfield** and **Jefferson Airplane**, this band from Sevilla is active since the end of the '60s emulating the psychedelic experience of their idols. The first sign of change arrives in 1970 when they meet producer Gonzalo Perayo and publish their debut *Glorieta De Los Lotos*, a compelling example of Spanish rock influenced by **The Moody Blues**, with hints of blues and flamenco tunes, all cooking in the brew of the best west coast psychedelia. The next album *We come to smash this time* of 1971 loses the flamenco-Rock identity, which was the pillar of their success, in favour of sonorities closer to **Canned Heat** and **Allman Brothers**. Consequently their notoriety diminishes bringing to a momentary breakup that following year, only to see them reunite and abruptly collapse once more due to the unexpected death of **Julio Matito**. Guitarist **Gualberto Garcia Perez** (see page 128) remains active and is still one of Spain's most famous musicians.

DISCOGRAPHY: **GLORIETA DE LOS LOTOS** (Philips, 1970) **WE COME TO SMASH THIS TIME** (Philips, 1971). C.A. & C.C.

TAPIMAN

José María Vilaseca "Tapi" - *drums*, **Pepe Fernández** - *bass*, **Max Sunyer** - *guitar*.

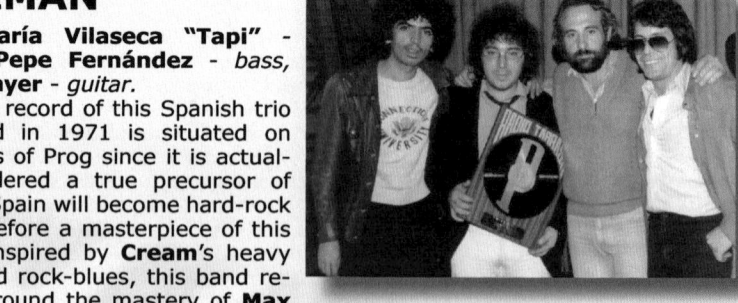

The only record of this Spanish trio published in 1971 is situated on the limits of Prog since it is actually considered a true precursor of what in Spain will become hard-rock and therefore a masterpiece of this genre. Inspired by **Cream**'s heavy blues and rock-blues, this band revolves around the mastery of **Max Sunyer**, whose guitar solos are like precious gems inserted into the rhythms paved by **Tapi**'s drumming and the powerful bass of **Pepe Fernandez**. They consciously play roughly with aggressive improvisations in order to sound more like a garage band, while converging various styles mixed to latin tunes just like **Carlos Santana** would. Lyrics are in English and sung with a Spanish accent that makes them even more fascinating. After the split, **Max** joins another band, the **Iceberg**.

DISCOGRAPHY: **TAPIMAN** (Edigsa, 1971). C.A. & C.C.

Europe: **SWEDEN**

ÄLGARNAS TRÄDGÅRD

Andreas Brandt - *violin, vocals, percussion, flute,* **Mikael Johansson** - *bass, handrum, zither, tablas, percussion,* **Dennis Lindh** - *drums, tablas, percussion, zinks, jews harp,* **Dan Söderqvist** - *guitars, percussion,* **Jan Ternald** - *piano, tastiere,* **Sebastian Öberg** - *cello, flute, sitar, tablas* **Margareta Söderberg** - *vocals.*

This band owes their place in the history of Progressive music thanks to their only album where they manage to combine prog and psychedelia to a marvel. *Framtiden Är Ett Svävande Skepp, förankrat I forntiden* (The future is a rocking ship, anchored in ancient times) of 1972 opens with spacey visions close to the German cosmic music and to **Pink Floyd**'s *Saucerful of secrets*, where a long track, performed with guitars, strings and keyboards, paints hallucinating landscapes. The following songs are flavored by folk melodies which transcend into ethnic-medieval dancing scenarios made even more surrealistic by the dreamy vocals of guest star **Margareta Soderberg**. In 2001 (almost thirty years later) this cult album was re-issued also containing previous unreleased tracks.

***DISCOGRAPHY:* FRAMTIDEN ÄR ETT SVÄVANDE SKEPP, FÖRANKRAT I FORNTIDEN** *(1972, Silence)* **DELAYED** *(2001, Silence).* M.G. & C.C.

ANEKDOTEN

Nicklas Berg - *guitar, mellotron, keyboards,* **Anna Sofi Dahlberg** - *cello, mellotron, keyboards, vocals,* **Jan Erik Liljeström** - *bass, vocals,* **Peter Nordin** - *drums, percussion.*

At the beginning of the '90s young Swedish bands like **Änglagård**, **Landberk** and **Anekdoten** look back upon **King Crimson** and all of his court, deriving great inspiration mainly from the material published between 1973 and 1974. As keen disciples they take this lesson and evolve it into their first two albums *Vemod* of 1993 and *Nucleus* of 1995, full of violent guitar riffs, powerful rhythms partly smoothed by mellotron and cello. The following albums are instead calmer, more linear, sometimes closer to a certain '90s post-rock, but keeping intact the melancholic trademark. Talented stage performers they also record two live albums: *Live In Japan* of 1998 and *Waking The Dead.*

***DISCOGRAPHY:* VEMOD** *(1993, Virta)* **NUCLEUS** *(1995, Virta)* **LIVE IN JAPAN** *(1998, Arcangelo)* **FROM WITHIN** *(1999, Virta)* **GRAVITY** *(2003, Virta)* **WAKING THE DEAD** *(2005, Arcangelo)* **A TIME OF DAY** *(2007, Virta).* M.G. & C.C.

ARBETE OCH FRITID

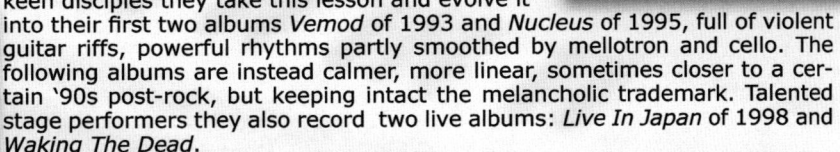

Ove Karlsson - *cello, bass, organ,* **Roland Keijser** - *winds, organ,* **Kjell Westling** - *violin, winds, guitar, piano,* **Torsten Eckerman** - *trumpet, percussion,* **Bosse Skoglund** - *drums,* **Bengt Berger** - *drums, percussion.*

Brilliant group of musicians from Uppsala, they form in 1969 calling themselves (translated) Work & Free-time. Their master-mind is the poly-instrumentalist **Ove Karlsson**, a polyhedral and genial musician that picked out other similar and versatile musicians, to create his particular and very personal genre made of ethnic, Tzigan (gypsy folk), circus and chamber music supported by a wave of psychedelia and also heavily inspired by dances like the tango and the Waltzer blended into a jazz mix of dramatic and dark or bright and fun atmospheres. The compositions result often to have confusing plots without a clear scheme, but presented as never before. The prevalent acoustic and traditional instruments are completed by social and political themes narrated by the lyrics.

***RECOMMENDED RECORDINGS:* ARBETE OCH FRITID** *(1970, SONET)* **ANDRA LP** *(1971, SONET).* M.G. & C.C.

Europe: SWEDEN

DICE

Leif Larsson - *keyboards, piano*, **Fredrik Vildö** - *bass*, **Robert Holmin** - *vocals, sax*, **Örian Standberg** - *guitar*, **Per Andersson** - *drums*.

Founded in 1972, this Swedish band starts recording their studio album in 1973 publishing it only five years later, in 1978, when all the surrounding world of Pop music had already completely changed. It is nevertheless a very beautiful symphonic rock album, inspired by **Yes** with continuous dialogues, sometimes playful duels, between the guitars and the keyboards, deeply influenced by the style of **Keith Emerson**. The outstanding final suite "Follies" is a twenty-two minute track divided into six movements of ever-changing atmospheres. Like many other bands of the '70s, **Dice** disappear soon after only to reunite during the '90s due to the reborn interest for the Prog genre. This brings to the release of a new album *The Four Riders Of The Apocalypse* in 1992 containing four long unpublished tracks derived from sessions recorded in 1977, but completely re-arranged.

DISCOGRAPHY: **DICE** *(1978, Marilla)* **THE FOUR RIDERS OF THE APOCALYPSE** *(1992, Belle Antique)* **LIVE** *(1993, Belle Antique)*. M.G. & C.C.

KEBNEKAISE

Kenny Håkansson - *guitar, vocals*, **Rolf Scherer** - *guitar*, **Bella Linnarson** - *bass*, **Pelle Ekman** - *drums*, **Mats Glengård** - *guitar, violin, vocals*, **Thomas Netzler** - *bass, vocals*, **Bah Hassan** - *percussion*, **Göran Lagerberg** - *bass, guitar*, **Gunnar Andersson** - *sax*, **Ingemar Böcker** - *violin*, **Åke Eriksson** - *drums*, **Per Lejring** - *keyboards, vocals*, **Pelle Holm** - *drums, vocals*.

Many northern European bands tried to mix prog and folk, **Kebnekaise** were among the best. In fact, their debut album *Resa Mot Okänt Mål* shows how talented they were in playing a rich contamination of rock, blues and Swedish folk. The line-up changes that follow contribute greatly to the next two albums *Kebnekaise* and *Kebnekaise III* (absolutely the best of their whole discography), where they manage to blend different styles inserting African percussions under the jazzy melodies. This sound is confirmed also in *Elefanten* of 1977, but when their leader **Hakansson** leaves, they stir toward an average symphonic rock.

RECOMMENDED RECORDINGS: **RESA MOT OKÄNT MÅL** *(1971, Silence)* **KEBNEKAISE** *(1973, Silence)* **KEBNEKAISE III** *(1974, Silence)* **LJUS FRÅN AFRIKA** *(1976, Silence)* **ELEFANTEN** *(1977, Silence)*. M.G. & C.C.

KULTIVATOR

Johan Hedrén - *keyboards*, **Jonas Linge** - *guitars*, **Ingemo Rylander** - *vocals, flute, piano*, **Stefan Carlsson** - *bass*, **Johan Svåed** - *drums*.

Barndomens Stigar is an absolute masterpiece, an original, complex, immense and well balanced album. Released in 1981, during one of the worst moments for prog music, this ensemble of talented musicians (some previously from the band **Tunnelbanan**) play with skill and enthusiasm, sparking Canterburian energy connected to Zeuhl influences, Swedish folk and psychedelic shades. Fantastic the guitar textures, well merged with both keyboards and flute, and the fascinating the female voice, singing in Swedish. This band couldn't survive the New Wave and punk hurricane that mesmerized audiences all over the world and had to put an end to their short career. Ten years later they however reunited to re-issue the album on CD adding two previously unreleased tracks. This was an auto-produced initiative that was barely noticed outside the niche, so they disband once again. Nowadays each members is still active on his own accord involved in different activities like Theatre, Club Music or as Teachers.

DISCOGRAPHY: **BARNDOMENS STIGAR** *(LP 1981, Bauta - CD 1992, APM)*. M.G. & C.C.

Europe: SWEDEN

KVARTETTEN SOM SPRÄNGDE

Fred Hellman - *keyboards*, **Finn Sjöberg** - *guitar, bass, flute*, **Rune Carlsson** - *drums, percussion*.

The band's curious name (the bursting quartet) is inspired by a book of **Birger Sioberg** published in 1924. Even though they publish only this one record, *Kattvals* (1973) deserves a place in history because of its overwhelming jazz rock contaminations, inspired by **Fläsket Brinner**, and the powerful instrumental solutions they adopt, like the fascinating vintage sound of an old hammond Organ well evidenced in the whole recording. They play a warm prog rock with psychedelic colours, performed with magnificent guitar and keyboard solos and effervescing rhythms that recall **Santana** (a particular reference to the Mexican guitarist is the splendid album cover, very similar to **Santana**'s first album). **Kvartetten Som Sprangde** also collaborate in **Bern Staf**'s record *Valhall*, a wonderful project though actually very distant from *Kattvals* sound. Worthy of mention **Finn Sioberg** solo album *Finn* in 1978.

DISCOGRAPHY: KATTVALS *(1973, Gump)*.

M.G. & C.C.

LANDBERK

Andreas Dahlbäck - *drums, percussion*, **Stefan Dimle** - *bass*, **Reine Fiske** - *guitars*, **Patric Helje** - *voce, guitars*, **Simon Nordberg** - *keyboards*, **Jonas Lidholm** - *drums*.

With a touch of Swedish folk, some psychedelic tunes, several hints from **King Crimson** and a heavy use of the mellotron, this is the recipe of **Landberk**'s debut album: although the sonorities of *Lonely Land/Riktig Akta* are very similar to *In the Court of Crimson King*, this is one of the most appreciated bands of the '90s. The following *One Man Tell's Another* is instead a more personalized album, more elegiac and with original melodies. Their detachment from the classic prog clichè will be completed with their fourth album *Indian Summer*: an underrated record where they are apparently playing a more simple pop-prog, yet still very intense, melancholic, with sublime results and of high quality.

DISCOGRAPHY: RIKTIGT ÄKTA *(1992, Record Heaven)* **LONELY LAND** *(1992, The Laser's Edge – versione inglese di Riktig Äkta)* **ONE MAN TELL'S ANOTHER** *(1994, Megarock)* **UNAFFECTED** *(1995, Melodie & Dissonanze)* **INDIAN SUMMER** *(1996, Record Heaven)*.

M.G. & C.C.

NOVEMBER

Björn Inge - *drums, vocals*, **Christer Stålbrandt** - *bass, vocals*, **Richard Rolf** - *guitars*.

November is born as a clone band of the more famous British trio **Cream**. Their success was definitely limited abroad by this fact and penalized by the use of Swedish lyrics, very hard to understand outside their country. Their debut album *En My Tid Ar Har* of 1970 is nevertheless very good and a perfect example of powerful hard blues with an outstanding lead guitar. The second recording *2:a November* is closer to the prog genre although their personality is still limited by this emulation. The last album entitled *6: e November* is finally a more mature and more personal one, with better structured melodies that alternate delicate to energetic and triumphant episodes. A powerful repertoire that improves their groove in concert.

DISCOGRAPHY: EN NY TID AR HAR...(*Sonet, 1970*) **2:a NOVEMBER** *(Sonet, 1971)* **6:e NOVEMBER** *(Sonet, 1972)*.

C.A. & C.C.

Europe: SWEDEN

RAGNARÖK

Peter Bryngelsson - *guitar*, **Peder Nabo** - *flute, guitar*, **Steffan Strindberg** - *bass*, **Stefan Ohlsson** - *drums, guitars*, **Henrik Strindberg** - *horns, guitars*, **Lars Peter Sörensson** - *drums, percussion*.

Being born in 1976, this second wave of prog did not serve them good as they were always compared to one or another band. Their delicately sad, sometimes jazzy yet very acoustic atmospheres, with soft flutes and arpeggios, actually do recall something like **Camel**, but the very Nordic style of their compositions make quite the difference: the slow flowing melodies bear within the sweet warmth of home. The first two albums are recorded with different line-ups but with good and similar results. The rest of their discography is instead more modern and with new-age inclinations. The recent reunion and consequent new album do not however reach the level of their beginnings.

RECOMMENDED RECORDINGS: RAGNARÖK *(1976, Silence)* **FJÄRILAR I MAGAN** *(1979, Silence)* **M.G. & C.C.**

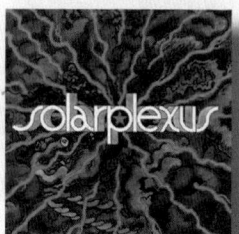

SOLAR PLEXUS

Monica Dominique – *keyboards, vocals*, **Carl-Axel Dominique** – *keyboards, flute, vocals*, **Georg Wadenius** - *bass, guitars, vocals*, **Tommy Borgudd** - *drums*.

A 1969 jazz-rock band with strong progressive elements founded by the classical background of siblings **Monica** and **Carl-Axel**, together with bassist **Wadenius** and drummer **Borgudd** (both from the jazz-prog band Made in Sweden). Their sound results to be strangely similar to the contemporary English jazz-prog of those years. A first homonym double LP is released in 1972 with instrumental parts in between **Nucleus** and **Egg**, but with a new folk and beat taste also given by the great vocal arrangements. **Wadenius** is replaced by **Bosse Haggstrom** and **Tommy Korberg**, joins in on voice and guitar for a good second album which lacks the amazing force of the previous. The rest of their material will be more oriented to an ethnic-folk jazz that still maintains a high level of originality.

RECOMMENDED RECORDINGS: SOLAR PLEXUS *(1972, Odeon)* **SOLAR PLEXUS 2** *(1973, Odeon)* **M.G. & C.C.**

TRÄD GRÄS OCH STENAR

Bo Anders Persson - *guitars, vocals, violin*, **Arne Ericsson** - *keyboards, cello, flute*, **Torbjörn Abelli** - *bass*, **Tomas Mera Gartz** - *drums*, **Jacob Sjöholm** - *guitars*.

Born from the ashes of **Pärson Sound**, **International Harvest** and **Harvest**, pioneers in psychedelic and minimalist sonorities, this band is the Swedish answer to kraut rock. The debut album starts off their career with the hypnotic and slow motion rhythms of **Velvet Underground** where we also find a version of "All along the Watchtower" filtered by **Terry Riley**'s moods. Following the Green Wave, they leave Stockholm and move to the country-side where they compose a new album full of long jam sessions and two live recordings. After a first breakup in the mid '70s, they will reunite once in 1979 and again during the '90s just to perform live for some concerts. Finally, in 2002 they decide to release a new album, *Ajn schvajn draj*, a convincing record, performed with modern sounds.

***DISCOGRAPHY*: TRÄD, GRÄS OCH STENAR** *(Decibel 1970)* **ROCK FÖR KROPP OCH SJÄL** *(Silence 1972)* **DJUNGELNS LAG** *(Tall 1972)* **MORS MORS** *(Tall 1974)* **AJN SCHVAJN DRAJ** *(Silence 2002)*. **M.G. & C.C.**

Europe: SWITZERLAND

CIRCUS

Roland Frei - *vocals, acoustic guitar, flute,* **Marco Cerletti** - *bass, bass pedals, guitars,* **Andres Grieder** - *flute,* **Fritz Hauser** - *drums, percussion, vibes.*

Considered as one of the best prog bands from Switzerland, they form in Basilea in 1975 with no keyboards in their line-up. This feature makes them even more fascinating as they develop a sound greatly inspired by **King Crimson** and **Van der Graaf Generator**, whereas the flute takes over a **Jethro Tull** style. Nevertheless their strong personality emerges in all three studio albums and in the excellent live recording: beautiful melodies and a rhythmic section of great technical skill. In particular the first two albums confirm a steady quality and coherence with incredible sax and flute solos which climax in the complex composition of the amazing 22 mins suite contained in the album *Movin'On*.

RECOMMENDED RECORDINGS: **CIRCUS** *(Zytglogge, 1976)* **MOVIN' ON** *(Zytglogge, 1977).*
M.G. & C.C.

FLAME DREAM

Peter Wolf - *vocals, winds,* **Roland Ruckstuhl** - *keyboards,* **Urs Waldispühl** - *guitars,* **Urs Hochuli** - *bass, vocals,* **Peter Furrer** - *drums, percussion.*

Swiss band formed near the German borders and oriented towards an English symphonic prog greatly inspired by **Yes**, especially in the use of vocals and guitar in the first 1978 album. Their excellent musical quality shines through the highly skilled interlacements between vocals, flute, guitars and keyboards supported by complex and ever changing rhythms. Guitarist **Waldispuhl** exits just after the first release and is not replaced: therefore the second recording will be characterized by the predominant keyboards, feature that will make their sound even more personal and original. *Out In The Dark* is also a good job yet sometimes slightly boring in the theme repetition derived both from **Genesis** or other Brit bands, or even from their own material and structural linearity. The rest of the discography is inferior to these three albums.

RECOMMENDED RECORDINGS: **CALATEA** *(Philips, 1978)* **ELEMENTS** *(Vertigo, 1979).*
M.G. & C.C.

ISLAND

Benjamin Jäger - *vocals, percussion,* **Güge Jürg Meier** - *drums, percussion,* **Peter Scherer** - *keyboards, vocals,* **René Fisch** - *sax, flute, clarinett, vocals.*

One glance at H.R. Giger's wonderful illustration on the cover of their one and only album *Pictures* and we know we are staring at a precious jewel from the crown of royal Prog: **Island** is a rose of very talented musicians playing a superlative symphonic rock, yet somewhat very distant from the common cliches. Their classical background bends Canterbury jazz and avant-garde to their will, creating amazing sounds also clearly influenced by the **VDGG**. Their music is severely marked by dark atmospheres, with screaming saxophones, bizarre percussions and a burning theatrical groove. The beautiful track "Zero" is the true fulcrum around which the whole record swivels screeching for more, but alas there is no further material for this Swiss band.

DISCOGRAPHY: **PICTURES** *(1977, Round).*
M.G. & C.C.

Europe: TURKEY

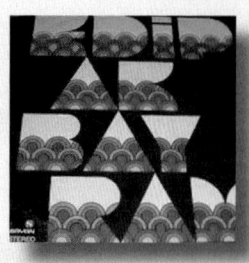

EDIP AKBAYRAM

Edip Akbayram is the main artist from the second wave of Anatolian pop, releasing wonderful albums characterized by the excellent mix of Turkish folk and progressive/psychedelic sounds inspired by both American and British prog bands. His backing group, **Dostlar**, is composed of some of the best and talented musicians whom play with him since 1973. The first two albums are probably his best although the whole discography is certainly a very interesting one. It's as if his voice screams in the darkness and this darkness is filled with the fuzz of the guitars playing wah wah effects together with local traditional instruments sounding as if Indian sitars were played by American psychedelic musicians. A very fascinating artist.

RECOMMENDED RECORDINGS: EDIP AKBAYRAM *(1974, Sayan)* **NEDIR NE DEGILDIR?** *(1977, Yavuz)* **NICE YILLARA GULUM** *(1982, Turkuola)* **DOSTLAR 1984** *(1984, Turkuola)* **1985** *(1985, Sembol Plak)* **YENI GELEN GUNE TURKU** *(1986 Sembol Plak)*. M.G.

ERSEN
(& Dadaslar)

During the '70s and despite the Turkish government's control over the censorship of the Arts, psychedelic rock still found its way in the weak music panorama of this country. **Ersen** was one of the first and best, already known and famous as a pop artist, he releases many hit singles that will be gathered in the album *Dunden Bugune* published in 1975. Although it is a collection of his greatest hits, the record overall is a very good example of garage rock with psychedelic influences derived from **The Doors**, with an ever present outstanding saxophone. The second *Ersen 2* of 1976 and the following *Bu Da Bizlerden* of 1979 are very similar projects, with songs performed in a **Procol Harum** style, using slightly heavier rhythms and good vocals supported by the melodic organ. **Ersen** never picked a political side and this limited his success with the younger generations for years. The original recordings are of course very rare to find and his music is now available on CD reprints.

DISCOGRAPHY: DUNDEN BUGUNE *(Uzunçalar, 1975)* **ERSEN 2** *(Uzunçalar, 1976)* **BU DA BIZLERDEN** *(Uzunçalar, 1979)*. C.A. & C.C.

MOĞOLLAR (Mogiòllar)

Cahit Berkay - vocals, guitars, traditional instruments, percussion , **Engin Yörükoglu** - drums, percussion, traditional instruments, **Taner Öngür** vocals, bass, **Serhat Ersöz** - vocals, keyboards, **Murat Ses** - keyboards.
Turkish band born in 1976 and still active, they are rightfully considered as the rock pioneers of their country. Originated as a folk band (the name means Mongols), they begin to insert influences from psychedelia, rock, jazz and prog without losing their strong identity, rooted in the Anatolian traditions and music of the Mediterranean area. As of today the 25 albums all have radically different lines-up: of prog interest those from 1971-72 featuring the temporary collaborations of singer and composer **Bariš Manço** and of **Cem Karaca**. The band pauses completely between 1976 and 1993, when they resume their career though their fame never wore out.

RECOMMENDED RECORDINGS: DÜM-TEK *(Coškun, 1975)* **MOĞOLLAR** *(Uzunçalar, 1976)*. M.G. & C.C.

Europe: **YUGOSLAVIA**

LEB I SOL

Vlatko Stefanovski - *guitar, vocals,* **Bodan Arsovski** - *bass,* **Nikola Dimushevski** - *keyboards,* **Dimitrije Cucurovski** - *drums.* **Gabaret Tavitijan** - *drums.*

Leb I Sol's popularity grew all over the ex-Yugoslavian areas and are one of the best and talented bands of the Macedonian music panorama. Founded in 1976, they were jazz rock lovers, attempting to blend different styles into this genre, including folk and Balcanic traditional sounds. The debut album released in 1977 is a good mix of jazz-rock which confirms how these musicians are more comfortable during the instrumental partitions of their songs, playing exciting improvisations and guitar-keyboards duets. Immediately after a second production follows full of compelling fusion atmospheres which prove their great talent, awarding them the title of "Band of the Year" by the press. Their prog phase ends with the release of what seems to be their best work, *Ruchni Rad* of 1979, a very appreciated album by the audience.

DISCOGRAPHY: **LEB I SOL** *(PGP-RTS, 1977)* **LEB I SOL 2** *(PGP-RTS, 1978)* **RUCHNI RAD** *(PGP-RTS, 1980).* **C.A. & C.C.**

TAKO

Djordje Ilijin - *keyboards, flute,* **Miroslav Dukic** - *guitars, vocals,* **Dusan Cucuz** - *bass, vocals,* **Slobodan Felekatovic** - *drums.*

Inspired by the very best of Pink Floyd's '70s material, their track "U verdi Za Spavanje" as a matter of fact sounds just like a new

version of "Shine on you crazy diamond". The whole album spreads through the smooth dreamy atmospheres of the mesmerizing keyboards that are sometimes aided by a delicate flute, but mainly the compositions are guided by a lead guitar strongly influenced by the great **David Gilmour**. Also **Tako**'s second album of 1980 follows this winning formula, although it is more pleasant and personal, closer to the romanticism of their idols **Pink Floyd** and of **Camel**. In 1983 **Djordje Ilijin** publishes a solo album of his own, that in a way continues the interrupted tale of this band.

DISCOGRAPHY: **TAKO** *(1978, RTV)* **U VRECI ZA SPAVANJE** *(1980, RTB).*
M.G. & C.C.

TIME

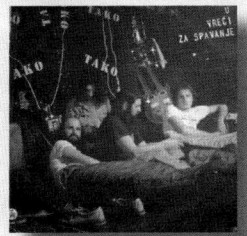

Dado Topic - *vocals,* **Tihomir Pop Asanovic** - *organ,* **Vedran Bozic** - *guitars,* **Mario Mavrin** - *bass,* **Ratko Divjak** - *drums,* **Brane Lambert Zivkovic** - *piano, flute.*

Creature of **Dado Topic** who

reunites a group of musicians to begin a brilliant adventure into the realms of the progressive world. Following the international standards established by bands like **Genesis**, **King Crimson** and **Gentle Giant**, their debut album of 1971 is a brave attempt to play rock in what used to be the Yugoslavian regime: the pleasant Hammond organ and flute interlacements are strongly influenced by jazz and by the American style of **Steely Dan**. After four years of silence a second release *Time II* comes out (1975) with a slightly modified line-up: despite the hard-rock trend of their new sound, it is still a good album with excellent melodic and romantic tunes. Every other future material thereafter leads very far way from the prog genre.

DISCOGRAPHY: **TIME** *(PGP-RTS, 1972)* **TIME II** *(PGP-RTS, 1975).* **C.A. & C.C.**

Indochina & North Asia: INDONESIA

DISCUS

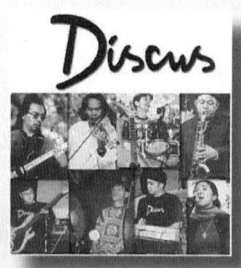

Iwan Hasan - guitars, harpguitar 21 strings, percussion, vocals, **Anto Praboe** - clarinet, flute, sax, vocals, suling, **Eko Paritur** - violin, electronics, vocals, **Fadhil Indra** - keyboards, vocals, **Hayunaji** - drums, percussion, vocals, **Kiki Caloh** - basso, vocals, **Krisna Prameswara** - keyboards, midi percussion programming, vocals, **Nonnie** - vocals.

One of the most fascinating prog bands in the whole wide word rises at the end of '90s in Indonesia: **Discus** is a strange but fascinating ensemble that debuts in 1999 with an astonishing record, *1st*, which blasts a personal symphonic rock into the universe of their local traditional sounds, all well juggled with a groovy jazzy attitude. The enchanting melodies of their fascinating female voice alternate with a male vocalist singing over compelling and rapid instrumental parts or electro-acoustic moments. A second release, *Tot licht*, although not at the same level of the previous, is still a powerful representation of their sound, starting from the same ingredients but pointing toward the rock-metal genre with avant-garde tunes and RIO elements.

DISCOGRAPHY: 1ST *(1999, Mellow Records)* **...TOT LICHT** *(2003, Musea)*.

M.G. & C.C.

FRAGILE

Henk Limaheluw - guitars, **Ferry Limaheluw** - guitars, **Chris Limaheluw** – bass, **Hank Oraille** - vocals, percussion, **Ted Tahapary** – drums.

A very particular band of Indonesian musicians coming from the Maluku Islands (ex-Dutch colony) and living in Holland. Founded in 1972 by the three **Limaheluw** brothers, they began playing the music they loved such as the hard blues of **Janis Joplin** and **Jimi Hendrix**. Their only album of 1976 was published in 500 copies and contained coarse unpolished sounds, rich of guitar fuzzes very similar to **Cargo** or the German **Baumstan**. The absence of keyboards unleashes the two guitars that run wild through the complex plots, often used to support the dramatic screams of lead singer **Oraille**. The long track contained on the second side, "So Sad", has a very interesting progression that goes from a slow blues to a **Santana** styled solo.

RECOMMENDED RECORDINGS: FRAGILE *(Private pressing LP, 1976 - CD Estrella 2004)*. M.G. & C.C.

GURUH GIPSY

Guruh Gipsy is a project born as the personal wimp of the Indonesian President's son, **Guruh Soekarno**. The former band, **Gipsy**, drew inspiration from the musical scene of the '60s and early '70s, playing covers from **Procol Harum**, **The Moody Blues** and **Faces**. When **Soekarno** joins in, he brings along his new ideas of ethnic contamination and western music, defining their style once and for all. The album is a compelling masterpiece which required over 16 months of recording sessions and employed a great deal of guest musicians, making its production very expensive. First issued on tape, it was published on vinyl subsequently. The strange mix of Indonesian folk and European prog rock is the strength of their music and their most important result, sometimes sounding as if **King Crimson** were playing with Asiatic instruments like the gentorak or the bajra.

DISCOGRAPHY: GURUH GIPSY *(Pramaqua, 1977)*. C.A. & C.C.

Indochina & North Asia: JAPAN

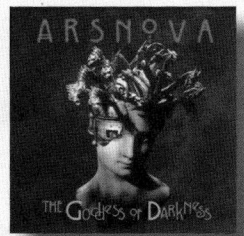

ARS NOVA

Satoshi Handa - *guitars*, **Keiko Kumagai** - *keyboards, Hammond Organ*, **Shinko "Panky" Shibata** - *bass*, **Hazime** - *drums*.

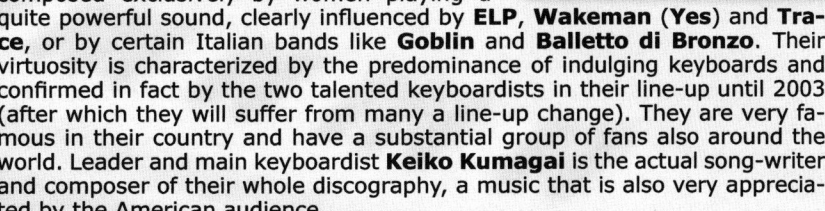

For a long time this Japanese quartet was composed exclusively by women playing a quite powerful sound, clearly influenced by **ELP**, **Wakeman** (**Yes**) and **Trace**, or by certain Italian bands like **Goblin** and **Balletto di Bronzo**. Their virtuosity is characterized by the predominance of indulging keyboards and confirmed in fact by the two talented keyboardists in their line-up until 2003 (after which they will suffer from many a line-up change). They are very famous in their country and have a substantial group of fans also around the world. Leader and main keyboardist **Keiko Kumagai** is the actual song-writer and composer of their whole discography, a music that is also very appreciated by the American audience.

RECOMMENDED RECORDINGS: **FEAR AND ANXIETY** *(1992, Nippon Columbia)* **TRANSI** *(1994, Nippon Columbia)* **THE GODDESS OF DARKNESS** *(1996, Nippon Columbia)* **THE BOOK OF THE DEAD** *(1998, Nippon Columbia)* **ANDROID DOMINA** *(2001, Nippon Columbia)* **LACRIMARIA** *(2001, Nippon Columbia)*.   M.G. & C.C.

FLIED EGG

Shigeru Marumo – *guitar, keyboards, vocals*, **Hiro Tsunoda** – *vocals, drums*, **Masayoshi Takanaka** – *bass, guitars, vocals*.

A Japanese power trio coming from the disbandment of **Strawberry Path** and **Brush** from which it derives a hard psychedelic prog of great force and impact, all sung in English. The guitar's harsh riffs merge into Brit-beat psychedelic rhythms where the Hammond intrusions are supported by a bass playing in the best **John Entwistle** (**The Who**) style. Both albums released in 1972 by Vertigo are rich of interesting parts greatly inspired by **Uriah Heep** and **Grand Funk Railroad**; yet the musicians manage a strange blend of '60s hippie psychedelia and '70s hard-prog with great skill, proving an originality that goes beyond a simple emulation.

RECOMMENDED RECORDINGS: **DR. SEIGEL'S FRIED EGG SHOOTING MACHINE** *(Vertigo, 1972)* **GOODBYE** *(Vertigo, 1972)*.   M.G. & C.C.

KIMIO MIZUTANI

Kimio Mizutani – *guitars*, **Masahiko Satoh** - *keyboards*, **Hiromasa Suzuki** - *electric piano*, **Hiro Yanagida** – *Hammond organ*, **Kayoko Isshu** – *vocals*, **Masaoki Terakawa** - *bass*, **Hideaki Takebe** – *bass*, **Takeshi Inomata** – *drums* + **Toyama String Quartet** + **Etoh Wood Quartet**.

Guitarist of great inventive and technique, **Kimio Mizutani** begins his career at the end of '60s playing in different bands, among which **Love Live Life + One**. As a soloist he releases only one excellent work in 1971 entitled *A Path through Haze*. This is a very personal and fascinating album of great quality with varied compositional surprises that pop up unexpected, such as the psychedelic experimentations of the amazing jazz-rock title-track "Sail in the Sky" (between **Mahavishnu**, **Zappa**, **Rundgren** and the Canterbury School) or the incredible hard-jazz blues of "Tell me what you saw" with its **King Crimson** inspired ending. A good number of famous Japanese musicians collaborate to this recording as special guests, particularly in the string and woodwind sections.

RECOMMENDED RECORDINGS: **A PATH THROUGH HAZE** *(1971, Polydor)*.   M.G. & C.C.

Indochina & North Asia: JAPAN

OUTER LIMITS

Shusei Tsukamoto - *keyboards*, **Takashi Kawaguchi** - *violin, guitar, viola*, **Tomoki Ueno** - *vocals, keyboards*, **Takashi Aramaki** - *guitars, bass, vocals*, **Noboyuki Sakurai** - *drums, percussion*, **Tadashi Ishikawa** - *bass*, **Sugimoto Tadashi** - *vocals, bass, cello, stick bass*.

Outer limits is one of those bands who intransigently pursued symphonic rock to the core. Founded in the middle of the '80s, their debut album of 1985, *Misty Moon*, was an immediate success, with its baroque keyboards and violin fugues constantly referring to **PFM** and **King Crimson**. The following albums *A boy playing the magical bugle horn* and *the scene of pale blue* are both good records, containing the same style and high quality of the previous. After a fourth 1989 album, recorded live in studio, *the silver apples on the moon*, they disappear for eight years without giving any explanation. Finally, in 2007 they return with a brand new album, *Stromatolite*, a mature and convincing record that confirms their characteristic sound.

DISCOGRAPHY: **MISTY MOON** *(1985, Made in Japan)* **A BOY PLAYING THE MAGICAL BUGLE HORN** *(1986, Made in Japan)* **THE SCENE OF PALE BLUE** *(1987 Made in Japan)* **THE SILVER APPLES ON THE MOON** *(1989, Made in Japan)* **OUTER MANIA** *(1989, Made in Japan)* **STROMATOLITE** *(2007, Musea).*
M.G. & C.C.

PAGEANT

Hiroko Nagai - *keyboards, vocals*, **Kazuhiro Miyatake** - *flute, guitars*, **Ikkou Nakajima** - *vocals, guitars*, **Hideaki Indou** - *drums*, **Nobuyuki Nagashima** - *bass*.

They begin to form in 1981 and expand the line-up as they play. In 1985 they are asked to participate in a compilation called *Progressive Battle*. This gives them some credibility and leads to the opportunity of a first recording the following year, the excellent symphonic prog album *La Mosaique De La Reverie*, with very rich and melodic atmospheres. Many are the **Genesis** references, though hints from **Renaissance** and other bands from the new English prog can be found as some guitar styles inspired by **Rush**. Strong characteristic female voice of **Nakajima**. The second album release of 1987, *Abysmal Masquerade*, re-elaborates themes from the first in a less complex manner, similar to the third and last work, even more simple and pop.

RECOMMENDED RECORDINGS: **LA MOSAIQUE DE LA REVERIE** *(Made in Japan, 1986).*
M.G. & C.C.

PRISM

Akira Wada - *guitars*, **Ken Watanabe** - *bass*, **Daisaku Kume** - *keyboards*, **Koki "Corky" Ito** - *keyboards*, **Katsutoshi Morizono** - *guitars*, **Toru "Rika" Suzuki** - *drums*.

In 1975 eighteen year old guitarist **Akira Wada** founds his band with jazz-rock intentions. During their 30 album life-span, the sound simplifies into a sweet and more simple fusion genre. Starting from the first homonym album in 1977, probably one of their best, they will maintain the same quality up to a fourth recording *Prism Live* of 1979. The debut features the collaboration of **Katsutoshi Morizono** (former guitarist of **Yonin Bayashi**), resulting in excellent acrobatic guitar solos and a very interesting double keyboard section, often played together with an electric piano or a string machine keyboard.

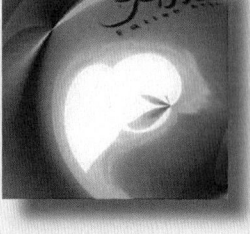

RECOMMENDED RECORDINGS: **PRISM** *(Polydor, 1977)* **SECOND THOUGHT/SECOND MOVE** *(Polydor, 1978).*
M.G. & C.C.

Indochina & North Asia: PHILIPPINES

ANAK BAYAN

Bing Labrador - *keyboards*, **Vic Naldo** - *guitars, vocals*, **Sonny Tolentino** - *bass*, **Edmond "Bosyo" Fortuno** - *drums, vocals*, **Alex Cruz** - *saxophones*.

'Pinoy Rock' is the name given to the genre of music produced in the Philippines, a country where the rock panorama is quite surprising. In fact we find many known names playing this 'Classic Pinoy Rock' genre like **Juan De La Cruz Band, Anak Bayan, Mike Hanopol**. These bands are of course influenced by prog rock yet actually they play a more personal mix, in-between western music and the local traditions. **Anak Bayan** was a splinter band created by the founder of **Juan De La Cruz Band**, drummer **Edmond Fortuno** aka '**Bosyo**', for the representation of *Tommy* where they played together with the Manila Symphony Orchestra. Bosyo was already famous abroad and in the early '70s he participates in **John Lennon** and **Yoko Ono**'s project, **the Plastic Ono Band**. The **Anak Bayan**'s one and only LP was recorded in 1973 but the tapes went lost by the studio and the official release postponed until four years later. This very hard to find original vinyl, presents us with a fresh album full of psychedelic sounds, fuzz guitars and effervescing rhythms. Recently it was remastered and reissued on CD but as of today all the original components, except for the saxophonist, are dead.
DISCOGRAPHY: ANAK BAYAN *(A&W Records, 1977).*   M.G. & C.C.

ASIN

Pendong Aban - *guitars, keyboards, strings, vocals*, **Lolita Carbon** - *vocals, acoustic guitar*, **Saro Bañares** - *percussion, vocals*, **Mike Pillora** - *bass, strings, vocals*.

This very particular band from the Philippines is practically unknown abroad, though very famous in their own country since the mid '70s. The name derives from **Joan Baez**'s song "Salt of the Earth": as a matter of fact, at first they used the entire title translated, reducing it later to simply **Asin** (salt). They cannot be considered literally as a true prog band since their music is more oriented towards a traditional folk genre. Yet the Anglo-Saxon contaminations both of the the metrical system and of the instruments used, simultaneously with other local ethnic ones, place their traditional melodies in a very interesting position, closer to prog than to any other genre of the times.

RECOMMENDED RECORDINGS: ASIN *(Vicor Records, 1978).*   M.G. & C.C.

JUAN DE LA CRUZ BAND

Wally Gonzales - *guitars, vocals*, **Rene Segueco** - *vocals, organ*, **Clifford Ho** - *bass, vocals*, **Romy Santos** - *horns*, **Bobot Guerrero** - *drums*, **Sandy Tagarro** - *lead vocals*. **Edmond "Bosyo" Fortuno**, **Joey "Pepe" Smith** - *drums*.

This "Filipino Rock group" formed in 1968 and pioneered what then became "Pinoy Rock' genre, fundamental to comprehend the musical evolution in this country. Founders are guitarist **Wally Gonzalez** and drummer **Edmond Fortuno** a.k.a. '**Bosyo**', two very well known and talented musicians. They first perform in the open air festival called "The Antipolo Rock Festival", after which, in 1971 they release a very successful first album, *Up in Arms*. That same year they are summoned to play together with the Manila Symphony Orchestra for the Philippine production of *Jesus Christ Superstar* (rock opera by **Tim Rice** and **Andrew Lloyd Webber**), at the "Cultural Center of the Philippines" where they will be crowned as the best band of their country.

RECOMMENDED RECORDINGS: UP IN ARMS *(1971, Vicor/Sunshine)* **HIMIG NATIN** *(1973, Vicor/Sunshine)* **MASKARA** *(1974, Vicor/Sunshine).*   M.G.

North America: CANADA

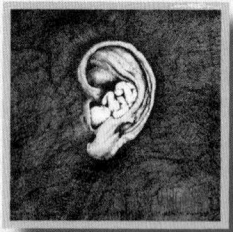

CONTRACTION

Robert Lachapelle - *keyboards*, **Yves Laferrière** - *bass*, **Richard Perrotte** - *drums*, **Christiane Robichaud** - *vocals*, **Robert Stanley** - *guitars*, **Christian St-Roch** - *drums*.

Among the best bands from Quebec in the early '70s, their very personal sound is characterized by hints of jazz that well preserve the avant-garde approach of musical research. Their first record is of a symphonic pop that tends to deep fusion contaminations and is released in two languages: first with beautiful French lyrics as a debut album, and then in English as a second version. Their unique style will be confirmed in the more mature second album *La Bourse Ou La Vie* of 1974: a small masterpiece that will unfortunately be their last due to internal disagreements between the musicians. **Christiane Robichaud**'s voice opens this album merging perfectly his vocals to **Stanley**'s immediately recognizable guitar and the wonderful keyboards of **Lachapelle**. The final breakup will officially date 1976.

DISCOGRAPHY: **CONTRACTION** *(Columbia, 1972)* **LA BOURSE OU LA VIE** *(Deram, 1974)*.

C.A. & C.C.

CONVENTUM

Jean-Pierre Bouchard - *acoustic guitar, flute*, **Bernard Cormier** - *violin, métallophone, percussion*, **André Duchense** - *acoustic guitar*, **Jacques Laurin** - *bass*, **René Lussier** - *guitars, mandolin*, **Alain-Arthur Painchaud** - *vocals*, **Jean Derome** - *flute*.

Another big name from the musical panorama of Quebec publishes a very good first album in 1977 called *A l'affut d'un complot*, containing a large predominance of acoustic sounds in which prog and chamber music are very close (something similar to the Belgian **Univers Zero**, but less darker and unsettling). Playing a large range of instruments, the band tries to merge feelings of novelty to antiquity, folk tunes and theatrical voices. This experiment works well and will be repeated in the following second, but last album, *Le bureau central des utopies*, a more mature an improved record than the previous one. **Conventum** is remembered as a band not easy to listen to, comparable to other European bands of RIO, but less complicated and less related to the political rage.

DISCOGRAPHY: **À L'AFFUT D'UN COMPLOT** *(1977, Le Tamanoir)* **LE BUREAU CENTRAL DES UTOPIES** *(1979, Les Disques Cadence)*. M.G. & C.C.

DIONYSOS

Paul-André Thibert - *vocals, engineering*, **Éric Clément** - *guitars*, **Jean-Pierre Legault** - *bass*, **Fernand Durand** - *bass*, **Robert Lepage** - *drums* **André Mathieu** - *keyboards*.

A band from Quebec who started as an ensemble of musicians playing cover versions of American hits released as singles in a French version. The path to become a true prog band with original and personal material begins with their debut album *Le Grand Jeu* of 1971, a record deeply influenced by these previous American rock blues experiences, but still not in English. Aware that this disconnection between the genre and the lyrics penalized the result, they release the following year, a new studio album, *Le Prince Croule* which will definitely be their best: the French lyrics well merge with a harder sound, influenced this time by **Atomic Rooster** and **Deep Purple** and their use of the compelling keyboards. They break-up soon after, reuniting four years later for a third more jazzy record, **Dionysos** (also known as *Changé D'adresse*). Although this was in fact a good work, it was not enough to save the situation and they definitively end their career in 1977.

RECOMMENDED RECORDINGS: **LE GRAND JEU** *(Jupiter, 1970)* **LE PRINCE CROULE** *(Zodiaque, 1971)* **DIONYSOS** *(DERAM, 1976)*. C.A. & C.C.

North America: CANADA

OCTOBRE

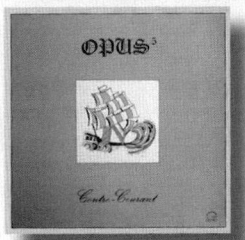

Pierre Flynn – *keyboards, vocals,* **Jean Dorais** - *guitar,* **Mario Légaré** - *bass,* **Pierre Hebert** - *drums.*

Canadian band from the area of Quebec, they begin playing together in 1972, releasing the following year a homonym debut album that, although still quite unrefined, results very interesting for the use of crossover situations, probably among the first, that distinguish their entire discography: a fusion genre that explores and blends french songwriting, symphonic prog, jazz and genuine avant-garde ideas. The following 1974 release is a good album but their real masterpiece is *Survivance* with the amazing "La Valse A Onze Temps" and its incredible change of rhythm from 3/4 to 11/8. Still great the next jazz-fusion album *L'Autoroute Des Reves* and its beautiful instrumental parts.

***RECOMMENDED RECORDINGS:* SURVIVANCE** (Trans World, 1975) **L'AUTOROUTE DES REVES** (CBS, 1977).
M.G. & C.C.

OPUS 5

Olivier Duplessis - *keyboards, vocals,* **Luc Gauthier** - *guitar, vocals,* **Serge Nolet** - *flute, vocals,* **Christian Leon Racine** - *bass, vocals,* **Jean-Pierre Racicot** - *vocals, percussion.*

Another good band from Quebec with great technical skills that do not linger in aesthetics but are always serving a functional purpose with devoted precision. Their sound recalls the Canterbury school with hints of **Gentle Giant** plots and Zeuhl echoes that explore the typical folk genre of their region through a rich and funny jazz-rock. Beautiful flute parts alternate with delicate melodies that are never trivial. Their first release in 1976 was titled *Volume 1*, though it took over 13 years to publish the sequel *Volume 2*: a posthumous album of rediscovered tapes gathered only thanks to the renewed interest of the Japanese market, not truly at the same level of their wonderful debut.

***RECOMMENDED RECORDINGS:* VOLUME 1: CONTRE COURANT** (Les Disques RCA, 1976).
M.G. & C.C.

SLOCHE

Réjean Yacola - *piano, keyboards, vocals,* **Martin Murray** - *keyboards, sax, vocals,* **Caroll Bérard** - *guitar, vocals,* **Pierre Hébert** - *bass, vocals,* **Gilles Chiasson** - *drums, vocals,* **André Roberge** - *drums, percussion,* **Gilles Ouellet** - *glassharmonica, percussion.*

Sloche's two albums are among the best of all Canadian prog rock, two authentic jewels. The first *J'un Oeil* of 1975 is a good mix of symphonic rock influenced by **Gentle Giant** and jazz rock sounds, a good record that builds up to the following (and best) second album, *Stadaconé*, which establishes their definitive sound, closer to **Mahavisnu Orchestra**, the Canterbury school and to some of their contemporary colleagues in Quebec. Their personality, fantasy, warm sounds and vivid arrangements emerge with the outstanding waves of keyboards and electric piano.

***DISCOGRAPHY:* J'UNOEIL** (1975, RCA) **STADACONÉ** (1976, RCA). M.G. & C.C.

North America: UNITED STATES

CARTOON

Scott Brazieal – *keyboards*, **Mark Innocenti** – *guitars*, **Gary Parra** – *drums, percussion*, **Herbert Diamant** – *horns*, **Craig Fry** – *violin, horns*.

While Prog waded through the decadence of the previous years, not many American bands kept it alive as these musicians from Phoenix. As a trio (keyboards, guitars and drums) they released a first homonym album with recordings from 1979 to 1981 before extending the line-up to become a quintet and publishing in 1983 a truer avant-guard prog of incredible musical force with inclinations to the R.I.O. movement: greatly inspired by **Samla Mammas Manna**, **Henry Cow**, **King Crimson** (like in the amazing "Ptomaine Poisoning") and **Stravinsky** (as in the long suite "Quote"), the rare vinyl was fortunately re-issued by Cuneiform yet without the song "Trio".

RECOMMENDED RECORDINGS: **SORTIE** *(Cuneiform, 1994)*   M.G. & C.C.

CATHEDRAL

Paul Seal - *vocals*, **Tom Doncourt** - *keyboards*, **Rudy Perrone, David Doig** - *guitars*, **Fred Callan** - *bass*, **Mercury Caronia IV** - *drums*.

One of the most symbolic prog bands from the USA who released one of the last great albums of the '70s: deeply influenced by **Gentle Giant**, **King Crimson** and **Genesis**, these New Yorkers have a very similar story to their Italian contemporaries, **Locanda delle Fate**, publishing one outstanding album before disappearing for decades due to the bad timing (decline of the genre) yet influencing other bands to come when the interest for prog rose again (like the Swedish New Prog band, **Änglagård**, in the early '90s). **Cathedral** is born from the ashes of the psychedelic band **Odyssey** in 1975, but their album came out only three years later, when the music world had already begun to change tastes in favour of punk and disco music. *Stained Glass Stories* is a cult album, (not as hard sounding as **Kansas** nor versatile like **Happy the Man**) arranged with a majestic use of mellotron and effervescing rhythms with dynamic textures that sometimes take too much from **Yes**. Reunited thirty years later, they issue a second studio album in 2007, *The Bridge*, confirming style and sound.

DISCOGRAPHY: **STAINED GLASS STORIES** *(Delta Records 1978)*, **THE BRIDGE** *(Cathedral, 2007)*.   M.G. & C.C.

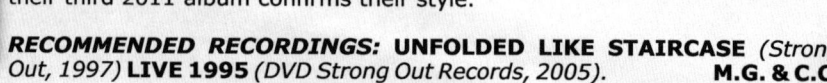

DISCIPLINE

Matthew Parmenter - *vocals, bells, keyboards, violin, saxophones, guitar, percussion*, **Matthew Kennedy** - *bass*, **Jon Preston Bouda** - *guitar*, **Paul Dzendzel** – *drums, percussion*, **David Krofchok** – *keyboards, vocals*.

Their main characteristic lies in the high visual and musical quality of the live performances also thanks to the histrionic and magnetic features of lead singer **Matthew Parmenter** (another **Peter Gabriel**'s disciple!). The first two studio albums are quite different from each other, the first of 1993 contains mostly short to medium song-like tracks with arrangements that result being not too redundant. The sound explosion of the second album released in 1997, *Unfolded like Staircase*, is greatly inspired by the atmospheres of **VDGG** and the tracks are this time perfectly structured long suites. Marvelous the live DVD of 1995 while their third 2011 album confirms their style.

RECOMMENDED RECORDINGS: **UNFOLDED LIKE STAIRCASE** *(Strong Out, 1997)* **LIVE 1995** *(DVD Strong Out Records, 2005)*.   M.G. & C.C.

North America: UNITED STATES

DREAM THEATER

John Petrucci - *guitars*, **Mike Portnoy** - *drums*, **John Myung** - *bass*, **Kevin Moore** - *keyboards*, **Charlie Dominici** - *vocals*, **James LaBrie** - *vocals*, **Derek Sheridian** - *keyboards*, **Jordan Rudess** - *keyboards*.

If prog rock rose again during the '90s, it is also due to the American band **Dream Theater**, born from the Heavy Metal genre (**Rush** and **Deep Purple**) and adding to their music symphonic arrangements, complex rhythms and long tracks in perfect prog style. This extends also to the introduction of a real concept album like *Metropolis 2* in 1999. Their second album, *Images and words* of 1992, is not only a cult but it is regarded as the one that established the standards of a whole genre for other bands like **Opeth** and **Tools**: Prog Metal. Today the band is still strong and active although their drummer **Mike Portnoy** left some years ago. All their works are full of exaggerated self indulging moments of long virtuosities especially during live performances, but their contribution to prog is undeniable.

RECOMMENDED RECORDINGS: **IMAGES AND WORDS** *(1992, ATCO)* **LIVE AT THE MARQUEE** *(1993, ATCO)* **SCENES FROM A MEMORY – METROPOLIS PART 2** *(1999, ATCO)* **OCTAVARIUM** *(2005, Atlantic).* M.G. & C.C.

FIREBALLET

Martyn Biglin – *bass, guitars, backing vocals*, **Ryche Chlanda** – *guitars, effects, backing vocals*, **Jim Cuomo** – *lead vocals, percussion*, **Brian Hough** – *keyboards, backing vocals*, **Frank Petto** – *keyboards, backing vocals*.

Two records for this New Jersey band, the first produced by **Ian McDonald** from **King Crimson**, a rich and busy album released in 1975, played with great skill and love for the prog genre, full of funny and interesting songs of excellent and very personal moments that alternate hints from the great prog masters such as **Genesis**'s "Seven Stones", **Yes**'s "Roundabout", **El&P**'s "Karn Evil 9", **George Martin**'s "Theme One" or **Mussorgskij**'s *Night on Bald Mountain* (the title track). Not very different in its intentions, yet certainly in the results, was their second album of 1976: they opt for more simplified solutions often disregarding the symphonic aspect to the advantage of a more immediate rhythmic and perception, orienting the melodies to semi-prog re-visitations of classic American pop songs.

RECOMMENDED RECORDINGS: **NIGHT ON BALD MOUNTAIN** *(Passport Records, 1975).* M.G. & C.C.

FRENCH TV

Mike Sary - *bass*, **Stephen Roberts, Bill Fowler, Paul Nevitt, Bob Ramsey, John Robinson, John Encifer, Warren Dale** - *keyboards*, **Artie Bratton, Dean Zigoris, Tony Hall, Chris Smith** - *guitars*, **Fenner Castner, Bob Douglas, Brian Donohue, Chris Vincent, Jeff Gard** - *drums*, **Clancy Dixon, Greg Acker, Steve Good** - *horns*.

A band from Kentucky among the most creative and the politicized of the last thirty years, perhaps the only true RIO band of the USA. They begin playing in the early '80s, deeply influenced by **Frank Zappa**, the Canterbury school and jazz-rock, using their music to communicate mocking and corrosive messages through their effervescing melodies. Their first four albums draw pictures of whirlwind of fantasies and vivid sounds: in 1997 **Mike Sary** and his band release their masterpiece *The Violence of Amateurs*, an overwhelming and lunatic jazz-rock album, one of the best of the last twenty years, that marks the following production *The Case Against Art* which represents a very innovative manifestation of classic Symphonic Prog with elements of jazz-fusion and prog-metal.

RECOMMENDED RECORDINGS: **FRENCH TV** *(Pretentious Dinosaur, 1984)* **THE VIOLENCE OF AMATEURS** *(PD, 1997)* **THIS IS WHAT WE DO** *(PD 2006).* M.G. & C.C.

North America: UNITED STATES

GRITS

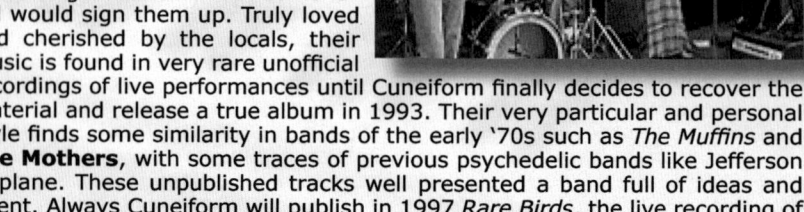

Tom Wright - *guitar, viola, vocals,* **Amy Taylor** - *vocals, bass, violin,* **Bob Sims** - *drums, percussion, vocals,* **Rick Barse** - *keyboards, vocals, bass.*

This band from Washington D.C. played through the '70s without ever publishing a real album since no label would sign them up. Truly loved and cherished by the locals, their music is found in very rare unofficial recordings of live performances until Cuneiform finally decides to recover the material and release a true album in 1993. Their very particular and personal style finds some similarity in bands of the early '70s such as *The Muffins* and **The Mothers**, with some traces of previous psychedelic bands like Jefferson Airplane. These unpublished tracks well presented a band full of ideas and talent. Always Cuneiform will publish in 1997 *Rare Birds*, the live recording of a concert held in 1976.

RECOMMENDED RECORDINGS : AS THE WORLD GRITS *(Cuneiform, 1993 - archive recordings from 1970-1975).* M.G. & C.C..

IT

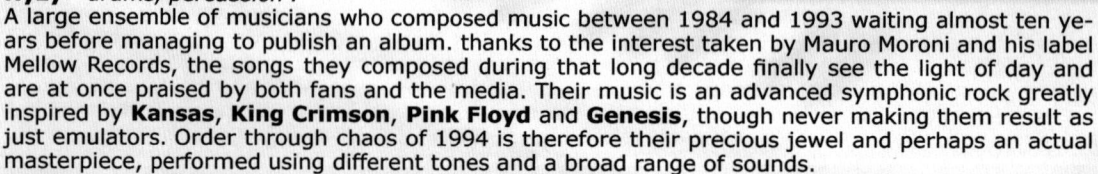

Todd Freeman - *guitars, bass, vocals,* **Scott Munson** - *guitars, keyboards, vocals,* **Mike Riseman** - *keyboards, piano,* **Darwin** - *vocals,* **Mark Stoffel** - *violin,* **John Hunter** - *drums, percussion,* **Jason Thomas** - *vocals,* **Ron Synovitz** - *sitar,* **Bill Lancaster** - *drums,* **Richard Banks** - *keyboards,* **Andy Hannon** - *keyboards,* **Nora O' Connor** - *backing vocals,* **Kevin Cox** - *flute,* **Lynda Killoran** - *contrabass,* **Chris Hyzy** - *drums, percussion .*

A large ensemble of musicians who composed music between 1984 and 1993 waiting almost ten years before managing to publish an album. thanks to the interest taken by Mauro Moroni and his label Mellow Records, the songs they composed during that long decade finally see the light of day and are at once praised by both fans and the media. Their music is an advanced symphonic rock greatly inspired by **Kansas**, **King Crimson**, **Pink Floyd** and **Genesis**, though never making them result as just emulators. Order through chaos of 1994 is therefore their precious jewel and perhaps an actual masterpiece, performed using different tones and a broad range of sounds.

DISCOGRAPHY: ORDER THROUGH CHAOS *(1994, Mellow Records).* M.G. & C.C.

IXT ADUX

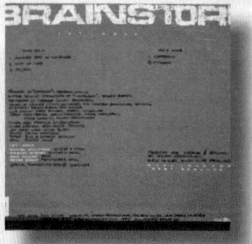

Daniel Williford - *guitar, vocals,* **Martin Austin** - *guitar, vocals,,* **Erik Miller** - *bass,* **Peter Mehit** - *drums, percussion.*

With their one and only album issued at the beginning of '80s, **Ixt Adux** made their way down the hall of fame of the American prog genre: *Brainstorm* was released in 1982 and is an impressive work of well arranged music, full of complex performances that echo sounds from the best of **Yes**, **Gentle Giant**, **Rush**, **King Crimson** and other American mainstream rock bands. The five elaborate compositions in the album whirl and twirl around the extensive use of guitars instead of the usual prog predominance of keyboards. The cutting-edge high-pitched and often loud guitars plunge into breathtaking solos and rarely pausing for the perfectly refined vocals which result as bizarre and unpredictable. Perhaps the only drawbacks to the sound are the unavoidable poor production available to such an independent and the resulting lack of tonal variation on the guitars. While the latter is mitigated by the sheer profusion of excellent playing, the former has to be taken as more indicative of the poor state of innovative music at this point in the 80s regardless of how much a detraction it seems now. Warts and all, this is a worthy release, particularly for the time.

DISCOGRAPHY: BRAINSTORM *(1982, Madame X).* M.G. & C.C.

North America: UNITED STATES

THE MARS VOLTA

Cedric Bixler-Zavala - *vocals*, **Omar Rodriguez-Lopez** - *guitars*, **Jon Theodore, Thomas Pridgen** - *drums*, **Juan Alderete** - *bass*, **Isaiah Owens** - *keyboards*, **Marcel Rodriguez** - *percussion*, **Pablo Hinojos-Gonzales** - *sound manipulation*.

This band confirms that different styles, sometimes in opposition, can cohabit or better, should work together. Born from the ashes of a pre-existing hard-core punk-rock '90s' band called **At The Drive In**, the magic couple **Rodriguez-Bixler** lead their new creature by maintaining the powerful and fast hard-core rhythms, adding compositions sometimes long as suites influenced by **Pink Floyd**, **King Crimson**, **Santana**, **Led Zeppelin** and psychedelia. The result is a devastating and overwhelming formula performed with high speed and post-core energy: in one word a prog-rock performed with punk-rock rhythms. The vocals sung by **Bixler** are deeply influenced by **Robert Plant** and other soul music singers, and the lyrics are sometimes in Spanish too. When performing live, these talented musicians play seemingly in absolute disorder their long and homogeneous compositions. Surprisingly creative in studio, the first two albums are recommended for they set the ground rules of all their following material.

RECOMMENDED RECORDINGS: DE-LOUSED IN A COMATORIUM *(Universal, 2003)* FRANCES THE MUTE *(Universal, 2005)*.   M.G. & C.C.

MIRTHRANDIR

Robert Arace - *drums*, **James Miller** - *bass, flute*, **Simon Gannett** - *keyboards*, **John Vislocky III** - *vocals, trumpet*, **Richard Excellente** - *guitars*, **Alexander Romanelli** - *guitars*.

A band founded in 1973 who belongs to those American groups deeply influenced by **Yes**, probably one of the best. In fact, their only album *For You the Old Women* of 1976 is a good record containing five tracks performed with intricate interlacing sounds and the complex textures of guitars and keyboards are inspired of course by their idols **Howe** and **Wakeman**. The warmth created by the use of certain vintage keyboards (moog, hammond organ, fender rhodes piano and mellotron) merges with both guitars and the fascinating flute melodies. Lyrics and vocals are refined and recall **Gentle Giant**. Due to the rising success of disco music during their short career, the band eclipses and fades away.

DISCOGRAPHY: FOR YOU THE OLD WOMEN *(1976, Mirthrandir)*.   M.G. & C.C.

OCTOBER

Pat Carson – *drums*, **Mark Krench** – *keyboards*, **Mark Sterling** – *keyboards*, **Jeff Rozany** - *bass, vocals*, **Brad Tolinski** - *violin, guitars*.

Symphonic space-prog band from Michigan, their music is full of acoustic guitars, outstanding keyboards and a powerful moog synth opening their first homonym album of 1979. The excellent *After the Fall*, is released the following year and is actually better than the previous, with a fascinating mellotron sounding like something from another planet and the watercolour artwork printed over the finest paper for the cover. As a whole the music is really enjoyable bringing to mind equal parts **Weidorje**, albeit a bit more melodic, and more symphonic bands like **Atoll** or **Ange**, perhaps even Harmonium's "L'heptade". There are very sparse vocals (just one track and not much of it) but the album in its integrity, would have benefitted from being completely instrumental. Although these two albums were published 'out of their time', at the end of '70s in a world far from the golden age of prog, the tracks are authentic gems that shine a light of their own through the use of a poised and skillful violin. The original LPs are almost impossible to find though recently they were both reissued (bootlegs) on CD by an unauthorized music label.

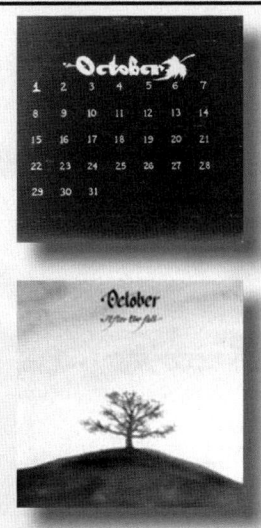

DISCOGRAPHY: OCTOBER *(Charisma Sound, 1979)* AFTER THE FALL *(Private Pressing, 1980)*.   M.G. & C.C.

North America: UNITED STATES

OREGON

Ralph Towner - *guitar, piano, keyboards,* **Paul McCandless** - *horns,* **Glen Moore** - *contrabass, violin, piano,* **Collin Walcott, Trilok Gurtu, Arto Tuncboyaciyan, Mark Walker* - *percussion.*

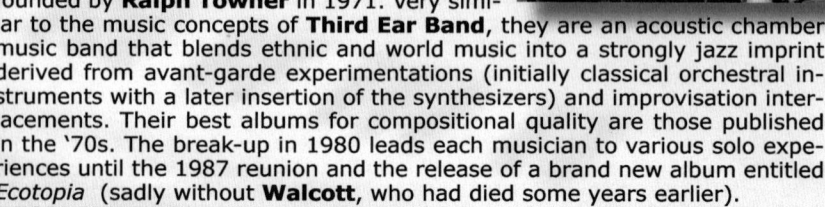

Authentic giants of jazz-prog, the ensemble is founded by **Ralph Towner** in 1971. Very similar to the music concepts of **Third Ear Band**, they are an acoustic chamber music band that blends ethnic and world music into a strongly jazz imprint derived from avant-garde experimentations (initially classical orchestral instruments with a later insertion of the synthesizers) and improvisation interlacements. Their best albums for compositional quality are those published in the '70s. The break-up in 1980 leads each musician to various solo experiences until the 1987 reunion and the release of a brand new album entitled *Ecotopia* (sadly without **Walcott**, who had died some years earlier).
RECOMMENDED RECORDINGS: MUSIC OF ANOTHER PRESENT ERA (Vanguard 1973) **DISTANT HILLS** (Vanguard 1973) **IN CONCERT** (live, Vanguard 1975) **ROOTS IN THE SKY** (Elektra 1979) **IN PERFORMANCE** (live, Elektra 1980) **ECOTOPIA** (ECM 1987) **ALWAYS, NEVER AND FOREVER** (Intuition 1991) **TROIKA** (Verabra 1994). M.G. & C.C.

POLYPHONY

Martin Ruddy - *vocals, bass,* **Christopher Spong** - *drums,* **Craig Massey** - *vocals, keyboards,* **Glenn Howard** - *vocals, guitars,* **Chatty Cooper** - *percussion, drums.*

When the Brits started their Prog revolution around 1968, they were looked upon by a world of artists in search of inspiration: emulated and copied, this new genre spread like a disease and as such was seen, at the turn of the century, by the fellow Anglo-Saxons of the American continent, whom did not seem to appreciate the invasion until the late 1973, when it was already cult. **Polyphony** is among the very few U.S. bands that began playing in these unfortunate early '70s, when the contamination was yet to be fully understood by the general audience. Their only album of 1971 was released and practically ignored, yet *Without Introduction* is probably one of the most classic symphonic rock albums of the American prog scene. Greatly influenced by **Keith Emerson, Nice** and **ELP** with some sprinkles of **Vanilla Fudge** and psychedelia, it is full of dynamic instrumental moments with frenzy rhythms, varied tempo changes and a complex crossfire of Hammond and guitar.
DISCOGRAPHY: WITHOUT INTRODUCTION (1971, Eleventh Hour). M.G. & C.C.

STARCASTLE

Terry Luttrell - *lead vocals,* **Gary Strater** - *bass, bass pedals, vocals,* **Stephen Tassler** - *drums, percussion, vocals,* **Herb Schildt** - *keyboards,* **Matthew Stewart** - *guitars, vocals,* **Stephen Hagler** - *guitars, vocals.*

They begin playing as the cover band (prog and rock classics) St. James in 1969, then change name in 1974 when they consolidate a more personal style that converges into their first successful debut album in 1976. Sounding very much like the British band Yes, both in the strong similarities of the solo voice and for the typical symphonic compositions, to which they differed only by inserting as a characteristic element a more pompous AOR attitude. After another three albums with the label Epic, good the first two, decidedly bad the third, they break-up in 1977. Many the attempts to reunite and create a new line-up due to Strater's death and Schidt's abandonment of the musical scene, when finally they publish Songs of Time in 2007.
RECOMMENDED RECORDINGS: STARCASTLE (Epic, 1976) **FOUNTAINS OF LIGHT** (Epic, 1977) **SONG OF TIMES** (ProgRock Records 2007). M.G. & C.C.

North America: UNITED STATES

STEELY DAN

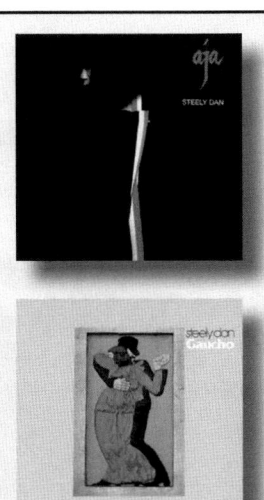

Donald Fagen - *keyboards, vocals,* **Walter Becker** - *bass, guitar, vocals,* **Denny Dias** - *guitars,* **Jeff "Skunk" Baxter** - *guitars, pedal steel guitar,* **Jim Hodder** - *drums,* **David Palmer** - *vocals.*

Donald Fagen and **Walter Becker**'s band is a strange creature that lived through many lives camouflaging into many a genre and never really being able to confine itself to something definite. Theirs is a story of continuous crossing borders and line-up changes according to the whips of the founding duo: from jazz to blues to rock, fusion and soul, with some refined touches of country music. Not only a gathering of very talented musicians (**Porcaro Bros**, **Larry Charlton**, **Brecker Bros**, **Michael McDonald** among many others), but also of the finest sound engineers, sometimes defined as the American **Pink Floyd** due to their extremely careful recording sessions. The whole discography is recommended but worthy of mention are *Aja* of 1977 and *Gaucho* of 1980 where they accomplish the perfect merge of all the above genres. Mainly a studio band with very few concerts and even shorter tours around the USA, in 1980 they take a long pause until their come back album in 2000 *Two Against Nature*, the reprise of a fascinating adventure.

RECOMMENDED RECORDINGS: AJA *(ABC, 1977)* **GAUCHO** *(ABC, 1980)* **TWO AGAINST NATURE** *(Giant, 2000).*   C.A. & C.C.

THINKING PLAGUE

Mike Johnson - *guitars, keyboards, percussion, vocals,* **Bob Drake** - *bass, drums, percussion, vocals, guitars, balalaika, keyboards.*

Founded in Colorado thanks to the two excellent minds of Mike Johnson and Bob Drake, the genial and introvert band begins to play in 1981 without a real line-up: essentially they were structured as an open-band where whoever arrived did his thing. Among the various collaborators are names like Fred Frith (Henry Cow), David Kerman (5 UU's) and Scott Brazieal (Cartoon). The 1984 debut strikes for the inventiveness and the force of their avant-guard pop, close to the R.I.O. movement and with hints of new wave. In the following albums they successfully mix influences derived from Zappa, Henry Cow, King Crimson, Gentle Giant, the Canterbury school and chamber music. The awareness of their talent and never ending creativity brings to the amazing 1989 third album In This Life. The band is apparently still active though nothing truly new has yet come forth.

RECOMMENDED RECORDINGS: IN THIS LIFE *(Recommended Records, 1989)* **IN EXTREMIS** *(Cuneiform, 1998).*   M.G. & C.C.

TOUCH

John Bordonaro - *drums, vocals,* **Don Gallucci** - *keyboards, vocals,* **Bruce Hauser** - *bass, voc,* **Jeff Hawks** - *vocals,* **Joey Newman** - *guitars, vocals.*

A very interesting "one shot" band representing the independent soul of Portland, managing to merge into their one and only album *Touch* (1969) all the different artistic experiences of the end of '60s. Born from the beat genre, they turn to performing a classic rock-blues mixing folk atmospheres with magnificent results. The strong vocal moments perfectly harmonize with the psychedelic guitars of **Joey Newman**, highlighting lyrics that treat contemporary topics like the war in Vietnam, for example. They breakup the following year never to reunite and the original version of this album becomes a known rarity for any collector. Reissued on CD it now contains previously unreleased added tracks.

DISCOGRAPHY: TOUCH *(Deram, 1969)*   C.A. & C.C.

North America: UNITED STATES

U TOTEM

Emily Hay - *vocals, flute*, **Sanjay Kumar** - *piano, keyboards, sitar*, **Eric Johnson** - *bassoon, sax*, **James Grigsby** - *guitars, bass, vibes*, **Dave Kerman** - *drums, percussion*.

This band founded in 1990 is another of **Dave Kerman**'s projects, like **Thinking Plague** and **5UU** of which **U Totem** is the probably most interesting and complete. Their music follows the great influence of the RIO movement, personalizing their sound still deeply influenced by **Henry Cow** and **Universe Zero**. In fact the songs are characterized by the use of unusual instruments that create a sort of modern symphony, sometimes with darker dissonances, strange rhythms and full blown experimentation. Another strength of this band is also the presence of a female vocalist who makes the music even more fascinating. Their production stops at a second album which is still appreciated worldwide.

DISCOGRAPHY: **U TOTEM** *(1990, Cuneiform Records)* **STRANGE ATTRACTORS** *(1994, Cuneiform Records).*   M.G. & C.C.

VICTOR PERAINO'S KINGDOM COME

Victor Peraino – *keyboards, percussion, vocals*, **John Laflotte** - *flute, guitars, vocals*, **David Christian** – *guitar*.

An American keyboardist who begins his career playing in England with **Arthur Brown's Kingdom Come**. He immediately stands out in their album of 1973, *Journey*, for the great quality of his talent, especially on the synths and mellotron. After the disbandment of this British band, he goes home and decides to perpetrate the name as a sort of legacy. In 1975 his **No Man's Land** is published as a crossover prog containing amazing tracks like "Empires of Steel" with its **Jethro Tull** atmospheres, or the symphonic "At Last a Crew" and "Lady of the Morning" rich of **King Crimson** styled mellotron moods. The excellent synth solo of "We're Next" is probably the only true prog part of this song, that for the rest appears to anticipate what will later be defined as disco music.

RECOMMENDED RECORDINGS: **NO MAN'S LAND** *(private press, 1975).*   M.G. & C.C.

YEZDA URFA

Brad Christoff - *drums, percussion*, **Phil Kimborough** - *keyboards, horns, vocals*, **Mark Tippins** - *chitarre, voce*, **Marc Miller** - *bass, vocals*, **Rick Rodenbaugh** - *vocals*.

Another band of almost unknown prog heroes who made

one good album in the middle of '70s disappearing immediately after. The rare *Boris* of 1975 is a record deeply influenced by **Yes** as by some other American bands. Their live performances contain many keyboards and guitar acrobatic textures that bring to very unpredictable results. The skillful musicians play high quality compositions and the instrumental parts are performed very fast and with a bizarre roundabout of sounds. There exists a second "lost" album, released 15 years later (*Sacred Baboon* of 1989) by a music label, which gathers old remastered recordings of 1976. The edition was probably due to the renewed interest in prog and by request of fans and collectors worldwide.

DISCOGRAPHY: **BORIS** *(1975, Private Pressing)* **SACRED BABOON** *(1989, Syn-Phonic).*   M.G. & C.C.

Oceania: AUSTRALIA

GALADRIEL

Gerry Adams - *guitar*, **Doug Bligh** - *drums*, **John "Spider" Scholtens** - *vocals*, **Gary Lothian** - *guitar*, **Mick Parker** - *bass, flute*.

A fascinating Australian band born and dead after only three years, which left us a wonderful album and a couple of 45RPM that have become very hard to find. The name and the cover illustration remind us of the fantastic world of Tolkien and the Ring Tales, misleading toward an idea of dreamy atmospheres and delicate music, yet **Galadriel** play a strange kind of hard-blues mixed with psychedelic sounds. The 1971 original record contains ten impressive songs where the talented quintet plays dynamic melodies and involving instrumental parts that blend with the smart use of lyrics and vocals. **Mick Parker**'s flute in the song "Standing in the rain" recalls the British **Jethro Tull** and the guitars of **Gerry Adams** and **Gary Lothian** (pictured right) are scratchy and loud, certainly less dreamy than expectations.

DISCOGRAPHY: GALADRIEL (1971, Polydor). M.G. & C.C.

HEADBAND

Chris Bailey - *bass, vocals*, **Joff Bateman** - *drums*, **Peter Beagley** - *keyboards*, **Mauri Berg** - *guitar*.

Not to be confused with **Tommy Adderley**'s rock'n'roll group from New Zealand, this band from Adelaide began playing in the early '70s releasing only one album and two 45RPM. They gained a discreet success and their live performances were excellent proving the great vocal skills of bassist **Chris Bailey** as a very talented front man. Their sound is a rock-blues oriented prog arranged with taste and personality, deeply influenced by **The Doors**, **Seeds** and **Jefferson Airplane**. Their pleasant but average album *A song for Tooley* was published in 1973 with a fascinating graphic designed cover: the approximate production affected the final result also by not properly acknowledging and giving the right amount of space to the keyboards of **Peter "head" Beagley**.

DISCOGRAPHY: A SONG FOR TOOLEY (Polydor, 1973). C.A. & C.C.

RAINBOW THEATRE

Julian Browning – *guitar, mellotron, keyboards*, **Frank Graham** - *horns*, **Graeme Carter** – *drums, percussion*, **Keith Hoban** – *vocals, organ*, **Ferg McKinnon** – *bass, chorus and orchestra arrangements*.

A powerful line-up of 14 elements gave birth to this Australian ensemble that occupied the better part of the mid '70s publishing two amazing and complex works, rich of symphonic prog elements taken from the an orchestral type of jazz and from the musical genre. A certain **King Crimson** tendency marks them, not just as a remake of the themes, but more as a model of inspiration. The first album, *The Armada*, sees the presence of an orchestra (Victorian Opera Company) and the added choruses result in a slightly over-emphatic pompousness. For the second, a series of new string and woodwind elements are introduced as is the incredible tenor voice of **Hoban** that gives a dramatic and lyrical intensity the vocal parts. Technically this is perhaps the best album ever published in the history of Australian prog.

RECOMMENDED RECORDINGS: THE ARMADA (*Clear Light of Jupiter, 1975*) **FANTASY OF HORSES** (*Clear Light of Jupiter, 1976*). M.G. & C.C.

South America: ARGENTINA

ALAS

Gustavo Moretto - *keyboards, flute, vocals,* **Alex Zucker** - *bass, guitars,* **Carlos Riganti** - *drums, percussion.*

Already in 1975 this trio was holding concerts way before recording their first album out that following year. **Gustavo Moretto**'s sound brought the keyboards and woodwinds to a particular blend between the symphonic style of **EL&P** and a jazz-rock inspired by **Weather Report**. The rhythmic section added to their charme the particular and personal use of the Argentinian tango. In 1977, during the recording of a second album, drummer **Carlos Riganti** decides to leave and the band breaks-up. The excellent material with incomplete drum parts were published posthumous in 1983. The reunion happens in 2003 with a fascinating studio album definable as avant-guard tango-jazz chamber music.

RECOMMENDED RECORDINGS: ALAS *(EMI, 1976)* PINTA TU ALDEA *(EMI, 1983)* MIMAME BANDONEÓN *(Epsa Music 2003, Sonoram, 2005).* **M.G. & C.C.**

AVE ROCK

Hector "Daddy" Antogna- *drums,* **Federico Sainz** - *vocals,* **Luis Borda** - *guitars, vocals,* **Oscar Glavic** - *bass, vocals,* **Osvaldo Caló** - *keyboards,* **Marcelo Sabarido** - *drums,* **Francisco "Pancho" Arregui** - *guitars, vocals,* **Jorge Liechtenstein** - *drums,* **Alberto Salamone** - *keyboards,* **Hector Ruiz** - *drums.*

This band started their career in 1974 releasing a first very interesting album, rich of personal ideas albeit the **Yes** references, complex rhythm changes and singular arrangements thanks to the talent of keyboardist **Osvaldo Caló** and for the compelling voice of **Federico Sainz**. The audience and the media proclaimed them as Argentine Symphonic Rock Pioneers, reinvigorating their efforts and inspiring a line-up change for the 1977 second release *Espacios*: unfortunately the vocal parts were penalized and the three very long suites contain excessive keyboard moments due to the protagonism of **Salamone**. Further more the absence of **Luis Borda**'s guitars weighed on the final results both of the album and of their future as a band. In fact, during their 1978 tour comes the final breakup.

DISCOGRAPHY: AVE ROCK *(Promusic, 1974)* ESPACIOS *(Promusic, 1977).* **C.A. & C.C.**

BUBU

Sergio Polizzi - *violin,* **Cecilia Tenconi** - *flute,* **Win Fortsman** - *sax,* **Petty Guelache** - *vocals,* **Eduardo Rogatti** - *guitar,* **Eduardo "Fleke" Folino** - *bass,* **Eduardo "Polo" Corbella** - *drums, percussion,* **Daniel Andreaoli** - *songwriter, arrangements.*

Another band who debuts with a phenomenal album and disappears immediately after the release: *Anabelas* of 1978 is an extraordinary record with only three long tracks where the melange between dreamy romantic atmospheres and jazz-rock is played with a mastery very close to the Canterbury school. The suite "El Cortejo de un dia Amarillo" covers the entire first side while "El Vape de Anabelas" and "Suenos de Maniqui" share the other. Best are the instrumental moments where the rich use of violins, horns, guitars and keyboards interlace the complex rhythms creating magical arrangements. **Bubu** is a band who remains in the legend of prog music and truly loved by collectors and fans.

DISCOGRAPHY: ANABELAS *(1978, Music Hall).* **M.G. & C.C.**

South America: ARGENTINA

CRUCIS

Gustavo Montesano - *bass, vocals*, **Pino Marrone** - *guitars, vocals*, **Gonzalo Farugia** - *drums, percussion*, **Anibal Kerpel** - *keyboards*.

One of the most respected bands of Argentina, this band released two good albums in the middle of the '70s with their effervescing rock made of aggressive moments alternated by the typical symphonic sounds. Both the homonym debut of 1975 and their second album *Los Delirios del*

Mariscal are performed with complex guitar and keyboard textures, rhythm changes and jazz-rock deviations, completed by Spanish lyrics and vocals that give a very beautiful latino touch. Deeply inspired by other Spanish prog bands as well as by **Deep Purple** and **Uriah Deep**, they yet manage to create their personal and unique style.

DISCOGRAPHY: **CRUCIS** *(1975/RCA)* **LOS DELIRIOS DEL MARISCAL** *(1976, RCA).*

M.G. & C.C.

MATERIA GRIS

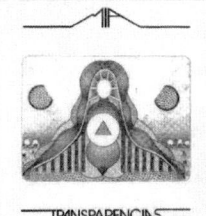

Carlos Riganti - *drums*, **Edgardo Rapetti** - *guitar*, **Julio Presas** - *guitar, vocals, flute*, **Omar Constanzo** – *bass*.

This band begins in 1970 emulating **The Beatles** until they start composing their own songs with more hard psychedelic forms: the only album of their career is published in 1972 and features two guitars and a complex rhythmic section. This is Argentina's first concept album, the first also to unite psychedelic jazz to a moderate hard prog with fast tempo changes. Therefore a unique work, divided into 16 short parts often characterized by melancholic vocals and theme reprises where the melodies conform to the Italian prog of the times. The album sees the collaboration of **Litto Nebbia**, **Bernando Baraj** and **Carlos Cutania** (**Carlos Riganti** in the above photo).

RECOMMENDED RECORDINGS: **OHPERRA VIDA DE BETO** *(EMI - Harvest, 1972).*

M.G. & C.C.

M.I.A.

Lito Vitale - *keyboards, piano, drums, percussion, flute, vocals*, **Liliana Vitale** - *vocals, drums, percussion, flute*, **Daniel Curto** - *guitar*, **Nono Belvis** - *bass*, **Juan Del Barrio** - *keyboards, drums*, **Alberto Muñoz** - *guitar, bass*, **Kike Sanzol** - *drums*.

Another fascinating band from South America, with three studio albums and one live recording: their debut album *Transparencias* of 1976 is full of elegant symphonic prog, a great use of keyboards recalling famous classical themes, but also full of original ideas, latin american atmospheres and folk traditional music. The following *Magicos Juegos del Tiempo* of 1977 is a more acoustic and intimate album, with more delicate moments. Their third album *Cornonstipicum* of 1978 returns to the symphonic origins, looking toward more avant-garde sonorities while the last, *Conciertos* of 1979, is a live triple LP with great space for long improvisations and researched sounds.

DISCOGRAPHY: **TRANSPARENCIAS** *(1976, Ciclo 3)* **MAGICOS JUEGOS DEL TIEMPO** *(1977, Ciclo 3)* **CORNONSTIPICUM** *(1978, Ciclo 3)* **CONCIERTOS** *(1979, Ciclo 3).*

M.G. & C.C.

South America: ARGENTINA

LITTO NEBBIA

Eclectic guitarist and very talented artist, **Felix Francisco Nebbia Corbacho**, nicknamed "**Litto**", became an authentic institution in Argentina as author of various hit singles and folk songs, also famous as a soundtrack composer. Since the late '60s he began playing with his own band **Los Gatos** during the Beat explosion, plunging into the exploration of very different musical genres. He approached the prog genre in 1972 by joining

the band **Huinca** in a record that resulted as the perfect attempt to mix Argentine folk with the overwhelming symphonic sounds coming from Europe and broadcasted by many radios of the time (**Genesis**, **Yes**, **ELP**). After this experience he starts his immense solo discography as **Litto Nebbia**, with two excellent albums: *Despertemos En America* and *La Muerte En Catedral*.

RECOMMENDED RECORDINGS: **HUINCA** *(1972, RCA)* **DESPERTEMOS EN AMERICA** *(1972, RCA)* **LA MUERTE EN CATEDRAL** *(1973, RCA)*.   **C.A.**

NEXUS

Lalo Huber - *keyboards*, **Carlos Lucena** - *guitar*, **Luis Nakamura** - *drums, percussion*, **Daniel Ianniruberto** - *bass*, **Mariela Gonzalez** - *vocals*, **Lito Marcello** - *vocals*.

Among some of the best symphonic prog artists from Argentina, this band is led by the talented **Lalo Huber**, an histrionic keyboardist greatly inspired by **ELP** (in fact considered **Keith**

Emerson's true heir) with the romanticism of **Genesis**. The two compelling albums sung in Spanish, *Détras del Umbral* and *Metanoia*, are proof of how he successfully blends his keyboards to more classical references. Their delicate and powerful lead singer **Mariela Gonzalez** decides to leave after the release of a 2002 live recording. Nevertheless the standard of their music remains excellent both in the participation to the Colossus project *Odyssey: The Greatest Tale* of 2005 and in the following studio-album of 2006 *Perpetuum Karma*.

DISCOGRAPHY: **DÉTRAS DEL UMBRAL** *(1999, Record Runner)* **METANOIA** *(2001, Record Runner)* **LIVE AT NEARFEST 2000** *(2002, Prog Media Records)* **PERPETUUM KARMA** *(2006, Record Runer)* **BUENOS AIRES FREE EXPERIENCE VOLUMEN 2** *(2007, Record Runner)*.   **M.G. & C.C.**

REDD

Juan Escalante - *vocals, drums, keyboards*, **Luis Albornoz** - *vocals, bass, guitar*, **Esteban Cerioni** - *vocals, bass, guitar, keyboards*.

Born from the ashes of a previous band called **Trìcupa**, they begin playing in 1977 as a trio, all excellent poly-instrumentalists. Their first concert was as the opening act of **Luis A. Spinetta**'s tour that same year. Then their first album *Tristes Noticias del Imperio* is recorded and released in 1979, an excellent work full of electro acoustic sounds in the style of **Genesis** and the early **King Crimson**, but with atmospheres recalling Italian bands such as **PFM** and **Celeste**. Escalante discovers to be seriously ill and has to abandon his musical career. The band therefore expands the line-up to five elements and finally publishes a second album in 1981, just slightly inferior than the previous and with richer symphonic sounds.

DISCOGRAPHY: **TRISTES NOTICIAS DEL IMPERIO** *(Priv. Press Cavoclo, 1979 – CD PRW 1995)* **CUENTOS DEL SUBSUELO** *(Priv. Press Cavoclo, 1981 – CD PRW 1995)*.   **M.G. & C.C.**

South America: BRAZIL

BACAMARTE

Mario Neto - *guitar, violin,* **Sergio Villarim** - *keyboards,* **Delto Simas** - *bass,* **Marco Verrissimo** - *drums,* **Márcus Moura** - *flute,* **Mr. Paul** - *percussion,* **Jane Duboc** - *vocals.*

Depois do Fim of 1983 shows how Italian prog deeply influenced all South American artists. This very interesting debut album proves them to be devoted

disciples of the **PFM** yet this Brazilian band finds its personal style creating an impressive mix of vibrant rock and symphonic sounds, merging electric moments to more delicate acoustic atmospheres coloured by keyboards, violin and flute, all topped by the compelling female vocals, although the lyrics are in Portuguese. The result is guaranteed. After a long pause the band returns in 1999, but the new album is less interesting than its previous.

DISCOGRAPHY: DEPOIS DO FIM *(1983, Som.Arte)* **SETE CIDADES** *(1999, Private Pressing).* **M.G. & C.C.**

LULA CÔRTES & ZÉ RAMALHO

This extraordinary duo is the result of the formidable interaction of musician and composer **Lula Cortes** and songwriter **Zè Ramalho**, who in 1975 release together the authentic masterpiece *Paebirù*: published as double album, it contains Brazilian traditional folk (strangely moving from tribal to a kind of

world music), marvelously combined to a heavy psychedelic atmosphere and the spaciest of German sounds, similar to **Amon Düül**. The four sides are named after the natural elements of Air, Water, Fire and Earth and the musical structure reminds us of certain Italian sonorities from **Alan Sorrenti**'s *Aria* and from **Aktuala**. Unfortunately the newly engraved vinyls caught fire and were in great part destroyed so the album became a rarity from its very beginnings! Many years later, a group of collectors produced a CD bootleg of this record and now, after the recent death of **Lula Cortes** in 2011 an official limited edition on both vinyl and CD format are available.

DISCOGRAPHY: PAÊBIRÚ - CAMINHO DA MONTANHA DO SOL *(1975, Rozenblitz).* **M.G. & C.C.**

QUATERNA REQUIEM

Elisa Wiermann - *keyboards, piano,* **Cláudio Dantas** - *drums, percussioni,* **Kleber Vogel** - *violin,* **Jones Júnior** - *guitar, viola,* **Marco Lauria** - *bass,* **Fabio Fernandez** - *bass, viola,* **José Roberto Crivano** - *guitar,* **Sérgio Dias** - *flute.*

A band based upon the duo **Elisa Wiermann** - **Claudio Dantas** and supported by other session men according to the compositions, playing a strange kind of classical music full of baroque and medieval sounds. Despite the complex combinations between keyboards, acoustic or electric guitars and the

violin create a fascinating and magical scenario, their genre tends strongly to the Pop side of prog, as in the debut album *Velha gravura* of 1992, a symphonic gem. The following LP *Quasimodo* of 1994, where the homonym suite lasts (only!) 39 minutes, is particularly delicate and reflective with its fascinating Gregorian chants. Also recommended, their live album *Livre* of 2000 and the last studio album *O Arquiteto* of 2002.

DISCOGRAPHY: VELHA GRAVURA *(1992, Faunus)* **QUASIMODO** *(1994, Private Pressing)* **LIVRE** *(2000, Private Pressing).* **M.G. & C.C.**

South America: BRAZIL

SOM IMAGINARIO

Wagner Tiso - keyboards, **Zè Rodrix** - organ, percussion, vocals, flute, **Roberto Silva** - drums, **Tavito** - guitars, **Luís Alves** - bass, **Laudir de Oliveira** - percussion, **Toninho Horta** - guitars, **Nivaldo Ornelas** - saxophones. An ensemble of talented musicians who were schooled by **Milton Nascimento**, grew up playing a music mixed with jazz, folk and classical influences and were less contaminated by the British prog invasion than their colleagues. Despite the truly broad Brazilian musical scenario, this band never emerged from the shadows. Their first two albums are deeply influenced by British and American pop, with psychedelic sounds and solid tracks that were good for their live performances. Only with their third remarkable album *Matanca do Porco* of 1972 will they somewhat manage to raise an interest in the jazz-rock elite: this completely instrumental album containing long suites is arranged with the help of the **Odeon Orchestra**, where the immense work on percussions supports the leading roles of guitars and piano. *Matanca do porco* is still among the best Brazilian prog albums ever!
DISCOGRAPHY: SOM IMAGINARIO (Odeon, 1970) **SOM IMAGINARIO II** (Odeon, 1971) **MATANCA DO PORCO** (Odeon, 1972).   C.A. & C.C.

TELLAH

Marconi Barros - bass, violin, guitars, synthesizers, vocals, **José Veríssimo** - bass, **Felipe Guedes** - batteria, **Cláudio Felicio** - guitars, vocals, **Denis Torre** - lead vocals, drums, percussion, synthesizers, **Rogério Peyroton** - keyboards.

A band from Brasilia playing a very similar music to **Deep Purple** which manages to create a great fan base even though the actual album release will take several years. In fact for a long time this band was employed as supporter or opening act to other more famous artists like **O Terço**, **Joelho Do Porco** and **Os Mutantes**. *Continente Perdido* of 1984 is a good album though sadly almost ignored by the press and the big distribution: deeply influenced by **Yes** and **Camel** (*Moonmadness*) with some references to **Rush** and resulting similar to certain contemporary Italian bands, this album is characterized by the large use of synth and organ with impressive and articulated arrangements for a simple trio. Frustrated by the weak response of the market, their activity fades until a last farewell concert where they played some unpublished tracks that will be included more recently in the remastered CD version.
DISCOGRAPHY: CONTINENTE PERDIDO (1984, Progressive Rock Worldwide).   M.G. & C.C.

TERRENO BALDIO

Roberto Lazzarini – keyboards, vibes, **João Kurk "Fusa"** – vocals, percussion, **Mozart Mello** – guitars, vocals, **Joãquim Correa** – drums, percussion, **João Rodolfo Ascenção** - bass.

Defined as the Brazilian **Gentle Giant**, this interesting band manages to unite their traditional music structures with European jazz and symphonic prog, both in the compositions and by the use of daring vocals, often in isostatic balance on the abyss of dissonance. Their ability and exemplary technique is confirmed in a first homonym album published in 1976 where the Portuguese lyrics underline these particular themes through the singing and the typical instrumentation of their country genres. Also good and maintaining this distinctive flavour is their second album of 1977, a repetitive and less incisive formula.
RECOMMENDED RECORDINGS: TERRENO BALDIO (1975, Pirata).   M.G.

South America: CHILE

EL CONGRESO

Fernando González *guitar*, **Fernando Hurtado** *bass*, **Sergio González** *drums, percussion*, **Francisco Sazo** *vocals, rondador, tarca*, **Renato Vivaldi** *flute, rondador, tarca*, **Joe Vasconcellos** *vocals, native percussion, trutruca, tarkas, pipes*.

Founded in 1970, this is something closer to a big ensemble than to a band, with many a line-up change, over more than fifteen different musicians that alternated for the recording of at least a dozen impressive albums (including the side project *Misa de Los Andes*, see below). Although they were not born as a politicized group, this big band was active during the darkest age in Chile's history and, as most artists were considered the true intellectuals of the country, they naturally stood up against the Pinochet government repression. Their prog-pop was deeply influenced by folk sounds due to the use of traditional instruments from the Andes which created compelling melodies interlacing the flute and acoustic guitar moments and adding a fascinating Latin American taste. Their topics were often developing religious and love themes through the beautiful voice of **Francisco Sazo**, a talented singer almost unknown abroad, but very emotional and delicate. This ensemble is still active today.

RECOMMENDED RECORDINGS: **EL CONGRESO** *(EMI, 1978)* **TERRA INCOGNITA** *(EMI, 1978)*.   C.A. & C.C.

LOS JAIVAS

Eduardo "Gato" Alquinta - *vocals, guitars, winds, percussion*, **Mario Mutis** - *bass, winds, percussion, vocals*, **Gabriel Parra** - *drums, percussion, winds, vocals*, **Claudio Parra** - *keyboards, percussion*, **Eduardo Parra** - *keyboards, percussion*.

This band from Chile is still active today even though now playing without co-founders **Alquinta** and **Gabriel Parra**. Born in the early '60s they were forced to run to Argentina due to the 1973 dictatorship

and recorded for many years abroad moving also to France where they lived for quite some time. Through the years their sound enriched exploring many of the various local influences and contaminations. Their prolific discography contains interesting things and probably their best period is published around the mid '70s. Strong in orchestral and symphonic compositions, they mix with ability elements of traditional folk and from popular songwriting, to classical music and symphonic rock, generating a particular and interesting personal style. The themes are tense and dramatic, but without neglecting melodies and more typical traditional vocal structures that recall the Andes folklore.

RECOMMENDED RECORDINGS: **LOS JAIVAS** *(EMI Odeón Argentina, 1975)* **ALTURAS DE MACHU PICCHU** *(SYM Chile, 1981))*.   M.G. & C.C.

MISA DE LOS ANDES

Main Singers: **Eduardo Castro** ("Paracas" Group), **Boris Gonzàlez, Mariela Gonzàlez, Gastòn Guzmàn, Natacha Jorquera, Juan Antonio Labra, Marìa Inès Navellàn,** "Paracas" Group, **Vìctor Sanhueza, Francisco Sazo** (from "Congreso").

Main musicians: **Raùl Di Blasio** - *piano*, **Arturo Gòmez** - *tarka*, **Rodrigo Herrera** - *oboe*, **Rodrigo Miranda** - *trumpet*, **Isabel Neira** - *flute*, **Joel Silva** - *french horn*, **Raùl Silva** - *cor anglais*, **Guillermo Soto** - *tenor sax*, **Carlos Vera** - *vibes*, **Patricio Vera** - *electric guitar*.

This rare album, released in 1978, is a parallel project of the band **El Congreso**: *Misa de Los Andes* is actually the name of the album written by **Jose Fernando Gonzalez** and **Sergio Tilo Gonzalez**. A beautiful work that almost went unknown abroad, composed for the Archbishop of Santiago based upon the official liturgical script of the Catholic Church. All the background parts were produced and performed by **El Congreso** (preserving their style), upon which the entire album is construed: almost impossible to compile a complete list of the musicians involved due to the participation of many unknown talented singers and performers. Worthy of note is the track "Zalo Reyes y Quiza" which has one of the most fascinating themes of the project. It has been reissued on CD only a few years ago but is still not distributed out of Chile.

DISCOGRAPHY: **MISA DE LOS ANDES** *(EMI, 1978)*.   M.G. & C.C.

South America: MEXICO

BANDA ELASTICA

Guillermo Gonzalez - *guitars*, **Zozimo Hernandez** - *bass, freetless bass*, **Rodolfo Nava** - *drums, percussion*, **Jose Navarro** - *percussion, timbales*, **Guillermo Portillo** - *horns*, **Jose Luis Romero** - *horns*, **Rosino Seranno** - *keyboards*.

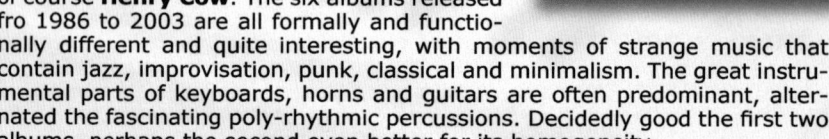

This band from 1983 represents one of the best avant-guard examples of R.I.O. movement in Mexico City. Their music is the perfect mix of many styles blended in such a way to recall **Frank Zappa**, **Miriodor**, **Nazca**, **Decibel** and of course **Henry Cow**. The six albums released fro 1986 to 2003 are all formally and functionally different and quite interesting, with moments of strange music that contain jazz, improvisation, punk, classical and minimalism. The great instrumental parts of keyboards, horns and guitars are often predominant, alternated the fascinating poly-rhythmic percussions. Decidedly good the first two albums, perhaps the second even better for its homogeneity.
RECOMMENDED RECORDINGS: BANDA ELASTICA *(CDDP, 1986)* BANDA ELASTICA II *(CDDP, 1991)*. M.G. & C.C.

CABEZAS DE CERA

Mauricio Sotelo - *stick, guitars, bass*, **Ramses Luna** - *flute*. **Francisco Sotelo** - *percussion*.

One of the most brilliant and intriguing bands of the new millennium, they began playing in Mexico city as trio of avant-garde rock, just like a kind of postmodern **King Crimson**, elaborating new and sharp sonorities. With their four albums, the Sotelo brothers reach a personal sound through the compelling textures of stick-bass and horns, open to improvising the industrial and fusion genres, similar to the new concrete music of **Centrozoon** and **Theo Travis**. Their second album *Metalmusica* of 2004 confirms the singularity of this band: curious sounding metal tools treated and amplified by electronic devices. Compared to other Mexican bands like **Cast** who play an old type of prog, **Cabezas de Cera** go beyond as futuristic cyber-prog pioneers.
DISCOGRAPHY: CABEZAS DE CERA *(CDC 2000)* ... UN SEGUNDO *(CDC, 2003)* METALMUSICA/ALEACIONES ALEATORIAS *(El Angelito, 2004)* HECHO EN MEXICO *(El Angelito, 2007)*. M.G. & C.C.

EL RITUAL

Gonzalo Chalo Hernández - *bass*, **Alberto Lalo Barceló** - *drums*, **Frankie Barreño** – *vocals, guitar, flute*, **Martín Mayo** - *keyboards*.

Very particular and unique Mexican band, they go beyond the satanic intentions of their name, uniting rock and psychedelic blues to strong jazz elements. In their only homonym album of 1971, strongly opposed and by the governing censorship, the excellent keyboards rule the scene and never stop even during the dynamic guitar fuzzing solos. The very original rhythms collocate them perfectly into their time, thanks also to a great dose of experimentation, partially derived from **Frank Zappa**, yet perhaps recalling a stranger mix of **Santana** and **Uriah Heep**.
RECOMMENDED RECORDINGS: EL RITUAL *(RAFF, 1971)*. M.G. & C.C.

South America: MEXICO

GALIE

Eugenio Barrantes - *bass, guitar,* **Leopoldo Cabieses** - *guitar,* **Ignacio Cordero** - *keyboards,* **Luis Diaz Torre** - *flute,* **Alfonso Portilla** - *drums,* **J. Ignacio Portilla** - *guitar,* **Gabriel Tellechea** - *piano, keyboards.*

Their superlative homonym album of 1980 is a beautiful example of symphonic rock where a warm energy ignites all the tracks, performed with passion. The acoustic instruments, like guitars, flute and piano, are outstanding and govern the music of keyboards with linear perfection. Inspiration derived from Italian bands like **PFM** and **Locanda delle Fate** are strong with also references to certain groups of Spanish prog and classical hints. However **Galie** is an instrumental band who releases other three enthusiastic albums following a progressive numeration (*Galie II, Galie III, Galie IV*) of good melodic taste and without exaggerated virtuosity.

DISCOGRAPHY: GALIE *(1980, Cheshire Records)* **GALIE II** *(1986)* **GALIE III** *(1990)* **GALIE IV** *(1992).*

M.G. & C.C.

NAZCA

Alejandro Sanchez - *violin,* **Carlo Nicolau** - *piano, cello,* **Carlos Ruiz** - *oboe, horns,* **Guauahtemoc Novelo** - *drums, percussion,* **Jorge Gaitan** - *bass, viola.*

After the break-up of **Decibel**, talented and creative violinist **Sanchez** founds in 1981 a new band with **Nicolau** and **Ruitz** (pictured right) in order to carry on the musical proposal of his previous group. In **Nazca**'s short life span, they produced two studio albums and a live recording (published posthumous). The 1985 debut resulted to be perhaps less bold than **Decibel**'s compositional style, but still reflected the typical structures of the R.I.O. movement, with many completely improvised parts that stayed well within more defined structures contaminated with jazz, ethnic and avant-garde chamber music, closer to **Univers Zero**. Qualitatively equivalent the second album of 1986, then the break-up.

RECOMMENDED RECORDINGS: NAZCA *(Discos Naja, 1985).*

M.G. & C.C.

NUEVO MEXICO

Carlos Mata - *guitar,* **Miguel Suárez** – *drums,* **Armando Suárez** - *bass,* **Jorge Reyes** - *flute.*

A band heavily opposed by the government's censorship, they begin as a trio with the particular name of **Abraham Lincoln** in 1971. With **Reyes**'s arrival they change their name and finally sign up for a first record in 1973, put on hold and released only later in 1975. Their style was full of those typical elements of the early '70s like acid and psychedelia, with parts of flute and singing similar to the **Jethro Tull** style of *Stand Up*. Also greatly inspired by other English and Italian prog bands, hints of which can be traced down to some **Pink Floyd** or **King Crimson** sounds, the traditional folk or Latino and pre-Hispanic music always blends to the mix generating a very personal and original genre: this first album is important for the development of Mexican prog.

RECOMMENDED RECORDINGS: HECHO EN CASA *(La Ciruela Eléctrica, 1975).*

M.G. & C.C.

South America: PERÙ

FRÀGIL

Octavio Castillo – *keyboards, violin, acoustic guitar, flute,* **César Bustamante** – *keyboards, violin,* **Luis Valderrama** – *guitars, mandolin,* **Arturo Creamer** – *drums, percussion,* **Andrés Dulude** – *vocals,* **Jean Pierre Magnet** - *saxophones.*

The most famous band of Peruvian prog, they start their career in the mid '70s composing symphonic tracks of open **Genesis** inspiration and also playing many of their covers in concert. Only in 1981 they manage to release a first album, *Avenida Larco*, in which the references to British symphonic rock are constant, though some local folk hints can still be found similarly added into the music like **Jethro Tull** would do. Then as the '80s developed, they changed drummer and approached more simple rhythms in their second work, *Serranio* (1990). This quest for an easy market success pushed them decidedly away from the initial prog style.
RECOMMENDED RECORDINGS: AVENIDA LARCO *(Rock Symphony, 1981)* **SERRANIO** *(Rock Symphony, 1990).* M.G. & C.C.

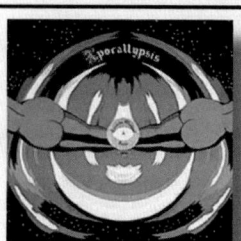

GERARDO MANUEL
Y EL HUMO

Gerardo Manuel Rojas - *vocals,* **Enrique "Pico" Ego Aguirre** - *guitars,* **Jorge "Coco" Pomar** - *bass,* **Freddy "Puro" Fuentes** - *drums.*

From Peru, this talented singer and great songwriter is supported by a personal backing band of musicians which play loud hard rock guitars with the typical fuzz and wah-wah sounds mixed to very funky rhythms. *Apocallypsis* of 1971 is a good album which has a consistent groove that recalls **Grand Funk Railroad**. "Where did you go?", "Apocallypsis" and "Are you ready?" are the three best moments while the weak parts are the cover versions and ballads, sometimes truly out of contest. Better results with *Machu Picchu 2000*, of 1972 which makes ample use of fuzz and funky sounds in the best jazz-prog rock style. "Machu Picchu Blues", "5.36 PM" and "December 31 1999" are the most beautiful tracks in it and are deeply influenced by **Tarkus**, also from this country. The music is fascinating and the lyrics are inspired by the ancestral history of the Incas, one of **Gerardo Manuel**'s favourites themes.
DISCOGRAPHY: APOCALLYPSIS *(1971, EMI)* **MACHU PICCHU 2000** *(1972, EMI).* M.G. & C.C.

TRAFFIC SOUND

Manuel Sanguinetti - *vocals, percussion,* **Willy Barclay** - *lead guitar,* **Freddy Rizo Patrón** - *guitars,* **Zulu** - *keyboards,* **Luis Nevares** - *drums,* **Jean Pierre Magnet** - *flute, saxophones.*

Among the most original bands of Peruvian pop music, they begin emulating **The Beatles** and certain other influences from Europe's beat movement. Then they turn toward the winds of acid psychedelia coming from the best **Pink Floyd**, **The Doors** and **Hendrix**. *Virgin*, *Traffic Sound aka III* and *Lux* are the results of this extraordinary union between Anglo-Saxon and Peruvian textures: a fascinating mix of dreamy atmospheres and highly technical performances, crowned by a balanced use of virtuosity. In fact **Traffic sound** is at the center of Peruvian live music and, even though they began to play less prog, they are still remembered as a powerful band with a great groove.

DISCOGRAPHY: VIRGIN *(Essex, 1969)* **TRAFFIC SOUND AKA III OR TIBET SUZETTES** *(Mag, 1970)* **LUX** *(Sono Radio, 1971).* C.A. & C.C.

South America: VENEZUELA

VYTAS BRENNER

Vytas Brenner - *keyboards, guitar,* **Pablo Manavello** - *guitar,* **Carlos Acosta** - *bass,* **Frank Rojas** - *drums,* **Jesús Chinchilla** - *drums, percussion,* **Angel Melo** - *percussion,* **Ramón Hernández** - *harp,* **Alfredo Rojas** - *percussion.*

German born artist and composer, he moves to Venezuela at the age of two. His delicate qualities and elegant musical taste manages to unite European symphonic prog to South-American music and a folk genre of different origins: Spanish and Italian traditional themes are present being countries in which he lived with his family for some time. Nine albums are his legacy before the unfortunate death in 2004 after a heartache. All excellent for quality, the most progressive is probably the 1973 debut album *La Ofrenda de Vytas Brenner*, unforgettable for **Brenner**'s beautiful keyboard playing and the great contribution of **Manavello**'s guitar.

RECOMMENDED RECORDINGS: **LA OFRENDA DE VYTAS BRENNER** *(Suramericana/Anes, 1973).*   M.G. & C.C.

EQUILIBRIO VITAL

Marcos Chacón – *guitar, vocals,* **Guillermo González** – *bass, flute, vocals,* **Carlos Serga** – *rhythm guitar, vocals,* **Laureano Rangel** – *drums,* **Arnoldo Serga** – *bass, percussion,* **Elena Prieto** – *vocals.*

Born in Maracay in 1980, they release a first record in 1983 which is quite hard to collocate in the prog panorama. The structure, maybe more traditionally symphonic, sometimes even new prog, hosts some hard, almost metal parts recalling **Led Zeppelin** and **Rush**, with powerful guitars solos and rough dry rhythms. Two lead singers, one male and one female. Rare, but incredible the flute intrusions just like **Focus** or **New Trolls**. Other than the two official albums, another two very rare audio tape recordings dated 1987 and 1990 can be found before the band disappears. Recent rumors of a come-back float around even though their leader **Chacòn** already passed away.

RECOMMENDED RECORDINGS: **EQUILIBRIO VITAL** *(Color Records, 1983 - Reissued on CD by Musea 2003).*   M.G. & C.C.

ESTRUCTURA

Marisela Pérez - *vocals,* **David Maman** - *keyboards, vocals,* **Antonio Rassi** - *guitar,* **Maria E. Ciliberto** - *guitar,* **Agni Mogollon** - *bass, vocals,* **Domenico Prioretti** - *drums,* **Walton de Jongh** - *percussion, effects.*

A band from Venezuela who released two beautiful albums at the end of the '70s: *Mas allà de tu Mente* (1978) is one of the most significant symphonic prog records for this country and it's absolutely their best. The magnificent keyboards pave the way to the wonderful guitar inspired by **Steve Hackett**'s style. The textures between the instruments are balanced and some tracks are also deeply influenced by **Yes** and **Rick Wakeman** with an added classical touch. The Spanish lyrics share the warmth of the intense latino atmospheres comparable to certain Argentine groups like **MIA** or of some Italian '70s prog bands. This continuous floating between pomposity and delicate melodies is the main characteristic of their second (and last) album, although of high quality it is less intense and far from the heights of the previous one.

DISCOGRAPHY: **MÁS ALLÁ DE TU MENTE** *(1978, Grabaciones Mundiales)* **ESTRUCTURA** *(1980, Grabaciones Mundiales).*   M.G. & C.C.

INTERNATIONAL COOPERATIONS

CENTIPEDE

Wendy Treacher, John Trussler, Roddy Skeping, Wilf Gibson, Carol Slater, Louise Jopling, Garth Morton - *violin*, **Michael Hurwitz, Timothy Kramer, Suki Towb, John Rees-Jones, Katherine Thulborn, Catherine Finnis** - *cello*, **Peter Parkes, Mick Collins, Ian Carr** - *trumpets*, **Mongezi Feza, Mark Charig, Elton Dean, Ian McDonald, Gary Windo, Karl Jenkins** - *horns*, **John Marshall, Tony Fennell, Robert Wyatt** - *drums, percussion*, **Maggie Nicols, Julie Tippetts, Mike Patto, Zoot Money, Boz Burrell**, *vocals*, **Roy Babbington Jill Lyons, Harry Miller, Jeff Clyne, Dave Markee, Brian Belshaw** - *bass*, **Brian Godding** - *guitars*, **Keith Tippett** - *piano- orchestration*, **Robert Fripp** - *producer*.

Among the collection of bizarre records, *September Energy* of 1971 is the masterpiece of **Keith Tippett**, former **King Crimson** and appreciated British jazz player. **Tippett**'s composed the entire project and gathered fifty talented musicians ('centipede' = one hundred feet = 2 per man) to execute it supported by **Robert Fripp** as executive producer. The musicians involved came from the best Canterbury schools and among them are the complete line-ups from **Soft Machine** and **King Crimson** till 1978. The record was published as a double album where the single long suite covered all four sides, having a length of 20 minutes for each of the 4 episodes. The music results as a perfect example of what is intended as experimental jazz-prog with Canterbury-rock shades. Keith Tippett died the 14th june of 2020 after a long illness.

DISCOGRAPHY: SEPTOBER ENERGY *(RCA, 1971)*   M.G.

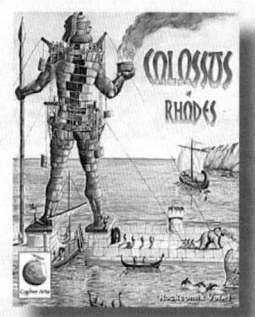

COLOSSUS OF RHODES

CD1: LEVIATHAN *(Italy)* **GREENWALL** *(Italy)* **SINKADUS** *(Sweden)* **CD2: MAD CRAYON** *(Italy)* **VELVET DESPERADOS** *(Finland)* **REVELATION** *(Italy)*

The magazine Colossus was funding a series of musical projects like the successful album *Odyssey: The Greatest Tale* (where various artists arranged songs with topics from Omero's epic) or the also fortunate *Kalevala* (Nordic mythology). *Colossus of Rhodes* (2005) is yet another attempt to repeat this winning formula of releasing a double CD through the label Musea with the cover illustrated by **Paul Whitehead** (reissued and repackaged as double CD + Comic book by Cypher Arts, California). The producers' hope was of bridging comic fans and progsters by using the advantage of **Whitehead**'s incredible art-work and fame, the same artist who painted the covers of **Genesis** and **VDGG** and many other albums of international prog-rock. However even if it started as the usual international project, it turned out to be an almost an exclusive Italian product due to the fact that not only the illustrations inside were of an Italian cartoonist, but also the music was mainly performed by Italian bands like **Leviathan** and **Greenwall**, leaving only two tracks to Scandinavian bands. The lyrics and the story-script inside the book were deeply inspired by the homonym film of Sergio Leone, leaving the bands free to sing both in Italian and English. The result is slightly confusing on a production level but the music performed is close to the great '70s prog genre.

DISCOGRAPHY: COLOSSUS OF RHODES *(Colossus/Musea, Cypher Arts, 2005)*   M.G.

KALEVALA

CD1:1. HAIKARA *(Finland)* **2. OVERHEAD** *(Finland)* **3. SIMON SAYS** *(Sweden)* **4. SINKADUS** *(Sweden)* **5. MOONGARDEN** *(Italy)* **6. IL CASTELLO DI ATLANTE** *(Italy)* **7. MAGENTA** *(Uk)* **8. SUBMARINE SILENCE** *Italy)* **9. METAPHOR** *(Usa)* **10. CLEARLIGHT** *(Usa-Fra)* **CD2: 1. ORCHARD** *(Norway)* **2. GREENWALL** *(Italy)* **3. REVELATION** *(Italy)* **4. SCARLET THREAD** *(Finland)* **5. MAD CRAYON** *(Italy)* **6. MUSEO ROSENBACH** *(Italy)* **7. LEVIATHAN** *(Italy)* **8. MALIBRAN** *(Italy)* **9. SOFIA BACCINI** *(Italy)* **10. ELEGANT SIMPLICITY** *(UK)* **CD3: : 1. QADESH** *(Uk)* **2. CANTINA SOCIALE** *(Italy)* **3. GRAND STAND** *(Sweden)* **4. GERMINALE** *(Italy)* **5. AARDVARK** *(Finland)* **6. THONK** *(Switzerland)* **7. GROOVECTOR** *(Finland)* **8. WHOBODIES** *(Finland)* **9. RANDONE & TEMPORE** *(Italy)* **10. CAFEÏNE** *(France)*.

Another project from the magazine Colossus, it is probably the best collective prog album released during the last twenty years. Over four hours of good music performed by great names from the international scene included more for their musical skills than for the notoriety: the Finnish **Haikara** and the resurrected Italian **Museo Rosenbach** play side by side tracks with other emerging bands of the '90s. The greater part of the artists contained are actually from Finland, since **Kalevala** is in fact a Nordic epic poem belonging to the Finnish mythology. Sometimes the track sequence seems a bit discontinued but the final result is still fascinating and convincing.

DISCOGRAPHY: KALEVALA *(Colossus/Musea, 2003).*   M.G.

TROOPERS
Chapter Three

Jethro Tull - *The Witch's Promise*

Europe: AUSTRIA

EELA CRAIG

Hubert Bognermayr – *keyboards, vocals,* **Gerhard Englisch** – *bass,* **Frank Hueber** - *drums,* **Alois Janetschko** - *engineer,* **Will Orthofer** – *vocals ,* **Fritz Riedelberger** – *guitar, keyboards, vocals ,* **Hubert Schnauer** – *keyboards, flute,* **Harald Zuschrader** – *keyboards, flute, guitar.*
One of the most famous and important Austrian bands formed in 1970 and dissolved officially in 1988 after several break-up, sometimes quite long. Their first homonym album published in 1971 found the critics enthusiastic for the force of the symphonic prog, psychedelic hard blues and dynamic structured jazz-rock. *One Niter* released in 1976 and *Hats of Glass* the following year are considered their best works, both played with a powerful trio keyboards. Their sound contained also electronic music and some contacts with space rock, though always strongly maintaining a distinctive symphonic style. *Missa Universalis* is good to, then they eventually shift to a pure electronic pop genre.
RECOMMENDED RECORDINGS: ONE NITER *(Vertigo, 1976)*   **M.G. & C.C.**

KYRIE ELEISON

Gerard Krampl - *keyboards,* **Manfred Drapela** - *guitar,* **Norbert Morin** - *bass,* **Karl Novotny* - *drums, percussion,* **Michael Schubert** - *vocals.*
Many artists attempted to emulate the distinctive sound of **Peter Gabriel**'s **Genesis**: one of the best results was achieved with *The Fountain Beyond the Sunrise*, a compelling masterpiece of romantic rock. Intense, dramatic, with plenty of mellotron arrangements, inspiring instrumental grooves, meditational vocals and hints of **VdGG**. *The Blind Window Suite* is instead an archive recording of 1975, released posthumous in 1994 with a different style, in between psychedelia and prog. Available today is a three-CD box containing both studio albums and a rare live recording.
DISCOGRAPHY: THE FOUNTAIN BEYOND THE SUNRISE *(1976, Merlin)* **THE BLIND WINDOW SUITE** *(1994, Indigo Music)* **THE COMPLETE RECORDINGS 1974-1978** *(2002, Mio Records).* **M.G. & C.C.**

ISAIAH

Gerd Raabe - *lead vocals, flute, guitars percussion,* **Michael Bornhorst** - *winds,* **Hans Gasser** - *bass,* **Walter Reschauer** - *drums, percussion,* **Edu Weber** - *guitar, vocals,* **Hubertus Nolte** - *keyboards, vocals.*
A great Austrian prog album of jazzy taste with an extraordinary lead guitarist. All the instruments are played with an out-standing talent though flute and sax come out more strongly than the rest in this homonym and solitaire work of 1975, often considered to be a simple photocopy of British jazz-prog, but in fact it is quite the opposite: a unique and true gem that deserves greater attention. Very difficult item to find in its original vinyl format, it has been finally made available in 2006 on its CD version.
DISCOGRAPHY: ISAIAH *(1975, LP - CBS, 2006, CD - MSI Music).*   **M.G. & C.C.**

PATERNOSTER

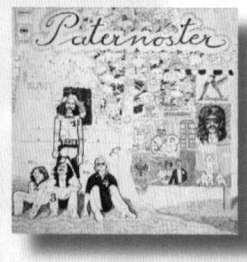

Gerhart Walenta - *drums,* **Gerhard Walter** - *guitar, vocals,* **Franz Wippel** - *organ, vocals,* **Heimo Wisser** - *bass.*
Another one-shot album band from Vienna that became a cult in its own right. The style of this 1972 work is unique, magnificent and solemn, with the overwhelming church organ playing sometimes in a psychedelic and slow crescendo, with bizarre vocals, both for the way they are conveyed and for how they hover over the solemnity of the organ partitions. Only the sharp sounding guitars push harder into a very kraut-rock dimension.
DISCOGRAPHY: PATERNOSTER *(1972, Ohrwaschl).*   **M.G. & C.C.**

Europe: **BELGIUM**

BURNING PLAGUE

Michael Heslop – *guitar, vocals,* **Roger Carlier** - *bass,* **Alex Capelle, Alain Pire** - *guitars,* **Willy Stassen, Paul Vandevelde, Marc Ysaye, Mario Zola** – *drums.*

Hard-blues band born at the end of the '60s as a Belgian response to the Brit-blues. Their style evolves quickly into much more interesting sounds, extending into the jazz-rock genre. Always at the edge of prog, they are among those pioneers who blazed through the musical sky as new comets, pushing the boundaries of creativity to higher levels. They released a first album in 1970 only to vanish and reappear in 1992 playing in concert. A second album was published in 1995 and they still perform live in several festivals.

DISCOGRAPHY: BURNING PLAGUE *(CBS, 1970)* **TWO** *(MMS, 1995)* **LIVE AT LAST** *(Roadrunner, 1999).*
M.G. & C.C.

DRAGON

Bernard Callaert - *guitar, vocals, bass,* **Christian Duponcheel** - *keyboards, piano, flute, sax,* **Jean-Pierre Houx** - *keyboards, bass, vocals,* **Georges Vanaise** - *drums, vibes, flute,* **Jean Vanaise** - *guitar, vocals.*

After ten years of hard work they finally release a first album, Dragon, in 1976. Greatly influenced by Pulsar and a space-rock that recals **Hillage** or the German cosmic music (**Amon Düül II**, **Agitation Free**), sadly this work is completed in the wrong era since at the end of the '70s punk music had taken over, forcing them to put their career on hold. They return with a second album Kalahen in 1988, on the wake of the reborn interest in the prog genre. Though not well-produced, it is full of inventive and containing the same quality of ideas of their previous.

DISCOGRAPHY: DRAGON *(1976, Acorn)* **KALAHEN** *(1988, Ficrivan).*
M.G. & C.C.

FINNEGANS WAKE

Jean-Luc Aucremanne, Marcilio Onofre - *keyboards,* **Henry Krutzen** - *vocals, keyboards, winds,* **Alain Lemaitre** - *bass, keyboards, percussion,* **Michael Ouckisky, Pierre Quinet, Alexandre Moura-Barros** - *guitars,* **Celine T'Hooft, Richard Redcrossed** - *vocals.* **Alexandre Johnson** - *winds.*

Among the best prog bands from Belgium, excluding the experimental attitude, they have little in common with their colleagues **Univers Zero** and **Present**. This group of musicians plays an intense art-rock, strictly connected with the Canterbury style and not too distant from **Isildurs Bane**'s atmospheres. All four albums recorded from 1994 to 2004 contain a well structured chamber rock with hints of very evolved fusion and of contemporary classics. The fourth release is rich of avant-garde inventive, yet somewhat resulting more accessible in sound. At the end of 2008 they release Blue with special guests like **Guy Segers**, **Reginald Trigaux** and **Morgan Agren**.

DISCOGRAPHY: YELLOW *(Mellow Records, 1994)* **GREEN** *(Mellow Records, 1996)* **PICTURES** *(Musea, 2001)* **4TH** *(Carbon 7, 2004)* **BLUE** *(AltRock, 2008).*
M.G. & C.C.

FLYTE

Lu Rousseau - *lead vocals, percussion,* **Ruud Worthman** - *guitars,* **Jack van Liesdonck** - *keyboards,* **Leo Cornelissens** – *keyboards, vocals,* **Hans Boeye** – *drums, percussion,* **Hans Marynissen** – *percussion,* **Peter Dekeersmaeker** - *bass, vocals.*

A Dutch-Belgian band that lives on the border of both countries, in Breda. Founded in 1972 they will undergo several line-up changes for the next five years until German lead singer **Lu Rousseau** arrives, characterizing the rest of their career with his voice. Greatly inspired by **Camel**, **Fruupp** or **Machiavel**, with a singing very close to the French theatrical style, they eventually record in Belgium for a Dutch label their first symphonic prog album released in 1979 as *Dawn Dancer*. After this the band breaks-up.

RECOMMENDED RECORDINGS: DAWN DANCER *(Don Quixote, 1979).*
M.G. & C.C.

Europe: BELGIUM

ISOPODA

Dirk De Schepper - *lead vocals,* **Arnold De Schepper** - *bass, guitars, flute, vocals,* **Walter De Berlangeer** - *guitars, vocals,* **Geert Amant** - *piano, keyboards,* **Marc Van Der Schueren** - *drums, percussion.*

Their 1978 album Achrosticon is greatly inspired by the sound of **Genesis** during the **Peter Gabriel** era (1970/76). Not simply a copycat band, they release excellent songs and melodies with strong rhythmic variations and a very elegant instrumental mix of electric and acoustic devices. Unfortunately released at the end of the '70s, they faced all the difficulties posed by the arrival of punk, yet the following 1981 Taking Root is still a good work, although less inspiring than the first.
DISCOGRAPHY: **ACHROSTICON** *(1978, Twinkle)* **TAKING ROOT** *(1981, Lark).*   M.G. & C.C.

JULVERNE

Pierre Coulon – *flute,* **Dirk Descheemaker** – *clarinet,* **Michel Berckmans** – *tuba,* **Laurence Cornez** - *piano, percussion,* **Jeannot Gillis** - *violin, horns,* **Edith Heudens** – *viola,* **Claudine Steenackers** – *cello,* **Andre Klenes** – *double bass.*

The line-up of this band changes radically from one album to another, maintaining only two of the original elements of 1979 (**Coulon** and **Gillis**) in the last. With no drum section, but well equipped with chamber music elements, which is exactly what they play: Avant-garde symphonic prog with new sounds. Of course **Univers Zero** had already done this kind of music, but here there is no darkness and the drama is limited. Sunny, joyful, warm atmospheres where the piano interlaces themes with the flute and the strings, never tense or harsh. They are the other face of prog, not the best perhaps, but certainly different.
RECOMMENDED RECORDINGS: **A NEUF** *(Crammed, 1980).*   M.G. & C.C.

LAURELIE

Pierre Raepsaet - *bass, guitar, vocals,* **Christian Boissart** - *guitars, vocals,* **Yvon Hubert** - *piano, organ, vocals,* **Francis Dozin** - *flute, vocals,* **Andre Marquet** - *drums.*

First generation prog band in Belgium, with strong roots of blues and '60s psychedelia, they were greatly inspired by **Traffic**, **Cressida**, **Barclay James Harvest**, **Jethro Tull** and some hints of **The Moody Blues**. In fact, **Laurelie**, their only release of 1970, is very well packed with soft sounds, elegant and well defined compositions with very little space for improvisation. Some members pursued different careers in other bands after this experience.
DISCOGRAPHY: **LAURELIE** *(Triangle, 1970).*   M.G. & C.C.

MACHIAVEL

Albert Letecheur – *keyboards, percussion,* **Roland De Greef** – *bass, cello, guitars, percussion, winds, tape effects, vocals,* **Marc Ysaye** – *drums, vocals, percussion,* **Mario Guccio** - *vocals, flute, saxophones, clarinet,* **Jean-Paul Devaux** – *guitars, vocals.*

This band can be seen as a Belgian precursor of new prog when true prog was still high and shining. In fact they started in 1976 with a music apparently not too linked to the classical structure of the mainstream. They understood and anticipated the winds of punk which can be also found in embryo in their compositions, as well as other genres of more easy listening. Their best period is full of the pop or heavy rock contained in their first three albums, always in a style that can be cross-referenced with the English pop-prog of **Supertramp**, **Elton John** and **David Bowie**.
RECOMMENDED RECORDINGS: **JESTER** *(Harvest, 1977).*   M.G. & C.C.

Europe: BELGIUM

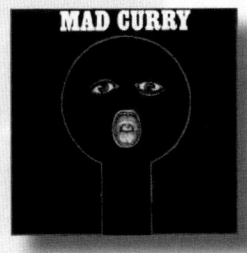

MAD CURRY

Viona Westra - vocals, percussion, **Giorgio Chitschenko (Joosk Geeraerts)** - saxophones, **Dany Rousseau** - keyboards, **Jean "Andore" Vandooren** - bass, **Eddy "Kane" Verdonck** - drums.

Belgium prog one-shot band of 1970, with no guitars and a taste for jazz. The talented musicians play with a beautiful dose of madness and spontaneous creativity where a main coherence is highlighted by unexpected moments. Every song in this album is a world a part, full of charming and original ideas. The sound richness is determined by the keyboards and sax, while **Westra** sings unifying it all with an unmatched fluidity. The precise rhythmic session, often essential for a jazz lightheartedness, is another distinctive element. After this each members pursued a different career (jazz, blues, funky) and in 2006 they reunite for a concert.
RECOMMENDED RECORDINGS: MAD CURRY *(Pirate's, 1970)*. **M.G. & C.C.**

KANDAHAR

Karel Bogard - keyboards, **Jeff de Visscher** - guitar, vocals, **Jacky Eddyn** - sax, flute, **Jean-Pierre Claeys** - bass, vocals, **Etienne Dlarye** - drums, percussion, cello, vocals.

The 1974 debut Long live the sliced ham is an album which mixes jazz, rock and fusion sometimes in a Canterbury school style and sometimes finding more experimental solutions like through traces of zeuhl. *In the court of Catharina Squeezer* (1975) and *Pictures from the past* (1978) follow the same line and recall the nice and fresh attitude of **Supersister**. Kicking rhythms, good performances, large instrumentation and a complex structure characterize the work. After ten years of silence they resume their career in 1991 with another album, *Ghent, Somewhere in Europe*, an average recording which adds nothing to the previous. Again in 2011 the surprise with a music cassette entitled *Spel*, more oriented towards new age.
RECOMMENDED RECORDINGS: LONG LIVED THE SLICED HAM *(1974, Dwarf)* **IN THE COURT OF CATHARINA SQUEEZER** *(1975, Dwarf)* **PICTURES FROM THE PAST** *(1978, Gip)* **M.G. & C.C.**

RECREATION

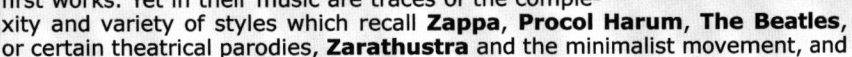

Jean-Jacques Falaise – organ, **Jean-Paul VanDen Bossche** - bass, guitar, **Francis Lonneux** – drums, percussion.

Their sound is greatly inspired by Canterbury elements especially from bands like **Egg** and **Khan** or the amazing **Obsolete** of **Dashiell Hedayat**, and to **Kevin Ayer**'s first works. Yet in their music are traces of the complexity and variety of styles which recall **Zappa**, **Procol Harum**, **The Beatles**, or certain theatrical parodies, **Zarathustra** and the minimalist movement, and also **Debussy**, **Stravinsky**, **Mahler**. They sometimes rearrange famous songs completely distorting them in a whirl of chaos rare for the prog genre. *Don't Open* of 1971 and *Music or not Music* of 1972 are two revolutionary album published during two also revolutionary years regarding the music world.
RECOMMENDED RECORDINGS: DON'T OPEN *(Triangle, 1970)* **MUSIC OR NOT MUSIC** *(Barclay, 1972)*. **M.G. & C.C.**

WATERLOO

Dirk Bogaert – vocals, flute, **Gus Roan** – guitar, **Marc Malyster** – organ, **Jacky Mauer** - drums, **Jean-Paul Janssens** – bass, **John Van Rymenant** – saxophones.

Devotion to both Nice and Arthur Brown, they develop a form of well arranged jazz-prog. After a beginning in clubs and little venues collecting good reviews, their first release First Battle is published in 1970 with an illustrated cover of Napoleon. The impressive opening track "Meet again" was an immediate hit single broadcasted by many radios supporting the distribution of the album in several nations. At the end of that same year they acquire a bizarre and ingenious saxophonist, John Van Rymenant who manipulates his instrument into creating a new style recalling sounds belonging to Coltrane and Miles Davis. They disappeared after releasing some other singles.
DISCOGRAPHY: FIRST BATTLE *(1970, CD Musea, 1999)*. **M.G. & C.C.**

Europe: BULGARIA

DIANA EXPRESS

Mitko Shterev - *keyboards*, **Ivan Lazov** - *bass*, **Ivan Hristov** - *drums*, **Licho Stones** - *guitar*.
A very popular group in Bulgaria, they obeyed the Socialist regime and their three albums, released between 1974 and 1979, had the merit of exporting Bulgarian folk abroad, at first in the communist region and later across the Iron Fence. Their style is as mentioned a folk-prog based on the massive use of keyboards played with good taste and personality. They maintained their fame also after the fall of the regime as the music kept evolving with them. Many important collaborations from musicians of their country, like with special guest **Vassil Naydenov**.
DISCOGRAPHY: **MITKO SHTEREV** (Balkanton, 1974) **DIANA EXPRESS 2ND** (Balkanton, 1975) **PRAYER FOR RAIN** (Balkanton, 1979).
C.A. & C.C.

FSB

Konstatin Tsekov - *keyboards*, **Rumen Boyadzhiev** - *keyboards*, **Alexander Baharov** – *bass*, **Petur Slavov** - *drums*, **Ivan Lechev** – *violin*.
Formation Studio Balkanton is the explained acronym of this Bulgarian band born in 1974 by excellent professional musicians formed at the national Academy of Music. In the second half of the '70s they played in Scandinavia as **Free Sailing Band** maintaining the initials. Their first three releases are good symphonic prog albums with synthesizers and string arrangements recalling **PFM**, **Yes**, **Camel** and **Genesis**. Then in the early '80s they abruptly turn to a low quality disco music following the desperate desire to capture the interest of the new generations.
DISCOGRAPHY: **FSB** (1975, Balkanton) **NON STOP** (1977, Balkanton) **FSB II (ROCK-CINFONICO)** (1978, Balkanton) **78 R.P.M.** (1981, Balkanton) **TEN YEARS AFTER** (1984, Balkanton).
M.G. & C.C.

SHTURZITE

Peter Ghyouzelev – *guitar, vocals*, **Kiril Marichkov** – *bass, keyboards, vocals*, **Vladimir Totev** – *keyboards, guitar, vocals*, **Georgr Totev** – *drums*.
Bulgary's answer to **The Beatles** (their name means **The Crickets**), the band began playing together in 1967 for a student's party. After some singles and unofficial recordings, they vanish and reappear in 1974. Their first homonym album of 1976 contains an interesting pop-rock psychedelia similar to **The Beatles** with hints of heavy-rock. An important band to understand the evolution of progressive this country.
DISCOGRAPHY: **SHTURZITE** (1976, Balkanton) **20TH CENTURY** (1980, Balkanton).
M.G. & C.C.

SIGNAL

Yordan Karadjov – *vocals*, **Christo Lambrev** – *bass*, **Roumen Spassov**, **Alexander Marinovsky** – *guitar*, **George Kokalanov**, **Vladimir Zakhariev** – *drums*.
During the spring of 1971 singer **Yordan Karadjov** aka "Rancho" founds the **Golden Strings**, a legendary Bulgarian pop band with strong psychedelic sonorities. Under this name they release some singles and a rock opera called *The legend of the Thracian treasure*, which is performed live but still has never been officially released. In 1978 this band breaks-up and half of the musicians reunited as **Signal**, always in a psychedelic context yet perhaps more pop-rock. Guitarist **Alexander Marinovsky** replaces **Spassov** who prefers to work as a producer behind the mixer. Sometimes in disagreement with the socialist government (until the early '80s), their golden years go from 1979 to 1992.
RECOMMENDED RECORDINGS: **SIGNAL** (1979, Balkanton).
M.G. & C.C.

Europe: **CZECHOSLOVAKIA**

AKU AKU

Slavek Neuhöfer – *violin, vocals,* **Jan Peclinovsky** – *guitar, vocals,* **Ludek Zednik** – *bass, keyboards,* **Vladimir Saska** – *drums, keyboards, vocals.*
Formed in the late '80s in Teplice, northern Bohemia, the four excellent and accurate musicians tend to play complex and technically demanding songs, with a rather aggressive and sharp style. Strongly inspired by **King Crimson** and **Rush**, they largely use an odd tempo with a wicked bass marking heavy rhythms, sometimes inclining to more dark and acid rock with gothic tones and an underground feeling, closer to the polish **SBB**. The vocals are very theatrical and sung in Czech, at times with a very powerful martial touch of dramatic effects. Their 1990 debut *Humanquake* is followed by the live album *Aku Aku Knaak* of 1992. Last, but not good as the previous, *Mezi Psem a Vlkem*, released in 1995. After almost ten years from their breakup *Cekání Na Slunce* is released in 2003 as a collection of previously unpublished tracks recorded in 1988.
RECOMMENDED RECORDINGS: HUMANQUAKE *(Guerilla Records, 1990).*   M.G. & C.C.

COMBO FH

Daniel Fikejz - *keyboards, marimba, percussion, vocals,* **Bolivoj Suchý** - *Saxophones, strings, piano, percussion,* **Milan Sládek** - *tuba, piano, percussion,* **Richard Mader** – *guitars, piano, percussion,* **Václav Pátek** – *bass,* **Tomáš Suchomel** – *drums, percussion, vocals, piano.*
A Czechoslovak ensemble who plays a particular form of avant-garde jazz, rich of Canterbury references, R.I.O. forms and **Zappa** styled sonorities, but also of contemporary classical music such as **Bartok**. Their sound is complex and articulated with structures similar to **Henry Cow** of *LegEnd*, sometimes even recalling **Samla Mammas Manna**, especially in the use of the drums. Another characteristic is how they inserted all the above never exaggerating, in a way that allowed simpler and more accessible schemes. In their first record *Vèci* of 1981, a series of short tracks are held together by a dynamic and pyrotechnic guideline. In 1986 a second and very different work.
RECOMMENDED RECORDINGS: VÈCI *(Panton, CBS France, 1981).*   M.G. & C.C.

DOMÁCÍ KAPELA

Karel Vavrinek, Roman Koucy Kuna - *bass, guitars,* **Jan Brabec** - *drums,* **Martin Kontra** - *keyboards, guitars,* **Karolina Hejdukovà** - *vocals.*
Another great band born during the '80s listening to the German new wave genre: as it often occurred in this period, the rebel pioneers would begin surfing the new current and then very quickly change their style into a strange form of new prog, in their case, melancholic and with dark influences. In Great Britain **Japan** and **Ultravox** are another example, but **Domàci Kapela** go beyond. Their only album *Nedele* comes out in 1992 with a mix of male and female vocals in Czech, close to the results of **Art Zoyd** and **Univers Zero**. The track "Indiani milujou hory" (Indians loves the Mountains) is a clear representation.
RECOMMENDED RECORDINGS: NEDELE *(Levnè Knihy, 1992).*   M.G. & C.C.

ENERGIT

Ivan Khunt - *vocals,* **Jaroslav "Erno" Šedivý** - *drums,* **Luboš Andršt** - *guitar,* **Emil Viklický** - *piano, moog,* **Rudolf Tichálek** - *saxophones,* **Jan Vytrhlík** - *bass.*
A spin-off band from **Flamengo**, this Czech band starts with strong live performances of average hard rock. The original ideas and explicit lyrics procures them the consequent censorship by the government's regime, so their first album moderates tunes and lyrics through the beautiful keyboards of **Viklicky**. The line-up changes several times and their sound turns into a kind of western European jazz, well mixed to rock and funky fresh rhythms.
DISCOGRAPHY: ENERGIT *(Supraphon, 1975)* PIKNIK *(Panton, 1978).*   C.A. & C.C.

Europe: **CZECHOSLOVAKIA**

PRUDY

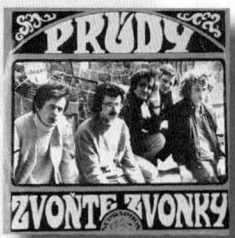

Pavol Hammel - *vocals, guitar,* **Peter Saller** - *guitar,* **Vladimír Kaššay** - *bass,* **František Machats** - *drums,* **Marián Varga** - *keyboards.*

Although is not a true progressive band, more psychedelic-beat given the time-frame, this band from eastern Europe is important to the understanding of the development of Prog in Czechoslovakia. The 1967 English psychedelic wave reached this country in 1969 and the first result is **Prudy**. Their first album *Zvonte Zvonky* is the perfect merge between the experiences of **Zombies** and **Bee Gees**, with more dynamic and powerful rhythms. Unfortunately sung in Czech, a language that ill connects to this genre, the piano played by **Marian Varga** still manages to justify the quality to this album.

DISCOGRAPHY: **ZVONTE ZVONKY** *(Supraphon, 1969).*   **C.A. & C.C.**

STROMBOLI

Michal Pavlicek – *guitars, bass, vocals,* **Vladimir Kulhanek** - *bass,* **Klaudius Kryspin** – *drums,* **Bara Basikova** – *vocals,* **Vendula Kasparkova** – *synth Yamaha,* **Vilem Cok** - *vocals, bass,* **Michael Kocab** – *vocals,* **Iva Bittova** – *violin,* **Jan & Michal Pavlicek Jr.** – *vocals.*

Poly-instrumentalist **Pavlicek** chose this name picturing the volcanic power of his intentions and the explosive music generated by this talented ensemble led by an intense and sensual female singer. The band started playing live around 1985 and these concerts were released in a first homonym album the following year: like **Pink Floyd**'s 1969 *Ummagumma* it was a double album containing a live recording and a studio album all in one. The concert is a mix of poignant and personal progressive jazz with powerful and difficult improvisations, while the studio album of a more simple kind of rock with electronic sounds. Unfortunately in 1989 their second release, *Shutdown*, is an average work and very far from their wonderful debut.

RECOMMENDED RECORDINGS: **STROMBOLI** *(Panton, 1987).*   **M.G. & C.C.**

SYNKOPY (Sinkopy 61)

Jiri Rybar – *drums, vocals,* **Pavel Pokorny** – *vocals, violin,* **Petr Smeja** – *guitars, vocals,* **Milos Orsag** – *accordion,* **Petr Fischer** – *clarinet,* **Michal Polak** - *vocals,* **Oldrich Vesely** - *keyboards, vocals.*

A band born in 1960 as **Synkopy 61**, they start off by performing in ballrooms inspired by the American sound of **Beach Boys** (and in fact support the Czech tour of their idols in 1969). Between 1968 and 1972 they change sound and release **Uriah Heep** songs sung in Czech. **Vesely** then leaves for five years to join **Modry Efekt**, returning in 1980 and shortening the band's name to **Synkopy**. They release three Prog albums of which *Slunecni Hodiny* (1981) is probably their masterpiece, placing their style close to the sound of the American **Kansas**. The band seems to retire in 1990 though they reunite in 1992 for a last concert.

RECOMMENDED RECORDINGS: **SLUNECNI HODINY** *(Panton, 1981).*   **M.G. & C.C.**

DEŽO URSINY

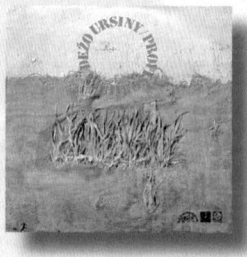

Dezo Ursiny – *guitars, vocals,* **Jaroslav Filip** – *keyboards, tubular bells,* **Vladimír Kulhánek** – *bass,* **Jaroslav Šedivý** - *drums,,* **Jirí Kaniak** - *oboe.*

Singer and guitarist, **Dezider** (**Dežo**) **Ursiny** was also a film screenwriter and director. Considered as one of the most important personalities of Slovak rock and popular music, he belongs to a wide group of Czechoslovak beat legends that began playing already in the early '60s. With the musicians of a band called **Flamengo**, he releases his first solo album *Provisorium* in 1972 (the Czech answer to *In the Court of the Crimson King* of **King Crimson**) where he sings trying to emulate the style and vocals of **Greg Lake**. "Christmas Summer" and "Apple Tree in Winter" are truly beautiful with regards to the other less important tracks, like **Jaroslav Šedivý**'s too long drum solo. However, still a good album though the sound quality and cohesion sometimes feels weak.

RECOMMENDED RECORDINGS: **PROVISORIUM** *(Supraphon, 1972).*   **M.G. & C.C.**

Europe: ESTONIA

IN SPE

Peeter Brambat – *flute,* **Riho Sibul** - *guitars,* **Erkki-Sven Tüür** – *keyboards, flute, vocals,* **Arvo Urb** - *drums,* **Anne Tüür** - *keyboards,* **Mart Metsala** - *keyboards,* **Toivo Kopli** - *bass,* **Priit Kuulberg** –*effects, vocoder.*

A symphonic electro-acoustic prog band with strong classical, melodic and evocative components. They record with different line-ups two amazing albums: in 1983 the symphonic homonym debut with strong references to the English founding fathers, to a certain wave of new prog and also to the Finnish current of the genre. Quite different and simpler in rhythms is their second album of 1985, recalling **Gentle Giant** and the Canterbury sound. Among the instruments pops the singular noise of a typewriter and **Terje Terasmaa** playing the vibraphone.
RECOMMENDED RECORDINGS: IN SPE *(Melodiya, 1983).* M.G. & C.C.

LINNU TEE

Indrek Patte - *vocals,* **Madis Lepasoo** - *keyboards,* **Margus Kliimask** - *bass,* **Toomas Vanem, Endel Jigi, Raul Jaanson** - *guitar,* **Juri Mazurchak** - *drums.*

All former musicians in previous bands playing during the '70s, they gather together when in 1989 the Soviet regime cuts some slack to the musical culture of the time. Their only testimony is a self-titled album which well represents the pompous AOR derivation in Estonia, recalling the sound of bands like **Asia**, **Toto** and the **Yes** of *90125*. One of the top bands in the country they were asked to participate in a compilation of various artists released in 1990. Unfortunately weakened by the constant line-up changes, they disappear until 2002, year of the **Kuri Proge Festival** in which they perform for the last time.
DISCOGRAPHY: LINNU TEE *(1989, Melodiya)* 11 : ROCK- ELAGU IGAVENE SUVI **(various artists)** *(1990, Compilation Melodiya).* M.G. & C.C.

KASEKE

Peeter Malkov - *flute,* **Ain Varts** - *guitar,* **Riho Sibul** - *guitar,* **Priit Kuulberg** - *bass,* **Andrus Vaht** - *drums,* **Tonu Naissoo** - *keyboards,* **Mart Metsala** - *tastiere.*

Unlike other colleagues, this Estonian supergroup finds its golden age under the official Soviet label in the early '80s. Formed by very talented musicians coming from bands such as **In Spe**, **Ruja** and **Mess**, they publish an EP, *Sõnum*, and the studio album *Põletus*, two powerful works of fusion prog with broad instrumental moments seldom self-indulgent where the guitars interlace in compelling duels also with the keyboards and flute.
DISCOGRAPHY: SÕNUM *(1981, Melodiya)* PÕLETUS *(1983, Melodiya).* M.G. & C.C.

RUJA

Andrus Vaht - *drums,* **Tiit Haagma** - *bass,* **Jaanus Nõgisto** - *guitar,* **Rein Rannap** - *keyboards,* **Urmas Alender** - *vocals.* **Juhan Viiding** – *lyrics.*

A prog-rock band born in 1971 in an Estonia deeply subdued by the Soviet Regime. Their display of devotion to the British musical invasion already was daring, but to sing in the Estonian language brought them to be immediately censored by communist government, forcing the band to delay the release of their first EP to 1980. They break-up in 1988 although, as for many others, a one off reunion is held in 1994 since in their country they are cherished and still quite appreciated.
DISCOGRAPHY: RUJA (EP) *(1979, Melodiya)* RUJA *(1981, Melodiya)* KIVI VEEREB *(1987, Melodiya)* PUST BUDET VSJO *(1988, Melodiya)* MUST LIND *(1994, CD).* M.G. & C.C.

Europe: **FINLAND**

GIANT HOGWEED ORCHESTRA

Antti Aalto - *guitars,* **Mika Muinonen** - *guitars,* **Jyri Träskelin** - *flute,* **Turo Sinkkonen** - *bass, piano,* **Jaakko Kakko** - *drums, percussion.*
Additional players: Teemu Niemelä - *moog,* **Mikko Tuominen** - *trumpet,* **Alpo Nummelin** - *didjeridoo.*

There's absolutely no connection to the famous song by **Genesis** in this band of intense instrumental psychedelic prog, very compelling and hypnotic. Yet another one-shot band, their only recording (published in 2004 by an Italian label) is one of the best Finnish examples of the genre, with its extraordinary and monumental twenty minute suite "Halogen". The excellent interlacing of guitars and flute intersect with the occasional trumpet, moog and didjeridoo creating an dreamy sound vortex which reprises in a contemporary way **Pink Floyd** and **Gong**.
DISCOGRAPHY: **THE GIANT HOGWEED ORCHESTRA** *(2004, Mellow Records).* **M.G. & C.C.**

HÖYRY KONE

Jukka Hannukainen - *vocals, keyboards, programming,* **Teemu Hänninen** - *drums,* **Tuomas Hänninen** - *guitars,* **Jussi Kärkkäinen** - *guitars,* **Nina Lehos** - *oboe,* **Topi Lehtipuu** - *vocals, violin,* **Marko Manninen** - *cello,* **Jarno Sarkula** - *bass, flute.*

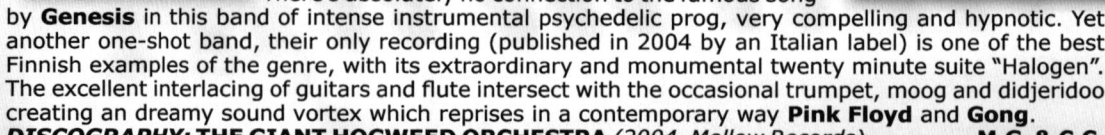

A talented Finnish band, very distant from any easy listening solution, they release two albums in the second half of the '90s containing a music very close to the R.I.O. movement, full of avant-garde and experimental sounds with a touch of the contemporary classical genre: dissonances, electric noises, folk hints and weird melodies lead the band toward some of the best examples of a brainy song-writing with no compromises or rules and no intention of following any trend but their own.
DISCOGRAPHY: **HYÖNTEISIÄ VOI RAKASTAA** *(1995, Ad Perpetuam Memoriam)* **HUONO PARTURI** *(1997, Ad Perpetuam Memoriam).* **M.G. & C.C.**

JUKKA HAURU

Great prog-rock artist from Finland, he seems to be sadly forgotten nowadays due to the similarities with **Wigwam**, **Piirpauke** and **Pekka Pohjola**. **Jukka Hauru** is a greatly enlightened musician and a powerful guitarist. In his first 1971 album Information his ingenious sense of humor finds musical solutions close to the ones of **Gong** (the **Daevid Allen** era), full of psychedelic sounds, fusion and jazz and of course greatly inspired by his idol **Jimi Hendrix**. His second and last record Episode is published in 1973, still a good album but somewhat repetitive and with no real novelty. After this he will simply accept collaborations as a guest musician in other projects adding nothing to his solo career.

DISCOGRAPHY: **INFORMATION** *(Love records, 1971)* **EPISODE** *(Love records, 1973).* **M.G. & C.C.**

KAAMOS

Peter Strohlman - *guitars,* **Eero Munter** - *bass,* **Eero Valkonen** - *drums,* **Ilkka Poijärvi** – *keyboards,* **Jimmy Lewman** – *voce,* **Ilpo Murtojärvi** – *guitars,* **Johnny Gustafsson** – *vocals, drums,* **Kyösti Laihi** – *keyboards,* **Eric**

Typical band of the early '70s with interesting ideas that publish late in the decade, when punk and disco were the new kids on the block, obfuscating all the rest from the music business until a new reprise of the genre in the '90s. They begin playing in clubs in 1973, undergoing more than a line-up changes and finding it hard to sign up for their album. Finally released in 1977, *Deeds and Talks* is an album of classical music with echoes of medieval sounds and folk prog similar to **Jethro Tull** without a flute. They are and remain dead and buried although twenty years later the new resurrection of prog leads to the reissue of their album on CD.
DISCOGRAPHY: **DEEDS AND TALKS** *(M&T Production 1977).* **M.G. & C.C.**

Europe: FINLAND

KALEVALA (Kalevala Orchestra)

Harri Saksala, "Limousine" Leppänen – *vocals*, **Olli Ahvenlahti** – *piano*, **Matti Kurkinen** – *guitar*, **Remu Aaltonen** - *drums*, **Juha "Lido" Salonen** – *bass, guitars*.

A band born in 1969 as a project of bass player **Juha 'Lido' Salonen**, who takes the name from the epic saga Kalevala about Finland's creation. Their first psychedelic-prog album *People No Names* is released in 1972, although interesting it results weak in certain instrumental solutions. The songs were originally composed to be sung in Finnish, hence the issues of adapting the new English lyrics by singer **Harri Saksala** (a voice recalling **Jan Anderson** of **Jethro Tull**). The following two albums in fact feature a different lead singer and the third album is published without **Kurkinen**, who died in a car crash. This last work has a beautiful artwork on the cover which well represents the hermetic surrealism of the time.

RECOMMENDED RECORDINGS: **PEOPLE NO NAMES** (Finnlevy, 1972) **BOOGIE JUNGLE** (Hi-Hat, 1975) **ABRAHAM'S BLUE REFRAIN** (HILP, 1977). M.G. & C.C.

KUUSUMUN PROFEETTA
(Moon Fog Prophet)

Imika Ratto - *keyboards, vocals*, **Teemu Majaluoma** - *guitar, vocals*, **Mikko Elo**: *bass*, **Veli Nuorsaari** - *drums*.

The **Moon Fog Prophet**, known in Finland as **Kuusumun Profeetta**, is a cosmic fury band. Born in 1994, they retire to a hut in Pori in order to unleash their visionary jams by mixing some ideas from **Van Der Graaf Generator** with a powerful psychedelia. Their five recordings contain all the best influences and variations, full of dramatic stuff, wild instrumental moments and lunatic lyrics similar to the work of **Robert Wyatt**. The epic album of 2002 is a theatrical show soundtrack.

RECOMMENDED RECORDINGS: **DIM DUM SING THE SUN** (Metamorphos, 1998) **WHEN THEY OPENED THEIR PARACHUTES... SILENCE** (Metamorphos, 1999) **MERN3336** (Metamorphos, 2001) **TAUNTING TIN BELLS THROUGH THE MAMMAL VOID** (Mellow Records, 2002). M.G. & C.C.

PIIRPAUKE

Sakari Kukko - *piano, winds*, **Hasse Walli** - *guitars*, **Antti Hytti** - *bass*, **Jukka Wasama** - *drums*

This band formed in 1974 around the visionary figure of musician and globe trotter **Sakari Kukko**. Still active after 34 years of line-up revolutions, they start their prolific discography in 1975 with an avant-garde sound strongly affected by folk and ethnic jazz, precursors of what today is called World Music. **Kukko**'s experimentations explore the very different styles coming from traditions of the countries all over the planet, Finnish, Turkish, African, south-American, Balkan, Andalusian, Mediterranean and more. The first period is probably the most prog, especially the first two records with their traversal and eclectic ideas that find some analogies in the American band Oregon.

RECOMMENDED RECORDINGS: **PIIRPAUKE** (Love Records, 1975). M.G. & C.C.

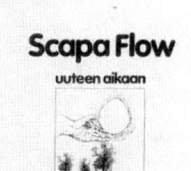

SCAPA FLOW

Ismo Järvinen - *vocals, sax, flute*, **Timo Seppänen** - *guitar*, **Pia-Maria Noponen** - *vocals, keyboards*, **Eero-Pekka Kolehmainen** - *keyboards*, **Asko Ahonen** - *bass*, **Leevi Leppänen** - *drums*.

A minor but fascinating prog band from Finland that release their official debut in 1980, *Uuten Aikan* (sung in Finnish), to prove how, even if punk and disco were already capturing all the attention, a record could still find ways of being published. Even though it's magic lasts only for 33 minutes, the very compelling arrangements are full of the romanticism of a keyboard playing stylish classical music with cool rock guitars and a dreaming flute.

DISCOGRAPHY: **UUTEN AIKAAN** (1980, Kompass). M.G. & C.C.

Europe: **FINLAND**

TABULA RASA

Heikki Silvennoinen - *guitar*, **Jukka Leppilampi** - *vocals*, **Tapio Suominen** - *bass*, **Asko Pakkanen** - *drums*, **Jarno Sormunen** - *flute*, **Jim Pembroke** - *piano*, **Jarno Sinisalo** - *piano, keyboards*, **Jukka Aronen** - *drums, percussion*.

Important band of the '70s Finnish musical scene, they play a very romantic kind of prog with deep roots in the traditional northern folk genre. The finesse of the delicate instrumental solutions draw inspiration from the sounds and styles of **Camel** and **Wigwam**, while the Finnish lyrics are perfectly merged into the melodies. Beautiful the acoustic moments where the flute inserts itself creating the misty atmospheres of their homeland. Both albums are similar in concept and music, compelling and tightly knotted into the country's identity.

DISCOGRAPHY: **TABULA RASA** *(1975, Love Records)* **EKKEDIEN TANSSI** *(1976, Love Records).* **M.G.**

UZVA

Heikki Puska - *guitar, piano, accordion, percussion*, **Lari Latvala** - *violin*, **Heikki Rita** - *clarinett*, **Pekko Sams** - *bass*, **Olli Kari** - *drums, percussion*, **Lauri Kajander** - *guitar*, **Tuure Paalanen** - *cello*, **Hanne Eronen** - *flute*, **Inka Eerola** - *violin*, **Antti Lauronen** - *flute, sax*, **Timom Kortemäki** - *winds*.

Three good albums for this Finnish band that is not easily describable: their music is more like an instrumental prog containing sounds of jazz-rock seasoned by influences from the Canterbury school and mixed with a little touch of folk. Some acoustic tonalities recall a certain kind of never too serious chamber music carried out with a dynamic and well balanced instrumentation and of course, their great personality.

DISCOGRAPHY: **TAMMIKUINEN TAMMELA** *(2000, Ylösmatka Records)* **NITTOAIKA** *(2002, Silence)* **UOMA** *(2006, Silence).* **M.G. & C.C.**

VIIMA

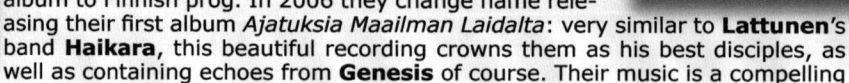

Päivi Kylmänen - *vocals*, **Kimmo Lähteenmäki** - *keyboards, drums*, **Jarmo Kataja** - *bass*, **Mikko Uusi-Oukari** - *guitars, flute*.

Born in 1999 as **Lost Spectacles**, they participate to the collective album *Tuonen Tytar* in 2001, a tribute album to Finnish prog. In 2006 they change name releasing their first album *Ajatuksia Maailman Laidalta*: very similar to **Lattunen**'s band **Haikara**, this beautiful recording crowns them as his best disciples, as well as containing echoes from **Genesis** of course. Their music is a compelling electro-acoustic groove with classical and folk tastes all sung in Finnish. After another participation in a collective epic project, *Kalevala* (see page 278), they publish a last album in 2009.

DISCOGRAPHY: **AJATUKSIA MAAILMAN LAIDALTA** *(2006, Viima).* ***Partecipations:*** **TUONEN TYTAR** *(2001, Mellow Records)* **Kalevala** *(2008, Musea, bonus track of the definitive edition remastered).* **M.G. & C.C.**

XL

Jarmo Saari - *guitar*, **Arttu Takalo** – *vibes*.

Formed in Helsinki in 1992 by famous Finnish jazz musicians all from the Sibelius academy, **DJ Bunuel** will later join to close the definitive line-up, taking care of the sound effects and widening the band's horizons. An interesting mix of folk transposed in eclectic contemporary forms through modern jazz, rock and electronic grooves. Composers **Takalo** and **Saari** release five great studio albums (and a live recording) of very personal jazz-prog with intense and dreamy atmospheres. The acoustic and technological sonorities mix skillfully to contemporary classical music creating good energy and feelings. They disband in 2004 though the talented musicians are still active and collaborate with important names of the musical scene like **Pekka Pohjola**.

RECOMMENDED RECORDINGS: **XLENT** *(SKU, 1994)* **JETI** *(SKU, 1999)* **VISUAL** *(SKU, 2003).* **M.G. & C.C.**

Europe: FRANCE

ACINTYA

Philippe de Canck - *keyboards*, **Philippe Clesse** - *violin, guitar*, **Jean-Louis Tauvel** - *bass*, **Bernard Petite** - *drums, percussion*.

La Cité des Dieux Oubliés is a decent instrumental album of symphonic prog rock with traces of vaguely kraut space-rock where and the combined keyboards and violin always stand out. Both instruments lead all three compositions with elements that recall **Wapassou**. The rhythmic section is also very creative, although the deeply classical parts often seem to linger on to cover more space than quality. One of longest tracks is "Espoir" with musical solutions close to the German **Eloy**, while the title-track contains interesting patterns of very compelling piano and violin.

DISCOGRAPHY: LA CITÉ DES DIEUX OUBLIÉS *(1978, SRC).*

M.G. & C.C.

ARACHNOID

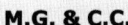

Patrick Woindrich - *bass, vocals*, **Nicolas Popowski** - *guitar, vocals*, **François Faugieres** - *keyboards, vocals*, **Pierre Kuti** - *keyboards*, **Bernard Minig** - *drums*, **Marc Meryl** - *lead vocals*.

These Frenchmen start playing for a couple of years before publishing their only record in 1978, which will result as one of the fundamental albums of the French prog scene. A fascinating style of creepy and dark symphonic prog which opens with two powerful tracks: the almost 14 minutes of the theatrical "La Chamadére", similar to some works of **Ange** and "Piano Caveau" led by a piano that plunges into an instrumental classical composition of its own. However, the rest of this album is just as good.

DISCOGRAPHY: ARACHNOID *(1978, Divox).*

M.G. & C.C.

ARCHAÏA

Pierrick Le Bras - *guitar, keyboards, vocals*, **Michel Munier** - *bass*, **Philippe Bersan** - *vocals, keyboards, percussion*.

The second half of the '70s gives birth to one of the most fascinating and peculiar creatures of French prog. Declared **Magma** fans, they courageously and uncommonly choose to use only percussions instead of the usual drums. Their only album is a gem of the genre, characterized by a vibrating jazz-rock with tense and dark atmospheres, very close to zeuhl. They unleash an overwhelming energy and a very original personality through obsessive rhythms, a powerful bass, dreamy vocals, spacey keyboards and psychedelic guitars. Brave, obscure, even Lovecraft would have chosen their music as a soundtrack for his tales.

DISCOGRAPHY: ARCHAÏA *(1977, CC).*

M.G. & C.C.

ARIEL KALMA

In the French pop rock panorama he is known for his experimental and avant-garde music explorations: fearlessly arrangements with sonorities of unknown or lost (and found) instruments. Of his several albums, the first two auto-produced in 1975, *Ariel* and *Le Temps Des Moissons*, are homemade experiments with sounds deriving from any sort of musical instrument. The first recording is probably the best: deeply influenced by one of his travels to India, he merges together tunes apparently long gone to his personal European background; each album cover is hand-drawn and duly numbered by he himself, probably to reduce the expenses.

DISCOGRAPHY: ARIEL *(private pressing, 1975)* **LE TEMPS DES MOISSONS** *(private pressing, 1975)* **NOISES (OSMOSE with Richard Tinti)** *(Beta Lactam Ring, 1978)* **INTERFREQUENCE** *(Montparnasse, 1979).*

C.A. & C.C.

Europe: FRANCE

ASIDE BESIDE

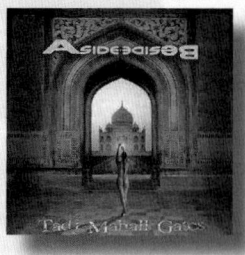

Lionel Giardina - *lead vocals, guitar,* **Frédéric Woff** - *keyboards, drums, percussion, contrabbasso,* **Vincent Chevalier** - *vocals, keyboards, piano,* **Pascal Riaux** - *guitars,* **Tristan Péan** - *bass.*
Their only record *Tadj Mahall Gates* of 2002 is both a delicate recording and a vigorously compelling work of lulling Canterbury school dreams. In fact the strength of this album is its colorful and polymorphic mix of smart prog contaminations of all kinds, like symphonic prog, jazz and space rock, **Wyatt**-styled vocals and elements from **Oldfield**, **Echolyn** and **King Crimson**, obtaining a surprisingly positive final result. Sadly after this a good release the band disappears. Their official web-site is full of info and pictures, as if still waiting for them to publish something new.

DISCOGRAPHY: **TADJ MAHALL GATES** *(2002, Musea).*   M.G. & C.C.

AVARIC

Lionel Baillemont - *guitars, bass, vibes, keyboards,* **Frank Lopez** - *vocals, dulcimer, flute, guitars,* **Jean-Marie Noël** - *percussion,* **Patrick Aubailly, Eric Milhiet** – *vocals, flute, organ.*
Interesting but not so known, this is a project of the poly-instrumentalist **Lionel Baillemont**. Very similar to **Malicorne**, the talented musicians play beautiful melodies adorned with delicate vocals. The three albums published from 1979 to 1981 are all very compelling, but of course pay the price of being released during a very difficult moment for this kind of genre. From album covers to the very lyrics, everything recalls a suspended realm between medieval sounds and a sadness rich of poetic elegy. A complete re-edition of their works with other added unreleased tracks has been issued recently.

DISCOGRAPHY: **AVARIC** *(private pressing, 1979)* **PAUVRE SENS ET PAUVRE MEMOIRE** *(private pressing, 1980)* **ROTROUENGES DU MÉCHANT AMOUR** *(private pressing, 1981)*   M.G. & C.C.

EMMANUEL BOOZ

This timid musician starts his career at the end of 1969 with his French version of **Arlo Guthrie**'s *Alice's Restaurant*, demonstrating an extraordinary talent, but unfortunately of no real commercial impact. His following albums *Le jour où les Vaches* and *Clochard* are rich of experimentations where he mixes different styles with his very own sense of melancholy. In 1979 *Dans quelle etat J'erre* is recorded with the collaboration of excellent session men like **Jean Louis Mahiun** on the bass. A well balanced recording with a very high quality of predominant electric and acoustic guitars, probably his best album.

DISCOGRAPHY: **AU RESTAURANT D'ALICE** *(Barclay, 1969)* **LE JOUR OU LES VACHES** *(Atlantic, 1970)* **CLOCHARD** *(Atlantic, 1976)* **DANS QUEL ETAT J'ERRE** *(Polydor, 1979).*   C.A. & C.C.

CAFEINE

Christophe Houssin - *keyboards,* **Patrick Jobard** - *guitar, backing vocals,* **Philippe Ladousse** - *vocals,* **Jean-Christophe Lamoreux** - *bass, sitar,* **Herve Morel** - *drums e percussion.*
Both good albums are important to the French new prog genre. The first *La Citadelle* is very pleasant and well structured, a well arranged symphonic prog with violin and flute that give it its mysterious medieval atmospheres. The second, *Nouveaux Mondes*, takes six years to see the light and will be defined by the French Press as a good answer to **Alan Parsons Project**. Interesting ho each song alternates different singers. All the lyrics are sung in French.

DISCOGRAPHY: **LA CITADELLE** *(Musea, 1994)* **NOUVEAUX MONDES** *(Musea, 2000).*   C.A. & C.C.

Europe: FRANCE

CARPE DIEM

Christian Truchi - *keyboards, vocals,* **Claude-Marius David** - *sax, flute, percussion,* **Gilbert Abbenanti** - *guitar,* **Alain Berge** *bass,* **Alain Faraut** - *drums.*
This French band from Nice began playing in 1969 but will eventually published a first album, *En Regardant Passer Le Temps*, only in 1976, and a second, *Cueille Le Jour* one year later. Both albums are above average quality and their style is based on a romantic symphonic rock, rather well constructed especially in the instrumental parts which are mainly led by the keyboards. Horns and guitars also find their space and the overall musical structure shares some similarities with bands like **King Crimson**, **Genesis** and **Camel**. At times the vocals recall the typical French theatrical style common to Ange and to other bands of the French prog rock arena.
DISCOGRAPHY: EN REGARDANT PASSER LE TEMPS *(1976, Arcane)* **CUEILLE LE JOUR** *(1977, Crypto).* M.G. & C.C.

CHÊNE NOIR (Théâtre du Chêne Noir)

Gérard Gelas - *musical director, drums, percussion,* **Nicole Aubiat** - *vocals, percussion,* **Bénédicte Maulet** - *vocals,* **Pierre Surtel** - *flute, saxophones, vocals,* **Guy Paquin** - *cello, trumpet, vocals,* **Daniel Dublet** - *guitar, vocals, percussion,* **Jean Marie Redon** - *flute, vocals.*
Also called **Théâtre du Chêne Noir**, this band of 1966 was born as a theatrical ensemble led by the genial artist **Gelas**. In 1971 he decides to start recording their music, a complex and fascinating avant-garde with jazz elements similar to other bands that were experimenting in that period. Greatly inspired by **Coltrane** and **Mingus**, the band manages to arrange their compositions in a more minimal and experimental style close to the concrete music of **Pierre Henry**. Of course the four operas published lack the visual element of their representations, a detail that must be kept in mind, yet the result is still very involving like the charming *Aurora*.
RECOMMENDED RECORDINGS: AURORA *(Futura, 1971)* **CHANT POUR LE DELTA, LA LUNE ET LE SOLEIL** *(Chêne Noir Disques, 1974).* M.G. & C.C.

CLIVAGE

André Fertier - *guitar, keyboards,* **Armand Lemal** - *percussion,* **Patricio Villaruel** - *tabla,* **Jean-Pierre de Barba** - *saxophones,* **Claude Duhaut** - *bass,* **Mahmoud Tabrizi-Zadeh** - *violin,* **Jean Querlier** - *winds,* **Michel Delaporte** - *tabla,* **Claude Salmieri** - *drums,* **Brigitte Toulson** - *vocals,* **Christian Gentet** - *bass.*
A jazz-rock band who inserts the typical progressive rock influences of Indie for their extraordinary debut album, *Regina Astris* of 1977. The second *Mixtus Orbis* is a reprise of the previous themes in a more symphonic key, always tightly linked to very ethnic atmospheres. Six years after this release of 1979 **Fertier** organizes the publishing of a new record entitled *Kassiopee*, a good album but quite distant from the previous two.
DISCOGRAPHY: REGINA ASTRIS *(Gratte Ciel, 1977)* **MIXTUS ORBIS** *(Gratte Ciel, 1979)* **KASSIOPEE** *(Rumeur, 1985).* C.A. & C.C.

ECLAT

Alain Chiarazzo - *guitar, vocals,* **Fabrice Di Mondo** - *drums,* **Pascal Versini, Thierry Massé** - *keyboards,* **Laurent Thomann, Bruno Ramousse, Philippe Troisi** - *bass.*
Pet creature of **Alain Chiarazzo**, this powerful guitarist founds the band in 1989 and deserves a role in the history France's new prog. Constant trademarks are the elegance and melodic skills of each musician, finally proven by the debut album *Eclat De Vers* that was recorded only in 1991. Greatly inspired by **Camel** and **Hackett** (**Genesis**), their music moves smoothly through poetic and symphonic structures and spreads fresh jazz-rock arrangements with grace up to the limits of folk and new age.
DISCOGRAPHY: ECLAT DE VERS *(MSI, 1991)* **ECLAT II** *(Musea, 1992)* **VOLUME 3** *(Musea,1997)* **ECLAT EN CONCERT 1998 MARSEILLES/TOKYO** *(live, Musea 1999)* **LE CRI DE LA TERRE** *(Musea, 2002)* **L'ESPRIT DU CERCLE** *(Musea, 2012).* M.G. & C.C.

Europe: FRANCE

EDEN ROSE

Jean-Pierre Alarcen - *guitar*, **Christian Clairefond** - *bass*, **Henri Garella** - *hammond organ*, **Michel Jullien** - *drums*.

This very skillful and talented quartet from Marseille starts its career at the beginning of '70s with a good album *On The Way To Eden* of symphonic rock music on the wake of **Procol Harum**'s success. They add the personal touch of certain interesting jazz-rock experiments that improve the over-all vigor and results to have a more fresh effect. This album was not a success for the general audience probably due to the fact that it is a completely instrumental. The very impressive Hammond organ perfectly blends with the guitar of **Pierre Alarcen**, who will later transforms this band into the famous **Sandrose**.
DISCOGRAPHY: **ON THE WAY TO EDEN** *(Katema, 1970).*   C.A. & C.C.

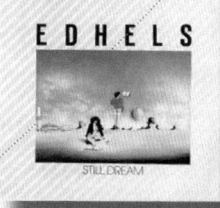

EDHELS

Marc Ceccotti - *guitars, keyboards, bass, vocals*, **Noel Damon, Philippe Peratonerre, Jean-Marc Bastianelli** - *keyboards*. **Jean-Luis Suzzoni** - *guitars*, **Sandrine Brisson** - *violin*, **Jacky Rosati** - *drums*.
A true institution of French prog with a very interesting discography, almost monitoring the evolution of new prog in Europe. The band born in 1980 and still active today even if they have been quiet for some time now, recalls the Italian **Malibran** or **Notturno Concertante**. Their founder **Marc Ceccotti** is a very talented poly-instrumentalist from Monte Carlo, who leads them through six studio recordings and a live album of symphonic rock, new age, fusion, Canterbury sounds, unplugged and brainy art-rock music. In 1993 **Ceccotti** starts his own parallel solo career of other nine intriguing productions, while *Saltimbanques* of 2003 is the last album at the moment for the band.
RECOMMENDED RECORDINGS: **THE BURSTING** *(Edhels, 1981)* **ORIENTAL CHRISTMAS** *(Musea, 1985)* **ASTRO-LOGICAL** *(Edhels, 1991)* **SALTIMBANQUES** *(Mellow Records, 2003).*   M.G. & C.C.

EDITION SPÉCIALE

Mimì Lorenzini - *guitar, vocals*, **Ann Ballester** - *keyboards, vocals*, **Josquin Turenne Des Press, Francois Grillot** - *bass, vocals*, **Francois Bouchet D'Angely, Alan Gouillard** – *drums*, **Mireille Bauer** - *percussion*.

Typical jazz-rock band of the mid '70s, they were greatly inspired by the sound of **Brand X**, **Al Di Meola** and **Santana**. Guitarist and founder **Mimì Lorenzini** began playing professionally since the early '70s, until he meets singer and keyboardist **Ann Ballester** thus gathering up an impressive line-up (**Mireille Bauer** from **Gong**) and releasing three albums of polyphonic melodies of good taste, with elegant soft tunes and delicate hints of funky, creating a style that results close to the Canterbury School and to **Gong**'s album *Shamal*.
DISCOGRAPHY: **ALLÉE DES TILLEULS** *(United Artists, 1976)* **ALIQUANTE** *(RCA, 1977)* **HORIZON DIGITAL** *(RCA, 1978).*   M.G. & C.C.

EMERAUDE

Bernadette Simonet - *piano*, **Gilles Escoffier** - *guitar*, **Dominique Falchon** - *guitar*, **Gilles Baud** - *bass, vocals, guitar*, **Didier Chas** - *drums*, **Jean Paul Ansart** - *keyboards*.

Among the musical gems of the French '80s, *Geoffroy* is small masterpiece in its own right, work of sublime grace, led by the electro-acoustic sounds of piano, guitars and keyboards. Full of melancholic poems and delicate melodies that surround the compositions with a magic aura. A very particular album of delicate soft symphonic rock with medieval and folk ideas, all sung in English. The second album entitled *Voyageur* will be released only in 2000 and is quite short of the little miracle of twenty years back.
DISCOGRAPHY: **GEOFFROY** *(1980, private pressing)* **VOYAGEUR** *(2000, private pressing).*   M.G. & C.C.

Europe: FRANCE

EMERGENCY EXIT

Robert Latxague – *guitar, vocals,* **Pierre Maggioni** - *bass, acoustic guitar,* **Michel Lacrouts** – *electric piano, percussion,* **Roger Levy** – *drums, percussion,* **Pierre Camy** - *flute.*

A band with a very short life, and with an unique album, the **Emergency Exit** recorded in 1976 *Sortie De Secours*, witb a clear inspiration to the jazz rock of Canterbury, united to the sound characteristics of the French period of the first 70's, and so with the use of psychedelic sounds, French singing and some links to the zeuhl and the avanguardian jazz. The album was composed by three long pieces, quite homogeneous between them, and well documented by the potentiality of the band, perfectly inserted in an excellent composition's field. We can find a strong differences with the band of the same nationality, in the extended use of the singing parts, often well united to the flute, so that they could not have harmonic problems. Some member of the band stayed in the French jazz field.

RECOMMENDED RECORDINGS: SORTIE DE SECOURS *(Pole Records, 1976).* M.G. & C.C.

ERGO SUM

Lionel Ledissez – *vocals, percussion,* **Jean Guerin** – *flute, keyboards,* **Michel Leonardi** - *guitars,* **Roland Meynet** – *violin, acoustic guitar,* **Max Touat** – *bass, acoustic guitar,* **B. B. Brutus** – *drums, percussion.*

Authors of an album entitled *Mexico* published in 1971, they were playing together already since 1968 when **Ledissez** and **Guerin** began experimenting contaminations of jazz and blues with the psychedelic-rock genre. The English lyrics were sung by **Ledissez** with a strong blues acid and raucous voice similar to **Roger Chapman** of **Family**; yet his true crystal vocals shine brightly in other tracks, decidedly more melodic. Never too long, the songs were a good concentrated mix of singing and instrumental parts, with excellent solos between jazz and more traditional rock.

RECOMMENDED RECORDINGS: MEXICO *(Thélème, 1971).* M.G. & C.C.

EX VITAE

Jean Lars - *bass,* **Jacques Lars** - *lead guitar,* **Jean-Michelle Philippe** - *guitars,* **Jean-Loup Marlaud** - *saxophones, horns, flute,* **René-Marc Bini** - *keyboards,* **Marc Millon** - *drums, vibes, percussion,* **Alain Labarsouque** - *viola.*

A band from Limoges who auto-produced an only album entitled *Mandarine* in 1978. This private publishing was never re-issued therefore rendering the few existing copies an incredibly rare item. The four tracks within are in an open jazz of clear prog-rock trend, broadly using the Canterbury and avant-garde themes. The technique is very valid, comparable to certain virtuosities of **Soft Machine** or **Moving Gelatine Plates**, with classic jazz-rock hints and sometimes zeuhl cues. Beautiful violin parts, electric piano waterfalls, the incredibly talented rapidity of the bass, all converge into dreamy flutes or into the sax solos, often similar to **Elton Dean**'s style.

RECOMMENDED RECORDINGS: MANDARINE *(Private Press, 1978).* M.G. & C.C.

NINO FERRER

Giorgio Giombolini – *organ,* **Slim Pezin** – *guitar,* **Lucien Dobat** - *drums,* **Donald Rieubon** – *drums,* **Allan Reeves** - *keyboards,* **Jean Mandengué** – *bass,* **Les Krapoutchick** - *backing vocals,* **Pierre Dutour** – *trumpet,* **Nino Ferrer** – *vocals.*

Nino Ferrer (Agostino Ferrari) is an Italian born but naturalized French citizen, who became famous with some successful pop songs at first in Italy during the early '60s and then in his home country. *Metronòmie* of 1971 should be considered as his masterpiece, with the long instrumental prog-rock compositions, very well performed, and greatly contaminated by soul and jazz. "La Maison près de la Fontaine" is his most famous hit single (half a million sold copies of the 45RPM format which came out in parallel although already in the album). This and his other works are almost unknown to the general public for he is best remembered as the beat-troubadour who committed suicide in 1998.

RECOMMENDED RECORDINGS: METRONÒMIE *(1971, Riviera).* M.G.

Europe: **FRANCE**

FLAMEN DIALIS

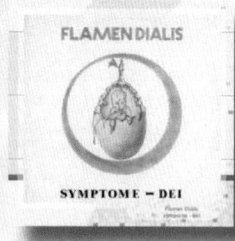 

Y.H. Le Gallic – *keyboards, vocals,* **D. Le Gallic** - *keyboards, drums,* **M. Le Saout Chant** – *guitars,* **A. Ernouf** – *vocals, flute, tuba,* **B.B. L'Helgouch** - *vocals,* **J.J. Chenn** – *vocals.*

Their only album of 1979, *Symptome-Dei*, is a very personal and inventive work, full of electronic experiments reprising classical themes like the particular blend of **Pink Floyd** and **Ravel**. Many choral voices accompany the sometimes repetitive and obsessive middle-eastern sounds, or the epic and evocative sequences dominated by a strong rhythmic section which can also be absolutely missing. The particular merging of Mellotron and modern synths with some German electronics of the early '70s, creates surreal and dreamy atmospheres that seem to spark the intense and beautiful instrumental improvisations. An unique and charming work.

RECOMMENDED RECORDINGS: **SYMPTOME - DEI** *(FLVM, 1979).* **M.G. & C.C.**

PATRICK FORGAS

Patrick Forgas – *drums, vocals, percussion, guitar, bass, organ,* **Jean-Pierre Fouquey** – *keyboards,* **Gérard Prévost** – *bass,* **Laurent Roubach** – *guitar,* **Patrick Tilleman** – *violin,* **Patrick Lemercier** – *violin,* **François Debricon** – *saxophones, flute,* **Bruce Grant** - *saxophones.*

Greatly inspired by **Wyatt** (considered his French alter-ego), he is strongly devoted to the Canterbury sounds and in his first album *Cocktail* of 1977 he also very well mixes other forms of avant-garde, never too heavy nor over the line. After a long pause, he still shows his desire to surprise with other albums not always of prog, restarting again his solo career in 1990. Alone he publishes altogether four albums, but on the side he creates a parallel project named the **Forgas** Band **Phenomena** with other four releases: among these, *Soleil 12* of 2005 is the prog come-back, with his typical elegance and the excellency of the musical styles contaminated.

RECOMMENDED RECORDINGS: **COCKTAIL** *(Gratte-Ciel, 1977)* **SOLEIL 12** *(Cuneiform, 2005).* **M.G.**

GRIME

Didier Duval - *guitar, vocals,* **Thierry Duval** - *keyboards, lead vocals,* **Marc Nion** - *saxophones, flute, vocals,* **Nick Vicente** - *bass,* **Didier Morando** - *drums.*

Although born at the end of '70s and disbanded in 1982, they published only one auto-produced homonym album in 1979 of French classic symphonic prog, with theatrical singing and calm atmospheres. The very personal style recalls the works of **Atoll** and **Ange**, but also the less famous *Skryvania* share certain sound affinities. The short tracks develop in a traditional manner with choral or sung parts often recited and the perhaps not too generous use of keyboards is counterbalanced by broad sax partitions and hints of **King Crimson**. Recently re-issued by Musea, the CD contains other 6 bonus live tracks recorded in 1981.

RECOMMENDED RECORDINGS: **GRIME** *(stampa privata, 1979 - Rist. Musea, 1992).* **M.G. & C.C.**

HALLOWEEN

Gilles Coppin - *keyboards, vocals,* **Jean-Philippe Brun** - *violin, guitars, lead vocals, bass,* **Philippe Di Faostino** - *drums, percussion,* **Yann Honoré** - *bass,* **Jean-François Delcamp** - *acoustic guitar, lute, bass,* **Geraldine Le Cocq** - *lead vocals,* **Jena-Pierre Mallet** - *guitars,* **Christophe Dagorn** - *bass,* **Stéphane Kerihnel** - *guitar,* **Emmannuel Martre** - *bass.*

Their debut of 1988 is still characterized by the '80s new-prog style but with a darker vein and the gloomy sound of a violin. With the third album of 1994 *Merlin* they finally turn to a more personal shady symphonic rock through a very classical reinterpretation of King Arthur's myth (with strings and woodwinds) and full of creepy magical atmospheres. Also interesting the live recording *Silence.. au dernier rang!* of 1998 while their last of 2011, *Le Festin*, is not at the same level.

RECOMMENDED RECORDINGS: **MERLIN** *(1994, Musea).* **M.G. & C.C.**

Europe: FRANCE

IRIS

Tony Carbonare - *bass, vocals,* **Alain Carbonare** - *keyboards, vocals,* **Gilbert Henry** - *drums,* **Gerard Carpagli** - *guitars.*
This mysterious and almost unknown band founded by brothers **Tony** and **Alain Carbonare** (the latter will later join **Wurtemberg**) produced only one album in 1972 entitled Litanies, a fresh and pleasant progressive folk similar to some works of **Ange**. The excellent guitars and keyboards of "Jus de Citron", probably the best track in the album, or "Oracle" and the aleatoric atmospheres of dreamy folk which ignite "Ballade pour une Minette Plastique" as well as all the other songs. Recently reissued also on CD.
DISCOGRAPHY: LITANIES *(Sonopresse, 1972).*   C.A. & C.C.

JANNICK TOP

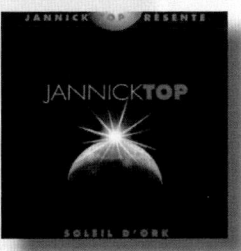

Greatly respected for the powerful sound of his excellent and innovative bass style (**Magma** musician), his solo career begins in 1975 with the compelling single Utopia Viva containing two zeuhl tracks reissued later in *Soleil d'Ork*, a CD published in 2001 by Utopic Records, the label he owns and under which most of his discography falls. Among the many projects he entertains, the **Utopic Sporadic Orchestra** is probably one of the best with its huge line-up, almost twenty musicians also from **Magma**: a temporary overnight Zeuhl band which played in the festival of Nancy Jazz Pulsations on October 1975 a spectacular version of "De Futura". The only record of this incredible orchestra came out only in 2001 as *Nancy 75* with Jannick's other live sessions or rehearsals as bonus tracks.
RECOMMENDED RECORDINGS: Jannick Top: SOLEIL D'ORK *(2001, Utopic Records)* **Utopic Sporadic Orchestra: NANCY 75** *(2001, Utopic Records) .*   M.G. & C.C.

MANU LANNHUEL

A small masterpiece for the French acid-folk genre with its spectral and absolutely gloomy prog atmospheres, this homonym debut of 1976 is an Breton folk album of great songs with an ever present and intensely emotional voice singing stunning psychedelic tunes. With hardly any kind of instrumental breaks, the fuzzing rock guitar leads through the melodies supported by a very inventive and jazzy drummer. The artist will release other albums but never as magical and not of prog.
RECOMMENDED RECORDINGS: MANU LANNHUEL *(Iris, 1976).*   M.G. & C.C.

MALICORNE

Gabriel Yacoub, Marie Yacoub, Hughes de Courson, Laurent Vercambre – *Hurdy-Gurdy, guitars, dulcimer, percussion, flute, vocals.*
Gabriel Yacoub was a former musician in **Alan Stivell**'s band, but after many artistic divergences due to the leader's Celtic tendencies, he decides to leave and publishes in 1973 a first album, Pierre de Grenoble, with his wife **Marie Sauvet**, known also as **Marie Yacoub** or **Marie de Malicorne**. Immediately after, they form **Malicorne** together with **Hughes de Courson** and **Laurent Vercambre**, a folk band which constantly uses traditional acoustic instruments like the Hurdy Gurdy, the auto-harp and the dulcimer. The delicate and complex arrangements create atmospheres that belong to the best folk-prog galaxy, gently merging with the electric guitar and the powerful vocals of the magical singing duo. In 2011 a reunion concert for the nostalgics and released in DVD.
RECOMMENDED RECORDINGS: MALICORNE *(1974, Hexagone)* **EN PUBLIC** *(1979, CBS).*   M.G. & C.C.

Europe: FRANCE

ALAIN MARKUSFELD

Alain Markusfeld - *guitar, bass, piano, keyboards,* **Joel Dugreneau** - *basso,* **Geza Fenzl** - *drums,* **Laurent Thibault** - *electric piano,* **Dominique Blanc - Francart** - *synthesizer.*
Poly instrumentalist but above all guitarist of incredible technique who began his career influenced by the psychedelia at the end of the '60s. Le Monde En Etages was published in 1970, a very lysergic work with fascinating songs recalling the early **Pink Floyd** and based on his particular guitar style, rhythmic and always filling in all the gaps. More complex the following album, Le Son Tombè du Ciel, with its interesting ethnic and hard space-rock intrusions, sometimes even similar to **Led Zeppelin**'s the third album. Different yet still good is also his second phase which goes from 1977 to 1981: 4 other albums with jazz-fusion elements and traces of ethnic and middle-eastern hints.
RECOMMENDED RECORDINGS: LE SON TOMBÉ DU CIEL *(Barclay, 1971)* PLATOCK *(Egg, 1978).*
M.G. & C.C.

MEMORIANCE

Jean-Francois Perier - *keyboards, vocals,* **Didier Guillamat** - *lead vocals,* **Jean-Pierre Boulais** - *guitars, vocals,* **Michel Aze** - *bass, vocals,* **Didier Busson** - *batteria, percussion,* **Claude Letaillenter** - *rhythm guitar, sound engineer.*
A symphonic prog band singing in their mother tongue a music that often results very far from the French characteristics, although the vocals maintain them completely through the theatrical lyrics also sometimes recited similarly to **Ange**. Their first album of 1976 contains two long and two short tracks with a quite articulated sound, decidedly nearer to English bands such as **Pink Floyd** and **Procol Harum**. Here the predominant guitars share the roles of rhythmical and solo instrument, sometimes recalling **Gilmour**, sometimes **Hackett**'s style. Less appreciated their second album with shorter tracks and decidedly more rhythm though maintaining beautiful melodic lines and the dramatic atmospheres.
RECOMMENDED RECORDINGS: ET APRÉS *(Eurodisc, 1976).*
M.G. & C.C.

MOSAÏC

Yves Brebion - *guitar, piano, vocals,* **Hubert Brebion** - *drums,* **Jean-Yves Escoffier** - *guitar, keyboards,* **Philippe Lemongne** - *bass, synthesizers.*
French progressive avant-garde band, they formed around the personalities of **Yves** and **Hubert Brebion** leaving only one record to testify their great instrumental skills. Published in 1978, Ultimatum is a pleasant mix of styles very near to jazz-rock, trespassing into fusion and with an obvious tribute to the Canterbury sounds and to classical music. Echoes of **Hatfield & the North** and some harmonies from **King Crimson** are present here and there, but the most impressive thing is the powerful virtuosity in certain free-jazz textures like "Un trop" or the meditative moments of "Souvenirs". Recently it was reissued on CD in 2003 with added unpublished tracks.
DISCOGRAPHY: ULTIMATUM *(Ekimoz, 1978)* ULTIMATUM...PLUS *(MIO, 2003).*
C.A. & C.C.

NADAVATI

Jaques Liot - *guitar, percussion,* **Patrice Freequentin** -*saxophones, flute,* **Mico Nissim** - *keyboards,* **Alain Lecointe** - *bass, percussion,* **Didier Hauck** - *drums, percussion.*
Another one shot band whose sound tends more to jazz and fusion than to real prog, they were considered a sort of Chicago clone from which they emulate perfectly the use of woodwinds and keyboard arrangements. The 1978 Le vent de l'esprit souffle où il veut is a typical jazz-rock album with few zeuhl elements stolen from **Mahavishnu Orchestra** and mixed with compelling horn solos (a very impressive flute) led by composer **Jacques Liot**'s electric guitar. High energy and passionate playing with the fabulous bass lines of **Alain Lecointe** (**Serge Bringolf's Strave**, **Alain Eckert**, **Hamsa Music**), the record also features stars like **Richard Raux** (**Magma**) and **Lionel Ledissez** (**Ergo Sum**).
DISCOGRAPHY: LE VENT DE L'ESPRIT SOUFFLE OU IL VEUT *(IPG, 1978).*
C.A. & C.C.

Europe: FRANCE

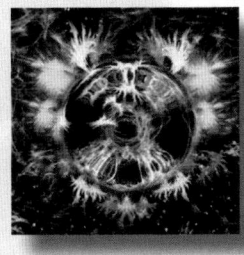

NEBELNEST

Cyril Malderez, Sébastien Carmona - *guitars*, **Michael Anselmi** - *drums*, **Gregory Tejedor** - *bass*, **Olivier Tejedor** - *keyboards*.

This quartet formed in 1997 is one of the top European avant-garde rock bands that prove prog can mix multiple styles and still be aggressive, metal, and zeuhl with a psychedelic guitar and the symphonic keyboards. Their first stunning self-titled debut of 1999 impresses the international music world albeit being at the same time quite difficult to listen to for the dark, storming flames between a mid '70s **King Crimson**, **Magma** and **High Tide**. The following work improves the formula but with less concentrated creativity. The third album is published in 2006 with a line-up change and a forth is yet to come.
DISCOGRAPHY: NEBELNEST *(Cuneiform, 1999)* **NOVA EXPRESS** *(Cuneiform, 2002)* **ZEPTO** *(Cuneiform, 2006)*.
M.G. & C.C.

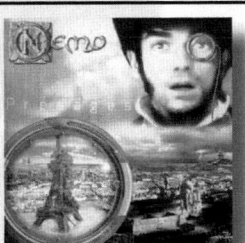

NEMO

Pascal Bertrand - *drums, percussion*, **Pierre Louveton** - *guitars, vocals*, **Guillaume Fontaine** - *keyboards*, **Benoit Gaignon** - *bass*.
Not to be confused with the homonym 70's French eclectic-prog band, this new-prog group of 1999 releases a first record of 2002 entitled *Les Nouveax Mondes*. Yet it is with their second album *Présages* that they achieve a true success all around the world, with sounds very similar to **Rush**. The strong keyboard arrangements tend toward jazz-rock, with stunning instrumental breaks and atmosphere changes typical of the classic prog genre. A great discography with beautiful artworks on the covers of their albums which helped largely to promote them in the most famous prog festivals.
RECOMMENDED RECORDINGS: LES NOUVEAUX MONDES *(Musea, 2002)* **PRÈSAGES** *(Musea, 2003)* **IMMERSION PUBLIQUE - LIVE** *(Musea, 2005)* **SI PARTIE 1** *(Musea, 2006)*.
M.G.

NOETRA

Jean Lapouge - *guitar*, **Christian Paboeuf** - *flute, oboe*, **Daniel Renault** - *drums*, **Denis Lefranc** - *bass*, **Pierre Aubert** - *violin*, **Pascal Leberre** - *horns*, **Francis Michaud** - *horns, flute*, **Denis Vollet** - *cello*, **Claude Lapouge** - *horns*, **Laurent Tardif** - *flute*.

An amazing line-up led by **Lapouge**, who was able to mix in an excellent way chamber music and avant-garde with progressive jazz-rock in Canterbury style. Only two albums, the first *Neuf Songes* of 1992, rich of melodic pathos, delicate harps, flutes and strings charmingly move through the soft oboe parts recalling **Soft Machine** with **Nucleus** tonalities and the finesse of certain violin passages similar to **Mahavishnu Orchestra** or even **After Crying**. The second album *Definitivement Bleus* is the recovery of material recorded from 1978 to 1982, confirming how this is not an impromptu band who came out of nowhere despite the limited discography.
RECOMMENDED RECORDINGS: NEUF SONGES *(Musea, 1992)*.
M.G. & C.C.

NYL

Michel Peteau - *guitar*, **Stephane Rossini** - *drums*, **Bernard Lavialle** - *guitars*, **Patrick Fontaine** - *bass*, **Elizabeth Wiener** - *vocals*, **Loy** - *keyboards*, **Ariel Kalma, Patrick Quentin** - *saxophones*, **Jannick Top** - *bass*.
A French rock commune, creature of guitarist **Michel Peteau**, enfant prodige from **Cheval Fou** that managed to gather many musicians and form, together with his drummer and alter-ego **Stephane Rossini**, this band during the early '70s. Their only album published by Urus in 1976, is the result of a pleasant recording session, arranged with care, sometimes recalling the early **King Crimson**. The music is affected by the incurable chronic psychedelia of this skillful ensemble sailing through the acid swamps in the attempt of adding a progressive touch to the whole with the presence of **Jannick Top** (**Magma** bass player). Sadly they disbanded immediately after but luckily this amazing piece of history was recently reissued in a CD version with bonus tracks in 2011.
DISCOGRAPHY: NYL *(Urus, 1975)*.
C.A. & C.C.

Europe: FRANCE

OCARINAH

Jean-Michel Valette - *keyboards, guitars*, **Marc Perdirx** - *bass*, **Charles Bevand** - *drums*.

A French space-rock band deeply inspired by the experimental sonorities of the Canterbury school. Their only album of 1978 is a remarkable instrumental work, very close to the saturated keyboards of **Egg**, with a fascinating Hammond Organ and its compelling distortions that somewhat recall the more spacey **Gong** and **Soft Machine**. Sometimes their avant-garde and jazz-rock style is constellated with sparks of clear zeuhl influences. This stunning trio find skillful instrumental solutions rendering their music an unpredictable job of fantasy and acrobatic rhythms.
DISCOGRAPHY: PREMIÈRE VISION DE L'ÉTRANGE *(1978, Calypsia).* **M.G. & C.C.**

ORION

Franck Mamosa - *guitar*, **Janusz Tokarz** - *keyboards*, **Laurent Delenne** - *flute, vocals*.

French theatrical symphonic band who publish at first a 45RPM in 1977 called Folie and then in 1979 the album *La Nature Vit, L'homme Lui, Critique...* also containing the previous single. Their very dramatic and original style results even more magnificent than **Ange** and more melodic than **Camel**: well rooted in their country's folk-pop music, they also touch ecologist themes unusual for the times, yet the insertion of more trivial songs often damaged the global picture. Although good and well appreciated they do not survive the raging novelties and disband soon after the LP release. Their keyboardist resumes the name and with a different line-up recently published another two albums in 2013 and 2015.
DISCOGRAPHY: LA NATURE VIT, L'HOMME LUI CRITIQUE *(Sofrason, 1979).* **C.A. & C.C.**

OSE

Hervé Picart - *moog, organ, guitar, bass*, **Richard Pinhas** - *moog, ARP & EMS synthesizers*, **Francois Auger** - *drums*.

Musical critic and poly-instrumentalist **Picart** joins forces with two **Heldon** musicians, **Pinhas** and **Auger**, and together they release in 1978 the electronic album *Adonia*. Greatly inspired by the styles of Wright and **Gilmour**, the references are quite obvious like in the suite "Approche Sur A" where **Pink Floyd**'s *Shine On You Crazy Diamond* is openly quoted. A classy work of great intelligence with typical cosmic moments of the German space genre, like certain incursions similar to **Fripp**'s guitar playing and the cyber grooves created by sequencers, mini-Moog and the drone music of the synths.
RECOMMENDED RECORDINGS: ADONIA *(Egg, 1978).* **M.G. & C.C.**

PATHAPHONIE

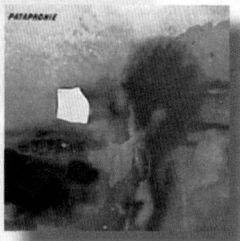 

Pierre Demouron – *bass*, **Gilles Rousseau** - *drums percussion*, **André Viaud** – *guitars*, **Bernard Audureau** – *keyboards (first album only)*.

Born in the early '70s, they produced two albums in the style of **Soft Machine**'s Third with the jazz-rock and avant-garde of **Henry Cow** and fragments which recall certain solo works of **Hugh Hopper**. The predominance of improvisation and the insertion of experimental elements from kraut and zeuhl, go from **King Crimson** the classical world of **Debussy**, determining a more open and personal fusion. The first record *Pataphonie* of 1975 is a collection of live recordings from 1972 to 1975, often completely improvised, while the second *Le Matin Blanc* of 1978 (similar to **Hathfield and the North**) was reissued in a CD version in 1999 with some bonus tracks of more recent concerts.
RECOMMENDED RECORDINGS: LE MATIN BLANC *(Féerimusic, 1978).* **M.G. & C.C.**

Europe: FRANCE

PERCEPTION

Yochk'o Seffer – *saxophones, clarinet*, **Siegfried Kessler** - *piano*, **Didier Levallet** - *bass*, **Jean-My Truong** - *drums*.
Their leader **Seffer** is probably more famous for his future **Magma** and **Zao** career, or as a soloist, yet with this band he lays down the grounds of an excellent avant-garde jazz-rock. Not simple to listen to, the first homonym album of 1971 is a bridge between the British jazz experimentations (London and Canterbury) of **Nucleus** and **Soft Machine** and that of **Miles Davis**. His strong personality develops very serious pieces, structured for technique and destructured in the compositions, often free and improvised. The 300 copies of *Perception & Friends* (1972) confirm the previous high level and quality as does the live album *Mestari* of 1974, both reissued on CD.
RECOMMENDED RECORDINGS: PERCEPTION (Futura, 1971). M.G. & C.C.

PHILHARMONIE

Frédéric L'Epée - *guitars, piano*, **Laurent Chalef** - *guitars*, **Bernard Ros** - *guitars, bass, stick*.
Previous **Shylock** member, **Frèdèreic L'Epèe** is a devoted **Fripp** fan, so when in the late '80s he gets together with another two guitarists to form this particular all-sting-trio, it feels right but quite strange. Their first album of 1999, *Beau Soleil*, clears the skies of any remaining doubt: the ideas and plots of **King Crimson** inspiration merge to jazz, classical and minimalist chords, resulting incredibly charming and personal. Even better after signing up with label Cuineform. Changes in the line-up with added instruments do not interfere with the band's style and sound as in the fascinating and complex *Le Dernier Mot* of 1998.
RECOMMENDED RECORDINGS: LE DERNIER MOT (Cuneiform, 1998). M.G. & C.C.

POTEMKINE

Charles Goubin – *guitars, vocals*, **Michel Goubin** – *keyboards, vocals*, **Dominique Dubuisson** – *bass*, **Philippe Goubin** – *drums, percussion*.
In 1971 the **Goubin** brothers form a band playing songs from the **Rolling Stones** and from other famous rock groups. Then after listening to **Weather Report** and **Miles Davis** in 1973, they finally undertake a more personal path towards jazz-prog, close to **Magma**'s zeuhl matrix. The following year they publish a 45 RPM and in 1975 their first album *Foetus*, also auto-produced and later distributed by Pole Records. Their sound, greatly inspired by the Canterbury school, is confirmed also in the second work entitled *Triton* (1977), recalling some of classical authors like **Varese** and **Bartock**, and indirectly **Frank Zappa**. *Nicolas II* of 1978 follows in the same steps.
RECOMMENDED RECORDINGS: TRITON (VST, 1977). M.G. & C.C.

PRIAM

Chris Casagrande - *guitars, synthesizers*, **Laurent Lacombe - Colomb** - *keyboards*, **Bertrand Hulin-Bertaud** - *bass*, **Emma M.** - *drums*.
A very underestimated French quartet playing an almost completely instrumental fusion, founded on the ashes of the late '80s prog-rock band **Arlequin**. *Three Distances... Irregular Signs* is their 1997 debut which blends fusion and symphonic rock with strong influences from **Pink Floyd** and **Robert Fripp** alternating electric and acoustic guitar moments with outstanding solos. In their second 2001 album *Diffraction* the musicians point toward new experimentation with marked **King Crimson** dissonances blended to avant-garde, ambient and electronic sounds with classical, jazz-rock or ethnic hints as well as a dose of retro space prog. Here they insert a real chorus and a female vocal quartet.
DISCOGRAPHY: ... 3 DISTANCES / IRREGULAR SIGNS (1997, Musea) **DIFFRACTION** (2001, Musea). M.G. & C.C.

Europe: **FRANCE**

RED NOISE

Patrick Vian - *guitar*, **Daniel Geoffroy** - *bass*, **Claude Senin** - *saxophones*, **Jean-Claude Cenci** - *saxophones*, **Philip Barry** - *drums*, **Marc Blanc** - *drums*, **Daniel Ceccaldi** - *bass*.

Criticized for emulating their idol **Frank Zappa**, their music is yet among the best examples of pioneers of the early '70s French pop avant-garde. Capable of unconventional sounds by mixing various genres and combining free-jazz with psychedelic rhythms and blues elements, they assembled into a single record all of these experiments: *Sarcelles Locheres* of 1971 is an album that tributes **Zappa** already from the artwork cover. Interesting the non-sense of the opening track "Cosmic toilet ditty" where the eclectic guitarist **Patrick Vian** wildly and thoroughly amuses himself, though today they may sound old, extreme, ironical and perhaps to heavily experimental.

DISCOGRAPHY: **SARCELLES LOCHERES** *(Futura, 1971).*   C.A. & C.C.

RIPAILLE

Patrick Audouin - *keyboards, percussion, vocals*, **Patrick Droguet** - *guitars, percussion*, **Michel Munoz** - *drums*, **Gérard Duchemann** - *lead vocals, keyboards*, **Jacquy Thomas** - *bass, keyboards, percussion, vocals*, **Robert Le Gall** – *violin*, **Jo Courtin** – *accordion*, **Pierre Holassian** – *saxophones*.

Another one shot band of 1977 that can be taken as a perfect example of symphonic prog with medieval and Renaissance elements which blending into a progressive folk with possible echoes of **Gryphon**. Short delicate tracks with soft and melodious singing parts, harps and electronic-acoustic waterfalls similar in certain points to *The Geese And The Ghost* by **Anthony Phillips**. Rare but interesting the jazz cues or the more complex instrumental parts, with alternating moments in which the vocal and the rhythmic elements recall **Gentle Giant** or some structures of **Magma** (without the zeuhl).

RECOMMENDED RECORDINGS: **LA VIEILLE QUE L'ON BRÛLA** *(Ballon Noir, 1977).*   M.G. & C.C.

WILLIAM SHELLER

Born as **William Hand**, this very open-minded musician finds few others like him in the entire world. Graduated at the Academy of Music in Paris, he applies his classical studies of harmony, counterpoint and the art of fugue to the pop genre (many the analogies with Italian composer **Franco Battiato**). Starting from the '60s Beat music he begins literally playing brainy games through his compositions with often escapades into the prog universe like in his first 1970 album *Lux Aeterna* which he writes for orchestra, chorus and rock band. The Baroque intro of "Le Nouveau Monde" (*Univers* of 1986) and his use of classical arrangements are another good representation: we will find him constantly rearranging his songs, old and new, like for vocals and orchestra one time and then for vocals, piano and string quintet the next.

RECOMMENDED RECORDINGS: **LUX AETERNA** *(CBS, 1970)* **UNIVERS** *(Mercury, 1987)* **CHEMIN DE TRAVERSE** *(Anthology, Mercury, 2005)* **AVATARS** *(Mercury, 2008).*   M.G. & C.C.

SOTOS

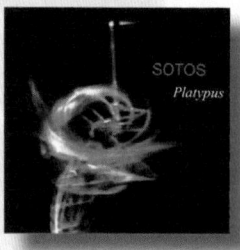

Nicolas Cazaux, **Nadia Leclerc** - *violin*, **Yan Hazera** - *guitars*, **Michael Hazera** - *drums*, **Bruno Camiade** - *bass*.

Heirs of **Magma** and **Univers Zero**'s French-Belgian tradition, this band moves under the label Cuneiform with two well-refined albums based upon strong doses of improvisation, echoes of **King Crimson** and a jazz-rock of wild and overwhelming sonorities. The excellent debut of 1999 and its 2002 sequel are both the result of **Yan** and **Michael Hazera**'s creative minds: a chamber-rock interpreted with dynamic vigor, especially in the second LP produced by Bob Drake. After the break-up the two brothers will move on to their next project, the R.I.O. avant-garde band **Zaar**.

DISCOGRAPHY: **SOTOS** *(Gazul, 1999)* **PLATYPUS** *(Gazul, 2002).*   M.G. & C.C.

Europe: FRANCE

SPEED LIMIT

George Jinda - *drums, percussion*, **Yochk'o Jeff Seffer** - *saxophones, flute, vocals*, **Jean-Louis Bucchi** - *keyboards, vocals*, **Joël Dud Dugrenot** - *bass*, **Shiroc** - *percussion*, **Jannick Top** - *bass, percussion, vocals*.

A jazz-rock quintet tending towards the jazz-prog of **Nucleus** due to the presence of **Magma** alumni with an attitude of ambitious experimentation. Their first album of 1974, Speed limit, is an instrumental record often criticized for being a bit too jazz, though it is actually a good example of the progressive vision of French jazz-rock with the stunning piano-sax duets of "Ballad to Laura Antonelli". In *Speed limit II* the experimental and dissonant atmospheres are more complex while the musical skills derive more from contemporary classical compositional structures (also adding a string quartet) like in the famous "Pastoral Idyl" similar to some works of **Pat Metheny**.

DISCOGRAPHY: SPEED LIMIT *(Le Chant Du Monde, 1974)* **SPEED LIMIT II** *(RCA, 1975).*   C.A. & C.C.

STEP AHEAD

Christian Robin - *guitar*, **Gerald Macia** - *acoustic guitar*, **Claudie Truchi** - *keyboards*, **Danny Brown** - *vocals*, **Claude Marius David** - *drums*.

In the wake of **Yes**, this French band is the pioneer version of what new-prog will become after the rise of the English **Marillion**. Their very personal style is also credited to the remarkable Irish singer **Danny Brown**. Their debut *Step Ahead* is published in 1982 (ante-**Marillion**) as a concept album narrating the adventures of a woman incarnating all the typical atmospheres of '70s called White Lady. A good and well balanced record with incredible guitar textures that blend perfectly with the keyboards in full **Yes** style. When the band seemed ready for a sequel (also noticed by **Alan Parsons**), they clashed with label RCA which deleted the contract killing any further project and the band itself.

DISCOGRAPHY: STEP AHEAD *(RCA, 1982).*   C.A. & C.C.

TAAL

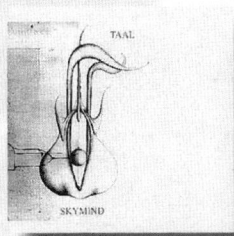

Anthony Gabard - *guitars*, **David Stuart Dosnon** - *bass*, **Loic Bernardeau** - *drums, vocals*, **Igor Polisset** - *percussion*, **Sebastien Constant** - *keyboards*, **Helene Sonnet** - *flute*, **David Lucas** - *vocals*.

French Prog band from Poitiers with two albums containing many music styles and turning them into a very surprising sound, with influences from jazz, metal, celtic, classical, baroque, electronic music, while playing a huge number of instruments. This ensemble of six musicians (including a string quartet) is structured like **Isildurs Bane** and their strength in the debut album of 2000 are of course the instrumental parts with very few lead vocals. The following album of 2003, *Skymind*, is one of the most ambitious and compelling works of Prog world in the last fifteen years, with a heavy use of the guitar work supported by the violin, sax and flute. Stylistically a classical symphonic album with some gypsy folk and metal hints.

DISCOGRAPHY: MISTER GREEN *(Musea, 2000)* **SKYMIND** *(Musea, 2003).*   M.G. & C.C.

TERPANDRE

Bernard Monerri - *guitar, percussion*, **Jacques Pina** - *keyboards*, **Michel Tardieu** - *keyboards*, **Patrick Tilleman** - *violin*, **Paul Fargier** - *bass*, **Michel Torelli** - *drums, percussion*.

Another one shot band for this classical influenced melodic progressive group of musicians whose only album was recorded in 1978 and self-released later in 1981 (reissued by Musea in 1988). It is a completely instrumental recording, a splendid concentrate of romanticism, class and feeling with great use of the keyboards: **Jacques Pina** and **Michel Tardieu** divide themselves between piano, electric piano, clavinet, mellotron and synthesizers. The guitar and electric violin play very compelling textures, well blending with the rest and sometimes adding some jazzy hints. A very fine and delicate record, similar to **Camel**, **Spring** and **Rousseau**.

DISCOGRAPHY: TERPANDRE *(1981, Dionysos).*   M.G. & C.C.

Europe: FRANCE

JACQUES THOLLOT

Jacques Thollot – *drums, keyboards, bass, percussion*, **Elise Ross** – *vocals*, **Jean-Paul Céléa** – *bass*, **Michel Grailler** - *clavinet*, **François Couturier** - *electric piano*, **Chris Howard** - *flute*, **François Jeanneau** - *saxophones*.

Prodigy child, he begins as a jazz drummer at only 13 in certain local french bands. Attracted by the usual sounds of avant-garde coming from the south of England, his style results between zeuhl, **Frank Zappa** and the Canterbury school. The debut produced by Futura in 1971 is a one man band album called *Quand Le Son Devient Aigu, Jeter La Giraffe A La Mer* with various experimental spacey-like electronics, fragile and imaginative compositions containing psychedelic and rock elements. Another 2 albums are published before his true masterpiece, *Cinq Hops* of 1978, a work not only influenced by Canterbury but also by the zeuhl of **Magma**, rich of ethereal atmosphere expressed through piano interlacements, complex rhythms and the chant-like singing of **Elisa Ross**.
RECOMMENDED RECORDINGS: **CINQ HOPS** *(Free Bird, 1978).*   M.G. & C.C.

TRAVELLING

Yves Hasselmann - *piano, Hammond organ, vocals*, **Jacques Goure** - *bass*, **Roger Gremillot** - *drums*.

This trio from Bison changed their name from **Le Point** because of another group using it. They play a jazz-rock close to the Canterbury School and wholly led by the keyboards of **Yves Hasselmann**, greatly inspired by Mike Ratledge's fuzzed-out organ. An only album released in 1973 with sounds and arrangements similar to **Moving Gelatine Plates**. The main composition is an 18 minutes title-track of great music influenced by Caravan and **Soft Machine**, where the voice recalls the singing of **Robert Wyatt**.
DISCOGRAPHY: **VOICI LA NUIT TOMBEE** *(1973, Futura).*   M.G. & C.C.

TRIANGLE

Mimi Lorenzini - *guitars*, **Gérard Fournier** - *bass, vocals*, **Jean-Pierre Prévotat** - *drums*, **François Jeanneau** - *keyboards, flute, saxophones*.

This is creative jazz guitarist **Mimi Lorenzini**'s first band before he plays with Edition Speciale. *Triangle* (1970) is an acid first debut with residues of heavy jazz, dadaism, psychedelic and lysergic blues similar to **Kevin Ayers**' style with **Traffic**, **Caravan**, **Moody Blues** and **Jethro Tull** moments. "Cameron's Complaint" is probably the best track here contained with its Canterbury atmospheres and a predominant flute that makes everything seem airy and simple. *Triangle II* (1972) is a more mature and complete album greatly inspired by bands like **Nucleus**. *Homonymie* (1973) is still a good album though less innovative.
RECOMMENDED RECORDINGS: **TRIANGLE II** *(Pathé, 1972).*   M.G. & C.C.

URBAN SAX

A 1977 project of French drummer, multi-instrumentalist and composer **Gilbert Artmann** (leader of **Lard Free**) who directs this multimedia ensemble which reunites eight sax players in several live events supported by some vocalists and a slim rhythm section. The line-up will soon grow to 16 saxes, adding also dancers, choruses and percussionists, to become a stage acting art-group. Their first homonym album is released in 1977 with only two tracks played with saxophones over an electronic pad. Not boring yet resulting very repetitive since the only listening is unable to recreate the live groove of the performances. All eight albums (the last studio album is of 2014) cross-pollinate jazz, classical, rock, contemporary avant-garde and systemic music, also employed to create atmospheres and background scores for official celebrations.
RECOMMENDED RECORDINGS: **URBAN SAX** *(Cobra, 1977).*   C.A. & C.C.

Europe: FRANCE

LAURENCE VANAY
(Jacqueline Thibault)

This musician, singer and song-writer starts in 1972 playing with **Nanajo** (only one song included in her first album two years later). As the wife of **Laurent Thibault** (**Magma** founder), his occasional cooperation helps create a sound of darker jazz-rock folk: under the alias **Laurence Vanay** a first 1974 album *Galaxies* linked to **Magma**'s prog-rock is released with more melancholic and delicate atmospheres. A year later she records *Evening Colours* under the alias **Gate Way**, an instrumental record more similar to a soundtrack than to prog. As **Maire Mennesson** she records an all-instrumental album *Magic Slows* in 1975 and then she dedicates to film scores and a collaboration in her husband's solo album of 1979. *Les Soleils de la Vie* published in 2015 was a project finished in 1977 and put on hold.
RECOMMENDED RECORDINGS: GALAXIES (*SFP, 1974*) **EVENING COLOURS (GATE WAY)**(*Galloway, 1975*) **LES SOLEILS DE LA VIE** (*Galloway, 1975*).
C.A. & C.C.

VERSAILLES

Guillaume de la Piliere - *vocals, guitars, flute*, **Benoit de Gency** - *drums*, **Oliver de Gency** - *bass*, **Alain de Lille** - *keyboards*.
A French symphonic band from the '90s with a distinct and dramatic keyboard-driven style similar to **Genesis** and **Yes**, with the theatricality of **Ange**. Their second album *Don Giovanni* of 1992 is representative of their sound full of a spacey but heavy mellotron, a heavily inflected guitar, dramatic French vocals and a flute, as is the following spectacular *Le Trésor de Vaillésres* and their last *Blaise et Benjamin*. After this they disband and the remaining act as a catalyst in reforming the theatrical '70s project of **Dominique le Guennec**, the band **Mona Lisa**, with whom they release a 1998 studio album and a live from their ProgFest 2000 appearance before fading once again.
DISCOGRAPHY: LA CATHÉDRALE DU TEMPS (*1991, Musea*) **DON GIOVANNI** (*1992, Musea*) **LE TRÉSOR DE VAILLÉSRES** (*1994, Musea*) **BLAISE ET BENJAMIN** (*1998, Musea*).
M.G. & C.C.

VISITORS

Bernard Torelli – *guitars*, **Patrick Attali** – *vocals, drums*, **Jean Pierre Massiera** – *keyboards, programming, sound engineer, producer*.
A 1974 project of musician, producer and sound engineer **Jean-Pierre Massiera**, with one studio recording never supported by concerts, mixing hard rock influences inspired by **Electric Prunes** and **Vanilla Fudge**, to synthesizer experiments, studio devices and tape manipulations. This concept-album of unusual prog compositions on extra-terrestrial contacts was played by nineteen musicians resulting in a truly eclectic psych-fusion with zeuhl elements, complex arrangements and often grandiose vocals: it failed miserably as did the 45 RPM "Dies irae" issued in parallel. In 1976 **Massiera** founds the disco-rock band **Rockets**, also produced by **Paul Lemoine**, and given their success he decides to resume a completely renewed **Visitors** project in 1981: a synth dominated mix of rock, pop and electronic sounds destined to fail again.
DISCOGRAPHY: VISITORS (*Decca, 1974*).
M.G. & C.C.

VOLAPÜK

Guigou Chenevier - *percussion, drums, sax, programming*, **Michel Mandel** - *clarinet*, **Guillaume Saurel** - *cello, flute*, **Takumi Fukushime** - *violin, vocals*.
Project of former **Etron Fou Leloublan** drummer **Guigou Chenevier**, the band plays an electro-acoustic Rock In Opposition genre of avant-garde taste but never forgetting the melodic aspects. After four good studio albums and a live recording, they are regarded as true progsters and heirs of the **Art Zoyd** and **Univers Zero** legacy. *Where is Tamashii* is their last album released in 2003, with a Japanese female violinist that brightens up the music with folk elements and her fine vocals, singing in Japanese.
DISCOGRAPHY: LE FEU DU TIGRE (*1995, Cuneiform Records*) **SLANG!** (*1997, Cuneiform Records*) **PÜKAPÖK** (*1999, Retort Media*) **POLYGLÖT** (*2000, Cuneiform Records*) **WHERE IS TAMASHII?** (*2003, Orkhestra*).
M.G. & C.C.

Europe: FRANCE

VORTEX

Jack Vivante - *bass,* **Jean-Pierre Vivante** - *keyboards,* **Maurice Sonjon** - *vibes, chime,* **Christian Boissel** - *cor anglais, keyboards,* **Alain Chaleard** - *xylophone, vibes,* **Jackes Guyot** - *sax,* **Gerard Jolivet** - *sax,* **Jean-Michel Belaich** - *drums.*
Two incredible albums (1975-1979) for these creators of a very rich jazz-rock of multiple shades. An overwhelming sound that unites the Canterbury school elegance of **Hatfield & The North** and **National Health**, the orchestral arrangements of **Frank Zappa** and the vibrations of the best **Magma** zeuhl sonorities. A really compelling mix with keyboards, sax and vibraphone chasing after each other into a labyrinth where each movement is carried out by powerful poly-rhythmic solutions. The second album *Les Cycles de Thanatos* is a stunning masterpiece.
DISCOGRAPHY: **VORTEX** *(1975, JBO)* **LES CYCLES DE THANATOS** *(1979, FLVM).* **M.G. & C.C.**

WURTEMBERG

Alain Carbonare - *dulcimer, harp, organ, piano, guitar,* **Bernard Maitre** - *keyboards,* **Michel Richard** - *guitars,* **Gilles Michault-Bonnet** - *winds,* **Alain Demeusy** - *bass,* **Jean-Marie Hausser, Jean-Pierre Garbin** - *percussion.*
Artisan lute maker and fine musician, **Alain Carbonare** is one of the most important names of the French folk genre: former founder of the 1972 band Iris, he is also famous for his collaborations with **Alan Stivell**. He then founds **Wurtemberg** in 1979 driven by the will of creating himself certain medieval and renaissance instruments with the intent of inserting them into a pop music context with electro-acoustic tracks. *Rock Fantasia Opus 9* is the only album they release in a time where prog was pronounced dead: delicate and poetic compositions of very suggestive and fascinating folk prog expressed with deep feeling. Disbanded shortly after with a come back in 2008 entitled *Rock Fantasia Opus 10*.
RECOMMENDED RECORDINGS: **ROCK FANTASIA OPUS 9** *(Sterne, 1980).* **M.G. & C.C.**

XII ALFONSO

Philippe Claerhout - *guitar, bass, keyboards, percussion,* **François Claerhout** - *keyboards, programming, percussion,* **Thierry Moreno** - *drums, percussion,* **Michael Geyre** - *keyboards.* **Plus guest musicians...**
A style converging classical music, medieval sounds, Celtic and French traditional folk and a little bit of electronics for this band from Bordeaux born in 1996. After two interesting albums, their third titled *Claude Monet vol. 1* of 2002 is where they final reach a certain maturity, doubled with the sequel published three years later. The stunning merge of these different styles does not create confusion with never too heavy long instrumental passages, some female vocals and an elegant Celtic-influenced atmosphere sometimes recalling **Mike Oldfield**.
DISCOGRAPHY: **THE LOST FRONTIER** *(1996, Musea)* **ODYSSÉES** *(2000, Musea)* **CLAUDE MONET VOL. 1** *(2002, Musea)* **THIS IS** *(2003, Musea)* **LE CHANT DE PIERRE** *(2003, Musea)* **CLAUDE MONET VOL. 2** *(2005, Musea).* **M.G. & C.C.**

ZOO

Michel Bonnecarrère - *guitar,* **Ian Bellamy** - *vocals,* **André Hervé** - *keyboards,* **Tony Canal** - *trumpet,* **Daniel Carnet** - *violin, sax,* **Joël Daydé** - *vocals,* **Christian Devaux** - *drums, percussions,* **Pierre Fanen** - *guitar,* **Michel Hervé** - *bass,* **Michel Ripoche** - *sax, violin, trumpet.*
French band, born in 1968 around the excellent and versatile guitarist **Bonnecarrère** (not to be confused with a homonym dutch group active in the same period), with a large line-up playing an experimental mix of psychedelia, jazz, pop, blues and soul. Their first 1969 album is good but the second of 1970 even better: *I shall be free* confirms their choice of a powerful horn section where each song gives large space to the instrumental brasses, sometimes simple, others with a funky groove, always well compensated by the interesting **Hendrix** styled guitar or by softer moments dominated by violin and organ.
RECOMMENDED RECORDINGS: **I SHALL BE FREE** *(Riviera Records, 1970).* **M.G. & C.C.**

Europe: GERMANY

AMENOPHIS

Stefano Rössman - *drums, keyboards*, **Michael Rössman** - *guitars, keyboards*, **Wolfgang Vollmuth** - *bass, guitars, keyboards, vocals*, **Elke Möhrle** - *vocals*, **Kurt Poppe** - *keyboards*, **René Kius** - *drums*.

Founded in 1978, they start off with a good prog debut inspired by **Yes**, **Genesis** and **Camel** (recorded in their own apartment in 1983) where delicate and airy passages move through compelling acoustic arrangements. In 1987 their second album *You and I* and the 2 years tour which followed, confirm the attempt of a lighter product yet maintaining their prog background and characteristic sound. The disappointing sales forced them to sell all of the equipment, thus breaking up the band. Their commitment to a complex prog genre kept them from continuing with careers in the musical panorama.

DISCOGRAPHY: **AMENOPHIS** *(1983, Pallas Records)* **YOU AND I** *(1988, Pallas Records).*   M.G. & C.C.

ANABIS

Holger Sann – *lead vocals, flute, guitar, percussion*, **Erhard Waschke** – *guitars*, **Bert Beck** - *bass, percussion, kazoo, vocals*, **Roland Dörr** – *keyboards*, **Mike Morkel** – *drums, percussion, vocals*, **Peter Müller** – *guitars*.

Formed in 1978 as a symphonic prog band of **Genesis** imprint with heavy and psychedelic keyboards and new wave inserts flowing into an 80's new prog format. The debut album of 1980, *Heaven on Earth*, is sung in English by **Sann** (a voice very close to **Gabriel**'s) and made more personal by the harder guitar playing and the simple rhythms. In 1982 the second album *Wer Will* was published on the same line of the first, but this time with German vocals and cynical lyrics and some softer parts of flute creating more atmosphere. Their last record *Theatre* of 1988 features a different line-up and is a more contemporary rock album, essentially pop, with English vocals as well as an infusion of horns and the heavy guitar sound.

RECOMMENDED RECORDINGS: **HEAVEN ON EARTH** *(PM Records, 1980).*   M.G. & C.C.

BIRTH CONTROL

Bernd Noske – *drums, percussion, vocals*, **Bruno Frenzel** – *guitar, vocals*, **Bernd Koschmidder** - *bass*, **Wolfgang Neuser** – *keyboards, percussion, vibes*.

It is difficult to list a line-up for this band which throughout the 16 studio albums never stayed the same, if not for drummer **Noske**. Formed in a very open way at the end of the '60s in Berlin playing a hybrid jazz-rock, mainly instrumental, with psychedelic and experimental shades that led them to a symphonic hard rock of kraut elements. Their best period is probably from 1971 to 1975, especially with the heavy rock and subtle jazzy arrangements of *Operation* (1972) and *Hoodoo Man* (1972). Certain commercial musical choices and the inclusion of more jazz elements do not favor the sales and they seem to end the adventure in the early '80s. With a complete revolution of line-up, the band reforms again in 1993 with a form of kraut-fusion and are still active today.

RECOMMENDED RECORDINGS: **HOODOO MAN** *(CBS, 1972).*   M.G. & C.C.

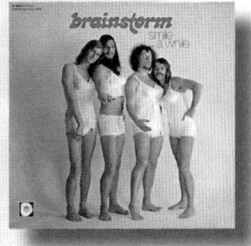

BRAINSTORM

Roland Schaeffer - *guitars, winds, keyboards*, **Eddy Von Overheidt** - *keyboards*, **Rainer Bodensohn** - *flute, bass, vocals*, **Joe Koinzer** - *drums*, **Enno Dernov** - *bass*.

Among the closest German bands of the early '70s to derive inspiration from the Canterbury school, these musicians arrive from two different groups: **Fashion Pink** (former **Fashion Pricks**) and Baden-Baden. In their debut album *Smile A While* of 1972, the fusion quintet confirms their particular vision of instrumental jazz-rock close to certain cyclic solutions by **Soft Machine** mixed to the bizarre open structures of **Frank Zappa**. The same formula of unusual and highly complex harmonies, sax, flute and (distorted) organs, is repeated in their second album of 1973, *Second Smile*. The disappointing sales force label Spiegelei to break the contract therefore disbanding the group.

DISCOGRAPHY: **SMILE A WHILE** *(Spiegelei, 1972)* **SECOND SMILE** *(Spiegelei, 1973).*   M.G. & C.C.

Europe: GERMANY

BRAVE NEW WORLD

Reinhart Firchow - *flute, ocarinas, xylophone, vocals*, **Lucas Lindholm** - *bass, fiddle, keyboards*, **Dicky Tarrach** - *drums, percussion*. **Herb Geller** - *flute, saxophones, oboe, piano*. **John O'Brien-Docker** - *guitars, keyboards*, **Esther Daniels** - *vocals*.
An almost entirely instrumental band which published one of the most interesting kraut-rock albums of Germany: this 1972 concept album entitled Impressions on Reading Aldous Huxley contains elements of folk, psychedelic rock and electronics with peculiar percussion patterns where the flute, saxophones and a stylophone endow their music with a certain special otherworldly sound, creating mysterious hallucinations and dreamy atmospheres throughout all the episodes of this long composition. Sadly, after the release they dissolve into thin air.
DISCOGRAPHY: **IMPRESSIONS ON READING ALDOUS HUXLEY** (Vertigo, 1972). C.A. & C.C.

DIES IRAE

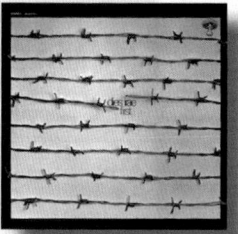

Cord Wahlmann - *vocals, harmonica*, **Robert J. Schiff** - *bass*, **Harald H.G. Thoma** - *guitar, vocals*, **Andreas F. Cornelius** - *drums*.
This German quartet born in the early '70s released only one album of good and original ideas expressed by mixing various styles through a very hard electric blues close to the sounds of **Deep Purple** and **Black Sabbath**. Not to be confused with the several metal bands which used the same name (from the latin Day Of Wrath, referring to judgment day), this prog band with lyrical references to the occult were playing psychedelic electronics and free jams which included a heavy blues guitar and harmonica with long instrumental parts. In 1972 they split into two separate bands, **Lucy Gang** and **Green Wave** and will take different directions until the '90s when they attempt to reform the original band. In 1993 the final break-up.
DISCOGRAPHY: **FIRST** (Pilz, 1971). C.A. & C.C.

DROSSELBART

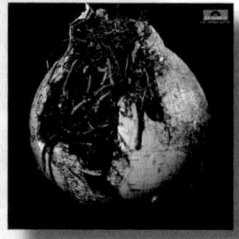

Peter Randt - *vocals, guitar*, **Jemina** - *vocals*, **Christian Trachsel** - *keyboards*, **Dietmar Mainka** - *guitar*, **Werner Schuler** - *bass*, **Martin Honemeyer** - *drums*.
Another original and eccentric one shot band from Germany's kraut-rock trenches similar to **Uriah Heep**'s style but with psychedelic tunes tending toward a harder rock genre. Their 1971 album is a keyboard driven sound full of church organ passages that create magical atmospheres through the Hammond organ or the ethereal synthesizers. The beauty infused by the aggressive riffs of a heavy rock guitar does not however compensate the melodic vocals of **Jemima** that often result as shrieks of exhibitionism which clash with the arrangements and with the dark German lyrics on religious themes.
DISCOGRAPHY: **DROSSELBART** (Polydor, 1970). C.A. & C.C.

EDEN

Anne Dierks, Annette Schmalenbach - *vocals*, **Mario Schaub** - *winds*, **Dirk Schmalenbach** - *violin, keyboards, vocals*, **Hans Fritzsch** - *guitar*, **Michael Dierks** - *keyboards, vocals*, **Michael Claren** - *vocals, bass*, **Hans Müller** - *drums*, **guest musicians**...
A minor band formed in 1977 who released the following year a good album *Erwartung* containing the most notorious elements of German melodic prog: rich sounds, ethnic instruments (like the sitar) a good presence of flute, saxophones, violin and arrangements driven by the keyboards with scratchy guitar riffs and the predominant male and female vocals. *Perelandra* of 1980 is their second album but with nothing new to add. Very surprising instead the third album, *Heimekehr* with clear influences from **Pink Floyd**.
DISCOGRAPHY: **ERWARTUNG** (Lord, 1978) **PERELANDRA** (Lord, 1980) **HEIMEKEHR** (Pila, 1981). C.A.

Europe: GERMANY

EILIFF

Rainer Bruninghaus - *keyboards*, **Bill Brown** - *bass*, **Houschang Nejadepour** - *guitars, sitar*, **Herbert J. Kalveram** - *saxophones*, **Detlef Landmann** - *drums*.
Another great instrumental band of German rock from the late '60s, among the best of north-European jazz-rock. Similar to **Brainstorm**, they play a fusion featuring the classy Canterbury-style with bass, guitar and keyboards and some ethnic instruments (mostly the sitar). Their first album of 1971 is recorded and engineered by the great **Conny Plank**: killer keyboards (electric piano), a wild guitar and sax interplay with very complex grooves and extended jams. The second more psychedelic album *Girlrls* is even more improvisational and jammy with a stunning electric jazz of oriental tastes (due to the guitarist's Persian origins).
DISCOGRAPHY: EILIFF *(Philips, 1971)* GIRLRLS *(Philips, 1972)*. M.G. & C.C.

EMTIDI

Dolly Holmes - *acoustic guitars, kazoo, vocals*, **Maik Hirschfeldt** - *guitars, flute, vocals*.
While in Germany the mainstream of the early '70s was into electronic and experimental sounds, this duo publishes an acid and psychedelic folk rock album greatly inspired by the music of **Bob Dylan**, with acoustics and the insertion of unusual musical instruments (kazoo, bouzouki, flute) that sometimes recall **Jefferson Airplane**. More pleasant the second and last album of 1972, *Saat*, where Dieter Dierks production directs them to pastoral folk atmospheres, more suitable for both musicians, with lots of mellotron and keyboards with guitar intros close to **Klaus Shulze**. The record is sung in English except for the track "Die reise" sung in German.
DISCOGRAPHY: EMTIDI *(Thorofon, 1971)* SAAT *(Pilz, 1972)*. C.A. & C.C.

EPIDERMIS

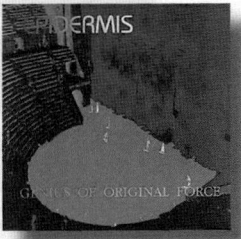

Reiner Neeb - *drums, percussion, flute, vocals*, **Wolfgang Wünsche** - *bass, vocals*, **Rolf Lanz** - *guitars, flute, vocals*, **Michael Kurz** - *keyboards, vocals*.
1977 *Genius Of Original Force* is a prodigy of fantastic and stunning music which pays a large tribute to the style of **Gentle Giant**, but not only: this first album is a very dense and complex prog with the multi-layered vocal arrangements of their idols and some more dynamic instrumental parts closer to **Yes** and **King Crimson**. A mix of rock, classical and jazz which create a moving sonic dreamscape with unexpected rhythm and mood changes, and the bizarre vocals. They record a second album in the early '80s called *Muster-Burger* and a third in the early '90s with the same line-up and some special guests.
DISCOGRAPHY: GENIUS OF ORIGINAL FORCE *(1977, Kerston)* MUSTER-BURGER *(1982)* FEEL ME *(1991)*. M.G. & C.C.

EPITAPH

Cliff Jackson - *vocals, guitar*, **James McGillvray** - *drums, vocals*, **Bernd Kolbe** - *bass, keyboards, vocals*, **Klaus Walz** - *guitar, vocals*, **Achim Wielert** - *drums*, **Norbert Lehmann** - *drums*, **Heinz Glass** - *guitar*, **Harvey Janben** - *bass*, **Michael Karch** - *keyboards*.
Founded in Dortmund in 1969, their debut album already sees them as a mature heavy prog band performing a scratchy sound similar to some works of **Uriah Heep**, **Patto**, **May Blitz**, yet open to sweeter delicate moments of mellotron. The result is more British due to the two English musicians playing with this natural born German band. The following albums *Stop, Look & Listen* (1972) and *Outside The Law* (1974) are both in line with the previous. Line-up changes and contract squabbles cause a slow disbandment that reunites in 2004 for another series of albums and concerts.
RECOMMENDED RECORDINGS: EPITAPH *(1971, Polydor)* STOP, LOOK & LISTEN *(1972, Polydor)* OUTSIDE THE LAW *(1974, Billingsgate Records)*. M.G. & C.C.

Europe: **GERMANY**

FAITHFUL BREATH

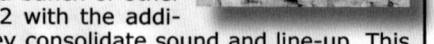

Manfred von Buttlar - *keyboards, piano, guitars, vocals,* **Heinz Mikus** - *guitars, lead vocals,* **Jurgen Meritz** - *drums, percussion, vocals,* **Horst Stabenow** - *bass, guitars, vocals.*
Founded by former **Magic Power** musicians **Heinz Mikus** and **Horst Stabenov** in 1967 with a bunch of other talented colleagues, it is only after 1972 with the addition of keyboardist **Von Buttlar** that they consolidate sound and line-up. This German symphonic rock band debuts with a fine album titled *Fading Beauty* in 1973, full of the typical keyboards spread over three compact and solemn long tracks with contemplative mellotron backgrounds and arrangements very near to classical music. In 1977 they start recording *Back On My Hill*, finished and published in 1980, just before the first break-up. **Mikus** and **Stabenov** will continue together and with **Uwe Otto** (drums) they revive the old band's name, but playing a distinct heavy metal from then on.
RECOMMENDED RECORDINGS: **FADIN BEAUTY** *(1973, Sky)* **BACK ON MY HILL** *(1980, Sky).* **M.G.**

FLYING CIRCUS

Falco Kurtz - *drums,* **Michael Dorp** - *vocals,* **Michael Rick** - *guitar,* **Lorenz Gelius-Laudam** - *guitar,* **Harald Krause** - *keyboards,* **Markus Erren** - *bass.*
A good German band with a rich personality although filled with derivations from the '70s top European prog-rock. After many years of gigs in clubs, pubs and festivals, they release a first album *Seasons* in 1998 with a good combination of kraut-rock and hard rock inspired by **Deep Purple**. In 2000 *Out Of The Waste Land* represents the synthesis of all the influences converged into their music, from **Pink Floyd** to **Rush** passing through the space rock of **Hawkwind** and the symphonic prog of **Yes**. Less original the third of 2004, *Pomp*, where the tribute to **Rush** is sometimes too much.
DISCOGRAPHY: **SEASONS** *(Early Birds, 1998)* **OUT OF THE WASTE LAND** *(Early Birds, 2000)* **POMP** *(Rockwerk, 2004).* **C.A. & C.C.**

HIGH WHEEL

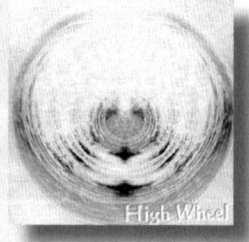
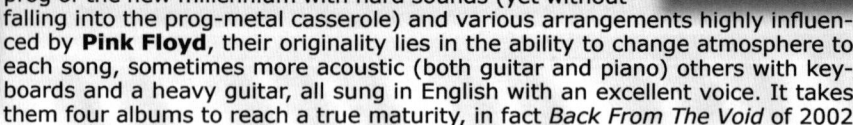

Wolfgang Hierl - *guitar, flute, vocals,* **Eric Kogler** - *bass,* **Uli Jenne** - *drums,* **Andreas Lobinger** - *keyboards.*
This Bavarian symphonic prog quartet reinvents the new prog of the new millennium with hard sounds (yet without falling into the prog-metal casserole) and various arrangements highly influenced by **Pink Floyd**, their originality lies in the ability to change atmosphere to each song, sometimes more acoustic (both guitar and piano) others with keyboards and a heavy guitar, all sung in English with an excellent voice. It takes them four albums to reach a true maturity, in fact *Back From The Void* of 2002 is probably their best work, a quite metaphysical and powerful progressive rock incorporating exquisite acoustics (even metal).
DISCOGRAPHY: **1910** *(High Wheel, 1993)* **REMEMBER THE COLOURS** *(Rockwerck, 1994)* **THERE** *(Ipso Facto, 1996)* **BACK FROM THE VOID** *(High Wheel, 2001)* **LIVE BEFORE THE STORM** *(live, Progress, 2006).* **M.G. & C.C.**

IBLISS

Rainer Buechel - *winds,* **Wolfgang Buellmeyer** - *guitars, percussion,* **Norbert Buellmeyer** - *bass, percussion,* **Andreas Homann** - *drums, percussion,* **Basil Hammoudi** - *percussion, flute, vocals.*
One shot band, their stunning album *Supernova* of 1972 puts them among the best kraut-rock bands of Germany: jams impregnated with jazz-rock and fusion and only some hints of the '60s psychedelia. Distinctive the predominant percussion arrangements, oriented to compelling ethnic sounds sometimes with hypnotic effects, prelude to the music of **Weather Report**. Guitar and sax solos complete the compositions for a final result of evocative tribal fusion. Sound engineer for the album was **Conny Plank**, yet this little gem went barely noticed by the critics and the audience.
DISCOGRAPHY: **SUPERNOVA** *(Spiegelei, 1972).* **C.A. & C.C.**

Europe: GERMANY

IKARUS

Wulf-Dieter Struntz - *keyboards*, **Lorenz Köhler** - *vocals*, **Jochen Petersen** - *guitars, flute, vocals*, **Wolfgang Kracht** - *bass, vocals*, **Bernd Schroder** - *drums, percussion*, **Manfred Schulz** - *guitars, vocals*.

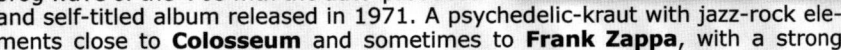

Shady German one shot band among the first prog wave of the '70s with the auto-produced and self-titled album released in 1971. A psychedelic-kraut with jazz-rock elements close to **Colosseum** and sometimes to **Frank Zappa**, with a strong tendency towards space rock or light symphonic overtures, with keyboards similar to **VDGG** or **Raw Material**. Great emphasis is given to the guitar and organ interplay, though the use of flute, saxophone and clarinet add more color to their compositions. Today it may seem old and slightly childish, but overall sincerely funny and decidedly pleasant to hear.
RECOMMENDED RECORDINGS: IKARUS (Private Press, 1971 - Reissued by Second Battle Records 1995). **M.G. & C.C.**

INDIGO

Martin Ernst - *keyboards, vocals*, **Gerhard Huber** - *drums, percussion, acoustic guitar*, **Wolfgang Krieg** - *guitars, vocals*, **Reinhart Kunstmann** - *bass*.
A mid '70s German band (not to be confused with the Austrians of the next decade) which release their first concept album in 1977 thanks to an independent label: inspired by the life of Sylvia Plath, the dramatic German lyrics are sung with sonorities sometimes inspired by **Procol Harum**; the dark and more underground sound is due to a rawer guitar tone and probably the low-budget production. A quite simple symphonic genre with hard prog keyboards and broken rhythms recalling themes by **Camel** and **Novalis**, or a **Hackett** styled guitar, especially in the instrumental parts. After this work follow three other albums, on the same line, the last of 1988.
RECOMMENDED RECORDINGS: MEER DER ZEIT (Hiddenhall Music Produktion, 1977). **M.G. & C.C.**

ISKANDER

Klaus-Jürgen Knüppel – *keyboards*, **Hajo Kann** - *drums*, **Michael Pichmann** - *guitars*, **Gabi Stolz** - *guitars*, **Ulrich Mennenöh** - *bass*, **Bernd Weißbach** - *vocals*.
In 1973 **Peter Tassius**, **Gabi Stolz** and **Klaus Jürgen Knüppel** decide to form their own band and for some years play live undergoing several line-up changes until they seem to consolidate as a quartet in 1977, with characteristic long improvisations on all instruments and complex rhythms, harmonies and melodies. A year later **Tassius** is replaced by **Pichmann** (although in 1981 he records an album with them) and they start inserting elements of jazz, rock, classical and electronics, blending them into a personal fusion genre. Also of 1981 *Boheme 2000*, a jazz-ballet project. In 1984 singer **Bernd Weißbach** joins in and appears in the 1987 album *Mental Touch*, probably their masterpiece, before leaving the band. Songs became shorter, structured and more dense in the 1990 album. In 2010 a come-back tour but no real novelties.
RECOMMENDED RECORDINGS: MENTAL TOUCH (Iron Curtain, 1988). **M.G. & C.C.**

IVORY

Ulrich Sommerlatte – *keyboards*, **Thomas Sommerlatte** - *keyboards*, **Christian Mayer** – *vocals, guitars*, **Goddie Daum** - *guitars*, **Charly Stechl** - *bass, flute*, **Fredrik Rittmüller** - *drums*.
Band born in 1979 around keyboardist, orchestral director and composer of classical derivation, **Ulrich Sommerlatte**. *Sad Cypress* is a symphonic prog album of 1980, close to the sound of **Genesis** like in "My Brother", but also rich of personal cues such as "In Hora Ultima" sung in latin and played by two keyboards (with his father). The long pause after this work is interrupted by surprise in 1996 when **Urlich** reforms the band keeping only **Mayer** from the old line-up. The album resulting is entitled *Keen City*, an ambient work with psychedelic elements distant from the previous one.
RECOMMENDED RECORDINGS: SAD CYPRESS (Jupiter label, 1980). **M.G. & C.C.**

Europe: GERMANY

KIN PING MEH

Werner Stephan - *lead vocals, guitar,* **Kalle Weber** - *drums, percussion,* **Torsten Herzog** - *bass,* **Fritz Schmitt** - *keyboards,* **Joachim Schäfer** - *guitar,* **Willie Wagner** - *guitar,* **Alan Wroe** - *bass,* **Gagey Mrozeck** - *guitar,* **Geff Harrison** - *vocals, guitar.*
Not a typical kraut-rock band, they are closer to an art-rock form of hard-prog which deeply recalls **Deep Purple**. Formed in 1970 in Mannheim, the quintet performs covers of famous songs until discovered by Polydor and produced by **Achim Reichel** (see page...). Of the six studio recordings made within 1977, the first two of 1971 and 1972 are powerful albums blending very effectively prog and hard rock, after which they descend into a commercial pop rock (even more British or American sounding), with good arrangements but no personality. They were also a stunning live act, in fact in 1991 a concert recorded in 1973 is issued posthumous: *Hazy Age On Stage*.
RECOMMENDED RECORDINGS: **KIN PING MEH** *(Polydor, 1971)* **KIN PING MEH 2** *(Polydor, 1972).* **C.A.**

JANE

Klaus Hess - *lead guitar,* **Charly Maucher** - *bass, vocals,* **Werner Nadolny** - *organ,* **Peter Panka** - *drums,* **Bernd Pulst** - *vocals.*
At the end of 1970, **Justice Of Peace** dissolves and regroups as **Jane**, oscillating between prog and a more energetic form of hard rock with spacey hints. This band from Hannover releases in 1972 *Together*, already a masterpiece from the cover artwork (very visionary) to the content. Sung in broken English with a heavy blues guitar and a hypnotic drum beat that makes it more an underground work and probably underrated for this reason. Also the second is very good though somewhat more harmonious and with the addition of synths that provided spacier atmospheres. The dark ballad "Out in the rain" is perhaps the best and most famous of their songs. Although they publish more in the following years (the last in 2009 as a tribute to the late **Peter**), nothing is at the same level of these first two.
RECOMMENDED RECORDINGS: **TOGETHER** *(Brain, 1972)* **HERE WE ARE** *(Brain, 1973).* **C.A. & C.C.**

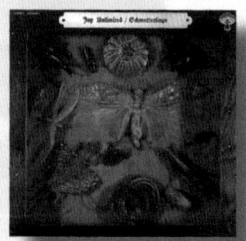

JOY UNLIMITED

Joy - *vocals,* **Hans W. Herkenne** - *drums, percussion,* **Albin Metz** - *trumpet, bass,* **Roland Heck** - *keyboards, vibes, marimba, percussion, vocals,* **Dieter Kindl** - *bass, guitar, percussion,* **Gerd Köthe** - *winds,* **Klaus Nagel** - *guitar, percussion, flute,* **Hans Lingenfelder** - *guitar.*
Also known as **Joy and the Hitkids**, this blues-band starts an official career in 1970 with the inspired debut *Overground* that mixed psychedelia, jazz-rock, kraut and soul with certain pop elements (**The Beatles**) and elegant sounds from the newborn American funk. Led by the extraordinary voice of female singer **Joy Fleming**, the success brought to an English version titled *Turbolence* for the UK market and *Joy Unlimited* for the US market. In 1971 their second stunning album *Schmetterlinge* (butterflies) deviate to a more simple electronic kraut, never too far from their pop and blues roots.
DISCOGRAPHY: **OVERGROUND** *(Polydor, 1970)* **SCHMETTERLINGE** *(Pilz, 1971).* **C.A. & C.C.**

LIFT

Stephan Trepte - *vocals,* **Franz Bartzsch** - *keyboards, vocals,* **Michael Heubach** - *keyboards,* **Henry Pacholski** - *vocals,* **Hans Wintoch** - *vocals, violin,* **Konrad Burkert** - *drums,* **Jürgen Heinrich** - *guitars,* **Till Patzer** - *flute, saxophone,* **Manfred Nytsch** - *trombone.*
Based in Dresden, they form after the disbandment of the **Dresden Sextett** in 1973, with many a concert all over their halved country (behind the wall). A first record of pale symphonic pop all sung in German is released in 1977 based upon excellent keyboards and mellotron, where the guitars and bass are less important and merged into the arrangements. After some line-up changes, a slightly more commercial second work of 1979, *Meeresfahrt*, is published featuring good lyrics and a balanced romantic symphonicism with hints of funky and light jazz influences led by a great dual keyboard with dominant mellotron waves, distinctive organ, electric piano and powerful clavinet parts.
DISCOGRAPHY: **LIFT** *(Amiga, 1977)* **MEERESFAHRT** *(Amiga, 1979).* **C.A. & C.C.**

Europe: GERMANY

MESSAGE

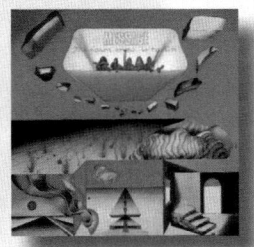
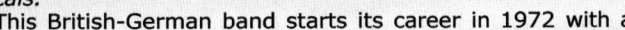

Allan Freeman - *vocals, synthesizers,* **Gunther Klinger** - *drums,* **Tom McGuigan** - *vocals, keyboards, mellotron,* **Allan Murdoch** - *guitars,* **Gerhard Schaber** - *percussion,* **Horst Stachelhaus** - *bass,* **Billy Tabbert** - *guitars, vocals.*

This British-German band starts its career in 1972 with a sophisticated heavy folk rock articulated around complex keyboards arrangements and a dynamic guitar playing. Their debut *The Dawn Anew Is Coming* well suits all the atmospheres of a very melodic and original European prog with balanced sounds and good lyrical compositions. The sequel *From Books And Dreams* is darker, mainly instrumental with heavier space-rock themes. Their two albums of 1975 and 1976 are instead a more conventional and easy listening heavy rock music, sometimes including jazzy hints, in search of a commercial response that never quite convinced, not even in the other three works, the last of 1980.
DISCOGRAPHY: **THE DAWN ANEW IS COMING** *(Bellaphon, 1972)* **FROM BOOKS AND DREAMS** *(Bellaphon, 1973).*
                                                                                                   C.A. & C.C.

NEUSCHWANSTEIN

Frédéric Joos – *vocals, acoustic guitar,* **Thomas Neuroth** – *keyboards,* **Klaus Mayer** – *flute, synthesizer,* **Roger Weiler** – *guitars,* **Rainer Zimmer** - *bass, vocals,* **Hans-Peter Schwarz** - *drums.*

This proto-neo-prog band is maybe the best of the **Genesis** copy-cats due to the voice of their singer Joos whom sounds incredibly like **Gabriel**. Formed in 1974 as the winners of a musical contest with their German version of Lewis Carroll's 'Alice in Wonderland', they start a great live activity with the conceptual stage show: the demo recordings made in 1976 of the original visual performance were released only later in 2002 and then in an official 2008 English version. Therefore the actual true first album dates 1978: very near to the **Genesis** sound, *Battlement* adds a dark electronic edge through the organ, synths and moog, with sublime flute parts like in the famous "Intruders and the Punishment", while "Zartlicher Abschied" is the only track deriving from the quoted Alice opera.
RECOMMENDED RECORDINGS: **BATTLEMENT** *(Racket Records, 1978).*   M.G. & C.C.

NINE DAYS WONDER

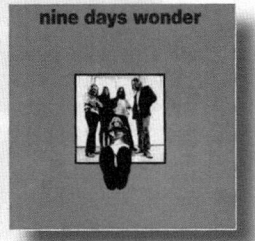

Walter Seyffer - *vocals, drums, percussion,* **Rolf Henning** - *guitar,* **Karl Mutschlechner** - *bass,* **John Earle** - *vocals, winds, guitar,* **Freddie Münster** - *saxophones, keybords,* **guest musicians....**

An international quintet formed in 1966 which record a wild debut album in 1971, between **Frank Zappa**, **Captain Beefheart** and the British Prog style of **Soft Machine**, **King Crimson** and **Deep Purple**, where the instruments appear and vanish from the arrangements without logic thus developing a creative chaos. After this they renew the line-up by 1973 and release a second more conventional prog record *We never lost control*. Then their sound becomes surprisingly more organic, surrendering to an anonymous pop rock as in *Only The Dancer* released in 1975, a straight rock album based mostly on sax (guest **David Jackson** from **VDGG**) and keyboards. The group's last album *Sonnet To Billy Frost* of 1976 was a press-dismissed rock opera.
RECOMMENDED RECORDINGS: **NINE DAYS' WONDER** *(Bacillus, 1971)* **WE NEVER LOST CONTROL** *(Bacillus, 1973).*   C.A. & C.C.

NOSFERATU

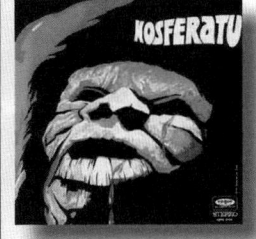

Michael 'Mick' Thierfelder - *vocals,* **Christian Felke** - *sax, flute,* **Michael 'Mike" Kessler** - *bass,* **Reinhard 'Tammy' Grohe** - *organ,* **Michael 'Xner' Meixner** - *guitar,* **Byally Braumann** - *drums.*

Contrary to other bands produced by **Conny Plank** their musical career was short and mysteriously lacked the recognition of a larger public. Sometimes compared to the British sound of **Gravy Train**, they actually play an original and personal music. Their only album of 1970 contains good strong lyrics, all sung in English, with deep and trippy atmospheres created by the long instrumental solos, crossing raw and aggressive guitars with predominant sax, flute and electric organs, for a fresh, enthusiastic and atypical jazzy rock, dominated by progressive folk arrangements. Last but not least the cover artwork which is simply wonderful.
DISCOGRAPHY: **NOSFERATU** *(Vogue, 1970).*   C.A. & C.C.

Europe: GERMANY

OCTAFISH

Wieland Braunschweiger - *vocals*, **Thomas Denzel** - *synthesizers*, **Frank Messmer** - *synthesizers, sequencers, programming*, **Hank Willers** - *guitars*, **K-J. Zickler** - *saxophones*.
They start their career as a cover-band of **Frank Zappa & The Mothers**, before turning to music of their own. Classifying themselves as 'industrial fake jazz', their fantastic genre gets better throughout the years: the second album *Hai Girls* (1998) is even better than the previous *Land Unter* (1995) because of the more focused arrangements near to a fusion jazz. Inside is also their version of **Zappa**'s "The torture never stops", performed with great intensity and mastery. Completely instrumental, they incorporate a strong backbeat with complex rhythms greatly inspired by the avant-rock of **King Crimson**, **Frank Zappa**'s jazzier material and hints from the New York experimental jazz scene (**Knitting Factory**). A last studio album in 2009 and more recently a tour in 2017 for this overwhelming music-machine.
RECOMMENDED RECORDINGS: **LAND UNTER** *(Octafish, 1995)* **HAI GIRLS** *(Sonic, 1999)*. C.A. & C.C.

OCTOPUS

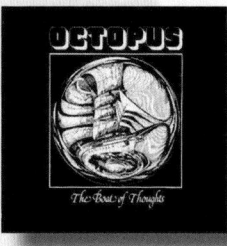

Pit Hensel - *guitars*, **Werner Littau** - *keyboards*, **Jennifer Hensel** - *vocals*, **Frank Eule** - *drums*, **Claus D. Kniemeyer** - *bass*.
Formed in Frankfurt in 1973 by guitarist **Pit Hensel** and bassist **Claus Kniemeyer**, this symphonic prog band inspired by **Eloy** and **Camel**, play a more personal genre with a large use of Mellotron and organ (**Banks** or **Emerson**) and the particular gritty voice of their female singer **Jennifer Hensel**, similar to **Janis Joplin** but without the typical scratchy blues sound. Perhaps leaning more towards rock, they mix classic prog elements (multiple rhythm changes) with a little bit of blues through the predominant searing guitars. Probably their best work is their 1976 *The Boat Of Thoughts*, though the second *An Ocean Of Rock* also results just as good. *Rubber Angel* of 1979 and *Hart Am Rand* of 1981, featuring a male singer, both shift to a more commercial style.
RECOMMENDED RECORDINGS: **THE BOAT OF THOUGHTS** *(Sky Records, 1976)*. M.G. & C.C.

ODYSSEE

Volker Franke – *drums, percussion*, **Silvio Dalla-Torre** - *bass*, **Friedhelm Wolff** – *keyboards*, **Werner Kiente** - *piano, guitars, vocals*, **Rainer Schön** – *guitar, vocals*.
Not to be confused by the late '90s homonym German band, this particular group of musicians begin playing together in school and continued after years of hard practice until they decide to produce their own album in 1978. *White Swan* is a one shot work printed on vinyl and never officially reissued afterwards (perhaps some bootleg CDs), making it a very rare item. The simple shorter songs well balance the extended and copiously symphonic title-track. Greatly inspired by the **Genesis** of *Wind & Wuthering*, **Yes**, **Camel** and **Neuschwanstein**, they nevertheless enrich their sound with an open stream of fusion, jazz and groovier tones making them a particularly unique symphonic jazz-prog German band.
DISCOGRAPHY: **WHITE SWAN** *(Private pressing, 1978)*. M.G.

OS MUNDI

Udo Arndt - *guitar, vocals*, **Christoph Busse** - *drums, vocals*, **Dietrich Markgraf** - *winds*, **Andreas Villain** - *bass*, **Wolfgang "Buddy" Mandler** - *drums, percussion*, **Raimund "Mikro" Rilling** - *cello, bass*.
This group formed in 1970 with a psychedelic heavy rock version of a latin church mass, following the example of **Electric Prunes**. An extraordinary example of classic kraut-rock, performed with an **Amon Düül** style of dark atmospheres where the organ is the main instrument of the ensemble. Their second effort *43 Minuten* of 1972 was a sequel stripped of the psychedelia and sung with a female jazz pop vocalist, **Ute Kannenberg**: a globally average symphonic jazz album, of which the song "A Question Of Decision" is probably the best track. In 1980 they held a sold out revival concert of strong jazz orientation and later in 2004 will publish an album with some of these live recordings.
DISCOGRAPHY: **LATIN MASS** *(Metronome, 1970)* **43 MINUTEN** *(Brain, 1972)*. C.A. & C.C.

Europe: GERMANY

PANCAKE

Günther Konopik - *drums*, **Walter Negele** - *guitar*, **Tommy Metzger** - *guitar*, **Werner Bauer** - *bass*, **Hampy Nerlich** - *vocals*, **Biggi Zmierczak** - *vocals*, **Uli Frank** - *keyboards, vocals*, **Ralf Scheibe** - *bass, vocals*.

A typical classy tripped-out kraut rock oddity formed by **Werner Bauer** with a first album released in 1975: *Roxy Elephant* is a German classic prog with British inspirations, where a massive use of guitars and the complete absence of keyboards still managed to mix epic heaviness with majestic arrangements and powerfully emotional songs. In the second album *Out of the Ashes* of 1977, they modify their sound to a prog oriented pop rock harshly criticized by the press. The third and last work of this band, *No illusions*, is a record of 1979 and does not belong to the prog genre at all. These albums have been recently reissued by Garden of Delights.
RECOMMENDED RECORDINGS: ROXY ELEPHANT *(Private pressing, 1975)* **OUT OF THE ASHES** *(Blubber lips, 1978)*.   C.A. & C.C.

THE PEROTIC THEATRE

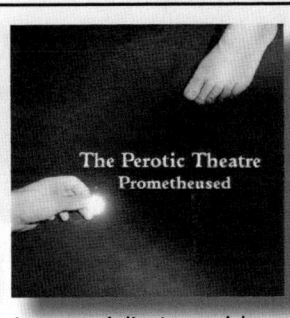

Niklas David - *piano, moog synthesizers*, **Alex Wiemer** - *vocals, guitar*, **Mathias Both** - *vocals, guitar*, **Rudi Leitchle** - *drums*.

An atypical symphonic prog band with avant-garde elements from Stuttgart, they belongs to the new wave of German Prog in the early '90s. Two albums after a long experience of live performances, both self-produced. Their best is probably *Prometheused* with well distributed and balanced sounds between innovation and the attempt to bring back the past prog mainstream, without self-indulgent devices. Very good at entertaining the audience, they maintain ever delicate and harmonized arrangements with long suites (tribute to the masters of British prog) with English lyrics sung with an accent.
DISCOGRAPHY: PROMETHEUSED *(Private pressing, 1995)* **DRYVE** *(Private pressing, 1996)*. C.A. & C.C.

POSEIDON

Horst Meinzer - *vocals, bass, guitar*, **Tony Mahl** - *keyboards*, **Wilfried Sahm** - *guitar*, **Theo Metzler** - *guitar*, **Rudi Metzler** - *drums*.

Also known as **Prussic Acid**, this German prog band swims against the great current of krautrock, producing a sound closer the American wave instead: their only self-produced album of 1975, *Found my way*, contains soft tunes, in open contrast with the typical kraut rock standard of their place and time, with organ and guitar textures which develop a delicate music balance. The recording passed unobserved given the absence of a more commercial track that could stand out in some way. Drummer **Rudi Metzler** is at the moment the only still active musician playing with the psychedelic rock band **Trigon**.
DISCOGRAPHY: FOUND MY WAY *(self production, 1975)*. C.A. & C.C.

REBEKKA

Marion Weldert - *vocals*, **Hubert Schneider** - *guitar, flute*, **Martin Schneider-Weldert** - *saxophones*, **Peter Laubmeier** - *keyboards, piano*, **Joachim Zscheile** - *bass*, **Christoph B. Imler** - *drums, percussion*.

Perhaps less famous than other German bands, their beautiful symphonic rock album *Phoenix* of 1982 still deserves the appropriate attention: compared to Renaissance due to a romantic classicism and the presence of a female soprano vocalist, **Marion Weldert**, their music mixes acoustic folk with the melodic, sometimes dreamy soundscapes of rising synths and electric guitars, to flute parts, acoustic percussions and spectacular guitar solos that recall the best of Andy Latimer. A last album was released in 1984 titled *Labyrinth*.
DISCOGRAPHY: PHOENIX *(1982, Heute)* **LABYRINTH** *(1984, Ohrwurm Records)*. M.G. & C.C.

RELEASE MUSIC ORCHESTRA

Manfred Rurup - keyboards, **Norbert Jacobsen, Gunther Reger** - winds, **Bernd Kiefer, Holger Dunkel, Frank Fischer** - bass, **Wolfgang Lindner, Wolfgang Thierfeldt** - drums, **Margit Maya Haberland** - percussion, vocals.

A group born on the ashes of **Tomorrow's Gift**, they release five good albums in the second half of the '70s. RMO were never a stable line-up and their sound tends to a more commercial and streamlined US jazz-fusion with each new work. Their first album Life of 1974 includes live recordings of their first concert but their particular jazz-rock stands out better in the 1975 release *Garuda*, with impressive electric piano arrangements and funky hints mixed to the vivid horns that justify the last part of the name, in affinity with **Mahavishnu Orchestra**, even though they end up as a quintet of average quality, similar to the experience of the Italian band **Nova**.

DISCOGRAPHY: LIFE (Brain, 1974) **GARUDA** (Brain, 1975) **GET THE BALL** (Brain, 1976) **BEYOND THE LIMIT** (Brain, 1978) **NEWS** (Brain, 1979). M.G. & C.C.

ROUSSEAU

Ali Pfeffer - drums. **Jorg Schwartz, Christoph Masbaum, Uwe Schilling** - guitars, **Rainer Hoffmann** - keyboards, **Christopher Huster** - flute, guitars, **Georg Huthmacher, Dieter Beermann** - bass, **Herbert G. Ruppik, Dieter Muller** - vocals.

This art-rock symphonic band forms in 1977. Their first album of 1980, *Flower in Asphalt*, is full of unusual pathos for its time, also thanks to the instrumental textures and enchanting melodies of the melodic guitar, the flutes and the romantic lyrics. Thanks to a certain success they decide to release *Retreat* in 1983, greatly influenced by the Canterbury teachings, but the line-up changes and the harsh musical moment lead both this and the 1987 album to result as less inspired. 16 years later the reunion in 2002, with another album, this time more classical: *At The Cinema* is published by the French label Musea, who also re-issued all their old material.

DISCOGRAPHY: FLOWER IN ASPHALT (Streyer Disco, 1980) **RETREAT** (Siebenpunkt, 1983) **SQUARE THE CIRCLE** (Musea, 1987) **AT THE CINEMA** (Musea, 2002). M.G. & C.C.

RPWL

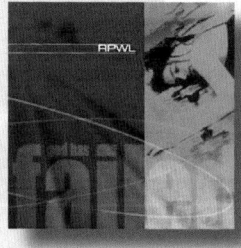

Hyogi Lang - vocals, keyboards, **Chris Postl** - bass, **Kalle Wallner** - chitarra, **Manfred Müller** - drums, **Phil Paul Rissettio** - drums, **Stephan Ebner** - bass, **Andreas Wernthaler** - keyboards, **Markus Jehle** - keyboards.

Risettion Postl Wallner Lung - the band members - is a still active German progressive rock group formed in 1997 as a **Pink Floyd** cover band. Their stunning evolution lies in how after three years they begin to write their own music, transforming their career into one of the most interesting products of the new-progressive market. The original **Pink Floyd** influence is ever present but most surprising is the freshness and the energy in their concerts.

In 2005 the studio album *World Through My Eyes* features former **Genesis** and **Stiltskin** vocalist **Ray Wilson** singing "Roses". In 2008 they publish The *RPWL experience*, a work that diverts from the previous with a new form of rawer adult pop of unpolished sounds.

RECOMMENDED RECORDINGS: GOD HAS FAILED (Tempus, 2000) **THE RPWL EXPERIENCE** (Inside Out, 2008) **THE RPWL LIVE EXPERIENCE** (Metalmind, 2009). C.A. & C.C.

SAHARA

Henner Hering - keyboards, **Holger Brandt** – drums, percussion, **Michael Hofmann** - synthesizer, guitar, flute, vocals, **Günther Moll** – guitar, vocals, **Stefan Wissnet** – lead vocals, bass, acoustic guitar.

Born as **Subject ESQ** with a good and complex album of 1972, they change name with the arrival of keyboardist **Hennes Henring** (**Out Of Focus**) and release a first work in 1974 called *Sahara Sunrise*. Deep and dynamic symphonic instrumental parts with some jazz inserts and vocals between beat and country, this album is dominated by a long title-track suite of 27 minutes characterized by continuous changes; less fascinating the rest of the record. More compact and coherent the 1975 record *For all the Clowns* which confirms the good impact of **Wissnet**'s voice.

RECOMMENDED RECORDINGS: FOR ALL THE CLOWNS (Ariola, 1975). M.G. & C.C.

Europe: GERMANY

SECOND MOVEMENT

Harald Kesselhack - *vocals*, **Siggi Zeidler** - *keyboards*, **Thomas Mockl** - *guitars*, **Manni Greiner** - *bass*, **Mathias Helk** - *drums*, **Manni Bierbach** - *winds*.

Kraut rock band oriented to a symphonic fusion with delicate horn arrangements for two excellent albums: the first of 1976, *Blind Man's Mirror*, inspired by **Eloy** with sounds of space rock and British Canterbury hints; the skillful and precise ensemble has the downside of sounding sometimes too cold and mechanic, often embellishing with heavy *Santana* like lead breaks or some extended keyboard passages, a wandering bass and the dreamy flute of **Manni Bierbach**. The last album of 1981 *Movements* completely changes style to a more mainstream '80s sound.
RECOMMENDED RECORDINGS: BLIND MAN'S MIRROR *(Castle records, 1976)*.   C.A. & C.C.

SIXTY NINE

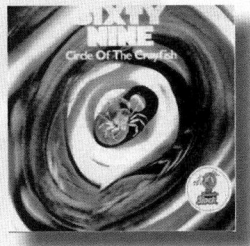

Armin Stöwe - *organ, piano, synthesizers, vocals*, **Roland Schupp** - *drums, percussion*.

A German symphonic prog rock duo formed in 1969 by **Armin Stöwe** (organ, piano, synthesizer, guitar, vocals) and **Roland Schupp** (drums, percussion, gongs). Their first album of 1972, *Circle of the Crayfish*, is a studio recording based on keyboards and synth arrangements with compelling sounds and a cautious approach to certain electronic tunes. The second album *Live* of 1974 contains the recordings from the 1973 tour: losing part of the studio devices it still gains in groove and energy. It's a pity they disband immediately after.
DISCOGRAPHY: CIRCLE OF THE CRAYFISH *(Philips, 1972)* **LIVE** *(Philips, 1974)*.   C.A. & C.C.

STREETMARK

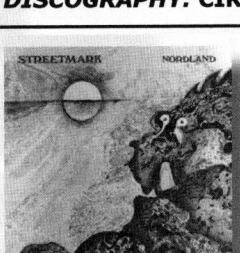

Dorothea Raukes - *keyboards, vocals*, **Thomas Schreiber** - *guitar, vocals*, **Georg Buschmann** - *vocals*, **Wolfgang Westphal** - *bass*, **Hans Schweiß** - *drums*, **Wolfgang Riechmann** - *vocals, synthesizers*.

Founded in 1968 by keyboardist **Dorothea Raukes** and guitarist **Thomas Schreiber**, they played as a cover band in Dusseldorf's underground clubs for several years. At the turn of the decade they develop their own style, influenced by Procol Harum, Focus and ELP, and in 1975 they finally issue the cosmic album *Nordland* produced and recorded by **Connie Plank**: a brilliant debut with the usual weak point of the English sung vocals. In 1977 the album *Eileen* sees **Wolfgang Riechmann** (tragically murdered in 1978), a solo recording artist who joined in on vocals and keyboards. This second release is re-issued in 1979 with the new title **Wolfgang Riechmann and Streetmark** with a bonus track "Dreams". The last two works are oriented to a form of adult pop.
DISCOGRAPHY: NORDLAND *(Sky, 1975)* **EILEEN** *(Sky, 1977)* **DRY** *(Sky, 1979)* **SKY RACER** *(Sky, 1981)*.   C.A. & C.C.

TETRAGON

Hendrik Schaper - *keyboards, vocals*, **Jürgen Jaehner** - *guitars*, **Rolf Rettberg** - *bass*, **Joachim Luhrmann** - *drums*.

The band set up a primitive recording facility in an old farm and recorded live all the tracks of their one and only album *Nature* which was released in 1971. The absence of a personal style (since they usually performed covers of other songs with their original impros) is deeply evident, however it remains a good and pleasant instrumental album with few vocal parts well oriented to blues and jazz. *Stretch* is a posthumous (2009) studio album recorded in 7 days in Dec 1971 but never released officially by the band while *Agape* is the recording of a 1973 concert issued in 2012. Soon after they vanish but the strength of the first album led it to be re-released several times over the years, even more recently on CD.
DISCOGRAPHY: NATURE *(Soma, 1971)*.   C.A. & C.C.

Europe: GERMANY

TIBET

Jürgen Krutzsch – *guitar, percussion,* **Kalus Werthmann** – *lead vocals,* **Deff Ballin** – *keyboards, percussion,* **Dieter Kumpakischkis** – *keyboards,* **Karl Heinz Hamann** - *bass, percussion,* **Fred Teske** – *drums.*

Born in 1972 by **Jürgen Krutzsch** with the initial intent of playing Tibetan instruments (tabla, violin, zither, flute), he quickly abandons this though the band retains a certain pseudo-mystic feel. A series of sampler recordings of this early period were released with a 16 year-old singer known as **Maggie**. The band tours extensively, opening occasionally for **Kraan**, and will publish only one album in 1979: recorded in three separate sessions (1976 to 1978) and primarily in sung English, the sound is a complex fusion of astral rock, jazz, classical music and Tibetan sounds, heavily keyboard-driven (Hammond, mellotron) and compared to **Eloy, Camel, Genesis, Amenophis** and even to **Uriah Heep** and other bands of symphonic space or of AOR rhythms. Disbanded after the final concert in 1980, apparently the master went lost so for the re-issuing on CD by Musea in 1994, it had to be re-recorded entirely.
RECOMMENDED RECORDINGS: TIBET *(Musea, 1979).* M.G. & C.C.

TRILOGY

Jochen Kirsten – *keyboards,* **Guido Harding** – *keyboards,* **Detlef Deeken** – *guitars,* **Ludger Samson** – *bass,* **Martin Breuer** - *drums.*

Name derived from the album of their idols **ELP**, this only instrumental symphonic and super-keyboardy band releases in 1979 a first album titled *Here it is,* with organ and a large use of Mellotron recalling also sounds from **Genesis** (**Trespass** and **A Trick of the Tail**) like in the long suite "Crowded". Well received in their country, some copies reach the British market where it becomes a sort of cult due to the few copies available. In 1982, with a different line-up, they publish *Nachtlichter,* a mostly unknown second opera with more short and nervous tracks, but still of good interest. Then they simply vanish.
RECOMMENDED RECORDINGS: HERE IT IS *(Cain, 1979).* M.G. & C.C.

TRIUMVIRAT

Jürgen Fritz - *keyboards,* **Hans Pape, Helmut Köllen** – *bass, guitars, vocals,* **Hans Bathelt** – *drums, percussion.*

This band was often heavily accused of copying ELP. Their first semi-conceptual LP of 1972, *Mediterranean Tales* opens with the 16 minutes of "Across the Waters" and is an immediate success. During the recording of the *Illusions on a Double Dimple* (1973) **Hans Pape** is replaced by **Helmut Köllen**. With this conceptual album on depression and personal relations, they go international. Their third work of 1975, *Spartacus,* even makes it to the USA due to the blend of elaborate tracks and beautiful ballads. A first non-conceptual album, *Old Love Dies Hard,* is then released but not on the same level. Popularity decreases leading to the alleged suicide of **Helmut** after which **Jürgen** renames the band **The New Triumvirat** and issues *Pompeii,* but the magic was gone. Not ready to let it go he seeks the collaboration of several guests like **Curt Cress, Jeff Porcaro,** and **Steve Lukather** releasing other two works of scarce interest.
RECOMMENDED RECORDINGS: ILLUSIONS ON A DOUBLE DIMPLE *(EMI/Harvest, 1973).* M.G. & C.C.

ULYSSES (Neronia)

Gerard Hynes – *vocals,* **Mirko Rudnik** – *guitars,* **Thomas Diehl** – *keyboards,* **Ender Kilic** – *Bass,* **Robert Zoom** – *drums,* **Tracy Hitchings** – *vocals*.

In 1993 **Ulysses** releases a first album titled **Neronia**, but for legal reasons, the band has to change name and chose the album's title. The themes are close to **Marillion** and **Pendragon**, but with a good dose of melodic personality, especially in the compositions. After a decade they finally issue in 2004 a second more epic and emphatic new prog work with strong rhythms and less complex vocals: *Nerotica* is a mixture of metal and neo-prog, nothing groundbreaking on the prog scale, as are all the following albums under the new name (not to be confused with Dutch **Ulysses**).
RECOMMENDED RECORDINGS: NERONIA *(PyraMusic, 1993).* M.G. & C.C.

Europe: GERMANY

VERSUS X

Arne Schaefer - *vocals, guitars,* **Ekkehard Nahm** – *keyboards,* **Stephan Dilley, Jorg Fischer, Thomas Keller** - *bass,* **Stefan Maywald, Uwe Voellmar** - *drums.*
A fascinating classic prog for nostalgics, yet annoying for certain art-rock fans, this creature of **Arne Schaefer** (other parallel projects of his are **Apogee** and **Flexable**) plays a modern symphonic and intricate progressive rock, influenced by classical music, heavy rock, jazz-rock and other contemporary classical composers. Versus X of 1993 is their first album, performed with mastery and resulting in a well balanced genre between communication and experimentation, with fusion and metal ideas and long suites written with a sense of proportion. Other three works stretch over the years like the recent 2008 album *Primordial Ocean*.
DISCOGRAPHY: **VERSUS X** *(Versus X, 1994)* **DISTURBANCE** *(Musea, 1996)* **THE TURBULENT ZONE** *(Musea, 2000)* **PRIMORDIAL OCEAN** *(Musea, 2008).* M.G. & C.C.

WERWOLF (Werewolf Art-Rock)

Peter Besting - *drums, vocals,* **Gerd Heuel** - *guitar,* **Burkhard Huckestein** - *bass,* **Wolfgang Unthan** - *keyboards,* **Gitta Löwenstein** - *vocals.*
Not to be confused with the German punk band, this group of musicians have a particular history: formed in 1970 after rehearsing in a self-built hut with freezing temperatures, they end up in drummer **Peter Besting**'s newly built house in Wenden in 1972. Often used as opening act of bands like **Eloy**, **Grobschnitt** and **Birth Control**, only in 1979 do they feel ready to record a 30 minute demo in search of a contract, without success. After several line-up changes they self-release a symphonic prog album *Creation* in 1982 as a limited edition of 1000 copies. In 1992 it was reissued in the USA with a new cover artwork by Lee Gaskins and three added tracks from the demo of 1979. In the mid '80s they split after releasing some songs in German, only to reunite as **Werewolf Art-Rock** with the 2014 album *Mystic Land*.
DISCOGRAPHY: **CREATION** *(1984, private pressing)* **MYSTIC LAND** *(2014, private pressing).* M.G. & C.C.

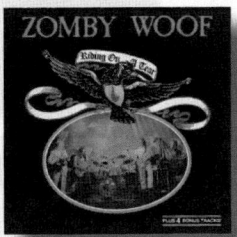

ZOMBY WOOF

Ulrich Herter, Heinrich Winter - *vocals, guitars, keyboards,* **Matthias Zumbroich** - *keyboards,* **Udo Kreuss** - *bass,* **Berthold Mayer** - *drums.*
The name is taken from **Zappa**'s album yet they have very little in common with his music: rooted in 1971 they play their first gig in the Hayinger Festival of 1974 and perform on TV in 1976, still with no label or record. Eventually Jupiter signs them up for an art-rock album (similar to **Epidaurus**, **Minotaurus** and **Ivory**), greatly inspired by **Yes** with good melodies, well arranged vocals and a vintage keyboard driven 24-carat symphonic rock, certainly a more European symphonic prog than of German derivation. A change in line-up sees the insertion of vocalist **David Hanselmann** (former **Message** and **Triumvirat** singer) and they record a second LP named *No Hero* in 1979, but remained unable to find a record company, so they disband after a last concert in 1980.
DISCOGRAPHY: **RIDING ON A TEAR** *(Jupiter, 1977).* M.G. & C.C.

RUFUS ZUPHALL

Gunter Krause - *guitars, vocals,* **Thoms Kittel** - *keyboards, guitar, bass,* **Klaus Gulden** - *flute, percussion,* **Manfred Spangenberg** - *bass,* **Udo Dahmen** - *drums.*
Band born in the late '60s from a psychedelic blues matrix and arrived to the publishing of a first record in 1970 with the album *Weiß Der Teufel*, the German answer to **Jethro Tull**. As a matter of fact many sounds had that same jazzy folk blues with hard psychedelic hints played by an acid **Hendrix**-styled guitar with a heavy use of flute. A good album, perfect prelude to the following *Phallobst* of 1971 which maintained the same sound, constructed better through more personal pieces. Recently a reunion concert is documented by the modest live *Colder Then Hell*.
RECOMMENDED RECORDINGS: **WEIß DER TEUFEL** *(Pilz, 1970)* **PHALLOBST** *(Pilz, 1971)* M.G. & C.C.

Europe: **GREAT BRITAIN**

AFTER THE FIRE

Peter Banks - *keyboards, vocals,* **Andy Piercy** - *guitars, vocals,* **Nick Battle** - *bass, violin, vocals,* **Ivor Twidell** - *drums.*

This living biblical quote (Kings 19:12) begins their career in 1971 as a Christian Rock band playing a keyboard-driven (**Peter Banks**) prog to Christian audiences in pubs and college circuits across the UK for over 6 years. In 1977 they hold a sell-out show yet still need to self-funded *Signs Of Change* in 1978, containing all the classical prog songs written throughout the years and inspired by **ELP**, **Camel**, **Genesis**, **Pink Floyd** and **Yes**. A sort of document album summarizing the previous period: therefore for the next album they change direction and adopt the new wave genre under the acronym **ATF**. This and other two albums released by CBS, along with several singles, lead them to a certain success on both sides of the Atlantic and to become the opening acts of **ELO**, **Queen** and in the USA **Van Halen**, before the disbandment in 1982. In 2003 they reunite as **ATF2** but with no real novelty.
RECOMMENDED RECORDINGS: **SIGNS OF CHANGE** *(Rapid Records & RoughMix, 1978).* **M.G. & C.C.**

ARCADIUM

Graham Best - *bass, vocals,* **Alan Ellwood** - *organ, vocals,* **John Albert Parker** - *drums,* **Robert Ellwood** - *guitar, vocals,* **Miguel Sergides** - *vocals.*

This late '60s psychedelic band formed by songwriter, guitarist and singer **Miguel Sergides** starts to play in clubs until the small label Middle Earth (owned by one of these typical underground clubs) decides to release in 1969 their only nightmarish album *Breathe Awhile* (lately reissued by Akarma). "I'm On My Way" is the long and creepy opening track of compelling dark psychedelia and ghostly blues with menacing slow motion atmospheres and powerful sound solutions: in a way one of the first bands to play gothic prog, inspiring even the more lunatic **Black Sabbath** songs.
DISCOGRAPHY: **BREATHE AWHILE** *(1969, Middle Earth).* **M.G. & C.C.**

ARENA

Mick Pointer – *drums,* **Clive Nolan** – *keyboards,* **Keith More, Steve Rothery, John Mitchell** – *guitars,* **Ian Salmon** – *bass,* **Tracy Hitchings, Rob Sowden** – *vocals.*

Super-group founded in the mid '90s by **Mick Pointer** (former **Marillion** drummer) and **Clive Nolan** (**Pendragon**'s keyboardist), with the sporadic collaboration of **Steve Rothery** (**Marillion** guitarist). They play an average prog rock saved by a more catchy hard rock as in the first two albums *Songs From The Lion's Cage* (1995) and *Pride* (1996). A third album *The Visitor* (1998) is instead a concept album closer to the sound of the later **Marillion** with a new heavier dimension. The following *Immortal?* (2000) with singer **Rob Sowden** shifts the band's sound towards hard prog but with no originality. *Contagion* (2003) is a powerful concept album on redemption while *Pepper's Ghost* (2005) results as a heavy and very symphonic metal music. *The Seventh Degree Of Separation* (2011) and *The Unquiet Sky* (2015) are more conventional.
RECOMMENDED RECORDINGS: **THE VISITOR** *(Verglas, 1998)* **M.G. & C.C.**

ARZACHEL

Steve Hillage – *guitars, vocals,* **Dave Stewart** – *keyboards,* **Mont Campbell** – *bass, vocals,* **Clive Brooks** – *drums.*

Embryo of a band later re-named **Uriel**, this first line-up was created by **Steve Hillage** and **Dave Stewart**, authors of a superlative psychedelic rock, that worked well as a transition to that high artistic expression named Canterbury School: in fact some musicians will later join future bands such as **Egg**, **Gong**, **National Health** and **Caravan**. High quality keyboards and guitar playing for the best explosive and full blown psychedelic prog rock in the British panorama, with other interesting influences from **Syd Barrett**'s **Pink Floyd** and from **Hawkwind**'s space-rock. First re-issue by Akarma in 2002.
DISCOGRAPHY: **ARZACHEL** *(Evolution, 1969).* **M.G.**

Europe: GREAT BRITAIN

BACK DOOR

Colin Hodgkinson - *bass, vocals,* **Ron Aspery** – *saxophones,* **Tony Hicks** – *drums,* **Dave MacRae** – *keyboards.*
A jazz-rock trio founded in 1971 by **Colin Hodgkinson** (bass), **Ron Aspery** (sax) and **Tony Hicks** (drums). They record some demos but none was interested in band with no guitarist and keyboard players (the lead instrument was the left-hander bass). They auto-produce in 1972 a self titled album, sold locally. This starts their live career and gains them the attention of Warner Brothers which re-releases the debut album and records a second in New York, *8th Street Nites*, produced by **Felix Pappalardi**. Keyboardist **Dave MacRae** joins in on the third but after a fourth unsuccessful work they split in 1976. In 1986 they reunite for a short tour and record some material which comes out only after the 2003 reunion in a new album. They tour until 2006 when **Tony** dies closing definitely the experience. In 2007 **Colin** forms his own trio and releases *Back Door Too!*
RECOMMENDED RECORDINGS: 8TH STREET NITES *(Warner Brothers, 1973).* M.G.

TONY BANKS

Tony Banks - *keyboards, guitars, bass, vocals,* **Kim Beacon** - *vocals,* **Chester Thompson** - *drums.*
Keyboardist of classical derivation with strong compositional skills and a distinct (and often emulated) style, he is one of the original **Genesis** founding members of 1965. After a successful but exhausting world tour, **Phil Collins** orders his colleagues at the end of 1978 a long pause. **Tony** uses this time to put together his first solo album *A Curious Feeling* published the following year: this is the only true prog album he writes, with interesting conceptual lyrics as well as the characteristic massive wall of keyboards that made his style so famous. Why this gifted musician strayed from his prog roots remains a mystery. Unfortunately he was never very successful on his own, both in his albums (an '80s pop digital/synthetic release and other three AOR ones) and in the film soundtracks he composes.
RECOMMENDED RECORDINGS: A CURIOUS FEELING *(1979, Charisma).* M.G.

CARDIACS

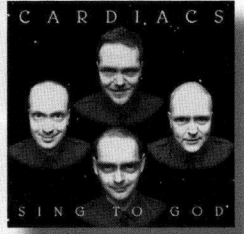

Tim Smith – *guitar, vocals, keyboards,* **Jim Smith** - *bass,* **William D. Drake** - *keyboards,* **Dominic Luckman** - *drums.*
Someone invented 'pronk' as a contraction of prog-punk to define them since their style was an interpretation of a generation born with punk, but nostalgic of prog, ready for the new wave, but with brains in the various avant-garde forms. Formed in 1977 (originally as **Cardiac Arrest**) by **Tim Smith**'s unique use of unusual chord progressions, **Zappa**-esque complexities, psychedelic overtones, catchy melodies and odd, often impenetrable lyrics, they go through several line-ups before settling on a first in 1984. Their sound evolves from the raw DIY punk of the early cassettes to the sumptuous psychedelic pop grandeur of their most recent works. A stroke in 2008 leaves **Tim** unable to continue his career: many a benefit concert to raise money for his care as well as the release of a tribute album. Today their music is available on iTunes: a good way to ensure **Tim** and the band receive some payment for their work.
RECOMMENDED RECORDINGS: SING TO GOD *(Alphabet Business, 1996).* M.G. & C.C.

CASTANARC

Marc Holiday - *vocals.* **David Powell, Steve Beighton** - *keyboards,* **Paul Ineson, Rick Burns** - *guitars,* **Neil Duty, Rob Clark** - *bass,* **Dave Kirkland, Vincenzo Lammi** - *drums.*
Obscure neo-prog band from the UK's mid '80s, all four albums are a good mixture of **Genesis**, **Yes** and **Camel** sounds with delicate atmospheres which recall somewhat **Pink Floyd**. The remarkable vocals of **Mark Holiday** draws the attention away from the prog genre and into a **John Waite**-like rock dimension but over-all the ensemble is capable of recreating a melancholy through their predominant and compelling keyboard playing. *Journey To The East* is their first 1984 album, a real cult prog classic and probably their best. The last is of 1998.
DISCOGRAPHY: JOURNEY TO THE EAST *(Peninsula, 1984)* RUDE POLITICS *(Khepra, 1988)* LITTLE GODS *(1989).* M.G. & C.C.

Europe: GREAT BRITAIN

CIRKUS

Paul Robson - *lead vocals*, **John Taylor** - *bass*, **Derek G. Miller** - *organ, piano, mellotron*, **Stu McDade** - *drums, percussion, backing vocals*, **Dogg** - *guitars*.

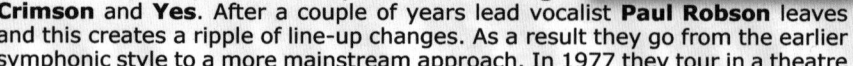

This quintet records in 1973 their debut album *Cirkus One*, greatly influenced by the music of **King Crimson** and **Yes**. After a couple of years lead vocalist **Paul Robson** leaves and this creates a ripple of line-up changes. As a result they go from the earlier symphonic style to a more mainstream approach. In 1977 they tour in a theatre production called 'Future Shock', based on the musical, and release with them an album of which they are not however authors. A year later the single "I'm On Fire" features on a *Battle Of The Bands* LP before a first break-up. In 1994 the album *Cirkus Ii The Global Cut* is published, where only **Derek Miller** features from the original line-up. The real reunion will take place in 1998 when the original line-up releases *Pantomyne*.
RECOMMENDED RECORDINGS: **CIRKUS ONE** *(Private Pressing, 1971)*   C.A. & C.C.

ENGLAND

Martin Henderson - *bass, vocals*, **Franc Holland** - *guitars, vocals*, **Robert Webb** - *keyboards, vocals*, **Jode Leich** - *drums, percussion, bass, vocals*.

This British prog-rock quartet releases its debut LP *Garden Shed* in 1977, a sound deeply influenced by **Yes**, **Genesis** and **Gentle Giant**. This record contains beautiful doses of Mellotron and sweet guitars arpeggios that fill with romanticism the melodies also thanks to the fascinating lyrics. For the twenty years anniversary, a second album is released in 1997, *The Last Of The Jubblies*, with unpublished works recorded between 1975 and 1976, therefore previous to their debut. With the help of **Gordon Haskell** and **The Forward Organisation**, keyboardist **Robert Webb** also manages to re-issue *Garden Shed* for the occasion.
RECOMMENDED RECORDINGS: **GARDEN SHED** *(Arista, 1977)*.   M.G. & C.C.

BRIAN ENO

Founder of ambient music, this glam rocker, expert in electronic devices and producer of **Peter Gabriel**, **U2** and **Talking Heads**, has influenced many a musician. He grows with Doo Wop and R&B, later fascinated by avant-garde composers like **John Cage** and **Terry Riley**. In 1971 he joins **Roxy Music** as the only one at the time to know how to operate a certain synth. His eclectic looks often eclipse Bryan Ferry's, leading to the eventual exit and solo career. *No Pussyfooting* of 1973 is an early ambient venture where **Robert Fripp** invents his *Frippertronics* system, so **Eno**'s first true solo album is actually *Here Come The Warm Jets*, followed by another 2 works and a couple of collaborations before he finally undertakes the prog genre with *Another Green World* of 1975, featuring guests including **Phil Collins**. The sequel of 1977, *Before And After Science*, is a more pop prog while afterwards he focuses on ambient like in the 2004 album, again with **Fripp**.
RECOMMENDED RECORDINGS: **ANOTHER GREEN WORLD** *(Islands, 1975)* **BEFORE AND AFTER THE SCIENCE** *(Polydor, 1977)*.   C.C.

FANTASY

David Read - *bass*, **Paul Lawrence** - *vocals, guitar*, **David Metcalfe** - *keyboards, vocals*, **Peter James** - *guitar, vocals*, **Peter Webster** - *drums, vocals*.
This band starts rehearsing in the family farmhouse of singer **Paul Petley** and after some line-up changes, they finally sign up with Polydor for their 1973 debut *Paint a Picture*. Greatly influenced by **The Moody Blues** and **Cressida**, their delicate prog sound is very well arranged resulting in pleasant melodies and elegant instrumental performances. The tapes for a next album recorded in 1974 were published posthumous by Audio Archives as *Beyond The Beyond* only in 1992: nine very refined tracks of absolute beauty with warm vocals, acoustic guitars and loads of Hammond organ and Mellotron. In 1994 *Vivariatum* is released as an anthology of archive recordings and unreleased tracks.
RECOMMENDED RECORDINGS: **PAINT A PICTURE** *(1973, Polydor)* **BEYOND THE BEYOND** *(1992, Audio Archives)* **VIVARIATUM** *(1994, Audio Archives)*.   MG & C.C.

Europe: **GREAT BRITAIN**

FISH

Born **Derek William Dick**, this scottish singer and songwriter grows up with **The Beatles** and then plunges into **Yes**, **ELP** and **Pink Floyd** wanting his own band, but he cannot play anything. So he decides to become a singer and practices on **Elton John** and **Deep Purple** songs. After an experience in a couple of bands, at the end of 1980 he answers an add from **Marillion** and auditions drunk with a **Genesis** repertoire. Impressed by his vocal skills (very like **Peter Gabriel**) their first gig together is in 1981. He writes most lyrics with **Steve Rothery** but often in disagreement with both colleagues and labels, in 1988 he exits starting his own career and label: *Vigil in Wilderness of Mirror*, *Raingods with Zippos*, *Fellini Days* and *A Feast Of Consequences*, among others. In the meantime he also becomes an actor.
RECOMMENDED RECORDINGS: **VIGIL IN A WILDERNESS OF MIRRORS** *(EMI, 1990)* **RAINGODS WITH ZIPPOS** *(Roadrunner 1999).*
M.G. & C.C.

MORGAN FISHER

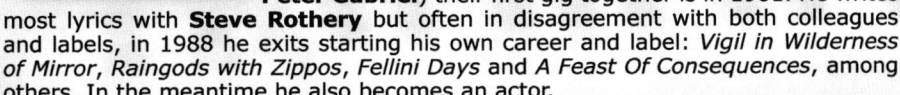

Keyboardist **Morgan Fisher** begins his career in 1966 with **The Soul Survivors** (later **The Love Affair** and then **L.A.**). In 1972 he forms **Morgan**: singer **Tim Staffel** from **Smile** (future **Queen** embryo line-up) joins also for the lyrics. Their debut *Nova Solis*, is a typical '70s prog with every type of keyboard and percussions imaginable. That same year he also records *Morgan Fisher's Hand Job* but RCA cancels for the explicit name and cover, so it is released only in 1984 as *Ivories*. The 1973 *Brown Out* is again released later in 1977 for the US and two years after in the UK as *The Sleeper Wakes*: a mix of hysterical synth solos, high operatic vocals, pretentious pseudo-classical keyboard art-rock and experimental song structures. Then he joins **Mott The Hoople** (soon to become **British Lions**) and is still active with many collaborations more focused on ambient.
DISCOGRAPHY: **MORGAN: NOVA SOLIS** *(Polygram, 1972)* **BROWN OUT** *(Passport, 1977)* **MORGAN FISHER: IVORIES** *(Strike Back, 1984).*
M.G. & C.C.

FRESH MAGGOTS

The one shot duo **Mick Burgoyne** and **Leigh Dolphin** publish in 1971 their only album *Fresh Maggots* with RCA, a particularly personal acid-folk prog that goes from English classic folk like **Amazing Blondel**, to the most adventurous psychedelia and heavy elements like **Free**'s fuzz guitars, switching from guitars to violin to glockenspiel to guitars again. The release was delayed for years and when it finally came out the music had turned to other horizons so it did not obtain the forecasted success. Apparently still unreleased are the BBC session recordings and the demo tracks for their projected second album.
DISCOGRAPHY: **FRESH MAGGOTS** *(RCA, 1971)*
C.A. & C.C.

FRUUPP

Stephen Houston - *keyboards, oboe, vocals,* **Peter Farrelly** - *bass, flute, vocals,* **Vincent McCusker** - *guitar, vocals,* **Martin Foye** - *drums, percussion.*
Perhaps the only Irish symphonic prog band, they form in Belfast in 1970 thanks to guitarist, singer and writer **Vince McCusker**. After signing with Dawn Records they publish *Future Legends* in 1973, an album of great personality with ample use of strings and jazzy inserts.
In the following years they produced three other studio albums combining several styles and instruments like classical music (oboe), folk (acoustic guitars) and symphonic (interplay of electric guitar and organ). The poetic melodies, symphonic moments, fast structural changes and complex tracks of *The Prince Of Heaven's Eyes* are perhaps the apex of their career.
RECOMMENDED RECORDINGS: **THE PRINCE OF HEAVEN'S EYES** *(Dawn Record, 1974).*
M.G. & C.C.

Europe: **GREAT BRITAIN**

GALAHAD

Roy Keyworth - *guitars, bass, tape effects,* **Stuart Nicholson** - *vocals,* **Spencer Luckman** - *drums, percussion,* **Dean Baker** - *keyboards, programming,* **Neil Pepper** - *bass.*
Born in 1985, they took form in the centre of the new prog era, when bands like **IQ** and **Marillion** had already traced the lines of the reborn genre. Initially a cover band of **Genesis**, **Led Zeppelin**, **Rush**, and **U2**, from 1987 they

start fabricating a series of singles, audio tapes, auditions and promos, when finally in 1991 their first record *Nothing is Written* comes out. With good regularity the band has produced a wide discography and probably their best work is the 2002 album *Year Zero*, with **John Wetton** (**Asia**, **King Crimson**, **Family**) on guest vocals. Then their sound takes a more contemporary, metallic approach, winning them the 2007 Classic Rock Society awards with *Empires Never Last*.
RECOMMENDED RECORDINGS: **YEAR ZERO** *(Avalon Records, 2002).* M.G. & C.C.

GORDON GILTRAP

Excellent self-taught acoustic guitarist, sometimes recalling **Anthony Phillips** (**Genesis**) who shares his English country-side folk tastes. His first two albums have not much to do with prog, so it is with his third work of 1971 where he starts inserting certain elements from the genre. The best album of his discography is considered to be *Visionary* (influenced by William Blake) released in 1976, as well as the

album *Perilous Journey*, produced the following year with his own band and awarded by the Sunday Times as the best album of 1977. *Fear of the Dark* is also a fascinating project of 1978, one of the last with true prog elements. His last album is in fact a potpourri of styles published in 2004.
RECOMMENDED RECORDINGS: **PERILOUS JOURNEY** *(Voiceprint, 1977).* M.G. & C.C.

GIZMO

Dave Radford – *guitars, vocals,* **Brian Gould** - *keyboards, vocals,* **Maurice Memmott** – *keyboards, violin,* **Steve Wise** - *drums, percussion.*
Interesting and underestimated band formed in the full punk new wave era, their style, very anchored to the times, is controversially labeled under the prog umbrella for all the wrong reasons: their sound instead manages to unite the typical prog themes with the electronic new wave with incredible balance. In 1975 young singer-songwriter from Canterbury **David Radford** is noticed by the President Records and signed up with his band (**Gizmo**) for a first single. Then some line-up changes will mold their sound until the release of 1979's demo tape and the following first real album *Just Like Master Bates*. Published in 1981, *Victims* is a more average work that will lead to a first break-up until the reunion of 1992 with *They're Peeling Onions in the Cellar*, probably their best album so far.
RECOMMENDED RECORDINGS: **THEY'RE PEELING ONIONS IN THE CELLAR** *(Canterbury Records, 1992).* M.G. & C.C.

GOLIATH

Linda Rothwell – *vocals,* **Malcolm Grundy** – *guitars,* **Joseph Rosbotham** - *horns,* **John Williamson** – *bass,* **Eric Eastman** – *drums, percussion.*
In 1970 this band releases with CBS its one and only self titled album with elements of rock, folk and blues, as well as an Eastern touch, for a lighter jazz-infected crossover prog sound similar to **Jethro Tull** but with

a female singer: the vocals of **Linda Rothwell** are sensational and compelling, recalling the voice of **Grace Slick** (**Jefferson Airplane**). A band strictly linked to the 1970s playing an interesting and very pleasant proto-folk prog with funky bass arrangements and fusion hints.
DISCOGRAPHY: **GOLIATH** *(CBS, 1970).* M.G.

Europe: GREAT BRITAIN

GRACIOUS

Alan Cowderoy - *guitars, vocals,* **Martin Kitcat** - *piano, keyboards, vocals,* **Robert Lipson** - *drums,* **Tim Wheatley** - *bass,* **Paul Davis** - *guitar, vocals.*
Another fine band from the early British prog-rock movement formed around keyboardist **Martin Kitcat**, so impressed by **King Crimson**'s Mellotrons that he immediately incorporates them into their sound. The first album of 1970 features symphonic songs paved with Mellotron and breaks of pure electric rock alternating baroque sounds and lunatic melodies recalling **Pink Floyd**. A year later their second album is a much better work due to the stunning mellotron often in captivating interplay with the electric guitar mixing blues, rock, classical and symphonic with pleasant atmospheres. The end comes nevertheless until a new and final album in 1996.
DISCOGRAPHY: GRACIOUS *(1970, Vertigo)* **THIS IS... GRACIOUS** *(1972, Philips)* **ECHO** *(1996, Centaur).*
M.G. & C.C.

GRAVY TRAIN

Norman Barratt - *guitars, vocals,* **Barry Davenport** - *drums,* **J.D. Hughes** - *keyboards, vocals, horns,* **Lester Williams** - *bass, vocals.*
Formed in 1970 by guitarist and vocalist **Norman Barratt**, they sign up at first with Vertigo for two good solid prog-rock folk albums with plenty of wonderful flute playing: the first (1970) is an average work despite the excellent guitar playing and the powerful vocals of **Barratt**, and the second (1971) entitled *(Ballad of a) Peaceful Man* is probably their best. The next two albums are instead published by Dawn (1973, *Second birth*, and 1974 *Staircase To The Day*, with the fine art-work cover by **Roger Dean**) but the label seemed more interested in launching the new glam-rock artists instead of the quality of these productions.
DISCOGRAPHY: GRAVY TRAIN *(Vertigo, 1970)* **(BALLAD OF A) PEACEFUL MAN** *(Vertigo, 1971)* **SECOND BIRTH** *(Dawn, 1973)* **STAIRCASE TO THE DAY** *(Dawn, 1974).*
C.A. & C.C.

JOHN GREAVES

Deeply rooted in the Canterbury teachings, he is an excellent bass player of jazz-rock writing a delicate traditional music close to the chanson française (the French Chansons of 2004). With **Peter Blegvad** (**Henry Cow/Slap Happy**, 1974) he records in 1977 the *Kew Rhône* project with singer **Lisa Herman**, an example of R.I.O. mastery. Then he joins **National Health** in parallel playing also with **Soft Heap**. After many collaborations he publishes a first solo album *Accident in Paris* (1982) and forms a touring band for the album *Parrot Fashion* (1984). Meanwhile playing as a session man, he starts his new project *Songs* of 1995, with **Robert Wyatt** singing a few tracks. In 1998 he begins the electric *The Caretaker*, released only in 2001, featuring him on lead vocals and bass. His last live concert of 2015 *Piacenza* confirms his ongoing activity.
RECOMMENDED RECORDINGS: ACCIDENT *(1982, Europa Records)* **PARROT FASHIONS** *(1984, Europa Records)* **SONGS** *(1995, Resurgence)* **THE CARETAKER** *(2001, Resurgence-Voiceprint)* **John Greaves-Peter Blegvad-Lisa Herman: KEW. RHÔNE** *(1977, Virgin).*
M.G. & C.C.

GREENSLADE

Dave Greenslade – *keyboards,* **Dave Lawson** - *vocals, keyboards,* **Andy McCulloch** - *drums, percussion,* **Tony Reeves** – *bass.*
When Colosseum disbands, **Dave Greenslade** and **Tony Reeves** decide to found their band with **Andrew McCulloch** (**King Crimson**) and **Dave Lawson** (**Web**). The two keyboard line-up preludes to a great symphonic flow of Mellotron, with strings and jazz elements, choirs, hard blues and the strong use of a clavinet in the solo parts, lacking the longness and self-indulgent epic scores. They debut in 1973 with a total of four studio albums before ending the band. In *Bedside Manner Are Extra* the song "Drum Folk" greatly represents their style. They reunite in 2000 with some concerts and new releases where the omnipresent keyboard dual-play (here with **John Young**) is always very exciting.
RECOMMENDED RECORDINGS: GREENSLADE *(Warner Bros, 1973)* **BEDSIDE MANNERS ARE EXTRA** *(Warner Bros, 1973).*
M.G. & C.C.

Europe: GREAT BRITAIN

HANNIBAL

Alex Boyce – vocals, **Jack Griffiths** - bass, **Bill Hunt** – keyboards, **Adrian Ingram** – guitars, **John Parkes** – drums.

An only album of 1970 which starts out fairly slow but builds in quality as it moves along, sometimes recalling **Atomic Rooster** with echoes of **Edgar Broughton Band**: this is an interesting heavy prog ensemble with a taste for jazz, a great lead guitar and keyboards, with a lot of saxophone, but penalized by their technical inability to develop the songwriting and the performances. Even if it is a product of **Tony Stratton Smith**'s Charisma (**Genesis** and **VDGG**'s same label), there seems to be a void in the production and mixing desk at the recording studios. Perhaps with more promotional guidance they could have made a less average music. Nevertheless still further proof of all the chances offered to the emerging bands in the '60s and '70s.
DISCOGRAPHY: HANNIBAL (Charisma, 1970).   M.G.

HOME

Laurie Wisefield – guitars, **Mick Stubbs** – vocals, **Mick Cook** – drums, **Cliff Williams** – bass.

Founded in London in 1970 by guitarist **Laurie Wisefield** and singer/song-writer **Mick Stubbs**, this band released three albums between 1971 and 1973. The third (and last) entitled *The Alchemist*, is probably their masterpiece: a concept album of supernatural events. **Stubbs** exits when all the others join **Al Stewart** as his support band in 1974. **Wisefield** will later join **Wishbone Ash** (today he is touring in the musical version of War of the Worlds) while **Williams** becomes the official bass player in **AC/DC**. Rumors of an fourth album were never confirmed and since both **Stubbs** and **Cook** have passed away this will remain just a dream.
RECOMMENDED RECORDINGS: THE ALCHEMIST (CBS, 1973).   M.G.

HORSLIPS

Barry Devlin – bass, vocals, **Sean Fean** – lead guitar, vocals, **Eamonn Carr** – drums, vocals, **Charles O'Connor** – violin, mandolin, vocals, **Jim Lockhart** – flute, tin whistle, keyboards, vocals.

Irish quintet from Dublin formed in 1970, they are very famous in their home country for inventing a personal Celtic folk prog-rock which sometimes recalls the style of **Steeleye Span** and **Fairport Convention**. With almost a dozen albums, the first four are probably their best. Disbanded in 1980, the pressure of the fans forced the to the reunion of the original band, with the new album of 2004, *Roll Back*, a record containing re-arrangements of their old songs with rich acoustic treatments or performed in the original style but completely reinvented.
RECOMMENDED RECORDINGS: DANCEHALL SWEETHEARTS (Oats, 1974) **BOOK OF INVASIONS: A CELTIC SYMPHONY** (Oats, 1976).   M.G.

ICE

Mick Rutherford – vocals, **Andy Radek** – guitars, **Colin Richardson** – Bass, **Steve Sheldon** – drums, **Paul Watts** – guitars.

One shot band formed in 1978 by the musicians of **Willow**, all except the keyboardist. Their only psychedelic rock album of 1979, *Saga Of The Ice King*, is a concept inspired by Icelandic mythology with an elegant combination of electro-acoustic sounds, symphonic parts, pastoral vibes, a melodic singing and simple even hard rock elements in **Black Sabbath** style. Recorded in **Colin Richardson**'s tool-shed, the quality is obviously not excellent and it was remastered and issued by Kissing Spell on CD in 2004, with also a better cover illustration. They toured around until 1982 when, after an attempt to compose new material, the band decides to disband. **Richardson** sadly passed away in 2006.
RECOMMENDED RECORDINGS: SAGA OF THE ICE KING (Storm Records, 1979).   M.G. & C.C.

Europe: **GREAT BRITAIN**

IF

Dick Morrissey – *saxophones, flute,* **Terry Smith** – *guitars,* **Dave Quincy** – *saxophones,* **Dennis Eliott** – *drums,* **John Mealing** – *keyboards,* **Jim Richardson** – *bass,* **J.W. Hodkinson** – *vocals.*

A seminal jazz rock band formed in 1969 by **Dick Morrissey** and **Terry Smith**, often seen as the British answer to the American **Blood, Sweat and Tears** and **Chicago**: the main difference was that they did not have a trumpet or trombone player and featured two saxes instead. Reputed too jazz for prog and too rock for jazz, their first homonym album of 1970 hit both US and UK charts in no time. Another three albums follow with exhausting tours, culminating in the apparent break-up of 1972, after **Morrissey**'s exit due to medical issues. Essentially a live band, probably the only jazz-rock at the time to feature solos by all band members.
RECOMMENDED RECORDINGS: IF *(Island/Capitol, 1970)* IF 2 *(Island/Capitol, 1970)* IF 3 *(Island/Capitol, 1971)* IF 4 "Waterfall"*(Island/Capitol, 1972).* M.G.

INDIAN SUMMER

Malcom Harker – *bass, vocals,* **Paul Hooper** – *drums,* **Bob Jackson** – *keyboards, lead vocals,* **Colin Williams** - *guitars.*

Very interesting scottish quartet, their only album of 1971 was not adequately promoted (even if with the same management of **Black Sabbath**) to the success it deserved. Fairly long keyboard driven hard rock songs with lots of instrumental interplay, merged into the mainstream groove of their age. The great vocal skills of singer **Bob Jackson** (a powerful voice similar to **Ian Gillan**) often wrongly led to comparisons with **Deep Purple** and **Uriah Heep**, since they had a very personal style. The label shuts down thus closing also any future projects for this band. **Jackson** will continue his career in other groups until recently.
DISCOGRAPHY: INDIAN SUMMER *(Neon, 1971).* M.G.

IONA

Dave Bainbridge - *guitars, keyboards,* **Dave Fitzgerald, Mike Haughton, Troy Donockley** - *horns, vocals.* **Joanne Hogg** - *vocals, keyboards,* **Nick Beggs, Tim Harries, Phil Barker** - *bass,* **Terl Bryant, Frank Van Essen** - *drums, violin.*

If the Roman quote 'Nomen omen' is true (destiny in the name), this scottish band's choice of calling itself like an Hebrides island proves their music to be just as misty and shady as the name. Worthy heirs of **Renaissance**, **Strawbs** and **Clannad**, they are among the most interesting prog-folk bands of '90s: formed in 1989, and still active, their first album is released the following year with great attention to the Celtic and acoustic sonorities. Interpreters of feeling and melody performed though mature arrangements, all six albums are full of spirituality among new age and jazz-fusion, with the smooth and sweet voice of **Joanne Hogg**.
RECOMMENDED RECORDINGS: IONA *(What Records, 1990)* BOOK OF KELLS *(What Records, 1992)* HEAVEN'S BRIGHT SUN *(live, Authentic, 1997)* OPEN SKY *(Authentic, 2000).* M.G. & C.C.

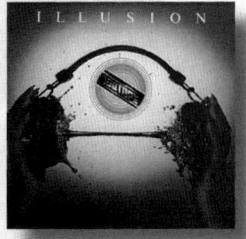

ISOTOPE

Gary Boyle - *guitars,* **Nigel Morris** - *drums,* **Laurence Scott** - *keyboards,* **Hugh Hopper** - *bass.*

Fusion jazz-rock quartet with strong progressive elements formed in 1972 by guitarist **Gary Boyle**, with hand picked musicians from the London jazz arena. A first homonym album of 1974 inspired by **Nucleus** and the Canterbury school, yet losing a certain spontaneity for a boring overall result. After a line-up change of keyboards and bass (**Hopper** from **Soft Machine** joins in), they release that same year a much more complete album titled *Illusion*. In 1975 *Deep End* arrives also with a change of musicians, guest staring **Morris Pert**. In 1977, with only **Boyle** as original member, the new line-up never goes beyond rehearsals, recording just a couple of radio sessions later published on CD in 2008. **Boyle** pursues his prolific solo career (the last three albums are published in Denmark, where he is still active).
RECOMMENDED RECORDINGS: ILLUSION *(Gull Records, 1974).* M.G. & C.C.

Europe: **GREAT BRITAIN**

IT BITES

Francis Dunnery - *guitar, lead vocals,* **John Beck** - *keyboards, vocals,* **Bob Dalton** - *drums, vocals,* **Dick Nolan** - *bass, vocals.*
Born in 1985, they release their debut the following year blending reggae, pop and new age into a metal foreground of direct melodies. The band matures in 1988 with a more prog-rock album *Once Around the World*, its 15-minute title track. They belong to that field of new prog oriented to less structured and complex forms, with models closer to real songs and harder rhythms recalling **IQ** (**Menel** period), especially in **Dunnery**'s guitar playing, composer and singer with a voice similar to **Gabriel**'s. From the '90s each members starts on other important collaborations until the abandon of **Dunnery** replaced by **John Mitchell** (**Arena**) for the last three studio albums.
RECOMMENDED RECORDINGS: ONCE AROUND THE WORLD *(Geffen, 1988).* M.G. & C.C.

JONESY

John Jones - *guitars, vocals,* **Trevor "Gypsy" Jones** - *vocals, bass,* **Jamie Kaleth** - *vocals, keyboards,* **Alan Bown** - *trumpet, horns,* **Richard "Plug" Thomas** - *drums, percussion.*
Brothers **John** and **Trevor Jones** start playing together and compose pieces while abroad living with their parents (Tasmania). Once back in London they start moving through the music scene and manage to release a first single only in 1972 followed by three great albums: *No Alternative, Keeping up* and *Growing*. Their sound is identifiable to a beat blues connected to prog for the important structures of some pieces, the use of hard elements (similar to **Led Zeppelin**), jazz and sometimes also funky, with a good quantity of Mellotron partitions greatly influenced by **King Crimson**. Re-issued in 1995 on CD by a Korean, they return with a new album only in 2003, *Sudden Prayers Make God Jump*.
RECOMMENDED RECORDINGS: KEEPING UP *(Dawn Records, 1973).* M.G. & C.C.

JULIAN'S TREATMENT

John Dover - *bass,* **Jack Drummond, Roger Odell** - *drums,* **Cathy Pruden** - *vocals (1969-70),* **Julian Jay Savarin** - *vocals, keyboards (1969-73)* **Del Watkins, Nigel "Zed" Jenkins** - *guitar, flute,* **Lady Jo Meek** - *vocals.*
Born in Dominica and established in the UK during the '60s, **Julian Savarin** forms his own band to develop his sci-fi trilogy releasing a first album *A Time Before* This in 1970: a fascinating record with the beautiful vocals of **Cathy Pruden** and the compelling keyboards of **Julian** playing organ and Mellotron. Due to budget problems and a lack of promotion the group disbands until 1972 when a label signs them up for the next gotic-psychedelic work, *Waiters On The Dance*. Once again the total lack of promotion and exposure force him to leave the music business and to dedicate his career to writing novels of worldwide success.
DISCOGRAPHY: A TIME BEFORE THIS *(Youngblood, 1970)* **WAITERS ON THE DANCE** *(Birth Records, 1973).* M.G.

KARDA ESTRA

Richard Wileman - *guitar, keyboards, percussion,* **Ileesha Bailey** - *vocals,* **Rachel Larkins** - *viola, violin,* **Zoe King** - *flute, saxophones, oboe.*
A horror symphonic project started in 2000 by multi-instrumentalist **Richard Wileman**, for a prog of orchestral arrangements very close to the classical genre, with a large use of keyboards, strings and horns, as well as a series of exotic instruments, supported by the weird and sometimes scary voice of **Illesha Bailey**. Terror is the recurring theme and *Eve* (2001) is probably the best among the prolific discography. Based on *The Future Eve* written in 1886 by August Villiers de L'Isle Adam, it narrates the story of a scientist who creates a fiance for his friend. The forth album *Voivode Dracula* (2004), based of course on Bram Stocker's novel, and *The Age of Science and Enlightenment* (2006) are also very particular. Still active this very day.
RECOMMENDED RECORDINGS: EVE *(2001, Cyclops)* **CONSTELLATIONS** *(2003, Cyclops)* **VOIVODE DRACULA** *(2004, Cyclops).* M.G. & C.C.

Europe: GREAT BRITAIN

KESTREL

Dave Black - *guitar, vocals,* **John Cook** - *guitar, synth, keyboards,* **Tom Knowles** - *lead vocals,* **Fenwick Moir** - *bass,* **Dave Whitaker** - *drums, percussion.*
Born as a college gig quintet they caught the attention of producer John Worth who releases their only album and masterpiece in 1975. It didn't sell too well so they all went their separate ways. Nevertheless this band has a very particular sound between English prog and American soul, sometimes crossing into funky or the more complex jazz-rock. Eight simple and straightforward tracks of a symphonic prog use of the instruments (lots of Mellotron) with the beautiful soul vocals of **Knowels**'s very emotional singing recalling the voice of **Steve Walsh** (**Kansas**).
RECOMMENDED RECORDINGS: KESTREL *(Cube, 1975).* M.G. & C.C.

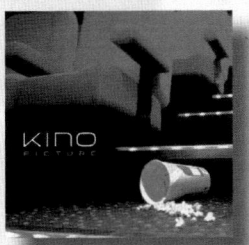

KINO

John Mitchell - *guitars, vocals,* **Pete Trewavas** - *bass,* **John Beck** - *keyboards,* **Chris Maitland** - *drums, percussion.*
Not to be confused with the Russian punk band, this super group is formed by four musicians reunited from very different bands: guitarist **John Mitchell** (**Arena, It bites**), bass **Pete Trewavas** (**Marillion, Transatlantic**), keyboardist **John Beck** (**It bites**) and drummer **Chris Maitland** (**Porcupine Tree**). Their 2005 album *Picture* is an unadventurous neo-prog of 10 tracks (the 9 minute opening "Losers' Day Parade") with highly melodic and catchy pop elements of skillful guitar play, a steaming rhythmic section and some quieter keyboards moments. **Mitchell**'s vocals crown a hard-oriented prog of no real inventive. That same year a compilation with added bonus tracks.
RECOMMENDED RECORDINGS: PICTURE *(Dawn Records, 2005).* M.G.

MAGENTA

Rob Reed - *keyboards,* **Christina Maria Booth** - *vocals,* **Chris Fry** - *guitar,* **Daniel Fry** - *bass,* **Colin Edwards** - *guitar, keyboards,* **Kieran Bailey** - *drums.*
Born in 2001 as a one album project by keyboardist and composer **Rob Reed** (Cyan, Fyreworks, Trippa, Othello Syndrome) and singer **Christina Murphy** (Booth): *Revolutions* is a double concept album on moments that changed humanity (small revolutions), with four suites and two short tracks greatly recalling **Yes**, **Genesis** and **Renaissance**. Recorded initially with the aid of session musicians, the demand for live concerts was such to need a permanent band. In 2004 another concept album on the seven capital sins, less symphonic. A total of 8 studio albums of which the last in 2017 for this truly prog band.
RECOMMENDED RECORDINGS: REVOLUTIONS *(2001, F2 Music)* **SEVEN** *(2004, F2 Music)* **ANOTHER TIME ANOTHER PLACE** *(2004, F2 Music)* **HOME** *(2006, F2 Music)* **NEW YORK SUITE** *(2006, F2 Music)* **METAMORPHOSIS** *(2008, F2 Music)* **CHAMELEON** *(2011, Tiger Moth).* M.G. & C.C.

MAGNA CARTA

Chris Simpson – *guitars, vocals,* **Lyell Tranter** – *guitars,* **Glenn Stuart** – *vocals.*
Acoustic folk band formed in 1969 by **Chris Simpson** (only surviving member), greatly influenced by **Simon & Garfunkel**'s soft and gentle music, often with a traditional feel, augmented with orchestral arrangements and good vocal harmonies; also inspired by artists like **Fairport Convention**, **The Moody Blues**, **Amazing Blondel**, **Kevin Ayers**, **Caravan** and other bands of Canterbury school derivation. The music itself is not truly prog but albums like *Seasons* (1970) and *Lord Of The Ages* (1975) have a certain epic featuring mythic medieval themes and lyrics which set them apart from regular folk. With **Glen Stuart**'s exit (voice) in 1977 the magic seems lost until in 1983 **Chris** meets and marries **Linda Taylor** (voice) continuing as a duo until 2009. Last studio album in 2015.
RECOMMENDED RECORDINGS: SEASONS *(Vertigo, 1970)* **LORD OF THE AGES** *(Vertigo, 1975).* M.G.

Europe: **GREAT BRITAIN**

MANDALABAND

David Rohl - *synths*, **David Durant** - *vocals*, **Tony Cresswell** - *drums*, **Vic Emerson** - *keyboards*, **John Stimpson** - *bass*, **Ashley Mulford** - *guitars*.
In 1967 composer, producer and keyboardist **David Rohl** founds the band **Sign of Life**, renamed **Ankh** for the first demo with **Eric Stewart** (**The Mindbenders, 10cc**), and a contract with Vertigo in 1968, which the label eventually refuses to release. In 1974 he creates **Mandalaband**, signing with Chrysalis, which prevents him from being the producer, so he quits mid recordings and they finish without him. Dissatisfied the label asks him to do the final remix: a highly complex first album on the Chinese invasion of Tibet (with Tibetan lyrics) with often dissonant musical structures. **Rohl** leaves and the band reforms as **Sad Café** with the 1977 album *Fanx Ta-ra*. Once back Rohl closes the decade with the Tolkien inspired *The Eye Of Wendor*, released in 1978 featuring stunning guest stars. In 2009 and 2011 another two good albums.
DISCOGRAPHY: **MANDALABAND** *(Chrysalis, 1975)* **THE EYE OF WENDOR: PROPHECIES** *(Chrysalis, 1978).*
M.G. & C.C.

MARSUPILAMI

Dave Laverock – *guitars, vocals*, **Leary Hasson** – *keyboards, percussion*, **Mike Fouracre** – *drums, percussion*, **Fred Hasson** – *vocals, percussion, harmonica*, **Richard Hicks** – *bass*, **Jessica Stanley-Clarke** – *flute, vocals*.
English dark proto-prog band relocated to the Netherlands and playing a complex mixture of blues, experimental jazz with hints of folk, unusual for the time. They debut with a first album in 1970 and a second work, *Arena*, the following year, both well representing the particular compositional structure, rich of weird melodies and harmonies, lots of heavy keyboards, electric guitar and flute (sometimes off-key) with a pounding percussionist. In particular the latter was produced by **Peter Bardens** (**Camel**) who amplified their stylistic beauty with dreamy jazz saxes and classical flute elements along with the good vocal partitions for a sound greatly inspired by **King Crimson, Jethro Tull, Strawbs** and **East of Eden**. Singer **Fred Hasson** forms a new line-up with the purpose of carrying out some concerts.
RECOMMENDED RECORDINGS: **ARENA** *(Transatlantic, 1971).*
M.G. & C.C.

NICK MASON

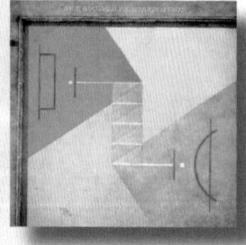

Carla Bley - *keyboards*, **Robert Wyatt** - *vocals*, **Karen Kraft** - *vocals*, **Steve Swallow** - *bass*, **Chris Spedding** - *guitar*, **Gary Windo, Gary Valente, Mike Mantler** - *Saxophones, flute, trombone, trumpets*, **Nick Mason** - *drums*.
Pink Floyd's drummer never really had a solo career of his own, in fact this only album is actually a **Carla Bley** creation, to which **Mason** agreed to put his name on. This free jazz pianist, known for her wild experimentations, was the ideal partner for an ambient effects seeker like **Nick**. *Fictitious Sports*, entirely recorded in 1979 but published by the label only two years later, is a Canterbury School jazz pop prog written and composed by **Carla** with the clashing voice-duo of **Robert Wyatt** (**Soft Machine**) and **Karen Kraft**. The songs flows along as a teetering, grooving mass of weirdness in which everyone at hand is clearly having a lot of fun; a good example are the hilarious lyrics and arrangements of "I'm A Mineralist". Probably the only **Floyd**-ian sonorities can be found in the song "Hot River".
DISCOGRAPHY: **FICTITIOUS SPORTS** *(1981, Harvest).*
M.G.

MAY BLITZ

James Black - *vocals, guitar*, **Reid Hudson** - *bass*, **Tony Newman** - *drums*.
Formed by vocalist and guitarist **Jamie Blackmix** in 1969, they release two incredibly heavy, powerful and psychedelic albums with strong blues undertones and progressive tendencies, despite the lack of keyboards. Their 1970 debut documents the development of heavy music, with unpredictable crushing riffs occasionally diverting to ambient, a hybrid keyboardless sound between **Black Sabbath**, **High Tide** and **Pink Fairies**, built on well structured blues-oriented guitar solos (similar to **Uriah Heep**) and bass with outstanding and strong vocals. The second album of 1971, *The 2nd of May*, is a less interesting work despite the wonderful song "For Madmen only".
DISCOGRAPHY: **MAY BLITZ** *(Vertigo, 1970)* **THE 2ND OF MAY** *(Vertigo, 1971).*
C.A. & C.C.

Europe: GREAT BRITAIN

McDONALD & GILES

Ian McDonald - *vocals, guitars, keyboards, winds, harp...* **Michael Giles** - *drums, percussion, vocals,* **Peter Giles** - *bass,* **Steve Winwood** - *piano, hammond,* **Michael Blakesey** - *trombone,* **Peter Sinfield** - *lyrics.*
The musical press credits **Robert Fripp** as only true founder of the project **King Crimson**, labeling him as the 'king'. Without denying his genius, it is also true that if it were not for his companions, there would be no court and therefore, no king. In 1970, multi-instrumentalist **Ian McDonald** and drummer **Mike Giles** decide to leave this Super group and start a project of their own by recording an interesting homonym album that soon become a cult. **McDonald** (already fundamental pillar in the songwriting of *In the Court of the Crimson King*) had written some tracks meant for the sequel of **KC**'s first album, but given some disagreements and the final exit of both musicians, he takes his songs with him and together with his new partner, they write this compelling work that **Fripp** himself recommends (coupled with the second **KC** album *In the wake of Poseidon*). Featuring guest star on keyboards: **Steve Winwood** from **Traffic**.
DISCOGRAPHY: McDONALD AND GILES *(Island, 1970).* M.G.

MELLOW CANDLE

Alison Williams - *vocals,* **Clodagh Simonds** - *keyboards, vocals,* **David Williams** - *guitars, vocals,* **Frank Boylan** - *bass,* **William A. Murray** - *drums, percussion.*
Irish singers **Alison Williams** and **Clodagh Simonds** were both students in a convent and formed in 1963 with another friend the band **Gatecrashers**, initially imitating re-known folk groups and songs from **The Beatles**. When **Richard Coughlan** (**Caravan**) joins and the line-up expands, they change name and sign up with Deram for their only true album *Swaddling Songs* produced by **David Hitchcock** in 1972. This debut album is a sonic marvel of simple melodies, with Gaelic folk prog ballads constructed perfectly on delicate plots of piano and guitars and of course the incredible blend of these two beautiful voices. In 1996 an album called *The Virgin Prophet* is published as a recovery of alternative versions or unpublished tracks from the previous 1972 recordings.
RECOMMENDED RECORDINGS: SWADDLING SONGS *(Deram, 1972).* M.G. & C.C.

MOSTLY AUTUMN

Bryan Josh – *vocals, guitars,* **Heather Findlay** – *vocals, guitars, percussion,* **Iain Jennings** – *vocals, keyboards,* **Bob Faulds** - *violin,* **Liam Davison** – *vocals, guitars,* **Stuart Carver** - *bass,* **Angela Goldthorpe** - *horns,* **Rob McNeil** – *drums.*
A powerful atmospheric rock band formed in the late '90s with a Celtic edge that goes from the initial electro-acoustic folk prog to a more recent pop with softer prog connotations. The large number of musicians and the vocal ensemble creates a rich and full sound clearly inspired by **Pink Floyd** as well as **Steve Hackett** (**Genesis**) uses of the guitar (two in this band), with extensive flute parts, low and penny whistles, violins and vocal harmonies. A total of thirteen studio-albums from 1998 to 2010, of which the second and third are probably their most mature.
RECOMMENDED RECORDINGS: THE SPIRIT OF AUTUMN PAST *(Cyclops Records, 1999).* M.G. & C.C.

NIRVANA

Patrick Campbell-Lyons, Ray Singer - *guitars, vocals,* **Alex Spyropolous** - *keyboards,* **Brian Henderson** - *bass.* **Peter Kester, David Preston** - *drums.*
A band created by Irish guitarist **Patrick Campbell-Lyons** and Greek keyboardist **Alex Spyropolous**, with a first album in 1967, *The Story Of Simon Simopath*, a visionary concept. The sound is a melodic late '60s pop with classical chamber music elements due the orchestrations. In 1968 the song "Rainbow Chaser" hits the charts with the first-ever British recording to feature the 'phasing' audio technique. After a third LP, **Alex** leaves and **Patrick** is alone. In 1992 the quarrel with the homonym American band was settled out-of-court and led to the inclusion of "Lithium" in the English band's last album *Orange and Blue*, containing previously unreleased tracks.
RECOMMENDED RECORDINGS: THE STORY OF SIMON SIMOPATH *(Island, 1967)* ALL OF US *(Island, 1968)* DEDICATED TO MARKUS III *(Pye, 1970)* M.G. & C.C.

Europe: **GREAT BRITAIN**

NO MAN

Tim Bowness - *vocals*, **Steve Wilson** - *guitars, keyboards, programming*.

This intriguing parallel project of duo **Steve Wilson** (singer and guitarist of **Porcupine Tree**) and vocalist **Tim Bowness** starts in 1986 with a first album published only in 1993, a beautiful mix of psychedelia, experimental prog, jazz and pop-rock, rich of dubs and techno sounds. An uncompromising approach that connects rock and pop through a myriad of influences from neo-classical and jazz to dub and techno: a late '80s bridge between prog and New Wave recalling the works of artists like **Japan**, **Ultravox** and **Talk Talk**, with the best things from the '70s experimental prog that punk never managed to delete. Their masterpiece is probably the 1994 *Flowermouth*, an album featuring all star guests like **Robert Fripp**, **Richard Barbieri**, **Steve Jansen**, **Ian Carr**, **Mel Collins**.
RECOMMENDED RECORDINGS: FLOWERMOUTH *(One Little Indian, 1994).* M.G.

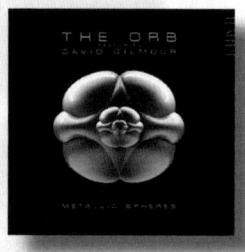

THE ORB

Alex Paterson, Jimmy Cauty, Thomas Fehlmann – *keyboards, synthesizers, computers, studio devices, samples, loops,* **plus special guests...**

Since the essence of Progressive music remains that of escaping the beaten paths to explore new sonorities, instead of simply emulating the old gods, this techno-trance-electropop group is somewhat the imaginary continuity of **Pink Floyd** if they had ever pursued the electronic genre. Founded in 1988 by two London DJs, **Alex Paterson** and **Jimmy Cauty**, their music manipulates with craft the electronic spheres inspired by Ambient artists like **Brian Eno** and **Kraftwerk**. Surprisingly psychedelic and chill-out, also thanks to the use of samples from mysterious sources, their lysergic power conquers **David Gilmour** who gladly collaborates in their album *Metallic Spheres* published in 2010 (other famous collaborations in previous works are **Steve Hillage** and **Simon Phillips**).
RECOMMENDED RECORDINGS: ADVENTURES BEYOND THE ULTRAWORLD *(Big Life, 1991)* U.F.Orb *(Big Life, 1992)* POMMEFRITZ *(Island, 1994)* METALLIC SPHERES *(EMI, 2010).* M.G.

PALLAS

Ronnie Brown - *keyboards*, **Euan Lowson** - *vocals*, **Niall Mathewson** – *guitar*, **Derek Forman** – *drums, percussion*, **Graeme Murray** – *bass, vocals*.

This Scottish '80s prog band in the style of **IQ** and **Marillion** forms at the end of the '70s with an EP of rock very close to metal. The first true album, *Arrive Alive*, is published only in 1981 as a self-produced tape of harder symphonic and keyboard sounds and AOR pop forms. The following work of 1984 entitled *The Sentinel* is probably their best for the variety technical ability, centered on melodic hooks, loud sounds and a great voice. A change in line-up brings another 2 albums before vanishing for over 12 years: *Beat the Drum* is a 72 minutes album with epic accents, rock rhythms and ballads released in 1998 and followed by the wonderful *The Cross And The Crucible* in 2001 with its atmospheric keyboards, great guitar tunes and a well working rhythm section.
RECOMMENDED RECORDINGS: THE SENTINEL *(EMI, 1984).* M.G. & C.C.

PINEAPPLE THIEF

Bruce Soord – *guitar, vocals, programming*, **Steve Kitch** – *keyboards*, **Jon Sykes** - *bass, vocals*, **Wayne Higgins** – *guitars, vocals*, **Keith Harrison** – *drums, vocals*.

Former guitarist of **Vulgar Unicorn**, **Bruce Soord** starts his solo career under the name PT with a proposal of ancient sounds in a modern disguise recalling the space rock of the '70s, especially by **Pink Floyd**. The typical soft starting tracklead to explosive crescendos and '80s styles like **Talk Talk** and **King Crimson**, or to the more safe rock guitars, but on melodic and conceptually accessible themes, with fascinating atmospheres and melancholy psychedelic moments. Balance, beauty, and modernity also in the second release of 2002, with a frenzy guitar pattern and acoustic sets.
RECOMMENDED RECORDINGS: WHAT WE HAVE SOWN *(Cyclops Records, 2007).* M.G. & C.C.

Europe: **GREAT BRITAIN**

RARE BIRD

Graham Field - *keyboards,* **Steve Gould** – *vocals, bass,* **Dave Kaffinetti** - *keyboards,* **Mark Ashron** – *drums, vocals.*
Five albums from 1969 to 1974 for a quartet that, although strongly remaking the well-known schemes of **Procol Harum**, and in part of **Pink Floyd**, Traffic and Doors, managed to unite in a personal and positive way the heterogeneous styles of the new late '60s psychedelic sound, generating excellent ballads or more complex and defined pieces, often with jazz inclinations. The initial particularity of having two keyboardists and the strong voice of **Gould** characterized their sound despite the addition of a guitarist in the future shifting to a harder rock with some funky lines. **Nic Potter** (**VDGG**) played on two albums of the second line-up and **John Wetton** (**King Crimson**) guested on one.
RECOMMENDED RECORDINGS: **RARE BIRD** *(Command/Probe, 1969)* **AS YOUR MIND FLIES BY** *(ABC/Dunhill, 1970).*
M.G. & C.C.

RAW MATERIAL

Colin Catt – *vocals, keyboards,* **Mike Fletcher** – *saxophones, flute, vocals,* **Dave Green** – *rhythm guitar,* **Phil Gunn** – *bass,* **Cliff Harewood** – *lead guitar,* **Paul Young** – *drums, percussion.*
Two albums for this standard prog quartet (plus front-man **Mike Fletcher** on horns) of typical prog rock, slightly jazz and psychedelic with heavy, dark and apocalyptic plots: their debut album in 1970 has some great moments (the longer tracks on side 1) but ends in a bizarre poem recitation with string arrangements. Superior the second work *Time Is ...* published the following year, a more defined and mature, elegant and with folk elements, excellent vocals and flute parts. The line-up here adds a second guitarist (**Harewood**) for a more '70s sound with lots of instrument interplay.
RECOMMENDED RECORDINGS: **TIME IS ...** *(RCA Neon, 1971).*
M.G. & C.C.

ROOM

Steve Edge - *guitars,* **Chris Williams** - *lead guitar,* **Bob Jenkins** - *drums, percussion,* **Jane Kevern** - *vocals, tambourine,* **Roy Putt** - *bass.*
A group of friends playing together in clubs and pop festivals since 1968, which after winning a prize finally sign up with Deram for their only record *Pre-Flight*, published in 1970: merging heavy psychedelic rock, progressive jazz and full orchestrations, the female vocals are very compelling, evoking delicate atmospheres, while the guitar duo is a mastery of invention and unpredictable energy. Adventurous and rather accomplished, considered very ahead for its time, the band was not understood by the audience and critics. Re-released in 2008 by Esoteric/Cherry Red.
DISCOGRAPHY: **PRE-FLIGHT** *(Deram, 1970).*
C.A. & C.C.

MIKE RUTHERFORD

Mike Rutherford – *guitars, bass,* **Anthony Phillips** – *keyboards,* **Noel Mc-Calla** - *vocals,* **Morris Pert** – *percussion,* **Simon Phillips** – *drums.*
As for **Tony Banks**, when **Phil Collins** hits the pause button in 1978 after the tour, also **Michael Rutherford** (**Genesis** bassist and guitarist who also founds the mid '80s pop band **Mike & The Mechanics**) decides to apply for his solo career with a first debut of his own in 1980: *Smallcreep's Day*, recorded with '**Ant' Phillips** (former **Genesis** guitarist) on keyboards and singer **Noel Mc-Calla** (met during the auditions for replacing **Gabriel**'s role), is a half-concept album on the adventures of a worker who dares to travel beyond the closed factory doors and into a hidden world. Of course the similarities to the mother-band are obvious but **Mike** manages to blend his prog style to straight rock tunes. The second work abandons prog for a hard-rock punk and new wave, with the screamed out vocals of **Mike** himself.
RECOMMENDED RECORDINGS: **SMALLCREEP'S DAY** *(Passport Records, 1980).*
M.G. & C.C.

Europe: **GREAT BRITAIN**

SKID ROW

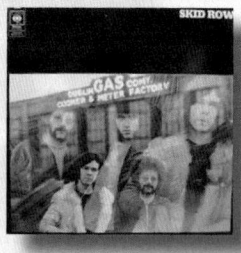 

Gary Moore - *guitars*, **Paul Chapman** – *guitars*, **Bernhard Cheevers** – *guitars*, **Nollaug "Noel" Bridgeman** - *drums*, **Phil Lynott** – *bass, vocals*, **Brush Shiels** – *bass, vocals*.

An Irish hard-rock blues band with Prog shades founded in 1967 by **Brendan 'Brush' Shiels** and **Ben Cheevers**, with **Phil Lynott** as their singer before leaving to create his own band, **Thin Lizzy**. At the end of 2006 the demo tapes featuring **Phil** were discovered after being presumed lost for decades. **Shiels** takes over the singing and 16 year old guitarist **Gary Moore** joins for the debut album produced by CBS in 1970: *Skid* was recorded in only 11 hours. The second release *34 hours*, inspired by the time-lapse given by the label, was published the following year. **Gary Moore** leaves and **Paul Chapman** takes over the guitars for a third album when the label decides to put everything on hold. **Gary Moore** dies in 2011.
RECOMMENDED RECORDINGS: SKID (*CBS, 1970*) 34 HOURS (*CBS, 1971*). M.G. & C.C.

SKIN ALLEY

Thomas Crimble – *bass, keyboards, vocals*, **Nick Graham** – *bass, flute, keyboards, vocals*, **Bob James** – *guitars, saxophones, flute*, **Krzysztof Henryk Justkiewicz** – *keyboards, trumpet, vocals*, **Alvin Pope** – *drums, percussion*.

Perfect example of a band that covered the transition from the '60s beat to the '70s psychedelia, they form as a quartet in 1968's West-London developing a different kind of rock that drew much from jazz and blues. Spotted by the legendary DJ **John Peel**, they sign up for two albums in 1969, of which the second is probably their best, *To Pagham and Beyond*, with jazz moments in **Nucleus** style, flutes that sometimes present **Jethro Tull** sounds and the coupled mellotron-organ that duet with a dirty sax recalling **King Crimson**, but with more classic blues vocals. A total of 4 studio albums of which their last in 1973.
RECOMMENDED RECORDINGS: TO PAGHAM AND BEYOND (*CBS, 1970*). M.G. & C.C.

SKY

John Williams - *guitars*, **Francis Monkman** - *keyboards*, **Herbie Flowers** - *bass, tuba*, **Tristan Fry** - *drums, percussion*, **Kevin Peek** - *guitars*.

Classical rock band formed in London in 1978 by guitarist **John Williams** and keyboardist **Francis Monkman** (**Curved Air** and **801**). Their style of combining prog to rock with easy-listening songs quickly gained them a large success. Their first two albums repeat this formula which tends to become less original in time, since their eyes seemed to be more on the market than on the music: both *Sky* (1979) and the sequel double album *Sky 2* (1980) confirm the high technical quality with very funny to virtually symphonic compositions, sometimes with too average or standard arrangements. Then **Monkman** quits, replaced by a more jazz oriented **Steve Gray**. The third album decidedly lessens the interest as for the rest of their discography in studio, yet the album *Sky Five Live* of 1983 proves their skills in concert.
RECOMMENDED RECORDINGS: SKY 2 (*Arista, 1980*). M.G. & C.C.

SPIROGYRA

Barbara Gaskin – *vocals*, **Julian Cusack** – *violin*, **Martin Cockerham** – *guitar, vocals*, **Steve Borrill** – *bass*, **Dave Mattacks** – *drums, percussion*.

From Canterbury but absolutely not Canterburian, this folk prog band publishes its first album *St-Radiguns* in 1971 with a huge success: very moody, politically conscious songs full of good interplay and with a great duo (**Martin Cockerham** and **Barbara Gaskin**) singing in a style that recalls **Comus** and **Jefferson Airplane**. The following year already a second album, *Old Boot Wine*, yet not obtaining the same appreciation, while the third album, *Bells, Boots and Shambles*, manages to return on track yet not to save them from the break-up. **Barbara** became backing-vocals for *Hatfield and the North* and later with **National Health** and **Bill Bruford** and **Dave Stewart**. In 2009 a partial comeback with a couple of new albums.
DISCOGRAPHY: ST-RADIGUNS (*RCA, 1971*) OLD BOOT WINE (*RCA, 1972*) BELLS, BOOTS AND SHAMBLES (*RCA, 1973*). M.G. & C.C.

Europe: GREAT BRITAIN

STRING DRIVEN THING

Chris Adams - *vocals, guitars,* **Pauline Adams** - *vocals,* **John Mannion** - *percussion,* **Graham Smith** - *violin,* **Billy Fairley** - *drums,* **Colin Wilson** - *bass, guitars.*

A Scottish folk prog band formed in 1967 which despite the support from their label obtained less success than their predecessors **Incredible String Band** and **Pentangle**. A self-produced debut album of 1970 is credited to **Chris** and **Pauline Adams** with the help of guitarist **John Mannion**. Only two years later will it be re-recorded and released by Charisma along with a second, *The Machine that Cried* of 1973, probably their best work: the perfect mix of vocals and violin arrangements by **Graham Smith** (later **V.D.G.G.**) produce melancholic atmospheres together with the psychedelic guitar playing. Due to health-related issues, **Chris** and his wife quit, leaving **Graham** alone for the next two albums: a more AOR rock that had no real distinction except for the violin. In the mid '90s **Chris** reforms the band releasing a live album in 1998.
RECOMMENDED RECORDINGS: **STRING DRIVEN THING** *(Charisma, 1972)* **THE MACHINE THAT CRIED** *(Charisma, 1973).*
C.A. & C.C.

STUD

Jim Cregan – *guitars, vocals,* **John Weider** – *violin, keyboards, guitars, vocals,* **Bob James** – *guitars, saxophones, flute,* **Richard "Charlie" McCracken** – *bass,,* **John Wilson** – *drums, percussion,* **Poli Palmer** – *vibes.*

Bass player **Richard MacCracken** and drummer **John Wilson** (both formerly playing in **Rory Gallagher**'s **Taste**), found this band with guitarist **Jim Cregan** (former **Blossom Toes**) on vocals in 1970, joined the following year by keyboardist and violinist **John Weider**. The result is a strange folk-prog of brave improvisations with strong jazz flavours supported by the musicians' mastery. Their homonym album published in 1971 is mostly a progressive rock sound with lots of jazzy elements and the jam band style with minor psychedelic influences. Thanks to the good success obtained in Germany, they manage to publish a second album with BASF in 1972 before the break-up.
DISCOGRAPHY: **STUD** *(Deram, 1971).*
M.G. & C.C.

SYNANTHESIA

Dennis Homes - *vibes, guitars, vocals,* **Dennis Homes** - *vibes, guitars, vocals,* **Jim Fraser** - *saxophones, oboe, flute,* **Les Cook** - *guitars, congas, violin, mandolin, vocals.*

Yet another one shot band of soft acid folk with jazz-prog tastes and some great sax playing by **Jim Fraser** in the style of **David Jackson** (**V.D.G.G.**). Founded in 1968 by guitarist **Leslie Cook**, they perform in and around the London area, home to **David Bowie**'s Arts Lab (rumors see them briefly as **Bowie**'s backing band before the Hype), until they manage to sign up with RCA in 1969 for their only album. Penalized with an almost total lack of radio airplay, the label was not interested enough to promote them adequately so they eventually split leaving this beautiful work which recalls the sounds of **Forest**, **Incredible String Band** and **Jan Dukes de Grey** with a hint of **Audience** and **Van Der Graaf Generator**.
DISCOGRAPHY: **SYNANTHESIA** *(RCA, 1969).*
M.G. & C.C.

T2

Keith Cross - *guitars,* **Peter Dunton** - *vocals, drums,* **Bernard Jinks** - *bass.*

Evolved from the earlier band **Neon Pearl**, led by drummer **Pete Dunton**, this trio plays a form of psychedelic proto-prog rock, inspired by **Jimi Hendrix** and **Cream**, with a powerful hard rock blues sound of jazz rock tastes. Formed and managed by **John Morphew**, he signs them up with Decca for their 1969 debut *It'll All Work Out In Boomland* which grants them to perform in the Isle of Wight Festival. Sadly the tension among the musicians disbands the group in 1972, while recording material for their second album. The break-up causes the unfinished album to be shelved for more than twenty years and to be finally published by a German label in 1992, along with another two works with only **Dunton** as original member.
RECOMMENDED RECORDINGS: **IT'LL ALL WORK OUT IN BOOMLAND** *(Decca, 1969).*
M.G. & C.C.

Europe: **GREAT BRITAIN**

TANGENT

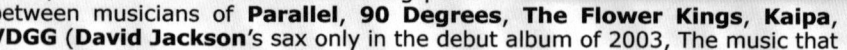

Andy Tillison, Guy Manning, Sam Baine - *keyboards, vocals,* **Roine Stolt, Jakko Jakszyk** - *guitars,* **Jonas Reingold** - *bass,* **David Jackson, Theo Travis** - *winds,* **Zoltan Czorz, Jaime Salazar** - *drums.*
Initially intended to be an **Andy Tillison** solo effort, it became a worldwide meeting point between musicians of **Parallel, 90 Degrees, The Flower Kings, Kaipa, VDGG** (**David Jackson**'s sax only in the debut album of 2003, The music that died alone), often featuring **Jakko Jakszyk** from the forth 2008 release *Not As Good As The Book*. Their debut sound begins as a pleasant and fresh prog of vintage taste that already in the next works tends to an old school conventional prog, a modern but average and predictable Istitutional Art-Rock.
DISCOGRAPHY: THE MUSIC THAT DIED ALONE *(Inside Out, 2003)* **THE WORLD THAT WE DRIVE THROUGH** *(Inside Out, 2004)* **PYRAMID AND STARS** *(live, Inside Out 2005)* **A PLACE IN THE QUEUE** *(Inside Out, 2006)* **NOT AS GOOD AS THE BOOK** *(Inside Out, 2008).*   M.G. & C.C.

TEMPEST

Allan Holdsworth - *guitar, violin, vocals,* **Mark Clarke** - *bass, keyboards, vocals,* **Paul Williams** - *vocals, guitars, keyboards,* **Jon Hiseman** - *drums, percussion.*
Not to be confused with the homonym US band, this is an English bunch of friends catalyzed by **Jon Hiseman** after the first disbandment of **Colosseum**, dedicated to a more dynamic and complex heavy prog with jazz rock tints, full of hard and dirty blues atmospheres recalling **Cream**. Their first album of 1973 contains one of the first appearances of the late **Allan Holdsworth** (**Gong, UK, Soft Machine**) but despite **Hiseman**'s efforts in songwriting and arranging, the record doesn't sell. Same for the following *Living In Fear*, more of a **Deep Purple** hard-rock jazz than a progressive album.
DISCOGRAPHY: TEMPEST *(Bronze, 1973)* **LIVING IN FEAR** *(Bronze, 1974).*   C.A. & C.C.

TIME

Joe Dolly – *drums, vocals,* **Alex Johnson** – *guitars, vocals,* **Gary Margetz** – *guitars, vocals,* **Torris Margetz** - *bass.*
Not to be confused with the prog band from Yugoslavia, these musicians play a complicated hard-prog heavily influenced by **Yes** despite the emphasis on dual guitars and very few keyboards. Formed by previous members of **Spontaneous Combustion**, brothers **Garry** and **Triss Margetts** (on guitar/keys/voice and bass/voice respectively), this quartet is sometimes compared to **Peter Banks' Flash**, though more complex due to the guitar solos of front-man Alec Johnson (later singer of Nightwing). In 1975 they record a one and only self-titled album, also thanks to Bulk Records and under the precious guidance of famous German producer **Conny Plank**. Favourites are songs like "Dragonfly", "Turn Around" for the long ones, and "Shady Lay", "Violence" or "Liar", for the shorter tracks.
DISCOGRAPHY: TIME *(LP, 1975 Buk, CD reissue Bulp, 2005).*   M.G.

TITUS GROAN

Stuart Cowell - *keyboards, guitar, vocals,* **John Lee** - *bass,* **Tony Priestland** - *sax, flute, oboe,* **Jim Toomey** - *drums.*
Inspired by Mervyn Peake's gothic fantasy trilogy novel, this quartet led by **Stewart Cowell** and **Tony Priestland** releases an album in 1970 entitled *...Plus*. Their proto-prog sound often fronted by the horn section is a mix made of English psychedelia, hard blues and folk keyboard prog: the dilated blues of "It's wasn't for you", the psychedelic 12-mins medieval jam suite "Hall of Bright Carvings", the almost country **Beatles**' ballad "It's all up with us" or the **Jethro Tull** "I can't change" make their music quite varied in the form of a compilation of single hits.
RECOMMENDED RECORDINGS: ... PLUS *(Dawn, 1970).*   M.G. & C.C.

Europe: GREAT BRITAIN

TONTON MACOUTE

Chris Gavin - bass, guitars, **Dave Knowles** - sax, flute, clarinett, vocals, **Paul French** - piano, keyboards, vibes, vocals, **Nigel Reveler** - drums, percussion.
Obscured by other great and more famous contemporary bands, this is nevertheless a very interesting one shot band, born from the ashes of **Windmill**, disbanded after the death of their front-man. For some unknown reason the name derives from the Haitian dictator Papa Doc Duvallier's brutal presidential guard of 1959: their style instead is a breezy and pleasant music recalling **Camel**'s soft and melodic jazz blues fusion of inspired British jazz-rock, with the long instrumental interplay of compelling keyboards, guitars and flute. Their only and brilliant album was published by RCA's shortlived progressive Neon label in 1971, now a rarity and re-issued on CD in 1994.
DISCOGRAPHY: TONTON MACOUTE (1971, Neon).

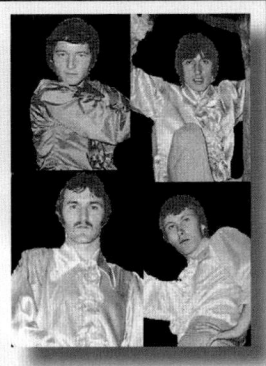

M.G. & C.C.

TUDOR LODGE

John Stannard, Lyndon Green - vocals, guitars, **Ann Stewart (1969-71, 1981)**, - vocals, winds, **Linda Peters [aka Linda Thompson], Lynne Whiteland (dal 1982)** - vocals, acoustic guitars.
This singing guitar-trio (who adds some piano and flute to their sound with ancient music here and there) is an overall average folk rock band with hints of hippy-ness, pastoral ambiances and just enough virtuosity to arise the proghead's interest. Their debut is published in 1970 by Vertigo for a stunning quality of medieval sprinkled psych-folk with electric and acoustic sounds. The unusual employment of winds and horns ingeniously enriches the groove. Plus the astoundingly beautiful fold-out artwork makes it a little gem hard to duplicate, though re-issued successfully also in the artwork. In 1997 the two men return with a new lady singer and record 5 studio-albums, the last of 2006.
DISCOGRAPHY: TUDOR LODGE (Vertigo, 1970).

C.A. & C.C.

TYRANNOSAURUS REX

Marc Bolan - vocals, guitars, **Steve Peregrine Took** - vocals, bongos, kazoo, talking drum, gong, assorted percussion, **Mickey Finn** - backing vocals, moroccan drums, tabla, bass, cymbals.
Before his more famous glam-rock project **T. Rex**, guitarist **Marc Bolan** begins his career in this hippy-folk duo together with percussionist **Stephen Porter**, AKA **Steve Peregrin**  Took. The music of their four studio albums contains the great psychedelic and ethnic sonorities (proto-world music) written by **Bolan** and supported by the eclectic **Steve**'s rythms, who then leaves after a third album to pursue his own glam career. Replaced by **Mickey Finn** who augmented the ethnic sounds in their last 1970 album *A Beard of Stars*, before changing musical direction and becoming **T. Rex** until **Bolan**'s death by car crash in 1977.
RECOMMENDED RECORDINGS: UNICORN (1969, Regal Zonophone) **A BEARD OF STARS** (1970, Regal Zonophone).

M.G.

WARM DUST

Alan Solomon - keyboards, saxophones, **John Surguy** - saxophones, guitars, **Paul Carrack** - vocals.
A sextet oriented to horn sounds playing a solid psychedelic prog led by sax players **Alan Solomon** and **John Surguy** (also guitar) and featuring **Paul Carrack** (future singer for **Mike and Mechanics**, **Steve Hackett** and **Roger Waters**'s Berlin 1990 concert *The Wall*). They release a 1970 debut as a double album, *And It Came To Pass*, with long compositions, thought-provoking lyrics and plenty of instrumental interplays of sax, flute, organ and guitars. The best is probably the concept album of 1971, a frightening recount of the horrors of war which in Germany came out abbreviated to *Peace For Our Times* and published by BASF. Their career ends with a third homonym album remarkable only for the long full-blown prog in "Blind Boy".
DISCOGRAPHY: AND IT CAME TO PASS (*Trend, 1972*) **PEACE FOR OUR TIMES** (*BASF, 1973*) **WARM DUST** (*BASF, 1974*).

M.G.

Europe: GREAT BRITAIN

THE WEB

Dave Lawson - *keyboards, vocals,* **Lennie Wright** - *drums, percussion, vibes,* **Kenny Beveridge** - *drums, percussion,* **Tom Harris** - *flute percussion,* **Tony Edwards** - *guitars,* **John Eaton** - *bass, percussion.*
Born in 1967 as a proto-prog jazz-blues act rich of psychedelia and attempts of avant-garde experimentation, the powerful voice of African-American **John L. Watson** and the presence of two guitarists in the first studio albums *Fully Interlocking* (1968) and *Theraphosa Blondi* (1970) mark their initial sound, that after the exit will become a more profound prog with sophisticated vibes. In fact their third album *I Spider*, also of 1970, is superior and probably their masterpiece (in a prog sense), released by a new label and with the Canterbury sound of keyboardist **Dave Lawson**. The last album is not under their name, at first as **Web** and then officially as **Samurai**.
RECOMMENDED RECORDINGS: I SPIDER *(Polydor, 1970).*
M.G. & C.C.

DARRYL WAY'S WOLF

Darryl Way - *violin, viola, keyboards,* **Ian Mosley** - *drums,* **Dek Messecar** - *bass, vocals,* **John Etheridge** - *guitars.*
After the disbandment of **Curved Air**, their violinist **Darryl Way** decides to recruits other fellow musicians such as drummer **Ian Mosley** (later in **Trace**, **Steve Hackett**'s band and **Marillion**), guitarist **John Etheridge** (later with **Soft Machine**) and **Dek Messacar** on bass (later with **Caravan**). Their debut *Canis Lupus* of 1973 contains good melodic songs recalling his previous band, with instrumental compositions of classical inspiration and the predominant string arrangements like the wonderful viola in "McDonald's Lament". Other two albums follow, less inspired but still very pleasant: *Saturation Point* (1973) and *Night Music* (1974).
DISCOGRAPHY: CANIS LUPUS *(1973, Decca)* **SATURATION POINT** *(1973, Decca)* **NIGHT MUSIC** *(1974, Decca).*
M.G. & C.C.

RICHARD WRIGHT

17 year old keyboardist **Richard William Wright** was a student when he meets future **Pink Floyd** companions **Waters** and **Mason**, starting the band in the early 1966 for which he writes and sings too. In 1978 he begins a parallel solo career publishing his first album *Wet Dream* (which of course recalls some of the atmospheres from works in *Dark Side Of The Moon* and *Wish You Were Here*). In 1984 he and **Dave Harris** work on the project **Zee**, releasing the techno-pop-experimental *Identity* (recently re-issued on CD in summer 2018). In 1996 his second solo album *Broken China* features special guests like **Sinéad O'Connor**, **Pino Palladino** and **Manu Katchè**. This masterpiece confirms his previous contributions to **Pink Floyd**'s music and is full of his characteristic ambient sounds and dreamy atmospheres. He also collaborates on **Gilmour**'s solo album *On an Island* a couple of years before passing away for cancer in 2008.
DISCOGRAPHY: WET DREAM *(1978, Harvest)* **BROKEN CHINA** *(1996, EMI).*
M.G.

801

Phil Manzanera - *guitars,* **Brian Eno** - *keyboards, guitars, vocals,* **Lloyd Watson** - *slide guitar, vocals,* **Francis Monkman** - *keyboards,* **Bill MacCormick** - *bass, vocals,* **Simon Phillips** - *drums, percussion.*
During his career in **Roxy Music**, guitarist **Phil Manzanera** involves some of his colleagues for a side project of his own in 1972, with more experimental and psychedelic intentions inspired by the Canterbury school teachings: initially called **Quiet Sun** he teams up with bassist **Bill Mc Cormick** (**Matching Mole**) and later will also include **Brian Eno** changing the name to **801** and publishing two albums, *Live* of 1976 containing two covers of **Beatles** and of **Kinks** songs, some of **Manzanera**'s and **Eno**'s repertory and also **Quiet Sun** tracks such as "East of Asteroid"; in 1977 *Listen Now* is released, again with **Eno** and 16 other musicians (**Mel Collins** on sax, **Eddie Jobson** on electric piano and **Rhett Davies** on Hammond) for a dark and moody jazz pop fusion.
RECOMMENDED RECORDINGS: 801 Live *(Polydor, 1976)*
M.G.

Europe: GREECE

IRAKLIS & LERNAIA HYDRA

Iraklis Triantafyllidis - *vocals, guitars, violin, mandolin, harmonica, fife, percussion,* **Dimitris Zafirelis** – *guitar, vocals,* **Giorgos Sieras** – *guitar, vocals,* **Vasilis Stamatiadis** - *drums,* **Nikos Doikas** - *bass,* **Giorgos Gavalas** – *flute, vocals,* **Nikos Sakelis** - *keyboards,* **Nikos Milionis** - *harmonica,* **Marianna** – *vocals + orchestra.*
A band revolving names (**DNA**, **Lernaia Hydra**) and cast, playing as support of the Greek poet, singer and musician **Iraklis Triantafyllidis** from 1972, with a blend of traditional folk, psychedelic rock and classical elements. Of their albums, the double concept LP of 1976 *Se Allous Kosmous* (in other worlds) is probably the best, rich of guitars and traditional Greek and Mediterranean instruments (beautiful the interplay of flute and violin), with more rock, psychedelia and some jazzy moments which generate an interesting local pop prog. Still active today with some sporadic live performance.
RECOMMENDED RECORDINGS: SE ALLOUS KOSMOUS *(EMI, 1976).* M.G. & C.C.

PETE & ROYCE

Ilias Porfiris - *bass,* **Vassilis Ghinos** - *keyboards,* **Fontas Hatzis** - *drums,* **Peter Tsiros** - *guitars, vocals.*
Founded in 1978 by painter and guitarist **Panagiotis Pete Tsiros** and keyboardist **Vassilis Ghinos**, this band home-records what will be Greece's first self-released record, *Suffering of Tomorrow* in 1980: a concept-album dedicated to the tragic death of **Pete**'s brother, merged into a visionary and typical **Pink Floyd** atmosphere with a rock structure. The following year they release Days of destruction containing songs directly confronting the political realities of Athens in 1981: more of a song-oriented folk rock album, raw and purposely amateurish, the political protest consisted in creating an apolitical artistic purity, rather than consciously protesting for something. Apparently a third album oriented to funk exists in a demo version yet never published. Only **Vassilis** is still active today.
DISCOGRAPHY: SUFFERING OF TOMORROW *(Octoichos, 1980)* **DAYS OF DESTRUCTION** *(Ocean, 1981).* C.A. & C.C.

PURPLE OVERDOSE

Costas Constantinou - *guitar, vocals,* **George Papageorgiades** - *bass,* **George Nikas** - *drums,* **Michael Vasiliou** - *organ,* **Apostolos Labouris** - *flute,* **plus guest musicians...**
Formed in 1987 by song-writer, guitarist and singer **Costas Constantinou**, this Greek band recreates the psychedelic atmospheres of the mid '60s blending hard rock with psychedelia for a curious mixture of blues or jazz elements, oriental influences and folk with flower-power English lyrics of an idealistic naturalism and freedom of spirit. Their best work is probably their fifth album *Reborn*, released in 1999 with its long spacier compositions variety of styles, showing the band's full maturity. For a panoramic overview the compilation *Painting The Air* consists of material from the earlier years, as well as three previously unreleased tracks.
RECOMMENDED RECORDINGS: REBORN *(Action, 1999)* **PAINTING THE AIR** *(On Stage, 2004).* C.A.

WILL O' THE WISP

Takis Barbagalas – *guitars,* **Angelos Gerakitis** – *vocals,* **Costas Pagonas** – *bass,* **Kostas Kostopoulos** – *drums,* **Amalia Kountouri** – *flute,* **Vagelis Stefanopoulos** – *piano, organ,* **Tasos Papastamou** – *violin,* **Markela Dounezaki** – *vocals.*
This Greek prog-rock sextet formed in 1997, plays a significant '70s psychedelic music recalling **Camel** and **Caravan**. With a name derived from Irish folk, the English lyrics are inspired by the tales of these lands, supported by a soft space-rock with very personal instrumental parts rich of flutes and violins, creating dark atmospheres through the organ, or sunnier moments through the rhythmic guitars. In 1999 they release their first self-titled album with a beautiful double cover also dedicated to Tolkien. While recording the third work they set up their own music company, Wow Records, under which *Ceremony Of Innocence* is published in 2004. After this, the last 2007 CD.
RECOMMENDED RECORDINGS: A GIFT FOR YOUR DREAMS *(Sound Effect, 2007).* M.G. & C.C.

Europe: HOLLAND

AURORA PROJECT

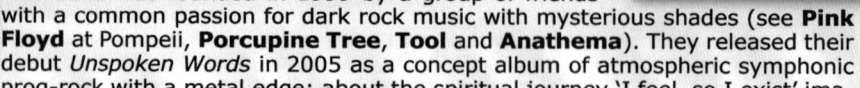

Dennis Binnekade - *vocals*, **Joris Bol** - *drums*, **Marc Vooijs** - *guitars*, **Marcel Guyt** - *keyboards*, **Remco van den Berg** – *guitars, backing vocals*, **Rob Krijgsman** – *bass*.
This band was founded in 1999 by a group of friends with a common passion for dark rock music with mysterious shades (see **Pink Floyd** at Pompeii, **Porcupine Tree**, **Tool** and **Anathema**). They released their debut *Unspoken Words* in 2005 as a concept album of atmospheric symphonic prog-rock with a metal edge: about the spiritual journey 'I feel, so I exist' imagined by guitarist **Marc Vooijs**, accompanied by the deep synth-lines, a storyteller-singer and backed by an entire choir. The self-produced artwork and multimedia software attached (the CD contains a game which links to the band's website) is completed with videos illustrating the construction of the lyrics and live footage of the band. Their second album *Shadow Border* of 2009 and the most recent *World of grey* confirms the quality of their style.
RECOMMENDED RECORDINGS: **UNSPOKEN WORDS** *(DVS, 2005)* M.G.

AVALANCHE

Rob Dekker - *keyboards*, **Daan Slaman** - *guitar*, **Jan Blom** - *voce, mandolin, guitar, bass*, **Marcella Neeleman** - *flute*, **Fred Dekker** - *bass*, **Johan Spek** - *drums*.
A band playing at ceremonies of the Protestant Church, led by multi-instrumentalist **Jan Blom** who records the tracks with the help of some friends and releases them as an early '70s sounding masterpiece in 1979: the original tape titled *Perseverance Kills Our Game* (done on a four track tape recorder, so the sound is fairly poor) seems to have gone lost but a CD version is available since 2015; probably a CD bootleg can be found. The first side is primarily a medieval-flavored folk rock acoustic instrumental work (only 1 song contains dreamy vocals) with gorgeous archaic flutes, a mandolin and the soaring and spiritual electric guitar work: unbelievably pretty yet somehow very sad. The second half expands the sound to include psychedelia and more progressive arrangements with very long instrumental tracks and dueling guitars.
DISCOGRAPHY: **PERSEVERANCE KILLS OUR GAME** *(LP Starlet, 1979).* M.G.

AYREON

Arjen Anthony Lucassen - *vocals, guitars, keyboards, bass*.
Arjen Anthony Lucassen's recordings are ambitious works, usually concept albums having almost ridiculous sci-fi themes carried out with the collaboration of many artists of prog and heavy metal like **Fish**, **Bruce Dickinson**, **James LaBrie**, **Mikael Akerfeldt** (**Opeth**) and **Neal Morse**. He starts around 1994 from the need to create rock operas but the commercial failure of the first two albums *The Final Experiment* and *Actual Fantasy* (probably due to the lack of special guests) leads him to seek help. Everything goes better with the following *Into the Electric Castle: A Space Opera* and the two chapters of *Universal Migrator Part 1 & Part 2*. Not satisfied he starts other parallel projects like **Ambeon** and **Star One**, releasing other two albums similar to his other works. Then back with **Ayreon** he finally publishes a new album on human emotions, *The Human Equation* of 2004. Still active and prolific on many fronts.
RECOMMENDED RECORDINGS: **INTO THE ELECTRIC CASTLE: A SPACE OPERA** *(Inside Out, 1998)* **THE HUMAN EQUATION** *(Inside Out, 2004)* M.G.

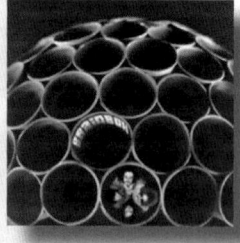

BRAINBOX

Jan Akkerman - *guitar*, **Pierre Van Der Linden** - *drums*, **Andre Reynen** - *bass*, **Kaz Lux** - *vocals, percussion*, **Herman Meyer** - *guitar*.
A blues, folk and heavy edged psychedelic rock-prog band formed in 1968 when enfant-prodige **Jan Akkerman** and drummer **Pierre Van Der Linden** join 19 year-old singer **Kazmierz 'Kaz' Lux** for a couple of demos: **Lux**'s voice (similar to blues rocker **Rory Gallager** and **Joe Cocker**) with **Jan**`s distinctive rock guitar (inspired by jazz and classical sources) give them their uniqueness, topped with **Tom Barlage**'s flute in some tracks of their first self-titled debut. Then **Jan** leaves in 1969 to form **Focus** (with **Thijs Van Leer** later joined by **Pierre**), so they recruit **Herman Meyer** for a more jazzy sound. Also **Lux** leaves in 1971 and yet they still issue *Parts* lacking the chemistry and soul of their beginnings. In 1982 and 2003 some concert reunions and a last album in 2011, *The 3rd Flood*.
RECOMMENDED RECODINGS: **BRAINBOX** *(Imperial, 1969)* **PARTS** *(Harvest, 1972).* C.A.

Europe: HOLLAND

CLIFFHANGER

Gijs Koopman – *bass, keyboards*, **Dick Heijboer** – *keyboards*, **Rinie Huigen** – *guitars, vocals*, **Hans Boonk** – *drums, percussion*.

Splendid dutch band of symphonic prog founded by keyboardist **Dick Heijboer** releasing demo tapes and albums from 1993 to 2001 among the best of this genre. Their first album album *Cold Steel* is very compelling, almost a masterpiece, as is the following *Not to Be Or Not to Be* with more instrumental tracks strongly keyboard-driven. Their music combines busy and intricate playing with subtle melodic moments with a good interplay. In 1997 **Dick** performs with them for the last time, replaced by **Ronald Van De Weerd** for a couple of albums but by the next spring they split since also **Gijs** quits and joins **Dick** in the band **Android** (which dissolved shortly after). In 1999 all ex-**Cliffhanger** members put their heads together again recording a new album in 2001, the musically weak *Circle*, before a final break-up.
DISCOGRAPHY: COLD STEEL (*Musea, 1995*) **NOT TO BE OR NOT TO BE** (*Musea, 1996*) **CIRCLE** (*Musea, 2001*). M.G.

FLAMBOROUGH HEAD

Andre Cents - *guitars*, **Marcel Derix** - *bass*, **Koen Roozen** - *drums, percussion*, **Edo Spanninga** - *keyboards*, **Siebe Rein Schaaf** - *vocals, keyboards*, **Eddie Mulder** - *guitar*, **Margriet Boomsma** - *vocals, flute*.

Formed in a region of north-Holland with its own dialect, anthem, traditional sports and banner. **Edo Spanninga** meets the **Wolf** brothers and the trio decides to form a band. Both brothers quit so they reform deriving their name from the rocky British coast winning a contract for the debut in 1998, *Unspoken Whisper*. Theirs is a very melodic symphonic rock (**Marillion**, **Pendragon**) proposed with taste and skill and with some romantic touches inspired by **Camel**. The third work of 2002, *One for the Crow*, is wonderfully mature and alternating keyboards compositions with strong electric guitar-work (rocky riffs and moving solos), beautiful classical guitar, some cheerful tin whistles and quite powerful vocals for a blend of classical, rock, folk, symphonic and neo-prog.
RECOMMENDED RECORDINGS: UNSPOKEN WHISPER *(1998, Cyclops)* **DEFINING THE LEGACY** *(2000, Cyclops)* **ONE FOR THE CROW** *(2002, Cyclops)* **TALES OF IMPERFECTION** *(2005, Cyclops)*. M.G.

GAMMA

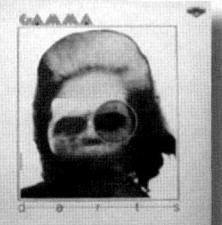

Ed Starink - *guitar, organ, piano, vocals*, **Frans Te Spenke** - *piano, vocals*, **Jan Willem Ludolph** - *bass*, **Kees Moolhuizen** - *guitar*, **Paul Poulissen** - *keyboards, saxophones*, **Ton Van Dijk** - *drums, percussion*.

A jazz prog-rock session-group born in 1970 as the project of **Paul Poulissen** and inspired by **Focus** and the typical '70s' sound. Their self-produced debut album *Alpha* of 1973 contains a sound dominated by the keyboards of **Poulissen** who demonstrates skill also as a saxophonist and twisting the style into a brass rock recalling **Ekseption** too. Singer **Frans Te Spenke** has an unusual mood that spoils the overall brightness, but luckily it is mostly an instrumental album ranging from horns and saxes to the jazzy interplay with piano, bass and drums, **Jan Akkerman** sounding guitars and a great flute work of slight psychedelic shades. The second album released in 1974, *Darts*, is even more perfect than their previous work.
DISCOGRAPHY: ALPHA (*LP GA, 1973*) **DARTS** (*LP GA, 1974*). M.G.

GOLDEN EARRING

Barry Hay - *vocals, guitar, flute, saxophones*, **George Kooymans** - *vocals, guitars*, **Rinus Gerritsen** - *bass, synth, keyboards*, **Cesar Zuiderwijk** - *drums, percussion*, **Eelco Gelling** - *guitars*, **Frans Krassenburg** - *vocals (1964-67)*.

In 1961 teenagers **George Kooymans** (age 13) and **Rinus Gerritsen** (age 15) form **The Tornados** and hit the top of the national charts with a couple of singles in 1965. In 1969 multi instrumentalist and singer **Barry Hay** joins them and they become *Golden Earring* (inspired by a 1947 song of **Marlene Dietrich**) when they discover a homonym group. Also their music changes towards a hard rock blues with many instrumental parts that in albums like *Moontan* - containing their most famous track "Radar Love" - brings the band near to prog and to the international market, opening **The Who**'s 1972 European tour and as support for **Santana** and **The Doobie Brothers** in the US. The band performed almost continuously since their foundation and is still active today.
RECOMMENDED RECORDINGS: MOONTAN *(Track-Polydor, 1973)*. M.G.

Europe: HOLLAND

KNIGHT AREA

Gerben Klazinga – keyboards, **Mark Smit** – vocals, **Pieter van Hoorn** – drums, **Gijs Koopman** - bass, Moog Taurus, **Mark Vermeule** - guitars. Born in 2004 as the musical project of keyboardist **Gerben Klazinga**, after the release of *The Sun Also Rises* as session-men, they become a 'proper' seven-piece band establishing themselves as a live act (in fact the success of this recording wins them the invite to Nearfest in 2005): this first concept album centers around a boy searching for his identity and discovering how to cope with his emotions. Carrying on in the spirit of their debut, *Under A New Sign* is published in 2007 recalling **Pendragon** and **IQ** with its lush keyboards and whirling song structures. More in general their neo-prog is a symphonic hard-rock with **Marillion**, **Arena** and **Dream Theater**'s influences, alternated with strong melodic moments.
DISCOGRAPHY: THE SUN ALSO RISES (Laser's Edge, 2004) **UNDER A NEW SIGN** (Laser's Edge, 2007) **REALM OF SHADOWS** (Laser's Edge, 2009). **M.G.**

KRACQ

Bert Vermijs – synthesizers, keyboards, vocals, **Jos Hustings** – guitar, vocals, **Cees Michielsen** – drums, percussion, **Twan van der Heiden** - bass, **Charlotte Rutten** - vocals, **Toni Guarracino** – vocals, sound engineer.
Mysterious band coming from the dutch underground, recording a good album in 1978 influenced by space rock, psychedelic avant-garde and RIO. **Kracq** (a pun of the names **King's Ransom** and **Carmine Queen**) formed in 1977 and disbanded in 1980 before the reunion in 2005 for some albums that lack the greatness of their beginning. Their only album *Circumvision* is kind of a historic document for dutch music, a heroic recording published at the end of the '70s prog era, the worst moment for this genre. Their production in fact belongs to the world of independent labels, with the unfortunate low quality sounds as a result. The following albums, originally self-produced separately, were recently reissued as unique CD.
DISCOGRAPHY: CIRCUMVISION (Polymnia, 1978, CD, 2004) **MIXED EMOTIONS & CELLAR TAPES** (Polymnia, 1979, CD, 2004). **M.G.**

LADY LAKE

Leendert Korstanje – keyboards, **Fred Rosenkamp** – guitars, **Jan Dubbe** - drums.
The first line-up in 1973 is a progressive blues-oriented band known as Session which did not last long, reforming in later in 1976 when keyboardist **Korstanje** (from Delay) meets **Rosenkamp** (guitarist and founder) then changing to a name inspired by **Gnidrolog**'s second album. In 1977 they record No Pictures, a symphonic prog album, with the very simple plots and very charming echoes from **Camel**, **Focus**, **Fruupp** and **Caravan** running from psychedelia to a hard-rock similar to **Kansas**. In 1995 the label Musea is able restore the master tapes adding some material from 1979 and later and issuing in 1997 a new version of this old classic. The 2005 reunion album *SuperCleanDreamMachine* is on the same line.
RECOMMENDED RECORDINGS: SUPERCLEANDREAMMACHINE (Musea, 2005). **M.G.**

LIKE WENDY

Bert Heinen – guitar, keyboards, vocals, **Marien**, **Mark-Jeroen Heek** – drums, percussion, keyboards.
A Multi-instrumentalist duo who after a couple of demos in 1995-96 (*Dream Of The Falcon* was reissued in 2016), debuts with *The Storm Inside*, an album released in 1998 and mainly influenced by the new prog of **Marillion**, **Pendragon** and **Genesis**. The second work of 1998 *Rainchild* continues on the same lines while *Tales from Moonlit Bay* is probably their best with the 21 minutes epic masterpiece opening-track "Falcon Suite" and its **Hackett** sounding guitar. The following two works are a down-path until **Marien** decides to leaves and in 2005 and **Bert Heinen** engages a new partner, another multi-instrumentalist called **Mark-Jeroen Heek**, to release the last pale episode with the sad title of *Endgame*.
RECOMMENDED RECORDINGS: THE STORM INSIDE (LabraD'Or, 1998) **RAINCHILD** (LabraD'Or, 1999) **TALES FROM THE MOONLIT BAY** (LabraD'Or, 2001). **M.G.**

MAYFLY

Gustaaf Verburg - *vocals, guitar, piano*, **Onno Verburg** - *vocals, guitar*, **Ide Min** - *vocals, synthesizers*, **Maarten Min** - *vocals, drums*, **Huub Nijhuis** - *bass, cello*, **Arie de Geus** - *piano, violin*.

The 1970 ensemble **Guruperide** changes name a year later developing a good live activity and signing up for some singles with a full LP in the bargain. The founders **Gustaaf** and **Ide** suddenly disagree, jeopardizing the entire operation. Producer Martin Doyceur accepts their idea of writing the record at home and these six energetic madmen lock themselves up in **Ide**'s attic and create their homonym album published in 1973: short songs performed with intense emotion, the vocals creating an incredible atmosphere of delicate and magical sounds, written over a pad of bass and piano coloured by an absolutely ingenious acoustic guitar and touches of violin for a fascinating taste of folk. A combination of the melodic pop of **The Beatles**, the exquisite folkloric vignettes of Magna Carta and impressionistic lyrics on the contemplation of nature and human aging.
DISCOGRAPHY: MAYFLY (Ariola, 1973).   C.A.

MIRROR

Kees Walravens - *guitars*, **Paula Mennen** - *keyboards, vocals*, **Philip de Goey** - *horns*, **Johan Saanen** - *bass*, **Peter Fransen** - *drums*.

This Dutch symphonic prog band formed by high school friends in 1972 with only one self-produced album titled *Daybreak*: recorded in six days at the Stable Studio in Arnhem, it was released in 1976 just before the break-up. The music is mainly instrumental and influenced by bands like **Focus**, **Yes** and **Pink Floyd** with the usual keyboards and organ, adding a horn section (saxophone, oboe, flute) that gives a pleasant originality. Very fascinating the female vocals which find their space in the complex structure of the long four tracks. After the publication, the band tours Holland extensively until some internal disagreements bring to the exit of **Johan Saanen** and the consequent split, merging into a new band called **Lethe** in 1978.
DISCOGRAPHY: DAYBREAK (Private pressing, 1973).   C.A.

PANTHEON

Ruud Wouterson - *keyboards, piano, vocals*, **Albert Veldkamp** - *bass, guitar*, **Hans Boer** - *flute, sax, vocals*, **Rob Verhoeven** - *drums, percussion*.

High school band formed in 1971, winners of the national talent contest of Rekreade Festival: a recording session with Phonogram. No one was more than 21 when they record their first single (the B side initially censored) which led to a series of live performances, and a second single that was broadcasted on radio and TV. Phonogram producer Tony Vos signs them up for an album in 1972, *Orion*, the band's only LP before they disband: a compelling romantic soul music mixed with the Canterbury jazz-rock influences by **Focus**. **Ruud Wouterson** leads the band with his keyboards, well supported by horn player **Hans Boer**, for a mainly instrumental work of unleashed melodies, relaxing atmospheres and intriguing solos. Lacking a financial insight they end breaking up. They played at various revival concerts with the original line up until 1992.
DISCOGRAPHY: ORION (1973, Vertigo).   M.G. & C.C.

SAGA (aka US)

Paul van Velzen – *vocals, drums*, **Jos Wernars** - *guitars*, **Guido Goebertus** - *keyboards*, **Ernest Wernars** - *bass, guitar*, **Alex Eeken** - *drums*.

This band from The Netherlands starts its career in 1975 with brothers **Jos** and **Ernest Wernars**, drummer **Paul van Velzen**, and later **Guido Goebertus** on keys. Wanting to sound as during their concerts they record *To Whom It Concerns* with clean and elegant melodies, uncomplicated instrumental parts of symphonic and direct schemes, aiming for simplicity without losing the excellent changes of atmospheres. A lovely use of Mellotron and intelligent and balanced acoustic guitar harping, recalling **Genesis**'s **Anthony Phillips**; also many echoes to **The Moody Blues** in the singing parts. In 1998 they reunite changing name to **US** and recording a ten other works with excellent, controlled keyboards, organ, mellotron, a very good lead singer and strong electric doses of guitar. Still active today with a recent album just out in 2017.
RECOMMENDED RECORDINGS: TO WHOM IT CONCERNS (UAP, 1979).   M.G. & C.C.

Europe: HUNGARY

LOCOMOTIV GT

Gábor Presser - *keyboards, vocals,* **Tamás Barta** - *guitars, vocals,* **Károly Frenreisz** - *bass,* **József Laux** - *drums,* **Tamás Somtó** - *saxophones, bass, vocals,* **János Karácsony** - *guitars.*

This is a band who sold more of a million of their many albums in Hungary, with tours through the Anglo-Saxon countries and during the last of these, as support for **Grand Funk Railroad**. Founded in 1971 by former members of **Omega** like **Gábor Presser** and **Jószef Laux**, they tended towards a prog-rock inspired by **Traffic**, with strong jazz tints and heavy blues inserts. Their debut was considered experimental and hazy in Hungary, but the West saw it as the best new music that could come from the East and in 1972 they were invited to open for **Joe Cocker** and **Genesis**. They also spent the year in London, recording a second album, *Ringasd El Magad*, or producing several music projects. A clash with the Communist Government banned their fifth album but did not really stop them to this very day.

RECOMMENDED RECORDINGS: **LOCOMOTIV GT** *(1971, Pepita)* **RINGASD EL MAGAD** *(1972, Pepita)* **III - BUMMM!** *(1973, Pepita).*

M.G.

MINI

Török Ádám - *flute, vocals,* **Németh Károly** - *keyboards,* **Jeno Balogh** - *drums,* **Laszlo Kunu** - *guitar,* **Alajos Nemeth** - *bass.*

Founded in 1968 by vocalist and flutist **Ádám Török**, playing an early **Jethro Tull**-like styled music for a while before becoming jazzier. Their first album of 1978, *Vissza A Városba* (Back Into the City), features space rock, jazz rock and soft **Camel** inspired songs with no guitar, a lot of flute, Fender Rhodes, floating string synths and a very precise rhythmic section. The second album, *Úton A Föld Felé* (Toward the Earth) released the following year is similar to the first one, while in 1983 *Dzsungel* (Jungle) was easier and lighter. **Ádám** begins other projects until reuniting the band for another five albums since 1998 under the name **Török Ádám & Mini**. The 2001 album *A Szél Nomádja* (Nomad of the Winds) is an instrumental prog rock album, very close to the music of **Solaris**.

DISCOGRAPHY: **VISSZA A VAROSBA** *(Pepita, 1979)* **UTON A FOLD FELE'** *(Pepita, 1980)* **MINI KONZERT** *(Pepita, 1980)* **DZSUNGEL** *(Pepita, 1982)* **25 EV ROCK** *(Pepita, 1983).*

C.A.

KORÁL

Ferenc Balázs – *keyboards, vocals ,* **László Fischer** - *guitars,* **Zsolt Scholler, Tibor Fekete** – *bass,* **Péter Dorozsmai** – *drums.*

Another band that released the debut album in the worst moment for prog since disco music and punk were flourishing on all the radio stations. Born in 1974 playing a pompous symphonic rock comparable to some things from **Journey**, **Asia** or **Styx**, although not at the same level. This aspect justifies their contemporaneity to that AOR still present in the Western music charts as melodic and conventional music, but very pleasant and appreciated by the audiences. Their style is greatly inspired by **Omega**, though sounding more mid-'70s, with notable **Eloy** and **Pink Floyd** influences, and even heavy rock touches which recall **Deep Purple** even in their look.

RECOMMENDED RECORDINGS: **KORÁL I** *(1980, Pepita).*

M.G.

PANTA RHEI

András Szalay - *bass,* **Sándor Szalay** - *guitar,* **Kálmán Matolcsy** - *keyboards,* **Csaba Béke** - *drums,* **Enikö Ács** - *vocals,* **András Schmidt** - *drums,* **András Laár** - *vocals, guitar.*

Hungarian band born in 1974, starting with a record of variations over the music of **Bela Bartòk** arranged with the same approach of **ELP**'s first albums. Unfortunately this recording was stopped from the heirs of the famous musician before the official release, although a bootleg can be found. After improving their style, they move on to release a self-titled album in 1980 of symphonic rock interpreted with the progressive taste of compelling keyboards and guitars with good synthesizer inserts. In 1983 they come back as **P.R.Computer** with a fascinating homonym electronic album (They also design and build their own synths).

DISCOGRAPHY: **PANTA RHEI** *(Pepita, 1980)* **P.R.COMPUTER** *(Pepita, 1983).*

C.A.

Europe: HUNGARY

PIRAMIS

Som Lajos - *bass*, **Rèvesz Sàndor** - *vocals, guitar*, **Gallai Péter** - *keyboards, vocals*, **Köves Miklós** - *drums*, **Závodi János** - *guitar*.
One of the most important pop bands in this country, born in 1973 and occasionally entering the progressive territory without much conviction. Their music followed an absolutely hard-rock style since their beginnings, influenced by the more bloody **Black Sabbath** (**Lajos Som** declared himself as his faithful disciple). Having a sound characterized by easy listening compositions, with simple structures and an obsessive drumming that perfectly interplay with the guitar of talented **Janos Zavodi**, great performer of spectacular solos during the live acts of this band. *Erotika* is definitely their prog album, otherwise the rest of the discography is simply definable as hard rock.
RECOMMENDED RECORDINGS: EROTIKA (Pepita, 1981).   C.A. & C.C.

RUMBLIN' ORCHESTRA

Bela Ella - *keyboards*, **Beatrix Ella** - *flute*, **Kitty Ella** – *cello*, **Attila Ella** - *trombone*, **Daniel Ella** - *Oboe*, **Miklos Ella** – *violin*, **Justin Szabo** - *bass, drums, vocals*.
A symphonic-prog band, or a classical orchestra in love with rock music? An ensemble formed in the second half of the '90s with outstanding musicians all belonging to the **Ella** family. A magnificent symphonic genre not 100% prog, sometimes recalling **The Alan Parsons Project** and **ELP** as well as **After Crying**. Their first album *Spartacus* of 1998 is influenced (even in the name) by Triumvirat with some English vocals (strong foreign accent), more of a neo-classical work. The second work *The King's New Garment* is instead more balanced, alternating classical and rock moments. After this 2000 release, nothing else.
RECOMMENDED RECORDINGS: SPARTACUS (Periferic, 1998).   M.G.

SYRIUS

Zsolt Baronits – *saxophones, vocals*, **Miklos Orszaczky** – *vocals, bass, guitar, violin*, **Lazlo Pataki** - *piano, organ*, **Mihaly Raduly** – *saxophones, flute*, **Andras Veszelinov** – *drums, percussion, vocals*.
A legendary group formed by **Zsolt Baronits** in 1962 mainly to play beat music changing around 1970 when they start playing prog-rock and jazz-rock fusion. They are signed up by an Australian label and issue their debut *Devil's Masquerade* in English there first, before Hungary. This album is a mix of jazzy prog-rock, influenced by **Bela Bartòk** and other great names of British Prog, all stirred together in a big pot of complex rhythms. For unknown reasons they couldn't go back to Australia and some members left the band shortly afterward. The new line-up releases *Széttört álmok* (Broken Dreams) in 1976, yet on the same line with the previous' complex sounds. Disbanded in 1978 they reunite in the 2000 for a last concert (recorded and released) in 2001.
DISCOGRAPHY: DEVIL'S MASQUERADE (1971, Festival Spin) **AZ ÖRDÖG ÁLARCOSBÁLJA** (Devil's Masquerade Hungarian version, 1972, Pepita) **SZETTORT ALMOK (Broken Dreams)** (1976, Pepita).   M.G.

TOWNSCREAM

Csaba Vedres - *keyboards*, **Péter Ács** - *bass*, **Gábor Baross** - *drums*, **Béla Gál** - *cello, sinthesizers*.
A band founded in 1995 by **Csaba Vedres** (former of **After Crying** keyboardist) with **ELP** influences, folk and other classical elements. The debut album *Nagyvárosi Ikonok* proves evident skill in the construction of keyboard textures and classical sounds with hints of trumpets and flutes, a fine and compelling product with just a few weak moments. The band was working on another record called *Zsoldosok* which would have been made up of studio and live recordings, but they disbanded around 1999 and the project was shelved. **Vedres** carried on his career composing classical music unrelated to progressive rock.
DISCOGRAPHY: NAGYVÁROSI IKONOK (Periferic Records 1997).   M.G.

Europe: ICELAND & GREENLAND

EIK

Magnús Finnur Jóhansson - *vocals, flute*, **Thorsteinn Magnússon** - *guitar, keyboards, vocals*, **Pétur Hjaltested** - *keyboards*, **Ásgeir Óskarsson** - *drums, percussion*, **Lárus Halldór Grímsson** - *keyboards, flute, vocals*, **Haraldur Thorsteinsson** - *bass*, **Tryggvi Július Hübner** - *guitars, vocals*.

Seven musicians playing together from 1971 to 1978, with only two albums of predominantly symphonic prog, with space/avant moments, elements of rock, blues, jazz and funk, groovy bass lines and tempo changes, all infused with the essence of Iceland. Their album of 1977 *Hrislan Og Stramurinn* (the twig and the stream) opens with a classical piano ready to unleash the compelling keyboards and guitar arrangements of **Hübner**. Their style is a combination between **Camel**, **Yes** and **Wigwam** with beautiful vocal harmonies and some jazz influences. The first album *Speglun* has English lyrics while the second is sung in their mother tongue.

DISCOGRAPHY: SPEGLUN *(1976, Steinar)* **HRISLAN OG STRAMURINN** *(1977, Steinar).*   M.G.

HINN ISLENSKI THURSAFLOKKUR

Egill Ólafsson – *vocals, keyboards*, **Tómas Tómasson** – *bass*, **Þórður Árnason** - *guitar*, **Ásgeir Óskarsson** – *drums*, **Karl J. Sighvatsson** - *keyboards*, **Rúnar Vilbergsson** – *bass tuba*.

For a name that means 'Those Icelandic Hobgoblins', this band's first album of 1978 sounds more like a spin-off from **Gentle Giant**'s music, combining perfectly folk passages, eclectic parts and progressive elements of skillful instrumental parts and choirs. The second release of 1979, *Thursabit* instead takes a distance from the previous style (also abbreviating the name to **Thursaflokkurinn**) and concentrates more on their Icelandic folk roots, mixing influences from **Hatfield and the North** and **National Health**, especially into the vocals arrangements, all sung in their mother tongue. They disband after the 1982 album.

RECOMMENDED RECORDINGS: HINN ÍSLENSKI THURSAFLOKKUR *(Spor, 1978)*   M.G.

ICECROSS

Axel P. J. Einarsson - *guitar, vocals*, **B. Ómar Óskarsson** - *bass, vocals*, **Ásgeir Óskarsson** - *drums*.

Hard psychedelic prog-rock band founded by **Axel Einarsson** and **Ásgeir Óskarsson** in 1972, their only album is recorded in Denmark but issued only in Iceland, with a disturbing cover, prelude to the dark doomsday sounds recalling **Black Sabbath**'s works. The guitar is the absolute protagonist with its riffs and speed, pushing towards harder sonorities that sometimes break into delicate ballads such as "A Sad Man's Story". The use of sustained rhythms contributes greatly to their success yet in 1974 they change name to **Ástarkveðja** relocating in the USA and permanently disbanding in 1975.

DISCOGRAPHY: ICECROSS *(1972, Private pressing).*   M.G. & C.C.

MÁNAR

Cólafur Thórarinsson - *vocals, guitar, flute*, **Björn Thórarinsson** - *organ*, **Gudmundur Benediktsson** - *vocals, piano*, **Smári Kristjánsson** - *bass*, **Ragnar Sigurjónsson** - *drums*.

A multi-faceted song-oriented compact sound, with traces of folk, great organ tunes united to the typical symphonic prog flute harmonies and the hard-psychedelic guitar moods. This band formed in 1967 publishes a fascinating album in 1971, full of smooth Scandinavian melodies and a mix of styles which confirms the magic of early '70s, where creativity and fantasy seemed to be unlimited, sometimes recalling bands like **Junipher Greene** and **Thor's Hammer**.

DISCOGRAPHY: MÁNAR *(1971, Steinar).*   M.G. & C.C.

Europe: ICELAND & GREENLAND

NATTURA

Shady Owens - *vocals*, **Björgvin Gí-slasson** - *guitar*, **Karl J. Sighvatsson** - *keyboards*, **Sigurdur Árnason** - *bass*, **Ólafur Gardarsson** - *drums*.

From Iceland, this band formed in 1969 becomes very popular with gigs in local clubs until 1971, when a substantial line-up change occurs leaving only **Gislason** and **Arnason** from the initial core and adding female singer Shady Owens and keyboardist Karl Sighvatsson. Their only album *Magic Key* is recorded independently in London the following year with a prog rock very close to the contemporary English proposals (**Curved Air, Deep Purple, Czar, Affinity, Cressida, Gravy Train**) translating into a psychedelia of folk influences fairly rooted in a typical guitar-organ driven model and the melodic teachings of **The Beatles**.
DISCOGRAPHY: MAGIC KEY (1972, Private pressing). M.G. & C.C.

SUME

Malik Høegh - *guitars, vocals*, **Hans Fleischer** - *drums*, **Emil Larsen** - *bass, vocals*, **Sakio Nielsen** - *organ*, **Nikolaj Steenstrup** - *mellotron, percussion*.

A band born in 1972 (meaning "Where ?") from Greenland which releases its first album *Sumut* ("Which way?") a year later with an unusual prog made of pure modern folk (or World music) all sung in Inuit on the stories of their people in defense of their rights: the phonetic properties work very well with the '70s music style and rock instrumentation. Another two good albums of the same period and then nothing until the early '90s with the 1994 live recording *Persersume*, and in 2014 the release of a documentary film retracing their history: *Sume - Lyden af en Revolution*.
RECOMMENDED RECORDINGS: SUMUT (ULO, 1973). M.G.

SVANFRIDUR

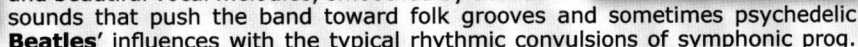

Birgir Hrafnsson - *guitars*, **Pétur Kristjánsson** - *vocals*, **Gunnar Hermansson** - *bass*, **Sigurdur Karlsson** - *drums*, **Con Sigurdur Jónsson** - *keyboards, violin, flute, vocals*.

Another band from Iceland with one good album released in 1972 for a heavy prog made of guitars and beautiful vocal melodies, smoothed by acoustic sounds that push the band toward folk grooves and sometimes psychedelic **Beatles**' influences with the typical rhythmic convulsions of symphonic prog. *What's Hidden Here?* is recorded in London and contains these interesting examples of heavy prog-rock mixed to local folk with the original and inventive use of violin and Moog synthesizers, courtesy of guest musician and arranger **Sigurdur Johnsson**. The album was recovered from obscurity by Graham Brook, founder and owner of the label Hi-Note, and released on CD in 1995.
DISCOGRAPHY: WHAT'S HIDDEN HERE? (1972, Private pressing). M.G. & C.C.

TRÚBROT

Shady Owens - *vocals*, **Gunnar Þórðarson** - *guitar, flute, vocals*, **Karl Sighvatsson** - *organ, piano*, **Rúnar Júlíusson** - *vocals, bass*, **Gunnar Jökull Hákonarson** - *drums, vocals*, **Magnús Kjartansson** - *piano, organ, vocals*.

A band from Iceland formed in 1969 that will later lend members to **Náttùra**, like the young American singer **Shady Owens**. Their first self-titled album is totally sung in their mother tongue, featuring some organ-based pop song covers (**The Beatles**) strongly influenced by the beat-hippy era with traces of psychedelia and a five-minute opera titled 'Elskaðu Náungan'. Keyboardist **Karl Sighvatsson** and singer **Shady** leave before the second work, more prog oriented, while *Lifun* of 1971 is a concept album between prog and other sounds such as **Bee Gees**. Mandala is released in the summer of 1972 as their last album for they disbanded the next year. A part from the first album, the rest contain also songs in English, a controversial issue for this country.
RECOMMENDED RECORDINGS: LIFUN (Geimstenn, 1971). M.G. & C.C.

Europe: ISRAEL

TRESPASS

Igil Stein - *keyboards, vocals, flute*, **Roy Bar-Tour** - *bass*, **Gabriel Weissman** - *drums*.

This young trio captures the best international reviewers' interest using some of the best solutions derived from **ELP**, **Quatermass**, **Le Orme** and other keyboard-driven bands, avoiding nostalgic tunes and tending towards a more modern symphonic sound with a musical playfulness seldom heard in the progressive rock genre: in both albums they perform a dynamic brand of prog-baroque-jazz-blues-folk sung in English with large instrumental compositions also recalling **Focus**, **UK** or **The Nice**. *Morning Lights* is probably their best although jazzier than the previous.
DISCOGRAPHY: IN HAZE OF TIME *(Musea, 2002)* **MORNING LIGHTS** *(Musea, 2006)*.   M.G.

TUNED TONE

Shem-Tov Levy - *flute, vocals, piano, percussion*, **Haim Romano** - *guitars, congas, mandolin*, **Shlomo Gronich** - *keyboards, vocals*.

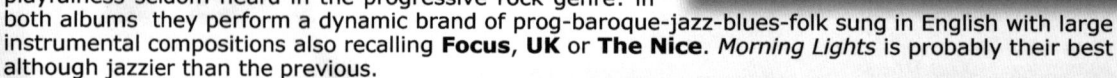

This Jewish one-shot band is a trio founded by former **NoNames** colleagues and talented musicians **Shem Tov Levy** and **Slomo Gronich**, together with guitarist **Haim Romano** from **Churchills** (and other special guests from the Israeli rock and post-beat musical scenario, see page 223). Their only homonym album is released in 1979 and declared a Pop record with folk-rock hints and a fascinating flute; it also contains some moments of samba and the remarkable guitar playing, both acoustic and electric, of **Haim**. The song "White Days" is written by the famous female poet **Lea Goldberg** and is probably one of the most beautiful songs coming from this country.
DISCOGRAPHY: TUNED TONE *(1979, Hed-Arzi)*.   M.G.

YOSSI PIAMENTA

Orthodox Jewish singer, songwriter and guitarist highly influenced by **Jimmy Hendrix** and known for introducing the electric guitar to Hebrew folk and religious music. **Yossi Piamenta** creates his own band in 1974 with his brother **Avi**, a flutist, called **Piamenta** playing live for several years and recording some singles/demos until 1977, when saxophonist **Stan Getz** (touring in Israel at the time) hears them and decides to help record an album that combined heavy metal, jazz and Arabic/oriental elements. This very unique effort was unfortunately never released officially, and **Yossi** follows **Stan** on a US tour and again back to Israel where he holds also many religious concerts on his own (the **Piamenta Band** was one of the most-requested groups of musicians for Jewish weddings over the last century). **Yossi** dies of cancer in 2015.
RECOMMENDED RECORDINGS: SONGS OF THE REBBES *(1992, Moni Piamenta Productions)*.   C.C.

ZINGAL'E

Yonatan Stern - *vocals*, **Ady Weiss** - *keyboards*, **David Rosental** - *keyboards*, **Ehud Tamir** - *bass*, **Tony Brower** - *violin, mandolin*, **Efraim Barak** - *guitar*, **David Shanan** - *drums*, **David Hofesh** - *vocals*.
The band forms in 1974, named after the Hebrew slang word for 'joint' and are the first Israeli prog group to use theatrical elements in their concerts (masks, lights). Since the first singles in Hebrew failed, they decide to publish their first album in English and as a mostly instrumental work: *Peace* was ready at the end of 1975 but released only in 1977 in Israel. A brilliant progressive structure with articulated arrangements in which the tracks succeed one after the other seamlessly forming two long suites. The music is swift and sparkling, recalling sometimes **Gentle Giant** or **Supersister**, especially in intricate passages where multiple instruments interact with each other (mainly keyboards and violins) resulting in a kind of original prog-fusion.
DISCOGRAPHY: PEACE *(1977, Ilanot Music)*.   M.G. & C.C.

Europe: ITALY

ABIOGENESI

Sandro Immacolato - *drums*, **Patrick Menegaldo, Marco Cimino** - *keyboards*, **Roberto Piccolo** - *bass*, **Toni D'Urso** - *guitars, vocals*.
Born in the mid '90s around the figure of guitarist, songwriter and vocalist **Toni D'Urso**, brother of **Salvatore 'Ursus' D'Urso** (leader of the '80s neo-psychedelic **No-Strange**), this quartet from Turin records five albums of hard-prog with gothic atmospheres, (similar to the '70s style of **Black Widow**): a constant symphonic rock mixed with heavy elements and modern arrangements blending the vintage taste of psychedelia through the use of instruments typical of those years. The Italian label Black Widow immediately signs them up for a first album in 1995 featuring long pieces, effects and complex atmospheres of instrumental psychedelia and acoustic rock, also described as crossover prog. Their third work *Le Notti di Salem* is released in 2000 with the contribution of the late **Clive Jones** (former Black Widow).
RECOMMENDED RECORDINGS: ABIOGENESI *(1995, Black Widow)* **IO SONO IL VAMPIRO** *(2005, Black Widow).*
M.G.

ACQUA FRAGILE

Bernardo Lanzetti - *vocals, guitar*, **Gino Campanini** - *guitar, vocals*, **Maurizio Mori** - *keyboards, vocals*, **Franz Dondi** - *bass*, **Pier Emilio Canavera** - *drums, vocals*.
Born in 1967 as **Gli Immortali** (with the 45RPM "Il tempo dell'amore") they become officially **Acqua Fragile** (meaning fragile water) in 1971 and are best remembered for their singer, **Bernardo Lanzetti**, before he joins **PFM** in 1976. Greatly inspired by **Gentle Giant**, **Yes** and **CSN&Y** for the vocal harmonies, also similar to the voice of **Roger Chapman** from **Family**, **Lanzetti**'s pretty good English accent is due to his time in the US: they wanted to sing in English but this made it more difficult to find a label that would produce them. Both albums are very interesting, especially their second work of 1974, *Mass Media Stars*, which managed to be released also in the USA. Recently reunited in studio, they are working on a new project soon to be published.
DISCOGRAPHY: ACQUA FRAGILE *(1973, Numero Uno)* **MASS MEDIA STARS** *(1974, Ricordi)* **LIVE IN EMILIA** *(1994, Prehistoric).*
M.G. & C.C.

ALBEROMOTORE

Maurizio Rota - *vocals, percussion*, **Adriano Martire** - *keyboards*, **Fernando Fera** - *guitars*, **Glauco Borrelli** - *bass, vocals*, **Marcello Vento** - *drums*.
Meaning 'crankshaft', this quintet forms in the early '70s playing in clubs and festivals until 1974 when they released a first album *Il Grande Gioco*, after being discovered by singer and guitarist **Ricky Gianco** (who is also the author of their lyrics). He signs them up with Intingo (specialized in Italian folk) when their original label, Car Juke Box shuts down and they re-lease the debut once more: among the eight tracks, "Israele" is a song supporting the Palestinian cause, sung by **Maurizio Rota**'s strong voice (often compared to **Joe Cocker**) while the overall sound of the band is more influenced by an American styled blues more than by symphonic prog. The following year they release the single "Messico lontano" before disbanding and pursuing each their own career: **Marcello Vento** marries **Jenny Sorrenti** and together they bring reunite the band Saint Just; **Glauco Borrelli** starts a solo career while **Marcello Vento** dies in 2013.
RECOMMENDED RECORDINGS: IL GRANDE GIOCO *(1974, CAR- Juke Box).*
M.G.

GLI ALLUMINOGENI

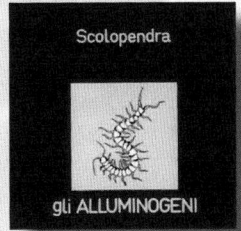

Patrizio Alluminio - *vocals, keyboards*, **Enrico Cagliero** - *guitars, bass*, **Daniele Ostorero** - *drums, percussion*.
Five friends playing together since 1966 during their holidays that, after calling themselves in various ways (**Green Grapes**), derive their name from singer **Patrizio Alluminio**, combining it to the hallucinatory substance (allucinogeno). From 1970 they sign up with Fonit Cetra for a series of singles, also participating in various festivals and supporting **Gentle Giant** on their Italian tour. They finally release their first concept album *Scolopendra* in 1972, an interesting progressive work with many guitar solos, keyboards and rhythmic changes (beautiful "La stella di Atades"). Unhappy with the final mix, the disagreement breaks them up. They recently reunite for an album in 1993, *Geni Mutanti*, and a 1994 collection of unreleased material, *Green Grapes*. A project called *Metafisico* was rumored in 2008 but only 4 songs came out on Spotify.
RECOMMENDED RECORDINGS: SCOLOPENDRA *(1972, Fonit-Cetra).*
M.G.

Europe: ITALY

ALUSA FALLAX

Augusto "Duty" Cirla - *vocals, drums, flute,* **Guido Gabet** - *guitar, vocals,* **Massimo Parretti** - *keyboards,* **Mario Cirla** - *flute, saxophone, french horn, vocals,* **Guido Cirla** - *bass, vocals.*

Formed in Milan in 1969 by keyboardist **Massimo Parretti** in search of musicians for a song he'd been commissioned: he meets **Gli Adelfi** which after the recording change their name into this band. After the release of another two pop singles they change style for the album *Intorno Alla Mia Cattiva Educazione (about my bad manners)* in 1974, opting for a more complex classical structure (13 tracks divided into two long suites) with great flute and keyboard atmospheres, an outstanding rhythmic section and occasional jazz influences. They continued their career performing live for a decade through not in the prog genre (disco) releasing a single under the name **Blizzard** before finally splitting up in 1979.
DISCOGRAPHY: **INTORNO ALLA MIA CATTIVA EDUCAZIONE** *(1974, Fonit).* M.G. & C.C.

ANALOGY

H. J. "Mops" Nienhaus - *drums,* **Jutta Taylor Nienhaus** – *vocals,* **Nicola Pankoff** - *keyboards,* **Mauro Rattaggi, Wolfgang Schoene** – *bass,* **Martin Thurn Mithoff**– *guitars, flute, percussion.*

In 1968 **Martin Thurn** founds **Sons of Giove** later renamed **Joice** (and due to a misprint, **Yoice**) and in 1971 some singles with newcomer **Nikola Pankoff**. For their first 1972 LP as **Analogy**, the label chose a nude pic in which **Rattaggi** is hidden since he was away with the army. The sound is a psychedelic blues with open kraut folk prog supported by **Jutta Nienhaus**'s dark voice. In 1973 **Thurn** composes a long piece entitled *The Suite* (published only in 1993). **Jutta** and **Martin** go to London in 1975 and form **Earthbound** with **Dick Brett** and **Scott Hunter** and in 2009 **Earthbound** members with the original trio **Nienhaus, Thurn, Rattaggi** (plus 'Hunka Munka' **Roberto Carlotto**) reunite under the name **Analogy** for concerts and the 2012 live *Konzert*.
RECOMMENDED RECORDINGS: **ANALOGY** *(Dischi Produzioni Ventotto, 1972)* **THE SUITE** *(Ohrwaschl Records, 1993)* **KONZERT** *(AMS-BTF, 2013).* M.G.

ANATROFOBIA

Alessandro Cartolari - *horns, tape effects,* **Luca Cartolari** - *bass, tape effects,* **Andrea Biondello** - *drums,* **Mario Simeoni, Gianni Trovero** - *horns.*

This band from Turin forms in 1991 and names itself after the phobia for ducks derived from the famous American comic strips (Anatidaephobia): it consists of a trio playing intense and almost mystical live acts where they develop a sound made of stylistic changes, from fanfare to silence, through jazz, RIO and electronic music. Six studio albums of which the first released in 1997 and the last in 2007 for a decade of hard work and prize winning awards from the record industry. In their last work *Brevi Momenti Di Presenza* their sound changes moving from the previous fusion to a more electronic and free improvisational approach.
DISCOGRAPHY: **FRAMMENTI DI DURATA** *(CMC 1997)* **RUOTE CHE GIRANO A VUOTO** *(Zzz 1999)* **UNO SCOIATTOLO IN MEZZO AD UN'AUTOSTRADA** *(Wallace 2001)* **LE COSE NON PARLANO** *(Wallace 2001)* **TESA MUSICA MARGINALE** *(Wallace 2004)* **BREVI MOMENTI DI PRESENZA** *(Wallace 2007).* M.G. & C.C.

ANTARES

Marco Tessitore - *keyboards,* **Ennio Barone** - *bass,* **Joseph Kalì** - *guitars,* **Lorenz Shulze** - *drums.*

Not to be confused with the German symphonic group of the same name, this minor Italian band of the late-seventies releases only one album, Sea of Tranquillity, in 1979, a conceptual work recorded in Oslo with a mixed line-up of Italian and foreign musicians, based on the Apollo 11 moon landing. It's a largely instrumental work and the few lyrics are sung in English blending mainstream pop with spacey atmospheres and electronics. The presence of **Antonio Bartoccetti** (**Jacula, Antonius Rex**) as co-songwriter of the tracks "My girlfriend" and "Galaxy" makes up for the use of cheap instruments playing poor sounds, sadly typical of this era. **Antares** do not have a great deal in common with other Italian artists of the same time and tends to draw comparisons with **Eloy** and **Pink Floyd**. The album was reissued on CD in 1994.
DISCOGRAPHY: **SEA OF TRANQUILLITY** *(1979, LP Unifunk - CD Mellow Records).* M.G.

Europe: ITALY

ANTONIUS REX (Including JACULA)

Antonio Bartoccetti composes two singles with **Doris Norton** aka '**Fiamma dello Spirito**' as they decide to call themselves **Jacula**, releasing a first scary album in 1969, *In Cauda semper stat Venenum*, based on guitar and pipe-organs, spectral voices, long instrumental litanies and occult verses with no drums. The second *Tardo Pede In Magiam Versus* of 1972 is more rock-oriented. Then **Antonio** spins off and creates his new project in 1974, **Antonius Rex**, which inherits all the unreleased materials of the previous band. After Vertigo aborts the attempt of an outrageously diabolic album *Neque Semper Arcum Tendit Rex* (published in 2002 by the label Black Widow), the first real **Antonius Rex** album *Zora* is released in 1977, with old and new versions from the **Jacula** repertory. Recently **Bartoccetti** releases in 2009 *Per Viam* as **Antonius Rex** and in 2011 *Pre Viam* as **Jacula**. All his concepts are rarely performed live, so in 2005 an official video was published as *Magic Ritual*.
RECOMMENDED RECORDINGS: Antonius Rex: **NEQUE SEMPER ARCUM TENDIT REX** (Black Widow, 2002) Jacula: **IN CAUDA SEMPER STAT VENENUM** (Private Pressing, 1969 - Black Widow, 2001) **TARDO PEDE IN MAGIAM VERSUS** (Rogers, 1972).   M.G.

ARCANSIEL

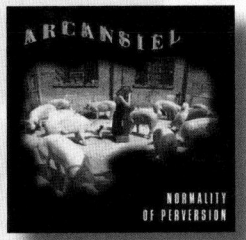

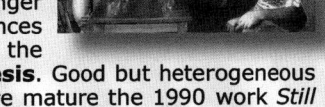

Marco Galetti - *keyboards, vocals*, **Gianni Opezzo** - *guitars*, **Nici Clerici** - *bass*, **Gianni Lavagno** - *drums*, **Sandro Marinoni** - *saxophones, flute, keyboards*.
Formed in 1986 by keyboardist, composer and singer **Marco Galetti**, combining symphonic rock influences with modern pop styles, their music is close to the '80s British neo-prog of **IQ**, **Marillion** and **Genesis**. Good but heterogeneous the first record, *Four Daises* of 1988; much more mature the 1990 work *Still Searching*, with its excellent suite and the shorter tracks of more evident derivations with a lot guitar-keyboard overlapping, some overt symphonic tendencies and a full range of acoustic-electric expressions. In 1993 **Galletti** is replaced by **Paolo Baltaro** for the less prog yet interesting album *Normality of Perversion*. After 10 years the reunion and a compilation of greatest hits with re-arranged tracks and an unpublished work.
RECOMMENDED RECORDINGS: STILL SEARCHING (Contempo Records, 1990).   M.G. & C.C.

AREKNAMÉS

Michele Epifani - *keyboards, vocals, flute*, **Piero Ranalli** - *bass*, **Mino Vitelli**, **Luca Falsetti** - *drums*, **Stefano Colombi** - *guitars*.
Led by composer, producer, vocalist and multi-instrumentalist **Michele Epifani**, the name derives from their idol **Franco Battiato**'s song of 1973: this quartet is strongly influenced by the dark and heavy style of **VDGG** and the Canterbury scene, with hints of **Gnidrolog** and **Indian Summer**, twisting through the sepulchral **Black Sabbath** they successfully manage to keep a very personal style. Two albums of long and throbbing songs, guided by an outstanding arsenal of analogical keyboards, mellotron along with some heavy guitars, the dramatic mood changes constantly alternating between melodic parts and furious passages, classic symphonic rock and outright doom-prog. The second album love hate round trip won the ProgAwards 2006. A third work of 2010 features the 20-minute track "The very last Chamber".
RECOMMENDED RECORDINGS: AREKNAMÉS (Black Widow 2004) **LOVE HATE ROUND TRIP** (Black Widow 2006) **LIVE AT BURG HERZBERG FESTIVAL** (live, Herzberg Verlag 2008).   M.G. & C.C.

ARIA PALEA

Egidio Marullo - *drums, percussion*, **Gianluca Milanese** - *flute*, **Apollonio Tommasi** - *bass*, **Gigi De Giorgi**, **Fiorino Calogiuri**, **Marilù Calogiuri** - *vocals*, **Emanuele Lucci**, **Dario Margiotta**, **Palmiro Durante** - *guitars*.
Two albums in the mid '90s for a sound combining dynamic changing moods to create delicate moments and powerful sections of fusion, jazz-rock, delicate and fine songwriting mixed with traditional music: *Zoicekardia* of 1996 recalls somewhat **Jethro Tull**, **Dalton**, **Finisterre**, **Mary Newsletter** and **Delirium** for the folk atmosphere of certain tracks with an emphasis on the guitar/flute interplay. Good use of clarinet and sax with derivations from **Area**. *Danze d'Ansie* of 1998 is a more original album between prog-folk and the theatrical avant-garde approach of **Osanna**, with lyrics in the southern Italian dialect Griko.
DISCOGRAPHY: ZOICEKARDIA (Lizard Records 1996) **DANZE D'ANSIE** (Lizard Records 1998). M.G.

Europe: ITALY

ARIES

Simona Angioloni - *vocals*, **Fabio Zuffanti** - *bass, acoustic guitar, dulcimer*, **Roberto Vigo** - *keyboards*, **Fabio Venturini** - *guitars*, **Carlo Barreca** - *flute*, **Pierpaolo Tondo** - *drums*.
Among the multitude of projects by multi-instrumentalist and composer **Fabio Zuffanti**, this is his most romantic and light-symphonic side with warmer atmospheres than most of his previous works: in fact the difference with **Hostsonaten** (former band) are the softer and more melodic themes, sometimes with a mild trace of folk recalling **Renaissance** and **Iona** also for the ethereal voice of **Simona Angioloni**. The first homonym album of 2005 contains six good compositions with the 17 sparkling minutes of the stunning closing-track "When Night is Almost Done". This intricately arranged project distinguishes itself from most Italian symphonic prog band for the atmospheric art-rock.
DISCOGRAPHY: **ARIES** *(2005, Mellow Records),* **DOUBLE REIGN** *(2010, AMS Records).*   M.G. & C.C.

ATON'S

Pietro Ratto – *keyboards, guitars, vocals*, **Vito Frallonardo** – *bass*, **Massimo Trasente** – *drums, percussion*.
Formed in 1977 by Italian writer, musician **Pietro Ratto** as his answer to the rise of punk and new wave: initially a punk-rock band, they gradually tend toward a more melodic genre arriving to prog in its more lighter version drawing inspiration from classical and folk atmospheres. Their first recording of 1985 results in the hour-long rock opera "H", which blends traditional acoustic instruments with synths and drum machines. Born as a video, it was first issued on tape but released only later in 1993. Therefore the first studio album is actually *A.I. 2984* of 1988, quite an interesting work, simple and linear, sometimes extremely melodic. Decidedly more prog the complex and articulated *Caccia Grossa* of 1991. Another two albums before **Ratto** concentrates on his parallel solo career, so the last album for this band is *Capolinea* of 2002.
RECOMMENDED RECORDINGS: **CACCIA GROSSA** *(Contempo, 1991).*   M.G.

AUFKLÄRUNG

Michele Martello, **Fabio Guadalupi** - *guitars*, **Marco Mancarella** - *keyboards*, **Luciano Rubini** - *bass*, **Massimo Mignini** - *drums*, **Edoardo Lecci** - *flute*, **Chicco Grosso** - *vocals*.
It may have begun in the '90s, but this band's sound is classic '70s somewhere between **Genesis**, **ELP**, the Italian '70s prog and a touch of **Pink Floyd**. Formed in 1990 from members of another group called **The Eclipse**, they opt for an enlightening name to confirm the intent of cultural break by revisiting a musical movement of the past: **Marco Mancarella**'s band starts off with a first demo, "Jetho Van Hall", in 1990, and by 1994 they had enough material for a real album, *De' La' Tempesta ... L'Oscuro Piacere*, released in nine CD copies strategically distributed. Nothing paid off like good press and they were finally contacted by Pick Up records that releases the album in 1995; the same year they are invited to participate in the Amnesty International prog festival of Terni.
DISCOGRAPHY: **DE LA TEMPESTA... L'OSCURO PIACERE** *(Lizard/Pick Up, 1995).*   M.G.

AVIOLINEE UTOPIA

Christian Logli - *saxophones*, **Giuliano Lott** - *vocals, percussion*, **Nancy Parrillo** - *bass*, **Andrea Pergher** - *guitars*, **Giacomo Plotegher** - *piano, keyboards*, **Michele Tecilla** - *drums, percussion*.
Of the few Italian prog groups (**Deus Ex Machina**) dedicated to jazz-rock during the '90s, this sextet obtained great results even if with an only album published in 1997. A very elaborate music, never too complicated, with hyperbolic instrumental textures which avoid the cold technicalities or mannerisms by combining a compelling fusion similar to both **Deus** and **Area**, with a little symphonic prog à la **BMS** and **PFM** thrown in. The album features aggressive guitar parts, searing saxes and passionate, raging vocals which never lose the melodious feel, alternating between soft, almost ambient passages to frenzy moments of euphoria. They disbanded right after this masterpiece.
DISCOGRAPHY: **AVIOLINEE UTOPIA** *(1997, Mellow Records).*   M.G.

Europe: ITALY

IL BACIO DELLA MEDUSA

Simone Cecchini - *vocals, acoustic guitar,* **Federico Caprai** - *bass,* **Eva Morelli** - *flute, saxophones,* **Simone Bronzetti** - *guitars,* **Carlo Barreca** - *flute,* **Diego Petrini** - *drums, mellotron,* **Daniele Rinchi** - *violin.*
Born in 2002 (meaning Medusa's Kiss), this is a typical Italian '70s sound similar to **PFM** but also to hard rocking groups like **Osanna** or **De De Lind**. The self-tiled debut album released in 2004 is an art-rock music with few keyboards and a more predominant use of flute, saxophone and accordion, for a Renaissance/Baroque taste that confers more personality to their sound. The musical and artistic attention takes great care in the lyrics and arrangements. In 2005 **Daniele Rinchi** joins the band with his outstanding violin style and they record a second album in 2008, *Discesa Agl'inferi D'un Giovane Amante*, with new instruments and the mellotron of **Petrini**. A last new album was released after a live recording of 2016 and published in 2017 as *Deus Lo Vult*.

DISCOGRAPHY: **IL BACIO DELLA MEDUSA** *(2004, Private Pressing),* **DISCESA AGL'INFERI D'UN GIOVANE AMANTE** *(2008, Black Widow)* **LIVE** *(2016, AMS)* **DEUS LO VOULT** *(2017, AMS).* **M.G.**

BAROCK PROJECT

Luca Zambini - *keyboards,* **Giambattista Giorgi, Francesco Caliendo** - *bass,* **Eric Ombelli** - *drums,* **Marco Mazzuoccolo** - *guitars.*
Founded in 2002 by pianist **Luca Zabbini**, a great fan of **Keith Emerson**, his intentions were to revive the '70s prog through a perfect classical structure (mainly Baroque) blended to a good mix of jazz rock. In 2007 they perform in Bologna with a string quartet and release the DVD *Rock in Theater*. That same year they also publish their first album *Misteriose Voci* with good success. But it is with the third album, *Coffee in Neukölln*, with English lyrics that they become known also abroad winning the nomination in the Prog Awards 2012. After a line-up change they start recording their fourth album, *Skyline* featuring the flute of **Vittorio De Scalzi** (**New Trolls**) and the art-work cover of **Paul Whitehead** (illustrator of **Genesis** and **VDGG** albums). The new 2017 album *Detachment* comes out after another internal change.
RECOMMENDED RECORDINGS: **MISTERIOSE VOCI** *(Musea, 2007)* **COFFEE IN NEUKÖLLN** *(Musea, 2012)* **SKYLINE** *(Artalia, 2015)* **DETACHMENT** *(Artalia, 2017)* **M.G & C.C.**

BARROCK

Valter Poles, Giuseppe Vendramin - *keyboards, guitars,* **Maurizio Poles** - *drums,* **Graziella Vendramin, Paola Poles** - *vocals,* **Giampaolo Poles** - *bass.*
This symphonic prog band from Friuli-Venezia Giulia is born 1982 greatly influenced by the Italian **BMS**. They began with a homonym self-produced tape recorded in 1985 of polyphonic styles where every track sounds like a chamber concert of very complex proposals, blending concrete music with the Renaissance, Baroque and Medieval keyboards of **Vendramin** and **V.Poles** recalling folk influences from **Renaissance** though maintaining their personal touch. The classical Italian vocals of the two female singers glide through the difficult arrangements similar to **Opus Avantra**. At the end of the '80s a Japanese label signs them up and published worldwide their debut album as *L'Alchimista* in 1991. Another two albums close this decade before vanishing for good.
DISCOGRAPHY: **L'ALCHIMISTA** *(Moon Witch, 1991)* **OXIAN** *(SI Music, 1994)* **LA STREGA** *(Mellow Records, 1999).* **M.G.**

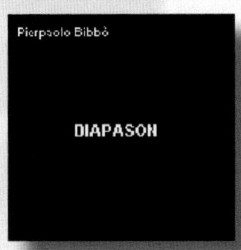

PIERPAOLO BIBBÒ

Multi-instrumentalist, singer, arranger and producer, this musician from Sardinia starts his official career in a time considered too late for the genre; nevertheless his debut album *Diapason* of 1980 contains a collection of good romantic songs with outstanding delicate instrumental arrangements. Surrounded by good and well prepared musicians (he even opens his own recording studio) he records it composing everything himself and playing guitars, bass, synths (and vocals), while the others give a reasonable 'band' feel through the added keyboards, drums, violin and flute. During the '80s he plays and writes songs for an electro-pop band called **Segno**. In 2012 he finally returns to prog with his new album *Genemesi* and six years later with *Via Lattea*.
RECOMMENDED RECORDINGS: **DIAPASON** *(1980, LaStrega)* **GENEMESI** *(2012, MPRecords).* **M.G&C.C.**

Europe: ITALY

BUON VECCHIO CHARLIE

Luigi Calabrò - *guitars, vocals,* **Richard Benson** - *vocals, acoustic guitar,* **Sandro Centofanti** - *keyboards,* **Sandro Cesaroni** - *saxophones, flute,* **Paolo Damiani** - *bass,* **Rino Sangiorgio** - *drums.*

This one shot band, precursor to **BMS** and **PFM**, plays an Italian symphonic prog recalling **Colosseum**, **King Crimson**, **Genesis**, **ELP** and **The Nice**. Recorded in 1971 their only album is released only in 1992 by Melos: all three suites start with a classical tune that develops into melodic rock with hard-prog or jazz tendencies, like the first track opened by a flute playing Grieg's "Hall of the Mountain King". Their music alternates between calmer folk parts and the grand symphonic flights of keyboards and organ, with both acoustic and electric guitars, flute and sax, plus a the few sporadic vocals of **Richard Benson** (today soloist in the goth-metal genre). In 1999 the label Akarma also re-issues it with two extra unpublished tracks. In 1972 some members feature in **Beppe Palomba**'s LP *A Rosa, A Giovanna E Alle Altre* and in 1974 **Benson** participates (using the band's name) and wins the Villa Pamphili festival award.
DISCOGRAPHY: **BUON VECCHIO CHARLIE** *(1992, Melos)* **GHENT SESSIONS** *(1999, Akarma).* **M.G.**

ROBERTO CACCIAPAGLIA

Perfect synthesis between **Terry Riley**'s minimalism, classical music and **Tangerine Dream**, **Philip Glass** and **Mike Oldfield**, his studies in orchestral art, electronic sounds and avant-garde computer-based music land him in the court of Rolf Ulrich Kaiser (label Ohr) for which he records in 1974 the beautiful sympho-cosmic vocal-electro album *Sonanze*. In parallel he begins a long and ongoing collaboration with **Franco Battiato** (*Pollution*, 1973) also starting to work with several TV networks for musical soundtracks and he plays with some German electronic-rock bands (**Popul Vuh**) with whom he concerts through the '70s. In 1986 his masterpiece: *Generazioni Del Cielo*, an ethereal album, spiritual and dreamy with celestial rhythms. The '90s see him working on commissioned material for the theatre and ballet, but never forgetting to enrich his discography almost every year.
RECOMMENDED RECORDINGS: **SONANZE** *(PDU, 1975)* **GENERAZIONI DEL CIELO** *(Fonit, 1986)* **ARCANA** *(BMG, 2001)* **QUARTO TEMPO** *(Universal, 2007)* **CANONE DEGLI SPAZI** *(Universal, 2009).*
M.G & C.C.

CALLIOPE

Rinaldo Doro – *keyboards, celtic harp,* **Massimo Berruti** – *vocals,* **Gianni Catalano** – *drums,* **Mario Guadagnin** – *guitars, vocals,* **Enzo Martin** – *bass.*

Formed in 1989 this keyboard-driven quartet plays a traditional Italian '70s prog in the style of **Latte & Miele**, **Le Orme** and **PFM**. When **Rinaldo Doro** meets producer **Beppe Crovella** (keyboardist in Arti e Mestieri), he signs them up with his label Vinyl Magic and publishes their debut album in 1992, *La Terra Dei Grandi Occhi*. Strongly anchored to the '70s symphonic sound thanks to the ample use of analogical keyboards (Hammond and Mellotron), they release a second album the following year, on the same line of the previous but with a few harder tints. The real change, also in line-up, comes with their third work, *Il Madrigale Del Vento*, with more classic and folk inclinations realized with pieces that **Doro** actually composed for a solo project.
RECOMMENDED RECORDINGS: **IL MADRIGALE DEL VENTO** *(Vynil Magic, 1995).* **M.G & C.C.**

I CAMALEONTI

Tonino Cripezzi - *vocals, keyboards,* **Livio Macchia** - *guitar, vocals,* **Paolo De Ceglie** - *drums,* **Dave Sumner** - *guitar,* **Gerry Manzoli** - *bass.*

An Italian beat band formed in 1962 that approached prog during the mid '70s in two of their many albums: their fourth work of 1973, *Amicizia & Amore*, was a concept album meant as a blend of selected and harmonic melodies alternating to a more underground rock genre. Instead the label CBS, worried about a sales' factor, distorted the ultimate release through heavy orchestral arrangements, thus upsetting the musicians very much. Three years later they manage to release *Che Areo Stupendo...La Speranza*, their last work with CBS due to the same reasons, but this time a little bit more faithful to their ideas. After these two experiences the band diverts once more to their chart-hits with renewed success. They are still active today.
RECOMMENDED RECORDINGS: **AMICIZIA & AMORE** *(CBS, 1973)* **CHE AEREO STUPENDO...LA SPERANZA** *(CBS, 1976).*
C.A. & C.C.

Europe: ITALY

CAMERA ASTRALIS

Davide Sgorlon - *guitars, 12 strings guitar,* **Renato Cavallero** - *vocals, keyboards, drums, percussion,* **Andrea Starnini** - *piano, electric piano,* **Gianni Giannella** - *bass,* **Franco Vassia** - *lyrics.*
This **Genesis** clone (the after-**Gabriel** period of *A Trick of the Tail* and *Wind and Wuthering*) both in the musical arrangements and in the incredibly **Phil Collins** sounding voice of **Renato Cavallero**, comes with none of the boring triviality that copy-cats usually have: their only self-produced album of 1998, *I Supplicanti*, is a stunning experiment of Italian lyrics (magistrally written by **Franco Vassia**) sung as if the 'singing drummer' himself had a Mediterranean incarnation. The band's personal touch lies in a somewhat richer melodic charge due to the keyboard-driven compositions (piano and synths) and to the powerful guitar solos and acoustic guitar arpeggios in **Steve Hackett**'s style.
DISCOGRAPHY: I SUPPLICANTI *(1998, private pressing).*   M.G.

JURI CAMISASCA

Guitarist, singer and song-writer **Roberto 'Juri' Camisasca** meets **Franco Battiato** during army services: this long lasting friendship and collaboration begins in the early '70s when he starts experimenting musically through the use of the vocal 'instrument' in its every sound variation. His first solo album of 1974, *La Finestra Dentro*, is a complex work rich in metaphors, hallucinated and claustrophobic lyrics with **Juri**'s excellent acid-folk songwriting and his unique vocals. **Battiato** features in the line-up on VCS3 synths and as co-producer too, lending some of his musicians as session-men. They also carry out the avant-garde project **Telaio Magnetico** together, a shortlife supergroup with **Mino Di Martino (I Giganti)** and **Terra Di Benedetto (Albergo Intergalattico Spaziale)**, afterwhich he retires to a Benedectin convent for 11 years. In 1988 he returns with a new album of rearranged Gregorian chants called *Te Deum*. As a song-writer his best are probably "Il Carmelo di Echt" and "Nomadi".
RECOMMENDED RECORDINGS: LA FINESTRA DENTRO *(Bla Bla, 1974)* IL CARMELO DI ECHT *(EMI, 1991)* ARCANO ENIGMA *(Mercury, 1999).*   M.G & C.C.

CAPSICUM RED

Red Canzian - *vocals, guitar,* **Paolo Steffan** - *vocals, bass, piano,* **Mauro Bolzan** - *keyboards, piano,* **Roberto Balocco** - *drums.*
After a couple of commercial singles this quartet from Treviso publishes a first truly prog album in 1972, *Appunti Per Un'idea Fissa*. Formed in 1970 by singer and guitarist **Bruno 'Red' Canzian**, this only record of average Italian melodies on British models (**Procol Harum, Moody Blues, ELP**), contains an interesting version of Beethoven's "Patetica". The band disbands shortly after and **Red Canzian** joins **Osage Tribe** for a while before becoming the official bass player in the super famous **Pooh**, while **Paolo Steffan** forms a country-inspired duo called **Genova & Steffan** releasing only on album in 1975.
DISCOGRAPHY: APPUNTI PER UN'IDEA FISSA *(1972, Bla Bla).*   M.G & C.C.

ALEX CARPANI

Keyboardist and composer **Alex Carpani** during a convalescence composes, arranges, performs and records all the parts of his debut concept album called *Waterline* (2007). At first conceived as an instrumental work he sends a demo to singer **Aldo Tagliapietra (Le Orme)** who accepts to take on the lead vocals of this classic symphonic and romantic prog of excellent melodies with the vintage sounds of a compelling keyboard. The **Alex Carpani Band** was supported by very capable American session-men for an overall result greatly influenced by **Genesis, ELP, Camel, Le Orme** and **Locanda delle Fate**, though nothing extremely new or innovative. **Paul Whitehead**'s artwork is featured on the cover of both this and the second album of 2011, *The Sanctuary*.
RECOMMENDED RECORDINGS: WATERLINE *(2007, Cypher Arts)* THE SANCTUARY *(2011, Ma.Ra. Cash).*   M.G & C.C.

Europe: ITALY

IL CASTELLO DI ATLANTE

Roberto Giordano - *keyboards, vocals,* **Dino Fiore** - *bass,* **Aldo Bergamini** - *guitars, vocals,* **Paolo Ferrarotti** - *drums, vocals,* **Massimo Di Lauro** - *violin.*
Dino Fiore asks his friend **Paulo Ferrarotti** to form a band in 1974, that has not really changed over the years. After a self-produced 45RPM in 1983 they encounter producer **Beppe Crovella** (keyboardist of **Arti & Mestieri**) with whom they collaborate until he signs them up with Vinyl Magic and finally publishes in 1993 their first debut album *Sono Io Il Signore Delle Terre A Nord*, an interesting mix of new prog and symphonic elements from the '70s: highly emotional Italian lyrics full of allegories and metaphors, the music is built around keyboards and choral effects, with violin and soaring guitar solos. *L'ippogrifo* in 1995 is a more mature and complete work re-elaborating old material of the past 16 years while *Come Il Seguitare Delle Stagioni* of 2000 is the first album to consist of entirely new material. *Tra Le Antiche Mura* is probably their masterpiece, based on a literary concept with each song presented as a book and nominated for the Italian Prog Awards in 2009.
RECOMMENDED RECORDINGS: **Capitolo 7: TRA LE ANTICHE MURA** (*Electromantic, 2009*). **M.G.**

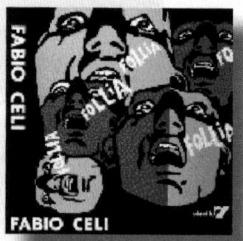

FABIO CELI & GLI INFERMIERI

Fabio Celi - *keyboards, piano, vocals,* **Ciro Ciscognetti** - *keyboards, piano,* **Luigi Coppa** - *guitar, harmonica,* **Rino Fiorentino** - *bass,* **Roberto Ciscognetti** - *drums, percussion.*
Antonio Cavallaro AKA **Fabio Celi** founds his band **Gli Infermieri** (the nurses) in 1968 near Naples, initially as **Fabio Celi & I Pop**. After a couple of singles, they change name and publish their only album in 1969 entitled *Follia* (Craziness): a revolutionary recording between prog and psychedelia with beat resonances. All six tracks are longer more than five minutes each with two keyboards (Farfisa organ modified to sound like the Moog) and an acid guitar that sound absolutely outstanding. The bizarre and irreverent lyrics were censored by the official Italian broadcasting due to the contents. If the 1969 release date claimed by **Celi** is accurate, then this should be considered one of the earliest transitional albums moving from pop and beat to the classic prog period. Drummer **Ciscognetti** is the only active musician today.
DISCOGRAPHY: **FOLLIA** (*1969, Studio 7*). **M.G & C.C.**

IL CERCHIO D'ORO

Franco Piccolini - *keyboards ,* **Giuseppe Terribile** - *lead vocals, guitar, bass,* **Gino Terribile** - *drums, vocals,* **Maurizio Bocchino, Piuccio Pradal, Roberto Giordana** - *guitar,* **Giorgio Pagnacco** - *keyboards.*
This symphonic prog band formed in 1974 with brothers **Gino** and **Giuseppe Terribile** and **Franco Piccolini** actively gigging around Savona but never managing to secure a contract. The only recordings from this early phase are some singles from the late '70s published before the break-up. In 1999 Mellow Records dusts off 12 of their 1976 unpublished recordings and releases a self-titled album adding their first singles to the mix. Another label also decides to publish in 2005 some demo quality material and covers of songs by **The Trip**, **Le Orme** and **New Trolls**: *La Quadratura Del Cerchio* is printed only on vinyl. Consequently they decide to reunite and with two new guitarists they record *Il Viaggio Di Colombo* in 2008 produced by Black Widow. They recently published another two works and are still performing live.
RECOMMENDED RECORDINGS: **IL VIAGGIO DI COLOMBO** (*2008, Black Widow*) **M.G.**

CIRCUS 2000

Silvana Aliotta - *vocals, percussion,* **Marcello Quartarone** - *guitars, vocals,* **Gianni Bianco** - *bass, vocals,* **Johnny Betti, Franco "Dede" Lo Previte** - *drums, percussion.*
The homonym LP of 1970 presents this band's sound as greatly inspired by the Californian psychedelic blues of **Jefferson Airplane** and **Grateful Dead**, with not much of a personal touch (except for **Silvana Aliotta**'s amazing voice). After a line-up change where drummer **Johnny Betti** is replaced by **'Dede' Lo Previte**, their second and last album is released a couple of years later: *An Escape From A Box* is a very different and decidedly more prog work where the complex compositions still maintain the elaborate psychedelic atmospheres and blues moments, switching from softer moods to quicker parts, even of folk. All lyrics are in English. After the disbandment **Quartarone** and **Betti** form the band **Living Life**, while **Lo Previte** joins the project **Duello Madre**.
RECOMMENDED RECORDINGS: **AN ESCAPE FROM A BOX** (*RiFi, 1972*) **M.G.**

Europe: ITALY

CITTÁ FRONTALE

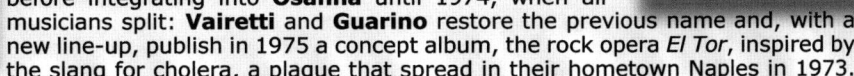

Lino Vairetti - *vocals, guitars, keyboards,* **Massimo Guarino** - *drums,* **Enzo Avitabile** - *horns,* **Rino Zurzolo** - *bass,* **Paolo Raffone** - *keyboards,* **Gianni Guarracino** - *guitars.*

In 1970 a band with this name formed for a short time before integrating into **Osanna** until 1974, when all musicians split: **Vairetti** and **Guarino** restore the previous name and, with a new line-up, publish in 1975 a concept album, the rock opera *El Tor*, inspired by the slang for cholera, a plague that spread in their hometown Naples in 1973. Predominantly acoustic, it is melodic to the point of sounding too commercial and often criticized for this aspect; **Enzo Avitabile**'s flute and saxophone give the Mediterranean folk compositions a slight hint of fusion, while **Vairetti**'s spirited vocals sing lyrics that underline social and political issues of a society torn apart by exploitation and oppression. The album's jazz-rock and West-Coast ballads prelude to the future sound of **Osanna**'s new album *Suddance* when they reunite three years later.
DISCOGRAPHY: EL TOR *(Fonit Cetra 1975).* M.G & C.C.

CONQUEROR

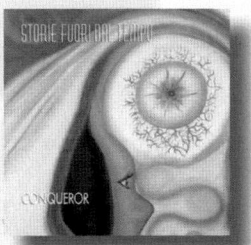

Natale Russo - *drums,* **Simona Rigano** - *keyboards, vocals,* **Tony Rose, Fabio Ucchino, Daniele Bambino** - *bass,* **Sabrina Rigano** - *vocals, winds,* **Gaetano Scarcella, Tino Nastasi** - *guitars.*

Sicilian conventional new prog quintet formed in 1994, they undergo a series of line-up changes before finally publishing their debut *Istinto* in 2003: a music containing compelling magical sounds derived from the golden age of the genre with a mix of horns, keyboards and guitars that create atmospheres greatly influenced by **Pink Floyd**, with the pleasant female voice of **Simona Rigano**. The band has released almost an album every year, among which the 2005 *Storie Fuori Dal Tempo* that gained them an international distribution, and the 2010 concept album on the life of the Mata Hari, *Madame Zelle*. More recently their last studio album is of 2014 entitled *Stems*.
DISCOGRAPHY: ISTINTO *(Conqueror 2003)* **STORIE FUORI DAL TEMPO** *(Maracash 2005)* **74 GIORNI** *(Maracash 2007).* M.G & C.C.

CONSORZIO ACQUA POTABILE

Paul Rosette - *vocals,* **Romolo Bollea** - *keyboards,* **Maurizio Venegoni** - *keyboards,* **Massimo Gorlezza** - *guitars,* **Riccardo Roattino** - *guitar,* **Pippo Avondo** - *drums.*

CAP is a quintet formed in 1971 and rediscovered only many years later by the label Kaliphonia who publishes in 1993 their live recording entitled *Sala Borsa Live '77*. The band therefore reunites with four of the original members, for a brand new album that same year, *Nei Gorghi del Tempo*, practically their first studio work: an elaborated, symphonic rock with complex pieces of typical Italian prog (similar to **BMS** or **PFM**) and some classical influences as well. Lyrics are all in Italian and sung by the intense voice of **Paul Rosette**. In 2016 their last album *Coraggio e Mistero* featuring singer **Alvaro Fella** (**Jumbo**).
RECOMMENDED RECORDINGS: ROBIN DELLE STELLE *(Kaliphonia, 1998)* **CORAGGIO E MISTERO** *(Black Widow, 2016).* M.G.

CONTRAPPUNTO

Adelaide Loru, Sara Arrigone – *vocals,* **Andrea Cavallo** – *keyboards,* **Sebastiano Di Paola** – *giutars,* **Denis Fiori** - *bass,* **Denis Militello** - *drums.*

Late 90's symphonic band emulating the '70s prog in the style of **Arrakeen** or the **Marillion** of *Clutching at Straws*, with a touch of added jazz. Mainly driven by **Andrea Cavallo**'s piano, their first album *Subsidea* of 1999 merges skillfully Moog and Hammond with a mix of moody instrumental rock through the few good guitar solos and the voice of **Sara Arrigone** featuring only here. The following album, *Lilith* of 2001, is in fact sung by **Adelaide Loru**, not the only novelty: no more vintage sounds, but more oriented towards **Fish**'s last era and the addition of further jazzy moments. The last 2005 *Elegie D'inverno* is an instrumental work credited to **Contrappunto Project**, rich of wind instruments and greatly influenced by **Stravinski**, **Gerswin** and **Piazzolla**, resulting more like a solo project of **Cavallo**.
RECOMMENDED RECORDINGS: SUBSIDEA *(Progressive Rock Worldwide, 1999)* M.G.

Europe: ITALY

CORTE AULICA

Gus Pasini - *drums*, **Nicola Gasperi** – *keyboards*, **Luca Saccenti** - *guitars*, **Emanuele Jaforte** – *bass*.

This symphonic ensemble from Brescia formed in 2006 with a mission: <<to create music which recalls the Canterbury setting of the '70s>> greatly inspired by **Camel**, **Caravan** and **Hatfield and the North**, yet still managing their own strong personality into the smooth melodic compositions adapted to our times. An interesting sound produced by Mellow Records and with two great musicians, the experienced **Emanuele Jaforte**, multi-instrumentalist (here bass player) and part of the jazz-rock project **Ypsilon**, and **Gus Pasini** (former drummer of **Notabene**) who wrote and composed almost all the material, as well as the fabulous artwork on the cover, of their only album *Il Temporale e l'Arcobaleno*.
DISCOGRAPHY: IL TEMPORALE E L'ARCOBALENO *(Mellow Records 2006)*. M.G.

CORTE DEI MIRACOLI

Graziano Zippo - *vocals*, **Alessio Feltri** - *keyboards*, **Michele Carlone** - *keyboards*, **Gabriele Siri** - *bass*, **Flavio Scogna** - *drums, percussion*, **Riccardo Zegna** - *keyboards*.

The only true studio album for this traditional keyboard-based symphonic prog band is a homonym work released in 1976 of very melodic and Baroque tunes mixed to jazz-rock and greatly diverting from the Anglo-American influences of the time. Sometimes heavy, sometimes lighter, usually lyrical and moderately complex, their sound combines certain aspects of **Genesis**, **VDGG** and **PFM**. The album also features **Vittorio De Scalzi** (**New Trolls**) on guitars and mixer. Mellow Records published in 1993 *Dimensione Onirica*, a record containing previous unreleased recordings from 1973-74, and the following year a powerful live album of a 1976 concert entitled *Live at Lux* (unfortunately with low quality audio).
DISCOGRAPHY: CORTE DEI MIRACOLI *(1976, Grog)* **DIMENSIONE ONIRICA** *(1992, Mellow Records)* **LIVE AT LUX** *(1993, Mellow Records)*. M.G & C.C.

COURT

Luigi Bonacina - *bass*, **Paolo Lucchina** - *vocals*, **Mosè Nodari** - *guitars, piano, oboe, flute*, **Ayron R. Silva** - *piano*, **Francesco Vedani** - *drums, percussion*, **Andrea Costanza** - *guitar*, **Alberto Biroldi** - *percussion*, **Giorgio Salvetti** - *piano, flute, keyboards*, **Marco Strobel** - *guitar, mandolin*.

Formed in 1990, this psych-folk band signs up with an indie label for a debut album of fascinating archaic atmospheres led by guitars with good flute and oboe inserts and an evocative singing. Their symphonic prog has strong classical influences despite the limited keyboards, and the acoustic instruments give an almost chamber-like characteristic to their sophisticated romantic art-rock. In 1997 their second work *Distances* is released as an impressive folk masterpiece: <<Court filters prog, folk and ancient music traditions, generating a new, original sound, completely detached from the very concept of song. Their music develops with unlimited creativity, explicitly trying to overcome any boundary>>. After many other albums and concerts around the world, they are still active today.
RECOMMENDED RECORDINGS: DISTANCES *(1997, WMMS)*. M.G & C.C.

DIK DIK

Pietro Montalbetti - *guitars, bass, vocals*, **Erminio Salvaderi** - *guitar, vocals*, **Giancarlo Sbriziolo** - *vocals, guitar*, **Sergio Panno** - *drums*, **Roberto Facini** - *guitars*, **Joe Vescovi, Roberto Carlotto** - *keyboards*, **Nunzio 'Cucciolo' Favia** - *drums*.

This famous pop-beat band since 1965 has only one true progressive effort in their entire discography: the 1972 *Suite Per Una Donna Assolutamente Relativa*, a concept album with the lyrics of **Herbert Pagani** and composed by **Mario Totaro**. Co-produced by **Maurizio Vandelli** (leader and guitarist of **Equipe 84**), it was released at a time when labels were more interested in sales and hit singles. In fact they soon go back to the Italian Pop, but only after publishing the next *Storie e Confessioni*, in which traces of prog can be still found due to the special guest musicians in the line-up.
RECOMMENDED RECORDINGS: SUITE PER UNA DONNA ASSOLUTAMENTE RELATIVA *(Ricordi, 1972)* **STORIE E CONFESSIONI** *(Ricordi, 1973)*. C.A. & C.C.

Europe: ITALY

DIVAE

Alessandro Costanzo, Lino Vairetti - *vocals,* **Enzo Di Francesco, Gianni Leone, Marco Vantini** - *keyboards,* **Luis Dragotto Moraleda** - *guitars,* **Ugo Vantini** - *drums,* **Romolo Amici** - *bass,* **Jerry Cutillo** - *flute.*
Excellent new-prog band from Rome, formed in 1995 with only one album and many a concert. The roaring symphonic sounds (Hammond, Mellotron, e-piano, synthesizers) integrate some heavy rock inserts and delicate Italian vocal parts, which make *Determinazione* an astounding work of compelling styles greatly influenced by **Genesis, Deep Purple** and **Gentle Giant**, guest-starring on vocals **Lino Vairetti** (singer of **Osanna**) and **Gianni Leone** (**Balletto di Bronzo** keyboardist). Sadly the project dies immediately after the release and each member follows a new career: drummer **Ugo Vantini** joins at first **Balletto Di Bronzo** and then **Ezra Winston** before founding **VuMeters**.
DISCOGRAPHY: DETERMINAZIONE (Progressivamente 1995). **M.G & C.C.**

DONO CELESTE

Antony Graham Milner - *vocals,* **Ignazio Serventi** - *guitars,* **Alessandro Buzzi** - *drums, percussion,* **Giampaolo Piras** - *bass,* **Enrico Ghezzi** - *piano, keyboards.*
This band from Genova of 1999 attempts to deviate from any kind of prog they can, trying to propose something more personal, smart and seducing, yet resulting in a certain form of kraut-rock and modern psychedelia in their one shot album entitled *So Linger*. Sadly the record went almost ignored although it is an incredible work with an undefined structure and compositional paths which move in slow motion creating moods and landscapes surrounded by the cosmic nature of **Pink Floyd** tunes and an indolence expressed through solutions later emulated by post-rock bands like **Sigur Ros**. Fifty-five bright minutes of visionary melancholy.
DISCOGRAPHY: SO LINGER (1999, Mellow Records). **M.G & C.C.**

DORACOR

Corrado Sardella - *keyboards.*
Anagram and alias of keyboardist and drummer **Corrado Sardella** since his debut album of 1997. His prolific discography is mainly a primarily-instrumental symphonic and melodic prog based on influences from **Keith Emerson** and **Rick Wakeman**. A very capable musician handling most of the instruments himself and writing long tracks and suites supported by good session men that complete his compositions through the sounds of guitars, sax and violin. *Transizione* (2001) is probably his masterpiece although also *Evanescenze* (2005) and *Onirika* (2007) are excellent representations of his music. The drum machine results slightly cold and mechanic, luckily dropped in the more recent recordings like the 2008 album *Lady Roma*.
RECOMMENDED RECORDINGS: TRANSIZIONE (2001, Mellow Records) **EVANESCENZE** (2005, Mellow Records) **ONIRIKA** (2007, Mellow Records) **LADY ROMA** (2008, Mellow Records). **M.G.**

EAZYCON

Carl Lee (Carlo Musso) - *vocals, guitars,* **Frankie Partipilo** - *saxophones, percussion,* **Ustad Partipilo** - *sitar, flute, tablas.*
Formed in Turin in the early '80s by **Carlo Musso** AKA '**Carl Lee**' and **Frankie Partipilo**, this 'open' band duo is still very actively dedicated to any form of experimentation in all the realms of free music, making their sound not easily classifiable: especially contaminated by jazz, psychedelia and new wave, they insert a wide range of styles like tex-mex, world music (sitar and flutes) and theatrical expressions that contain very strong ideas, although resulting overall confusing. Their only album *In the tradition* of 1987, is all but traditional and Partipilo's sax solos make him sound like the Italian incarnation of **David Jackson**(**VDGG**). Occasionally supported by friends and guest musicians, they recently published their new album *Fear and Pleasure* in 2014, a recovery of old unpublished tracks and newly remastered songs.
DISCOGRAPHY: IN THE TRADITION (Toast, Oliphant, 1987) **FEAR AND PLEASURE** (Spittle, 2014). **M.G.**

Europe: ITALY

EDGAR ALLAN POE

Beppe Ronco - *guitars,* **Giorgio Foti** - *keyboards, vocals,* **Marco Maggi** - *bass,* **Lello Foti** - *drums.*
Nothing to do with the novelist, this band forms in 1972 from the ashes of **Angelo & the Spacemen**, playing covers and originals for years around Milan. In 1974 they manage to release their debut album *Generazioni* in a limited edition recorded in only three days (later published by Vinyl Magic in 1991 and world wide in 2004): the melodic approach and dynamic sound of guitars and keyboards well support the lyrics on political themes of the time. Their manager convinces them to give away the copyright in exchange of promotion and concerts (that will never happen). In 1975 they re-arrange the Spielberg film soundtrack *Jaws*, distributed for free at the movie premiere. Sony then contacts them but the timing is wrong since their keyboardist had army services; when he comes back disco music had hit the planet and they were no more.
DISCOGRAPHY: GENERAZIONI (STORIA DI SEMPRE) *(Kansas, 1974).* M.G & C.C.

EGOBAND

Alessandro Accordino - *vocals, keyboards,* **Alfonso Capasso** - *bass,* **Fabio Cioni** - *drums,* **Massimo Fava** - *guitar,* **Andrea Brogi** - *drums,* **Simone Coloretti** - *guitar,* **Jacopo Giusti** - *drums.* **Davide Matteucci** - *sax, oboe.*
Given the little information and the fact they never seem to perform live, this probably is more of a project than a real band, with **Accordino** and **Capasso** as the only steady members. Five albums that develop from purely new prog with heavy AOR tendencies, to the Canterbury School style. Their debut of 1991 is titled *Trip in the Light of the World*, more of a heavy prog approach, while the second of 1993 *Fingerprint* has more of a blues' influence. Their sound evolution starts with *We Are...* released in 1995, where the hard-blues inserts and influences from **VDGG** tend to psychedelia. After five years they publish in 2000 the album *Earth*, with strong references to the Canterbury School. More recently a surprise last album of 2016 *Tales From The Time*, which seems to close the circle back to a neo symphonic prog which recalls **Marillion**.
RECOMMENDED RECORDINGS: WE ARE... *(1996, Mellow Records)* **EARTH** *(1999, Mellow Records).* M.G.

ENEIDE

Gianluigi Cavaliere - *lead vocals, guitar,* **Adriano Pegoraro** - *guitar, flute, vocals,* **Carlo Barnini** - *keyboards, vocals,* **Romeo Pegoraro** - *bass, vocals,* **Moreno Diego Polato** - *drums, percussion, vocals.*
This quintet from Padova starts off as **Eneide Pop** back in 1970. Still teenagers they sign up with Trident after performing as supporting act for **VDGG**. Their only album was recorded and scheduled for release in 1972 but never saw the light so *Uomini Umili Popoli Liberi* is self-published (by their own label LPG) only in 1990 and finally by Mellow Records in 1993. It's a good album with well structured and short songs, alternating hard rock and Mediterranean melodies which recall **PFM**, **Jumbo**, **Osanna** and **Nuova Idea** with hints of **The Trip**. The whole recording is characterized by a good mix between guitar, keyboards (mostly Hammond and moog), flute and some highly dramatic vocals.
DISCOGRAPHY: UOMINI UMILI POPOLI LIBERI *(1990, LPG).* M.G & C.C.

EQUIPE 84

The prog phase of **Equipe 84**, a famous Italian beat band from Modena which started off in the mid '60s, comes around at the end of the decade after several line-up changes. Their leader and guitarist **Maurizio Vandelli** is influenced, as many other Italian musicians, by the new born genre and in their fourth work of 1970, Id, they insert ethnic instruments and other unusual devices for a pop album, with many special guests such as bass player **Mike Shepstone** (**Rokes**), keyboardist **Mario Totaro** (**Dik Dik**), singer **Donatello** and drummer **Franz Di Cioccio** (**PFM**). With *Dr. Jeckyll & Mr.Hide*, **Vandelli** writes a concept album, which unfortunately does not sell. The real prog chapter is the 1974 *Sacrificio*, a complex record blending prog-rock to the melodic Italian songs. They split around 1977 and will reunite for an album in the late '80s.
RECOMMENDED RECORDINGS: ID *(Ricordi, 1970)* **CASA MIA** *(Ricordi, 1971)* **DR.JECKYLL & MR.HIDE** *(Ariston, 1972)* **SACRIFICIO** *(Ariston, 1973)* C.A.

Europe: ITALY

ERIS PLUVIA

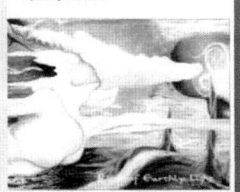

Alessandro Serri - *guitars, vocals*, **Edmondo Romano** - *winds*, **Paolo Raciti** - *keyboards*, **Marco Forella** - *bass*, **Martino Murtas** - *drums*.
Rings Of Earthly Light is the birth of the new 90's Italian art-rock, one of the few compared to the masterpieces of the '70s with its sumptuous and refined symphonic rock of Canterbury style and folk inserts. This debut of 1991 features a very melodic prog with an orchestral style and good folk and pastorals moments, where the acoustic instruments (flute, soprano sax, acoustic guitar and violin) result in a very Baroque sound recalling **Camel** and **Rousseau**. The vocals are in English. They disband immediately after as the musicians are involved in new projects (**Ancient Veil, Avarta, Narrow Pass**) and collaborations (**Finisterre, Höstsonaten**) until the reunion after almost twenty years, with a 2010 album titled *Third Eye Light* and a last more recent work of 2016 *Different Earths*.
DISCOGRAPHY: RINGS OF EARTHLY LIGHT *(Musea Records, 1991)* **THIRD EYE LIGHT** *(AMS, 2010).*
M.G & C.C.

ERRATA CORRIGE

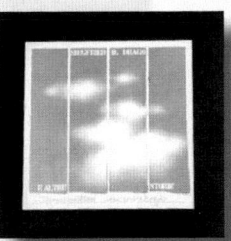

Mike Abate - *guitar, vocals*, **Marco Cimino** - *flute, keyboards, piano, cello*, **Gianni Cremona** - *bass, vocals*, **Guido Giovine** - *drums, vocals*.
A one shot Italian prog band from Turin that released a good LP in 1976 of complex dreamy prog, mainly acoustic, with flute, cello, piano and guitars well supported by the keyboards and recalling somewhat **Celeste**. *Siegfried, il Drago e altre Storie* is an excellent debut album close to the style of **PFM, Locanda Delle Fate** or **Il Volo**, where the ample symphonic compositions blend to the poetic Italian lyrics through the superb, gentle vocal harmonies of the band. Punk and new wave set the new course so they soon disband until a partial reunion in 1992 with a compilation of previously unreleased tracks (recorded before and after their first album) entitled *Mappamondo*.
DISCOGRAPHY: SIEGFRIED, IL DRAGO E ALTRE STORIE *(1976, EC)* **MAPPAMONDO** *(1992, Mellow Records).*
M.G & C.C.

ESAGONO

Claudio Montafia - *flute*, **Gianni Cinti** - *oboe*, **Marco Gallesi** - *bass*, **Marco Cimino** – *keyboards, cello*, **Giorgio Diaferia** - *drums*.
After the first break-up of the jazz-prog band **Arti & Mestieri**, the former musicians will pursue two different projects, that for certain aspects may be considered as spin offs from the mother group: **Esagono** born in 1976 as an excellent jazz-rock band characterized by the attempt of inserting classical sounds into a fusion groove, and **Venegoni & Co.** founded in 1977 by guitarist **Gigi Venegoni** ND which will receive better appreciation. As **Esagono** they nevertheless produce three very interesting albums, the 1977 debut *Vicolo*, re-issued by **Beppe Crovella**'s label Electromantic Music in 2002 (that sparks the reunion), the 2006 second album *Due* and the latest *Apocalypso* of 2008.
DISCOGRAPHY: VICOLO *(MU Records, 1976)* **DUE** *(Electromantic, 2006)* **APOCALYPSO** *(Electromantic, 2008).*
M.G.

FANCYFLUID

Fabrizio Goria - *vocals*, **Max Gotta, Pietro Ratto** - *guitars*, **Sandro Bruni** - *keyboards*, **Paolo Annone** - *bass*, **Roberto Pasquino** - *drums, percussion*.
Band of Italian new prog born in 1988 and signed up with label Musea for all three albums before fading away: their debut of 1990 *Weak Waving* is an attempt to emulate some English schemes (early **Marillion**) through a good use of violin, flute and sax, but penalized by the heavily accented English singing of **Fabrizio Goria**. The second work of 1992, *King's Journey*, is a concept with more elegant and complex textures also due to the use of unconventional instruments and the participation of guests such as the late **Rodolfo Maltese** (**Banco del Mutuo Soccorso**). In 1995, their last episode *The Sheltering Sea*, an average record with excellent arrangements which create a sophisticated music through delicate atmospheres.
DISCOGRAPHY: WEAK WAVING *(1990, Musea)* **KING'S JOURNEY** *(1992, Musea),* **THE SHELTERING SEA** *(1995, Musea).*
M.G.

Europe: ITALY

FESTA MOBILE
(Including BARICENTRO)

Giovanni Boccuzzi, Francesco Boccuzzi - *keyboards*, **Tonio Napolitano** - *bass*.

Festa Mobile is a symphonic prog fantasy-concept band and album, with some jazz influences, where the fast paced space prog-rock blends perfectly into the Italian style of **PFM**, **Le Orme** and **BMS**. Their 1973 debut *Diario Di Viaggio Della Festa Mobile* (Diary of a Moveable Feast) is a naive work with ample keyboards, good vocals and a guitar greatly influenced by **Robert Fripp**. After this project, brothers **Giovanni** and **Francesco Boccuzzi** (from Bari) move on and found in 1976 their own band **Baricentro**, another jazz-rock group playing an instrumental fusion in funky **Weather Report** style but maintaining the Mediterranean sounds in both their works of 1976 and 1978. Their jazz-rock results in a very compelling prog with very percussion-oriented rhythms creating unusual African & Latino atmospheres.
DISCOGRAPHY: Festa Mobile:DIARIO DI VIAGGIO DELLA FESTA MOBILE *(RCA, 1973)* Baricentro:SCONCERTO *(EMI, 1976)* TRUSCIANT *(EMI, 1978)*. M.G & C.C.

FIABA

Bruno Rubino – *drums*, **Giuseppe Brancato** – *vocals*, **Massimo Catena** – *guitar*, **Carlo Bonfiglio** – *guitar*, **Giuseppe Capodieci** – *bass*.

Founded by drummer **Bruno Rubino** in 1991, this Sicilian quintet mixes a rather harsh and uncomplicated prog metal with medieval folk in the style of **Magellan**, **Rush**, **King Crimson** and **Angelo Branduardi** (musician, songwriter and medieval song restorer). Of their five albums, the third *Lo Sgabello Del Rospo* is the most particular: a rock-opera divided in eight parts and sung in Italian with good moments, including riffs recalling **Iron Maiden**. The music alone wouldn't probably pull it off, if not for **Giuseppe Brancato**'s dramatic and theatrical chameleon-like vocalizations influenced by **Demetrio Stratos** (**Area**) and **Alberto Piras** (**Deus Ex Machina**): an interesting 'one-man' prog metal opera for this incredible singer, and of course also thanks to **Rubino**'s complex and overwhelming drum playing.
RECOMMENDED RECORDINGS: XII L'APPICCATO *(1994, Mellow Records)* IL CAPPELLO HA TRE PUNTE *(1996, Pick-Up)*, LO SGABELLO DEL ROSPO *(2001, Lizard)*. M.G.

FLOATING STATE

Gigi Ferri - *guitars*, **Mimmo Ferri** - *keyboards*, **Beatrice Birardi** - *drums*, **Francesco Antonino** - *bass*, **Grazia Stella** - *horns*, **Michele Moschini, Marco Esposito** - *vocals, flute*.

This art-rock band from Puglia is founded in 1995 by **Gigi** and **Mimmo Ferri** who pursue the '70s British prog sonority of **Genesis** and the folk-rock atmospheres of **Jethro Tull** and **Strawbs**, mixed with the sparkling rock of **Osanna** and the jazz energy of **Caravan** majestically sung by **Michele Moschini**. It takes several years to consolidate a line up (after 1999 drummer **Beatrice Birardi** and sax **Grazia Stella** join for their first demo-cassette) before managing to publish the debut album *Thirteen Tolls At Noon* (2003), an enchanting world where fairy tales, mysticism, anarchy and folkish medieval atmospheres run freely in the best romantic tradition. Some hard-rock and dynamic parts are featured in the 45 minute suite "Pilgrimage To Nowhere". No further albums but only a few participation in collective projects.
RECOMMENDED RECORDINGS: THIRTEEN TOOLS AT NOON *(Lizard 2003)* M.G & C.C.

FOGLIE DI VETRO

Daniele Bronzetti - *vocals, drums, flute, percussion*, **Matteo Benvenuti** - *guitars*, **Marco Marchetti** - *bass, vocals, tablas*, **Carlo Pari** - *piano, keyboards*, Guest musician: **Valerio Barbieri** - *saxophones*.

'The glass leaves' is yet another one shot band in the Italian prog panorama of the mid 90's publishing only one beautiful self-titled album in 1996 with a blend of the best '70s symphonic prog tradition of **BMS, PFM, New Trolls, Le Orme, Celeste, Quella Vecchia Locanda, Locanda delle Fate**. Initially they recorded a four-track demo, later included in the debut which expanded to eight tracks of melodic symphonic rock with an intense lyrical approach and romantic instrumental parts. The dominating piano of **Carlo Pari** fill the arrangements with smooth slightly classical parts while **Daniele Bronzetti** sets the mood with his warm and expressive voice singing in Italian.
DISCOGRAPHY: FOGLIE DI VETRO *(1996, Mellow Records)*. M.G & C.C.

Europe: ITALY

GARDEN WALL

Alessandro Seravalle - *guitar, vocals, programming,* **Mauro Olivo** - *keyboards,* **Camillo Colleluori** - *drums,* **Raffaello Indri** - *guitars,* **Pino "McKenna" Mechi** - *bass, stick.*

Alessandro Seravalle starts this project in 1992 as a demo-tape simply titled *Garden Wall*, managing thus to sign up for the recording of a symphonic heavy prog debut called *Principium* the following year. *Path Of Dreams* is their second album of 1994, dedicated to the discovery of extreme experiences through the pathos of **Peter Hammill** inspired vocals and walls of sound made of psychedelia and a visionary technicalities. Their prog-metal is a mystery zone full of hallucinatory experimentation, probably the only Italian band capable of mixing '70s art-rock with metal or goth and classical avant-garde music with electronic sounds. During the years the band's sound hardens to an extremely violent and heavy rock with rare moments of ethno-jazz.

DISCOGRAPHY: PRINCIPIUM *(WMMS, 1993)* **PATH OF DREAMS** *(WMMS, 1994)* **CHIMICA** *(WMMS, 1995)* **THE SEDUCTION OF MADNESS** *(WMMS, 1997)* **FORGET THE COLOURS** *(Mellow, 2002)* **TOWARDS THE SILENCE** *(Mellow 2004)* **ALIENA(C)TION** *(Mellow, 2008)* **ASSURDO** *(Lizard, 2011).* **M.G & C.C.**

GATTO MARTE

Nino Cotone - *violin, viola,* **Giuseppe Brancaccio** - *bassoon,* **Maximilian Brooks** - *piano, keyboards, vocals,* **Pietro Lusvardi** - *contrabass.*

The Italian answer to the Hungarian **After Crying** although they prove their own strong personality oriented to a sort of chamber music which combines traditional progressive and RIO jazz to Italian folk, classical and world music. Their ten albums released from 1997 to 2014 are all on the same line with an ample use of strings and influences from **King Crimson**'s *Lizard* or *Islands*. Although tending towards an avant-garde closer to RIO, it is not dark but instead cheerful with a funny and sparkling verve.

DISCOGRAPHY: DANAE *(1997, private-pressing)* **GIOCO DEL MAGO** *(2000, Lizard)* **PIEROINO** *(2001, Music Center)* **LEOLOMBRICO** *(2003, Music Center)* **MARACHELLE** *(2005, Marac)* **FAUST** *(2006, Music Center)* **SOGNI DI BIMBA** *(2007, Music Center)* **MARTE SULLA LUNA** *(2012, BTF).* **M.G.**

GENFUOCO

Marco Borgogni - *vocals, flute, guitar,* **Tarcisio Bratto** - *guitar, sax,* **Franco Cecchi** - *keyboards, piano,* **Giovanni De Luca** - *bass,* **Paolo De Luca** - *guitar,* **Marco Naldini** - *drums, percussion.*

Excellent Italian band from the late '70s which publishes its only album in 1979 called *Dentro l'Invisibile*: a record of soft tunes between **Celeste** and **Locanda delle Fate** with symphonic prog, fusion, prog pop and relaxed jazz influences or acoustic parts. A music capable of classical influences, rock and Mediterranean melodies with electro-acoustic combinations and very compelling solutions. Although nothing truly original, the synths and sax combine perfectly with a good use of flutes (soprano and alto) at times, as well as some folk instruments. A reunion in 2000 for some concerts and with the release of an interesting live album with added archive unpublished recordings of performances in the '70s.

DISCOGRAPHY: DIETRO L'INVISIBILE *(1979, Città Nuova)* **LIVE** *(2001, Proposta Genfuoco).* **M.G.**

GERMINALE

Marco Masoni - *bass, vocals,* **Alessandro Toniolo** - *flute, sax, vocals,* **David Vecchioni** - *drums, percussion,* **Gabriele Guidi** - *keyboards,* **Saverio Barsali** - *guitar,* **Salvo Lazzara** - *guitar, vocals,* **Andrea Moretti** - *keyboards,* **Matteo Amoroso** - *drums, percussion.*

A band born in Pisa in 1991 that after a very pleasant 1994 debut album releases a truly extraordinary work entitled *...e il Suo Respiro Ancora Agita le Onde...* containing several compositions which recall the Italian Prog of the seventies full of improvisation and shifting moods recalling somewhat **Gentle Giant**. Their refined arrangements and songwriting prove a great personality: in their 2001 album *Cielo e Terra* they explore a cultural path which better defines what they call Evolutional Rock. *Scogli di Sabbia* is a splendid compilation of unreleased tracks published in 2005.

RECOMMENDED RECORDINGS: GERMINALE *(1994, Mellow Records)* **... E IL SUO RESPIRO ANCORA AGITA LE ONDE...** *(1996, Mellow Records)* **CIELO E TERRA** *(2001, Mellow Records).* **M.G.**

Europe: ITALY

I GIGANTI

Giacomo Di Martino - *vocals, guitars,* **Francesco "Checco" Marsella** - *keyboards, vocals,* **Sergio Di Martino** - *bass, vocals,* **Enrico Maria Papes** - *vocals, drums.*

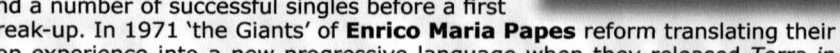

Famous quartet from Milan which begins as a beat band in 1964 with a couple of hit album and a number of successful singles before a first break-up. In 1971 'the Giants' of **Enrico Maria Papes** reform translating their pop experience into a new progressive language when they released *Terra in Bocca* in 1971, a brave and very interesting concept-album based on the chronicles of crime and mafia in Italy: this half electric and half acoustic rock opera is led by Italian sung or spoken lyrics that range from softly melodic to highly dramatic. Produced and arranged by **Vince Tempera** (**Il Volo**), the compositions features guest musicians like guitarist **Marcello Della Casa** (**Latte e Miele**) and bass player **Ares Tavolazzi** (**Area**). The group disbands soon after.
RECOMMENDED RECORDINGS: **TERRA IN BOCCA** *(Ri-Fi, 1971)*   **C.A & C.C.**

GOAD

Maurilio Rossi - *vocals, bass, keyboards, guitars,* **Gianni Rossi** - *guitar,* **Roberto Masini** - *violin, guitar,* **Francesco Diddi** - *flute, violin, saxophones, moog, guitars, bass,* **Paolo Carniani** - *drums.*
A band founded near Florence at the end of the '70s by brothers **Gianni** and **Maurilio Rossi**, with a couple of albums during the mid '80s of electronic disco music covers. In 1994 they start a tribute project dedicated to **Edgar Allan Poe**, released the following year: a more atmospheric and evocative brand of dark prog rock similar to **Jacula** or **Black Sabbath**. Their next album *Glimpse* of 1998 undergoes numerous cuts and a mix not approved by the **Rossi** so they decide to quit the label. Since then they record many albums with a darker and more sophisticated prog sound of symphonic and hard rock which combines the solemnity of the early **King Crimson** with **Led Zeppelin**'s harsh energy.
RECOMMENDED RECORDINGS: **TRIBUTE TO EDGAR ALLAN POE** *(1995, Violet-Multipromo)* **THE WOOD** *(2006, Mellow Records)* **MASQUERADE** *(2011, Black Widow).*   **M.G.**

GREENWALL

Andrea Pavoni - *keyboards.*
Keyboardist **Andrea Pavoni** creates his pet project in the early '90s with the help of other musicians and vocalists of course, but mainly a one man band of new-age like music. *Il Petalo del Fiore e Altre Storie* is an average symphonic prog published in 1999 with interesting keyboard improvisations, alternately recalling **Camel**, **Rick Wakeman** and **Mike Oldfield** and with frequent classical references like to **Mozart**'s *Figaro*. The following *Elektropuzzles* is between prog and new-age while *From The Treasure Box* of 2005 is a more mature instrumental work, elegant and direct. His best works are probably the ones contained in the collective projects of *Kalevala* and *The Colossus of Rhodes* (see page 278).
DISCOGRAPHY: **IL PETALO DEL FIORE E ALTRE STORIE** *(1999, Mellow Records)* **ELEKTROPUZZLES** *(2001, Mellow Records)* **FROM THE TREASURE BOX** *(2005, Rock Revelation)* **Partecipazioni:** **KALEVALA** *(2003, Musea)* **THE LETTERS** *(2004, Mellow Records)* **THE COLOSSUS OF RHODES** *(2005, Musea, Cypher Arts).*   **M.G & C.C.**

HORUS

Beppe Bellussi - *drums,* **Roberto "Pacio" Freggiaro** - *bass, acoustic guitar,* **Battista Leone** - *vocals,* **Antonino Valenti** - *keyboards, vocals,* **Italo Vercellina, Willy Fugazza** - *guitars.*
This band from Turin starts with a nice single, released back in 1978 which went relatively unnoticed probably due to the punk and disco tidal wave. They never had a chance to release a full album before disappearing from the scenes but in 1993 Mellow Records digs up the old tapes of 1978 and combines them with the single on a short 30 minutes CD entitled *Stelle di Battaglia*. Their sound recalls some Italian symphonic elements from **Locanda delle Fate**, **PFM**, **BMS**, Processione and **Le Orme** with spacey-fusion jamming and the occasional folk-rock moments. Before disbanding they become the official backing band for **Tito Schipa jr.** in his Italian tour of 1980 with the late **Willy Fugazza** on guitar.
DISCOGRAPHY: **STELLE DI BATTAGLIA** *(1993, Mellow Records).*   **M.G & C.C.**

Europe: ITALY

HÖSTSONATEN

Fabio Zuffanti - *bass, keyboards, guitars, vocals.* **Stefano Marelli** - *guitars.* **Boris Valle, Osvaldo Giordano, Agostino Macor, Alessandro Corvaglia** - *keyboards.* **Edmondo Romano, Francesca Biagini** - *horns.* **Federico Foglia, Maurizio Di Tollo** - *drums.*

After starting his very prolific career in the band **Finisterre**, bassist and composer **Fabio Zuffanti** moves solo and publishes the complex *Merlin-The Rock Opera* (with the collaboration of **Victoria Heward** for the lyrics) before creating a new parallel project as an 'open' group under the name **Höstsonaten**, taken from a very famous movie by Ingmar Bergman: a prog-rock, jazz, folk and ethnic sound inspired by **Anthony Phillips**, **Barclay James Harvest** and **Jethro Tull** for a delicate and bucolic symphonic prog from majestic to pastoral pastel tints, with Celtic inserts, good flute passages and a certain new age echoing some works from **Camel**. The 'Seasoncycle Suite project' is an ambitious concept in four parts released from 2002 to 2011, each CD dedicated to one of the four seasons.
DISCOGRAPHY: **HÖSTSONATEN** *(Mellow Records 1997)* **MIRRORGAMES** *(Mellow 1998)* **SPRINGSONG** *(Sublime 2002)* **WINTERTHROUGH** *(AMS 2008).*
M.G & C.C.

HUNKA MUNKA

Roberto Carlotto is the mind behind this project which in the future will become his nickname. Still young he works with international stars like **Rod Stewart** and **Colosseum** in England, Germany and Switzerland, while in Italy he had previously played with **Big 66, I Cuccioli** and **Ivan Graziani** in **Anonima Sound** (in 1970, before his solo career). Wonderful keyboardist, he manipulates with great mastery synth sounds and early examples of tape-loops with first generation drum machines. Unforgettable his solo album *Dedicato a Giovanna G* recorded in 1971: an experimental soft-prog featuring **Nunzio 'Cucciolo' Favia** (former **Osage Tribe** drummer) and **Ivan Graziani** on guitar. In 1973 he joins **Dik Dik** and features as session man in some collaborations. As **Karl Otto** he releases the electronic EP *Promise Of Love* in 1984 and recently is taking part in the reunion of **Analogy**.
DISCOGRAPHY: **DEDICATO A GIOVANNA G** *(1972, Ricordi)*
M.G.

INDACO

Rodolfo Maltese – *guitars, bouzuki, mandolin, sitar,* **Pio Mancini** – *violin,* **Luca Barberini** – *bass,* **Carlo Mezzanotte** – *keyboards,* **Pierluigi Calderoni** – *drums, percussion,* **Massimo Alviti** – *vocals, guitars,* **Gabriella Aiello** – *vocals.* **Daniele Sepe, Paolo Fresu, Lester Bowie** – *horns.*

Italy is not a land of super-groups, but his project is an exception: created in 1991 by guitarist **Rodolfo Maltese** (**Banco del Mutuo Soccorso**) and violinist **Mario Pio Mancini**, it features a parade of guest musicians such as **Francesco Di Giacomo** and **Vittorio Nocenzi** both from **BMS**, **Mauro Pagani** (**PFM**) and the late **Andrea Parodi** (**Tazenda**), and international jazz stars like **Fresu, Sepe** and **Lester Bowie**. The sound is a warm jazz-prog with ethnic instruments in a very original Mediterranean World Music. A first 1997 album of Middle-Eastern and Indian flavours (sitar) is followed by probably their best work, *Amorgòs* (mandoline, bouzuki, violins and trumpet) and the 2002 *Terra Maris*, from Irish folk ballads to jazzy accents with the torrid Spanish vocals of **Gabriella Aiello**.
RECOMMENDED RECORDINGS: **AMORGÒS** *(1999 – il Manifesto).*
M.G.

INGRANAGGI DELLA VALLE

Davide Noè Savarese - *vocals,* **Flavio Gonnellini** - *guitars, vocals,* **Mattia Liberati** - *keyboards, vocals,* **Shanti Colucci** - *drums, percussion,* **Antonio Coronato** - *bass,* **Marco Gennarini** - *violin, vocals,* **Alessandro Di Sciullo** - *guitars, keyboards, bass synth, vocals.*

Young prog-rock group formed in Rome in 2010 by **Mattia Liberati** and **Flavio Gonnellini**. After consolidating the new line-up and finding their front-man (singer **Igor Leone**) in 2012, they sign up for their first concept album *In Hoc Signo*, set in the First Crusade, a true manifesto of their music and philosophy: a '70s symphonic-prog open to fusion, ethnic and jazz-rock influences with special guests such as drummer **Mattias Olsson** (**Änglagård**), singer **Angelica Sauprel Scutti** and **David Jackson** (VDGG) on sax. Their second album *Warm Spaced Blue* is published in 2016 featuring **Fabio Pignatelli** (**Goblin**) on bass. At the moment a new album is soon scheduled to be released.
RECOMMENDED RECORDINGS: **WARM SPACED BLUE** *(2016, Black Widow).*
M.G.

Europe: ITALY

JET LAG

Saverio Autellitano - *keyboards*, **Luca Salice** - *vocals and flute*, **Fabio Itri** - *guitars*, **Marco Meduri** - *bass*, **Bruno Crucitti** - *drums*.

A symphonic prog band founded in 1996 from the extreme South of Italy, Reggio Calabria, playing a sparkling jazz-rock linked to the Italian Prog tradition (**DFA** and **Deus Ex Machina**) and to the atmospheres of **King Crimson**, **Pink Floyd** and **Medeski Martin & Wood**. The name is a tribute an album by **PFM** and their impeccable sound is given by the choice of an analogic recording that maintains the typical instrumental groove of the '70s fusion genre, hard to find in the contemporary Italian panorama, even rarer for southern Italy. In 1998 they self-produce the EP Difference and sign up for an only album entitled *Delusione Ottica*, released in 2001 by Lizard Records. In 2004 they take part in a **King Crimson** tribute published by Mellow Records (*The letters, an unconventional guide to King Crimson*), with the song "Pictures of a City".
DISCOGRAPHY: DELUSIONE OTTICA (Lizard, 2001).   M.G & C.C.

LA COSCIENZA DI ZENO

Alessio Calandriello - *vocals*, **Stefano Agnini, Andrea Lotti, Luca Scherani** - *keyboards*, **Davide Serpico** - *guitars*, **Gabriele Guidi Colombi** - *bass*, **Andrea Orlando** - *drums*, **Stefano Agnini** - *lyrics, keyboards*, **Domenico Ingenito** - *violin*.

This is a prog band born in 2007 that derives its name from Italo Svevo's psychoanalytical novel *Zeno's Conscience* on the paradoxes of human behavior. Influenced by **Yes**, **BMS** and other prog giants. In 2008 the keyboardist **Stefano Agnini** (soon replaced by **Lotti**!) inspires them for a song included in Mellow Records' prog compilation and in 2011 they finally manage to release a self-titled debut sold-out in a few months. The following year keyboardist **Luca Scherani** (also playing in **Höstsonaten**, **Il Segno del Comando**, **Trama** and **Periplo**) replaces **Lotti** and they issue a second record *Sensitività*, produced this time by Fading Records. In 2013 violinist **Domenico Ingenito** joins in for a third good work titled *La Notte Anche Di Giorno*.
RECOMMENDED RECORDINGS: SENSITIVITÁ (2013, Fading Records).   M.G.

BERNARDO LANZETTI

Bernardo Lanzetti is one of the most famous Italian prog vocalists still around. He starts in 1971 singing in the band **Acqua Fragile** and later in 1976 as **Premiata Forneria Marconi**'s front-man, before finally releasing his first solo album in 1979. His discography is of an average pop rock with a voice recalling **Roger Chapman** (**Family**) and **Peter Gabriel**, and a good English accent due to some time spent in the US. In 1998 he decides to release a completely new album, probably inspired by the work of the late **Demetrio Stratos**' *Cantare La Voce* of 1978: *I Sing The Voice Impossibile* is a very experimental album of extreme vocal sounds that he will repeat in the 2008 *Eclecticlanz*. Later he joins **Mangala Vallis** and consequently is involved in the project **Cavalli Cocchi-Lanzetti-Roversi** with their album of 2011.
RECOMMENDED RECORDINGS: I SING THE VOICE IMPOSSIBLE (1998, MP Records) **ECLECTICLANZ** (2008, AMS-BTF)   M.G.

LATTE E MIELE

Alfio Vitanza - *drums*, **Oliviero Lacagnina, Mimmo Damiani, Luciano Poltini** - *keyboards*, **Marcello Della Casa, Massimo Gori** - *bass, vocals*.

A keyboard-driven trio from Genova with strong classical influences formed by guitarist **Marcello Della Casa** and drummer **Alfio Vitanza**, then only 16. Greatly inspired by **ELP** or **Le Orme**, their first 1972 album *Passio Secundum Mattheum* has a Bach-inspired music and lyrics based on the Gospel while *Papillon* has **Beethoven** derived compositions. After some concerts they disband and reform in 1976 for a third work more jazz-rock oriented in 1976 titled *Aquile e Scoiattoli*. A mostly pop-rock album recorded in 1979 is also released only in 1992 as *Vampyrs*, not comparable with the band's previous works. **Vitanza** joins **New Trolls** until 2006 and in 2008 the original trio reunites for the brand new album *Marco Polo, Sogni e Viaggi*.
RECOMMENDED RECORDINGS: PASSIO SECUNDUM MATTHEUM (Polydor, 1972) **PAPILLON** (Polydor, 1973) **AQUILE E SCOIATTOLI** (Magma, 1976) **MARCO POLO...** (Aereostella, 2009).   M.G.

Europe: ITALY

LEVIATHAN

Andrea Amici - *piano, keyboards,* **Alex Brunori** - *vocals,* **Giorgio Carana** - *guitars,* **Andrea Moneta** - *drums, percussion,* **Sandro Wlderk** - *bass, basspedals.*

Italian neo-prog trio formed in Rome in 1985 with **Sandro Wlderk** credited for all the compositions and **Alex Brunori** for all the lyrics. In 1987 their definitive lineup is completed and after a two-track demo they decide to self-produce the album *Heartquake* (re-issued officially by Musea the following year), which for many is the first neo-prog Italian release: clearly influenced by **Genesis**, **Marillion** and **Pendragon**, its lyrical and melodic roots are deeply cut into the Italian symphonic style of **PFM** or **BMS**. In 1989 another auto-produced work, *Bee Yourself* (once again released by a label the year after), where the neo-prog tendencies blend with an exquisite jazzy vibe. After a series of concerts they take a long pause until 1998 when they publish *Volume* for Mellow Records, the first to be sung in Italian by **Paolo Antinori** (while the previous ones where in English). In 2003 the participation to the prog compilations *Kalevala* and *Colossus of Rhodes* (see page 278).
RECOMMENDED RECORDINGS: BEE YOURSELF *(Contempo Records, 1989).* **M.G.**

LIVING LIFE

Johnny Betti - *drums, keyboards, vocals,* **Gianni Cinti** - *oboe,* **Flavio Capello** - *flute, sax,* **Aldo Valente** - *keyboards,* **Marcello Quartarone, Daniele Pintaldi** - *guitar,* **Roberto Savarro** - *bass, vocals,* **Sandro Gianotti** - *percussion.*

After leaving the psychedelic band **Circus 2000**, drummer **Roberto 'Johnny' Betti** spends a few years touring Europe with jazz musicians until his trip in Afghanistan for a year. Once home, in 1975 he creates the project **Living Life** in Turin and founds his own record label Shirak, which will release both albums ranging from a jazz-rock influenced by folk music for the first, to a more symphonic prog on the second, involving four keyboard players. On the debut of 1975, *Let: From Experience to Experience*, he is joined by guitarist **Marcello Quartarone** (also former **Circus 2000**). *Mysterious Dream* is released after 6 years containing more complex and dreamy compositions featuring avantgarde and electronic sounds between Canterbury School and the German cosmic couriers.
RECOMMENDED RECORDINGS: MYSTERIOUS DREAM *(1981, Shirak).* **M.G & C.C.**

LUNA

Danilo Rustici – *guitars,* **Joe Amoruso** – *keyboards,* **Dario Franco** – *bass,* **Sebastiano Romano** – *drums.*

Former **Osanna** guitarist **Danilo Rustici** founds his new band in 1977 with other three great musicians, releasing two 45 RPM in the late '70s and another one in 1980 under the name **Tunnel**. After returning to the original name, they record a self-titled debut and only album in 1981 for Splash label: a melodic '80s light pop-rock with some good guitar riffs and elegant piano paces, with little value for prog fans who probably expected something more out of a prog hero like **Rustici**. True also that the project was out-grown by the time, since the arrival of new musical trends put an end to many bands and musicians between 1977 and 1980.
DISCOGRAPHY: LUNA *(1981, Splash).* **M.G.**

LUNA INCOSTANTE

Valerio Bianco - *vocals, sax, keyboards,* **Rinaldo Doro** - *bass,* **Mario Arietti** - *guitar,* **Maurizio Arietti** - *guitar,* **Dante Garimanno** - *drums,* **Patrizia Rucli** - *vocals, keyboards,* **Vittorio Bianco** - *saxophones, flute.*

They start off during the early '80s playing a mix of new wave and punk, then developing a style closer to prog and finally releasing a demo recorded at **Beppe Crovella**'s studio. By the beginning of the '90s their sound had become a full-blown quirky heavy prog act with one foot in traditional '70s Italian prog and the other exploring more innovative paths of discreet symphonic inspirations and extremely lyrical vocal moments. A first self-released tape *Senza titolo* in 1992 leads them to sign up with Mellow Records and publish their next album *Senzasanti* the following year. All compositions are written by guitarist **Roberto Grimaldi** and have strong influences from **Frank Zappa** and **King Crimson**. On the same line their last album *Luna Incostante* of 1998.
RECOMMENDED RECORDINGS: SENZASANTI *(Mellow Records, 1993).* **M.G.**

Europe: ITALY

MAD CRAYON

Daniele Agostinelli – *keyboards*, **Alessandro Di Benedetti** – *keyboards*, **Mario Spinetti** – *drums*, **Luca Cleri** – *guitar*, **Daniele Vitalone** – *bass*, **Stefano Fabiani** – *drums*, **Federico Tetti** – *guitar, saxophones*.

Born in 1986, they sign up with Cygnus records (Vinyl Magic) in 1993 and release the following year *Ultimo Miraggio*, an excellent Italian prog album admittedly influenced by **Genesis** and featuring complex writing with bright vocals around frequent breaks and clever solos. After performing as opening act for **Banco del Mutuo Soccorso**, they issue a second album in 1999 called *Diamanti* and in 2009 their most formidable album, the modern and eclectic *Preda*, for a more **Porcupine Tree** and **Ozric Tentacles** styled sound with hints of prog-fusion. During the years between the last two works they participate in various collective projects such as the tribute album *Zarathustra's Revenge* dedicated to Italian '70s prog artists, and in 2003 in the *Kalevala* and *Colossus of Rhodes* compilations (see page 278).
DISCOGRAPHY: ULTIMO MIRAGGIO *(1993, Cygnus Records-Vinyl Magic)* **DIAMANTI** *(1999, Mellow Records)* **PREDA** *(2009, AMS Records)*.   **M.G.**

MALAAVIA

Pas Scarpato - *vocals, guitars, bass.* **Oderigi Lusi, Fabrizio Garofoli, Sebastiano Mazzoleni** - *keyboards.* **Lucio Fontana, Giacomo Leone** - *drums*, **Mena Casoria, Helena Biagioni** - *vocals*, **Joe La Viola** - *horns*, **Egidio Napoletano** - *percussion*.

Malaavia - Carovana Eterea are a melodic symphonic band greatly inspired by **Le Orme**, **PFM**, **Osanna** and **Saint Just**, blending it with ancient and classical music and Mediterranean folk hints similar to **Renaissance**. The not-dogmatic spirituality of the lyrics recalls the eclectic **Franco Battiato** and **Juri Camisasca**. The excellent debut-album of 2003 is a luxurious fresco with Arabic tints and modern experimental sounds that transcend their music into a fusion of different expressions. **Lino Vairetti** features as special guest in the song "Danze D'Incenso". The second more balanced album of 2008 is a synthetic work with echoes of jazz, Neapolitan melodies and Italian pop songwriting.
RECOMMENDED RECORDINGS: DANZE D'INCENSO *(Maracash, 2003)* **VIBRAZIONI LIQUIDE** *(Multiforce, 2008)*.   **M.G. & C.C.**

MALIBRAN

Giuseppe Scaravilli - *guitars*, **Giancarlo Cutuli** - *flute, sax*, **Angelo Messina** - *bass*, **Benny Torrisi** - *keyboards*, **Jerry Litrico** - *guitar*, **Alessio Scaravilli** - *drums*.

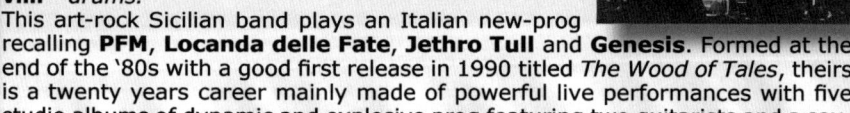

This art-rock Sicilian band plays an Italian new-prog recalling **PFM**, **Locanda delle Fate**, **Jethro Tull** and **Genesis**. Formed at the end of the '80s with a good first release in 1990 titled *The Wood of Tales*, theirs is a twenty years career mainly made of powerful live performances with five studio albums of dynamic and explosive prog featuring two guitarists and a sax-flute player. The strong symphonic arrangements allow them to engage in a complex interplay between all six musicians. Probably their most mature work is the 2001 album *Oltre l'Ignoto*.
DISCOGRAPHY: THE WOOD OF TALES *(Pegaso, 1990)* **LE PORTE DEL SILENZIO** *(Mellow Records, 1993)* **LA CITTÀ SUL LAGO** *(Mellow Records, 1998)* **IN CONCERTO** *(live, Mellow Records, 2000)* **OLTRE L'IGNOTO** *(Mellow Records, 2001)* **TRASPARENZE** *(Electromantic, 2008)*.   **M.G. & C.C.**

MANGALA VALLIS

Gigi Cavalli Cocchi – *drums*, **Bernardo Lanzetti** – *vocals*, **Mirco Consolini** – *guitars, bass*, **Enzo Cattini, Matteo Stocchino, Cristiano Roversi** – *keyboards*, **Riccardo Sgavetti, Roberto Tiranti** – *bass, vocals*, **Nicola Milazzo** – *guitars*.

Drummer **Gigi Cavalli Cocchi** collaborates since 1989 with **Luciano Ligabue**, **Clan Destino** and **Consorzio Suonatori Indipendenti** (**CSI**). In 2001 he founds Mangala Vallis with some excellent musicians and very careful arrangers of new prog with the classic sound of the early '70s mixing **Genesis**, **Gentle Giant**, **Spock's Beard** and **Marillion** influences. The debut album of 2002 *The Book of Dreams*, is dedicated to Jules Verne. **Bernardo Lanzetti** (former **Acqua Fragile** and **PFM**) here features in the closing song and in 2005 as their lead singer for the second work *Lycanthrope*, with **David Jackson** (VDGG) on sax. **Roberto Tiranti** is the new vocalist in their last effort *Microsolco*.
RECOMMENDED RECORDINGS: LYCANTHROPE *(Maracash, 2005)*   **M.G. & C.C.**

Europe: ITALY

MAURY E I PRONOMI (Aquael)

Maurizio Galia - *keyboards, vocals,* **Nicola Guerriero** - *guitar,* **Enrico Testera** - *bass,* **Aldo Leone, Sergio Ponti, Carlo Bellotti, Ivano Granero** - *drums,* **Sergio Cagliero** - *keyboards,* **Marco Giacone Griva** - *lead guitar.*
Born in 1979 as **Aquael**, this pop band from Turin gigs around the region for years until, in 1995 **Maurizio Galia** spins off solo to auto-produce his material as **Maury e i Promemoria**: in 1997 the debut *Ziqqurat nel Canavese* and in 1999 a second work, *Tanganica, il Passato e il Futuro*, this time as **Maury e i Pronomi**, both sung together with the powerful voice of **Silvia Delfino**. This second album contains previous **Aquael** out-takes with only a few new songs and thus will lead to a reunion of the original line-up and a Mellow Records' contract for the album of 2005 *(Ec)Citazioni Neoclassiche*, a more classic Italian Prog close to the sound of **Le Orme**, with the superlative flute of **Dino Pelissero**. In 2008 they finally restore the name **Aquael** and after a couple of participations in prog tributes, they are now publishing an anthology supervised by **Lino Vairetti**.
RECOMMENDED RECORDINGS: **(EC)CITAZIONI NEOCLASSICHE** *(Mellow Records, 2005)* **AQUAEL ANTHOLOGY** *(Toast, 2020).* C.C.

MEMORIA ZERO

Stefano Acunzo - *bass,* **Marco Della Rocca** - *drums,* **Antonio Acunzo** - *guitar, vocals,* **Federica Santoro** - *vocals, keyboards,* **Ettore Scandale** - *vocals, horns,* **Mauro "Parapilla" Montecchiani** - *vocals.*
This is an avant-garde jazz-fusion Zeuhl, RIO band for a highly experimental prog-rock played essentially live since 1995. Winner of the **Demetrio Stratos** Award in 1999, after a couple of demos of highly complex rhythms and eclectic arrangements, they manage to publish *Free Sdraio* in 2001, an album of micro-suites, **Frank Zappa** cabaret and nonsense with experiments of dub and psychedelia echoing **Peter Hammill**, **Gong** or **Duke Ellington**'s *Caravan*: an Italian answer to French TV with a particular attention to fragmentation and extravagant flashes recalling **John Zorn**'s experiments. Vocal parts performed with a strange combination of traditional harmonious and angular structures, dissonant solos of sax and the overall mysterious atmosphere are the most memorable aspects of the album. In 2012 they seem to have self-produced Between.
DISCOGRAPHY: **FREE SDRAIO** *(Lizard 2001).* M.G. & C.C.

MEN OF LAKE

Maurizio Poli - *keyboards,* **Mauro Borgogno** - *guitars,* **Marco Gadotti** - *bass,* **Claudio Oberti** - *drums.*
Formed under previous band names since 1977, their prog incarnation takes the form of **Men of Lake** only in 1987 with a series of demos which land in the realm of label Musea, that produces their first homonym album, published in 1991. Their sound is of clear '70s psychedelic inspiration with the classic English symphonic heavy prog and melancholic atmospheres similar to **Rare Bird, Raw Material, Procol Harum, King Crimson** and the Canterbury School. The second 1993 album *Out of the Water* has a cleaner prog approach with dark vocals and superb keyboards with some **Peter Hammill** atmospheres, while the third and last work of 1998 follows certain **Pink Floyd** structures. Overall a good mix of psychedelia, jazzy-pop and blues.
RECOMMENDED RECORDINGS: **MEN OF LAKE** *(Musea, 1991).* M.G. & C.C.

MO.DO.

Valerio Cherubini - *guitar, flute, vocals,* **Gianantonio Merisio** - *keyboards, vocals,* **Stefano Barzaghi** - *guitars,* **Roberto Colleoni** - *bass,* **Walter Locatelli** - *drums.*
This Italian symphonic prog band formed in 1978 has the misfortune of starting at a time when prog is put aside by punk, but the musicians nevertheless carried out this progressive project against all the odds. Despite releasing only one album in the early '80s, *La Scimmia Sulla Schiena del Re* is a very good symphonic record of electro-acoustic arrangements interlacing various instruments which feature mostly guitars and keyboards with a few sparse vocals sung in Italian. The typically smooth and classic sound similar to **Premiata Forneria Marconi** prevails through the use of flute, acoustic and soft electric guitars, while a more aggressive organ and odd-timed rhythms will recall the sound of **Gentle Giant**.
DISCOGRAPHY: **LA SCIMMIA SULLA SCHIENA DEL RE** *(1980, Iaf).* M.G. & C.C.

Europe: ITALY

MURPLE

Pino Santamaria - *guitar, vocals,* **Piercarlo Zanco** - *vocals, keyboards,* **Mario Garbarino** - *bass,* **Duilio Sorrenti** - *drums.*

Formed in 1971 this four-piece group from Rome is a typically symphonic Italian prog band inspired by classical music. Their only '70s release *Io Sono Murple* is a concept-album about a penguin published in 1974, with average but well performed arrangements spread across one long suite fragmented by atmosphere changes and compelling instrumental spaces, with intense prog moments and a predominant electric guitar. Before they split, the band performs as backing band for the famous pop-beat singer **Mal (Primitives)** during his 1975 tour in Iran. Lead by the drummer **Duilio Sorrenti** (cousin of **Alan** and **Jenny Sorrenti**) they reunite after all these years with two new albums: in 2008 *Quadri Di Un'esposizione* and in 2014 *Il Viaggio*.

DISCOGRAPHY: **IO SONO MURPLE** *(1974, Basf)* **QUADRI DI UN'ESPOSIZIONE** *(2008, BTF-AMS).* **IL VIAGGIO** *(2014, BTF-AMS).* **M.G. & C.C.**

NAPOLI CENTRALE

James Senese - *sax, vocals,* **Franco Del Prete, Agostino Marangolo** - *drums,* **Mark Harris, Ciro Ciscognetti, Pippo Guarnera, Savio Riccardi** - *electric piano,* **Tony Walmsley, Pino Daniele, Kelvin Bullen, Gigi De Rienzo** - *bass.*

After disbanding the second incarnation of the proto jazz-prog band **Showmen 2** in 1972, sax player **James Senese** and his former drummer **Franco Del Prete**, form this vibrant electric jazz-rock band in the typical mid '70s manner, with a dominating sax, electric piano and few vocals. The 1975 debut album, inspired by **Miles Davis** and **Nucleus** mixed to Neapolitan melodies and southern Italy folk tints, was a success and led to a Italian tour in which **Pino Daniele** plays the bass. The next two albums that followed until 1978 are more or less on the same line. Then **Senese** puts the project on hold until he publishes from 1984 to 2016 as **James Senese - Napoli Centrale**.

RECOMMENDED RECORDINGS: **NAPOLI CENTRALE** *(Ricordi, 1975)* **MATTANZA** *(Ricordi, 1976)* **QUACCOSA CA NUN MORE** *(Ricordi, 1977).* **M.G. & C.C.**

NOTABENE

Daniele Manerba - *keyboards,* **Silver Pes, Gianpiero Maccabiani** - *guitars,* **Gianluca Avanzati** - *bass,* **Gustavo Pasini** - *drums,* **Andrea Alberici** - *vocals,* **Rocco Vitiello** - *violin, trumpet.*

After the break-up of the prog metal band **Lithos** in 2003, drummer and bassist reunite under this name inserting to the line-up other musicians among which the blues singer **Andrea Alberici**, for two albums of vintage Italian '70s prog in the spirit of **Museo Rosenbach, BMS, Balletto di Bronzo, Paese Dei Balocchi, Maxophone** and **Giro Strano**: a symphonic rock with jazz sounds (**Rocco Vitiello**'s trumpet and violin), particularly in their second and more mature work of 2007 *Sei lacrime d'Ambra*, where the interesting themes develop complex compositions with jazz tunes and a good songwriting. During the 2007 drummer **Gus Pasini** leaves to found **Corte Aulica**, a more Canterbury styled band (see pag.356).

DISCOGRAPHY: **NOTABENE** *(Mellow Records, 2005)* **SEI LACRIME D'AMBRA** *(Mellow Records, 2007).* **M.G. & C.C.**

NOTTURNO CONCERTANTE

Lucio Lazzaruolo - *guitars, keyboards,* **Raffaele Villanova** - *guitars, vocals,* **Giancarmine Tammaro, Betty Iandolo** - *vocals,* **Enzo Abbondandolo** - *bass,* **Michele Iacoviello, Paolo Picone** - *drums.*

A band named after a musical piece by XIX-century Italian composer Ferdinando Carulli, formed in Avellino around 1985. Their debut album in 1990 titled *The Hiding Place*, is considered one of the best progressive rock albums of the Italian panorama. **Lazzaruolo** and **Villanova** are an art-rock guitar duo 'open band' inspired by **Phillips, Hackett** and **Giltrap**, who make ample use of the acoustic guitar in all their 6 albums, also contributing to several prog tribute albums. *Riscrivere Il Passato* of 2001 is a surprising ethno-rock album, while more recently they published a new work in 2012, *Canzoni allo Specchio*, transcending into chamber music.

RECOMMENDED RECORDINGS: **THE HIDING PLACE** *(Musea 1990)* **EREWHON** *(Mellow Records, 1993)* **RISCRIVERE IL PASSATO** *(Mellow Records, 2002).* **M.G. & C.C.**

Europe: ITALY

NOVA (Including UNO)

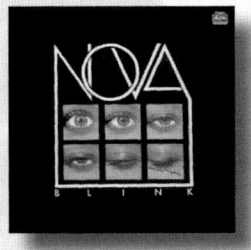

Corrado Rustici, Danilo Rustici - *guitars, vocals,* **Elio D'Anna** - *winds,* **Luciano Milanese, Barry Johnson** - *bass,* **Renato Rosset** - *keyboards,* **Franco 'Dede' LoPrevite, Ric Parnell** - *drums.*
After the 1974 break-up of the Neapolitan band **Osanna**, **Danilo Rustici** and **Elio D'Anna** move to London and found **Uno** publishing that same year one good homonym album of jazz-prog with **Pink Floyd** influences. The following year the duo joins **Rustici**'s brother **Corrado** (former **Cervello** guitarist) in the US and they develop into a fusion jazz-rock inspired by **Brand X** and **Mahavishnu Orchestra**. Under the name **Nova** they release a first album in 1975 featuring **Brand X** percussionist **Morris Pert**. The success is immediate, yet **Danilo Rustici** quits the project (reuniting with **Osanna** in 1978) while they record a second work called *Vimana* the following year with special guests such as **Phil Collins, Percy Jones** and **Narada Michael Walden** for a funky prog album. Another two good works for this open project of super-musicians.
DISCOGRAPHY: Uno: **UNO** (Fonit-Cetra, 1974) Nova: **BLINK** (Ariston, 1976) **VIMANA** (Ariston, 1976) **WINGS OF LOVE** (Ariston, 1977) **SUN CITY** (Ariston, 1978). M.G. & C.C.

NUOVA ERA

Walter Pini - *keyboards,* **Ivan Pini** - *lyrics,* **Enrico Giordani** - *bass,* **Gianluca Lavacchi** - *drums,* **Alex Camaiti** - *guitar, vocals,* **Claudio Guerrini** - *vocals.*
One of the first Italian neo-prog bands, this symphonic quartet's style is greatly influenced by the '70s classic sound of **BMS, PFM, Le Orme** and **Museo Rosenbach** yet performed with a modern technology and deriving material from medieval stories rich of fantasy tales. After the good debut album *L'Ultimo Viaggio* published in 1998, the next two, *Dopo l'Infinito* and *Io e il Tempo* are probably better representative of their great skills as suite composers. *Il Passo del Soldato* of 1995 is still a good record although not at the same level of the previous three. They disband immediately after this release only to reunite in 2016 for a new dreamy prog album called *Return to the Castle*.
DISCOGRAPHY: L'ULTIMO VIAGGIO (1989, Contempo) **DOPO L'INFINITO** (1989, Contempo) **IO E IL TEMPO** (1992, Contempo) **IL PASSO DEL SOLDATO** (1995, Pick Up). M.G. & C.C.

NUOVA IDEA

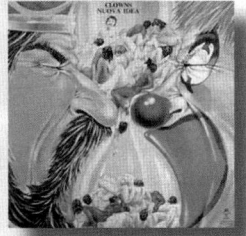

Marco Zoccheddu - *guitar, vocals,* **Claudio Ghiglino** - *guitar, vocals,* **Giorgio Usai** - *keyboards, vocals,* **Enrico Casagni** - *bass, flute, vocals,* **Paolo Siani** - *drums, vocals,* **Antonello Gabelli** - *guitar, vocals,* **Arturo "Ricky" Belloni** - *guitar, vocals.*
Formed in 1970 with a debut album out the following year, *In the Beginning* contains a very interesting heavy classical rock with predominant keyboards, choirs and beautiful melodies which recall **Città Frontale** and **Le Orme** for the percussive rhythms, vibrating guitar solos and vocals, also close to **Vanilla Fudge**. The suite "Come, Come, Come" is the only English song with compelling duels between cut-edge guitars and symphonic keyboards. The following work *Mr. E. Jones*, is a concept album similar to the early **Camel** and to the early **New Trolls**. *Clowns* is probably their best work, more magnificent, less hard and with good keyboard parts echoing **Keith Emerson**. In 2010 their drummer publishes a couple of albums as **Paolo Siani feat. Nuova Idea**.
RECOMMENDED RECORDINGS: IN THE BEGINNING (1971, Ariston) **CLOWNS** (1973, Ariston). M.G.

OBSCURA

Massimo Tabai - *keyboards, songwriter,* **Matteo Cavallari** - *guitars, lyrics,* **Matteo Pinfari** - *bass,* **Marcello Ricci** - *drums,* **Barbara Mazzola** - *flute, vocals,* **Luca Palleschi , Davide Cagnata** - *vocals.*
A very interesting Neo-prog Italian band born in 1996 playing live for nearly a year until they gather in **David Cremoni**'s house (Moongarden guitarist) to record their first tracks for the album *Le Città Invisibili*, inspired by book of Italo Calvino. Before finishing the instrumental parts singer **Luca Palleschi** joins the band **Moongarden** replaced by **Davide Cagnata**. The recordings are put in stand by while the musicians continue their live activity until in 2004 the master of their almost completed CD is recovered by **Cagnata** and given to Mauro Moroni, producer for Mellow Records. The 'lost' album is finally issued in 2007, for a very good vintage music full of mellotron and bass pedals and a balanced mix of male and female singing.
DISCOGRAPHY: LE CITTÁ INVISIBILI (Mellow records, 2007). M.G.

Europe: ITALY

ODESSA

Lorenzo Giovagnoli - *keyboards, vocals,* **Boris Bartoletti, Giulio Vampa** - *guitars,* **Valerio De Angelis** - *bass,* **Federico Filonzi, Marco Fabbri** - *drums.*
Formed in 1998 by keyboardist **Lorenzo Giovagnoli**, the band was completed with three prog musicians on guitar, bass, and drums, playing original compositions as well as cover versions of their idols from the Italian golden age of prog such as **Area, The Trip** and **Rovescio della Medaglia**. This quartet released only two albums, ten years apart from each other: the 1999 *Stazione Getsemani* is one of the most famous records of the progressive '90s, a happy mix of art-rock, hard sounds and experimental solutions, with an interesting bluesy keyboard solo executed on Hammond organ. **Lorenzo**'s strong voice singing in Italian recalls the great **Demetrio Stratos** from **Area**. Their last LP of 2009, *The Final Day*, is less surprising.≤
DISCOGRAPHY: **STAZIONE GETSEMANI** *(Mellow Records, 1999)* **THE FINAL DAY – IL GIORNO DEL GIUDIZIO** *(Lizard, 2009).*   M.G & C.C.

ODISSEA

Roberto Zola - *vocals,* **Luigi 'Jimmy' Ferrari** - *guitars,* **Enrico Cinguino** - *keyboards,* **Alfredo Garone** - *bass,* **Paolo Cerlati** - *drums.*
Born as Pow-Pow in 1970 as support group for the pop singer **Michele**, they change to **Odissea** in 1972 after the entrance of guitarist **Luigi 'Jimmy' Ferrari**, converting to an Italian melodic rock-inspired prog style. The group had a good live activity, even supporting **Genesis**'s 1972 Italian tour. Produced by Alessandro Colombini and with the precious graphic design of Mario Convertino, their only album is a convincing combination of symphonic rock and melody, close to **Le Orme** (but without **Aldo Tagliapietra**'s dreamy voice): **Roberto Zola**'s harsh vocals recalls **Alvaro Fella** (**Jumbo**) without the vocal and lyrical excesses. The following year **Zola** quits and the musicians go back to being **Michele**'s backing band and playing for a while with **La Famiglia degli Ortega** for some US concerts. In 1976 they re-form with a line-up change for some concerts in Switzerland and breaking up once more shortly after.
DISCOGRAPHY: **ODISSEA** *(RiFi 1973).*   M.G & C.C.

OSAGE TRIBE

Marco Zoccheddu - *guitars, vocals,* **Nunzio "Cucciolo" Favia** - *drums.* **Bob Callero** - *bass, vocals.*
Founded in 1971 by young **Franco Battiato** (composer, avant-garde songwriter and famous pop singer) who together with drummer **Nunzio 'Cucciolo' Favia**, guitarist **Marco Zoccheddu** (former **Nuova Idea** and **Gleemen**) and bass player **Bob Callero**, start recording a first single "Un Falco Nel Cielo", before **Battiato** quits for a solo contract with label Bla Bla. The remaining trio veers toward a more aggressive sound and release their masterpiece *Arrow Head* in 1972: a hard rock style with strong prog influences and some jazzy moments. Immediately after both **Zoccheddu** and **Callero** leave to found **Duello Madre** with **Franco 'Dede' Lo Previte**, while 'Cucciolo' will later join the band **Dik Dik**. **Callero** also play with **Il Volo** and for **Lucio Battisti**. In 2007 they reunite for a live concert and in 2013 **Callero** and 'Cucciolo' publish an album under the band's name of old and new songs called *Hypnosis*.
DISCOGRAPHY: **ARROW HEAD** *(Bla Bla, 1972).*   M.G & C.C.

MAURO PAGANI

Multi-instrumentalist, composer and producer, **Mauro Pagani** grew up with a passion for music and for the violin. His begins in fact in 1970 playing this instrument in **Fabrizio De Andrè**'s forth album *La Buona Novella*. During this period he meets the musicians with whom he co-founds the famous Italian band **Premiata Forneria Marconi** in which he stays until 1976. His solo discography begins with a first self-titled album released in 1978 containing Mediterranean, jazz, avant-garde, Balcanic, Arabian and oriental sounds. His six studio albums feature many of the best Italian musicians of that time including members from **Area, PFM** and singer **Teresa De Sio**. In 1984 he collaborates again with **De Andrè** for the arrangements of two amazing albums in Italian dialects (he will make his own version of *Crêuza de Mä* - Church by the Sea - in 2004, with some added instrumental and unreleased tracks).
RECOMMENDED RECORDINGS: **MAURO PAGANI** *(Ascolto, 1978)* **CRÊUZA DE MÄ 2004** *(Officine Meccaniche, 2004).*   M.G & C.C.

Europe: ITALY

PANNA FREDDA

Angelo Giardinelli - *guitar, vocals,* **Giorgio Brandi** - *keyboards, guitar, vocals,* **Carlo Bruno** - *bass,* **Filippo Carnevale** - *drums, guitar,* **Lino Stopponi** - *keyboards,* **Pasquale "Windy" Cavallo** - *bass,* **Roberto Balocco** - *drums.*
The beat band **I Figli Del Sole** were gigging since 1966 in Rome's nightclubs. After listening to the music of **Vanilla Fudge, Hendrix, The Moodies** and **Pink Floyd**, leader and composer **Angelo Giardinelli** decides to create a rock band and forms **Panna Fredda** somewhat behind the backs of the horn section, that considered this a madness. Contacted by label Vedette, the new line-up starts to record in 1970 an album shelved by the production who wanted them to release hit singles. They finally manage to have their way and publish *Uno* the following year: almost as if it were an episode from Canterbury School, their style spreads from the sonorities of **Egg** to **Caravan** with a very effective guitar-keyboard interplay of evident classical influences. **Panna Fredda**'s lone work is one of the earliest pioneers of symphonic prog with a distinct baroque twist and an emphasis on experimentation, but given the times, they did not manage a sequel.
DISCOGRAPHY: UNO (Vedette, 1971 - Vynil Magic, 2000). M.G & C.C.

LA PENTOLA DI PAPIN

Ferruccio Bettini - *vocals, keyboards,* **Angelo Lenatti** - *guitar, vocals,* **Dory Dorigatti** - *bass,* **Bruno Stangoni** - *drums.*
This one shot band from the end of the '70s is an interesting project due to the fact that their only album *Zero-7* was released in 1977 with all the flavours of a genre in vogue seven years before. Not a real masterpiece of its own, nor for the genre, the groove of this band is of posthumous interest due to the wave of re-discovery that hit the '90s and they were re-issued by the label Vinyl Magic in 1993. Overall a fairly good album all sung in Italian with slight classical influences, very strong keyboard partitions and an organ played in the best **Jon Lord** style (**Deep Purple**). The fuzz guitar contributes largely to this vintage early '70s atmospheres that may recall something from **Premiata Forneria Marconi**.
DISCOGRAPHY: ZERO-7 (Disco Più, 1977). M.G & C.C.

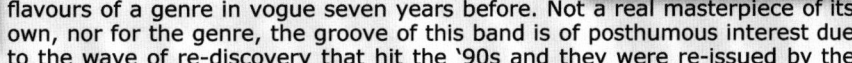

PHOLAS DACTYLUS

Paolo Carelli - *vocals,* **Eleino Colledet** - *guitars,* **Maurizio Pancotti** - *keyboards,* **Valantino Galbusera** - *keyboards, vocals,* **Rinaldo Linati** - *bass,* **Giampiero Nava** - *drums.*
Particular, personal and innovative Italian avant-garde band formed in 1972 around guitarist **Eleino Colledet**. Thanks to the strong interest of **Vittorio De Scalzi** (**New Trolls**), they managed to sign up with the label Magma for their debut of 1973 called *Concerto delle Menti*: for over thirty years this was the only Italian prog album where the vocals were entirely recited as if acting in a theatrical performance. This unique feature combined with an apocalyptic and hallucinatory music between **King Crimson**'s jazz experimentation and more lyrical and calm sounds recalling **Jethro Tull**, led to a genius yet upsetting traditional Italian prog of avant-garde, jazz, krautrock and jams. The group disbands after this album and apparently none of the members continued their careers as professional musicians.
RECOMMENDED RECORDINGS: CONCERTO DELLE MENTI (Magma, 1973). M.G & C.C.

PRESENCE

Sophya Baccini - *vocals,* **Enrico Iglio** - *keyboards,* **Sergio Casamassima** - *guitars, bass.*
Not to be confused with the UK band, this very capable ensemble has an original sound characterized by a dark hard-prog mixing rock to classical and opera music. In particular **Sophya Baccini**'s voice is outstanding. They self-produce the first two albums, of which the experimental concept EP of 1990 called *The Shadowing*. In 1994 label Black Widow final signs them up for the concept album *The Sleeper Awakes*, sung mostly in English with additional lyrics in French, German and Latin and recorded partially with the string section of the Naples' Symphonic Orchestra. The 1996 *Black Opera* is released and is probably their masterpiece with its new versions of four romanzas written by **Giuseppe Verdi** (*Trovatore, Rigoletto, La Forza del Destino* and *La Traviata*). Their last work is the 2016 *Masters and Following*, a double studio and live album.
RECOMMENDED RECORDINGS: BLACK OPERA (1996, Black Widow) M.G.

Europe: ITALY

PROWLERS

Laura Mombrini - *vocals,* **Alfio Costa** - *keyboards,* **Stefano Piazzi** - *guitar,* **Marco Premoli** - *bass,* **Giovanni "Giana" Vezzoli** - *drums,* **Flavio Costa** - *guitar,* **Alan Ghirardelli** - *bass.*

They start in playing in 1985 influenced by the blues and hard rock of the early **Pink Floyd** (Syd Barrett era), yet in 1987 they release a punk pop album as **The Prowlers**, called *Living Outside the Law*. After many live concerts in northern Italy, in 1989, they record eight tracks with an old Fostex recorder for the demo tape *Morgana*: their first prog and psychedelic work re-issued by Mellow Records in 1994. The following year *Mother and Fairy* is an even more prog double concept album, mixed by producer **Ciro Perrino** (drummer of **Il Sistema**, **Celeste**), full of keyboard-guitar duels and **Laura**'s beautiful voice recalling **Annie Haslam** (**Renaissance**). The quality leap in sound and production is the truly new-prog *Sweet Metamorfosi* published in 1997, a colossal rock suite about the story of the band written by **Alfio** and inspired by the Italian Prog masters.

RECOMMENDED RECORDINGS: **MORGANA** *(1994, Mellow Records)* **MOTHER AND FAIRY** *(1996, Mellow Records)* **SWEET METAMORFOSI** *(1998, Mellow Records).* M.G & C.C.

PSYCHONOESIS

Gabriele Tartaglino, Federico Daidone - *guitars,* **Michele Nastasi** - *trumpet,* **Davide Ponzini** - *bass,* **Mattia Nelli** - *drums.*

Coming from Milan, they start as a quintet in 1996 with a good live activity before deciding to produce a self-titled debut in 2002, released by Rock Revelation, and an even more convincing sequel. Experts in creating sonic soundscapes and intricate atmospheres, always in balance between rich and smoother parts, they combine elements of post-rock, jazz-rock, lounge jazz, horn-rock and ambient mixing their music with different medias, including graphic arts. The strong use of trumpets, the shifting moods, the somber backgrounds and the distorted **Robert Fripp**-styled guitars recall the **King Crimson** experiments organized with visionary and undefined moods, trespassing into an enigmatic after-hours jazz. After this experience some continued as valid session men or collaborators in other Italian prog and modern jazz recordings.

DISCOGRAPHY: **PSYCHONOESIS** *(Rock Revelation, 2001)* **SUPERFLUALISMO** *(BTF, 2005).* M.G.

QUASAR LUX SYMPHONIAE

Roberto Sgorlon - *guitars, vocals,* **Paolo Paroni** - *keyboards, piano,* **Fabrizio Morassutto** - *drums, percussion,* **Italo Cigainero** - *bass,* **Paolo Maestrutti** - *bass,* **Fabio Giacomello** - *guitar,* **Annalisa Malvasio** - *vocals,* **Marco Bertolissi** - *vocals.*

This symphonic prog band with huge operatic vocals formed in 1976 by around guitarist **Roberto Sgorlon**. The tapes of their first work recorded the following year were titled *Dead Dream* and went lost until 1984, when they are released as the melodic hard-rock album *Night Hymn*. Soon they turn to a more classical sound, with a real first album published only in 1994. This double concept album is a rock opera entitled *Abraham* and inspired by the Bible tales. Mainly led by piano and keyboards, with good orchestral moments, impressive choruses and dramatic atmospheres, with Gregorian, Rennaisance and Baroque influences. Also their third work of 2000, *Mit*, is another concept album.

DISCOGRAPHY: **ABRAHAM – ONE ACT ROCK OPERA** *(1994, WMMS)* **THE ENLIGHTENING MARCH OF THE ARGONAUTS** *(1997, WMMS)* **MIT** *(2000, Mellow Records).* M.G & C.C.

RACCOMANDATA RICEVUTA RITORNO

Luciano Regoli - *vocals, acoustic guitar,* **Nanni Civitenga** - *guitars,* **Stefano Piermarioli** - *keyboards,* **Francesco Froggio Francica** - *drums, percussion,* **Manlio Zacchia** - *bass,* **Damaso Grassi** - *sax, flute.*

This band from Rome formed in 1972 with a concept album, *Per... un mondo di Cristallo* (for... a world of crystal), about an astronaut returning after a long trip: a hard rock, jazz, classical, melodic, pastoral and even an ample use of flute, sax, keyboards (especially organ), and acoustic/electric guitar recalling **Osanna**, **Semiramis** and **Il Balletto di Bronzo**. **Luciano Regoli**'s voice (similar to **Freddie Mercury**'s) gives good personality to their music, full of compelling instrumental moments. A surprising revival in 2010 gathers **Regoli** and **Civitenga** under the new name **Nuova Raccomandata Ricevuta Ritorno** for an interesting album called *Il Pittore Volante*.

DISCOGRAPHY: **PER UN MONDO DI CRISTALLO** *(1972, Fonit)* **IL PITTORE VOLANTE** *(2010, BTF/AMS).* M.G & C.C.

Europe: ITALY

I RAMINGHI

Franco Mussita - *bass, vocals,* **Angelo Sartori** - *keyboards,* **Angelo "India" Serighelli** - *guitar,* **Romeo Cattaneo** - *drums,* **Valerio Cherubini** - *guitar, vocals,* **Titta Colleoni** - *Hammond organ, vocals,* **Michele "Gufo" Capogrosso** - *drums, vocals.*

This band from Bergamo forms around bassist and singer **Franco Mussita**, a musician playing already in the early '60s and in love with **Deep Purple, Vanilla Fudge, Blue Cheer** and **Uriah Heep** to the point of wanting to record music like this. The name means The Wanderers, appropriate for a sound completely contaminated by the times where you actually hear the change as it happens from an Italian perspective instead of through the Californian pioneers like **The Doors, Jefferson Airplane** and **The Grateful Dead**. After two singles in 1970, they release their only album *Il Lungo Cammino dei Raminghi* (The Wanderers' Long Journey) later in 1971: a form of proto-proto-prog of everything that came immediately before (acid psychedelia, hard blues and hard rock), almost the Italian version of **Quicksilver Messenger Service**.

DISCOGRAPHY: IL LUNGO CAMMINO DEI RAMINGHI *(Bentler, 1971).*

M.G.

REALE ACCADEMIA DI MUSICA

Enrique Topel Cabanes - *vocals,* **Federico Troiani** - *keyboards,* **Nicola Agrimi** - *guitars,* **Pierfranco Pavone** - *bass,* **Roberto Senzasono** - *drums.*

A band born in 1972 on the ashes of **Fholks** (**Jimi Hendrix**'s support band in his 1970 Italian tour), this is one of the most important groups of the Roman scene. Their debut album, produced by **Maurizio Vandelli** (guitarist of **Equipe 84**), is a good blend between the dreamy atmospheres of King Crimson and the melodic style of **BMS** and **Locanda delle Fate**, with a great **Federico Troiani** on keyboards. Their second album of 1974 features singer and songwriter **Adriano Monteduro** and they result as his backing band. Disbanded shortly after, in 2008 **Monteduro** releases his new album using them again but without the original line-up (in fact **Troiani** dies in 2000 after three solo albums of his own).

RECOMMENDED RECORDINGS: REALE ACCADEMIA DI MUSICA *(Ricordi, 1972)* ADRIANO MONTEDURO & REALE ACCADEMIA DI MUSICA *(RCA, 1974)* IL LINGUAGGIO DELLE COSE *(Delta Italiana, 2008).*

M.G & C.C.

CLAUDIO ROCCHI

He begins playing bass with **Stormy Six**, participating on their debut before moving on to his solo career: after the early experimental-folk period (Italian folk mixed to eastern influences, mainly from India, psychedelia, pop and electronic music), he publishes material veering towards pop and later of electronic experimentations. His debut in 1970 is the soft album *Viaggio* containing songs between ballads and acid explorations of pacifism and the hippy culture. *Volo Magico N.1* (1971), the improvised and meditative *Essenza* (1973) and the electronic *Suoni di Frontiera* (1975) are probably his best. In the late '70s he retires to a Hare Krishna community for several years and collaborates with many musicians like the psychedelic pioneer **Lodovico Ellena** (**Effervescent Elephants** guitarist), **PFM** violinist **Mauro Pagani**, **Osanna** saxophonist **Elio D'Anna**, **I Giganti** guitarist **Mino Di Martino** and **Area** guitarist **Paolo Tofani** for their solo projects. He unfortunately passed away in 2013.

RECOMMENDED RECORDINGS: VIAGGIO *(Ariston, 1970)* VOLO MAGICO N. 1 *(Ariston, 1971)* ESSENZA *(Ariston, 1973)* 1980)

M.G & C.C.

RUNAWAY TOTEM

Cahal De Betel - *keyboards, guitars, vocals,* **Tipheret** - *drums, keyboards,* **Virhur** - *keyboards,* **Giuseppe Buttiglione, Nezah** - *bass,* **Mihmir De Bennu** - *guitars,* **Giorgio Revelant, Ana Tores Fraile** - *vocals.*

Formed in 1988, this band from Trento is inspired by **Magma**'s zeuhl sound, they mix space and kraut- rock with esoteric themes, the energy of **King Crimson** with an **Amon Düül II** touch and even hints of **Gentle Giant**, using a rich instrumentation (keyboards, guitars) to create ethereal, romantic climates with grandiose backing vocals evoking **Area**: their first two exciting albums *Trimegisto* and *Zed* are released by Black Widow, while probably their best work is the third, *Andromeda*, published in 1999 by Musea and part of the 'Cicli Cosmici' trilogy. The last phase is called '4 Elementi 5' and starts with the 2007 *Exameron*, an original mix of concrete music and RIO.

RECOMMENDED RECORDINGS: TRIMEGISTO *(Black Widow, 1993)* ZED *(Black Widow, 1996)* ANDROMEDA *(Musea, 1999),* EXAMERON *(Runaway Totem, 2007).*

M.G & C.C.

Europe: ITALY

SAMADHI

Luciano Regoli - *vocals*, **Nanni Civitenga** - *guitars*, **Aldo Bellanova** - *bass, acoustic guitars*, **Stefano Sabatini** - *keyboards*, **Sandro Conti** - *drums*, **Ruggero Stefani** - *percussion*, **Stevo Saradzic** - *flute, sax*.

Italian group formed with some former members of the excellent **Raccomandata Ricevuta Ritorno** (singer **Luciano Regoli** and guitarist **Nanni Civitenga**) and from **Uovo di Colombo, Kaleidon, Teoremi** and **Free Love**, for an only album of symphonic pop with some progressive tendencies. A variety of styles arranged with organ, flute and some strings for their self-titled album of 1974 which appears to be more like a project of research and experimentation blended to pure melody of romanticism and Mediterranean jazz-rock. Seven well performed tracks with instrumental passages and great lyrics written by the actor and dramatist Enrico Lazzareschi (and sung by the powerful voice of **Regoli**).
DISCOGRAPHY: **SAMADHI** *(1974, Fonit).*

M.G & C.C.

TITO SCHIPA (Junior)

Son of the great tenor **Tito Schipa**, he starts in 1967 with a show based on a selection of 18 **Bob Dylan** songs, rearranged and put together to form a sort of rock-opera called *L'Opera Beat* (**Dylan** stops the project through his lawyer). In 1969 he begins to work on the first Italian rock-opera ever, based on Orpheus and a modern version of the Greek myth: performed on January 27th, 1970 for the first time at the famous Teatro Sistina in Rome, *Orfeo 9* was such a success that it led to an LP and a movie (first shown in 1975 for censorship issues) featuring **Loredana Bertè** as the narrator, **Tullio De Piscopo** on drums and **Renato Zero** in the role of the 'Happiness Seller' (Eurydice's pusher). In 1972 he publishes the single "Sono passati i giorni" and an actual double album the following year, *Io Ed Io Solo*, written mainly in a singer-songwriting style. In 1978 he returns to the pop-opera format with **Donizetti**'s *Don Pasquale*, re-titled *Er Dompasquale*. Still active but not on the music scenes.
RECOMMENDED RECORDINGS: **ORFEO 9** *(Fonit-Cetra, 1972)*

M.G.

IL SEGNO DEL COMANDO

Mercy - *vocals*, **Gabriele Grixoni** - *guitars*, **Matteo Ricci, Francesco La Rosa** - *guitars*, **Agostino Tavella, Franz Ekurn** - *keyboards*, **Diego Banchero** - *bass*.

The Sign of Command take their name from a 1970's novel by Giuseppe D'Agata and the Italian TV series of occult, reincarnation and supernatural events. Formed in 1995, they prefer evoking sadness, anxiety and fear through a dark prog of gothic sounds, spooky arrangements, nightmare soundscapes. Their second album of 2002 *Der Golem* is more complex than the homonym debut album of 1997, although the first is more prog oriented: here the atmosphere's of Kafka's Prague are recreated through the tale of this mud giant magically brought to life in defense of the Jewish people. The music is keyboard-driven (piano, Mellotron, organ and analogue synths for the authentic vintage sound) with a folky acoustic guitar (electric solos similar to **Antonius Rex** and **Camel**), heavy but never metal, and some psychedelic passages with modern electronic elements.
RECOMMENDED RECORDINGS: **DER GOLEM** *(2002, Black Widow).*

M.G & C.C.

SINESTESIA

Roberto De Micheli - *guitars*. **Alberto Bravin** - *keyboards*, **Paolo Marchesich** - *drums*, **Alessandro Sala** - *bass*, **Ricky de Vito** - *vocals*.

Formed in Trieste in 1997, they publish a first demo-tape in 2003 titled *Aquarium* and an album finally in 2007 thanks to Immaginifica label owner **Franz Di Cioccio** (**PFM** drummer). Theirs is a crossover prog mixed to heavy metal and a melodic use of the voice, blending typical '70s flavor with modern hard stuff similar to the style of **Dream Theatre, Opeth, Rush** and **Pink Floyd**. Immediately after the release they tour Italy playing with bands such as **BMS** and **La Maschera di Cera**, taking part in main live events like Gods of Metal in Milan. Two years later *The Day After Flower* is published leading to a participation in the Prog Exhibition in Rome.
DISCOGRAPHY: **SINESTESIA** *(2007, Aereostella/btf)* **THE DAY AFTER FLOWER** *(2009, Aereostella/ EDEL)* **PROG EXHIBITION boxset** *(2011 Immaginifica-Aereostella).*

M.G.

Europe: ITALY

LA SORGENTE

Pino Carella - *keyboards, vocals*, **Franco Rossetti** - *drums*, **Bruno Raia** - *guitars*, **Daniele Giuliani** - *Violin, Viola*, **Walter Destri** - *bass*, **Raffaele Giuliani** - *flute*.

The Catholic Church reformed in Italy during the '60s by celebrating a 'beat' mass' to appeal to young people. It spread during the '70s resulting in a series of albums inspired by the Gospel produced by religious labels. Christian prog bands, such as **Messaggio 73**, **Genfuoco** and **Quel Giorno di Uve Rosse**, developed and the 1979 album *Trasparente* of **La Sorgente** is one of the finest and most prog with its delicate acoustic-based fusion of chamber-pop and Mediterranean folk. The music is a classic combination of flute, violin and piano with a synthesizer and organ which occasionally play to a 12-string guitar. After the disbanding **Pino Carella** pursued a career as appreciated composer and songwriter for famous italian pop stars like **Fausto Leali** e **Laura Pausini**. Today he is planning a rebirth of the band under the new name **La Sorgente 2.0**.
DISCOGRAPHY: TRASPARENTE (1979, EUN). M.G. & C.C.

SPIROSFERA

Giorgio Brugnone - *bass, keyboards*, **Johnny Berto** - *drums*, **Nicola Pavan** - *vocals*, **Mirko Baruzzo** - *keyboards*, **Nicola Genovese** - *horns*.

Yet another one shot band this time from the Veneto region of the early '90s, which signed up with Lizard for an only album of 1996 strongly influenced by the '70s Italian Prog mixed with hard rock, jazz rock and psychedelia, often compared to **Deus Ex Machina** and **Area**: *Umanamnesi* is a lunatic and complex LP of heavy music with pyrotechnic vocals and a metal tinged guitar work with electric riffs of apparent heavy rock which develop into jazzy rhythms and symphonic arrangements. The vocals (in Italian) are delivered with energy and conviction through **Nicola Pavan**'s voice which definitely recalls **Demetrio Stratos**.
DISCOGRAPHY: UMANAMNESI (Lizard 1996). M.G. & C.C.

STORMY SIX

Carlo de Martini - *strings, mandolin, acoustic guitar, vocals*, **Franco Fabbri** - *vocals, guitars, percussion*, **Umberto Fiori** - *vocals, acoustic guitar*, **Salvatore Garau** - *drums*, **Tommaso Leddi** - *mandolin, violin, guitars, piano*, **Luca Piscicelli** - *bass, vocals*.

Formed in 1966 playing pop, folk and psychedelia with strong left wing political protest songs. After two average works they release *Guarda Giù Dalla Pianura* in 1974 and start a more serious live activity. Their music becomes more complex and the prog vein starts to show in the following year's work *Un Biglietto Del Tram*, finally maturing in *L'apprendista* of 1977, an album between avant-guard, chamber music and pop songwriting. In contact with **Chris Cutler** and his RIO movement, they start recording *Macchina Maccheronica*, released in 1980 and completely in the ranks of the prog army. Their career pauses in 1983 after the publication of the pop electronic *Al Volo*, reuniting for a concert later in 1993 and for the 2013 collaboration with **Moni Ovadia**, *Benvenuti nel Ghetto*.
RECOMMENDED RECORDINGS: MACCHINA MACCHERONICA (L'Orchestra, 1980). M.G. & C.C.

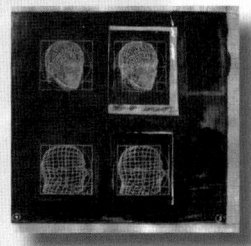

SUNSCAPE

Marco da Rold - *guitar, vocals*, **Matteo Curcio** - *bass, keyboards*, **Tony Fucci** - *drums*, **Carlo Soppelsa** - *flute, keyboards*, **Marinella Mastrosimone** - *vocals*.

Formed in 1993 in Milan with an experimental sound far from the typical neo-prog bands of the time, their style is a heavy sound influenced by psychedelia and space rock greatly inspired by **Pink Floyd**, **Porcupine Tree**, **Hawkwind** and **Ozric Tentacles**, with some krautrock hints as well. Mellow Records releases their homonym debut work in 1999 (and records a second album in 2001, never yet published): a fascinating album of modern and magnetic guitars, flute and keyboards interlacing with clean and bright tunes which create melancholic and dreamy atmospheres.
DISCOGRAPHY: SUNSCAPE (1999, Mellow Records). G.D.S.

Europe: ITALY

SYNDONE

Nik Comoglio – *keyboards,* **Paolo Sburlati, Paolo Rigotto** - *drums, percussion* **Fulvio Serra, Federico Marchesano** – *bass,* **Marta Caldara, Francesco Pinetti** – *vibes, keyboards and Timbales,* **Riccardo Ruggeri** – *vocals, flute.*
Keyboardist **Nico 'Nik' Comoglio** forms 'Shroud' in 1989 with two good albums produced by **Beppe Crovella** (**Arti & Mestieri**). This keyboard-driven ensemble plays with no guitars, resulting in a richly jazz-rock mix with light Latin inserts. Their debut of 1990 *Spleen* is a concept on a young man affected by spleen (sad mood) because of his inability to adapt, while *Inca* is an acoustic prog styled composition with the use of vintage '70s keyboards (two keyboardists on Hammond, Moog and other synths with an ELP sound). **Nik** quits for a while, later establishing his own studio in Turin where he records scores for adds, theatre, movies, and even a solo album. In 2010 the band reunites with **Riccardo Ruggeri** singing in opera style and featuring special guests on their last work of 2016 *Eros & Thanatos*, **Steve Hackett** (**Genesis** guitarist) and **Ray Thomas** (**The Moody Blues**) on flute.
RECOMMENDED RECORDINGS: **ODYSSEAS** *(Fading, 2014)* **EROS & THANATOS***(Fading, 2016).* **M.G.**

ALDO TAGLIAPIETRA

For over forty years (1966 - 2009) he played bass, guitar and fronted with his distinctive melancholic falsetto voice the famous Italian band **Le Orme**. The 1982 break-up leads him to release his first solo album, the 1984 pop work...*Nella Notte*. In 1986 his mother-band reforms and he re-joins the line-up, managing to publish another solo album of his own in 1990 called *Radio Londra* and again in 2008 for the album *Il Viaggio* recorded ten years before and based on his experiences in India, featuring him on the sitar. The following year he quits **Le Orme** definitely (briefly singing at the Prog Exhibition of 2010 with his former band mates **Toni Pagliuca** and **Tolo Marton** in Rome), publishing a couple of unplugged albums before he finally records his two truly prog works titled *Nella Pietra e Nel Vento* and *L'Angelo Rinchiuso*.
RECOMMENDED RECORDINGS: **IL VIAGGIO** *(Il Giardino, 2008)* **NELLA PIETRA E NEL VENTO** *(SELF, 2010)* **L'ANGELO RINCHIUSO** *(SELF, 2016).* **M.G.**

TAPROBAN

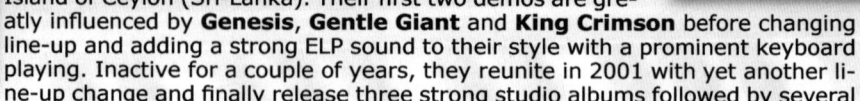

Gianluca De Rossi - *keyboards, guitar, vocals,* **Davide Guidoni** - *drums, percussion,* **Guglielmo Mariotti** - *bass, guitar, vocals.*
Formed in 1996 in Rome, theirs is the ancient name of the Island of Ceylon (Sri-Lanka). Their first two demos are greatly influenced by **Genesis**, **Gentle Giant** and **King Crimson** before changing line-up and adding a strong ELP sound to their style with a prominent keyboard playing. Inactive for a couple of years, they reunite in 2001 with yet another line-up change and finally release three strong studio albums followed by several contributions to the **Colossus Project** albums. The debut album recalls classic Italian prog groups like **BMS**, and the beautiful sequel is full of **Emerson**-styled keyboard. The third record of 2006, *Posidonian Fields*, is a sparkling and fascinating album closer to **Yes**, with more personality and good ideas.
DISCOGRAPHY: **OGNI PENSIERO VOLA** *(2001, Musea)* **OUTSIDE NOWHERE** *(2004, Mellow Records)* **POSIDONIAN FIELDS** *(2006, Mellow Records).* **M.G. & C.C.**

IL TEMPIO DELLE CLESSIDRE

Elisa Montaldo – *keyboards,* **Stefano "Lupo" Galifi** – *vocals,* **Fabio Gremo** – *bass, acoustic guitar,* **Giulio Canepa** - *guitar,* **Paolo Tixi** – *drums.*
Keyboardist **Elisa Montaldo** contacts in 2006 **Stefano 'Lupo' Galifi**, singer in **Museo Rosenbach**'s album **Zarathustra**, to create a cover band of this album (the name is in fact inspired by the instrumental closing section of the first part) and to perform live shows based upon this work. After a while they start writing their own songs inspired by the '70s Italian prog, and finally in 2010 a first album is released by the label Black Widow. Great attention is paid to the integration between the music and the lyrics, with particular reference to the emotional sphere, nature and tradition. This self-titled album was a success and led to many a participation in festival and concerts also abroad. In 2013 they release a second album, *AlieNatura*, with singer **Francesco Ciapica**. Still active their last album *Il-lûdĕre* is published in 2017.
RECOMMENDED RECORDINGS: **IL TEMPIO DELLE CLESSIDRE** *(2010, Black Widow).* **M.G.**

Europe: ITALY

THEATRE

Ricky Tonco - *vocals, guitars,* **Silver Sancio** - *keyboards,* **Pietro Foi** - *guitar,* **Piero Ottanà** - *bass,* **Giorgio Bartoloni** - *drums.*
Struggling Italian band from Milan initially named **Brainstorm** and founded in 1987 with three demo tapes over a span of six years. Many a line-up change before releasing their full-length only album (nearly the entire original line-up) *No More Rhymes But Mr. Brainstorm* in 1993 with Mellow Records. Inspired by the powerful sound of **Genesis** and the early **Marillion**, the final result is a very compelling symphonic oriented style with a careful use of synthesizers, intense organ-led passages and the melodic guitar solos. Greeted with enthusiasm by the prog fans worldwide, after the break-up, **Ricky Tonco** joins **Cristiano Roversi** to form **Moongarden**.
DISCOGRAPHY: **NO MORE RHYMES BUT MR. BRAINSTORM** *(1993, Mellow Records).*   M.G. & C.C.

TNR

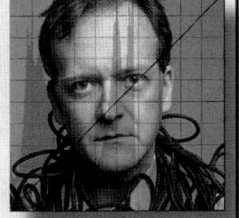

Ohm (Marco Olivotto) - *keyboards, guitars, vocals,* **Fabrizio Daicampi** - *guitars,* **Emanuele Martini** - *bass,* **Sergio Zuanni** - *drums.*
TNR is the abbreviation of **The Noisy Room** aka **Ohm & The Fall Band**, a project that began in the '80s with **Marco 'Ohm' Olivotto** (one of the best prog Italian sound engineers) and **Fabrizio Daicampi**, as a possible compromise between the world of songwriting and the sophisticated arrangements of art-rock. Their music is between **Talk Talk** and **David Sylvian** and after two demos the duo finally releases *The Chessboard* in 1992 with guest star **Peter Hammill** as author of the song "The beat of a different Drummer". The following *Samsara* is a mature concept album featuring **David Lord** on keyboards (**Peter Gabriel**'s former producer), **Stuart Gordon** on violin (**Peter Hammill**'s former musician) and singer **Paolo Benvegnù**.
DISCOGRAPHY: **THE CHESSBOARD** *(TNR, 1992)* **SAMSARA** *(Mellow Records, 1994).*   M.G. & C.C.

LA TORRE DELL'ALCHIMISTA

Michele Mutti - *keyboards,* **Davide Donadoni** - *bass,* **Michele Giardino, Elena Biagioni** - *vocals, keyboards,* **Norberto Mosconi, Michelangelo Donadini** - *drums,* **Silvia Ceraolo** - *flute.*
Their name is taken from one of the most famous tracks of the band **Area** meaning the Alchimist's Tower, these boys from Bergamo play a radical symphonic prog based upon the powerful performances of young keyboard-wizard **Michele Mutti**. Their first eponymous album of 2001 seems to have come out of the '70s with its keyboard-driven sound and where the acoustic guitar and flute replace the electric guitar. Invited to participate in the 2002 NearFest, they release a live album before proceeding towards a new excellent studio album entitled *Neo* published in 2007 always focused on a twin keyboard attack with the strong lead flute and confident warm Italian vocals.
DISCOGRAPHY: **LA TORRE DELL'ALCHIMISTA** *(Kaliphonia, 2001)* **USA... YOU KNOW?** *(live, Maracash 2005)* **NEO** *(Maracash, 2007).*   M.G. & C.C.

IL TRONO DEI RICORDI

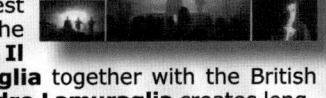

Alessandro Lamuraglia - *keyboards,* **Erik Landley** - *bass, sax,* **Stefano Cupertino** - *tape effects, programming,* **Paolo Lamuraglia** - *guitars,* **Alberto Mugnaini** - *vocals.*
Symphonic band formed in 1990 as one of the best keyboard-oriented symphonic rock bands of the Italian '90s: inspired by the Italians **BMS, PFM, Il Balletto di Bronzo** and **Rovescio della Medaglia** together with the British counterparts **Yes** and **ELP**. Their leader **Alessandro Lamuraglia** creates lengthy keyboard compositions with strong epic themes in the best **Rick Wakeman** style. Tempo changes, atmosphere variations, well chosen tunes and open melodies with Baroc hints that never falls into kitsch. The lyrics are in English and inspired by **William Blake**'s poems.
DISCOGRAPHY: **IL TRONO DEI RICORDI** *(1994, The Laser's Edge).*   M.G. & C.C.

Europe: ITALY

UBI MAIOR

Lorenzo Marotta, Mario Moi - *vocals*, **Stefano Mancarella, Stefano Mansueto, Marcella Arganese** - *guitars*, **Gabriele Manzini** - *keyboards*, **Walter Gorreri** - *bass*, **Alessandro Di Caprio** - *drums*.
Formed in 1999 mixing symphonic prog and hard rock and touring until 2005 as guests in many a festival, compilation or tribute albums (to **King Crimson** and **The Moody Blues**). They produced very interesting tracks over six years, without ever releasing a real debut album (in 2001 they record their first demo *Frontiere* and then **Gabriele Manzini** also joins **The Watch**). After some spring gigs they record a new demo called *Atto Primo - Atto Secondo* featuring new versions of old tracks, and a new, longer composition which paved the way for their debut in 2005, Nostos, containing good and well performed songs with a cover version of **Balletto di Bronzo**'s famous song "La tua casa comoda". Four years later a second powerful album Senza Tempo and their latest work of 2014 *Incanti Biomeccanici*.
RECOMMENDED RECORDINGS: **NOSTOS** *(2005, BTF)* **SENZA TEMPO** *(2009, BTF)*. **M.G.**

UNREAL CITY

Emanuele Tarasconi - *keyboards, lead vocals*, **Francesca Zanetta** - *guitars, mellotron*, **Dario Pessina** - *bass, bass pedals, vocals*, **Marco Garbin** - *drums, percussion*, **Matteo Bertani** - *violin, keyboards, vocals*.
Formed in 2008 by keyboardist **Emanuele Tarasconi** and guitarist **Francesca Zanetta** from Parma, they start as strange power trio based upon guitar, keyboards and drums, adding new musicians along the way and developing their style into a more complex and technical '70s prog through the use of vintage instruments like the Minimoog, Mellotron, Hammond and church organ, violin and lute. A self-released EP is released in 2012 capturing producer **Fabio Zuffanti**'s (**Finisterre, La Maschera Di Cera**) attention and leading to their debut album *La Crudeltà Di Aprile* the following year. The lyrics touch dark themes of psychological conflict and personal growth. Recently they issued the 2015 album *Il Paese del Tramonto* and soon they are to release *Frammenti Notturni* proving them still active and also well-known abroad too.
RECOMMENDED RECORDINGS: **LA CRUDELTÁ DI APRILE** *(Mirror/BTF, 2013)*. **M.G.**

L'UOVO DI COLOMBO

Enzo Volpini - *keyboards, acoustic guitars, vocals*, **Elio Volpini** - *bass, guitar, vocals*, **Ruggero Stefani** - *drums, percussion, vocals*, **Toni Gionta** - *lead vocals*.
A musical project started in 1972 by brothers **Enzo** and **Elio Volpini**, this band was strongly penalized by a great lack of promotion from their label EMI Records. Their only homonym album of 1973 unites two different models of symphonic prog: the British prog of **Emerson Lake & Palmer** and the Italian melodic prog of **Le Orme**. Electric organ-driven, their compositions feature fantastic instrumental performances, well balanced and arranged with good taste, crowned by the outstanding voice of **Toni Gionta**. **Elio** will join **Etna**, his brother carried on as session-man while **Ruggero** joins **Gli Alunni del Sole**.
DISCOGRAPHY: **L'UOVO DI COLOMBO** *(1973, EMI)*. **M.G. & C.C.**

VENEGONI & C.

Gigi Venegoni – *guitars*, **Marco Astarita** – *percussion*, **Ciro Buttari** – *percussion*, **Ludovico Einaudi** – *keyboards*, **Paolo Franchini** – *bass*, **Beppe Sciuto** – *drums, percussion*.
Formed by **Luigi 'Gigi' Venegoni**, former guitarist of **Arti & Mestieri**, this open band counts over twenty musicians who collaborated with them during the years. They debut with the 1977 album *Rumore Rosso*, a jazz rock music with instrumental pieces, also very long, guided by Gigi's guitar who took part of the previous band style and refined it through Mediterranean and middle-eastern sounds, also thanks to the large use of ethnic and traditional percussions. Their best work is probably the following *Sarabanda*, out two years later. After a decade of silence, the revival: in 1989 *Nocturne*, in 2001 *Mosaico* and in 2007 *Planetarium* featuring **Furio Chirico** on drums (former band mate from **Arti & Mestieri**). Recently they are both active in **A&M**'s new projects.
RECOMMENDED RECORDINGS: **SARABANDA** *(Cramps, 1979)*. **M.G. & C.C.**

Europe: ITALY

IL VOLO

Vince Tempera, Gabriele Lorenzi - *keyboards,* **Alberto Radius, Mario Lavezzi** - *guitar, vocals,* **Bob Callero** - *bass,* **Gianni Dall'Aglio** - *drums.*
This studio project was put together by some very popular musicians, all coming from famous Italian bands: **Radius** and **Lorenzi** from the rock band **Formula Tre**, **Lavezzi** from the pop group **Flora Fauna e Cemento**, and **Dall'Aglio** from the beat band **I Ribelli** and **Callero** from the only true prog formation **Osage Tribe**. A sort of super-group featuring as double keyboardist the famous composer Vince Tempera, and the lyrics written **Lucio Battisti**'s personal songwriter **Giulio Rapetti** aka **Mogol**. The first homonym work is released in 1974 by **Battisti**'s label Numero Uno (most of the musicians participate to his projects as session-men), for a somewhat jazz-fusion of melodic symphonic prog structured on two keyboards with great vocals and very interesting percussions. Their second album *Essere O Non Essere* (to be or not to be) is a soft instrumental work with some majestic keyboards flights recalling **King Crimson**.
DISCOGRAPHY: IL VOLO *(Numero Uno, 1974)* ESSERE O NON ESSERE? *(Numero Uno, 1975).* **M.G.**

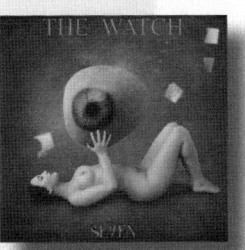

THE WATCH

Simone Rossetti – *vocals, flute,* **Ettore Salati** – *guitars,* **Marco Schembri** – *bass,* **Gabriele Manzini** – *keyboards,* **Roberto Leoni** - *drums.*
Simone Rossetti was already the charismatic front man of his previous group from 1993 **The Night Watch**. This great vocalist and flute player has a voice very similar to **Peter Gabriel** and so the sound of the new band of course follows the early **Genesis** style with some reminiscences of **Marillion**, **Spock's Beard** and **Änglagård**. Formed in 2000 after the disbandment, they mainly began as a cover band of the early **Genesis** before beginning to write their own material, sung in English and often criticized for emulating with no personal touch. The debut of 2001 titled *Ghost* contains instead very interesting personality and magnificent Mellotron work, that, yes, sounds like outtakes between *Nursery Crime* and *Selling England By The Pound*, but still is <<*the best album Genesis NEVER made!*>>. Still actively on the same line today.
RECOMMENDED RECORDINGS: VACUUM *(Lizard/Pick Up, 2004)* SEVEN *(Pick Up, 2017).* **M.G.**

YLECLIPSE

Alessio Guerriero - *guitar, vocals,* **Andrea Picciau** - *keyboards, vocals,* **Andrea Iddas** - *bass, vocals,* **Federico Bacco** - *drums,* **Roberto Diomedi** - *drums.*
From Cagliari (Sardinia) they form in 1998 as **Eclisse** for a debut album titled *Mercury and Sulfurus* before changing to **Yleclipse**. Despite their roots (islanders tend to be very patriotic) they fall deeply in love with a from of eclectic progressive rock with Celtic atmospheres (Irish and Scottish folk in particular) and some Medieval influences. The rest of their discography is published by Mauro Moroni's Mellow Records for a total of five albums dedicated to the musical research oriented to broaden their horizons with a wide range of styles: from ragtime to ambient and evocative slow-air tunes, arranged with the typical '90s unplugged taste. Influences vary form **Genesis**, **Steve Hackett**, **Anthony Phillips**, **Marillion**, **IQ**, **Pendragon**, **Yes**, **ELP**, **PFM**, **Rush**, **Jethro Tull** and even from **The Rolling Stones**.
RECOMMENDED RECORDINGS: OPUS *(2006, Mellow Records).* **M.G.**

ZAUBER

Liliana Bodini – *lead vocals, percussion,* **Massimo Cavagliato** – *drums, percussion,* **Mauro Cavagliato** - *bass, guitars, keyboards, percussion, vibes, vocals,* **Gianni Cristiani** – *flute,* **Paolo Clari, Oscar Giordanino** - *keyboards.*
Formed in the mid '70s they publish a first excellent homonym album in 1978 (re-issued in 1989 as *Il Sogno*) of a prog similar to **BMS**. Their third 1992 record *Phoenix* is a mix of new and old songs (from 1976-77) with short electro-acoustic parts of strongly classically influenced melodies (**Bach**) augmenting their sound with chimes, xylophone, glockenspiel, flute, harmonica, viola, cello, recorder and oboe, close to **Jethro Tull** or **Fruupp** but more Baroque. In parallel **Clari** and **Cristiani** form the new age project **Clarion** with the other **Zauber** musicians as guests. **Michele Tale** instead forms his own band **Tale** for one very sophisticated symphonic prog album in 1994 (also with other **Zauber** musicians) titled *Senza Frontiere*.
RECOMMENDED RECORDINGS: ZAUBER (Il Sogno) *(MU, 1978).* **M.G.**

Europe: NORWAY

AKASHA

Sverre Svendsen - vocals, mellotron, **Kjell Evensen** - drums, **Arild Andreassen** - bass, **Jens Ivar Andreassen** - guitars, mellotron, synthesizers, piano, organ, **Tor-Jonny Hansen** – lyrics.
An underground Scandinavian prog quintet born in 1970 from Finn-mark, a tiny village somewhere beyond the Arctic Circle, which records one strange but fascinating album in a hotel bomb cellar unfortunately penalizing it for the low quality sound. This self-titled album dates 1977 and the English science-fictional lyrics are sung with a style recalling **Greg Lake**, while their music is full of Mellotron in its orchestral tunes and a heavy use of Moog in its space sonorities, as in the track "Electronic Nightmare" greatly inspire by the early **Genesis** and **The Moody Blues**. The highly experimental analog sounds and noises done with filters and oscillators relegate the guitars to a secondary role. In 1995 the album was re-issued on CD by the Swedish label APM after re-mastering and de-noising the old tapes.
DISCOGRAPHY: **AKASHA** *(Bat, 1977).*

M.G.

AIRBAG

Bjørn Riis - guitars, keyboards, **Jørgen Hagen** - keyboards, **Joachim Slikker** – drums, **Anders Hovdan** - bass, **Asle Tostrup** – vocals, keyboards.
These high school friends were already playing together since 1994 yet the line-up consolidates only five years later releasing a first EP only in 2005: *Sounds That I Hear* blends influences from **A-Ha**, **Porcupine Tree** and **Pink Floyd**, allowing people to freely download it from their website thus creating a good international fan base. In 2007 a second EP *Safetree*, and their performing as opening for acts for **Pineapple Thief**, **Gazpacho** and **Riverside** finally brought them a contract for their 2009 album with Karisma Records, *Identity*, and later in 2011 a second and more powerful work entitled *All Rights Removed*, containing the fascinating suite "Homesick" which recalls **Pink Floyd**'s "Shine on you crazy diamond". Other two recent albums always on the same line for this rock-prog band.
RECOMMENDED RECORDINGS: **ALL RIGHTS REMOVED** *(Karisma Records, 2011)*

M.G.

AMPERA

Hanne Tangstad – vocals, **Trygve K. Jensen** – guitars, **Kåre Helleve** – bass, **Jostein Henanger** – drums, **Per Einar Dahl** – keyboards.
An alternative prog band with great expectations, formed sometime around 2004 with a first auto-produced demo of four tracks until a label from Chile called Mylodon Records decides to release their debut album *A Vulcanized Mingle* in 2006.
This only work contains a sound heavily influenced by **Anekdoten** with random inserts of **King Crimson** passages and the fascinating female voice of **Hanne Tangstad**, who sings in English with her cold tones, closer to certain alternative tendencies than to the prog moods and atmospheres, providing a halo of originality not comparable to other Norwegian group these days. Apparently still active, yet no new novelty on the horizon.
DISCOGRAPHY: **A VULCANIZED MINGLE** *(Mylodon Records, 2007).*

M.G.

FLAX

Hermod Falch – lead vocals, **John Hesla** – guitar, flute, **Lars Hesla** – keyboards, **Arve Sakariassen** – bass, **Bruce Rasmussen** - drums.
Band of hard rock origins born in 1972, they start off publishing in 1975 an album simply titled One before the break-up. A first debut greatly inspired by **Deep Purple** and **Led Zeppelin** with hard blues parts and excellent guitar solos. Their singer **Falch** has very theatrical inclinations, like when he wears a skeleton disguise on stage, using many changes of tone and vocal impositions, sometimes recalling **Queen**, **Cargo** and **Angel**. Three years after the debut and following disbandment, they reform with a consistent line-up change and publish *Monster Tapes* in 1980, picking up from where they had left: a heavier hard rock with discreet symphonic colors, evident blues inspirations and high-pitched vocals for a complex guitar-driven music full of energy, tempo shifts and the jazzy hints of an electric piano/clavinet.
RECOMMENDED RECORDINGS: **ONE** *(Vertigo, 1976).*

M.G.

Europe: NORWAY

FRUITCAKE

Pål Søvik - *drums, vocals*, **Tore Bø** - *bass, keyboards*, **Helge Skaarseth** - *keyboards, mandolin*, **Siri M. Seland** - *keyboards, bass*, **Gunnar Bergersen** - *bass*, **Jens G. Sverdrup** - *guitars*, **Steffen Holthe** – *guitars*, **Robert Hauge** - *guitars, backing vocals*, **Olav Nygård** - *bass*, **Nina C. Dahl** – *flute*.

Born in 1990 as **The Stinking Rich**, they change to **Fruitcake** two years later and record a self produced album titled *Fool Tapes* in 1992. Guitarist **Steffen Holthe** had to join the armed forces and although they initially decide to wait for him, a good contract leads them to proceed in publishing *How To Make It* in 1994: delicate songs with extended instrumental parts crossing over into the **Pendragon**, **IQ** and **Jadis** vein with hints of **Änglagård** and **Anekdoten**. Pressure from the record company makes them follow-up with a second studio album in 1995, *Room For Surprise*, probably their best work, and after another three good releases, **Steffen** finally joins them on a last album of 2004 entitled *Man Overboard*.
RECOMMENDED RECORDINGS: HOW TO MAKE IT (Cyclops 1994) **ROOM FOR SURPRISE** (Cyclops 1997). M.G.

GARGAMEL

Jon Edmund Hansen - *guitars*, **Bjorn Viggo Andersen** - *keyboards*, **Geir Tornes** - *bass*, **Morten Tornes** - *drums, vocals*, **Tom Uglebakken** - *guitars, vocals, flute*, **Leif Erlend Hjlmen** - *cello*.

Formed in the spring of 2001 they hold a concert and record two songs the following year. Cello player **Leif Erlend Hjelmen** joins in and they record another three tracks which all together will be released as their debut album *Watch for the umbles* in 2006: an old fashioned and evocative prog-rock full of fresh ideas and fluid solutions with experimental dark atmospheres, melancholic moods and psychedelia recalling somewhat **King Crimson** and **VDGG** with a blend of kraut-rock. Their sound is drenched with heavy Hammond organs, a gloomy mellotron and the sophisticated jazzy electric piano, combined with classical instruments like cello, flute and saxophone. Their last work dates 2009.
DISCOGRAPHY: WATCH FOR THE UMBLES (Transubstans, 2006). M.G.

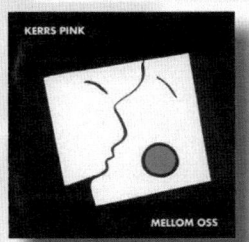

KERRS PINK

Harald Lytomt – *guitar, flute, keyboards*, **Jostein Hanse** - *bass, guitar, vocals*.

Formed in 1972 as **Cash Pink**, they become **Kerrs Pink** and publish 5 studio albums always with different line-ups up to seventeen elements. Their real debut of 1980 is a homonym album of Nordic folk well balanced by many electric parts of **Camel** influence, especially for the guitar, but maintaining the traditional sonorities. The second *Mellom Oss* is released the following year and together with the debut can be considered their best material: beautiful atmospheres with some **Pink Floyd** influences for a prog rock which blends Scandinavian folklore and refined English art-rock through the fabulous dialogues between three guitars, a flute and two keyboards. Their 2002 album *Tidings* is the last and features a new lead singer and great female backing vocals.
RECOMMENDED RECORDINGS: MELLOM OSS (Pottiskiver /Polygram, 1981). M.G.

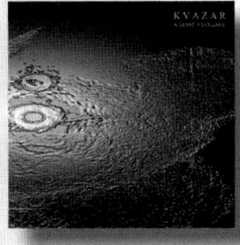

KVAZAR

Andre Jensen - *vocals, piano, keyboards, acoustic guitar*, **Endre Tønnesen** - *bass, vocals*, **Ronny Johansen** - *keyboards*, **Alexander Knøsmoen** - *guitars*, **Kim A. Lieberknecht** - *drums*.

Formed in 1997 with a couple of demos (some of this material is included in their first album) with Kvarts Records while working on their eponymous debut released in 2001 by Musea Records. Greatly influenced by **Änglagård**, **King Crimson**, **Genesis** and **Anekdoten** they create well balanced and melancholic atmospheres with Nordic features and fascinating compositions. Their second release in 2005 is called *A Giant's Lullaby*, with almost a completely new lineup and a female guest vocalist named **Trude Bergli**: they move from the Scandinavian symphonic genre to a beautiful blend of styles and sounds that combine their original atmosphere with fusion, jazz, folk rock and some traces of **Pink Floyd**.
DISCOGRAPHY: KVAZAR (2000, Musea) **A GIANT'S LULLABY** (2006, Musea). M.G.

Europe: NORWAY

PANZERPAPPA

Knut Tore Abrahamsen - *guitars*, **Steinar Børve** - *horns, keyboards*, **Trond Gjellum** - *drums, percussion*, **Jørgen Skjulstad, Anders Krabberød** - *bass, guitars, keyboards*.
In 1996 **Trond Gjellu** records some demos under the name Panzerpappa based on the prog rock of **Samla Mammas Manna** and **Univers Zero**. He plays the drums in a Tolkien project and meets Steinar with whom he founds the band in 1998 adding **Abrahamsen** and **Skjulstad** to the line-up. They debut live in concerts until finally managing to record the self-produced album *Passer Gullfisk* in 2000: a synthetic rock orchestra playing a creative avant-rock with very dynamic and complex songs inspired by the fun side of **Frank Zappa**. Another five works and in 2013 they are invited to play at the Rock In Opposition festival in France. Trond undergoes surgery but he continues to write material for their last album *Pestrottedans* (dance of the plague rat) for AltrOck Records in 2015.
DISCOGRAPHY: **PASSER GULLFISK** *(Panzerpappa, 2000)* **HULEMYSTERIET** *(Panzerpappa, 2002)* **FARLIG VANDRING** *(Avant Audio, 2004)* **KORALREVENS KLAGESANG** *(Hangar, 2006).* **M.G.**

POPOL ACE (Popol Vuh)

Pete Knutsen - *keyboards, guitar*, **Arne Schultze** - *guitar*, **Jahn Teigen** - *vocals*, **Terje Methi** - *bass*, **Thor Andreassen** - *drums*.
Born in 1959 as **The Scavers**, they change to **Arman Sumpe Dur Express** during the '60s and in 1970 become **Popol Vuh**. After a couple of singles they record in 1972 a first album of symphonic prog, jazz rock and some hard blues parts in assonance with **Aunt Mary**. Also *Quichè Maya* stays on good levels before a halt caused by the homonym German band that forced them to change name to **Popol Ace** in 1975. *Stolen From Time* is the first album under the new name: a concept strongly influenced by **Genesis**, but too rigidly produced to gather the hoped-for international success. Singer **Jan Teigen** leaves for his own pop career so in 1978 they hire a new vocalist for a last unnecessary album before the break-up.
RECOMMENDED RECORDINGS: **POPOL VUH** *(Polydor, 1972).* **M.G & C.C.**

SAFT

Ove Thue - *vocals*, **Trygve Thue, Rune Walle** - *guitar*, **Tom Harry Halvorsen** - *keyboards, flute*, **Magne Lunde** - *bass*, **Rolf Skogstrand** - *drums*.
This heavy prog and pop rock band from Bergen is active since 1969 as one of the first to sing in Nynorsk (a rural dialect, one of four official languages in Norway). Brothers **Ove** and **Trygve Thue** are the only constant members of the various line-up changes, and begin with a musical set-up of *Hår* (Hair) recorded in 1970. After a major line-up change their style shifts to folk and country rock (Hardanger fiddle) and they release a first self-titled debut all in English (except for "Fjøsvise"): "All the Time" had the US military slogan from the Vietnamese war (Fighting for freedom is like fucking for virginity) in the chorus and was beeped out by the BBC. Winners of the European Pop Jury in 1971 with "People in Motion", the band's biggest hit, they issue thereafter other singles and albums before slowly disbanding in 1974. From the late '90s some reunions albums but never at the same level of their first one.
RECOMMENDED RECORDINGS: **SAFT** *(Polydor, 1971).* **M.G.**

TANGLE EDGE

Ronald Nygård - *guitar*, **Tom Steinberg** - *drums*, **Hasse Horrigmoe** - *bass*.
Formed around 1980 by **Ronald Nygård** (guitars and keyboards) and **Hasse Horrigmoe** (bass guitar and 12-string acoustic guitar), they release four CD's since 1989 touring England, Russia, Italy, Denmark, Sweden and Norway. Strongly influenced by German prog, especially **Amon Düül II**'s sound, their first album *In Search of a New Dawn* sounds so old and psychedelic that it seems recorded in Germany during 1972. A Norwegian answer to the **Ozric Tentacles** with a spacey psychedelic guitars, Moog synths, hippy percussion, bongos and tubular bells. Same for the following second album *Entangled Scorpio Entrance*, purely instrumental as the previous mixing improvisation with written parts. A prolific discography up to the most recent 2016 album proves them to be still active.
RECOMMENDED RECORDINGS: **IN SEARCH OF A NEW DAWN** *(Mushroom, 1990)* **ENTANGLED SCORPIO ENTRANCE** *(Mushroom, 1992).* **M.G.**

Europe: **NORWAY**

THULE

Steve Riise Jensen - *guitar, vocals,* **Peer-Einar Pedersen** - *bass, vocals,* **Jens Morten Søreide** - *vocals,* **Einar Jan Larsen** - *guitars,* **Even Gaare** - *drums,* **Jens Haugan** - *drums,* **Pål Valle** - *keyboards, vocals,* **Hugo Barbala** - *drums, percussion.*
Band founded at the end of the '80s as a faithful replica of the contemporary **Pink Floyd** period, their bizarre and interesting prog rock contains also references to the Swedish **Trettioåriga Kriget** (rock orientation, strong bass presence) and to Rush.
Although all their discography is very interesting, their albums *Ultima Thule* and *Natt*, are the most representative with a dark, gloomy goth sound. Instruments are the usual guitar, keyboards, bass and drums. Obvious the similarities to **Pink Floyd**, given the intents of their beginnings, mostly in the **Gilmour** styled guitar and the use of space music and atmosphere. The gothic hints are enhanced by, for example, spoken text over howling winds and an overall dark aura that pervades all their songs.
DISCOGRAPHY: ULTIMA THULE *(Arktisk, 1987)* **NATT** *(Arktisk, 1990).*   M.G.

UTOPIAN FIELDS

Tom-Inge Andersen - *bass,* **Tor Dahl** - *guitars,* **Lars Fredriksen** - *vocals,* **Atle Byström Olsen** - *guitars,* **Tor Øyvind Folleggg** - *keyboards,* **Geir Wetle Holtan** - *drums, percussion,* **Kjersti Thunem** - *flute,* **Ronny Byström Olsen** - *harmonica.*
Formed in Skien in 1988 and disbanding around 1991 after three records, the last of which recorded the year of the break-up and still never yet published by anyone. Their style is a moderate neo-prog of symphonic, psychedelic and folk shades sung in English and recalling **Pink Floyd**, **Wishbone Ash** and the early Canterbury school themes. Their self-titled debut of 1989 has probably the best and more involving atmospheres. Singer **Lars Fredriksen** quits soon after the publication, replaced by **Bård Tufte Johansen** - later to become a well known comedian and TV personality - for the follow-up album *White Pigeon, You Clean...* released in 1990.
RECOMMENDED RECORDINGS: UTOPIAN FIELDS *(Colours, 1989).*   M.G & C.C.

WHITE WILLOW

Jacob C. Holm-Lupo - *guitar,* **Jan Tariq Rahman** - *keyboards,* **Tirill Mohn** - *violin,* **Sara Trondal** - *vocals,* **Eldrid Johansen** - *vocals,* **Alexander Engebresten** - *bass,* **Sylvia Erichsen** - *vocals,* **Mattias C. Olsson** - *drums, percussion,* **J Ketil Vestrum Einarsen** - *horns,* **Sigrun Eng** - *cello.*
Formed in 1992 around **Jacob Holm-Lupo**, their first album *Ignis Fatus* of 1995 is a mid paced melancholic and beautiful mellotron-led folk-prog with brilliant acoustic guitar moments, flute and strings. The next three years they reformed with **Sylvia Erichsen** as vocalist for *Ex Tenebris*, evolving into goth. The line-up changes again for a third album *Sacrament* of 2000, sounding more a symphonic prog band and less folk. Vintage keyboard wizard **Lars Fredrik Frislie** joins for the 2004 *Storm Season*: folk is gone while the symphonic streak duets with an almost heavy metal guitar. *Signal to Noise* returns them to a more modern prog while the 2011 album *Terminal Twilight* exhibits vintage keyboards.
RECOMMENDED RECORDINGS: IGNIS FATUS *(1995, The Laser's Edge)* **SACRAMENT** *(2000, The Laser's Edge)* **STORM SEASON** *(2004, The Laser's Edge).*   M.G.

VANESSA

Knut Værnes – *guitar,* **Jan Erik Pedersen** – *bass,* **Frank Aleksandersen** – *drums,* **Brynjulf Blix** – *keyboards,* **Haakon Graf** - *keyboards,* **Svend Undseth** - *flute, saxophones, clarinet, winds.*
Among the first jazz rock bands in Norway, formed in 1971 by **Sven Undseth** playing gigs in Club 7 in Oslo while recording their first album, *City Lips*, issued in 1975: technically perfect it recalls **Mahavishnu Orchestra** and the Canterbury school blending rock music with jazz improvisations and funky lines through beautiful guitar parts, a dominant clarinet and sax solos throughout. The second album, *Black and White*, is more strong, defined and mature, with a different line-up, but not different from the propose of playing a good jazz rock with plenty if references to the Canterbury sound, especially to **Hugh Hopper** and **Pierre Moerlen**.

RECOMMENDED RECORDINGS: BLACK AND WHITE *(Compendium, 1976).*   M.G & C.C.

Europe: POLAND

COLLAGE

Tomek Rozycki - *vocals,* **Przemek Zawadzki** - *bass,* **Mirek Gil** - *guitars,* **Wojtek Szadkowski** - *drums, percussion,* **Jacek Korzeniowski** - *keyboards,* **Robert Amirian** - *vocals, guitar,* **Pawel Zajaczowski** - *keyboards,* **Ania Milewska** - *piano,* **Jurek Barczak** - *guitar.*

One of the best heirs of **Marillion** and **IQ**, this band is formed in 1985 although their debut **Basnie** is published only in 1990. Only **Gil** and **Szadkowski** remain after a line-up change, so to test the new singer they release a cover album, *Nine Songs of John Lennon*, in 1993 followed a year later by *Moonshine*, perhaps one of the greatest symphonic prog-rock works of the modern era with its wonderful melodies, blending heavy keyboard backgrounds with extremely melodic guitar and vocals: an original style with intricate tempo changes which differentiate this band from the competition. Lyrics are in Polish and English depending on the album. Their adventure continues as **Satellite** by initiative of **Wojtek Szadkowski** after the disbandment in the late '90s.

DISCOGRAPHY: **BASNIE** *(1990, Inter Sonus/Ars Mundi)* **NINE SONGS OF JOHN LENNON** *(1993, Ars Mundi)* **MOONSHINE** *(1994, SI Music)* **SAFE** *(1995, Ars Mundi)* **CHANGES** *(1995, Ars Mundi).* **M.G.**

EXODUS

Andrzej Puczyñski - *guitar,* **Wojciech Puczyñski** - *bass,* **Wladyslaw Komendarek** - *keyboards,* **Pawel Birula** - *vocals, guitar,* **Zbigniew Fyk** - *drums,* **Marek Wójcicki** - *guitar,* **Kazimierz Barlasz** - *vocals,* **Jacek Olejnik** - *keyboards,* **Bogdan lol** - *guitar,* **Joanna Rosiñska** - *vocals.*

Founded in 1976 with the intention of creating a rock music strongly influenced by the classical genre. An extraordinary symphonic rock expressed with rare personality and modern taste, born as the perfect support of their theatrical acts where the delicate and powerful voice of **Pawel Birula** (the Polish answer to **Yes**) has nothing to envy to the more famous British and American singers. By the mid '80s they had toured in the USSR and West Germany, recording TV programs and radio broadcasts with a few singles, the 1980 first album *The Most Beautiful Day* and the 1982 the second work *Supernova*. A reunion in 2008 for the last album *Hazard*.

DISCOGRAPHY: **THE MOST BEAUTIFUL DAY** *(Polskie Nagrania Muza, 1980)* **SUPERNOVA** *(Polskie Nagrania Muza, 1981)* **HAZARD** *(Metal mind, 2006)* **NADZIEJE NIEPOKOJE** *(2006).* **C.A.**

EXTRA BALL

Jaroslaw Smietana - *guitars,* **Wladyslaw Sendecki** - *keyboards,* **Jan Cichy** - *bass,* **Benedykt Radecky** - *drums.*

Born in 1974 while playing in a club full of automatic billiards pools which granted a bonus for good play with an 'extra ball'. The debut as an official band took place in a jazz festival that same year winning the second prize, so the following year they kept playing in contests and even toured the USSR. Birthday is their first album containing a technically high level of melodic jazz-rock, some East-European folk dance themes (**Bela Bartok**) and a touch of blues in one track. Particular the harmonic balance between the guitar of **Smietana** and the keyboards of the eclectic **Sendecki**, better evidenced in the live album *Aquarium live N°3* of 1976. They continue their career more or less on the same line until the break-up after 1983.

DISCOGRAPHY: **BIRTHDAY** *(Poljazz, 1976)* **AQUARIUM LIVE N°3** *(Poljazz, 1977)* **MARLBORO COUNTRY** *(Poljazz, 1978)* **GO AHEAD** *(Poljazz,1979).* **C.A.**

GARGANTUA

Marcin Borowski – *drums,* **Justyn Hunia** - *keyboards,* **Leszek Mrozowski** - *bass,* **Bartek Zeman** – *guitar,* **Pawel Kubica** – *keyboard,* **Tylda Ciolkosz** – *violin.*

Polish musicians bound to the middle-East tradition and the Russian masters like **Stravinsky** and paying attention to **Steve Reich**'s experimental music, they start their career in 2003 with a first homonym album of fusion and strong jazz inputs with literary digressions inspired by the RIO movement. The musicians describe their sound as <<Stravinsky's deaf illegitimate son romancing Reich's sleepy gorilla while rocking a decapitated doll in a banana-peel cradle and listening to the new Univers Zero hit single on Radio Dada>>. *Kotegarda* is released in 2007 after a line-up change for a music with no marketing compromises. A career in development that hopefully may still reserve some surprises.

DISCOGRAPHY: **GARGANTUA** *(Ars Mundi, 2003)* **KOTEGARDA** *(Roadkill Music, 2007).* **M.G.**

Europe: POLAND

MAREK GRECHUTA

Born in 1945, **Marek Grechuta** begun to play piano at 7. He meets **Jan Kanty Pawlukiewicz** and they start a cabaret group called **Anawa** (mimicking the french words 'en avant' meaning 'forward'). His first album *Marek Grechuta & Anawa* of 1970 presents an original mix of cabaret, pop and prog elements with neo-baroque sounds. The following year his masterpiece entitled *Korowód* is published with real musical hymns, and **Marek** becomes a star (creating friction with **Jan**, so they break-up). He continues with a new band called **Wiem** (acronym of W Innej Epoce Muzycznej - in another musical era) and issues *Droga Za Widnokres* in 1972 and *Magia Obloków* in 1974, milestones for Polish prog-rock containing a poetic art-rock with jazz influences. After 1976 he makes peace with **Jan** and reactivates the previous project for a while. Other albums follow until his premature death in 2006.
RECOMMENDED RECORDINGS: KOROWÓD *(1971, Muza/Polskie Nagravia)* MAGIA OBLOKÓW *(1974, Pronit).*   M.G.

KLAN

Marek Alaszewski - *guitar, vocals,* **Maciej Gluskiewicz** - *piano, organ,* **Roman Pawelski** - *guitar, bass,* **Andrzej Poniatowski** - *drums, vocals.*
Between the end of the '60s and the early '70s the Polish panorama starts experimenting a new form of rock in motion and this band is one of these proto-prog bands: a Warsaw fusion quartet born in 1969 and led by guitarist **Marek Alaszewski** playing a psychedelic jazz-rock with references to **Vanilla Fudge**, orchestral inputs, acid instrumental jams (between **Santana** and **Grateful Dead**), fine melodic breaks and similarities to **Niemen**. After a self-titled EP in 1970, lyricist **Marian Skolarski** joins and composes a ballet called *Mrowisko*, a majestic, psychedelic concept with a very underground feel, full acid leads and fuzz-guitar solos, some violin and some jazzy parts. They reunite in 1992 and are apparently still active with other concerts and albums... not at the same level.
DISCOGRAPHY: MROWISKO *(1970, Muza)* PO CO MI TEN RAJ *(1992, Dig).*   M.G & C.C.

LIZARD

Damian Bydliński - *vocals,* **Andrzej Jancza** - *keyboards,* **Mariusz Szulakowski** - *drums, percussion,* **Janusz Tanistra** - *bass,* **Miroslaw Worek** – *guitars,* **Krzysztof Maciejowski,** *violin, keyboards.*
Formed in 1990 playing a music between **King Crimson** (*Lizard* is **KC**'s 3rd album) and the Polish neo-symphonic prog vibes, for many years they performed live, releasing a demo and a first record later in 1997, *W Galerii Czasu* (In the gallery of time): a mix of **KC**, **Marillion**, **UK** and **Bill Bruford**'s *Gradually Going Tornado*, with the excellent voice of **Bydlinski** (between **Belew** and **Berlin**). The music generally is pretty dramatic and sinister in all their discography, with more romantic overtones in particular moments, as the band avoids approaching to melodic themes and prefers to offer rhythmic, dark or atmospheric variations and experimental touches recalling mid-'70s **Genesis** and even **SBB** influences in the instrumental and vocal passages, with nice and heavy guitar moves or evolving piano and synth lines.
RECOMMENDED RECORDINGS: W GALERII CZASU *(Ars-Mundi, 1997).*   M.G & C.C.

ORKIESTRA ÒSMEGO DNIA

Jan A. P. Kaczmarek, Grzegorz Banaszak, Maciej Talaga, Ewa Išykowska, Agnieszka Dondajewska, Robert Nakoneczny, Olga Szwajger, Krzesimir Dêbski, Krzysztof Ścierański - *various instruments.*
An ensemble formed in 1977 and disbanded in 1989, the 'Eighth Day Orchestra' released a beautiful first album written by **Jan A. P. Kaczmarek** with assorted arrangements composed by the musicians: traditional music mixed with rock, experimentation and East European folk, including from Russia, with a feeling of being performed by a military band doped with mescaline. Multiple reed and string instruments create an otherworldly landscape that today may be labeled as mentally disturbing new age: this is not soft, meditative and relaxing music, but true psychedelia and timeless ritualistic sounds resulting in three very fascinating works of the first half of the '80s and a reunion album of 1995.
RECOMMENDED RECORDINGS: MUZYKA NA KONIEC *(1981, Muza/Polskie Nagravia).*   M.G.

Europe: POLAND

OSSIAN (aka Osjan)

Jacek Ostaszewski – *flute, vocals,* **Wojciech Waglewski** – *guitars, vocals,* **Radoslaw Nowakowski** - *drums, congas, bata,* **Milo Kurtis** – *drums, winds, Jewish harp, vocals.*

Formed as **Ossian** (with over ten great albums from 1971 to 2008) by **Jacek Ostaszewski, Marek Jackowski** (former **Anawa** musicians) and **Tomasz Holuj**, they change name to the polish **Osjan** (a fictional character from a poem by Bolesław Leśmian) due to a homonym band in Scotland. In 1975 **Jackowski** abandons to form the rock band **Maanam** with Greek percussionist **Milo Kurtis**, later invited to join **Osjan**. Heavily influenced by the music of India, they are predecessors of what will become world music later even if they prefer describing their ethnic music instead as the research of the most basic and universal elements of music, a multi-cultural language. In fact elements from Africa, Arabia and Asia mixed with the folk music of the Native Americans can be found too, blended to classical and jazz.

RECOMMENDED RECORDINGS: **OSSIAN** *(1973, Poljazz)* **OSJAN: ROOTS** *(1983, Pronit).*   M.G.

QUIDAM

Zbyszek Florek - *keyboards,* **Maciek Meller** - *guitar,* **Radek Scholl** - *bass,* **Rafal Jermakow** - *drums, percussion,* **Emila Derkowska** - *vocals,* **Ewa Smarzynska** - *flute,* **Jacek Zasada** - *flute,* **Bartek Kossowicz** - *vocals,* **Mariusz Ziolkowski** - *bass.*

Formed in 1991 as the rock blues band **Deep River**, they change name only in 1995 while recording their album *Quidam*, changing style into a melodic, text-based symphonic rock influenced by **Marillion** and **Camel**, blending harmonies, refined neo-prog arrangements and diversity of orchestrations (keyboards, cello, flute, oboe, strings) to the delicate and fascinating female vocals of **Emila Derkowska**. The following recordings increase slightly the pop-prog components, until the abandonment of their singer after *The Time Beneath the Sky* of 2002, replaced by **Bartek Kossowicz**. Their last album *Saiko* of 2012 bears the transformation with lyrics in the Polish and updates the sound.

RECOMMENDED RECORDINGS: **QUIDAM** *(1996, Ars Mundi)* **POD NIEBEM CZAS – THE TIME BENEATH THE SKY** *(2002, Rock Serwis).*   M.G.

REPORTAZ

Andrzej Karpinski, Piotr Lakomy - *various instruments.*

A project founded in 1982 by vocalist and percussionist **Andrzej Karpinski** on the ashes of an amateur punk-rock band called **Sten**. Initially influenced by the British New Wave genre, their musical style changed radically: every concert became an especially prepared and never repeated twice theatrical-musical show with long compositions influenced by groups like **The Residents, Zamla Mamas Mamma** or **Cabaret Voltaire**, including elements of jazz, classical and folk music, for a very limited number of concerts. Promoted by **Chris Cutler** and rated as the best Polish avant-garde rock of the '80s, they have a representative discography like the 1988 *W Gr Rzeki* (Up The River), heavily based on critics of political situation in Poland. In 1990 **Karpiski** emigrates from Poland for some years and the band disbands until 2000. They will return as his solo project of free form improvisational lyrics playing again in theatres (Muzyka do Taca and Gulasz z Serc) and a new last album *Bezsensory/Nonsensors* in 2005.

DISCOGRAPHY: **REPORTAZ** *(Recommended Records, 1987).*   M.G.

SATELLITE

Robert Amirian - *vocals,* **Sarhan Artur Kubeisi** - *guitars,* **Mirek Gil** - *guitars,* **Darek Lisowski** - *keyboards,* **Krzysiek Palczewski** - *keyboards,* **Przemek Zawadzki** - *bass,* **Wojtek Szdkowski** - *drums,* **Jarek Michalski** - *bass.*

Initially **Wojtek Szadkowski**'s solo project as he begins to write and plan his career during 2000, after the **Collage** disbandment. He recruits **Sarhan Kubeisiis** and is later joined by former band-mates **Robert Amirian, Mirek Gil** for a classic English new-prog. Although not at the same level of the previous group incarnation, *A Street Between Sunrise And Sunset* debuts in 2003, followed by *Evening Games* in 2006, which led to their participation a year later to the famous Baja Prog Festival in Mexico. Yet another two albums until 2009, with **Amirian**'s absolutely sensational vocals and **Gil**'s immediately recognizable guitar playing.

RECOMMENDED RECORDINGS: **A STREET BETWEEN SUNRISE AND SUNSET** *(2003, Metal Mind)* **EVENING GAMES** *(2005, Metal Mind).*   M.G.

Europe: PORTUGAL

ANANGA RANGA

Firmino Luis - *vocals, guitar,* **Alvaro** - *bass, vocals,* **Manuel Barreto** - *piano, vocals,* **Necas** - *drums,* **Rui Pedroso, Vasco Alves** - *keyboards,* **Pantera** - *percussion.*
Ensemble of prog-oriented jazz-rock formed in 1976 with a name inspired by the Indian love manual, similar to the Kamasutra. They start with fake pop singles in order to acquire a contract: smart move that worked out in 1979, leading them to release their jazz-rock fusion LP *Regresso As Origens* with sax **Manuel Garcia** and violinist **Carlos Zingaro**: a full blown instrumental work with a very typical '70s sound and obvious influences from **Mahavishnu Orchestra** and **Return To Forever**. Their second album *Privado* tried to appeal to both pop and jazz-rock audiences, so the result was a confusing work that led to the decision of some musicians to quit, thus actually breaking up the band for good.
DISCOGRAPHY: REGRESSO AS ORIGENS *(MetroSom, 1980)* **PRIVADO** *(MetroSom, 1981).* **M.G.**

BANDA DO CASACO

Nuno Rodrigues - *guitare, percussion,* **Armindo Neves** – *guitars,* **Mena Amaro** - *violin, vocals, bells,* **Celso de Carvalho** – *bass, cello, xilophone,* **António Pinho** - *vocals, percussion,* **António Pinheiro da Silva** – *guitar, flute,* **Miguel Coelho** – *violin, winds,* **Jorge Paganini** – *violin.*
Born in 1973 as a psychedelic folk band evolving into prog rock. Their very interesting debut of 1975, *Dos Benefícios de um Vendido no Reino dos Bonifácios*, is a real provocation to the Establishment. The second *Coisas do Arco da Velha* takes their satirical lyrics even further as in the song "É triste não saber ler" (A sad thing, not knowing how to read). The third is their most famous experimental work, *Hoje há Conquilhas, Amanhã não Sabemos* of 1977 featuring guitarist **António Pinheiro da Silva** and multi-instrumentalist **Rão Kyao**. The next works become more rock (*No Jardim da Celeste*, with singer **Né Ladeiras** and **Jerry Marotta**, **Gabriel**'s former drummer).
RECOMMENDED RECORDINGS: HOJE HÁ CONQUILHAS, AMANHÃ NÃO SABEMOS *(Imavox, 1977)* **NO JARDIM DA CELESTE** *(EMI, 1980).* **M.G.**

SAGA

José Luis Tinoco - *piano, keyboards, guitars,* **Zé da Ponte** - *bass, guitars,* **Fernando Fallé** - *drums.*
Creature channeling the creativeness of composer and musician **José Luis Tinoco**, this one shot musical project expresses itself in lone album of 1976 titled *Homo Sapiens*: an excellent work in collaboration with multi-instrumentalist **Zé Da Ponte** (although mainly a bass player who will pursued his career as appreciated session man) with strong jazz-rock progressive roots with breaks of symphonic rock mixed to latino attitudes; all sung in Portuguese with male and female vocals, the electric piano, guitars and horns create complex elegant textures recalling some Italian bands like **Arti & Mestieri**, **Baricentro** and **Kaleidon**. Technically impeccable, the performers after this experience all become appreciated sessionmen for other projects while keyboardist **Tinoco** develops a brilliant solo career of his own.
DISCOGRAPHY: HOMO SAPIENS *(1976, Movieplay).* **M.G & C.C.**

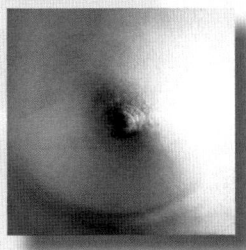

SATURNIA

Luis Simões - *guitar, sitar, theremin, vocals,* **Eduardo "M. Strange" Vasconcelos , Vasco Pereira, Francisco Rebelo** - *keyboards.*
Born in 1998 as an extraordinary complex duo of artistic research, they mainly evolve around the figure of guitarist and singer **Luis Simões** and, at first, of keyboardist **Eduardo Vasconcelos** aka 'M. Strange'. Originally meant to be a free art communal project of several artistic areas such as literature, photography, design, painting and music, the name came from the merge between the saturnia butterfly, the planet saturn and saturnalia. They record a first homonym album in 1999, after which **M. Strange** is replaced by **Vasco Pereira**, a space rock synth organist: in 2000 the duo plays live, but the keyboardist role is replaced again by **Francisco Rebelo**. Other albums of space and psychedelic prog have been published until very recently, by now considered more like **Simões** solo project.
RECOMMENDED ECORDINGS: SATURNIA *(PT, 1999)* **THE GLITTER ODD** *(Cranium, 2001).* **C.A.**

Europe: ROMANIA

FFN

Cristian Mandolciu – vocals, percussion, **Gabriel Litvin** – guitar, vocals, **Silviu Olaru** - bass, **Doru Donciu** - flute, vocals, **Florin Dumitru** – drums, **Lucian Rusu** – drums.

This is the acronym of **Formația Fără Nume** (Band Without a Name), a Romanian hard-rock and art-rock band formed in 1971 playing a typical prog from the '70s and giving particular care to the guitar riffs . Three albums all released in the second half of the '70s justify the heavy use of flute and recalls greatly names like **Jethro Tull** and **Gravy Train**. Probably the first album *Zece Pași* of 1976 is their best, more fresh and convincing also due to the good timing with which it was published.
DISCOGRAPHY: ZECE PAȘI *(1975, Electrecord)* **ZI CU ZI** *(1977, Electrecord)* **UN JOC** *(1981, Electrecord).*
M.G.

PROGRESIV TM

Harry Coradini - vocals, **Ladislau Herdina** - guitar, vocals, **Helmuth Moszbruker** - drums, **Zoltan Kovacs** - bass, **Ilie Stepan** - bass, **Stefan Péntek**- organ, **Liviu Tudan** - bass, piano, vocals, **Florin Ochescu** - guitar, **Ion Cristian** - drums, vocals, **Gheorghe Torz** - flute, **Mihai Farcal** - drums.

Unfairly penalized from a social and political situation, not suitable to host artistic innovation, this band formed in 1972 initially as **Classic XX**, managed to publish nevertheless two albums rich of original spirit and fresh energy: *Dreptul de-a visa* is their 1973 debut album, featuring skilfully composed hard-rock tunes with plenty of melody and a strong emphasis on vocal harmonies, enhanced by flute interludes somewhat reminiscent of the Italian **Delirium**. Their line-up evolves into a second release *Puterea Muzicij* four years later, with less energetic groove and more elaborate structures supporting Romanian lyrics (which don't sound too weird) through the presence of piano and, occasionally, strings. Unfortunately they disband soon afterwards.
DISCOGRAPHY: DREPTUL DE A VISA *(Electrecord, 1973)* **PUTEREA MUZICIJ** *(Electrecord, 1979).* **C.A.**

SEMNAL M

Iuliu Merca – guitar, vocals, **Stefan Boldijar** – bass, vocals, **Chita Ciolac** – keyboards, **Solomon Francisc** – drums.

Formed around 1976 by guitarist **Iuliu Merca** and bassist **Stefan Boldijar**, they rehearse through the following year publishing a single and aiming for their debut album *Trenul Cursa De Persoane Apahida* released soon in 1978 by Electrecord. Determined to conquer a larger audience, the LP contains mixed tempos of basic soft and hard rock with an almost **Doobie Brothers** aura surrounding their compositions, dominated by groovy lines, melodic solos, light psychedelic influences and a few bluesy references in a couple of tracks. They published a total of three albums before disbanding after the last in 1982. Their approach to prog- rock, although weak, holds up mostly thanks to the strong folk core. During 1991 they reunite with a completely new line-up built around original member **Iuliu Merca** for average easy-listening pop-rock.
DISCOGRAPHY: CÎHTECE TRANSILVANENE *(1979, Electrecord)* **TRENUL CURSA DE PERSOANE APAHIDA-CLUJ NAPOCA** *(1981, Electrecord)* **PLANETA VISURILOR NOASTRE** *(1982, Electrecord).* **M.G.**

SFINX

Comeliu Bibi Ionescu - bass, **Mihai Cernea** – drums, **Dan Andrei Aldea** – guitar, keyboards, vocals, **Dan Badulescu** – keyboards, **Nicolae Enache** – keyboards, **Sorin Chirifiuc** - guitar, vocals, **Doru Apreotesei** - keyboards, vocals.

Founded during the '70s by the guitarist **Dan Andrei Aldea**, the **Sfinx** became one of the most attractive bands by the prog audiences worldwide. Their first album *Lume Alba* it's an high quality pop-rock recording with Folk tastes evidenced by a gipsy violin and pleasant vocal arrangements. the following second album is the more related with Prog, in fact *Zalmoxe* is their best work that belongs to the history of symphonic rock, inspired by **Gentle Giant**, **Yes**, **Genesis** and **Pink Floyd**. The third album released during the eighties is their weakest work.
DISCOGRAPHY: LUME ALBA *(1975, Electrecord)* **ZALMOXE** *(1978, Electrecord)* **SFINX** *(1984, Electrecord).*
M.G.

Europe: RUSSIA

THE ALEATORICA ORCHESTRA

Andrey Feofanov – *guitar,* **Sergey Vasiljev** – *bass,* **Sergey Sopov** – *drums, percussion,* **Igor Sharankov** – *guitars,* **Kirill Zinovjev** – *keyboards,* **Alexandr Voronin** – *soprano saxophone ,* **Dmitry Pronin** – *lead guitar,* **Liza Feofanova** – *vocals.*
Brainchild of Boheme Music owner, guitarist and composer **Andrew Feofanova**, a short-lived Russian collective of the early '90s playing intellectual music with an only album in 1993, *Vakavilia*: nine instrumental compositions of progressive fusion with a touch of psychedelia and something subtly oriental. Remote analogies can be made with the work of **Alexey Kozlov** and **Arsenal**, as well as with **Djam Karet** of *The Devouring*. Several things stand out from the general outline, like in "March" and "Liakhn Lia" where fragments of ballet combine elements of the symphonic avant-garde with guitar jazz-rock. Extremely unusual release, listening to this large group of musicians searching for an experimental music, sometimes trespassing into new age, light mood but with rhythm resulting in a strange jazz-rock coloured with prog.
RECOMMENDED RECORDINGS: VAKAVILIA *(f Records / RDN, 1993).* **M.G.**

ALLEGRO ENSEMBLE

Nikolai Levinovsky – *keyboards,* **Alexander Fisher** – *trumpet,* **Vyacheslav Nazarov** –*Trombone,* **Igor Butman** – *saxophones,* **Victor Dvoskin** – *bass,* **Evgeni Guberman** – *drums,* **Yuri Genbachev** - *percussion.*
An intriguing jazz orchestra from the Soviet Union formed as a personal project by composer and keyboardist **Nikolai Levinovsky** in 1980, playing compositions rich of progressive sounds and animated by a truly admirable interior creativity. The first edition of his four albums (all of the first half of the '80s) are rare, and although under the Iron Curtain, they were nevertheless promoted world wide, appreciated with real interest by American and Western audiences. In fact, two of them, *In this World* and *Sphinx* were reissued on CD in America under the direct supervision of the **Levinovsky**, the both sold out very soon. He continued a prolific solo career and is to this day active on the jazz scene.
RECOMMENDED RECORDINGS: IN THIS WORLD *(Melodyia, 1981).* **M.G.**

ARIEL

Valeriy Yarushin - *bass, vocals,* **Sergej Antonov, Lev Gurov** - *guitar,* **Rostislav Gepp** - *keyboards,* **Boris Kaplun** - *drums.*
From Tchelyabinsk, somewhere near the Ural mountains, they are active from 1971 to 1974 recording at least five unknown albums of keyboard-driven folk-based music, close to that of **Pesnyary**, but with an electric sound that resulted more pop-rock with some prog elements. The 1974 self-tilted debut features the eight minutes long "Otdavali Molodu" (Given In Marriage), a truly beautiful prog-folk track. Their second LP *Russian Pictures* of 1976 is probably their most complex work, quite difficult to access without the proper folk knowledge. Three other records and a rock opera called *Masters* and dedicated to the tragic story of the builders of the most beautiful church in Moscow. Sadly, no recorded copies of it are known to exist.

DISCOGRAPHY: ARIEL *(Melodyia, 1975)* **RUSSKIE KATRINKY** *(Melodyia, 1977)* **ARIEL** *(Melodyia, 1980)* **KAZHDY DEN' TVOI** *(Melodyia, 1981)* **UTRO PLANETY** *(Melodyia, 1983)*. **M.G.**

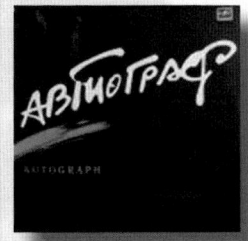

AUTOGRAPH (Autograf)

Arthur Berkut – *vocals,* **Alex Sitkovetsky** - *guitar,* **Leonid Guthin** - *bass,* **Ruslan Valonen** - *keyboards,* **Sergei Masayev** – *saxophones,* **Victor Mikhalin** – *drums.*
Formed in 1979 by **Alexander Sitkovetsky** at the end of the '70s: an art-rock band with songs (lyrics by Margarita Pushkina) rich of complex instrumental parts influenced by classical music. In 1983 the Communist Party increased censorship so they played more popular (or instrumental) music. In 1985 they participate in **Bob Geldof**'s Live Aid: this finally brings them a first official album the following year, and tours in West Europe and the US. Due to political changes they were reputed too close to the Establishment and started to lose popularity in their motherland. Trying to adapt their style to AOR (**Journey**), they recorded a US album changing name to **Autograf** to avoid confusion with the homonym American heavy-metal band. Disbanded in 1990.
RECOMMENDED RECORDINGS: AUTOGRAPH *(Melodyia, 1985).* **M.G.**

Europe: **RUSSIA**

EPOS

Alexander Stedin – *synthesizers, vocals,* **Anatoliy Molotov** – *vocals, musical director,* **Irina Nikolaitchuk** – *vocals,* **Anna Dudanova** - *vocals,* **Nikolay Ryzhov** - *percussion,* **Alexander Tsyganov** – *bass,* **Peter Akimov** – *cello,* **Tatiana Frenkel** - *violin,* **Galina Klokar** - *violin.*

Formed in 1986, their career was probably damaged by the political disaster on local culture after the end of Soviet Union. They publish a first album in 1989, *Рок-былина "Илья" (Epic-rock "Ilya")* and a second *Джордж Победоносец George Victorious* in 1991, though the first is the most representative since they were at the time seemingly unaware of a band called **Magma** and the cosmic utopia of 'Kobaia': their sound is like a vocal-heavy zeuhl concert held within a Russian Orthodox Church, steeped with Russian folk music traditions; a beautiful rock-opera with lots of classical moments and arrangements, choruses and ancient atmospheres. The bass-playing and drumming particularly as well as the repetitive chanting (in Russian) could easily be mistaken for 'Kobaian'.

RECOMMENDED RECORDINGS: **ELIJAH (Ilya)** *(Melodya, 1989, CD Boheme Music).* **M.G.**

LITTLE TRAGEDIES

Gennady Ilyin - *keyboards, vocals, programming, percussion,* **Igor Mikhel**, **Alexander Malakhovsky**- *guitars* **Yuri Skripkin** - *drums,* **Oleg Babynin** - *bass, vocals,* **Aleksey Bildin** - *saxophone, 2000-present.*

Formerly called **Pardox**, this band is formed by keyboardist and composer **Gennady Ilyin** and guitarist **Igor Mihel** in 1988 plays a form of prog art-rock without recording an album until after 1999 when they changes name. **Ilyin** travels for his studies between Germany and home, always writing material for this future project, managing a trilogy of albums around the works of the poet **Nikolay Gumilyov** (dedicated to his memory). The first two albums *Passions on Titanic* and *Porcelain Pavilion* (1st of the trilogy) are based on rhythm programming and a heavy use of analog recorded vintage synths and Hammond organ and Minimoog. *Солнце Духа (Sun of the Spirit)* and *Возвращение (Return)* are the 2nd and 3rd parts of the trilogy, the latter is finally more the product of a real symphonic-rock band, with ELP inspirations. They are still publishing and active today.

RECOMMENDED RECORDINGS: **ВОЗВРАЩЕНИЕ (RETURN** *(Musea, 2004).* **M.G.**

MARIMBA PLUS

Lev Slepner - *marimba, percussion,* **Ilya Dvoretsky** - *flute, percussion,* **Andrey Krasinikov** - *saxophones,* **Sergey Nankin** - *clarinet, vocals,* **Nikolay Solonovich** - *cello,* **Anton Chumachenko** - *bass,* **Alexander Zinger** - *drums, percussion,* **Timur Nekrasov** - *saxophones,* **Pavel Kovan** - *drums.*

Russian band active since 1999 driven by an African instrument called the marimba and playing jazz fusion world music. The band is led by the award-winning marimba player and composer **Lev Slepner**, also performing covers from **Richard Galliano, Lalo Schifrin, Horace Silver, Herbie Hancock** and **Stevie Wonder**. Their songs tell stories and paint images of eastern philosophy and African holidays, French elegance and Russian dance, *Celestial Elephants* and the Song of the Nibelungs, movie adventures and cosmic travels. Their latest project, *Flight Over the World*, is in fact about traveling the globe to pick up different musical cultures and colours.

RECOMMENDED RECORDINGS: **MARIMBA PLUS** *(2001, private pressing)* **CELESTIAL ELEPHANT** *(2007, private pressing).* **M.G.**

YURI MOROZOV

Multi-instrumentalist, composer **Yuri Morozov** is the Russian psychedelic prog-rock inventor, employed by the Soviet studios Melodija as sound-engineer, so all his over 50 albums have an enviable quality sound too. Also author, his novels were published only after the fall of the Regime. His music style is very creative and psychedelic, with great skill in handling tapes, expert of synthesizers comparable to **Hawkwind** or **Faust**, while his voice sound like **Caetano Veloso** but with the inexplicable Russian pop aspect of a blood-curdling falsetto singing. The **Hendrix** dedicated album *Вишневый Сад Джими Хендрикса (The cherry garden of Jimi Hendrix)* of 1973 is the mostly instrumental and far more acidic compilation *Земля гномов* of 1976 is better representative of his early psychedelic period. *Svad'ba kretinov* of 1976 and *In Rock* 1981 also can be singled out according to taste. He died in 2006.

RECOMMENDED RECORDINGS: **THE CHERRY GARDEN OF JIMI HENDRIX** *(Melodyia, 1973)* **SVADBA KRETINOV** *(Melodyia, 1976)* **SVET MOJ ANGEL** *(Melodyia, 1982).* **M.G.**

Europe: RUSSIA

OLEG KIREYEV
ORLAN ETHNO JAZZ BAND

Siberian saxophonist, pianist and composer **Oleg Kireyev** is the first musician in Bashkiria to practice ethnic jazz incorporating folk instruments and guttural singing techniques: he considers himself a mix of Russian, Tatar and Bashkir, influenced by the powerful heritage of bebop and traditional jazz, combined with African rhythms, Latin jazz music and Asian and Moldavian free jazz music, yet developing his own unique style paradigm. He founds his band in 1985, an ensemble oriented to the discovery of old traditions, officially indicated as world music. Their first album *Bashkir Legends* of 1989 is a masterpiece of ethnic oriented jazz with vocal experiments and the use of kurai (wind instrument) and kubyz (Jewish harp). Other cross-cultural projects include **Feng Shui Jazz Theatre**, collaborations with African musicians and **Mandala** (Jazzheads).
RECOMMENDED RECORDINGS: BASHKIR LEGENDS *(Melodyia, 1989).* **M.G.**

SEZON DOZHDEI (Rainy Season)

Boris Bardash – vocals, **Andrei Lavrinenko** – bass, **Alexei Petrov** – drums, percussion, **Maxim Pshenichny** - guitar, keyboards, flute, percussion.
A space prog-rock band born in Leningrad (St. Petersburg) in 1979, recording a first album in 1986 taht was mysteriously unpublished. After a line-up changes their debut *Return* is released in 1992 with a sound between **Pink Floyd** and **Gong**: the blurriness of mature psychedelia and the avant-garde detailed specifics of Rock In Opposition in the confluence give it a curious psychological thriller effect. A kind of progressive ethno-ambient recalling **Jade Warrior** of trans-folk psychedelic lines with distant mystical vocalizations. The second album is translated *The Album of Herbs*, a good sequel that carries the signs of a close finale: a third live album *Nostalgia* in 1997 and recorded between 1988-1989 signs their break-up probably already occurred years before.
DISCOGRAPHY: RETURN *(Boheme Music, 1992)* **THE ALBUM OF HERBS** *(Boheme Music, 1993)* **NOSTALGIA** *(SoLyd Records, 1997).* **M.G.**

DAVID TUKHMANOV

David Fedorovich Tukhmanov is a refined Russian composer, very popular in his country for arranging music for official State ceremonies during the '70s and '80s. His first album *Как Прекрасен Мир (How Beautiful Is The World)* of 1972 is a baroque prog art-pop, to put it mildly. After another album he releases in 1975 *По Волне Моей Памяти - Po Volnie Moyey Pamiaty (Sailing Through The Seas Of My Memory)* blending Russian folk to **Frank Zappa** and the early **Gong** of *Camembert Electrique*. Some songs are up to level while others feature awkward sounding female vocals of domestic popular music trying to sing with a deviation from academic standards, mixed to electric guitars and resulting in a sort of café chantant crowd-pleaser from a high-school dance of some kind. A 10 year pause and a come back in 1985, then in 2001 and 2004 for the very curious of this Eastern styled attempt.
RECOMMENDED RECORDINGS: PO VOLNIE MOYEY PAMIATY *(Melodyia, 1975).* **M.G.**

VERMICELLI ORCHESTRA

Sergey Schurakov – accordion, **Mikhail Ivanov** – bass, **Vitaliy Semenov** – drums, **Nail Kadirov** - guitars, **Maria Schurakova** – mandolin.
Brainchild of composer and accordionist **Sergei Shchurakov** (1960 - 2007), formed in 1996, the collective was in fact an extensive trial field for his polystylistic experiments with an overwhelming philharmonic instrumentation, the rhythms of rock music and a considerable ethnic component. All this is fully represented in their second album *Byzantium* of 1999: an entirely instrumental concept record that creates with ingenuity a tale based upon the ancient Byzantine Empire. Ballad-like songs such as "The Dancing Sphinx" narrated through a brisk accordion in dialog with a playful flute, or "Byzantium" with the gentle cooing of brass, spattering busts of acoustics and in the overall melodic pattern, orchestral rock splashes in the "Zakateka", where jerky guitar overtones play with virtuoso mandolin parts, flute and powerful cello.
RECOMMENDED RECORDINGS: BYZANTIUM *(Boheme Music, 1999).* **M.G.**

Europe: SPAIN

ALAMEDA

José Roca - *guitar, vocals*, **Rafael Marinelli** - *keyboards*, **Manuel Marinelli** - *keyboards*, **Manuel Rosa** - *bass*, **Luis Moreno** - *drums*.

This band from Sevilla was founded in 1977 crossing into the fertile ground of flamenco-prog with fairly good results. In 1979 they record a demo-tape in Ricardo Pachon's studio which gets them noticed by CBS Gonzalo Garcia Pelayo who signs them up for an album illustrated by **Maximo Moreno**, known for his artworks for other Spanish musicians as **Triana** and **Miguel Rios**: it remains their best and more original work with keyboards and synths blending to a gloomy latino-jazz. Between 1979 and 1983 they publish other three studio albums, the latter entitled *Noche Andaluza* also featuring flamenco player **Paco De Lucia**. The band splits in 1983 reuniting in 1994 for another three albums. The last are a live-CD, a registration from their 20th Anniversary concert in 1999 and an ultimate studio album *Calle Arriba* of 2008.
RECOMMENDED RECORDINGS: ALAMEDA (Epic, 1979) **MISTERIOSO MANANTIAL** (Epic, 1980) **AIRE CALIDO DE ABRIL** (Epic, 1981) **NOCHE ANDALUZA** (Epic, 1983). C.A.

AMAROK

Robert Santamaria - *guitars, keyboards, percussion*, **Lidia Cerón, Marta Segura, Candela Casas** - *vocals*, **Alfredo Arcusa, Manuel Sesè, Paul Zanartu, Renato Di Prinzio** - *drums, percussion*, **Joan Morera** - *violin*, **Alan Chehab** - *bass*, **Kerstin Kokocinski, Manel Mayol, Mirela Sisquella, Miguel Angel Ortin** - *horns*, **Asy Guerrero, Carlos Gallego** - *guitars*.

The name come from the Eskimo for 'wolf', a prelude for this mainly acoustic duo formed in 1994, pet project of multi-instrumentalist (and paleontologist) **Robert Santamaria** with vocalist **Lidia Cerón** (replaced by **Marta Segura** in since 2000). Their material explores new age, electronic, folk, ethnic and progressive sounds with calm keyboard sequences and **Enya**'s style vocals creating atmospheric melodies of Medieval European Minstrel: rock, jazz and world music recalling **Dead Can Dance** and the romantic rock of **Genesis** and **Camel**. The most prog of their six albums is probably *Mujer Luna* of 2002 while *Quentadharken* of 2004 is a bit more neo than purely prog.
RECOMMENDED RECORDINGS: MUJER LUNA (Musea 2002). M.G.

AZABACHE

Gustavo Ros - *keyboards*, **Jorge "Skinny" Barrall** - *bass*, **Daniel Henestrossa** - *guitar, vocals*, **Ricardo Valle** - *drums*.

Spanish band in the symphonic sub-genre with an impressive quality, borderline to neo-prog. After their participation in another project called **Azahar**, keyboardist **Gustavo Ros** and Uruguayan bass-player **Jorge 'Flaco' Barrall** aka **Skinny** join guitarist **Daniel Henestrossa** and drummer **Ricardo Valle** to form a new band in 1978, during the rise of punk and disco. They managed nevertheless to release two albums, *Dias de Luna* (Moon Days) in 1979 and *No Gracias* (No Thank You) in 1980, with a moderate success, perhaps because their sound resulted too soft for traditional prog and too challenging for the mainstream audience: their symphonic prog lacked the appropriate energy and that certain ingenious peak, although well orchestrated and with brilliant keyboards and vocal parts.
DISCOGRAPHY: DIAS DE LUNA (Movieplay, 1979) **NO GRACIAS** (Movieplay, 1980). C.A.

COTÒ EN PÈL

Carles Pico - *guitar*, **Pep Llopis** - *keyboards, vocals*, **Vicent Cortina** - *drums, percussion*, **Paco Cintero** - *bass, horn, vocals*.

An excellent Spanish one-shot band with an only album released in 1978 titled *Holocaust*. Their sound is strongly prog-related inspired by the great British artists of the '70s, with a fascinating mellotron recalling the best **King Crimson**, although some atmospheres are more influenced by **Pink Floyd**. Keyboard-driven, the **Fripp** styled guitar tends to flamenco, with breathless rhythm accelerations, languid instrumental parts and Catalan vocals in mild crescendos. They disappear quietly at the end of the '70s, although drummer **Vicent Cortina** did play with a number of Mediterranean-inflected bands, including the jazz/fusion project **Son Mediterraneo** and most recently as a member of the folk group **Al Tall**. **Pep Llopis** composed or produced some award-winning Spanish contemporary dance songs and is still active on the Spanish musical scene.
DISCOGRAPHY: HOLOCAUST (1978, Nevada). M.G.

Europe: SPAIN

CRACK

Rafael Rodriguez - *guitars*, **Alex Cabral** - *bass*, **Manolo Jimenez** - *drums*, **Alberto Fontaneda** - *guitar, flute, vocals*, **Mento Hevia** - *keyboards, vocals*.
Formed in 1978 and disbanded immediately after the publication of their only album *Si Todo Hiciera Crack* in 1980, they mix the power of rock with blazing rhythms and cutting guitars, blending the elegance of classical music with acoustic and orchestral sounds (a lot of mellotron) and adding the Mediterranean heat of the vocal parts (sung in Spanish) and a flute that inevitably recalls **Jethro Tull** with the **Genesis** romanticism (sensitive piano chords and moving Mellotron waves). A Latino-rock prog with articulated instrumental parts spread over seven tracks, all containing beautiful harmonies but with that typical Spanish climate complicating the compositions for an enthralling and emotional experience.
DISCOGRAPHY: SI TODO HICIERA CRACK *(1979, Chapa)*. M.G.

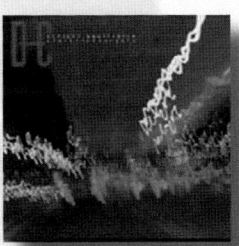

DIFICIL EQUILIBRIO

Alberto Diaz - *guitar*, **Sisco Artacho, Enric Gisbert, Joan Francisco** - *bass*, **Luis Rodriguez** - *drums*.
This Spanish ensemble formed in 1995 mixing a nervous art-rock and Canterbury jazz-fusion with a hard and psychedelic approach greatly inspired by **King Crimson** and **Soft Machine**. They debut in Barcelona playing a slightly more cutting-edged and meditated formula evolving into the elaborated futuristic heavy-prog of intricate textures (**Fripp**) of the last works. A total of seven studio albums from 1997 to 2013 for this trio (guitar, bass and drums-percussions) of powerful instrumental prog-rock, beautifully structured like in the album *Trayecto* published in 2000 or in *Simetricanarquia* of 2003.
DISCOGRAPHY: DIFICIL EQUILIBRIO *(Liquid, 1997)* TRAYECTO *(Musea, 2000)* SIMETRICANARQUIA *(Musea, 2003)* FLOOD *(Musea, 2006)*. M.G & C.C.

ERROBI

Beñat Amorena - *drums, vocals*, **Mikel Ducau** - *vocals, guitars, keyboards*, **Anje Duhalde** - *guitars, vocals*, **Mikel Halty** - *bass*.
After Franco's death in 1975, Spain started enjoying a cultural revolution: a full explosion of the progressive movement occurred in the second half of the decade in the different regions of Spain, now making obvious references to their musical traditions. One of the regions that suffered worst the Regime was the Basque province, which flooded with folk artists soon, and with a few groups that mixed folk music into the rock format: bands like **Izukaitz**, **Haizea**, **Itoiz**, **Itziar** and **Errobi** exploited this moment of cultural Renaissance, these last were playing since 1973 and finally debuted with a first album in 1975 as if just waiting for it to happen. Sumptuously prog is their work *Ametsaren Bidea* with full blown guitars and keyboards, hints of jazz cues and some **King Crimson** tints.
RECOMMENDED RECORDINGS: AMETSAREN BIDEA *(Xoxoa, 1979)*. M.G & C.C.

GALADRIEL

Jesús Filardi - *vocals, keyboards*, **Manolo Macia** - *guitar*, **Oscar Pérez** - *drums*, **Pablo Molina** - *bass*, **David Alfaro** - *keyboards*.
This sophisticated neo-prog band forms in 1976 singing both in English and Spanish, pretty much with a **Jon Anderson** style, but playing a music that recalled an interesting mix of **Yes**, **Marillion** (**Fish** era) and **Twelfth Night** (**Geoff Mann**). A soft and very well elaborated sound with dynamic changes and nice acoustic passages more similar to certain Italian prog bands like the early **PFM**, for example. *Chasing the Dragonfly* combines ethnic flavors with a very mundane '80s neo-prog. **Bautista**'s guitar mixes with skill **Howe** and **Hackett** for a blues like jazzy soul. Their last album of 2008 is unfortunately not at the same level of their previous works, with nothing new or innovative to the instrumental layers, maybe slightly more pop.
DISCOGRAPHY: MUTTERED PROMISES FROM AN AGELESS POND *(Musea, 1988)* CHASING THE DRAGONFLY *(Musea, 1992)* MINDSCAPERS *(Musea, 1997)*. M.G.

Europe: SPAIN

GOMA 2

Manuel Uhia Bea - *bass, bagpipes,* **Carlos Carballa Besada** - *drums, percussion,* **"Xerardo" González Bea** - *keyboards, bagpipes,* **J. Ramón Chouza López** - *vocals, bagpipes,* **Samuel Oonsion Piñeiro** - *guitar, bagpipes.*
This is a totally different band from the other **Goma** of 1975. Always Spanish and always with an only album, published in 1979 this time and reissued on CD in 1999, this interesting psychedelic group from Galicia play a strange kind of rock'n'roll mixed with bagpipe sounds taken from their Celtic tradition (Galicia was inherited by Spain from the Celts), singing Galician lyrics and thus trespassing into the prog genre. An exceptional band that practices a mixture of folk-progressive with some spark of psychedelia and jazz in very small doses. The song "Shadow in the night" is a slow theme with good psychedelic guitar and bagpipes that give a very interesting prog touch. Another good track, "Enough Xa!" with its traditional folk gaita and guitars. A true prog gem is "Fusion" with more than 9 minutes of very good keyboards, guitar and incursions in jazz-rock.

DISCOGRAPHY: **GOMA 2** *(LP - Private pressing, 1979, CD - Fonomusic, 1999).*   M.G.

GÒTIC

Rafael Escoté - *bass,* **Jordi Marti** - *drums, percussion,* **Jep Nuix** - *flute,* **Jordi Vilaprinyo** - *piano, keyboards.*
This Spanish symphonic band formed in 1975 by **Rafael Escote, Jep Nuix, Jordi Vilaprinyo** and **Jordi Marti** recording two albums in 1978, but releasing only one at the time. *Escenes* is a record full of light and optimistic romantic rock that gently combines the warm and relaxing sound of **Camel** with the early **PFM**, some Catalan ethnic folk and forms of fusion that recall the jazz-symphonic sound of **Chick Corea**'s keyboard (*Return to Forever*) with certain solutions closer to **Gentle Giant**. The other album stayed an unofficial bootleg for all these years and was finally published in 2016 thanks to the band itself: *Gegants I Serpentines* is a bit more typical for the fusion genre, but with flute, keyboards and guitar still as front and center pieces.
DISCOGRAPHY: **ESCENES** *(1978, Movieplay).*   M.G.

GUADALQUIVIR

Javier Mora - *keyboards,* **Louis Cobo** - *guitars,* **Andrés Olaegui** - *guitars,* **Pedro Ontiveros** - *winds,* **Larry Martin** - *drums,* **Jaime Casado** - *bass.*
Formed in 1978 by **Andrés Olaegui** and **Luis Cobo**, two veteran guitarists and long-time friends with a huge experience in Flamenco, folk and fusion, the band took its name from the largest river in that area of Spain. Even though they were in charge of writing the band's material, it was not a guitar-dominated ensemble: the solid presence of the rhythmic section and the melodic adornments delivered by flute and sax player **Pedro Ontiveros** gave them jazz-rock and world music characteristics for a Flamenco-oriented prog. In many occasions they played as opening acts for **Triana** or shared the stage with other prog bands of the time and from 1984 to this day, all ex-members played as session-men, some of them launched in prolific solo careers of their own. In 2008 the one-off 30 years concert anniversary.

RECOMMENDED RECORDINGS: **GUADALQUIVIR** *(EMI Harvest, 1978).*   M.G & C.C.

HAIZEA

Xabier Lasa - *guitars,* **Gabriel Barrena** - *bass, contrabass,* **Xabier Irondo** - *flute, acoustic guitar,* **Amaia Herrikoia** - *vocals,* **Carlos Busto** - *drums, percussion, xylophone,* **Txomin Artola** - *guitar, vocals.*
Basque progressive folk group signed up with the label Elkar, this five-piece band playing a psychedelic electric folk is composed by guitar (sometimes two), bass, drums, flute, assorted percussive objects and the captivating voice of **Amaia Herrikoia**. Both albums are very interesting: their self-titled debut of 1975 is more intimate and more **Fairport Convention**-like, while the second album titled *Hontz Gaua* is a classic free-folk prog with some Gregorian elements, a beautiful atmospheric double bass and nice female vocals, a remarkable work with compelling example short acoustic ballads related to the traditions of their land, and also a spectacular title-track of 14 minutes of mixed sounds creating a sprint of acid psychedelia.
DISCOGRAPHY: **HAIZEA** *(1975, Ioio)* **HONTZ GAUA** *(1976, Ioio).*   M.G & C.C.

Europe: SPAIN

KOTEBEL

Carlos Plaza - *keyboards, bass, percussion,* **Adriana Plaza** - *keyboards,* **Omar Acosta** - *flute, EW5,* **Carlos Franco** - *drums, percussion,* **Jaime Pascual** - *bass,* **César Garcia Forero** - *guitars,* **Carolina Prieto** - *vocals,* **Miguel Rosell Arreaza** - *cello.*

Formed in Madrid around 1999 by Venezuelan pianist and composer **Carlos Plaza**, their main structure is basically classical and symphonic (**Rachmaninoff**, **Ravel** or **Debussy**), with added influences, especially their typical fusion touch provided by piano and synthesized violin, which creates a spectacular balance between the acoustic instruments and the modern synths. After a first album titled Structures taht same year, the project becomes an actual band and from 2000 they record and publish another six good albums (the last just recently) with **EL&P** and **PFM** sonorities, but also greatly inspired by **Camel**, **The Enid**, **Hackett** and **Genesis**, all blending with the usual fusion that characterizes them and a very complex mix of Flamenco and Moorish sounds due to their provenance.

RECOMMENDED RECORDINGS: OMPHALOS (Musea, 2006). M.G. & C.C.

KOZMIC MUFFIN

Pedro Granell – *guitar, vocals,* **Enrique Otero** - *keyboards,* **Pablo Rega** – *guitars, vocals,* **Javier Vaamonde** – *bass,* **Patxi Valera** – *drums.*

They began around 1992 in Galicia when guitarist **Pedro Granell** starts to listen to blues, classical music (**Satie**, **Mussorgsky**) and the '70s prog of **King Crimson**, **Hawkwind**, **Manfred Mann**, **Soft Machine** and **Pink Floyd**. He quits the dark garage band **Eskios** (after a couple of EPs) for a more psychedelic-oriented sound he writes for himself. After meeting bassist **Javier Vaamonde** and drummer **Patxi Ortega**, both from **Balowsky**, they join forces and record *Nautilus*, published in 1994, a record that became legend in collector circles throughout Europe. After **Granell** leaves, some old songs and rearrangements, along with some new material, were used for a second album, *Space Between Grief and Comfort* (1997). Due to the new rock twist, **Gonzalez** and **Vaamonde** also leave in 1999 to form the jammy oriented **Triceratops**.

DISCOGRAPHY: NAUTILUS (Man Records, 1994) **SPACE BETWEEN GRIF AND COMFORT** (Man Records, 1997). M.G.

IBIO

Ito Luna - *drums,* **Dioni Sobrado** - *guitars,* **Lily Alegría** - *bass,* **Mario Gómez Calderón** - *keyboards,* **Adolfo Gómez Calderón** - *guitars.*

An excellent band deftly mixing equal parts of folk and symphonic prog and singing with a marked Southern European accent. This quartet from Cantabria (land of the famous Caves of Altamira) released only one LP back in 1978 before mysteriously disappearing. Despite some Italian symphonic overtones brought on by the lush keyboard work, the mostly instrumental album titled *Cuevas de Altamira* never forgets its Iberian origins through the typical Spanish melodies with a generally upbeat tempo, the strong presence of an acoustic guitar and a few but emphatic vocals (perhaps a little overwrought for some tastes). The abundance of Moog, synths and mellotron, the complex drumming and the mildly distorted and phased electric guitar make it a 100% prog.

DISCOGRAPHY: CUEVAS DE ALTAMIRA (Fonomusic, 1978). M.G.

IZUKAITZ

J.M. "Pototo" Aranburu - *bass,* **Odile Kruzeta** - *keyboards, flute, percussion, vocals,* **Fran Lasuen** - *violin, alboka, percussion, vocals,* **Aurelio Martínez** - *horns,* **Bixente Martínez** - *guitars, vocals.*

An assorted ensemble of Basque folk-ethno prog that is more world music than actual prog. The ethnic elements, medieval sounds and other fascinating tunes (flutes, Basque bagpipes, violins) with few electric instruments supported by percussion are comparable to some works by **Gryphon**, **Steeleye Span**, **Pentangle**, **Itoiz** and **Fairport Convention**. They integrate many prog elements to their sound (especially on their second album *Otsoa Dantzan*), with male and female vocalists alternately singing solo or in chorus. The local Basque instruments such as goxoak and xirula are balanced by an usual guitar/keyboard/bass set with some flute, fiddle and plenty of acoustic guitar. Their first eponymous album is instead an excellent Celtic folk work with rock tinges.

DISCOGRAPHY: IZUKAITZ (Xoxoa, 1978) **OTSOA DANZAN** (Xoxoa, 1980). M.G.

Europe: SPAIN

LISKER

Julian Alberdi - *guitar,* **Jabier Zabala** - *bass,* **Jesus Gil** - *flute,* **Ernesto Gomez** - *guitar,* **Jose Antonio Salado** - *drums.*
This quintet is one of the least ethnic sounding Basque bands, closer to **De De Lind**'s style of hard rock, offset by some delicate flute playing inspired by **Ian Anderson**. Their only, short (barely 35-minute) LP entitled *Lisker* was released in 1979 resulting in a rather open and space-rock style with this bright and melodic flute which contrasts the rougher, bluesy, scratchy guitar riffs. Although there are a couple of vocal ballads sung in Basque, the rest of the songs are mainly constellated with hard solos and some aggressive fuzzy guitar (five high quality tracks in total) with speedy rhythms which sometimes start off in delicate acoustic moments of folk, arriving to open instrumental parts where the duets/duels between guitar and flute are the absolute protagonists.
DISCOGRAPHY: LISKER (1979, Xoxoa). M.G. & C.C.

MÚSICA DISPERSA

J. Manuel Brabo – *mandolin, flute, guitar,* **Selene** – *piano, percussion, vocals,* **Josep M. Vilaseca** – *drums,* **Albert Batiste** – *bass, organ, harmonica, vocals,* **Jaume Sisa** – *acoustic guitar, vocals.*
Interesting ethnic-folk psychedelic acid-jazz band from Barcelona who debuts with an album in 1970 of avant-garde sounds, hypnotic rhythms of un-distorted electric guitars and attempts to recreate the German space-rock. Initially singer **Jaume Sisa**'s solo project, the vocal arrangements sing without real words, in contrast with the main theme, on another melody of their own, built from onomatopoeia, unintelligible canturreos, snorting and nonsensical muttering, setting the tone for an album that uses vocals as another instrument rather than as a vehicle for lyrics. In the absence, for the most part, of a traditional drum kit, the bass player binds the music together with some beautifully engaging rhythms. Various hand percussion, slaps and claps add rhythmic texture throughout.
DISCOGRAPHY: MÚSICA DISPERSA (Diabolo, 1970 - Edigsa, 1979). M.G.

OM

Toti Soler - *guitar,* **Jordi Sabatés** - *keyboards,* **Jordi Soler** - *guitar,* **Romá** - *horns,* **Doro Montaberry** - *bass,* **Josep Polo** - *drums.*
Pioneers of Catalan jazz-rock featuring very prestigious musicians like Toti Soler on guitars and Jordi Sabatés on keyboards. They publish a first poorly recorded acid-folk work in 1970 as a collaboration titled *Dioptria* as **Pau Riba acompanyat per OM**, before their homonym album in 1971 with only two tracks per side, presenting many analogies with **Soft Machine**, **Colosseum** and other similar British bands. Theirs is a sweet instrumental jazz-rock with excellent guitar work throughout, some more avant-garde tracks and hand-clapping stomping happiness. A next album *La Mariposa de la Muerte* followed before the break-up, although it has never been published yet. Soler will continue as a soloist and session man, also collaborating with **Orquestra Mirasol**.
RECOMMENDED RECORDINGS: OM (Edigsa, 1971). M.G.

OMNI

Michael Starry - *guitars, keyboards,* **Juan Rios** - *rhythm guitar,* **Jesùs Cabral** - *bass,* **Pepe Torres** - *winds,* **Alberto Märquez** - *keyboards,* **Ismael Colón** - *drums, percussion,* **Rocío Piña** - *vocals.*
The original line-up formed in 1989 as a trio with guitarists **Mike Starry** and **Salvador Velez** and **Josè Luis Algaba** on bass. Greatly inspired by the symphonic prog of **Camel** and **Genesis**, they are of course influenced by the local folk flavours of Flamenco with added middle-east sounds and latino jazz fusion. All their music is mainly instrumental in all four albums (the first is actually a selection of demos recorded between 1990 and 1993 with good jams recalling some late '70s German bands). *El Vals de Los Duendes* of 2002 is still firmly rooted in the '70s classically-oriented style with beautiful keyboards and delicate guitar parts, to really heavy bits, and even a sax. On the same line the other works after overcoming a bit of an adjustment in the line-up.
RECOMMENDED RECORDINGS: EL VALS DE LOS DUENDES (Rock Progresivo Andaluz, 2002). M.G.

Europe: SPAIN

ONZA

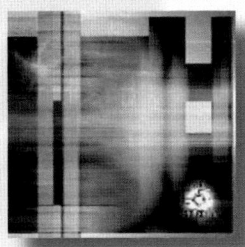

Jaime Padilla - *guitar, vocals,* **Lali Belza, Alejandro Perez** - *keyboards,* **Alfonso Romero** - *bass,* **Josè Maria Colon, David Navarro** - *drums.*
Andalusian trio active since 1989, mixing art-rock of the '70s with jazz-fusion, space-rock, new age and Spanish folk. A good debut album followed by an unexplained long pause, *Reino Rocoso* is one of the first European new prog albums from the '90s. Thirteen years later **Jaime Padilla** comes back with a new line-up publishing *Zona Crepuscolar*, presented at the Minnuendo Festival in 2004. A new last album of 2007 titled *Paradigma* containing native vocals, beautiful melodies, symphonic keyboards and rocking guitars: a compact art-rock, strongly influenced by **Pink Floyd**'s suffused sounds, characterized by modern patterns similar to other contemporary artists like RPWL and Inquire.
DISCOGRAPHY: REINO ROCOSO *(Musea, 1990)* **ZONA CREPUSCOLAR** *(Mellow Records, 2003)* **PARADIGMA** *(Margen, 2007).*   M.G.

PAN Y REGALIZ

Guillermo Paris - *vocals, flute,* **Alfons Bou** - *guitars,* **Artur Domingo** - *bass,* **Pedro Van Eeckout** - *drums, percussion.*
Mainly a **Guillermo Paris** project with musicians from the suburbs of Barcelona formed at the end of the '60s, formerly playing in a folk group called Els Mussols before changing name, first to **Aqua De Regaliz** (1969) under which they released some singles, and finally to **Pan Y Regaliz** (1971). Their homonym debut album of 1971 was reissued entitled I can fly in 1979 (making them one of the earliest Spanish rock groups to release an album under Franco's Regime, together with **Smash, OM, Musica Dispersa, Sisa, Maquina** and **Tapiman**): a work definitely inspired by the early **Jethro Tull**, the album is full of blues atmospheres and acid tunes throughout, with the psychedelic guitar of 'Muiti' **Alfonse Bou** and **Paris**'s delicate flute playing.
DISCOGRAPHY: PAN Y REGALIZ *(Reissued as I CAN FLY - Ekipo, 1971).*   C.A.

STORM

Luis Genil – *keyboards, vocals,* **Ángel Ruiz** – *guitars, vocals,* **Diego Ruiz** – *drums, vocals,* **José Torres** – *drums, vocals.*
Formed in Seville in 1969 by brothers **Angel** and **Diego Ruiz**, they released their self-titled debut only in 1974, an energetic link between late '60s psychedelic fuzz and the bluesy '70s metal sound with strong hard-prog Hammond sounds similar to **Deep Purple**. Vocals and performances are at the same level of **Atomic Rooster**, sung in English with an heavy Spanish accent. Plagued by censorship issues (which led the band to record its debut in English), the tensions grow after a second album (this time in Spanish) in 1979, *El Día De La Tormenta*, heavily criticized for dropping many of the debut's merits, and is their final work. Since the death of **Genil** in 2004, the chances of a reunion record seem slim, although the band has since reunited on stage.
RECOMMENDED RECORDINGS: THE STORM *(Basf, 1974).*   M.G.

TABLETOM

"Rockberto" **Roberto Gonzalez** – *vocals,* **Jesús** – *bass, violin,* **Pedro Ramirez** - *guitar,* **Denis** - *saxophones,* **Jose Ramirez "Pepillo"** – *flute, saxophones,* **Antonio** – *drums.*
From the hippy community of Malaga, they form around 1976, led by singer **Roberto Gonzalez** and brothers **Jose Ramirez** (flute) and **Pedro Ramirez** (guitar). The 1980 debut *Mezclalina* contains a powerful rock blues filled with fusion and outstanding vocal textures. Special guest: guitarist **Lito** with his fantastic solos and refined works. Penalized by the lack of support of label RCA, they decide to continue their career against all odds through three decades and to this very day. Initially an Andalusian version of **VDGG** minus the dark atmospheres, they make an ample use of of flutes and saxes, featuring plenty of jazzy combinations with Flamenco-styled rhythms and narcotic, psychedelic instrumentals with sporadic vocals.
RECOMMENDED RECORDINGS: MEZCLALINA *(RCA, 1979).*   M.G.

Europe: SPAIN

TARANTULA

Rafael Cabrera - *vocals*, **Emilio Santonja** - *drums*, **Manolo Peydró** - *guitar*, **Vicente Guillot** - *keyboards*, **José Pereira** - *bass*, **José Vicente** - *guitars*, **Ana María González Pazos** - *vocals*, **Enrique Alfonso Almiñana** - *vocals*, **Manuel Grau Faerna** - *guitars*, **Francisco Domingo** - *bass*, **Juan Torres** - *drums*.

A keyboard-driven quintet from the second half of the '70s led by **Vicente Guillot** supported by a good rhythm, folk elements, classical music, blues and occasional hard rock inserts. The debut of 1976 recalls the Italian Symphonic-Prog of **BMS** and **Le Orme** thanks to the dramatic voice of **Rafael Cabrera** (singing only in this first album) and the Germans **Jane** and **Ramses** for the harder-edged guitar and powerful organ runs. Their second work of 1978 comes with a line-up change and consequently losing a big part of their magic. *Tarantula 2* seems to lead to a strange kind of heavy rock and adding a female voice coupled with the new singer for a little weird touch and a dark sound recalling more **Uriah Heep**. **Vicente Guillot** is the only remaining original member.
DISCOGRAPHY: TARANTULA 1 *(Si Wan, 1976)* **TARANTULA 2** *(Si Wan, 1977)*. **M.G.**

VAINICA DOBLE

Carmen Santonia, Gloria Van Aerssen - *vocals, acoustic guitars*.
This is a female pop-prog duo from Spain made of two hippy girls **Carmen Santonia** and **Gloria Van Aerssen** who manage to merge perfectly the contemporary atmospheres of European psychedelia, totally sung in Spanish, with emotional orchestral arrangements, christian rock and children lullabies. Their activity produces three albums per decade from 1971 to 2000, when unfortunately **Carmen** dies. Their debut produced is censored at once by Franco's Regime: a wonderfully dated music with naughty goblins, a frenzied cat, a lonely girl, then a hymn against whale killing, stories about mischievous birds, a blind lover, sunny christian psych-rock tracks with bold acid guitars, an occasional scream and beatific rock & roll. "Caramelo de Limón", one of their greatest hits, is a psych-spanish-rock filled with exhilarating guitar riffs, incredible drumming and gorgeous female ha-ha-ha-ha's; "Dime Félix" has a background of female's whispering that sounds creepy and it's about a pigeon killed by a raged husband.
***RECOMMENDED RECORDINGS:* VAINICA DOBLE** *(Columbia, 1971)* **HELIOTROPO** *(Ariola, 1973)*. **M.G.**

VEGA

Tomás Vega – *guitar*, **Guty López** – *bass*, **Larry Martín** – *drums*, **Pedro Ample** - *percussion*, **Rafael Guillermo** – *keyboards*, **Jorge Pardo** - *saxophones* **Enrique Carmona** – *guitar*.
Tomàs Vega previously played with **Los Grimms** along with **Jorge Pardo**, also collaborating in a couple of **Dolores** (**Pedro Ruy Blas**) records. He founds this intense and interesting ensemble oriented towards an instrumental jazz-rock prog with powerful guitars and a sax. They release three albums between 1978 and 1981, each accompanied by a single, blending Andalusian traditional flamenco, folk and jazz with English progressive tendencies, often resulting in a colorful and rich fusion sound. The first two albums are in fact heavily drenched with flamenco-driven fusion compositions, while the last release *Sol de Oscuridad* seems to be more intended as an attempt at commercial success. The band was already in its death throes by the time the third album released.
DISCOGRAPHY: ANDALUZA *(Dro East & West, 1978)* **JARA** *(Dro East & West, 1979)* **SOL DE OSCURIDAD** *(Dro East & West, 1981)*. **M.G.**

ZEBRA

Joan Bibiloni - *vocals, guitars*, **Agustí Fernández** - *keyboards*, **Albert Candela** - *bass*, **David Walmsley** - *guitars*, **Manolo Marí** - *drums*, **Tony Anderson** - *vocals*.
A band born from the gathering of former musicians of other Spanish groups, all with different backgrounds. Their sound is based upon the outstanding guitar of **Joan Bibiloni**, with only one album release of 1976: a beautiful and very interesting work with pleasant pop music very close to progressive, and even a version of "Imagine" by **John Lennon** arranged with **Yes** influences, as **Bibiloni** plays with a **Steve Howe** style. The songs contain a typical '70s melodic rock, some reggae with Californian rock influences or garage and hard rock references, and the endless directionless 6 minutes jamming in one of the tracks. **Tony Anderson** features as special guest on vocals. A rumor says that **Jon Anderson** from **Yes** was present during the album's mixing.
DISCOGRAPHY: ZEBRA *(Private-pressing, 1976)*. **M.G.**

Europe: SWEDEN

ÄNGLAGÅRD

Thomas Johnson - *keyboards, piano,* **Jonas Engdegård** - *guitars,* **Tord Lindman** - *vocals, guitars,* **Johan Högberg** - *bass,* **Anna Holmgren** - *flute,* **Mattias Olsson** - *drums, percussion.*
Formed in 1991 by guitarist and lead vocalist **Tord Lindman** and bassist **Johan Högberg**, their symphonic rock blended **King Crimson**'s dissonances and **Genesis**' romanticism with heavy doses of mellotron and flute (**Anna Holmgren**). Although not so original (similar to the American Cathedral or the french **Shylock**), both *Hybris* and *Epilog* are yet extremely fascinating, dramatic and melancholic albums. The debut was followed by an American tour which included an appearance at the 1993 Progfest in Los Angeles. By 1994 the band had released their second and final album followed again by an appearance at Progfest: this would prove to be their final performance recorded and released in 1996 as the live requiem *Buried Alive*. **Lindman** went on to a career in the film business while the remaining members reformed briefly in 2003, but are currently on indefinite hiatus.
DISCOGRAPHY: HYBRIS *(1992, Mellotronen)* **EPILOG** *(1994, private press)* **BURIED ALIVE** *(1996, Musea).*   M.G. & C.C.

ASOKA (Taste Of Blues)

Robban Larsson - *guitars,* **Patrick Erixcon** - *vocals, bongos,* **Claes Ericsson** - *piano, hammond organ,* **Tjobbe Bengtson** - *bass,* **Daffy Bengtson** – *drums.*
Born in 1967 as the kraut-rock group called **Taste Of Blues** with the 1969 album *Schizofrenia*, a psychedelic influenced prog-blues hard-rock, with guitar, organ and English vocals. **Claes Ericsson** (organ, violin) and **Patrik Erixson** (drums) spin off into this new group with a 1971 album rich of powerful guitars, Hammond and a lot of percussions, with a good Swedish singer and lyrics full of irony ("Svensson Blues" is in a dialect). Some songs recall the latino rythms of **Santana**, others are more hard prog rock with fuzzy pre-metal sounds and some psychedelic elements added here and there, bluesy distorted guitars and over driven-bass playing and even a jazzy piano moment. The instrumental work is solid and good but nothing extraordinary, perhaps recalling **Booker T & The MGs**. In 2007 they publish 36 Years Later and another last work in 2009.
DISCOGRAPHY: ASOKA *(Sonet, 1971).*   M.G.

ATLAS

Björn Ekbom - *keyboards, piano,* **Erik Björn Nielsen** - *keyboards, piano,* **Janne Persson** - *guitars,* **Uffe Hedlund** - *bass,* **Micke Pinotti** - *drums.*
Swedish symphonic-prog group that released a single studio album in 1979 entitled *Blå Vardag* (Daily Blues) which sounds like an unreleased work from **Yes**: however they are not a clone band since they insert into their instrumental proposal the typical Swedish symphonic mood and a certain **Camel** romanticism, largely instrumental fusion passages with an emphasis on guitar and dual keyboard interplay, also compared to an instrumental version of **Genesis** and **Bo Hannson**. They disband soon after while guitarist **Janne Persson** start in 1980 a rather personal project under the name **Mosaik**, involving a couple of other band members, keyboardist **Erik Bjorn Nielsen** and bassist **Ulf Hedlund**. The 1982 record is full of folk elements and melodic symphonic rock with softer jazz and some Avant-Garde minimalism tendencies.
DISCOGRAPHY: BLÅ VARDAG *(1979, Bellatrix).*   M.G. & C.C.

BLACK BONZO

Nicklas Ahlund - *keyboards ,* **Patrick Leandersson** - *bass,* **Magnus Lindgren** - *vocals,* **Joachim Karlsson** - *guitars,* **Mike Israel** - *drums, percussion.*
Born on the ashes of hard rockers **Gypsy Sons Of Magic**, they form in 2003 proposing a music strongly rooted in the '70s, such as **Deep Purple, Uriah Heep, Jethro Tull**, but also **The Beatles, Cream, Traffic, Genesis, Gentle Giant**, and using only vintage instruments for the charming debut of 2004. Their art-prog album *Lady of the Light* of 2004 adds depth to their style through the mellotron, piano and Hammond organ, with an intense drumming, the intricate guitar work, the firm but steady bass lines, the complex song structures and their vocalist (who sounds like **David Byron**), a mix greatly recalling **Uriah Heep**. Another two albums close the century with no real novelty.
RECOMMENDED RECORDINGS: LADY OF THE LIGHT *(B&B, 2004).*   M.G. & C.C.

Europe: SWEDEN

BLÅKULLA

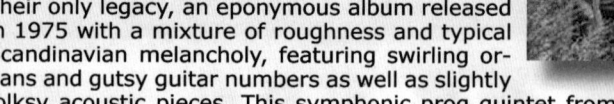

Dennis Lindegren - *vocals*, **Mats Öhberg** - *guitar*, **Bo Ferm** - *organ, piano*, **Hannes Råstam** - *bass*, **Tomas Olsson** - *drums*.

Their only legacy, an eponymous album released in 1975 with a mixture of roughness and typical Scandinavian melancholy, featuring swirling organs and gutsy guitar numbers as well as slightly folksy acoustic pieces. This symphonic prog quintet from Gothenburg sing in Swedish, greatly inspired by the hard blues rock of **Cream** and **Deep Purple**, with the hard riff guitar reminiscent of **Steve Howe**, but more fuzzy and distorted, the acoustic phrases of folk taste, well supported by the warm sound of organ and piano recalling **Yes** or **Rick Wakeman**. In 1997 a cd version was finally made available with three previously unreleased demos from 1974 added, featuring the harder, more blues-oriented material of their early days for a heavy vintage Swedish prog.
DISCOGRAPHY: **BLÅKULLA** *(1975, Anette).*   M.G. & C.C.

ENERGY

Alvaro Is - *keyboards*, **Amedeo Nicoletti** - *guitars*, **Björn Inge** - *drums*, **Bosse Norlén** - *bass*, **Luis Adugdo** - *slagverk*.

Formed from the ashes of the hard rock group **November** (1969/72), this heavy fusion incarnation is a spin off of drummer **Björn Inge**, heavily influenced by bands like **Inner Mounting Flame**, **Between Nothingness** and **Mahavishnu Orchestra** performing a very strong jazz-rock. Featuring Spanish keyboard master **Alvaro Is** (later in Iceberg), their only album of 1974 is contaminated by various elements, touching the tunes preferred by the German kraut-rock, with short trespassing into Latino and fusion themes.
DISCOGRAPHY: **ENERGY** *(Harvest, 1974).*   C.A. & C.C.

ENSEMBLE NIMBUS

Hakan Almkvist - *guitars, bass, vocals*, **Hasse Bruniusson** - *percussion*, **Kirk Chilton** - *violin*, **Lars Bjork** - *horns*, **Stefan Karlsson**, **Tomas Bodin** - *keyboards*.

An unconventional music quartet (keyboards, clarinet, viola and percussions) created in 1992 by two great Swedish musicians, **Hakan Almkvist** and **Hasse Bruniusson** (ex-**Zamla Mammaz Manna**) on drums, great RIO performers with a debut album in 1994. Sided among those artists like **Univers Zero**, **Etron Fou** e **Art Zoyd**, although the Scandinavia's orchestral-grade progressive-rock has a brighter approach, they are open to the East and to free jazz: the other side of Swedish new prog. **Almkvist** is also active with his ethnic music in **Orient Squeezers** and **In The Labyrinth** while **Bruniusson** is also a member of **Roine Stolt**'s The Flower Kings.
DISCOGRAPHY: **KEY FIGURES** *(APM, 1994)* **SCAPEGOAT** *(TAP, 1998)* **GARMOMBOZIA** *(TAP, 2000).* M.G.

FLOWER KINGS

Roine Stolt - *guitar, vocals*, **Tomas Bodin** - *keyboards*, **Michael Stolt** - *bass*, **Hasse Fröberg** - *vocals, guitar*, **Jaime Salazar** - *drums*, **Hasse Bruniusson** - *percussion*.

Formed in 1993 by **Roine Stolt** (former guitarist of **Kaipa**), for a first symphonic prog solo album of 1994 called *The Flower King*, after which they consolidates into a real band and publish the following year their debut as such: *Back in the World of Adventures*, recalling **The Moody Blues**, **Genesis**, **Jethro Tull** and **Yes**, borrowing ideas but not music, closer to neo-prog. A very prolific discography full of interesting works (*Retropolis, Stardust We Are, Unfold the Future*) or more boring albums (*Space Revolver, The Rainmaker, Adam & Eve*). In 1999 Stolt is replaced by **Jonas Reingold** for the 2000 album *Space Revolver*.
RECOMMENDED RECORDINGS: **THE FLOWER KING** *(1994, Foxtrot,);* **RETROPOLIS** *(1996, Foxtrot)* **STARDUST WE ARE** *(1997, Foxtrot)* **UNFOLD THE FUTURE** *(2002, Inside Out).* M.G.

Europe: **SWEDEN**

GROVJOBB

Jerry Johansson - *guitars*, **Jesper Jarold** - *bass*, **Ola Wolfhechel Jensen** - *drums*, **Simon Krarup Jensen** - *flute*.

Formed in the summer of 1995 playing a mix between Swedish folk music and progressive jazz-rock, with spacey psychedelic influences. Their first record of 1998, *Landet Leverpastej*, is in fact a particular mix of psychedelia, Nordic folk, symphonic prog, soft jazz and '70s sounds. On the same line the following two albums both out one year after the other. Of their three records their second *Vättarnas Fest* is probably the best with the instrumental psychedelic and progressive folk, a prominent flute (like a Swedish version of **Jethro Tull**) and an eastern-influenced 19 minute long suite. A more meditative music with deep roots in India for they don't have keyboards: the only instruments are guitar, drums, flute, bass and an occasional sitar.
RECOMMENDED RECORDINGS: VÄTTARNAS FEST *(Garageland Records, 1999)*. **M.G. & C.C.**

IBIS

Gösta Nilsson - *piano*, **Island Östlund** - *drums*, **Olle Nilsson** - *guitar*, **Tommy Johnsson** - *bass*.

Started out in a previous band called **Vildkaktus** mixing rock with jazz and folk and some similarities to **Traffic**, they release three albums before disbanding in 1972. On these ashes the musicians start the new project with a self-titled debut released in 1974. The more jazzier direction recalling **Soft Machine** (after **Wyatt**) and the soft atmospheres of **Mahavishnu Orchestra**, with symphonic inserts and traces of the Canterbury scene as well, in both albums published as *Ibis*. During the publications, sax player **Ed Epstein** also collaborates to **Kornet**'s album *Fritt Fall* while after the disbandment some members join the avant-garde jazz group **Bitter Funeral Beer Band**.
RECOMMENDED RECORDINGS: IBIS *(Ljudspår, 1974)*. **M.G. & C.C.**

IN THE LABYRINTH

Peter Lindahl, Hakan Almkvist - *sitar, guitars, percussion, horns, keyboards*. **Mikael W. Gejel** - *guitars, horns*. **Karin Langhard-Gejel, Ulf Hansson, Fareidoum Nadimi** - *percussion*, **Kirk Chilton, Micke Lövroth** - *violin*.

Alchemist of images and sounds (their album covers illustrate woods, fires and trees with gnomes), finest sitarist, hippy hermit of the Swedish forests, this is an experimental musical project of **Peter Lindahl** in which he channels his interior world as a modern evolution of the magical acid-folk influenced by the **Incredible String Band**. Three albums sometimes predictable and similar to each other, of which *Dryad* is a lesson of progressive-folk, mixing styles to create a symbiosis almost like the early **Pink Floyd**, with classical and oriental overtones. Mystery and melancholy, often broadened by rich arrangements that feature diverse instrumentation and sometimes vocals, with an emphasis on beauty: it took almost eight years to create this little masterpiece.
DISCOGRAPHY: THE GARDEN OF MYSTERIES *(APM, 1994)* **WALKING ON CLOUDS** *(TAP, 1999)* **DRYAD** *(TAP, 2002)*. **M.G. & C.C.**

LIFE

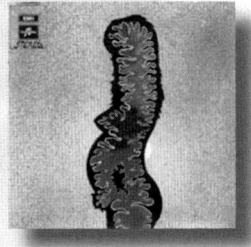

Anders Nordh - *guitar, piano, bass, vocals, synthesizer*, **Paul Sundlin** - *bass, piano, vocals, electric piano*, **Thomas Rydberg** - *drums*.

Formed in 1970 by **Tomas Rydberg, Anders Nordh** and **Paul Sundlin**, the last two formerly in a band called **Trolls**, they are inspired by **Tear Gas** and **Leafhound** for a hard prog rock sang in a clean and traditional way mixing hard blues, jazz, beat and psychedelia with some references to **The Moody Blues**, **Procol Harum** and **Mecky Mark Man**. Their 1970 debut album origin was in Swedish and prepared for the next year in an English version. They disband in 1972 as the members converged in other minor bands, not always linked to the prog. 34 years later the reunion for a concert with a new line-up and a new album titled *After A Life*, finally released in 2014.
RECOMMENDED RECORDINGS: LIFE *(EMI - Columbia, 1970)*. **M.G. & C.C.**

Europe: SWEDEN

MYRBEIN

Janders Lönnkvist - *drums, xylophone, vocals*, **Bo "Bosse" Lindberg** - *guitar, trumpet, organ, vocals*, **Johan von Sydow** - *bass, trombone*, **Mats Krouthén** - *keyboards, clarinett, vocals*.

Formed in 1977 as a **King Crimson** cover band, the trio called 'ant leg' was technically excellent, yet their only release *Myrornas Krig* (the ants' war) of 1981 is an album that does not represent their value: the best moments in fact are the pure instrumental parts not manipulated in studio, with excellent horns (**Henry Cow**, **Wasa Express**, **Samla Mannas Manna**), albeit too obsessive, unquiet and deliberately ironic and humorous, constantly between the jokes and the more mature avant-garde experiments, bizarre and unconventional sense and silly, frenzied vocals. A Scandinavian cocktail of fuzz guitar, electric piano, organ, bass and drum, with the occasional saxophone or clarinet, their compositions are the result of a collective process of complex arrangements, quirky mood turnabouts and changing time signatures, the music never stays long in one place.

DISCOGRAPHY: MYRORNAS KRIG *(LFM, 1981)*. C.A. & C.C.

KUNDALINI

Arne Jonasson - *guitars, bouzouki, saz, cümbüs, nyckelharpa, mey, zurna, näverlur, etc...* **Patrick Sundqvist** - *drums, percussion*, **Gunna Olofsson** - *bass*.

Created as a showcase for the fusion of multi-instrumentalist **Arne Jonasson**, known for his psychedelic space-rock group **Holy River Family Band**, along with drummer Patrik Sundqvist and bassist **Gunnar Olofsson**, they release a jazz-prog rock instrumental album in 1997 titled *Asylum For Astral Travellers*. Twenty short tracks of good fusion electro-acoustic flavors created by guitars, bouzouki, sax, horns and other ethnic instruments over fresh rhythms where oriental sounds and dreaming melodies are the mainstream. Another good record of 1999 titled *Luminous Morning* was published by **Jonasson** and **Sundqvist** as the duo **Chameleon**.

DISCOGRAPHY: ASYLUM FOR ASTRAL TRAVELLERS *(1996, Mellow Records)*. M.G. & C.C.

PAATOS

Stefan Dimle - *bass*, **Reine Fiske** - *guitars*, **Huxflux Nettermalm** - *drums, percussion*, **Petronella Nettermalm** - *vocals, cello*, **Johan Wallen** - *keyboards*, **Peter Nylander** - *guitar*.

In 1999 **Landberk** guitarist **Reine Fiske** is asked to play with the famous Swedish folk rock singer **Turid** and chooses to team up with band mate **Stefan** together with **Ricard** and **Johan** from **Agg**. The creation of a new band is the natural consequence. **Turid** contributes with a song called "Tea", recorded live in studio along with "Perception" and issued in 2001. Then they compose and perform live the music to the silent movie *Nosferatu* for a one and a half hour long event, before finding time to record the modern jazz-rock debut *Timeloss*, four elegant tracks with soft tunes and northern atmospheres. *Kallocain* and *Silence of Another Kind* are more direct, full of feeling with an involving and bright groove. The band is still releasing and active.

RECOMMENDED RECORDINGS: TIMELOSS *(2002, Stockholm Records)* **KALLOCAIN** *(2004, Inside Out)* **SILENCE OF ANOTHER KIND** *(2006, Inside Out)*. M.G. & C.C.

PANDORA

Björn Malmquist - *bass*, **Peter Hjelm** - *vocals*, **Åke Rolf** - *guitar*, **Jan-Erik Dockner** - *piano, keyboards*, **Leif Hellquist** - *guitar*, **Bertil Jonsson** - *drums*.

Formed in 1971 and from Norrkoping, Sweden, by drummer **Bertil Jonsson** and guitarist **Urban Gotling**, they release an album in 1974 titled *Measures Of Time*. The music is well played, with symphonic touches recalling **Beggar's Opera**, **Genesis**, **Camel**, **Gracious** and **Cressida**, with nice keyboards and a pleasant English singing overall. The whole album holds good quality levels, with well structured songs, compelling instrumental parts lead by a Moog and electric guitars, fascinating melodic tunes and interesting jazz-rock inserts. They held good concerts also as opening act for **Kaipa** and **Trettioariga Kriget**. The band disbands around 1981 for different reasons and disagreements between the musicians (some had already left for other musical realms).

DISCOGRAPHY: MEASURES OF TIME *(1974, SMA)*. M.G. & C.C.

Europe: SWEDEN

PANTA REI

Thomas Arnesen - *guitars, keyboards, percussion,* **Leif Östman** - *guitars, percussion,* **Cary Wihma** - *bass, percussion,* **Tomo Wihma** - *drums, percussion,* **Georg Trolin** - *vocals, percussion,* **Göran Freese** - *saxophones, percussion,* **Gunnar Lindqvist** - *flute.*
Swedish psychedelic-prog and space-rock band that released one fantastic self-titled album in 1973 which features a eye catching cover that still manages to scandalize despite the passing of over four decades. Full of tripped out and blistering fuzz guitar, the jazzy flair is completed by flutes, saxophone and various percussion and drumming. A one shot album with strong hippy tastes released by Harvest with great instrumental parts for five long tracks that seem coming from a typical American acid jazz-rock jamming at the end of '60s. Complex textures and atmospheres, today described as music for busted minds, for a lot of improvisation, full exposure of the Flower Power philosophy through some quite modern solutions for the time.
DISCOGRAPHY: PANTA REI *(Harvest, 1973).*   C.A.

RESAN

Anders Nordh - *guitars, keyboards, vocals,* **Hasse Jonsson** - *guitar, vocals,* **Lasse Finberg** - *guitar,* **Marion Noel** - *flute vocals,* **Benny Svensson** - *keyboards,* **Paul Sundlin** - *bass, keyboards, vocals,* **Stefan Höglund** - *bass,* **Thomas Rydberg** - *drums, vocals,* **Pelle Holm** - *drums, percussion, vocals.*
Formed in 1973 on the ashes of the hard rock band **Life**, they quickly turn into dreamy cosmic pieces and the general sense of psychedelia, sung in Swedish. The turbulent late '60s create a musical phenomenon that swept all over Europe, and in Stockholm specifically it gave rise to a Flower Power counterculture: *Resan* (the trip) was surprisingly released on the Swedish CBS subsidiary label Epic with a cover clearly adhering to the exciting life of a typical Hippy community and the album represents a unique and almost hidden part of the most intellectually stoned psychedelic Swedish history: a blissful but at times dark atmosphere of full electric instrumentation, perfect but peculiar mix of preaching hippy-naivety rooted in the early '70s. Reissued as limited edition on vinyl in 2012.
DISCOGRAPHY: RESAN *(LP Epic 1973, Subliminal Sounds, 2012).*   M.G.

SAGA

Christer Stålbrandt – *vocals, bass,* **Kenny Bülow** – *guitar, vocals,* **Mats Norrefalk** - *guitar, vocals,* **Sten Danielsson** – *drums,* **Sylvia Olin** - *piano,* **Björn Isfält** - *cello,* **Christer Eklund** – *saxophone.*
Hard and heavy prog rock band, with delicate instruments like horns and strings, founded in 1973, when the best prog from the worldwide scenes was almost exhausted: their only album suffers the comparison to the bigger bands also damaged by futile lyrics supported by the melodramatic and pompous vocals. Sounding like a more psychedelic prog version of **November**, with emphasis on creating Nordic-styled atmospheres and mixing different influences like fusion, folk and blues, the album lacks consistency because every track has a different style. Instrumental moments feature some decent to good guitar parts, the folkier cello, the jazzy sax lines, acoustic textures and electric explosions which all result in an incoherent musical proposal. They disband soon after the release.
DISCOGRAPHY: SAGA *(Sonet, 1974).*   M.G.

THE SPACIOUS MIND

Jens Unosson – *keyboards, tape effects vocals,* **Henrik Oja** – *guitars, percussion, vocals,* **Thomas Brännström** -*guitars, e-bow, winds, vocals,* **David Johansson** – *drums, percussion.*
Together since 1991, they have become famous as one of the world's leading psychedelic bands greatly inspired by the acid haze of the San Francisco ballrooms of the late '60s. Their 1993 first album, *Cosmic Minds at Play*, is a very brilliant and charming debut, with long pieces and explosive jams similar to **Hawkwind** for a psychedelic space-rock with **Pink Floyd** atmospheres and kraut rock inserts: the twin guitars battle over a steady drum and bass background, while the atmospheric keyboards swirl in and out of the mind, creating melancholic tapestry of sounds delivering the message of Love. A prolific discography of 14 albums, the recent last in 2014.
RECOMMENDED RECORDINGS: COSMIC MINDS AT PLAY *(Garageland, 1993).*   M.G. & C.C.

Europe: SWEDEN

SPLASH

Christer Holm - *horns,* **Christer Jansson** - *guitars, violin, vocals,* **Gösta Rundqvist** - *keyboards,* **Håkan Lewin** - *flute, saxophones,* **Jan Erik Westin** - *drums,* **Kaj Söderström** - *bass, vocals,* **Leif Halldén** - *horns,* **Lennart Löfgren** - *horns,* **Henrik Hildén** - *drums,* **Thomas Jutterström** - *keyboards, violin, vocals,* **Torbjörn Carlsson** - *flute, saxophones.*
This jazz-rock group from Söderhamn was active from 1969 to 1979, with several band members met as being part of a pop band called **Why**. By 1973 they released a first album and stabilized the line-up which lasted up to the end of '70s, evolving their sound into longer and more instrumental compositions contaminated by a fusion genre influenced by folk music, resulting in a psychedelic prog with a strong use of horns arrangements (saxophones, trumpet and trombones) bearing interesting and original ideas that sounded as if Chicago were playing after coming from a very trippy party. Three good albums from this decade that never achieved a true commercial success. For some time they even had their own record label called Splash Records.
DISCOGRAPHY: UT PÅ VISHAN *(Polydor, 1971).* M.G.

TWIN AGE

Johan Hansson - *vocals,* **Carl Johan Kilborn** - *keyboards,* **Jörgen Hanson** - *drums,* **John Löwenadler** - *guitars,* **Petter Pettersson** - *bass.*
Strongly influenced by the music of **King Crimson** with some neo-prog traits, the vocals recall **Gabriel**'s singing with the symphonic keyboards of **Genesis** and **Hackett** guitar licks as in their

first 1996 album *Month of the Year*, where the good romantic textures of guitars and keyboards look back but with a modern and updated sound. Great melodies and fairly complex arrangements which also recall **Manticore** or **I.Q.** (vocals) and the early **Marillion** symphonic splashes. Their neo-prog continues in the following *Lialim High*, a good sequel with a more refined and inspired ideas. The third *Moving the Deckhairs* is not at the same level.
DISCOGRAPHY: MONTH OF THE YEAR *(1996, Altair Music)* **LIALIM HIGH** *(1997, Altair Music)* **MOVING THE DECKHAIRS** *(2000, Record Heaven).* M.G.

UNICORN

Peter Edwinzon – *keyboards, vocals,* **Anders Måreby** – *guitars, cello, vocals,* **Dan Swanö** – *lead vocals, drums, percussion,* **Frida Bergström** - *vocals,* **Tom Nouga** – *bass, saxophones.*
Not to be confused with the '70s British band produced by **David Gilmour**, this is one of **Dan Swanö**'s projects (other band names like **Edge of Sanity**, **Nightingale**, **Bloodbath**, **Pan.Thy.Monium**, **Karaboudjan**). He also released an outstanding pop-prog solo album titled *Edge of Sanity*, influenced by **Marillion** and **IQ**. It is hard to believe that a dedicated metal-head like **Dan** would found a neo-progressive rock band: along with guitarist **Anders Mareby** they initially were called **Ghost**, then **Icarus** and from 1987 as **Unicorn** they publish 4 demos until 1992, all exceptional in terms of quality (*The Weirdest of Tales, A Collection of Worlds Pt. 1 & 2* and *After Before*). Their debut album comes in 1993 along with other works of mature neo-prog.
RECOMMENDED RECORDINGS: EVER SINCE *(1993, Mellow Records).* M.G.

VILDKAKTUS

Gösta Nilsson - *piano,* **Island Östlund** - *drums,* **Olle Nilsson** - *guitar,* **Tommy Johnsson** - *bass.*
Formed in 1970, this band from Stockholm plays a rock genre mixed to jazz and folk with some similarities to **Traffic**. Their best album *Vindarnas Vägar*, is almost the twin of the contemporary *The Yes Album* by **Yes**, though side B side reveals an extraordinary haunting jazz-rock closer to the early **Nucleus**, and tripped out

ethnic-rock jams filtered by the cultural Scandinavian tradition that gives them their peculiar sound. The first two albums feel like a Swedish **Crosby Stills and Nash**, with some jazzy sections and Swedish lyrics. Three albums of which the last recorded in 1972 and released in 1974, a year after the disbandment, when they had already moved on and into a band called **Ibis**.
DISCOGRAPHY: VINDARNAS VÄGAR *(Polydor, 1971)* **NATTEN** *(Polydor EFG, 1972).* M.G.

Europe: SWITZERLAND

AGAMEMNON

Urs Ritter – *drums,* **Erich Kuster** – *vocals, guitar, organ,* **Walter Rothmund** – *bass, keyboards,* **Werner Kuster** – *keyboards, guitar, flute.*
A Swiss band from the German canton with one original LP privately released, recorded in 1981. A traditional sound rooted between the '60s and the '70s, for a keyboard dominated space, psychedelic prog full of symphonic elements and kraut recalling **Pink Floyd** and **Procul Harum**. The English lyrics are about the life of Greek hero **Agamemnon**, divided into two long suites with very dark keyboards and organ similar to the work of **VDGG**, or reminiscent of **Minotaurus**, **Epidaurus** and in some parts **Kyre Eleison**. The singer instead has a voice close to **Cat Stevens**'.
RECOMMENDED RECORDINGS: AGAMEMNON PART I & II *(Private pressing, 1981).*   M.G. & C.C.

CLEPSYDRA

Aluisio Maggini - *vocals,* **Gabriele Hofmann** - *guitar,* **Philip Hubert** - *keyboards,* **Pietro Duca** - *drums,* **Andy Thommen** - *bass.*
Excellent neo-prog band active from 1989 with four records greatly inspired by English bands such as **IQ**, **Fish**-era **Marillion** and **Pendragon**. The outstanding voice of **Aluisio Maggini** singing in English recalls **Deyss** also for the timber assonance. *More Grains of Sand* is a very typical melodic rock but the third album of 1997 titled *Fears* is probably their best, oriented to modern sounds with a large use of the keyboards. The line-up features a guitarist change from **Hofmann** to **Marco Cerulli**, but the sound maintains its style with the bass and the dynamic drumming and some stunning guitar playing.
RECOMMENDED RECORDINGS: FEARS *(Private pressing, 1997).*   M.G. & C.C.

DOCMEC

Louis Crelier – *vocals, keyboards, flute,* **Olivier Vuille** – *bass, vocals,* **Dominique Bettens** – *guitars,* **Jean-Philippe Amadruz** – *drums.*
Another one-shot band represented by a symphonic rock album that sounds like a prog soup of ingredients stolen from the most famous albums of this genre (**Genesis**, **Pulsar**, **Yes**): *Objet Non Identifié* was released in 1976 and probably recorded partially in a local university due to the poor production, while the other side was properly done in studio and recalls the **Ange** fairy-tale atmospheres with sweet and melancholic atmospheres and a bit of **Jethro Tull**. English lyrics delivered by strong vocals supported by piano and synthetic strings, numerous Moog synth leads, a sparkling guitar and the very heavy bass playing.
DISCOGRAPHY: OBJET NON IDENTIFIE *(Private pressing, 1976).*   M.G.

DRAGONFLY

René Bühler - *vocals, percussion,* **Markus Husi** - *keyboards,* **Marcel Ege** - *guitars,* **Klaus Mönnig** - *bass,* **Beat Bösiger** - *drums.*
Formed around 1974 by school mates **Markus Husi** (**Yes**, **Genesis** and **ELP** fan) and **Marcel Ege** (strongly influenced by **Hendrix**, **Deep Purple** and **Santana**), by 1975 **Briggitta Fischer** had joined providing band name and lyrics to their instrumentals. In 1978 the line-up consolidates and they release their one and only self titled release that can be described as a classic symphonic prog with strong hard rock edges and a hint of Italian symphonic influence like from **PFM**. A late '70s sound, prelude to new-prog, with a large employ of keyboards (Hammond organ, synthesizer, Honer clavinet, piano) and a **Hackett** guitar style. Reissue on CD with two high quality bonus-tracks.
DISCOGRAPHY: DRAGONFLY *(1982, Highfly).*   M.G.

Europe: **SWITZERLAND**

ERTLIF

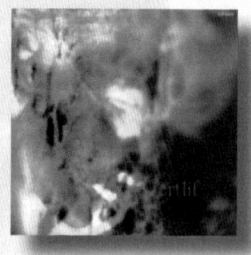

Danny Andrey - *guitars*, **Teddy Riedo** - *bass*, **James Mosberger** - *keyboards*, **Hanspeter "Bölle" Börlin** - *drums, percussion*, **Richard John Rusinski** - *vocals*.
Born in 1970 by **Andrey** and **Riedo** from **Egg&Bacon**, the band records in 1972 their debut over only three days, for a good mix of pop, psychedelic rock and gloomy progressive-garage recalling **Rare Bird**, **Uriah Heep**, **The Moody Blues**, **Pink Floyd**, **Procol Harum** and **Toad**. The song "Classical Woman" is very symphonic and emotional with beautiful organ arrangements and a surreal kind of psychedelic rhythms. In 1973 they record the song "Plastic Queen" and in 1978 they disband reappearing later in 1993 with a line-up change and the new studio album *Illusion* of 2001 (*Relics from the Past: Unreleased Recordings 1974-1975* was recently issued).
RECOMMENDED RECORDINGS: ERTLIF (Tell Record, 1972).

M.G. & C.C.

EXIT

Andy Schmid - *guitar, vocals, harmonica*, **Edwin Schweizer** - *bass*, **Roman Portail** - *keyboards*, **Kafi Kaufmann** - *drums, percussion*.
Formed 1972, they produced only a homonym album in 1975, with a limited edition of 350 copies. Their sound is similar to others of the same region with roots in American psychedelic rock, recalling sometimes The **Doors** or **The Yardbirds**, with a more kraut taste, generating a sort of psychedelic symphonic uniqueness through the decidedly interesting keyboards. The static singing, not perfectly in tone, in fact, probably derives by having recorded in just a few days on a simple cassette tape: a Swiss space-prog close to **Eloy** and **Grobschnitt**, but more amateurish.
RECOMMENDED RECORDINGS: EXIT (Boing Records, 1975 - Black Rills, 2008).

M.G. & C.C.

GALAAD

Pierre-Yves Theurillat - *vocals*, **Gianni Giardiello** - *keyboards*, **Sebastien Froidevaux** - *guitars*, **Gerard Zuber** - *bass*, **Laurent Petermann** - *drums, percussion*.
Formed in 1988 and led by charismatic singer **Pierre-Yves Theurillat**, they release a self-titled demo in 1991 for an official debut later the following year: *Premier Fevrier* is a compelling classic symphonic prog album closer to new prog with its majestic keyboards. The French vocals gives a theatrical touch to the music recalling **Ange**. The songs are of full of shifting moods, aggressive singing, complex rhythms, impressive and slightly distorted guitar playing, fantastic Moog lines, beautiful pastoral flute and piano duets. *Vae Victis* is a just as good and almost diverting to a more techno prog-metal.
DISCOGRAPHY: PREMIER FÉVRIER (1992, Musea) **VAE VICTIS** (1996, Here We Go, issued as Cd only in Japan).

M.G. & C.C.

KROKODIL

Hardy Hepp - *vocals, piano, violin*, **Düde Dürst** – *vocals, drums, percussion*, **Walty Anselmo** – *sitar, lead guitar, vocals*, **Terry Stevens** – *bass, guitars, vocals*, **Mojo Weideli** – *harmonica, flute, percussion*.
German-Swiss band with **Terry Stevens** coming form England, they form in 1969 as a rock-blues group regarded as the Swiss version of the **Groundhogs** (due to their first album). Already from the 2nd work they begin to insert a slight psychedelic-prog into their sound, very much dominant on the next, *Invisible World Revealed*, with mellotron, organ, harmonica and flute all backed up by an acoustic guitar completed by the exotic and stoned feel of eastern and Indian influences introduced by sitar and tabla. They disband in the mid '70s issuing some unpublished archival works thereafter.
RECOMMENDED RECORDINGS: AN INVISIBLE WORLD REVEALED (United Artists, 1971).   M.G.

Europe: SWITZERLAND

PACIFIC SOUND

Chris Meyer - *vocals*, **Mark Treuthardt** - *guitar, bass*, **Diego Lecci* - *drums*, **Roger Page** - *keyboards*.
Tripped out bluesy-krautrock band from Switzerland formed in 1970, relatively unknown due to the short career: this quartet recorded one album called *Forget Your Dream* in 1971 for a stoned, propulsive sound including heavy psychedelic guitars and crazy Hammond organs. An aggressive pop with strong acid hard blues rich of fuzz and distortion generating heterogeneous pieces, passing from simple rock'n'roll ("Drive my Car") to the blues keyboard of "Gates of Hell". Recently re-issued on CD with bonus tracks. Their heavy accented English vocals and the poor recording penalize its already weird style.
DISCOGRAPHY: FORGET YOUR DREAM! *(Splendid, 1972).* M.G.

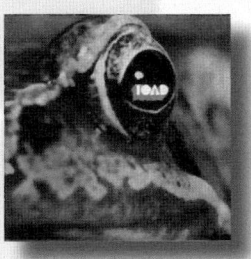

TOAD

Benj Jäger - *vocals*, **Vic Vergeat** - *guitars*, **Werner Froelich** - *bass*, **Cosimo Lampis** - *drums*.
Formed in 1970 with **Cosimo Lampis** from the band **Brainticket** and **Vittorio 'Vic' Vergeat** from **Hawkwind**, this Italian-Swiss project published in 1971 their art-rock debut album, including a highly guitar driven sound with lots of heavy psychedelic rock elements and blues influences recalling **Led Zeppelin** and **Deep Purple**. *Tomorrow Blue* is more elaborate and thanks to the presence of the violin, it has a more mature and versatile style. *Dreams* is not far from the last things from **Atomic Rooster**. They reunite in 1993 for a brand new album entitled *Stop this Crime*, reissued with a different title (*Hate To Hate*) after their disbandment in 1995. And again, a 1994 concert published years later in 2006 with alternate versions of early tracks from **Toad**'s career, a few of which appeared on their debut album.
RECOMMENDED RECORDINGS: TOAD *(Halleluiah, 1971)* **TOMORROW BLUE** *(Halleluiah, 1972).* M.G.

WELCOME

Bernie Krauer - *keyboards, vocals*, **Tommy Stebel** - *drums, percussion, acoustic guitar, vocals*, **Francis Jost** - *bass, vocals*.
Formed in 1975, this keyboard-driven band features the analogic sounds of **Krauer**, former **Landscape** musician. As a trio they record a first homonym album with very similar and typical **Yes** sonorities, characterized by sometimes wavering vocal harmonies, heavy mellotron and Hammond parts and rather sparse guitar work. They hold some live shows in the attempt of promoting it but with no real success. Bassist **Francis Yost** is replaced by **Helmi Erdinger** and they issue a less good 1978 work, *You're Welcome*, with still an excellent suite. The band reportedly records a third album in the late '70s but this was never released. They disband in 1981.
RECOMMENDED RECORDINGS: WELCOME *(EMI, 1976).* M.G.

YOLK

Markus Furst, Rémi Sträuli - *vocals, drums, keyboards*, **Beat Burkhardt** - *bass*, **Chasper Wanner, Willi Riechsteiner** - *guitars*, **Stefan Hugi, Thomas Moser** - *horns*.
Not to be mistaken with the French homonym band, this Swiss trio follows the example of bizarre-like **Gong** and French TV: formed in 1991 they belong to the more radical side of avant-rock, proposing sounds between **Zappa**, **Syd Barrett** and the more liquid jazz-rock of RIO, making a principle out of breaking conventional rules and exploring different styles and sounds, changing line-up frequently, as an open group. In 1999 they more or less disband when **Riechsteiner** and **Hugi** decide to close this chapter of their musical history. The last recordings from the same year are re-issued as *Die Vierte* by label Fazzul Music in 2003.
DISCOGRAPHY: DIE ERSTE *(Yolk, 1993)* **DIE ZVOTE** *(Yolk, 1994)* **DIE DRITTE** *(Yolk, 1997)* **OKSIVINIS** *(Triceratop, 2000)* **DIE VIERTE** *(Fazzul, 2003).*
M.G. & C.C.

Europe: TURKEY

BÜLENT ORTAÇGIL

Bülent Ortaçgil, Onno Tunc, Atilla Ozdemiroglu - *guitars, vocals, keyboards, ethnic percussion.*

Bülent Ortaçgil is a Turkish composer, guitarist and singer born in 1950, publishing a first LP *Anlamsız* (Meaningless) while in college. His first real debut is the album *Benimle Oynar Misin* (Will You Play with Me?) of 1974, a rare example of psychedelic-folk prog from Turkey blending of western prog-rock with Turkish traditions: a coherent album, a song cycle of quiet everyday moments and objects with arrangements for acoustic guitar and piano, the occasional harpsichord. He returns to music after a long pause and his next album is released ten years later, for a consistently intriguing discography.

RECOMMENDED RECORDINGS: **BENIMLE OYNAR MISIN** (Label 1 Numera, 1974). **M.G.**

CEM KARACA

He starts playing with an **Elvis Presley** cover band, slowly improving into a mix of traditional folk blended with the new sounds coming from Europe. In 1972 he joins **Moğollar** writing some songs for them, then he founds his own band, **Dervisan** in 1974 and after this, a prog-oriented band named **Edirdahan**, publishing his masterpiece *Safinaz*. After 1980 he escapes to Germany because his Marxist political views, returning after an amnesty in 1987. *Merhaba Gençler ve Her zaman Genç Kalanlar* (Hello to anyone young and to anyone who feels young) is one of his best come back albums. **Karaca** dies in February 2004.

RECOMMENDED RECORDINGS: **SAFINAZ** (Kalan, 1978). **M.G.**

HARDAL

Sukru Yuksel – *vocals, guitar,* **Aydin Sencan** - *bass,* **Alper Karamahmutoglu** - *guitar,* **Zafer** - *drums,* **Ozkan Turgay** - *keyboards.*

Formed in 1979 mixing progressive rock with psychedelia and some hard rock and resulting in a very nice debut album published the following year: *Nasil Ne Zamman* is a excellent work as it really doesn't sound like any classic progressive group oriented to a very elaborated pop-rock with funky rhythms and outstanding electric guitars with a good fuzz sound, nice synths, even some piano and some pop hints. The Turkish lyrics merged perfectly with the Anglo-Saxon music textures. It finally is reissued on CD in 2009 for the first time. Another two good albums and then they disappear.

RECOMMENDED RECORDINGS: **HEREDEN HEREYE!** (Underground Masters, 1980) **NASIL NE ZAMMAN** (Underground Masters, 1982). **M.G.**

ILHAN IREM

Born in 1955, he records some tapes in the early '70s before publish a real first album in 1979: a beautiful and romantic voice (albeit the typically sexist lyrics in their conception of love), a good production sometimes enriched with orchestral arrangements very near to the progressive genre, compared to the **Alan Parsons Project**. Not strictly prog, his pop music is both simple and sophisticated at the same time with keyboards and synthesizers supported by drum machines. The best material is published between 1981 and 1987 and the album *Romance* of 1994.

RECOMMENDED RECORDINGS: **ROMANCE** (Diskotür-Yavuz, 1984). **M.G.**

Europe: TURKEY

IHTIYAÇ MOLASI

Mark Dahlgren - *keyboards, vocals,* **Joe Guarino** - *bass, vocals,* **Mike Novak - Tolga Cebi** - *keyboards, violin,* **Taner Sarf** - *guitars,* **Sinan Gursoy** - *bass,* **Murat Gullu, Cevdet Erek** - *percussion.*
Formed in 1995, these four musicians, all with different musical tastes, play an intellectual art-rock with joyful and colorful tints, varied and accessible. They declare that their differences broaden their style to a large musical approach described as 'play what you feel'. They perform singing in English and Turkish with plenty of instrumental moments. Both albums contain moments of symphonic rock with a modern new prog, but their main feature is this strange kind of jazz-oriental rock with a frequent use of ethnic instruments. A third recent work in 2015.
DISCOGRAPHY: **MILAD** (Zihni, 2000) **1.5** (Can, 2004). M.G. & C.C.

NEKROPSI

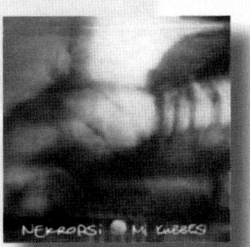

Cem - *guitar, vocals,* **Cev** - *drums, vocals,* **Patrick Chartol , Cenk Turanli, Ker**- *bass, vocals,* **Gök** - *guitars,* **Tol** - *guitar, vocals, samplers.*
Formed in 1990 by drummer **Cevdet Erek** and guitarist **Erem Tanyeri**, they start playing a very chaotic thrash-metal genre releaseing a first demo titled *Speed Lessons Part 1*. Soon they evolve into a more creative and rich style of guitar improvisations for a prog folk derived from Turkish popular music. Their first album of 1996, *Mi Kubbesi*, contains fast rhythmic drums, heavy bass lines and ferocious guitar duels close to a death metal album with **King Crimson** influences and the **Pink Floyd** spaciness blending to Middle-Eastern tunes. The strange song with German lyrics "Papa" is inspired by the industrial electronic pop of D.A.F.
DISCOGRAPHY: MI KUBBESI (Musea, 1996). M.G.

REPLIKAS

Gökçe Akçelik, Barkın Engin, Orçun Baştürk Selçuk Artut, Burak Tamer - *guitars, vocals, keyboards, samplers, drums, ethnic percussion.*
Founded in 2000, this innovative and fresh rock band with psychedelic and Anatolian Middle-Eastern rhythms mixes avant-prog, eclectic, heavy and post-rock with incredible artistic perception. The eclectic debut *Köledoyuran* recorded in 2000 ranges from alternative to traditional or cultural folk. *Dadaruhi* of 2001 is more conceptual, with guest musicians and a chorus, adding electronic elements to the chemistry of traditional instruments (ney, zuma, Ramadan drum). The third album *Avaz*, released in 2005 is based upon tracks born from true jam sessions, full of improvisations though with less experimentation.
DISCOGRAPHY: KÖLEDOYURAN (Ada Music, 2000) **DADARUHI** (Ada Music, 2002) **AVAZ** (Doublemoon Records, 2005) **ZERRE** (Peyote, 2008) **BIZ BURADA YOK IKEN** (Ada Music, 2012). M.G.

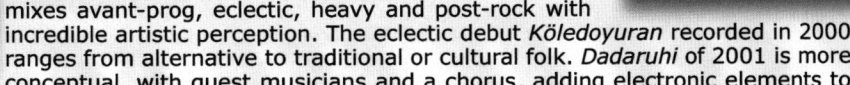

21 PERON

Haluk Öztekin – *guitar,* **Harun Kapancioglu** – *drums,* **Yusuf Örnek** – *vocals,* **Sinan Hasertürk** – *bass,* **Andreas Wildermann** – *organ.*
They begin in 1970 as a college cover band of **Creedence Clearwater Revival** and **The Who** (mainly) until by 1975 they had recorded five tracks by themselves with influences from **Frank Zappa, Gentle Giant** and **Genesis**, mixing everything with a personal ethnic Anatolian connotation and some typical Arabian tunes with traces of psychedelic and classical music. In 1975 they record a homonym album with these symphonic and experimental styles, released only in 2003 by Arkaplan label for they never got the right support. In 1979 they win the Eurovision Song contest and were supposed to represent Turkey but were refused entry to Israel due to the oil crisis. Just before disbanding they record an average pop album entitled *Seviyorum*. Surprisingly they came back recently with a renewed line up for a brand new album *Tapon* of 2014.
RECOMMENDED RECORDINGS: **21 PERON** (Arkaplan (1975), 2003) **TAPON** (Arkaplan, 2014). M.G.

Europe: YUGOSLAVIA

AERODROM

Jura Paden - *guitar, vocals,* **Zlatan Zivkoviae** - *vocals, percussion,* **Remo Krstanoviae** - *bass,* **Mladen Krajnik** - *keyboards,* **Paolo Sfeci** - *drums.*

Formed in 1978 by guitarist, vocalist and composer **Jurica Paden** who previously worked with several important bands from Zagreb music scene, their prog debut album *Kad Misli Mi Vrludaju* is greatly inspired by **Yes**, **Genesis** and **Rick Wakeman**, resulting in a very pleasant record with magnificent arrangements. Already from the second album they are seduced by the new wave, developing a commercially successful mainstream pop-rock expression, which only occasionally contained some neo-prog-crossover elements. They disband in 1987 following other projects and reunite in 2000 for the come-back album *Na Travi*, and another couple of less interesting works.

RECOMMENDED RECORDINGS: **KAD MISLI MI VRLUDAJU** *(Jugoton, 1979)* **TANGO BANGO** *(Jugoton, 1981).*
C.A.

DAG (aka Trio Dag, Grupa Dag)

Dragan Popovic - *guitar, vocals,* **Aleksandar Milanovic** - *guitars, vocals,* **Grujica Milanovic** - *vocals, percussion.*

Formed in 1972, their name is the acronym of guitarists **Dragan Popovic**, **Aleksandar Milanovic** and percussionist **Grujica Milanovic**. This acoustic trio releases their only album *Secanja* in 1974, a recording which doesn't represent them fully as live performers, with its mix of acoustic and dynamic electric moments (sitar, flute, Hammond). A very original progressive rock and acid folk work with references to the Californian psychedelic folk or to the British Canterbury scene. The lack of commercial response led to their premature dissolution the following year, leaving behind also three 7" singles.

DISCOGRAPHY: **SECANJA** *(PGP RTB, 1974).*
M.G. & C.C.

DRUGI NAČIN

Branko Pozgajec – *vocals, keyboards,* **Halil Mekic, Danijel Velican** – *guitars,* **Zeljko Mikulcic, Bozo Ilic** – *bass,* **Ismet Kurtovic** – *vocals, flute, harp.* **Miroslav Budanko, Boris Turina** – *drums, lyrics.*

Formed in 1975 by members of a previous band called **Zlatni Akordi**, they release a single in 1973 before acquiring the new name derived from a poem by F. G. Lorca (In Another Way). The homonym debut of 1975 is a rare example of Hippy concept album, talking about love and solitude, for a well performed hard rock with strong progressive colours, characterized by the interplay between twin guitars and twin flutes, inspired by **Deep Purple**, **Wishbone Ash** and **Jethro Tull**. Disbanded a first time until 1978, the totally renewed line-up issues a second album *Ponovno Na Putu* without the same success of the first. They return again in 1992 with a third album of their '70s singles re-arranged. In 2000 they act as support group for **Jethro Tull**'s concert in Zagreb.

RECOMMENDED RECORDINGS: **DRUGI NAČIN** *(PGP RTB, 1975)* **PONOVNO NA PUTU** *(PGP RTB, 1978)* **DRUGI NAČIN** *(Croatia Records, 1993).*
M.G.

GALIJA

Nenad Milosavljevic - *vocals, acoustic guitar,* **Goran Ljubisavljevic** - *electric guitar,* **Predrag Brankovic** - *bass,* **Boban Pavlovic** - *drums,* **Ljubodrag Vukadinovic** - *keyboards,* **Predrag Milosavljevic** - *vocals, tambourine.*

Nenad Milosavljevic is a hippie-influenced singer and songwriter who also composed music for theatrical plays. In 1977 he founds this band named after the coffee bar where they went. They played a highly sophisticated symphonic prog rock (although sometimes not too original) and theatrical Baroque-pirate look, along with **Nenad**'s surprising voice in between **Ian Anderson** and **Peter Gabriel**. From the mid '80s they shift to a more polished (and less rocking) art pop-rock with occasional fusion of Balkan folk and a frequent use of local poetry. The first three albums are considered their best yet today they are active but not on the prog front.

RECOMMENDED RECORDINGS: **GALIJA GRUPA** *(PGP, 1979)* **DRUGA PLOVIDBA** *(PGP, 1980)* **IPAK VERUJEM U SEBE** *(PGP, 1982).*
C.A.

Europe: **YUGOSLAVIA**

GRUPA 220

Drago Mlinarec - *vocals, guitar,* **Vojko Sabolovic** - *vocals, guitar,* **Vojislav Mišo Tatalovic** - *bass,* **Ranko Balen** - *drums,* **Branimir Civkovic** - *keyboards.*
A beat band formed in 1966 importing the flower-power movement in Yugoslavia. They record some singles of success and are the first to publish an album back in 1968 in Zagreb (present Croatia), probably the first ever rock music album for their country: *Nasi Dani* contains all the elements of the future European prog genre, from the well assorted keyboards and guitars to the strong vocals and compelling melodies contaminated with classical sounds. A first line-up change in 1970 and **Mlinarec** plans a new album, but instead decides to issue it under his own name: *A Ti Se Ne Daj* of 1971, marking the beginning of his solo career. After some concerts and a last album they disband definitively in 1975.
RECOMMENDED RECORDINGS: NASI DANI *(Jugoton, 1968).* C.A.

INDEXI

Slobodan A. Kovacevic - *guitars,* **Davorin Popovic** - *vocals,* **Fadil Redzic** - *bass,* **Djordje Kisic** - *drums,* **Nenad Jurin** - *keyboards.*
Also known as **Indeksi**, this Bosnian band is synonymous of the Sarajevo pop-school scene, beginning in 1962 with a pop rock with many influences of local folk. Contaminated in time, they went through phases of beat, psychedelia, hard rock and prog, issuing a series of singles from 1967 as per request of their label. They toured extensively playing a music characterized by the dominant organ and guitar, mirroring influences from **Procol Harum**, **The Beatles** or the early **Deep Purple**. Finally a first concept album in 1978, *Modra Rijeka*, based on the lyrics of poet Mak Dizdar, containing a symphonic-style prog similar to **Yes**, others with delicate harps and almost folk singing and the psychedelic guitar style of **Hendrix**. The second album of 1999 *Kameni Cvjetovi* is instead a more mainstream rock. In 2001 singer **Popovic** dies and they disband with a final posthumous double live CD *Poslednji Koncert U Sarajevu*.
RECOMMENDED RECORDINGS: MODRA RIJEKA *(Jugoton, 1978).* M.G.

IZVIR

Marko Bitenc – *vocals, percussion,* **Marjan Lebar** - *bass,* **Slavko Lebar** - *guitar,* **Andrej Petkovic** - *drums,* **Franc Opeka** - *guitar,* **Davor Petric** – *guitar,* **Andrej Konjajev** – *organ, piano, vocals.*
Jazz-rock band with progressive colours born in Ljubljana (Slovenia) in 1971, they record only one album in 1977, plus some singles: a very interesting dose of disco-prog and hard rock that sounds more like an early '70s than late '70s release, with a fascinating art work on the sleeve. The spacey psychedelic opening recalls **Igra Staklenih Perli**, but oddly enough confined to the lengthy first track while moving on towards a funky fusion direction. Somewhere between **Santana**, **Camel** and **Fermata**, with sounds resulting as a Slovenian **Malo**, with lots of clavinet and funky inserts. After the split some musicians join other bands of Slovenian jazz-rock, like **Predmestje**.
DISCOGRAPHY: IZVIR *(RTV, 1977).* M.G.

OPUS

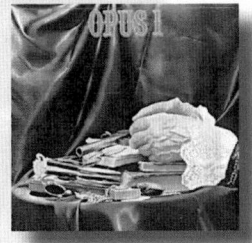 

Miodrag Okrugic - *keyboards,* **Miodrag Kostic, Milan Matic** – *guitar,* **Dusan Cucuz, Slobodan Orlic** – *bass,* **Ljubomir Jerkovic, Zelimir Vasic** – *drums.*
Formed in 1973 by keyboardist **Miodrag Okrugic**, the original line-up included guitar player **Miodrag Kostic** and bassist **Dusan Cucuz**, but soon they split. They were named after **Okrugic**'s composition "Opus No. 1" which he scored while playing in a former band called **Yu Grupa**. **Okrugic** re-forms **Opus** in 1975 with a new line up and the strong voice of **Dušan Prelević**: soon they record their self-titled symphonic rock debut album which failed to draw attention and so they split again and then for good in 1977. In addition to their only LP album, they record three singles added as bonus tracks to the re-issue on CD in 2003.
DISCOGRAPHY: OPUS 1 *(Jugoton, 1975).* M.G.

Europe: YUGOSLAVIA

POP MAŠINA

Robert Nemecek – *bass, vocals,* **Zoran Bozinovic** - *guitar, vocals,* **Rasa Djelmas** - *drums,* **Sava Bojic** – *guitar, vocals,* **Mihajlo Popovic** – *drums.*
Founded in 1972 playing extended progressive heavy acid rock jams for free, they record a good debut the following year: *Kiselina* (acid) is a strange concept album on drugs and psychedelic trips, blending the early '70s heavy metal roots with post-hippie psychedelic ballads. Another two albums, *Na Izvoru Svetlosti* and the live recording *Put Ka Suncu* (the first live album for Yugoslavia) before the first disbandment in 1976, leaving **Zoran Bozinovic** as the only original member to continue with a change towards jazz-rock, but after one unsuccessful single they disbanded for good. **Robert Nemecek** renews the band under the name **Rok Masina** in early 1980s but they also failed to chart, leaving two unnoticed records.
DISCOGRAPHY: **KISELINA** *(PGP-RTB, 1973)* **NA IZVORU SVETLOSTI** *(RTV, 1975)* **PUT KA SUNCU** *(RTV, 1976).* **M.G.**

SEPTEMBER

Tihomir Pop Asanovic - *keyboards,* **Janez Boncina** – *keyboards, vocals.* **Petar Ugrin** – *trumpet, violin,* **Ratko Divjak** - *drums,* **Karel Charlie Novak** – *bass,* **Braco Doblekar** – *saxophones, percussion.*
Band from Ljubljana, Slovenia, formed in 1975 by experienced musicians, among the best Yugoslavian jazz-rock artists. After the release of their first fusion album *Zadnja Avantura*, they renew the line-up for a second album published in 1978, *Domovina Moja* (my homeland) with a very AOR sound and more mainstream oriented, containing the homonym hit single. Their style is as a mellow form of jazz-rock with accessible and relatively short songs, characterized by the good vocals of **Boncina** and the excellent instrumental skills of the band. Although they were greatly influenced by **Kansas** and the southern American style, they still were one of the best Balkan jazz-rock bands of the time. They broke-up in the late 1979: both **Asanovic** and **Boncina** led parallel solo careers.
DISCOGRAPHY: **ZADNJA AVANTURA** *(PGP/RTB, 1976)* **DOMOVINA MOJA** *(PGP/RTB, 1978).* **M.G.**

SMAK

Radomir "Točak" Mihajlovic – *guitar,* **Slobodan Stojanovic** - *drums,* **Zoran Milanovic** – *bass,* **Boris Arandjelovic** - *vocals,* **Lazar Ristovski** – *keyboards.*
Formed 1971, this band is famous for their guitarist **Mihajlovic** aka **'Točak'** (The Wheel), from the **Hendrix** and **Page** school of solo playing, with a style that mixed hard rock, prog, fusion and jazz rock with blues. They released very appreciated albums on the western market, helped by the English version releases and the high quality of their vocalist **Arandjelovic** and his falsetto often used as an instrument rather than real singing. "Ulazak u harem" is a folk-inspired instrumental issued as hit-single in 1975. Disbanded for the first time in 1981, they reunite in 1986 for another album and then disband again only to resurrect one more time in 1992, dropping all the Prog references in favour of a simple hard rock genre.
RECOMMENDED RECORDINGS: **CRNA DAMA (Black Lady)** *(RTV, 1975).* **M.G.**

YU GRUPA

Dragi Jelic - *guitar ,* **Zika Jelic** - *bass,* **Miodrag Okrugic** – *organ,* **Velibor Bogdanovic** – *drums.*
A Serbian group formed in 1970 with some successful singles that conquered a big audience and the particular attention of British label CBS who signs them up for a concert in London's the Marquée. Becoming thus a Balkan rock symbol, they release a first self titled debut in 1973, for a hard rock with elements of local folk. Unfortunately some internal disagreements led, first to line-up changes and then to the final separation in 1981. **Goran Bregovic** was one of their fans and supported their reunion in 1987. The ballad "Crni leptir" is famous for being sung by bass-guitarist **Žika Jelić** (along with "Dunavom šibaju vetrovi" from their 1988 album *Ima nade*).
RECOMMENDED RECORDINGS: **YU GRUPA** *(Jugoton 1973)* **KAKO TO DA SVAKI DAN?** *(Jugoton 1974)* **YU GRUPA** *(Jugoton 1975)* **MEDU ZVEZDAMA** *(Jugoton 1977).* **M.G.**

Indochina & North Asia: JAPAN

ASTURIAS (Yoh Ohyama)

Yoh Ohyama - *programming, synths, guitars, bass, percussion,* **Yoshihiro Kawagoe** - *piano,* **Misa Kitatsuji** – *violin,* **Kaori Tsutsui** - *clarinet.*

Two different incarnations for this project formed in 1987 by **Yoh Ohyama**, a multi-instrumentalist in love with **Mike Oldfield**'s music. Being a sound engineer, he releases three albums as solo works found under **Electric Asturias**. The commercial failure forces **Ohyama** to a ten years pause until he decides to reunite a band with a completely renewed image: **Acoustic Asturias** becomes a quartet formed by classical musicians recording *Bird Eyes View* in 2004, a 25 minutes symphonic album with **Yoshihiro Kawagoe** playing piano as the best **Rick Wakeman**'s style, and *Marching Grass On The Hill* in 2006 featuring **Ito Kyoko** on the violin. Then in 2008 he plans another solo album with the previous style, *In Search Of The Soul Trees*.
RECOMMENDED RECORDINGS: BIRD EYES WIEW *(Musea/Poseidon, 2004).* M.G.

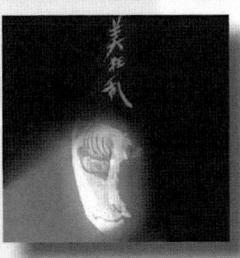

BI KYO RAN

Masaaki Nagasawa - *drums,* **Masahide Shiratori** - *bass,* **Kunio Suma** - *guitar, vocals,* **Akihito Suzuki** - *percussion, vocals,* **Kotomi Osuka** - *piano, keyboards,* **Kazuya Mizoguchi** - *guitar,* **Masato Taguchi** - *percussion,* **Kouji Tazawa** - *vocals.*

One of the most important Japanese progressive rock bands, formed in 1973 playing a music that sounded like outtakes of **King Crimson**'s *Red* era. The guitar sounds like a **Fripp** clone too, although sometimes it gains a bit in originality, very well executed with an added violinist. Their album of 1997, *Kyobo Na Ongaku (A Violent Music)*, is instead more aggressive and recalling **Anekdoten**, but without the same brightness. They record also some interesting live albums, one of them dedicated exclusively to **King Crimson** covers. Still active, the recent *Anthologies* are a re-issue of their earliest and best songs featuring guitarist and leader **Kunio Suma** and drummer **Masaharu Sato**.
RECOMMENDED RECORDINGS: BI KYO RAN *(1982, King Records)* PARALLAX *(1983, King Records)* A VIOLENT MUSIC *(1998, Musea)* ANTHOLOGY Vol.1 *(2002, Gohan).* M.G.

CINEMA

Hiromi Fujimoto - *vocals, piano,* **Tohru Ohta** - *guitars, bouzouki,* **Yoshihiko Kitamura** - *synths, ocarinah,* **Tokiko Nakanishi** - *violin, viola,* **Masaki Massimo** - *bass,* **Hirokazu Taniguchi** - *drums, electronic percussion.*

The reincarnation of the former 12 years symphonic project **Fromage**, they re-form in 1994 with a totally new prog sound of the '90s made of complex orchestral arrangements featuring three keyboardists playing together and the typical guitars. Traditional Asian percussions give a touch of originality to the delicate arrangements, compared to other chamber-leaning symphonic groups such as **Verdun** or **Virginia Astley**. **Hiromi Fjimoto** is their female lead singer with a very smooth and elegant voice. They tour mostly in Asia and release material sporadically from the debut of 1995 to 2004, with only three studio albums to their credit in the past twelve years.
RECOMMENDED RECORDINGS: INTO THE STATE OF FLUX *(Belle Antique, 1994)* M.G.

DEJA VU

Motoi Sakuraba - *keyboards,* **Tetsuya Nagatsuma** - *bass, vocals,* **Genta Kudoh** - *drums, percussion, vocals.*

Formed at the Meiji University of Tokyo in 1984 under the name **Clashed Ice** (soon changed), this trio is based upon the outstanding keyboard arrangements of **Motoi Sakuraba**, clearly influenced by **ELP**, **Balletto di Bronzo** and **Gerard**. During the next three years they tour and record their own material, gaining fame and international recognition, but it's not until 1988 that they are able to release their only album *Baroque in Future*, reissued by Musea in 1998 with two bonus tracks of a 1989 concert where they played with the French iconic band **Atoll**. This work confirms the ultra-symphonic and powerful rock of the band played with music exaggerations pointed towards exhibitionism and kitsch solutions. During the recording sessions of a second album, they split due to disagreements on the musical direction.
DISCOGRAPHY: BAROQUE IN THE FUTURE *(1988, Made in Japan).* M.G.

Indochina & North Asia: JAPAN

FANTASMAGORIA

Miki Fujimoto - *violin,* **Junpei Ozaki** - *guitars,* **Ryuichi Odani** - *keyboards,* **Naoki Kitao** - *bass,* **Masataka Suwa** – *drums.*
It all started with the excellent violinist **Miki Fujimoto**, a woman playing the typical neo-symphonic prog revival of **King Crimson** and **Curved Air** with jazz-rock and fusion blends. This instrumental rock band released a self-titled live demo and then spent the following four years touring the entire world. The eleven tracks of their 2009 debut album *Day And Night* confirm their enormous talent: apparently a spacey alternative art-metal with this incredible violin and good acid guitars, where the keyboards (astral strings, harpsichords, and old fashioned organs) are not forgotten for an integrated symphonic touch and completed by a powerful rhythmic section.
RECOMMENDED RECORDINGS: **DAY AND NIGHT** *(Musea, 2008).*

M.G.

HIRO YANAGIDA

Born in 1949, he starts playing with **The Floral** in 1966: in 1969 they change name to **Apryl Fool**, becoming a famous psychedelic rock jam band, but disbanding soon after recording their debut album. He joins **Food Brain** and **Love Live Life + One,** and also releases four solo albums of his own in the early '70s, all bearing the fascinating textures of guitars (also featuring **Kimio Mizutani**) and Hammond organ with compelling inserts of flute, sax and violin. A music richly keyboard-oriented, sometimes experimental, never self-indulgent. He returned recently after the dark and difficult '80s, revealing a renewed strength and other new interesting albums, also playing as a session musician and composing various songs for TV jingles or commercials.
RECOMMENDED RECORDINGS: **MILK TIME** *(Liberty, 1970)* **HIRO YANAGIDA** *(Atlantic, 1971)* **HIRO** *(URC, 1972)* **HIROCOSMOS** *(CBS, 1973)* **UFO** *(CBS, 1978)* **MA-YA** *(Substance, 2003).*

M.G.

KBB

Akihisa Tsuboy - *violin, guitar,* **Toshimitsu Takahashi** - *keyboards,* **Dani** - *bass,* **Shirou Sugano** - *drums.*
Active since 1992 with a debut album released only 8 years later, this instrumental fusion band represents a good answer to the jazz-rock prog of **Mahavishnu Orchestra**, **Dixie Dregs**, **King Crimson** and **UK**. Led by the superlative violin of **Akihisa Tsuboy**, their albums are rich of tenses, powerful and dynamic music, intense and complex, yet melodic and surprisingly accessible. A very compact and overwhelming progressive-fusion with references to **Kenso** and the compelling melodic structures, improvisations and rich songwriting recalling the early '70s **Robert Fripp**, all with a top-notch production.
DISCOGRAPHY: **LOST AND FOUND** *(Musea 2002)* **FOUR CORNER'S SKY** *(Musea, 2003)* **LIVE 2004** *(live, Musea 2005)* **PROOF OF CONCEPT** *(Musea 2007).*

M.G.

KOHENJI HYAKKEI

Tatsuya Yoshida - *drums, vocals, keyboards,* **Ryuichi Masuda** - *guitars, vocals,* **Aki Kubota** - *keyboards, vocals,* **Shigekazu Kuwahara** - *bass, vocals,* **Jin Harada** - *vocals, guitar,* **Kengo Sakamoto** - *vocals, bass,* **Oguchi Kenichi** - *keyboards,* **Nami Sagara** - *vocals,* **Miyako Kanazawa** - *keyboards, vocals.*
Drummer **Tatsuya Yoshida** and his love for **Christian Vander** ignite this project of zeuhl sounds with violent and outstanding songs of an invented language (close to kobaian), almost clones of **Magma**. Frenzy and furious recordings performed with an impressive prog musical roller-coaster exploding with flashy keyboard lines, intricate guitar riffs, speedy, convoluted bass/drum patterns, operatic female vocals that border on apocalyptic war cries combined with a superhuman technique and catchy, complex arrangements. Only their last 2005 album *Angherr Shisspa* is less brutal.
RECOMMENDED RECORDINGS: **HUNDRED SIGHTS OF KOENJI** *(1994, God Mountain)* **ANGHERR SHISSPA** *(2005, Skin Graft Records).*

M.G. & C.C.

Indochina & North Asia: JAPAN

MAGICAL POWER MAKO

Behind the band is **Makoto Kurita**, versatile avant-garde artist born in 1958 with a natural piano talent and for composing music: he starts his adolescent career recording tapes and trying to find new sounds. Only eighteen he publishes a first album in 1973, *Magical Power*, milestone in the birth of a Japanese avant-garde, psychedelic, and prog movement: he blends freely acid folk with doses of avant psychedelia assorted with local kraut. Another two excellent works: the techno-pop *Super Record* (1975) and the more rock oriented *Jump* (1977), before plunging into a more psychedelic pop genre. Interesting the recovery of the 1972/75 works reissued in a 5 CD version called *Hapmoniym*. **Mako** can play more than a hundred instruments and his songs are filled with eccentricity.
RECOMMENDED RECORDINGS: **SUPER RECORD** *(Polydor, 1975).*

M.G. & C.C.

CARMEN MAKI & OZ

She starts her musical career as a fairly typical chanteuse before joining a theatrical company in 1968 after which she joins **Kazuo Takeda**'s **Blues Creation**, publishing an LP rich of inventive ideas, **Carmen Maki & Blues Creation**, recalling singers like **Janis Joplin** and **Maggie Bell**. During the early '70s things become totally different: she forms the prog-oriented band **Carmen Maki & Oz** in 1972, finally source of a good commercial success with unforgettable albums full of hard-rock tunes and soft folk moments. Yet their 1975 debut is a bit too mainstream for the majority of Jap-rock fans and the band breaks-up a couple of years later after another two albums.
RECOMMENDED RECORDINGS: **CARMEN MAKI & OZ** *(Polydor, 1975)* **TOZASRETA MATI** *(Polydor, 1976)* **III** *(Polydor, 1977)* **LAST LIVE** *(Polydor, 1978)*.

M.G.

MIDAS

Kazuo Katayama - drums, percussion, **Eishyo Lynn** - piano, keyboards, **Katsuaki Mishima** - bass, **Eigo Utoh** - vocals, violin, guitars, **Kenjiro Kawakatsu** - drums, percussion, **Shohei Matsura**, bass, stick.
Formed in 1983 playing a more traditional Japanese rock during their first fourteen years. In 1988 they release the progressive rock debut *Beyond the Clear Air*, a masterpiece of symphonism guided by outstanding keyboards and a burning and elegant electric violin inspired by **PFM**, **UK** and **Camel** but more classical and closer to jazz-rock tendencies. The following chapters are distant from the beauty of their debut album with a more modern, aggressive sound, often with Japanese folklore leanings in their lyrical compositions. The newer sound combines elements of jazz and classical music with the peculiar modern Japanese interest in complex electronic and dance music, and even adds a heavier rock to the multiple layers of keyboard and violin with a scarce electric guitar.
RECOMMENDED RECORDINGS: **BEYOND THE CLEAR AIR** *(1988, Made in Japan).* M.G. & C.C.

MUGEN

Masaya Furuta - drums, percussion, **Katsuhiko Hayashi** - keyboards, flute, **Akira Kato** - bass, guitar, **Takashi Nakamura** - vocals, keyboards, **Takashi Kawaguchi** - violin.
Formed in 1978 by two keyboardists, **Katsuhiko Hayashi** and **Takashi Nakamura**, both in love with British and Italian Prog. After some demos they sign up for a debut album in 1984, *Sinfonia della Luna*, a very mellow sound with classical guitar, beautiful waves of Mellotron and sensitive electric guitar solos. The second album, *Leda et la Cygne* (1986), is considered as their best also thanks to contributions by **Takashi Kawaguchi** on violin (**Outer Limits**), **Kazuhiro Miyatake** on flute and **Ikkou Nakujima** on acoustic guitar (both from Pageant). The 1988 *The Princess of Kingdome Gone* is more disappointing.
RECOMMENDED RECORDINGS: **SINFONIA DELLA LUNA** *(1984, Made in Japan Records)* **LEDA ET LE CYGNE** *(1986, Kings Records)*

M.G.

Indochina & North Asia: JAPAN

NOVELA

Hisakatsu Igarashi - *vocals* , **Terutsugu Hirayama** – *guitar, vocals*, **Mototsugu Yamane** - *guitar*, **Eljiro Akita** - *drums*, **Toshio Egawa** - *keyboards*.

Formed in 1979 by former **Scheherezade** and **San Sui Kan** musicians blending symphonic prog and hard rock, recalling a mix of **Rush** and **Genesis**, yet still singing in their mothertongue. The debut album *La Songerie* of 1980 includes the beautiful heavy prog keyboards of famous **Toshio Egawa** and multi-instrumentalist **Terutsugu Hirayama**. *Requiem* (1981), *Paradise Lost* (1981) and *Sanctuary* (1983) are their next good and much more proggier works. The activity of this band goes on until the mid '80s, then **Hyrayama** follows **Teru** joins **Teru's Symphonia** in 1985 while **Egawa** had already started on his project **Gerard** in 1983.

RECOMMENDED RECORDINGS: **PARADISE LOST** *(King Records, 1981).*   **M.G. & C.C.**

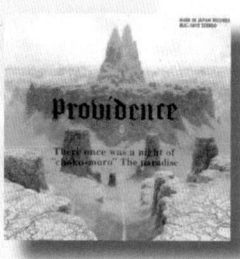

PROVIDENCE

Madoka Tsukada - *keyboards*, **Satoshi Ono** - *guitar*, **Yasuyuki Hirose** - *bass*, **Yŏko Kubota** - *vocals*, **Yuichi Sugiyama** - *drums*.

One of the most important band of the Japanese neo-prog period, formed in 1985 with some demo tapes and various line-up consolidations. Their first album *And I'll Recite An Old Myth...* of 1990 is considered great for quality and the variety of themes: **Madoka Tsukada** composed all songs with a touch of jazz and hard rock and the voice of **Kubota**, who sings in Japanese with great elasticity between the high and dry notes and the more low and melodic tones. The album features the collaboration of **Christian Beya** from **Atoll**. After replacing some members in 1991, they become more active on stage and publish *Rare Tracks* the following year, and in 1996 *There Once Was A Night Of "Choko-Muro" The Paradise*. They performed live around their country until 2002.

RECOMMENDED RECORDINGS: **AND I'LL RECITE AN OLD MYTH...** *(BSP/King Records, 1990).* **M.G.**

SPACE CIRCUS

Yoshikazu Ogawa - *drums*, **Yukinao Sano** - *guitars*, **Hajime Okano** - *guitars, bass, synth*, **Takashi Toyoda** - *synths, polymooog, mini moog, sequencers*, **Vincenzo Panormo** - *ARP strings machine*.

A Japanese clone of the British band **Camel**, not very original but still a pleasant melodic band, who managed to published in 1978 (a difficult moment for the prog genre) with label BMG their first album and then another after switching keyboard players, thus changing also their sound from the classic fusion of *Funky Caravan* to a space rock tendency of *Fantastic Arrival*. **Okano Hajim**e's guitar playing is very reminiscent of **Andrew Latimer**, and it is thanks to him that these excellent albums have been reissued in 2008 with some added bonus live material.

RECOMMENDED RECORDINGS: **FANTASTIC ARRIVAL** *(BMG, 1979).*   **M.G.**

TIPOGRAPHICA

Tsuneo Imahori - *guitar*, **Naruyoshi Kikuchi** - *sax*, **Osamu Matsumoto** - *trombone*, **Akira Minakami** - *keyboard*, **Hiroaki Mizutani** - *bass*, **Akira Sotoyama** - *drums*.

Active from 1986 to 1998, they released four beautiful albums, with particular mention to *God Says I Can't Dance* issued in 1996. They perform a completely instrumental music, basically a rhythmically complex type of very free jazz-rock with classic RIO and Canterbury school-inspired elements, avant-garde and **Frank Zappa** formulas, for a style recalling the early **Henry Cow**, **Picchio Dal Pozzo** and **Hartfield & The North**. The compositions feature blazing guitars, honking sax and horn textures and compelling super tight arrangements for a music that never results as self-indulging.

DISCOGRAPHY: **TIPOGRAPHICA** *(God Mountain, 1994)* **THE MAN WHO DOES NOT NOD** *(Pony/Canyon, 1995)* **GOD SAYS I CAN'T DANCE** *(Mellow, 1996)* **FLOATING OPERA** *(Sistema, 1997).***M.G.**

Indochina & North Asia: KOREA

MAGMA

Cho Ha-Moon - *bass, vocals*, **Kim Kwang-Hyun** - *guitar*, **Moon Young-Sik** - *drums*.
A very energetic band formed in 1980, homonym of the famous French group lead by **Christian Vander**, but absolutely different and far away from those experimental solutions. The Korean **Magma** were a trio of young rockers who released a very good record in 1981 of hard rock with great instrumental spaces inspired by the typical Anglo-Saxon prog mainstream: great guitar solos or soft pop rock moments and inventive parts of brilliant instrumental hard rock. They were also a University rock band and entered one of the contests, big at the time during those years, winning it. The supervisor of the contest was MBC (a Korean broadcasting TV station) which sponsored their song in the compilation released soon after, "Folkie Jin".
DISCOGRAPHY: MAGMA (Vertigo, 1981).   M.G.

RUN WAY

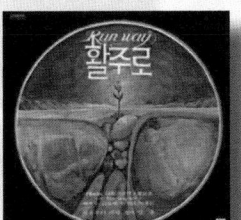

Kim Jong Tae - *keyboards* **Bae Chul Su, Chi Deok Yeop, Han Yeong-Soo, Park Soo-Bok, Kang Won-Ho,** - *various intruments.*
Formed in 1968 naming themselves after the university where they met (Korea Aerospace University), it took them over 10 years to decide to record their first album, published finally in 1979. Reason why *Whal Ju Loh* has a well consolidated sound by the time it is realized, between the early psychedelic genre and the newly branded garage rock. Many tracks end with a rigid, rehearsed full-stop, rather than fade-outs. Keyboardist **Kim Jong Tae**'s great Hammond organ, the acid guitars which never reach the rude distortion of "Sinawe", long tracks and out of tune vocals which recall some works of **San Ul Rim**, although more concise: a compelling experience for this guitar and organ driven quartet which alternate between flower power psych-lite and pure '70s arena rock. **Bae Chul Su** and **Chi Deok Yeop** will later form **Songolmae**, completing their evolution from the '60s psychedelia to legitimate large-scale rockers.
DISCOGRAPHY: WHAL JU LOH (Jigu, 1978).   M.G.

SANULLIM (San Ul Rim)

Kim Chang-Wan – *vocals, lead guitar*, **Kim Chang-Hoon** – *bass, guitar, keyboards*, **Kim Chang-Ik** – *drums*.
Band composed by three **Kim Chang** brothers, formed 1976 proposing a psychedelic beat with folk tints and progressive elements. Their discography is very large and various, the first two albums are the most prog thanks to the interesting musical mix of vocals, typical of the region. Also the third is still pertinent with it s 18 mins jam, though more rock. With the arrival of disco and dance music, they change completely style. Specialized in fuzz guitars and vintage organ sounds, playing spacey instrumental tracks of clear psychedelia influence like from **The Electric Prunes, Blues Magoos, The Chocolate Watchband, Iron Butterfly** and **The Doors**. They are incredibly good at creating melancholy moods which sound joyful. Two of the brothers left the music business to pursue their careers, only the eldest, **Wan** carried on until 2008.
RECOMMENDED RECORDINGS: VOL 2 = AS LAYING CARPET ON MY MIND (Seo ra beol / SRB record company, 1978).   M.G.

SHIN JUNG HYUN

The great Old Man of Korean pop-rock. At the end of the war, in 1955 he was playing rock'n'roll for the USA Troops, with a first LP in 1959. His backing band changes name through the years, starting with 1962's beat band **Add 4** (1964-68), then re-recording his first album with **Lee Jung Hwa** as **Shin Jung Hyun & Donkeys** in 1969 with added strings; in 1972 as **Golden Grapes**, the following year another two albums considered as precursors of psychedelic rock for **Shin Jung Hyun and The Question**s, and three albums between 1972/73 as **Shin Jung Hyun and the Men** always in the psychedelic rock format. In 1974 two versions of the Korean masterpiece album under the name **Shin Joong Hyun & Yup Juns** were published, the promo version is more raw and features greater space within the songs for instrumental interplay.
RECOMMENDED RECORDINGS: SHIN JUNG HYUN AND THE MEN - WOMAN OF THE EVENING SUN (Universal, 1972).   M.G.

North America: CANADA

A NEW PLACE TO LIVE
(Robert John Gallo)

This American artist recorded many albums for little labels, changing name and country (currently in Canada) producing and arranging a first album released in 1965 by a band called The 'You Know Who' Group, a strange beat record in which the masked band members go under false name. Most likely an exploitative joke as a calculated attempt to capitalize on the British Invasion, they actually managed a small hit with "Roses Are Red, My Love" and their exaggerated fake British accent, being all from NY. Irreverent to the institutions he creates his own label (Mandala) under which he publishes as a solo artist, changing name many times and many times founding other labels (Guinness) to fraud taxes and government control. *A New Place to Live* was released in 1972 as well as *Painted Poetry* (both from Canada), the latter reissued in 1977 as *A Place To Live* using the nickname **Snowball**.
RECOMMENDED RECORDINGS: A NEW PLACE TO LIVE *(Mandala, 1972).* M.G.

AQUARELLE

Pierre Lescaut –keyboards, **Stéphane Morency** – *guitars*, **Pierre Bournaki** – *violin*, **Anne-Marie Courtemanche** – *vocals*, **Jean-Philippe Gélinas** - *saxophones, flute*, **Michel De Lisle** – *bass*, **André Leclerc** – *drums, percussion*.
This symphonic jazz-rock band released only one energetic fusion-type album, that led them to be invited to the International Festival of Montreux in Switzerland, where they recorded live their concert publishing it the following year. Their only album *Sous Un Arbre* is a hard jazz-rock, dominated by piano and/or the violin with more commercial ethnic and rhythmic parts of grove funk and latino tints. Progressive fusion in Quebec particularly often featured a pastoral quality, with some British influence (**Gentle Giant**) and more generic influences from different jazz artists around the globe, for this band specifically **Jean Luc Ponty** and **Maneige**. Keyboardist **Pierre Lescaut** is the composer of all seven pieces while the whole band is credited for the music, rather brilliantly executed. After the disbandment he will change to new age compositions.
RECOMMENDED RECORDINGS: AQUARELLE (Aka: Sous Un Arbre) *(WEA, 1978).* M.G. & C.C.

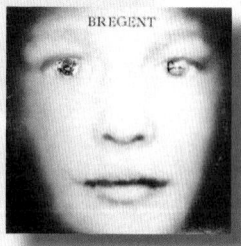

BRÉGENT

Michel-Georges Brégent - *keyboards*, **Jacque Brégent** - *vocals*, **Vincent Dionne** - *percussion*.
Brothers **Michel-Georges** and **Jacque Brégent** start their own rock group with two saxes, illustrating musically the texts of French poets Baudelaire, Verlaine and Villon, and also songs from **Léveillé**, **Leclerc** and the semi-anarchist **Léo Ferré**. A very dynamic singing ranging from whispering to yelling supported by jazzy, gothic, improvs, quite innovative for the times. Their first album of 1972 *Poussières Des Regrets* has dark and sometimes gothic tunes, alternated to psychedelic sounds. In the mid '70s **Michel Georges** teams up with percussionist **Vincent Dionne** for two albums mixing krautrock and electronic prog on the level of **Kraftwerk**. The new duo reunite with **Jacque** in 1979 for a second **Bregent** album titled *Pour Partir Ailleurs* which repeats the formula of their debut pointing slightly to a more avant-prog pop-rock with free-jazz inserts and lyrics wrote by the Canadian songwriter **Felix Leclerc**.
DISCOGRAPHY: POUSSIERE DES REGRETS *(RCA, 1972)* **POUR PARTIR ALLIEURS** *(CAM, 1979).* C.A.

CANO

André Paiement - *guitar, vocals*, **Rachel Paiement** - *vocals*, **Marcel Aymar** *guitar*, **David Burt** - *guitar*, **John Doerr** - *bass*, **Michel Dasti** - *drums*, **Wasyl Kohut** - *violin*, **Michel Kendel** - *keyboards*.
Acronym for **Coopérative des Artistes du Nouvel-Ontario**, they form in 1971 in a semi-hippy-pastoral commune and developing into theater, poetry, writing and a whole bunch of other arts and craftsmen-ships on a 320 acres Buffalo ranch. A band born as arrangers of old melodies from the French tradition with a renewed taste: a debut album in 1976, *Tous Dans L'meme Bateau*, and another, *Au Nord De Notre Vie*, more mature and recalling the sound of **Renaissance**. The third album *Eclipse* of 1978 has some English songs too. Unfortunately **Andrè Paiement** commits suicide at the end of the year while violinist **Wasyl Kohut** died of illness soon after.
DISCOGRAPHY: TOUS DANS L'MEME BATEAU *(A&M, 1976)* **AU NORD DE NOTRE VIE** *(A&M, 1977)* **ECLIPSE** *(A&M, 1978)* **RENDEZ VOUS** *(A&M, 1979)* **SPIRIT OF THE NORTH** *(A&M, 1980).* C.A.

North America: CANADA

CONCEPT
(aka The Humanist Advent Concept)

Peter Riden – *guitars, vocals,* **Robert C. Schwelb** – *keyboards, vocals,* **Marc Ulus** - *bass, guitars, flute, vocals,* **Pier Heiken** - *drums, keyboards, vocals.*

Also known as the **Humanist Advent Concept**, this is the musical journey of **Peter Riden** and some long time friends who developed into great musicians (**Robert C. Schwelb**, **Pier Heiken** and **Marc Ulus**) and disciples of the underground following that grew along with them: preacher of the Concept of Humanism brought to all the open-minded believers of true freedom through a music that fries your brain without the use of drugs. *Invasion* was published in 1979 with ingenious mastery, playing acid and weird guitars as if under the influence of LSD. The music transports you on a trippy experience that sucks you into a whirlwind of deformed sensations. In fact it was released with the warning 'don't take drugs when You play it'. Another two albums also re-issuing unpublished recordings.
RECOMMENDED RECORDINGS: INVASION *(Reveal, 1979).*   M.G.

CONNIVENCE

Paul Pugnaire - *guitar, vocals,* **Marc Sommer** - *bass, vocals,* **Jean-Luc Gotteland** - *keyboards, flute, vocals,* **Thierry Durbano** - *drums, percussion,* **Lionel Dugas** - *vocals, guitar.*

Not really band, but more of a collective name for artists (Legault and Soucy) or groups (Oasis and Nous Autres) from the same region that found cheaper to share recording costs and release in 1977 on the same record their personal tracks, but also playing on each other's works: echoes of the early **Genesis**, of **Anhony Phillips** in the soloist works, some elements of French folk, a bit jazz and a bit avant-garde for the softer pieces. Dramatically different styles for three albums (until 84) with different line-ups, none of which released in Cd format yet. On the same line the second compilation with numerous strings, horns and a female voice, while in the third the component of the electric sounds increases.
RECOMMENDED RECORDINGS: CONNIVENCE *(Kebec Disc, 1977).*   M.G.

ROBERT CONNOLLY

Author, film producer, journalist and eccentric musician expert in ancient archaeological mysteries (as per the titles of his works) and close encounters with aliens, he publishes a fascinating 1978 album titled *Plateau*, good but not essential: a very light prog inspired by the '70s sound, well supported by keyboards, Hammond organ and synthesizers, with a good female voice, orchestra and chorus included. A sci-fi concept coming with a comic book around the story for an underground prog with cosmic and space moods diminished by the low-cost effect distortions of a home production. Side 1 mixes narration, female vocals, acoustic ballads to prog, while Side 2 is where **Connolly** focuses entirely on the keys for a more traditional progressive rock, though the vocals tend towards AOR, typical of the region. Still not officially reissued on CD.
RECOMMENDED RECORDINGS: PLATEAU *(Tube, 1977).*   M.G.

FRANCK DERVIEUX

An interesting Canadian indie-rock performer playing jazzy fusion gigs whom, after a cancer diagnose, records *Dimension M* in 1972, an album completely dedicated to his doctors and with the participation of guests like **Yves Laferrière** and **Christian St. Roch**. The opening title-track kicks off with a bizarre avant-psych prog instrumental before turning into a more psychedelic guitar solo, followed by pieces of grand piano souring from jazz to complex symphonic organ and a solid rhythm section, ending with **Robichaud**'s wordless singing, or the violin soloing of **Terry King**. Sadly **Dervieux** dies shortly after the release, thus leaving this as his only legacy.
DISCOGRAPHY: DIMENSION M *(CBS, 1972).*   M.G.

North America: CANADA

EDEN
Jean-Bernard Borja - *bass, vocals*, **Robert Boileau** - *keyboards*, **Gilles Favreau** - *guitar*, **Jean Remillard** - *drums*.
Another obscure one-shot band from Quebec with a homonym 1978 album, greatly influenced by **Yes**, with sparkling keyboards and synthesizers well interlaced to compelling guitar and bass works. French vocals and symphonic prog released during the decline of the genre did not help this standard keyboard-driven quartet with nothing extraordinary other than perhaps the early '70s styled artwork. Pleasant and rare album since it has not been yet reissued on CD, and cannot be found in any bootleg version either.
DISCOGRAPHY: **EDEN** (Zik zak, 1978).

C.A.

ET CETERA
Marie Bernard Pagé - *keyboards, vocals*, **Denis Chartrand** - *keyboards, winds, vibes, vocals*, **Pierre Dragon** - *drums, percussion*, **Robert Marchand**- *guitars*, **Alain-Yves Pigeon** - *bass*.
Not to be confused with the Germans led by **Dauner** or the homonym Danish symphonic-prog band of the '90s, this French-Canadian **Gentle Giant** copy-cat published only one album in 1976, 36 minutes short. The soft and sensual vocals of **Marie Bernard Pagé**, a female vocalist with a beautiful voice singing in French, combined with a rather romantic symphonic prog also recalling **Sandrose** or **Apoteosi**, bring a lightness to the music of the **ELP**-esque synths or the **Yes** inspired piano riffs. There are airy pastoral segments that sound like the early **Genesis** and vibraphone parts which add jazz fusion into the mix. Curious their use of a synthesizer prototype called **Ondes Martenot**, an fairly unknown instrument similar to the theremin that they played in tandem with the synthesizers.
DISCOGRAPHY: **ET CETERA** (Apostrophe, 1976).

C.A.

ETERNITE'
Claude Péloquin - *vocals*, **Michel Le François** - *guitar, keyboards*.
A project of singer **Claude Péloquin** and multi-instrumentalist **Michel Le François**, for one good symphonic-prog record very close to some things by **Pulsar** and maybe by **Claude Leveillee**. Their only album *les Chants De L'éternité* was recorded in 1977 with the help of guests like **Maneige** and **Contraction**'s drummer **Richard Perrotte**. Their dark, lyrical style has a few complex ideas, very pleasant echoes of folk and many spacey keyboard parts with acoustic breaks: pretty much song-driven yet with an overall progressive flavor covering the entire album, leading into the dramatic tracks with instrumental and poetic finesse.
RECOMMENDED RECORDINGS: **LES CHANTS DE L'ETERNITE** (Polydor, 1977).

M.G.

FM
Cameron Hawkins - *vocals, sinthesizers*, **Martin Deller** - *drums, percussion, sinthesizers*, **Nash the Slash** - *electric violin, mandolin, glockenspiel, vocals*.
Not to be confused with the British AOR band, this very particular band from Toronto was lead by a crazy violinist by the name of **Nash The Slash** playing dressed as a mummy. Their first Lp of 1976 is a weird sort of hard-rock with strange studio tampering, space-pop hooks, instantly memorable choruses, highly syncopated arrangements, swaths of instrumental workouts, lazer synths and sequencers, with exciting inserts of electric violin. Unfortunately, their crazy front-man opts for a solo career, so the remaining duo replaces him with **Ben Mink**, never managing to regain the magic of their first album. *Headroom: Direct to Disc* is an album recorded live, probably the best example of the deep harmony among the musicians.
RECOMMENDED RECORDINGS: **BLACK NOISE** (Passport, 1977) **HEADROOM: DIRECT TO DISC** (Labirynth, 1978).

C.A.

North America: CANADA

HORN

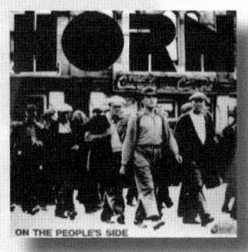

Les Clackett - *vocals*, **Bruce Burron** – *guitars*, **Gary Hynes** – *guitars*, **Alan Duffy** – *bass*, **David De Launay** – *keyboards*, **Wayne Jackson** – *trumpet*, **Bill Bryans** - *drums*.

This group released only one album in 1972 and then stopped all their activities: *On The People's Side* is a strong jazz and R&B oriented work with compelling guitar and bass playing, good vocals and a progressive swing attitude due to the horn section. A septet featuring drummer **Bill Bryans** and trumpeter **Wayne Jackson** among others. Their music is a nice example of Canterbury fusion psychedelic pop with soft arrangements and a solid drumming that ignites with a slight **King Crimson** aura. **Bryans** later joins some new wave bands like **Government** and **The Parachute Club**, while **Wayne Jackson** features on **Peter Gabriel**'s famous track "Sledgehammer".
DISCOGRAPHY: ON THE PEOPLE'S SIDE *(1972 Special Records).* M.G.

CHARLES KACZYNSKI

Violinist **Charles Kaczynski** guests on **Conventum**'s first album in 1977 before releasing his solo masterpiece *Lumière De La Nuit* in 1979, playing all the parts thanks to the technology of modern multi-track recorders: not only did he write the music, the lyrics and the musical and orchestral arrangements, but this talented multi-instrumentalist played every single instrument on this album, including violin, alto violin, cello, acoustic bass, acoustic guitar, 12-string guitar, piano, organ, melodica, flute, recorder, percussions, and vocals. A progressive chamber music, epic with medieval, celtic, baroque and folk themes, bearing similarities at times with **Jean-Luc Ponty** and **Mike Oldfield**, though the musical concept is quite unique. A rare album with a rarer English version recently reissued on CD in 2005.
DISCOGRAPHY: LUMIERE DE LA NUIT *(Private pressing 1979 - CD Progquebec, 2004).* M.G.

KAOS MOON

Bernard Ouelette - *vocals, keyboards, guitars, drums*, **Sylvain Provost** - *guitars*, **Norman Lachapelle** - *bass*, **Magella Cormier** - *drums*.

Keyboardist and drummer **Bernard Ouellette** is the founder and inspiring soul of this high quality melodic rock quartet together since 1985 and greatly influenced by **Marillion**. The romantic pop element is the main characteristic of their sound, with attempts of funky, some hard rock inserts and brilliant instrumental pieces intermingled with the vocals all sung in English. Both albums (the debut arrives only in 1994) are very good although not too original, probably their second of 2004, *The Circle of Madness*, is more pleasant, less experimental and more immediately accessible.
DISCOGRAPHY: AFTER THE STORM *(Kozak, 1994)* **THE CIRCLE OF MADNESS** *(Unicorn, 2004).* C.A.

INDISCIPLINE

Jean-Philippe Goulet - *keyboards, violin*, **Louis Pelletier** - *drums, percussion*, **Martin Poirier** - *bass*, **Francois Therriault** - *guitars, vocals*, **Bernard Baribeau** - *saxophones*.

When the band's name is **Indiscipline** you know there has to be a **King Crimson** flavour to their music: these Canadian musicians play prog inbetween metal and heavy rock with driving guitars and a powerful rhythmic section. They publish a first album in 1994 titled *A Non Obvious Ride*, with good combinations of bass and drums, proposing some melancholic saxophones inserts into the more involving tracks. Their second album *Vixit* released in 1998 contains paler tunes where the darker atmospheres reside in wild and frenzied instrumental moments yet far from being labeled as symphonic. This record contains another tribute, this time to the **Van Der Graf Generator** (*Darkness*). All their songs are sung in English and French.
DISCOGRAPHY: A NON OBVIOUS RIDE *(Belle Antique, 1994)* **VIXIT** *(Orange, 1998).* C.A.

North America: CANADA

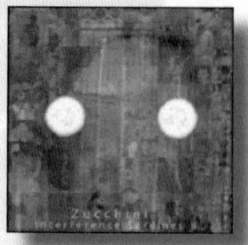

INTERFERENCE SARDINES

Philippe Venne – *guitars,* **Frédéric Lebrasseur** – *drums,* **Andrée Bilodeau** – *violin,* **Sébastien Doré** - *bass,* **Marc Gagnon** – *violin.*
The most important element of music is imagination: the extraordinary capacity to operate without preconceived schemes ignites the RIO movement and avant prog experimentations for a genre born to bear no labels. These young musicians from Québec City play a very violin-oriented prog between rock and contemporary music, between jazz and traditional folk, with strong influences of artists like **Henry Cow**, **Univers Zero**, **Jean Luc Ponty** and **Aksak Maboul**. The 1988 debut, *Mare Crisium*, and their 2001 masterpiece, *Zucchini*, are both a perfect example of these eclectic and absurd compositions, impregnated with wild imagination. The third and last album comes out seven years later, in 2008: *Spot De Rue* contains still excellent and unexpected solutions.
RECOMMENDED RECORDINGS: **ZUCCHINI** *(Ambiances Magnétiques, 2001).* M.G.

LE MATCH

Jacques Lauzon - *drums,* **Francis Leduc** - *violin, flute,* **Pierre-Yves Migneron** - *guitar, vocals,* **Gaétan Rousseau** - *bass,* **Normand Théroux** - *keyboards, vocals.*
La Nouvelle Frontiére was a 7-piece band that split due to the fact that twins **Marie-Claire** and **Richard Séguin** were heavily into folk whereas their keyboardist **Normand Théroux** wanted a heavier sound: the twins formed the duo **Les Séguin** while **Théroux** formed in 1974 **Le Match**. Their only album *Lègendes* is still strongly influenced by traditional Quebec folk, mixing a more commercial AOR with a distinct **Gentle Giant** complexity. Heavy vocals with French lyrics and lots of keyboards; the violin and flute confer a certain originality through the medieval atmospheres they create, rich of melody and dramatic touches. The most famous track "Le soleil des plants d'huile" is a song about Montreal's east-end oil refineries.
DISCOGRAPHY: **LÈGENDES** *(Sonogram, 1974).* C.A.

L'INFONIE

Formed in 1967 in a versatile rock commune, the ensemble was led by **Walter Boudreau** and **Raôul Duguay**. Their first album, published in 1969, is a pastiche of various styles: avant-garde and extreme experimentation influenced by **Zappa** and **Beefheart** with many jazz and ethnic references. Their obsession for the number 3 characterizes all their discography (The first album *Volume 3* contains 33 musicians, the second is entitled *Volume 33 - Mantra*, the third *Volume 333*) containing a strange psychedelic chamber-jazz in the vein of the late '60s mixed with pop and experimental fusion. **Raôul** will later start his solo career as a poet, author and songwriter so without him, **Walter** completes the "Paix" project as their last production named *Volume 3333* in 1974.
DISCOGRAPHY: **L'INFONIE VOLUME 3 (Andrè Perry presente l'Infonie)** *(Polydor, 1969)* **VOLUME 33 (Mantra)** *(Polydor, 1971)* **VOLUME 333** *(Kotai, 1972)* **VOLUME 3333** *(Kotai, 1974).* C.A.

MICHEL MADORE

Michel Madore is an artist involved with various media: mainly a sculptor and painter, in the mid '70s he enters the musical world to acquire new emotions. Helped by some amateur musicians, in 1976 he releases *Le Komuso a Cordes*, an album containing various styles of psych/prog with Moogs and a **Gong**-like sax, mixed with good experimentation (the track "Juggernaut" is remarkable with its space effects), filtered with an orchestration similar to **Jan Michel Jarre**'s. In the second album, **Madore** plays everything himself for a much different fusion-folk result, recalling the works of **Bregent**. From the '80s he abandons music and focuses on his painting and sculptures.
DISCOGRAPHY: **LE KOMUSO A CORDES** *(Kebek, 1976)* **LA CHAMBRE NUTIALE** *(Kebek, 1979).* C.A.

North America: CANADA

NATHAN MAHL
Guy Le Blanc - *keyboards*, **Mark Spènard, Jose Bergeron** - *guitars*, **Claude Prince** - *bass*, **Dan Lacasse, Alain Bergeron** - *drums*, **Jean-Pierre Ranger** - *vocals*.
Keyboardist **Guy Leblanc** is the creator of this project, started in 1981 and playing a form of fusion jazz-rock partly rooted in symphonic prog (not neo-prog) with a first album issued in 1983. The following year they disband due to **Guy**'s personal issues. After a long period of reprises and demises with many a line-up changes, they still manage to record some tracks. In 1997 **Guy** founds his own label, Mahl Productions, and they record another album released in 1999, *The Clever Use of Shadows*: mainly an instrumental work along the lines of **Happy The Man** with heavy influences from **Allan Holdsworth, UK** and **Gentle Giant**. In parallel **Guy** also played with **Camel**, yet he manages to produce an extensive discography as **Nathan Mahl**.
RECOMMENDED RECORDINGS: **PARALLEL ECCENTRICITIES** (Hit! Records, 1983) **THE CLEVER USE OF SHADOWS** (Mahl, 1999) **HERETIK VOL. 1: BODY OF ACCUSATION** (Mahl, 2000) **HERETIK VOL. 2: THE TRIAL** (Mahl, 2001).
M.G.

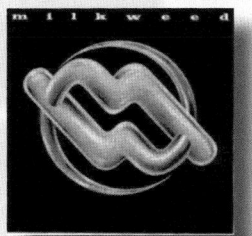

MILKWEED
Sergio Gonclaves - *keyboards*, **Louise Caffope** - *oboe*, **Edouardo Couto** - *guitar*, **Nelson Gamboa** - *bass*, **Marcel Lapointe** - *saxophones*, **Gerard Masse** - *drums*, **Pierre Nadeau** - *vocals, piano*, **Jocelyn Sheehy** - *guitar*.
More likely a project than an actual band, deliver their multi-discipline art in the form of a progressive recording situated in the symphonic rock mainstream with dark atmospheres obtained playing an oboe performed with the help of a powerful keyboard and the English recitation singing of **Pierre Nadeau** (penalized by his slightly French accent and the fairly average and dated poetry on most of the tracks). Their only album *Milkweed* of 1978 is a good work nevertheless that should have deserved a sequel. After the release this dark ensemble of musicians disappears leaving no trace, except for **Nadeau** who becomes an appreciated pianist before his death in 2004. The album has been re-issued in the nineties by SynPhonic Records.
DISCOGRAPHY: **MILKWEED** (Syn-Phonic, 1978).
C.A. & C.C.

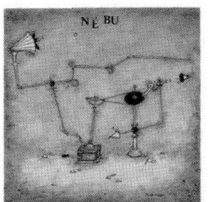

NÉBU
Jean Derome - *flutes, vocals*, **Pierre Saint-Jacques** - *piano, percussion, vocals*, **Claude Simard** - *contrabass, bass*.
From Québec they form in 1978 with the help of **René Lussier** from **Conventum** and also thanks to Solstice which are actually the managers of Cadence Records, the label that will publish both their albums. This trio merges jazz to classical inspirations with a heavy progressive accent. Among the first to play at the Festival Jazz of Montreal in 1980 and founders of the organization **Ensemble de Musique Improvisé de Montréal** (EMIM), a group of jazz players gigging frequently in little bars and clubs (an album titled *Danses* will be released by this Ensemble in 1979). Their debut album is an atmospheric smokey jazz with flute, piano, and stand-up bass while the second work, *Motus* of 1980, has a unique illustration by **Derome** on its cover.
DISCOGRAPHY: **NÉBU** (Cadence, 1978) **MOTUS** (Cadence, 1980).
M.G.

NIGHTWINDS
Mike Gingrich – *basso*, **Gerald O'Brien** – *tastiere*, **Terry O'Brien** – *chitarre*, **Mike Phelan** - *batteria*, **Sandy Singers** - *voce*.
Discovered at the end of '70s by another contemporary band called **Klaatu**, the quintet was persuaded to record an album: many a dispute during the sessions that led to the disbandment before the eventual release of 1979, which did not take place. In 1991, the two former components of **Klaatu**, **Dee Long** and **Terry Draper**, recover the old tapes and release this lost album with an excellent work of digital mastering and post-production under the label Laser's Edge. It's a classic symphonic prog album that recalls the **Genesis** of *A Trick of the Tail* with references to **Yes** and a lot of catchy tunes. Keyboard dominated it also features some incredible drum and bass interplay as well as strong songwriting and solid musicianship.

DISCOGRAPHY: **NIGHTWINDS** (Laser's Edge, 1991, posthumous release).
M.G.

North America: CANADA

OFFENBACH

Pierre Harel – vocals, lyrics, **Gerry Boulet** – keyboards, **Breen Le Boeuf** – bass, **Robert Harrison** – drums, **John Mc Gale** – guitar, saxophones.

Born on the left overs of the psychedelic **Les Gants Blancs** led by the Boulet brothers, they become Offenbach Soap Opera in 1969 singing in French but in time musically more oriented towards **Pink Floyd**, **Uriah Heep**, **Atomic Rooster** and **Deep Purple**. The first LP of 1971 has scarce success, so they accept to present a Mass for the dead at the St-Joseph Oratory in Montreal, a project aimed to gain some notoriety, in fact attracting 5000 people to an eclectic performance of rock mixed with liturgical Latin Gregorian chants recorded on a 16 track and released in 1973 as *Saint-Chrône-de-Néant*. They also release a documentary called *Tabarnac* with filmmaker Pierre Harel. In 1976 their first LP completely in English, *Never Too Tender* and after a few lineup changes and 2 albums in French they win a first Felix Award in 1979 with *Traversion*. The last concerts in 1985 then **Gerry Boulet** leaves to pursue a solo career until his death in 1991.
RECOMMENDED RECORDINGS: SAINT-CHRONE DE NEANT *(Barclay, 1973, Live)* OFFENBACH *(A&M, 1977)* TRAVERSION *(RCA, 1979).*
M.G.

PANGÉE

Thierry B. Gateau - bass, clarinet, guitars, bass pedals, **Jean-Francois Bergeron** - keyboards, **Julien Bilodeau** - guitars, **Jean-Vincent Roy** - percussion, **Pierre-Olivier Nadeau** - violin.

Their name comes from the original super-continent at the birth of planet Earth, later split into Laurasia and Gondwanna. Their only album is a concept inspired by mythology and entirely instrumental, released in 1995. A mainly guitar-driven quintet with strong **King Crimson** and **Yes** references, but the use of synths links them to the modern prog era. A pleasant album with delicate arrangements, good instrumentation and elaborate tracks which offer good progressive touches of innovative and highly challenging music, between a free-hearted psychedelic rock and the more symphonic-jazz with emphasis on the **Djam Karet**-like guitar tricks (ambient, robotic tones turning into complex and atmospheric leads) and the dreamy keyboards and violins.
DISCOGRAPHY: HYMNEMONDE *(Musea, 1995).*
C.A.

POLLEN

Jacques Tom Rivest - vocals, bass, acoustic guitar, keyboards, **Sylvain Coutu** - drums, vibraphone, percussion, **Claude Lemay** - keyboards, flute, vibraphone,, bass, vocals, **Richard Lemoyne** - guitars, keyboards, bass.

Formed in 1972, they became famous a couple of years later when **Gentle Giant** chose them to open their concerts in the Canadian tour, giving them large visibility and a discographic contract. Their only album of 1976 is a romantic symphonic prog (distant from the usual folk tendencies of their colleagues) with French lyrics and open references to **Genesis**, **Yes**, **Ange**, **Carpe Diem**, **BMS** and **PFM**. The vocals of **Jacques Tom Rivest** are emotional and theatrical, a very good performer, while three of the four members play the keyboards, with nice solos, an acoustic guitar and some nice flute and vibraphone passages. After the disbandment in 1976 some members begin their solo careers or as producers.
RECOMMENDED RECORDINGS: POLLEN *(Kébec Disc, 1976).*
M.G.

ROUGE CIEL

Nemo Venba - trumpet, drums, percussion, **Antonin Provost** - guitars, **Simon Lapointe** - keyboards, winds, **Guido Del Fabro** - violin, turntables, mandolin.

High school friends **Guido Del Fabbro** and **Antonin Provost** started the band as a duo in 1996 expanding over the years to an avant-garde quartet with RIO tendencies. Their eponymous debut of 2001 is full of improvised jazz and prog rock, with complicated dissonant parts to groovy passages and even Folk touches here and there. The complex interplay of violin, trumpets and electric piano give way to plenty of individual solos, even with a heavy use of mandolin, ranging across an **Art Zoyd** and **Univers Zero** sound with buoyant **Miriodor** jaunts, pastoral fusion, pyrotechnic prog-fusion, crazed free jazz violin solos, pedestrian avant-jazz, post-Kagel deconstructionism and a sort of Eastern-European jazz-rock. Another two albums more or less on the same line of the first for a band that still may reserve a surprise.
RECOMMENDED RECORDINGS: VEUILLEZ PROCEDER *(MFMV, 2005).*
M.G. & C.C.

North America: CANADA

SYMPHONIC SLAM

Timo Laine - *guitar synth, guitars, lead vocals,* **John Lowery** - *drums, vocals,* **David Stone** - *keyboards, vocals.*

Timo Laine, from Finland but raised in California, started as a guitar teacher and playing with **Zebra** for some demos. In 1974 he joins Canadian **Neil Merryweather** on his 1974 project/album *Space Rangers* and shortly after he buys himself a prototype gadget which hooked up six individual synthesizers to his guitar, one for each string. He relocates to Toronto where he teams up with **David Stone** and **John Lowery** to play on his own project/album *Symphonic Slam*, released in 1976, blending prog-rock and jazz with psychedelic tones. When the label asks him for a disco album, he quits them and founds Lady Records for his next project, published in 1978 as **Timo** and titled *Symphonic Slam II*, for a trippy sequel of the previous. In the '80s he participates in other musical projects, as well as dedicating to painting and entomology (bugs). Finally back, in 2005 he releases his first true solo album, *Monotrim Project*, and decides to start on a third **Symphonic Slam** album, *Hey Fire* (initially supposed to be titled *Cave Canem*).
RECOMMENDED RECORDINGS: SYMPHONIC SLAM *(A&M, 1976).*   M.G. & C.C.

TERRACED GARDEN

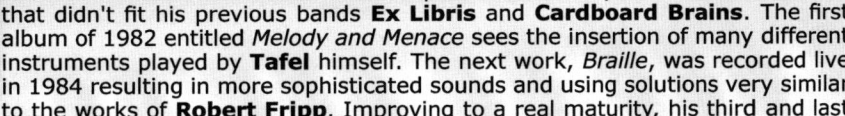

Carl Tafel - *keyboards, bass, guitar,* **Scott Weber** - *drums,* **Jody Mitchell** - *guitar,* **Darrell Flint** - *bass.*

Born in 1981 as the solo project of **Carl Tafel**, who hit a studio to record material he had composed over the years that didn't fit his previous bands **Ex Libris** and **Cardboard Brains**. The first album of 1982 entitled *Melody and Menace* sees the insertion of many different instruments played by **Tafel** himself. The next work, *Braille*, was recorded live in 1984 resulting in more sophisticated sounds and using solutions very similar to the works of **Robert Fripp**. Improving to a real maturity, his third and last album of 1988, *Within*, is richer in ideas, class and quality. **Life** and circumstance prevented any further efforts so the band fades away while **Tafel** join **Station Twang** as a bass player in 2000, occasionally holding solo concerts over the years.
DISCOGRAPHY: MELODY AND MENACE *(CT, 1983)* BRAILLE *(CT, 1984)* WITHIN *(Melody & Menace, 1988).*   C.A.

TRUE MYTH

Tom Treumuth - *keyboards,* **Tony Cook** - *guitars,* **Steve McKenna** - *bass, slide guitar,* **Brian Bolliger** - *drums,* **Bruce Cummings** - *vocals.*

Born as a college project in Fanshawe's music school, their keyboardist **Tom Treumuth** secures a deal with Warner Bros for the 1979 debut, the first digital album recorded in Canada and the second in the world (the first being **Stevie Wonder**'s *Secret Life Of Plants*). This homonym album contains great melodic singing parts delivered by **Cummings**' voice, able to touch surprisingly high notes, without falsettos. A lot of piano, but also Mellotron and synths for a **Yes** and **Genesis** feel, but very much similar to **Kansas**. Tom soon opens his own record label, Hypnotic, signing up his band mates for their second work, *Telegram*, in 1981, a modest AOR style with the dragging and sunny prog of his keyboard playing.
RECOMMENDED RECORDINGS: TRUE MYTH *(WEA, 1979).*   M.G.

VISIBLE WIND

Luc Hébert - *drums,* **Louis Roy** - *bass, bass pedals,* **Stephen Geyster** - *keyboards, flute, vocals,* **Claude Rainville** - *guitars.*

Originated from the trio **Herbert-Roy-Geyster**, this band has an ever changing line-up which causes the consequent sound, different from record to record, alternating instrumental and vocal parts sung in English and French of mainly new-prog but with the prevalent use of a vintage instrumentation to obtain a '70s symphonic feel. Their debut *Catharsis* of 1988 is a melodic album recalling **Marillion**'s style with AOR cues. The second shifts towards **Genesis** before passing to the **King Crimson** and **Camel**-like symphonic, well balanced and interesting *Narcissius Goes To The Moon*. Just a little bit inferior the last, *Barb-À-Baal-A-Loo* of 2000 with **Jethro Tull** flutes. In 2006 they participate to the BajaProg festival mixing virtuosity with a more contemporary sound.
RECOMMENDED RECORDINGS: NARCISSIUS GOES TO THE MOON *(Musea, 1996).*   M.G.

North America: UNITED STATES

ALBATROSS

Mark Dahlgren - *keyboards, vocals,* **Joe Guarino** - *bass, vocals,* **Mike Novak** - *vocals,* **Paul Roe** - *guitar,* **Dana Williams** - *drums, percussion.*

Classic symphonic rock band greatly sounding like **Yes'** keyboard parts with the typical mellotron, Hammond or Moog. Their strength lied in the experimentation and the good guitar-synth duets. The 1976 album contained tracks like "Four Horsemen of the Apocalypse" that they were already performing live since 1971: an independent effort (unusual for the time) produced to promote the band in some way. But sales were bad so they tried some changes shortly after, with **Jethro Tull** costumes or by holding free concerts, but disco music was rising and nothing really helped thus disbanding about 18 months after their only album release. The band members go their separate ways: singer **Mike Novak** joins **The Blues Hawks** in 1996.

DISCOGRAPHY: ALBATROSS *(1975, Anvil).* M.G.

ASTRË

Bill Tankersley - *bass, bass pedals, keyboards,* **Mark Loveless** - *keyboards, guitar,* **Les Mobley** - *drums, vocals.*

Formed in 1978 and releasing their only album in 1981: no secret why this band was so horrendously under-produced given the attention to the new rising and shining musical genres of the time. Yet, their debut *Foresight* was a prestigious convergence of styles with its superbly complex prog-rock lying behind the mess (a reissue may help to revive it all together). Influenced by **Genesis**, **King Crimson**, **Gentle Giant** and closing with a joking tribute to **ELP** and **Yes**, the definitely symphonic sounds are very well performed with a skillful mix of keyboards and guitars with a touch of AOR. After the publishing of their record the band kept holding concerts and touring in the US, until 1983 when their activities almost ceased completely and in 1984 they officially disbanded.

DISCOGRAPHY: FORESIGHT *(Akustic Records, 1981),* C.A.

ATLANTIS PHILARMONIC

Joe Di Fazio - *keyboards, piano, guitar, bass, vocals,* **Royce Gibson** - *drums, percussion.*

A symphonic rock duo formed in 1971 strongly driven by organ, piano and mellotron, pushing the music to majestic sounds influenced by **ELP** or **Yes**, and blending it with some fusion, psychedelia, pop or Moody Blues moments, while the guitar invents rocky riffs directed to more hard-rock solutions similar to **Uriah Heep**, **Deep Purple** or **Atomic Rooster**. Their debut album of 1974 released by the label Deutsche Harmonia Mundi, is eclectic work with a clear classical orientation (as their name clearly suggests), with excellent vocals and rhythmic changes, a perfect showcase of these talented musicians. In 1975 they record a second album before the break-up, published as *Grand Master* only in 2008.

DISCOGRAPHY: ATLANTIS PHILARMONIC *(1974, Dharma Records).* M.G.

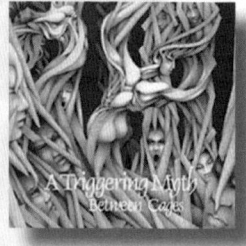

A TRIGGERING MYTH

Rick Eddy - *keyboards, guitars, percussion,* **Tim Drumheller** - *keyboards, percussion.*

Formed in 1989 by **Rick Eddy** and **Tim Drumheller**, an American duo of multi-instrumentalists for a heavily based keyboard prog (especially the piano), curiously mixing jazz, rock and classical symphonic music with mysterious overtones of tension-filled suspense. Influenced by **Gentle Giant**, **VDGG** and **ELP** though their style remains a unique contemporary sound of its own. The homonym debut of 1990 improves throughout their production from a form of modern fusion jazz (**Perigeo**, **National Health**, **Frank Zappa**, **Area**, **Happy the Man**) to more complex compositions. Among the great collaborators are **Bonetti** and **Piras** of **Deus Ex Machina**, and **Akihisa Tsuboy** from the Japanese band **KBB**.

RECOMMENDED RECORDINGS: THE REMEDY OF ABSTRACTION *(The Laser's Edge, 2006).* M.G.

North America: UNITED STATES

 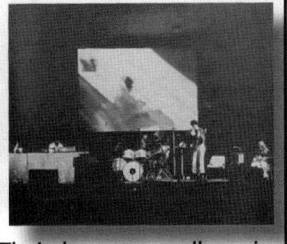

BABYLON

Rick Leonard - *bass, vocals*, **Doroccus** - *vocals, keyboards*, **Rodney Best** - *drums, percussion*, **J. David Boyko** - *guitars*, **G.W. Chambers** - *keyboards, piano*.
Formed in 1976 with influences of the early **Genesis** and **Gentle Giant**, this wonderful band plays an excellent '70s prog with hard rock driven passages, great analogue keyboard work, **Hackett** styled guitar playing and extraordinarily adept musicianship. Their homonym album in 1978 contains the refined voice of **Doroccus** with theatrical vocals, great instrumental parts and broad melodies. They released only this work and broke up that same year. During 1989, after a good restoration done by label Syn-Phonic, two good live recordings of 1978 were released as posthumous live albums, containing their entire track list plus several songs which were not on that original release.
DISCOGRAPHY: BABYLON (1978, Mehum Music) **NIGHT OVER NEVER** (1989, Syn-Phonic) **BETTER CONDITIONS FOR THE DEAD** (1989, Syn-Phonic).
M.G.

BRIMSTONE

Gregg Andrews - *vocals*, **Ken Miller** - *bass*, **Bernie Nau** - *keyboards*, **Jimmy Papatoukakis** - *drums*, **Christopher Wintrip** - *guitar, vocals*.
Formed in Ohio by **Chris Wintrip** in the early '70s, they went through many line-up changes changes throughout the years. Their only album was published in 1973 and entitled *Paper Winged Dreams* (available on CD). It has long instrumental parts in which the keyboards and guitar alternate their roles on the first side, while the second is a suite in five parts with vocal solos, vocal harmonies and pleasant guitar playing, an outstanding use of the Hammond organ, well managed in a delicate atmosphere. They kept touring during the '80s with some new members replacing those who left and holding concerts as close to home as possible.
DISCOGRAPHY: PAPER WINGED DREAMS (Brimstone Records, 1973).
C.A.

 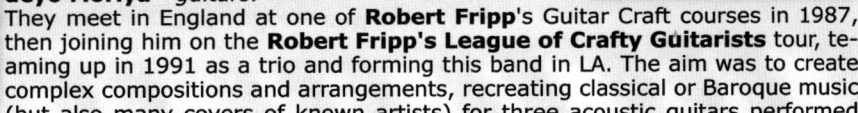

THE CALIFORNIA GUITAR TRIO

Bert Lams - *guitars*, **Paul Richards** - *guitars*, **Hideyo Moriya** - *guitars*.
They meet in England at one of **Robert Fripp**'s Guitar Craft courses in 1987, then joining him on the **Robert Fripp's League of Crafty Guitarists** tour, teaming up in 1991 as a trio and forming this band in LA. The aim was to create complex compositions and arrangements, recreating classical or Baroque music (but also many covers of known artists) for three acoustic guitars performed with a modern approach and never overdubbed. They sign up with label Discipline Global Mobile and in 1993 release *The Yamanashi Blues*, an incredible debut album with various genres like pop, rock, Californian surf music and jazz. Their best selling album *Pathways* includes compositions by **Bach**, **Beethoven** and **Stan Funicelli** among others.
RECOMMENDED RECORDINGS: INVITATION (2001, DGM) **PATHWAYS** (2001, DGM).
M.G.

CHAKRA

Nigel Redman - *keyboards*, **Tom Maxwell** – *drums*, **John Ugarte** - *bass*, **David Lamb** – *vocals*, **Mark Blumenfeld** – *guitars*.
American symphonic prog band from the late '70s who managed to publish an album with the worst timing possible: this self-titled release of 1979 consists of 8 tracks absolutely dominated by **Nigel Redmon**'s keyboards (maybe even abusing them) creating instrumental passages and atmospheres that are way too similar to the early **Genesis** or even more so to the work of **Yes** and **Emerson Lake & Palmer**. The distinct classical quality is self-indulging especially the grand piano managed with originality, good skills and heavy tendencies of symphonic rock coupled with the original lyrics sung by the majestic voice of **David Lamb**, oriented over disputed religious themes. Overall an average album but still quite pleasant.
DISCOGRAPHY: CHAKRA (Brother Studio, 1979).
C.A. & C.C.

North America: UNITED STATES

CLEARLIGHT
(Cyrille Verdeaux)

This project was started in France in 1973 by song-writer, pianist and composer **Cyrille Verdeaux**, who signed up with Virgin for his debut of 1975 titled *Clearlight Symphony* with special guests like **Didier Malherbe** from **Gong**. A blend of classical romanticism and prog-rock experimentation which led him to be enrolled as **Gong**'s support artist. Although the project was born in France, he moved with his family to California, where he releases the rest of his works. After many good albums, a family tragedy brings him to a quest for interior peace and he leaves to study Yoga in India. Once back this French artist published a series of new age albums where he conceptualizes his experiences with Indian music. *Infinite Symphony* of 2003 is a good symphonic prog album with a **Paul Whitehead** illustration on the cover.
RECOMMENDED RECORDINGS: CLEARLIGHT SYMPHONY (Virgin, 1975) **INFINITE SYMPHONY** (Clearlight 888 Music, 2003).
M.G.

COMPANION

Brit Warner - *vocals, guitars, keyboards,* **Wain Bradley** - *vocals, bass, keyboards,* **Mike Russell** - *keyboards,* **Andy Tate** - *guitars,* **Shof Beavers** - *drums.*
Prog-rock band Leviathan disbands in 1974, yet Brit Warner and Waine Bradley continue to work together and create this project recording one album that same year, mostly distributed to the press and media: Reap the lost dreamers veers towards folk, opened by a beautiful version of The Beatles' track "Blackbird" while and the rest are delicate melodies and typical '70s arrangements, acoustic ballads or hard-prog recalling The Moody Blues, Pink Floyd and CSN&Y. The arrangements are highly eclectic with spacey synthesizers and light psychedelic vibes, mainly performed on acoustic guitars with a few electric vibes reminding Yes, while the lead vocals come closer to Jon Anderson's style. Lovely string work too for a more bucolic feel. Bradley now runs his own label.
DISCOGRAPHY: REAP OF THE LOST DREAMERS (Akarma, 1974).
M.G.

COVENANT

David Gryder - *keyboards, percussion, programming,* **Bill Pohl** - *guitar, bass.*
Musical project of **Dave Gryder**, multi-talented musician who starts his career as drummer and vocalist in trash metal bands. His only album *Nature's Divine Reflection* has nothing in common with these early years: a sumptuous example of symphonic prog in the style of **Wakeman**, without too many disguises for a very sincere and proud record, rich of drums and keyboards with complex and decidedly well played scores spread over two long suites and a short linking piece. It is an instrumental album where **Gryder** plays virtually all the the instruments including vintage keyboards like Hammond organ, Prophet 5, Mellotron, ARP and Korg synths, digital drums overdubbed with both digital and analog tracks. Guitar and bass are played by **Bill Pohl** in the first suite. Shortly after he joins **Blood Of The Sun** and **Storm At Sunrise**.
RECOMMENDED RECORDINGS: NATURE'S DIVINE REFLECTION (Syn-Phonic, 1993).
M.G.

EARTHRISE

Kenn Pierog – *bass, vocals,* **Bill Drobile** - *keyboards, vocals,* **Greg DiDonato** – *drums.*
The year is 1975, the first golden era of prog is at it's peak and three American musicians decide to form a band named after a **Camel** song though they are more an **EL&P** clone, with a massive use of Hammond Organ and keyboards, still quite an original and fresh. They start to play mostly live and in 1977 they manage to release a first self-titled album of symphonic, instrumental prog, with some sounds reminding the Italians **Le Orme** and some jazzy keyboards recalling the Canterbury school. They split in 1979 without recording a new album and in 1998 a reunion for some concerts sends the message they plan on a second release. In the meantime the original tapes of their debut went sadly lost so they remaster them from an old vinyl. In 2008 *Earthrise Day Two* was finally released.
RECOMMENDED RECORDINGS: EARTHRISE (Arceden, 1977).
M.G. & C.C.

North America: UNITED STATES

EASTER ISLAND

Mark Miceli - *guitar, vocals, synthesizer,* **Rick Bartlett** – *vocals,* **Ray Vogel** - *keyboards,* **Park Crain** - *bass, synth pedals, percussion,* **Mark Hendricks** - *drums.*
Originally formed in 1973 by excellent guitarist **Mark Miceli**, they began playing with emphasis on the minimoog and Mellotron works as well as the guitar, like most prog bands from the mid '70s seemed to do, influenced by **King Crimson**, **Yes** and **ELP**, with heavy doses of world music in the rhythms and some good songwriting. Their self-titled debut of 1979 was re-issued as *Now and Then* in 1991 in CD-format. The band is summoned from the dead in 1999 for a second album, *Mother Sun*, but with a much more modern cut, also thanks to a very good work of keyboardist **Vogel**: the previous style adds long AOR cues and good keyboard and guitar interplay, uniting complex rhythms to more melodious moments resulting in effects that are often superb and epic.
RECOMMENDED RECORDINGS: NOW AND THEN *(Private pressing, 1991).*   M.G.

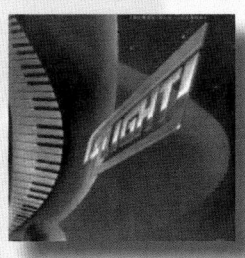

FLIGHT

Pat Vidas - *trumpet, saxophones.* **Jim Yaeger** - *keyboards,* **John De Nicola** - *bass,* **Ted Karczewsky** - *guitars,* **Steve Shebar** - *drums.*
Eclectic jazz-rock band from Florida led by American musician and singer Pat Vidas, who also played brass instruments, which made their music very accessible, not like a regular fusion band, but sounding more like the brass rock of **Chicago** inspired by **ELP** or **Gentle Giant**. Formed in the mid '70s, they released three albums (the first two are an exceptional mixture of jazz rock with some symphonic influences) for a pop rock between fusion and prog, equipped with an exquisite instrumental technique decidedly avant-garde, especially in the second 1976 album *Incredible Journey*: a nice romantic setting with not only a guitar in the leading role. If the first two are quite similar in intent and structure, the third work of 1980, *Excursion Beyond*, the band veers to a clear jazz rock with great improvisations and the exquisite solos that still makes it a masterpiece.
DISCOGRAPHY: FLIGHT *(Capitol, 1975)* **INCREDIBLE JOURNEY** *(Capitol, 1976)* **EXCURSION BEYOND** *(Motown, 1980).*   C.A.

FLYING ISLAND

Bill Bacon - *drums,* **Jeff Bova** - *keyboards,* **Fred Fraioli** - *violin, flute,* **Tom Prely** - *bass,* **Ray Smith** - *guitar.*
Connecticut based jazz rock fusion band led by violinist **Fred Fraioli**, with keyboardist **Jeff Bova** and drummer **Bill Bacon**, sign a 5-year contract with Vanguard Label and in 1975 they released a first self-titled album with very rich and elaborated sounds and also featuring **Joe Farrell** from **Return to Forever**. Their sound contains strong references to the progressive and fusion of **Frank Zappa** and some echoes of **Mahavishnu Orchestra** too, amongst others. Their second and actually last work, *Another Kind Of Space*, maintained the decent levels of the previous. After the band dissolves, the musicians join other projects: **Bacon** with **Material**, **Curlew** and then in one of the **Gong** incarnations; **Fraioli** contributes to **Fates Warning**; **Bova** becomes a studio musician and record producer.
RECOMMENDED RECORDINGS: FLYING ISLAND *(Vanguard, 1975)* **ANOTHER KIND OF SPACE** *(Vanguard, 1976).*   M.G.

FOLLY'S POOL

Doug Carlson - *vocals, guitar, keyboards,* **Jeff Carlson** - *guitars, vocals,* **Ray Haney** - *bass,* **Jeff Bryon** - *drums,* **Darren Devaurs** - *keyboards,* **Steve Ono** - *guitars.*
Formed in 1974 playing a folk genre with roots buried in country music, they soon evolve into a sound based upon tunes very close to the early **Eagles**, but shaded with progressive moods. It features flute, good guitar, nice vocal harmonies and well crafted songs. Despite this positive prelude, the press reviewed their debut album of 1977 as a pale copy of **Loggins and Messina**'s records, without understanding the prog propulsion and the delicate contamination of typical American styles. Probably the production is to blame for having released a record aiming for broadcasts instead of concerts. The next two works have nothing prog to them (*Bathing Caps Required*, 1985 and *Road Through Independence*, 2008) so that was that.
RECOMMENDED RECORDINGS: FOLLY'S POOL *(Century Records, 1977).*   C.A.

North America: UNITED STATES

GABRIEL BONDAGE

Rex Bundy - *vocals, acoustic guitars*, **Jeff Krueger** - *lead guitar*, **Ron Schwartz** - *keyboards*, **Tony Stram** - *bass*, **PJ Shadowhawk** - *drums, backing vocals*.

Chicago-based and religiously inclined art-rock band formed in 1973, recording a first album titled Angel dust in 1975: Christian-inspired lyrics with plenty of biblical references and a rather soft progressive rock of commercial leanings, mainly dominated by rural influences. The music is a spacey organ and keyboard driven pop rock that never fully convinced neither the critics nor the public, albeit their symphonic approach in the debut. The next work Another Trip To Earth was released in 1977 and went slightly better. Bands members also had various other side projects up until 1984. They reunited recently working on new material, some of which is available on their facebook and myspace websites.

DISCOGRAPHY: **ANGEL DUST** *(Dharma, 1975)* **ANOTHER TRIP TO EARTH** *(Dharma 1977).* **C.A.**

GLASS HAMMER

Fred Schendel - *keyboards, guitar, flute, vocals, drums*, **Steve Babb** - *keyboards, bass, guitars, vocals*.

Symphonic-progressive rock band formed in 1992 when multi-instrumentalists **Steve Babb** and **Fred Schendel** began to write and record *Journey of the Dunadan*, a concept album released the following year and based on the story of **Aragorn** from J.R.R. Tolkien's *Lord of the Rings* trilogy. To their surprise, the album sold several thousand units and this was the first of nearly twenty albums over the past 25 years. Many musicians and singers (**Jon Anderson** provided backup vocals on two songs in 2007's *Culture of Ascent*) have featured in their works as guest: lyrically inspired mostly by their love of literature for Victorian prose and medieval mythology, they lean towards a '70s strong Hammond-driven music in the tradition of ELP, **Yes**, **Genesis** and **Camel**.

RECOMMENDED RECORDINGS: **JOURNEY OF THE DUNADAN** *(1993, Arion Records)* **THE INCONSOLABLE SECRET** *(2005, Arion Records)* **CULTURE OF ASCENT** *(2007, Arion Records).* **M.G.**

SHAUN GUERIN

Shaun Guerin - *vocals, drums, keyboards, guitar, bass*, **John Thomas** - *guitars*, **Matt Brown** - *keyboards, vocals*, **Dan Shapiro** - *bass*.

Poly-instrumentalist and singer from LA unfortunately passed away in 2003, **Shaun Guerin** was the son of **John Guerin**, **Frank Zappa** and **Joni Mitchell**'s drummer. After playing in a couple of bands he took a soloist career and published two albums of his own: the first in 2002 titled *By The Dark Of The Light* and the second *The Epic Quality Of Life* published just before his death. Both records are illustrated by **Paul Whitehead** and are influenced by the music of the early **Genesis**, **King Crimson** and **Yes**, with some jazz fusion hints. **Shaun** plays the drums, keyboards, guitars, bass and sings all by himself in the debut while with some of his **Cinema Show** bandmates in the latter, making this cd less of a solo effort and giving it more of a band feel. In 2003 he participates to **Clearlight**'s *Infinite Symphony* playing drums and percussion and contributing vocals for one track.

RECOMMENDED RECORDINGS: **THE EPIC QUALITY OF LIFE** *(Clearlight 888 Music, 2003).* **M.G.**

HOLDING PATTERN

Tony Spada - *guitar, vocals*, **Tony Castellano** - *bass*, **Robert Hutchinson** - *drums*, **Mark Tannebaum** - *keyboards*.

Project of eclectic guitarist **Tony Spada**, the band was co-founded with drummer **Robert Hutchinson** in the late '70s conquering great interest for their energy during the live performances. Their self-titled debut of 1981 was an EP that along with other tracks recorded over the years, was reissued as the 1991 album *Majestic*. Oriented to symphonic prog, although with more dynamic sounds, they were on the same line of **Camel**. After a long pause, in 2007 their unexpected come back album *Breaking The Silence*, where the only progressive element is the art-work on the cover done by **Paul Whitehead**, while the sounds are a pale memory of their glorious past.

DISCOGRAPHY: **HOLDING PATTERN** *(Cleefo, 1981 EP)* **MAJESTIC** *(Art Sublime, 1991)* **BREAKING THE SILENCE** *(Surveillance, 2007).* **C.A.**

North America: UNITED STATES

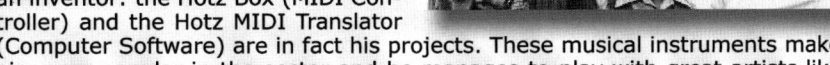

JIMMY HOTZ

Jimmy Hotz - *vocals, keyboards, guitars, engineering, producer, computer programmer plus* **guest musicians**...
Besides his career as musician, he is an inventor: the Hotz Box (MIDI Controller) and the Hotz MIDI Translator (Computer Software) are in fact his projects. These musical instruments make him very popular in the sector and he manages to play with great artists like **Fleetwood Mac**, **Chicago**, **Leon Russell**, **Jon Anderson** and **Stevie Winwood**. His debut comes late after all these experiences, but it is a high quality and original product based upon space rock and dominated by keyboards with hints of hard rock inspirations, as testify the wonderful guitars of *Beyond the Crystal Sea*, released in 1980. A record considered one of the best examples of early art-rock, in which many good musicians from Texas and California feature playing compelling performances.
DISCOGRAPHY: BEYOND THE CRYSTAL SEA (Vision, 1980). C.A.

HOWEVER

Peter Mark Prince - *vocals, keyboards, bass, guitar, percussion, violin,* **Bobby Read** - *vocals,, keyboards, horns,* **Bill Kotapish** - *guitars, bass, percussion, vocals,* **Joe "Stellar" Prince** - *drums, percussion,* **Annie Gadbois** - *cello*.
East coast band formed in 1972 with strong Canterbury school tendencies and RIO influences greatly inspired by **Muffins**, **Happy The Man**, **Henry Cow**, **Frank Zappa**, **Gentle Giant**, especially for the vocals. For years they gave concerts in university campuses, clubs and assembly halls until the core duo became a true live quartet around 1980. These four extraordinary poly-instrumentalists publish the 1981 debut *Sudden Dusk*, resulting in a mix of complex and charming progressive eclectic jazz, dark RIO/chamber rock, changing styles all the time, rich of evolving ideas sometimes to the extreme by using dissonances, with smart experimental themes, rich in wind instruments, acoustic guitars and many vintage keyboards. There are also some nice female vocals on a few compositions. On the same line their second and last work *Calling* of 1985.
RECOMMENDED RECORDINGS: SUDDEN DUSK (Random Radar Records, 1981). M.G.

KALABAN

David Thomas - *vocals,* **Randy Graves** - *guitars, vocals,* **Michael Stout** - *keyboards,* **Kent Underwood** - *bass, vocals,* **Gary Stout** - *drums*.
Compelling new-prog band from Utah, formed in 1975 and previously called **Procyon's Demise**. In 1985 they release their self-titled debut as an independent cassette production before managing to publish it (only in 1990) as *Don't Panic*: the textures between guitars and keyboards are typical of **Dream Theater** while the instrumental characteristics are greatly influenced by **Yes** and **Genesis** (four tracks out of six) although the bright singing of "Between The Lines" makes it the best from the album. Three years later, a second album follows, but without the same energy: *Resistance is Useless* saw the light in 1993, more eclectic with some clear fusion passages and ethnic sounds from India. The band disappears from 1999 to 2013 with a recent come-back album in 2017 (available only as downloadable digital file!) to prove they are not yet over.
DISCOGRAPHY: DON'T PANIC (Syn-Phonic 1990) **RESISTANCE IS USELESS** (Syn-Phonic 1993). M.G.

MIKE KENEALLY

Keyboardist and excellent guitarist (former **Zappa** musician in his last band between 1987 and 1993), he moves to San Diego and plays in several local bands, recording albums from 1983 (age 22) till recently for an endless discography, all very worth listening to. Simultaneously he forms **Mike Keneally & Beer For Dolphins** among other important musical collaborations as guest or session man. Influenced by **The Beatles** and **Frank Zappa**, in his 1992 album *Hat* he develops his own unique style of jazz fusion carried out also in the next two works. He was also a great producer and was nominated as National Music Director of The Paul Green School of Rock Music in 2006. In 2009 he was in tour with a new trio formed by **Bryan Beller** on bass and **Marco Minnemann** on drums.
RECOMMENDED RECORDINGS: HAT (Immune Records/Exowax, 1992) **BOIL THAT DUST SPECK** (Immune Records/Exowax, 1993) **THE MISTAKES** (Immune Records/Exowax, 1995). M.G.

North America: UNITED STATES

ILÙVATAR

Gary Chambers - *drums, percussion, backing vocals,* **Glenn McLaughlin** - *vocals, percussion,* **Dean Morekas** - *bass, backing vocals,* **Dennis Mullin** - *guitars,* **Jim Rezek** - *keyboards.*

Born in 1983 as the cover band **Sojourn**, they finally start writing their own pieces and become the neo-prog band in 1992, named after the deity in Tolkien's Middle Earth (recalling how **Marillion** took theirs from the same book by chopping 'Sil' off from **Silmarillion**). Quite obviously influenced by the symphonic music of **Marillion** and **IQ**, with one eye on **Genesis** and the other on the AOR of **Styx** or the hard rock of **Rush**, they debut with a homonym album the following year containing from the '70s soft symphonic rock to the more accessible '80s British prog. Absolutely better, more complex and structured, the second and the third albums *Children* and *Sideshow*. Their career ends with the last two more modest works, *A Stormy Two Days Wide* of 1999 and *From the Silence* of 2014.

RECOMMENDED RECORDINGS: CHILDREN *(Kinesis, 1995)* **SIDESHOW** *(Kinesis, 1997).*   **M.G.**

LIFT

Chip Gremillion - *keyboards,* **Cody Kelleher** - *bass,* **Chip Grevemberg** - *drums,* **Chris Young** - *guitar,* **Courtenay Hilton** - **Green** - *vocals,* **Richard Huxen** - *guitars,* **Laura "Poppy" Pate** - *vocals,* **Tony Vaughn** - *bass.*

Formed in New Orleans in 1972 by keyboardist **Chip Gremillion**, bassist **Cody Kelleher** and drummer **Chip Grevemberg**, they hold frequent concerts for university events and in local clubs playing songs from **Genesis**, **Led Zeppelin**, **The Beatles**, **Uriah Heap**, **Robin Trower**, **ELP**, **Yes**, **King Crimson**, **The Moody Blues** and other southern bands, gradually introducing some original material of their own as it was composed. In 1974 producer Sonny Fox helps them record four songs titled *Caverns of Your Brain* (barely 19 at the time they were capable of a form of symphonic rock that will be developed with more success by **Yes** some years later) and suggests to relocated to Atlanta, where nothing really goes as it should, disbanding finally in 1979.

DISCOGRAPHY: CAVERNS OF YOUR BRAIN *(Guinness, 1974).*   **C.A.**

THE LOAD

Dave Hessler - *bass, guitar,* **Sterling Smith** - *keyboards,* **Tommy Smith** - *drums, percussion.*

A trio formed in 1973 with a great experience as cover band in the little clubs of Ohio: **Hessler** builds himself a double-neck guitar with a bass on the bottom and six strings on top, while **Sterling** acquires a Minimoog synth, allowing him to switch from bass to synth. They become partial owners of Owl Studios and Owl Records, allowing the band to record a first LP at their own pace in 1976, *Praise the Load*, deeply inspired by European prog. Their exploration of American pop avant-garde sounds leads them to a sequel entitled *Load have Mercy*, recorded in 1978 but shelved until 1996. They then relocate to LA working as session musicians (mostly with **The Beach Boys**) so by 1979 they return home.

DISCOGRAPHY: PRAISE THE LOAD *(OWL Intermedia, 1976);* **LOAD HAVE MERCY** *(OWL Intermedia, 1977).*   **C.A. & C.C.**

MAC ARTHUR

Ben MacArthur, guitarist, keyboardist and singer releases two albums recorded with the typical '70s prog groove characterized by the sound of synthesizers and his self-indulging guitar playing. The band forms in 1977 while their debut is released in 1979 with an anonymous sleeve and the name **MacArthur** as sticker (reissued as the bootleg *The Black Forest*). In 1982 the second album with a form of very technical AOR and keyboards influenced by **ELP**. Reformed in 2006 they seem to be working on new material recording and releasing new material yet nothing has yet seen the light of day.

DISCOGRAPHY: MAC ARTHUR (Reissued as THE BLACK FOREST) *(R.P.C., 1977)* **MAC ARTHUR II** *(Bay Music, 1982).*   **M.G.**

North America: UNITED STATES

MAELSTROM

Robert Owen – *guitar, saxophones, piano, mellotron, vocals,* **Mark Knox** - *keyboards,* **Paul Klotzbier** – *bass,* **James Larner** – *flute, piano, percussion, harmonica ,* **Jeff McMullen** – *vocals, guitar,* **Jim Miller** – *drums, percussion*
Formed in 1972 they record their first album the following year, released as **On The Gulf**, mixing '70s psychedelia, Canterbury sounds and symphonic prog with instrumental fusion, organ and sax evoking **Egg**, **Khan**, **King Crimson**, the early **Gong** and **Vanilla Fudge**, as well as multiple breaks, odd rhythms and complex interplay recalling **Gentle Giant** for both moods and vocals. Some darker movements and exquisite flowing sax solos in **VDGG** style and beautiful atmospheres of flute and coral echoes reminiscent of **Gnidrolog** and **Marsupilami**. Yet these seemingly disparate styles manage to remain symphonic throughout, alternating between quiet songs and highly experimental passages. The second work of 1975, *Paradigms*, is more of an avant-garde and European free jazz/free improvisation styled music, with occasional diversions into something highly chaotic, mostly acoustic jazz-rock, 100% instrumental.
RECOMMENDED RECORDINGS: MAELSTROM *(Black Moon Productions, 1973).* M.G. & C.C.

MASTERMIND

Bill Berends - *guitars, keyboards, vocals,* **Rich Berends** - *drums, percussion,* **Phil Antolino** - *bass,* **Jens Johansson** - *keyboards,* **Lisa Bouchelle** - *vocals.*
Formed in 1986, they played a keyboard-oriented prog, initially cloning **ELP** in their first album of 1990. With *Volume Two - Brainstorm* they add prog-metal elements to their music and the result is without doubt an advantage: heavy metal, jazz fusion and progressive hybrid of breathtaking speed. Their third release features **Phil Antolino** on the bass leading into a more original prog with long and complex instrumental developments where it's hard to believe that they are only a trio. The entirely instrumental album *Excelsior!* Features keyboardist **Jens Johansson**, with lots of jazzy influences, while *Angels of the Apocalypse*, sung by a compelling female vocalist, completes their transition to prog metal, although still open to contaminations with other genres.
RECOMMENDED RECORDINGS: VOLUME TWO – BRAINSTORM *(1992, Cyclops Records)* **EXCELSIOR!** *(1998, Inside Out)* **ANGELS OF THE APOCALYPSE** *(2000, Inside Out).* M.G.

NETHERWORLD

Denny Gordon – *vocals,* **Randy Wilson** – *keyboards,* **Kirk Long** – *bass, guitars,* **Robin Belvin** – *guitars, oboe,* **Dave Kump** – *drums,* **Scott Stacy** – *guitars,* **Peter Yarbrough** – *bass.*
Formed in 1975 when **Kirk Long** answers **Randy Wilson**'s add to create a band playing covers from **Yes**, **Genesis**, **King Crimson**, **The Doors**, **Hendrix** plus some of their own material. Gradually their live-act becomes more spectacular (with lasers, liquid lights, projections and a singer with a hooded cape and led eyes, cloning his idol **Peter Gabriel**) - **Denny Gordon** is a powerful vocalist with references to heavy metal singers - In 1981 they release their only album called *In the Following Half-Light*, disbanding in 1984 only to reunite later in 1992 with a song on the double-compilation LP *Past-Present-Future*: a 10 minutes instrumental track titled "Cumulo Nimbus" that was added as bonus track on the reissue of their debut by Musea in 2002.
DISCOGRAPHY: IN THE FOLLOWING HALF-LIGHT *(Private pressing, 1981)* **NETHERWORLD** *(Musea, 2002, Reissue of the previous one with bonus tracks added).* M.G.

THE NEW AGE

Personal project of **Jordan Oliver** who records this interesting concept album in 1980 resulting in a very fine symphonic prog, strongly keyboard-oriented and completely instrumental, although with rock shades. This work is entitled *Neptuned* and contains only one track distributed along both sides. The story is of a dream journeying through the author's childhood: in fact the music is rich of dreamy references and fantasy dimensions, all well connected to prog. Reissued on CD by Unipeg Records without crediting the band but only **Jordan**, leader, keyboardist and main songwriter, aided by a fine cast of musicians including a very present violinist who is all over the music in duet with the thick keyboards, giving it a strong classical feel recalling the best **Curved Air**, **Pavlov's Dog** and **Darryl Way's Wolf**.
DISCOGRAPHY: NEPTUNED *(1980, Unipeg Records).* M.G.

North America: UNITED STATES

NORTH STAR

Glenn Leonard - *drums, marimbas, keyboards,* **Kevin Leonard** - *keyboards, flute, guitars, bass,* **Joe Newman** - *vocals, bass, guitars.*

The trio was formed by **Glenn Leonard** and **Dave Johnson** in 1976 with a first successful demo and an EP of three tracks recorded in 1982. The true debut album occurs in 1984: *Triskelion* was a symphonic early **Genesis** and **EL&P** sounding work with good instrumental parts. **Johnson** decides to quit during the recordings so bassist/singer **Joe Newman** replaces him on guitar. Better the 1985 second album *Feel the Cold*, moving backwards in terms of sound, now more vintage and as always much inspired by the classic **Genesis** era, much more keyboard-driven compared to the debut, with **Newman**'s voice performing again in a very expressive and lyrical way with a **Peter Nichols** shade. *Power* was recorded in 1991, **Johnson** back on guitars, and published in 1993, is a slightly more **Marillion** oriented sound, while the 2004 *Extremes* takes the sound back to their symphonic debut.

RECOMMENDED RECORDINGS: **FEEL THE COLD** *(Syn-phonic, 1985)* **POWER** *(Space Monster Optional Entertainment, 1993)* **EXTREMES** *(Space Monster Optional Entertainment, 2004).* **M.G.**

NOW

Jon Ernst – *guitar,* **Gary Morrell** – *guitar, vocals,* **Barb Crawford** - *drums* **Nick Peck** – *keyboards.*

Not to be confused with the Belgium band, this Californian group was formed in 1981 by **Eric Kampman**, **Gary Morrell** and his friend **Jon Ernst** with a first single out in 1985. The following year they debut with their most progressive album entitled *Everything is Different Now*: very influenced by **Genesis**, **King Crimson** and vocals recalling **Derek Shulman** from **Gentle Giant**, with **Crawford**'s powerful drums contributing largely to create a very strong and compact sound, lots of guitar, many twists and turns and odd-time signatures. Three different songwriters for a variety of styles, ranging from symphonic prog to straight-ahead rock. The second and the third album, although good and well produced, are not at the same level, directed to new audiences with a more direct, more commercial sound. They disband in 1993 for internal divergences, musical differences and personality conflicts.

RECOMMENDED RECORDINGS: **EVERYTHING IS DIFFERENT NOW** *(Syn-Phonic, 1986).* **M.G.**

ORCHESTRATOR

Michael Wise - *vocals, 12 strings guitar,* **Gary Ortleib** - *keyboards, vocals,* **guest musician:** **Brian Lemons** – *drums.*

A delicate duo, very perfectionist on sound production and playing pastoral vibes closer to the new age genre. Their homemade 1984 album *New World Music* though, contains progressive passages recalling somewhat the works of **Jimmy Hotz**: a very outdated, epic-sounding full-scale pop romanticism or soft art-pop, strongly reminiscent of **The Moody Blues** with the necessarily faceless/warm sensitive vocals and a spacey mix of acoustic/electric/programmed aural surfaces. The album is a remarkably ambitious work with six tracks of good synths and rhythms with the softer **Pink Floyd** or **Alan Parsons** atmospheres for a stiff shot of universal energy.

DISCOGRAPHY: **NEW WORLD MUSIC** *(Private Pressing, 1984).* **M.G.**

OZZ KNOZZ

Jack Alford - *drums, flute, guitar, vocals,* **Bill Massey** - *bass, guitar,* **Duane Massey** - *keyboards,* **Richard Heath** - *guitar,* **Marty Naul** - *drums,* **Milton Coronado** - *vocals, keyboards,* **Roberto Guinea** - *guitars.*

A keyboard-driven band formed in 1969 from Texas, with an album published in 1975 and printed in limited edition, entitled *Ruff mix*. There are voices about the direct involvement in studio during the recording sessions of musicians from **Lucifer's Friend** who could have inspired their heavy progressive sound: not comparable to other examples of the genre, their music here is very rich of energy and original ideas and was finally reissued on CD in 1984. In 2008 they reunite with an AOR hard-rock style, completely different from the beginnings, and two albums *10,000 Days & Nights* and the 2011 work *True Believers*.

DISCOGRAPHY: **RUFF MIX** *(Private pressing Houston, 1975; PID Black Rose, reissued on CD, 1984).* **C.A.**

North America: **UNITED STATES**

PENTWATER

Tom Orsi – drums, percussion, vocals, **Mike Konopka** – guitars, flute, violin, vocals, percussion, **Ken Kappel** - keyboards, theremin, vocals, **Ron LeSaar** - bass, vocals.

Interesting Chicago combo formed by school mates in 1970 as **Pentwater River** and initially playing a psychedelic symphonic rock later influenced by **Yes, Genesis, ELP, King Crimson** and **Gentle Giant**. Gigs, radio broadcasts and several tracks followed until **Goldman** quits in 1975, replaced by **Ron Fox**. This new quintet produces a self-titled debut in 1977 on their own Beef Records: a somewhat complicated prog with multiple changes, polyphonic harmonies and sudden breaks supported by a lyrical violin and a bewitching flute and characterized by an abuse of polyphonic vocals and counterpoints. Their high-decibel rock effectively utilizes contemporary classical elements for a good symphonic prog, also inspired by **Zappa**'s irony. Not willing to conform to the production's request, they produced about 55 tracks until the break-up in 1978, some released on the 1992 archival album *Out of the Abyss*, others in *A-Dul* of 2007.
RECOMMENDED RECORDINGS: **OUT OF THE ABYSS** *(Beef Records, 1992).* M.G.

PRE

Alfred Collinsworth - vocals, 12 strings guitar, **Larry Collinsworth** – guitars, **Brian Paulson** - keyboards, **Steve DeMoss** - bass, vibes, glockenspiel, **Dwight Dunlap** – drums, percussion.

Formed in Kentucky, they record a full album in 1973, disbanding after a few months without ever releasing their work. During the '90s **Steve Roberts** discovers the tapes and publishes them, issued on CD in 1994 including bonus tracks for a 60 minutes of very good music: the American answer to **Yes** (especially *The Yes Album* and *Fragile* but a little more compact and urgent). It has it all, the heavy organ, a loud woody bass playing, great guitar leads, complex rhythms and passionate vocals. The best tracks are the longest, "Ascetic Eros" and "Ballet for a Blind Man", with a quality of the recording of a major label studio with a large budget. A mystery why it was shelved.
DISCOGRAPHY: **PRE** *(1973. posthumous release 1994, CD ZNR).* M.G.

MICHAEL QUATRO

Recording artist, composer, pianist & singer/songwriter, **Michael Quatro**'s production is more of a well done pop with some albums which crossover to the realm of prog. Born in Detroit, he began a classical pianist at the age of just seven, also playing for the Detroit Symphony Orchestra. In 1969 he also started a talent scout agency which helped develop the careers of **Iggy Pop, Alice Cooper** and **Funkadelic**, to name but a few (his sister was rock'n'roll singer **Suzi Quatro**). Renowned for unusually releasing albums recorded in single takes, the 1975 *In Collaboration With The Gods* and the 1995 *Vision* are probably his best from a prog point of view, where he plays keyboards mainly inspired by **Nice** and **ELP**.
RECOMMENDED RECORDINGS: **IN COLLABORATION WITH THE GODS** *(UA, 1974)* **DANCERS, ROMANCERS, DREAMERS AND SCHEMERS** *(Prodigal, 1976)* **VISION** *(Prodigal, 1995).* C.A.

QUILL

Keith Christian - vocals, bass, guitars, **Ken DeLoria** - keyboards, **Jim Sides** - vocals, drums, percussion.

A keyboard-oriented trio formed in 1975 with the intention of creating an original and epic music, full of mood shifts and orchestral-oriented structures: their power-trio formation allowed **DeLoria**'s keyboard inputs to take center stage in the melodic department, focused on the meticulously melodic approach similar to **Yes, Genesis** and the early '70s **Rick Wakeman**. A symphonic prog concept-album that combines the magic of fairy tales and the affirmation of the self, recorded with private funding at a resort studio in 1977. *Sursum Corda* contains two suites, one for each side, developed with linearity and performed with no forced changes of tempo. They also managed to record the yet unreleased 54 minutes suite titled "The Demise of the Third King's Empire" before disbanding a couple of years later.
DISCOGRAPHY: **SURSUM CORDA** *(1977, Cotillion).* M.G.

North America: UNITED STATES

RASCAL REPORTERS

Steve Gore – drums, **Steve Kretzmer** – keyboards.
High school friends **Steve Gore** and **Steve Kretzmer** start to write their music in 1974 publishing only in 1980 a tape as *Freaks Obscure*: full of Canterbury sounds, RIO and **Frank Zappa** inspirations with elegant and harmonic pieces rapidly destroyed by sound effects, weird distorted vocals and schizophrenic atmospheres (dull, cartoon-like vocals take over a weird musicianship, sometimes led by repetitive keyboards, others by distorted guitar sounds, programmed sounds and unbearable tape effects). The true debut album of 1984, *Ridin' On A Bummer*, features **Fred Frith** and **Tim Hodgkinson** (former **Henry Cow**) as special guests. Their masterpiece is the following *Happy Accidents*. They even open their label Hebbardesque and release a 12-CD box-set of unpublished tracks from the mid '70s (neither can read or write music, composing by ear and rote-repetition: basically two one-man bands working together).
RECOMMENDED RECORDINGS: RIDIN' ON A BUMMER (Landmark, 1984) **HAPPY ACCIDENTS** (Landmark, 1988). **M.G.**

SHADOWFAX

G.E.Stinson - guitar, sitar, vocals, **Doug Maluchnik** - keyboards, **Chuck Greenberg** - lyricon, flute, clarinet, **Phil Maggini** - bass, cow bell, **Stuart Nevitt** - drums, percussion.
Born as a blues band in Chicago in 1972, they begin to contaminate their music with jazz and rock. So already in their 1976 first album titled *Watercourse Way* they feature a powerful guitar jazz-rock, with sweet and soft piano and flute playing, ethnic jazz and folk percussions with a deep crescendo of Mellotron. The band disappears for a few years after this debut and then resurfaces on the Windham Hill label in 1982 with a self-titled album of new material. From the second album onward they however start to lose the prog component, crossing into ambient, new age, bar-style jazz and so on.
RECOMMENDED RECORDINGS: WATERCOURSE WAY (Passport, 1976). **M.G & C.C.**

SIGMUND SNOPEK III

He started by playing with the pioneering psychedelic prog-rock band **Bloomsbury People** (which performed in Atlanta's Pop Festival along with '60s pop-rock icons such as **Jimi Hendrix**). They were innovative, combining elements of baroque pop, psychedelia, classical music, pop & rock, electronic music and avant-garde in their only self-titled album of 1970. Then as a solo artist he releases three good albums of non conventional prog with references to **Zappa**, avant-garde and modern dissonances, greatly varying in styles, and also writing a number of operas and symphonies in a post-modern key. In 1978 he forms **Snopek** with another two LPs where he plays flute, oboe, clarinet, saxophone, horns, as well as his battery of keyboards and vocal duties. Then he goes back to publishing under his own name for other five works.
RECOMMENDED RECORDINGS: FIRST BAND ON THE MOON (1980, CD Musea, 2002) **ROY ROGERS MEETS ALBERT EINSTEIN** (1982, CD Musea, 2001). **M.G.**

THE SMASHING PUMPKINS

Billy Corgan - vocals, guitars, orchestral arrangements, **James Iha** - guitars, **D'Arcy Wretzky** - bass, **Jimmy Chamberlin** - drums, percussion.
Not a progressive band at all, this post-grunge American band formed in 1988 actually released a beautiful concept album in 1995 called *Mellon Collie & The Infinite Sadness*: published as double CD of two long hours, it is a wonderful record that unveils **Billy Corgan**'s deepest interest towards the progressive genre. However the dirty grunge sound is ever present here as well, but merged into the melodies which echo greatly the works of **Genesis**, **Fleetwood Mac** and **Pink Floyd** (*The Wall*). Everything is performed with fresh energy and in the spirit of young disciples respecting the master's teachings.
RECOMMENDED RECORDINGS: MELLON COLLIE AND THE INFINITE SADNESS (1995, Virgin). **M.G.**

North America: UNITED STATES

SPOCK'S BEARD
Neal Morse - *keyboards, guitars, vocals,* **Ryo Okumoto** - *keyboards,* **Alan Morse** - *guitars,* **Dave Meros** - *bass,* **Nick D'Virgilio** - *drums, voce.*
Formed in 1992 by **Neal Morse**, who wrote all the band's material along with being their lead singer, keyboardist and guitarist. They played a nostalgic '70s golden age prog, not so original and heavily influenced by **Gentle Giant**, **Yes** and **Genesis**, full of elaborated neo-prog instrumental developments with jazz-rock inserts. A good 1995 debut album and an interesting live-act for a prolific discography of which a last album of only a couple of years ago. After the first two releases, their albums start to sound too American and linked to past models. During the 2002 **Neal** quits them and is replaced on vocals by drummer **Nick D'Virgilio** from their eighth work *Feel Euphoria*: a new beginning that lasted for another pair of LPs until he also quits and goes solo, replaced by former **Enchant** vocalist **Ted Leonard** in their last two works.
RECOMMENDED RECORDINGS: **THE LIGHT** *(Syn-Phonic 1995)* **BEWARE OF DARKNESS** *(Radiant 1996)* **DAY FOR NIGHT** *(Inside Out, 1999)* **DON'T TRY THIS AT HOME** *(live, Inside Out 2000)* **V** *(Inside, Out 2000)* **SNOW** *(Inside Out, 2002)* **OCTANE** *(Inside Out, 2005).* **M.G.**

SUNBLIND LION
Keith Abler - *vocals,* **David Steffen** – *guitar,* **Dave Hassinger** – *drums,* **Steve Orschesky** – *bass,* **Duane Abler** – *keyboards,*
Formed in 1974 by musicians coming from other late '60s and early '70s bands such as **Love Society** and **Phase III**. Although their four works are distinctly different one from the other, they are all characterized by smart lyrics, impressive guitar playing and grandiose keyboard work. *Observer* of 1976 was their most progressive effort with lengthy, synthesizer-adorned, conceptual pieces. *Above and Beyond* followed a couple of years later, a more basic rock approach with the exception of "The King and His Parliament" a sophisticated **Kansas** meets **Jethro Tull** track. *Live Lion* was a collection of previously unrecorded songs performed live with no-frills and a rock & roll sound and released in 1980, before a long pause. The 1989 reunion concert was filmed and published as VHS videotape while the 2014 *The Sanatorium* is their last published work proving them still active.
RECOMMENDED RECORDINGS: **OBSERVER** *(Private pressing, 1976).* **M.G.**

STEVE TIBBETTS
Multi-instrumentalist with great skills as record engineer and very capable of creative experimentation, his first album was published while he was still in college in 1977: a record based upon overdubs of electronic keyboards, tape loops and guitars, performed exclusively by him alone, for an electronic prog with space tastes, comparable somewhat to the German kraut-rock. His second album is re-released by ECM and is probably what got him noticed, especially for the electric guitar parts. A total ten works all featuring the characteristic overdubs with the insertion of exotic drums, kalimba, special effects guitars and synths. *Exploded View* near to rock and for the first time ever he inserts vocal parts (without actual lyrics) for a more energic result. In the mid '80s he travels extensively through Nepal, where he meets **Chöying Drolma**, a Tibetan Buddhist monk with whom he collaborates releasing two albums: *Chö* of 1987 and *Selwa* in 2004.
RECOMMENDED RECORDINGS: **YR** *(Private pressing, 1980)* **NORTHERN SONG** *(ECM, 1982)* **EXPLODED VIEW** *(ECM, 1986).* **M.G.**

TOOL
Maynard James Keenan - *vocals,* **Adam Jones** - *guitars,* **Justin Chancellor** - *bass,* **Danny Carey** - *drums, percussion.*
Formed in 1990, they release an EP titled *Opiate* in 1992 before their debut album *Undertow* the following year: a raw, straight-forward art-metal sound of alternative heavy metal prog. The sequels confirm the intents of unifying musical experimentation and visual arts, incorporating them to the very long and complex songs as an act of style-transcending and part of the prog-psychedelic-art rock genre. *Aenima* and *Lateralus* are full of heavy sounds, dark atmospheres, esoteric lyrics and rich inventions of strong contents. They hit the top of the charts, winning three Grammy Awards and opening the 2003 American Tour dates of **King Crimson**, that were curiously promoting their last album with sounds close to the ones of **Tool** themselves. After their last album in 2006, rumors of a new album have never yet come true.
RECOMMENDED RECORDINGS: **LATERALUS** *(2001, Music for Nations-BMG).* **M.G.**

North America: UNITED STATES

TRANSATLANTIC

Neil Morse - vocals, keyboards, guitars, **Mike Portnoy** - drums, backing vocals, **Roine Stolt** - vocals, guitars, **Peter Trewavas** - bass, backing vocals.

Four musicians from the most famous new prog bands, **Marillion, Dream Theater, Flower Kings** and **Spock's Beard**, bound together into a project of classic progressive rock which starts in 1999. The result is a super group playing a collection of recognizable symphonic rock with long tracks, melodic sounds, predictable rhythm changes and large instrumental space. Their first album *SMPTe* is very compelling - the best track is a cover version of the suite "In Held (Twas) In I" by **Procol Harum** - while the sequel *Bridge Across Forever* is a more average work. Each member of the band gets a shot at singing and the vocal harmonies are outstanding. 2009 album *The Whirlwind* is probably their best work: a long symphonic prog concept with elements of fusion, rock guitars and at times massive multiple layers of various keyboards (the organ adding that vintage '70s sound). **Neal** gets them back for a last avoidable 2014 album.

RECOMMENDED RECORDINGS: SMPTe *(2000, Inside Out)* LIVE IN AMERICA *(2001, Inside Out)* THE WHIRLWIND *(2009, Inside Out).*

M.G & C.C.

ULTIMATE SPINACH

Ian Bruce-Douglas - vocals, keyboards, guitars, horns, **Barbara Hudson** – vocals, guitar, **Geoffrey Winthrop** – guitar, **Jeff Baxter** – guitar (1969), **Richard Nese** – bass.

Previously a club band called **Underground Cinema** (with some demos recorded from 1965 to 1968 yet released only in 1996) they become **Ultimate Spinach** when in 1967 **Alan Lorber** announces his plan to make Boston the new centre of the arts, attempting to create a Boston sound (Bosstown Sound) parallel to San Francisco's west coast style. Despotically directed by their ingenious leader **Bruce-Douglas**, author of compositions with broad instrumental parts, their first two albums *Ultimate Spinach* and *Behold and See* are both gems of the American hippy genre, even if the second is more elaborate and less direct. Internal disputes force **Bruce** to leave and the entrance of **Baxter** signs a third last album in 1969 before the break-up.

RECOMMENDED RECORDINGS: ULTIMATE SPINACH *(MGM, 1968)* BEHOLD & SEE *(MGM, 1968).* M.G.

VOLARÉ

Patrick Strawser - keyboards, **Steve Hatch** - guitar, mandolin, **Richard M. Kesler** - bass, saxophones, **Brian Donohoe** - drums, percussion.

Formed in 1994 by three students, **Patrick Strawser, Jon-Fredrik Nielsen** and **Steve Hatch**, they undergo some line-up changes before recording a 5-track self-titled demo in 1996 followed by their first album called *The Uncertainty Principle* the following year. Both are excellent works of Canterbury jazz-rock performed with a strange kind of fusion recalling **Hatfield and the North, National Health** and **In Cahoots**. Shifting moods, sudden breaks, slick melodies and flexible passages composed with a heavy use of electric piano and synths blending to a frenetic guitar work. The slight modern edge, mainly in a fast tempo, allows each member to emerge also individually. Nothing very original or ground-breaking, but still a high level quality.

DISCOGRAPHY: THE UNCERTAINTY PRINCIPLE *(1997, The Laser's Edge)* MEMOIRS *(2003, Pleasant Green).*

M.G. & C.C.

YETI

Jon Teague – drums, **Eric Harris** - guitar, **Doug Ferguson** – keyboards, **Tommy Atkins** – bass.

Formed in 1999 as an entirely instrumental band that unite prog and punk ranging from slow, drifting moods, to frantic, powerful and blasting sounds. The heavy feel is more dominant, with a thick, pounding rhythmic section, some wailing synths, a distorted guitar and acrobatic bass lines. A bit of **Magma** and a little **King Crimson**, recalling all things Zeuhl, RIO and the hard core Punk of **Discharge**. Present in various festival such as ProgDay 2001, their sound is dirty, with complex rhythms, vocal guttural parts, gargles, vomit, strong bass tunes, guitars that seem dog barks and other difficult to manage proposals. After the first album *Things to Come*, keyboardist **Ferguson** dies. The band continues with another two albums, calling their music 'Doom in Opposition', yet it has been described as a blend between **Ozzy Osbourne** and **Magma**.

RECOMMENDED RECORDINGS: THINGS TO COME *(Private pressing, 2000).* M.G.

Oceania: AUSTRALIA

BAKERY

John Worrall - *vocals, flute,* **Peter Walker** - *guitar,* **Mal Logan** - *keyboards,* **Eddie McDonald** – *bass,* **Hank Davis** - *drums.*
A hard prog-rock band formed in 1970 playing a balanced mix of hard-rock and country with jazz sounds and excursions into the typical light-prog areas of ambient music. Their debut *Momento* switches from gentle acoustic passages to booming assaults within the same song. The second LP is a live recording of a mass at St George's Cathedral in 1971 titled *Rock Mass For Love*: one of the first Australian musicals preceding the first Aussie production of *Jesus Christ Superstar* by almost a year (the Jesus Rock genre, or God Rock, begins in 1963 with **Sister Luc-Dominique** AKA **Jeanine Deckers** and her hit single called "Dominique". In 1970 **Tim Rice** and Andrew **Lloyd Webber**'s *Jesus Christ Superstar* culminates this pop mass event movement in which composers communicate the Christian message through music). Some line-up changes and festival performances follow until the break-up in 1975.
DISCOGRAPHY: **MOMENTO** *(Astor, 1971).*   M.G.

BEE GEES

Barry Gibb – *vocals, guitar,* **Robin Gibb** – *vocals,* **Maurice Gibb** – *vocals, keyboards, guitars, bass.*
Formed in 1958 with a first album out in 1965, this incredibly famous band is caught playing a baroque pop or psychedelic pop at a certain moment of their career before taking on disco music and becoming the titans they are today. Probably the most relevant, the 1969 fifth album *Odessa* is a double vinyl, originally intended as a concept on the loss of a fictional ship in 1899. This ambitious project created tension and internal disagreements, leading to **Robin Gibb**'s temporary estrangement to the group. An orchestral, almost liturgical album, symphonic and with amazing vocals, yet not well received and led to a decline in the group's fortunes until their Disco period of the '70s. *Odessa* is the last work in the band's original incarnation, including guitarist **Vince Melouney**.
RECOMMENDED RECORDINGS: **ALL OVER THE WORLD (IDEA)** *(Ex-Libris, RSO, 1968)* **HORIZONTAL** *(RSO, 1968)* **ODESSA** *(RSO, 1969).*   M.G. & C.C.

BUFFALO

Dave Tice , Alan Milano – *vocals,* **John Baxter, Norm Roue, Karl Taylor** – *guitar,* **Peter Wells** - *bass,* **Paul Balbi, Jimmy Economou** – *drums.*
In 1968 the Heavy psychedelic blues-rock band Head formed and published one album the following year before disbanding. Singer **Dave Tice** spins off taking bass player **Pete Wells** along with him to form this pre heavy-metal band in 1971. After a training in many pubs, still playing rock-blues, they improve their style, evolving to a vibrating harder sound, rich of psychedelia and more progressive too. Surprisingly among their fans we find **AC/DC**. The strength of their sound impresses **Black Sabbath** who will have them as supporting band, leading them to a contract with Vertigo Records. Five total albums before disbanding in 1977: *Volcanic Rock* and *Only Want You For Your Body* are a cult for hard-rock/prog-metal lovers. Then after 1975 they undergo some line-up changes resulting in a more commercial sound, thus the break-up.
RECOMMENDED RECORDINGS: **DEAD FOREVER...** *(Vertigo, 1972)* **VOLCANIC ROCK** *(Vertigo,1973)* **ONLY WANT YOU FOR YOUR BODY** *(Vertigo, 1974).*   M.G.

CHETARCA

Bruce Bryan - *synthesizers,* **Geoff Gallent** - *drums,* **Paul Lever** - *vocals, harmonica,* **Ian Miller** – *guitar,* **John Rees** - *bass, violin,* **Andrew Vance** - *keyboards, vocals.*
Born in 1972 from the ashes of a band called **Langford Lever**, their swirling bluesy jams and grooves added some progressive values in the instrumental sections with **ELP** keyboard tendencies. Their only record of 1975 is an interesting and personal work presenting a symphonic prog with blues, hard rock and also rock'n'roll connotations (**Lever** still decidedly blues oriented in a **Tom Jones** style), a double keyboard and no guitarist in the line-up. The sound is a mix of superficial keyboard and piano experiments and well-structured vocal sections creating a chaotic combination of psychedelic, jazzy and classical features. The bassist will be seen later in the '80s playing with **Men at Work**.
RECOMMENDED RECORDINGS: **CHETARCA** *(WEA/Atlantic, 1975).*   M.G. & C.C.

Oceania: AUSTRALIA

CHRIS NEAL

Chris Neal – *keyboards, guitars, bass, drums, drum machine, percussion, mandolin, harmonica, flute,* **Bill Graham** - *bass,* **Laurie Kemp** - *drums.*

Australian musician, songwriter, television and film music composer, he starts playing the classical piano followed by an intensive period of progressive jazz. He ends the '60s writing a flower-power rock musical called *Manchild*, which toured Australian capital cities during 1971-72, creating several box-office records. Then he publishes his first solo prog-rock album in 1974 called *Winds Of Isis*, the keyboard fugues and symphonic moments recalling somewhat **Mike Oldfield**, both for the dynamic structure and the melodic lightness. The electronic musical score for **Fritz Lang**'s silent classic *Metropolis* came next, followed by concerts featuring the soundtrack played live on the first commercially available microprocessor-based digital sequencer (The Roland MC-8). By the '80s he made a career in film scoring, setting up his recording studios.

RECOMMENDED RECORDINGS: **WINDS OF ISIS** *(M7, 1974).*   M.G.

CYBOTRON

Steve Maxwell Von Braund - *synth, electronic percussion, alto sax,* **Geoff Green** – *keyboards,* **Gil Matthews** – *drums, recording engineer,* **Harry Vyhnal** – *electric violin,* **Jim Keays** - *vocals.*

Experimental electronic music duo formed in Melbourne by German **Steve Maxwell Von Braund** aka 'Steve Braund' and **Geoff Green** in 1975. Steve had just published a first solo kraut-rock work titled *Monster Planet*, considered Australia's first electronic rock album, already featuring **Geoff**, but also **Gil 'Rats' Matthews**, **Jim Keays** and violinist **Harry Vyhnal**. Their second album (first under the band name) followed a year later presenting a strong and powerful electronic music also confirmed in the other three sequels *Saturday Night Live*, *Colossus* (maybe refined by the more regular use of the acoustic drums) and last album in 1980 called *Implosion*. Five tracks of a fourth album (*Abbey Moor*) were recorded in 1981 and published as bonus tracks on the 2005 re-issue of *Implosion* since this last work was never completed.

RECOMMENDED RECORDINGS: **COLOSSUS** *(Champagne Records, 1978).*   M.G.

MACKENZIE THEORY

Rob MacKenzie – *guitars,* **Cleis Pearce** – *electric viola,* **Paul Wheeler** – *bass,* **Greg Sheehan** – *drums,* **Peter Jones** - *piano.*

Formed in Melbourne by lead guitarist **Rob MacKenzie** in 1971, playing a symphonic jazz-rock, very rich in melody and technique. The early gigs were mainly as supporting acts for other artists and the annual Sunbury Pop Festivals of 1972-73-74. Their only album was published in 1973 titled *Out of the Blue*, recorded live in studio before the break-up. Actually their final live concert together was recorded and released as *Bon Voyage*, against the wishes of **Mackenzie**, who felt that the performance captured on the album was below-par.

RECOMMENDED RECORDINGS: **OUT OF THE BLUE** *(Mushroom, 1973)* **BON VOYAGE** *(Mushroom, 1974).*   M.G.

KAHVAS JUTE

Dennis Wilson – *lead vocals, guitars,* **Bob Daisley** – *bass, vocals,* **Tim Gaze** – *guitars, piano, vocals,* **Dannie Davidson** – *drums.*

Formed in 1970 and playing a hard psychedelic rock with underground elements and blues and jazz inserts, without any keyboards and the exceptional guitar work of **Wilson** and of **Daisley** on bass (true innovator later playing with **Ozzy Osbourne**, **Gary Moore**, **Uriah Heep**, **Rainbow**). Their only album *Wide Open* was released in 1971 and re-issued adding five tracks taken from the reunion concert (with different line-up) of 2005 at The Basement in Sydney: a DVD and album pack entitled *Then Again: Live at the Basement* was published in 2006. They acted as supporting group for **Bo Diddley**'s second in 1973, reuniting for the first time only in 1991.

RECOMMENDED RECORDINGS: **WIDE OPEN** *(Infinity, 1971).*   M.G. & C.C.

Oceania: NEW ZEALAND

AIRLORD

Steve MacKenzie - *vocals, guitar*, **Ray Simenauer** - *vocals, guitar*, **Brad Murray** - *bass, vocals*, **Alan Blackburn** - *keyboards*, **Rick Mercer** - *drums*.
Born in 1976, they are one of the many New Zealand bands who headed for Australia to recorded their album *Clockwork Revenge*, published the following year. A fairly symphonic sound with typical theatre singing lines, a predominant hard rock guitar and variable, but not complex, rhythms. **Steve MacKenzie** sounds a lot like **Peter Gabriel** when he slips into the correct register, but he spends much of the album singing in a wispier tone: in fact, apart from the crazed title-track (practically **Genesis** meets **Pavlov's Dog**) the majority instead is a less sentimental version of **Barclay James Harvest** or **Fantasy**. The other songs keep the theatricality in the multiple voices, yet have a knack for memorable melodies: every track distinguishes itself from the pack, but apart from the title track, fails to offer anything truly original. They disband in 1978.
RECOMMENDED RECORDINGS: CLOCKWORK REVENGE *(Private pressing, 1977).*   M.G.

LUTHA

Graham Wardrop – *lead guitar, vocals*, **Garry McAlpine** - *percussion, vocals*, **Peter Edmonds** – *drums*, **Peter Fraser** – *bass, vocals*, **Kevin Foster** – *keyboards*.
Formed in 1970, all five musicians came from previous top local bands like **Throb** and **Pussyfoot**. They were insistent on remaining a Dunedin based band even after attracting considerable national interest. Both albums were recorded in 1972 with HMV, the self-titled debut and *Earth*, containing a rock style quite rich of psychedelic tunes and prog spreads. EMI organizes and records a concert at the end of 1972 at the James Hay Theatre in Christchurch: here they perform 3 tracks along with other bands (**Blerta**, **Quincy Conserve** and **Desna Sisarich**) and the album is released only after they disband in 1973.
DISCOGRAPHY: LUTHA *(HMV, 1972)* **EARTH** *(HMV, 1972)* **LIVE** *(EMI, 1973).*   M.G.

SCHTÜNG

 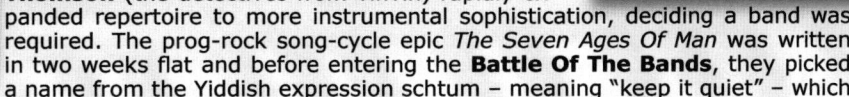

Andrew Hogan – *keyboards*, **Morton Wilson** – *keyboards*.
Formed in late 1972 by **Andrew Hagen** and **Morton Wilson**, this duo named **Thompson and Thomson** (the detectives from TinTin) rapidly expanded repertoire to more instrumental sophistication, deciding a band was required. The prog-rock song-cycle epic *The Seven Ages Of Man* was written in two weeks flat and before entering the **Battle Of The Bands**, they picked a name from the Yiddish expression schtum – meaning "keep it quiet" – which somehow become *Schtüng*. Their self-titled debut of 1977 (only a couple of songs survived from *The Seven Ages Of Man*, testifying the fast-paced songwriting of **Hagen** and **Wilson**) features two keyboardists supported by an orchestra with influences of **Pink Floyd, The Moody Blues** and **Supertramp**. The second side of the album is more Canterbury jazz with a strong presence of sax and flute.
DISCOGRAPHY: SCHTÜNG *(Atlantic, 1977).*   M.G.

THINK

Alan Badger – *bass*, **Phil Whitehead** – *guitar*, **Neville Jess** – *bass*, **Don Mills** – *keyboards*, **Ritchie Pickett** – *vocals*.
Typical prog rock band, reproducing sounds and elements from the past mainstream experiences of Anglo-Saxon cliches, similar to **Cressida**, the early **Yes, Beggar's Opera, Fantasy** and **Gypsy**. Very melodic with a dominating Hammond organ and guitar and the occasional Moog synthesizer, they publish only one album in 1976, *We'll Give You A Buzz*, and two singles shortly after, before breaking-up in 1979. **Phil Whitehead** and **Don Mills** came from the disbanded **Beam**, with **Phil** actually having a short stint with **Human Instinct** in-between. **Kevin Stanton** was also a member at one time but later went on to play with **Mi-Sex**.
DISCOGRAPHY: WE'LL GIVE YOU A BUZZ *(Atlantic, 1976).*   M.G.

South Africa: SOUTH AFRICA

ABSTRACT TRUTH

Kenny Henson – *guitar, vocals,* **Sean Bergin** - *saxophones, flute,* **Peter Measroch** – *keyboards, flute, vocals,* **George Wolfaardt** - *bass, flute, drums, vocals.*

Kenneth Edward Henson was playing with **Leeman Ltd** in 1965. The following year he and **Ramsay MacKay** joined ex-**Navarones** musicians **Colin Pratley** and **Nic Martens** in **Freedom's Children**. Henson joins The Bats and later a jazz group called **The Sounds** with sax-player **Sean Bergin**. In 1969 he is asked to play the sitar with other musicians to back up a belly dancer in Hotel Totum's disco-pub: to fill the rest of the evening they took on a hybrid fusion of blues jazz, folk-rock and Eastern-type of jams. *Totum* thus took form, recorded over a single weekend using a 4-track machine and released in 1970, followed soon by another work titled *Silver Trees* as an attempt to record a more structured music: featuring no cover versions like the previous one, all tracks were composed by the various members of the band, rich of flute, beat and hippie sounds with very light singing parts and the typical African percussions. They imploded in 1971.

DISCOGRAPHY: SILVER TREES *(EMI, 1970)* **TOTUM** *(Uptight, 1970).* M.G.

FREEDOM'S CHILDREN

Ramsay Mackay - *bass,* **Colin Pratley** - *drums,* **Kenny Henson** - *guitar,* **Nic Martens** - *keyboards,* **Julian Laxton** - *guitar,* **Brian Davidson** - *vocals.*

Formed in 1966, they publish their psychedelic debut *Battle Hymn of the Broken Hearted Horde* in 1968, followed by *Astra* and *Galactic Vibes* at the turn of the decade: the latter is probably their most progressive release, featuring a mix of strong guitar driven acid hard rock and symphonic space prog, supported by a deliberately underground and unconventional voice for pop music. The early single was credited to **Fleadom's Children** since the word 'freedom' was censored at the time. Unable to legally work in certain places due to issues surrounding Apartheid, they couldn't break through, especially outside their country. A come-back album was issued in 1990.

DISCOGRAPHY: BATTLE HYMN OF THE BROKEN HEARTED HORDE *(Parlophone, 1968)* **ASTRA** *(Parlophone, 1970)* **GALACTIC VIBES** *(Parlophone, 1971)* **A NEW DAY** *(Victory, 1990).* C.A.

STEVE LINNEGAR'S SNAKESHED

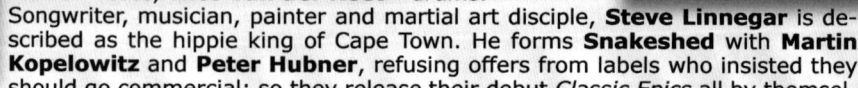

Steve Linnegar – *guitar, vocals,* **Martin Kopelowitz** – *guitar, vocals,* **Colleen Breel** – *keyboards,* **Trevor Muller** - *bass,* **Nico van der Reet** – *drums.*

Songwriter, painter and martial art disciple, **Steve Linnegar** is described as the hippie king of Cape Town. He forms **Snakeshed** with **Martin Kopelowitz** and **Peter Hubner**, refusing offers from labels who insisted they should go commercial: so they release their debut *Classic Epics* all by themselves in 1982 on their own private label, featuring a crafty mix of folk, psychedelic, progressive and AOR with cool Tao-inspired lyrics. In 1984 they wrote *The Music Of Shogun* inspired by the tv series and soundtrack, yet probably their best work is the following *Karate Moves*.

RECOMMENDED RECORDINGS: CLASSIC EPIC *(Snake Records, 1982)* **THE ART OF MIST** *(Snake Records, 1984).* M.G.

DUNCAN MACKAY

Born in the UK in 1950, he moves to South Africa in the late '60s with his family. In 1970 he tours Brazil with **Sergio Mendes**' band. Once back he forms the **Tricycle** in 1973, resident band at The Branch Office club, playing **Peddlers**, **Nice** and **ELP** material as well as **Duncan**'s own compositions: *Chimera* was recorded virtually live in studio during 1974, as a result of this experience. He returns to England joining several bands like **Baker Gurvitz Army**, **Hiseman**'s newly reformed **Colosseum 2** and **Cockney Rebel**, while recording and releasing his second solo album of 1977, *Score*, probably his masterpiece. He features on **Kate Bush**'s first three albums and playing with **Camel**, **The Alan Parsons Project** and **Budgie** before recording a third work in 1980, *Visa*. After a fourth album he returns to South Africa and founds in 1993 the Down South Recording studio. His last solo work *The Bletchley Park Project* was published in 2017.

RECOMMENDED RECORDINGS: SCORE *(EMI, 1975).* M.G.

South America: ARGENTINA

AGNUS

Luis Saéz - *guitar*, **Cacilia Gloria, Laura Fazzio** – *flute, keyboards,* **Enrique Shussler** – *violin,* **Ricardo Bonetto** – *drums,* plus guest musicians...
More of an organization than a regular band, this Argentinian act was formed in 1973, refusing to adapt to any label and constant line-up change over the years, resulting in up to 10 musicians and singers by the end of the decade with only **Luis Saez** remaining from the original crew and an army of guitars, bass, flutes, keyboards and violin. Their only album *Pinturas y Expresiones* was recorded in 1980 exhibiting a romantic symphonic rock with strong folk inserts recalling the Italian prog of **PFM** with links to **M.I.A.** (Músicos Independientes Asociados), **Pink Floyd**, **Jethro Tull** and **Focus**. Their own style featured the slightly improvised guitar solos between the symphonic sections and the solid singing parts, led by beautiful female choirs. After some tours and concerts they disband.
DISCOGRAPHY: PINTURAS Y EXPRESIONES *(Private Press,1980).* M.G.

ANACRUSA

José Luis Castiñeira de Dios - *musical director,* **Susana Lago** - *vocals, keyboards,* **Julio Pardo** - *flute,* **Bruno Pizzamiglio** - *oboe,* **Daniel Sbarra** - *guitars,* **Jorge Trasante** - *drums, percussion,* **Juan Mosalini** - *gaita,* **Phillipe Pages** - *keyboards.*
Formed in 1972 with a first record released the following year, they are very rooted in South American traditional and folk music: Peruvian, Bolivian, Argentinean ballads, boleros, milongas, tango and the insertion of some traditional string instruments such as the charango and the cuatro. A relaxed chamber folk fusion with pastoral and well-crafted arrangements. Their line-up changes from one album to another, keeping as a constant **Lago**'s voice, sweet and velvet or scratchy and aggressive. With the fourth record *El Sacrificio* of 1978, the folk parts give in to a more prog composition of the songs, saving the melodic aspect and inserting very charming instrumental moments with many jazz incursions. Their last album was published in 2005.
RECOMMENDED RECORDINGS: EL SACRIFICIO *(Philips, 1978).* M.G. & C.C.

ANIMA

Octavio Stampalia - *keyboards,* **Alejandra Hamelink** - *vocals,* **Santiago Aynacioglu** - *drums,* **Daniel Spinelli** - *bass,* **Marinno Battaglin** - *guitars.*
Only one record released in 1989 featuring a symphonic art-rock with some rather subtle elements of prog-metal in most tracks, about half of them instrumental. Vocals by **Alejandra Hamelink** are very good and strongly operatic, sometimes supported by a choir. Blending the musical tastes of the late eighties to an imaginary mix of **Yes** and **Le Orme**, this is probably one of the best Argentine prog albums of that decade. The song "Ciudad Sin Tiempo" is a great example of good balance between guitars, keyboards and the powerful drums, alternating harsh and symphonic textures, dynamic and soft, lushly orchestrated arrangements with frequent changes of musical direction, tempo and moods.
DISCOGRAPHY: ANIMA *(Viajeiro, 1989).* C.A. & C.C.

AQUELARRE

Emilio Del Güercio - *bass, vocals,* **Héctor Stark** - *guitar, vocals,* **Hugo González Neira** - *keyboards, vocals,* **Rodolfo Garcia** - *drums, vocals.*
Meaning witches nocturnal meeting with the devil, they form on the ashes of **Almendra** in 1970 with a first studio album released in 1972: the cover was illustrated by their bass player, who will become a graphic designer later on. The music is a sophisticated psychedelic rock blues folk, with very impressionistic moments, artistic arrangements, surrealistic themes, space elements and a jazzy rhythmic section. Another three albums, one a year, their last released in Spain in 1975 followed by a tour before their 1977 goodbye concert in Argentina without **González Neira**, who stayed in Spain. After their dissolution **Rodolfo Garcia** joined **Tantor** and **Emilio del Güercio** started his solo career.
RECOMMENDED RECORDINGS: CANDILES *(Trova Industrias Musicales, 1973).* M.G. & C.C.

South America: ARGENTINA

AUCÁN

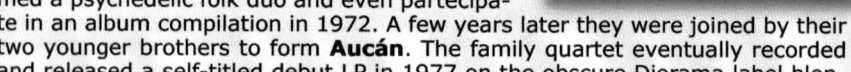

Eugenio Perez – *guitars*, **Miguel Perez** – *guitars*, **Diego Perez** – *drums*, **Pablo Perez** – *bass, keyboards, vocals*.

A family band started as a duo back in 1970, when brothers **Eugenio** and **Miguel Perez** formed a psychedelic folk duo and even partecipate in an album compilation in 1972. A few years later they were joined by their two younger brothers to form **Aucán**. The family quartet eventually recorded and released a self-titled debut LP in 1977 on the obscure Diorama label blending symphonic rock with traditional music and classical influences similar to the sounds of **Camel**, **Sagrado**, **Le Orme** and **Celeste**. Their second album all together titled *Brotes del Alba* came out a couple of years later, supported also by other guests playing oboe, cellos, English horn, harmonica and baroque flutes. Smooth, well-structured melodies with frequent folk incursions, lots of acoustic instrumentation, elegant guitar passages and the predominant keyboards, while the lyrics are in Spanish.
DISCOGRAPHY: AUCÁN *(Music Hall, 1977)* **BROTES DEL ALBA** *(Music Hall, 1980)*. **M.G.**

BAUER

Gabriel Ardanaz – *vocals, guitars*, **Ezequiel Esposito** – *bass*, **Martin Mykietiw** – *keyboards*, **Julian Paz** – *guitars*, **Federico Perez Losada** – *drums, percussion*.

Formed around 2002, they debut shortly after with an EP of 6 songs entitled *Klee*, their music inspired by the most experimental works of **Pink Floyd**, **Porcupine Tree** and **Massive Attack**. The first self-released album is issued in 2004, *Astronauta Olvidado*, considered a sequel sung in Spanish of **Radiohead**'s *Ok Computer*. A very fascinating record where slide guitars are well mixed with spacey keyboards and vintage sounds, like the use of a real Mellotron. 12 songs all starting slow and mellow, building up into a hypnotizing cosmic space and accelerating gradually into swelling eruptions. The Spanish vocals fit perfectly the often melancholic atmospheres. *En otra ciudad* released in 2006 confirms their quality.
DISCOGRAPHY: KLEE *(EP. Private Press, 2002)* **ASTRONAUTA OLVIDADO** *(Private Press, 2004)*. **M.G.**

COLOR HUMANO

Edelmiro Molinari – *guitar, vocals*, **Gabriela Molinari** – *vocals*, **Rinaldo Rafanelli** – *bass, vocals*, **David Lebón**, **Oscar Moro** – *drums*.

When **Almendra** disbands, **Edelmiro Molinari** tries to set up a band called **Viento** which didn't work out so in 1971 he teams up with **David Lebón** and **Rinaldo Rafanelli** creating a trio influenced by **Cream**, although there arrangements are more folk jazz with instrumental fugues dominated by the guitar. They release three rare albums without a real title. **David** is replaced by **Oscar Moro**, shifting their sound; they present the second volume as a double record to the label which rejects the idea and divides it in two, thus publishing them separately. They disband in 1974 with a 1995 concert recorded live to celebrate the anniversary.
DISCOGRAPHY: COLOR HUMANO *(Microfón, 1972)* **COLOR HUMANO** *(1°LP, Talent, 1973)* **COLOR HUMANO** *(2°LP, Talent, 1973)*. **M.G.**

CONTRALUZ

Carlos Barrio - *guitar*, **Néstor Barrio** - *drums*, **Freddy Prochnik** – *bass*, **Alejandro Barzi** – *vocals, flute*, **Jaime Fernández Madero** – *vocals, keyboards (since 1995)*.

Formed in 1969 as a beat band, they change name from **Lemon** to **Celofan** before consolidating a final style imitating **Jethro Tull** then developing a more personal mix of rock and national folk (Tango rhythms from the Pampa). Their presence in several concerts, festivals and competitions earned them wider recognition and in 1973 they recorded *Americanos* for EMI Records with **Alvaro Canada** on vocals and **Alejandro Barzi** on flutes. Their 1974 single "Que tu voz escuche" is a carnavalito-rock that, had it not been for the censorship, could have been a success, perhaps avoiding the break up. They reunite in the late '90s publishing three albums in the new century.
DISCOGRAPHY: AMERICANOS *(EMI, 1973)* **EL PASAJE** *(Private pressing, 1998)*. **M.G. & C.C.**

South America: ARGENTINA

EL RELOJ

Luis Alberto Valenti - *keyboards, vocals*, **Juan Esposito** - *drums, vocals*, **Willy Gardi** - *guitar, vocals*, **Osvaldo Zabala** - *guitar*, **Eduardo Frezza** - *bass, lead vocals*.
Originally formed by **Eduardo Frezza** and **Willy Gardi** in 1970 from the ashes of two previous bands called **Lagrima** and **Los Angeles Salavjes**, they release a couple of singles from 1973 that lead them to their 1975 self-titled debut clearly influenced by **Deep Purple** and **Uriah Heep**, with an angry Hammond organ dominating the sound touched alternatively by jazz and blues. Their second album results more symphonic and less direct inserting some echoes of **King Crimson**, but also with the chromatic sensibility of some Italian prog bands like **The Trip**. Tensions rise inside the band so after some tours and concerts they break-up and reunite several times during the years, each resulting in an album before taking a pause once more (the last two works being more prog metal oriented).
RECOMMENDED RECORDINGS: EL RELOJ II *(RCA, 1976)*.   M.G. & C.C.

ESPIRITU

Fernando Bergé – *vocals*, **Osvaldo Favrot** – *guitar*, **Carlos Goler** - *drums*, **Claudio Martinez** – *bass*, **David Lebon, Gustavo Fedel, Ciro Fogliatta** – *keyboards*.
Formed in 1973 on the ashes of **Onda Corta**, a band from 1969 founded by **Fernando Bergé** and **Osvaldo Favrot**. After a series of gigs they released a single entitled "Soy la Noche" before managing to publish an album in 1974 titled *Crisalida*: a fine symphonic rock record with echoes from **Yes** and **Genesis**. Their second album *Libre y Natural* resents some internal disputes among the members leading to the disbandment after its publishing in 1976. Reformed by the two founding members in 1982, they issue a couple of albums more before the band becomes the solo project of lonely **Favrot** who releases *Fronteras Magicas* in 2003, a last work helped by his son.
RECOMMENDED RECORDINGS: CRISALIDA *(1975)*.   M.G. & C.C.

ETERNIDAD

Claudio Pedra - *keyboards, sax, flute*, **Daniel Méndez** - *guitar, harmonica, vocals*, **Robi Massarotto** - *bass, vocals*. **Luis Yanes** - *drums, percussion*, **Roberto Méndez** - *guitar, vocals*.
Formed in 1971 as a folk rock duo by brothers **Daniel** and **Roberto Mendez**, they evolve into a 5-piece line-up around the mid '70s, recording their only album *Apertura* quite late, in 1977, when the market was preparing for punk and disco music. A compelling self-produced debut of symphonic rock mixed with folk elements, some fusion and strong melodies, not a masterpiece but featuring impressive changes between electric leads and acoustic experiments with flute and mandolin, often overpowered by the symphonic-oriented keyboard work of **Claudio Pedra**. After the album's release they seem to have changed the line-up only to disband anyway in 1978.
DISCOGRAPHY: APERTURA *(Private pressing, 1977)*.   M.G.

INVISIBLE

Luis Alberto Spinetta – *guitars, vocals*, **Hector Lorenzo** – *drums*, **Carlos Rufino** – *bass*.
A power trio of rockers founded by **Luis Alberto Spinetta**, former guitarist of **Pescado Rabioso** who starts in 1973 with influences from **Hendrix**, **Led Zeppelin** and **Black Sabbath**. This is what results from their homonym debut album, while the second, *Durazno Sangrando*, improves their sound to a powerful prog rock and becoming their masterpiece: the title translates to bleeding peach, a concept with lyrics inspired by Carl Jung and Richard Wilhelm's book, *The secret of the golden flower*. Their most popular album is the following *El Jardin del Los Presentes* where new guitarist **Tommy Gubitsch** plays a **King Crimson** blend of Argentine Tango-like folk. Sadly after this work of 1976 the band splits up for good.
DISCOGRAPHY: INVISIBLE *(Sony, 1974)* DURAZNO SANGRANDO *(Sony, 1975)* **EL JARDÍN DE LOS PRESENTES** *(Sony, 1976)*.
M.G. & C.C.

South America: ARGENTINA

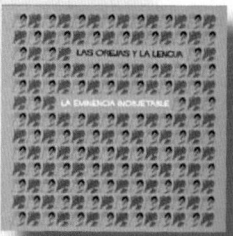

LAS OREJAS Y LA LENGUA

Nicolas Diab - *bass*, **Fernando De La Vega** - *drums*, **Rogelio Corte, Diego Suarez** - *horns*, **Diego Kazmierski** - *keyboards*, **Gate Leiras** - *guitars*, Founded in 1992 as a pop-rock band, **Diego** and **Rogelio** augment the sound gradually to a more complex and weirder style, with more improvisational-based ideas, psychedelic rock, electronic tunes (inspired by kraut) and curious Canterbury jazz incursions. It takes ten years for their debut album to be published: *La Eminencia Inobjetable* was actually recorded as a stable quintet in 1996, but it could only be released in 2002. One year later their second work *Error* is published, but the sound has become a bit harsher and with less fusion elements, considering the time lapse between the recordings it is more than plausible.
DISCOGRAPHY: LA EMINENCIA INOBJETABLE (Viajero Inmovil, 2002) **ERROR** (Viajero Inmovil, 2003).
M.G. & C.C.

MAQUINA DE HACIER PAJAROS

Charly Garcia - *keyboards, acoustic guitar, vocals*, **Jose Luis Fernandez** - *bass, acoustic guitar, vocals*, **Oscar Moro** - *drums, percussion*, **Gustavo Bazterrica** - *guitars, vocals*, **Carlos Cutaia** - *keyboards*.
Formed by **Charly Garcia** in 1975 on the ashes of **Sui Generis** but abandoning the folk side and turning to the more complex symphonic sound of progressive rock, mixed with pop, hard rock and South-American elements. There are definite influences from **Genesis** (smooth acoustic guitars) and most obviously **Yes** (keyboards acrobatics, sudden breaks and changing rhythms), but there is also some sort of Italian prog flavor in the multi-vocal poppish parts blended with acoustic guitars. Two excellent albums where he gives way to the magniloquent organs with two simultaneous keyboardists mixing **Yes** and **PFM** to **Mahavishnu Orchestra**'s speed playing, **Gentle Giant**'s tempo changes and Latin rhythms. They disband after the second album of 1977.

RECOMMENDED RECORDINGS: **LA MAQUINA DE HACIER PAJAROS** (Microfon, 1976).
M.G.

SUI GENERIS

Charly García – *keyboards, guitar, vocals*, **Nito Mestre** – *acoustic guitar, production, vocals*, **Rinaldo Rafanelli** – *bass, guitars, vocals*, **Juan Rodríguez** – *drums*.
Formed in 1969 by the merging of two bands, **To Walk Spanish** led by **Carlos Alberto 'Charly' García Moreno** and **The Century Indignation** led by **Carlos Alberto 'Nito' Mestre**. Originally experimenting with psychedelic music in the '60s, they change to folk rock in their second work *Confesiones de Invierno* in 1973, with more detailed arrangements surrounding the omnipresent piano-acoustic guitar and the frequent flute. Then **Garcia** discovers the magical world of keyboards and incorporates more musicians to record *Pequeñas Anécdotas Sobre las Instituciones* in 1974, a much more prog album sung in Spanish. They disband in 1975 to form another more symphonic band. In 2000 the come back album with a concert in Boca Juniors' Stadium in Buenos Aires.
RECOMMENDED RECORDINGS: **PEQUEÑAS ANÉCDOTAS SOBRE LAS INSTITUCIONES** *(1974, CD Sony Music, 1994).*
M.G.

JORGE PINCHEVSKY

Born in 1943, he begins to play the violin at the age of six. In 1964 he tours South America with a number of different bands like **La Cofradia de la Flor Solar** and **Billy Bond y La Pesada**. His only album *Su violín mágico y La Pesada* is a blues and hard rock approach with a leading violin for not quite 30 minutes of music of low quality sound. He also participates to *Pequeñas Anécdotas Sobre Las Instituciones* of **Sui Generis**. After joining a community in the mountains he moves to Paris, where plays with **Clearlight** in 1975 supporting **Gong**, whose ranks he joins soon after recording *Shamal*. Returning to Argentina in 1985 he is involved in many projects (the rock opera *La hija de la lágrima* by **Charly Garcia** in 1994) and issues a second album with **The Samovar Big Bang**. He dies in 2003, after a bike accident.
RECOMMENDED RECORDINGS: **SU VIOLÍN MÁGICO Y LA PESADA** *(Harvest, 1973).* M.G.

South America: ARGENTINA

JINETES NEGROS

Octavio Stampalia - *keyboards,* **Marcello Ezcurra** - *vocals,* **Pablo Robotti, Eduardo Penney** - *guitars,* **Christian Colaizzo, Ricardo Penney** - *drums,* **Marcelo Vaccaro, Charly Moreno** - *bass,* **Gerardo Pricolo** - *percussion.*
In 1999, **Anima**'s keyboardist **Octavio Stampalia** and vocalist **Marcelo Ezcurra** put together a new project with the help of a guitarist, a bassist and a drummer, the name is based on a poem by Nené Dinzeo meaning Black Riders. They release an accessible prog album in 2000, rather song based but nicely enhanced by the keyboards and the effective use of choruses provided by a dozen singers for a modern epic symphonic rock. Impressed by the calendar of Salvador Dali, published by his wife Gala, **Stampalia** decides create a concept album with a song dedicated to each monthly relative painting with surrealistic lyrics surrounding the music: released independently in 2001, *Chronos* had heavy prog sounds echoing **Saga, Kansas, New Trolls** and **Yes**.
RECOMMENDED RECORDINGS: **EL JINETE NEGRO** *(Viajero Inmovil, 2000)* **CHRONOS** *(Viajero Inmovil, 2001)* **OMNIEM** *(Mellow Records, 2007).*   M.G. & C.C.

PABLO EL ENTERRADOR

Jorge Antun - *keyboards,* **Marcelo Sali** - *drums,* **Jose Maria Blanc** – *guitars, bass, vocals,* **Omar Lopez** - *keyboards.*
A symphonic prog rock quartet formed in 1971 with two keyboardists, so obviously their style is quite keyboard-driven: two mysterious albums, both rumored to have been published later but recorded in the early '80s. Their first self-titled debut in fact is dated 1983, while there are resources that indicate its release somewhere in 1979/1980. The second, *Sentido De Lucha* of 1998 is said to have beed made somewhere in 1984, and given the coeherence with the first, this seemed worth mentioning. A romantic and melodic music dominated by the sensational vocals of guitarist **Jose Maria Blanc**. The heavy and constant use of an electric piano creates delicate and classical atmospheres, enriched by South-American melodies. A last come-back album was just issued in 2016.
RECOMMENDED RECORDINGS: **PABLO "EL ENTERRADOR"** *(Viajero Inmovil, 1983).*   M.G. & C.C.

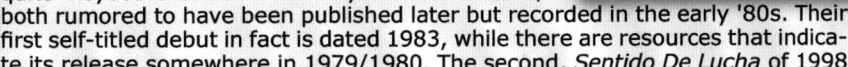

PASTORAL

Miguel Angel Erausquín - *guitar, vocals,* **Alejandro De Michele** - *guitar, vocals,*
Folk rock duo **Alejandro De Michele** and **Miguel Angel Erausquin** met in Buenos Aires at school in 1971. Their first self-titled album was released in 1974 without any promotion. The following year *En El Hospicio* was produced by **Litto Nebbia**. The success brought to a third work, *Humanos,* with the collaboration of many guests as **Charly García** who played keyboards and **Oscar Moro** who played drums. *Atrapados En El Cielo* of 1977 continued on the same line but by 1979, when they released *De Michele-Erausquin*, the differences between the two partners were many and the album was only completed because contractual obligations. They split, **Alejandro** joined **Merlín** and **Miguel** began his solo career publishing a record. They reunite in 1982 with a new album and some concerts but in 1983 **Alejandro** dies in a car crash.
RECOMMENDED RECORDINGS: **PASTORAL** *(Music Hall, 1974)* **EN EL HOSPICIO** *(Caball Records, 1975)* **HUMANOS** *(Caball Records, 1976).*   M.G.

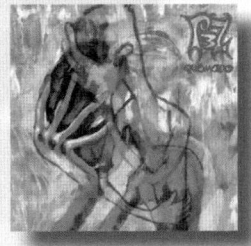

PEZ

Ariel Minimal – *guitar, vocals,* **Poli Barbieri, Iris Auteri** – *drums,* **Alez Barbieri, Franco Salvador** – *bass.*
Formed in 1993 by **Ariel Minimal**, they begin as a hard, experimental rock trio recording a first work called *Cabeza.* In 1995 a second, more progressive album *Quemado,* mixing tango, psychedelia, prog, bossa nova and rock. In 1996 **Ariel** joins **Los Fabulosos Cadillacs** as their guitarist and the band tours all over Argentina along with them too. During 1998 they self-release a third record titled *Pez,* a fast and heavy style that approached punk rock in an elaborate manner. In 2000 they create their own record label, Azione Artigianale, releasing their fourth album *Fragilinvencible,* the beginning of a very prolific discography: *Folklore* of 2004 is another very appreciated work, and their latest, *Rodar* of 2017, features **Litto Nebbia**.
RECOMMENDED RECORDINGS: **CABESA** *(Discos Milagrosos, 1994)* **QUEMADO** *(Discos Milagrosos,1996)* **RODAR** *(Melopea, 2017).*   M.G.

South America: BRAZIL

MARCO ANTONIO ARAUJO

Former guitarist of the band **Vox Populi** in 1968, he moves to the UK in 1970 to deepen his guitar studies. Once back in 1977 he studies the cello and even joins a symphonic orchestra before deciding to compose his own material. Influencias, published in 1980 with the support of some friends, is a compelling prog album while Quando A Sorte Te Solta Um Cisne Na Noite is more intimate and elaborate, with European harmonies and melodies mixed to Brazilian folk themes. The links with the pastoral side of Italian Prog are very strong (**PFM**) closer to chamber folk music with basically acoustic instrumentation, displaying his talent as a composer where strings and flutes come in evidence. He dies very young in 1986 with a total of 74 concerts, even performed in factories in front of the workers during their lunchtime.
DISCOGRAPHY: **INFLUENCIAS** *(Records, 1980)* **QUANDO A SORTE TE SOLTA UM CISNE NA NOITE** *(Records, 1980).*
C.A.

ARRIGO BARNABE'

Creative, outsider, introvert, an experimenter genius, **Arrigo Barnabè** is a great Brazilian musician and actor With his debut and masterpiece Clara Crocodilo, published in 1980, he starts a revolution: an orchestra directed as only **Frank Zappa** could have done, with a polyphonic rhythmic guide and a dodecaphonic manual always open. Elements from the samba tradition and south-American jazz converged into the songs, merging with zeul, kraut and RIO inserts. A music far from any commercial solution, with the direct transmission of feelings with no compromises. He has also written soundtracks for several Brazilian movies, hosts a radio show called Supertônicas at Rádio Cultura in São Paulo and is cited in the songs "Língua" by **Caetano Veloso** and "Eu Quero Saber Quem Matou" by **Rogério Skylab**.
RECOMMENDED RECORDINGS: **CLARA CROCODILO** *(TG, 1975).*
C.A.

CASA DAS MAQUINAS

Luiz Franco Thomaz - drums, percussion, **José Aroldo Binda** - guitar, vocals, **Carlos da Silva** - bass, vocals, **Mário Testoni Jr.** - keyboards, **Mário Franco Thomaz** - drums, vocals, **Carlos Roberto Piazzoli** - guitar, bass.
Born in 1974 from the disenchantment of glam-dance-pop musicians **Netinho** and **Aroldo** from **Os Incrìveis** who wanted to a less commercial style, they recruit three others and record a first self-titled album released soon after in plain old hard rock sung in Portuguese. Their second album Lar de Maravilhas (1975) however, is considered a national prog classic, with more sophisticated elements, stronger melodies, better arrangements and an emphasis on spacious, multi-layered symphonic keyboards (particularly the synths). The following work Casa de Rock sees them back to the hard rock formula, near to the sound of **Deep Purple**'s Fireball, rough and essential, immediate and overwhelming, featuring two drummers and no more spacey keyboards.
DISCOGRAPHY: **CASA DAS MAQUINAS** *(Cast, 1974)* **LAR DE MARAVILHAS** *(Cast, 1975)* **CASA DE ROCK** *(Cast, 1976).*
C.A.

DOGMA

Renato Coutinho - keyboards, **Daniel Mello** - drums, **Fernando Campos** - guitars, **Barao** - bass.
Only two albums somewhat recalling **Camel**, **Pendragon** and **Cyan** this very interesting Brazilian band (previously called Tempus Fugit) manages amazing keyboards, fine guitars, delicate acoustic sounds and light melodies with the collaboration of **Marcus Viana** from **Sagrado Coraçao Da Terra** on the violin. Their first neo-prog album of 1992 contains only instrumental music while Twin Sunrise is considered their best work: published a couple of years later it is more symphonic, powerful and melodic than the previous, yet a perfect sequel, with guitarist **Fernando Campos** sounding like a mix of **Steve Rothery**, **Mike Oldfield** or **Steve Hackett**.
DISCOGRAPHY: **DOGMA** *(1992, Progressive Rock Worldwide)* **TWIN SUNRISE** *(1995, Progressive Rock Worldwide).*
M.G.

South America: BRAZIL

MODULO 1000

Luiz Paulo Simas – keyboards, vocals, **Eduardo** - bass, **Daniel Cardona Romani** - guitars, **Candinho** - drums.

Formed in 1969 and disbanded two years later, they proposed a form of psychedelia with strong hypnotic elements, heavy and experimental sounds in balance between the early **Pink Floyd**, **Iron Butterfly**, **Grand Funk Raiload** and something from **Led Zeppelin**, in a very powerful and crazy mix. Precursors of the genre in Brazil, their only record *Não Fale Com Paredes*, published in 1971, contains hallucinated vocal lines, often repetitive and singing protest lyrics - probably one of the reasons why the album was ill-received by the media - the dramatic tones of a tearing organ and an FX guitar. At the end of the promotional tour, they broke up definitely.

RECOMMENDED RECORDINGS: NÃO FALE COM PAREDES (Top Tape, 1971). M.G. & C.C.

MOTO PERPETUO

Guilherme Arantes - vocals, keyboards, **Egídio Conde** - guitars, **Gerson Tatini** - guitars, **Cláudio Lucci** - bass, **Diógenes Burani** - drums.

The project ignited when **Guilherme Arantes** and **Claudio Lucci** met in 1973 creating a band to release this album/project of guitar harmonies and compelling keyboards. The scarce personality confirms the work as a sort of testing potentialities of the known with the very impressive arrangements of guitarist **Egidio Conde**. Strong songwriting over delicate vocal harmonies, intelligent arrangements and dreamy instrumental parts with elements of pop, folk and classical music all over, catchy choruses and a strong Latin character. **Guilherme** pursues his own long solo career. In 1981 three of the former members issue an album as **São Quixote**, with **Arantes** appearing as a guest musician.

DISCOGRAPHY: MOTO PERPETUO (Continental, 1974). C.A. & C.C.

QUANTUM

Fernando Costa - keyboards, **Paulo Eduardo Naddeo** - drums, percussion, **Reynaldo Rana Jr** - guitar, **Segis Rodrigues** - bass, **Felipe Carvalho** - bass, **Luiz Seman** - vocals, **Paulo Zinner** - drums.

Strongly inspired by **Camel** and **Genesis** with added elements of jazzy nature, which provided some peculiar swing to the overall symphonic sound, they release a beautiful instrumental prog album in 1983 performed with taste and great capability (good musicians and use of right tunes), disbanding soon after. The reunion ten years later with a new line-up for a second record in 1994 closer to neo prog, still good and compelling but less inspired than the previous. Rumor has it that an actual second album from the previous decade had been briefly circulating among collectors and fans in cassette format.

DISCOGRAPHY: QUANTUM (1983, private press) **QUANTUM 2** (1994, Record Runner). M.G. & C.C.

RECORDANDO O VALE DAS MAÇÃS

Fernando Pacheco - guitars, **Fernando Motta** – acoustic guitar, **Eliseu de Oliveira** – keyboards, vocals, **Ronaldo de Mesquita** - bass, **Milton Bernardes** – drums, percussion, **Moacir Amaral** – flute, vocals, **Luiz Aranha** – violin, **Lourenço Gotti** – drums.

Formed in 1973 and very inspired by the whole hippy philosophy and Flower Power movement of the early '70s, their first album was published only in 1977, *As Crianças da Nova Floresta* (The Children Of The New Forest), a perfect example of mellow symphonic prog sung in Portuguese, maybe not so original, but linked to Samba, **Vinicius De Moraes** and **Jobìm**. Besides the standard guitar and dual keyboards they include violin, flute and digital horn, with arrangements always very tastefully done, musically involved, and consistently interesting. Their first album is completely re-recorded and reissued with different arrangements and English lyrics in 1993. They seems to be still active today.

DISCOGRAPHY: AS CRIANÇAS DA NOVA FLORESTA (aka 1977-1982) (GTA, 1977). M.G.

South America: BRAZIL

SAGRADO CORAÇÃO DA TERRA

Alexandre Lopes, Chico Amaral – *guitars,* **Edson Plá, Caio Guimarães, Paulinho Carvalho** – *bass,* **Zé Arthur, João Guimarães** – *drums, percussion,* **Cristiana Ramos, Inês Brando, Giácomo Lombardi** – *keyboards,* **Marcus Viana, Vanessa Falabella, Carla Villar** – *vocals.*
When **Saecula Saeculorum** ceased to exist, **Marcus Viana** decides to start a new band in 1979, reuniting almost a small orchestra of first class musicians in order to create a new breed of Folk rooted symphonic music with evident Baroque and Celtic influences. 5 years later they release their debut album *Sagrado*, a fusion between new age and a weak form of neo-prog. Success took time and many a line-up change but gaining an assorted range of good musicians they created rich textures with tribal elements, prog rock, vocal crossings inspired by classic choral harmonies. The 1999 release *Farol da Liberdade* blends pristine symphonic prog to beautiful Brazilian Folk and from here on their quality maintained unaltered.
RECOMMENDED RECORDINGS: SAGRADO *(King Records, 1985)* **FLECHA** *(King Records, 1987)* **FAROL DA LIBERDADE** *(King Records, 1991)* **GRANDE ESPÍRITO** *(King Records, 1994).* **M.G.**

TEMPUS FUGIT

Andre Mello – *keyboards, vocals,* **Henrique Simões** – *guitars, vocals,* **Ary Moura** – *drums, percussion,* **Andre Luis** – *bass, acoustic guitar.*
Formed in 1989, they undergo many a line-up consolidation before being able to publish a first concept album in 1997, *Tales from a Forgotten World*, strongly influenced by the music of **Yes**, **Camel** and **Marillio**n, to which they blend their Brazilian elements. In 1999 the second studio album *The Dawn After The Storm* is a more mature work full of lush keyboards and fresh ideas leading to a roller coaster of tours and festivals since everybody liked their style that combined nostalgia for the golden symphonic era, with a modern twist. The third album recorded in 6 years proves that the band takes its music very seriously: published in 2008 *Chessboard* continues on the same path of extended, instrumental suites of classic symphonic prog and neo prog with a clear **IQ**, early **Genesis** and **Kyrie Eleison** references.
RECOMMENDED RECORDINGS: TALES FROM A FORGOTTEN WORLD *(RSLN, 1997)* **THE DAWN AFTER THE STORM** *(Rock Symphony, 1999).* **M.G.**

VIA LUMINI

Fernando Loia - *drums, percussion,* **Cézar Pacca** - *guitar,* **Edilson Rodrigues** - *vocals, acoustic guitar,* **Mauro Cannalonga** - *keyboards, piano,* **Marcelo Dias** - *bass,* **Silvio De Oliveira** - *flute.*
Formed as Aura in the late '80s by a quintet of young musicians interested in reviving classic '70s prog music in South America, they managed to secure a recording contract with a lengthy debut album published in 1991 called *Vôos e Sonhos* and a second work in 1995. Both records mix symphonic rock and new-prog inspired by **Yes**, **Genesis**, **Camel** and **Marillion**, with melodic latino atmospheres (helped by the use of Portuguese lyrics). Guitarist and vocalist **Edilson Rodrigues** left after the debut, replaced by flautist **Silvio De Oliveira**, giving the band an added dimension in sound, as well as another band to emulate (**Jethro Tull**) on their second and final release *What Have We Done About Us*. There is no clear record of when they break up.
DISCOGRAPHY: VÔOS E SONHOS *(1991, Progressive Rock Worldwide)* **WHAT HAVE WE DONE ABOUT US?** *(1995, Progressive Rock Worldwide).* **M.G. & C.C.**

VIOLETA DE OUTONO

Fabio Golfetti - *guitar, vocals,* **Claudio Souza, Joao Parahyba** - *drums,* **Angelo Pastorelli, Gabril Costa** - *bass,* **Fabio Ribeiro, Fernando Cardoso** - *keyboards.*
Psychedelic rock band formed in 1984 by guitarist **Fabio Golfetti** and drummer **Claudio Sousa**, both previously with **Zero**. Together with bassist **Angelo Pastorello** they publish a number of great psychedelic works until 2005, when they add keyboardist **Fernando Cardoso** to the line-up, also replacing Pastorello with **Gabriel Costa**. Their sound is very influenced by the early '70s British bands like **Caravan** or **Cressida**, **Pink Floyd**, **Gong**, **Hawkwind** and the psychedelic side of **The Beatles**, with light grooves and organ jams characterized by a melodic and dreamy sound, warm vocals, an ethereal piano and the leading guitar. A first debut on demo tape heavily broadcast, in 1986 a three-track EP, releasing their first album a year later.
RECOMMENDED RECORDINGS: VIOLETA DE OUTONO *(Invisivel, 1987).* **M.G. & C.C.**

South America: CHILE

AKINETÓN RETARD

Estratos Akrias, Petras Das Petren, Edén Carrasco - horns, **Leras Tutas, Lecta Celdrej** - bass, **Bolshek Tradib** - drums, **Tanderal Anfurness** - guitar.
Powerful avant-garde rock band playing a dynamic jazz-rock filled with culture and influenced by **Zorn, Kaiser** and **Soft Machine**. A real underground icon formed in 1994 proposing their loud punk formula of cheerful sounds based upon horns and guitars, elaborating ironic fanfares and implacable fugues. A first album in 1999 for a memorable debut followed by *Akranania*, a second RIO avant-garde project displaying their innovative and experimentalist style, close to the music of **Art Zoyd, Univers Zero, Present, King Crimson** and even **Jacula** (although they may not be aware of the similarities). And so on as they are still proudly active with a last album published in 2016.
RECOMMENDED RECORDINGS: AKINETÓN RETARD (Lizard 2001) **AKRANANIA** (Mylodon 2002) **21 CANAPES** (Mylodon 2003) **CADENCIA UMANA** (Mylodon 2006). **M.G. & C.C.**

MATRAZ

Diego Aburto - piano, keyboards, **Claudio Cordero** - guitar, **Inti Oyarzun** - vocals, bass, **Marcelo Stuardo** - drums, marimbas, **Loreto Chaparro** - vocals, **Jorje García** - bass.
A mainly instrumental band formed in 1996 and inspired by **Marillion** though orienting their sound to a more aggressive and heavy rock solution similar to the work of **Dream Theater**, blending prog metal with fusion as well as symphonic prog. Their first album *Tiempo* was recorded in 1999 and partly funded by the Chilean Goverment as an award for musicalizing the poem "Tiempo" by nobel winner and poet Gabriela Mistral: long suites and well performed improvisations full of keyboard virtuosisms mixed with overwhelming guitars. The second album *Gritarè* published in 2004 evolves, with a female singer and Spanish lyrics for a dazzling array of moods often within the same track.
DISCOGRAPHY: TIEMPO (Mylo, 2000) **GRITARE'** (Mylo, 2004). **C.A. & C.C.**

ANTONIO SMITH (Congregaciòn)

Antonio Smith - vocals, guitar, **Alejandro Rodríguez** - guitar harmonica, vocals, **Alberto Pradas** - bass, guitar, vocals, **Baltasar Villaseca** - percussion, guitar, vocals, **Carlos Vittini** - flute, percussion.
Antonio Smith forms Congregaciòn in 1970, also featuring guests such as **Eduardo** and **Gabriel Parra** from **Los Jaivas** and **Julio Numhause** (**Quilapayún, Amerindios**): in 1972 they release a first 33RMP titled Viene, a psychedelic bucolic work of incalculable cultural value, censored by the military dictatorship of Augusto Pinochet in 1973, who branded **Smith** as a "tenorino with nuances of homosexual". Exiled to Argentina they join a hippy community called Grupo Sol de Chile with a compilation recorded in 1974. Same year *Viene* becomes a full die-hard psych album, trippy and ethereal, and he issues a solo debut *Come Let's Be More*. A second solo work in 1975 titled *Somos El Mundo* before publishing albums under alias names like **Awankana** or **Anton Senchi**.
RECOMMENDED RECORDINGS: VIENE (IRT, 1974). **C.A. & C.C.**

TRYO

Félix Carbone - drums, vibes, marimbas, **Francisco Cortez** - vocals, bass, cello, **Ismael Cortez** - vocals, guitar.
Formed in the early '80s, they do not confine to the traditional roles of a PowerTrio: drummer **Felix Carbone** frequently switches his kit of assorted percussions, and bassist **Francisco Cortez** is also an excellent cello player; only **Ismael Cortez** maintains his spot alternating between electric and acoustic guitars. The result is an energic modern music, well arranged, well balanced albeit the surprising virtuosisms and symphonic pomp recalling **Yes**. The melodies of their third album *Patrimonio* are absolutely compelling, delicate and full of harmony, supported by outstanding and powerful drums with prog-folk passages and **Gentle Giant** reminiscences. *Dos Mundos* is more sophisticated, proposing acid jazz tastes merged in **King Crimson** combinations between heavy electric complex rhythms and subtle passages of acoustic voyages.
RECOMMENDED RECORDINGS: PATRIMONIO (Cantera, 1999) **DOS MUNDOS** (Cantera, 2002). **C.A.**

South America: MEXICO

CAST

Alfonso Vidales – vocals, keyboards, **Dino Brassea** – vocals, flute, **Antonio Bringas** – drums, **Claudio Cordero** – guitar, **Flavio Miranda** – banjo.

Born in 1978, when the golden era of progressive rock was already agonizing: keyboardist **Alfonso Vidales** decides to create a band reviving the symphonism of those pioneers though no information on their first 16 years is available. In 1994 they publish three self released albums: *Landing in a Serious Mind*, a debut sung in a strong accented English but sounding as freshmen of the genre and not as a band with so many years of experience. The second *Sounds of Imagination*, containing a full hour of more mature neo-symphonic rock, which strengthens a rumor claiming it all as material written between the 1978 / 1994 gap. This latter is clearly influenced by **Genesis**, **Marillion**, **Yes**, **Jethro Tull** and **ELP**, with AOR vibes recalling **Saga**, especially in the synth parts. A third work that year is openly declared being songs from their '80s repertoire and this the begining of more than 20 albums for a band still ferociously active today.
RECOMMENDED RECORDINGS: LANDING IN A SERIOUS MIND (ALF, 1994) **ANGELS AND DEMONS** (ALF, 1998) **IMAGINARY WINDOW** (FGBG, 1999).
M.G.

CHAC MOOL

Jorge Reyes - guitar, flute, **Carlos Alvarado** - keyboards, **Armando Suárez, Carlos Castro, Mauricio Bieletto** - various instruments.

Formed in 1979 for a 'space-rock meets Mexican folk meets orchestral rock' kind of trippy Prog, with well-written Spanish lyrics but perhaps lacking a better singer. Characterized by a strong use of keyboards, bass and flutes recalling **Ian Anderson** from **Jethro Tull**, their dark neo-prog style contains also random space/psychedelic moments for a great 'blue prog' deeply influenced by folk elements from their Mexican culture with musical ideas also inspired by **Pink Floyd**. A well balanced mix with pleasant results and simple textures. Three albums in the '80s and a come-back in 2000 confirming the space sounds and dreamy atmospheres of a classic symphonic prog with good melodies.
DISCOGRAPHY: NADIE EN SPECIAL (Philips, 1980) **SUENOS DE METAL** (Philips, 1981) **CINTAS EN DIRECTO** (Philips, 1982).
C.A. & C.C.

CODICE

David Martinez - drums, percussion, **Luis Maldonado** - vocals, **Mario Mendoza** - keyboards, **Arturo Garcia** - bass, **Marco Corono** - guitars, keyboards.

Began as a solo project of guitarist and keyboardist **Marco Corona** in Los Angeles, he moves to Monterrey, Mexico and recruits a band of classically-trained musicians in 1995. Granted funding from the Monterrey Council for the Arts in 1998 to produce their only album, *Alba Y Ocaso*. Mainly instrumental double CD with the dominating keyboards spreading compelling atmospheres and influences from **ELP** well mixed with guitars and horns. Echoes of new prog's acoustic breaks and **King Crimson** grooves blend with Latin-American emphasis. Many live performances from universities to major progressive festivals such as BajaProg III, MexProg 2000 and ProgFest 2000. They recorded tracks for a second album, still never published.
DISCOGRAPHY: ALBA Y OCASO (1999, Art Sublime).
M.G. & C.C.

DECIBEL

Jaime Castañeda, Moises Romero - drums, percussion, violin, vocals, **Carlos Robledo, Carlos Alvarado** - keyboards, winds, percussion, vocals, **Alejandro Sanchez** - violin, piano, bass, winds, percussion, vocals, **Walter Schmidt** - bass, guitar, keyboards, sax, vocals.

A Mexican chamber/RIO band formed in 1974 as the trio **Carlos Robledo, Moises Romero, Walter Schmidt**, that after 6 months was already a sextet with **Jaime Castañeda** replacing **Romero** on drums and **Carlos Alvarado** on keyboards. In 1978 they record a first album 1980 *El Poeta Del Ruido*, an interesting work, hectic and disorganized the feel, with influences from **Henry Cow, Faust, Karlheinz Stockhausen, Il Balletto Di Bronzo, Univers Zero, Art Zoyd** and **Magma**. Another two albums follow, with a live recording in 2000 and an album of previously unreleased material. The last time they played together was 2003 in ExCinema Teresa in Mexico City.
RECOMMENDED RECORDINGS: EL POETA DEL RUIDO (Orfeon, 1978).
M.G. & C.C.

South America: MEXICO

DELIRIUM

Amador Ramirez – keyboards, **Manolo Lhoman** - bass, **Alberto Herr** – drums, **Alfredo Flores** - violin, **Daniel Rivadeneyra** – guitar, **Oscar Saldana** - vocals.

This Mexican neo-prog act plays a surprisingly pleasant symphonic prog rock based upon the guitar-keyboard interplay performed with stunning mastery. The refined and delicate touches of violin create extraordinarily dreamy atmospheres. Both albums contain lots of improvised parts, mostly instrumental and very reminiscent of the '70s Italian sound - particularly of **PFM** and **Quella Vecchia Locanda**. The album first self titled album of 1985 was later released as *Primer Diálogo* in 1997 locally and as *El Teatro del Delirio*, with added tracks for a foregin distribution that same year. In 1991 they also record *Tomando Decisiones* a second work that went 'lost'.
RECOMMENDED RECORDINGS: TOMANDO DECISIONES *(Discos, 1991)* **EL TEATRO DEL DELIRIO** *(PCS. 1997)*.
C.A. & C.C.

FLÜGHT

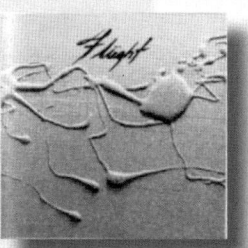

Sergio De Labra - piano, keyboards, **Víctor Ruiz** - guitars, bass **Jorge Pre za**- guitars, bass, **Armando Gonzalez** - bass,.

Formed as a duo in 1979 by keyboardist **Sergio De Labra** and guitar/bass player **Jorge Preza**, influenced mostly by the Italian prog of Le Orme, BMS and **Il Rovescio della Medaglia**. After some to and fro of guest musicians, guitarist **Victor Ruiz** replaces **Jorge** definately and they finally release a self-titled album in 1982. On bass it features **Armando Gonzalez**. Their music is a rooted in the German post-Krautrock of **Tangerine Dream** and **Mike Oldfield**, with symphonic shades inspired by **Yes**. A second release is published in 1989 entitled *Saraba*. This last album is less related with their previous one and more directed toward an interesting Jazz Rock with Fusion sounds.
DISCOGRAPHY: FLÜGHT *(OPCCD, 1982)* **SARABA** *(Exilio, 1989)*.
C.A.

THE HIGH FIDELITY ORCHESTRA

Jesus Gonzalez – guitars, synthesizers, piano, vocals, **Rene Romero** - guitars, **Raymundo Barajas** – drums, marimba, **Gilberto Gonzalez** - bass.

Solo project of multi-instrumentalist **Jesus Gonzales**, friend and collaborator of the band **Nazca**, he records a self-titled album in just a few days during September 1982 for a total of only 23 minutes of incredible cosmic acid rock played by a real hi-fi orchestra. Altough the first couple of tracks are a monotonous imitation of **King Crimson**, **Robert Fripp** and **Pink Floyd**, almost all the remaining pieces are not only free from imitation, but very original too, full of innovative ideas and complex arrangements. These five compositions (from 3 to 7) are so unique and interesting that they make this album worth the while.
DISCOGRAPHY: THE HIGH FIDELITY ORCHESTRA *(Smogless, 1984)*.
M.G.

ICONOCLASTA

Ricardo Moreno Echevaria - keyboards, **Héctor Hernández** - guitar, **Ricardo Ortegón** - guitars, **Alfredo Raigosa** - bass, **Víctor Baldovinos** - drums, percussion.

Formed in 1980 as a garage rock group, their sound soon turns towards a more progressive genre combining elements from rock, jazz, folk and classical music. They release a first eponymous debut under their own Rosenbach records in 1983 presenting a developing band still trying to find a style. The main instrument is the electric guitar, with the keyboards as a secondary actor, though frequently used. Their second album *Reminescentias* contains atmospheres influenced by **ELP** and **Yes**, while *Soliloquio* confirms their symphonic prog canons. The following *Adolescentia Cronica* is without doubt their best out of the eleven studio albums, of which the last in 2013.
RECOMMENDED RECORDINGS: ICONOCLASTA *(Discos Rosembach, 1982)* **REMINESCENCIAS** *(Discos Rosembach, 1985)* **ADOLESCENCIA CRONICA** *(Discos Rosembach, 1989)*.
C.A.

South America: MEXICO

METACONCIENCIA

Francisco Estrada – *acoustic and electric guitars*, **Ricardo Moreno** - *guitars, keyboards*, **José Ramon Porrua** - *bass*, **Carlos Bonequi** – *drums, percussion*.

Formed in 1996, this guitar driven band (two very capable guitarists, one of them also the keyboardist) combines classic rock, jazz, blues, and metal resulting in an interesting sound, transforming from **Genesis** to **King Crimson** sometimes with hard rock influences recalling **Dream Theater**. In 2003 they publish their only album *Bestiario*, a 61-minute all-instrumental album based on the interplay between solos of the art-rock electric guitar and bass and the acoustic guitar accompanied by a quite extraordinary drummer. Their compositions are unique and their arrangements inspired, venturing into the experimental side whilst pushing the traditional boundaries.

RECOMMENDED RECORDINGS: **BESTIARIO** (*Musea, 2003*). M.G.

MUSICANTE

Guillermo Diego – *classic guitar, songwriter*, **Norma Chargoy** – *percussion*, **Other musicians...**

A project of **Guillermo Diego** on classic guitars accompanied by percussionist **Norma Chargoy**, they start as a duo in 1982 playing modern chamber music with a folk oriented Prog mixed to a soft form of western rock, pre-Ispanic traditional tunes and the almost exclusive use of acoustic instruments. To add more emphasis, the arrangements are augmented through the use of horns, strings and an orchestra, some things recalling **Camel** and others very similar to the Belgian **Julverne**. Both albums are issued during the '80s and present this vibrant ethnic fusion, while **Diego** issues a solo album of his own in 2006.

RECOMMENDED RECORDINGS: **A LOS QUATRO VIENTOS** (*EMI, 1987*). M.G.

NIRGAL VALLIS

José Luis Fernández Ledesma Q. – *keyboards, jaranas, kalimba, guitar*, **Ramón Nakash B.** – *violin, mandolin*, **Alejandro Schmidt R.** –*guitars, bass*, **Claudio Martinez De Alba** – *vocals*, **Rafael González** – *drums, percussion*.

Born as school band trio in 1983, they manage to consolidate the line-up for an album in 1985 called *Y Muriò La Tarde*, reissued in 1995 by the label Musea, with a first side written by the band and the second written by **Arturo Meza**. Ten years later they reunite thanks to Musea and write four new tracks for the CD release. Their music is a compelling prog rock folk with symphonic tunes recalling Renaissance and Latin-American melodies. The groove is involving, the music well performed and sometimes the sounds are original and unusual. This band was **Jose Luis Fernandez Ledesma Q**'s first gig, now one of the most famous Mexican progressive musicians with many solo albums and collaborations with singer and composer **Alquimia**.

RECOMMENDED RECORDINGS: **Y MURIÓ LA TARDE** (*Gente de Mexico, 1985 – Musea 1995*). M.G.

NOBILIS FACTUM

Enrique Balderas Rodriguez - *keyboards, vocals*, **Jesus Padilla Lechuga**- *guitar, keyboards, vocals*, **Guillermo Nava Cerda** - *bass, guitar, keyboards, vocals*, **Miguel Caldera Moreno** - *drums, percussion, vocals*.

A progressive melodic group which started to play together in 1978 a synth dominated melodic prog (since all the band members played the keyboards) with many live appearances, leading them to win a scholarsahip from the local university, but then came to a first split. Officially named **Nobilis Factum** in the spring of 1980, they publish their only self-produced album a couple of years later called *Mutante*, very interesting though completely sung in Spanish, but suffering this predominant use of keyboards, sometimes compelling and sometimes very boring. In 1997 **Miguel Caldera Moreno** reforms the band publishing *Mutante* on CD and adding a bonus track of trivial techno-pop, supported by **Cesar M. Garduno** and **Roberto Eslava**.

RECOMMENDED RECORDINGS: **MUTANTE** (*Private pressing, 1982*). M.G.

South America: PERÙ

FLOR DE LOTO

Alonso Herrera - *guitar*, **Alejandro Jarrin** - *bass*, **Jorge Puccini** - *drums, percussion*, **Johnny Perez** - *flute, sequencer*.

Instrumental quartet formed by guitarist **Alonso Herrera** and bassist **Alejandro Jarrín** back in 1998. This excellent ensemble performs a prog full of traditional folk elements especially in their first homonym album of 2005: a completely instrumental album that won them the description of Peruvian **Jethro Tull**, although they prove to be really different. In fact their second album *Madre Tierra* (definitely their best record followed by other impressive works as well) shifts towards jazz fusion, yet maintaining the outstanding flute work with **Johnny Perez** later replaced by **Junior Pacora** in *Crescendo* of 2008. Their fourth album of 2011 is more prog-metal oriented, leaving their Andean folk behind for a while, catching up with another couple of records later on.
RECOMMENDED RECORDINGS : **MADRE TIERRA** *(Mylodon, 2006)*.   **C.A.**

LAGHONIA

Saúl Cornejo - *vocals, guitar*, **Alberto Miller** - *guitar*, **Eddy Zarauz** - *bass*, **Carlos Salom** - *Hammond organ*, **Manuel Cornejo** - *drums*, **Alex Abad** - *percussion*, **Ernesto Samamé** - *bass*, **David Levene** - *vocals, guitar*.

Perù's fertile psychedelic prog scenario counts great quality bands which would all gather at a **Laghonia** concert to watch the first South American Hammond B2 being played. Formed in 1965 by the **Cornejo** brothers and **Eddy Zaraus**, they were fans of classical music, especially **Tchaikovski**, when **The Beatles** hit the planet: so they found this band blending classical to beat and sounds from **The Yardbirds**, **The Zombies** (baroque), **The Animals** and later adding the **Hendrix/Santana** guitar riffs. The debut album *Glue* in 1968 is followed by *Etcetera* a year after. Both works have a poor production quality but their style is an honest psychedelic pop. Also a 2006 release with rare versions and previously unreleased material came out named *Unglue*. The **Cornejos** and **Carlos Salom** will then form **We All Together**, but that's another story.
RECOMMENDED RECORDINGS: **GLUE** *(RFR, 1971)* **ETCETERA** *(Essex, 1971)*.   **C.A.**

PAX

Enrique "Pico" Ego Aguirre - *guitar, keyboards, vocals*, **Miguel Flores** - *drums*, **Marc Aguillar** - *bass, piano*, **Jaime "Pacho" Orue Moreno** - *vocals*.

Formed on the ashes of a garage-psychedelic rock band called **Los Shain's** (1964-1969), this final incarnation issues only one album in 1970 with a very long title: *May God And Your Will Land You And Your Soul Miles Away From Evil*. A much more energic prog from the previous style, mixing psychedelia and the hard rock of **Deep Purple**, **Led Zeppelin** and **Black Sabbath**, resulting in a pleasant groove, with whirlwinds of guitars recalling **Jimi Hendrix**, a nice bass in the style of **Cream** or **Budgie** and some soft, orchestrated ballads.
DISCOGRAPHY: **MAY GOD AND YOUR WILL LAND YOU AND YOUR SOUL MILES AWAY FROM EVIL** *(Sonoradio, 1970)*.   **C.A.**

TARKUS

Walo Carillo - *drums*, **Guillermo Van Lacke** - *bass*, **Dario Gianella** - *guitar*, **Alex Nathanson** – *vocals, acoustic guitar*.

The heaviest of all hard rock/progressive bands from Peru, formed in 1971 when **Guillermo Van Lacke** approaches Telegraph Avenue musicians **Alex Nathanson** and **Walo Carrillo** who temporarily join for some concerts. The melodic element is filled by guitarist **Dario Ginella** and they debut in 1972 with an album of heavy rock and futuristic vision, probably too advanced so the label decides not to release it. They do it themselves without promotion and in limited copies: the heaviest and most extreme album to have dropped through that year, with raw early-metal riffs sometimes buried in the very late '60s acid hard-rock jamming sound. While the rest wanted to project a second work, **Dario** joins the religious congregation Los Niños De Dios. In 2008 the reunion for some concerts and an album of unrecorded songs from the early years.
RECOMMENDED RECORDINGS : **TARKUS** *(Mag LP, 1972)*.   **M.G.**

South America: VENEZUELA

ADITUS

George Henríquez – *keyboards*, **Alvaro Falcón** – *guitar*, **Sandro Liberatoscioli** – *bass*, **Valerio González** – *drums*.
Originally formed in 1973 by **Edgar De Sola**, **Sandro Liberatoscioli**, **Carlos Atilano** and **José Ignacio Lares** (who were soon joined by **Alvaro Falcón** and **George Henríquez**) as a prog band with jazzy tendencies. **De Sola** and **Lares** exit to form **Ficcion** in 1976, replaced by Valerio González for their debut *A Través De La Ventana*. Vibraphonist **Freddy Roldan** joins in consolidating their jazz-rock fusion sound in the following work while **Roldan** and **Falcón** also leave replaced by **Pedro Castillo** who, paradoxically, conducts them towards a more commercial music: thus *Fuera De La Ley* is their transitional third work and last prog album. Their three first albums (1977, 1977, 1981) are fairly unknown and actually progressive works recalling **Return to Forever**, **Mahavisnu Orchestra**, **Brand X**, **Santana**, **Saga** and **Asia**. The next nine albums still contain some proggy elements but nothing worth mentioning.
RECOMMENDED RECORDINGS: A TRAVES DE LA VENTANA *(GDR, 1977)*. M.G.

ENFASIS

Licio Lugarini Melloni – *guitars, drums, vocals*, **Blanca Pulido Quintana** - *vocals*, **Carolina Pulido Quintana** – *guitar, vocals*, **Ubaldo Vella** – *keyboards, drums*, **Tony Linares** - *bass*. **Donn Ángel Pérez** – *drums*, **Eva Delgado** - *vocals*, **Chupa Vaez, Oscar Vaez** - *percussion*.
New prog band with pop tendencies that published a first homonym album in 1983. Their second release titled *Vencer o Morir* confirms those tendencies and like many similar bands, they aim to ascend the charts and please. A last homonym Stereo 7 tape was published at the end of '80s before disappearing from the scenes. Led by guitarist and drummer **Licio Lugarini Melloni** and keyboardist **Ubaldo Vella**, the second vinyl is much closer to an energic AOR or Arena rock, with flashy keyboards, a solid female lead singer and hard guitar solos producing a bombastic atmosphere. The songwriting is rather conservative, with choruses and solos, but there are a few tracks with light symphonic touches and the overall mood is quite enjoyable.
DISCOGRAPHY: ENFASIS *(GDR, 1983)* **VENCER O MORIR** *(GDR, 1984)*. M.G.

TEMPANO

Pedro Castillo - *guitar, vocals*, **Julio César Della Noche** - *keyboards*, **Miguel Angel Echevarreneta** - *bass, acoustic guitar*, **Gerardo Ubieda** - *drums*.
Formed in 1977, their symphonic prog debut is published a couple of years later titled *Atabal-Yemal*: beautiful jazz intrusions, experimental touches rich of romantic lyrics and orchestrations with great overtures interrupted by an aggressive Canterbury jazz rock evoking **Return To Forever** or **Camel**, with the unusual sounds and breaks of **Happy The Man** blended to the typically warm, South American colours. Major line-up changes around **Gerardo Ubieda** slowly evolving from an early '80s **Asia** clone to a tasteless pop rock band via the next 5 albums. In 1999 the original line-up reunites for four excellent records: *Childhood's End / El fin de la infancia* features cellist **Peter Pejtsik** (from **After Crying**) for a darker chamber touch and a really great comeback. *The Agony And The Ecstasy* is even better and more melodic, still jazzy and Avant-Prog.
RECOMMENDED RECORDINGS: ATABAL YEMAL *(Vinyl Internacional - Musea, 1979)* **THE AGONY AND THE ECSTASY** *(Musea, 2002)*. M.G.

FERNANDO YVOSKY

Composer, singer and guitarist, he releases privately in 1975 an only album titled *Dos Mundos* under his name, yet credits also go to keyboardist, singer and flutist **Guillermo Mager**, who was the other composer of a work, that featured no less than 20 participants on bass, drums, guitars and wind/string instruments: a huge instrumental armour of acoustic instruments and keyboards, leading to depressive orchestrations, warm vocals, symphonic keyboard galore and rural soundscapes. Dreamy and often melancholic pastoral prog-folk, structurally executed in a symphonic matrix recalling the italian prog of **PFM**.
DISCOGRAPHY: DOS MUNDOS *(GDR, 1975)*. M.G.

South West Asia: EX-SOVIETIC REPUBLICS

ARTSRUNI

Vahan Artsruni - *guitar, vocals,* **Vahagn Amirkhanyan** - *guitar,* **Arman Manukyan** - *flute,* **Artur Molitivin** - *bass,* **Levon Hackverdyan** - *drums,* **Lilianna Hackverdyan** - *percussion.*
From Armenia, this sextet was formed in 2000 by composer, guitarist and vocalist **Vahan Artsruni** playing a smooth jazz fusion with middle-eastern accents and prog tints coloured by their own cultural background which give the music a genuine local flavour. The flute play recalls **Jethro Tull** and **Notturno Concertante** but the acoustic guitar also gives them an early **Camel** feel. Lacking a keyboard player, they fill the void with a jazzy effect for a romantic music and the instrumental verve of their live performances. In fact *Cruzaid* is their only studio album of 2002, while they actually debut one year before with a live called *The Lost and Found*: the energetic interaction between the flute and guitar is supported by an incredible bass playing and even parts featuring the Armenian Philharmonic Orchestra.
DISCOGRAPHY: THE LOST AND FOUND *(live, Musea, 2001)* **CRUZAID** *(Musea, 2002).* **M.G.**

BOOMERANG

Yury Parfionov – *trumpet,* **Victor Nikolayev** - *sax,* **Lev Lieplauk** - *piano fender,* **Tahir Ibragimov** – *percussion,* **Farhad Ibragimov** - *bass, tabla,* **Konstantin Lee** - *guitar.*
From Kazakhstan, the Jazz Ensemble **Boomerang**, aka **Bumerang**, was formed in 1973 by drummer **Tahir Ibragimov**. Their albums (1983-1985-1986) are all based upon a folk fusion jazz rock rich of oriental flavours coming from their country with a mix of Caucasian and Asian cultural roots, adding up to an original prog style of their own Their second work *Ornament* is probably the best with its compelling horn arrangements and a Rhodes piano recalling **Eumir Deodato**'s style. Yet their last album *Mirage* (thanks a reissue of Musea Records) is their most popular, and a little more commercial record, with atmospheres from **the Alan Parsons Project**, good but not at the same level of the previous two.
RECOMMENDED RECORDINGS: ORNAMENT *(Melodyia, 1985).* **M.G.**

ER. J. ORCHESTRA

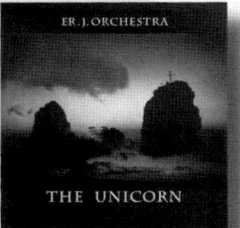

Alexei Alexandrov - *flute, piano, percussion,* **Victor Krisko** - *violin, viola,* **Sergei Hmelyov** - *vibes, marimba,* **Viktor Melezhik, Gregory Nemirovsky** - *horns,* **Vladimir Sorochenko** - *bass,* **Andrei Chuguyevets** - *guitar, domra, bayan,* **Dr. Kobtsev** - *vocals, percussion,* **Alexander Beregovsky** - *vibes, percussion, flute, drums.*
From Ukraine, they form as an actual small orchestra around 1989 by **Alexei Alexandrov**, intending to blend rock and jazz with Slavonic melodies and using ethnic instruments. The debut album *Gabrielius* was recorded in 1994/95 and released privately in 1998. The second release *On The Hill Again* was published in 2002: a wonderful record where they start from fusion, reaching into folk, World Music, prog and the contemporary classical genre with original solutions and adding part of their national identity into the sound. The *Unicorn* of 2004 is their last studio album, for a band wandering through styles and influences: too light to be Art Rock and too Prog to be ignored.
RECOMMENDED RECORDINGS: ON THE HILL AGAIN *(2002, Rostock).* **M.G.**

FIRYUZA

Dmitriy Manukyan - *drums,* **Dmitriy Sablin** - *keyboards,* **Sabir Rizaev** - *horns,* **Alif Nifchenko** - *bass,* **Yevgeny Nochevn, Mikhail Mamedov** - *guitar,* **Khana Ten** - *violin.*
From Turkmenistan formed in 1979 by **Dmitriy Manukyan** (from **Gunesh Ensemble**) for an instrumental music of fascinating jazz-rock fusion, soft prog, folk, oriental elements and sounds very similar to **Mahavishnu Orchestra**. The solos are mainly of violin and sax (played like **David Jackson** from **VDGG**). This seven piece ensemble releases their only album *Firyuza Instrumental Ensemble* featuring their traditional folk ethno-fusion through prog with a slightly psychedelic twist. The four long instrumental parts present electric guitars and a constant use of the folky violin and strong sax moments: more avant-garde than **Gunesh**, with emphasis on blending complex climate changes recalling **Kraan** and a certain zeuhl funk at moments..
DISCOGRAPHY: FIRYUZA (Инструментальный ансамбль Фирюза) *(1979, Melodyia).* **M.G.**

South West Asia: EX-SOVIETIC REPUBLICS

FROM.UZ

Andrew Mara-Novik - *bass*, **Vitaly Popeloff** - *guitar*, **Albert Khalmurzayev** - *keyboards*, **Vladimir Badirov** - *drums*.
From Uzbekistan, formed in 2004 when **Vitaly Popeloff** and **Andrew Mara-Novik** decide to team up and compose more complex music of an instrumental nature with arrangements recalling famous prog bands like **Yes** (great use of organ and synthesizers) and without the presence of a lead vocalist. There was no individual author in the group since each composition wanted to be the result of a common effort through the method of attempt and experimentation, a flight of fantasy and emotions: a few themes guiding each track with a tempo and rhythm fluctuating unpredictably. This for their first two albums: **Andrew** and **Vladimir Badirov** leave and some new members join **Vitaly** for their third work of 2010, with lyrics this time. Still a technical instrumental prog fusion but getting better with each record.
DISCOGRAPHY: **AUDIO DIPLOMACY** *(10T Records, 2007)* **OVERLOOK** *(10T Records, 2008)*. **M.G.**

GANELIN TRIO

From Lituania, **Vyacheslav Ganelin** is Russian-born Israeli musician moved here at the age of 4, becoming an excellent piano player and composer, experimenter of new musical languages, including synthesizers and computers coupled with classic instruments. In 1968 he forms his own ensemble with percussionist **Vladimir Tarasov** and saxophonist **Vladimir Rezitsky** (re-

placed in 1971 by **Vladimir Chekasin**), combining free jazz with folk elements and classical music. Their debut *Con Anima* was released in 1976 as the first of a dozen albums before the break-up of 1987, when **Vyacheslav** moves to Israel. A reunion tour in 2001 and the award form the Lithuanian Jazz School in 2016.
RECOMMENDED RECORDINGS: **CON ANIMA** *(1980, Leo Records)* **CONCERTO GROSSO** *(Leo Records)* **TTAANGO ... IN NICKELSDORF** *(1986, Leo Records)* **JERUSALEM FEBRUARY CANTABILE** *(1989, Leo Records)* **OPUSES** *(1990, Leo Records)*. **M.G.**

GUNESH ENSEMBLE

Rishad Shafi - *drums, percussion*, **Vladimir Belousov** - *bass freetles*, **Mikhail Loguntsov**- *guitar*, **Stanislav Morozov** - *sax*, **Kurban Kurbanov** - *tablas*.
From Turkmenistan, this free-jazz band formed in 1970 (later led by drummer **Rishad Shafi**) playing a form of ethnic-fusion recalling *Hot Rats* and *The Grand Wazoo* of **Frank Zappa**. The percussions are at the same level of **Bill Bruford**, with the insertion of a sitar and melodies coming from Vietnam, India and Indochina. The first two albums, released in 1980 and 1984, were reissued as *Rishad Shafi presents Gunesh* in 2000, with a brand new work titled *45° In A Shadow*, maybe more accessible. During the years the line-up changed so often that at least 65 musicians can be counted since their beginnings as a vocal group with supporting instrumentation, traditional mughams and jazz improvisations (a mugham is a very complex music combining classical poetry and musical impros in a modal system, as a collection of melodies).
RECOMMENDED RECORDINGS: **RISHAD SHAFI PRESENTS GUNESH** *(Reissue of the first two albums, Boheme Music, 2000)* **45° IN A SHADOW** *(Boheme Music, 2000)*. **M.G.**

KARFAGEN

Antony Kalugin - *keyboards, flute, percussion, vocals, guitars*, **Oleg Polyansky** - *keyboards*, **Kostya Shepelenko** - *drums*, **Sergey Kovalev** - *harmonica, bayan, bass*.
From Ukraine, **Antony Kalugin** formed this band in 1997 while he was studying in university. He teamed up with **Sergei Kovalev** (accordion and harmonica) for the project but in parallel issued a first solo work in 2002 titled *The Water*. This is how he found the funds to publish a first **Karfagen** album in 2006, titled *Continium*: the beginning of a prolific discography of symphonic prog with romantic colours inspired by **Camel** and blending classical music driven by piano and keyboards with elements of the Ukraine tradition. Refined sounds arranged with taste and melodies oriented to an elegant soft jazz-rock for a band that seems to be still currently active and coherent.
DISCOGRAPHY: **CONTINIUM** *(2006, Unicorn Records)* **THE SPACE BETWEEN US** *(2007, Unicorn Records)*. **M.G.**

South West Asia: EX-SOVIETIC REPUBLICS

OLIVE MESS

Denis Arsenin - *bass*, **Edgar Kempish** - *drums, percussion*, **Alexey Syomin** - *guitar*, **Sergey Syomin** - *guitar, archlute*, **Ilze Paegle** - *vocals*, **Lilia Voronova** - *keyboards*, **Vilnis Kundrats** - *sax*, **Maris Jekabsons** - *vocals, pipes*, **Elizaberh Perecz** - *keyboards*, **Julia Pecherskaya** - *vocals*.

From Lettonia, formed as a trio in 1998, the name chosen in honour of the French composer **Olivier Messiaen**. They blend Medieval-Renaissance references to **King Crimson** prog with Irish folk, avant-garde and RIO, a sort of **Univers Zero** but more eclectic and less dark. In 2001 they release a first recording *Live Without Audience*, which pretty much acted as a demo. After this, the line-up expands and they issue *Gramercy*, consisting in 5 long compositions with lyrics mainly focused on historical events in medieval France and a music shifting between traditional and avant-garde. The female singer **Ilze** has a stunning soprano voice that feels a bit out of place, singing sometimes theatrical, half-spoken, half-sung vocals. The second album *Cherdak* takes quite a while to come out, losing the female voice to a male's, singing in English with a terrible accent.

DISCOGRAPHY: GRAMERCY (2002, Soleil Zeuhl) **CHERDAK** (2008, Mellow Records). M.G.

PESNIARY

Vladimir Muliavin - *guitars, vocals*, **Leonid Bortkevich** - *vocals, lira*, **Anatoliy Kasheparov** - *vocals, bayan*, **Vladislav Misevich** - *horns*, **Valeriy Dayneko** - *vocals, violin*, **Leonid Tyshko** - *bass*, **Aleksander Demeshko** - *drums*, **Vladimir Nikolaev** - *keyboards, horns*, **Cheslav Poplavskiy** - *vocals, violin*, **Anatoliy Gilevich** - *keyboards*, **Vladimir Tkachenko** - *guitar, violin*.

From Bielorussia, formed in 1969 as a great ensemble of many musicians playing a multitude of various instruments. Five excellent albums during the '70s for a good folk-prog with traditional choirs and delicate sounds of horns (outstanding the sax solos). One of the few (and possibly the first) Soviet bands to tour in America in 1976, their Belarusian folklore often had various psychedelic rock elements. Some songs composed by **Alexandra Pakhmutova** and lyrics from poets of the past like **Yanka Kupala**, (*Song of Fate*, 1976 and *Guslar*, 1980, the latter also released as concept album). **Vladimir Muliavin** dies in 2003 and they split.

RECOMMENDED RECORDINGS: PESNIARY 4: BELARUS FOLK SONGS (Melodyia, 1978). C.A.

X-RELIGION

Antony Kalugin - *keyboards, flute, percussion, vocals, guitars, effects*, **Oleg Albert Khalmurzayev** - *keyboards*, **Vitaly Menshikov** - *bass, guitars*, **Valery Vorobjev** - *drums*.

From Uzbekistan, they form in 1996 thanks to musicians coming from two previous hard rock bands, **Edgar Poe** (**Vitaly Menshikov**) and **Rare Bird** (**Albert Khalmurzayev** aka **Al-Bird** and **Vladimir Badirov**). Their music is of pure symphonic nature inspired by **ELP**, but with a modern and more aggressive approach perhaps recalling the style of **Nathan Mahl**, blending keyboard-intensive passages sometimes approaching metal and interspersed with Russian classical influences. **Al-Bird** was already composing his *Sodom & Gomorra XXI* when they joined forces, yet it still came out as his solo effort in 2002. The band's other release *Dances of Gobelins* was recorded around the same time but as a truly collaborative work among all three members this time.

DISCOGRAPHY: SODOM & GOMORRA XXI (Released as Al-Bird, Musea, 2002) **DANCES OF GOBELINS** (Mellow Records, 2003). M.G. & C.C.

YALLA

Farrukh Zakirov – *songwriter, vocals*, **Rustam Iliasov** – *vocals, bass*, **Abbos Aliyev** – *arranger, vocals, keyboards*, **Javlon Tokhtayev** – *vocals, guitar*, **Alishier Tulyaganov** – *vocals, percussion*, **Ibraghim Aliyev** – *percussion*.

From Uzbekistan, they were formed in 1970 by **Farrukh Zakirov** playing a music between rock and ethnic sung in Uzbekian, Russian, Persian, Hindi, Nepalese and French, Arabic, German and Tatar languages. Their prog masterpiece is the second release *The Face Of My Sweetheart* of 1983, but they are remembered for the song "Uchquduc-tri kolodtsa", a very popular hit. Their music incorporates traditional ethnic folk tunes and poetry of Uzbekistan and other central Asian and Middle-Eastern cultures. They appeared on Soviet national television and elsewhere in the Soviet Union, and on concert tours and festivals in Europe, Africa, Asia and Latin America. **Zakirov** was employed as Vice-Minister of Culture in his country some years ago.

RECOMMENDED RECORDINGS: THE FACE OF MY SWEETHEART (Melodyia, 1983) M.G.

IT'S ALMOST PROG!

AFRO CELT SOUND SYSTEM

Simon Emmerson - *guitar, production*, **N'Faly Kouyate** - *kora, balaphon, ngoma drums, vocals*, **Moussa Sissokho** - *djembe, talking drum*, **James McNally** - *Bodhrán, accordion, whistle*, **Johnny Kalsi** - *dhol*, **Iarla Ó Lionáird** - *vocals*, **Emer Mayock** - *tin whistle, flute, uillean pipes*, **Martin Russell** - *keyboards, programming*.

This African folk band formed in 1995 in London. During a recording of **Baaba Maal**, **Simon Emmerson** was impressed by the similarity of the African melody with an Irish theme. This led to a project that started joining African and European musicians to mix different cultures through the use of technology: a blend of pop, rock, techno dance, African rhythms, drum'n'bass and Gaelic melodies, sung by **Iarla O'lionaird**. Classified more as World Music, they have produced nine albums since that day, the third *Further in Time* presents a cast of 20 guests featuring also **Peter Gabriel**, **Robert Plant**, **Pina** and **Demba Barry** for an electronic act with influences drawn from traditional Celtic (vocals) and African (rhythms and instrumentation).

RECOMMENDED RECORDINGS: **VOLUME 3: FURTHER IN TIME** *(Real World, 2001).* M.G.

THE BEATLES

John Lennon - *keyboards, piano, guitars*, **Paul McCartney** - *keyboards, piano, bass, percussion*, **George Harrison** - *guitars*, **Ringo Starr** - *drums, percussion*.

Formed in 1960, they had published a dozen albums when in 1967 *Sgt. Pepper's Lonely Hearts Club Band* is released: a masterpiece of psychedelic pop-rock. A constant of this band is the wide range of influences and styles that they assimilated into their own with a hunger for experimentation in style and sound. The urban legend of them influencing **Bob Dylan** in 1964 to use electric instruments, creating the fusion of folk and rock that would lead to the development of psychedelia. Then in 1966 their album *Revolver* already proves a leap in themes and experiments. One last tour and they concentrate on using the studio as an instrument, from *Sgt. Pepper* to *Abbey Road*, twisting and turning in a realm of proto-prog invention.

RECOMMENDED RECORDINGS: **REVOLVER** *(1966, Apple)* **SERGENT PEPPER'S LONELY HEART CLUB BAND** *(1967, Apple)* **THE MAGICAL MISTERY TOUR** *(1967, Apple).* M.G.

DAVID BOWIE

David Robert Jones aka **Bowie** starts as a sax player in the late '50s before becoming an artist in narrative story-telling & characterisation, non-standard song structures, musical eclecticism and a variety of singing styles. In 1967 his first solo album is a psychedelic pop and hall/cabaret music recalling **Anthony Newley**. A couple of years later *Space Oddity* is recorded for a folk prog music of acoustic ballads and psychedelic pop, featuring a line-up of session musicians and a 50 piece orchestra. Then the musical concept *Ziggy Stardust* and his glam-rock experimentation (introducing istrionic White Duke) and a funky krautrock-inspired electronic music that leads him to Germany and his collaboration in 1977 with **Brian Eno** on the Berliner Trilogy: *Low*, *Heroes* and *Lodger* continue the krautrock and avant-garde electronic industrial pop phase until dance comes along for his '80s more commercial moment. In 1995 a new collaboration with **Eno** results in the industrial sounding album *Outside*, with ambient and electronics experimentations.

RECOMMENDED RECORDINGS: **LOW** *(1976, RCA)* **HEROES** *(1977, RCA)* **LODGER** *(1979, RCA).* M.G.

JOHN CALE

John Davies Cale spends his twenties involved in the NY avant-garde music scene, collaborating in projects and performances such as **Erik Satie**'s 18 hour version of *Vexations*. He performs with **Dream Syndicate**, one of the first groups to combine serious concert hall sensibilities with rock and loud droning minimalism. In 1965 he co-founds **The Velvet Underground**, one of the first alternative and experimental rock bands influenced by avant-garde and minimalism (later settling on garage rock) thanks to his use of repeating minimalist figures, noise textures and droning hypnotic sounds. After two albums he exits to pursue his own solo career and in 1971 his encounter with **Terry Riley** results in a second album, *Church of Anthrax*. *Hobo Sapiens* of 2003 is another great proof of his inventiveness and continuous experimentation with art-rock.

RECOMMENDED RECORDINGS: **CHURCH OF ANTRAX** *(Columbia, 1971)* **THE ACADEMY IN PERIL** *(Reprise, 1972)* **HOBOSAPIENS** *(EMI, 2003).* M.G. & C.C.

IT'S ALMOST PROG!

DEAD CAN DANCE

Lisa Gerrard - *contralto vocals,* **Brendan Perry** - *baritone vocals, programming.*

In 1980 Australian guitarist **Brendan Perry** leaves the punk band **The Marching Girls** to experiment with electronic music, tape loops and rhythms. In 1981 he forms **DCD** with UK vocalist **Lisa Gerrard**, relocating to London as a duo, with many session musicians and collaborators helping them record in studio and perform live. Their 1984 debut contains British post-punk and gothic rock influences. Their second album, *Spleen and Ideal* inaugurates a different orientation: ethnic explorations which comprise aboriginal melodies combining elements of European folk - particularly from the Middle Ages and the Renaissance - with ambient pop and worldbeat flourishes inspired by symphonic prog and prog folk themes and using production techniques related to electronic prog and other experimental styles. Their masterpiece among many, is the 1993 *Into the Labyrinth*.
RECOMMENDED RECORDINGS: INTO THE LABYRINTH *(4AD, 1993).* **M.G.**

DEEP FOREST

Eric Mouquet & Michel Sanchez - *keyboards, piano, programming, percussion.*

Formed in 1991 as a French duo, **Eric Moquet** and **Michel Sanchez** go well beyond borders for an interesting project with songs full of ethnicity mixed with dance rhythms blending trance with all kinds of vocal samples and native chants from around the globe, intertwining them with contemporary rhythms and effects and presenting the resulting mixture as a world fusion music. Their first work *Deep Forest* is in fact regarded as the album that started the whole ethnic fusion movement, opening a bold new direction inside the new-age genre. In 1996 their album *Boheme* wins a Grammy ("While the heart sleeps" is sung by **Peter Gabriel**) and is characterized by the many Hungarian chants.
RECOMMENDED RECORDINGS: DEEP FOREST *(1992, Columbia)* **BOHEME** *(1995, Columbia)* **COMPARSA** *(1997, Saint George)* **PACIFIQUE** *(2000, Saint George).* **M.G.**

DEEP PURPLE

Ian Gillan - *vocals,* **Jon Lord** - *keyboards,* **Ian Paice** - *drums,* **Ritchie Blackmore** - *guitars,* **Roger Glover** - *bass.*

Formed in 1968 with a debut titled *Shades of Deep Purple*, their following two efforts were definitely more prog, especially their third, self-titled album, which saw Lord's masterful, classically-influenced use of the B3 Hammond organ steal the limelight. In 1969 bassist **Nick Simper** and vocalist **Rod Evans** exit, replaced by **Roger Glover** and **Ian Gillan**, for a second incarnation called **Deep Purple Mark II** and a live album, *Concerto for Group and Orchestra*, recorded with the Royal Philharmonic Orchestra (referenced in the italians' *Concerto Grosso per I New Trolls* and in some recent live projects by **Dream Theater**). The next titled *In Rock*, contains songs like "Child in Time" derived from this orchestral experience. Unfortunately, ego clashes and differences in musical directions caused a final spilt in 1976. The original **DPMKII** members reunite in 1984 beginning another bumpy musical venture and many album releases.
RECOMMENDED RECORDINGS: CONCERTO FOR GROUP AND ORCHESTRA *(1969, Harvest.* **M.G.**

DISSIDENTEN

Uve Müllrich, Marlon Klein, Friedo Josch, Elke Rogge, Esther Bertram - *various instruments, programming, percussion.*

This band from Berlin formed in 1981 traveling the world and researching different cultures and sounds: a first year in India results in their album *Germanistan* and a couple of years later they tour north Africa for the creation of *Sahara Electric* drenched in Arabic music, jazz and German new wave with krautrock tunes: a musical melting pot that opened new horizons for bands like **Afro Celt Sound System, Kunsertu, Orchestra di Piazza Vittorio** and **Republic Square**. A further trip to Canada will broaden their sound with native Indian American music. *The Jungle Book* of 1993 is their most avant-folk work while together with American composer **Gordon Sherwood** they create an opera in 2000, titled *The Memory Of The Waters*.
RECOMMENDED RECORDINGS: GERMANISTAN *(Schnellball, 1981)* **SAHARA ELECTRIC** *(Exil, 1984)* **THE JUNGLE BOOK** *(Exil, 1993).* **M.G. & C.C.**

IT'S ALMOST PROG!

ELBOW

Guy Garvey - *vocals, guitar*, **Craig Potter** - *keyboards*, **Richard Jupp** - *drums*, **Mark Potter** - *guitars*, **Pete Turner** - *bass*.
An English band formed in 1990 with Indie roots but with a complex music and the relative intelligent lyrics, sounding like a **Peter Gabriel**/**Talk Talk**/**The Blue Nile** mix. After a third prog art-rock work titled *Leaders of the Free World*, they are dropped by their label in 2005, yet decide to autoproduce a next album instead of breaking-up or going electronic. They explore their sound further, resulting in a diverse range of styles and instrumentation with a fourth album released in 2008 as *The Seldom Seen Kid*: full of prog influences, it is awarded the Mercury Music Prize. So they continue on the same lines with *Build A Rocket Boys!* Their singer **Guy Garvey** has a voice that recalls **Gabriel**'s vocal style, for a final touch.
RECOMMENDED RECORDINGS: **THE SELDOM SEEN KID** *(Polydor, 2008)* **BUILD A ROCKET BOYS!** *(Fiction, 2011)*. M.G.

JAPAN

David Sylvian - *guitar, vocals, programming*, **Steve Jansen** - *drums, drum-machines, programming*, **Mick Karn** - *bass, synths*, **Richard Barbieri** - *keyboards, synths*.
Formed in 1974 playing a sort of glam rock and soon becoming one of the most original and inventive examples of new wave in the early '80s. Inspired by **David Bowie**'s Berliner Trilogy mixed with **Brian Eno**'s instrumentalism, they blend western electronic sounds to traditional far east folk, enhanced by **Sylvian**'s haunting baritone voice. They fit in the prog definition of innovation and experimentation, with albums like *Gentlemen Take Polaroids* and *Tin Drum* setting the rules followed by many other artists later. However, personal conflicts escalate leading the band's demise at the end of 1982. After the split, the musicians went on to work on various solo projects, like **David Batt 'Sylvian'** who released some good albums collaborating with **Riuichi Sakamoto** and **Robert Fripp**. **Richard Barbieri** joins **Steve Wilson** founding **Porcupine Tree**.
RECOMMENDED RECORDINGS: **TIN DRUM** *(1981, Virgin)*. M.G.

JON & VANGELIS

Jon Anderson - *guitars, vocals*, **Vangelis Papathanassiou** - *keyboards*.
Jon Anderson, the famous singer and songwriter of **Yes**, meets **Vangelis Papathanassiou**, former **Aphrodytes Child**, in 1973 starting a collaboration and friendship that will last through the years in their respective solo projects.
This relation also produces a first album together and published in 1979 titled *Short Stories*, released after a lucky single called "I Here You Now": an adult pop prog and new-age ambient music that had a discreet success. Encouraged by the sales they decide to create other works like *The Friend Of Mr. Cairo* in 1981, *Private Collection* in 1983 (containing the famous suite "Horizon") and their last album *Page Of Life* of 1991.
DISCOGRAPHY: **SHORT STORIES** *(1979, Polydor)* **THE FRIENDS OF MR. CAIRO** *(1981, Polydor)* **PRIVATE COLLECTION** *(1983 Polydor)* **PAGE OF LIFE** *(1991, Omtown - Higher Octave)*. M.G. & C.C.

LED ZEPPELIN

Robert Plant - *vocals, percussion*, **Jimmy Page** - *guitars*, **John Paul Jones** - *bass, acoustic guitar, keyboards*, **John Bonham** - *drums, percussion*.
The New Yardbirds form in 1968 and shortly after the name change, they set to track the course of hard rock. Their bluesy debut contains "Dazed and Confused" with **Page**'s experimental use of a violin bow on guitar strings. The second work introduces rock'n'roll to Tolkien. The third plays with various styles from metal to blues to traditional folk, revealing an entirely acoustic side. 1971's truly prog fourth album is represented by the iconic "Stairway to Heaven". After *Houses of the Holy*, they retreat to the countryside and record the epic double album *Physical Graffiti* with a mobile studio. Then *Presence* ("Achilles Last Stand") and the last, most prog, *In Through the Out Door*, dominated by synths and keyboards, before the 1980 split.
RECOMMENDED RECORDINGS: **HOUSES OF THE HOLY** *(Atlantic, 1973)* **PHYSICAL GRAFFITI** *(Swan Song, 1975)* **IN THROUGH THE OUT DOOR** *(Swan Song, 1979)*. M.G. & C.C.

IT'S ALMOST PROG!

LOREENA McKENNITT

Her albums are real journeys, starting in 1984 with the Celtic folk of the first two albums and slowly incorporating a fascinating mix of other cultures, uniting East and West, Europa and Asia. Great harp player and fantastic singer, she is often mentioned in the same sentence with **Enya** (new age) or world music, ignoring the prog elements, closer to the ideas of **Dead Can Dance**: similar in sound, Spanish and Middle Eastern influences, as well as lyrics taken from literature. Her '90s works *The Mask And The Mirror* and *The Book of Secrets* are echoing Celts, Templars, Medieval legends and Sufis, surrounding the groove with engaging emotions.
RECOMMENDED RECORDINGS: **THE VISIT** *(Quinlan Road, 1991)* **THE MASK AND THE MIRROR** *(Quinlan Road, 1994)* **THE BOOK OF SECRETS** *(Quinlan Road, 1997)* **AN ANCIENT MUSE** *(Quinlan Road, 2006).*
M.G. & C.C.

MASSIVE ATTACK

Robert "3D" Del Naja - *vocals, programming, keyboards, sampler, producer,* **Grant "Daddy G" Marshall** - *keyboards, programming, sampler, producer, vocals,* **Andy "Mushroom" Vowles** - *producer, keyboards, sampler.*
Formed in 1987 with a first debut full of sampling the spatial ambient of **Billy Cobham**'s first album (also in the credits): *Blue Lines* was released in 1991 with its famous "Unfinished Symphony", a step into their career as pioneers of trip-hop. UK hip-hop in the '90s was jungle beats with 500bpm tempos and colorful, frantic sounds; they take the opposite route and slow everything down to the swirling, dreamlike instrumentation of *Mezzanine*, groudbreaking masterpiece like *OK Computer*. The incredible voices of **Elizabeth Fraser** and **Horace Andy** top with elegance a post punk or even gothic rock, blended with the cold and hypnotic power of electronics, more rock and less influenced by black music (soul and hip hop, although always present). Also *100th Window* is highly experimental.
RECOMMENDED RECORDINGS: **MEZZANINE** *(1998, Melankolic/Emi-Virgin).*
M.G. & C.C.

THE MUSE

Matt Bellamy - *vocals, guitars, keyboards,* **Chris Wolstenholme** - *bass,* **Dominic Howard** - *drums.*
Formed in 1994 (age 13) they release an EP in 1998 and a couple of singles before a first album titled *Showbiz*, helped by **Radiohead**'s producer John Leckie. Their pop-rock blends styles from the last 30 years for a trio that manages to sound grandiously prog. *Origin of Symmetry* is more experimental in the atmospheres (wind chimes, bones, llama claws and bubble wrap effects) while *Absolution* is a huge bombastic sounding work with piano-driven episodes and heavily effected guitars. *Black Holes and Revelations* ("Knights of Cydonia") is a hit and *The Resistance* of 2009 wins a first Grammy for Best Rock Album containing the suite "Exogenesis": symphony with up to 40 musicians playing in the recording process. Still alive and producing material, they have a more rock-pop edge at the moment.
RECOMMENDED RECORDINGS: **BLACK HOLES AND REVELATIONS** *(2006, Warner Bros.)* **THE RESISTANCE** *(2009, Warner Bros.)*
M.G. & C.C.

ALAN PARSONS PROJECT

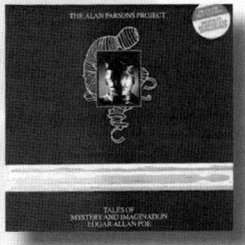

Eric Woolfson- *vocals, keyboards,* **Alan Parsons** - *vocals, keyboards, guitars, programming, mixing and production.*
Acclaimed **Beatles** and **Pink Floyd** producer and sound engineer, this is his personal electronic prog-rock project, carried out since 1975 with the help of songwriter **Eric Woolfson** and musical arranger **Andrew Powel**. Maniacs of sound engineering and complex pop-rock, they use the recording studios as powerful musical instruments, hiring session men, actors and various good singers (**John Miles** and **Orson Welles** among others). Ten great concept albums with themes inspired by Edgar Allan Poe, Isaac Asimov's robots or on the work of psychiatrist Sigmund Freud. Disbanded as duo in 1990, **Woolfson** passes away in 2009 leaving **Parsons** alone with his **Alan Parsons Live Project** playing their hits around the world.
RECOMMENDED RECORDINGS: **TALES OF MISTERY AND IMMAGINATION** *(Arista, 1976)* **I ROBOT** *(Arista, 1977)* **PYRAMID** *(Arista, 1978).*
M.G.

IT'S ALMOST PROG!

POOH

Dodi Battaglia - *vocals, guitars*, **Riccardo Fogli, Red Canzian** - *vocals, bass,* **Roby Facchinetti** - *vocals, keyboards,* **Stefano D'Orazio** - *drums.*
One of the most famous Italian pop bands still performing live, they form in 1962 as a beat band of easy listening love songs of melodic pop. Among the over 30 albums there are aome full blown works that belong to the Italian prog-rock panorama, especially of the early '70s, a movement that swept across Italy and that was not easy to ignore. In 1973 the arrival of bass player **Red Canzian** (former **Capsicum Red** guitarist) marks the orientation of *Parsifal* (the title track is a masterpiece of symphonic rock), although already *Opera Prima* of 1971 contains a music that seems to follow the trend. 1975 *Un Po' Del Nostro Tempo Migliore*, "La Gabbia" (soundtrack for a 1977 TV fiction) and *Dove Comincia Il Sole* (their last studio album of 2010) belong to this melodic and orchestrated side of the sub-prog genre .
RECOMMENDED RECORDINGS: **OPERA PRIMA** *(CGD, 1971)* **PARSIFAL** *(CGD, 1972)* **UN PÒ DEL NOSTRO TEMPO MIGLIORE** *(CGD, 1975)* **PALASPORT** *(Live, CGD, 1982)* **DOVE COMINCIA IL SOLE** *(CGD, 2010)*
M.G.

QUEEN

Freddie Mercury - *keyboards, piano, lead vocals,* **Brian May** - *guitars, vocals,* **John Deacon** - *bass, vocals,* **Roger Taylor** - *drums, percussion, vocals.*
Formed in 1967 when **Roger Taylor** and **Brian May** team up with **Tim Staffel** for the psychedelic hard rock group **Smile** (supporting **Yes** and **Pink Floyd** in their early years). **Farrokh Bulsara** aka **Freddie Mercury** had a vision for a new direction introducing flamboyance, bombast, glamour and visual presentation to their music and live shows, with albums blending the exaggerated pomp of prog rock and the energy of early heavy metal with Vaudeville, operatics and classical music devices. Initially anti-synths, they concentrate on rich and highly skilful vocal and guitar arrangements culminating in the outrageous and surprising "Bohemian Rhapsody" of the 1975's *A Night At The Opera*. After 1976, the only other strongly prog related work is their last *Innuendo* of 1991.
RECOMMENDED RECORDINGS: **A NIGHT AT THE OPERA** *(EMI, 1975)* **A DAY AT THE RACES** *(EMI, 1976)* **NEWS OF THE WORLD** *(EMI, 1977)* **INNUENDO** *(EMI, 1991).*
M.G.

MASSIMO RANIERI & EUMIR DEODATO

Massimo Ranieri – *vocals,* **Eumir Deodato** - *keyboards arrangements,* **Silvano Chimenti, Carlo Coppotelli** – *guitar,* **Maurizio Majorana** – *bass,* **Vincenzo Restuccia** – *drums.*
Gianni Calone aka **Massimo Ranieri** is a singer of traditional Neapolitan music and melodic love songs. Already a star in USA in the mid '60s as **Gianni Rock**, he returns to Italy and as **Ranieri** he starts releasing albums as well as participating in movies as an actor. During 1976 he collaborates with Brazilian jazz musician **Eumir Deodato**: *Meditazione* is a very melancholic art-rock and Italian easy-going pop-prog album containing famous classical and traditional themes re-arranged by **Deodato** with **Ranieri**'s beautiful voice sounding deeply emotional, supported by orchestral arrangements and a rather subdued guitar/rhythm section with dreamy orchestrations characterized by symphonic keys.
RECOMMENDED RECORDINGS: **MEDITAZIONE** *(CGD, 1976).*
M.G.

LOU REED

Lou Reed have a prolific solo discography apart from the albums with **Velvet Underground**: **Lou** meets classical music student **John Cale** in 1964, soon creating a band playing an experimental genre-less rock that would influence avant-rock, punk, new wave, garage and alternative rock. **Cale** leaves after the first two albums, when **Reed** goes commercial later quitting the band himself in 1970. **David Bowie** helps **Reed** on the album Transformer thus launching his career. The pure-noise inferno of *Metal Machine Music* is an obscure episode of electronic tunes and a confused attempt of ambient music, very distant to anything else. In 1990, **Reed** and **Cale** release *Songs for Drella*, a farewell tribute to **Andy Warhol**, keyboard-driven with a viola and **Reed**'s guitar-work. Also the collaboration with his wife **Laurie Anderson** is a remarkable experience into experimental music.
RECOMMENDED RECORDINGS: **METAL MACHINE MUSIC** *(RCA, 1975)* **SONGS FOR DRELLA** *(Sire, 1990)* **HUDSON RIVER WIND MEDITATIONS** *(Sounds True, 2007).*
M.G. & C.C.

IT'S ALMOST PROG!

TERRY RILEY

During the '60s he performs all-night solo concerts playing harmonium and sax through tape loop echo devices; during the break he would play them backwards. In *C of 1964* is often given credit for pioneering the musical style known as minimalism. More an improvising performer than a composer, he veered towards a more rock and jazz trend. His 1969 the overdubbed electronic *A Rainbow in Curved Air* massively influenced still developing psychedelic progressive and avant-garde rock music. Soon the sound of pulsing electronic synths and organs became a standard part of many young adventurous performers culminating in the German experimental collective known as **Tangerine Dream**. He continues to perform and compose to this day.
RECOMMENDED RECORDINGS: A RAINBOW IN A CURVED AIR *(CBS, 1968)* M.G.

ROBBIE ROBERTSON

Former guitarist of **The Band** (Bob Dylan's official backing group as well, disbanded in 1975 after the docu-film *The Last Waltz* directed by **Martin Scorsese**), Jaime Robert Robertson starts a solo career in the late '80s, after many collavorations and film/tv scores. In 1994 he releases a third album with **The Red Road Ensemble**, actually the soundtrack for a TBS documentary called *Songs For The Native Americans*. This introspective voyage begins with his mother being a Native American: a compilation of original songs performed by real American-Indian artists like **Rita Coolidge** and **Ulali**, yet not just a world music work given the pop-rock-country-folk inserts blended with ambient sounds.
RECOMMENDED RECORDINGS: SONGS FOR THE NATIVE AMERICANS *(Capitol, 1994)*. M.G.

THE SHADOWS

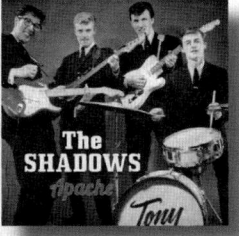

Bruce Welch - *guitars, vocals*, **Hank Marvin** - *guitars, keyboards, vocals*, **Brian Bennett** - *drums, vocals*, **Jet Harris** - *bass, vocals*.
This British instrumental rock ensemble is mostly associated with **Cliff Richard** or to a genre that has nothing to do with prog at all. Yet there is one song, one of their first songs, for which these four musicians are remembered as pioneers: *Apache*. It is September 1960, years before **The Beatles** and the so-called British invasion, when as **The Shadows** they publish this tribute to the native-American tribe, but with **Jerry Lordan**'s instrumental, all-twanging guitars pervading the tribal rhythms. One of the most sensational debuts (quite unfortunate they did not pursue this strand in their future works), credited among the most influential 45RMPs of the pre-**Beatles** era. The impetus for an entire generation of emulators, *Apache* was the major inspiration of many bands in the world. **Hank Marvin** himself has been cited as a master by more guitarists than most people could name.
RECOMMENDED RECORDINGS: 20 GOLDEN GREATS *(1977, EMI.)* M.G. & C.C.

SPARKS

Ron Mael - *keyboards*, **Russell Mael** - *vocals*.
L.A brothers **Ron** and **Russell Mael** formed their first band **Halfnelson** in 1970 inventing their often-copied, seldom-equaled brand of music. Along with brothers **Earle** and **Jim Mankey** and drummer **Harley Feinstein**, they change name in 1971 publishing a self titled debut produced by **Todd Rundgren**. The band goes to London and in 1974 begin recording (with producer Muff Winwood) the prog-glam album *Kimono-My-House*. Their glamorous art-rock, crossover, new wave cocktail mix of sound even ventured into disco in the late '70s/early '80s. Their most recent release of 2009, *The Seduction Of Ingmar Bergman*, is an eccentric and bizaar album, not dissimilar to a symphonic rock opera.
RECOMMENDED RECORDINGS: KIMONO MY HOUSE *(Island, 1974)* **THE SEDUCTION OF INGMAR BERGMAN** *(Lil' Beethoven, 2009)*. M.G. & C.C.

IT'S ALMOST PROG!

SUPERTRAMP

Roger Hodgson - *vocals, bass, guitars,* **Rick Davies** - *vocals, keyboards,* **John Hallywell** - *saxophones,* **Bob Miller, Bob Siebenberg** - *drums,* **Richard Palmer** - *guitars,* **Frank Farrell, Dougie Thompson** - *bass.*

A slow start with low sales for their first album full of prog tunes: the great songwriting skills of both **Davies** and **Hodgson** is confirmed in following albums like the keyboard-dominated *Crime Of The Century* and *Crisis? What Crisis?* or the melodic pop-rock of *Breakfast in America* and their absolute masterpiece *Even In The Quietest Moments*. Their style was actually more a variant of prog-rock, described as sophisto-rock, before they start to develop a more R&B-flavored music. This change in direction manifests in the 1982 *Famous Last Words*. In 1984 **Hodgson** leaves while they continued with occasional tours and another 4 albums, however less successful.
RECOMMENDED RECORDINGS: SUPERTRAMP *(A&M, 1970)* **CRIME OF THE CENTURY** *(A&M, 1974)* **EVEN IN THE QUIETEST MOMENTS** *(A&M, 1977)* **BREAKFAST IN AMERICA** *(A&M, 1979).* **M.G.**

TALK TALK

Mark Hollis - *guitars, lead vocals,* **Tim Friese-Greene, Simon Brenner** - *keyboards,* **Paul Webb** - *bass,* **Lee Harris** - *drums, percussion.*

Formed in 1981 by **Mark Hollis** playing a typical '80s synth pop, but with fine arrangements and a good songwriting. After the first two albums, producer and keyboardist **Tim Friese-Greene** joins in 1983 and they begin to experiment with jazz and classical music with echoes from **Can** and **Pink Floyd** creating a good chamber pop which at times sounded like jazz or ambient music, but actually was something essentially new. *The Colour of Spring* of 1986 was just a draft of what was to come in *Spirit of Eden* and *Laughing Stock*: a seemingly free-form and abstract soundscape, where each note - or moment of silence - is necessary and powerfully emotional. Not a standard prog act, yet full of instrumental exploration and willingness to abandon traditional structures.
RECOMMENDED RECORDINGS: THE COLOUR OF SPRING *(EMI, 1986)* **SPIRIT OF EDEN** *(EMI, 1988)* **LAUGHING STOCK** *(Polydor, 1991).* **M.G.**

TALKING HEADS

David Byrne - *guitars, vocals,* **Tina Weymouth** - *bass, vocals,* **Jerry Harrison** - *guitars, vocals,* **Chris Frantz** - *drums, Special guests:* **Robert Fripp** - *guitars,* **Brian Eno** - *sound effects, production.*

Formed in 1975 when **Byrne**, **Frantz** and **Weymouth** meet and move to NY playing in the punk club CBGB. After the addition of **Harrison** in 1976, they record a debut LP presenting a totally unique sound regarded as pop/art rock. The second *More Songs About Buildings & Food* had **Brian Eno**'s help, incorporating more electronic and accoustic instruments. He produces their third and fourth albums too, *Fear Of Music*, probably their true art-prog release full of funky, acid rock and African influences with **Fripp**'s contribution on "I Zimbra", and *Remain In Light*. They maintain the strong rhythms and frenzied guitars yet bend towards the commercial sound of *Speaking in Tongues*. The inventiveness was waning and the rest is forgivable.
RECOMMENDED RECORDINGS: MORE SONGS ABOUT BUILDINGS & FOOD *(1978, Sire)* **FEAR OF MUSIC** *(1979, Sire)* **REMAIN IN LIGHT** *(1980, Sire).* **M.G.**

ULTRAVOX

John Foxx - *vocals,* **Midge Ure** - *vocals, guitars, synths,* **Chris Cross** - *bass, synths, programming,* **Billy Currie** - *keyboards, synths, viola, violin,* **Warren Cann** - *drums, drum-machines, percussion.*

A band with two incarnations, the first having **John Foxx** as a singer with a sound linked to an interesting form of alternative punk-rock new wave produced by **Brian Eno**. The second life starts in 1980 with **Midge Ure** and their masterpiece *Vienna*: gothic symphonic keyboards, classical atmospheres, large use of viola and instrumental tracks. Intelligent pop, but pop nevertheless, in *Quartet* (produced by **George Martin**) as well as the reunion album of 2012 *Brilliant*. **John Foxx**'s solo career is very creative, but he tends to produce ambient albums that cannot quite be considered electronic prog at all.
RECOMMENDED RECORDINGS: VIENNA *(Chrisalis, 1980)* **QUARTET** *(Chrisalis, 1982).* **M.G.**

APPENDIX:
PROG ON STAGE, BIBLIOGRAPHY and WEBSITES, ARTISTS INDEX

Peter Gabriel - *Blood of Eden*

PROG ON STAGE
A Conversation with Libero Robba

After reading and consulting the parade of names, artists, events and records that contributed to change many people's lives, it is clear how the role of inventing a new genre was not only the privilege of those few that made it to a planetary Fame & Fortune, but also of the many that disappeared after one brief moment, often just recording a single album.

What do the Kings of Prog (**Pink Floyd, Genesis, King Crimson, Rush, Kansas, Yes**) have to do with Knights & Valets such as **After Crying, Gunesh, Pavlov Dog, Balletto di Bronzo** and **Museo Rosenbach**? They share a much forgotten common denominator: the stage. And it doesn't matter if this stage is not the same for everyone. It doesn't matter whether **Museo Rosenbach** ever had a colossal white brick wall like **Pink Floyd**, or the computerized lights of **Genesis**; they all had, one way or another, a stage, big or small, to perform on and reveal themselves to the world. Even those one night stands, born and gone after a single show, still had a stage.

Pink Floyd - 1981

All these artists sooner or later required the important work of the handful of invisible heroes defined as Roadies, the stage technicians. Yes, technicians, because ensuring the perfect outcome of a show is not just mere handy-work, but it needs the complete vision of each multiple aspect. To better explore this universe, **Libero Robba** will present his precious experience as an authentic stage professional, an old-times Turin 'Roadie' with a respectable curriculum and above all, who lived through the birth of Italian Prog.

<<I started my career as a drum-roadie, that is, by installing the drum kits on stage. Then I specialized in assisting all the musicians and solving stage issues through-out 3.300 concerts across Europe.>>

Libero went on Tour with names such as **Dire Straits, Weather Report, Ray Charles** and **BB King**; during his career he also worked for great Italian artists such as **PFM, New Trolls, Arti & Mestieri, Area** and **Banco del Mutuo Soccorso**, not to mention his childhood friendship with the members of **Procession**. His name can be found inside **PFM**'s double live album of 1981 *PerForMance*, or you can see him appear in many backstage pics with famous artists.

Yes - 2004

<<Dear Maurizio, I would like to recall all the great people who are long gone like Demetrio Stratos, Franco Mamone, Giulio Capiozzo, Gianfranco Gaza and the father of all managers Gianni Sassi, also founder of Cramps Records: names in this book that no one should forget for their talent, compassion, availability and humbleness. I learned a lot from them.>>

Too often the importance of people like **Libero** is forgotten. The evolution of this role started during the '60s in small clubs where often the band members would roll up their own sleeves and install the modest instrumentation, with perhaps a couple of guys fixing lights and amplification. Already in the early '70s the job grew to unthinkable levels

Libero Robba & Claudio Trotta

Genesis - 1974

with increasingly complex set designs (**Genesis**, **Yes** and **Pink Floyd**) that required real experts to materialize on stage the imaginary and fantastic visions contained in the records and in some of the incredible covers. New professional figures like *Sound Engineer, Light Engineer, Road Manager* or *Road Crew Manager* (coordinating all the Roadies, just like **Libero Robba**, with the responsibility of mounting the stage and assisting the musicians). As a matter of fact, in the last few decades the stage was designed and directed by engineers and architects.

Progressive Rock best incorporated and spread this way of living a concert, status that in more recent years has also become the way of any artist, even outside the genre. The rich theatrical performances of **Peter Gabriel**'s **Genesis**, the **Yes** album covers painted by **Roger Dean** and made three-dimensional in concert, **Gerald Scarfe**'s giant puppets created for **Pink Floyd** and appearing both real or projected on a 200 by 50 feet wall, these are not magic tricks but the hard work of technicians like **Libero Robba**.

To what extent has the music world given credit to these figures? **Libero Robba** today is actively unemployed yet, universally known for his generosity, he still lends a hand for free in many a concert of his hometown. The general sense of ingratitude that affects the entourage of the working stage people is immense.

Giancarlo Bertelle & Libero Robba

<<*Being a Roadie is the lifestyle chosen by dozens of my colleagues who put their passion into a job, their sweat and tears, the fatigue and satisfaction, priceless in terms of money. Of course we are paid, it's true. But we lead a life that often consists of a 20 hour shift, with working injuries to which a bunch of my very own friends gave their life or health, just to be soon forgotten.*

Today I proudly watch the triumphant return of artists whose career I helped since their beginnings and, with all due respect, I must sadly admit that not many paid the rightful attention to these hard workers without whom the final result would not be possible.

Nowadays just like before, many young people are thrown on or behind a stage to learn everything and as fast as humanly sustainable, come wind or cold, rain or shine, working very long hours in the weeny times of day.>>

Personally I too have a small experience as stage technician, so I attend every concert with a very different spirit: while watching my favorite artist perform I always imagine all those dirty, sweaty men, sometimes overweight for a disorderly life, that still manage to ensure the perfect outcome of every show.

<<*In the memory of: Franco Savio, Roberto Prizzon, Patrick Germanini, Fernando Scarpa, Mike, Mark, Nick Sizer, Martin, Spartaco, Ciccio, Woods "La Scossa", Massimo Pacilli "Dott. Bacillo", Ragno and Rodrigo Beccari. Some are by now long gone but we must keep them in our hearts.*>>

Maurizio Galia, Libero Robba

BIBLIOGRAPHY & WEBSITES

Dag Erik Asbjorsen, *Scented Gardens Of The Mind*, Borderline Books, 2000.
Dag Erik Asbjorsen, *Cosmic Dreams At Play - A Guide To German Progressive And Electronic Rock*, Borderline Books, 1995.
Dag Erik Asbjorsen, *Cosmic Dreams At Play - A Comprehensive Guide To German Progressive Of The 1970s*, Reggio Emilia, Strange Vertigo, 2008.
Barclay James Harvest - *All Is Safely Gathered In*, Eclectic Discs, 2005.
Graham Bennett, *Soft Machine: Out-Bloody-Rageous*, London, Saf Publishing, 2005.
Ian Carr, Digby Fairweather, Brian Priestley, *The Rough Guide to Jazz*, London, Rough Guides, 2004.
John Cavanagh, *The Piper At The Gates Of Dawn*, Vignola, Sublime Records & Books, 2005.
Stuart Chambers, *Yes - An Endless Dream Of '70s, '80s And '90s Rock Music*, Burnstown, GSPH, 2003.
Jim Christopulos, Phil Smart, *Van Der Graaf Generator - The Book*, London, Phil And Jim, 2005.
Julian Cope, *Krautrocksampler*, Roma, Lain, 2006.
Julian Cope, *Japrocksampler*, Roma, Arcana, 2008.
Ronald Couture, *Essential Mini-Guide To Progressive Rock Past & Present, 1966-2006*, Quebec, Prog Archives, 2006.
Nigel Cross, Michael Heatley, *Inside Pink Floyd - A Critical Review 1967-1996*, Classic Rock Productions, 2004.
Roger Dean, *Views*, Pomegranate 1993
Roger Dean, *Magnetic Storm*, Pomegranate 1993
Michel Delville & Andrew Norris, *Frank Zappa, Captain Beefheart and the Secret History of Maximalism*, Cambridge, Salt Publishing, 2005.
Jim DeRogatis, *Turn On Your Mind*, Milwaukee, Hal Leonard, 2003.
Keith Emerson, *Picture Of An Exhibitionist*, London, John Blake Publishing, 2004.
Alan Farley, *The Extraordinary World Of Yes*, Lincoln, IUniverse Inc., 2004.
Armando Gallo, *I Know What I Like*, Los Angeles, D.I.Y. Books, 1980.
Genesis Collectibles (by P. Vickers), Bangor, 2002.
Genesis Chapter & Verse (by P. Dodd), London, Orion Publishing Group, 2007.
Gentle Giant - Scraping The Barrel, Alucard, 2004.
Lukasz Hernik, *Genesis - W Krainie Muzycznych Olbrzymow*, Poznan, In Rock, 2007.
Philip Jackson, *Favourite All Time Progressive Rock Albums* - The Survey, Lyon, Acid Dragon, 1998.
Philip Jackson, *Favourite All Time Progressive Rock Albums - The Origins Of Progressive Rock*, Lyon, Acid Dragon, 1998.
Billy James, *Freak Out!! - Frank Zappa e i Mothers of Invention*, Roma, Arcana, 2003.
Tony Jasper & Derek Olivier, *The International Encyclopedia of Hard Rock and Heavy Metal*, London, Sidgwick And Jackson, 1986.
Michael King, *Falsi Movimenti. Una storia di Robert Wyatt*, Roma, Arcana, 1994.
Lewis Lapham, *I Beatles in India*, Roma, Edizioni E/O, 2007.
Mark E. Lawhon, *Classic Concerts Of The 1970s: The Encores Continue*, Leawood, Leathers Publishing, 2004.
Toby Manning, *The Rough Guide To Pink Floyd*, London, Rough Guides, 2006.
Nick Mason, *Inside Out- A personal history of Pink Floyd*, London, Chronicle Books, 2004.
Allan Moore, *Aqualung*, Vignola, Sublime Records & Books, 2007.
Louis De NY, *Le petit Monde du Progressif Italien - Une discographie amoureuse*, France, Camion Blanc 2015
Tobias Petterson, Ulf Henningsson, *The Encyclopedia of Swedish Progressive Music*, Stockholm, Premium Publishing, 2007.
Pink Floyd - Their Mortal Remains Official Catalogue – London, V&A Publishing, 2017
Gerald Scarfe, *The making of "The Wall"*, London, Onion Publishing 2010
Nick Sedwick, *In The Pink (Not A Hunting Memoir)*- London, V&A Publishing, 2017
Sid Smith, *In The Court Of King Crimson*, London, Helter Skelter, 2001.
Thierry Sportouche, Jacques Toni, *Storia Di Un Minuto - A Comprehensive Guide To The Italian Progressive Rock Of The 70's*, Lyon, Acid Dragon, 1994.
Thierry Sportouche, Jacques Toni, *The Brass Lizard - The Progressive Brass Bands From The British Blues To The Beginning Of Jazz Rock*, Lyon, Acid Dragon, 1995.
The Work Of Hipgnosis - 'Walk Away René' (edited by Storm Thorgerson), Lindsfield, Paper Tiger, 1978.
The PhotoDesign Of Hipgnosis - 'The Goodbye Look' (edited by Storm Thorgerson), London, Vermilion, 1982.
Dave Thompson, *"Turn It On Again" - Peter Gabriel, Phil Collins & Genesis*, San Francisco, Backbeat Books, 2005.
Storm Thorgerson, Peter Curzon - *Mind Over Matter - The Images Of Pink Floyd*, London, Sanctuary, 1998
Mark Wilkinson, *Shadowplay*, Denmark, Edition Brusen, 2009

progressive-rock websites:

Arlequins:
www.arlequins.it

Centro Studi Progressive Italiano:
www.centrostudiprogitaliano.it

Electrotheremin:
www.electrotheremin.com

GEPR - Gybraltar Enciclopedia of Progressive Rock:
www.gepr.net

Gnosis:
www.gnosis2000.net

Italian Prog:
www.italianprog.it

Making Time 1960s British Music:
www.makingtime.co.uk

Marmalade Skies:
www.marmalade-skies.co.uk/index.htm

Mellotron:
www.mellotron.com

MovimentiProg:
www.movimentiprog.net

Prog Archives:
www.progarchives.com

Uzbekistan Progressive Rock Pages
www.progressor.net

The Rotters' Club:
www.rottersclub.net

Sezione Musica:
www.sezionemusica.it

Strawberry Bricks –The Guide To Progressive Rock:
www.progressiverock.com

Israel Music:
www.israel-music.com

Turkish Rock Music:
www.weloveist.com/turkish-rock

Korean Rock Music:
www.krockisreal.com

Prog-Sphere:
www.prog-sphere.com

Pink Floyd Info & News:
www.brain-damage.co.uk

Greenland bands:
www.groenlandband.com

Greenland bands:
www.music.gl

Real World Music:
www.realworldrecords.com

ARTISTS INDEX

21 Peron: *pag.411*
801: *pag.338*
A New Place To Live (Robert John Gallo): *pag.420*
A Piedi Nudi: *pag.224*
A Triggering Myth: *pag.428*
Abiogenesi: *pag.349*
Abstract Truth: *pag.444*
Ache: *pag.183*
Acqua Fragile: *pag.349*
Acynthia: *pag.291*
Aditus: *pag.458*
Aerodrom: *pag.412*
Afrocelt Sound System: *pag.462*
After Crying: *pag.100*
After The Fire: *pag.320*
Agamemnon: *pag.407*
Agitation Free: *pag.36*
Agnus: *pag.445*
Airbag: *pag.382*
Ailord: *pag.443*
Akasha: *pag.382*
Akineton Retard: *pag.453*
Akritas: *pag.218*
Aksak Maboul: *pag.180*
Aktuala: *pag.224*
Aku Aku: *pag.285*
Alameda: *pag.394*
Alas: *pag.268*
Albatross: *pag.428*
Alberomotore: *pag.349*
Aleatorica Orchestra: *pag.391*
Aleph: *pag.168*
Älgarnas Trädgård: *pag.247*
Alice: *pag.187*
Allegro Ensemble: *pag.391*
Alluminogeni: *pag.349*
Almendra: *pag.174*
Alphataurus: *pag.224*
Alquin: *pag.219*
Alrune Rod: *pag.18*
Alusa Fallax: *pag.350*
Amarok: *pag.394*
Amenophis: *pag.307*
Amon Düül: *pag.37*
Ampera: *pag.382*
Anabis: *pag.307*
Anacrusa: *pag.445*
Anak Bayan: *pag.257*
Analogy: *pag.350*
Ananga Ranga: *pag.389*
Anatrofobia: *pag.350*
Anekdoten: *pag.247*
Ange: *pag.24*
Änglagård: *pag.401*
Anima: *pag.445*
Annexus Quam: *pag.194*
Antares: *pag.350*
Antonius Rex (Jacula): *pag.351*
Anyone's Daughter: *pag.194*
Aphrodite's Child: *pag.93*
Apocalypsis: *pag.218*
Apoteosi: *pag.225*
Aquarelle: *pag.420*
Aquelarre: *pag.445*
Arachnoid: *pag.291*
Aragon: *pag.168*
Araujo, Marco Antonio: *pag.450*
Arbete Och Fritid: *pag.247*
Arcadium: *pag.320*
Arcansiel: *pag.351*
Archaïa: *pag.291*
Arco Iris: *pag.175*
Area: *pag.103*
Areknames: *pag.344*
Arena: *pag.320*
Argent: *pag.204*
Aria Palea: *pag.351*
Ariel Kalma: *pag.291*
Ariel: *pag.391*

Aries: *pag.352*
Ars Nova: *pag.255*
Arsenal: *pag.240*
Art Zoyd: *pag.25*
Artcane: *pag.187*
Arti & Mestieri: *pag.104*
Artsruni: *pag.459*
Arzachel: *pag.320*
Asgard: *pag.225*
Ash Ra Tempel: *pag.38*
Asia Minor: *pag.187*
Asia: *pag.204*
Aside Beside: *pag.292*
Asin: *pag.257*
Asoka: *pag.401*
Astre: *pag.428*
Asturias: *pag.414*
Atila: *pag.128*
Atlantic Philarmonic: *pag.428*
Atlas: *pag.401*
Atoll: *pag.26*
Atomic Rooster: *pag.204*
Aton's: *pag.352*
Aucan: *pag.446*
Audience: *pag.205*
Aufklärung: *pag.352*
Aunt Mary: *pag.237*
Aurora Project: *pag.340*
Autograph: *pag.391*
Avalanche: *pag.340*
Avaric: *pag.292*
Ave Rock: *pag.268*
Aviolinee Utopia: *pag.352*
Axis: *pag.94*
Ayers, Kevin: *pag.57*
Ayreon: *pag.340*
Azabache: *pag.394*
Babylon: *pag.429*
Bacamarte: *pag.271*
Backdoor: *pag.321*
Bacio della Medusa: *pag.353*
Bakery: *pag.441*
Balletto Di Bronzo: *pag.105*
Banco Del Mutuo Soccorso: *pag.106*
Banda Do Casaco: *pag.389*
Banda Elastica: *pag.274*
Banks Tony: *pag.321*
Banzai: *pag.180*
Barclay James Harvest: *pag.205*
Baricentro (see Festa Mobile): *pag.362*
Barnabé, Arrigo: *pag.450*
Barock Project: *pag.353*
Barrock: *pag.353*
Battiato, Franco: *pag.107*
Battisti, Lucio: *pag.108*
Bauer: *pag.446*
Beatles (The): *pag.462*
Bee Gees: *pag.441*
Beggars Opera: *pag.205*
Bi kyo ran: *pag.415*
Bibbò, Pierpaolo: *pag.353*
Biglietto Per L'inferno: *pag.225*
Birth Control: *pag.307*
Black Bonzo: *pag.401*
Black Widow: *pag.206*
Blakulla: *pag.409*
Bloque: *pag.129*
Blossom Toes: *pag.206*
Boomerang: *pag.459*
Booz Emmanuel: *pag.292*
Bort Eduardo: *pag.241*
Bowie, David: *pag.462*
Brainbox: *pag.340*
Brainstorm: *pag.307*
Brand X: *pag.206*
Brave New World: *pag.308*
Breakout: *pag.238*
Bregent: *pag.420*
Brenner, Vytas: *pag.277*
Brimstone: *pag.429*

Bröselmaschine: *pag.194*
Brown, Pete: *pag.207*
Bubu: *pag.268*
Budka Suflera: *pag.238*
Buffalo: *pag.441*
Bülent: *pag.410*
Buon Vecchio Charlie: *pag.354*
Burning Plague: *pag.281*
Burning Red Ivanhoe: *pag.19*
Cabezas De Cera: *pag.274*
Cacciapaglia, Roberto: *pag.354*
Cafeine: *pag.292*
Cai: *pag.241*
Cale, John: *pag.462*
California Guitar Trio: *pag.429*
Calliope: *pag.354*
Camaleonti: *pag.354*
Camel: *pag.58*
Camera Astralis: *pag.355*
Camisasca, Juri: *pag.355*
Campo Di Marte: *pag.226*
Can: *pag.39*
Can Am Des Puig: *pag.188*
Canarios (Los): *pag.241*
Cano: *pag.420*
Capsicum Red: *pag.355*
Caravan: *pag.59*
Cardiacs: *pag.321*
Carpani Alex: *pag.355*
Carpe Diem: *pag.293*
Cartoon: *pag.260*
Casa Das Maquinas: *pag.450*
Cast: *pag.454*
Castanarc: *pag.321*
Castello Di Atlante: *pag.356*
Catapilla: *pag.207*
Catharsis: *pag.27*
Cathedral: *pag.260*
Celeste: *pag.226*
Celi Fabio e gli Infermieri: *pag.356*
Cem Karaca: *pag.410*
Centipede: *pag.278*
Cerchio D'oro: *pag.356*
Cervello: *pag.226*
Chac Mool: *pag.454*
Chakra: *pag.429*
Chene Noir (Theatre du Chene Noir): *pag.293*
Cherry Five: *pag.227*
Chetarca: *pag.441*
Churchills: *pag.223*
Cid, Josè: *pag.125*
Cinema: *pag.415*
Circus 2000: *pag.356*
Circus: *pag.251*
Cirkus: *pag.322*
Città frontale: *pag.357*
Clearlight: *pag.430*
Clepsydra: *pag.407*
Cliffhanger: *pag.341*
Clivage: *pag.293*
Cluster/Kluster: *pag.195*
Codice: *pag.454*
Collage: *pag.386*
Collegium Musicum: *pag.15*
Color Humano: *pag.446*
Colosseum: *pag.60*
Colossus Of Rhodes: *pag.278*
Combo Fh: *pag.285*
Companion: *pag.430*
Companya Electrica Dharma: *pag.130*
Comus: *pag.207*
Concept (The Humanist Advent Concept): *pag.421*
Connivence: *pag.421*
Connolly, Robert: *pag.421*
Conqueror: *pag.357*
Consorzio Acqua Potabile: *pag.357*
Contraction: *pag.258*
Contraluz: *pag.446*
Contrappunto: *pag.357*
Conventum: *pag.258*
Corte Aulica: *pag.358*
Corte Dei Miracoli: *pag.358*
Cos: *pag.180*

Cosmos Factory: *pag.148*
Coto En Pel: *pag.394*
Court: *pag.358*
Covenant: *pag.430*
Crack: *pag.395*
Cressida: *pag.208*
Crucis: *pag.269*
Culpeper's Orchard: *pag.183*
Curved Air: *pag.61*
Cybotron: *pag.442*
Dag (Trio Dag): *pag.412*
De De Lind: *pag.227*
Dead Can Dance: *pag.463*
Decibel: *pag.454*
Deep forest: *pag.463*
Deep Purple: *pag.463*
Deja Vu: *pag.415*
Delirium (Italy): *pag.227*
Delirium (Mexico): *pag.455*
Dervieux, Frank: *pag.421*
Deus Ex Machina: *pag.109*
Devil Doll: *pag.228*
DFA: *pag.228*
Diana Express: *pag.284*
Dice: *pag.248*
Dies Irae: *pag.308*
Dificil Equilibrio: *pag.395*
Dik-Dik: *pag.358*
Dionysos: *pag.258*
Discipline: *pag.260*
Discus: *pag.254*
Dissidenten: *pag.464*
Divae: *pag.359*
Djam Karet: *pag.159*
Docmec: *pag.407*
Dogma: *pag.450*
Domaci Kapela: *pag.285*
Dono Celeste: *pag.359*
Doracor: *pag.359*
Dragon (Belgium): *pag.281*
Dragon (New Zealand): *pag.172*
Dragonfly: *pag.407*
Dream Theater: *pag.261*
Drosselbart: *pag.308*
Drugi Nacin: *pag.412*
Dün: *pag.188*
Dzyan: *pag.195*
Earth & Fire: *pag.219*
Earthrise: *pag.430*
East Of Eden: *pag.208*
East: *pag.222*
Easter Island: *pag.431*
Eazycon: *pag.359*
Echolyn: *pag.160*
Eclat: *pag.293*
Eden (Canada): *pag.422*
Eden (Germany): *pag.308*
Eden Rose: *pag.294*
Edgar Allan Poe: *pag.360*
Edhels: *pag.294*
Edip Akbayram: *pag.252*
Edition Speciale: *pag.294*
Eela Craig: *pag.280*
Egg: *pag.208*
Egoband: *pag.360*
Eider Stellaire: *pag.188*
Eik: *pag.346*
Eiliff: *pag.309*
Ekseption: *pag.219*
Elbow: *pag.464*
El Congreso: *pag.273*
El Reloj: *pag.447*
El Ritual: *pag.274*
Electra: *pag.40*
Eloy: *pag.41*
Embryo: *pag.42*
Emeraude: *pag.294*
Emergency Exit: *pag.295*
Emerson, Lake & Palmer: *pag.62*
Emtidi: *pag.309*
Enbor: *pag.242*
Eneide: *pag.360*
Energit: *pag.285*

Energy: *pag.402*
Enfasis: *pag.458*
England: *pag.322*
Enid: *pag.209*
Eno, Brian: *pag.322*
Ensemble Nimbus: *pag.402*
Epidaurus: *pag.195*
Epidermis: *pag.309*
Epitaph: *pag.309*
Epos: *pag.392*
Equilibrio Vital: *pag.277*
Equipe 84: *pag.360*
Er. J. Orchestra: *pag.459*
Ergo Sum: *pag.295*
Eris Pluvia: *pag.361*
Errata Corrige: *pag.361*
Errobi: *pag.395*
Ersen: *pag.252*
Ertlif: *pag.408*
Esagono: *pag.361*
Eskaton: *pag.189*
Espiritu: *pag.447*
Estructura: *pag.277*
Et Cetera: *pag.422*
Eternidad: *pag.447*
Eternité: *pag.422*
Etna: *pag.228*
Etron Fou Leloublan: *pag.28*
Eulenspygel: *pag.196*
Ex Vitae: *pag.295*
Exit: *pag.408*
Exodus: *pag.386*
Extra Ball: *pag.386*
Ezra Winston: *pag.229*
Faithful Breath: *pag.310*
Family: *pag.63*
Fancyfluid: *pag.361*
Fantasia: *pag.185*
Fantasmagoria: *pag.416*
Fantasy: *pag.322*
Far East Family Band: *pag.149*
Faust: *pag.43*
Fermata: *pag.16*
Ferrer, Nino: *pag.295*
Festa Mobile: *pag.362*
FFN: *pag.390*
Fiaba: *pag.362*
Finch: *pag.220*
Finisterre: *pag.110*
Finnegans Wake: *pag.281*
Finnforest: *pag.185*
Fireballet: *pag.261*
Firyuza: *pag.459*
Fish: *pag.323*
Fisher, Morgan: *pag.323*
Flairck: *pag.220*
Flamborough Head: *pag.341*
Flame Dream: *pag.251*
Flamen Dialis: *pag.296*
Flamengo: *pag.182*
Flaskett Brinner: *pag.138*
Flax: *pag.382*
Flied Egg: *pag.255*
Flight: *pag.431*
Floating State: *pag.362*
Flor De Loto: *pag.457*
Flower Kings: *pag.402*
Flower Travellin' Band: *pag.150*
Flught: *pag.455*
Flying Island: *pag.431*
Flying Circus: *pag.310*
Flyte: *pag.281*
FM: *pag.422*
Focus: *pag.96*
Foglie Di Vetro: *pag.362*
Folly's Pool: *pag.431*
Forgas, Patrick: *pag.296*
Fragil: *pag.276*
Fragile: *pag.254*
Freedoms Children: *pag.444*
French TV: *pag.261*
Fresh Maggots: *pag.323*
Fripp, Robert: *pag.64*

From.Uz: *pag.460*
Fruitcake: *pag.386*
Frumpy: *pag.196*
Fruupp: *pag.323*
FSB: *pag.284*
Fusioon: *pag.131*
Gabriel Bondage: *pag.432*
Gabriel, Peter: *pag.65*
Galaad: *pag.408*
Galadriel (Australia): *pag.267*
Galadriel (Spain): *pag.395*
Galahad: *pag.324*
Galie: *pag.275*
Galija: *pag.412*
Gamma: *pag.341*
Ganelin Trio: *pag.460*
Garden Wall: *pag.363*
Gargamel: *pag.383*
Gargantua: *pag.386*
Garybaldi: *pag.229*
Gatto Marte: *pag.363*
Genesis: *pag.66*
Genfuoco: *pag.363*
Gentle Giant: *pag.67*
Germinale: *pag.363*
Giant Hogweed Orchestra: *pag.288*
Giganti: *pag.364*
Gila: *pag.196*
Giltrap, Gordon: *pag.324*
Giro Strano: *pag.229*
Gizmo: *pag.324*
Glass Hammer: *pag.432*
Gnidrolog: *pag.209*
Goad: *pag.364*
Goblin: *pag.104*
Golden Earring: *pag.341*
Goliath: *pag.324*
Goma 2: *pag.396*
Goma: *pag.242*
Gomorrha: *pag.197*
Gong: *pag.68*
Gotic: *pag.396*
Gracious: *pag.325*
Granada: *pag.242*
Gravy Train: *pag.325*
Greaves, John: *pag.325*
Grechuta, Marek: *pag.384*
Green Wall: *pag.364*
Greenslade: *pag.325*
Grime: *pag.296*
Grits: *pag.262*
Grobschnitt: *pag.44*
Groovector: *pag.185*
Group 1850: *pag.97*
Grovjobb: *pag.403*
Grupa 220: *pag.413*
Gryphon: *pag.209*
Guadalquivir: *pag.396*
Gualberto Garcia Perez: *pag.132*
Guerin, Shaun: *pag.432*
Gunesh Ensemble: *pag.460*
Guru Guru: *pag.45*
Guruh Gipsy: *pag.254*
Hackett, Steve: *pag.69*
Haikara: *pag.21*
Haizea: *pag.396*
Halloween: *pag.296*
Hammill, Peter: *pag.70*
Hannibal: *pag.326*
Hansson Bo: *pag.139*
Happy The Man: *pag.161*
Hardal: *pag.410*
Hardie, Sebastian: *pag.169*
Harmonium: *pag.154*
Harper, Roy: *pag.210*
Hatfield And The North: *pag.71*
Hawkwind: *pag.72*
Headband: *pag.267*
Heldon: *pag.29*
Henry Cow: *pag.73*
High Tide: *pag.210*
High Wheel: *pag.310*
High-Fidelity-Orchestra: *pag.454*

Hinn Islenski Thursaflokkur: *pag.346*
Hiro Yanagida: *pag.416*
Hoelderlin: *pag.46*
Holding Pattern: *pag.432*
Home: *pag.326*
Horizont (Gorizont): *pag.240*
Horn: *pag.423*
Horslips: *pag.326*
Horus: *pag.364*
Høst: *pag.237*
Höstsonaten: *pag.365*
Hotz, Jimmy: *pag.433*
However: *pag.432*
Höyry-Kone: *pag.288*
Hunka Munka: *pag.365*
Ibio: *pag.397*
Ibis: *pag.403*
Ibliss: *pag.310*
Ice: *pag.326*
Iceberg: *pag.133*
Icecross: *pag.346*
Iconoclasta: *pag.455*
If: *pag.327*
Ihtiyac Molasi: *pag.411*
Ikarus: *pag.311*
Illes Ensemble: *pag.222*
Iluvatar: *pag.434*
Imàn Califato Independiente: *pag.243*
In Spe: *pag.287*
In The Labyrinth: *pag.403*
Indaco: *pag.365*
Indexi: *pag.413*
Indian summer: *pag.327*
Indigo: *pag.311*
Indiscipline: *pag.423*
Interference Sardines: *pag.424*
Invisible: *pag.447*
Iona: *pag.327*
IQ: *pag.74*
Iraklis: *pag.339*
Irem, Ilhan: *pag.410*
Iris: *pag.297*
Irish Coffe: *pag.181*
Iron Duke: *pag.183*
Isaiah: *pag.280*
Isildurs Bane: *pag.138*
Iskander: *pag.311*
Island: *pag.251*
Isopoda: *pag.282*
Isotope: *pag.327*
It Bites: *pag.328*
It: *pag.262*
Itoiz: *pag.131*
Ivory: *pag.311*
Ixt Adux: *pag.262*
Izukaitz: *pag.397*
Izvir: *pag.413*
Jacula (see Antonius Rex): *pag.365*
Jade Warrior: *pag.210*
Jane: *pag.312*
Jannick Top: *pag.297*
Japan: *pag.464*
Jazz-Q: *pag.182*
Jenghiz Khan: *pag.181*
Jericho Jones (see Churchills): *pag.223*
Jet Lag: *pag.366*
Jethro Tull: *pag.75*
Jinetes Negros: *pag.449*
Jon & Vangelis: *pag.464*
Jonesy: *pag.328*
Joy Unlimited: *pag.312*
Juan De La Cruz: *pag.257*
Jukka Hauru: *pag.288*
Julian's Treatment: *pag.328*
Julverne: *pag.282*
Jumbo: *pag.230*
Juniper Greene: *pag.121*
Kaamos: *pag.288*
Kaczynski Charles: *pag.423*
Kada: *pag.222*
Kahvas Jute: *pag.442*
Kaipa: *pag.140*
Kalaban: *pag.433*
Kaleidoscope: *pag.211*

Kalevala Orchestra: *pag.289*
Kalevala: *pag.278*
Kandahar: *pag.283*
Kansas: *pag.162*
Kaos Moon: *pag.423*
Karda Estra: *pag.328*
Karfagen: *pag.460*
Kaseke: *pag.287*
Kayak: *pag.220*
KBB: *pag.416*
Kebnekaise: *pag.248*
Keneally, Mike: *pag.433*
Kenso: *pag.151*
Kerrs Pink: *pag.383*
Kestrel: *pag.329*
Khan: *pag.211*
Kimio Mizutani: *pag.255*
Kin Ping Meh: *pag.312*
King Crimson: *pag.76*
Kino: *pag.329*
Klan: *pag.387*
Klockwerk Orange: *pag.12*
Knight Area: *pag.342*
Kohenji Hyakkei: *pag.416*
Koral: *pag.344*
Koray, Erkin: *pag.145*
Korni Grupa/Kornelians: *pag.147*
Kotebel: *pag.397*
Kozmic Muffin: *pag.397*
Kraan: *pag.47*
Kracq: *pag.342*
Kraftwerk: *pag.48*
Krokodil: *pag.408*
Kultivator: *pag.248*
Kuusumun Profeetta (Moon Fog Prophet): *pag.289*
Kundalini: *pag.404*
Kvartetten Son Sprangde: *pag.249*
Kvazar: *pag.383*
Kyrie Eleison: *pag.280*
L'infonie: *pag.424*
Laboratorium: *pag.238*
La Coscienza di Zeno: *pag.366*
Lady Lake: *pag.342*
Lagger Blues Machine: *pag.181*
Laghonia: *pag.457*
Landberk: *pag.249*
Lannhuel, Manu: *pag.297*
Lanzetti Bernardo: *pag.366*
Lard Free: *pag.30*
Las Orejas Y La Lengua: *pag.448*
Latte E Miele: *pag.366*
Laurelie: *pag.282*
Le Match: *pag.424*
Leb I Sol: *pag.253*
Led Zeppelin: *pag.464*
Leviathan: *pag.367*
Life: *pag.403*
Lift (Germany): *pag.312*
Lift (U.S.A.): *pag.434*
Like Wendy: *pag.342*
Linnegar's Steve, Snakeshed: *pag.444*
Linnu Tee: *pag.287*
Lisker: *pag.398*
Little Tragedies: *pag.392*
Living Life: *pag.367*
Lizard: *pag.387*
Load: *pag.434*
Locanda Delle Fate: *pag.230*
Locomotiv Gt: *pag.344*
Los Jaivas: *pag.273*
Lula Cortez & Ramalho: *pag.271*
Luna: *pag.367*
Luna incostante: *pag.367*
Lutha: *pag.443*
M.L.Bongers Project: *pag.197*
Mac Arthur: *pag.434*
Machiavel: *pag.282*
Mackay, Duncan: *pag.444*
Mackenzie Theory: *pag.442*
Mad Crayon: *pag.368*
Mad Curry: *pag.283*
Made In Sweden: *pag.142*
Madore, Michel: *pag.424*
Maelstrom: *pag.435*

Magenta: *pag.329*
Magical Power Mako: *pag.417*
Magma (France): *pag.31*
Magma (Korea): *pag.419*
Magna Carta: *pag.329*
Mahl, Nathan: *pag.425*
Maki, Carmen & Oz: *pag.417*
Malaavia: *pag.368*
Malibran: *pag.368*
Malicorne: *pag.297*
Mammut: *pag.197*
Manar: *pag.346*
Manço, Bariš: *pag.146*
Mandalaband: *pag.330*
Maneige: *pag.155*
Mangala Vallis: *pag.368*
Manuel, Gerardo: *pag.276*
Maquina De Hacier Pajaros: *pag.448*
Maquina!: *pag.243*
Marillion: *pag.77*
Marimba Plus: *pag.392*
Markusfeld, Alain: *pag.298*
Mars Volta: *pag.263*
Marsupilami: *pag.330*
Maschera Di Cera (La): *pag.231*
Master's Apprentices: *pag.170*
Mastermind: *pag.435*
Mason, Nick: *pag.330*
Massive Attack: *pag.465*
Matching Mole: *pag.211*
Materia Gris: *pag.269*
Matraz: *pag.453*
Maury E I Pronomi (Aquael): *pag.369*
Maxophone: *pag.230*
May Blitz: *pag.330*
Mayfly: *pag.343*
McDonald & Giles: *pag.331*
McKennitt Loreena: *pag.465*
Medina Azahara: *pag.243*
Mellow Candle: *pag.331*
Melody: *pag.189*
Memoria Zero: *pag.369*
Memoriance: *pag.298*
Men Of Lake: *pag.369*
Mess (Sven Grünberg): *pag.20*
Message: *pag.313*
Metaconsciencia: *pag.456*
Metamorfosi: *pag.231*
Mezquita: *pag.244*
M.I.A.: *pag.269*
Midas: *pag.417*
Milkweed: *pag.425*
Mini: *pag.344*
Minimum Vital: *pag.189*
Minotaurus: *pag.198*
Miriodor: *pag.156*
Mirror: *pag.343*
Mirthrandir: *pag.263*
Misa De Los Andes: *pag.273*
Mo.do.: *pag.369*
Modry Efekt: *pag.17*
Modulo 1000: *pag.451*
Modulos: *pag.244*
Moğollar (Mogiòllar): *pag.252*
Mona Lisa: *pag.32*
Moody Blues: *pag.78*
Moongarden: *pag.231*
Morozov, Yuri: *pag.392*
Morse Code: *pag.157*
Mosaic: *pag.298*
Mostly Autumn: *pag.331*
Moto Perpetuo: *pag.451*
Moving Gelatine Plates: *pag.190*
Muffins: *pag.163*
Mugen: *pag.417*
Murple: *pag.370*
Muse: *pag.465*
Museo Rosenbach: *pag.112*
Musica Dispersa: *pag.398*
Musica Urbana: *pag.244*
Musicante: *pag.456*
My Solid Ground: *pag.198*
Myrbein: *pag.404*

Mythos: *pag.198*
Nadavati: *pag.298*
Napoli Centrale: *pag.370*
National Health: *pag.79*
Natschinski, Thomas: *pag.199*
Nattura: *pag.347*
Nazca: *pag.275*
Neal, Chris: *pag.442*
Nebbia, Litto: *pag.270*
Nebelnest: *pag.299*
Nebu: *pag.425*
Nekropsi: *pag.411*
Nektar: *pag.49*
Nemo: *pag.299*
Netherworld: *pag.435*
Neuronium: *pag.135*
Neuschwanstein: *pag.313*
New Age: *pag.435*
New Trolls: *pag.113*
Nexus: *pag.270*
Nice (the): *pag.80*
Niemen Czeslav: *pag.122*
Nightwinds: *pag.425*
Nimbus: *pag.186*
Nine Days Wonder: *pag.313*
Nirgal Vallis: *pag.456*
Nirvana: *pag.331*
No Man: *pag.332*
NoNames (Shlomo Gronich): *pag.223*
Noblis Factum: *pag.456*
Noetra: *pag.299*
North Star: *pag.436*
Nosferatu: *pag.313*
Notabene: *pag.370*
Notturno Concertante: *pag.370*
Nova (Italy): *pag.371*
Nova (Finland): *pag.186*
Novalis: *pag.50*
Novela: *pag.418*
November: *pag.249*
Now: *pag.436*
Ñu: *pag.136*
Nucleus: *pag.81*
Nuevo Mexico: *pag.275*
Nuova Era: *pag.371*
Nuova Idea: *pag.371*
Nyl: *pag.299*
O Terço: *pag.178*
Obscura: *pag.371*
Ocarinah: *pag.300*
Octafish: *pag.314*
October: *pag.263*
Octobre: *pag.259*
Octopus: *pag.314*
Odessa: *pag.372*
Odissea: *pag.372*
Odyssee: *pag.314*
Offenbach: *pag.426*
Old Man And The Sea: *pag.184*
Oldfield, Mike: *pag.82*
Olive Mess: *pag.461*
Om: *pag.398*
Omega: *pag.101*
Omni: *pag.398*
One Shot: *pag.190*
Onza: *pag.399*
Opus 5: *pag.259*
Opus Avantra: *pag.232*
Opus: *pag.413*
Orb (the): *pag.332*
Orchestrator: *pag.436*
Oregon: *pag.264*
Orion: *pag.300*
Orkiestra Òsmego Dnia: *pag.387*
Orlan Jazz Band (Oleg Kireyev): *pag.393*
Orme (Le): *pag.114*
Orquestra Mirasol: *pag.245*
Os Mundi: *pag.314*
Os Mutantes: *pag.177*
Osage Tribe: *pag.372*
Osanna: *pag.115*
Ose: *pag.300*
Ossian (Osjan): *pag.388*

Out Of Focus: pag.51
Outer Limits: pag.256
Outsiders: pag.221
Ozric Tentacles: pag.212
Ozz Knozz: pag.436
Paatos: pag.404
Pablo El Enterrador: pag.449
Pacific Sound: pag.409
Paese Dei Balocchi: pag.232
Pagani, Mauro: pag.372
Pageant: pag.256
Pallas: pag.332
Pan Y Regaliz: pag.399
Pan: pag.184
Pancake: pag.315
Pandora: pag.404
Pangee: pag.426
Panna Fredda: pag.373
Pantarei: pag.405
Panta Rhei: pag.344
Pantheon: pag.343
Panzerpappa: pag.384
Parsons Alan, Project: pag.465
Parzival: pag.199
Pastoral: pag.449
Paternoster: pag.280
Pathaphonie: pag.300
Patto: pag.212
Pavlov's Dog: pag.164
Pax: pag.457
Pekka Pohjola: pag.186
Pendragon: pag.212
Pentacle: pag.190
Pentola di Papin (la): pag.373
Pentwater: pag.437
Perception: pag.301
Pereira Gonçalo: pag.239
Perigeo: pag.116
Perotic Theatre: pag.315
Pescado Rabioso: pag.176
Pesniary: pag.461
Pete & Royce: pag.339
Petrus Castrus: pag.126
Pez: pag.449
Philarmonie: pag.301
Phillips, Anthony: pag.83
Phoenix: pag.127
Pholas Dactylus: pag.373
Picchio Dal Pozzo: pag.232
Pierrot Lunaire: pag.233
Piirpauke: pag.289
Pinchevsky, Jorge: pag.448
Pineapple Thief: pag.332
Pink Floyd: pag.84
Piramis: pag.345
PLJ Band/Termites: pag.95
Pollen: pag.425
Polyphony: pag.264
Pooh: pag.466
Pop Masina: pag.414
Popol Ace: pag.384
Popol Vuh: pag.52
Porcupine Tree: pag.213
Poseidon: pag.315
Potemkine: pag.301
Pre: pag.437
Premiata Forneria Marconi: pag.117
Presence: pag.373
Present: pag.13
Priam: pag.301
Prism: pag.256
Procession: pag.233
Procol Harum: pag.85
Progresiv Tm: pag.390
Progress Organisation: pag.182
Providence: pag.418
Prowlers: pag.374
Prudy: pag.286
Psychonoesis: pag.374
Pulsar: pag.33
Purple Overdose: pag.339
Q65: pag.221
Quantum: pag.451

Quarteto 1111: pag.239
Quasar Lux Symphoniae: pag.374
Quatermass: pag.213
Quaterna Requiem: pag.271
Quatro, Michael: pag.437
Queen: pag.466
Quella Vecchia Locanda: pag.233
Quidam: pag.388
Quill: pag.437
Raccomandata Ricevuta Ritorno: pag.374
Radiohead: pag.213
Ragnarok (New Zealand): pag.173
Ragnarök (Sweden): pag.250
Rainbow Theatre: pag.267
Raminghi: pag.375
Ranieri Massimo & Deodato Eumir: pag.466
Rare Bird: pag.333
Rascal Reporters: pag.438
Raw Material: pag.333
Reale Accademia Di Musica: pag.375
Rebekka: pag.315
Recordando O Vale Des Maças: pag.451
Recreation: pag.283
Red Noise: pag.302
Redd: pag.270
Reed Lou: pag.466
Reichel's machine, Achim: pag.201
Release Music Orchestra: pag.316
Renaissance: pag.86
Replikas: pag.411
Reportaz: pag.388
Resan: pag.405
Rialzu: pag.191
Riba, Pau: pag.245
Ribeiro Catherine: pag.191
Riley, Terry: pag.467
Rios, Miguel: pag.245
Ripaille: pag.302
Robertson Robbie: pag.467
Rocchi Claudio: pag.375
Room: pag.333
Rouge Ciel: pag.426
Rousseau: pag.316
Rovescio Della Medaglia: pag.234
RPWL: pag.316
Ruja: pag.287
Rumblin'orchestra: pag.345
Run Way: pag.419
Runaway Totem: pag.375
Rundgren, Todd & Utopia: pag.165
Ruphus: pag.237
Rush: pag.158
Rutherford Mike: pag.333
Saft: pag.384
Saga (aka US - Holland): pag.343
Saga (Portugal): pag.389
Saga (Sweden): pag.405
Sagrado Coração Da Terra: pag.452
Sahara: pag.316
Saint Just: pag.234
Samadhi: pag.376
Samla Mammas Manna: pag.143
Sandrose: pag.191
Sanullim(San Hul Rim): pag.419
Satellite: pag.388
Saturnia: pag.389
SBB: pag.123
Scapa Flow: pag.289
Schipa Tito, Junior: pag.376
Schtung: pag.443
Schulze, Klaus: pag.53
Second Hand: pag.214
Second Movement: pag.317
Secret Oyster: pag.184
Segno del comando: pag.376
Semiramis: pag.234
Semnal M: pag.390
Sensation's Fix: pag.118
Sepsis: pag.240
September: pag.414
Sezon Dohzdei: pag.393
SFF: pag.199
Sfinx: pag.390

Shadowfax: pag.438
Shadows: pag.467
Sheller, William: pag.302
Sheshet (Shem Tov Levy): pag.348
Shin Jung Hyun: pag.419
Shingetsu: pag.152
Showmen (Showmen 2): pag.235
Shturzite: pag.284
Shylock: pag.192
Sigmund Snopek III: pag.438
Signal: pag.284
Sinestesia: pag.376
Sisa, Jaume: pag.246
Sistema (Il): pag.235
Sithonia: pag.235
Sixty Nine: pag.317
Skaldowie: pag.124
Skid Row: pag.334
Skin Alley: pag.334
Sky: pag.334
Sloche: pag.259
Smak: pag.414
Smash: pag.246
Smashing Pumpkins: pag.438
Smith Antonio (Congregaciòn): pag.453
Socrates: pag.218
Soft Machine: pag.87
Solar Plexus: pag.250
Solaris: pag.102
Solution: pag.221
Som Imaginario: pag.272
Sorgente (La): pag.377
Sorrenti, Alan: pag.236
Sotos: pag.302
Space Circus: pag.418
Spacious Mind (the): pag.405
Sparks: pag.467
Spectrum: pag.171
Speed Limit: pag.303
Spirogyra: pag.334
Spirosfera: pag.377
Splash: pag.406
Spock's Beard: pag.439
Spooky Tooth: pag.214
Spring: pag.214
Standarte: pag.236
Starcastle: pag.264
Steely Dan: pag.265
Stelle Di Mario Schifano (Le): pag.119
Step Ahead: pag.303
Stern Combo Meissen: pag.54
Storm (The): pag.399
Stormy Six: pag.377
Strawbs: pag.215
Streetmark: pag.317
String Driven Thing: pag.335
Stromboli: pag.286
Stud: pag.335
Sui Generis: pag.448
Sume: pag.347
Sunblind Lion: pag.439
Sunscape: pag.377
Supersister: pag.98
Supertramp: pag.468
Svanfridur: pag.347
Symphonic Slam: pag.427
Synanthesia: pag.335
Syndone: pag.378
Synkopy (Synkopy 61): pag.286
Syrius: pag.345
T2: pag.335
Taal: pag.303
Tableton: pag.399
Tabula Rasa: pag.290
Tagliapietra, Aldo: pag.378
Tai Phong: pag.192
Tako: pag.253
Talk Talk: pag.468
Talking Heads: pag.468
Tangent: pag.336
Tangerine Dream: pag.55
Tangle Edge: pag.384
Tantra: pag.239
Tapiman: pag.246

Taproban: pag.378
Tarantula: pag.400
Tarkus: pag.457
Tasavallan Presidentti: pag.22
Tellah: pag.272
Tempano: pag.458
Tempest: pag.336
Tempio delle clessidre: pag.378
Tempus Fugit: pag.452
Terpandre: pag.303
Terraced Garden: pag.427
Terreno Baldio: pag.272
Tetragon: pag.317
Theatre: pag.379
Think: pag.443
Thinking Plague: pag.265
Third Ear Band: pag.215
Thirsty Moon: pag.200
Thollot Jacques: pag.304
Thule: pag.385
Tibbetts, Steve: pag.439
Tibet: pag.318
Time (U.K.): pag.336
Time (Yugoslavia): pag.253
Tipographica: pag.418
Titus Groan: pag.336
TNR: pag.379
Toad: pag.409
Tomorrow: pag.215
Tomorrow's Gift: pag.200
Tonton Macoute: pag.337
Tool: pag.438
Torre Dell'alchimista (La): pag.379
Touch: pag.265
Townscream: pag.345
Trace: pag.99
Träd Gräs Och Stenar: pag.250
Traffic Sound: pag.276
Traffic: pag.88
Transatlantic: pag.440
Travelling: pag.304
Trees: pag.216
Trespass: pag.348
Trettoåriga Kriget: pag.144
Triana: pag.137
Triangle: pag.304
Trilogy: pag.318
Triode: pag.192
Trip (the): pag.120
Triumvirat: pag.318
Trono Dei Ricordi: pag.379
Troya: pag.200
Trubrot: pag.347
True Myth: pag.427
Tryo: pag.453
Tudor Lodge: pag.337
Tukhmanov, David: pag.393
Tuned Tone: pag.348
Twelft Night: pag.89
Twenty Sixty Six And Then: pag.201
Twin Age: pag.406
Tyrannosaurus Rex: pag.337
U Totem: pag.266
Ubi Maior: pag.380
Ufo: pag.216
UK: pag.216
Ultimate Spinach: pag.440
Ultravox: pag.468
Ulysses: pag.318
Unicorn: pag.403
Univers Zero: pag.14
Universal Totem Orchestra: pag.236
Uno (see Nova): pag.371
Unreal City: pag.380
Uovo Di Colombo: pag.380
Urban Sax: pag.304
Uriah Heep: pag.217
Ursiny Dežo: pag.286
Utopian Fields: pag.385
Uzva: pag.290
Vainica Doble: pag.397
Van Der Graaf Generator: pag.90
Vanay, Laurence: pag.305
Vanessa: pag.385

Vega: *pag.400*
Venegoni & C.: *pag.380*
Vermicelli Orchestra: *pag.393*
Versailles: *pag.305*
Versus X: *pag.319*
Via Lumini: *pag.452*
Victor Peraino's Kingdom Come: *pag.266*
Viima: *pag.290*
Vildkaktus: *pag.406*
Violeta De Outono: *pag.452*
Virus: *pag.202*
Visible Wind: *pag.426*
Visitors: *pag.305*
Volapük: *pag.305*
Volarè: *pag.440*
Volo (Il): *pag.381*
Vortex: *pag.306*
Wakhevitch, Igor: *pag.193*
Wallenstein: *pag.56*
Wallenstein: *pag.56*
Walpurgis: *pag.201*
Waniyetula: *pag.202*
Wapassou: *pag.34*
Warm Dust: *pag.337*
Watch (the): *pag.381*
Waterloo: *pag.283*
Waters, Roger: *pag.217*
Weather Report: *pag.166*
Web (The): *pag.338*
Weidorje: *pag.193*
Welcome: *pag.409*
Werwolf: *pag.319*
White Willow: *pag.385*

Wigwam: *pag.23*
Will O' The Wisp: *pag.339*
Wind: *pag.202*
Wright, Richard: *pag.338*
Wolf Darryl Way's: *pag.338*
Wurtenberg: *pag.306*
Wyatt, Robert: *pag.91*
Xhol: *pag.203*
XII Alfonso: *pag.306*
XL: *pag.290*
X-Religion: *pag.461*
Yalla: *pag.461*
Yatha Sidra: *pag.203*
Yes: *pag.92*
Yeti: *pag.440*
Yezda Urfa: *pag.266*
Yleclipse: *pag.381*
Yolk: *pag.409*
Yonin Bayashi: *pag.153*
Yossi Piamenta: *pag.348*
Yu Grupa: *pag.414*
Yvosky, Fernando: *pag.458*
Zao: *pag.35*
Zappa, Frank: *pag.167*
Zarathustra: *pag.203*
Zauber: *pag.381*
Zebra: *pag.400*
Zingal'e: *pag.348*
ZNR: *pag.193*
Zombies: *pag.217*
Zomby Woof: *pag.319*
Zoo: *pag.306*
Zuphall Rufus: *pag.319*